Logic and Belief in Indian Philosophy

Logic and Belief in Indian Philosophy

Edited by
PIOTR BALCEROWICZ

MOTILAL BANARSIDASS
PUBLISHING HOUSE • DELHI
Email: naraina@mlbd.in • Website: www.mlbd.in
@mlbdofficial
+91 89 2999 9000

*2nd Reprint: Delhi, **2024***
First Edition: Delhi, 2010

Cover design: Piotr Balcerowicz
Layout design and fonts, typeset by: Piotr Balcerowicz

ISBN: 978-93-5760-544-1 (Hardcover)
ISBN: 978-93-5760-571-7 (Paperback)

Printed & Published by
Rajendra P Jain *for*
Motilal Banarsidass Publishing House
A-44, Naraina Industrial Area, Phase I,
New Delhi–110 028 (INDIA)
Email: naraina@mlbd.in Website: www.mlbd.in
Tel.: (+91-11)4751 1592
Showroom:
4637/20, F-2, Hari Sadan, First Floor, Ansari Road, Daryaganj
Delhi–110 002 (Opp. Fire Station) ***Tel.***: (+91-11)4559 7999

TABLE OF CONTENTS

Table of Contents 5

Preface 6

Contributors 11

MYTH, BELIEF AND APPEAL TO RATIONALITY

JOHANNES BRONKHORST:
What did Indian Philosophers Believe 19

CLAUS OETKE:
Pramāṇa, Logic and Belief 45

RAGHUNATH GHOSH:
Can There be Unbiased Epistemology in Indian Philosophy? 71

PETER FLÜGEL:
Power and Insight in Jain Discourse 85

GOD VIS-À-VIS PROOF AND BELIEF

FERNANDO TOLA and CARMEN DRAGONETTI:
The Distinction *in intellectu / in re*
in the Ontological Proof and in Bhartṛhari 221

JOHN VATTANKY, S. J.:
Theism—The Culmination of Nyāya Logic 237

PIOTR BALCEROWICZ:
What Exists for the Vaiśeṣika? 249

LOGIC AND BELIEF IN SĀṀKHYA AND YOGA

SHUJUN MOTEGI:
Early Concepts of Logic in Sāṁkhya 363

PHILIPP A. MAAS:
Valid Knowledge and Belief in Classical Sāṁkhya-Yoga 383

LANGUAGE, GRAMMAR AND BELIEF

ASHOK AKLUJKAR:
Grammarians' Leaving Logic at the Door 395

HIDEYO OGAWA:
Bhartṛhari on Unnameable things 415

LOGIC AND BELIEF IN INTERPRETATION AND TRANSLATION

DIWAKAR ACHARYA:
Major Points of Vācaspati's Disagreement with Maṇḍana 433

STEPHEN H. PHILLIPS:
From the *Tattva-cintā-maṇi* by Gaṅgeśa:
The *kevala-vyatireki-prakaraṇam*: Negative-Only Inference
(Annotated Translation and Commentary) 447

LOGIC, REALITY AND BELIEF IN BUDDHIST TRADITION

HORST LASIC:
A Hot Dispute About Lukewarm air: Dignāga on *Āpta-vāda* 521

DAN ARNOLD:
On (Non-semantically) Remembering Conventions:
Dharmakīrti and Dharmottara on *Saṁketa-kāla* 539

VINCENT ELTSCHINGER:
Studies in Dharmakīrti's Religious Philosophy:
4. The *cintā-mayī prajñā* 565

KLAUS-DIETER MATHES:
The 'Principle of True Nature' (*dharmatā-yukti*)
as a Justification for Positive Descriptions of Reality
in Mahāyāna Buddhism 605

HIROSHI NEMOTO:
Tsong kha pa on the Three Times:
New Light on the Buddhist Theory of Time 617

KAORU ONISHI:
The *Bodhi-caryâvatāra* and Its Monastic Aspects:
On the Problem of Representation 627

BELIEF, HOPE AND GAMBLING

IRMA PIOVANO:
Sociological and Juridical Aspects of Dice-Play in Ancient India 657

GENERAL INDEX 675

Preface

The present volume explores a theme which has so far rarely received the attention it legitimately deserves, although its fundamental importance to proper understanding of the true nature of Indian philosophical enquiry and intellectual heritage seems unquestionable. Whether in Indian social and historical context or throughout the history of Western thought, the relations between logic, belief and philosophy have always been very complex and multifaceted.

The general theme of the enquiry presented here is adequately reflected in the title of the volume: *Logic and Belief in Indian Philosophy*, which aptly highlights the *yukti-āgama* dimension. In particular, it focuses on various aspects of Indian thought, and Indian logic in particular, with special emphasis on the relationship, and tension, between rational examination and belief in Indian philosophical tradition.

The selection of papers by world-acclaimed specialists in Indian philosophy deals with a broad spectrum of problems such as the real nature and status of reason and faith in India, their rational, or otherwise, grounding or the extent to which their correlation is bipolar or interdependent. A number of vital philosophical questions stimulated the discussion in the volume: Can we speak of the symbiosis or, rather, tension between philosophy, logic in particular, and religion in Indian context? How do sound proof and irrefutable evidence relate to the bequeathed body of dogmas? To what degree did Indian thinkers consider logical means of enquiry independent of belief? How can logic itself be rationally validated without a recourse to assumptions sanctioned by tradition and belief? What is the place of scepticism or mystic experience vis-à-vis rational method and logical tools? How did Indian logicians try to accommodate the idea of irrationality and religious belief in the scheme of *pramāṇa*? These questions do not only concern the relationship between the phenomena of religiosity and religion, on the one hand, and rationality and rational justification, on the other. They are also applicable to the spheres of ritual, religious-social practices, or even gambling, as well as to various ways of how behaviour and religious acts were rationalised.

The contributions were grouped in thematic sections, the titles of which are self-explanatory. Some articles probe deeply into very detailed and intricate doctrinal aspects of selected Brāhmaṇical philosophical schools and of Jaina and Buddhist traditions, whereas others attempt synthetic conclusions as well as methodological and theoretical reflection concerning the very nature of Indian philosophy and its religious background. The reader will also find an English translation of 'The chapter on the negative-only inference' (*Kevala-vyatireki-prakaraṇa*) of Gaṅgeśa's *Tattva-cintā-maṇi*, a ground-breaking work that revolutionised mediaeval Indian logic.

Some of these contributions were directly presented by the authors during the International Seminar 'Logic and Belief in Indian Philosophy—The Impact of Indian Thought in Asia and Europe' (for the programme see below, p. 9), held between 30 April and 5 May 2006 in Białowieża, one of the most beautiful and picturesque spots in Poland, in the heart of the great Białowieża Forest, supposedly the largest primeval forest in Europe. The Seminar 'Logic and Belief in Indian Philosophy' was organised by Piotr Balcerowicz, Marek Mejor and Monika Nowakowska.

On this occasion, on behalf of the organisers of the Seminar, I would like to extend most sincere thanks to UNESCO, to the Polish National Commission for UNESCO and the Rector of the University of Warsaw for their much appreciated financial support, without which the Seminar could not have taken place.

I also wish to express my deepest gratitude to my colleagues Marek Mejor and Monika Nowakowska of the Faculty of Oriental Studies, the University of Warsaw, for their organisational efforts that made the Seminar possible.

The present volume appears as Volume Three of the Series *Warsaw Indological Studies* by the arrangement with Motilal Banarsidass Private Limited, Delhi. When I met my friend Narendra Prakash Jain, the Director of Motilal Banarsidass, in December 2006 and mentioned the plans to publish the proceedings of the Seminar 'Logic and Belief in Indian Philosophy', he enthusiastically greeted the idea. I personally feel deeply obliged to him for his readiness to accept the publication for print and his efforts to make the contributions included in this volume available to a wider readership.

Piotr Balcerowicz
Warsaw, July 2008

SESSION PROGRAMME OF THE INTERNATIONAL SEMINAR
'LOGIC AND BELIEF IN INDIAN PHILOSOPHY'
Warsaw–Białowieża, Poland
30 April – 5 May, 2006
University of Warsaw

1 May, 2007 (Białowieża): Session 1, 2 [chairmen—Karl Potter, Hiroshi Marui]:

Johannes Bronkhorst: 'What Did Indian Philosophers Believe?'

Ashok Aklujkar: 'Grammarians' Leaving Logic at the Door'

Carmen Dragonetti and Fernando Tola: 'The Ontological Proof and Bhartṛhari'

John Vattanky, S. J.: 'Theism: The Culmination of Nyāya Logic'

2 May, 2007 (Białowieża): Sessions 3, 4 [chairman—Jonardon Ganeri]:

Raghunath Ghosh: 'Can there be Unbiased Epistemology in Indian Philosophy?'

Claus Oetke: '*Pramāṇa*, Belief and Decision'

Shujun Motegi: 'Early Concepts of Logic in Sāṁkhya'

Philipp Maas: 'Valid Knowledge and Belief in Classical Sāṁkhya-Yoga'

3 May, 2007 (Białowieża): Sessions 5, 6 [chairmen—Ashok Aklujkar, Johannes Bronkhorst]:

Karl Potter: 'Should Dharmakīrti have given in so easily to Yogâcāra?'

Dan Arnold: 'On Semantics and Saṁketa: Thoughts on a Neglected Problem with *Apoha*'

Vincent Eltschinger: 'Studies in Dharmakīrti's Religious Philosophy: The *Cintā-mayī Prajñā*'

Horst Lasic: 'A Hot Dispute About Lukewarm Air: Dignāga on *Āpta-vāda*'

Stephen Phillips: 'Sensitivity to Defeaters (*bādhaka*) as Intrinsic to Knowledge of Inference-Warranting Concomitance (*vyāpti*)'

Toshihiko Kimura: 'Imperfect Reduction to Absurdity in the Proofs of Indian Metaphysics'

4 May, 2007 (Białowieża): Sessions 9, 10 [chairman—Stephen Phillips]:

Taisei Shida: 'On the Distribution of Validity and Invalidity at the Origination of Cognition: What is the "General Cause of Cognition" and the "Causal factor for Validity"?'

Peter Flügel: 'Power and Insight in Jain Discourse'

Hiroshi Marui: 'Considering the 'Six Tarkas' in the *Nyāya-mañjarī*'

Piotr Balcerowicz: 'What Exists for the Vaiśeṣika?'

Contributors

Diwakar Acharya studied in Kathmandu and Benares, and wrote his Ph.D. dissertation on Vācaspatimiśra's *Tattva-samīkṣā* at the University of Hamburg. He taught at Nepal Sanskrit University and worked for the Nepalese-German Manuscript Cataloguing Project and the Nepal-German Manuscript Preservation Project in Hamburg and Kathmandu. His areas of interest are Indian philosophy and religion, early Tantra, *kāvya*, and epigraphy. He is currently teaching as visiting lecturer at the Graduate School of Letters, Kyoto University, Japan.

Ashok Aklujkar received his M.A. degree in Sanskrit and Pali from the University of Poona and his Ph.D. degree in Sanskrit and Indian Studies from Harvard University. He taught courses in Sanskrit language and in the related *belles lettres* and mythological and philosophical literatures at the University of British Columbia from 1969 to 2006 (and, when invited as a visiting professor, at Hamburg, Rome, Cambridge (Massachusetts, Harvard University), Kyoto, Paris and Oxford). He is now Professor Emeritus at the University of British Columbia. His published research is mostly in the areas of Sanskrit linguistic tradition and poetics. Advanced students have worked under his guidance in the areas of Buddhist and Brahmanical philosophy, religion, and mythology. He is probably most well-known for his book *Sanskrit: an Easy Introduction to an Enchanting Language* .

Dan Arnold (daarnold@midway.uchicago.edu) is Assistant Professor of Philosophy of Religion in the Divinity School at the University of Chicago. His first book, *Buddhists, Brahmins, and Belief: Epistemology in South Asian Philosophy of Religion* (Columbia University Press, New York 2005), won an American Academy of Religion Award for Excellence in the Study of Religion. His articles have appeared in such journals as *Philosophy East and West*, *the Journal of Indian Philosophy*, *Journal of the International Association of Buddhist Studies*, and *Asian Philosophy*.

Piotr Balcerowicz (www.orient.uw.edu.pl/balcerowicz), presently teaching at the University of Warsaw (Department of South-Asian Studies) and professor of Social Sciences and Humanities (Asian Studies and Department of International Relations), specialises in Indian philosophical tradition, with emphasis on Indian epistemological thought and Jainism. He lectures on Indian philosophy and Indian religions as well as on intercultural relations and contemporary history of Asia, esp. South-Asia, Central Asia and the Middle East. He received his M.A. degree in Indology from the University of Warsaw in 1990 and his Ph.D. degree in Sanskrit and Indian Studies from Hamburg University in 1999. He studied Sanskrit, Prakrits and Pāṇini at Banaras Hindu University in 1987–1988 and Western philosophy at postgraduate level at Polish Academy of Sciences, Warsaw in 1990–1994. He earned his 'Habilitation' (post-doctoral degree) in Eastern philosophies in 2005 from Polish Academy of Sciences with his postdoctoral thesis (*History of Classical Indian Philosophy. Part One: Beginnings, Analytical Trends and Philosophy of Nature*. Warsaw 2003). He published extensively on Indian philosophy, but also on the Middle East and Central Asia, and authored a number of books on Indian philosophy, Jainism and history of Afghanistan.

Johannes Bronkhorst (johannes.bronkhorst@unil.ch) has been professor of Sanskrit and Indian studies at the University of Lausanne (Switzerland) since 1987. His research has so far concentrated on the history of Indian thought in the broadest sense, covering Buddhism, Jainism and Brahmanism. The interrelationship between these three, and their *Sitz im Leben*, receive special attention.

Carmen Dragonetti (cldragon@mail.retina.ar), Dr. Phil., Universidad Nacional Mayor de San Marcos (Lima, Perú); Research Fellow of the CONICET (National Council for Scientific Research) in the highest category; President of the Foundation Institute of Buddhist Studies (Argentina); and Fellow 2004 of the John Simon Guggenheim Memorial Foundation (USA). She is the author of a number of books and articles, in English and in Spanish, about Indian culture, especially on Indian philosophy, alone or in collaboration with her husband Fernando Tola, of which two recent ones are: Being as Consciousness (Motilal Banarsidass, New Delhi 2004) and On the Myth of the Opposition between Indian Thought and Western Philosophy (Georg Olms Verlag, Hildesheim 2004).

Vincent Eltschinger (b. 1970; Vincent.Eltschinger@assoc.oeaw.ac.at, v.eltschinger@bluewin.ch) studied Indology and Buddhist Studies at the University of Lausanne, where he wrote a Ph.D. thesis on Dharmakīrti's polemics against Brahmanical orthodoxy. Since 2003 he has been a research fellow at the Austrian Academy of Sciences (Vienna). He has taught at the universities of Lausanne, Zurich, Paris (École Pratique des Hautes Études) and Vienna. Current research interests include the religious and apologetical dimensions of late Indian Buddhist philosophy, the intellectual genealogy of the Buddhist epistemological school as well as the Buddhist elites' strategies of self-assertion in post-Gupta time.

Peter Flügel is Lecturer in the Study of Religions and Chair of the Centre of Jaina Studies at the Department of the Study of Religions in the School of Oriental and African Studies, University of London. He has published extensively on the history and anthropology of contemporary Jain schools and sects, Jain *stūpa*s, Jaina-Vaiṣṇava syncretism, and on the social history of the Jain tradition. Recent publications include the edited volumes *Studies in Jaina History and Culture: Disputes and Dialogues* (Routledge, London 2006) and (with Gustaaf Houtman) *Asceticism and Power in South-and Southeast Asia* (Routledge, London 2009). He is the editor of the *International Journal of Jain Studies* (www.soas.ac.uk/ijjs), co-editor of *Jaina Studies—Newsletter of the Centre of Jaina Studies* (www.soas.ac.uk/jainastudies/newsletter), and series editor of *Routledge Advances in Jaina Studies*.

Raghunath Ghosh (raghunbu@yahoo.co.in), Professor of Philosophy, University of North Bengal, Siliguri, W.B. specialises in Indian Philosophy (classical and modern). He has published ten books, one hundred fifteen papers in different professional journals and edited a number of volumes. Ghosh has widely travelled and lectured in different universities in the Netherlands, France, England, Japan, Germany, U.S.A., Poland, Finland, Singapore, Malaysia and Bangladesh and researched with Professor Kuno Lorenz, University of Saarland, Germany under the auspices of DAAD. He was a Visiting Fellow in the Universities of Puna, Jadavpur, Rabindra Bharati and Midnapur and a recipient of Best Book Award conferred by Indian Council of Philosophical Research, New Delhi. He is at present Dean of Faculty of Arts, Commerce & Law, University of North Bengal and Director of Buddhist Study Centre, NBU.

Horst Lasic (lasic@oeaw.ac.at) studied Tibetology, Buddhist Studies and Indology at the University of Vienna, where he received his Ph.D. degree with a study on Jñānaśrimītra's *Vyāpti-carcā* in 1999. He has been working since 1995 as a research fellow at the Institute for the Cultural and Intellectual History of Asia of the Austrian Academy of Sciences and has been a lecturer for Tibetan and Sanskrit at the University of Vienna since 1999. Currently he is working on editions of Jinendrabuddhi's *Pramāṇa-samuccaya-ṭīkā* and of Candrakīrti's *Madhyamakâvatāra*, as well as on a reconstruction of Dignāga's *Pramāṇa-samuccaya*, Chapter 2.

Philipp A. Maas received his Ph.D. from the University of Bonn, Germany. He works as a full-time post-doc researcher on a first critical edition and annotated translation of the *Vimāna-sthāna* section of the *Caraka-saṁhitā* in research projects at the Institute for the Cultural and Intellectual History of Asia, Austrian Academy of Sciences, Vienna and at the Institute for South Asia, Tibet and Buddhist Studies, University of

Vienna. He has published, among other things, a first critical edition of the *Pātañjala-yoga-śāstra*'s initial chapter and papers on the textual history of this work as well as on the structure of different yoga meditations.

Klaus-Dieter Mathes works as a Tibetologist at the Asia-Africa Institute at the University of Hamburg. His research deals with the Indian origins of Tibetan *mahāmudrā* traditions. He obtained a Ph.D. from Marburg University (Germany) with a study of one of the five treatises of Maitreya, the *Dharma-dharmatā-vibhāga* (a subtle analysis of the distinction made between the ordinary phenomenal world and the true nature of these phenomena). In his Habilitation thesis he focused on 'Gos Lo tsā ba gZhon nu dpal's (1392–1481) extensive commentary of the *Ratna-gotra-vibhāga* (*Uttara-tantra*). The study was recently published under the title: *A Direct Path to the Buddha Within: Gö Lotsāwa's Mahāmudrā Interpretation of the Ratna-gotravibhāga* (Wisdom Publications, Boston 2008).

Shujun Motegi (motegis@shinshu-u.ac.jp) is Professor of Ethics in the Department of Education at Shinshu University, Nagano, Japan. He lectures the history of ethical thoughts of Japan in the relation with Buddhism. He received his M.A. degree in philosophy from Kyoto University in 1977, after studying abroad at Banaras Hindu University in 1973-1975. He published the first volume of the critical edition of the *Yukti-dīpikā* in co-operation with Albrecht Wezler in 1998. His recent concern is in the early history of Sāṁkhya and Yoga found in the *Mokṣa-dharma* section of the *Śānti-parvan* of the Great Epic of India.

Hiroshi Nemoto is a research fellow of the Japan Society for the Promotion of Science and a Ph.D. candidate at the Graduate School of Hiroshima University. He obtained his M.A. in Indian Philosophy from the Graduate School of Hiroshima University in 2004. From 2004 to 2006, he worked with Tibetan scholars at Drepung Gomang Monastic College in Mundgod, South India.

Claus Oetke studied Indology, Philosophy and Sinology at the University of Hamburg (Germany), where he received a doctorate in 1973. From 1973–1983 he was a lecturer (*wissenschaftlicher Assistent*) at the Institute for Culture and History of India and Tibet in Hamburg. His Habilitation in 1983 and professorship at the same institute was followed by short term professorships on deputation in Vienna (Austria) and Kiel (Germany). From 1987 to 1992 he held a *Heisenberg Professur* of the Deutsche Forschungsgemeinschaft (DFG), which led to visiting professorships at the University of Pennsylvania (Philadelphia, USA), The Australian National University in Canberra (Australia) and the University of Texas at Austin (USA). Since 1993, he has been Head of the Department of Indian and Tibetan

Studies at the University of Stockholm. His main topics of research include: Tibetan translations from Chinese Buddhist texts, problems of person and self in the Indian philosophical tradition, studies in early Mādhyamaka-Buddhism, Indian theories of inference and proof ('Indian Logic'), theoretical issues of interpretation and linguistic semantics. Some of his major publications are: *'Ich' und das Ich. Analytische Untersuchungen zur buddhistisch-brahmanischen Atmankontroverse* (Stuttgart 1987), *Zur Methode der Analyse philosophischer Sūtratexte. Die Pramāṇapassagen der Nyāyasutren* (Reinbek 1991), *Studies on the Doctrine of Trairupya* (Wien 1994), *Logic Matters in the Prasannapāda. A Study on Reasoning and Proof in Metaphysics* (Stockholm 2006).

Hideyo Ogawa (hogawa@hiroshima-u.ac.jp) was born in Japan in 1954. He received a doctorate in letters from Hiroshima University in 2002. He studied Pāṇinian grammatical works also in India. Since 1990, he has been teaching Indian philosophy at Hiroshima University. His main work is *Process and Language: A Study of the Mahābhāṣya ad A 1.3.1 bhūvādayo dhātavaḥ*, published from Motilal Banarsidass in 2005.

Kaoru Onishi is lecturer in Buddhist Studies at Kansai University in Osaka, Japan. His research interests focus on the discourse of Mahāyāna Buddhist texts as well as on the history of Buddhist Studies in modern Japan.

Stephen Phillips teaches at the University of Texas at Austin with a dual appointment in Philosophy and Asian Studies. A Sanskritist and translator of, in particular, the Navya-nyāya ('New Logic') school of Udayana (c. 1000) and Gaṅgeśa (c. 1300), Professor Phillips has written widely on classical Indian philosophies. His translation and commentary on the perception chapter of Gaṅgeśa's *Tattva-cintāmaṇi* ('Jewel of Reflection on the Truth about Epistemology') with N.S. Ramanuja Tatacharya (New York 2004), is being published this year in a revised Indian edition by Motilal Banarsidass, Delhi. His *Classical Indian Metaphysics* (Chicago 1995), which is a study of the controversy, in particular, between Advaita Vedānta and Nyāya, is also published in an Indian edition by Motilal Banarsidass (1998). Columbia University Press is publishing his *Yoga, Karma, and Rebirth* (forthcoming, May 2009) which includes fresh translations of classic yogic texts all the way back to the Upanishads.

Irma Piovano (irmapiovano@cesmeo.it) has been the Scientific Director of CESMEO (Torino) since its foundation and is the Regional Director (for Romance-speaking countries of Europe) of the IASS. She is a Member of the Scientific Committees of *Indologica Taurinensia* and *Corpus Iuris Sanscriticum* (CIS) and the President of their Editorial Boards. She is a Member of various Academies and was awarded the Degree of 'Vachaspati' D.Litt. (Honoris Causa) by the Shri Lal Bahadur Shastri Rashtriya Sanskrit Vidyapeeth (2007). Her fields of research are Indian legal tradition, Indian and Southeast Asian Literatures and the history of Indian studies in Italy. Besides many articles and essays on these subjects, she edited and translated the *Dakṣa-smṛti* (CIS, Torino 2002).

Fernando Tola (cldragon@mail.retina.ar), Dr. Lit., Universidad Nacional Mayor de San Marcos (UNMSM), Professor Emeritus UNMSM (Lima, Perú); he was Research Fellow of the CONICET (National Council for Scientific Research) in the highest category (retired today), and Professor of Sanskrit and Indian Philosophy in the University of Buenos Aires, Argentina. At present he is Vice-President and Director of Research of the Foundation Institute of Buddhist Studies (Argentina). He is the author of a number of books and articles, in English and in Spanish, alone or in collaboration with his wife, Carmen Dragonetti.

John Vattanky is emeritus Professor of Indian Philosophy and Sanskrit at Gnandeepa-Vidyapeeth, Pune. He was educated at Oxford and Vienna and in the rigorous ways of traditional Indian learning. He has specialised in Navya-nyāya and published several books on the subject, the main ones are: *Gaṅgeśa's Philosophy of God* (1984), *The development of Nyāya Theism* (1993), *Nyāya Philosophy of Language* (1995) and *A System of Indian Logic: the Nyāya Theory of Inference* (2002). He is continuing his researches and publications.

Myth, Belief and Appeal to Rationality

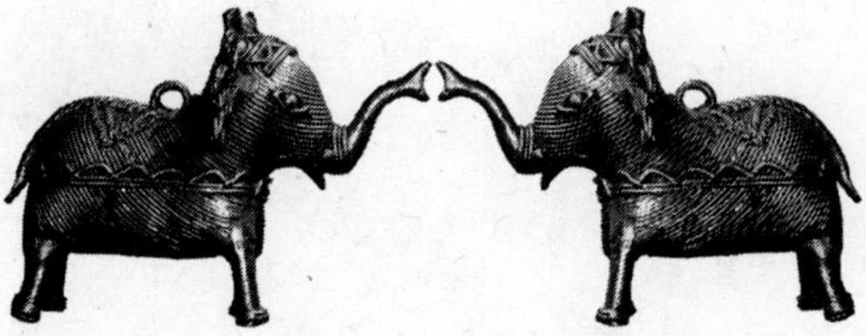

What Did Indian Philosophers Believe?

JOHANNES BRONKHORST

1. Did the Indians believe their myths?

1.1. Introduction

Popular writers about Christianity sometimes maintain that only modern fundamentalist Christians take the Biblical creation story literally; no one in pre-modern days, they say, ever thought of doing so. Karen ARMSTRONG represents this view in various publications, in one of which she states (2005b): 'Until the advent of the modern period, nobody would have regarded the six-day creation story [of the Bible] as a literal, historical account.'[1] She is not the only one to maintain such a position. Some scholars of religion hold quite generally that myths were not taken literally in earlier days.[2] Ninian SMART (1996: 138), to mention but one example, has the following to say about myths in general and about the way they are understood at present and in the past:

> '[It] seems ... that we are moving out of the age of what may be called "fanciful" myth into that of "factual" myth. I do not mean by this that the more fanciful myths have not been believed in some sense to be factual: describing reality. But now there is a more earthbound understanding of what is factual. So Adam and Eve have to be real persons: or if they are not they have to be symbolic representations of a real human condition that can be described metaphysically or existentially.'

---

[1] She elaborates these ideas in ARMSTRONG (2005a).

[2] An example of a philosopher who holds similar views is Mary MIDGLEY (2006: 51): 'For a long time this kind of language [i.e. mythical language—JB] was reasonably well understood. Since the mid-nineteenth century, however, there has been a disastrous attempt to get rid of it, keeping only literal statements of fact.'

Logic and Belief in Indian Philosophy
Warsaw Indological Studies 3 (2010) 19–44.

And again (SMART (1996: 161)):

> 'As we move towards another century and into it, the divergence, considered phenomenologically, between the old myth and the new history tends to fade away. Legends of Moses and Krishna and the Buddha and Confucius tend to solidify. Since historicity is regarded as a plus, there is a trend towards thinking of the legendary as historically real. In any case, it becomes a problem to distinguish between the two.'

These passages suggest that, at least according to Smart, there was a time when myths were not understood to be true in an earthbound factual manner, not historically real. Unfortunately he does not elaborate or clarify this suggestion, and nor does he give any specification as to the date or period during which the important transition toward the new understanding of myths took place. Why should such a change take place? And what is it that supposedly pushes 'us' to change our understanding of myths? Neither Smart nor Armstrong propose answers to these questions.

Some support for the position of Smart and Armstrong may be derived from a well-known article by Raffaele PETTAZZONI (1954 /1984), whose original Italian version came out in 1948. It points out that many societies described by ethnographers distinguish between 'true stories' and 'false stories', with creation myths typically belonging to the 'true stories'. However, as PETTAZZONI (1954 /1984: 102) points out, 'myth is true history because it is sacred history, not only by reason of its contents but also because of the concrete sacral forces which it sets going.' The truth of myths 'has no origin in logic, nor is it of a historical kind; it is above all of a religious and more especially a magical order' (p. 103). These myths remain 'true' as long as the world they are part of remains by and large the same. However, PETTAZZONI (1954 /1984: 108) observes, 'a day will come when the myths of beginnings too will lose their "truth" and become "false stories" in their turn ... This will occur when their world, built up on the ruins of the first one, collapses in its turn to give place to a later and different structure.'

Pettazzoni's remarks are interesting, but strictly speaking they only concern 'truth' in inverted commas. If I understand them correctly, 'truth' in inverted commas may be paraphrased with the help of some such word as 'applicability'. Pettazzoni's remarks leave open the question whether or not members of the societies involved literally believe even their 'true' stories ('true' in inverted commas). They suggest that these people may normally not bother about their ordinary truth, they may never think about it. The question whether they believe their stories may therefore be misplaced, inapplicable in the situation.

This reflection is related to a known difficulty in anthropology, whose description I borrow from the philosopher Daniel C. DENNETT's book *Breaking the Spell* (2006: 161):

> 'Many anthropologists have observed that when they ask their native informants about "theological" details—their gods' whereabouts, specific history, and methods of acting in the world—their informants find the whole inquiry puzzling. Why should they be expected to know or care anything about *that*? Given this widely reported reaction, we should not dismiss the corrosive hypothesis that many of the truly exotic and arguably incoherent doctrines that have been unearthed by anthropologists over the years are artefacts of inquiry, not pre-existing creeds. It is possible that persistent questioning by anthropologists has composed a sort of innocently collaborative fiction, newly minted and crystallised dogmas generated when questioner and informant talk past each other until a mutually agreed-upon story results. The informants deeply believe in their gods—"Everybody knows they exist!"—but they may never before have thought about these details (maybe nobody in the culture has!), which would explain why their convictions are vague and indeterminate. Obliged to elaborate, they elaborate, taking their cues from the questions posed.'

The suspicion that some myths may be artefacts of inquiry rather than pre-existing creeds gains in interest in the light of the recent and much discussed claim that the Pirahã, a people of Amazonian hunter-gatherers, have no creation myths at all.[3]

It may not be justified to extrapolate directly from anthropological literature to societies with sophisticated intellectual traditions, but it may make us aware of possible difficulties. These latter societies may preserve ancient myths by means of writing or refined mnemonic devices well beyond their sell-by date. How do educated readers or listeners consider them?

Scholars of classical Greece have repeatedly addressed the question whether the ancient Greeks believed their myths. The question is complicated and cannot, it turns out, be answered with a simple yes or no.[4] It is yet justified to ask the question, if for no other reason than that classical Greece witnessed the coming into being of a tradition of critical reflection. It would certainly be interesting to know whether there were issues that were considered beyond questioning, and the realm of myths might conceivably be one of those.

---

[3] See EVERETT (2005), DOUGLAS (2006).

[4] See VEYNE (1983), LLOYD (1990: 44 f.).

This way of formulating the problem shows that the exact meaning of the word 'myth' is of little importance for its solution. It does not matter here whether myth is a meaningful or useful concept in and outside ancient Greece, nor whether the Greeks themselves had a concept corresponding to it. All that counts here is that critical reflection in ancient Greece was sooner or later confronted with traditional forms of knowledge, usually presented in narrative form. Was this confrontation experienced as one by the individuals involved? And what was its outcome? These questions are interesting, even if—as appears to be the case—their answers are multiple and complex.

Some thinkers point out that Judeo-Christian religion distinguished itself, already in Antiquity, from Greek and other religions in that reflexive thought about myth became an integral part of it. The requirement of truth in religion, it is claimed, pervades all of ancient Christian thought.[5] This, if true, would distinguish the Judeo-Christian tradition from other religions.

I have already pointed out that it is not clear whether or to what extent myths—I use the word again in its broadest sense—are believed to be true in societies which have no strong tradition of critical reflection. One can easily imagine a society many of whose members, even though thoroughly familiar with its myths, have never asked themselves the question whether they are true or not. One thing seems however clear. In a society in which there *is* a tradition of critical reflection, at least some members will sometimes ask this question. Some of them will answer in the positive, and hence be conscious believers; others will decide that some of these myths, or all of them, are not, or probably not, literally true.

1.2. An Indian creation myth[6]

Classical India, like classical Greece, had many myths, and a tradition of critical reflection that expressed itself primarily in its philosophies. A number of thinkers, many of them belonging to different philosophical schools, were engaged in an ongoing debate, in which each tried to improve his own system in the light of the criticism he received or might receive from others. The consequences of this debate were far-reaching, and various school doctrines appear to have been adopted, even invented, for no other reason than to improve the inner coherence and consistency of the different philosophies.

---

[5] STROUMSA (2005: 34–36), with a reference to ASSMANN (1997: 1–8).

[6] This section and the following one use material found also in BRONKHORST (2001); see further BRONKHORST (2007: 212 ff.).

What attitude did these philosophers have with regard to their myths?[7] This question is important, for it may enable us to understand these thinkers better. For when classical Indian philosophers defend their positions against each other, they normally defend the philosophical aspects of their beliefs, leaving other aspects—such as the 'mythical' ones—out of the discussion. Yet there is at least one myth which is so often referred in the surviving literature that some conclusions can be drawn about it.

This myth is particularly important in the Brahmanical context. It is a creation myth which tells us not only about the creation of the world, but also about that of the different classes (*varṇa*) in human society.[8] It is important for Brahmanism, for the division of society into these four classes is the cornerstone of their vision of society. No doubt for this reason it is told or referred to in many texts, not always in exactly the same form. The story finds its classic, and as far as we know earliest, exposition in the *Puruṣa-sūkta* of the *R̥g-veda* (RV 10.90). This hymn recounts how the world and its inhabitants came about as a result of a sacrifice in which the primordial giant, Puruṣa, is dismembered. The hymn does however more: it also explains how the proper hierarchy of human beings came about.[9] The for us most important parts read, in the (slightly adjusted) translation of Wendy DONIGER O'FLAHERTY (1983: 30–31):

> '[1] The Man has a thousand heads, a thousand eyes, a thousand feet. He pervaded the earth on all sides and extended beyond it as far as ten fingers. [2] It is the Man who is all this, whatever has been and whatever is to be. He is the ruler of immortality, when he grows beyond everything through food. … [6] When the gods spread the sacrifice with the Man as the offering, spring was the clarified butter, summer the fuel, autumn the oblation. … [11] When they divided the Man, into how many parts did they apportion him? What do they call his mouth, his two arms and thighs and feet? [12] His mouth became the Brahmin; his arms were made into the Warrior, his thighs the Common man, and from his feet the Servant was born.'

---

[7] The question what story is to be counted as myth, and which not, will not be addressed here. The Indian epics constitute a marginal case. Note here that the sixteenth-century commentator Maheśvaratīrtha states, with regard to Vālmīki's *Rāmāyaṇa* (ad 2.41.10 vulg.), that everything that happened in it was absolutely real; see POLLOCK (1993: 279).

[8] Note that this is not the only creation myth that accounts for the origin of the classes; for other examples, see MUIR (1972).

[9] OBERLIES (1998: 381–382): 'In dem diese Opferung beschreibenden Sūkta … wird nicht nur die Entstehung der Welt und der sie bevölkernden Wesen—im weitesten Sinne—erklärt, sondern auch die Ordnung der Gesellschaft.'

It is not obvious how exactly the composer and early listeners of this hymn believed this process to have taken place. It may not be all that difficult to imagine such a sacrifice, even though its size exceeds that of the world. However, some of the details pose serious challenges to our power of imagination. How, for example, does one use spring as clarified butter, summer as fuel, autumn as fuel in a sacrifice? And there are serious problems related to the division in which the primordial giant's mouth became the Brahmin, his arms the Warrior (*rājanyà*), his thighs the Common man (*vaíśya*), and his feet the Servant (*śūdrá*). These four classes of human beings—this seems to be the first mention of the four *varṇa*s in Indian literature—are referred to in the singular. Do we have to conclude that just one Brahmin, one Rājanya, one Vaiśya and one Śūdra were created at that time? In that case one could wonder where they found partners so as to procreate. Should we perhaps understand the text differently, in the sense that all Brahmins were created out of the mouth of primordial Man, all Rājanyas from his arms, all Vaiśyas from his thighs, and all Śūdras from his feet?

It might be objected that myths should not be read like this. No cosmogonic myth, it could be maintained, was ever understood in such a literal fashion. It cannot be questioned or analysed in the way a modern scientific theory is subjected to questioning and analysis. Myths have to be interpreted and should not be taken at face value. When a Bororo individual says 'I am a parakeet' this must be understood to mean—according to some anthropologists—'As a man, I am to other men what a parakeet is to other birds.'[10] With regard to the *Puruṣa-sūkta*, M. Sunder Raj points out that it 'is an allegory, a poetic vision, and is not to be taken in a literal sense.'[11]

The hymn to Puruṣa is, in the words of Louis RENOU (1965: 8), 'the major source of cosmogonic thought in ancient India'; elsewhere he says (1956: 12):

> 'Il n'y a guère de poème cosmologique de l'Atharvaveda où l'on ne retrouve quelque allusion voilée au mythe du Géant sacrifié et au schéma évolutif qui en résulte … C'est encore le thème du Géant qui sous les traits de Prajâpati 'le seigneur des Créatures' ressurgit dans les Brāhmaṇa et en commande la plupart des avenues.'

Jan GONDA (1968: 101) calls it 'the foundation stone of Viṣṇuite philosophy'. Especially the part concerning the creation of the four main divisions of society, the four *varṇa*s, has been taken over in numerous texts belonging both to the Vedic and to the classical period. We find it, for example, in the *Taittirīya-saṁhitā* (7.1.1.4–6), the *Mahā-bhārata* (3.187.13; 8.23.32; 12.73.4–5; 12.285.5–6), the *Rāmāyaṇa*

---

[10] WEINER (1994: 573), who ascribes this recast to Lévi-Strauss.

[11] DANDEKAR (1993: 27).

(3.13.29–30), but also in the first chapter of the *Manu-smṛti*. The Lord, we there read, created, 'so that the worlds and people would prosper and increase, from his mouth the Brahmin, from his arms the Kṣatriya, from his thighs the Vaiśya, and from his feet the Śūdra.'[12] Elsewhere the same text refers to this myth as common background knowledge, used as an alternative way of speaking about the four *varṇas*.[13] The *Puruṣa-sūkta* remains important in later literature and practice.[14]

These and many other references to the myth of the *Puruṣa-sūkta* do not allow us to decide with certainty whether the authors concerned took this myth literally. They do however show that this myth remained 'true' in Pettazzoni's sense in remaining relevant to a social situation that continued to prevail, or that should prevail according to those primarily concerned, the Brahmins. But did they think that the myth was true in the sense of corresponding to reality? The answer, it seems, was yes for at least some Brahmanical thinkers. There is indeed evidence that Indian thinkers, or at least some of them, did take the myth of the creation of the four *varṇas* out of the initial giant quite seriously, i.e. literally—as being literally true. Part of the story is retold in the *Padārtha-dharma-saṁgraha*, also known as *Praśastapāda-bhāṣya*, which is the classical surviving treatise of the Vaiśeṣika philosophy, written by Praśasta, alias Praśastapāda. The passage concerned reads:[15]

---

[12] MDhŚ 1.31:

> *lokānāṁ tu vivṛddhy-arthaṁ mukha-bāhûru-pādataḥ /*
> *brāhmaṇaṁ kṣatriyaṁ vaiśyaṁ śūdraṁ ca niravartayat //*

The translation follows, with modifications, DONIGER–SMITH (1991). The *Bhaviṣya-purāṇa* has the same verse, see LÁSLÓ (1971: 117).

[13] MDhŚ 10.45:

> *mukha-bāhûru-pajjānāṁ yā loke jātayo bahiḥ /*
> *mleccha-vācaś cârya-vācaḥ sarve te dasyavaḥ smṛtāḥ //*

Tr. DONIGER–SMITH (1991: 241):

> 'All of those castes who are excluded from the world of those who were born from the mouth, arms, thighs, and feet (of the primordial Man) are traditionally regarded as aliens, whether they speak barbarian languages or Aryan languages.'

See also MDhŚ 1.87, 92–94; 8.270; 10.45.

[14] See SHENDE (1965), GONDA (1977: 98–105 (390–397)).

[15] PBh, p. 11: *evaṁ samutpanneṣu caturṣu mahā-bhūteṣu mahêśvarasyâbhidhāna-mātrāt taijasebhyo 'ṇubhyaḥ pārthiva-paramâṇu-sahitebhyo* (variants: *pārthivâdi-paramâṇu-sahitebhyo, pārthivâṇu-sahitebhyo*) *mahad aṇḍam ārabhyate* (some editions read: *utpadyate*). *tasmiṁś catur vadana-kamalaṁ sarva-loka-pitāmahaṁ* (variant: *catur-vadana-kamala-sakala-loka-pitāmahaṁ*) *brahmāṇaṁ sakala-bhuvana-sahitam utpādya prajāsarge viniyuṅkte* (variant: *niyuṅkte*). *sa ca mahêśvareṇa viniyukto* (variant: *niyukto*) *brahmā 'tiśaya-jñāna-vairāgyâiśvarya-sampannaḥ prāṇināṁ* (variant: *sarva-prāṇināṁ*) *karma-vipākaṁ viditvā karmânurūpa-jñāna-bhogâyuṣaḥ sutān prajāpatīn mānasān manu-deva-ṛṣi-pitṛ-gaṇān* (variant: *manūn deva-°*) ***mukha-bāhûru-***

> ‘When in this way the four composite elements have come into existence, a great egg is formed, caused solely by God’s meditation/volition, out of atoms of fire with an admixture of atoms of earth (i.e. gold). In it [God] creates Brahmā, with four faces like so many lotuses, the grandfather of all worlds, and all worlds; he then enjoins him with the duty of creating living things. That Brahmā, thus enjoined by God, and endowed with abundant knowledge, complete absence of passion and absolute power, knows the effects of the deeds of living beings; he creates the Prajāpatis, his mind-created sons, with knowledge, experience and span of life in accordance with their [past] deeds; [he also creates] the Manus, Devas, Ṛṣis and groups of Pitṛs, the **four *varṇa*s out of his mouth, arms, thighs and feet [respectively]**, and the other living beings, high and low; he then connects them with *dharma*, knowledge, absence of passion and power in accordance with their residue of past deeds.’

In order to correctly evaluate this passage, it is important to realise that the *Padārtha-dharma-saṁgraha* is no book of stories and myths, and nor is it meant to be read as literature. Quite on the contrary, it is a very serious treatise about the constitution of reality, of which it presents a coherent and systematic explanation. It is hard to believe that any passage of this serious work, including the one just cited, was not meant to convey reality, not metaphorically, but in a most literal manner. It is true that the contents of this passage may not have been part of the Vaiśeṣika philosophy during the time preceding Praśasta. There are reasons to believe that the very notion of a creator God may have been introduced into the system by this author, and that he borrowed this notion from the religious current to which he may have belonged, that of the Pāśupatas. This does not, however, mean that this notion is to be taken less seriously than the remainder of the *Padārtha-dharma-saṁgraha*.[16]

The explicit mention of the creation of the four varṇas out of the mouth, arms, thighs and feet respectively of the creator in a work as serious and reality-oriented as Praśasta’s *Padārtha-dharma-saṁgraha* strongly suggests that at least one participant in the tradition of critical reflection accepted this myth as literally true. It seems likely that there were other Brahmanical intellectuals of that period who did the same.

pādataś caturo varṇān anyāni côccâvacāni bhūtāni (variants: *bhūtāni ca*; *anyāni côccâvacāni ca sṛṣṭvā*) ***sṛṣṭvā***, *āśayânurūpair dharma-jñāna-vairāgyâiśvaryaiḥ saṁyojayatīti*.

[16] On the philosophical reasons underlying the introduction of the notion of a creator God into Vaiśeṣika, see BRONKHORST (2000: § 7, esp. p. 37 f.); further BRONKHORST (1996).

As is well known, the Buddhists did not accept the Brahmanical division of human society into four classes, nor did they accept the myth that lent credence to it. A number of Buddhist authors criticise the very same myth which Praśasta (and probably many others with him) explicitly accepted, the myth that the four *varṇa*s were originally created out of the mouth, arms, thighs and feet of the original being. They do so by showing that it is incoherent, or that it has implications which even the Brahmins would not be willing to accept.[17]

We find such criticism already in the *Aggañña-sutta* of the *Dīgha-nikāya*. The Brahmin Vāseṭṭha here reports the position of his fellow-Brahmins, according to whom 'only the Brahmins are the real sons of Brahmā, born from his mouth, born from Brahmā, produced by Brahmā, heirs of Brahmā.'[18] The Buddha responds that they maintain this position, 'forgetting what is old' (*porāṇaṁ assarantā*). This expression has been variously interpreted by the commentators: some speak of an old tradition,[19] others of ancient history.[20] The context however favours a third interpretation: these Brahmins forget the past, that is to say, the relatively recent past of their own birth. This is shown by what follows.[21] According to the Buddha it is undeniable that the wives of Brahmins (*brāhmaṇānaṁ brāhmaṇiyo*) have their periods, become pregnant, give birth and feed; in spite of being thus born from a human womb, the Brahmins maintain that they are born from Brahmā.[22] In doing so, these Brahmins insult (*abbhācikkhanti*) Brahmā.[23] This criticism is obviously based on the most literal interpretation of the Brahmanical myth. The claim of the Brahmins of being born from Brahmā is in conflict with their birth from a human mother. In other word, the Brahmins are credited with the belief of having been born, at the beginning of their present life, from the mouth of Brahmā.

A somewhat more recent text, the *Vajra-sūcī*, proceeds in a similar manner. One finds here the following argument:

[17] For the following paragraphs, see ELTSCHINGER (2000), RENOU (1960: 43).

[18] DN III, p. 81: *brāhmaṇā va brahmuno puttā orasā mukhato jātā brahma-jā brahma-nimmitā brahma-dāyādā.* Cp. MEISIG (1988: 80 f.) for the Chinese parallels.

[19] WALSHE (1987: 408): 'ancient tradition'; RHYS DAVIDS (1921: 78): 'ancient lore'.

[20] Sv III, p. 862: *porāṇan ti porāṇakaṁ aggaññaṁ lok'uppattiṁ cariya-vaṁsam*; FRANKE (1913: 275) 'es ist nicht uralte Erinnerung an eine wirkliche Tatsache.'

[21] The following remarks also occur in the *Assalāyana-sutta* (MN II, p. 148).

[22] DN III, pp. 81–82: *dissanti kho pana vāseṭṭha brāhmaṇānaṁ brāhmaṇiyo utuniyo pi gabbhiniyo pi vijāyamānā pi pāyamānā pi, te ca brāhmaṇa yonijā va samānā evam āhaṁsu: brāhmaṇā va ... brahmuno puttā orasā mukhato jātā brahma-jā brahma-nimmitā brahma-dāyādā.* Cp. MEISIG (1988: 86 f.).

[23] This last remark does not occur in the *Assalāyana-sutta*.

> 'There is another defect [in your proposition]. If the Brahmin is born from the mouth, where is the Brahmin woman born from? Certainly from the mouth. Alas! Then she is your sister! So, you do not regard the convention of licit and illicit sexual intercourse! But that is extremely repugnant to the people of this world.'[24]

The *Śārdūlakarṇâvadāna* states essentially the same:

> 'If this world has been created by Brahmā himself, the Brahmin woman is the sister of the Brahmin, the Kṣatriya woman the sister of the Kṣatriya, the Vaiśya woman [the sister] of the Vaiśya, or the Śūdra woman [the sister] of the Śūdra; in case she has been created by Brahmā, [a woman of the same class], being a sister [of her husband], will not be a suitable wife.'[25]

This is not the place to investigate how the Vaiśeṣikas answered, or might have answered, the criticism of the Buddhists. It must here be sufficient to note that the three classical commentaries on Praśasta's *Padārtha-dharma-saṁgraha*—the *Vyomavatī*, the *Nyāya-kandalī*, and the *Kiraṇâvalī*—dedicate in this connection long discussions to the question as to the existence of a creator God, but do not say a word about how this particular myth is to be interpreted so as to avoid contradictions. The discussion stays on a highly abstract, 'philosophical', level, where inferences and logical analyses have their place. The details of the myth, on the other hand, do not receive attention.

Note that a number of Jaina texts, too, criticise the myth of the primordial giant, along with other Brahmanical myths. These texts are part of what may have been a micro-genre of Jaina literature that uses satire to make fun of these stories. Jean-Pierre Osier has recently studied four of these texts that have survived: two versions of the 'Ballad of the rogues' (*Dhūrtâkhyāna*, *Dhuttakkhāṇa*)—one in the Cūrṇi of

---

[24] VSūc$_1$, p. 225 l. 6–8, VSūc$_2$, p. 9 [JJ]: *anyac ca dūṣaṇaṁ bhavati. yadi mukhato jāto brāhmaṇo brāhmaṇyāḥ kuta utpattiḥ. mukhād evêti cet hanta tarhi bhavatāṁ bhaginī-prasaṅgaḥ syāt. tathā gamyāgamyaṁ na sambhāvyate. tac ca loke 'tyanta-viruddham*. Tr. MUKHOPADHYAYA (1960: 20).

[25] Divy(V) no. 33, verses 76–77, p. 332:

yadi tāvad ayaṁ loko brahmaṇā janitaḥ svayam /
brāhmaṇī brāhmaṇa-svasā kṣatriyā kṣatriya-svasā //
atha vaiśyasya vaiśyā vai śūdrā śūdrasya vā punaḥ /
na bhāryā bhaginī yuktā brahmaṇā janitā yadi //

the *Niśītha-sūtra*, the other one by Haribhadra—and two 'Examinations of Dharma' (*Dharma-parīkṣā*), by Hariṣeṇa and Amitagati respectively.[26]

What can we conclude from the above? One gets the impression that those in the Brahmanical tradition were inclined to accept the creation story considered (and other myths) literally, in spite of the difficulties this entailed. One might be tempted to conclude, with Ninian Smart and Karen Armstrong, that perhaps in those pre-modern days no one would dream of understanding a myth literally. This position is however undermined by the fact that the Buddhists (and the Jainas) had no difficulty whatsoever to interpret the myth so literally that they could make fun of it. They had no difficulty imagining all Brahmins being born, literally, from the mouth of the primordial giant, and they drew absurd consequences from this. But if the Buddhists could interpret this myth literally, so could the Brahmins, or at least those Brahmins who had trained themselves as philosophers and debaters. Some of these Brahmins may have silently discarded a literal interpretation of the myth, but some, among them apparently Praśasta, did not, and included the myth, literally understood, in their analytical vision of the world.

1.3. Mīmāṁsā

The Mīmāṁsakas are probably the most orthodox upholders of the Vedic tradition. They present their school of thought as a school of hermeneutics, i.e. textual interpretation. These Mīmāṁsakas were therefore directly involved in the question we are studying: do we have to take everything in the *Veda* literally?

These Vedic hermeneuts are aware of the difficulties that may arise, and they discuss it in their classical text, the commentary by Śabara on the *Mīmāṁsā-sūtra*. Śabara points out that certain Vedic statements are hard to accept if interpreted literally. Śabara gives the following examples: 'The trees sat down for a sacrificial session'; 'The snakes sat down for a sacrificial session'; 'The old bull sings mad [songs].'[27] These statements are in conflict with our experience. Śabara does not ask us to accept them. On the contrary, he proposes a form of Vedic interpretation that allows us not to accept any descriptive statement at its face value.

The justification for this radical position lies in the Mīmāṁsā conception of what the *Veda* really is. It is a corpus of texts, to be sure. But it is a corpus of texts that has no beginning in time, and therefore no author. The reasoning is simple. An

[26] OSIER (2005: 45, 80 f.) for the myth of the primordial giant; see also OSIER (2000) and OSIER–BALBIR (2004: 76).

[27] ŚBh 1.1.32: *vanas-patayaḥ sattram āsata; sarpāḥ sattram āsata; jarad-gavo gāyati mattakāni.* None of these three citations seems traceable in the *Veda* as we know it.

author, any author, composes his text at a specific moment of time. A text that was always there can have no author, because it has no beginning. Such a text cannot refer to any historical event either, for such a reference can only be made after the event. Śabara pronounces himself on this issue in connection with the Vedic statement which says that the god Prajāpati extracted his omentum.[28] Śabara discusses this statement and observes: 'If a historical event were to be referred to, the *Veda* would be open to the charge of having a beginning.'[29] Similarly, the Vedic statement 'We grasped your right hand, o Indra'[30], if taken literally, would be open to the same charge.[31] Elsewhere (1.1.31) Śabara is obliged to give different interpretations to expressions such as *prāvāhaṇi* and *auddālaki*, which normally signify 'son of Pravāhaṇa' and 'son of Uddālaka';[32] of course, the *Veda* cannot refer to historical personalities or their sons.

This procedure is radical, as I pointed out already. It does not permit a literal interpretation of large portions of the Vedic texts. The creation myth which we discussed above falls by the wayside, as do all other stories, whether mythical or historical. In the end Śabara and his co-Mīmāṁsakas decide that only injunctions are to be taken literally. Mīmāṁsakas like Śabara did not believe any of the Vedic myths. The criticisms uttered by the Buddhists against a Vedic creation myth was no threat to them.

One may wonder whether there were really many Brahmins in ancient India who spent their lives performing complex and demanding rituals that were not accompanied by myths, in whatever way understood. We will return to this question later on. Theoretically the classical Mīmāṁsā position is coherent: Yes, Vedic rituals have to be performed, but no, the myths and other stories that are told in those same *Veda*s should not be taken literally. One wonders how many people were satisfied with ritual obligations that would, so to say, be hanging in the air.

It is yet noteworthy that the custom to give metaphorical interpretations to myths continued undeterred in India, particularly so in connection with the stories told in the *Rāmāyaṇa* and *Mahā-bhārata*. Christopher MINKOWSKI (2005) draws attention to the seventeenth century commentator Nīlakaṇṭha, who interprets the whole *Mahā-bhārata* in a non-dualist manner. The story of Manu and the Flood, for example, is about the ontological possibility of *jīvan-mukti*, i.e. the possibility of con-

---

[28] TaitS 2.1.1.4: *sa ātmano vapām udakkhidat.*

[29] ŚBh 1.2.10: *vṛttāntânvākhyāne 'pi vidhīyamāne ādimattā-doṣo vedasya prasajyeta.*

[30] RV 10.47.1 etc.: *jagṛbhmā te dakṣiṇam indra hastaṁ.*

[31] ŚBh 9.1.9: *athâivam ucyate, tasyâitad vacanaṁ yo gṛhītavāṁs tasya hastam iti. ucyate. nâitad adhyavaseyam. ādimattā-doṣo vedasya prasajyate.*

[32] POLLOCK (1989: 608) refers to this passage in an article that draws attention to the non-historical nature of much of Sanskrit literature, possibly in imitation of the *Veda*.

tinuing embodied life after spiritual enlightenment. Manu, seen this way, is the mistaken egoism (*ahaṁkāra*); the fish that saves him is the *jīva*; the boat that Manu builds is his last human embodiment etc. And Nīlakaṇṭha was not alone in providing such allegorical interpretations.

1.4. Purāṇic versus Siddhāntic astronomy

At the beginning of this lecture I talked about the Biblical creation myth that, if taken literally, is in conflict with the findings of science. The Vedic creation myth which we subsequently considered was not accused of being in conflict with science, and yet it was criticised for being in conflict with common sense, or with propriety. We do not normally associate difficulties that arise within Indian religions with a presumed conflict with science, but this is too simplistic a position, as the following example with show.

The Vedic corpus was not the only corpus which was invested with canonical status within the Brahmanical tradition. A subsequent stage of this tradition found expression in the *Purāṇa*s, a large number of texts of great length, and contrary to the *Veda* the texts in this corpus *were* read by numerous Hindus.[33] These *Purāṇa*s present a view of the universe that has been summarised as follows by Christopher MINKOWSKI (2001: 81):

> 'The Purāṇas are consistent in presenting a model of the cosmos in which the earth is a flat horizontal disk in a vertical, egg-shaped universe, in which there are seven heavens above and seven underworlds below. Mount Meru stands at the centre of this disk, and above Meru are suspended a series of wheels, with the Sun, Moon, nakṣatras, Mercury, Venus, Mars, Jupiter, Saturn, and the Saptarṣi stars, in that order, riding on them. Above the Saptarṣi is the pole star. The rising and setting of the Sun, Moon, nakṣatras and planets is explained by the enormous height of Mt. Meru, behind which in their circular rotations above us the celestial bodies are blocked from our sight.
>
> Viewed from above, the disk of the Earth is made up of seven concentric continents with seven intervening oceans. The central continent

[33] These texts contain contradictions, and some of them are aware of it. McComas Taylor (Indology discussion forum, 2 March 2007) draws attention to some relevant passages in the *Śiva-purāṇa*: before this *Purāṇa* arises in the world, 'all the śāstras will contradict one another' (1.2.7), and 'all [other] *Purāṇa*s will clamour on the surface of the earth' (1.2.10); there will be disputes among *tīrtha*s, *mantra*s, places of pilgrimage, *pīṭha*s (seat, throne, sacred place), donations, *deva*s and doctrines (*siddhānta*) (1.2.11–17).

> with Meru at its centre is called the Jambūdvīpa, which is surrounded by the salt ocean. The southernmost portion of Jambūdvīpa is the location for the land of Bhārata. As far as distances are concerned, Mt. Meru is 84,000 yojanas high, Jambūdvīpa is 100,000 yojanas in diameter, the Bhāratavarṣa is 9,000 yojanas in extent, while the disk of the earth as a whole, including all seven continents and seven oceans, and what lies outside them, is 50 crores or 500 million yojanas in diameter.
>
> … this account of the cosmos is found in a number of Purāṇas and can be traced to a common source, which Pingree has argued was probably completed in the latter half of the 2nd century C.E. (Kirfel, 1954: 7–49; Pingree, 1990: 275).'

Besides this mythological model of the universe, there existed in India also a tradition of astronomy which had undergone strong Hellenistic influence. It found expression in a number of texts called *Siddhānta*s. MINKOWSKI (2001: 81) summarises the Siddhāntic view of the universe in the following words:

> 'In the Siddhāntic model of the cosmos the earth is a fixed, non-rotating sphere at the centre of a series of interesting spheres on which the sun, moon, and the various planets and stars revolve around the earth. In this model the planets are ranged above the earth in this order: Moon, Mercury, Venus, Sun, Mars, Jupiter, Saturn, and all the Stars. In this model the diameter of the earth is calculated to be about 1600 yojanas, with a circumference of about 5000 yojanas. This is the model articulated already in the *Paitāmahasiddhānta* of the fifth century, and it is the model taken up in all other astronomical Siddhāntas in India, regardless of their other differences (Pingree, 1990: 276–78).'

It will be clear that these two models of the universe are very different from each other, and that one might say that here a religious point of view was in conflict with a scientific one. The inconsistencies between the Purāṇic and Siddhāntic cosmologies do indeed strike the eye: in the former the earth is flat, while in the latter it is a globe; in the first it has a huge size, in the second it has a manageably small size; etc.[34]

What happened when the two met? MINKOWSKI (2001: 82) gives the following brief résumé:

[34] MINKOWSKI (2001: 82).

> 'As far as we know, [the] mutual inconsistency [between the Purāṇic and Siddhāntic cosmologies] passed largely undiscussed until the mid-ninth century, when the astronomer Lalla turned to a critique of the Purāṇic model in his Siddhānta, the *Śiṣyadhīvṛddhidatantra*. Lalla did attempt to accommodate some elements of the Purāṇic model to the globular earth of the Siddhāntas: Mt. Meru is made the axis inside the earth on which the earth revolves; all the other oceans and continents of the Purāṇic model are assumed to be south of the equator; and the power that drives the interesting spheres is still the Pravaha wind, which is the force that makes the planets and stars revolve around Meru in the Purāṇic model.
>
> Nevertheless Lalla explicitly rejected the improbable Purāṇic assertions that eclipses are caused by Rāhu; that night is caused by Meru blocking the Sun; that the Moon wanes because the gods are drinking the Soma in the moon; that the Moon is higher in the heavens than the Sun is; and that the earth is flat and rests on a support. These criticisms are repeated in later Siddhāntas, especially in Bhāskara II's very influential work, the *Siddhāntaśiromaṇi*, of the 12th century ...'

So far there is a rather clear parallel with the Christian scientist who reinterprets certain Biblical passages and rejects others so as to leave space for his scientific convictions. What happened next in India invites a comparison with the creationism of today. From the sixteenth century onward astronomers and some others started writing treatises to show that there is no contradiction between the Purāṇic and the Siddhāntic models, and that the *Purāṇa*s are right. I cite once again MINKOWSKI (2001: 83–84):[35]

> 'Since the Purāṇas must be true, therefore, it is in their proper interpretation, and in the proper construal of the Siddhāntas, that contradictions can be removed. Typically it is asserted that the Siddhāntas describe only some limited part of the real, Purāṇic world, or else that they describe some alternative, and less actual world, or that the Siddhāntic model is simply a convenient fiction, not literally believed even by the astronomers, but useful for making calendars and calculating the relative latitudes and longitudes of places in our local range of knowledge.'

Here, then, there can be no doubt that the authors concerned believed their myths, literally and not symbolically. It is remarkable that the two different models seem to

[35] See further MINKOWSKI (2000), (2002a), (2002b), (2004).

have coexisted peacefully for a number of centuries. Following this, some professional astronomers made critical remarks with regard to Purāṇic cosmology. Only during the last few centuries did the upholders of tradition strike back with force. Do we have to conclude from this that people had started to attach more value to their traditions, that they had perhaps started to read their traditional texts ever more literally?

The disputes between the upholders of the Purāṇic and the Siddhāntic views of the universe were fierce, and became even more so when Lancelot Wilkinson, the British Political Agent to the court of Bhopal from 1829 to 1841, acted on the belief that the best way to introduce the modern Copernican system of astronomy to learned Indians was through the medium of Sanskrit, and in particular through the instrumentality of the Siddhāntic model of the cosmos. This led to a vivid exchange of pamphlets and treatises, surveyed by MINKOWSKI in a recent publication (2001). The details do not interest us at present. It is however clear that the literal interpretation of ancient religious teachings were at the heart of this debate.

2. Did the Indians believe their philosophies?

It might be argued that the myths we have considered so far—the myth of creation out of a primordial giant, the myth of singing bulls, the mythical concept of the universe—are not part of the core beliefs of Brahmanism, about which unshakeable faith should be expected. To make a comparison with Christianity once again, those who reject, or reinterpret, the creation myth of Genesis may yet remain good and convinced Christians. Their belief, these Christians may think, centres on more vital issues than some stone age myths. The same might be thought of Indian philosophers, who made great efforts to base their philosophical claims on sometimes elaborate arguments, but did not use their reasoning skills (at least not in the surviving philosophical literature) to prove the correctness of the myths of their religions.[36] What is more, these philosophers, while criticising each others' views, never attacked each others' myths. Yet these myths would have been easy targets, if they had been seriously believed in. This may be taken as an indication that, say, Buddhist philosophers did not think that their Brahmanical opponents took the Brahmanical myths seriously, and vice-versa.

[36] LO TURCO (2005) argues that stories, too, can be arguments, and cites a number of modern philosophers to support this claim. Unfortunately the Indian thinkers we are interested in had not read these philosophers. As a result they persisted in their (positivist?) ways and tried to prove their positions with arguments rather than stories. This is even true where this position is a subjective illusionism which denies the existence of the world; see BRONKHORST (1999).

Which are the vital issues of Brahmanism? Or rather: which knowledge did the Brahmins consider vital? It is possible to answer this question, for certain types of knowledge are for many Brahmins an essential precondition for reaching the highest religious goal: liberation from the cycle of rebirths. Philosophers have made efforts to formulate this liberating knowledge as clearly as possible. There are different schools of Brahmanical philosophy, to be sure. This is due to the fact that there were differences of opinion as to what exactly constitutes this liberating knowledge. The Sāṁkhya philosophers, for example, claimed that knowledge of Sāṁkhya was a precondition for reaching the highest goal. The Vaiśeṣika philosophers had a rather different vision of the world, knowledge of which was essential *for them*. And so there were other schools of thought, with equally high claims.

Knowledge of the right philosophy, seen in this way, is extremely important in the Brahmanical tradition (similar applies to Buddhism). Reaching such knowledge was not just a matter of life and death, but far more important: a matter of being liberated from, or hopelessly enmeshed in, the endless cycle of rebirths. Here the certainty of the beliefs concerned could not be taken lightly. There would be no possibility to treat this kind of knowledge in the same way as mythological 'knowledge'. This, at least, is what one would expect.

However, this expectation is confronted with some difficulties.[37] There is a long list of commentators who wrote on philosophies which were clearly not their own. The most famous example is Vācaspatimiśra I (tenth century), who wrote important works in the fields of Advaita Vedānta, Nyāya, Sāṁkhya, Mīmāṁsā and Yoga. Scholars may be tempted to think that Vācaspati changed his convictions several times over, i.e. experienced several conversions, but there is no indication in his works to suggests this (as far as I am aware). One rather has the impression that Vācaspati, by writing all those works, established himself as an authority in all those fields; what he privately believed was not part of this exercise.

Vācaspati does not stand alone.[38] Several Jainas wrote commentaries on Buddhist logical texts: Mallavādin and Durvekamiśra on Dharmottara's *Nyāya-bindu-ṭīkā*, Haribhadra on Śaṅkarasvāmin's *Nyāya-praveśa*. Another Jaina, Abhayatilaka, wrote a commentary on Nyāya, the *Nyāyâlaṅkāra*. Various authors of Mīmāṁsā works quietly dissent from a number of key premises of the tradition, most notably its

[37] Eli Franco and Lawrence MacCrea alerted me to the phenomenon described in what follows. Franco also shared with me his impression that mostly Jainas and Vedantins wrote on other systems. See further below.

[38] It is quite unusual in the history of Indian thought to find members of one school writing commentaries on a text of another school with an eye to refuting its arguments, yet this happened in the case of Śrīharṣa's *Khaṇḍana-khaṇḍa-khādya*, which was in this way attacked by Naiyāyikas and Navya-Naiyāyikas. See POTTER (1977: 15–16).

strict atheism. MacCrea mentions in particular Murāri Miśra, author of the *Aṅgatva-nirukti*, a Mīmāṁsā work, and Lakṣmaṇa, author of the *Tantra-vilāsa*, both in the eighteenth century CE. But already Kumārila-bhaṭṭa (seventh century CE) begins his *Śloka-vārttika* with a dedicatory stanza to Śiva,[39] a feature which his commentator Pārthasārathi Miśra makes an attempt to explain away.[40] Inscriptional evidence from the end of the first millennium CE, too, shows that there were Brahmins who claimed expertise in various incompatible schools of philosophy. The Malhar stone inscription of Jājalladeva, for example, speaks of a Brahmin who 'had no rival in the doctrine of Kāśyapa and in the Sāṁkhyas. He completely mastered the two Mīmāṁsās. He had for his eyes the teaching of Akṣapāda.'[41]

A quick glance at the bibliography of Karl Potter's *Encyclopedia of Indian Philosophies* (EIPh) creates the impression that the more we advance in time, the more scholars felt free to write commentaries on altogether different schools of philosophy; it contains numerous names of authors who appear to have commented on works belonging to different schools. A famous example is Nāgeśa Bhaṭṭa, also known as Nāgoji Bhaṭṭa (around 1700), who made his reputation as a grammarian, but also wrote commentaries in the fields of Nyāya, Sāṁkhya, Yoga, and Advaita Vedānta. I myself have had the privilege of learning from a traditional teacher, Śrīnivāsa Śāstrī, who was a recognised expert in the field of Navya-nyāya, but personally committed to Advaita Vedānta. This double (or triple, or quadruple) allegiance of a large number of traditional scholars has never been made the object of a study, as far as I am aware. It seems however clear that for many of them philosophy did not exhaust their religious commitment. It is hard to obtain precise information, but there is reason to think that many Nyāya philosophers had links with Śaivism, the worship of the god Śiva. A number of thinkers of the 'old' Nyāya-Vaiśeṣika schools are known to have been Śaivas, or even more specifically Pāśupatas; this is true of Praśastapāda (probably), Uddyotakara, Bhāsarvajña, Vādi

---

[39] MŚV, Pratijñādhikaraṇa, 1:

viśuddha-jñāna-dehāya tri-vedī-divya-cakṣuṣe /
śreyaḥ-prāpti-nimittāya namaḥ somârdha-dhāriṇe //

There are further indications suggesting that Kumārila may have been concerned to integrate 'Hinduistic' elements, such as his acceptance of the idea of liberation (see MESQUITA (1994); there is no reason to think that earlier Mīmāṁsakas had accepted this idea, cp. BRONKHORST (2000: 100)). See further below.

[40] Cp. BIARDEAU (1964: 145): 'Est-ce ... que la Mīmāṁsā épuise la croyance religieuse des brahmanes qui l'enseignent ou qu'elle l'ait jamais épuisée? Pour l'époque contemporaine, il est certain que non: les rares Mīmāṁsaka d'aujourd'hui se disent généralement *smārta* et se rattachent donc aux disciples de Śankara.'

[41] GUPTA (1983: 30), with a reference to *Epigraphia Indica* I, p. 44.

Vāgīśvara.[42] Other philosophers may have had other religious convictions which however have left no traces in their works.

Most of the examples here talked about are relatively recent. But the knowledge that there were many recent authors who wrote about more than one system of thought raises questions about early authors who did the same. The most famous example is no doubt Vasubandhu, who is supposed to have converted to the Yogācāra school of Mahāyāna Buddhism, having been a Sautrāntika before. Robert KRITZER (2005) has recently collected numerous passages that show that Vasubandhu's presumably early *Abhidharma-kośa-bhāṣya* was already strongly influenced by the *Yogâcāra-bhūmi*, one of the most prominent early texts associated with the Yogācāra school. This suggests that the legend about Vasubandhu, too, may be in need of renewed reflection.

What, then, did Indian philosophers believe? It appears that, also in the Indian situation, it may not be possible to generalise. Some, it would seem, were willing to believe at least a number of their traditional myths quite literally, others would rather avoid being associated with these improbable tales. Some took the philosophies they wrote about quite literally, others took their distance with regard to at least some of them.

It is tempting, and I think illuminating, to recall in this connection what Wilhelm Halbfass had to say about the Sanskrit doxographies, texts which offer a survey of 'all' or 'six' systems or doctrines. The most well-known of these texts is the *Sarva-darśana-saṁgraha* of Mādhava-Vidyāraṇya (fourteenth century CE), the oldest known is the *Ṣaḍ-darśana-samuccaya* of Haribhadra (eighth century), but there are many others. HALBFASS (1988: 351 ff.) draws attention to the fact that the Indian doxographic literature is largely the work of two religio-philosophical groups—the Jainas and the Advaita Vedāntins. This may not be coincidence. The Jainas had developed a way of presenting non-Jaina points of view in such a way that they appear as partial truths within a context of comprehensive perspectivism. Advaita Vedānta viewed other doctrines as stages on the way to its absolute truth, which was tantamount to their subordination to Advaita Vedānta. To quote HALBFASS (p. 356):

> 'The two traditions (i.e. Jainism and Advaita Vedānta) claim to include and fulfil other doctrines—as a perspectivistic or a hierarchically subsuming inclusivism. They claim that in their ultimate and perhaps hidden meaning these doctrines converge in what is clearly and explicitly

[42] On Praśastapāda, see BRONKHORST (1996); on Uddyotakara, see the final colophon of the *Nyāya-vārttika*; INGALLS (1962: 284); on Bhāsarvajña, see SARMA (1934); on Vādi Vāgīśvara, see RAGHAVAN (1942). See also GERSCHHEIMER (2007: 240): 'l'on regroupe le Nyāya et le Vaiśeṣika sous une même étiquette—parfois *tarka*, ou *śaiva*.'

> taught in Advaita Vedānta (or in Jainism according to the Jainas). This is expressly stated in the introductory verse of the *Sarvasiddhānta-saṁgraha* of Ps.-Śaṅkara: that which, in a variety of forms, all philosophical doctrines express, is the *one* Brahman which is taught by the Upaniṣadic Vedānta.'

But also Bhavya, a Buddhist author of the Madhyamaka school, has an inclusivist attitude with regard to the other schools of thought he describes. As he put it:[43]

> 'The Blessed One has taught the very existence (*astitva*) of the Self (*ātman*) in order to divert (i.e. to remonstrate) those who grasp non-existence and advocate non-existence, [and] those whose minds are impaired by the view (*dr̥ṣṭi*) which negates (*apavāda*) causality (*hetu-phala*). He attracts those and in order to stop attachment to the grasping of a Self (*ātmagraha*) among the adherents of a Self (*ātmavādin*), he teaches: "The Self does not exist" (*ātmā nâsti*). Conventionally (*saṁvr̥titaḥ*), he teaches the abandonment of the Self, and to those who are endowed with receptivity (*kṣānti*) for the vast and profound doctrine (*dharma*), he teaches that in ultimate reality (*paramārthataḥ*) there is neither Self (*ātman*) nor non-Self (*anātman*). Thus the very teachings in the many preachings (*pravacana*) of the Blessed One are taught in accordance with relative (*saṁvr̥ti*) and absolute (*paramārtha*) [truth (*satya*)], so there is no contradiction (*virodha*).'

It can easily be seen that several religio-philosophical groups allowed, even encouraged, their followers to study other systems of thought in detail. It would be worth a separate study to see whether and to what extent the history of Indian philosophy manifests a development from confrontation to subordination. Whatever the outcome of such a study, it seems clear that the answer to our riddle may have to be looked for in the peculiar nature of Jainism, Advaita Vedānta, Madhyamaka Buddhism, and perhaps other schools, which took a wider view of reality, in which there was also place for alternative philosophical positions.

---

[43] *Tarka-jvālā* on *Madhamaka-hr̥daya-kārikā* 8.88, as translated by Qvarnström (1989: 106–107); cited in Kiblinger (2005: 51).

BIBLIOGRAPHY

ARMSTRONG 2005a = Armstrong, Karen: *A Short History of Myth*. Canongate, Edinburgh–New York–Melbourne 2005.

ARMSTRONG 2005b = Armstrong, Karen: Review of RUSE (2005). *New Scientist* 30 July (2005) 42–43.

ASSMANN 1997 = Assmann, Jan: *Moses the Egyptian. The Memory of Egypt in western monotheism*. Harvard University Press, Cambridge (Massachusetts)–London 1997.

BIARDEAU 1964 = Biardeau, Madeleine: *Théorie de la connaissance et philosophie de la parole dans le brahmanisme classique*. Mouton, Parin–La Haye 1964.

BRONKHORST 1996 = Bronkhorst, Johannes: 'God's arrival in the Vaiśeṣika system', *Journal of Indian Philosophy* 24 /3 (1996) 281–294.

BRONKHORST 1999 = Bronkhorst, Johannes: *Langage et réalité: sur un épisode de la pensée indienne*. Bibliothèque de l'École des Hautes Études, Sciences Religieuses 105, Brepols, Turnhout 1999.

BRONKHORST 2000 = Bronkhorst, Johannes: *Karma and teleology: a problem and its solutions in Indian philosophy*. Studia Philologica, Monograph Series, International Institute for Buddhist Studies, Tokyo 2000.

BRONKHORST 2001 = Bronkhorst, Johannes: 'The origin of Mīmāṁsā as a school of thought: a hypothesis', in: Klaus Karttunen, Petteri Koskikallio (eds): *Vidyārṇavavandanam. Essays in Honour of Asko Parpola*. Studia Orientalia 94, Helsinki 2001: 83–103.

BRONKHORST 2007 = Bronkhorst, Johannes: *Greater Magadha. Studies in the culture of early India*. Handbook of Oriental Studies, Section 2 South Asia 19, E.J. Brill, Leiden–Boston 2007.

DANDEKAR 1993 = Dandekar, R.N.: *Vedic Bibliography, Fifth Volume*. Government Oriental Series, Class B, No. 17, Bhandarkar Oriental Research Institute, Poona 1993.

DENNETT 2006 = Dennett, Daniel C.: *Breaking the Spell. Religion as a natural phenomenon*. Allen Lane, London 2006.

DhP = Amitagati: *Dharma-parīkṣā*. Pt. Balchandra Shastri (ed., tr.): *Amitagati-acharya's Dharmaparīkṣā*. Jain Saṁskriti Saṁrakshaka Sangha, Sholapur 1978.

Divy(V) = *Divyâvadāna*. P.L. Vaidya (ed.): *Divyāvadāna*. Buddhist Sanskrit Texts 20, Darbhanga 1959.

DN = *Dīghanikāya*. T.W. Rhys Davids, C.A.F. Rhys Davids, J.E. Carpenter (eds.): *Dīghanikāya*. 3 Vols, Pāli Text Society, London I: 1890, II: 1903, III: 1911.

DONIGER–SMITH 1991 = Doniger, Wendy; Smith, Brian K. (tr.): *The Laws of Manu*. Penguin, Harmondsworth 1991.

DONIGER O'FLAHERTY 1983 = Doniger O'Flaherty, Wendy: *The Rig Veda: an anthology. One hundred and eight hymns, selected, translated and annotated.* Penguin Books, Harmondsworth 1983.

DOUGLAS 2006 = Douglas, Kate: 'Lost for words', *New Scientist* 18 March (2006) 44–47.

EIPh = Potter, Karl H. (ongoing): *Encyclopedia of Indian Philosophies, Bibliography*. http: //faculty.washington.edu /kpotter

ELTSCHINGER 2000 = Eltschinger, Vincent: *'Caste' et philosophie bouddhique. Continuité de quelques arguments bouddhiques contre le traitement réaliste des dénominations sociales.* Wiener Studien zur Tibetologie und Buddhismuskunde 47, Arbeitskreis für Tibetische und Buddhistische Studien Universität Wien, Wien 2000.

EVERETT 2005 = Everett, Daniel L.: 'Cultural constraints on grammar and cognition in Pirahã: another look at the design features of human language', *Current Anthropology* 46 /4 (2005) 621–646.

FRANKE 1913 = Franke, R. Otto: *Dīghanikāya, das Buch der langen Texte des buddhistischen Kanons, in Auswahl übersetzt.* Vandenhoeck & Ruprecht, Göttingen—J.C. Hinrichs'sche Buchhandlung, Leipzig 1913.

GERSCHHEIMER 2007 = Gerschheimer, Gerdi: 'Les "six doctrines de spéculation" (*ṣaṭtarkī*): sur la catégorisation variable des systèmes philosophiques dans l'Inde classique', in: Karin Preisendanz (ed.): *Expanding and Merging Horizons. Contributions to South Asian and Cross-Cultural Studies in Commemoration of Wilhelm Halbfass.* Österreichische Akademie der Wissenschaften, philosophisch-historische Klasse, Denkschriften, 351. Band, Beiträge zur Kultur- und Geistesgeschichte Asiens Nr. 53, Austrian Academy of Sciences Press, Vienna 2007: 239–258.

GONDA 1968 = Gonda, Jan: 'The Mudgalopaniṣad', *Wiener Zeitschrift für die Kunde Südasiens* 12–13 (1968 /1969) 101–113 [1968: Beiträge zur Geistesgeschichte Indiens, Festschrift für Erich Frauwallner].

GONDA 1977 = Gonda, Jan: 'Vedic cosmogony and Viṣṇuite bhakti', *Indologica Taurinensia* 5 (1977) 85–111 [reprinted: *Selected Studies*. Volume VI.1, E.J. Brill, Leiden 1991: 377–403].

GUPTA 1983 = Gupta, Chitrarekha: *The Brahmanas of India. A study based on inscriptions.* Sundeep Prakashan, Delhi 1983.

HALBFASS 1988 = Halbfass, Wilhelm: *India and Europe. An essay in understanding.* State University of New York Press, Albany 1988.

INGALLS 1962 = Ingalls, Daniel H.H.: 'Cynics and Pāśupatas: The Seeking of Dishonor', *Harvard Theological Review* 55 (1962) 281–298.

KIBLINGER 2005 = Kiblinger, Kristin Beise: *Buddhist Inclusivism. Attitudes towards religious others.* Ashgate, Hants (England)–Burlington (USA) 2005.

KIRFEL 1954 = Kirfel, Willibald: *Das Purāṇa vom Weltgebäude (Bhuvanavinyāsa). Die kosmographischen Traktate der Purāṇa's: Versuch einer Textgeschichte.* Bonner Orientalistische Studien, Neue Serie,

Bd. 1, Selbstverlag des Orientalischen Seminars der Universität Bonn, Bonn 1954.

KRITZER 2005 = Kritzer, Robert: *Vasubandhu and the Yogācārabhūmi. Yogācāra elements in the Abhidharmakośabhāṣya*. Studia Philologica Buddhica, Monograph Series 18, The International Institute for Buddhist Studies, Tokyo 2005.

LÁSLÓ 1971 = Lásló, Franz: *Die Parallelversion der Manusmṛti im Bhaviṣyapurāṇa*. Abhandlungen für die Kunde des Morgenlandes XL,2, Franz Steiner Verlag, Wiesbaden 1971.

LLOYD 1990 = Lloyd, Geoffrey Ernest Richard: *Demystifying Mentalities*. Cambridge University Press, Cambridge 1990 [reprinted: 1993].

LO TURCO 2005 = Lo Turco, Bruno: 'The metaphorical logic of the Mokṣopāya', in: Jürgen Hanneder (ed.): *The Mokṣopāya, Yogavāsiṣṭha and Related Texts*. Geisteskultur Indiens, Texte und Studien 7, Shaker, Aachen 2005: 131–138.

MDhŚ = *Mānava-dharma-śāstra* [*Manu-smṛti*]. Patric Olivelle (ed.): *Manu's Code of Law: A critical edition and translation of the Mānava-dharmaśāstra*. Oxford University Press, Oxford 2005.

MEISIG 1988 = Meisig, Konrad: *Das Sūtra von den vier Ständen. Das Aggañña-Sutta im Licht seiner chinesischen Parallelen*. Freiburger Beiträge zur Indologie 20, Otto Harrassowitz, Wiesbaden 1988.

MESQUITA 1994 = Mesquita, Roque: 'Die Idee der Erlösung bei Kumārilabhaṭṭa', *Wiener Zeitschrift für die Kunde Südasiens* 38 (1994) 451–484 [Festschrift Oberhammer].

MIDGLEY 2006 = Midgley, Mary: 'Imagine there's no heaven', *New Scientist* 7 October (2006) 50–51.

MINKOWSKI 2000 = Minkowski, Christopher Z.: 'Nīlakaṇṭha's cosmographical comments in the Bhīṣmaparvan', *Purāṇa* 42 (2000) 24–40.

MINKOWSKI 2001 = Minkowski, Christopher Z.: 'The paṇḍit as public intellectual: the controversy over *virodha* or inconsistency in the astronomical sciences', in: Axel Michaels (ed.): *The Pandit. Traditional scholarship in India*. Manohar, New Delhi 2001: 79–96.

MINKOWSKI 2002a = Minkowski, Christopher: 'The "Bhūgolavicāra": a cosmological manuscript from Jaipur', in: G. U. Thite (ed.): *Subhāṣiṇī: Dr. Saroja Bhate Felicitation Volume*. Prof. Dr. Saroja Bhate Felicitation Committee, Pune 2002: 250–263.

MINKOWSKI 2002b = Minkowski, Christopher: 'Astronomers and their reasons: working paper on Jyotiḥśāstra', *Journal of Indian Philosophy* 30 (2002) 495–514.

MINKOWSKI 2004 = Minkowski, Christopher Z.: 'Competing cosmologies in early modern Indian astronomy', in: Charles Burnett, Jan P. Hogendijk, Kim Plofker and Michio Yano (eds.): *Studies in the History of the Exact Sciences in Honour of David Pingree*. Islamic Philosophy, Theology and Science 54, E.J. Brill, Leiden–Boston 2004: 349–385.

MINKOWSKI 2005 = Minkowski, Christopher: 'What makes a work traditional? On the success of Nīlakaṇṭha's Mahābhārata commentary', Federico Squarcini (ed.): *Boundaries, Dynamics and Construction of Traditions in South Asia.* Firenze University Press/ Munshiram Manoharlal, Florence/Delhi 2005: 225–252.

MN = Trenckner, V.; Chalmers, R. (eds.): *Majjhima-Nikāya.* 3 Vols, Pāli Text Society, London 1888–1899.

MS = Jaimini: *Mīmāṁsā-sūtra.* Subbah Śāstrī (ed.): *Mīmāṁsā-darśanam.* Ānandāśrama Sanskrit Series 97, Poona 1973–1984.

MŚV = Kumārila Bhaṭṭa: *Mīmāṁsā-śloka-vārttika.* Svāmī Dvārikādāsa Śāstrī: *Ślokavārttika of Śrī Kumārila Bhaṭṭa, with the commentary Nyāyaratnākara of Śrī Pārthasārthi Miśra.* Ratna Publications, Varanasi 1978.

MUIR 1972 = Muir, John: *Original Sanskrit texts on the origin and history of the people of India, their religion and institutions. Volume first: Mythical and legendary accounts of the origin of caste, with an enquiry into its existence in the Vedic age.* 3d edition, rewritten and greatly enlarged. Oriental Publishers, Delhi 1972 [first edition: 1890].

MUKHOPADHYAYA 1960 = Mukhopadhyaya, Sujitkumar: *The Vajrasūcī of Aśvaghoṣa. A study of the Sanskrit text and Chinese version.* Revised second edition. Visvabharati, Santiniketan 1960.

OBERLIES 1998 = Oberlies, Thomas: *Die Religion des Ṛgveda. Erster Teil: Das religiöse System des Ṛgveda.* Publications of the De Nobili Research Library 26, Gerold/Motilal Banarsidass, Wien/Delhi 1998.

OSIER 2000 = Osier, Jean-Pierre: 'Une critique satirique des normes brahmaniques chez les jaina: Dhūrtākhyāna de Haribhadra et Dharmaparīkṣā de Hariṣeṇa', in: Marie-Luce Barazer-Billoret, Jean Fezas (ed.): *La norme et son application dans le monde indien.* École française d'Extrême-Orient, Paris 2000: 139–153.

OSIER 2005 = Osier, Jean-Pierre: *Les jaïna. Critiques de la mythologie hindoue.* Cerf, Paris 2005.

OSIER–BALBIR = Osier, Jean-Pierre; Balbir, Nalini: *Haribhadra, Ballade des coquins.* Flammarion, Paris 2004.

PBh = Praśastapāda: *Praśastapāda-bhāṣya* (*Padârtha-dharma-saṁgraha*). Johannes Bronkhorst, Yves Ramseier (eds.): *Word Index to the Praśastapādabhāṣya: A complete word index to the printed editions of the Praśastapādabhāṣya.* Motilal Banarsidass, Delhi 1994.

PETTAZZONI 1954 /1984 = Pettazzoni, Raffaele: 'The truth of myths' (English translation), in: Raffaele Pettazzoni: *Essays on the History of Religions*, Leiden 1954: 11–23 [reproduced in: Alan Dundes (ed.): *Sacred Narrative.* University of California Press, Berkeley 1984: 98–109; Italian original: 'Verità del mito', *Studi e materiali di storia delle religioni* 21 (1947–48) 104–116].

PINGREE 1990 = Pingree, David: 'The Purāṇas and jyotiḥśāstra: astronomy', *Journal of the American Oriental Society* 110 /2 (1990) 274–280.

POLLOCK 1989 = Pollock, Sheldon: 'Mīmāṁsā and the problem of history in traditional India', *Journal of the American Oriental Society* 109 (1989) 603–610.

POLLOCK 1993 = Pollock, Sheldon: 'Rāmāyaṇa and political imagination in India', *Journal of Asian Studies* 52 /2 (1993) 261–297.

POTTER 1977 = Potter, Karl H.: *Encyclopedia of Indian Philosophies, II: Indian Metaphysics and Epistemology. The tradition of Nyāya-Vaiśeṣika up to Gaṅgeśa.* Motilal Banarsidass, Delhi 1977.

QVARNSTRÖM 1989 = Qvarnström, Olle: *Hindu Philosophy in Buddhist Perspective. The Vedāntatattvaviniścaya chapter of Bhavya's Madhyamaka-hṛdayakārikā.* Lund Studies in African and Asian Religions 4, Plus Ultra, Lund 1989.

RENOU 1956 = Renou, Louis: *Hymnes spéculatifs du Véda.* Connaissance de l'Orient, Gallimard /Unesco, Paris 1956.

RENOU 1960 = Renou, Louis: *Études védiques et pâṇinéennes, tome VI: Le destin du Véda dans l'Inde.* Publications de l'Institut de Civilisation Indienne 10, E. de Boccard, Paris 1960.

RENOU 1965 = Renou, Louis: *The Destininy of the Veda in India.* Motilal Banarsidass, Delhi 1965 [English translation of RENOU (1960)].

RHYS DAVIDS 1921 = Rhys Davids, T.W.; Rhys Davids, C.A.F. (tr.): *Dialogues of the Buddha—translated from the Pāli of the Dīgha Nikāya.* Part III, The Pāli Text Society, Oxford University Press, London 1921 [reprinted: 1977].

RUSE 2005 = Ruse, Michael: *The Evolution-Creation Struggle.* Harvard University Press, Cambridge (Massachusetts)–London 2005.

RV = *Ṛg-veda-saṁhitā.*

RAGHAVAN 1942 = Raghavan, V.: 'The works of Vādi Vāgīśvara', *Adyar Library Bulletin* 6/1 (1942) 34–40.

SARMA 1934 = Sarma, Dasaratha: 'The name of the author of the Nyāyasāra', *Indian Historical Quarterly* 10 (1934) 163–164.

SHENDE 1965 = Shende, N. J.: *The Puruṣa-sūkta in the Vedic literature.* Publications of the Centre of Advanced Studies in Sanskrit, Class A No. 4, University of Poona, Poona 1965.

SMART 1996 = Smart, Ninian: *Dimensions of the Sacred. An anatomy of the world's beliefs.* HarperCollins, London 1996.

STROUMSA 2005 = Stroumsa, Guy G.: *La fin du sacrifice. Les mutations religieuses de l'Antiquité tardive.* Odile Jacob, Paris 2005.

Sv = Buddhaghosa: *Sumaṅgala-vilāsinī, Dīgha-nikāya-aṭṭha-kathā.* T.W. Rhys Davids, J.E. Carpenter, W. Stede (eds.): *Sumaṅgala-vilāsinī, Dīghanikāya-aṭṭhakathā.* 3 volumes, Pāli Text Society, London 1886–1932.

ŚBh = Śabara-svāmin: *Mīmāṁsā-śābara-bhāṣya*. See: MS.

TaitS = *Taittirīya-saṁhitā*. Ānandāśrama edition.

VEYNE 1983 = Veyne, Paul: *Les grecs ont-ils cru à leurs mythes? Essai sur l'imagination constituante*. Éditions du Seuil, Paris 1983.

VSūc = *Vajra-sūcī*. (1) See: WEBER (1860). (2) See: MUKHOPADHYAYA (1960).

WALSHE 1987 = Walshe, Maurice (tr.): *The Long Discourses of the Buddha. A translation of the Dīgha Nikāya*. Wisdom, Boston 1987 [reprinted: 1995].

WEBER 1860 = Weber, A.: 'Über die Vajrasūcī (Demantnadel) des Açvaghosha', *Abhandlungen der königlichen Akademie der Wissenschaften zu Berlin*, philos.-histor. Kl., 3, 1859 (1860) 205–264.

WEINER 1994 = Weiner, James F.: 'Myth and metaphor', in: Tim Ingold (ed.): *Companion Encyclopedia of Anthropology*. Routledge, London–New York 1994: 591–612.

Pramāṇa, Logic and Belief

CLAUS OETKE

— 1 —

Unlike many papers read on conferences about Indian philosophy the present essay will not primarily deal with something which is found in texts but something which is not found, or more exactly with something which is conspicuous by its absence. The idea of belief or some comparable notion can hardly be encountered as a topic in textual passages in which epistemological issues are discussed, and this holds good in particular for passages dealing with the so-called *pramāṇa*s as well as those which focus on matters that are commonly considered as topics of logic in its Indian variety. This is a remarkable fact even if hardly anybody has found that circumstance surprising. But the topics of *pramāṇa*s and of 'Indian Logic' in particular are in fact essentially related to the issue of belief, and objective connections between those phenomena exist in various regards.

An adequate assessment of the relations between *pramāṇa*, logic and belief requires, however, a terminological clarification or more precisely an elimination of possible misconceptions as far as belief is concerned. Presumably there are intuitions that suggest a contrast between the notions of logic and belief. Those who feel that logic is intimately connected with truth and knowledge whereas belief has its place in religion or generally in areas in which safe knowledge can hardly be attained are probably influenced by such intuitions. But what is the basis of these impressions? I remember that in school I once gave an explanation of 'belief' which reads as follows:

> Belief is if one regards something as true without knowing that it is true.

Nowadays I regard this definition as incorrect and I believe to know why that error arose. A concise description of the mistake is that the idea that lack of a certain ingredient is an essential feature of a concept had been amalgamated with the idea that lack of a certain feature is an essential ingredient of a concept. In other words, from the fact that something is not implied by a term it had been inferred that the term

Logic and Belief in Indian Philosophy
Warsaw Indological Studies 3 (2010) 45–70.

implies the exclusion of the pertinent semantic ingredient. Such a derivation is surely illegitimate. Using linguistic terminology one can say that 'believe' is in contrast to 'know' a 'non-factive' verb. By attributing to a person a belief one does not presuppose that that which is believed is true. But although it is indeed correct to say that somebody might believe something without knowing it this does not entail that nobody can both believe and know one and the same thing (at the same time). As far as one can see the only reasons which are suited to induce the impression that believing something excludes knowledge are connected with presumably universal principles of linguistic behaviour but not with the conceptual content of 'belief' and 'knowledge'. It might be noted in passing that precisely this circumstance could partly explain why belief has not been made topical in Indian theories of *pramāṇa* because of the mistaken idea of a contrast between belief and knowledge. At any rate, I adopt here a view which is widely accepted nowadays, namely that knowledge entails belief but not vice versa, or to put the point in a more stylish manner: 'NN knows that p' entails 'NN believes that p' but not the other way around. The tenet of entailment between knowledge and belief could arouse feelings of uneasiness in view of phenomena of 'implicit knowledge'. Perhaps we should say that every competent speaker of English knows that the following sentence

(i) If everybody go to this meetings then he are not happy.

is grammatically incorrect. But is it equally correct to say that every native speaker of English believes that the above cited sentence is incorrect? Nevertheless, in the present context complications of this sort can be set aside because it suffices to assume that according to a standard way of using terms of knowledge an implication between knowing and believing holds true.

Against the background of the preceding conceptual elucidations one can easily convince himself of the fact that posing questions concerning relations between logic and belief *can* be important and relevant. Two examples suffice for an illustration of this point:

(Q1) If (a proposition) P logically implies (a proposition) Q, does it hold true for everybody that if he knows P he believes Q?

(Q2) If (a proposition) P logically implies (a proposition) Q, does it hold true for everybody that if he knows P and believes Q he knows Q?

A negative answer to Q1 casts a light on the common concept of belief, whereas an affirmative answer would be suited to arouse questions concerning some pertinent concept of belief or logical implication or both. The high relevance of Q2 can be gathered from the consideration that if, given identical concepts of knowing and believing, different answers could be legitimately given to the question, the difference would necessitate the supposition of deviant concepts of logical implication. One can thus *a priori* establish that if an affirmative answer would be suitable with respect to (a number of) logical theories of the Western tradition whereas a negative answer would be appropriate to (a number of) doctrines that are commonly acknowledged as logical theories of the Indian tradition, then the concepts of the notion of logical implication and presumably the import of the term 'logical' must be essentially different in both cases, provided that the deviant verdicts concerning Q2 result on the basis of identical concepts of belief and knowledge. That suffices for a justification of the claim that the mutual connection of the notions of logic, knowledge and belief is an issue of fundamental importance for the assessment and understanding of the area which is often designated by the term 'Indian Logic' and that this holds good independently of empirical details.

— 2 —

Before assessing the question of the treatment of belief in textual sources a further terminological specification concerning the noun 'belief' and the verb 'to believe' is required. The verb occurs both in contexts such as

(ii) Karl believes in acupuncture.

as well as in

(iii) Karl believes that Kathmandu is the capital of Bhutan.

Only the usage of 'believe' in the last example and the corresponding notion of belief will be the topic of the present discussion. It can be set apart from other possible uses of the word by the criterion that 'to believe' is replaceable by 'to regard as true' and the corresponding concept could be distinguished by a term such as 'T-belief', where 'T' signals the specific connection between believing something and regarding something as true. Nevertheless, in the subsequent paragraphs the word 'belief' or 'believe' will be used throughout, so that one must be aware of the fact that a conceptual specification is involved here. It might be worthwhile to note in passing another factor that could have contributed to an unwarranted neglect of the notion of 'belief' in epistemological treatises of the Indian tradition: Philosophically relevant notions or concepts are often not made available by words of a language in a ready made form but must be distilled from current usages of linguistic expressions.

The following examples serve as illustrations and should convey a clearer idea of the exact manner in which the phenomenon of belief in the sense of regarding as true without involving any commitment about actual truth has been disregarded. In the *Praśastapāda-bhāṣya* in which the relevant items acknowledged in the Vaiśeṣika school of philosophy have been systematically classified mental entities, in particular mental events or states have been relegated to the domain of the category 'Quality' (*guṇa*). In this treatise six mental qualities are made topical, five of which, namely 'pleasure' (*sukha*), 'pain' (*duḥkha*), 'desire' (*icchā*), 'dislike' (*dveṣa*) and 'effort' (*prayatna*), cannot be equated with belief in any sense of the word and relate to clearly distinct phenomena of the mental realm. In contrast to these the item which the text mentions in the first place, namely *buddhi*, exhibits an undeniable connection with the cognitive sphere. The two most fundamental statements concerning *buddhi* which the text makes are the following: 1) The terms *buddhi, upalabdhi, jñāna* and *pratyaya* are equivalent (*paryāya*). 2) There are two main varieties of *buddhi*, namely 'knowledge' (*vidyā*) and 'non-knowledge' (*avidyā*). It is easy to see that the term *buddhi*, which might be rendered here by 'cognition', exhibits a significant trait which it shares with the concept of belief as explicated above. Both belief and *buddhi* have in common that they lack entailments with respect to actual truth or more precisely: the extent to which those terms refer to mental states involving a relation to something that can be true the existence of that relation does not presuppose the factual truth of the pertinent relatum. But *buddhi* in the sense of the *Praśastapāda-bhāṣya* represents a more general concept and can never be equated with belief. There are two items belonging to the non-knowledge variety of *buddhi* which obviously do not involve that something is regarded as true by anybody, namely 'doubt' (*saṁśaya*) and 'non-ascertainment' (*anadhyavasāya*). The latter term is significant insofar as it is explained by examples in which persons who are in a perceptual position which could permit them to classify certain objects do in fact not classify them in some pertinent regard. Accordingly, they suggest a close affinity between the correlating non-negated term *adhyavasāya* and the concept of 'judgement' which has played and sometimes still plays a prominent role in Western philosophy. The latter term is significantly related to the concept of belief inasmuch as judging that something is the case represents a typical manner of acquiring a belief. Nevertheless, although the term *adhyavasāya* explicitly occurs in the section that deals with non-ascertainment the text provides no clue as to whether it denotes a mental act that presupposes the truth of some object of ascertainment or not. Everything which the *Praśastapāda-bhāṣya* says in connection with *adhyavasāya* or *anadhyavasāya* is, so far as one can see, perfectly compatible with the assumption that the root from which it is derived is a factive verb and thus belongs to the same category as 'know', 'regret' etc. The same holds true regarding the term *nirṇaya* that appears in the *Praśastapāda-bhāṣya* in connection with an assessment of the outcome of the operation of the two *pramāṇa*s 'perception' and 'inference'. To be sure, there is no definite evidence that could rule out that those words or particular occurrences of certain other terms such as *avadhāraṇa* are meant to denote acts of judgement that do not presuppose truth. But the very fact that those terms are left undetermined seems to betray that non-factive notions like believing or judging had not evoked the interest of the author. The same diagnosis can be given regarding the *Tarka-saṁgraha*, a work which represents the later tradition of Nyāya-Vaiśeṣika. According to this text 'cognition', represented by the terms *buddhi* as well as *jñāna*, comprises two varieties, namely (1) 'remembrance' (*smṛti*) and (2) 'experience' (*anubhava*). Since the text declares concerning the latter term that it comprises two varieties, namely a) 'corresponding to an object' (*yathârtha*) and b) 'not corresponding to an object' (*ayathârtha*) one could be tempted to believe that the pertinent notion exhibits an affinity to that of belief inasmuch as it specifically relates to acquisitions of new beliefs concerning some object irrespective of whether the concerned beliefs are true or false. However, the elucidations that are given in connection with the *ayathârtha*-type suffice to show that this equation must be erroneous. For according to the text there are three varieties of this type, namely (i) doubt (*saṁśaya*), (ii) error (*viparyaya*) and (iii) counterfactual reasoning (*tarka*). The occurrence of the first sub-variety makes it impossible to equate *anubhava* with either judgement or belief. The last variety on the other hand excludes an identification of *yathârtha* with 'true'. For according to the *Tarka-saṁgraha*, *tarka* is instantiated by counterfactual deliberations such as 'If fire would not occur then smoke would not occur either'. According to a natural understanding, counterfactual propositions like the cited one can be true, and it appears evident that the term *yathârtha* possesses a restricted import corresponding to its compositional semantic value 'as an object' or 'as its object' so that it can only refer to judgements which ascribe to really existing entities attributes which they in fact possess. Although the terms *buddhi*, *jñāna* and *anubhava* according to the elucidations which the text provides subsume a range of phenomena that could be plausibly considered as involving acquisitions of beliefs, none of them can be equated with notions like 'judgement', 'belief' or 'acquisition of belief'. On the one hand they are too general, because of the inclusion of states of doubt, and on the other hand they are too restrictive, because they do not provide room for other types of hypothetical judgements apart from a special variety of counterfactual deliberations or other non-hypothetical judgements apart from those that pertain to atomic subject-predicate propositions. Sources of the Nyāya-school, such as the *Nyāya-sūtras* and the *Nyāya-bhāṣya*, reveal a similar lack of interest concerning notions equivalent to 'judgement' or 'belief'. The terms *buddhi* and *jñāna* occur equally in many places in the *Nyāya-sūtras* (NS), and those items even occupy a prominent place because in NS 1.1.9 *buddhi* is explicitly mentioned as a member of the category 'objects of cognition' (*prameya*) and NS 1.1.15 declares that *buddhi*, *upalabdhi* and *jñāna* are equivalent (*buddhir upalabdhir jñānam ity anarthāntaram*). However, in view of NS 1.1.10 which says that desire, dislike, effort, pleasure, pain and cognition are the characteristic of the soul (*icchā-dveṣa-prayatna-sukha-duḥkha-jñānāny ātmano liṅgam*) one should suspect that in a similar manner as in the Vaiśeṣika *jñāna* is a general notion that is meant to comprise all mental phenomena which are neither volitional nor emotional or sensational. Since *jñāna* in its technical sense should relate to mental entities that possess the duration of a single moment, this term is at any rate unsuited to represent a dispositional state like belief. On the other hand various occurrences of *upalabdhi* show that the term refers to mental acts that have concrete objects, such as material substances or qualities as objects, see e.g. NS 3.1.10, 3.1.26 etc. And the same holds probably good for a number of uses of the terms that are declared to be its equivalents, see e.g. NS 3.2.33. The term *nirṇaya*, which occurs in the enumeration of the Nyāya-categories in NS 1.1.1, seems to represent a notion that is closer to the ideas of judgement and belief insofar as it apparently denotes an attitude which concerns objects that are capable of being true. Nevertheless the definition provided by NS 1.1.41 which says that *nirṇaya* is the ascertainment of a matter after deliberating over it by means of a position and a counter-position (*vimṛśya pakṣa-pratipakṣābhyām arthâvadhāraṇaṁ nirṇayaḥ*) betrays that the term can refer to judgements at best with respect to specific situations occurring in debates. In the *Nyāya-bhāṣya* this problem is recognised and at the end of his explanation of NS 1.1.41 the author of the *Nyāya-bhāṣya* states that the same sort of ascertainment equally occurs without deliberations concerning a thesis and a counter-thesis as a result of perception (*na câyaṁ nirṇaye niyamaḥ vimṛśyâiva pakṣa-pratipakṣābhyām arthâvadhāraṇaṁ nirṇaya iti. kintu indriyârtha-sannikarṣôtpanna-pratyakṣe 'rthâvadhāraṇaṁ nirṇaya iti*). A reference to belief itself could be assumed in the definition of 'example' (*dṛṣṭānta*) which is given in NS 1.1.25 and which reads: *laukika-parīkṣakānāṁ yasminn arthe buddhi-sāmyaṁ sa dṛṣṭāntaḥ*. For a natural translation of this sentence could be: 'An object regarding which there is an agreement of beliefs/opinions/views of ordinary men and experts is an example.' Nevertheless, neither here nor in the preceding passage of NS 1.1.14 is it absolutely certain that the pertinent terms *nirṇaya*, *arthâvadhāraṇa* and *buddhi* are meant to represent non-factual concepts like 'judgement' and 'belief'. For the hypothesis that translations such as '*Nirṇaya* is the true ascertainment of a matter after deliberating over it by means of a position and a counter-position' or 'An object regarding which there is an agreement of true beliefs of ordinary men and experts is an example' represent the intended import of the concerned statements is not at all eccentric and commentaries like the *Nyāya-bhāṣya* do not disconfirm such an understanding. The fact that the words *nirṇaya*, *avadhāraṇa* and *buddhi* do not embody a factual import by virtue of their linguistic meaning can surely not refute that supposition. As far as I can see there is only one unambiguous reference to a non-factive notion of belief or conviction which occurs in NS 2.1.3 *viprattipattau ca saṁpratipatteḥ*. For there is no reason to question the interpretation suggested by the *Nyāya-bhāṣya*, at least to the extent that this phrase expresses the thought that situations in which differences of opinions exist are situations in which different persons have in common that they are convinced of contrary propositions. Since among contrary propositions at least one of them cannot be true the term *saṁpratipatti* cannot represent a factive notion and the assumption that it should relate to states of belief or conviction appears very plausible. At the same time, however, one must acknowledge the fact that the statement of NS 2.1.3 occurs in the context of a deliberation about the origins of doubt and this is a topic which is at best remotely connected with that of logic in any defensible meaning of this term.

Seen in this light one could be tempted to ask: 'What have belief and logic in common in Indian philosophy and what could justify a symposium with the title 'Logic and Belief in Indian Philosophy'?'

— 3 —

It appears advisable to transcend the narrow framework of a purely immanent perspective. For even if it should turn out that the Indian tradition itself has nothing or little significant to say about relations between logic and belief in some sense of those two terms it does not follow that nothing significant *can* be said. Let us therefore have a closer look at the issue as to whether the subject-matter associated with the denomination 'Indian Logic' is *objectively* connected with the phenomenon of belief if one hypothesises the notion of 'belief' that has been explicated in the first chapter.

The topic of 'Indian Logic' appears under an internal perspective as a component of the comprehensive area of epistemology and in particular of the theory of *pramāṇa*s. Given the assumption that this outlook is not completely erroneous it emerges that logic in its Indian variety and belief are in fact significantly related and that this holds even true in various respects. The expression *pramāṇa* is rendered by 'means of knowledge', 'means of (right) cognition', and in the German tradition often by 'Erkenntnismittel' or even 'Mittel gültiger Erkenntnis'. All these expressions suggest that *pramaṇa* is instrumental in the acquisition of knowledge and one could even surmise that 'means of acquisition of knowledge' would be a very apt rendering of this expression. But if it is true that a *pramāṇa* is instrumental for the acquisition of knowledge it must equally hold good that a *pramāṇa* is a means for the acquisition of belief given the above claimed entailment between knowledge and belief. Nevertheless, this fact alone cannot suffice for a vindication of the contention that one should explicitly attribute to *pramāṇa*s a function with respect to belief. Inasmuch as an accelerator is an instrument for an increase of speed it is also an instrument for the change of speed, but the characterisation of an accelerator as a means to increase speed appears more significant than to characterise it as a means for changing speed. By the same token one could argue that a characterisation of *pramāṇa*s as a means for the acquisition of beliefs is less significant than its characterisation as a means for the acquisition of knowledge. It could therefore appear that emphasising links between logic and belief in Indian philosophy is more misleading than revealing. This objection could be set aside if one were able to show that, even given that the equation between *pramāṇa* and 'means of knowledge' is at least roughly correct, the notion of *pramāṇa* is connected with the notion of belief in other ways than merely by the circumstance that anything that applies to knowledge equally applies to belief because every state of knowledge is a state of belief.

The claim that *pramāṇa* is related to belief in a more significant manner than the one depicted above rests on the theses that (1) *pramāṇa*s themselves, i.e. items designated by the term *pramāṇa*, are related to states of belief not only by some sort of instrumental relation, (2) theories of *pramāṇa* are linked with belief on account of methodological connections and (3) an *objectively* proper explication or definition of the term *pramāṇa* would contain reference to belief as an ingredient. The first two points possess a special significance because they manifest different respects in which empirical knowledge is relevant for philosophical undertakings. Inasmuch as the contention of a significant relation between logic in its Indian variety and belief is concerned, it can be vindicated on account of three sorts of connection that are correlates of (1)–(3), namely (a) belief is a relevant object of cognitive processes which are an object of concern in 'Indian logic', (b) acquisition of belief constitutes a phenomenon that is methodologically important for the establishment of theories of the concerned type and (c) the ideas of belief and acquisition of belief are needed for a description of the nature of pertinent logical doctrines.

Ad (1)

In the context of doctrines of *pramāṇa* belief comes into play as a relevant object in two regards. Belief is a possible object of a most significant variety of *pramāṇa* and it is an important type of object of that variety. The fact that inference (*anumāna*) plays a central role in doctrines of *pramāṇa* is beyond any reasonable doubt. It is equally plain that 'inference' in this context must be taken to represent a broad notion allowing for a subsumption of inferential activities taking place in everyday practice. If one poses the question as to what types of entities are the most common objects of inferences in common life, the following answer appears indisputable: states of beliefs are typical objects. Even against the background of an immanent perspective it is appropriate to assign to beliefs a distinguished status among the possible objects of inference. The tenet that states of beliefs of other people cannot be directly observed by ordinary men is, as far as one can see, universally acknowledged in the Indian philosophical and non-philosophical tradition. On the other hand, recognition of unobservable objects is at various places in the textual sources depicted as a distinguishing mark of inference.

The fact that knowledge of states of belief can be equally considered as a result of verbal communication in combination with the circumstance that some textual sources suggest such a view does not refute the contention that belief represents a most important kind of objects of central varieties of *pramāṇa*. Even against the background of statements that assign to the *pramāṇa* 'word' or 'linguistic communication' (*śabda*) a particular relevance for the recognition of unobservable entities, the assignment of a prominent status to beliefs as objects remains valid. On the one hand, with the exception of the minority group which acknowledges only perception as a *pramāṇa*, it is generally assumed that the importance of certain varieties of means of knowledge lies in their capacity to make imperceivable objects recognisable, irrespective of variations of detail as far as the question is concerned as to whether the concerned objects can be even imperceivable in principle. Accordingly, it is at most of secondary importance what the varieties of *pramāṇa* performing such a function are called and how they are described. It is anyway doubtful whether the debates concerning the sub-classification of *pramāṇa*s and their exact number concern a substantial issue. For without the lack of explicit criteria for the identity of types of *pramāṇa* it is not sure that deliberations of this sort possess significance and even if explicit criteria were stipulated it would not follow that a number of alternatives cannot be equally legitimate. At any rate, given that the standard type of inference that is explicated in the framework of 'Indian Logic' as well as in the context of *pramāṇa*-theories concerns the acknowledgement of facts which can be derived from certain data on the additional supposition that some pertinent case does not deviate from a norm (in some or the other sense of the term), an extension to the area of linguistic communication is apposite. The same considerations which have been put forward as arguments supporting the claim that acts of linguistic communication create under certain conditions a basis for the recognition of facts which are communicated can be equally used to support the claim that acts of linguistic communication are suited to convey the existence of particular beliefs on the part of communicating subjects. The basis is in all cases an assumption of compliance with regularities. In fact, the descriptions offered by the texts usually suggest that the existence of situations described by linguistic expressions can only be validly derived on the hypothesis of a corresponding belief. As a matter of fact, one can hardly dispute that if an act of communication, say an assertion of NN to the effect that P, constitutes a valid basis for the acquisition of the knowledge that P on the part of some other person, a recognition of a corresponding belief of the speaker on the part of the recipient is at least sometimes, if not even regularly, an indispensable requirement.[1] Moreover, it is plain that acts of verbal communication are not the only basis for knowledge of other person's belief; the common basis of such knowledge is behaviour in general in combination with assumptions concerning wishes, desires or preferences of other beings.

The circumstance that beliefs are not only possible but even important objects of pieces of inferential reasoning is due on the one hand to the pervasiveness of their occurrence in human beings and on the other hand to the importance of knowledge about beliefs for the acquisition of knowledge of other matters such as states-of-affairs which other people consider as true, of actual or possible behaviour of people, of human character, of the import of acts of communication etc. For such reasons belief deserves to play a central role in the humanities. Knowledge of the mechanisms of belief acquisition is particularly important for making predictions in the realm of social life.

Belief as an object of knowledge possesses even epistemological relevance under the aspect of the issue as to how knowledge about belief can be attained in special cases. Concerning the question as to what is generally required for having knowledge of other persons' beliefs a natural answer would be that an essential requirement is the existence and knowledge of some piece of evidence, in particular some linguistic or non-linguistic (way of) behaviour. This is a picture which is equally suggested, although as far as one can see not explicitly stated, in Indian epistemological treatises. But is that true? The issue which is at stake is crucial because it affects the methodology of historical studies on philosophy. According to an alternative view, which I consider as correct, the above depicted 'behavioural evidence' account of knowledge of belief is inadequate because in certain instances possession of adequate evidence is insufficient. What is acquired in addition is the possibility of providing a plausible account of why and how a considered possible belief could have been adopted. An important reason for advocating a stricter standard of knowledge concerning belief is rooted in the phenomenon of linguistic indeterminacy. It happens that even in view of contextual features different and non-equivalent hypotheses concerning interpretation are admissible and that the ascription of non-equivalent beliefs on the basis linguistic acts are equally compatible with all fea-

[1] Here one can leave out of account the doctrine that the eternal words of the *Veda* constitute valid means for the recognition of certain (non mental) facts, because on the one hand this opinion is merely shared by certain groups and on the other hand even the proponents of this doctrine allow for the possibility of acquiring knowledge by ordinary acts of communication.

tures of linguistic behaviour. If the pertinent interpretations and the corresponding belief-ascriptions differ regarding the possibility of providing a plausible account of their origination or the rationality of their adoption, a decision between the alternatives would have to rely on those considerations. Or one could say, more cautiously, that if definite knowledge of beliefs is possible in such cases then considerations pertaining to behavioural evidence must be supplemented by considerations pertaining to rational intelligibility. Is thus explicability or rationality a means of knowledge on the same par with perception, inference etc.? In the context of linguistic communication one could provide additional support for such a view by referring to cases in which speakers employ linguistically indeterminate forms of expression in connection with expectations to the effect that interpreters will apply considerations of intelligibility including considerations pertaining to the explicability and rationality of beliefs for an interpretation of their utterances. It is not necessary to pursue this issue deeper here. But the point should be noted that this phenomenon manifests that considerations pertaining to empirical matters, such as the way in which linguistic communication is related to belief and knowledge about belief, are potentially relevant for the detection of problems arising in philosophical investigations.

If belief possesses so much epistemological significance merely as a possible object of knowledge one could wonder why many if not the overwhelming majority of textual sources fails to assign to belief a special significance in the above discussed respects. Why did authors writing on *pramāṇa* miss the opportunity to highlight the importance of their topic by stressing the fact that their investigations pertain to the methodological equipment of acquiring knowledge about other person's beliefs? On the one hand, this omission can appear intelligible in view of the fact that in the context of the philosophical literature *pramāṇa*s were naturally brought in connection with the ascertainment of theoretical propositions, in particular tenets that belong to the field of metaphysics and sometimes also to religion. Under such a perspective it is natural to think that one should ascertain in the first place how the world really is rather than what individual people believe about it. On the other hand, however, functions are attributed to *pramāṇa*s which are objectively related to successful practice—and this connection has been even explicitly acknowledged in the Indian philosophical tradition. Since at least in the social sphere success of practice is intimately connected with knowledge of what people believe, the degree of lack of attention regarding belief exhibited by treatises on *pramāṇa* is by no means a matter of course. The relevance of knowledge about beliefs of people exists independently of whether the concerned beliefs are true or not. The same holds true for knowledge pertaining to the mechanisms which are at work in the acquisition of beliefs. It is a well known fact that success on the stock market crucially depends on the ability of recognising not only what other people believe but also of predicting what people will believe irrespective of the truth of their beliefs. What matters is a sufficiently firm grasp of the mechanisms which are actually at work in the acquisition of beliefs. Possibly the overwhelming emphasis on knowledge in theories of *pramāṇa* has favoured a neglect of all the aspects of belief which are not immediately related to the *contrast* between (mere) belief and knowledge.

It has to be admitted that from the circumstance that some topic is objectively important it does not follow that it deserves to occupy a prominent place in epistemological theories. Moreover, given the existence of momentous divergences between the modern world and the world which the creators of theories of *pramāṇa* experienced, there is no *a priori* basis for being surprised if our attributions of importance to phenomena and those of past writers radically differ. Therefore the fact is significant that the preceding considerations do not yet provide an exhaustive account of the issue. One reason is that the very nature of the undertaking of elaborating a theory of means of acquisition of knowledge bestows importance to adoptions of beliefs. Given the correctness of the previously suggested explication of *pramāṇa*, the attribution of vital relevance to the phenomenon of belief-acquisition can be immanently derived from the idea of a doctrine of *pramāṇa*s.

Ad (2)

It is the methodological aspect that establishes a most significant relationship of relevance between a philosophical theory of *pramāṇa*, taken as something involving a specification of possible means of acquisition of knowledge or of possible justifications for knowledge claims, on the one hand and investigations of actual ways of acquiring beliefs on the other. A main reason lies in the comprehensive, and, so to speak, topic-neutral character of such a theory. A philosopher wanting to investigate the nature of knowledge will surely not be satisfied by listing everything which in his opinion is an instance of this notion. But even if he did, he would not be well advised to begin with collecting items which instantiate that term because a crucial problem lies in the fact that his personal opinions about what counts as knowledge and what does not might not be shared by everybody. Moreover, an adversary could rightly object that if an enumeration of all items satisfying a term should specify its import or nature then the question becomes vital whether our philosopher counts as knowledge his personal opinions about knowledge and whether he allocates his belief about the correctness of the outcome of his own investigations to the realm of knowledge. Thus a vicious circle threatens. On the other hand, it cannot be a satisfactory procedure to pick out certain items which are commonly acknowledged as instances of the notion of knowledge. For the general and comprehensive nature of the envisaged investigation forbids one to start with a partial selection and on the other hand one could expect from a philosophical investigation concerning knowledge that it does not merely tell us what people generally believe to be an instance of knowledge but also embodies a critical examination whether or not the concerned beliefs are justified and conveys some idea about what does not fall under the notion and why this should be so. Isn't it therefore recommendable to tackle the pertinent problem by investigating properties of a notion that deviates from knowledge exactly by lacking the commitment of truth which is inherent in that notion? Belief exhibits this feature. Moreover, a reliable assessment of what people actually believe does not appear unrealistic. There is no need to enumerate all instances of this notion. The general and topic neutral nature of the project entails merely that all relevant types of belief occurring in all areas of possible knowledge are accounted for. To be sure, it cannot be *a priori* guaranteed that actual accounts using this method fail to be exhaustive in this regard. It is even conceivable that lack of exhaustiveness is unavoidable due to the circumstance that relevant types of belief have not occurred in the society which is accessible to the investigator, and a glimpse on the Indian intellectual tradition seems to show that this is not merely a theoretical possibility. Nevertheless, all those impediments also affect a procedure starting from the notion of knowledge. Therefore the advantage of avoidance of circularity characterising the approach by belief is decisive.

To be sure, in a philosophical context not every *a posteriori* investigation and classification of actually occurring beliefs and their possible objects is meaningful. But *some* classifications are in fact philosophically relevant. At the beginning of the *Nyāya-bhāṣya* it is stated that an agent of cognition after having apprehended an object by means of knowledge desires either to acquire or to get rid of that object (*pramāṇena khalv ayaṁ jñātârtham upalabhya tam artham abhīpsati*—variant reading: *tam īpsati vā jihāsati vā*). Apparently the writer of the text thinks here that an 'apprehension' of an object represents something which is brought about by a *pramāṇa* as a means, and the object can hardly be something else than a concrete particular because otherwise it would be hard to see how that could become an object of desire or aversion. In the light of the general conception of *pramāṇa* as a means of (the acquisition) of knowledge this is puzzling given that this characterisation appears to rule out from the outset knowledge pertaining to abstract entities. If somebody recognises that the number 321 can be divided by three, does he thereby develop a desire to acquire or get rid of that object? Maybe, the remark concerning the alleged consequences of 'apprehensions' by a *pramāṇa* are not really essential, but another component of the pertinent conception, namely that *pramāṇa*s are means of apprehending objects seems to be a vital ingredient of such theories. As we had seen before, the *Tarka-saṁgraha* distinguishes between experiences that are in accordance with the object (*yathârtha*) and experiences which are not (*ayathârtha*). The four *pramāṇa*s acknowledged in this work are viewed as instruments for the former type of cognition, which is according to the text designated by the term *pramā*. Such experiences are defined as cognitions classifying objects as they really are, for example a cognition (*jñāna*) with respect to a piece of silver that it is silver. Regarding the other type the author of the work remarks that it is an experience that classifies something as something which it is not and that the cognition with respect to a conch-shell 'this is silver' represents an example. (*tad-vati tat-prakārako 'nubhavo yathârthaḥ. yathā rajata idaṁ rajatam iti jñānam. sa eva pramêty ucyate. tad-abhāva-vati tat-prakārako 'nubhavo 'yathârthaḥ. yathā śaktāv idaṁ rajatam iti jñānam*—the second and the last sentence is missing in some manuscripts). This shows two things: (1) The expression *jñāna* appears (in this passage and elsewhere) as a non-factive term, applying to *yathârtha* experiences such as 'this is silver' with respect to silver as well as to *ayathârtha* experiences such as the above cited one. (2) Both types of 'experiences' appear to correspond to a three place relation between a subject, an object and some mode of conceiving an object that could be represented by a sentence-scheme such as 'A apprehends B in the manner C'. Accordingly, the nature of this experience must be closely akin to the states that are described by sentence-forms such as 'A regards B as (a) C' and 'A believes B to be (a) C'. Irrespective of whether we even identify the pertinent cognitions as beliefs or acquisitions of beliefs or not, the following question is relevant: 'Must belief always be analysed as a relation that holds good between a subject, an object and a way of viewing an object?' There is no doubt about the correct answer: 'This is not true'. Cases exist in which belief *cannot* be analysed in this way. People can believe that Hanuman fought against Rāvaṇa, and for the existence of this belief it is absolutely immaterial that Hanuman and Rāvaṇa probably never existed, so that such a belief cannot consist in a relation of viewing-as concerning certain objects on the part of a subject. It is equally difficult to see how a conception of belief as a relation between a believer and a particular object can do justice to beliefs pertaining to non specified objects, i.e. states of beliefs which are ascribed to some believing subject by sentences such as 'A believes that a/some cat is on the mat' (according to their most natural reading) and how those theories can account for the difference between such a belief and a belief which would be expressed by 'A believes that his cat is on the mat.' We had seen above that the *Tarka-saṁgraha* itself mentions counterfactual propositions like 'If fire did not exist, smoke would not exist either.' Those who persist in thinking that such sentences should be understood as expressing relations between (real) fire and (real) smoke should also consider counterfactuals such as: 'If a second sun existed it could be much warmer.' There should be no need to elaborate in more detail that there are a lot of actual or possible beliefs that cannot be analysed in the manner suggested by the *Tarka-saṁgraha*, the *Nyāya-bhāṣya* and other sources. If one wants to specify a more general form and simultaneously wishes to preserve the conception of belief as a relation it would be more suitable to analyse it as a relation between a subject and an abstract entity that can be denoted by 'that'-clauses, but is surely not well suited as an object of acquisition or avoidance or of corresponding desires.

The upshot is that an analysis of belief reveals in a more immediate manner than an analysis of knowledge why theories of *pramāṇa* are threatened by crucial deficiencies. An advocate of the *pramāṇa*-tradition might argue that one should refrain from classifying as knowledge propositional attitudes pertaining to fictions. After all, the writer of the *Tarka-saṁgraha* explicitly assigns 'experiences' referring to counterfactual propositions to the realm of *tarka* which is subsumed under the category of experiences that do not correspond to an object, i.e. which are *ayathârtha*. But against the background of belief such a move turns out to be futile. The fact that beliefs can pertain to fictions is undeniable. It can equally be hardly denied that such beliefs can be true.—After all, if Hanuman did not exist, the belief that Hanuman did not exist should be true.—Accordingly, the question as to which factors either guarantee or increase the probability that if beliefs occur they are also true, irrespective of whether or not they are *de re* beliefs, i.e. beliefs about actually existing objects, is not spurious. If 'knowledge' were defined in such a manner that in principle all true beliefs could be classified as knowledge, then it follows that the question as to which factors might guarantee or enhance the probability of the occurrence of knowledge cannot be solved by taking only *de re* beliefs into consideration. If, on the other hand, one defined knowledge in some narrower sense then the aim of specifying all relevant factors for its existence might be attainable even if one restricted one's attention to particular varieties of belief, but in this case the *relevaṇce of achieving* the pertinent aim becomes questionable. By considering the phenomenon of belief without supposing an artificially restricted meaning of the term the entire range of phenomena can be discerned which any theory of means of knowledge or means of acquisition of knowledge must account for if it should be both correct and relevant.

Not only accounts of the nature of belief, but also a survey of manners of acquisition of beliefs is methodologically relevant for a theoretical account of means of knowledge. A first question that should be posed is: (a) 'Are *all* beliefs acquired?'. This question is not spurious because the view that there are innate beliefs is not absurd. Another question that must be equally considered is: (b) 'Are *all* beliefs that are acquired, acquired by experience?'. Obviously the notion of acquisition of a belief is vague to some extent. Nevertheless, there is a legitimate reading of the term according to which one could say that a person can acquire the belief that, say Peano's second axiom, which reads

$$(x)(Nx \rightarrow (\exists y)((Ny \ \& \ Syx) \ \& \ (z)(Szx \rightarrow z = y))$$

and which means in ordinary language

'Every natural number has exactly one successor'

is true. Is such a belief, if it is acquired, acquired by experience? Maybe, a staunch defender of *pramāṇa*-theories of the sort of the doctrine propagated in the *Tarka-saṁgraha* would be inclined to bring the *pramāṇa* 'verbal communication' (*śabdà*) into play and point out that ordinary people adopt the belief that Peano's second axiom is true by reading books written by competent mathematicians. But it is not difficult to discern that such a reply misses some most vital points. First one cannot reduce the problem to the acquisition of the *de dicto* belief, that Peano's second axiom is true. Most people who understand the axiom will not merely come to the conclusion that there was some person called 'Peano' who stated some mathematical truth, but they will rather, possibly 'triggered' by reading some book, come to believe that that which the axiom says is true. Should one nevertheless say that persons who believe that it is true that every natural number has exactly one successor after having read a book have adopted their belief by experience? Obviously a distinction must be drawn here. On the one hand one could admit that experiences like reading a book might stimulate persons to grasp the pertinent thought that every natural number possesses just one successor. But this does not entail that a person who has grasped the thought must rely on experience in order to believe it or to recognise that he is justified to believe it because it is true. As a matter of fact, in this regard considerations of trustworthiness of the conveyor of a verbal message, which have usually been considered as an essential ingredient of verbal communication in *pramāṇa*-theories, are quite irrelevant. Acknowledgement of mathematical axioms or proofs only because of the trustworthiness of a person is a deficient manner of adopting a mathematical belief. If anything essentially matters it is insight into the content of a message and not assumptions regarding a conveyer of a message. In view of these facts it could appear natural to retort that theories of *pramāṇa* are meant to account for just one of two aspects of acquisition of knowledge and argue that doctrines like the one proposed in the *Tarka-saṁgraha* are fully adequate because they specify a decisive factor, namely verbal communication, that causes persons to grasp a true thought. But in the final analysis this move is futile. For verbal communication can only serve to impart something which some person—or maybe some god—has recognised as true without being informed by acts of verbal communication. One should note that this view is in complete agreement with statements that can be found in the textual sources about verbal communication as a *pramāṇa*. Accordingly, both grasping the thought which the above cited or some other axiom expresses and recognising its truth—provided it is true—should be possible without relying on any verbal communication as a means of knowledge. The most plausible supposition is that knowledge is at stake which can be acquired without any experience. Anyhow, the question as to whether beliefs pertaining to mathematical axioms or theorems are acquired by experience requires a differentiated answer embodying a reference to the distinction between grasping or entertaining a thought and judging it to be true. Even if acts of grasping thoughts are caused by experiences it does not follow that beliefs in their truth depend on experience. Thus an analysis of certain varieties of belief are suited to reveal crucial distinctions which in their turn throw a different light on the notion of a means of knowledge. This result has not only a bearing on the issue that emerged in the preceding paragraph as to whether 'rationality' or terms involving reference to rationality, such as 'rational intelligibility' etc., could designate something possessing the status of a means of knowledge. It possesses equally potential relevance for an explication of the notion of a means of knowledge—and the question of the equivalence between 'means of knowledge' and *pramāṇa*.

It had been suggested earlier that accounts of ways of acquiring beliefs might be bound to remain deficient due to 'social' circumstances because of the fact that a community in which a philosopher was active ignored certain sorts of cognitive practice. Now one can see, why this problem is not merely theoretically conceivable. In contrast to the Western tradition knowledge of mathematical axioms and mathematical proofs was not a central topic in Indian philosophy. The most plausible reason is that mathematical reasoning did not play the same role in ancient Indian communities as in ancient Greek society. This sort of limitation is, however, not peculiar to accounts of acquisitions of beliefs but affect accounts of knowledge and theories of *pramāṇa*, too.

Nonetheless, even under an Indian perspective certain aspects of acquisition of beliefs which are not retrievable from theories of *pramāṇa* could have been detected. The pertinence of the above formulated question, viz. 'Are *all* beliefs acquired?', can be recognised without taking special areas of knowledge into consideration. For it is in the first place observation of the world of everyday practice and common sense which undermines confidence in an affirmative answer. Is it reasonable to assert that people at some time acquire the belief that they are living or that other things apart from themselves exist? Perhaps one should even here observe a distinction which has been suggested in the preceding paragraph. For it seems implausible to maintain that very small children grasp the thought that they live or exist. In some sense at least, which involves the idea of grasping a thought, one might say that people acquire the belief that they exist. In another sense it seems apposite to ascribe even to small children a belief in their existence as well as the existence of an external world, because they behave in ways which (seems to) betray some grasp of a difference between their own existence and that of other persons and objects and because their behaviour could not be regarded as reasonable if the pertinent beliefs were not true. At any rate, given that a person grasps thoughts pertaining to her own existence or the existence of an external world, it appears doubtful that additional experiences are needed in order to make valid assessments of their truth. This suggests the idea that there might be beliefs such that entertaining the thought (proposition) which is their content is sufficient for their truth and beliefs such that a recognition of the truth of their content cannot rely on additional experiences apart from grasping the pertinent content. Beliefs about one's own existence or the existence of an external world are by no means the only candidates for such a status; believing that something is the case and recognising that one is believing this or the proposition expressed by substituting 'thinking' for 'believing' in the preceding sentence could be other examples. At any rate, if one admits that there can be true beliefs classifiable as knowledge which do not require any experiences apart from grasping certain thoughts for a recognition of their truth, one might consider either the act of grasping thoughts as a means of knowledge or accept that states of knowledge occur which do not depend on any means of knowledge. Neither alternative has been accepted in any *pramāṇa*-theory, as far as one can see. It appears even that the latter alternative of knowledge not relying on means of knowledge has been (almost?) unanimously rejected in the Indian philosophical tradition. Seen in the light of the preceding considerations this appears astonishing. One might accordingly think that a different idea has been associated with the term *pramāṇa* and that the possibility of assigning to acts of grasping thoughts the status of a *pramāṇa* should be rejected because *pramāṇa*-theories ask for the primary causes of states of knowledge and therefore cannot recognise that acts of grasping a thought which are caused by different factors are means of knowledge in the pertinent sense. However, this move threatens to be self-defeating. All theories accepting inference as a *pramāṇa*—and this is the overwhelming majority—acknowledge that inferences can and usually are 'triggered off' by acts of perception. As long as not the entire canon of *pramāṇa*s is reduced to perception, it needs to be admitted that mental processes that take perceptual data as inputs can in principle occupy the position of a *pramāṇa*. In view of the above mentioned examples of presumably true beliefs or other common examples such as truly believing that one does not experience a severe tooth-ache at present, it is by no means immediately plausible that inference or indicators permitting valid inferences should be a means of knowledge but not processes of grasping a thought, of becoming aware of something, of interpreting data etc. or their respective objects. Seen from a purely immanent perspective it could be objected that the notion of *pramāṇa* is intimately connected with the notion of the acquisition of new information, so that e.g. acts of obtaining awareness might not appear as suitable candidates for the status of means of knowledge in the relevant sense. However, the notion of new information is affected by crucial vagueness. It is notorious that Dharmakīrti accepted as valid inferences derivations such as 'A is a tree' from 'A is an oak.' Given that this philosopher accepted also the tenet that a means of knowledge must impart new knowledge that did not exist before, it follows that the proposition that something is a tree must represent new information with respect to the proposition that the entity concerned is an oak. This is by no means a matter of course but might be accepted given a suitable understanding of 'new information'. The problem is, however, that precisely on this understanding of the notion it becomes difficult to see why subsuming perceptual data under concepts or other varieties of interpretation of data are denied the status of a separate means of knowledge. One could point out that problems of consistency of Dharmakīrti's theory must not affect in the same way other doctrines of *pramāṇa* because they permit the hypothesis of a stronger reading of 'new information', according to which information is new relative to some (set of) data only if its recognition requires additional experience apart from experience of the pertinent data. Accordingly, something can be a *pramāṇa* only if it plays an instrumental role for the acquisition of beliefs which are new in the strong sense. This, however, leads us back to a problem which had been encountered before: Internal consistency might be saved, but this has the price of diminishing the relevance of the entire theory as a general account of knowledge and acquisition of knowledge.

The methodological relevance of accounts concerning belief rests on purely systematic grounds and possesses two facets. First a registration of actually existing types of belief and an analysis of actual ways of belief acquisition constitute a relevant heuristic device for detecting properties of possible knowledge and its acquisition. On the other hand any account that involves a specification of possible sources of knowledge can be effectively controlled by testing whether some pertinent inventory of sources of knowledge exhibits the property that for every variety of belief there is at least one source exemplifying a type occurring in the inventory. Even if a negative result does not immediately necessitate a rejection of the concerned knowledge account it either yields reasons for putting its adequacy into doubt or furnishes motives for specifying some regard in which the account *would* be adequate. Accordingly, the topic of belief and belief acquisition is in principle also relevant for the understanding of theories of *pramāṇa*. Questions of detail as those mentioned in the preceding sections only illustrate the systematic connections.

Ad (3)

The preceding considerations are compatible with the assumption that theories of *pramāṇa* specify factors which are decisive for the possession or acquisition of certain true beliefs. They do not refute the conditional saying that every belief is such that if it has been acquired by means of a *pramāṇa* then it is true and possibly an instance of knowledge. The arguments of the preceding paragraph concern only the contention that the reverse, namely that everything which is an instance of knowledge has been acquired by means of *pramāṇa*s, is most probably false and that therefore the methodological relevance of belief casts a critical light on 'really existing doctrines of *pramāṇa*'. But can one admit that the Indian doctrines of *pramāṇa* identify factors for which it holds true that every belief that depends on those factors is also true and can be classified as an instance of knowledge? My claim is that this is not only not true but that certain textual sources even betray an implicit recognition of this fact.

In the second half of the comments on NS 1.1.3 the *Nyāya-bhāṣya* deals with the question as to whether the different *pramāṇa*s pertain to different or to identical objects. The position of the *Nyāya-bhāṣya* is that although certain objects can only be vindicated by one specific *pramāṇa* various cases exist in which different *pramāṇa*s can have common objects. An example is, among others, the acquisition of knowledge of the occurrence of fire at some place. Somebody might be informed (by a trustworthy person) that fire exists somewhere, somebody might infer the occurrence of the same fire because he perceives smoke and somebody might have a perceptual experience of the fire itself. These different ways of ascertaining the existence of objects might even occur regarding one and the same person. In this connection the *Nyāya-bhāṣya* remarks, however, that some sort of priority needs to be attributed to perception. This is illustrated by the example that somebody first ascertains an object about which he has a desire to acquire knowledge on the basis of verbal cognition but desires to ascertain it also by inference and after this task has been performed still wants to ascertain it by perception. Only after the object has been perceived, the 'desire to know' vanishes, according to the opinion of the author (*sā cêyaṁ pramitiḥ pratyakṣa-parā. jijñāsitam artham āptôpadeśāt pratipadyamāno liṅga-darśanenâpi bubhutsate, liṅga-darśanânumitaṁ ca pratyakṣato didṛkṣate, pratyakṣata upalabdhe 'rthe jijñāsā nivarttate*). The significant fact is that the writer expresses the view that both after verbal communication and after inference a desire to know can persist. To be sure, one *could* interpret this remark as a result of the consideration that a subject might be unsure whether something which appears to him to be based on a *pramāṇa* is really based on a *pramāṇa*. This means that the initial ascertainment by linguistic communication leaves room for the doubt whether that which the subject cannot distinguish from valid linguistic communication and which would under the hypothesis that it is an instance of valid linguistic communication furnish an appropriate reason for believing that some communicated state of affairs is the case exhibits in fact the property which it appears to exhibit, i.e. whether it really is an instance of valid linguistic communication. Nevertheless, whereas such an interpretation might be acceptable regarding the stage of verbal cognition because misjudgements concerning the reliability of what other people say is not uncommon, a similar diagnosis appears little plausible as far as the stage of inference is concerned. In view of the fact that the standard inference of fire from smoke is pertinent in the present context one must ask: If even in standard cases of inference doubt can persist whether the inference is really valid, how could one rely on inference at all? To be sure, one could imagine that the writer of the *Nyāya-bhāṣya* had in mind that in the context of an inference a person can be subject to a perceptual error by considering something as smoke which is not smoke. But if perceptual error is a relevant issue here, then it is hard to understand why the author of the text categorically declares that after perception desire to know comes to an end. The idea that the curiosity is satisfied by perception in particular because in a perceptual situation one recognises a number of characteristic features of an object which cannot be ascertained by means of communication or inference should not be decisive here because the remarks appear in the broader context of a discussion of the phenomenon that different means of cognition can pertain to the same object. Therefore the most plausible hypothesis is that the writer of the text intuited that both verbal communication and inference are relatively fallible and felt that perception possesses a higher degree of reliability. This could be true even if this view militated against the general theoretical outlook of the author. For whenever theoretical tenets are concerned which appear intuitively doubtful it can happen that in some context somebody expresses thoughts that do not fully harmonise with his theory. Perhaps it is no accident that later commentators such as Uddyotakara and others employ the more neutral term *ākāṅkṣā* 'desire' instead of 'desire to know' (*jijñāsā*).

The recognition of the phenomenon that inferences can be blocked either by other inferences or by other means of cognition is attested by sources of various periods. Even relatively late treatises, such as the *Tarka-saṁgraha*, admit this possibility notwithstanding the fact that such a position probably implies a rejection of certain earlier tenets, in particular those of Dharmakīrti and his successors, and a reintroduction of views which were prevalent at still earlier periods. The *Tarka-saṁgraha* explicitly stipulates that among the fallacious reasons a variety, called *sat-pratipakṣa*, and another variety, called *bādhita*, exist. The first one is exemplified in cases in which an inference or inferential argument is counterbalanced by a different inference or inferential argument employing a different 'reason' (*yasya sādhyâbhāva-sādhakaṁ hetv-antaraṁ vidyate sa sat-pratipakṣaḥ*). The second one occurs if the outcome of an inference or inferential argument militates against some proposition that is vindicated by some other means of cognition (*yasya sādhyâbhāvaḥ pramāṇântareṇa niścitaḥ sa bādhitaḥ*). Although it is plain that these as well as other fallacious reasons or pieces of reasoning do not qualify for the status of a *pramāṇa*, those phenomena possess relevance for the assessment of inference as a means of knowledge. For the manner in which they are treated strongly suggests that *if* the same pieces of reasoning would not be counterbalanced in the mentioned ways, then they would qualify for the status of a *pramāṇa*.

We may well abstain from investigations concerning the 'real intentions' of writers of works on *pramāṇa*. For if one assesses the issue from an objective point of view the verdict should be that inferences, even if they are valid, do not guarantee truth. According to many theories of inference (*anumāna*) compliance with the criteria for the validity of a reason leaves room for the possibility that the criteria are fulfilled and the outcome is false precisely because some pertinent case exhibits a unique exception to an otherwise general regularity. The examples which are commonly discussed in 'Indian Logic' only allow the diagnosis that that which is at stake is a derivation of some proposition from certain data under the premise that the pertinent data do not exhibit a deviance from a norm. Given that this is true, one must draw the conclusion that Indian theories of inference attempt to account for pieces of defeasible reasoning. It follows from this fact that the account of inferential reasoning that is represented by the tradition of Dharmakīrti is misleading. Although inferences employing so-called *svabhāva-hetu*s could be considered as pieces of reasoning in which from given data propositions are derived which can be recognised as true without bringing other experiences into play, the variety of the *kārya-hetu*s corresponds to pieces of reasoning in which the data do not license the derivation of the conclusion without bringing propositions relying on other data of experience into play. Whereas the first variety corresponds to acquisitions of beliefs which need not rely on any knowledge except knowledge of pertinent data, the second variety corresponds to acquisitions of beliefs which can never be licensed by knowledge of data without relying on additional experiential knowledge concerning regularities. The issue of the correct answer to the above formulated query (Q2), namely

> If (a proposition) P logically implies (a proposition) Q, does it hold true for everybody that if he knows P and believes Q he knows Q?

is quite intricate as far as 'Indian Logic' is concerned. If the phrase '(a proposition) P logically implies (a proposition) Q' is interpreted in the sense of '(a proposition)

Q can be established by a faultless *anumāna* on the basis of (a proposition) P as a datum' an affirmative answer to the question might well correspond to views held by a number of writers even outside the tradition of Dharmakīrti's school. On the other hand, however, it is questionable whether such a stance is objectively adequate and it is even possible that a negative answer harmonises better with internal theoretical elements of doctrines advocated in the Indian epistemological tradition.

Knowledge imparted by verbal communication as defined in textual sources is equally defeasible because even if all the stipulated requirements of reliability of a verbal communication are met the fact that the linguistic data of a message need to be interpreted by a recipient of a message introduces an ingredient of fallibility that cannot be eliminated.

The proposition that defeasible reasoning is a primary concern of Indian Logic would alone suffice for a falsification of the above formulated conditional that whenever a belief has been acquired by means of a *pramāṇa* then it is true and a possible instance of knowledge. Means of acquisition of new beliefs which, applied in a correct manner, guarantee true outcomes, might in fact exist. Arithmetical operations could be a suitable example. One could also mention phenomena such as the capacity to make safe predictions about possible outcomes of particular situations in certain games or the ability of competent speakers of a language to identify possible meanings of sentences not encountered before. But precisely examples like these are conspicuous by their absence in discussions on *pramāṇa*. (The discussions on the *pramāṇa sambhava* in the *Praśastapāda-bhāṣya* or the *Nyāya-bhāṣya* do not invalidate this statement.) On a more general level the problem is that doctrines of *pramāṇa* are meant to provide an account of empirical knowledge. In this context it is doubtful whether a specification of means playing an instrumental role for the acquisition of states of beliefs or criteria that could be invoked for a justification of claims of knowledge, such that their existence or satisfaction guarantees truth, is possible and meaningful at all. For on the one hand considerations of relevance demand that the range of possible belief and knowledge should not be restricted to trivial and completely uncontroversial propositions, and on the other hand the desideratum that the account should be significant calls for a specification of means of knowledge that is not overtly or covertly circular. If it were stated e.g. that knowledge could be acquired by entertaining arbitrary thoughts and simultaneously ascertaining in oneself a feeling of well being of some type and if the danger of the fallibility of such a criterion were averted by *stipulating* that a feeling of well being exhibits the relevant type only under the condition that the entertained thought is in fact true, then the provided specification would evidently trivialise the account. Similar consequences threaten if the concepts of perception, inference etc. were manipulated in such a way that they imply the truth of some concerned content.

If theories of *pramāṇa* have neither achieved an exhaustive account of the acquisition of true beliefs nor a non question begging specification of criteria such that beliefs complying with those criteria are guaranteed to be true, one might wonder whether those doctrines possess any value at all. Should we say that the Indian epistemological tradition including Indian Logic was an aberration in the history of philosophy? In order to recognise that this verdict is not justified we should reverse the perspective by looking at certain outcomes and pose the question in which respect those results could be useful. Let us only take the Nyāya doctrine of the four *pramāṇa*s, 'perception', 'inference', 'comparison' and 'verbal communication', as an example and let us set aside the third *pramāṇa* 'comparison' which usually plays a marginal role. Bearing in mind that *pramāṇa*s are classified as instruments (*karaṇa*) in textual sources, this means that we should ask whether perception, inference and verbal communication can be regarded as relevant factors for the acquisition of true beliefs in *some* respect. Or let us address the issue like this: 'Which question concerning belief or knowledge would exhibit the property that a specification of perception, inference and verbal communication as instruments would provide a significant reply to it?' There is at least one promising answer to this question which demands though to give up the quest for a connection between *pramāṇa*s and individual beliefs or individual pieces of knowledge. The proposal is: Perception, inference and verbal communication possess an exceptional relevance as instruments for the regulation of systems of beliefs. The term 'regulation of systems of beliefs' refers here to processes of acquisition of new beliefs, abandonment or suspension of previous beliefs as well as the replacement of old beliefs by new beliefs in the framework of a structure of a multitude of (partly interconnected) beliefs, representing a totality of beliefs held by an individual person or even a social community. If an individual or a group of individuals regularly employs perception, inference and verbal communication as a means of acquiring new beliefs and of controlling inherited or previously adopted beliefs he boosts the chances to better his 'score of knowledge', both in the sense that the amount of true beliefs is augmented and in the sense that the proportion between true and false beliefs is improved. This does not entail that the employment of those means of knowledge guarantees truth in each individual case. Their function is merely to contribute to increase of knowledge in the longer run. It is not any more assumed that those means fulfil only an instrumental role for acquisitions of beliefs because, in contrast to the view suggested in theories of *pramāṇa*, it is acknowledged here that their employment might equally possess an abandonment of previous beliefs without an adoption of a different opinion as a result.

Against this background it is even possible to appreciate the adoption of verbal communication as a separate *pramāṇa* in Nyāya. For verbal communication is the only *pramāṇa* which hints at the dimension of social control of the adoption and preservation of beliefs of individuals. Notwithstanding the fact that historical examples show that the actual manner in which opinions of individuals are influenced by social communities is sometimes disastrous, the possibility of social control is immensely significant. An important way of detecting perceptual error is the knowledge, most often imparted by verbal communication, that other persons who are in a similar perceptual situation have divergent perceptual experiences. This also reveals the importance of the adoption of a plurality of means of cognition. In this light one can recognise the questionable nature of the arguments of philosophers advocating a rejection of certain *pramāṇa*s or a reduction of their number on the basis of the allegation that the concerned *pramāṇa*s do not always generate true beliefs. By reducing the number of *pramāṇa*s one diminishes the chances of mutual control. It is the conception of means of acquisition of knowledge which invariably generate true beliefs alone by themselves which deserves to be rejected rather than the admittance of instrumental factors that cannot perform such a task in isolation.

To be sure, as an account of instrumental factors enhancing increase of knowledge in general theories of *pramāṇa*s in the form encountered in the texts are presumably deficient. It can hardly be doubted that the prevalent conception of inference explicated in the framework of Indian Logic is too narrow and that this diminishes the significance of those theories for a general account of increasing knowledge by inferential means. The textual sources betray the intention to single out as relevant inferences relying on the hypothesis of regularities to which no exceptions are known. Thereby the possible relevance of hypotheses concerning regularities to which exceptions *are* known is ignored. As far as the general question is concerned, as to precisely when and why extrapolations of regularities can be employed for the acquisition of new beliefs or of knowledge, it seems that some clues can be got from Dharmakīrti's works, but these represent at best a beginning. The role of an *a priori* component in the acquisition of belief and knowledge is completely ignored in *pramāṇa*-theories. In addition to this, they provide no clue which instrumental function should be attributed to actions, such as sending someone to see what is happening, placing something on scales or making an experiment. Theories which simply declare that *pramāṇa*s are mental entities do not provide a satisfying reply. The decisive problem is *why* non-mental activities must be precluded and in this connection answers relying on doctrinal tenets such as that in reality there are no entities except mental ones are hardly convincing. As far as the question of the factors relevant for 'improving the score of knowledge' is concerned, remembrance can surely not be ruled out as irrelevant. Judgements such as the one expressed by the sentence

(iv) He is now much bigger than last year

are only justified on a basis which involves acts of remembrance. Notwithstanding those and other problems, regarding the question as to how human beings are able to increase knowledge pertaining to the world of experience by bettering the score of true beliefs in the longer run, both theories of *pramāṇa* and Indian Logic provide relevant answers, and this holds true despite the fact that those teachings were developed under a different perspective. Therefore the results of Indian doctrines of *pramāṇa* possess significance under the aspect of the question of how human beings can extend their realm of knowledge. One might even characterise *pramāṇa*s, such as perception, inference of the sort of an Indian *anumāna* or verbal communication, as means or instruments of knowledge as long as one bears in mind that the pertinent concept of the vague notion of a means of knowledge is that of a tool by which human beings are able to increase their knowledge both on the individual and on the collective level. The above mentioned items are suited as tools for increase of knowledge in two different ways: (a) They can function as quite reliable sources for the acquisition of new beliefs, such that individual beliefs that are adopted on their basis possess a fairly good chance of being true. (b) They can be employed as means of controlling possible beliefs in the manner that they are used as criteria for assessing the truth of (the contents of) potential beliefs either in the way of questioning the basis on which beliefs have been actually adopted or in the way of examining whether or not the propositional contents of possible beliefs are in accord with other possible experiences. This is a much more modest role than the one which is suggested concerning *pramāṇa*s in many textual sources of the Indian tradition. One might wonder what should explain such a divergence. To this question at least a partial answer can be offered: Competing schools of thought in Ancient India were eager to establish their own doctrinal tenets and defend them against rival contentions and detected in the idea that their tenets can be vindicated by *pramāṇa*s a useful device for validating their claims. Against this background every account of *pramāṇa*s that emphasises aspects of fallibility must appear unattractive.

Inquiries on belief in Indian philosophy will presumably yield quite meagre results as long as they only investigate what explicit statements occurring in textual sources, and in particular treatises on *pramāṇa* and inference, tell us about belief. Nonetheless, a pursuit of the question of belief in Indian philosophy can render an immense help for a better understanding of the subject-matter which was a concern of logic and epistemology in Ancient India.

Can There be Unbiased Epistemology in Indian Philosophy?

RAGHUNATH GHOSH

In this paper an effort is made to show that epistemology (*pramāṇa-śāstra*) as available in Indian philosophical systems is not unbiased, but is vitiated through various metaphysical or ontological presuppositions, though it is claimed by Indian philosophers that through a means of knowing (*pramāṇa*) a knowable entity (*prameya*) is substantiated. Gradually we will see that this principle of *mānâdhīnā meya-siddhiḥ* is a myth, because *pramāṇa* itself is not untouched by the scheme of *prameya* admitted by them.

— 1 —

The Naiyāyikas have accepted means of knowing (*pramāṇa*) as a first category, depending on which the other factors involved with it become meaningful. According to Vātsyāyana, if *pramāṇa* remains in its true form, such concepts as knower (*pramātṛ*), knowable entity (*prameya*) and valid cognition (*pramiti*) become meaningful. In fact, the meaningfulness of all these depends on that of *pramāṇa*.[1] That is why *pramāṇa* and *pramāṇa-śāstra* receive so much importance in this system. How do we know that a *pramāṇa* is a genuine one? In reply, it is said that the genuine nature of it is substantiated on the strength of its successful inclination.[2] In fact it is itself a form of inference in which *arthavattva* ('capability of being meaningful') is the *sādhya* ('probandum'), *pramāṇa* ('means of knowing') is *pakṣa* ('subject of inference') and *pravṛtti-sāmarthya* ('efficacy to successful inclination') is the *hetu* ('probans'). The genuinity of a *pramāṇa* is proved in terms of another *pramāṇa*, i.e. inference, which ultimately leads to infinite regress (*anavasthā*). In spite of this the Naiyāyikas are very much concerned with proving the genuinity of *pramāṇa* with the help of its efficacy to successful inclination (*pravṛtti-sāmarthya*) after keeping

[1] NBh 1.1.1: *arthavati ca pramāṇe pramātṛ prameyaṁ pramitir ity arthavanti bhavanti.*

[2] NBh 1.1.1: *pramāṇataḥ artha-pratipattau pravṛtti-sāmarthyād arthavat pramāṇaṁ.*

Logic and Belief in Indian Philosophy
Warsaw Indological Studies 3 (2010) 71–83.

the theory of *parataḥ-prāmāṇya* ('extrinsic validity of proof') in view. Whether something is a *pramāṇa* or a pseudo-*pramāṇa* (*pramāṇâbhāsa*) is dependent on its successful inclination, which leads to the supposition that the theory of *pramāṇa* on which a *meya* ('provable object') is substantiated is not free from the influence of *meya*-related presuppositions.

— 2 —

Each and every system of Indian Philosophy has got some metaphysical presuppositions that are reflected in their theories of knowledge. That is the only reason which gives rise to the principle of *mānâdhīnā meya-siddhiḥ* ('the substantiation of the knowable entities depends on the source of knowing'). This principle is true in the sense that knowable entities or categories are different in different philosophical systems. Hence, the definitions are formulated in such a way so that their presupposed entities can be proved. One could raise the problem of *circularity* in these cases. When a philosopher of a particular school is framing a definition of *pramāṇa*, it is to some extent 'subjective', but not objective in the sense that he bears some presuppositions. Whatever may be the reasons the philosophical systems particularly in India are not free from this defect of biasness. The point will be clearer if I put forth some definitions of perception (*pratyakṣa*) accepted by different systems.

The definition of perception given by the older Naiyāyikas is as follows: 'The perceptual knowledge is a cognition arising out of the contact of the sense-organ with an object, which cannot be described through language, which is non-deviating (*avyabhicārin*) and non-erroneous (*vyavasāyâtmaka*).'[3] This definition was accepted by the older Naiyāyikas because it was formulated in such a way so that their accepted theories of indeterminate perception (*nirvikalpaka-pratyakṣa*), indicated by the inclusion of such terms as 'something inexpressible by words' (*avyapadeśya*), 'contact' (*saṁnikarṣa*) between sense-organs and the object, 'non-erroneous character' (*vyavasāyâtmaka*), 'non-deviating character' (*avyabhicārin*) etc. be preserved. To them an object (*artha*) was a kind of category accepted by them and capable of being perceived (*yogya*). There did not arise any question of perceiving an absurd entity, as the categorical scheme admitted by them did not permit us to do so. The Nyāya did not admit an entity which could not be included under the accepted seven categories. In this case the term *artha* was included so that an absurd object not belonging to the set of admitted categories did not find entry in the scheme of perception.

[3] NS 1.1.4: *indriyârtha-sannikarṣôtpannaṁ jñānaṁ avyapadeśyaṁ avyabhicāri vyavasāyâtmakaṁ pratyakṣaṁ.*

Let us have a look towards the Advaita theory of perception. According to the Advaitins, the whole world is nothing but the manifestation of Brahman or Ātman or Consciousness (*caitanya*). Under this situation Dharmarāja Adhvarīndra, a follower of the Advaita school, thinks that mere connection (*saṁnikarṣa*) between sense organ and an object may not be the cause of perceptual cognition. If the whole world is Consciousness (*caitanya*), object (*artha*) is something covered by this Consciousness. Other object, like our sense organs etc., are the consciousness limited by objects, sense organs etc. Though Consciousness (*caitanya*) is one, it may have limiting adjuncts (*upādhi*) such as consciousness of an object (*viṣayâvacchinna-caitanya*), consciousness of the mental mode (*antaḥ-karaṇa-vṛtty-avacchinna-caitanya*) and consciousness of the knower (*antaḥ-karaṇâvacchinna-caitanya*). These limiting adjuncts of one Consciousness are called *viṣaya-caitanya, pramāṇa-caitanya* and *pramātṛ-caitanya* respectively. Being one, it has limiting adjuncts just as time, though one, has limiting adjuncts (*upādhi*s) in the form of hours, days, week, fortnight, month, year etc.[4] After keeping these metaphysical presuppositions in mind Dharmarāja Adhvarīndra accepted two criteria of perceptuality: perceptuality of knowledge (*jñāna-gata*) and perceptuality of object (*viṣaya-gata*). To him when there is a union between consciousness of a means of knowing (*pramāṇa-caitanya*) and consciousness of an object (*viṣaya-caitanya*), then it is the case of the perceptuality of knowledge (*jñāna-gata-pratyakṣatva*). It is to be borne in mind that they Advaitins have made a distinction between perception of the knowledge of a jar and perception of a jar. In the case of the perception of the knowledge of a jar there is the union between *viṣaya-caitanya* ('consciousness of an object') and *pramāṇa-caitanya* ('consciousness of a means of knowing') but *pramātṛ-caitanya* ('consciousness of the knower') will remain isolated in the sense that it maintains its separate existence by playing the role of an agent (*kartṛ*). How is such union of these two *caitanya*s possible? Dharmarāja Adhvarīndra left no stones unturned to make us convinced with the following reasoning. When our mind, after issuing from the body reaches to the object with the help of sense organs and assumes the shape of the object, then it is called mental mode (*vṛtti*), which is also a form of the consciousness.[5] To them the

---

[4] VPar (*Pratyakṣa-pariccheda*), p. 13: *siddhānte pratyakṣatva-prayojakaṁ kiṁ iti cet, kiṁ jñāna-gatasya pratyakṣatvasya prayojakaṁ pṛcchasi, kiṁ vā viṣaya-gatasya? ādye pramāṇa-caitanyasya viṣayâvacchinna-caitanyâbheda iti brumaḥ. tathā trividhaṁ caitanyaṁ viṣaya-caitanyaṁ pramāṇa-caitanyaṁ pramātṛ-caitanyaṁ cêti. tatra ghaṭâdy-avacchinnaṁ caitanyaṁ viṣaya-caitanyam antaḥ-karaṇa-vṛtty-avacchinnaṁ caitanyaṁ pramāṇa-caitanyam antaḥ-karaṇâvacchinnaṁ caitanyaṁ pramātṛ-caitanyam.*

[5] The luminous mind, issuing through the eye etc. essential for perception of an external object only (happiness etc. being perceived inwardly), goes to the space occupied by objects like a jar etc. and is modified into the form of a jar. This modification is called mental mode (*vṛtti*).

Advaitins the mind (*antaḥ-karaṇa*), like liquid substance, has no shape of its own, but assumes the shape of the object just as water assumes the form of the container. If this were the case, the consciousness of an object (*viṣaya-caitanya*) becomes identified with its corresponding mental mode (*antaḥ-karaṇa-vṛtti*). The union of these two limited forms of consciousness gives rise to the perception of the knowledge of the object.[6] The *pramātṛ-caitanya* ('consciousness of the knower') which, being a knower, remains isolated and *perceives* the knowledge of an object (*jñāna-gata-pratyakṣa*). In this case there is the distinction between a knower (*jñātṛ*) and a known object (*jñeya*). That is why it is the perceptuality of knowledge of an object (*jñāna-gata-pratyakṣatva*).

But there is another case of perception, which is called perceptuality of an object (*viṣaya-gata-pratyakṣatva*). For having a cognition of an object the existence of a knower is a precondition, insofar as the cognition of an object without the knower is impossible. If it is said that there is the perceptuality of object, it should be treated as different from the perceptuality of knowledge of an object (*jñāna-gata-pratyakṣa*). It is *not* knowledge which is perceived, but the *object only*. Such a situation cannot give rise to knower–known relationship (*jñātṛ-jñeya-bhāva*). Hence Dharmarāja Adhvarīndra says that in such cases there is only the knower in the form of consciousness (*pramātṛ-caitanya*); but other two, i.e. consciousness of the mental mode (*antaḥ-karaṇa-vṛtti*) and consciousness of an object, are united in the knower (*pramātṛ*). This situation is described by him as *pramātṛ-sattâtirikta-sattākatvâbhāva* ('an absence of the existence of other forms of consciousness excepting the existence of the knower').[7] Herein lies some sort of metaphysical presupposition. In this case Dharmarāja is dealing with metaphysics in disguise of epistemology. When a person thinks himself identified with the whole world, it is the stage of liberation due to the absence of reality of more than one (*advaita*). In this case an object is *not mere an object* but a *subjectified object*. Though there is no difference in saying 'subjectified object' and 'objectified subject' as evidenced in the *Bhagavad-gītā* (BhG 6.29: *sarva-bhūta-stham ātmānaṁ sarva-bhūtāni câtmani*, i.e. extension of self to others and bringing others under self), Dharmarāja preferred to use 'subjectified object', since *pramātṛ* ('knower') only remains at this stage. There is the absence of the existence of other objects excepting the existence of knower (*pramātṛ*). Is it not a state of liberation? Such a state is generally realised temporally at the time of aesthetic enjoyment (*rasa*). In KĀ, p. 92, Abhinavagupta has ex-

---

[6] VPar, p. 14: *tatra yathā taḍāgodakaṁ chidrān nirgatya kulyâtmanā kedārān praviśya tadvad eva catuṣ-koṇâdy-ākāraṁ bhavati, tathā taijasam antaḥ-karaṇam api cakṣurâdi-dvārā nirgatya ghaṭâdi-viṣaya-deśam gatvā ghaṭâdi-viṣyâkāreṇa pariṇamate sa eva pariṇāmo vṛttir ucyate.*

[7] VPar, p. 25: *ghaṭâder viṣayasya pratyakṣaṁ tu pramātr-abhinnatvam ... pramātr-abhedo nāma na tāvad aikyaṁ kintu pramātṛ-sattâtirikta-sattākatvâbhāvaḥ.*

plained this state of 'subjectified object' as 'the melting of the state of the knower' (*pramātṛ-bhāva-vigalana*). Just as an object when liquidified covers many areas, in the like manner the knower can expand himself in such a way so that all objects are included in him. At this stage he is not confined within himself but expands himself to all the objects and hence objects have no other existence other than that of the knower. That is why an individual can enjoy aesthetic pleasure (*rasa*) as he considers the pathos etc. belonging to characters of the novel or drama as his own due to his emotional involvement. This sharing of others' feelings is called by Abhinavagupta (KĀ, p. 84) *tan-mayī-bhavana* ('becoming one with other'). It may be asked to the Advaitins whether it is the case of epistemology or metaphysics. Whatever may be their reply, we have shown that a set of metaphysical presuppositions has led Dharmarāja Adhvarīndra to formulate such a definition of perception.

If we turn to the Buddhists in general and Dharmakīrti in particular, they are also not free from some basic presuppositions such as theories of momentariness, dependent origination, causal efficacy (*artha-kriyā-kāritva*) etc. as a characteristic feature of being (*sat*) etc. Keeping these in view Dharmakīrti has formulated the definition of perception: 'perceptual cognition is the non-erroneous cognition of an entity free from mental ascriptions.'[8] Is it not true that such a definition is given keeping some presuppositions in mind?[9]

Hence there is hardly anything in different systems of Indian philosophy which may be described as 'pure epistemology' or 'unbiased epistemology'. Perhaps this is the characteristic feature of all branches of philosophy. Behind the formulation of this definition Dharmakīrti has two presuppositions in mind: (1) the mark of an existent entity is its causal efficacy (*artha-kriyā-kārtitva-lakṣaṇaṁ sat*) and (2) whatever is existent is momentary (*yat sat tat kṣaṇikam*). An object endowed with mental ascriptions is not momentary due to its conceptualisation and hence it loses its unique singular (*sva-lakṣaṇa*). That is why the perceptual entity is described as free from mental ascriptions so that its unique momentary character is preserved.

While discussing the Buddhists definition of perception one could easily remember the affinities between *sva-lakṣaṇa*-character of an object and indeterminate perception (*nirvikalpaka-pratyakṣa*). Regarding the acceptance of a *sva-lakṣaṇa* ('unique singular') entity there are problems. As for example, an unique singular (*sva-lakṣaṇa*) entity is existent (*sat*) by virtue of its causal efficacy (*artha-kriyā-kāritva*).

---

[8] NB 3: *tatra kalpanâpoḍham abhrāntaṁ pratyakṣaṁ*.

[9] The presuppositions like an entity's momentary (*kṣaṇika*) and unique singular character (*sva-lakṣaṇa*) lead the Buddhists to formulate the definition of perception in such a manner so that this momentary and unique singular character of an entity is protected. In this context the question of circularity may be raised but it is of the virtuous type because no theorisation is possible without these presuppositions.

How can the causal efficacy of it be judged with a moment (*kṣaṇa*), the minutest particle of time? At the same time I would like to state that the Navya-nyāẏa theory of indeterminate perception (*nirvikalpaka-pratyakṣa*) in its turn is not free from some problems either. I would suggest one or two problems that the acceptance of the theory of indeterminate perception as admitted by the Nyāya poses. These problems occur due to the inconsistency of the presuppositions of the Naiyāyikas. First, Viśvanātha in his *Bhāṣā-pariccheda* (verse 51) and *Siddhānta-muktâvalī* has accepted that presentative cognition (*anubhava*) may be valid (*yathârtha*) and invalid (*ayathârtha*). The valid presentative cognition (*yathârthânubhava*) is of four types: perceptual cognition, inferential cognition, cognition through similarity and verbal testimonial cognition. The instruments of these are the four *pramāṇa*s, i.e. perception (*pratyakṣa*), inference (*anumāna*), comparison (*upamāna*) and verbal testimony (*śabda*). The perception is of two types: determinate (*savikalpaka*) and indeterminate (*nirvikalpaka*). Viśvanātha has accepted indeterminate perception as a form of perception but subsequently he remarks: 'the cognition which is indeterminate is beyond our sense-organ.'[10] If it is beyond the reach of our sense organ, how can it be called a form of *laukika-pratyakṣa* (ordinary perception)?[11] For, there is the lack of conditions of being perceptual due to not having the contact of the sense organ with the object (*indriyârtha-saṁnikarṣa*). Secondly, there arises the problem of determining its validity (*prāmāṇya*). If it is a form of perception, it must be true. But afterwards it is said that the truth-value cannot be assigned to it. It is neither true nor false. If it is so, it can never be a case of perceptual knowledge. Thirdly, if it is accepted that it is true how can *prāmāṇya* be ascertained? The Naiyāyikas believe in the extrinsic validity of truth (*parataḥ-prāmāṇya*), which cannot be applied to the indeterminate perception. Viśvanātha's position cannot be taken for granted due to the absence of feasibility of applying the extrinsic validity of truth which will go against the Naiyāyikas basic presuppositions. In this way we judge the justifiability of a theory through the spectacle of the ontological presuppositions, which proves that there is hardly any room for independent reasoning developed afterwards.

That the Naiyāyikas are bound with the ontological presuppositions is evidenced from the acceptance of the *prameya*s ('knowable entities'). The Nyāya admits twelve *prameya*s: the self (*ātman*), body (*śarīra*), sense-organ (*indriya*), object (*artha*), cognition (*buddhi*), mind (*manas*), inclination (*pravṛtti*), defect (*doṣa*), rebirth (*pretya-bhāva*), result (*phala*), suffering (*duḥkha*) and liberation (*apavarga*), the real

[10] BhPar 58: *jñānaṁ yan nirvikalpâkhyaṁ tad atīndrayaṁ iṣyate*.

[11] It may be argued that there are certain perceptions like *yogi-pratyakṣa* (transcendental perception) and *ārṣa-pratyakṣa* (seer perception), which are non-sensuous (*atīndriya*) in character caused by the contact of *ātman* and *manas*. But it should be kept in mind that these are not ordinary forms of perceptions but extra-ordinary (*alaukika*).

cognition of which leads us to realm of *apavarga*. From the false cognition an individual is entangled with this worldly affair leading to suffering and hence the real cognition of twelve *pramaya*s leads us to the world of liberation. Among these *prameya*s self is fundamental. Wrong cognition of the self arises where the self is understood as the non-self. Ordinary human beings consider the non-selves such as the body, sense organ and mind as selves and take new birth and death again and again. So long as there is no separation of the self from the body etc. an individual cannot be absolutely free from suffering. As soon as the wrong notion of the self in non-self vanishes, an individual attains liberation in the form of absolute cessation of suffering due to the loss of the cause of suffering. Hence, the realisation of the self is the real cause of liberation and hence the self is mentioned at the outset among the *prameya*s.

The right cognition of the categories leads us to the attainment of mundane and transcendental well-being (*dṛṣṭa* and *adṛṣṭa niḥśreyasa*). The right cognition of the categories such as *pramāṇa*, *vāda*, *jalpa*, *chala*, *hetv-ābhāsa* etc. leads us to the mundane well-being, because they are beneficial for defeating others and defending our own stand point. If an individual is well conversant with the categories and their application, he can easily understand the points of defeat (*nigraha-sthāna*), 'quibble' (*chala*) and 'pseudo-reason' (*hetv-ābhāsa*) in others argument, which can lead him to the world of victory in the field of philosophical debate. In the same way, the right cognition of the self, one of the *prameya*s, can conjoin us with the transcendental well-being (*adṛṣṭa-niḥśreyasa*), i.e. the attainment of liberation.[12] The true cognition of the self can remove ignorance or wrong notion (*mithyā-jñāna*), which again removes suffering, aversion and attachment (*rāga-dveṣa*) caused by the wrong notion. If there is non-attachment, there cannot be inclination (*pravṛtti*) towards an object. Due to the absence of inclination the merit and demerit cannot be generated. Owing to the lack of *dharma* and *adharma* there is no possibility of rebirth, which is meant for the enjoyment of the result of *karma* by an individual being. The absence of birth leads to the absence of suffering, which is the state of liberation according to Nyāya.[13]

This type of philosophical procedure of attaining liberation through self-realisation in primarily due to the Naiyāyikas first belief in the authority of the *Veda* and *Veda*s. Though the Nyāya is taken to be a realistic philosophy, yet it is not free from the influence of *Veda* or *Veda*s at the grass root level of their philosophy. Like the Vedāntins they also believe that the realisation of the self ultimately leads to the

---

[12] NS 1.1.1, vol 1, p. 65.

[13] NS 1.1.2: *duḥkha-janma-pravṛtti-doṣa-mithyā-jñānānām uttarôttarâpāye tad-antarâpāyād apavargaḥ*.

realm of liberation. Though the Naiyayīkas have mentioned *pramāṇa* as the first category to prove the existence of *prameya*, yet it cannot be ignored that the application of *pramāṇa* is to know the self truly (*tattva-jñāna*), otherwise there is a chance of misapprehension of self. When *pramāṇa* is applied, the total end-in-view of applying it, i.e. to conjoin an individual to liberation through self-realisation, is in the background. Hence *pramāṇa* is not 'objective', because of an agent cannot apply it 'freely', but 'subjective' or teleological, in the sense that it cannot be unbiased. That the Naiyayīkas are bound with the Upaniṣadic self etc. is evidenced from the example of *jahad-ajahad-lakṣaṇa* ('quasi-inclusive implication') taken by Annambhaṭṭa as *tat tvam asi* ('Thou art that'). Is it a case epistemology in the true sense of the term? Certainly not, because it is mixed with the metaphysics, which has been taken as an indeterminate perception (*nirvikalpaka-pratyakṣa*) by the Advaitin. In this case the testimonial cognition is based on some notion of self which is metaphysical.

Let us explain the same in the following way.

The indeterminate perception or *nirvikalpaka-pratyakṣa* is accepted in the case of the recognitive cognitions, such as 'This is that Devadatta' (*so 'yam devadattaḥ*) or 'That art thou' (*tat tvam asi*), on account of the fact that it does not reveal the relation between the two, i.e. this and that Devadatta or That and thou. It has been interpreted by the Advaitins that the sentence conveys the sense that Devadatta exists in Devadatta himself or an individual self exists in himself in the form of Brahman. But they do not admit any relation between the two by the term *vaiśiṣṭyânavagāhin* ('absentee of knowledge apprehending relatedness of the qualificand and qualifier'). If the meaning of the aforesaid sentences is pondered upon, it will be revealed that these are not actually relation-free. In other words, like other components the relation is also revealed in such cases due to the following reasons. First, how do we know that Devadatta exists in himself without the assumption of the relation of identity between them? Any type of recognitive cognition presupposes the relation of identity (at least in the sense of similarity) between two existing earlier or at present time. To the Advaitins identity (*tādātmya*) is the vital relation in the phenomenal cognition. In fact, they admit *tādātmya* in the places where there is a part-and-whole relation (*avayavâvayavi-bhāva-sambandha*) etc. Hence *tādāmya* has very often been accepted as a relation. To the Advaitins *tādātmya* ('identity') is taken in the sense of similarity as found in colour and the possessor of it. In the cases cited above there must be a relation of identity (*tādātmya*) in the sense of similarity between this and that Devadatta. That is why the recognitive knowledge (*pratyabhijñā*) is possible. Secondly, though there is no absolute identity between this Devadatta and that Devadatta or an individual being and Brahman, there must be an essential identity (*svarūpa-tādātmya*) between them. Otherwise, the sentences could not provide the intended meaning. Lastly, the cognition coming through the sentences are called relational in character, as it is sentential in nature. A sentence becomes meaningful if there is a word, its meaning and their relation. It may be asked whether in the words and their meaning there is signifier–signified relationship (*vācya-vācaka-bhāva*) or not. If the answer is in positive, relation is accepted between them. If not, the sentences cannot provide the desired meaning due to the lack of signifying character (*vācakatva*) of the words. In fact, Dharmarāja Adhvarīndra has accepted the meaningfulness of the sentences, which entails the existence of the relation in them. Hence the definition of *nirvikalpaka* perception as formulated by the Advaitins is hardly adequate. At least this type of definition apparently fails to justify *nirvikalpaka* cognition. The problem has been well taken by the Advaitins by giving a fresh interpretation of the above-mentioned sentence. To them the meaning of the sentences such as *so 'yaṁ devadattaḥ* or *tat tvam asi* etc. is indivisible (*akhaṇḍârtha*). When the sentences produce right cognition without being related to the relation among the words, it is called indivisible meaning. Only the stem (*prātipadika*), which are free from the suffixes causing relation, can give rise to indivisible meaning. In the case of the *nirvikalpaka-pratyakṣa* there is no relation between the meanings of the terms, but it gives an indivisible meaning after ignoring the individual ones.[14] Such statement is dependent on some metaphysical presuppositions, such as the phenomenon of *śabda-brahman* or *sphoṭa* in *Vedānta-paribhāṣā* (VPar).

Two types of perception, apart from the previously mentioned one, are *jīva-sākṣin* and *īśvara-sākṣin*. It has been mentioned in the *Vedānta-paribhāṣā* that the distinction between an individual being (*jīva*) and witness in self (*jīva-sākṣin*) lies on the status of internal sense-organ (*antaḥ-karaṇa*). If consciousness is limited by mind or inner organ it is called *jīva* (*antaḥ-karaṇâvacchinnaṁ caitanyaṁ jīvaḥ*). If the same *antaḥ-karaṇa* remains as a limiting adjunct (*upādhi*) in a *jīva*, it is called *jīva-sākṣin*. In the same way, the consciousness qualified by *māyā* is called *īśvara* or God (*māyâvacchinnaṁ caitanyaṁ paramêśvaraḥ*). When the same *māyā* remains as a limiting adjunct (*upādhi*) of consciousness, it is called witness in God (*īśvara-sākṣin*). The property, which is related to the predicate (*kāryânvayin*) and becomes a distinguisher (*vyāvarttaka*), being present (*vartamāna*) in a possessor of property, is called *viśeṣaṇa* while something, which cannot be related to the predicate (*kāryânanvayin*) and becomes a distinguisher (*vyāvarttaka*), being present (*vartamāna*) in the possessor of property, is called *upādhi*. Though the distinction between *viśeṣaṇa* and *upādhi* has been shown clearly, it is very difficult to understand the

[14] VPar (*Pratyakṣa-pariccheda*), p. 35: *idam eva tat tvam asi ity-ādi-vākyānāṁ akhaṇḍârthaṁ yat saṁsargânavagāhi-yathârthâjñāna-janakatvaṁ iti*.

exact position whether the inner organ (*antaḥ-karaṇa*) remains in an individual being as an adjunct or limiting adjunct. In the same way the position or status of *māyā* in consciousness (*caitanya*) cannot be known with the help of the reason. Without the help of intuition it is very difficult to have an idea about the status of mind in an individual being or the status of *māyā* in a consciousness. It needs *vision* to know the same. If these are known transcendentally, why are they called the forms of perception? The phenomena of *jīva-sākṣin* and *īśvara-sākṣin* are more metaphysical in character than epistemological. Hence the Advaitins cannot do 'pure epistemology' without the help of metaphysics.

In connection with the immediate awareness (*aparokṣa-jñāna*) Dharmarāja Adhvarīndra has pointed out that such perceptual awareness may sometimes arise from the testimony also, which is called perceptual awareness generated through verbal testimony (*śābda-janya-pratyakṣa*).

It has been argued by the Advaitins that, when an individual comes to know of his happiness through the utterance of the sentence 'You are happy' (*tvaṁ sukhī*) by somebody else, would it be considered as perceptual? The answer is in the positive, to the Advaitins. They have put forward an example of perceptual awareness through some testimonial cognition. A leader of a team is counting the members of his team to confirm that nobody is left behind. Among the ten members every time he is counting nine members but not ten, not including himself due to his absent-mindedness. Being pointed out by some body else he comes to know that he has not counted himself. Ultimately the person pointed him out as the tenth person and said: 'You are the tenth' (*daśamas tvam asi*). This is a case of perception, no doubt, which is generated through the utterance of the sentence by some body else.[15] Actually this type of awareness suggests a great area of the Advaita philosophy. To the Advaitins an individual being is always free, but he does not know it. When it is pointed out that he is free from suffering through the injunction of the *śāstra* or *āgama* or through hearing (*śravaṇa*), reflection (*manana*) and meditating (*nididhyāsana*), he suddenly sees himself free. This freedom is not new to him, but it is acquirement of what is acquired (*prāptasya prāptiḥ*). An individual's liberation or freedom is not at all a new achievement, but awareness of something, which is already known. This knowing of the known is possible through the testimonial statement as found in different *śruti*s. The function of the testimony in the form of *śruti* is to make someone aware of his own position and status. It provides the true picture of the human being, his freedom etc. about which he did not know. Hence, perception in the field

---

[15] VPar (*Pratyakṣa-pariccheda*), p. 19: *na câivam api vartamāna-daśāyāṁ tvaṁ sukhī ity ādi-vākya-janya-jñānasya pratyakṣâpattiḥ syād iti vācyam iṣṭatvāt, daśamas tvam asi ity-ādau sannikṛṣṭa-viṣaye śabdād apy aparokṣa-jñānâbhyupagamāt.*

of freedom or liberation is generated through the āgamic statement *tat tvam asi*, which is very much significant in Indian Philosophical systems. In order to highlight this metaphysical aspect they have introduced a specific type of *pratyakṣa* called *śabda-janya-pratyakṣa* ('perceptual cognition generated through verbal testimony').

Indian theories of error called 'error theory' (*khyāti-vāda*) as admitted by different systems are based on purely metaphysical structure. The Vijñāna-vādin and Śūnya-vādin schools of Buddhism propagate consciousness-centric error theory (*ātma-khyāti-vāda*) and non-existent error theory (*asat-khyāti-vāda*) respectively after keeping the theory of consciousness in the form of *vijñana* (consciousness) and *śūnyatā* (voidness) in view. Such is the case with the indescribable theory of error (*anirvacanīya-khyāti-vāda*). In this case the represented object or the mistakenly known object is admitted as different from existent or non-existent (*sad-asad-vilakṣaṇa*), because it (i.e. the snake in the case of rope) is neither existent due to its sublation by the latter cognition nor non-existent due to having its apparent awareness (*prātibhāsika-sattā*). The Mīmāmsaka who do not believe in the existence of erroneous cognition formulates the theory of no error theory (*akhyāti*) presupposing it in view.

The Naiyāyikas admit that more than one *pramāṇa* can be applied to know a single object, which is called the theory of *pramāṇa-samplava*. The nature of an object is not a factor for applying *pramāṇa*. As for example, 'fire' can be known through perception, inference or verbal testimony. But so far as the Buddhist view is concerned, a particular nature of an object determines the particular means of knowing (*pramāṇa*) through which alone it is revealed. An object having a unique characteristic (*sva-lakṣaṇa*) is revealed by perception alone. A *sva-lakṣaṇa*-entity ('unique singular') cannot be revealed by inference and in the same way the *sāmānya-lakṣaṇa*-entity ('entity characterised by generality') can be known by inference alone, but not capable of being known by perception. This metaphysical presupposition leads them to admit the system of a specific fixed means of knowing (*pramāṇa-vyavasthā*). The Buddhists may say that if more than one *pramāṇa* is applied in a certain case, the object may be seen as having contradictory nature. To them if perception, inference and verbal testimony have a common object, the object should have been of similar type. But actually we find 'fire' for example, perceived in proximity is different from that existing in a remote distance. If an object is seen from a distance, it is seen as associated with some general features. When it comes near, the same object seems to have some other special features. Hence, perception, inference and verbal testimony differ from each other regarding the object grasped by them.

But the Naiyāyikas stick to their decision that many modes of knowing (*pramāṇa*) can be applied to the same object. They assert that a locus having diverse properties is one and the same. Jayanta (NMa, p. 33) has referred to the paradigm case of applying various *pramāṇa*s in a particular situation. From the words of a trustworthy person an individual can know of the existence of fire in a distant place. He goes towards the locus of fire. When he goes certain distance, he sees smoke arising from a place by which he infers the existence of fire. When he goes nearest to the fire, he perceives the same with his own.

— 3 —

From the above-mentioned arguments it can be concluded that *pramāṇa-śāstra* is not free from metaphysical or ontological commitment. In fact, when a particular epistemic theory is propagated by a particular system, the philosophers belonging to the school keep the ontological presupposition in view. Being influenced by this they formulate an epistemic theory, which can ultimately prove these presuppositions. Before a particular epistemic theory is formulated, its formulation is influenced by the presuppositions. The ontological commitment guides a philosopher remaining in him in the form of proposition (*pratijñā*). The same ontology or *prameya* is proved through the *pramāṇa*, which is in the substantiated form as we find in the case of conclusion (*nigamana*). When it is said that '*prameya* is established through *pramāṇa*' (*mānâdhīnā meya-siddhiḥ*), Indian philosophers talk of the latter type of function occupying the position of *nigamana*. The above-mentioned point may be highlighted again following the Advaitic line. In the beginning of the *Adhyāsa-bhāṣya* Śaṅkara has given the definition of superimposition (*adhyāsa*) as 'the appearance of the previously seen object in a different place, which has affinities with memory is called superimposition.'[16] This definition is in the description level, which has no relation with the actual realisation of the same. This is not the result of experience. When the self is realised, an individual can realise the truth of the statement describing *ādhyāsa* ('superimposition'). This description is the starting point to reach the realm of realisation. The true nature of the illusoriness of the world (*adhyāsa*) can be realised just after self-realisation has been attained. The first introduction with the concept of *adhyāsa* is taken as proposition (*pratijñā*) and the realisation of the same at the end is the conclusion (*nigamana*). Though the proposition and conclusion seem to be the same, there is a gulf of difference between the two. The former is a mere description given by somebody else from his experience while the latter is the result of an individual's own realisation. Such is the case with other theoretical enterprises. But it should be kept in view that these probable entities (*meya*) are working in the brain of the philosophers before the theoretical formation of knowledge starts. Hence, theory of knowledge can never be unbiased in the true sense of the term.

[16] ABh, p. 4: *āha—ko 'yaṁ adhyāso nāma iti. ucyate—smṛti-rūpaḥ paratra pūrva-dṛṣṭâvabhāsaḥ.*

BIBLIOGRAPHY

ABh = Śaṅkara: *Adhyāsa-bhāṣya*. Srimohan Tarkatirtha (ed.): *Brahma-sūtra-śāṅkara-bhāṣya Bhāmatī*. Sanskrit Pustak Bhandar, Calcutta 1980.

BhG = *Bhagavad-gītā*. Jayadayal Goyandaka (ed., Hindi tr.): *Śrīmad-bhagavad-gītā. With Śāṅkarabhāṣya*. Gita Press, Gorakhapur 1938.

BhPar = Viśanatha: *Bhāṣā-pariccheda*. Krishnaballabh Acharya (ed.): *Nyāya-siddhānta-muktâvalī*. Chowkhamba Sanskrit Series Office, Varanasi 2003.

KĀ = *Kāvyâloka*. Sudhir Kumar Dasgupta (ed.): *Kāvyāloka* . Vol. I. A. Mukherjee & Co., Calcutta 1386 (Bengali Saṁvat).

NB = Dharmakīrti: *Nyāya-bindu*. Gangopadhyaya, Mrinalkanti (ed.): *Nyāya-bindu-ṭīkā*. Indian Studies, Kolkata 1971.

NBh = Vātsyāyana Pakṣilasvāmin: *Nyāya-bhāṣya*. See: NS.

NMa = Jayanta-bhaṭṭa: *Nyāya-mañjarī*. Pt. Surya Nārāyaṇa Śukla (ed.): *Nyāyamañjarī of Jayanta Bhaṭṭa*. Part 1. *Kashi Sanskrit Series* 106, Chowkhamba Sanskrit Series Office, Varanasi 1971.

NS = Akṣapāda Gautama: *Nyāya-sūtra*. Phanibhūṣaṇa Tarkavāgīśa (ed.): *Nyāya-darśana*. Vol. I, West Bengal State Book Board, Calcutta 1989.

VPar = Dharmarāja Adhvarīndra: *Vedānta-paribhāṣā*. Swami Madhavananda (ed.; English tr.): *Vedānta-paribhāṣā with Sanskrit Text*. Belur Math 1972.

Power and Insight in Jain Discourse*

PETER FLÜGEL

In contrast to earlier Jainological emphasis on the unchanging and dogmatic nature of doctrinal Jainism, recent historical-philological and anthropological scholarship focuses predominately on historically changing, syncretic and hybrid features of Jain beliefs and practices, and on the role of agency in the construction of socioreligious identity.[1] Contrary to culturalist self-images and academic representations, it is widely recognised that the 'differences which separate Jainism from Hinduism and Buddhism ... are largely differences of emphasis for all are built from common material' (WILLIAMS (1983: xxii));[2] and that 'even though Jainism is a distinct religion and not a sect of Hinduism, still it is a fact that in the past [and present] many Jains used to regard themselves as Hindus and were also regarded by others as Hindus' (SANGAVE (1980: 3)). This raises questions about the characteris-

---

* This essay was originally conceived as a *prolegomenon* to my paper *Worshipping the Ideal King: On the Social Implications of Medieval Jain Conversion Stories*, which will be published under this title. Earlier versions of this paper were presented to the 'Hindu Studies Seminar' at the School of Oriental and Africa Studies in London, 25 November 1992, and to the 'Jains in Indian History and Culture Workshop' at Amherst College, 25 June 1993. A version of the *prolegomenon* written up for publication in 1996 was presented, essentially unchanged but updated and expanded, to the Conference 'Logic and Belief in Indian Philosophy' in Bialowieza, Warsaw University, 5 May, 2006. I am indebted to the participants of these fora for feedback, and particularly to Kornelius Krümpelmann, who commented on the manuscript. I also wish to express my gratitude to the Deutsche Forschungsgemeinschaft (DFG) and the Arts and Humanities Research Board (AHRB) in Britain for supporting my participation in the conferences in Amherst and Bialowieza.

[1] It is impossible to define a religious tradition, such as Jainism through a list of unchanging attributes. LÉVI-STRAUSS (1970: 3 ff.) prefers to talk about crystallisation of secondary differences within syncretic fields. Another viable strategy is to analyse contextually changing self-attributions. FOUCAULT (1981: 69) investigates discourse diachronically as a 'regular and distinct series of events' rather than positing a 'tradition' which might be 'behind discourse'. See also LUHMANN (1982). CARRITHERS (1990) and GOMBRICH (1996: 7), similarly, opt for the study of religious tradition as 'a chain of events'.

[2] Because of this common heritage, contemporary Jain 'orthodoxy' classifies only originally non-Indian traditions, such as Judaism, Christianity, and Islam, as truly heretical. See JAINI (1979: 314, n. 63). In the following I will focus on the relationship between 'Hindu' religions and Jainism only.

Logic and Belief in Indian Philosophy
Warsaw Indological Studies 3 (2010) 85–217.

tic features and the politics of Jain discourse, the principle medium of Jain cultural synthesis.[3] DUMONT (1980: 210) once stated that the Jains, like any non-Hindu group in India, 'cannot be regarded as independent of the environment in which it is set, as really constituting a society by itself, however strongly its own values push it in this direction.' Yet, whether, or to what extent, the Jains 'derive their *raison d'être* from their distinctive ways of manoeuvring within a [hierarchical] structure that they share with the whole society' (MARRIOTT (1976: 131)) needs further research.[4] LAIDLAW (1985), (1995: 95), in one of the few studies of Jain discourse to date,[5] argues that 'Jain cultural distinctiveness does not rest on rituals or practices in which people are marked as different and counted in or out' but on 'a range of practices and relationships through which Jains *participate* in Hindu public culture in India, and do so as Jains.' Jain culture is defined as a shared ethical life-style, or 'class psychology', grounded in 'a set of processes and practices which cluster around the ownership, management, funding, and use of property' (LAIDLAW (1985: 147, cf. 349 f.)). Socioreligious group formations beyond the institutions of family, caste and religious trusts are seen as ephemeral and dependent on instrumental processes of strategic mass mobilisation by individual lay leaders. CARRITHERS (1992: 118) studied how in conventional settings Jain public speakers 'create, manipulate, and transform' connections between listeners (*śrāvaka*), in particular through the narration of religious stories in communal rhetoric.[6] LAIDLAW's (1985: 55 f.) theory

[3] The single defining criterion that is universally accepted within the Jain tradition is the reference to the Jinas, especially Mahāvīra. To a lesser extent, the notions of practising *ahiṁsā* and vegetarianism, which is nowadays shared with many 'Hindus' and Buddhists, are used as reference points. On problems of Jain identity see FLÜGEL (2005), (2006a), (2006b).

[4] In spite of their differences, DUMONT and MARRIOTT both rely on the code-model of classical structuralism. However, MARRIOTT (1976) and his followers posit a multiplicity of incongruent cultural codes and/or rule-oriented strategies in order to investigate 'surface' phenomena as products of their interaction. The unity of 'Hindu society' or 'culture' is no longer presupposed, 'rather it is an empirical observation to be analyzed' (BURGHART (1978b), (1978a: 38)) in terms of competing groups which 'regulate their interaction on the basis of their own code of hierarchy' (BURGHART (1978a: 36)). The essentialism of 'society' is thus replaced by the essentialism of competing 'strategic groups' or '(sub-) cultures' (within a territorial state).The unity of a system as a whole is then generated through (a) mutual incorporation of elements of other codes, and (b) temporary agreements on the code of interaction (BURGHART (1978a: 37)). BURGHART (1983), (1985), in his outline of the study of intra-cultural 'arenas of interpretation', first noted points of transition between the multiple code-model and HABERMAS' (1980–81) theory of communicative action (which however avoids *a priori* reification of 'groups' altogether by merely presupposing universal interactional competencies).

[5] LAIDLAW (1985) offers an analysis of the relationship between Jain '*mokṣa*-discourse' and '*puṇya*-discourse', on which see CORT (1989) and BABB (1996), who do not explicitly use discourse-analytical approaches.

of the Jain 'language game' and CARRITHERS' (1991: 262) work on the 'rhetoric of *samāj*' both successfully move away from essentialist notions of communal identity. But they achieve this only at the price of recurring to instrumentalist definitions of community formation, disregarding the key dimensions of felt togetherness and shared belief and custom.[7]

In this essay, I propose to avoid both *a priori* definitions of socio-cultural identity and instrumentalist theories of community formation by analysing the stated principles of Jain religious discourse itself. I will compare and contrast these principles with the categories of Jürgen HABERMAS' (1980–81), who in his *Theory of Communicative Action* offers a seemingly non-reductionist interpretation of linguistically mediated processes of socio-cultural synthesis. In contrast to the explicit normative ideals of the Jains, rooted in an ontology of karman, Habermas' theoretical investigation presents itself as a non-ontological reconstruction of regulative ideals implicitly presupposed by all actual human discourse.[8] Some preliminary remarks on the architecture of his theory are necessary.

Habermas' model seeks to transcend the false alternative of 'community' and 'society'—which still dominates the sociology of Indian religions—by focusing on the relationship between 'lifeworld' and 'system' instead, as differentiated in contemporary modern society. 'Lifeworld', a term imported from phenomenology, is defined as the horizon or context of linguistically mediated communicative action.[9]

---

[6] See CARRITHERS (1992: 106) on the importance of the setting for processes of negotiation of Jain identity through the medium of cultural narratives; and FLÜGEL (1993) on the significance of self-referentiality in conversion stories narrated in settings, such as sermons, similar to those described in the narrative itself, thus generating self-verification. BOURDIEU (1991a), in FAUCONNIER (1981: 202 n. 8), demonstrated that self-verification must be distinguished from the success of an intended perlocutionary effect. See also FAUCONNIER's (1981: 185) analysis of the 'principle of incorporation', the description of a rite within the rite.

[7] See TÖNNIES' (1887) classical work on community and society.

[8] HABERMAS' analysis of discourse is influenced by the work of Karl-Otto APEL (1973) and the analysis of the 'colonisation' of discourse by generalised media of communication by the neo-Parsonian social systems theory of LUHMANN (1979) , etc. 'Discourse' is here used in the general sense of a set of verbal or written statements. HABERMAS (1980: 71) / (1984–1987 I: 42), (2005: 20) understands 'discourse' in a more restricted (and old-fashioned) sense as 'reasoning', i.e. the rational exchange of arguments for or against contested claims. In his terms, 'discourse' is the reflective form of 'communicative action' which is distinguished from mere 'communication'. LUHMANN (2002: 42 n. 37) points out that 'capacity for reasoned elaboration' is a traditional definition of 'authority'. See *infra* 106 f.

[9] Following Peirce and Royce, Apel and Habermas presuppose the ideal of an 'infinite community of interpretation' as the 'collective subject'. The resulting contrast between the 'real community of communication' and an implicitly presupposed 'ideal community of communication' has been criticised, for instance by WELLMER (1986: 68 f., 81–102) and ALBERT (2003: 30, 50

It is, in his view, constituted by language and has three components or actor-world relations, in which communications are simultaneously embedded: cultural symbols, social norms, and personal aims. Lifeworlds are conceived as thematic resources for the intersubjective construction of social situations though symbolic or communicative action.[10] In case of disagreement, situations are ideally defined rationally and consensually, through co-operative processes of interpretation based on the rejection or acceptance of claims of objective truth (cognition oriented), normative rightness (action oriented), and subjective sincerity (person oriented). The limited explanatory scope of the lifeworld perspective conceded, HABERMAS (1981: 180) / (1984–1987 II: 118) defines society as a whole 'simultaneously as a system and a lifeworld': 'societies are *systematically stabilised* complexes of action of *socially integrated* groups' (1980–1981: 228) / (1984–1987 II: 152). This definition acknowledges that society is not constituted through symbolic or communicative action alone, but also—and increasingly so—through systemic processes, i.e. the unintended consequences of action and interaction mediated by 'steering media' such as money or power rather than by language. Habermas thus situates the social role of discourse within a theory of differentiation of system and lifeworld. The degree of differentiation determines the extent to which social integration can/must be achieved through symbolic or communicative action alone.[11] Habermas argues that lifeworld and system perspectives are mutually incompatible. His proposed synthesis (chided as 'eclectic' by his critics) prescribes a systematic alternation of the two perspectives, thus addressing the problem in a similar way as Jain perspectivism. Within this framework, Habermas' contribution to discourse analysis results from a single conceptual move: the substitution of the pivotal concept of subjective 'intentionality'

Royce ff.), who advocate for a fallibilistic notion of consensus and deny a general interest in infinite discussion (ALBERT (2003: 70)). For a similar conceptual structure see, however, the Buddhist (and Jain) distinction between 'real' and 'ideal' *saṅgha*, analysed for instance by BECHERT (1961: 23 f., 35). HABERMAS (1991: 133) conceded that the normative content of universal pragmatic presuppositions can not be equated with obligatory norms of interaction. Anticipating presuppositions are normative in 'a wider sense', enabling practice, without regulating it. In his recent revision of his epistemic universal pragmatic concept of truth, HABERMAS (2004: 50–55, 256 f.) renounced the concept of a 'final consensus', because it is beyond the necessity and problems of discourse, and distinguishes now between truth and legitimation.

[10] Communicative action is defined as the reflexive form of symbolic interaction.

[11] HABERMAS (1981: 219) / (1984–1987 II: 145): 'Universal discourse points to an idealized lifeworld reproduced through processes of mutual understanding that have been largely detached from normative contexts and transferred over to rationally motivated yes/no positions. This sort of growing autonomy can come to pass only to the extent that the constraints of material reproduction no longer hide behind the mask of a rationally impenetrable, basic, normative consensus, that is to say, behind the authority of the sacred.'

(championed by Weberian, Husserlian or Wittgensteinian variants of interpretive sociology)[12] with the notion of intersubjective 'communication' (*Verständigung*), which in his view is the inherent *telos* of human language.[13] The intersubjective alternative to conventional subject-philosophical approaches[14] enables Habermas to criticise empirical discourses of power, based on 'instrumental action', as 'deviations' from an 'original' mode of unconstrained 'communicative action', implicitly presupposed by all interlocutors.

Habermas' characterisation of the constitutive role of implicit idealisations for linguistically mediated interaction by the term 'ideal speech situation' has been widely criticised (in similar ways as Chomsky's 'ideal speech community'), since, by definition, ideal situations are rarely, if ever, empirically encountered, and not even consciously contemplated by the majority of interlocutors.[15] Though it is a truism that ideals can only influence behaviour if they differ from it, a society which relies entirely on explicit consensus is both a modern utopia and a nightmare, since everything can become problematic under the imperative of rational control in an ideal world of unconstrained intersubjectivity. To avoid the 'cost' of social reflexivity, social life has to rely on traditions, habits, routines and systemic processes (mediated by institutions or markets) which are taken for granted, until questioned. This is recognised by the model. Habermas insists, however, that the fundamental unspoken expectations underlying all social interaction can be analytically reconstructed. Conflict, for instance over values, can only be peacefully resolved if the normative presuppositions of communicative action, such as common interest in the avoidance of violence, are implicitly observed.[16] Hence, rather than dismissing Habermas' 'utopianism' outright,[17] it may be more fruitful to ask whether the prin-

---

[12] See HABERMAS (1984: 35–82, 307–50) on three types of intentionality: fundamental intentionality of consciousness, strategic intentionality, and intentionality of non-deliberate actions. Phenomenological 'intentionality of consciousness' (not to be confused with Weber's 'strategic intentionality' or Searle's concept of subjective 'meaning intentionality') can be usefully compared with Jain concepts of consciousness and intentionality. An intentionalist stance alone can, however, not account for social processes of acceptance or definitions of acceptability of actions or arguments. APEL (1993: 41) stressed, rightly in my view, the 'reciprocal dependence of a priori of consciousness and linguistic a priori'.

[13] HABERMAS (1984: 461). *Verständigung* is itself an ambiguous word, combining 'understanding' (something, someone) and 'coming to an agreement' or 'reaching understanding'.

[14] See HABERMAS (1985) for an analysis of the *aporias* of 20th century philosophy.

[15] E.g. ALEXY (1996: 155 ff., 412 ff.).

[16] HABERMAS (1991: 169) derives the normative presuppositions of communicative action from the notion of 'common interest'. In (neo-)Parsonian sociology, the condition that the interacting units know that both could also act differently is known as 'double contingency'.

[17] ALBERT (1994: 259) chides the analytical projection of such an ideal into 'pre-theoretical knowledge' as 'normative essentialism'.

ciples of discourse identified by Habermas function indeed as universal presuppositions of communicative action or are merely one set of possible idealisations amongst many. The question is pertinent, since 'communicative action', according to Habermas, is predicated on the implicit recognition of the values of individual autonomy and equality, and the existence of domination-free social spaces and interactional competencies, which are rarely given in any concrete situation. Does Habermas' model, then, merely impose modern European ideals or is his theory indeed of universal relevance?[18]

This question can be explored by comparing Habermas' dialogical model of the 'ideal speech situation' with other models of highly idealised speech situations of a similar level of abstraction, such as the Jain theory of speaking, which, at first sight, seems to be predicated on hierarchical, or subject oriented, rather than egalitarian, or intersubjective, normative presuppositions.[19] From Habermas' perspective, the principles informing hierarchical systems, even if culturally dominant, cannot be universalised, since they themselves are predicated on the principles of communicative action which are (from the perspective of analytical reconstruction) consciously or unconsciously presupposed in all linguistically mediated interaction. Conversely, from a Jain perspective, the ontology of soul, non-soul, karman and the principle of non-violence are implicitly presupposed in all universally acceptable actions. In

---

[18] KEENAN's (1976) ethnographic critique of the postulated universality of Grice's conversational maxims has been extended to Habermas by PRATT (1986: 70). Disregarding criticism of Keenan's arguments, for instance by PRINCE (1982), she argues that Habermas' 'ideal speech act' merely reflects dominant Western standards of normality used to criticise 'deviations' as 'systemic distortions'. Following Nietzsche, FOUCAULT (1981: 56) had earlier criticised the 'will to truth' as a 'machinery of exclusion' of 'false discourses'. See also LINKENBACH's (1986: 108 n. 43) anthropological critique of Habermas 'objective hermeneutics'. HABERMAS (1983: 88 ff.) / (1990: 78 ff.) responded to objections to his 'ethnocentrism' in his work on discourse ethics, distinguishing 'moral' questions of 'common interest' or 'justice', orienting his own work, from 'ethical' questions of 'the good life' or 'self-realisation' which are culturally specific (HABERMAS (1983: 118).

[19] Normative presuppositions in Indian theories of language have been discussed by GANERI (1999: 17), who pointed to differences between the subject-centred epistemological conception of language in Nyāya and information transmission theories which, in contrast to the Nyāya theory of 'direct, non-inferential assent', assume that 'assenting to another's utterance is never direct, but always depends on the hearer's awareness of the speaker's intentions.' The proposal that the 'normativity of meaning' by divine decree in Gadādhara's (Navya-nyāya) semantics can 'partially' be defended in terms of the notion of tacitly shared 'conventional semantic theories' as 'the standard of correctness' within a specific linguistic community, rather than recurring to Matilal's 'ideal hearer' concept (GANERI (1999: 44)), presupposes an intersubjective solution of 'the co-ordination problem'. For the use of 'optimal standpoints' for reconstructing the presuppositions of Jain many-valued logic see also GANERI (2002: 271).

both cases, moments of 'insight' can be generated through the acceptance[20] and situational projection of the respective model.[21] It is debatable whether any comparison between contrasting philosophical or religious models implies a dialectical third perspective which will 'always be more general than the most general postulates of a religion and the most general rules of investigation itself' (PIATIGORSKY (1985: 210)) or is simply an addition without being 'higher or lower' (MURTI (1955: 127)). Frequently cited examples of overarching perspectives that are not predicated on specific comparisons are the dialectic of the categories of reflection (Hegel), the politics of cultural hegemony (Gramsci), or indeed the Jaina conception of a disjunctive synthesis of differences or alternatives (*anekânta-vāda*), which according to MURTI (1955: 128) is 'more a syncretism than a synthesis'. A non-relativistic scenario is plausible if one model is able to reconstruct another on its own terms in a non-reductive way, or if it improves the other model, without losing information, while the reverse is not possible. In such a case, the analytical superiority of one model over the other must be conceded in principle.

A peculiar feature of Habermas' universal pragmatic theory is that it can only be operationalised by 'reversing step by step the strong idealisations' of the concept of

[20] See for instance the extensive literature in analytical theology, following WITTGENSTEIN (1953), on the role of models for religious insight. For example RAMSEY's (1967: 37) analysis of the 'disclosure situation', based on religious commitment: 'So we see religious commitment as a total commitment to the whole universe; something in relation to which argument has only a very odd function; its purpose being to tell such a tale as evokes the "insight", the "discernment" from which the commitment follows as a response. Further, religious commitment is something bound up with key words whose logic no doubt resembles that of words which characterise personal loyalty as well as that of the axioms of mathematics, and somehow combines the features of both, being what may be called "specially resistant" posits, "final" endpoints of explanation, key-words suited to the whole job of living—"apex" words.' See further SMART (1965), HICK (1969), and others.

[21] The concept of 'insight' is used somewhat ambiguously in this article, referring both to cognitive insight in the sense of Habermas (*Einsicht*) and to Jain religious insight (*samyaktva* or *samyag-darśana*). This can be justified by pointing to similar ambiguities (a) in Habermas' use of *Einsicht* referring both to understanding and acceptance (close to Skt. *saṁjñā*, agreement, understanding, harmony), and (b) in the Jain usage of *samyaktva* which can refer to cognitive insight and acceptance of the 'rightness' of Jain doctrine, but mainly describes the 'direct experience' of the soul/self; see JAINI (1979: 80). The understanding of doctrine and self may or may not be linked, for instance in conversion experiences (FLÜGEL (1993)), which can be interpreted as a 'realization and internalization of important dogmatic subjects' (BRUHN (1997–1998, V.1)), though this conception does not account for the 'self-reported' enlightenment experiences of the Jinas. See SCHMITHAUSEN (1981: 199 n. 3) on similar ambiguities of the term 'insight' in early Buddhist scriptures. Generally on the problem of communicating 'experience' in Buddhist contexts see SCHMITHAUSEN (1981: 200 ff.), and for ideological uses FAURE (1991) and SHARF (1995). On Buddhist insight meditation, see GRIFFITHS (1981) and HOUTMAN (1999), amongst others. For observations on Buddhist and Jain meditation see BRONKHORST (1993b).

communicative action to approximate the complexity of natural situations. Because most methodological provisions and theoretical assumptions have to be dropped in this process, universal pragmatics becomes, for all practical purposes, indistinguishable from empirical pragmatics, except for the additional conceptual sensitivity 'needed to recognise the rational basis of linguistic communication in the confusing complexity of the everyday observed' (HABERMAS (1980: 444)/(1984–1987 I: 331).[22] What is gained is the ability to discover different levels of the linguistically represented reality, and communicative pathologies, such as veiled power relationships or systemic distortions of rational communication through the use of generalised media of communication.[23] For formal pragmatic investigations of South Asian discourse the fundamental empirical question is not whether, for instance, *mantras* or ritual language can be considered as 'speech acts', or in which sense.[24] The question is rather, as Richard BURGHART (1996: 301) put it, 'how does non-distorted speech communication take place in hierarchical structures'? BURGHART (1983), (1985) was the first South Asianist to tentatively explore the possibilities of the theory of communicative action for an understanding of religious and political discourse in South Asia. Since his premature death, few advances have been made in rendering Habermas' highly abstract theory fruitful for South Asian studies.

In this essay, I make a fresh attempt in exploring the analytical potential of Habermas' communication theoretical approach for South Asian Studies by contrasting Habermas' discourse ethics, the reflective form of communicative action, with Jain discourse ethics, a reflective form of non-violent action. I will focus particularly on their respective theorisation of the subtle role of power in processes of indirect communication. Habermas opened up a new critical perspective by studying the constitutive role of idealisation in discourse and its exploitation. Alternative approaches, such as FOUCAULT's (1981) and BOURDIEU's (1991a), by contrast, emphasise the ubiquity and institutionalised nature of power. This view exerts a strong influence on current empirical investigations of Jain processes of social self-

[22] On the difference between formal and empirical pragmatics see HABERMAS (1980: 440–52) / (1984–1987 I: 328–37).

[23] Talcott Parsons was the first to argue that symbolically generalised media of communication, steering media, such as power, money, status and value commitment, are the functional equivalents of sacred symbols in co-ordinating actions in societies not dominated by tradition: 'Instead of negotiating to consensus ... men rely on symbols <promising> the experience of meaning as a statistical probability over many acts. They are freed from the efforts to negotiate basics all the time' (BAUM (1976) on Parsons, cited by HABERMAS (1981: 393) / (1984–1987 II: 262).

[24] The potential of speech-act theory for South Asian studies has been explored by POTTER (1970), (1984), WHEELOCK (1982), DESHPANDE (1990), FINDLEY (1989), TABER (1989), GÖHLER (1995a), (1995b), amongst others.

identification.[25] In comparing Habermas' and Jain theories of discourse, I pursue three main arguments as far as the principles of Jain discourse is concerned:

(a) Despite being differently constructed, the Jain theory of speech plays a similar role within Indian philosophy as Habermas' theory of communicative action does within Western philosophy. Both aim at the integration of a variety of perspectives, proclaim the primacy of morality over truth and logic, and predicate critical analysis of typical speech acts, especially latent strategic speech acts (perlocutions), on idealised normative presuppositions.[26]
(b) The orientation towards, and mastery of, the principles of Jainism generates interactional competencies regarding the non-violent resolution of conflicts, and cognitive distancing effects, which enable competent agents to intentionally create ambiguous symbols (utterances and gestures), and to manipulate identities through the re-interpretation of culturally normative or conventional presuppositions. The same can be said of the cognitive functions of modern theories of communication.
(c) The perceived plurivocality or multifunctionality of symbols—one of the main features of syncretism and socio-cultural synthesis in general—is in the Jain case not only a feature of rule-application, or a consequence of external imposition or extrinsic borrowing etc.,[27] but also a consequence of religious knowledge, which can generate effects of insight *qua* (re-) interpretation of any given content. From the conventional point of view of communicative action, the principles of Jain hermeneutics produce systematically distorted communication, albeit one that is ideally oriented to salvific rather than material ends.

My basic contention is that philosophy (and logic), whether preoccupied with questions of universal validity, scepticism or pluralism, is always embedded in socio-cultural milieus which it both reflects and influences in varying degrees. Philosophy is always not 'merely philosophy', but a form of social discourse with social functions, manifest or latent. Philosophy does not merely consist in sets of propositions and logical or argumentative procedures but has also, directly or indirectly, pragmatic and expressive dimensions, and presupposes matching lifeforms

---

[25] See LAIDLAW (1985), (1995), and CORT (1989), (2001: 11, 171), who invokes Eliade's rather then Foucault's theory of power. See FLÜGEL (1997), (2006b: 108 f.).

[26] Citing examples, GÖHLER (1995b: 66) noted, similarly, the 'überraschende Gegenstandsgleichheit der Untersuchungen der Mīmāṁsā und der "Sprechakttheoretiker"' Austin and Searle: 'In etwas anderer Fassung finden sich diese Kategorien auch in der Mīmāṁsā' (GÖHLER (1995b: 69)).

[27] On extrinsic borrowing see DUMONT (1980: 194). For a Jain example see MISRA (1972: 16) on the merely 'nominal adoption' of the local South Indian culture by (Rājasthānī) Śvetâmbara Jain merchants in Bangalore.

and institutions for its social recognition.[28] The comparison between two expressly non-absolutist universalist theories, the theory of communicative action and the Jain theory of language usage, in my view, demonstrates that philosophies are intrinsically connected with a selective range of matching life-forms, while recognising that most socio-cultural milieus are culturally hybrid and contain elements which are universally acceptable. To what extent procedures and contents of 'rational inquiry'[29] are influenced by and influence social context is a question for empirical research.

The aim of this essay is to outline a new approach for the analysis of religious discourse in South Asia, and to prepare the ground for future critical sociolinguistic studies of Jain discourse. For this purpose key theoretical issues of philosophical pluralism and cross-cultural comparison are explored in a heuristic way. The essay is in eight parts. First, I am going to review the general problematic of Jain syncretism (I) and the existing academic literature on Jain rhetoric and discourse (II), followed by an overview of Habermas' theory of communicative action (III) and aspects of the work of Grice and Brown and Levinson, which will prove useful for operationalising Habermas' theory (IV). To prepare the ground for empirical investigation, I will then propose a typology of characteristic social settings of Jain religious discourse, and discuss their normative implications (V). Thereafter, I analyse the key features of the Jain theory of speech (VI), and of Jain discourse ethics in form of the Jain tetrad of the modes of speech (VII). Finally, I draw some general conclusions by comparing and contrasting the normative presuppositions of the theory of communicative action and the Jain theory of speech, which both in their own way offer critical analytical perspectives on the role of power and violence in human communication (VIII).[30]

— I —

One of the key arguments of this essay is that Jainism, as a meta-philosophy whose social efficacy is predicated on the systematic reinterpretation of conventional perspectives, constitutes a form of discourse which produces syncretic patterns. At present, syncretism is predominantly understood as a transitional phase

[28] See LUHMANN (1990). HABERMAS (1991: 25): 'Moralische Einsichten müßten für die Praxis in der Tat folgenlos bleiben, wenn sie sich nicht auf die Schubkraft von Motiven und auf die anerkannte soziale Geltung von Institutionen stützen könnten. ... jede universalistische Moral ist auf entgegenkommende Lebensformen angewiesen.'

[29] BRONKHORST (1999: 23 f.).

[30] Readers who are not interested in the discussion of the relevant theoretical context and literature are advised to move straight to section V.

within an overall dialectical process of religio-historical development—syncretisation or acculturation—which often involves parallel processes of linguistic syncretism and/or group formation.[31] PYE (1994: 220), for instance, defines the 'syncretic situation' as 'the temporary ambiguous existence of elements from diverse religions and other contexts within a coherent religious pattern.' He locates syncretism between a 'mere mixture' and a 'coherent mixture' or 'synthesis':

> 'If coherent mixture, or synthesis, represents the conclusion to a process which is thereby completed, syncretism by contrast is to be understood as dynamically open and indeed patent of resolutions other than synthesis. These might be, in particular, the outright dominance of one strand of meaning by another (assimilation), or the avoidance of synthesis through the drawing apart of the distinct elements and the consequent collapse of the syncretism (dissolution).'[32]

Earlier, BECHERT (1978: 20–3) had proposed a similar typology of syncretic phenomena, i.e. of 'the different forms in which religious traditions have influenced each other', associating them with particular ideological or cultural systems: (1) The marginal acceptance of single elements (e.g. Jains), (2) proper syncretism 'where elements from different religious traditions gain equal weight' (e.g. Nepal, Bali, Sri Lanka), (3) full integration (Neo-Hinduism), (4) perfect synthesis (e.g. Sikhs). According to Bechert, Jainism (in general) is an example of type one, because its 'essential characteristics' are not touched by the assimilation of new elements. Bechert's assessment of Jainism was probably influenced by BRUHN's (1954: 136) remarks on the lacking 'mixture of traditions' and the prevalence of a combinatorial coexistence of elements from diverse traditions in Jain literature. BRUHN (1987a: 109) later pointed to the frequent co-occurrence of various syncretic phenomena within a single tradition. He distinguished, for instance, between 'syncretism' and 'import' in Jain literature. In contrast to Bechert and Pye, in his view 'syncretism' denotes the end product of the process of syncretisation, i.e. a 'real' synthesis of elements (from the participants point of view), whereas 'import' describes a situation of 'unreal' synthesis, where new elements are incorporated but not yet properly integrated (danger of disintegration). Bruhn also suggested distinguishing more clearly between different sources and periods, in order to achieve greater realism. In this context belong analytical distinctions between (a) the 'hinduised' (WILLIAMS

[31] COLPE (1987: 220 f., 226).

[32] PYE (1994: 220). Structural-functionalist models of acculturation artificially limit the role of ambiguity and change to a 'liminal' phase between presumably static extremes (e.g. TURNER (1986: 93)). So called post-modern approaches try to invert this scheme by defining identity itself as a limit case.

(1983: xx)) or 'pseudo-jainised' (JAINI (1974: 335), (1979: 291–4) ritual and literature of (post-) medieval temple-worshipping Jain traditions, (b) the 'islamicised' (JAINI (1974: 314 n. 63)) iconoclastic reform movements which emerged in the Mughal period, and (c) contemporary 'westernised' developments.[33] Whatever the merit of such typologies, which contrary to WEBER (1988) are often based on the supposition of 'essential characteristics', it is apparent that one of the main ambitions of present research is the construction of comprehensive classifications of various forms of syncretisation and their strategic uses.[34]

An important debate between GOMBRICH (1971: 49) and BECHERT (1978: 20–4) on the question of the relation between literary syncretism (eclecticism) and the syncretism of popular religious practice in contemporary (Theravāda) Buddhism is also relevant for the understanding of similar phenomena amongst the Jains. Gombrich describes non-monastic forms of Buddhism as 'accretive' or corrupted forms. Bechert, on the other hand, criticises his devaluation of popular beliefs and of the political role of religion as 'elitist'. Instead, he interprets Buddhist 'cultures' as 'systems' or organic totalities, encompassing both *saṅgha* and society. TAMBIAH (1977), too, focuses less on Buddhist doctrine and the *saṅgha* and more on cultural history, emphasising especially the constitutive role of local cosmologies ('pantheons') which are implicated in the cults of Buddhist kingship. This approach, which favours a typified 'common man's' view from within and privileges 'hierarchisation' ('hegemony' or 'totalisation') as the most important strategy of acculturation, was pioneered by DUMONT (1980: 427 n. 6, 433 n. 19), who argued that historically the 'worldly religion' of 'Hinduism' emerged as a product of cumulative interactive processes between the 'two ideal types' of Brāhmaṇism and Jainism/Buddhism which superimposed an 'individual religion ... on to the religion of the group [caste]' (DUMONT (1980: 275)).[35] From the perspective of an individ-

[33] See the somewhat different ideal-typical distinction between 'canonical', 'classical', 'protestant' and 'modern' types of Jainism in FLÜGEL (2000: 37–40), to which 'mystical' Jainism (Digambara Mysticism) needs to be added.

[34] The following strategies have been suggested for instance: addition, parallelism, identification, hierarchical subordination (inclusion), re-interpretation. See HACKER (1985: 12), DUMONT (1980: 260), COLPE (1987: 223), PYE (1994: 222), BECHERT (1978: 23), BRUHN (1993: 38). With few exceptions, research on syncretism has been restricted to the comparative study of the semantics of cultural ideologies. This article, by contrast, utilises the analytical tools of rhetorics and pragmatics.

[35] The theoretical appropriation of 'the participant's point of view' generated much confusion in South Asian Anthropology because of the ambiguous status of the key Neo-Kantian concept of 'value-realisation', which, on the one hand, reifies culture, and, on the other hand, claims to achieve greater empirical adequacy by representing the 'native's point of view' (HABERMAS (1981: 340–3, 351) / (1984–1987 II: 226–8, 234)). DUMONT (1980) oscillates ambiguously between two interpretations: Hinduism (1) as a mixture between two literary ideal types, and (2) as a

ual, GUMPERZ (1972: 230 f.) pointed out, superposed structures demand a wider socioreligious repertoire, including role compartmentalisation and perspective variation. Dumont's view that, from a lay participant's point of view, soteriological cults appear as religions of individual choice which are superimposed upon worldly religion, lends support to both accretionary and syncretistic interpretations. It also highlights the marginal historical role of Jainism in India, which, for want of political support, was nowhere able to achieve a culturally dominant position comparable to Buddhism in the countries of Theravāda Buddhism, and consequently not forced to develop its own (hegemonic) social system. Jainism always remained primarily a monastic religion which relied on the institutions of Hinduism and the state to legislate for society. Jain philosophical syncretism conceives merely of a negative totality based on the disjunctive synthesis of differences within an infinite horizon of plural perspectives. Yet, negative philosophical forms of syncretism are to be distinguished from positive linguistic or socioreligious forms of syncretism, which are less prominent in Jain discourse, but dominant in practice.[36]

The Jain case shows that it is an empirical question whether a given form of popular religion appears to be predominantly accretic or syncretic. It also underlines the crucial importance of configurations of power for competitive processes of doctrinal syncretism and socio-cultural synthesis. The religious status of 'popular Jainism'—'deviation', 'cultural bedrock' or 'modern political essentialisation'—is the subject of ongoing disputes between rivalling Jain leaders. Epistemologies and religious rituals for Jain laity were constructed intentionally by Jain monks. Yet, the

---

form of popular religious practice, resulting from the hierarchical incorporation of tribal cults, textual Brāhmaṇism, and 'the great heresies' (cf. DUMONT (1980: 428 f. n. 10)), through (a) Brāhmaṇic mediation, and/or (b) popular extrinsic borrowing of social signs from superiors without functional transformation (DUMONT (1980: 194)). The elitist *Brāhmaṇa*-centredness of this approach has attracted much criticism. Dumont himself indicated that his approach is not much different from the one of the philologist (DUMONT (1980: 433 n. 19)). The problem is that the 'common man' is usually treated as a literary type—'the Buddhist king' (Tambiah) or 'the Brāhmaṇic householder' (Dumont)—which mediates between doctrine and practice in a normatively prescribed way. By contrast, GLUCKMAN (1955: 128), for instance, appeals to the universal rationality or 'reasonableness' of common sense: 'The concept of the "reasonable" measures the range of allowed departure from the highest standards of duty and absolute conformity to norm, and the minimum adherence which is insisted on.' 'Reasonability' can be normalised, but, strictly speaking, it refers to empirical conditions.

[36] On the Jain philosophical 'syncretism' of *anekânta-vāda* and *syād-vāda* see for instance MURTI (1955: 127 f.) and GANERI (2001: 147), (2002: 279): 'In moving from pluralism to syncretism, the Jainas commit themselves to the claim that we are led to a *complete* account of reality by integrating of all the different points of view' (ib. GANERI (2002: 279)). It has to be noted, though, that this approach does not tolerate 'invalid' (*apramāṇa*) points of view. Hence, not every statement is conditionally true.

extent to which social life is regulated by Jain social philosophy varies locally and from sect to sect, and from caste to caste. Iconoclastic Jain sects rely on the Hindu social system alone, whereas temple-worshipping sects accept the 'hinduised/ jainised' practices of popular Jainism as an integral part of Jain religion,[37] while communal reformers demand the 'eradication of every non-Jain element from the Jaina community' (SANGAVE (1980: 410)) in order to form entirely new social entities. Present political attempts to ethnicise the 'Jain community' by propagating intra-religious, trans-sect and trans-caste marriages are unlikely to succeed, however, because of ongoing internal sectarian rivalries, exclusive caste and class affiliations of the laity, and the continuing existence of mixed religious castes. Effectively, Jain communalism contributes to the strengthening of the cultural self-consciousness of an important faction of the new Indian business class, but does not alter the hierarchical structure of the society itself.

Jain laity usually practises 'Jain' and 'Hindu' rituals side by side, combining soteriological religion with worldly religion without mixing the two, as described by Dumont.[38] Even the lay followers (*śrāvaka*) of contemporary Jain reformist groups (e.g. 'Jain communalists') cannot avoid combining 'Jain' and 'Hindu' religious practices, because of lacking Jain life-cycle rituals.[39] Sometimes popular practices are 'jainised' by ascetics, and in this way legitimately incorporated into Jain religion. 'Jain marriages' for instance, and similar life-cycle rituals, are created simply by adding a Jain *mantra* to customary local procedures; and 'Jain *pūjā*s' are rendered possible if interpreted as forms of *dāna*, i.e. without expectation of return etc. (WILLIAMS (1983: xx–xxv, 216)). Re-interpretation and modification through addition etc., are essential techniques for incorporating elements from other traditions and for constructing cosmologies and embryonic Jain social systems along the lines of pre-existing Hindu and Buddhist models. Yet, only few elements of 'Hindu' popular religion have been fully integrated, predominantly into the ritual corpus of

---

[37] See JAINI (1991: 187).

[38] MAHIAS (1985: 96 f., 287), GOONASEKERE (1986: 185 f.), CORT (1989: 433), and others, talk about the Jain layman's 'oscillation' between 'alternative' Jain (or Jain and Hindu) 'realms of value'. The social function of Jain practices for legitimising status-mobility within Indian society remains to be studied.

[39] 'Jain practices' are considered to be forms of temporary renunciation which are derived from the code of conduct for individual Jain mendicants, like the six obligatory rites (*āvaśyaka*), asceticism (*tapas*), meditation (*dhyāna*), plus, for the laity, the obligatory giving of alms to the ascetics (*dāna*); whereas all social rituals mediated by the *Brāhmaṇa*s, such as life-cycle rituals (*saṁskāra*s) or the worship (*pūjā*) of gods other than the Jinas, are regarded as 'Hindu practices'. Of course, 'Jain practices' are considered to be hierarchically superior by Jains, although 'Hindus' regard them as 'heretical' deviations from standard practice, because they are neither predicated on the authority of the *Veda*s nor on the mediation of the *Brāhmaṇa*s.

temple-worshipping sects. Aniconic Jain sects do not practice socioreligious rituals to the same degree as image-worshipping sects, and thus have a less clearly defined socioreligious identity. Structure and semantics of the ritual terminology correspond to socioreligious structure. The paradigmatic case of an apparently 'non-Jain' popular ritual which was appropriated and re-interpreted by medieval Jain ascetics to build up a Jain system of lay rituals is *pūjā*.[40] Its ambiguous status between soteriological and world-affirming orientations is reflected in the intentional multivocality of the religious terminology employed in this and similar lay rituals, as WILLIAMS (1983), LAIDLAW (1985) and CORT (1989), (1991) demonstrated.[41] The socioreligious dimension constituted by a system of jainised lay rituals seems to be predicated on generalised indirectness.

— II —

Modern writers on Jainism have often noted the abundance of similes and double meanings (*śleṣa*) in Jain narrative and ritual literature,[42] and their strategic use to infuse conventional language and popular stories with different meanings, derived from Jain ethics.[43] WILLIAMS (1983: xviii–ix) was the first scholar to highlight the ways in which medieval Jain writers, such as the Digambara *ācārya* Jinasena (9th CE), instrumentalised śaivaite terms (amongst others) as 'vehicles' for the indirect communication of their own religious views:

> 'Jain writers have shown a remarkable aptitude for the subtle handling of words ... The polyvalence of certain expressions even within the limits of the same text is often disconcerting: *guṇa* in particular is greatly overworked and so are *kriyā* and *karman*. Indeed one is led to wonder whether the double meanings given to many words and their

[40] It is an open question whether Hindus or indeed Jains or Buddhists first introduced *pūjā* rituals in Indic religion. Jain *pūjā* manuals are comparatively late.

[41] The fact that the status of *pūjā* as a 'Jain ceremony' is disputed within the Jain tradition diminishes the relevance of HUMPHREY–LAIDLAW's (1994: 41 f.) 'cognitive-psychological' analysis of Jain *pūjā*, as they point out themselves (LAIDLAW (1994: 137)). See FLÜGEL (2006b) for a review of this issue.

[42] E.g. WINTERNITZ (1920 II: 303–5), BLOOMFIELD (1923: 262 f.), SCHUBRING (2000: 268, § 150), BALBIR (1983), BRUHN (1993: 36) etc.

[43] E.g. HERTEL (1922: 8), JAIN (1981: 11), MONE (1987: 324 f.) etc. The social implications of the possibility that the multivocalities in Jain texts are intentional have, however, only reluctantly been considered by textual scholars to date, not least because of the unclear status of the element of necessary violence it implies (cf. BALBIR (1984: 37), GRANOFF (1992)).

> formal identity with Hindu terms may not be voluntary. Examples of such coincidences (with the Jaina meanings noted in parentheses) are: *śiva* (*mokṣa*), *liṅga* (the monks symbols such as the *rajo-harana*), *guṇa-traya* (the *ratna-traya*), *paśupati* (the Jina) *mahā-deva* (the Jina) whilst on the other hand the word Digambara itself can be an epithet of Śiva.'

WILLIAMS (1983: xix) sees the reasons for the intentionally multivocal use of terms in the political assertiveness of 'Hinduism' in medieval South Indian society which forced the Jains to conceal their 'heterodox' beliefs behind a conformist public facade as a way of social self-protection:

> 'It may be that such resemblances were intended to render Jaina doctrines attractive to śaivas or that śaiva persecution made it desirable to give to certain Jaina texts an innocuous aspect. Certainly the Jaina's concept of *asatya*[44] would make it easy for them to adopt an attitude similar to that of those Shiite sectarians who in the early days of Islam maintained an outward conformity by concealing their real beliefs under forms of words.'

Numerous studies on diglossia, multilingualism/multifaithism and code-switching demonstrated in the meantime that the strategy of 'outward conformity and inward dissent', based on the method of differentiating hierarchical levels/ media of discourse, is not limited to a certain historical period in South Asia or to the Jains in particular, but a universal feature, especially of dependent subaltern groups, minorities, or elites. DUMONT (1980: 194) analysed the method of 'extrinsic borrowing' 'from superiors of certain features as social signs and not as functional features' in terms of a theory of acculturation, which distinguishes three contemporary types of cultural interaction:[45] 'rejection, mixture, in which traditional and modern features exist happily side by side, and combination, which unites them intimately in new forms of a hybrid nature and ambiguous orientation' (DUMONT (1980: 229)).[46] Oth-

---

[44] See *infra* (p. 194) on *satyâsatya*: something may be true as well as false (*satya-mṛṣā*) or neither true nor false (*a-satya-mṛṣā*).

[45] Cf. FERGUSON's (1972: 244 f.) definition of diglossia: 'DIGLOSSIA *is a relatively stable language situation in which, in addition to the primary dialects of the language (which may include a standard or regional standard), there is a very divergent, highly codified (often grammatically more complex) superimposed variety, the vehicle of a large and respected body of written literature, either of an earlier period or in another speech community, which is learned largely by formal education and is used for most written and formal spoken purposes but is not used by any sector of the community for ordinary conversation*' [author's italics].

[46] See FLÜGEL (1995–6: 170 f.) on the relationship between conventional indirectness and 'mixed' and 'combined' strategies of integration.

ers emphasised the political implications of counter-hegemonic adaptive strategies. SEAL (1968), RUDOLPH–RUDOLPH (1984), HAYNES (1991), and JAFFRELOT (1993), for instance, investigated the paradoxical effects of double-strategies employed by political mediators in (colonial) South Asia, which used 'modern language' in the public sphere, i.e. institutions of the state and print media, and 'traditional language' within their own community. Sociolinguistic theories of discourse and multilingualism will prove useful for the future study of the interaction of different levels within Jain religious language and of Jain discourse being superimposed on different contexts.[47] In Jain literature, DERRETT (1980: 144) identified 'double standards'. CARRITHERS (1991: 266 f.) showed how the multivocal 'political rhetoric' of the leaders of Jain lay communities (*samāja*) gains persuasive force only if indirectly tapping into a 'diffuse realm of religious sentiments'. LAIDLAW (1985: 60) and CORT (1989: 449–70) suggested, conversely, that the official renunciatory 'religious ideology' of the Jains implicitly relies on a 'diffuse Jain ideology of wellbeing', and how 'symbolically rich' multivalent concepts, such as *lābha* or *maṅgala* which can mean either 'profit' or 'power' both in the world and in the religious sphere, 'bridge the two ideologies' (CORT (1989: 465)). The merit of Carrithers', Laidlaw's and Cort's approaches lies in the attempt to interpret the implicit links between the Jain religious discourse and the socio-economic sphere in terms of a theory of symbolisation.[48] But they suffer from an exclusive focus on the

[47] GUMPERZ (1972: 225) distinguishes two types of relationships between variants: '*dialectal* and *superposed*'. On 'seemingly intentional processes of distortion' by argots and on the use of implicit language to claim in-group membership and to maintain group boundaries see GUMPERZ (1961), (1972: 221–3, 227 f.). Most authors in a recent volume on religious discourse edited by OMINIYA and FISHMAN (2006) derive their inspiration from the classic papers of FERGUSON (1959/1972: 232 f.) and FISHMAN (1967) on diglossia and bilingualism in exploring situational uses of either two varieties of a (religious) language, or of two distinct (related or unrelated) languages side by side throughout a speech community, each with a clearly defined role. Jain heteroglossia is discussed, with varying success, by PANDHARIPANDE (2006), with the additional help of BOURDIEU's (1991: 107) institutional theory of the power of language. See also DESHPANDE (1979) on Jain claims of Ardhamāgadhī being a prestigious 'Āryan' language.

[48] Cf. STRECKER (1988). For similar descriptions of the 'dual purposes' of the Jain cult, see WEBER (1920/1978: 217), HUMPHREY–LAIDLAW (1994: 171 f.), LAIDLAW (1995: 354), JOHNSON (1995b: 310), and BABB (1996: 98–101). However, as WILLIAMS (1983) indicated, there is nothing particularly 'Jain' about the 'undefinable symbolic realm of wellbeing' (CORT (1989: 455)). Wellbeing as a religious value is generally associated not with Jainism but with 'Hinduism' or interpreted as a general social value (CORT (1989: 458)), SANGAVE (1980: 409), MAHIAS (1985: 109, 287), GOONASEKERE (1986: 185 f.)). In the Jain context it might as well be interpreted as a mere contextual condition of success of ascetic life. FLÜGEL (2006b: 104), therefore, proposed to distinguish between well-being A (socioreligious) and well-being B (material). See also contemporary

laity and from the artificial treatment of Jain communities as quasi-ethnic groups isolated from the wider context of Indian society, which makes a critical analysis of the contextual relationships between Jainism and society, Jainism and power etc.—masked by the use of multivalent symbols—virtually impossible.[49] 'Clearly', writes CORT (2001: 11), 'most scholars of ideology view power as ubiquitous.' LAIDLAW (1995), following Foucault, shares this view. However, while Williams' remarks need to be qualified, I think he and his successors posed the crucial question for an understanding of the characteristic 'syncretic', 'hybrid' or 'parasitic' form of much Jain narrative literature and lay ritual, by pointing to the intentional multivocality of basic concepts of popular Jainism, invented by ascetics, and their political-rhetorical function within contexts of competitive religious proselytisation. Williams did not pursue this line of research further, but confined himself to the sociologically less interesting search for the precise entailments of single terms. In order to handle the potentially boundless increase of investigations of such terms, BRUHN (1983: 61) proposed to limit 'rhetorical studies' to specific Jain genres, and most of Williams' successors followed this path.

I chose a different strategy in this article, turning away from the description and analysis of literary genres and doctrinal semantics (a task for the philologist) to the investigation of the pragmatics of Jain discourse. The limited aim of this study is to explore the methodological preconditions for an investigation of contextual implications of intentional multivocal utterances in Jain religious language. To accomplish this, a prior comparative analysis of the constitutive principles of Jain discourse and its typical normative contexts is required. Particularly significant is the question of the ways in which the specific ethical principles of Jain discourse interlink both with contextual norms and with universal moral presuppositions of communication *per se*, upon which intentional language usage indirectly relies, if Habermas is to be believed. I will seek to demonstrate that critical reflection on language usage on a level of abstraction similar to universal pragmatics is doctrinally prescribed for Jain ascetics, who need to consider the ethical implications of their own religious rhetoric in different contexts.[50] Because the social implications

---

Terāpanth reformist attempts to disambiguate the concepts of Jain popular religion, i.e. to separate clearly between religion and society.

[49] See the first principle of FISHMAN's (2006: 14) decalogue of theoretical perspectives for the sociology of language and religion: 'The language (or 'variety') of religion always functions within a larger multilingual/multivarietal repertoire.' The notion of 'religious repertoire' is derived from GUMPERZ's (1972: 230) definition of the 'verbal repertoire' of a speech community (or individual) as 'the totality of dialectal and superposed variants regularly employed.'

[50] The notion of univocality has to be used with great care, because of its association with positivistic ideal language theories. In practice, perceived univocality is always relative to a his-

of the Jain rules of speech themselves are hardly illuminated in Jain hermeneutical literature,[51] I will start my investigation with a theoretical analysis of characteristic Jain hermeneutical procedures and discursive strategies in typical situations of linguistically mediated interaction.

The social function of Jain theories of speech, I argue, can be understood from the perspective of a theory of interactional competence. The term interactional competence encompasses cognitive, linguistic and rhetorical ability, and hence the capacity to use language both for the pursuit of power and insight. Interestingly enough, the use of mental and linguistic violence is a necessary requirement for accomplishing both aims. Power and influence are intrinsically connected with violence. It is one of the most intriguing questions how power works through discourse. Power has been defined by Max WEBER (1972: 28), from an intentionalist perspective, as the 'opportunity existing within a social relationship which permits one to carry out one's own will even against resistance and regardless of the basis on which this opportunity rests.'[52] Rhetoric has similarly been characterised as a competence-based social technique by means of which a minority, or an elite, may gain or exercise social influence, personal prestige or persuasive power, over a majority. Its capacity to influence is often predicated on the measured violation of a conventional structure by means of the manipulation of linguistic and non-linguistic media of communication; i.e. it presupposes a 'deviance' from what is culturally felt as being 'normal' without threatening the co-operation of the listeners. Influence is further

---

torical background of implicit contextual knowledge and cannot be explicated merely by referring to logical or grammatical rules. Strictly speaking, common-sense knowledge cannot be described exhaustively at all, because ultimately the whole world is implicated in every expression.

[51] See in particular the canonical *Aṇuogaddārāiṁ* (AṇD).

[52] HABERMAS (1981: 400–12) / (1984–1987 II: 267–77) adopts both Weber's definition of power as 'instrumental action' and Parsons' theory of money and power as 'codes' or 'generalised media of communication', distinguished from the codes of influence and value commitments. Parson's theory of power was further developed by LUHMANN (1975)/(1979) and HABERMAS (1981) / (1984–1987 II). Power as code is explained as follows: 'The power code schematises alter's possible responses in a binary fashion: he can either submit to or oppose ego's demands. A preference for compliance is built into the code through the prospect ego holds out for sanctioning later in case the latter fails to carry out orders. Under those conditions, the person in power can condition the responses of those subordinate to him, without having to depend primarily on the willingness to co-operate. From both sides is expected an objectivating attitude toward the action situation and an orientation to the possible consequences of action' (HABERMAS (1981: 401) / (1987: 268)). Habermas thus implicitly operates with two notions of power: power as a code in the sense of Parsons and Luhmann, and as instrumental action in the sense of Max Weber. In this article the instrumental definition of power is predominately referred to. For a discussion of Jain conceptions of power, see FLUGEL (forthcoming).

strengthened through commitment and dogmatism on the side of the proponent.[53] By such means, a speaker may exert a disproportionate influence on individuals and society at large and stimulate changes in a pre-meditated direction. Social influence is rooted in conflict and striving for a new consensus: 'Conflict is ... at the root of influence, either because it arises from the presence of a difference or because the existence of a disagreement brings it into the open' (MOSCOVICI (1985: 353)).

Rhetoric has another, ethical-pedagogical, side: it may not only serve as an instrument of power and manipulation, but (from the perspective of the addressee) also as a critical analytical method of truth-finding and insight. Both aspects are often intrinsically related and can only be dissected analytically.[54] The ways in which Jain ascetics play with the two aspects of rhetoric, how they use multivocal language strategically as a means of normative influence and religious conversion, are interesting questions for sociological research.[55] If, as Williams argued, the multivocal categories of/for popular Jainism are intentionally constructed by proselytising ascetics, and if this is done to generate effects of religious insight (*samyag-darśana*) in the audience, for instance through the rhetorical provocation of *vairāgya*-shocks (aversion leading to renunciation),[56] how then does Jain philosophy account for the element of violence which is necessarily implied in acts of persuasion? In other words, if social influence can only be achieved through strategic acts of violence, how do ascetics conceive of the moral paradox involved in the violent production of non-violent attitudes?

— III —

For the analysis of the role of violence in rhetoric, or speech acts in general, a standard of non-violent speech is required. Such a standard is offered in the Jain scriptures. It will be discussed in Chapters V–VII. Comparable paradigms in contemporary Western philosophy are the conversational maxims of GRICE (1975) and the universal pragmatic validity claims of HABERMAS (1980), both echoing Kant rather than Carnap. A comparison with the Jain model promises to elicit key differences and highlight the specific nature of the principles of Jain discourse. In the following discussion of the two models, I adopt HABERMAS' (1980–1981: 440 ff.) /

---

[53] LUHMANN (1982) and ALEXY (1996: 326 ff.).

[54] See HABERMAS (1981: 270 ff., 414–18/1984 II: 181 ff., 280) on trust (based on possession of valid knowledge and autonomy), and punishment and reward (based on property and means of inducement and deterrence) as distinct—rational and empirical—sources of generalised acceptability.

[55] SONTHEIMER's (1991: 201) observation that codified 'Hinduism had [has] only persuasive power and was no law in the western sense' equally applies to doctrinal Jainism.

[56] BRUHN (1983: 32).

(1984–1987 I: 328 ff.) suggestion to treat empirical pragmatic models as if they were conscious operationalisations of universal pragmatics.[57] The latter claims to be a more general than the former since it does not only theorise principles of linguistic exchange but also the morally binding force of rational argument and the socially constitutive function of rationally constituted consensus. Contrasting claims to universality of the models of Habermas and the Jains, the former would claim (on debatable grounds), can be tested through comparative analysis.

In his *Theory of Communicative Action*, HABERMAS (1980: 384–88) / (1984–1987 I: 284–89) distinguishes between 'communicative' and 'strategic' types of linguistically mediated interaction to be able to discriminate between consensus-oriented and manipulative forms of language usage. The key variable in his model is the dominant social orientation informing language usage.[58] Communicative action is orientated towards consensus through rational argumentation, understanding and insight, whereas strategic action (success-oriented action) is orientated towards power and the pursuit of self interest through the manipulative use of speech.[59] Despite the ambiguity of his key terms *Verständigung* ('communicative understanding') and *Einsicht* ('insight'),[60] Habermas differentiates clearly between linguistic and normative aspects of communicative action, that is, the understanding of the meaning of a speech act and the acceptance of implicit validity claims. In contrast to speech act theoreticians such as Austin, Grice, and others, Habermas does not privilege the intention of the speaker as determinative of the social meaning of a

---

[57] This approach goes back to Pierce, Royce and Mead, and was revived by Apel.

[58] HABERMAS (1980: 442 n. 84) / (1984–1987 I: 444 f. n. 84). This formulation is still intentionalist. The artificial segregation of perlocutions from the other components has been criticised, as well as Habermas' original equation of perlocutions with latent strategic action, his exclusive attribution of teleological goal-oriented behaviour to strategic action, and the logocentric ideal type of rationality. In response to criticism, HABERMAS (1986: 401 n. 60) later accepted the 'basic teleological structure of all actions' and proposed a combination of 'actor-orientation' (success vs. understanding) and 'types of coordination of action plans' (influence vs. agreement) as a replacement. This formula was necessary to save his definition of 'proper illocutions' being dependent not only on subjective conditions of satisfaction of the meaning of a speech act, but also on intersubjective conditions (reasons for the acceptance of validity claims). In reality, strategic action always appears to be intermingled with communicative action (HABERMAS (1986: 443)), and perlocutionary effects are not only consequences of strategic action but also of communicative action. Cf. HABERMAS (1980: 397) / (1984–1987 I: 295 f.) versus SEARLE (1993: 98 f.).

[59] Most critics of Habermas rejected his strict distinction between *poesis* and *praxis*.

[60] HABERMAS (1996: 339): '"Insight" signifies that a decision can be justified on the basis of "epistemic" reasons', that is, when practical reflection 'extends beyond the subjective world to which the actor has privileged access ["pragmatic" reasons] to the [implicitly known] contents of an intersubjectively shared social world.'

speech act, which he sees as negotiable, but focuses on the (contextually varying) conditions of acceptability, that is, the implicit or explicit reasons on which the validity claims of a speech act are based, which can be accepted or rejected in processes of intersubjective communication. The question is: What does it mean to understand a speech act? Not: What does it mean to understand an intention? Habermas expands AUSTIN's (1962) distinction between 'locutionary', 'illocutionary' and 'perlocutionary' speech acts, which he re-labels, partly following SEARLE's (1979: 12–20) terminology, as 'constatives', 'regulatives' and 'expressives' in analogy to his three universal validity claims 'truth', 'rightness' and 'truthfulness', by focusing not so much on speech acts themselves but on the social function of speech for the co-ordination of action. The advantage of Habermas' distinction between 'speech acts' and 'linguistically mediated interaction', prefigured in the work of sociolinguists such as GUMPERZ (1964), (1972) and HYMES (1972b),[61] is that it allows to analyse the contextual moral and legal implications of language usage, i.e. the socially binding force of the validity claims implied in illocutionary speech acts, which cannot be reduced to the 'power of words' themselves nor to the underlying intention of the speaker.

'Communicative action' is not the same as 'communication'. It refers to a situation where the intersubjective co-ordination of action-plans is reached by way of rational agreement, that is, where an explicit consensus is constitutive for social integration (HABERMAS (1998: 396–98)). 'Strategic action' (success- / influence-oriented action), on the other hand, refers to a situation of exploitation, because it is not able to generate new normative consensus through rationally motivated acceptance of reasons itself, but only through the force of pre-existing norms and institutional or other configurations, which are external to the communicative process.[62]

[61] GUMPERZ (1972: 381): 'Verbal interaction is a social process in which utterances are selected in accordance with socially recognized norms and expectations. It follows that linguistic phenomena are analyzable both within the context of language itself and within the broader context of social behavior.'

[62] HABERMAS (1984: 313–5) distinguishes between cognitive and expressive intentions; arguing that the illocutionary goal of speech acts, that is, consensus, can be reached either through the intersubjective recognition of power claims (perlocutionary effects) or of validity claims (illocutionary effects) (HABERMAS (1980: 385 ff.) / (1984–1987 I: 286 ff.), (1981: 107 ff.) / (1984–1987 II: 69 ff.)). Cf. his comparison between imperatives (directives), e.g. commands, and regulatives (commissives), e.g. promises (HABERMAS (1980: 427 ff.) / (1984–1987 I: 319 ff.)): both commissives, and directives (and declaratives) imply normative conditions by referring to situations that OUGHT to be, whereas assertives merely represent situations as they ARE.

Acts of social self-commitment to do something in the future or to give reasons for a validity claim, by way of promises, oaths and contracts, and acts aiming at committing others through directives (commands, injunctions), by instrumentalising existing obligations, are both focal elements of Jain discourse. The difference between the models of Habermas and the Jains is that the former rely on universal moral justifications, whereas the latter require only socially valid norms

Hence, by defining communicative action as the original mode of language usage, directly oriented towards normative agreement, Habermas is able to criticise strategic action as a success orientated mode of language usage, which is parasitic on the former, because it is only indirectly orientated towards communicative understanding. The whole purpose of Habermas' theory lies in the analysis of the conditions of the possibility of a consensual constitution of social order, without grounding the emancipatory potential of discourse either in metaphysical postulates or in institutional configurations of power as suggested by FOUCAULT (1981), BOURDIEU (1991a), (1991b), or BLOCH (1975). The critical emancipatory interest which informs the theory of communicative action is directed against (illegitimate) power and in favour of consensual (and non-violent) forms of conflict resolution and institution building. HABERMAS (1998: 449) argues that the emancipatory potential of language is not a metaphysical ideal, but manifest in the 'unconcealed idealising surpluses of an *innerworldly* transcendence' in form of the universal validity claims implicitly presupposed in all processes of communication, as the vanishing points (*Fluchtpunkte*) of infinite processes of open intersubjective interpretation.[63]

How can we explain the power of non-institutionally bound illocutionary acts to produce feelings of normative obligation? What motivates a listener freely to submit him/herself to normative constraints if not self-interest or external force? At first sight, HABERMAS' (1980) argument that illocutionary binding effects are the product of processes of rational understanding, i.e. of insight into the validity of reasons (e.g. common values and convictions), seems to rely on the pre-existence of an implicit normative consensus and of the rhetorical ability of the speaker (HABERMAS (1980: 386)). However, like other proponents of formal pragmatics (Apel, Allwood, Grice),[64] Habermas attempts to circumvent both normative reductionism and subjectivism, by not focusing on the local 'ethical' context of specific empirical cases, but on the general 'moral' presuppositions of communication, that is, the universal normative conditions of intersubjective recognition which must be fulfilled for a speech act to be accepted. He states that 'we understand a speech act, if we know, what makes him acceptable' (HABERMAS (1980: 400)). Crucially, he assumes that every linguistically mediated interaction presupposes a set of idealisations on the side of the interlocutors

as conditions for their acceptability. Expressives are a different case altogether. They are not predicated on truth claims nor on claims of rightness, and therefore not redeemable by argument. Legitimacy is entirely based on sincerity and redeemable by practice only (HABERMAS (1981: 97–100) / (1984–1987 II: 62–4). For differing views on the structure and interrelationship of the various components see APEL (1993: 45–9), HABERMAS (1993), and SEARLE (1989), (1993).

[63] Remarks on religious communication can be found in HABERMAS (1988: 23, 34, 60, 185), and HABERMAS (2005). See also ARENS (1991: 174–6).

[64] On the history of formal pragmatics see APEL (1993: 43) and HABERMAS (1993: 21–5).

themselves. He explicates these implicit basic conditions of communicative action in terms of a model of three universal pragmatic[65] validity claims underlying all grammatically comprehensible utterances: (1) (propositional) truth, (2) (normative) rightness, and (3) (expressive) sincerity.[66] Habermas argues that the binding power of rea-

[65] Cf. HABERMAS (1984: 354 f., 440). With some exceptions (HABERMAS (1980: 418 f.) / (1984–1987 I: 312 f.)) his validity claims correspond closely to Grice's cooperative principle and conversational maxims (see *infra*) (and more generally to Searle's conditions of success and non-defective performance). However, one of the great misconceptions of speech act theory is the assumption that almost all social actions are communicative actions, and that communication is more or less identical with conversation. The cooperative principle of speech exchange should not be mixed up with consent to social co-operation (HABERMAS (1980: 397) / (1984–1987 I: 295)). Another mistake is to assume that only intentional communicative actions have communicative effects. SEARLE (1993: 89) was the first to criticise Grice's 'meaning-nominalism' with counter-examples showing that even non-intentional statements can have an effect, which demonstrates that conventional propositional content of words, i.e. representation, is more fundamental than speaker intention, and that Grice, by concentrating exclusively on the transfer and decoding of information, ultimately 'confuses meaning with communication.' In other words, understanding an utterance cannot be regarded as a perlocutionary effect. Critics of Grice denounce the infinite regress involved in the inference of speaker's intentions, and the vagueness and arbitrariness (incompleteness and incoherence) of the maxims. HABERMAS (1984: 333–48, 362), (1980: 371, 418) / (1984–1987 I: 274 f.) and APEL (1993: 32) criticise Grice's (etc.) mentalist 'intentional semantics' as treating understanding exclusively in terms of strategic action, *á la* Weber and economic game theory, by reducing meaning to the perlocutionary effect of the intentions of an isolated individual, not taking into account community context and conventional intersubjectivity and understanding through consensual agreement by condemning the hearer to passivity.

From HABERMAS' (1993: 18 f.) perspective, Searle offers an intermediary approach between intentional semantics and universal pragmatics: 'From my point of view, a speech act, which the speaker uses in order to come to an agreement with the addressee about something, expresses simultaneously (a) a certain speaker intention, (b) a certain state of affairs, and (c) an interpersonal relationship. According to the original intentionalist view [Grice, P.F.], the whole communication process can be explained from the perspective of the speaker and his intentions in such a way that (c) and (b) are derived from (a). … Searle modifies his explanatory strategy to the effect that successful communication now depends on the successful representation of states of affairs, namely that both (c) and (a) are derived from (b).'

[66] Habermas' validity claims are grounded in Popper's 'three world' theory of subject, object, and society. See ALBERT's (1994: 240) critique of this 'ontology' from a 'one world' perspective. Cf. Searle's five 'conditions of successful speech' (essential condition, preparatory condition, propositional content, sincerity), three of which correspond to Habermas' validity claims (truth = essential condition, rightness = preparatory condition, sincerity = sincerity), whereas one (propositional content) is unique to Searle. On the basis of the idealised 'standard form' of rational communicative action, HABERMAS (1980) generates a complex system of analytical categories, by correlating the validity claims and the two dominant social orientations, consensus and power, with four 'basic' types of speech acts (imperatives, constatives, regulatives, expressives). The aim is to discriminate between consensual and latent strategic forms of language usage. The resulting

sons, that is, of rationally motivated validity claims whose acceptance implies weak normative obligations,[67] is not rooted in content but in procedural form, i.e. in the guarantee of the speaker, if necessary, to justify his/her claims in terms of these three types of validity claims and to give reasons which can be criticised and rejected (only) with better reasons (HABERMAS (1980: 406)).[68] Precondition is the principal autonomy of the interlocutors, their ability to say 'no'. Only under this provision does acceptance imply voluntary agreement. For Habermas, who follows Kant and Durkheim here, the socially constitutive power of discourse is predicated on the independence of interdependent interlocutors, who co-operate on the basis of negotiated agreement. This, critics object, is the logic of the modern market based on functional division of labour.[69]

HABERMAS (1981: 62 f.) / (1984–1987 II: 38 f.), (1991: 25, 44) acknowledges, the readiness to accept the binding power of agreed normative claims, instead of traditional authority, is itself a product of processes of social conditioning and presupposes specific forms of life and socialisation. The development of moral consciousness is predicated on the internalisation of the perspective of the generalised other or threatening or factually exercised sanctions. Moreover, the social manifestation of the ideal-typical 'standard form' of rational argumentation presupposes situations or institutions where unconstrained rational argumentation between equals plays a constitutive role for society, such as the public sphere, the parliament, the courts of justice, or the university.[70] According to Habermas, modern social milieus such as these are the product of evolutionary processes of social differentiation generating an increase in both inter-

'pure types of linguistically mediated interaction' are summarised in Figure 16 of *Theory of Communicative Action* (HABERMAS (1980: 439) / (1984–1987 I: 329).

[67] They concern the present discourse of norm legitimation, not norm application. In updated versions of his theory HABERMAS (1991: 131–42) distinguishes two steps of argumentation: (1) related to moral judgement (legitimation) and (2) to moral action (application); i.e. *Begründungsdiskurs* and *Anwendungsdiskurs*.

[68] 'The binding effect of illocutionary forces comes about, ironically, through the fact that participants can say 'no' to speech-act offers. … A hearer can be "bound" by speech-act offers because he is not permitted arbitrarily to refuse them but only to say "no" to them, that is, to reject them for reasons' (HABERMAS (1981: 114) / (1984–1987 II: 73 f.). GADAMER (1993) objected that co-operation in communication does not automatically imply submission to the power of the better argument, at least not without considering the relevance of reasons. FOUCAULT (1981), BLOCH (1975: 21) and BOURDIEU (1991a: 107) similarly reject the idealisations of speech act theory in terms of institutional theories of discursive or symbolic power: 'The power of words is nothing other than the delegated power of the spokesperson' (BOURDIEU (1991a: 107)). For HABERMAS (1980: 418) / (1984–1987 I: 311 f.), (1985) these arguments apply only to empirical pragmatics.

[69] For instance R. Bubner, and A. Wellmer. See HABERMAS (1991: 32, 86 f., 166 f., 15).

[70] On the difference between informal and institutionalised 'ideal speech situations' see HABERMAS (1991: 132).

dependence and individual autonomy and responsibility through a progressive universalisation of law and acquisition of moral competence. He argues that in cases where communicative action is consciously used for the production of normative consensus and social co-operation, discourse takes over the social function of ritual, and becomes a second order ritual (HABERMAS (1981: 86)).[71] With reference to the apparently increasing importance of explicit negotiation in processes of social self-identification, Habermas defines this process of rationalisation as the 'linguistification (*Versprachlichung*) of the sacred', and argues that it goes hand in hand with the progressive 'technicisation' or 'colonisation of the lifeworld' by systemic processes.

How to analyse Jain discourse from the point of view of the theory of communicative action? Generally, religious discourse is depicted by HABERMAS (1980–1981) as a form of communication based on structures of traditional authority in which status rather than argumentation functions as a medium of generalised acceptability.[72] The role of power and insight in Jain discourse could be analysed in these terms. But one has to be aware of the fact that the 'rational reconstruction' of the universal normative presuppositions of linguistic exchange projects its own idealisations into human reality. The theory of communicative action itself contains a religious element in its notion of the 'unconscious innerworldly transcendence' that is implicitly presupposed in communicative action. A deeper analysis of the differences between the theory of communicative action and the Jain doctrine of speech therefore requires a comparison between the normative ideals underlying Habermas' theories of communicative action and discourse ethics[73] with those of Jain discourse ethics (to my knowledge there are no Jain attempts to rationally reconstruct implicit rules), supplemented by comparative analyses of rules and discourses of norm application in typical speech situations (See infra section V–VI).

The daily sermon (*pravacana*) of Jain ascetics is a good example for a transitional ritual, where discourse serves both as an instrument for the reproduction of the traditional authority of the *saṅgha*, and for the eventual production of new normative consensus via the evocation of religious insight amongst yet unconverted listeners. A

[71] Cf. WEBER (1978) on 'ethicisation', and FOUCAULT (1981: 62 f.) and LUHMANN (1982: 144 f.) on the progressive substitution of ritual through discourse. An evolutionary theory of religious development as increasing manifestation of communicative competence has been proposed by DÖBERT (1973: 152). For a critique see PEUKERT (1992: 231 f.).

[72] HABERMAS (2005) pointed out that within the public sphere religious arguments function in same way as other arguments, as reasons to be accepted or rejected.

[73] HABERMAS (1983: 103, cf. 76) / (1990: 93, cf. 66) defines the basic principle of discourse ethics (D), the reflective form of communicative action, as follows: 'Only those norms can claim to be valid that meet (or could meet) with the approval of all affected in their capacity as participants in a practical discourse.'

Jain discourse of conversion presupposes mutual independence of interlocutors and creates new consensus via the unconstrained acceptance of validity claims. The main difference compared with the ideal situation of communicative action is the institutionalised one-sidedness of a monological discourse and its coded semantic form which does not allow for a negotiated modification of the religious dogma itself, at least not in the short run. Because insight and power go hand in hand in tradition-based religion, conversion discourses always take the form of strategic action, producing insight (psychological and verbal acceptance of the dogma) as a perlocutionary effect predicated on the intentional deconstruction of the pre-existing conventional normative consensus.[74] In this case, latent strategic action serves as the vehicle for both communicative action or even mythopoetic world disclosure, and for the unquestioned reproduction of the hierarchy of power. In practice, the two fundamental ways of interpretation are irreducible to each other. But they can be analytically differentiated. In the following, I analyse the plurivocality of Jain discourse primarily in terms of its social implications—as a form of latent strategic action—though multiple ambiguities can be distinguished in every speech act in a conventional speech situation.

It is an open question to what extent the theory of communicative action falls under this verdict as well.[75] HABERMAS (1986: 383), who after all regards communicative action as the original or constitutive mode of language usage, insists on the empirical inevitability of indirect violence and power in the initial stages of the historical evolution of abstract norms. He distinguishes two developmental phases of communicative co-operation and social integration: Communicative action, he argues, is originally embedded in contexts of latent strategic action, because, initially, situation definitions do not sufficiently overlap. The participants therefore have to use indirect communication 'following the model of intentional semantic approaches (Grice)', in order to avoid a breakdown of co-operation. In the opening phases of all processes of co-operation indirect communication plays an important role for the creation of overlapping definitions of the situation, as an alternative of meta-communication: the speaker makes the hearer understand something qua perlocutionary effects, i.e. latent strategic speech acts, whose contextual implications are not directly expressed, and need to be inferred by the hearer.[76] However,

---

[74] This creates paradoxical consequences once communicative action as a value becomes itself topical.

[75] SEARLE (1993: 99).

[76] On perlocutionary effects and latent strategic speech acts see HABERMAS (1980: 393–7) / (1984–1987 I: 292–5).

these strategic sequences are embedded within the general context of communicatively oriented speech.[77]

For HABERMAS (1980: 402–8) / (1984–1987 I: 298–304), (1981: 57–63) / (1984–1987 II: 34–9), as for SEARLE (1993: 91, 99), normative authority is originally embedded within imperative authority, and takes the form of context-specific intentions and speech acts of particular individuals. This fits the case of the Jain sermon. However, Habermas' evolutionary theory of the genesis of norms is highly speculative and certainly the weakest part of his conceptual system. Moreover, he has not elaborated his theory of latent strategic language usage. But he indicates the systematic role of latent strategic action within a typology of social actions,[78] and shows how shared convictions may serve as sources of legitimate power. Power enters unnoticeable into the pores of everyday-life communication via two forms of pseudo-communication concealing strategic intent under the facade of consensual action: (a) conscious deception or manipulation, and (b) systematically distorted communication (HABERMAS (1984: 548)).[79] In cases of manipulation, at least one actor intentionally deceives others by hiding the fact that s/he does not comply with the three universal pragmatic validity claims. In cases of systematically distorted communication at least one of the participants deceives him/ herself about the fact that s/he acts strategically, while maintaining the external appearance of communicative action (HABERMAS (1984: 461)). In both cases a deviation from universal pragmatic presuppositions takes place, through the splitting up or doubling of communication. In the first case, a competent speaker generates intentionally multivocal expressions for social purposes. In the second case, the internal organisation of speech is distorted by way of a privatised use of language. In psychoanalysis this is regarded as a process of de-symbolisation. According to Habermas it is symptomatic for a loss of interactional competence (which may or may not be culturally normalised) (HABERMAS (1984: 251–4)). He argues that distorted forms of communication often occur in situations of social dependency, where they serve as unconscious defence mechanisms concealing conflict smouldering beneath surface consensus (HABERMAS (1984: 232, 264–9)).[80] A manipulative, intentionally symbolic usage of language, on the other hand, creating conflict artificially for the sake of influence, is to be expected in situations of social dominance, and requires cognitive and communicative competencies. We will see that ambiguous language can be used for religious purposes as well.

---

[77] HABERMAS (1980: 444) / (1984–1987 I: 331).

[78] HABERMAS (1980: 446) / (1984–1987 I: 333).

[79] For Durkheimian criticisms of psychological theories of 'rationalisation' see TURNER (1986: 36, 56).

[80] Cf. JAIN (1929: 72), GOONASEKERE (1986).

It could be asked whether the structural multivocality generated by Jain discourse, superposed on varying contexts, can from different viewpoints be interpreted either as a form of latent strategic action or of systematically distorted communication. The perceived ambiguity of certain terms or utterances in Jain discourse is a function of processes of religious interpretation. Depending on circumstances, they may involve forms of symbolisation as well as the expression of latent structural conflicts, resulting for instance from the typical position of many Jains as subaltern elites within the hierarchical structure of Indian society. On the one hand, Jain ascetics use the strategy of intentional re-interpretation of dominant forms of discourse and popular rites, thus creating a private language for competent members of their religious community. On the other hand, the propagation of Jainism through proselytising renouncers eventually triggers effects of moral insight amongst some listeners, by providing a language for example for the explanation and expression of diffuse feelings or implicit conflicts, which may explain part of its appeal. It is important to note that the Jain tradition itself provides a yardstick for the critique of self-deceptions and symptoms of alienated modes of life with its ideal of non-violence. The authenticity associated with such a life-project could be understood as a higher-level validity claim, in analogy to the claim to truthfulness in expressive speech acts.[81] However, better analytical categories are required to investigate the empirical diversity of forms of concealed strategic action. As Habermas indicates, some of them are provided by the intentional semantic approaches of Grice and Searle.

— IV —

One of the most interesting contributions to the theory of linguistic communication and rhetoric is GRICE's (1975) analysis of the communicative function of 'conversational implicature'. In his article *Logic and Conversation*, Grice provides a pragmatic description of how multiple meanings are purposefully generated. He investigates what he calls 'implicature', that is, instances in which 'a speaker deliberately says something which is not, in fact, what he means' (GRICE (1975: 43 f.)). Grice's analysis is based on the fundamental pragmatic postulate that there is a assumption by all conversationalists of the rational and efficient nature of talk—a supposition, which can be formally stated in terms of a set of counterfactual principles and maxims concerning the efficient and univocal transmission of information, given that both parties co-operate and are interested to continue the conversation. Against this assumption polite, multivocal ways of speaking appear as deviations, requiring ra-

[81] HABERMAS (1996: 341).

tional explanation on the part of the recipient, who finds in considerations of politeness reasons for the speaker's apparent irrationality or inefficiency. Given the speaker's rationality of expression, and the hearer's willingness to co-operate, unclear, ambiguous language forces the hearer to work out the implied suppositions of a multivocal statement. The latter must ask her/himself why a speaker, who can express her/himself unambiguously, has chosen not to say directly what s/he means, but rather speaks in a veiled language. In such cases, Grice argues, the hearer (interpreter) will assume that the speaker has deliberately 'flouted' the mutually presupposed conversational principles to 'force an implicature' onto the hearer, who then has to infer what the speaker intended without saying so openly. Particularly interesting are cases in which someone deliberately violates a maxim, not to mislead, but to influence others by getting another message across. Strategically constructed 'deviations' such as these, which are 'parasitic' to direct communication, are particularly successful in achieving social influence, because they induce the necessary element of conflict in a manifestly non-violent form, not breaching social norms openly but only indirectly via implicit 'exploitation' or 'flouting' of presupposed conversational principles. It is precisely this 'non-violent' form of social influence which I regard as central to Jain rhetoric.

The construction of implicatures is one of the foremost rhetorical and poetical devices. Yet, only under certain contextual conditions will a conversational act of flouting lead to social consequences. Without the hearer's willingness and ability to co-operate, and to invest the effort to work out or to grasp intuitively the implications of an ambiguous statement, rhetorical communication with the help of implicature would not be effective. The uses of implicatures presupposes the invocation of contextual knowledge or common experiential ground on the part of the hearer, who is forced to generate a meaningful interpretation in response to the speaker's deliberate violation of the principles of conversation, which implicitly forces on the hearer a choice between deference to the veiled imperative or discontinuation of the communication. The efficacy of this kind of indirect communication is ultimately based on ego's exploitation of alter's willingness to adhere to the general cooperative principle of language exchange under given normative conditions. Accordingly, the principal means of physically 'non-violent' resistance is non-cooperation.[82]

Grice's theory of language usage is, in itself, of limited use in anthropological research. Theories of information processing cannot sufficiently account for the empirical role of conventional meaning and contextual knowledge, as HYMES (1972a), (1972b) convincingly argued.[83] BROWN'–LEVINSON's (1978) theory of politeness,

[82] SHARP (1960), (1973).

[83] In his summary critique of Grice's intentionalist semantics, DAVIS (1998: 174) notes that 'common interests sustaining indirect speech act conventions are much deeper than mere politeness.' However, 'A common interest need not be universally shared to sustain a common practice.'

which builds upon Grice's principles, therefore links the theory of conversational implicature with Goffman's theory of social self-identity or 'face' (self-esteem or public self-image). It argues that talk exchange can be related to contextual, that is, institutional, variables by considering the relative social position of speaker and hearer, which decisively influences choices of politeness strategy. 'Face' is relationally defined, 'that is, normally everyone's face depends on everyone else's being maintained, and since people can be expected to defend their faces if threatened, and in defending their own to threaten others' faces, it is in general in every participant's best interest to maintain each other's face' (BROWN–LEVINSON (1978: 66)). Two kinds of 'face wants' are distinguished: 'negative face wants' (to be unimpeded by others)—often achieved by strategies of non-interaction (which Marriott regards as typical for Jains, and *vaiśya*s in general)—and 'positive face wants' (to be desirable to others) (BROWN–LEVINSON (1978: 66)). 'Face threatening acts' (FTA's) are illocutionary acts which might cause a loss of face by way of orders, requests, threats, offers, suggestions etc. They run contrary to particular face wants, and motivate certain strategies of politeness, employed to minimise the threat, and to maintain face in a particular situation (BROWN–LEVINSON (1978: 70–3)).

BROWN and LEVINSON distinguish four main strategies of politeness: (a) 'bald on record' (being as clear as possible), (b) 'positive politeness' (the expression of solidarity), (c) 'negative politeness' (the expression of restraint), and (d) 'off record' (the avoidance of unequivocal impositions) (BROWN–LEVINSON (1978: 73–5)).[84] Any of the four strategies may satisfy the opponent's face wants to avoid conflict and to minimise threat. Yet, politeness is also used in order to stimulate conflict in a calculated way. Positive politeness and negative politeness—the dominant Jain strategy— I

'Speaker meaning' and the 'actual linguistic conventions of language communities' should be studied: 'Rather than trying to deduce arbitrary practices from some general psychosocial principles, we must look at the social functions that particular conventions serve.'—'In sum, Gricean theory fails because speaker implicature is a matter of intention, sentence implicature is a matter of convention, and neither is calculable from or generated by psychosocial principles. Conversational rules instead codify social goals motivating intentions and sustaining conventions' (DAVIS (1998: 190)).

[84] Examples for positive politeness are familiar and joking behaviour. Negative politeness is mainly concerned with self-determination. It is at the heart of respect behaviour and corresponds to Durkheim's 'negative rites', that is, rituals of avoidance, which are typical for Jains. Characteristic examples of negative politeness are: conventional indirectness, question/hedge, be pessimistic (don't coerce, don't assume other's willingness to co-operate), minimise imposition, give deference, apologise (beg forgiveness), impersonalise, state FTA as a general rule, nominalise, go on record as incurring a debt, or as not indebting the hearer (BROWN–LEVINSON (1978: 134–216)). There are certain similarities between these strategies and Searle's and Habermas' illocutionary components, although Brown and Levinson's categories reflect the inconsistency of Sahlins' well known scheme of reciprocities, which was obviously influential.

would argue, are primarily strategies of conflict avoidance. The most interesting strategy, also often used in Jain discourse, is to go off-record, that is, to construct intentionally multivocal statements: 'A communicative act is done off record if it is done in such a way that it is not possible to attribute only one clear communicative intention to the act. In other words, the actor leaves himself an "out" by providing himself with a number of defensible interpretations; he cannot be held to have committed himself to just one particular interpretation of this act. Thus if a speaker wants to do a FTA, but wants to avoid the responsibility for doing it, he can do it off record and leave it open to the addressee to decide how to interpret it' (BROWN–LEVINSON (1978: 216)). The purpose of off-record strategies is to make the addressee responsible for decoding the intentions. An FTA, like any word, rule or symbolic act,[85] gains its meaning through context and becomes threatening only through its realisation via 'wrong or correct' interpretation.[86] The near universal usefulness of off-record strategies for purposes of persuasion and social influence is aptly expressed by STRECKER (1988: 114): 'To go off-record is one of the most pervasive strategies in social interaction whenever actors want to avoid harsh confrontation and the possibility of conflict, and when they want to persuade others, to influence them so that they do what they cannot be openly coerced to do. All this is done by means of indirect message construction.' Important for my argument is that politeness and symbolisation is used to avoid open conflict. A great deal of politeness and symbolisation is therefore to be expected from the Jains.

BROWN–LEVINSON (1978: 254–6) conclude their discussion of politeness phenomena with a typology of characteristic patterns of strategy distribution in speaker/hearer relationships regarding the contextual variables of power (P) and social distance (D) (which could be associated with 'active' directive and 'passive' commissive orientations respectively). In this way, they try to tie Grice's concept of conversational implicature into a context-sensitive social theory of linguistically mediated interaction.[87] They predict that in a situation where one of the interlocutors has high social power over another, and where social distance is low, the speaker with high social power will predominately use on-record strategies, and the speaker with low social power will use negative politeness and off-record strategies. STRECKER (1988: 165 f.), however, notes that individuals in an inferior position are generally not allowed to force an implicature upon the socially powerful (only *vice versa*). He suggests that the dominant pattern of strategy distribution in asymmetri-

[85] Cf. CASSIRER (1923–1929).

[86] Cf. BROWN–LEVINSON's (1978: 219) depiction of off-record strategies as violations of the Gricean maxims.

[87] Cf. BROWN–LEVINSON's (1978: 255) chart of dyadic strategy types.

cal social contexts is the combination of off-record strategies on the part of superiors and on-record strategies and negative politeness on the part of inferiors.

The still unresolved discrepancy between Brown and Levinson's and Strecker's interpretation provokes the question whether it makes sense at all to link types of socially-purposeful language usage to certain 'social positions', given the wide range of contextually acceptable strategy choices. Off-record strategies, in fact, can be used for many purposes: for purely aesthetic reasons, for the negotiation of unclear social relationships, for the veiling of heavy FTA's or forms of control, or for the stabilisation of asymmetrical social relationships. More importantly, a statement in itself does not force a reader/listener to adopt a particular type of interpretation (and no particular action follows from it in any structured way). Everything, in fact, depends on the wider social context, particularly on the informal or institutionalised norms and social conventions of a given field of discourse, which sanction the way in which language is used and which interpretations are regarded as feasible. As Habermas shows, it is only in situations where social pressures and normative sanctions are attached to language usage, that normative claims can be enforced through extra-linguistic sanctions. It is impossible to force anybody to comply with pragmatic conditions for the fulfilment of an implication, in the Gricean sense, without implicitly presupposing an institutional context and referring to a set of known social sanctions attached to the specific norms of a particular discursive field.[88]

This point has evaded most linguistic theories of politeness, because—as Habermas points out—they do not clearly distinguish between co-operation in conversation and the role of speech acts for social co-operation. Therefore they cannot explain, for instance, how, in certain situations, superiors may rely on contextual pressures to force inferiors to decode their veiled speech and to fulfil the indirectly communicated demands. It is not the power of the words themselves nor the speaker's intentions which inform the 'calling in' of conversational implicature, but the role of the presupposed norms and sanctions which assure the perpetuation of social systems which, for instance, force inferiors to infer unequivocally the indexical meaning of intentionally ambiguous statements of their superiors, and to practically fulfil their unspoken commands without questioning the normative basis of their social co-operation.[89] Because

[88] Strategies can be conventionalised and ossified into norms of dominance, and compliance can be legitimately enforced. See HABERMAS (1984: 253).

[89] In the technical linguistic and philosophical literature the term 'implication' is used in different ways and still awaits clarification as BROWN–LEVINSON (1978: 216 f.) note. For recent work see HORN (1973), (1985), (2001), DAVIS (1998), LEVINSON (2000), HORN–WARD (2004), ATLAS (2005). In the following I will call the process of fulfilling accepted validity conditions the 'social implication' of a speech act, in contrast to the 'logical' or semantical implication of a communicative act, and to its psychological 'conditions of satisfaction'. The social implications of a speech act are the possi-

they accept the unnecessary constraints of Grice's theory of information processing, even Brown and Levinson and Strecker cannot avoid reductionist interpretations of language usage in terms of pre-existing 'social positions' and differential 'power'. Habermas' distinction between communicative and success orientated language usage, however, seems to open a path for a non-reductionist understanding, for instance, of the social function of positive politeness, which, in the words of Brown and Levinson, can only 'express' but not 'generate' solidarity. Reductionism can only be avoided if not merely the reflexive but also the constitutive function of discourse for the construction of social identities is considered. From this perspective, strategies of negative politeness and off-record appear to have greater power than positive politeness or on-record strategies, particularly in social situations where coercion cannot succeed and where co-operation is primarily engendered through indirect communication.

— V —

Any empirical analysis of conversational implicatures requires a careful description of the discursive field and conventional ways of speaking in different 'speech situations' which form part of the 'communicative competence' (HYMES (1972b))[90] and 'repertoire' of the members of a particular 'speech community' (GUMPERZ (1964), (1972)).[91] From an observer's point of view, there are four formal contexts,

ble actions which may follow from it, if its validity claims are explicated through context-sensitive processes of interpretation of indexical meaning, and accepted. Cf. WEBER (1988: 95, 125) on the social function of 'noetic' interpretations of the social motives of ambiguous commands (in contrast to the objective understanding of the meaning of a statement) either (a) in terms of/for practical purposes, or (b) in terms of value-relations and for purposes of scientific understanding.

[90] See GUMPERZ's (1995: 209) definition: 'Communicative competence can be defined in interactional terms as "the knowledge of linguistic and related communicative conventions that speakers must have to create and sustain conversational cooperation", and thus involves both grammar and contextualization.'

[91] GUMPERZ (1964: 137) defined 'speech community' first as 'any human aggregate characterized by regular and frequent interaction over a significant span of time and set off from other such aggregates by differences in the frequency of interaction.' Later he added the criterion of compartmentalisation (GUMPERZ (1972: 231)) and emphasised the role of social norms for the definition of a speech community: 'any human aggregate characterized by regular and frequent interaction by means of a shared body of verbal signs and set off from similar aggregates by significant differences in language usage. ... Regardless of the linguistic differences among them, the speech varieties employed within a speech community form a system because they are related to a shared set of social norms' (GUMPERZ (1972: 219 f.). See also GUMPERZ–HYMES (1986) and HABERMAS (1980: 382 f.) / (1984–1987 I: 283). HYMES (1972b: 55) tries to 'bypass' the difficulties of defining 'community' by stating: 'The essential thing is that the object of description be an integral social unit.' The problem of essentialism does not pose itself at all in the more

or 'speech situations'[92] and associated 'speech events' and 'genres', which are relevant in the case of Jain discourse: (a) the religious debate (*vivāda*[93] or *prayoga*),[94] for instance at a royal court or modern court of law, (b) the public sermon (*pravacana*),[95] (c) the interaction between ascetics and non-ascetics in informal settings (*bhāṣā*), and (d) the interaction between ascetics (*vinaya*).[96] Each of these settings involves a different set of social and stylistic conventions, norms and expectations.[97] The agonistic debate at a royal court or a court of law for instance is a highly pragmatic affair whose outcome might decide the fate of a particular monastic group. Here, the contextual rules are defined by the king or the state, and classical

---

abstract theory of communicative action and Jain theories of speech (Hymes (1972b: 56), (1983: 167));—despite Albert's (1994: 259 n. 41) objections. See footnotes 10, 18, 67, 142.

[92] 'Such situations may enter as contexts into the statement of rules of speaking as aspects of setting (or of genre). In contrast to speech events, they are not in themselves governed by such rules throughout' (Hymes (1972b: 56)).

[93] Ṭhāṇ 6.67 lists six empirical types of debate, and Ṭhāṇ 10.95 ten special faults of debate. On Indian traditions of rational inquiry and theories of debate see, for instance, Bronkhorst (1999), Prets (2004).

[94] Carrithers (1992: 112 f.) singles this setting out as particular significant; while emphasising the universal principle of free negotiation of situations (Carrithers (1992: 105 f.)).

[95] Cf. Weber (1978: 213 f.) on the role of politeness in the proselytisation of Jainism, and Williams (1983: 45 f.) on the 'spreaders of religious faith' (*prābhāvaka*).

[96] Obviously, this is not an exhaustive taxonomy of all typical situations of language usage in Jain culture. I do not discuss examples of formulaic language, such as *mantra* or *japa*, or political oratory, which have already been exhaustively treated in the literature, but concentrate on those types of ritualised interaction where religious discourse is the predominant form of language usage. There are many different classifications of speech situations in the Jain scriptures, which deserve further investigation. For example, the four types of speech appropriate for an ascetic performing *bhikṣu-pratimā*s listed in Ṭhāṇ 237 (4.22): (1) requesting speech, used in the context of the begging round (*jāyaṇī bhāsā* <*yācanī bhāṣā*>), (2) questioning speech, used in the context of the studying the meaning of the scriptures, or path-finding (*pucchaṇī bhāsā* <*pracchanī bhāṣā*>), (3) speech used for seeking permission, for example to stay at a certain place (*aṇuṇṇavaṇī bhāsā* <*anujñāpanī bhāṣā*>), (4) speech used in the context of question-answer dialogues (*puṭṭha-vāgaraṇī bhāsā* <*praśna-vyākaraṇī bhāṣā*>). Ṭhāṇ 4.274 specifies also four situations in which it is permitted for monks and nuns to talk to each other.

[97] Hymes (1972b: 55–66) proposed the following useful analytical categories: language field, speech situation, speech event, speech act, speech styles, ways of speaking, components of speech (message form, message content, setting [physical], scene [psychological/cultural], purpose [outcome], purpose [goal], key, channel, forms of speech [varieties], norms of interaction [social structure], norms of interpretation, genres). They roughly correspond to Malinowski's earlier distinction of dogmatic context, ritual context, and sociological context, as well as structure and mode of recitation (Hymes (1972b: 64)). The interrelation of genres, events and acts and other components in Jain settings is worth studying further (Hymes (1972b: 65)).

philosophical and political rhetorical skills are in demand. The public sermon, on the other hand, is comparatively informal, despite its conventional setting and asymmetrical structure. It conveys religious content, inspiration and insight in an entertaining manner, and is often followed by casual discussions at the end. The fundamental norms of comportment are defined by the monastic community itself. The interactions between ascetics and non-ascetics ideally take place within a hierarchical context of worship of ascetic purity, and are sometimes highly ritualised.[98] However, there are also informal interactions, which require greater discriminatory skills on the part of the ascetics for not transgressing the norms of non-violent interaction. The code of polite interaction within the monastic order itself is derived from the principles of ascetic seniority (*dīkṣā-paryāya*) and group leadership, and operates in a similar manner.

I have ordered these four ritualised types of discourse sequentially in terms of their increasing coincidence with Jain ideals, starting with political rituals, then conversion rituals, interaction rituals, and finally monastic rituals. Other forms of classification are possible; for instance in terms of degrees of formality, social setting (assembly or individual contact),[99] or regarding the relative importance of discourse in ritual.[100] How-

---

[98] CARRITHERS (1992: 106) notes that in Jain (Indian) settings, the free negotiation of meaning is constrained by socio-cultural norms: 'There is a bias towards the authoritative pronouncement, that is, towards a relationship of unquestioning domination of the instructor. ... If we substract the authoritarian flavour, the telling of Siddhasagar's story [his example, P.F.] still retains an essential element, the creating of a common meaning by working jointly, interactively, to establish which interpretation is to be accepted.'

[99] TAMBIAH (1968: 177 ff.) and BLOCH (1975: 19) also distinguish between the 'primary function of language', as a vehicle for communication, and certain types of 'ritual language' (e.g. *mantra* or formalised oratory), which violate the communication function by being formal, unintelligible, and/or private (see also WHEELOCK (1982: 57); and HUMPHREY–LAIDLAW's (1994: 89) psychological variant). However, both ignore the constitutive function of language, and do not distinguish between speech acts and linguistically mediated interaction. Hence, they are forced to resort to reductionist interpretations of the social function of ritual language either in terms of institutions of power (BLOCH (1975: 24)) or paradigmatic cultural ideas (TAMBIAH (1985: 154)). Bloch's singular, BERNSTEIN (1964) inspired, emphasis on formality as (a) the decisive and (b) restrictive attribute of political and ritual discourse in contexts of traditional authority, can neither account for the Jain emphasis on content rather than form, nor on their insistence on ethics and the generative power of restraint. Tambiah criticises Bloch for not taking into consideration a number of factors: the intelligibility of ritual language derived from cosmological ideas, the role of ritual functionaries, and social context. Despite emphasising intellectual content of sacred language (in Buddhism), and similarities between sacred and profane language, Tambiah himself only discusses cases of popular 'magical' usage of language (e.g. *mantra*), and accepts emic 'power of words' theories as empirical fact, without discussing the role of discourse in ritual and emic theories of language (e.g. Vedic: RENOU (1955), Navya-Ṇyāya: GANERI (1999); the power of words to signify is also recognised by Jain philosophers).

ever, for our primarily sociological purpose, the crucial variable is 'interactional competence', that is, the knowledge and ability to use rules and moral judgement for interaction in specific situations. Interactional competence presupposes 'cognitive competence' (PIAGET (1937)), 'linguistic competence' (CHOMSKY (1965)),[101] 'communicative competence' (HYMES (1972a)), including 'oratory skill' (BLOCH (1975)). HABERMAS (1984: 187 ff., 231 f.) defines interactional competence more specifically as the universal pragmatic ability to regulate social conflict consensually through rational agreement, even in situations of severe discord, in accordance with the three universal pragmatic validity claims. He distinguishes further between the intuitive or conscious knowledge of specific grammatical and socio-cultural rules and contexts, and the mastery of the universal pragmatic conditions of the possibility of mutual understanding (*Verständigung*).[102] Because Habermas' notion of 'communicative competence', a composite of cognitive, linguistic and interactional competencies (in a more narrow sense),[103] is more abstract and formal than Hymes' sociolinguistic notion of 'communicative competence', it circumvents the problem of analytical reification of 'speakers' or of 'speech communities'. Building upon HABERMAS' (1991: 111–3) distinction between two levels of competencies, also reflected in his differentiation between universal 'moral' and cultural specific 'ethical' principles, and HYMES' (1972b: 57 f.) notion that knowledge of grammatical rules and of determinate ways of speaking together form the communicative competence of a particular speech community or individual, I propose to differentiate further between general 'interactional competence' and specific 'Jain interactional competence', that is, the formal procedural knowledge necessary for constituting discourse in agreement with Jain principles.[104]

---

[100] TAMBIAH (1968: 176) poses the interesting question of the relationship of words to actions in ritual, noting the predominance of words and intelligible language in healing and initiation rites addressing human beings, in contrast to rites of mass participation and rites addressing supernatural beings or forces of nature. He also discusses the problem of alternation between various types of language in ritual, and reformist attempts to destroy the ritual formalism of sacred language in favour of increased accessibility and understanding. Both observations apply to contemporary Jainism.

[101] See also DURBIN (1970).

[102] HABERMAS (1975: 3).

[103] To distinguish the two kindred notions of communicative competence, I privilege the term interactive competence here. The usefulness of HYMES's (1972a), (1972b) approach for the empirical investigation of ways of speaking has frequently been highlighted by HABERMAS (1975: 5), (1980: 440) / (1984–1987 I: 328). Habermas first used 'interactional competence' and later preferred 'communicative competence'. I use the term interactional competence in the broader sense of social coordination of actions through linguistic and non-linguistic means.

[104] This application of the theory of social competence was first outlined in FLÜGEL (1994), (1995–6: 165). For theories of religious competence (often combined with theories of religious socialisation) see SAMARIAN (1969), LUHMANN (1982), WAARDENBURG (1979), and GLADIGOW

Jain interactional competence is informed by general 'Jain religious competence', which can be defined as the sum total of Jain religious knowledge learned by an individual. In addition to general 'Jain interactional competence', religious rules and contextual knowledge necessary for navigating specific contexts can be studied, and the 'Jain religious repertoire' of a specific population or individual analysed (as part of a particular 'socio-cultural repertoire').

General 'interactional competence' refers to the ability of a flexible reflective regulation of total conduct in terms of universal moral presuppositions, contrasting with institutionalised settings, which, through their formal properties, relieve the individual to some extent from the task of defining the situation and from difficult moral choices. 'Jain interactional competence' varies with the degree of knowledge and the internalisation of general and cultural specific (sectarian etc.) It is necessary to distinguish Jain principles and their contextual rules of use; that is, the cognitive and non-cognitive (motivational, emotional etc.) know how to act in accordance with abstract and specific doctrinal principles in different socio-cultural circumstances. Jain principles and rules of application, of varying degrees of specificity.[105] General Jain principles are characterised by constitutive rules, generative of the field of Jain discourse as a whole. They are exemplified by ideal Jain speech events. Jain interactional competence is context-sensitive. The corresponding rules are deliberately constructed to enable a performer to react flexibly to emergent properties of a specific speech situation, and to shape it in accordance with Jain principles. Since principles and rules only negatively determine the field of pragmatic possibilities, speaking the Jain way, or avoiding interaction altogether, are creative acts, performances, which

(1997). The latter noted that the ability to orient oneself in complex religious contexts, to distinguish between different situations, to develop a 'religious identity', and to act appropriately cannot be taken for granted: 'Die Kompetenz, in einer polytheistischen Religion zu leben, sie angemessen zu benutzen, wird von modernen Interpreten einfach unterstellt' (GLADIGOW (1997: 105)). Following Luhmann and Waardenburg, he advocates for the semiotic analysis of religious pantheons as 'languages' which can be learned and selectively used (GLADIGOW (1997: 106)).

[105] Cf. SINGER's (1961: 96–138) distinction between principles and rules: 'I argued that moral principles are to be distinguished from moral rules by the fact that the former hold in all circumstances and do not admit of exceptions; that principles are always relevant whereas rules are not; that principles are invariant and do not vary with changes in circumstances or conditions; and by the fact that it is impossible for moral principles to conflict with each other. … I distinguished between fundamental rules, local rules, and neutral norms. Local rules … depend on local conditions in a way that fundamental rules do not, and hence are peculiar to, and differ with, different groups and communities—that is to say, different circumstances. Neutral norms are local rules that are conventional in a way that other rules are not ['it would make no moral difference if their opposites were adopted' (SINGER (1961: 113))], but both neutral norms and local rules depend on social needs or purposes that are advanced by general observance and would be frustrated or defeated by their general violation' (SINGER (1961: 327 f.)). On levels see also HARE (1981: 35 ff.).

ideally transform any speech event into a Jain discourse. Actual speech performances, or Jain 'speech styles' in the terms of HYMES (1972b: 57), I would argue, can not be sufficiently understood in terms of statistical features of overt behaviour, or as deviations from a general norm or ideal, but only as constitutive acts dependent on 'qualitative judgements of appropriateness' of selected features in a given situation.[106]

Theoretically, the required interactional competence of the ideal 'pure ascetic' (*śuddha-sādhu*) increases with the degree of informality of the interactional situation, because ascetic self-control, in accordance with Jain principles, is the price for freedom from external (social and ritual) control. In practice, Jain ascetics try to prevent rule-transgressions due to insufficient procedural knowledge with various methods: for example, by teaching context-sensitive rules not in abstract, but through exemplary cases, or by keeping inexperienced ascetics away from morally overcomplex situations through strict supervision. Similar competencies are outlined for the Jain laity. An ideal lay person is characterised, for instance by Hemacandra (YŚ 1.47–56), as one who is listening (*śravaṇa*), memorising (*dhāraṇā*), showing respect (*vinaya*), being an expert in sacred lore (*pravacana-kuśala*), and also avoiding religiously unprofitable speech (*sat-kathā*) etc. (WILLIAMS (1983: 265–72)). Thus, it is always the Jain interactional competence, the religious and cultural repertoire of an individual or group, which generates the capacity of defining or judging situations in terms of Jain principles, of imposing or inferring implicatures, and determining the relevant type of rhetoric or hermeneutic procedure.[107]

Once the settings and the required competencies are considered, the social implications of Jain discourse can be analysed in terms of the conditions and presuppositions of the acceptability of particular validity claims in Jain intersubjective hermeneutics. These can be discovered by negating speech acts as a whole.[108] The question is always: What are the social implications of a religious claim in this particular context? 'What makes a religious statement acceptable?'[109] Ultimately, such a question can only be answered by the participants themselves, because only they can determine on which grounds to accept or to reject a particular claim. In other words, the explication of implications can never be achieved objectively, for instance by explaining the 'cogency of ideas' through a description of 'the structure of

[106] On appropriateness and general features of discourses of rule application see also WELLMER (1986), and HABERMAS' (1991: 137–42) discussion of K. GÜNTHER (1988).

[107] Non-literal speech-acts can only work if their implications are understood (and accepted). BRUHN (1987b: 67), for instance, writes: 'The fact that everybody knew the basic pattern [of Jain soteriological sequences, P.F.] made it rather simple to find suitable words for a lecture or a sermon.' Cf. GLUCKMAN (1955: 24) on degrees of 'flexibility or of moral implication' of legal concepts.

[108] HABERMAS (1993: 26).

[109] Cf. GOMBRICH's (1988: 10) question: 'What makes a religious innovation acceptable?'

a problem situation' alone, as GOMBRICH (1988: 11) suggests, but is always an outcome of specific intersubjective processes of socio-cultural self-interpretation.[110]

Classical performative approaches to ritual or ritual language, for instance, which made use of Grice's or Searle's analysis failed to investigate this (like Grice and Searle themselves). In fact, they neglected the role of discourse in ritual altogether, in favour of either cultural determinism (Tambiah) or mental (Humphrey and Laidlaw) or material reductionism (Bloch). Following Searle's and Habermas' interpretation of the dual (illocutionary and propositional) structure of the speech act, TAMBIAH (1985: 153) argues that, because ritual action appears to mediate between (cultural) ideas and (political) practice, it can be interpreted as a performative matrix of 'indexical symbols (and indexical icons) as duplex structures carrying semantic and pragmatic meanings':

> 'The duality thus points in two directions at once—in the semantic direction of cultural presuppositions and conventional understandings and in the pragmatic direction of the social and interpersonal context of ritual action, the line-up of the participants and the process by which they establish or infer meanings. We note that the sense in which I imagine actors to infer indexical meaning is similar to Grice's formulation of "conversational implicature", in that by saying or enacting something a certain meaning is implicated, which can be readily understood (conventional implicature) or is capable of being "worked out" (non-conventional implicature), given certain contextual features and certain common understandings' (TAMBIAH (1985: 154)).

Although he treats ritual acts as speech acts (thus identifying action and his own action description), speech itself is curiously absent in Tambiah's conception (and where he talks about it, he returns to the traditional 'power of words', *śabda-śakti*, theory). Moreover, the propositional component of the ritual act, its symbolism, is not treated in terms of specific validity claims whose debatable normative implications may or may not be acceptable, but identified with timeless and incontestable cultural paradigms. Tambiah's performative analysis is therefore still oriented towards the theological model of textual hermeneutics, that is, the dogmatic explication (*phronesis*) of contextual implications of mythic paradigms or sacred texts. His approach assumes that the knowledge embodied in texts is superior to the interpreter's, and has to be accepted.[111] Because his performative analysis does not clearly distinguish between ritual acts and ritually mediated forms of social interaction, it must assume socially binding effects emerge automatically from the experi-

[110] Cf. GARFINKEL–SACKS (1970).

[111] Cf. HABERMAS (1980: 193–6) / (1984–1987 I: 134–6).

ence of ritual acts themselves, and that the authority of traditional ritual form should always be accepted, without question. The underlying notion of ritual enactment, a variation of the Neo-Kantian model of value realisation, cannot account for processes of intersubjective negotiation of conditions of acceptability and for the contextually varying social implications of ritually communicated validity claims. The presumed timelessness of mythical paradigms re-produces the characteristic pseudo-concreteness of Durkheimian functionalist studies of ritual performance, positing social integration both as a presupposition and result of ritual, without investigating the constitutive role of discourse in and about ritual itself.

Tambiah's theory does not throw light on Jain religious discourse, which appeals to reason and insight, instead of formulaic repetition, and whose contextually specific normative claims are constantly challenged and revised by the Jain *ācārya*s, under the threat of failure to appeal. In sum, because of the lacking theory of social constitution and cultural change, and the absence of sociolinguistic interest, Tambiah's approach cannot assist analysing the problem of contextual ambiguity of indexical meaning, which I deal with later in this essay. As an alternative, I suggest investigating Jain ritual discourse through the analysis of the Jain discourse ethics and traditional interpretative procedures for negotiating social meaning; to avoid falling into the same trap as Bloch, who identifies an increase of formality generally with a loss of meaning, which Tambiah rightly criticises.

Even if the idealist limitations of universal pragmatic or culturalist discourse analysis could be overcome, there is still the problem of how to analytically reconstruct implicatures in specific cases in a methodical way. This question is particularly prominent in theological, juridical and moral-philosophical debates concerning the status of rule application, that is, of interpretative processes that are involved in the specification of principles and rules through the explication of the contextual implications of given principles and rules.[112] As language in general does,[113] explicit normative principles and rules always entail an anonymous indexical element. That is, they implicitly refer to a range of possible situations as their field of applicability, which we must know and accept, if we wish to act accordingly. To explicate general conditions of applicability, one has to refer to paradigmatic situations. Paradoxically, the range of applicability diminishes with the increasing specification of the conditions, and increases with the diminishing specification.[114] In other words, the problem is the principal vagueness and ambiguity of the indexical meaning of symbolic forms, which, as GLUCKMAN (1955: 293) and TURNER (1986: 44) argued,

[112] GADAMER (1993: 107), WELLMER (1986).

[113] APEL (1993: 41).

[114] WELLMER (1986: 28, 35 f.).

is in fact a positive functional feature of abstraction, because it secures the adaptability of general principles to changing contexts.[115] An exhaustive characterisation of merely negatively determined situations, therefore, cannot and, indeed, should not be achieved once and for all by participants, even if a principle itself is accepted.[116]

The contextual meanings and social implications of symbolic forms (and the forms themselves) are always underdetermined and hence negotiable.[117] They can only be established temporarily through use and agonistic intersubjective interpretative processes, whose outcome is always open, even if methods of argumentation and discursive procedures are conventional,[118] and predicated on idealised universal pragmatic presuppositions. I therefore suggest supplementing standard descriptions of ritual, or action in general, by an analysis of the discursive procedures which define situations and establish relevance and contextually acceptable social meaning. The discursive field surrounding rituals and other social settings should be the main focus for an investigation of social dimensions of ritual efficacy. Conventional analyses of ritual focus almost exclusively on the given ceremonial setting and on the performative experience itself, and tend to give undue weight to the procedural knowledge of ritual functionaries, textualised cultural ideas, and articulated subjective experience. The resulting meaning reductionism can be avoided by investigating discursive negotiations of validity claims *in situ*,[119] including possibly the relationship between general, for instance moral, language games and institutionalised forms of reflexivity, such as theology and the social sciences. The analysis[120] of implicit judgements invoked in everyday practices of moral justification, moral utterances and moral disputes, can also demonstrate how cultural resources are used as potential reasons for claims of validity. From this perspective, social solidarity does not only emerge exclusively as a consequence of partaking in 'effervescent' rituals, to use Durkheim's expression, but primarily—and increasingly so—as the result of the participation in socially constitutive discourses of norm legitimation and shared definitions of situations.

---

[115] *Pace* BLOCH (1975: 17). On the function of general principles see also HARE (1981: 41).

[116] On the impossibility of an objective description of indexical meaning of Jain religious terminology see CORT (1989: 93), (1992: 178), HUMPHREY–LAIDLAW (1994: 101), and FLÜGEL (2006b).

[117] General principles or rules are generally combined with more specific rule of application. See WITTGENSTEIN (1953). 'Keine Norm enthält die Regeln ihrer eigenen Anwendung' (HABERMAS (1991: 24)).

[118] They may include culturally specific discourse etiquettes and formalised interpretative procedures, such as the (monological) forms of Jain scholastic exegesis (*niryukti*) described by BALBIR (1993: 56).

[119] See the pioneering work of TURNER (1986: 45). Lately, HABERMAS (2004: 53) conceded that all discourses are embedded in lifeworld practices, because they have the function to restore partially distorted background consensus (as analysed by TURNER).

[120] HABERMAS (1996: 335) used the term 'critical understanding' through 'reconstructive translation'.

The paradigmatic example of practical hermeneutical explications of implied indexical meaning, are intentionally multivocal forms of communication within 'master-slave' relationships; often discussed either in terms of formalisation of discourse, and of understanding implicit directives (e.g. commands), or in terms of the instrumentalisation of interpretation as such by the rhetoric of spiritual power in contexts of traditional authority. Building on the work of Brown and Levinson and Strecker on the influence of social structure on discourse, DRECHSEL (1994: 50), for instance, draws an analogy between the relationship of off-recordness and on-recordness in politeness theory, and the relationship of the ambiguous symbolism of 'sacred' kingship and the unequivocal social and material implications of royal pomp, which, he suggests, have to be worked out by the lower strata of society qua unspoken command. Although mere compliance or non-compliance with implicit directives in no way shows that they are legitimate or illegitimate,[121] the explanatory problem of this institutional theory is the same as in Habermas' analysis of latent strategic action in terms of universal normative presuppositions. The king's dual socially constitutive role, as a living symbol of society and as an individual with its own specific interests, involves his subjects in a paradoxical double-bind situation.[122] Because the king is the condition of socio-cosmic existence, royal power appears not primarily 'exploitative', but 'attractive', to the extent that the subjects try to read the king's mind and, ideally, to fulfil his unsaid wishes. Because the king is the condition of social order everyone is forced to identify with him. In fulfilling his wishes, the subject reproduces the conditions of its own social existence as a social being. A good example is the relationship between the king and his officials in the context of the 'polite society' of the court, and their characteristic mutual strategic orientation: the characteristic ambiguity of the king's role forces the officials to work out the 'implications' of royal gestures, and to fulfil his unspeakable material needs in form of service, presents etc.[123] Even a cursory glance at the vast literature on South Asian kingship shows the empirical significance of such phenomena, first theorised by HEGEL

[121] APEL (1993: 49).

[122] BURGHART (1996: 306): 'In a "Government of one", conventionally called monarchy, everyone else leads double lives. They lead a life as dictated by the will of their lord and master, and they lead a life of their own.'

[123] See also ALI (2004). LUHMANN (1979: 36) argued that the efficacy of power in general is predicated on the mutual desire to avoid anticipated possibilities of open conflict and brute force. Obedience is usually not the result of explicit commands but based on the avoidance of expected sanctions in case of the non-performance of desired behaviour: 'Der Machthaber braucht gar nicht erst zu befehlen, auch seine unbefohlenen Befehle werden schon befolgt. Sogar die Initiative zum Befehl kann auf den Unterworfenen verlagert werden; er fragt nach, wenn ihm unklar ist, was befohlen werden würde. Explizite Kommunikation wird auf eine unvermeidbare Residualfunktion beschränkt. In gewissem Umfange geht mit dieser Form der Machtsteigerung Macht auf den Machtunterworfenen über…' A classical European text on this phenomenon is LA BOÉTIE (1983: 136).

(1981: 145–77) in his analysis of the dialectic of recognition, and investigated by ELIAS (1983) in his sociological study of the French court and KANTOROWICZ (1957) on the ideology of European kingship.[124] BURGHART (1996: 308) found similar mechanisms within the political discourse under the Hindu monarchy in Nepal of the 1980s, combining arguments from Habermas and Bloch: 'The king cannot speak informally to the body politic: rather he must speak formally to everyone, for he represents everyone. Little that he utters, therefore, can be taken at face value, and one treats Governmental speech with some suspicion. It is, as a matter of course, something distorted.'

The relationship between a king and his subjects is structurally homologous to the relationship between senior and junior Jain ascetics, and to the relationship between ascetics and laity (*śrāvaka*s, 'listeners', or *upāsaka*s, 'servants'). In Jain scriptures, the junior partners in both relationships are characterised by the combined virtues of politeness (*vinaya*) and serving the guru (*vaiyāvṛttya*) (Uttar 30.30–7). From the point of view of Jain laity, even the relationship between Jains and Non-Jains should be analogous to the relationship between ascetics and Jain-laity (ascetics : laity :: laity : non-Jains). Similar (on/off record) strategic orientations are therefore to be expected. From an anthropological perspective, the crux of politeness theory is that functional contributions for the maintenance of public self-image are not coerced but received through processes of deliberate 'fulfilment' of face-wants of speakers of superior status by 'hearers' of inferior status; particularly the 'faces' of legitimate public figures, which condense the sense of identity in wider social circles. Social power operates here indirectly through the medium of free will and consent, if only under the implicit threat of social sanctions in the case of non-satisfaction of face-wants. In the words of TURNER (1986: 30), ritual in general is a mechanism that 'converts the obligatory into the desirable.'[125]

— VI —

It is essential for my argument to investigate Jain conceptions of pragmatic language usage, and to compare them with the theories outlined in the previous sections. The central question concerns the applicability of the theory of communicative action and

[124] On indirectness see for instance VELUTHAT (1978), BURGHART (1983: 297), BALBIR (1993: 267–9). In his work on *bhakti*, LORENZEN (1995: 3) recalls Gramsci's notion of 'hegemony', i.e. 'that the ideology (or ideologies) of privileged classes may exert, by a combination of persuasion and coercion, a "hegemony" over the ideology (or ideologies) of nonprivileged classes in the same society.'

[125] GÖHLER's (1995b: 72 f.) discussion of Kumārila's explanation of the 'impersonal' injunctive force of Vedic words whose propositional content can only be realised under certain conditions could be reinterpreted in similar terms.

its forms of operationalisation to the Jain context; particularly the role of the 'universal' validity claims and of the Gricean maxims. I have argued that the Jain theory of speech plays a similar role within Indian social philosophy as Habermas' theory of communicative action does within Western philosophy, because both proclaim the primacy of morality and ethics in language usage. Underlying Habermas' theory of communicative intent (*verständigungsorientierter Sprachgebrauch*) is not only the notion that, by definition, in the immediate context of communication all participants must have a common interest in the maintenance of linguistic exchange, and hence implicitly presuppose the ideal of non-violence, at least of the avoidance of physical violence, but also that they are implicitly oriented toward reaching agreement.[126] In this regard, Habermas' notion of infinite consensus represents a functional equivalent of the Jain notion of infinite knowledge leading to salvation (see infra, p. 129 f.). Moreover, universal pragmatic validity claims can be usefully compared and contrasted with the Jain vows of *ahiṁsā* and *satya*. On lower levels of abstraction, the Jain doctrine of the ways of speaking (*bhāṣā-jāta*), as exposed already in the older texts of the Śvetâmbara scriptures, can be usefully compared and contrasted with the conversational maxims of Grice; and conversational implicatures in Jain discourse, theorised in Jain literature, can be analysed as forms of latent strategic action in terms of Brown and Levinson's typology of FTAs. I do not argue that there is an exact correspondence between these modern and ancient Jain schemes of interpretation. Nor do I believe that there is only one way of reconstructing the social implications of Jain theories of language from the point of view of modern social philosophy and logic. But the comparison generates new perspectives on both Jain and Western philosophy , in particular on the ways in which fundamental ontological distinctions or questions can function as codes for the constitution of different discourses.

The principal difficulty of this enterprise is the apparent incompatibility of dialogical and monological perspectives; of the—quasi-legal—intersubjective and egalitarian normative underpinnings of the theory of communicative action and the self-centred and hierarchical normative foundations of the Jain theory of speech, that is, their different ontological commitments.[127] Habermas' differentiation between universal 'moral' and culturally specific 'ethical' presuppositions undermines from the outset the claim to universality of any religious ethical system. Since the legitimacy of Jain religious speech is rooted in the traditional authority of the

[126] Cf. HABERMAS (1991: 17, 173). HABERMAS (2004: 49) distinguishes four idealised presuppositions of argumentation: (a) public inclusion of all concerned individuals, (b) equal distribution of rights to communicate, (c) non-violence in the discourse situation, (d) truthfulness of all participants.

[127] See GERT (1973: Ch. 5–6) on the ways in which ego-centred legitimations of moral rules can be universalised; and critical comments of WELLMER (1986: 41 f.) and HABERMAS (1991: 173 f.) from the point of view of dialogical ethics.

speaker (*āpta*), that is, his/her Jain religious competence, rather than the procedural form of communicative action (*śabdânuśāsana*),[128] from the perspective of the theory of communicative action, its claims to universality can only gain acceptability in an open field of discourse to the extent that it articulates phenomena for which no other language is available.[129] Jain authors have also formulated a principles of discourse intended to transcend cultural boundaries. These principles can, however, only claim universality to the extent that they fulfil the condition of universal acceptability. Yet, this criterion is not foregrounded in Jain texts. A rational defence of the universality of Jain ethics will need to reconstruct the presuppositions of the egological Jain ethical perspective from the point of view of general interest. Conversely, discourse ethics rooted in formal pragmatics has only weak regulative force and needs to be supplemented by obligatory norms of action. The reduction of religion to morality and ethics and the epistemic approach, which Habermas inherited from Kant, are however shared, to some extent, by Jain doctrine. The following comparative study of Jain discourse ethics begins with the question of the status of religious language in Jain philosophy, especially intentionally multivocal language, which, at first sight, appears to violate the fundamental norms of universal pragmatics.

The main difficulty in understanding Jain concepts of religious language derives from the paradoxical, direct and indirect, nature of Jain religious knowledge (*āgama*). The problem is that, doctrinally, every utterance can be interpreted both from the transcendental or ultimate point of view (*niścaya-naya* or *pāramârthika-naya*) (henceforth PN), and from the practical point of view (*vyavahāra-naya*) (henceforth VN).[130] For a participant, ultimate and relative points of view are not necessarily absolutely distinct, but complementary, hierarchically related modes of orientation, which mutually implicate one another (like *noesis* and *noema* in

[128] Cf. UPADHYAYA (1987: 448).

[129] HABERMAS (2005). Christian theologians such as ARENS (1989: 11, 17 ff.) criticised this point already. ARENS (1991: 191) follows PEUKERT's (1984) views: 'In einer politisch-theologischen Kritik an Habermas ist Religion selbst als kommunikative Praxis zu begreifen, die "als Praxis, also im kommunikativen Handeln, Gott für die anderen behauptet und im Handeln zu bewähren sucht".' ARENS (1995: 150) proposes to see the 'church as a community of communication' in a double sense: 'Jesus Christ is communicated in the church and through the church's mediation.'

[130] Although influenced by the Nyāya school and by Nāgārjuna, within Jainism this terminological distinction goes back to Kundakunda, a South Indian Digambara ascetic of the c. 1st–8th century CE, who gives the following definition: 'From the *vyavahāra* point of view, conduct, belief and knowledge are attributed (as different characteristics) of the Knower, the Self. But from the real point of view there is no (differentiation of) knowledge, conduct and belief, in Pure Self' (SSā 1.7). Cf. MATILAL (1981: 43), CAILLAT (1984: 71 n. 54). The paradoxes generated by the PN/VN distinction gave rise to an extensive commentary literature which cannot be reviewed here.

Husserl's notion of intentionality). We are thus confronted with a conception of stages of religious insight and corresponding ways of using and interpreting language, measured in terms of degrees of insight (*jñāna*) and restraint (*saṁyama*), i.e. practice of non-violence (*ahiṁsā*).[131]

The Jain tradition uses the term *āgama* ambiguously.[132] It refers primarily to the ultimate truth, which Mahāvīra, the last Tīrtha(ṅ)kara, had experienced directly and preached to the world, and in a second sense to 'canonical' Jain scriptures, which still form the doctrinal basis for sermons and writings of present day ascetics (MĀLVAṆIYĀ (1968: 10–13).[133] In classical Jainism, knowledge of ultimate religious truth and reality can only be gained through meditation (*bhāvanā*). However, in the present 'unhappy' time cycle (*duṣamā avasarpinī*) direct insight cannot be achieved anymore. Instruction through the words or testimony (*śabda* or *āgama*) of Mahāvīra, handed down by the religious authorities (*ācārya*), is the only way of gaining religious knowledge at all. The doctrinal primacy of cognition over language explains why Jains (and Buddhists) 'have tried to preserve the meaning of the words concerned and not (like the Brahmins—P.F.) words themselves' (MĀLVAṆIYĀ (1968: 1)). Jainism teaches that, ultimately, all words—and indeed: doctrines—are neutral; it is the attitude of the knower alone that turns them into means of valid cognition (*pramāṇa*).[134] Conversely, for the knower, each word of the Jain scriptures appears to condense the teachings of Mahāvīra in a summary fashion. This is part of its evocative power:

> 'The Jainas maintain that the meanings of one single sentence, grasped by different hearers, are innumerable in accordance with their innumerable capacities … a sentence in the *āgama* has the power to suggest in various ways innumerable meanings' (MĀLVAṆIYĀ (1968: 12)).[135]

It is crucial for any understanding of Jain attitudes to language that, from the ultimate point of view (PN), sensuous cognition (*mati*) and words (*śruta* or *āgama*)[136]

---

[131] Cf. CAILLAT (1991: 10).

[132] Cf. AṇD 51, 467–70.

[133] The *āgamas* (scriptures) are not merely texts (HUMPHREY–LAIDLAW (1994: 199 f.)) but transmitted 'words of the omniscient' (Mahāvīra), that is, of trustworthy authority (*āpta*). They are considered as the vital force of Jain religion (MĀLVAṆIYĀ (1968: 1). *Āgama* can be roughly translated as knowledge or testimony (MĀLVAṆIYĀ (1968: 9)).

[134] SHAH (1966: 211), TULSĪ (1985: 190 f.).

[135] Cf. WITTGENSTEIN (1953) on word meaning and contexts of use.

[136] DUNDAS (1996: 77) translates *śruta-jñāna* both as 'knowledge *of* religious scripture' and as 'knowledge *located within* scripture', which needs to be revealed through interpretation. On the

are both forms of indirect, mediated knowledge (*parokṣa*) (TS 1.11).[137] This is why Digambara Jains insist that the sermons of a Jina take the form of a miraculous sound (*divya-dhvani*), which radiates the meaning (*artha*) of his teachings instantaneously, not mediated through words. As there is no language for the unspeakable (*avaktavya*) ultimate truth, any language can be used to express it.[138] As a consequence, 'from the absolute standpoint, the validity of a word or sentence is not intrinsic but extrinsic. That is, it depends on the merit of the speaker as well as of the listener' (MĀLVAṆIYĀ (1996: 2)). The conventional perception that 'there is no possibility whatsoever of any faults or defects in the content of the Agamas' thus rests entirely on the dogmatic belief that 'the speakers of the Jain Agamas were self-realized (i.e. omniscient, P.F.) persons' (MĀLVAṆIYĀ (1968: 3)). The normative basis of traditional hermeneutics euphemistically stated: 'In substance, this means that the absolute standpoint mainly keeps the listener in view while determining the

---

role of scriptures in Jain discourse see also FOLKERT (1993) and GRANOFF (1993). I am less concerned with the problems of textual hermeneutics here than with the pragmatics of religious discourse.

[137] According to TS 1.9–35, valid knowledge (*pramāṇa*) is of two types, direct (*pratyakṣa*) and indirect (*parokṣa*). Direct knowledge (PN) is based on immediate intuition. It includes *kevala* (omniscience), *manaḥ-paryāya* (mind reading), and *avadhi* (clairvoyance). Indirect knowledge (VN) is based on mediated intuition. It includes *mati* (empirical knowledge, acquired through the senses and the mind) and *śruta* (knowledge acquired through instruction). *Mati* is subdivided into four subcategories: *smṛti* (memory), *saṁjñā* (recognition), *cintā* (reasoning), *abhinibodha* (perception). *śruta*, scripture, is knowledge communicated with the help of material symbols such as words and gestures. There are a variety of views in Jain philosophy how the following four conventional means of knowledge derived from Nyāya philosophy relate to *mati* and *śruta* (mostly they are associated with the latter): *paccakkha* <*pratyakṣa*> (perception), *aṇumāna* <*anumāna*> (inference), *ovamma* <*upamāṇa*> (analogy), and *āgama* (verbal testimony of a person of authority, or scripture) (Ṭhāṇ 4.504, AṇD 436). See NYAYAVIJAYA (1998: 327 n. 1), TATIA (1951: 27–80), also TULSĪ (1985: 26 ff., 177–81).

[138] Generally, Jain ascetics use the local vernacular. They reject the idea of the intrinsic sacredness of Sanskrit or other liturgical languages. However, with the canonisation of the scriptures, Ardhamāgadhī gained an equivalent esoteric status. Many later Jain writings were composed in Sanskrit, the language of the Brāhmaṇic elite. The *āgama*s are in need of interpretation through a person of authority, i.e. an individual who knows the language and who has privileged access to religious insight (*darśana*). Initially, only the authority of Mahāvīra was accepted, the presumed author of the teachings in most transmitted texts, but later also the authority of the *śruta-kevalin*s, and of the *ācārya*s, who now interpret the *āgama*s for their disciples. The Jain doctrine of testimony thus legitimates the institutional hierarchy of religious authority. However, there are numerous problems, because Jains are also realists acknowledging the power of words as sources of valid knowledge, because they are connected with things, as well as with a speaker's intentions, and linguistic conventions. The logical arguments which were put forward, for instance by the NSā 5–8 or by MĀLVAṆIYĀ (1996: 2), to support the idea that the moral authority of the speaker is always more important than the content of his speech are, however, debatable (cf. SHAH (1966: 226 f.)). On the role of normative authority in Nyāya theories of testimony see GANERI (1999: 38 ff.).

validity of the scriptures, and the empirical standpoint mainly keeps the speaker in view while determining the same' (MĀLVAṆIYĀ (1968: 2)).[139]

Although *kevala-jñāna* (omniscience), the highest form of *pāramârthika* knowledge according to Jain doctrine, cannot be achieved in the present age, even today's ascetics are supposed to have mind reading (*manaḥ-paryāya*) and clairvoyance (*avadhi*) capacities. Through their training in non-identification they are expected to be capable of switching perspectives between *pāramârthika-naya* and *vyavahāra-naya*, and, thus, to look at the same phenomenon both directly and indirectly (note that from PN, VN appears as a form of indirect cognition). This has significant consequences for the apprehension of verbal utterances. From the religious point of view (PN), language appears merely as a superficial ornament, which disguises the essential truth and beauty of the inner soul, of pure consciousness, which can be experienced through meditation only.[140] In other words, the ambiguity of the concept of *āgama* is itself understood in terms of the 'absolute' and 'practical' points of view, which permit distinguishing clearly between ultimate religious meaning and linguistic means.[141] The main consequence of this perspective is the cognitive desubstantialisation of everyday conceptions of language. From the worldly point of view (VN), the propositional content of a word (*śabda*) depends on convention (and on its power of signification).[142] The semantic, and pragmatic, implications of a grammatically correct verbal utterance vary according to context. Speaker's intention (*abhiprāya*) is one of the contextual conditions of meaning. Yet, it is rarely discussed in the context of objectivist Jain (and Nyāya) semantics.

My general argument is that the doctrinal distinction between practical and transcendental orientations, and the learned ability of reversing perspectives, informs both the discernment and the systematic generation of plural, multivocal meanings in Jain discourse.[143] In my view, the cognitive competence of perspective alternation

[139] Cf. Matilal's theory of the 'ideal hearer' discussed by GANERI (2006: 115 f.).

[140] Examples are discussed by RYAN (1998: 77) and FLÜGEL (1993).

[141] Cf. PYE (1991), FAURE (1993: 209, 213) and GOMBRICH (1996: 24) on the Buddhist doctrine of skilful means (*upāya*).

[142] Similar relationships between 'authentic knowledge' (*jñāna*) and 'discursive/reflective knowledge' (*vijñāna*) can be found in Buddhism. Cf. LAMOTTE (1992: 21), BHARATI (1975: 169), SEYFORT RUEGG (1985: 309–12).

[143] In a modified form, the argument also applies to Mādhyamika Buddhism, and can be extended to any context informed by universalistic two truth theories. Cf. KOKOSZYNSKA (1936) on absolute truth (ideal language) and relative truth (everyday language). See ALBERT (1991: 124 ff.), (2003: 128) for Popperian criticism of (a) double truth theories, (b) of Cartesian recourse to 'god', and (c) Apel's and Habermas' recourse to the 'hermeneutical god' of the 'ideal community of communication' as guarantors of certainty instead of a real, fallible consensus. Albert argues that all double-truth theories are dogmatic 'immunisation strategies': 'Particular viewpoints are intro-

is a fundamental presupposition of Jain hermeneutics and rhetoric, and can be used both for the pursuit of insight and power.[144] Rooted in Jain ontology, the distinction between empirical and transcendental perspectives was an implicit feature of Jain doctrine even before its philosophical conceptualisation. The fundamental religious problematic of Jainism, framed by the asymmetrical soul/body, non-violence/violence codes, creates paradoxes and pragmatic ambiguities which require interpretation and contextual specification/conditioning with the help of additional coding.[145] How to translate these asymmetrical codes into practice? Many Jain texts address this problem. According to classical Jain philosophy of standpoints (*anekântavāda*), the epistemic tension created by the basic soul-body dualism of Jain doctrine, can only be resolved, if at all, by a process of perpetual alternation of PN-VN perspectives.[146] In Kundakunda's *Samaya-sāra* (SSā), this epistemic necessity is endowed with a soteriological function. The technical Jain *syād-vāda* philosophy, the conditionalisation of assertions, by contrast, is based on the conventional point of view (VN).[147] How do these two types of Jain perspectivism deal with the problem of multivocality? The Jain religious point of view (PN) infuses all phenomena with

duced that supposedly allow the separation of some problem areas from others, with the intention of eliminating any possibility of criticism from that direction; in short, one applies *dogmatic shielding principles*' (ALBERT (1991: 126). DUMONT's (1980) theory of the complementary opposition of status and power in Hinduism could be cited as another example of a dualism thesis.

144 For different interpretations of the (potential) social functions of Jain perspectivism see for instance MATILAL (1981), and JOHNSON (1995b), (1999). Cf. HOUTMAN (1999) for the political functions of insight meditation (*vipassanā*) in Buddhist Burma.

145 See LUHMANN's (1982) theory of 'steering differences' which tend to have the form of 'distinctions directrices', applied to the Jain context in FLÜGEL (1995–6: 164 f.). LUHMANN (1990: 215) argues that binary codes, which define self-referential systems in an unequivocal functional way, and ambiguous semantics are complementary: 'Durch semantische Ambiguität wird die Willkür in der Schließung des Systems und in der Ausschließung aller weiterer Werte aus dem Code des Systems berücksichtigt. Ambiguität ist gleichsam das kommunikationsinterne Korrelat für das, was im Beobachten und Beschreiben "zwischen" die Pole der Unterscheidung, besonders zwischen "wahr" und "unwahr" fällt. Die Ambiguität entspricht der Stille, die nicht mitspricht, wenn man spricht, oder auch die Weiße des Papiers, auf das man schreibt, und sie vertritt im System all das, was an Stelle dieser Leere eigentlich der Fall ist. Der Widerspruch von Eindeutigleit und Mehrdeutigleit kann auf diese Weise durch Differenzierung aufgelöst werden.'

146 Cf. JAINI (1979: 90 f.).

147 JOHNSON (1995a: 252 f.) argues that there is 'a fundamental incompatibility between *syād-vāda* and the absolute *vyavahāra-niścaya* distinction. The former is essentially an intellectual strategy for evading confrontation ... The latter, on the other hand, has ... a soteriological function.' For GANERI (2001: 133) *anekânta-vāda* and *syād-vāda* are complementary: the former provides the epistemology and the latter the semantics. On the technical definition of alternation (*anyataratvâdinā*) in *syād-vāda* theory see p. 143 f.

new meaning by re-coding them in terms of the doctrinal body/soul distinction. I shall designate this type of systematic distortion or appropriation of conventional meaning which at the same time opens up new semantic space, 'ontological ambiguity', in contrast to 'linguistic ambiguity',[148] in a wider sense, including expressions whose implications are semantically and/or pragmatic underdetermined (vagueness, indexicality, indirectness, presupposition etc.). Ontological ambiguity is not the same as linguistic ambiguity. But it can only be expressed in linguistic form. Therefore, both can be easily confused. Systematically distorted communication qua doctrinal re-coding and latent strategic communication are both predicated on the intentional creation of multiple meanings. Like latent strategic communication, ontological codes imply disguised generalised indexicality in form of the asymmetry of the binary code. Hence, from a practical point of view, both are social practices of symbolisation. Only their purposes, and perspectives, are different. From the point of view of Jain philosophy, the estranged view of the everyday world, which is intentionally created by the transcendental Jain perspective, is a product of discriminating knowledge, not of deliberate deception. This does not mean that it is unambiguous. LUHMANN (1990) argues, in my view convincingly, that every binary distinction creates at the same time clarity on one level, and ambiguity on another, *ad infinitum*. Different types of ambiguity become visible in the light of different distinctions. For instance, for someone applying the dogmatically prescribed Jain philosophical standpoints (*naya*) (TS 1.34), and the corresponding procedures for disambiguating contextual meaning, plurivocality becomes problematic in the light of conventional univocality, etymology etc.

More research is required to delineate different types and functions of multivocality in Jain discourse. However, one aspect of the Jain analysis of ambiguity deserves to be mentioned at this point. According to Jain logic, linguistic ambiguity[149] should not be confused with vague or incomplete description, which Jain *naya* philosophy contrasts with the epistemic ideal of definite description.[150] The problem of definite description has recently been discussed by HARE (1981: 40–3) regarding the media-

[148] Cf. HEIDEGGER (1925) on the difference between 'ontological' and 'ontic' perspectives; and LUHMANN (1990) on the difference between 'code' and 'semantics'.

[149] Analytical philosophers such as DONOVAN (1976: 1) broadly define religious uses of language as 'oblique' and 'evocative' or 'expressive', in contrast to plain 'informative' language (DONOVAN (1976: 11)): 'In very broad terms, what happens in religious interpreting can be described thus: the kinds of things in life found in one way or another to be religiously significant by those who practice religions are taken to have meanings over and above their scientific, historical or every-day meanings. These distinctively religious meanings they attempt to grasp and to communicate through the use of words, concepts, imagery, or stories drawn from the traditions of religious belief' (DONOVAN (1976: 100)).

[150] GANERI (2001: 133 ff.), BALCEROWICZ (2003: 46 ff.).

tion of general principle and specific situation, e.g. moral conflict.[151] Hare advocates a variant of the two-level theory of ethics. He argues that an exhaustive description of a particular situation from the point of view of intuitive *prima facie* principles is impossible, because they must be very general and simple. To inform moral choices, *prima facie* principles need to be supplemented by exceptions, or by critical principles, which 'can be of unlimited specificity'.[152] Both *prima facie* principles and critical principles are universal prescriptions. However, critical principles can only be universalised on condition of unlimited processes of specification by an infinite intelligence, that is, an omniscient being. Because a superhuman 'ideal observer'[153] can only serve as a theoretical vanishing point for finite cognition, the need for *prima facie* principles and exceptions arises (HARE (1981: 44 ff.)).[154] HARE's (1981: 58) characterisation of the cognitive preconditions of 'the rigor of pure prescriptive universality' enables us to recognise the similarities between the Jain ideal of definite description, as a standard against which incomplete or vague propositions can be measured, and Habermas' ideal consensus of an infinite community of interpretation, against which both systematically distorted and latent strategic communication can be assessed. The subject-philosophical role of 'omniscience' and the universal pragmatic role of 'infinite discourse' are functionally equivalent.[155] The comparison suggests also that the Jain ideal of omniscience is a logical consequence of Jain epistemology, and not a mere product of fanciful religious speculation.[156] The question whether in specific contexts vague utterances are ambiguous or

[151] Cf. supra, the discussion of rule-specification. See the critical discussion by WELLMER (1986: 32–7), who argues that the problem of exceptions can only be solved in concrete situations on the basis of 'reasons', not through processes of unlimited norm specification of 'principles', in analogy to unlimited processes of specification of causal laws in the natural science. In human history, the idea of a complete description does not even make sense as a regulative idea. Therefore, this attempt to synthesise universal principles and specific situations cannot solve problems of practical ethics. WELLMER (1986: 31)) himself derives secondary moral norms by way of negation of non-universalisable maxims.

[152] HARE (1981: 41): 'Briefly, generality is the opposite of specificity, whereas universality is compatible with specificity, and means merely the logical property of being governed by a universal quantifier and not containing individual constants. The two principles "Never kill people" and "Never kill people except in self-defence or in cases of adultery or judicial execution" are both equally universal, but the first is more general (less specific) than the second.'

[153] The term was introduced by Adam Smith.

[154] HARE (1981: 40): 'Critical thinking consists in making a choice under the constraints imposed by the logical properties of the moral concepts and by the non-moral facts, and by nothing else.'

[155] Infinite discourse also presupposes infinite knowledge (Lafont, in HABERMAS (2004: 256)).

[156] This observation applies mainly to the historically later concept of 'absolute omniscience' as opposed to 'complete self-realisation'.

merely semantically underspecified[157] cannot be rationally determined from a non-omniscient perspective. From a participant's point of view, under given normative conditions, any utterance can be created or perceived as an intentionally plurivocal symbol, even if the implicit indexical meaning or normative command can be inferred unequivocally. Everything depends on the pragmatic context.

A peculiarity of the Jain theory of speech, derived from the Jain *karman* theory, is that utterances are seen as material substances which stick to the impure soul but not to a pure one. In fact, speech as a technique of social influence is not only an important subject for proselytising ascetics, trying to attract followers (systematic distorted and latent strategic action are identical in this case),[158] but also an explicit topic of the Jain doctrine of *karmic* bondage, that is, the mechanism of binding (*bandha*) the soul of a listener, through the medium of his/her passion (*kaṣāya*) and desire (*rāga*), via an influx (*āsrava*) of insight-generating pure matter (*śuddha-pudgala*) (cf. TS 5.22). It is not necessary to recall the details and history of this doctrine, because SCHUBRING's (2000: 174, § 84) authoritative depiction of Jain cosmology implicitly operates with a theory of Jain rhetorical influence. Schubring shows, for instance, how processes of possession, which are considered to be the reverse of insight, are explained in certain texts in terms of the sending of inauspicious atoms (*aśubha-pudgala*) (SCHUBRING (2000: 151, § 69)); and how individuality (which increases with social standing) and thus, ideally, the degree to which *karman* is felt, generates the power of acting upon others, and to influence and bind people by imprinting (*dhāraṇā*) certain *karmic* perceptions onto their soul via the ejection of *pudgala* (SCHUBRING (2000: 181–7, § 87–91)):

> 'This process [of speech] is, to put it briefly, the ejaculation (*nisarai*, *nisr̥jati*) of substances (*davva*) taken in (*geṇhai*) previously (now being ready either for use or in store). They consist of ∞ atoms (*aṇanta-paesiya*), occupy the space of ¿ units, last for 1 *sam.* and own all qualities possible with reference to colour, smell, taste and sensation. Their reception is meant to bring about a close contact (*puṭṭha*, *ogāḍha*), i.e. with the units of the soul (*ātma-pradeśa*, Prajn.), and to it both fine and coarse particles (*aṇu* and *bāyara*) are subjected, which is discussed circumstantially. The reception takes place either with or without interruption (*antara*) in that either reception *or* ejaculation, or both reception *and* ejaculation occur within 1 *sam.*, and then, by the way (267a), they will belong to the same content of speech (true, false etc.) for which they were taken in. Their destiny depends on the inten-

[157] A question raised by GANERI (2001: 133 ff.), and answered in the negative

[158] Cf. SUNAVALA (1922: 26).

sity of speech. As we learn from Prajn. on Pannav. 262b. and from Vy. on Vij. 621b, when speaking [in a] low [voice] the particles of speech leave the mouth in coarse portions (*abhinna*), but they do not reach far and will perish soon, whereas when speaking loud they are finely divided (*bhinna*), and in this case speech will increase infinitely and reach the boundaries of the world' (SCHUBRING (2000: 149, § 68).

The strategic production of religious influence via *karmic* binding is of course not the primary concern of Jain *karman* theory, but certainly one of the possible consequences of the application of Jain categories to worldly problems. From the conventional point of view (VN), Jain scriptures describe speech as a potential weapon (*duppautta-maṇo-vāyā* <*duṣprayukta-mana-vacana*>) (Ṭhāṇ 10.93): 'Speech, so Pannav. 255b says, originates in the soul, while it becomes manifest in the body in the shape of a thunderbolt … [and] exists only the moment when being spoken' (SCHUBRING (2000: 148 f., § 68).[159] Yet, fundamentally (PN) it is described only as an external ornament of the soul without any intrinsic power, except the power of signification:

> '[1] Speech is different from the self (*no āyā bhāsā, annā bhāsā*). It is concrete (lit. fashioned, *rūviṁ*), devoid of consciousness (*acitta*) and inanimate (*ajīva*) though peculiar to living beings (*jīvāṇaṁ bhāsā, no ajīvāṇaṁ bh.*). [2] Speech exists and is divided' (*bhijjai*) neither before nor after but only during actual speaking. … .' (Viy 621a = 13.7.1ab, summarised by DELEU (1970: 199 f.)).[160]

If the hearer is aware of this s/he cannot be bound. Both interpretations derive from the dualistic doctrinal distinction between soul and body, and their asymmetrical hierarchical relationship.[161]

We can conclude from the foregoing discussion that, from the point of view of Jain doctrine, both linguistic conventions and intentional language are *vyavahāra*—worldly oriented—and ultimately of no religious value. Any pragmatic use of language, even for purposes of religious instruction, has only relative value, because the speaker is forced to orientate him/herself toward the external world, and to turn away from the ideal meditative focus on the potentialities of the soul. From this perspective, one can hardly speak of a Jain concept of 'religious language' at all. Jains never fully acknowledged the religious significance of *mantra*s and other types of

---

[159] Cf. Viy 102b, 621a, MĀLVAṆIYĀ (1971: 321–6).

[160] Cf. Āyār 2.4.1.5. JACOBI (1884: 150 n. 3) points out that the commentator uses categories of Vaiśeṣika philosophy to explain the meaning of this verse.

[161] Cf. HUMPHREY–LAIDLAW (1995: 214) on the paradoxes generated by the Jain *karman/jīva* code; and GANERI (2001: 137) on Jain 'discourse pluralism … organised in a vertical hierarchy.'

mystical utterances, which could be distinguish as 'religious' from 'non-religious' language. This applies even to Ardhamāgadhī, the liturgical language of the oldest scriptures. The only religious 'languages' which Jains clearly recognise are silence and meditative sounds, like Mahāvīra's legendary *divya-dhvani*.[162]

Because Jain (and most Buddhist) philosophers recognise that language is rooted in convention and mainly used for everyday communication, and other practical purposes, discourse theoretical perspectives promise a useful new angle on the neglected question of the socially constitutive function of Jain discourse. Studies of the Jain philosophy of language to date focus almost exclusively on Jain semantics, in particular on the seven *naya*s and the *sapta-bhaṅgī*, that is, pre-defined (but in principle infinite) perspectives for the analysis of the semantics of words or sentences under different contextual conditions. However, MATILAL (1981: 60 f.), JOHNSON (1995a: 253), and GANERI (2001: 137), (2002: 275, 279 f.), following earlier 20th century authors, interpret the Jain *naya*-schemes as models of 'discourse pluralism', intended to integrate different perspectives in a syncretic and ultimately, that is, from the perspective of unlimited perspectives, 'complete account'. The underlying theory of 'intellectual *ahiṁsā*' is doubted by CORT (2000: 341) with reference to (a) scriptural examples of the 'history of Jain struggles with non-Jains', and (b) criticism of the assumption that omniscience is 'the sum total of all possible *naya*s': 'The Jains posit that there is an *absolutely* true perspective' (CORT (2000: 332)). The argument could be strengthened by a slight modification. Mistaking the 'partial truth' of a one-sided (*ekānta*) statement for the 'whole truth' is not the only way of being wrong (*durnaya*) (CORT (2000: 331)) according to Jain philosophy. Jain perspectivism is only concerned with the relationship between partially and wholly true testimony (*pramāṇa*), not with entirely false testimony (*apramāṇa*), which is excluded at the outset.[163] Hence, it is not admissible to say that, by definition, ALL statements contain an element of truth. Strictly speaking, Jain *naya* doctrines are not theories of discourse, since they are focused exclusively on semantics. Yet, the Jain scriptures and commentaries dealing with the practicalities of ascetic life contain a general theory of the pragmatics of language usage, based on Jain discourse ethics, and show how Jain principles applied to worldly problems generate unique analytical possibilities of perceiving and manipulating speech. In contrast to Jain semantics, which privileges the perspective of the listener, Jain pragmatics privileges the perspective of the speaker.

---

[162] On the systemic function of monastic silence and paradoxical language in general see FUCHS (1989: 37).

[163] Cf. BALCEROWICZ (2003: 46). The negative truth value (f) in the *sapta-bhaṅgī* relates only to (underdetermined) existential predicates, not to statements that are doctrinally 'false', and exposed as such in the polemical Jain literature.

— VII —

Although Jain ascetics use the vernacular of their local followers, and reject the Brāhmaṇical idea of the intrinsic sacredness of certain words (MDhŚ 4.256), they do maintain a clear distinction between religious and non-religious ways of USING a given language, that is, the intrinsic structural (not metaphysical) features, intentions and functions of an expression.[164] In accordance with their basic religious principles, they emphasise not the religious (*dharmika*) qualities of a language *per se* but of speaking (and writing) as a social practice, and of the importance of the underlying rules as well as the intention and function of speech.[165] Already in the early canonical scriptures, Jain ascetics developed a normative doctrine of religious language usage, a discourse ethics supplemented by casuistic context-sensitive rules, which, as I will now show in greater detail, shares certain concerns and features with universal pragmatics.

Normative principles and rules of speech are constitutive for Jain discourse to the extent that they are used by speech communities, both to generate and to interpret speech. The way in which actual communication is informed by these principles is a matter of empirical investigation. Characteristically, Jain norms of speech are presented in the form of hierarchical levels of universality and corresponding competence of judgement and restraint of the speaker. Principles and rules of speech inform practice in varying degrees, according to their level of abstraction. For the following presentation, I distinguish four relevant dimensions of Jain doctrinal reflection on and prescription of ways of speaking:[166]

(1) Principles and criteria for religious speech (*ahiṁsā* and *satya*);
(2) General rules and clauses for language usage (*bhāṣā-jāta*);

[164] BALCEROWICZ (2003: 53) observes: 'No utterance is simply either true or false. In order to ascertain its truth-value one has to ascribe it to its specific viewpoint type, that supplies the contextual information that is lacking.' Similarly, no utterance is simply religious or non-religious.

[165] Interestingly, speaker's intention is not included in the list of Jain philosophical standpoints.

[166] The underlying method of specification is akin to Jain methods of progressive specification through fixed standpoints. See GANERI (2001: 133) for an analysis of the Jain view that linguistic expressions are contextually 'underspecified' and contain 'a hidden indexical element' which Jain dialecticians seek to systematically expose through the methods of *syād-vāda*, using actual values or quantifiers such as *syāt* (GANERI (2001: 139)). For another example of the ways in which Jain logicians contextualise utterances through a method of 'progressive indexication' of formalised conditionally valid viewpoints (*naya*) or 'context indicators' which gradually specify the relevant context in a controlled way see BALCEROWICZ (2003: 44 ff.). In contrast to the analysis of implications offered by universal pragmatics, Jain scholastic hermeneutics is based on dogmatically fixed viewpoints considered in form of a monological pluralism.

(3) Context-sensitive rules for proper ways of speaking;
(4) Examples (considering *karmic* and social implications) (*dṛṣṭānta*).

(Ad 1) The main criteria for identifying 'religious' language-usage are (a) non-violence (*ahiṁsā*), and (b) truth (*satya*), that is, the first two of the five great and small vows (*mahā-vrata* and *aṇuvrata*) of Jainism,[167] which have to be accepted by anyone who wants to be formally recognised as a practising Jain.[168] 'Non-religious' language is characterised by the opposite qualities—violence (*hiṁsā*) and non-truth or from the point of view of the agent (the two perspectives are not clearly differentiated): non-truthfulness (*asatya*).[169]

(Ad a) *Ahiṁsā* is the most important criterion for religious language usage. Jains, like Buddhists, regard speech as an active force and a potential weapon which, if misused, implies violence and negatively affects the *karman* of the one who handles it.[170] However, they also emphasise the fundamental connection between pure speech and spiritual advancement, which the Buddhist *Subhāsita-sutta*[171] seems to deny.[172] In order to minimise violence, Jain *ācāryas*, like other South Asian legislators (cf. MDhŚ 4.138 f.), laid great emphasis on the rules concerning proper speech, which they systematised probably for the first time in Indian philosophy:[173] 'the Jains insist on the absolute necessity of refraining from directly or indirectly aggressive speech' (CAILLAT (1984: 67)).

(Ad b) Truthfulness or truth (*satya*) is the one fundamental Jain principle that is directly related to language use. Its importance for the Jains is indicated by the fact that it is second only to the all-encompassing *ahiṁsā-vrata*, whereas it is given fourth place in the Buddhist *dasa-sīla* list. The Āyār II, one of the oldest texts of the Jain tradition, gives the following wording of the *satya-vrata* (in Jacobi's translation):

> 'I renounce all vices of lying speech (arising from anger or greed or fear or mirth). I shall neither myself speak lies, nor cause others to

---

[167] 'All the prohibitions and injunctions included in the two relevant lessons of Āyār and Dasav can be shown to proceed from the above fundamental principles, observance of truth based on *saṁjama*, and observance of *ahiṁsā*' (CAILLAT (1991: 10)).

[168] Most laity treats the *aṇuvratas* only as regulative ideals.

[169] Cf. BRUHN (1987a: 110), (1993: 28).

[170] CAILLAT (1984: 64).

[171] On well spoken language: 'O Bhikkhus, the Bhikkhu speaks well-spoken (language), not ill-spoken; he speaks what is right (dhamma), not what is unrighteous (adhamma); he speaks what is pleasing, not what is unpleasing; he speaks what is true, not what is false. O Bhikkhus, the speech that is provided with these four requisites, is well-spoken, not ill-spoken, both faultless and blameless to the wise' (SN 3.3).

[172] CAILLAT (1991: 14).

[173] CAILLAT (1984: 61).

speak lies, nor consent to the speaking of lies by others. I confess and blame, repent and exempt myself of these sins in the thrice threefold way, in mind, speech, and body' (Āyār 2.15.3.1–5).[174]

Noticeable in this statement is, firstly, that lying is 'renounced', i.e. the possibility is explicitly recognised, but deliberately excluded. Truth is not defined positively but negatively, through the exclusion of what it is not; which has been a popular approach in South Asian philosophy in general. Secondly, the vow refers to contexts of communication (speech acts such as consenting, causing others to do something). Thirdly, speaking the truth and lying are conceived as effects of the emotions which motivate the speaker's intentions (as the clauses indicate). Truth is here not primarily perceived in terms of the representational function of language, as a propositional relationship between words and things, but in terms of the expressive and regulative functions of language. After all, the intention of Jain authors was not primarily to produce a sound semantic theory of truth, but a pragmatic method for the liberation of the soul. The expressive aspect of speech, or truthfulness, is related to the character of the speaker, that is, his/her 'purity' of insight and sincerity:[175] 'truth means the state of being true' (TULSĪ (1985: 84)). The ethical and social dimensions of language are addressed in Āyār 2.4 and DVS 7.11 (see *infra* p. 161 and 162) in terms of the dispositions of the speaker and the effects of language on speaker and hearer. Viy 25.1.4.a (854b) reflects on fifteen kinds of activity (*joga*) which are affected by the four modes of inner sense (*maṇa*) and of speech (*bhāsā*), which are seen as intrinsically connected.[176] In all cases, pivotal importance is given to avoiding violence.

It is worth noting that both the Jain theory of speech and the theory of communicative action privilege pragmatic notions of truth. Habermas' analysis of validity claims focuses on the interplay of the dimensions of propositional truth, sincerity of expression and intersubjective rightness. Separately, these aspects are also distinguished in Jain texts on ways of speaking. The multi-functional nature of utterances, the context-relativity of truth values *cum* truth acts,[177] and the relationship between belief and meaning,[178] etc., requires further investigation. In his analysis of intermodal transfer of validity between speech acts, HABERMAS (1981: 442 f.) / (1984–1987 I: 444 f.), (1984: 105–12, 126)) demonstrates that performative and ethical or aesthetic statements also contain propositions, which can be questioned by interlocutors. Vows, for instance, are expressives which also carry a strong normative element; while most

[174] Cf. DVS 4.12.

[175] SCHUBRING (2000: 157, § 74).

[176] DELEU (1970: 267) points to the parallel in Paṇṇ 317a where *joga* is replaced by *paoga*.

[177] See FAUCONNIER (1981: 183) etc.

[178] See DAVIDSON (1984: 153) etc.

commissives and declaratives cannot work without emphasising the expressive component.[179] Declarations of sincerity, however, cannot be redeemed by argument but only through behavioural practice. This observation makes us aware that one of the functions of Jain ascetic practice is the public validation of sincerity, which is converted into generalised acceptability *qua* prestige and moral authority.[180]

(Ad 2) The principles of *ahiṁsā* and *satya* are too abstract to be useful for judging actual behaviour. This is why Jains have added further, lower order rules of language usage, which supplement the general principles and facilitate translating them into practice (speaking and writing). Two of the 'senior' canonical Jain texts deal with language usage in greater detail—the chapter on modes ('species') of speech (*bhāsā-jāya* <*bhāṣā-jāta*>)[181] in the Āyār 2.4.1–2 and later parallels in the canon,[182] and the chapter on pure speech (*vakka-suddhi* <*vākya-śuddhi*>) in the *Dasa-veyāliya* (*Daśa-vaikālika*, DVS 7), which is probably derived from the Āyār, but offers further clarifying statements.[183] In addition, there are several passages in the *Viyāha-pannatti* (*Bhagavatī*, Viy),[184] and the more systematic but on the whole 'strikingly ill-assorted'[185] explanations of the modes of speech (language) in Chapter 11 of the *Pannavaṇā* (*Prajñāpanā*, Paṇṇ) which, according to tradition, was composed c. 79–37 BCE by an ascetic called Ārya Śyāma. The relevant passages of the *Pannavaṇā* and its principal commentary, Ācārya Malayagiri's (c. 1131–1203) *Prajñāpanā-ṭīkā* (PaṇṇṬ), were summarised by SCHUBRING (2000: 148 f., § 68; 157 f., § 74), MĀLVAṆIYĀ (1971: 321–26) and, in passing, by CAILLAT (1991: 10 ff.).[186] The

[179] APEL (1993: 49).

[180] Cf. HABERMAS (1981: 270 f.) / (1984–1987 II: 181 f.).

[181] Sanskrit *chāyā* of Prakrit words is indicated by the symbols < >.

[182] Uttar 24.22, Ṭhāṇ 4.23 (238) [183b/464b].

[183] SCHUBRING'S (2000: 157 n. 2, § 74) opinion that the DVS version is derivative from the Āyār has been challenged by GHATAGE (1938: 137), who tried to prove the reverse. OKUDA (1975: 126) distinguishes between the Uttar (= Āyār which is not mentioned) and DVS variants. Cf. CAILLAT (1991: 2).

[184] Viy 1.10 (103b), 10.3 (499b), 13.7 (621a).

[185] SCHUBRING (2000: 157, § 74).

[186] In addition to these key texts there are many scattered *śloka*s concerning proper speech in the DVS 7–9. These texts are concerned with 'humility' and relate to the monastic environment, i.e. the *guru-śiṣya* relationship. Similar passages can be found in the Āyār and other texts which deal with problems of monastic discipline, e.g. Uttar 1. They do not concern speech as such but rather contextual factors, which I will discuss in the next section. DIXIT (1978: 59) notes, that 'the problem of employment of speech … is conspicuous by its absence in the old *Cheda-sūtras*', and that speaking is rarely mentioned in the later literature (but see FLÜGEL (1994: 110–115)). There is, however, an extensive *śrāvakâcāra* literature, which specifies some of the old monastic rules of the Āyār and the DVS for the Jain laity. See WILLIAMS (1983: 71–8). I will refer to this literature

categories of speech of the *Āyāraṁga* (Āyār), and one of the lists of sub-categories of the *Pannavaṇā* appear also in *Mūlâcāra* (MĀc) 5.110–120 of the Digambara author Vaṭṭakera. This text is generally dated 1st–3rd century CE (OKUDA (1975: 12 f.)), and must have been composed after the *Pannavaṇā*.

The situations which are depicted in these texts as problematic invariably show individual ascetics interacting with the wider social environment, coinciding with our paradigmatic speech situation type c. They are distinctly different from situations of monastic politeness (*vinaya*), formal sermons (*pravacana*), or public debates (*prayoga*), which will be briefly discussed later.

The presentation of the *bhāṣā*-rules in the Āyār is hierarchically structured in accordance with Jain principles and ethos. It begins with the *satya-mahā-vrata*, explaining its various modes: referential truth, grammaticality, clarity of expression, the avoidance of doubt, and of false promises etc. Then, various modalities of the *ahiṁsā-mahā-vrata* are described, such as the avoidance of harsh words, politeness, and indirect affirmation of violent deeds of others.[187] In addition to the vow of *satya*, five general clauses are given to the neophyte. They explain how to avoid false speech. That is, to speak with deliberation, and not in anger, fear, or mirth, because these states of mind might move one to 'utter a falsehood' (Āyār 2.15.3.1–5). Two further maxims are important for the ascetics: the observance of the *bhāṣā-samitis*, the circumspection regarding all speech acts, and of the *bhāṣā-gupti*s, the controls of the four types of speech, which are laid down in the *Uttarajjhayaṇa* (*Uttarādhyayana*, Uttar) 24.[188] Like *ahiṁsā* and *satya*, they are intended to direct the attention away from violent speech, from the expression of desire, and ultimately away from speech at all. These maxims and rules are not linguistic in any technical sense, and not conventional or customary in a folkloristic sense. They rather resemble the Gricean postulates, and hence, I would argue, function within Jain philosophy in a manner similar to operationalisations of HABERMAS' (1980: 400) formal pragmatic presuppositions of communicative action. That is, as principles, or general interpretive procedures,

only in footnotes. Because I am interested in the pragmatic aspect of speech, I will not discuss the technicalities of the analytical-pedagogical *nikṣepa* (transferring epithet) method and similar purely exegetical devices of the Jains, which are used to delineate the true (intended) contextual sense of an utterance through elimination of unwanted multivocality. It is important to note that 'clear literal meaning' is an explicit aim in (VN) Jainism.

[187] *Ahiṁsā* is here not taken as a general principle, but only related to language. One could distinguish these two meanings as *ahiṁsā* I and *ahiṁsā* II. *Satya* takes precedence over *ahiṁsā* in this context, because it is necessary to spell out rules of truthful speech first if one wants to discuss ways of avoiding their violation. Cf. footnote 305.

[188] Uttar 24.2, 24.22–23. See also TS 9.4–5. For further canonical references see SCHUBRING (2000: 304 f., § 173).

which theorise the normative conditions of the acceptability of statements, and hence of the ability of language to avoid violence and to enable, or generate, both non-violence and social co-operation (which is therefore seen as problematic).

In the following, I will analyse and compare these Jain modes of speech, both with Habermas' validity claims of truth, truthfulness and rightness, which correspond to constative, representative, and regulative aspects of speech acts (which are differently weighted in different contexts), and with the Gricean postulates, which from the perspective of Habermas' model further specify empirical pragmatic conditions of validity claims. The discussion of some of the implications of the major *bhāṣā*-rules follows, for purely formal reasons, the sequential order of Grice's co-operative principle and conversational maxims, though a mode of presentation oriented towards Jain principles could have equally been chosen.

GRICE (1975: 45 f.) defines the 'cooperative principle' (CP), and the four main 'conversational maxims', which he labelled in analogy to the pure categories of understanding (*reine Verstandesbegriffe*) in KANT's (1974: 118 f.) transcendental logic, as follows:

CP: 'Make your conversational contribution such as required, at the stage at which it occurs, by the accepted purpose or direction of the talk exchange in which you are engaged.'

Quantity: 'Make your contribution as informative as required (for the current purpose of the exchange). Do not make your contribution more informative than is required.'

Quality: 'Try to make your contribution one that is true: Do not say what you believe to be false. Do not say that for which you lack adequate evidence.'

Relation: 'Be relevant.'

Manner: 'Avoid obscurity of expression. Avoid ambiguity. Be brief (avoid unnecessary prolixity). Be orderly.'

Although the Gricean postulates are widely accepted as a theory of general principles of human communication, it is clear that partners in a conversation have to resort to more than just the rules of their language and the cooperative principle. For instance, to (1) conventional meaning of words and context, (2) background meaning, such as common cultural assumptions etc. That is, dimensions such as those listed as the seven Jain *naya*s. What counts as an appropriate, informative, true (plausible), relevant, and unequivocal expression cannot be judged in abstract, but only by the participants in a specific discourse. But it is the task of the analyst to elicit both the unspoken conditions of communicative success and the social conditions of fulfilment of speech acts in concrete situations. Here, I only indicate similarities and differences between the Gricean conversational postulates and analogous categories of the Jain analysis of speech and discourse ethics, and attempt to elicit the implications for a comparison with the theory of communicative action.[189]

Cooperative principle—non-violence (*ahiṁsā*)

Grice regards the cooperative principle as fundamental for any conversation. His notion of 'appropriateness' corresponds to Habermas' more general notion of 'communicative intent', which presupposes a commitment to the universal validity claims of propositional truth, expressive truthfulness and normative rightness, in addition to the basic condition of linguistic comprehensibility. Despite their differences, both notions are grounded in Kantian moral philosophy, rather than in utilitarian principles.[190]

Interestingly, in the two key Jain texts mentioned, no equivalent to the cooperative principle *per se* can be found, nor, of course, is there any mention of a specific consensus orientation. This is in accordance with the individual- or *jīva*-centred attitude that is recommended from the 'ultimate point of view' (PN).

However, a passage in Kundakunda's *Samaya-sāra*, whose importance has been emphasised by CAILLAT (1984: 71 n. 54), clearly states the necessity to observe the 'accepted purpose of the talk exchange' (here: religious instruction), as maintained by Grice's principle. The purpose of this statement is to explain, why the teaching of (ultimately incommunicable) Jain doctrines forces ascetics to give up their ideal meditative silence temporarily to use worldly pragmatic language (VN) in agreement with conventional standards of comprehensibility and rightness:[191]

> 'Just as a non-Aryan (foreigner) cannot be made to understand anything except through the medium of his non-Aryan language, so the knowledge of the Absolute cannot be communicated to the ordinary people except through the *vyavahāra* point of view' (SSā 1.8).

[189] Amongst the few South Asianists who considered Grice's categories for understanding the nature of religious language are WHEELOCK (1982) and SEYFORT RUEGG (1985) and for text interpretation OETKE (1991: 61 ff.). The latter accepted the Gricean standards as cultural universals and as a tool for the methodical reconstruction of an author's 'original intention' (OETKE (1991: 35)), arguing that 'the Nyāyasūtras and the philosophical *Sūtra*-texts in general seem to be tailored to an application of the Cooperative Principle and Grice's conversational maxims' (OETKE (1997: 140)). See BRONKHORST (1993a). GÖHLER (1995b: 75), by contrast, argued that the speech act theories of Austin and Searle are hardly applicable to written texts.

[190] On Kant's influence on the theory of communicative action see HABERMAS (1991).

[191] The acceptance of linguistic conventions was generally taught in ancient India. See SCHARF (1995) on Patañjali.

The true insights of Jain teaching, it is stated here, cannot be understood by pupils and the wider public if ascetics do not orientate themselves towards the capacities and expectations of their audience and take a co-operative attitude. This is a Jain version of the theory of 'skilful means' (*upāya*).[192] The commentator Amṛtacandra explicitly states that ascetics should direct their utterances towards the pragmatic 'purpose of the discussion':

> 'The ultimate reality must be subjected to an intellectual analysis and the constituent elements so obtained must be selected and emphasised according to the interest of the student and also consistent with the purpose of the discussion. The variations in the context and the intellectual aim will naturally determine the nature of the descriptions adopted with reference to the reality studied. The method of selective description to suit the purpose of the context is the method adopted by the ordinary man … Since the method is determined by a purpose of practical interest, the investigation will be relevant only to that purpose and the conclusion obtained must therefore be partial … .' (Commentary on SSā 1.8; p. 18 of Chakravarti's rendition).

Supporting the spiritual quest of others is one of the duties of the (*thera-kalpa*) ascetic (DVS_1 9.4.5). Yet, ultimately, social co-operation is not seen as a religious value in itself, but as a hindrance for the process of self-purification. Teaching religion to others is merely a 'method determined by a purpose of practical interest', but not directly oriented towards salvation itself, and therefore akin to the attitude 'adopted by the ordinary man who is engaged in his pursuit in life' (SSā 1.8, Commentary p.18).[193]

The doctrine of the ultimately (PN) non-religious character of teaching religious knowledge is, I think, the prime reason for the conspicuous absence of any mention of a functional equivalent of the cooperative principle itself in the Āyār. From the 'practical point of view' (VN) co-operative intent is acceptable, and even assumes a religious function, if the objective of the conversation is the furtherance of non-violence. In fact, the only difference between worldly co-operation (*laukika-upakāra*) and religious instruction or supra-mundane co-operation (*lokôttara-upakāra*) is the purpose of co-operation itself; that is, either the pursuit of worldly aims, or of the purification of the soul.[194] The same holds true for the difference between 'worldly' and 'religious' rhetoric, as we will see later. One should, therefore, expect mentioning of the cooperative principle in the AS's discussion of pragmatic language

[192] For Buddhist notions see for instance PYE (1978).

[193] See the discussion of the 'maxim of relation' below.

[194] TULSĪ (1985: 174 f.).

usage as well. In order to explain its absence, I suggest an additional argument, derived from the observation that violence is the main threat to co-operation, and, conversely, that non-violence is its fundamental pre-condition. Thus, we find that the value of *ahiṁsā*, which ultimately promotes total non-action (*ayoga*) in the world, also reflects, on a secondary level, the potential of total (hierarchical and non-violent) co-operation, in the sense of opening spaces, refuges, for existence (*Seinlassen*). Accordingly, many Jain texts emphasise that the implication of *ahiṁsā*, non-violence, is *dayā*, compassion. The *ahiṁsā-mahā-vrata*, therefore, implies the sought-after cooperative principle, although it does not say so explicitly. Indeed, from a Jain point of view, it could be argued, with good reason, that the positive notion of communicative intent is merely an application of the more general negative moral principle of non-violence within the sphere of social life. This begs the question: How universal are the cooperative principle and the formal pragmatic validity claims? Does communicative intent presuppose a more fundamental commitment to an ethics of (physical) non-violence?[195] The cooperative principle, albeit apparently only concerned with straightforward information transmission from speaker to hearer, implies normative conditions such as physical non-violence (and of non-silence) to ensure ongoing linguistic co-operation. But it remains indifferent to the distinction between violent and non-violent aspects of overt speech (and of thought) itself. Communicative action considers form and content of speech also only under formal aspects, that is, acceptability, which may include violent communications. The Jain principle of *ahiṁsā*, by contrast, implies not only formal but also qualitative conditions for the perpetuation of co-operation.

Numerous examples of rules concerning violent speech in the Āyār and DVS implicitly refer to non-violence as a condition for co-operation and as form of co-operation, as in the following *śloka*:

> 'Revered is he who speaks not ill in one's absence, who uses not a sharp tongue in one's presence, who speaks not with assertion, nor uses words that are harsh' (DVS$_2$ 9.3.8–9).

It is not apparent from this statement why these attitudes should be revered, apart from general considerations of the detrimental effects of violence on the karmic

---

[195] Christian theologians attacked the self-limitation of universal pragmatics to formal conditions of social communication from similar vantage points. PEUKERT (1984), (1992), for instance, argues for the priority of the 'resource' of 'universal solidarity' in the lifeworld over communicative ethics. The objective idealist HÖSLE (1997: 248 ff.) complains about the moral indeterminacy of formal consensus (reasonable/unreasonable) and calls for a defence of ethics based on substantial values; as do other 'Neo-Aristotelians' discussed by HABERMAS (1983), (1991), who accepts this point and modifies his position in HABERMAS (2004).

constitution on the speaker. But it is clear by implication that one who avoids 'sharp tongue' etc., is revered also because, otherwise, the continuation of co-operation is threatened and might be terminated. This and many similar statements implicitly stress the value of completely avoiding 'face-threatening acts', although not saying so openly. They are presented in the form of negations of non-universalisable maxims.[196] The closest one can get to an explicit, positive postulate of a 'co-operative principle' are statements concerning the ascetic values of offering fearlessness (*abhaya-dāna*) and supra-mundane co-operation (*pāramârthikôpakāra*) for the upliftment of the soul, which are seen as the greatest gift to society, in fact, constituting its fundamental condition.

Paradoxically, however, the methods of liberation taught by Jain ascetics do not emphasise co-operation but its direct opposite: separation and non-interaction with the world. This paradox is the main obstacle for an understanding of the social implications of the principle of *ahiṁsā*. SEYFORT RUEGG (1985) addressed this problem in Gricean terms in an interpretation of the *Ābhiprâyika-* and *Neyârtha-sūtra*s of Tibetan Buddhism. He argues that the Buddha's way of teaching non-cooperation amounts to an act of 'flouting' not only of the conversational maxims, but of the co-operative principle itself. But because the Buddha's acts of 'flouting' are not intended for the achievement of worldly gains, but for the spiritual liberation of others, SEYFORT RUEGG introduces the terms 'salvific principle' and 'salvific violence' as religious supplements to the pragmatic Gricean 'cooperative principle':

> 'In fact Grice's Cooperative Principle yields in such *Sūtras* to what we might call a Salvific Principle put to use in a perlocutionary manner. Still, in conformity even with this Salvific Principle of the Buddha, 'flouting'—or more specifically *upāya*-governed salvific exploitation—of the Conversational Maxims are to be found in *Ābhiprāyika* and *Neyārtha Sūtras*, just as they have been recognized in Grice's second type of conversational implicature involving exploitation of conversational maxims' (SEYFORT RUEGG (1985: 317)).

SEYFORT RUEGG's remarks are useful for understanding salvific violence, which 'conquers violence'. At the same time, his analysis is problematic, because he does not clearly distinguish between linguistic co-operation and social co-operation. Even the Buddha (or Mahāvīra) was of course forced to observe the cooperative principle during his sermons, like everyone else who wishes to communicate (SEYFORT RUEGG (1985: 315)), even if esoteric Buddhist (and Digambara Jain) schools deny this. From a pragmatic point of view, the 'salvific principle' of insight creation

[196] Cf. WELLMER (1986: 24 f.).

through acts of symbolic violence appears merely as a culturally specific norm, a systematic distortion of communication which, indeed, as SEYFORT RUEGG (1985: 318) argues, cannot be inferred from the surface meaning of a communication, only elicited via a systematic hermeneutics of the doctrinal system as a whole. Yet, from an emic point of view, the non-motivated 'intentional ground' of socially 'purposeful' communication, cannot be simply identified with the codified doctrinal system of Buddhism, as SEYFORT RUEGG (1985: 314 f.) suggests, because it refers to the existential conditions of meaning *per se* which can be explored only through direct meditative experience. From an etic point of view, the Buddhist intention to put an end to intention as a value, compared for instance with the phenomenological theory of the constitutive role of the structure of intentionality of consciousness or *Dasein*, is one ideology amongst others, and must be communicated in a conventional way.[197]

The conundrum of ideal non-cooperation becomes clearer, if we consider not only discourse but also religious practice. The practice of renunciation, which Buddhist and Jain doctrines aim to stimulate, is a religiously sanctioned act of social separation and selective non-cooperation, which does involve what might be termed 'sacred violence', in opposition to 'physical violence' and 'symbolic violence' (flouting) in the two forms of latent strategic action and systematically distorted communication ('salvific violence'). Within a hierarchical system, renunciation is a paradoxical act of status encompassment which creates at the same time new asymmetrical social relationships (renouncer/renounced, guru/devotees) and symmetrical social relationships (between devotees). In this way, acts of social separation and religious self-limitation are socially constitutive and culturally regenerative. Renunciation does not necessarily violate the conversational 'cooperative principle'. But, as a one-sided act of transcendence and symbolic incorporation of already established links of social co-operation, it contributes to the legitimation of stratified systems of functional differentiation and moral divisions of labour. Following DUMONT (1980: 197) and SEYFORT RUEGG (1985), I therefore propose to distinguish between the 'salvific' violence of (Jain) religious rhetoric and the 'sacred violence' of the quasi-sacrificial act of renunciation itself.[198] Effectively, Jain renouncers do not live outside society, but 'unbound ... amongst the bound' (Āyār 2.16.7). After renunciation, linguistic co-operation is strictly regulated, but continues. Worldly social co-operation, however, is severed more radically, although only unilaterally, while the scope of social co-operation in religious contexts is actually widened.[199] Sacred violence differentiates the levels of institutional non-violence and violence, while conditioning the patterns of selective co-operation. The necessary violence

[197] See FAURE (1991), SHARF (1995).

[198] On 'sacred violence', see for instance GIRARD (1977) and his critics.

[199] FLÜGEL (2006a: 333 f.).

(*ārambhajā hiṁsā*) of the social world is always presupposed by Jain ascetics, in form of Brāhmaṇic household rites, the state and the socio-economic institutions and activities of their followers, which grant them one-sided material support:

> 'The lay estate ... cannot exist without activity and there can be no activity without the taking of life; in its grosser form this is to be avoided sedulously but the implicit part of it is hard to avoid' (Āśādhara's 13th CE *Sāgara-dharmâmṛta* 4.12 summarised by WILLIAMS (1983: 121)).

Institutionalised *ahiṁsā*, therefore, does not only imply *dayā*, but also *hiṁsā*, within a structure of moral division of labour. That is, conceptually as well as practically, it necessarily implies—even presupposes—its own opposite.

In all these cases, from the practical point of view (VN), the principle of co-operation is implicitly presupposed, if not constituted, by unconditional acts of one-sided renunciation, although only the avoidance of violence is expressed. From the transcendental point of view (PN), however, *ahiṁsā* requires total non-cooperation with the world. Both possibilities of action, co-operation and non-cooperation, are open only to an individual which, by positing renunciation as the norm, is able to 'offer cooperation', or withdraw it,[200] selectively. It is mainly because the interdependence (and potential conflict) between the renouncer and the world cannot be stated openly in systems of hierarchical co-operation, that the Jain principle of *ahiṁsā* fulfils the functions both of the linguistic cooperative principle and of the constitutive principle of social co-operation only implicitly: without saying so.[201] In fact, most Jain norms for well spoken language do not advocate positive values, but the avoidance of their violation. Negative principles such as these are of a different kind than positive prescriptions *à la* Grice, who demands 'do cooperate', whereas the Jains implicitly say, 'do not not cooperate'. Thus, co-operation is implied in *ahiṁsā*, but in a modalised form.

The method of universalisation of specific moral norms and maxims *qua* double negation has been defended by WELLMER (1986: 21–37),[202] against HABERMAS (1991: 167 f., 172 f.) objection that consequentialist concepts of universal morality, predicated on norms of prohibition *qua* single or double negation, are inspired by the restricted 'liberal' aim of creating spaces of negatively defined individual freedom, contrasted with positive maxims, which are oriented towards publicly negotiated common interest. According to Habermas, the individualist conception of morality is based on a

---

200 Cf. SHARP (1960), (1973).

201 DUMONT (1980: 44, 60).

202 WELLMER (1986: 21 f.) argues that because obligatory norms of specific content cannot be derived from the categorical imperative of Kant, secondary moral norms are necessary which can only be derived by way of negation of non-universalisable maxims. See also the work of SINGER (1961) and HARE (1981), critically discussed by Wellmer.

negative reading of the monologically applied categorical imperative. In contrast to positive duties, negative duties (and positive permissions) derive their plausibility from the qualities of apodictic prohibition: (a) unconditional validity, (b) determinateness of content, and (c) unequivocal specification of addressees. From the perspective of the potential victim, to every negative duty corresponds a right; for example, to the duty not to kill, the right to body and life. Yet, a principle of morality which permits only the legitimation of general norms of prohibition cannot serve as an unequivocal basis for the constitution of a positive common will. WELLMER (1986: 31 f.) and HABERMAS (1991: 170 f.) agree that neither positive nor negative duties can claim absolute validity, because every situation is different, and requires the invocation of different norms. In discourses of norm application, as opposed to norm legitimation, both negative and positive rights and duties can act as reasons for appropriate action,[203] though positive norms tend to be more unspecific. Yet, in concrete situations, moral norms themselves cannot be legitimated privately, only from the perspective of 'common interest', determining what is equally good 'for all'. While positive norms are burdened with discourses concerning concrete aims (problem of prognostics, performance, attribution of outcomes and unintended consequences, expectation and moral division of labour, evaluation of a result in terms of quantifiable aims), negative norms seem to remain aloof of problems of application, which cannot be avoided altogether though. Negatively defined principles can only protect the integrity and subjective freedom of the potential victim and, by implication, the freedom of the individual moral person itself. This may be the general principle underlying the Jain practice of deliberate renunciation of all violent action.[204]

The absence of positive principles in Jain ethics has frequently been criticised. In HABERMAS (1991: 166 f.) view, positive duties cannot be based on negative duties, but only on the principle of mutual recognition informing communicative action.[205] In

---

[203] HABERMAS (1991: 170): 'Die unwahrhaftige Auskunft, die einem anderen das Leben rettet, ist moralisch ebenso geboten, wie die Tötung in Notwehr oder die unterlassenen Hilfeleistung zur Vermeidung größerer übel moralisch erlaubt sind.'

[204] See the 'ten commandments' of GERT's (1973) 'minimal ethic', and C. FRIED (1978: 29) cited by HABERMAS (1991: 172): 'What we may not do to each other, the things which are wrong, are precisely those forms of personal interaction which deny to our victim the status of a freely choosing, rationally valuing, specially efficacious person—the special status of moral personality.'

[205] According to HEGEL (1981: 148 ff.) voluntary death is the absolute proof of freedom in the struggle for recognition. Liberation, both in a social and a religious sense, is also the positive implication of the Jain practice of *sallekhanā*, the culmination of the process of implementing the negatively formulated rule of non-violence. HABERMAS (1991: 173 f.), similarly, notes the fundamental nature of 'self-referential' norms which implicitly define the duty of fulfilling the pragmatic presuppositions of communicative action, i.e. the positive norms of preserving the physical integrity of the body and life and personal freedom which seems sometimes more important than death.

his conception of morality, private morality and public justice differ not in principle, only in terms of the types of institutionally mediated interaction. The positive normative equivalent of the apodictic prohibition of speaking the untruth ("you should not lie") from the communication theoretical perspective is phrased in the following way:

> 'Act with an orientation to mutual understanding and allow everyone the communicative freedom to take positions on validity claims' (HABERMAS (1991: 173) / (1993: 66)).

Interestingly, this is not a maxim of truthfulness, but a reformulation of the cooperative principle. Being truthful, does not only imply the renunciation of deception, but is a positive act which contributes to the constitution of a social relationship.

There is another, practical, reason for the negative formulation of the cooperative principle. A negative statement forces the 'user' or interpreter of such a principle to work out the implied positive contextual presuppositions. This process involves the personal experiences of the individual concerned, in such a way that the positive 'implied' meanings and/or functions of the formal principle appear to be generated from the inner pool of values and expectations of the individual itself, and not as an externally imposed rule. The realm of 'sociability' or of 'the social' itself is theorised as an aspect of personal character, and not as an independently existing dimension of intersubjectivity (as in modern law, moral philosophy and sociology). From the perspective of Jain ethics, positive rules are generally regarded as lower order specifications of negative rules, whose conditions of application are implicitly presupposed. Negative rules secure a higher degree of formality and universality than positive rules, and hence greater contextual adaptability.[206] These are some of the reasons why positive principles are seldom expressed explicitly in the *āgama*s, but left to the interpretative imagination of their users, who have to work out their conditions of fulfilment.[207] However, if *ahiṁsā* is the functional equivalent of the cooperation principle, likewise do the modalities of the *satya-mahā-vrata* correspond to the conversational maxims, to which I will turn now.

Quantity—restraint (*saṁyama*)

There is no equivalent Habermasian validity claim for Grice's quantity-maxim, although it could be easily constructed. Functional equivalents of the maxim among the Jain rules of speaking are the principles of deliberation, moderation, and restraint (*saṁjama* <*saṁyama*>). Even if something is true, but is not to be said

---

[206] Cf. GONDA (1959).

[207] Closest to Grice's formulation of this principle is Āyār 2.4.1.6–7 (examples: Āyār 2.4.8–11, cf. DVS 7.11, Āyār 2.4.2.19).

(*avattavva* <*avaktavya*>), because it may create harm, or if it cannot be understood, one should not say it. The purpose of the latter maxim is to avoid unintentional ambiguity due to ignorance of the listeners (cf. SSā 1.8).[208] The information processing aspect is expressed in Jain texts in general terms, such as 'speaking with precision' or 'straightforward' (*ṛju*). Often prescriptions are mixed with moral considerations, thus overlapping with the manner aspect, as the following example demonstrates:

> 'A monk or nun, putting aside wrath, pride, deceit, and greed, considering well, speaking with precision, what one has heard, not too quick, with discrimination, should employ language in moderation and restraint' (Āyār 2.4.2.19).[209]

There is no mention here of the recipient of an utterance, nor of the 'information' to be communicated. The reasons are similar as in the case of the 'cooperative principle' *ahiṁsā*. Restrained speech is regarded in Jainism primarily (PN) as an exercise in self-purification, to be measured in terms of the strength of the commitment to Jain values, and the degree of Jain interactional competence. Only indirectly (VN) is restrained speech regarded as a vehicle for the univocal transmission of information. This, again, derives from the fact that the realm of the 'social' is only presupposed as a background for the individual 'path of purification'.[210]

The problem of ambiguity resulting from the fact that, from the perspective of PN, VN might be taken as a 'mixture of truth and untruth' is important. Interestingly, it is discussed in the Āyār and DVS itself in the context of half-true speech, or *satyā-mṛṣā bhāṣā* (see *infra* pp. 162–169):

---

[208] Cf. CAILLAT (1975: 80). See VANDERVEKEN's (1993: 378) generalisation of this maxim in terms of the 'strength' of illocutionary acts, 'in the sense that they have more conditions of success, of non-defective performance … .' For similar Jain formulations see BALBIR (1993: 71). From the hearer's point of view (which is not mentioned in the Āyār sections on speech), the most important quality is the ability to 'conquer one's senses' and not to become restless through the 'lashes of words reaching the ears' (DVS_2 9.3.8).

[209] CARRITHERS (1990: 157–9) singles *saṁvara* out, as the singular 'aesthetic standard' 'underlying both the rules and the morality' of Jainism. This concept of aesthetics (which is linked, in a footnote, with the concept of habitus) does not account for the normative religious aspects of *saṁvara*. The same applies to LAIDLAW (1995: 159).

[210] BROWN–LEVINSON (1978: 218 ff.) suggest corresponding off-record strategies to Grice's quantity-maxim: understatement, overstatement, and tautologisation. STRECKER (1988: 194) sees silence as an extreme-form of the off-record strategy of understatement and thus as a violation of the quantity maxim. From the 'practical point of view' this may be correct. For Jains, silence is the prime vehicle of exercising restraint, as indicated by the *bhāṣā-gupti*, and counts as a form of penance. For instance, an ascetic who fasts for one month 'may express himself by four ways only: by begging for alms, by putting a question, by making a request for lodging and by giving an answer' (Ṭhāṇ 183b, in SCHUBRING (2000: 158, § 74).

> 'Speaks not the wise something which is not known, or which generates confusion—whether this or that sense is right' (DVS$_2$ 7.4).

Ideally, a mendicant should remain silent. Otherwise, straightforward speech should be used. All language that could be both truth and false should be avoided:

> 'In speaking (a monk) should use as few words as possible; he should not delight in another's foibles; he should avoid deceiving speech, and should answer after ripe reflection.—One will repent of having used the third kind of speech (which is both true and untrue—P.F.); a secret should not be made known. This is the Nirgrantha's command.—[A monk] should not call one names, nor "friend", nor by his Gotra; "thou, thou" is vulgar; never address one by "thou"' (Suy 1.9.25–27).

Quality—truth (*satya*)

The equivalent of Grice's quality-maxim is *satya*, or truth. VANDERVEKEN (1993: 377) has shown that the maxim of quality can be generalised to cover commissives and directives, as well as assertives. A maxim of truth is expressed in the *satya-mahā-vrata*, which Jain ascetics recite twice a day during their obligatory *pratikramaṇa* ritual (see *supra*).[211] However, in accordance with the preferred Jain method of negative determination, the general principle of truth is treated in this context only in terms of its characteristic violations (*aticāra*), that is, as the opposite of non-truth (*asatya*). The precise implications of the maxim of truth for language usage are specified elsewhere in form of a distinction of four types or 'species' of speech (*bhāsā-jāya* <*bhāṣā-jāta*>), which are at the centre of the Jain theory of discourse, which looks at speech primarily as an object, and not from the perspective of the speaker. These analytical categories should be known and utilised by mendicants (ideally by all Jains) to prevent both the preparation and performance of violence (*ārambha*):

> 'A mendicant should know that there are four kinds of speech: The first is truth; the second is untruth; the third is truth mixed with untruth; what is neither truth, nor untruth, nor truth mixed with untruth, that is the fourth kind of speech: neither truth nor untruth' (Āyār 2.4.1.4).[212]

---

[211] WILLIAMS (1983: 73) quotes Somadeva's (959 CE) 'casuistic analysis' of the *satya aṇuvrata* for the laity with the help of this tetrad as an original statement, although it is clearly only a restatement of Āyār 2.4.1.4.

[212] Āyār 2.4.1.4: *aha bhikkhū jāṇejjā cattāri bhāsā-jāyāiṁ, taṁ jahā—saccam egaṁ paḍhamaṁ bhāsa-jāyaṁ, bīyaṁ mosaṁ, taiyaṁ saccā-mosaṁ, jaṁ ṇ'eva saccaṁ ṇ'eva mosaṁ ṇ'eva saccā-mosaṁ—asaccā-mosaṁ ṇāma taṁ cautthaṁ bhāsā-jāyaṁ.* CAILLAT (1991: 8 n.4) located the following parallels to the above *sūtra* in the Śvetâmbara canon: Uttar 24.20–23, Ṭhāṇ 4.23 (238), Viy

Notably, the same scheme of four modes is applied to speech and to cognition (*maṇa* <*manas*>) or knowledge (*ṇāna* <*jñāna*>) (Viy 622b/8.7.1b, 874b/15.1.4). Hence, the four *bhāsā-gutti*s <*bhāṣā-gupti*s>, or controls of speech, and the four *maṇa-gutti*s <*mano-gupti*s>, or controls of the inner sense, are both characterised by the same terms in Uttar 24.19–23. The four modes, thus, represent general attitudes towards truth, both in mind and in speech:

1.	*saccā* <*satyā*>	truth
2.	*mosā* <*mr̥ṣā*>	untruth
3.	*saccā-mosā* <*satyā-mr̥ṣā*>	truth mixed with untruth
4.	*asaccā-mosā* <*asatyā-mr̥ṣā*>	neither truth nor untruth

The formal structure of the four alternatives (tetra-lemma) is known as *catuṣ-koṭi* in Buddhist literature, but used differently here.[213] As the frequent use of the four

13.7.1a (621a-b), Pannavaṇā 11 (860–866). See also Viy 16.2.2b (701a), 18.7.1 (749a), 19.8 (770b), Samavāya 13.1, and DVS 7.1–3. OHIRA (1994: 14, 155) is of the opinion that the four modes were first taught at the time of DVS 7, which she dates between 5th–4th century BCE.

[213] There is an extensive academic literature on the *catuṣ-koṭi* in Buddhist philosophy. See for instance SCHAYER (1933), RAJU (1954), MURTI (1955), BAHM (1957), ROBINSON (1957), STAAL (1962), SMART (1964), JAYATILLEKE (1967), CHI (1974), SEYFORT RUEGG (1977), WAYMAN (1977), JONES (1978), GUNARATNE (1980), (1986), BHARADWAJA (1984), SCHROEDER (2000), and others. STAAL (1962: 52 n. 4) suggests the earliest passage to be *Majjhima-nikāya* 63. Nāgārjuna's (2nd CE) positive formulation of the 'tetralemma' (ROBINSON (1957: 303)) in his *Mūla-madhyamaka-kārikā* 18.6 attracted most academic interest (even more so the negated forms): 'Everything is either true or not true, or both true or not true, or neither true or not true; that is the Buddha's teaching' (Translated by ROBINSON (1957: 302), cf. MMK 18.8). In contrast to the debate on the use of the *catuṣ-koṭi* in 'Buddhist logic', focusing largely on the 'negative dialectic' of Nāgārjuna, the cited Jain cases indicate that the *catuṣ-koṭi* was used (at least by Jains) as a quasi-systematic scholastic frame for the discussion of logical alternatives, without specific doctrinal implications being connected with the frame itself. MURTI (1955: 129) noted early on: 'Four alternative views are possible on any subject' (referring to Madhyamaka and Jainism: he also cites Haribhadra) (see also CHI (1974: 298)). Notably, the four alternatives in Āyār 2.4.1.4 etc., are disjunctive, not additive, as stereotypical representations of 'Jaina Logic' generally assume. Because Jain usage of *catuṣ-koṭi*s was ignored, and because of the almost exclusive focus on Nāgārjuna, Buddhist scholars compared the 'four-cornered negation' only with the 'Jain relativism' in general. They derived the *catuṣ-koṭi* either speculatively from Jain *syād-vāda* (GUNARATNE (1980: 232)) or vice versa (BAHM (1957: 128)), or (and) contrasted it with 'the relativistic logic proposed by the Jains, to which Buddhism was opposed' (JAYATILLEKE (1967: 82)). According to RAJU (1954), the mythical Sanjaya framed the four alternatives already in the 7th century BCE, negating all of them, whereas 'Jaina logicians saw a relative truth in each pole and thus adopted a more positive and determinate attitude toward our cognitions of the world.' For recent, less logocentric, views on Nāgārjuna, focusing on 'skillful means', see for instance JONES (1978), SCHROEDER (2000). A similar four-valued theory of truth was defended by the Megarians (PRIEST–ROUTLEY (1989: 13)), which demonstrates that no specific philosophical position is associated with the form itself, only with its uses.

alternatives (*catur-bhaṅga* or *catur-bhaṅgī*) as a classificatory scheme in Ṭhāṇ IV, for instance, indicates,[214] the *catuṣ-koṭi* is used in Jain scholasticism in a similar way as the *nikṣepa* pattern, described by BRUHN–HÄRTEL (1978: v) as a formal 'dialectical technique (often employed in a "pseudo-exegetical function")'.[215]

JACOBI (1884: 150 n. 2) understood the first three modes to refer to assertions and the fourth to injunctions. According to Paṇṇ 860 (255b), the first two modes are distinct (*pajjattiyā* <*paryāptā*>) ways of speaking, which can be analysed in terms of the true/false distinction, and the third and fourth are indistinct (*apajjattiyā* <*aparyāptā*>) ways of speaking, whose validity or non-validity is indeterminable. The sub-categories of distinct speech are true speech (*satyā bhāṣā*) and false speech (*mṛṣā bhāṣā*), and the sub-categories of indistinct speech are true-as-well-as-false speech (*satyā-mṛṣā bhāṣā*) and neither-true-nor-false speech (*asatyā-mṛṣā bhāṣā*). A *muni* should use only the first and the last mode of speech, and avoid the remaining two 'by all means' (DVS$_2$ 7.1) in order to minimise harm:

> 'A monk or a nun, considering well, should use true and accurate speech, or speech which is neither truth nor untruth (i.e. injunctions); for such speech is not sinful, blameable, rough, stinging, &c.' (Āyār 2.4.1.7).[216]

---

[214] See DUNDAS (2007: 50 f.) on the analogy between four types of armies and four types of ascetics in Ṭhāṇ 292 (4.280–1). ALSDORF (1966: 186 f., cf. 190 f.) discussed a different type of *catur-bhaṅgas* in Jaina literature, made up of combinations of two positive and two negative possibilities. He pointed out that the use of the 'fourfold combination' is 'very typical of the scholastic who never misses an opportunity to make a "caturbhanga", i.e. the four possible combinations of two positive and two negative possibilities…' (p. 186).

[215] Ṭhāṇ 3.239 offers also a trilemma: (1) to state the truth (*tavvayaṇa* <*tadvacana*>), (2) to state the untruth (*tadaṇṇavayaṇa* <*tadanyavacana*>), (3) to state something meaningless or negative (*no-avayaṇa* <*no-avacana*>); Ṭhāṇ 7.129 a heptalemma: (1) speech (*ālāva* <*ālāpa*>), (2) taciturnity (*aṇ-ālāva* <*an-ālāpa*>), (3) flattery (*ullāva* <*ullāpa*>), (4) insult (*aṇ-ullāva* <*an-ullāpa*>), (5) dialogue (*saṁlāva* <*saṁlāpa*>), (6) prattle (*palāva* <*pralāpa*>), (7) contradiction (*vi-ppalāva* <*vi-pralāpa*>).

[216] I do not give the original wording in all cases. In different words, the same teaching is expressed in DVS$_1$ 7.1–3, which may be the oldest text concerning this subject:

cauṇhaṁ khalu bhāsāṇaṁ parisaṁkhāya pannavaṁ /
doṇhaṁ tu viṇayaṁ sikkhe, do na bhāsejja savvaso // 1 //
jā ya saccā avattavvā saccāmosā ya jā musā /
jā ya buddhehi 'ṇāinnā, na taṁ bhāsejja pannavaṁ // 2 //
a-sacca-mosaṁ saccaṁ ca aṇavajjam akakkasaṁ /
samuppeham asaṁdiddhaṁ giraṁ bhāsejja pannavaṁ // 3 //

'[1] Of the four kinds of speech, the thoughtful monk] should, after consideration, learn the training in two, [but] should not use the other two ones at any occasion.

(α) Speaking truthfully can either be interpreted ethically, as straightforward and accurate talk (on-record), or ontologically, as an assertion of the way things are.[217] Both perspectives can be found in the Jain and non-Jain commentary literature alike,[218] often mixed together, as the identical characterisation of the four *gupti*s of mind and speech illustrates. *Satyā bhāṣā* refers both to the psychological and the normative conditions of truthfulness, that is, sincere, grammatically accurate and contextually acceptable speech, and to propositional truth.[219] It is explicitly recognised in the Jain scriptures (though not in these terms) that, as a speech act, propositional language has also an expressive and normative content. The normative, the expressive, and the propositional components of spoken language are altogether necessary to communicate something.

Paṇṇ 862 states that 'the truth or validity of the speech depends on various situations and conditions' (MĀLVAṆIYĀ (1970: 325)). Ten different dimensions or 'validity conditions' of truthful speech are distinguished[220] (the compound *-saccā* <*satyā*> can be translated as 'sincere' or 'true' 'according to the conventions of ____'):[221]

1.	*jaṇavaya-saccā* <*janapada-satyā*>	Country
2.	*sammata-saccā* <*sammata-satyā*>	Consensus
3.	*ṭhavaṇa-saccā* <*sthāpanā-satyā*>	Representation
4.	*ṇāma-saccā* <*nāma-satyā*>	Name
5.	*rūva-saccā* <*rūpa-satyā*>	Form

> [2] That [form of speech] which is true, [but] not to be uttered, that which is half-true, that which is [quite] untrue and which is not practised by the Jinas, the thoughtful monk should not use.
> [3] [But] he should, after deliberation, use a speech not exposed to doubt, [a speech] which is neither true nor untrue and [a speech] which is true, provided that it is not to be blamed [and] rough' (SCHUBRING (1932: 101)).

See Āyār 2.4.8–11 and cf. DVS 7.11, 7.2 for examples.

[217] Cf. HABERMAS' (1980: 419 ff.) / (1984–1987 I: 312 ff.) defence of his clear-cut distinction between claims to truth and claims to truthfulness.

[218] Mookerjee, in TULSĪ (1985: 107): 'Truthfulness is the revelation of truth. (Gloss) Truth means the straight-forwardness [ṛjutā] in deed (physical movement), intention and word, and non-discrepant behaviour. The revelation (disclosure) of that truth is called truthfulness.' '(Note) Here "truth", as an ethical principle, is defined and explained. Umāsvāti [*Tattvârtha-bhāṣya* 7.9], however has included revelation of ontological reality also as an aspect of truthfulness.'

[219] Ṭhāṇ 308 (4.349) gives the *nikṣepa* of *satya*: name, object, knowledge, knowledge and action according to truth. Ṭhāṇ 254 (4.102) distinguishes four types (aspects) of truth defined in terms of unequivocality or sincerity (*ujjuyayā* <*ṛjutā*>) of (1) gesture, (2) speech, (3) mind, (4) seamless combination of the three, with the intention not to deceive.

[220] See also Ṭhāṇ 10.89.

[221] JACOBI (1895: 160) translated *bhāva-satyā* as 'sincerity of the mind', and *yoga-satyā* as 'sincerity of acting'.

6. *paḍucca-saccā* <*pratītya-satyā*>	Confirmation
7. *vavahāra-saccā* <*vyavahāra-satyā*>	Custom
8. *bhāva-saccā* <*bhāva-satyā*>	Inner Meaning
9. *joga-saccā* <*yoga-satyā*>	Practice
10. *ovamma-saccā* <*aupamya-satyā*>	Analogy

The same list is given and explained in *Mūlâcāra* 5.111–116, with exception of *yoga-satyā*, which is replaced by category No. 8 *sambhāvanā-satyā*, translated by OKUDA (1975: 128) as 'truth of possibilities' (*Möglichkeitswahrheit*; see *infra* p. 161).[222] There is no apparent systematic connection between the categories in this list. Yet, the list is clearly informed by the four 'doors of disquisition' (*aṇuogaddāra* <*anuyoga-dvāra*>) of canonical hermeneutics (AṇD 75), especially by the method of contextual interpretation (*aṇugama* <*anugama*>) through progressive specification via fixed standpoints (*naya*) (AṇD 601–606).[223] The occurrence of the terms *nāma, sthāpanā* and *bhāva* indicates the deliberate incorporation of a variant of the 'canonical' *nikkheva* <*nikṣepa*>, as BHATT (1978: xv, 20) suggested, although the *davva* <*dravya*> standpoint is missing.[224] A *nikṣepa* is a scholastic scheme which delineates fixed perspectives for the analysis of the principal dimensions of the possible contextual meanings of a word (contemporary linguistics is still struggling to establish comparable categories). The original purpose of the list of ten, as a whole, may have been similar. That is, assessing the meaning of an utterance from several commonly relevant perspectives.[225]

Most categories are self-explanatory. Truthful utterances based on the linguistic conventions of a country are explained by the commentaries through the example that 'in Konkan *piccaṁ* is said for *payas* and that by the *gopāla* the lotus is called *aravinda* only' (SCHUBRING (2000: 157 n. 4, § 74)). Because terms such as these are synonyms, they are all equally true.[226] Similarly, what is accepted by many people, i.e. linguistic

---

[222] MĀc 5.111: *jaṇa-vada sammada ṭhavaṇā ṇāme rūve paḍucca-sacce ya sambhāvaṇa vavahāre bhāve opamma-sacce ya.*

[223] According to AṇD 605, contextual interpretation (*aṇugama*) of the meaning of a *sutta* should progress in the following sequence: 'Know that the characteristic features (of exposition) are sixfold, viz. (1) the (correct) utterance of the text (*saṁhitā*), (2) disjunction and parting (of words), (3) paraphrasing, (4) expounding of compound words, (5) anticipation of objections, and (8) establishment (of the correct meaning).'

[224] Cf. Ṭhāṇ 4.349.

[225] BHATT (1978: 14) emphasises that the *nikṣepa* in Paṇṇ 863 'has no execution in the canonical context.' The material is therefore likely to belong to 'post-canonical works from which it was taken before the canon acquired its present shape.' He lists similar passages in the canon and the commentary literature (BHATT (1978: 157)).

[226] PaṇṇU 81: *jana-pada-satyaṁ nāma nānā-deśī-bhāṣā-rūpam apy avipratipattyā yad ekârtha-pratyāyana-vyavahāra-samartham iti, yathôdakārthe koṁkaṇâdiṣu payaḥ piccaṁ nīram udakam ity-*

expressions, is conventionally true (*sammata-satyā*).[227] Pragmatic theories of truth would fall under this perspective. A figurative representation, such as a statue which is not god itself, may itself not be accurate, but that what it symbolises can be recognised as true (*sthāpanā-satyā*).[228] The same applies to a name such as Devadatta or 'given by god' (*nāma-satyā*) (MĀc 113).[229] Allusions to external appearance in form of prototypes such as 'white cranes' (not all cranes are white) are examples of *rūpa-satyā*.[230] According to the commentators Haribhadra (PaṇṇV) and Malayagiri (PaṇṇṬ), the term *pratītya-satyā* designates an utterance which is true only under certain conditions, and thus predicated on empirical confirmation.[231] Examples are relative size ('this is long') or the relative state of transformation of objects at a given time (cf. MĀc 114).[232] Like other conventional expressions which, under certain conditions, could equally be classified as 'truth-mixed-with-untruth', common or idiomatic utterances such as 'the *kūra* (i.e. the cooked rice) is cooking' (MĀc 114) are acceptable as customarily true (*vyavahāra-satyā*).[233] The Śvetâmbara commentators explain the inner truth (*bhāva-satyā*) expressed by certain utterances with the example of a 'white crane' (*śuklā balākā*),[234] which MĀc 113 uses to illustrate *rūpa-satyā*, whereas Vaṭṭakera interprets the term as designating the 'higher truth', i.e. saying something untrue in order to avoid injury to someone (MĀc 116). This perspective is also applied to

ādi, aduṣṭa-vivakṣā-hetutvān nānā-jana-padeṣv iṣṭârtha-pratipatti-janakatvād vyavahāra-pravṛtteḥ satyam etad iti, evaṁ śeṣeṣv api bhāvanā kāryā. PaṇṇṬ$_1$ 257a.1: *ity-ādi "jaṇa-vaya-saccā" iti taṁ taṁ jana-padam adhikṛtyêṣṭârtha-pratipatti-janakatayā vyavahāra-hetutvāt satyā jana-pada-satyā yathā koṅkāṇâdiṣu payaḥ piccam ity-ādi.*

[227] PaṇṇU 81: *sammata-satyaṁ nāma kumuda-kuvalayôtpala-tāmarasānāṁ samāne paṁkaja-saṁbhave gopālâdīnāṁ sammatam araviṁdam eva paṁkajam iti.*

[228] PaṇṇU 81: *sthāpanā-satyaṁ nāma akṣara-mudrā-vinyāsâdiṣu yathā māṣako 'yaṁ kārṣāpaṇo 'yaṁ śatam idaṁ sahasram idam iti.*

[229] PaṇṇU 81: *nāma-satyaṁ nāma kulama-varddhayann api kula-varddhana ity ucyate dhanam avarddhamāno 'pi dhana-varddhana ity ucyate, apakṣas tu pakṣa iti.*

[230] PaṇṇU 81: *rūpa-satyaṁ nāma tad-guṇasya tathā rūpa-dhāraṇaṁ rūpa-satyaṁ, yathā prapañcayateḥ pravrajita-rūpa-dhāraṇam iti.* PaṇṇṬ$_1$ 257a: *yathā dambhato gṛhīta-pravrajita-rūpaḥ pravrajito 'yam iti.*

[231] OKUDA (1975: 127) translates *pratītya-satyā* as 'relative truth'.

[232] PaṇṇU 81: *pratītya-satyaṁ nāma yathā anāmikāyā dīrghatvaṁ hrasvatvaṁ cêti, tathā hi tasyânaṁta-pariṇāmasya dravyasya tat tat-sahakāri-kāraṇa-sannidhānena tat tad-rūpam abhivyajyata iti satyatā.* PaṇṇṬ$_2$ 257a uses the expression *pratītya-āśritya*, recourse to confirmation. PaṇṇV 11.17 gives the synonym *apekṣā*, consideration or regard.

[233] PaṇṇU 81: *vyavahāra-satyaṁ nāma dahyate giriḥ galati bhājanaṁ anudarā kanyā alomā eḍiketi, giri-gata-tṛṇâdi-dāhe loke vyavahāraḥ pravarttate, tathôdake ca galati sati, tathā saṁbhoga-jīva-prabhavôdarâbhāve ca sati, lavana-yogya-lomâbhāve cêti.*

[234] PaṇṇU 81: *bhāva-satyaṁ nāma śuklā balākā, saty api paṁca-varṇa-saṁbhave.*

other contexts in the Śvetâmbara texts Āyār 2.4.1.6 and DVS 7.11. An example of truth based on association with practice (*yoga-satyā*) is to describe someone according to his/her activity, for instance the designation *chattrī* (a *kṣatriya* who should protect his realm performs *chattra-yoga*), or *daṇḍī* (who performs *daṇḍa-yoga* or punishment).[235] Instead of *yoga-satyā*, the *Mūlâcāra* 115 has *sambhāvanā-satyā*, which means that assuming the possibility of something is a valid condition of truthful language: 'If he wanted, he could do it. If Indra wanted, he could overturn the Jambudvīpa' (OKUDA (1975: 128)). As an example of speaking the truth, using comparison or analogy (*aupamya-satyā*),[236] MĀc 116 mentions the word *palidovama* <*palyôpama*>, literally 'like a sack of corn', which designates a high number.[237] *Aṇuogaddārāiṁ* (AṇD) 368–382 demonstrates the practical 'usefulness' of this simile through the *naya* method of progressive disambiguation.[238]

(β) Untruthful language or speaking untruthfully (*mṛṣā bhāṣā*) is the proscribed opposite of truth or truthfulness.[239] In contrast to the ten conditions of truth, featuring the semantics of propositional utterances, the ten conditions out of which untruth 'arises' (compound: *-nissiya* <*niḥsṛita*>), listed in Paṇṇ 863, are primarily psycho-physical conditions.[240] According to SCHUBRING (2000: 157, § 69), 'speech springing from emotion is by itself understood as *mosā*.'[241] Eight of the ten categories overlap with the standard Jain list of the eighteen sources of sin (*pāva-ṭhāṇa* <*pāpa-sthāna*>),[242] starting with the four passions (*kasāya* <*kaṣāya*>), and attachment and aversion, which in the Paṇṇ are the sole cause of karmic bondage, disregarding *yoga*, or activity (MĀLVAṆIYĀ (1970: 384)). Most types of untrue speech, conditioned by these factors, can be categorised as expressive utterances. The last two categories, *ākhyāyika-*

[235] PaṇṇU 81: *yoga-satyaṁ nāma chattra-yogāc chattrī daṇḍa-yogād daṁḍîty evam ādi.*

[236] Cf. UPADHYAYA (1987: 105–7) on Hemacandra's examples of *upācara*, secondary meaning of a word based on similarity.

[237] PaṇṇU 81: *upamayā satyaṁ nāma samudravat taḍāgaṁ.*

[238] The problem of the vagueness of the concept of 'heaps' is also addressed in the so-called sorites paradoxes attributed to Eubilides.

[239] Ṭhāṇ 254 (4.102) distinguishes four types (aspects) of untruth defined in terms of equivocality or insincerity (*aṇujjuyatā* <*anṛjukatā*>) of (1) gesture, (2) speech, (3) mind, (4) contradictory combination of the three, with the intent to deceive.

[240] According to Jain philosophy, cognitive and motivational factors are linked. See also HYMES (1972a: 283) notion of communicative competence: 'The specification of ability for use as part of competence allows for the role of non-cognitive factors, such as motivation, as partly determining competence. In speaking of competence, it is especially important not to separate cognitive from affective and volitive factors, so far as the impact of the theory on educational practice is concerned; but also with regard to speech design and explanation.'

[241] Arguably, conditions such as anger and pride can also evoke (painfully) true statements.

[242] Viy 1.9.1 (95a).

niḥsr̥ita[243] and *upaghāta-niḥsr̥ita*,[244] do not refer merely to an underlying negative psycho-physical state in general, but to the unspecified psycho-physical conditions of two specific types of self-referentially defined commonly untrue speech acts—hearsay and false accusation—with predominately constantive and regulative attributes.

1. *koha-nissiya <krodha-niḥsr̥ita>*	Anger
2. *māṇa-nissiya <māna-niḥsr̥ita>*	Pride
3. *māyā-nissiya <māyā-niḥsr̥ita>*	Deceit
4. *lobha-nissiya <lobha-niḥsr̥ita>*	Greed
5. *pejja-nissiya <premana-niḥsr̥ita>*	Attachment
6. *dosa-nissiya <dveṣa-niḥsr̥ita>*	Aversion
7. *hāsa-nissiya <hāsya-niḥsr̥ita>*	Ridicule
8. *bhaya-nissiya <bhaya-niḥsr̥ita>*	Fear
9. *akkhāiya-nissiya <ākhyāyika-niḥsr̥ita>*	Hearsay
10. *uvaghāya-nissiya <upaghāta-niḥsr̥ita>*	False Accusation

CAILLAT (1991: 11) observed that the Paṇṇ presents the *kaṣāya*s as the cause of untruth, not of injury, as in Āyār 2.4.1.1 and DVS 7.11. This change of perspective, from *ahiṁsā* to *-satya* as the main criterion, may reflect the shift of emphasis in classical Jain *karman* theory from act to intention. The ten categories seem to have in common that they refer to acts which, intentionally or unintentionally, produce unwholesome perlocutionary effects in the addressee (and the speaker as well). They are either factually false, ethically wrong or both.[245]

(γ) The category 'partially true speech'[246] or 'truth-mixed-with-untruth' (*saccā-mosā bhāsā <satyā-mr̥ṣā bhāṣā>*) should not be mixed up with the conditionally true standpoints of *syād-vāda*, which apply only to valid statements, not to false

[243] Following Haribhadra (PaṇṇU 82: *ākhyāyikā asaṁbhavyâbhidhānaṁ*) and Malayagiri (PaṇṇṬ$_1$ 258b.9: *ākhyāyikā-niḥsr̥tā yat-kathāsv-asambhāvyâbhidhānam*), *akkhāiya <ākhyāyika>* is usually understood as a narrative (*kathā*) of something non-existing or impossible, based on mere 'legend' or hearsay. See RATNACANDRA (1988 I: 59), and GHATAGE (1996 I: 64). This betrays the spirit of realism of Jain philosophy. Though, *kathā* may also refer to 'talk', 'discussion' or 'disputation'. Potentially negative consequences of knowledge based on mere hearsay are explained in Viy 9.31(430a–438a). Ṭhāṇ 7.80 lists seven types of gossip (*vi-kahā <vi-kathā>*).

[244] *Uvaghāya*/ *uvagghāya <upaghāta>* is explained by Malayagiri (PaṇṇṬ$_1$ 258b.10) through the example *cauras tvam* ('you are a thief'), understood here as *abhyākhyāna*—false and groundless accusation. The term *upaghāta* generally designates an act of violence, but here more specifically an insult. See also Āyār 2.4.8 for this and similar examples of 'sinful speech'.

[245] Ṭhāṇ 6.100 lists six types of unwholesome speech. Ṭhāṇ 6.101 lists six types of false accusations, related to the context of enumeration (*patharā <prastāra>*) in confession.

[246] See for instance NYAYAVIJAYA (1998: 343–5).

knowledge (*apramāṇa*). 'Truth-mixed-with-untruth' designates intentionally or unintentionally ambiguous or unclear speech, which is strictly prohibited.[247] The meaning of the term is explained by DVS 7.4–10:

> '4. But this and that topic which confines the Eternal within limits—
> this half-true speech the wise [monk] should avoid.
> 5. By a speech which is untrue, though its appearance is that of a true one, a man is touched by sin, how much more a man who speaks plain untruth!' (DVS$_1$ 7.4).[248]

Satyā-mṛṣā bhāṣā is sinful language, based on the whole on non-universalisable ethical principles. For instance, the language of heretical forest-monks, who do not abstain from killing, whose thought, speech and behaviour is not well controlled:

> 'They employ speech that is true and untrue at the same time: "do not beat me, beat others; do not abuse me, abuse others; do not capture me, capture others; do not torment me, torment others; do not deprive me of life, deprive others of life"' (Suy 2.2.21).

The ten types of truth-mixed-with-untruth listed in Paṇṇ 865[249] do not explicitly address expressive or regulative aspects of speech acts, but only propositional content; despite the fact that performatives can also be both true and untrue. According to the commentaries, all types deal with indiscriminate speech, and with semantic and logical fallacies, such as category mistakes regarding the quality or quantity of objects or temporal modalities which can be easily 'mixed up' (compound: *-missiyā* <*miśritā*>), for instance in utterances designating part-whole relationships.

1. *uppaṇṇa-missiyā* <*utpanna-miśritā*> Born
2. *vigaya-missiyā* <*vigata-miśritā*> Destroyed
3. *uppaṇṇa-vigaya-missiyā* <*utpanna-vigata-miśritā*> Born-Destroyed
4. *jīva-missiyā* <*jīva-miśritā*> Life
5. *ajīva-missiyā* <*ajīva-miśritā*> Matter
6. *jīvâjīva-missiyā* <*jīvâjīva-miśritā*> Life-Matter

---

247 On combinations of truth and untruth in behaviour (*vyavahāra*), intent (*pariṇata*), belief (*dṛṣṭi*) etc., for instance in succession, theorised in terms of character types, see Ṭhāṇ 241 (4.35–44). See CAILLAT (1965/1975: 80) on types of duplicity to be avoided.

248 DSV 7.4–5:

eyaṁ ca aṭṭhamannaṁ vā jaṁ tu nāmei sāsayaṁ /
sa bhāsaṁ sacca-mosaṁ pi taṁ pi dhīro vivajjae // 4 //
vitahaṁ pi tahāmottiṁ jaṁ giraṁ bhāsae naro /
tamhā so puṭṭho pāveṇaṁ, kiṁ puṇa jo musaṁ vae // 5 //

249 See also Ṭhāṇ 10.91.

7.	*aṇanta-missiyā <ananta-miśritā>*	Infinite
8.	*paritta-missiyā <parīta-miśritā>*	Separate
9.	*addhā-missiyā <adhva-miśritā>*	Time
10.	*addhâddhā-missiyā <ardhâdhva-miśritā>*	Halftime

The list of ten modalities evidently reflects general issues of particular concern for Jain doctrine. It can be thematically subdivided in two triplets and two pairs. The first triplet—*utpanna, vigata, utpanna-vigata*—addresses unclear distinctions concerning life and death. The commentators explain the meaning of *utpanna-miśritā* as speaking in non-specific ways about the born, mixed with references to the yet unborn; for instance birth occurring in this or that village or town, that ten or more or less boys were born ('ten boys were born in this village today') etc.[250] In the same way, *vigata-miśritā* refers to cases of 'stating mortality in an indefinite way, e.g. saying that ten people have died in this village, etc.' (RATNACANDRA (1988 IV: 400)).[251] *Utpanna-vigata-miśritā* refers to both true and false, or contradictory assertions (*visaṁvāda*) regarding manifestations of both birth and death.[252] The second triplet—*jīva, ajīva, jīvâjīva*—similarly addresses the problem of pointing in a general way to 'great numbers' of either living or dead beings, or quantities of mixed living and dead beings.[253] Life (*jīva*) in abstract and concrete form can be confused through vague language, such as the language of sets (*rāśi*), or other numerical expressions. The same applies to matter

---

[250] PaṇṇU 82: *saccā-mosā dasa-vihā uppaṇṇa-mīsaga-vigata-mīsagâdi, uddissa gāmaṁ vā nagaraṁ vā dasaṇhaṁ dāra-gāṇaṁ jaṁmaṁ pagāsaṁtassa ūṇesu ahiesu vā evam ādi uppanna-missiyā.* PaṇṇṬ$_1$ 258a: *"uppaṇṇa-missiyā" ity-ādi, utpannā miśritā anutpannaiḥ saha saṁkhyā-pūraṇârthaṁ yatra sā utpanna-miśritā, evam anyatrâpi yathā yogaṁ bhāvanīyaṁ, tatrôtpanna-miśritā yathā kasmiṁścit grāme nagare vā ūneṣv adhikeṣu vā dārakeṣu jāteṣu daśa dārakā asminn adya jātā ity-ādi.*

[251] PaṇṇU 82: *em eva maraṇa-kahaṇe vigaya-missiyā.* PaṇṇṬ$_1$ 258b: *evam eva maraṇa-kathane vigata-miśritā.*

[252] PaṇṇU 82: *jammaṇassa maraṇassa ya kaya-pariṇāmassa ubhaya-kahaṇe visaṁvādaṇe uppāeṇa-vigata-missitā.* PaṇṇṬ$_1$ 258b: *tathā janmato maraṇasya ca kṛta-pariṇāmasyâbhidhāne visaṁvādena côtpanna-vigata-miśritā.*

[253] PaṇṇU 82: *jīvaṁta-mayaga-saṁkhaṇagâdi-rāsi-darisaṇe aho mahaṁ jīva-rāsi tti bhaṇaṁtassa jīvaṁtesu saccā maesu mosa tti jīva-missitā, ettha ceva bahusu matesu aho mahaṁto 'jīva-rāsi tti bhaṇaṁtassa maesu saccā jīvaṁtesu musā iti ajīva-missiyā, saccaṁ mayam amayaṁ vā ubhayaṁ ṇiyameṇa avadhārayaṁtassa visaṁvāde jīvâjīva-missiyā.* PaṇṇṬ$_1$ 258b: [4] *tathā prabhūtānāṁ jīvatāṁ stokānāṁ ca mṛtānāṁ śaṅkha-śaṅkhanakâdīnām ekatra rāśau dṛṣṭe yadā kaścid evaṁ vadati—aho mahān jīva-rāśir ayam iti tadā sā jīva-miśritā, satyā-mṛṣātvaṁ câsyā jīvatsu satya tvāt mṛteṣu mṛṣātvāt,* [5] *tathā yadā prabhūteṣu mṛteṣu stokeṣu jīvatsu ekatra rāśī-kṛteṣu śaṅkhādiṣv evaṁ vadati—aho mahānayaṁ mṛto jīva-rāśir iti tadā sā ajīva-miśritā, asyā api satyā-mṛṣātvaṁ mṛteṣu satyatvāt jīvatsu mṛṣātvāt,* [6] *tathā tasminn eva rāśau etāvanto 'tra jīvanta etāvanto 'tra mṛtā iti niyamenâvadhārayato visaṁvāde jīvâjīva-miśritā.*

(*ajīva*), and both life and matter (*jīvâjīva*). The consequence of imprecise language may be unintentional violence against individual living beings (in a 'heap of dead beings'). According to *Āvassaya-nijjutti* (ĀvNi 8.56–100), one of the principal heretics of the canonical period, Rohagutta, committed the mistake of mixing up categories by positing a third principle, *nojīva* or the half-living, which mediates between *jīva* and *ajīva*. Hence, his heresy was called *terāsiyā*.[254] The pair *ananta* and *parīta* addresses indiscriminate language regarding aspects of finite-infinite, part-whole, or singular term-existence relationships. The commentaries explain *ananta-miśritā* with reference to the case of certain plants, for instance root vegetables such as radish (*mūlaka*), which have only one body, yet are composed of an infinite number of souls (*ananta-jīva*).[255] The category *parīta-miśritā* focuses, conversely, for instance on the independence and separateness of each individual element within a composite form of vegetation.[256] The two ontological levels of the relationship between one and many can easily be mixed up in these cases; which has potential ethical (karmic) consequences. One of the principle concerns of the *Pannavaṇā*, highlighted in Malayagiri's commentary, is the difference between the categories infinite (*ananta*) and uncountable (*asaṁkhyāta*).[257] With regard to *adhva*, time, speech is both true and untrue if one says, for some reason, that 'it is night' during the daytime, or 'get up, it is day' when it is night.[258] The same applies to the part of a measure of time, or *ardhādhva*, such as a

[254] See LEUMANN's (1885) article on the seven early schisms (*niṇhava*).

[255] PaṇṇU 82: *mūlakâdi aṇaṁta-kāyaṁ tasseva paḍirikkaya-paṁḍuṁ-pattehiṁ aṇṇeṇa vā vaṇassaikāeṇa missaṁ daṭṭhūṇa esa aṇaṁta-kāyôtti bhaṇaṁtassa aṇaṁta-missiyā.* PaṇṇṬ$_1$ 259a: *tathā mūlakâdikam ananta-kāyaṁ tasyâiva satkaiḥ paripāṇḍu-patrair anyena vā kenacit-pratyeka-vanaspatinā miśram avalokya sarvo 'py eṣo 'nanta-kāyika iti vadato 'nanta-miśritā.* Cf. GHATAGE (1996 I: 227). On the *ananta-kāyas* see WILLIAMS (1983: 113–6).

[256] PaṇṇU 82: *tam eva samudayaṁ karamette sarittāṇaṁ amilāṇaṁ rāsī-kayaṁ parittam iti bhaṇaṁtassa paritta-missiyā.* PaṇṇṬ$_1$ 259a: *tathā pratyeka-vanaspati-saṅghātam ananta-kāyikena saha rāśī-kṛtam avalokya pratyeka-vanaspatir ayaṁ sarvo 'pîti vadataḥ pratyeka-miśritā.*

[257] See MĀLVAṆIYĀ (1971: 271, 430). Ṭhāṇ 10.66 lists ten meanings of the word *ananta*.

[258] This characterisation cannot be related to the difference between experienced or conventional time (*samaya*) and imperceptible abstract time (*addhā*) explained in Viy 11.11.1 (532b) (DELEU (1970: 178)), because in this case the speech act would be neither-true-nor-false. As the authoritative work of Jain scholastic hermeneutics, the *Aṇuogaddārāiṁ* shows, Jains are careful to distinguish semantic ambiguity from philosophical perspectivism (*anekânta-vāda, syād-vāda, nikṣepa, naya* etc.), which is seen as an analytic instrument for disambiguation: 'Whereas in the fallacy of *chhal* (fraud), one word has two meanings, no word in this argument [of *syād-vāda*] is of such nature. … To declare the existence of an object from one point of view and to declare its non-existence from another point of view, is not to indulge in a *pun*, and thus to be guilty of this fallacy' (KANNOOMAL (1917: 16)). Cf. C. R. JAIN (1929: 8, 16–18), GANERI (2001: 133). It should be noted that similes and analogies are considered to be media of disambiguation and not convey-

prahara, a quarter of the bright or dark period of the day.[259] The statements may be true in as much as time in general is concerned, but false with regard to time in particular (i.e. it may be bright, although technically it is still night).[260]

Examples for a potential mix up of the modalities of time, which may have negative moral consequences in cases of promises for instance, are given in Āyār 2.4.2, and in DVS 7.6–10 as paradigmatic cases for *satyā-mṛṣā* speech. The illocutionary form of these sentences is not essential, since they can be transformed into propositions of the form: 'x promises (commands etc.), that p':[261]

> '6. Such speech therefore, as e.g. "we [shall] go", "we shall say", "we shall have to do that", or: "I shall do that", or "he shall do that", 7. uncertain in the future or with regard to a matter of the present [or] of the past, a wise monk] should avoid. 8.9. If [a monk] does not know, [or] has some doubt about, a matter which concerns past, present and future, he should not say: "it is thus"; 10. (this he should do only) when there is no room for doubt' (DVS_1 7.6–10).[262]

ors of mixed truth and untruth. Obviously, they can play both roles. On *chala*, features of 'god', 'bad debates' etc., especially in the *Nyāya-sūtra*, see MATILAL (1999, Chapters 2–3).

[259] RATNACANDRA (1988 I: 270 f., 268), GHATAGE (2001 II: 454, 461).

[260] PaṇṇU 82: *addhā kālo so divaso rabhī vā, jo tam-missiyaṁ kareti, paraṁ turiyāveṁto divasato bhaṇati-uṭṭhehi rattī jāyatti, esā addhā-missiyā, tasseva divasassa rātīe vā ega-padeso addhâddhā, taṁ paḍhama-porisi-kāle taheva turiyaṁto majjhaṇhī-bhūtaṁ bhaṇatassa addhâddha-missiyā.* PaṇṇṬ$_1$ 259a: [9] *tathā addhā—kālaḥ, sa cêha prastāvāt divaso rātrir vā parigṛhyate, sa miśrito yayā sāddhā-miśritā, yathā kaścit kaścana tvarayan divase varttamāna eva vadati—uttiṣṭha rātrir yātêti, rātrau vā varttamānāyām uttiṣṭhôdgataḥ sūrya iti,* [10] *tathā divasasya rātrer vā ekadeśo 'ddhâddhā sā miśritā yayā sā addhâddhā-miśritā, yathā prathama-pauruṣyām eva varttamānāyāṁ kaścit kañcana tvarayan evaṁ vadati—cala madhyâhnī-bhūtaṁ iti.*

[261] HABERMAS (1981: 97–117) / (1984–1987 II: 62–76), and others, showed that semantic content of normative sentences can be transformed into propositional sentences while the reverse is not always possible.

[262] DVS 7.6–10:

> *tamhā gacchāmo, vakkhāmo, amugaṁ vā ṇe bhavissaī /*
> *ahaṁ vā ṇaṁ karissāmi, eso vā ṇaṁ karissaī* // 6 //
> *evamāī u jā bhāsā esa-kālammi saṅkiyā /*
> *saṁpayāīyam aṭṭhe vā taṁ pi dhīro vivajjae* // 7 //
> *aīyammi ya kālammī paccuppannam aṇāgae /*
> *jamaṭṭhaṁ tu na jāṇejjā "evameyaṁ" ti no vae* // 8 //
> *aīyammi ya kālammi paccuppannam aṇāgae /*
> *jattha saṅkā bhave taṁ tu "evameyaṁ" ti no vae* // 9 //
> *aīyammi ya kālammi paccuppannam aṇāgae /*
> *nissaṅkiyaṁ bhave jaṁ tu "evameyaṁ" ti niddise* // 10 //

Somadeva, in his *Yaśas-tilaka* of 959 CE (YT, p. 349–350), mentions a similar example of a statement which is on the whole true but to some extent false, that is, when someone 'after promising to give something at the end of a fortnight, gives it after a month or a year' (HANDIQUI (1968: 265)). He also mentions the statement 'he cooks food or weaves clothes' as one which is to some extent true but on the whole false because 'properly speaking, one cooks rice etc. and weaves yarn'. A different example of mixed speech, mentioned in Viy 18.7.1 (749a), are utterances of someone who is possessed. The fact that this case, referring to an existentially mixed psycho-physical state rather than to semantic ambiguity, cannot be easily fitted into any of the ten categories illustrates that the list is not exhaustive. From other viewpoints, the examples may also fit the categories of the other lists.

All of the ten enumerated modalities seem to refer to utterances in which the universal and the particular, or modalities of time, quantifiers, or other categories,[263] are mixed up in an indiscriminate and hence ambiguous way.[264] Though the mistakes discussed in the texts seem to be primarily based on indiscriminate cognition, producing objectionable uncertainty (cf. Āyār 2.4.1–2), the ten categories are very broad and can cover a great variety of motives, logical and semantic conundrums, such as vagueness or paradoxes, and linguistic forms and discursive strategies, such as off-record uses of metaphor, similes, veiled speech and politeness, which Brown and Levinson have analysed as popular forms for saying one thing and meaning another.[265] These phenomena deserve more detailed analysis in future studies. For the purpose of this essay, a few comparative notes on the implications of the findings for the question of the stance of Jain philosophy on the law of non-contradiction must suffice.

For PRIEST–ROUTLEY (1989: 3), 'admission or insistence, that some statement is both true and false, in a context where not everything is accepted or some things are rejected, is a sure sign of a paraconsistent approach—in fact a dialethic approach', i.e. the assumption that 'the world is inconsistent'. The Greek word *dialetheia* (two-

---

[263] See the mixed true-false utterance 'The god of the sky' (Āyār 2.4.1.12–13) and similar examples of mislabelling discussed in footnote 293.

[264] In symbolic logic such problems are discussed under the labels such as 'no-item thesis', 'misleading form thesis', 'truth value gap thesis', and 'new truth-value thesis' (HAACK (1974: 47 ff.)). According to PRIEST (1987) the single rationale underlying the theory of different types of truth value gaps, derived from the correspondence theory of truth, is that 'for certain sentences, α there is no Fact which makes α true, neither is there a Fact which makes $\neg\alpha$ true', which are to be distinguished from *dialetheia*, or true contradictions such that both statement A and its negation, $\neg A$, are true. In his view, the argument fails, because 'if there is no Fact which makes α true, there is a Fact which makes $\neg\alpha$ true, viz. the Fact that there is no Fact which makes α true' (PRIEST (1987: 54)).

[265] See for instance BALBIR (1987: 9) and DUNDAS (1996: 62).

way truth) refers to a true contradiction facing both truth and falsity.[266] PRIEST–ROUTLEY (1983: 17) were the first to point out parallels between Jaina logic and modern discussive logic, but argue, like most logicians before them, that Jain perspectivism is predicated on the rejection of the law of contradiction.[267] However, GANERI (2002: 274) demonstrated in his re-construction of the assumptions underlying the method of seven-fold predication (*sapta-bhaṅgī*), based on an extension of discussive logic via modalised many-valued truth-tables, that Jain logic 'does not involve any radical departure from classical logic … The underlying logic *within* each standpoint is classical, and it is further assumed that each standpoint or participant is internally consistent.' The findings of BALCEROWICZ (2003: 64) on the contextual logic of the seven *naya*s concur with this general conclusion. Both authors show that Jain logic is context-sensitive and a quasi-functional system.

To *syād-vāda* and *anekânta-vāda* the Jain *catuṣ-koṭi* of the modes of speech can be added, as another example of 'Jain logic' which clearly operates within the confines of the law of non-contradiction, and does not need to be interpreted as a form of scepticism, nor of syncretism predicated on the notion of a total truth integration of all viewpoints, as MATILAL (1981) argues. Our brief glance at the Jain interpretation of the third mode of the so-called 'four-valued logic' of the *catuṣ-koṭi*, applied to language usage, that is, the explicit exclusion of the values 'false' and 'both true and false', showed that 'Jain logic' does not 'flatly deny'[268] the law of non-contradiction. The examples in Jain scriptures for modes of speech which are both-true-and-false, and their explicit rejection, demonstrate, on the contrary, that Jain philosophy is unequivocally opposed to violations of the law of non-contradiction. This conclusion is also borne out by the Jain analysis of the temporal aspects of action (Viy 1.1.1=13a, 9.33.2d = 484a), which explicitly denies the possibility that an action that is being performed is not equal to the completed action, as the heretic Jamāli held ('has the bed been made or is it being made'). The question of the identity of an action in time has important consequence for the evaluation of karmic consequences, also of speech-acts.

---

[266] PRIEST–ROUTLEY (1983: 14) cite Stoic and other authors from Greek antiquity defending this view.

[267] 'In this respect the Jains anticipate contemporary discussive logic, initiated by Jaśkowski, and they may similarly be interpreted in terms of integration of different worlds, or positions, reflecting partial truth … Naturally such a theory risks trivialisation unless some (cogent) restrictions are imposed on the parties admitted as having obtained partial truth—restrictions of a type that might well be applied to block amalgamation leading to violations of Non-Contradiction.

Unlike the Jains, the Mādhyamikas apparently affirmed the law of Contradiction. But this does not prevent a certain unity of opposites, e.g. in the negative dialectic of Nāgārjuna, a concept, such as Being, can become indistinguishable from its opposite, Non-Being' (PRIEST–ROUTLEY (1983: 17)).

[268] STCHERBATSKY (1958: 415), cited in PRIEST–ROUTLEY (1989: 16)).

Contrary to PRIEST–ROUTLEY's (1989) intuitions, it seems, the main technique of argumentation used by Jain philosophers in all these cases resembles Aristotle's refutation of Heraclitus and other 'paraconsistent' thinkers in ancient Greece:

> 'Key parts of his analysis involved the use of time to avoid contradiction—instead of saying that a changing thing was both in a given state and also not in that state, it was said that the thing was in that state at time t_1, but not in that state at a different time t_2—and the theory of potentiality—required to reunify these now temporarily isolated states as parts of the one (and same) change. The appeal to different temporal quantifiers illustrated the *method of* (*alleged*) *equivocation* used since ancient times to avoid contradiction and reinforce consistency hypothesis; namely, where both A and -A appear to hold, find a respect or factor or difference r such that it can be said that A holds in respect r_1 and -A in respect r_2. It can then be said that a contradiction resulted only by equivocation on respect or factor r. Often however the method of alleged equivocation does not work in a convincing way, and it breaks down in an irreparable way with the semantic paradoxes, as the Megarians were the first to realize' (PRIEST–ROUTLEY (1989: 8)).

Speech that is both-true-and-untrue is rejected in the Jain scriptures, because it mixes aspects which can be discriminated, if necessary with the help of the method of perspective variation in time. To what extent ancient Jain philosophers would have agreed with Aristotle on this point is a question which can only be clearly answered in a separate study. It seems to me that the Jain theory of time is fundamental, also for Jain perspectivism.

(δ) The most interesting of the four modes of speech (and cognition) is 'speaking neither truth nor untruth' (*asaccā-mosā*). That is, speech to which the true/false distinction is not applicable. Muni Nathmal (Ācārya Mahāprajña) characterised *asatyā-mṛṣā* language as *vyavahāra-bhāṣā*, or conventional speech (Ṭhāṇ 4.23, Hindī commentary). Twelve types of the *asatyā-mṛṣā bhāṣā* are distinguished in Paṇṇ 866 = Viy 10.3.3 (499b):[269]

[269] LALWANI's (1985 IV: 133 f.) rendition of Viy 10.3.34 reads as follows: '[Gautama speaks] *Bhante!* There are twelve forms of language—address, order, prayer, question, advice, refusal, consent, enquiry, conviction, confusion, distinct and indistinct. Now, when one says, I shall take lodge, I shall lie, I shall stand, I shall sit, I shall stretch, do these forms conform to the fifth type viz. advice, and it is correct to say that they are never false?—[Mahāvīra answers] Yes Gautama! They conform to the fifth type and they are never false.'

1.	*āmantaṇī* <*āmantraṇī*>	Address
2.	*āṇavaṇī* <*ājñāpanī*>	Order
3.	*jāyaṇī* <*yācanā*>	Request
4.	*pucchaṇī* <*pṛcchanī*>	Question
5.	*paṇṇavaṇī* <*prajñāpanī*>	Communication
6.	*paccakkhāṇī* <*pratyākhyānī*>	Renunciation
7.	*icchâṇulomā* <*icchânulomā*>	Consent
8.	*aṇabhiggahiyā* <*anabhigṛhītā*>	Unintelligible
9.	*abhiggahiyā* <*abhigṛhītā*>	Intelligible
10.	*saṁsaya-karaṇī* <*saṁśaya-karaṇī*>	Doubt-Creating
11.	*voyaḍā* <*vyākṛtā*>	Explicit
12.	*avvoyaḍā* <*avyākṛtā*>	Implicit

Nine of the twelve categories are also listed in MĀc 5.118–119. The categories 1–7 are identical in both texts. Of the last five, only *saṁśaya* (No. 10) is mentioned by Vaṭṭakera, and a category labelled *aṇakkhara* <*anakṣara*>, 'incomprehensible', which can be read as an equivalent of *aṇabhiggahiyā* <*anabhigṛhītā*> (No. 8, maybe also incorporating aspects of No. 12).[270]

Speaking neither-truth-nor-untruth is interpreted by JACOBI (1884: 150 n. 2, 151)[271] and MĀLVAṆIYĀ (1971: 325 f.) as referring to injunctions. However, considering the great variety of listed speech acts (only the first three are injunctions), it seems better to use AUSTIN's (1962) term 'performatives', which are by definition neither true nor false, to characterise the first seven terms.[272] The last five terms cover aspects which Grice discussed under the conversational maxims of relation ('relevance') and manner ('avoid obscurity'). In Austin's terminology, addressing,

[270] On articulated (*akkhara-suya*) evidence, composed of written and oral sources see SCHUBRING (2000: § 74).

[271] Āyār 2.4.1.4 n., 2.4.1.7.

[272] AUSTIN (1962) distinguishes between implicit and explicit, self-verifying, performatives. An 'explicit performative sentence', such as taking a vow, 'indicates that the issuing of the utterance is the performing of an action—it is not normally thought of as just saying something' (AUSTIN (1962: 6 f.))—this would be a 'descriptive fallacy' (AUSTIN (1962: 3)). 'None of the utterances cited is either true or false' (AUSTIN (1962: 3)). 'It is essential to realize that "true" and "false", like "free" and "unfree", do not stand for anything simple at all; but only for a general dimension of being a right or proper thing to say as opposed to a wrong thing, in these circumstances, to this audience, for these purposes and with these intentions. ... This doctrine is quite different from much that the pragmatists have said, to the effect that the true is what works, &c. The truth or falsity of a statement depends not merely on the meanings of words but on what act you were performing in what circumstances' (AUSTIN (1962: 144)). The problem of determining truth-values of performative utterances has been discussed, for example, by FAUCONNIER (1981: 182).

ordering, requesting, and questioning etc. are all illocutionary acts. Questions,[273] commands, and exclamations are not propositions, since they can not be asserted or denied; that is, they are neither true nor false. Imperatives (directives), such as orders and requests, and regulatives (commissives), such as consenting and renouncing (promising, vowing etc.), through which the speaker commits him/herself to perform certain actions in future, imply normative conditions which ought to be fulfilled, but which are not fulfilled yet. In this sense, the propositional content is also neither true nor false. Truth, and its opposite, falsity, are properties that belong only to propositions. Propositions are statements that either assert or deny that something is the case. Not all sentences are true or false, because not all sentences make such claims. Commands, questions, and expressions of volition neither assert nor deny that something is the case, and are, consequently, neither true nor false.

ARISTOTLE (PH 4) already noted that 'every sentence is not a proposition; only such are propositions as have in them either truth or falsity. Thus a prayer is a sentence, but is neither true nor false.' Problems related to the ontological and truth-functional status of future events and the grammatical future were also discussed in Greek philosophy, which may or may not have influenced Indian philosophy in this point.[274] In *De Interpretatione* (PH), ARISTOTLE offers the following solution to a paradox posed by Diodoros Cronus as to the truth-value of the sentence 'Will there be a sea battle tomorrow?' Any definite answer ('yes' or 'no') to this indecidable question is presently neither true nor false, but if in future one becomes true, then the other becomes false:

> 'One of the two propositions in such instances must be true and the other false, but we cannot say determinately that this or that is false, but must leave the alternative undecided. One may indeed be more likely to be true than the other, but it cannot be either actually true or actually false. It is therefore plain that it is not necessary that of an affirmation and a denial one should be true and the other false. For in the case of that which exists potentially, but not actually, the rule which applies to that which exists actually does not hold good' (PH 9).

For Aristotle, as for the Jains, it is both unethical and factually wrong to assume the future is determined, since actions evidently influence events. Although it is not entirely clear what exactly Aristotle and the Jain author(s) had in mind, in both cases the commitment to free will and to the logic of events overrules the logic of

---

[273] Ṭhāṇ 6.111 lists six types of question-contexts, not all of which can be categorised as neither-true-nor-false; e.g. *vuggaha-paṭṭha* <*vyudgraha-praśna*>, questioning an opponent.

[274] On ambiguities created by the use of the future tense see also FAUCONNIER (1981: 180 f.), and others.

propositions. Generally, empirical facts can neither be proven true nor false by logical necessity: 'Even if I say "It's raining now" when the sun is shining, I have not said something that is n e c e s s a r i l y false, just something that happens to be false' (HARNAD (1999: 1)).[275] From a purely logical point of view, Bertrand RUSSELL (1905) showed that all predicates with variables are not propositions to which a truth value can be attached in an unambiguous way. Hence they are neither true nor false. However, they can be transformed into propositions by replacing the variable with a value or a quantifier.[276] It is, of course, difficult to say to what extent ancient Jain philosophers already shared certain intuitions with modern logicians.

The first seven categories, sometimes combined, cover most speech acts a Jain ascetic would conventionally use in contexts of monastic life; for instance taking vows (*paccakkhāṇa*), requesting permission (*āpucchaṇā*), ordering (*ājñā*), confessing (*ālocanā*), begging forgiveness (*kṣamāpaṇā*) etc. *Āmantaṇī* <*āmantraṇī*> speech or language, for instance, is 'used for attracting somebody's attention, a vocative word or expression' (GHATAGE (2003 III.2: 1001)), for instance 'O Devadatta'.[277] MĀLVAṆIYĀ (1971: 325) gives the following examples of an address and an order: 'when a person wanting John to come near him says "O! John"' or 'when a person says to another person, "Go ahead".' However, not in all contexts are such expressions neither-true-nor-false. Under certain circumstances, the first example may represent or can be read as an 'indirect' or 'implicit performative' speech act clad in form of an address, and it could be argued that, in certain contexts, the second example does not correspond to the prescription in Āyār 2.4 for mendicants to avoid pragmatic interventions.

The last five terms of the list are of a different nature. The term *aṇabhiggahiyā* <*anabhigṛhītā*> refers to 'unintelligible or incomprehensible speech' (RATNACANDRA (1988 I: 156)), which is either 'irrelevant' (DELEU (1970: 169)) or/and 'unacceptable' (GHATAGE (1996 I: 237)), but neither-true-nor-false. Its antonym, *abhiggahammi boddhavvā*, intelligible instruction, refers to 'clear and intelligible

[275] HAACK (1974: 58 f., 73–90) criticises the 'modal fallacy' in Aristotle's argument on future contingents, but accepts it as valid if interpreted as a truth value gap theory.

[276] See further STRAWSON (1950) and the ensuing debate, on which see also HORN (1985), (2001: 362 ff.), and others.

[277] PaṇṇU 82 f.: "*āmantaṇī*" *ity-ādi, he deva iti āmantaṇī, eṣā kilâpravarttaka-nivarttakatvāt satyâdi bhāṣā-traya-lakṣaṇa-viyogataś câsatyâmṛṣêti, evaṁ sva-buddhayā anyatrâpi bhāvanā kāryêti, kajje parassa pavattaṇaṁ jahā imaṁ karehitti āṇavaṇī, katthai vatthu-visesassa dehitti maggaṇaṁ jāyaṇī, aviṇṇāyassa saṁdiddhassa vā atthassa jāṇaṇatthaṁ tad-abhijutta-codaṇaṁ pucchaṇī, viṇīyassa uvaeso jahā—pāṇavahāu ṇiyattā havati dīhâuyā arogā ya emādi paṇṇavaṇī paṇṇattā vīyarāgehiṁ*. PaṇṇṬ$_1$ 258b: "*āmantaṇī*" *iti tatra āmantraṇī he devadatta ity-ādi, eṣā hi prāg-ukta-satyâdi-bhāṣā-traya-lakṣaṇa-vikalatvān na satyā nâpi mṛṣā nâpi satyā-mṛṣā kevalaṁ vyavahāra-mātra-pravṛtti-hetur ity asatyā-mṛṣā*.

language' (RATNACANDRA (1988 IV: 351)), which is 'relevant' and 'acceptable', and neither-true-nor-false.[278] Malayagiri's commentary explains the difference between irrelevant and relevant speech through the following example: 'to the question "What shall I do now?" the answer "Do as you like" is *aṇabhiggahiyā*, the answer "Do this, do not that!" is *abhiggahiyā*' (DELEU (1970: 169)).[279]

It is not entirely clear why *saṁsaya-karaṇī bhāsā* <*saṁśaya-karaṇī bhāṣā*>, 'ambiguous language which causes doubt' (RATNACANDRA (1988 IV: 570)), is regarded as neither-true-nor-false, and therefore permissible. It must be assumed that only the use of strategically ambiguous messages for the purpose of creating *vairāgya*-shocks is seen as legitimate, but not language which creates doubt about Jainism in the minds of believers. He seems to follow Malayagiri (PaṇṇṬ), who argued that from the *niścaya-naya* not only *satya-mṛṣā* but also *asatyā-mṛṣā* statements are false—'if they are spoken with the intention of deceiving others'(MĀLVAṆIYĀ (1971: 346)). However, Viy 18.7.1 (749a) states that, by definition, the speech of a Kevalin, because it is harmless, can only be true or neither-true-nor-false.[280] The statement associates higher moral truth with this type of speech, which can thus be compared with the 'twilight-language' (*sandhā-bhāṣā*) of Tantric Buddhism, which is also characterised as neither-true-nor-false.[281] According to OKUDA (1975: 129), MĀc 119 explains *saṁsaya-vayaṇī* <*saṁśaya-vacana*> as 'speech which expresses doubt'. But its commentator Vasunandin (11th–12th century) interprets this as 'speech of children and old people' as well as the sounds of (five-sensed) 'roaring buffalos' etc., which cause doubt as to their meaning, while the Digambara authors Aparājita and Āśādhara and the Śvetâmbara Haribhadra commenting on DVS 7, read *saṁsaya-karaṇī* simply as 'ambiguous speech' (*anekârtha-sādhāraṇā*). Haribhadra classifies speech of children as *aṇakkhara* <*anakṣara*>, incomprehensible, which also figures as the ninth and last category listed in MĀc

[278] PaṇṇṬ$_1$ 259a: *abhigṛhītā prati-niyatârthâvadhāraṇaṁ, yathā idam idānīṁ karttavyam idaṁ nêti.*

[279] PaṇṇṬ$_1$ 259a: *anabhigrahā yatra na pratiniyatârthâvadhāraṇaṁ, yathā bahukâryeṣv avasthiteṣu kaścit kañcana pṛcchati—kim idānīṁ karomi?, sa prāha—yat pratibhāsate tat kurv iti.* See SPERBER–WILSON's (1986) arguments for considering 'relevance' as the key to communication and cognition.

[280] DELEU (1970: 241).

[281] Jambūvijaya's edition of the Ṭhāṇ 4.23 (238) contains the following commentary of Jinabhadra's *Viśeṣâvaśyaka-bhāṣā* (VĀBh) 376–7: *aṇahigaya jā tīsu vi saddo cciya kevalo asacca-musa.*

119, which Vasunandin reserves for expressions of animals of two-four senses, and for sounds created by snipping fingers etc. (OKUDA (1975: 129)).[282]

Vyākr̥tā bhāṣā refers to clear distinct speech with explicit unambiguous meaning (RATNACANDRA (1988 IV: 511)).[283] There is no example given by the commentaries for distinct speech which is neither-true-nor-untrue. *Avyākr̥tā-bhāṣā*>, refers to indistinct involuted or poetic speech consisting of obscure or unintelligible words 'with deep and profound meaning' (RATNACANDRA (1988 IV: 445), cf. GHATAGE (2001 II: 800)).[284] *Mantra*s or *sūtra*s may be fitting examples. The fact that the *Mūlâcāra* does not mention these two categories reinforces the suspicion that they are redundant, and overlapping with the category of incomprehensible language.

The most interesting case is *pannavaṇī-bhāsā* <*prajñāpanī-bhāṣā*>, explanation, the generic term which Mahāvīra himself employs in the scriptures[285] to designate his discourse, which also gives the *Pannavaṇā-suttaṁ* its name. Like all descriptions of speech acts, *pannavaṇī* is a somewhat ambiguous term, because it refers both to the illocutionary act, locutionary content, and perlocutionary effect of proclaiming something. This ambiguity is reflected in different translations of the word. SCHUBRING (2000: 158, § 69) and DELEU (1970: 169) translate *pannavaṇī* as 'communication' (*Mitteilung*). According to SCHUBRING (2000: 157 f., § 69), the examples for 'communication' given in Viy 10.3.3 (499b) = Paṇṇ 866, 'We want to [*wollen*] lie down' (*āsaissāmo*) etc., refer to 'expressions of an intention' (to do something). However, DELEU (1970: 169) and LALWANI (1985: 133) translate *āsaissāmo* <*āśayiṣyāmaḥ*> as 'we will lie down' and 'we shall lie down' respec-

[282] PaṇṇṬ$_1$ 259a: *saṁśaya-karaṇī yā vāk anekârthâbhidhāyitayā parasya saṁśayam utpādayati, yathā saindhavamānīyatām ity atra saindhava-śabdo lavaṇa-vastra-puruṣavājiṣu*. SCHUBRING (2000: 157 f., § 74): 'All animals with two to four senses and beings with five senses express themselves in the neither true nor wrong way, but the latter will employ the first three modes just as well (Pannav. 260a) provided they have learnt to do so or carry along with them a higher ability.'

[283] PaṇṇṬ$_1$ 259a: *vyākr̥tā yā prakaṭârthā*.

[284] PaṇṇṬ$_1$ 259a: *avyākr̥tā atigambhīra-śabdârthā avyaktâkṣara-prayuktā vā avibhāvitârthātvāt*.

[285] The Pāli equivalents of *pannavaṇā* and *pannatta* are *paññāpana*, *paññatta* (MĀLVAṆIYĀ (1971: 212)). The word *pannatti* <*prajñapti*>, teaching, information, instruction, is frequently used in the canon, for instance at Viy 2.1.90, or Viy 16.6 (709b) where the verbs *pannaveti parūveti* <*prajñāpayati prarūpayati*> are used in to describe Mahāvīra's preaching activity. Hence, his teachings are called *pannavaṇā* <*prajñāpana*>, exposition, or *parūvaṇa* <*prarūpana*>, explanation (AṇD 51, MĀLVAṆIYĀ (1971: 210)). The 'proclamations' (*Kundmachung*) or preachings of the unattached ones are also called *niggantha pāvayaṇa*/ *pavayaṇa* <*nirgrantha pravacana*> in Viy 2.5.5 (134b), 20.8.5 (792b) and Ṭhāṇ 176a. See SCHUBRING (2000: 73, § 37).

tively, that is, as the description of a future action or state.[286] MĀLVAṆIYĀ (1971: 211), who points to kindred views in the Pāli text *Puggala-paññatti*, prefers the word 'describing' as a translation of *pannavaṇī* which he renders as 'speech that intends to describe a thing'. In this, he follows the 13th century commentary of Ācārya Malayagiri who stated that *pannavaṇī* 'means the speech that intends to describe the thing (or event) [as it is]'.[287] It is a form of *asaccā-mosā* speech, 'a speech which has nothing to do with norm (validity or invalidity) but which only describes the thing (or event)': 'To be more explicit, the speech which has nothing to do with religious dos and do-nots but which simply describes the thing is called *Prajñāpanī*.'[288] MĀLVAṆIYĀ (1971: 212) cites the example quoted by the commentator Malayagiri's *Prajñāpanā-ṭīkā*, 'Those who refrain from killing living beings live long and enjoy good health (in the next birth)',[289] and notes: 'The *gāthā* in point contains no command "do not kill" but simply describes the fact that those who do not kill live long and remain healthy.' Such speech 'has nothing to do with religious dos and do-nots' (MĀLVAṆIYĀ (1971: 211)). Hence, it should be distinguished from implicit performative speech. But, of course, it may be interpreted as such by a listener who infers an 'ought' from the 'is'. MONIER-WILLIAMS' (1986: 659) *Sanskrit-English Dictionary* translates the causative *prajñāpana* as 'statement, assertion'.

---

[286] DELEU (1970: 169) writes: '*āsaissāmo* is *āśayiṣyāmaḥ*, not, as Abhay. says, *āśrayiṣyāmaḥ*.' According to the rules of speech in Āyār 2.4.1.5 and DVS 7.8–10 one should avoid such a statement if one cannot be entirely sure.

[287] PaṇṇṬ 249b: *yathâvasthitârthâbhidhānād iyaṁ prajñāpanī*, in MĀLVAṆIYĀ (1971: 211, cf. 346).

[288] Contrary to MĀLVAṆIYĀ's (1971: 211) view that *asatya-mṛṣā* speech 'has nothing to do with norm' it is obvious that by referring to situations that ought to be both imperatives, commissives (vows), and declaratives imply normative conditions, even if used by an enlightened being. Only assertives attempt to represent situations as they are. Searle showed that from the hearer's perspective even literal speech implies a contextual horizon to be intelligible (HABERMAS (1980: 452) / (1984–1987 I: 337)). According to Paṇṇ 246b, *asatyā-mṛṣā* speech signifies not only *ohāraṇī* <*avadhāraṇī*> or determinative expressions such as 'I believe' or 'I think', but all attempts to communicate transcendental truth through descriptive (*prajñāpanī*) speech, which is assumed to be context-free and thus by definition neither-true-nor-false (*satyā-mṛṣā*). The Paṇṇ accounts for the use of certain classificatory terms and words which express universals (e.g. masculine, feminine, neuter) without clearly specifying their contextual range of meaning. Imperatives such as 'go ahead' belong to this category too. For instance, we may 'order a person of any gender and this person may or may not carry out orders. … This *ajñāpanī* (imperative) speech too could not be held as false. It should be regarded as a case of *prajñāpanī* speech' (MĀLVAṆIYĀ (1971: 326)).

[289] PaṇṇṬ$_1$ 249b:

pāṇivahāu niyattā havaṁti dīhâuyā arogā ya /
emāī paṇṇattā paṇṇavaṇī vīyarāgehiṁ //

LALWANI (1985 IV: 133) apparently follows the *Illustrated Ardhamāgadhī Dictionary* of RATNACANDRA (1988 III: 443), based on Malayagiri, in using the word 'advice' (*upadeśa*).[290] What is probably meant by the term *pannavaṇī* is that from the conventional point if view, which underlies the Jain '*catuṣ-koṭi*' of language usage, the testimony of an authoritative person is neither true nor untrue, because its meaning may be incomprehensible for a hearer, similarly to unintelligible utterances of non-enlightened creatures. With imperatives and addresses expressing universal truths or ideals has in common that no referent exists *in re* at a given place and point of time (as for instance in Malayagiri's example which should not be read as a prediction relating to a specific individual). The multidimensional implications of a general statement or rule such as this cannot be understood entirely in an instant, as WITTGENSTEIN (1953: 53–55, § 138–40) noted in his remarks on the relation between meaning and use of a word (WITTGENSTEIN (1953: 190 ff., § 138 f.)). Moreover, the example given by the commentaries concerning the necessary link between non-violence and health cannot be proved or disproved from a conventional perspective. It must be accepted on the basis of the authority of the speaker. Interestingly enough, the two truth theory is not invoked by the commentaries in defence of the concept of transcendental speech, being neither-true-nor-false, in spite of its capability to immunise any statement against criticism.[291]

Paṇṇ 832–857 gives another example for speech which is neither-true-nor-false by discussing the question of the 'congruity of grammatical and natural gender and number' (SCHUBRING (2000: 158, § 74)). It argues that words such as *go*, cow, which express (genderless) universals but are employed in masculine singular, are not false or both-true-and-false, say, with regard to female cows, but neither-true-nor-false. The same applies to imperatives (*ājñāpanī*), since 'we may order a person of any gender and this person may or may not carry out our orders' (MĀLVAṆIYĀ (1971: 326)).[292]

The last of the four variants of *ohāraṇī-bhāsā* <*avadhāraṇī-bhāṣā*>, or determinate speech, is another example of speech which is neither-true-nor-false. Reflexive

[290] Uttar 28.16 ff. lists amongst the ten sources of right insight (*samyag-darśana*) communications such as *upadeśa*, instruction, *ājñā*, command, *bīja*, seed (suggestion), as well as *abhigama*, comprehension of the sacred scriptures, and *vistāra*, complete course of study (including proofs, *pramāṇa*, and perspectives, *naya*): *nisagguvaesa-ruī, āṇā-ruī sutta-bīya-rui-meva / abhigama-vitthāra-ruī, kiriyā-saṁkheva-dhamma-ruī //* .

[291] Cf. MURTI (1955: 129) on transcendental language which expresses truth which is beyond language; and GANERI (2002: 271) on the non-assertible (inexpressible) in classical Jain seven-valued logic (*sapta-bhaṅgī*), which may be conceptually related to incomprehensible speech.

[292] This example could be interpreted as an early version of the 'misleading form thesis' addressed by RUSSELL (1905) and others. See HAACK (1974: 53–55). By contrast, the example 'Devadatta, give me the cow', mentioned by GLASENAPP (1915: 46), is neither-true-nor-untrue as a simple performative.

expressions such as 'I believe' or 'I think' are said to be capable of expressing any of the four modes of speech, depending on whether they serve religion (*ārāhiya* <*ārādhita*>), in which case they are true by definition, harm religion (*virāhiya* <*virādhita*>), in which case they are false, both serve and harm religion, in which case they are true-as-well-as-false, or whether they do neither, in which case they are neither-true-nor-false (Paṇṇ 830–831 [246b]).[293]

The examples show that in the Jain philosophy of speech pragmatic efficacy, that is, non-violence, supersedes propositional truth:[294]

> 'It goes with the sphere of *ethics* that all four modes of speech, and consequently the mode of wrong speech as well, are admitted, provided they are employed in a pious way of mind (*āuttaṁ* =*samyak*), while even true speech coming from a sinner's mouth will count for nothing (Pannav. 268a)' (SCHUBRING (2000: 158, § 74).

Conversely, as mentioned before, 'a mode of speech springing from emotion is by itself understood as *mosā*' (SCHUBRING (2000: 157, § 74)). In other words, the speaker's beliefs, attitudes or intentions (if not his/her *Being*), and the specific pragmatic context is decisive, not the words themselves, or the propositional meaning. Arguments relating to the 'higher truth' of morality based on similar considerations. HANDIQUI (1968: 266) notes that the 10th century Digambara *ācārya* Somadeva is more concerned with ethics than with propositional truth:

> 'Somadeva appears in certain circumstances to attach greater importance to self-preservation and philanthropic considerations than to speaking the truth. He opines that the truth must not be spoken if it is likely to endanger others and bring inevitable ruin to oneself.'

Another example of this attitude is given by the Śvetâmbara Ācārya Hemacandra who, in his 12th century *Yoga-śāstra* (YŚ 2.61) and self-commentary, narrates that the sage Kauśika, who was famous for speaking the truth, 'went to hell because accurate information given by him led to the capture and killing of a band of robbers' (cited by HANDIQUI (1968: 266 n. 4)):

> 'On the other hand (*api*), even though a statement may be true, it should not be spoken if it causes affliction to others [This is] because,

[293] Cf. SCHUBRING (2000: 158, § 74), MĀLVAṆIYĀ (1971: 325 f.)).

[294] Cf. CAILLAT (1975: 80), QVARNSTRÖM (2002: 41 n. 4).

even if it is accepted [by all the people] in the world, Kauśika was sent to hell [on account of making such a statement]' (YŚ 2.61).[295]

The explanations of the four modes of speech in canonical Jain literature and its medieval Sanskrit commentaries show that they are conceived as meta-rules, on a level of abstraction comparable to the discourse ethics of universal pragmatics, while the sub-categories and examples correspond to the level of empirical semantics and pragmatics. The levels of abstraction of the lists of examples in the commentaries vary, since the Jain lists are relatively unsystematic, although some may have been intended as scholastic devices for cumulative indexication *qua* fixed analytical perspectives. From the point of view of comparative analytical philosophy, some examples could serve as illustrations for one or other of the conversational postulates *à la* Grice ('be relevant' etc.), Searle, or Habermas, while others can be related to the modern logical investigations of vagueness, category mistakes, quantifiers, or modalities of time in particular. In contrast to modern intentionalist semantics, Jain philosophers of language analyse examples of fundamental types of speech rarely with reference to the intention of the speaker, but prefer an objective or listener's standpoint. That is, they investigate the structure of the utterance as a whole, from the de-contextualised point of view of the four combinations of the basic true/false distinction, seen from the perspective of discourse ethics. The same perspective is preferred by universal pragmatics.

We can conclude from this brief discussion of the explanations of the four modes of speech in the Śvetâmbara canon and commentaries that the rules of Jain discourse are less concerned with referential truth than with the pragmatics of speech;[296] in particular with the expression of the 'higher truth' of religious insight gained through direct self-experience, and speaking in accordance with the ethics of non-violence. Yet, it would be a mistake to assume that truth in Jain discourse is always defined as an aspect of objective illocutionary force, depending on the form of the utterance and the intentional state of a speaker alone, without the need to be backed up by argument in processes of critical inquiry. The primacy of pragmatic ethical and moral considerations, considered from a monological perspective, makes the Jain theory of speech in many ways akin to Habermas' theory of communicative action. The analysis of the implications of the Jain maxim of truth for language usage show that it combines as it were the validity claims two, three and four:

[295] For discussion of the ethical implications of this dilemma, for instance in terms of appropriateness, see for instance GERT (1973), HARE (1981), WELLMER (1986: 26 ff.), and HABERMAS (1991: 170).

[296] GANERI (2002: 277) shows that the *sapta-bhaṅgī* is also 'not strictly truth-functional', but suggests a solution to this problem.

propositional truth, normative rightness, and expressive truthfulness. Despite the primacy of non-violence and sincerity of expression, there are numerous examples for rules concerning referential truth, the ideal of univocal or straight (*ṛju*) speech, and the avoidance of deception, especially Āyār 2.4.1.1, Āyār 2.4.2.19, and DVS 8.46.[297] Such rules of avoidance of false representations (including false references

[297] Interestingly, some *śloka*s are similar to the last of Grice's quality maxims: 'Do not say that for which you lack adequate evidence', which invokes questions of referential truth and of the relationship between representational and expressive functions of language. The definition of the concept truth and falsehood, or of aspects thereof, is a notoriously difficult problem for modern science and philosophy, whose discourse is constituted by this fundamental distinction according to FOUCAULT (1981) and LUHMANN (1990). It is therefore interesting to see how the Jains tackle this issue, which is one of their foremost concerns. There is a note by LALWANI added to DVS_2 4.12 which identifies three types of falsehood: '(i) to deny what is, (ii) to establish what is not, and (iii) to alter the meaning'. They can be illustrated by the following examples:

(i) Jains are epistemic realists. Hence, it is not surprising that there are explicit statements defending the ideal of objective truth in the scriptures, as opposed to mere appearance, opinion, or consensus. The following passage stresses the necessity for ascetics to use their faculty of judgement to discover the truth of a given phenomenon, and not to be deceived by false appearances: 'Employing their judgment, they should know something for certain and something for uncertain: (1) Having received food or not having received food, having eaten it or not having eaten it, has come or has not come, comes or does not come, will come or will nor come' (Āyār 2.4.1.1–2). This orientation toward the world, predicated on a realistic analysis of the modalities of time, is diametrically opposed to Brāhmaṇism and Vedântic concepts such as *māyā* etc. This is evident in the following passage, which implicitly criticises the confusion of natural phenomena with illusory imagery of divine agency: 'A monk should not say: "The god of the sky! the god of the thunderstorm! the god of lightning! the god who begins to rain! the god who ceases to rain! may rain fall or may it not fall! may the crops grow or may they not grow! may the night wane or may it not wane! may the sun rise or may it not rise! may the king conquer or may he not conquer!" They should not use such speech. … But knowing the nature of things, he should say: "the air; the follower of Guhya; a cloud has gathered or come down; the cloud has rained"' (Āyār 2.4.1.12–13).

(ii) False appearance and deception should be avoided by all means: 'A *muni* speaks of appearance, ignoring the truth, encounters a sin. Then what to speak of one who indulges in whole untruth [Note by LALWANI: When a woman is dressed as a man and if she be called a man, it is a falsehood, though in her dress she appears like a man …].' (DVS_2 7.5, cf. Āyār 2.4.1.3). Ways of 'establishing what is not', such as vague promises and speculation, are also seen indiscriminate or deceptive utterances, because of the confusion of past, present, and future. Language which may create doubt ('maybe or not') has to be avoided by all means: 'When one knows not true implication, in the context of the present, past, and future, says not one, "surely it's like this". When one is in doubt about implication, in the context of the present, past and future, says not one, "surely it's like this". "Surely it's so",—says one when one has not an iota of doubt of implication about the present, the past and future' (DVS_2 7.8–10, cf. DVS_2 7.6–7, Āyār 2.4.1.5). It is remarkable, that early Jainism already insists on the correct use of temporal modalities, which must be related to

to past, present and future) and non-deceptive speech etc., can be understood as expressions of a pragmatic anti-illusionist (anti-Brāhmaṇic) realism, that is, as anti-deception strategies. From the perspective of politeness theory, one could add that the underlying cognitive realism does not only serve as a strategy of self-protection, as WILLIAMS (1983: xix) argues, but also to calculate the karmic consequences of speech acts, and functional demands on social inferiors, who (have to) read and fulfil the pragmatic implications of intentionally ambiguous statements of social superiors.

Relation

The Gricean maxim of relation, concerning the relevance of a statement, is generally determined by the 'purpose of the talk exchange' as already stressed by the co-operative principle, of which it is but a mode[298] (and therefore absent in Habermas' scheme).[299] The principle of relevance is vital for the selection of appropriate contextual references of both utterances and standpoints of interpretation. In religious discourses, the implicit limitations inscribed in the semantic structure of the ideological system, enforced by a system of related institutional and social sanctions, play an important role in the discrimination of relevant contextual references.[300]

the philosophy of transmigration, but also with the critique of the Brāhmaṇic sacred-word theory: 'speech exists only the moment when being spoken' (SCHUBRING (2000: 149, § 68). The practical value of all the cited examples is the same: reducing illusory appearances to their 'real' content.

(iii) There are no further maxims concerning 'changing the meaning' in the texts on the ways of speaking. Effectively, however, Jain narrative literature is based on a method of 'changing the meaning' of Indian folklore (HERTEL (1922)). The combined systematicity and context-sensitivity of Jain rules and regulations is particularly obvious in the following statement of the Digambara author Vasunandin's (1100 CE) *Śrāvakâcāra* 209, which propagates not only the 'abstention from untruth spoken out of passion or hate' but 'from truth too, if it provokes the destruction of a living being' (cited in WILLIAMS (1983: 78)). This and similar examples illustrate how the hierarchically superior principle of *ahiṁsā* supersedes the maxim of truthfulness in cases of rule-contradiction. Cf. MĀLVAṆIYĀ (1971: 325) on the role of the (situational) conditions of truthfulness in the *Pannavaṇā*.

[298] Amṛtacandra's commentary on the *Samaya-sāra* (*supra* p. 147) states this implication openly. Similar references can be found with regard to public debates at the royal court etc. Cf. ĀyārD 4.2.

[299] HABERMAS (1980: 418) / (1984 I: 312) remarks that it is hard to establish the universality of this maxim.

[300] Śrīmad Rājacandra's rules of speech recommend avoiding controversial religious themes: '1. While you are talking of one thing, you may not, unless it is absolutely unavoidable, bring in another thing. 2. Listen attentively to what the other is saying. 3. You should answer it patiently and with a sense or propriety. 4. Only such words be uttered as do not involve you either in self-praise or self-abasement. 5. For the time being, the less you talk of religion the better. 6. Do not involve yourself with others on issues pertaining to religion" (in MEHTA (1991: 72)).

I have argued elsewhere,[301] that the ethical 'code' of *ahiṁsā/ hiṁsā* forces limitations and therefore an attitude of reflective distance onto those individuals who observe themselves self-referentially with the help of this semantic differential. Cognitive distance, in turn, generates the potential of a selective, discriminating relationship towards the world, i.e. it allows for choice, by presupposing the perceptibility of potentialities, the modalisation of perception, which—as we have seen—is generated through the practices of meditative introversion and perspective alteration.

In other words, the ways in which contextually relevant references are selected are negatively determined, and channelled, by Jain values and rules, given that they *de facto* orientate practice. Through its in-built directionality, the dominant ethical code of Jainism (*ahiṁsā/ hiṁsā*) regulates pragmatic choices in everyday life, to the extent of the religious commitment and power of judgement of the user. Conversely, any semantically coded generalised strategy of selective choice implies corresponding processes of exclusion of non-relevant references, which form the complementary horizon of the unsaid and the unspeakable of legitimate religious experience. The discriminative functions of implied references to background knowledge and pragmatic conditions of fulfilment of religious claims, can be socially exploited through the off-record strategies of 'presupposition, hint, give associative clues' etc., which are associated with the Gricean maxim of relation. Precisely these qualities are associated with the proverbial South Asian ability both to tolerate and to ignore, which HACKER (1985) called 'inclusivism'.

Manner

The last maxim is explicitly concerned with the phenomenon of intentional multivocal speech, stressing the necessity of grammatically correct and unambiguous speech. The correlates of this maxim are held in great esteem by the Jains. The Āyār refers several times to the necessity of using clear language:

> 'Well considering (what one is to say), speaking with precision, one should employ language in moderation and restraint: the singular, dual, plural; feminine, masculine, neuter gender; praise, blame, praise mixed with blame, blame mixed with praise; past, present, or future (tenses), the first and second, or third person' (Āyār 2.4.1.3).[302]

Not only referential truth, relevance, and the syntactically correct use of words is discussed in such contexts (cf. DVS 8.49), but also the orientation towards the intended effect of (religious) speech on the hearer. That is, not to create doubt, and

[301] FLÜGEL (1993), (1995–6: 163–5) *pace* JAINI (1979: 312).

[302] Cf. Āyār 2.4.1.7, 2.4.2.19. See also Ṭhāṇ 10.96 etc.

lack of clarity (DVS 7.4). Manner can be interpreted as a combination of the validity claims of truth and sincerity with the condition of grammatical comprehensibility. Such features are usually considered in conjunction with other aspects of ideal speech acts, such as key, tone, spirit or style.[303] Grammar is not singled out in the Jain equivalent of the manner-maxim and privileged over other aspects of communicative competence, as it is in modern linguistics, but presented together with other rules of use, such as stylistic rules of performance.

Jain ascetic rules of manner directly address the problem of implicit meaning, and the necessity to avoid the (manner related) off-record politeness strategies of 'vagueness, ambiguity, over generalization, or incompleteness' (BROWN–LEVINSON (1978: 230 f.)). The clauses stating that both politeness (Āyār 2.4.2.3–6) and speech which might harm (Āyār 2.4.2.1–2) is to be avoided at all costs, however, forces the exclusion of a wide range of topics onto the performer of 'pure speech'. This is what makes Jain doctrinal texts often so dry—most of the 'juicy bits' are 'potentialised', left out, remain unsaid, although they are implicitly presupposed. In fact this is the area, where the 'rhetoric' of silence is, as it were, forced upon the Jain ascetic, who has to select words carefully, in order to steer between the need to communicate with the world and the obligation to observe the principles of *satya* and *ahiṁsā*.

To briefly summarise the results of the comparison between the Jain rules of speech with Habermas' validity claims and the Gricean postulates, it is apparent that for all of the universal pragmatic principles and conversational postulates there are functional equivalences amongst the Jain principles and rules of speech, which are by no means 'primitive' and 'ill-assorted', as for instance the philologist SCHUBRING (2000: 157, § 74) believed. Jain principles and rules of discourse are not mere examples of a culture-specific 'particularistic ethics', as LAIDLAW (1995: 14) argues, but form a 'comparatively systematic code which is well-grounded in objective considerations' (CAILLAT (1991: 14)).[304] The Gricean maxims and the Jain rules of speech are similar, though not identical. The norms of unequivocal and grammatically correct signification and transmission of information are fundamental for the Jain understanding of proper language use, but not sufficient for an understanding of its primarily ethical concerns, which overlap with Habermas' theory of communicative action. The Jain texts deliberately avoid defining certain words as 'sacred'. However, for Jainism, too, 'correct speech is of religious value' (CAILLAT (1984: 71)) in so far as the foremost

[303] Cf. HYMES (1972b: 62).

[304] For an early universalistic ethical statement see the 'very difficult passage' JACOBI (1884: 31 n. 4) Āyār 1.3.3.1 equating self and world: *saṁdhiṁ logassa jāṇittā. āyao bahiyā pāsa. tamhā ṇa haṁtā ṇa vighāyae.* All beings intend to live. Knowing the intention, one should not be non-vigilant. Consider all other beings as thyself. Therefore, you should not kill them yourself, nor get them killed by others (ĀyārBh 3.51, p. 214).

requirement for the realisation of Jain norms is restraint (negative politeness) in mind, speech and action. The religious ideal of correct, truthful and non-violent manner of speech is summarised in the following passage, already quoted above:

> 'A monk or nun, putting aside wrath, pride, deceit, and greed, considering well, speaking with precision, what one has heard, not too quick, with discrimination, should employ language in moderation and restraint' (Āyār 2.4.2.19).[305]

What is manifest in this statement is that the Jain maxims themselves address the necessity of avoiding the violence and the consequential *karmic* results of 'flouting' the rules of proper speech by means of off-record strategies. At the same time, negative politeness (especially conventional indirectness) is regarded as mandatory for maintaining the vows of non-violence and truth in language usage. A different matter altogether is the 'salvific' use of off-record strategies in contexts of religious instruction which will be discussed below.

(Ad 3) In addition to the general principles and maxims of proper speech discussed thus far, much space of the language related sections in the Āyār and DSV is devoted to experience-near examples and practical rules for selection of what to say and what not to say in accordance with the *satya-vrata*. These regulations do not have the status of general principles or maxims, but are derivatives of the latter, and provide generalised examples or schemata for the interpretation of certain types of situation. Generally single utterances and types of speech-acts (strategies) are discussed in the manner of modern analytical philosophy, often focusing on negative examples (*asatya*). The respective passages are almost identical in both key texts (Āyār 2.4.2.7–16 = DVS 7.22–35). They can be summarised as follows: First and foremost, one should avoid interventions in worldly affairs, particularly those involving value-judgements, taking sides, practical advice, or demands. Recommended speech-strategies are usually forms of negative politeness, such as conventional indirectness, impersonalisation or nominalisation.[306] Impersonalisation by way of transforming directives and commissives

[305] Conversely: '[1.] The monks and nuns may not use the following six forbidden forms of speech: lying, sneering, insult, coarse speaking, worldly speech, or speech renewing atoned matters. 2. There are six cases of idle talk about right conduct: of speaking rashly in relation to others, of damaging living creatures, of untruthfulness, of forbidden appropriation, of a jade, a eunuch, or a slave. Whoever uses those six kinds of idle talk, without being able to prove them fully, ranks as one who has committed the transgression himself' (KS 6.1).

[306] Cf. BROWN–LEVINSON (1978: 134 ff.). In PaṇṇṬ folio 259 B cited by MĀLVAṆIYĀ (1971: 212), and discussed earlier, the positive karmic consequences of not killing are expressed in this way; avoiding commandments of the form 'do not kill' for example by saying: 'Those who refrain from killing living beings live long and enjoy good health (in the next birth).'

into assertives, that is, a second-person performative perspective into a third-person observer's perspective, is the preferred method; evidently, because in this way 'illocutionary force switches over into the propositional content and thereby loses, if not its meaning, at least its force' (HABERMAS (1993: 27)).[307]

For instance, one should not say 'this should be done', but 'this is'. And one should not speak about forbidden subjects, such as business-choices etc., at all. One should not ask householders to do something, or 'forecast', or make promises to them (DVS_2 7.46 f.; 51). Another example of depersonalisation and nominalisation is the 'avoidance of harsh words'. That is, (false) accusations, abuse, and other varieties of face-threatening acts, such as speaking about the other's negative attributes (instead one should select positive ones, without being polite) (Āyār 2.4.2.1–11), or flattery, compulsive requests and rejection.[308] The most general strategy of nominalisation is not to mention anything which might lead to violent acts:

> 'In the same manner, a muni who is wise, Says not "This cow is fit for being milked", or "this ox is catigable" Or "capable of drawing a plough or carrying a load" Or "of drawing a chariot". (But if need be) Permissible is the following vocabulary: "This is a milch cow" "The ox is young" "The bull is thick or short" Or "this is worthy of a chariot"' (DVS_2 7.24–5).

By the same token, a mendicant is not to say 'this is the murderer' or 'this is a thief' if such a person enters the house in the night, because if s/he gives a warning, either the thief or s/he him/ herself might get killed, or 'the householder will suspect the ascetic ... to be the thief' (Āyār 2.2.2.4). The reverse strategy is applied to past acts of violence, as evident in the recommendation not to say 'well done' about an accomplished worldly task but always to stress the amount of unavoidable *karman*-producing violence employed (Āyār 2.4.2.3–6).[309] The second generally recommended strategy is thus to avoid references which might imply the potential for future acts of violence in both worlds,[310] and to condone past and present acts of violence, in order to stimulate

---

[307] See also AUSTIN (1962: 4) and BOURDIEU (1991a: 109) on disguising a performative utterance as a descriptive or constative statement. For somewhat different reasons, the counter-intuitive nominal style is also preferred by scientists and philosophers, as JACOBI (1903) has shown with regard to scientific Sanskrit.

[308] SCHUBRING (2000: 308 f., § 176).

[309] See WILLIAMS (1983: 71–8) for a discussion of the parallel rules of the *śrāvakâcāra*s.

[310] Umāsvāti's *Śrāvaka-prajñapti* (ŚrPr) 264 says: 'the aim of speech should be the intelligent pursuit of what is best for both worlds and the avoidance of what may cause hurt to others or to oneself or both'; and Kārttikeya defined *satya* as 'the avoidance of harmful, harsh, cruel, or secret speech and the use of balanced language that gives satisfaction to all living creatures and expresses the sacred truth' (in WILLIAMS (1983: 77 f.)).

acts of repentance. The latter is the only case of assertiveness which is explicitly demanded from an ascetic. In fact, a sermon is not considered to be *asatya* by Amṛtacandra (c. 11th CE) and other medieval writers, even if unpleasing (*apriya*) (PASU 91–101),[311] in accordance with the general principle that determinate (*avadhāraṇī*) speech which enhances religion is true by definition.[312] The determining factor in the Jain literature on speech, rather than the semantics of words, is the non-violent function of the utterance, not the intention of the speaker. Because this would amount to a general absolution for the religious uses of symbolic violence.

There is only a fine line between unnecessary and necessary violent speech, however, especially in the *satyā-mṛṣā* and *asatyā-mṛṣā* modes. The avoidance of transgression requires great analytic skill (which explains why only senior ascetics are permitted to conduct sermons). The statement quoted above, about the required proper knowledge of 'true implication in the context of past, present and future' (Āyār 2.4.1.5)[313] is relevant here. An ascetic must be able to discriminate temporal modalities so as to avoid and to repent acts of violence. The ability to distinguish between modalities of time is also the general condition of strategic manipulation, of one's individual purity, for instance, or of others, and of the self-realisation of the individual in the context of the hierarchical Brāhmaṇical system, where 'the temporal is intellectually subordinate to the spiritual and enclosed in it' (DUMONT (1980: 196)).[314] Temporal modalisation, in particular, enables a competent individual to apprehend or create unequivocal speech, and strategic ways of instrumentalising implicitly presupposed background knowledge.[315] By means of the ideal standards of on-recordness, and of non-violence, a competent Jain can discriminate truth and falseness, and right and wrong,[316] as well as explicit and implicit meaning, and its facets of false judgement, unclear speech, ambiguity of meaning, and deceptive purpose. The cultural specific conceptualisation of the ideal of clear, unambiguous

[311] Cf. WILLIAMS (1983: 78).

[312] MĀLVAṆIYĀ (1971: 325).

[313] Cf. DVS 7.8–10. See p. 179 ff.

[314] Cf. JAINI (1979: 139, 145–7). CAILLAT (1991: 13) dismisses the 'trival remarks' on temporal modalisation as unimportant. However, Jains generally do not consider the 'social functions' of speech acts, but only the *karmic*, 'individual functions'. Hemacandra's YŚ 2.53–64 describes the consequences of *asatya* as follows: 'A liar may have his tongue and an ear cut off, may be beaten and imprisoned, treated with contumely, and deprived of his possessions. In another incarnation he may be afflicted with dumbness, speech defects, and fetid breath' (WILLIAMS (1983: 78)).

[315] Cf. HABERMAS (1981: 400 ff.) / (1984 II: 267 ff.).

[316] Cf. HARE (1972).

speech generates also its opposite—an awareness of the implications of speech and the option to exploit them through lies, deception and intentional multivocality.[317]

Compliance with Jain rules of unequivocal, non-violent speech requires reflective monitoring of speech and conscious analysis of conditions of acceptability. The ability to discriminate between various modes of speech renders linguistic and social co-operation as problematic and therefore as manipulable. Rule-generated reflexivity also creates the cognitive potential for the strategic manipulation of social meanings, for instance through the intentional construction of multivocal statements (as it were an instrumentalisation of *anekânta-vāda* and *syād-vāda*). The doctrinally promoted distancing from the world, and the resulting apperception of the variability of perspectives and meanings, can be exploited in many ways—for salvific purposes or for personal gain. There are numerous instances of conscious flouting of (Jain) maxims, for both purposes, for instance in Jain narrative literature. What distinguishes religious and worldly usage of language is, from the point of view of Jain doctrine, only the effect, not the intention of the speaker, nor the words themselves. The speaker has to construct the message from the objective viewpoint of its potential violent/non violent function, not from a instrumental means-ends perspective. In practice it is difficult to decide which intention prevails—speaker's intention or systemic intention (SEYFORT RUEGG). The Jains, too, have no other means for judging sincerity of expression, or orientation towards objectivity, but previous conduct. One has to investigate speech acts in context in order to understand the selection and the specific strategic value of certain generalised pragmatic strategies derived from general cultural value-orientations, and recurring functional imperatives. The analysis of isolated types of speech-acts has generally proved to be less fruitful, because it only leads to the proliferation of examples.

(Ad 4) Jains have a keen interest in the actual functioning of their principles (of speech) in particular contexts of speech and of action. Therefore they have added not only meta-rules (concerning the actual observance of rules) but also contextual examples (*dṛṣṭānta* or *udāharaṇa*) and regulations for specific situations to the general principles, maxims, and generalised strategies or types of speech. And here, too, we can find the discussion of the role of social norms and institutionalised contexts of language usage, which force a certain direction of interpretation and execution of unsaid social intentions of the speaker upon the hearer. GUMPERZ (1995: 130 ff.) coined the term 'contextualisation conventions' to analyse processes of negotiation of implicit socio-cultural presuppositions of different 'activity types' defined by a purpose or goal. In the opening stages of any conversation, he observed,

[317] One may talk about the 'invention' of the symbolical: of the poetic and of rhetorics in this context.

'contextualisation cues' are exchanged to create a platform for co-operation by signalling contextually relevant presuppositions and preferences regarding norm selection. These relational signals 'are inherently ambiguous, i.e. subject to multiple interpretations', and may or may not be accepted:

> 'Conversational inference is thus not a matter of assigning truth values to instances of talk. An inference is adequate if it is (a) reasonable given the circumstances at hand, (b) confirmed by information conveyed at various levels of signalling, and (c) implicitly accepted in the course of conversational negotiation' (GUMPERZ (1995: 208)).

The rhetorical and practical significance of examples has been recognised in the Jain scriptures from early on. Examples function as arguments in intersubjective negotiations of situation definitions. Different types of examples are distinguished for instance in Ṭhāṇ 4.499–503. At the same time, the texts reflect the awareness that general principles and rules cannot be legitimised with reference to examples alone. Ṭhāṇ 4.499 and 10.95 point to the common fault (*āharaṇa-tad-dosa* <*āharaṇa-tad-doṣa*>) of using too many examples and quotes during a debate, and to faulty ways of relating example (*udḥaraṇa*) and rule, amongst other mistakes in the way of speaking.

From a monological observer's perspective, four paradigmatic contexts of pragmatic 'religious' speech discussed in Jain scriptures have been distinguished in this essay. They all concentrate on language usage of ascetics, as paradigms of Jain culture, and presuppose established co-operation: (a) religious debates at royal courts, (b) public sermons of leading ascetics, (c) informal communication of an ascetic with non-ascetics, and (d) communication between ascetics in the context of the monastic hierarchy. I dealt with the third case thus far, and already discussed the implications of narratives presented in public sermons elsewhere.[318] For the purpose of the argument of this essay, it will suffice to briefly examine cases of hierarchical monastic communication and of public debate to indicate the role of institutionalised normative expectations of reading and fulfilling the social implications of formal language usage.

The discursive context which is most relevant for ascetics in day to day life is the monastic hierarchy. It has three dimensions which sometimes, but not always, overlap: seniority (*dikkhā-pariyāya* <*dīkṣā-paryāya*>), *guru-sīsa* <*guru-śiṣya*> relationship, and the administrative hierarchy.[319] *Qua* rule, it is the duty of lower-standing ascetics to serve higher-standing ascetics (as it is the duty of the laity to serve the ascetics). Non-compliance with this norm is sanctioned by elaborated judicial procedures which might lead to excommunication. That is, the social norms

[318] FLÜGEL (1993). See also CARRITHERS (1992) on mind-reading.

[319] FLÜGEL (2006a: 324).

themselves tend to force an implicature upon the juniors, and restraint upon seniors (ideally: silence). I have shown elsewhere in greater detail that a junior mendicant is expected to read the implications of the speech and minute gestures and conversational clues of the *guru*, and obliged to serve him/her politely, that is, to perform *sevā*, as it is the duty of the householder to serve all mendicants.[320] Hence, Jain householders are called *uvāsaga*s <*upāsaka*s>, or servants of the *samaṇa*s <*śramaṇa*s>.[321] Pragmatic intentions and demands are never stated openly within the *śramaṇa-saṅgha*. But it is a general rule that juniors are supposed to read the implications of seniors and should try to fulfil their unstated wishes:

> 'Guessing the teachers thought and the purport of his words, one should express one's assent, and execute (what he desires to be done). An excellent pupil needs no express directions, or he is (at least) quickly directed; he always carries out his duties as he is told' (Uttar 1.43 f.).[322]

The way of interpreting the implications of every gesture of superiors and serving (*veyāvacca* <*vaiyāvṛttya*>) them in accordance with the rules (*vinaya*), is defined as a religious act of internal asceticism (*abbhantara tava* <*abhyantara-tapas*>).[323] Immersing oneself in the mind of a senior and reading his/her unstated wishes is an act of self-purification *qua* identification with an officially more advanced soul, taken as an external symbolic manifestation of one's own inner potential, just like a statue in a temple. At the same time, the prestige of seniors who 'get things done without ever saying so' is strengthened by this conventional procedure, which through use of implicit language also reproduces a sense of in-group membership.[324] This example is a good illustration of the general fact that multi-functional public roles imply unforced functional contributions from inferiors.[325] The observation also applies to the laity's duty to serve the ascetics. The asymmetrical relationship between mendicants and laity is conceptualised as a relationship between speakers and hearers—the laity are called both *uvāsaga*s <*upāsaka*s>, servants, and *sāvaga*s <*śrāvaka*s>, hearers. In both cases, as I have argued above, it is not a particular form of language usage, but the force of the norms and sanctions of the speech situation which direct the Jains of lower status

[320] FLÜGEL (1994: 324).

[321] HOERNLE (1989: 1 n.1), in UD.

[322] Cf. *Vyavahāra-bhāṣya* 10.192, in JAIN (1981: 159).

[323] Cf. Uttar 30.30–7.

[324] 'The more work … hearers do to supply meaning, the deeper their understanding and the greater their sense of involvement with both text and author' (TANNEN (1989: 23)).

[325] Cf. VĀBh 1.927, 3, 2.54, 4–8, in BALBIR (1993: 267–9, 317–46).

to infer and fulfil the pragmatic intentions of their religious superiors, which are conventionally not openly expressed, but implicitly stated.

Speech situations for which Jain ascetics are especially trained are many. The two most important forms of non-ritualised language usage a Jain ascetic has to learn are the public sermon (*pavayaṇa* <*pravacana*>) to the laity and the art of debate (*paoga* <*prayoga*>) or disputation (*vivāda*) with other ascetics.[326] Both forms of discourse are primarily instruments of social influence, based on the idea of the superiority of the better argument in public discourse or agonistic dialogues, i.e. verbal battles. Polite formal exchanges within the context of a religious hierarchy (type d and c), by contrast, tend to conform with an ideal of 'speaking in concordance with the one who knows the truth' (GAEFFKE (1970: 34–8)). *Prayoga* was/is important for gaining or maintaining social influence at the royal courts etc., and played a major role in medieval South Asia. The way in which this art was taught in the more advanced stages of monastic education[327] resembles Aristotelian style rhetorical training, as the following citation from the *Āyāra-dasāo* <*Ācāra-daśāḥ*> (ĀyārD), a Jaina *Cheya-sutta* (*Cheda-sūtra*) text, illustrates:

> 'It is of four kinds: (a) application of one's knowledge after a complete assessment of one's own powers in debate, (b) application of one's knowledge in debate after a full assessment of the *parisā* (assembly), (c) application of one's knowledge in debate after a full appreciation of the environment (*khetta*) of the debate, (d) application of one's knowledge in debate after a full estimation of the nature of the adjudicators, the ability of the opponent and the attitude of the authorities, etc. (*vatthu*)' (ĀyārD 4.2, in TATIA–KUMAR (1981: 32)).

It is interesting to note the similarity between the four factors considered relevant for strategy selection in public debate, and BROWN–LEVINSON's (1978: 79 ff.) variables for the assessment of the seriousness of a FTA, that is, social distance and relative power in particular. The view that South Asians traditionally knew only poetry, but not rhetoric, because of the 'absence of the institution of public speech' (HACKER (1985: 13 f.)),[328] must be doubted in the light of the evidence presented. I would argue, on the contrary, that self-conscious pragmatic language usage, politeness, and the art of persuasion via the construction of implicatures, is one of the recognised arts of Jain ascetics (and laity).[329]

---

[326] Ṭhāṇ 350b, 364b, ĀyārD 4.

[327] Cf. CORT (2001: 339 f.).

[328] Cf. GAEFFKE (1970).

[329] See MATILAL (1999: 31) on rules and regulations for debates (*kathā* or *vāda*) in Indian philosophical texts.

— VIII —

In this essay, I proposed a theoretical interpretation of syncretic processes as forms of symbolic communication, broadly following Habermas' analyses of systematically distorted and latent strategic action, predicated on the work of Grice and sociolinguists such as Hymes, Gumperz, Fishman and Brown and Levinson. The advantage of this perspective, compared to classical hermeneutics, is that social processes within a religious tradition do not have to be understood in terms of an enactment or actualising appropriation of textual meaning, or of rule-specification, but can be investigated as open historical processes for which religious knowledge and linguistic repertoire serves as cognitive resource, which can be used for the pursuit of either power or insight. To the extent that cognition and discourse are historically relevant, production of social meaning and co-operation can be understood in terms of the conditions of acceptability of validity claims. Rarely do human insight and instrumental rationality take precedence over habit and contingencies of life. GADAMER's (1993: 244) objection to Habermas' 'idealisation of the critical power of reflection' and reasons in discourse is therefore justified. However, Habermas' theory of communicative action is more narrowly concerned with a critique of both latent strategic action and mediated systemic forms of social reproduction, without illusions about the overwhelming factual role of power and indeterminacy in contemporary social processes. FOUCAULT's (1981: 56) more radical attack on the repressive aspects of discourse as a form of power itself, especially discourses informed by the 'will to truth' backed up by exclusionary mechanisms, nevertheless puts its finger on a crucial problem in both moral philosophy and organised religion. Habermas' theory of communicative action certainly does not properly account for the poetic 'world-disclosing' function of language, nor for the historical conditions of the theorisation of the 'universal' validity claims itself, which it merely takes as a primitive given of 'successful' prosaic communication. Both SEARLE (1993: 91 f., 99) and APEL (1993: 52 f.), despite their differences, criticise the hidden essentialism of this approach as 'functionalist' (in an old-fashioned sense), and suggest that the acceptance of validity conditions is a contingent 'perlocutionary effect' of the strategic attempt of getting the hearer to agree—an attempt which initially only commits the speaker (as the Jain example shows). Moreover, Habermas' original approach privileges the educated classes, and neglects empirical cases of reaching agreement or dissent through open strategic uses of language. Yet, the alternative reduction of validity to an effect of universally present 'empirico-transcendental' power in Foucault's or similar theoretical scenarios currently *en vogue* in Jaina Studies forecloses the possibility of problematising legitimacy once and for all. This, however, seems unwise, not least because, empirically, the sources of power and legitimacy often do not coincide. This is one of the reasons why DUMONT's (1980: xxxi) distinction between (political) power (*pouvoir*) and (religious) potency (*puissance*) has gained currency in South Asia research.

Classical Jainism derives its legitimacy ontologically from the presumed direct meditative insight of its omniscient prophets (*tīrthaṅkara*) into the eternal truth of existence (*sat*), i.e. the difference between self (*jīva*) and non-self (*ajīva*). Those who know, who have experienced direct insight, it is said, share an experiential consensus which transcends discourse and rational argument. However, discourse and argument is necessary for the dispersion of religious knowledge amongst the ignorant, although, initially, it can only facilitate first experiences of insight (*samyag-darśana*) by providing some of its conditions through instruction, but not generate insight itself. For Jain doctrine, insight is a psychophysical event which is unexplainable, a mysterious transformation of consciousness, which may or may not occur, once *karmic* bondage is weakened and religious knowledge fuses with personal experience. Paradigmatic activating conditions of insight are temporary feelings of peace accompanied with 'instructing' experiences of loss, suffering, or the sight of a saint. Verbal instruction (*upadeśa*) and suggestion (*dhvani*) may also provoke sudden insight (as a perlocutionary effect).[330] In practice, it usually does so only after a previous history of interaction, involving rational argument and agonistic debate, which prepares the epistemic ground for 'true' or 'dogmatic' insight, which may then be triggered circumstantially, for instance by fitting experiences.

I have not discussed the metaphysics and the psychological conditions of religious experience in this essay,[331] especially not the hypothetical experiences of the Jinas, but confined myself to the analysis of the conditions of understanding and accepting Jain religious claims as legitimate (*Einsicht*) and of fulfilment of their pragmatic implications. My argument rests on the observation of a principal two-stage process of Jain religious conversion: first, largely through agonistic discourse, based on rational argument, and, second, largely through non-agonistic instruction.[332] Although, in principle, an initiated disciple 'cannot say "no"' (BLOCH (1975: 19)) to transmitted Jain doctrine anymore after the 'initial acceptance of the code' (BLOCH

[330] Uttar 28.16–27, JAINI (1979: 141 f.). Cf. UPADHYAYA (1987: 105–7) on Hemacandra's examples of *upācara*, secondary meaning of a word based on similarity.

[331] See JAMES (1982), and footnotes 21, 28, 29, 61, 143, 286.

[332] See FLÜGEL (1993, (1994: 217–346)). This scheme has been abstracted from documented conversions to monkhood. It corresponds to the textual ideal (e.g. Uttar 23), but does not necessarily cover the Jain *cliché* of lay conversion through miracle-working. Lay conversions are gradual affairs, often starting with taking limited vows after public sermons and subsequently adding more severe restrictions. Jain vows do not compel the adherent to reject his ancestral beliefs and practices—unless they are wholly incompatible—but lead to a re-evaluation of these practices.

(1975: 24)), and subsequently receives religious instruction from his seniors predominantly in the mode of unquestioned conformity to revealed fundamental truth,[333] debate and rational argument continue on the basis of the accepted ontological and organisational principles (TS 9.25). In other words, although it is predicated on the acceptance of the validity of ultimately incommunicable evidence or feelings, Jain religious discourse, too, is confined to the level of conventional truth (VN), because 'whatever is beyond the province of speech is inexpressible (or unspeakable)' (Tulsī (1985: 190)). According to the proposed model, Jainism appeals to rationality and insight in different ways on both idealtypical developmental stages of conversion, and constitutes a kind of therapeutic discourse, which thrives on the interpretation of experience through a pedagogical scheme of explanation, which runs contrary to everyday perceptions and opens up new perspectives, thus inevitably generating ambiguity by 'splitting the codes' (Turner (1986: 56))[334] and thereby producing the potential for a transformation of meaning and, subsequently, conduct.

Because the appeal to rationality is predominant in Jain discourse, which conventionally contrasts the three jewels (*ratna-traya*) of right insight (*samyag-darśana*), right knowledge (*samyag-jñāna*) and right conduct (*samyak-cāritra*) to 'blind ritualism',[335] it seemed legitimate to privilege the perspective of the ascetics in this essay, which are trained in Jain doctrine. The importance of their power of persuasion for the continuation of the Jain tradition is a universal *topos* of Jain narrative and biographical literature. There, the problem of the moral ambivalence of religious rhetoric is explicitly addressed as a form of necessary violence (*āvassaya-hiṁsā* <*āvaśyaka-hiṁsā*>), to be repented by means of the obligatory ascetic rites (*āvaśyaka*). I have not discussed technical Jain theories of suggestion, implication, figures of speech, or narrative genres, nor any particular linguistic exchange in the manner of the ethnography of speaking, but concentrated on the principles of Jain discourse itself, particularly the ones concerning the illegitimacy of 'unnecessary violent' (*anāvassaya hiṁsā* <*anāvaśyaka-hiṁsā*>) speech. In this way, I hope to have shown how structures of traditional authority together with the constraints of given circumstances directly or indirectly pre-empt processes of negotiated meaning by channelling them in a certain direction. Even if the principles of rational inquiry are upheld by Jain doctrine,[336] open critical inquiry as defined by the theory of communicative action in not possible within the confines of the traditional religious institutions.

[333] Cf. Gaeffke (1970: 34–8), Balbir (1993: 40).

[334] Cf. Bloch (1975: 26 f.).

[335] Statement of a young Jain in London in conversation with the present author.

[336] Cf. Bronkhorst (1999).

The comparison between the theory of communicative action and Jain discourse ethics showed nevertheless significant similarities. Both approaches are rule-oriented, not goal-oriented. That is, they are concerned with the general interest of many, not with the eudaemonic perspective of a single actor, despite the fact that the methods of universalisation are different. The respective ideals of consensus and non-violence mutually implicate each other. Basic non-violence is presupposed by communicative action, and the general interest of all is presupposed by universal non-violence. Though the criterion of generalisability, equal interest, is not theorised in Jain philosophy, and only touched upon with reference to specific negative rights such as the privileged case of the universal interest in avoiding pain,[337] the scope of the moral universe is extended from humanity to all living beings, whose essential spiritual equality is a fundamental principle of Jaina philosophy.[338] The vanishing points of both theories, the ideal consensus of an infinite community of interpretation and the ideal omniscient observer, presuppose absolute knowledge and absolute consensus. Yet, there are two significant differences. The main difference between the transcendental pragmatics of mutual recognition and the monadological Jain ethics of non-violence concerns the nature of the fundamental principles. The former is predicated on positive norms and the latter on norms of prohibition.[339] The implicit method of universalisation of Jain ethics is the double negation, that is, the negation of non-generalisable statements. The resulting priority of physical non-action as a theoretical limiting case (not as a practical maxim) unburdens the doctrine of discussions of specific dilemmas of norm application, thus safeguarding both generalisability and contextual determinateness, while maintaining a perspective of disengagement with the world and non-specific positive duties. The second main difference between the two types of discourse ethics concerns the moral division of labour presupposed by Jain norms of discourse, which does not permit equal communicative freedom to take positions on validity claims, but privileges institutionally verified competent speakers (*āpta*).[340] Having emerged

[337] Cf. GERT's (1973) 'minimal ethic'.

[338] See DUMONT's (1977), (1980) works.

[339] The general difference of the two approaches has been pointedly expressed by SCHOPENHAUER (1977: 262, § 121) in his critique of the formalism of Kant's theory of morality and of state-oriented positive concepts of law from a perspective of Indic conceptions of morality. 'Der Begriff des R e c h t s ist nämlich, eben wie auch der der F r e i h e i t , e i n n e g a t i v e r : sein Inhalt ist eine bloße Negation. Der Begriff des U n r e c h t s ist der positive und ist gleichbedeutend mit V e r l e t z u n g im weitesten Sinne, also *laesio*. ... Hiernach sind dann die M e n s c h e n r e c h t e leicht zu bestimmen: Jeder hat das Recht, alles Das zu thun, wodurch er Keinen verletzt.'

[340] Habermas is often accused of the same for somewhat different theoretical reasons.

under historical conditions of normative inequality, Jain discourse ethics is not at all concerned with questions of human justice, only with negative individual freedom.

Dumont and Marriott posed the question whether Jainism, built from the same materials as other South Asian religions, can be interpreted as a blueprint for the formation of 'strategic groups', for instance by being connected with a set of specific procedures or dominant strategies, which are derived either from the structure of its dominant ideological codes *jīva/ajīva* and *ahiṁsā/hiṁsā* and/or the characteristic social position of its dominant lay-followers. Put in this way, any answer of the question must be vulnerable to the critique of socio-cultural 'essentialism' as 'ahistorical' and 'reductionist'. But to ask which principles and procedures the Jains themselves regard as 'essential' for the validation of their own politics of cultural synthesis remains indispensable. At least five derivative, and still accepted, paradigmatic pragmatic orientations for contexts of interaction between mendicants and non-mendicants can be isolated on the basis of the Āyār and the DVS: (1) impersonalisation, (2) nominalisation (objectivation), (3) degrees of non-speech, silence, and selective non-interaction, and (4) avoiding disagreement by presupposing common ground. All these strategies leave a speaker with a number of defensible interpretations which are technically neither true nor false (*satyâsatya*) and therefore useful to gloss over gaps between the often contradictory doctrinal and contextual implications of a speech act. The first three strategy types are those of negative politeness, which generally emphasise the mutual autonomy and non-interference of the interlocutors, for instance, by transforming directives into assertives. The last strategy type is a specific instance of positive politeness strategies, which are used to avoid conflict (and thus violence). For the same purpose off-record strategies are employed, which are considered as legitimate forms of symbolic violence, if used for the furtherance of religious insight. The overall result of this preliminary investigation of Jain discourse resonates with PAINE's (1981: 3) and BRENNEIS'–MYERS' (1984: 12) observation that in many societies, especially in those without elaborated hierarchies or structures of open coercion, conflict or contradiction, while often endemic, is rarely discussed openly, and expressed confrontation or coercion avoided through indirect speech, oriented toward the creation or maintenance of co-operation and the attainment of basic consensus, without saying so. Of course, not only particular speech acts but even the Jain maxims themselves can be read as generalised strategies, because they embody a certain directionality or orientation toward the world. The *differentia specifica* between the elements of Jain ontology and those of the culturally dominant religious systems of Hinduism, then, opens up negatively determined spaces for a distinct style of communicative action and rhetorical manipulation with characteristic multiple ambiguities and syncretic effects to be studied by future sociolinguistic investigations of Jain discourse.

BIBLIOGRAPHY

ALBERT 1991 = Albert, Hans: *Traktat über kritische Vernunft*. Fünfte erweiterte und verbesserte Auflage. J.C.B. Mohr (Paul Siebeck), Tübingen 1991 [first edition: Tübingen 1968. English translation: *Treatise on Critical Reason*. Translated by Mary V. Rorty. Princeton University Press, Princeton 1985].

ALBERT 1994 = Albert, Hans: *Kritik der reinen Hermeneutik*. J.C.B. Mohr (Paul Siebeck), Tübingen 1994.

ALBERT 2003 = Albert, Hans: *Transzendentale Träumereien: Karl-Otto Apels Sprachspiele und sein hermeneutischer Gott*. Hoffman & Campe, Hamburg 1975 [reprinted in: *Kritik des transzendentalen Denkens*. J.C.B. Mohr (Paul Siebeck), Tübingen 2003: 7–128).

ALEXY 1996 = Alexy, Robert: *Theorie der juristischen Argumentation: Die Theorie des rationalen Diskurses als Theorie der juristischen Begründung*. Dritte Auflage. Suhrkamp, Frankfurt am Main 1990 [first edition: 1983. English translation: *A Theory of Legal Argumentation*. Translated by Ruth Adler and Neil MacCormick. Oxford University Press, Oxford 1989].

ALI 2004 = Ali, Daud: *Courtly Culture and Political Life in Early Medieval India*. Cambridge University Press, Cambridge 2004.

ALSDORF 1966 = Alsdorf, Ludwig: *The Āryā Stanzas of the Uttarājjhāya. Contributions to the Text History and Interpretation of a Canonical Jaina Text*. Abhandlungen der Geistes- und Sozialwissenschaftlichen Klasse Jahrgang 1966 – Nr. 2, Verlag der Akademie der Wissenschaften und der Literatur in Mainz in Kommission bei Franz Steiner, Wiesbaden 1966: 154–220.

AṇD = *Aṇuogaddārāiṁ* [*Anuyoga-dvāra*]. T. Hanaki (English tr.): *Aṇuogaddārāiṁ (English Translation)*. Prakrit Jain Institute Research Publications Series Vol. 5, Vaishali 1970.

APEL 1973 = Apel, Karl-Otto: *Transformation der Philosophie*. 2 Bände, Suhrkamp, Frankfurt am Main 1973 [English translation (selection): *Towards a Transformation of Philosophy*. Routledge and Kegan Paul, London 1980].

APEL 1993 = Apel, Karl-Otto: 'Is Intentionality more Basic than Linguistic Meaning?' In: LEPORE–VAN GULICK (1993: 31–56).

ARENS 1989 = Arens, Edmund: 'Theologie nach Habermas: Eine Einführung', in: Edmund Arens (ed.): *Habermas und die Theologie*. Patmos, Düsseldorf 1989: 9–38.

ARENS 1991 = Arens, Edmund: 'Kommunikative Rationalität und Religion: Die Theorie des kommunikativen Handelns als Herausforderung politischer Theologie', in: Edmund Arens(ed.): *Erinnerung, Befreiung, Solidarität: Benjamin, Marcuse, Habermas und die Politische Theologie*. O. John & P. Rottländer. Patmos, Düsseldorf 1991: 145–200.

ARENS 1992 = Arens, Edmund: 'Domination and Communication', in: REIMER (1992: 247–62).

ARENS 1995 = Arens, Edmund: *Christopraxis: A Theology of Action*. Fortress Press, Minneapolis 1995 [first edition: *Christopraxis: Grundzüge theologischer Handlungstheorie (Quaestiones disputatae)*. Herder, Freiburg 1992].

ARISTOTLE = See PH.

ATLAS 2005 = Atlas, Jay David: *Logic, Meaning, and Conversation: Semantic Underdeterminacy, Implicature, and their Inference*. Oxford University Press, Oxford 2005.

AUSTIN 1962 = Austin, John Langshaw: *How to Do Things with Words. The William James Lectures delivered at Harvard University in 1955*. Clarendon Press, Oxford 1962.

ĀvNi = *Āvassaya-nijjutti* [*Āvaśyaka-niryukti*]. Edited with Haribhadra's *Ṭīkā*. Agamodaya Samiti, Bombay 1918.

Āyār = *Āyāraṁga-sutta* [*Ācārāṅga-sūtra*]. (1) [English translation:] JACOBI (1884: 1–216). (2) [Original Ardhamāgadhī-Text:] Tulsī, Ācārya, Muni Nathmal (eds.): *Aṅgasuttāṇi*. Vol. 1. Second Edition. Jain Viśva Bhāratī, Lāḍnūṁ 1992: 1–248 [first edition: 1974].

ĀyārBh = *Ācārâṅga-bhāṣya*. Ganadhipati Tulsi (Vācanā Pramukha), Acharya Mahaprajna (Bhāṣyakāra), Nathmal Tatia, Muni Dulaharaj, Muni Mahendra Kumar (English Rendering): *Acharanga-Bhasyam. English Translation of the Original Text of Ayaro together with its Roman Transliteration and Bhasyam (Sanskrit Commentary)*. Jain Vishwa Bharati, Ladnun 2001.

ĀyārD = *Āyāra-dasāo* [*Ācāra-daśāḥ*]. Schubring, Walter; Caillat, Colette: *Drei Chedasūtras des Jaina-Kanons. Āyāradasāo, Vavahāra, Nisīha*. Alt- und Neuindische Studien 11, De Gruyter, Hamburg 1966

BABB 1994 = Babb, Lawrence A.: 'The Great Choice: Worldly Values in a Jain Ritual Culture.' *History of Religions* 34,1 (1994) 15–38.

BAHM 1957 = Bahm Archie J.: 'Does Seven-Fold Predication Equal Four-Cornered Negation Reversed?' *Philosophy East and West* 7,3–4 (1957) 127–130.

BALBIR 1983 = Balbir, Nalini: 'The Micro-Genre of *Dāna*-Stories in Jaina Literature: Problems of Interrelation and Diffusion.' *Journal of the American Oriental Society* 11 (1983) 145–61.

BALBIR 1984 = Balbir, Nalini: 'Normalizing Trends in Jaina Narrative Literature', *Indologica Taurinensia* 12 (1984) 25–37.

BALBIR 1987 = Balbir, Nalini: 'The Perfect Sūtra as Defined by the Jainas.' *Bulletin D'Études Indiennes* 3 (1987) 3–21.

BALBIR 1993 = Balbir, Nalini: *Āvaśyaka-Studien. Introduction Générale et Traductions*. Alt- und Neuindische Studien 45,1. Franz Steiner Verlag, Stuttgart 1993.

BALCEROWICZ 2003 = Balcerowicz, Piotr: 'Some Remarks on the *Naya* Method', in: Piotr Balcerowicz: *Essays in Jaina Philosophy and Religion*. Motilal Banarsidas, Delhi 2003: 37–70.

BAUM 1976 = Baum, Rainer C.: 'On Societal Media Dynamics', in: Jan J. Loubser, Rainer C. Baum, Andrew Effrat, Victor Meyer Lidz (eds.): *Exploration in General Theory in Social Science. Essays in Honor of Talcott Parsons*. The Free Press, New York 1976: 579 ff.

BECHERT 1961 = Bechert, Heinz: 'Aśokas "Schismenedikt" und der Begriff *Sanghabheda*.' *Wiener Zeitschrift für die Kunde Südasiens* 5 (1961) 18–52.

BECHERT 1978 = Bechert, Heinz: 'Introduction: Report on the Symposion', in: Heinz Bechert: *Buddhism in Ceylon and Studies on Religious Syncretism in Buddhist Countries*. Vanderhoeck & Ruprecht, Göttingen 1978: 13–27.

BERNSTEIN 1964 = Bernstein, Basil: 'Elaborated and Restricted Codes: Their Social Origins and some Consequences.' *American Anthropologist* (*N.S.*) 66, 6, II (1964) 55–69.

BERNSTEIN 1971 = Bernstein, Basil: *Class, Codes, and Control: Theoretical Studies Towards a Sociology of Language*. Vol. 1. Routledge and Kegan Paul, London 1971.

BERNSTEIN 1996 = Bernstein, Basil: 'Vertical and Horizontal Discourse: An Essay', in: Basil Bernstein: *Pedagogy, Symbolic Control and Identity: Theory, Research, Critique*. Taylor and Francis, London 1996: 155–74.

BHARADWAJA 1984 = Bharadwaja, V. K.: 'Rationality, Argumentation and Embarrassment: A Study of Four Logical Alternatives (*catuṣkoṭi*) in Buddhist Logic.' *Philosophy East and West* 34,3 (1984) 303–319.

BHARATI 1975 = Bharati, Agehananda: 'On Intentional Language (Sandhābhāṣā).' *The Tantric Tradition*. Rider & Company, London 1975: 164–84.

BHATT 1978 = Bhatt, Bansidhar: *The Canonical Nikṣepa. Studies in Jaina Dialectics*. E. J. Brill (Indologica Berolinensa 5), Leiden 1978.

BLOCH 1975 = Bloch, Maurice: 'Introduction.' *Political Oratory in Traditional Society*. In: Maurice Bloch (ed.): Academic Press, London 1975: 1–28.

BLOOMFIELD 1923 = Bloomfield, Maurice: 'The Śālibhadra Carita: A Story of Conversion to Jaina Monkhood.' *Journal of the American Oriental Society* 43 (1923) 257–312.

BOURDIEU 1991a = Bourdieu, Pierre: 'Authorized Language: The Social Conditions for the Effectiveness of Ritual Discourse', in: Pierre Bourdieu: *Language and Symbolic Power*. Polity Press, Cambridge 1991: 107–16 [English translation by Gino Raymond and Matthew Adamson; most essays previously published in: *Ce que parler veut dire: l'economie des e'chnages linguistiques*. Librairie Arthème Fayard, Paris 1982].

BOURDIEU 1991b = Bourdieu, Pierre: 'On Symbolic Power', in: Pierre Bourdieu: *Language and Symbolic Power*. Polity Press, Cambridge 1991: 163–170 [first edition: Cambridge 1977].

BRENNEIS–MYERS 1984 = Brenneis, Donald L.; Fred R. Myers: 'Introduction.' Eds. D. L. Brenneis, F. R. Myers (eds.): *Dangerous Words: Language and Politics in the Pacific*. New York: University Press, 1984: 1–29.

BRONKHORST 1993a = Bronkhorst, Johannes: 'Review: Oetke 1991.' *Asiatische Studien* 47,3 (1993) 501–11.

BRONKHORST 1993b = Bronkhorst, Johannes: 'Remarks on the History of Jaina Meditation', in: SMET–WATANABE (1993: 151–162).

BRONKHORST 1999 = Bronkhorst, Johannes: *Why is there Philosophy in India? 1998 Gonda Lecture*. Royal Netherlands Academy of Arts and Science, Amsterdam 1999.

BROWN–LEVINSON 1978 = Brown, Penelope & Levinson, Stephen: 'Universals in Language Usage: Politeness Phenomena', in: E. Goody (ed.): *Questions and Politeness. Strategies in Social Interaction*. Cambridge University Press, Cambridge 1978: 56–310.

BRUHN 1954 = Bruhn, Klaus: *Śīlāṅkas Cauppaṇṇamahāpurisacariya. Ein Beitrag zur Kenntnis der Jaina-Universalgeschichte*. De Gruyter, Hamburg 1954.

BRUHN 1983 = Bruhn, Klaus: 'Repetition in Jaina Narrative Literature', *Indologica Taurinensia* 11 (1983) 27–75.

BRUHN 1987a = Bruhn, Klaus: 'Das Kanonproblem bei den Jainas', in: A. & J. Assmann (eds.): *Kanon und Zensur. Beiträge zur Archäologie der Literarischen Kommunikation II*. Wilhelm Fink Verlag, München 1987: 100–12.

BRUHN 1987b = Bruhn, Klaus: 'Soteriology in Early Jainism', in: Harry Falk (ed.): *Hinduismus und Buddhismus. Festschrift für Ulrich Schneider*. Freiburg 1987: 61–86.

BRUHN 1993 = Bruhn, Klaus: 'Sectional Studies in Jainology II.' *Berliner Indologische Studien* 7 (1993) 9–58.

BRUHN 1997–98 = Bruhn, Klaus: "Five Vows and Six Avashyakas: The Fundamentals of Jaina Ethics." Ed. C. Geerdes, 1997–1998 [http://herenow4u.de/eng/spr/religion/Bruhn.html].

BRUHN–HÄRTEL 1978 = Bruhn, Klaus; Herbert Härtel: 'Editors' Foreword', in: Bansidhar Bhatt: *The Canonical Nikṣepa: Studies in Jaina Dialectics*. Indologica Berolinensa 5, E. J. Brill, Leiden 1978: v–vi.

BURGHART 1978a = Burghart, Richard: *The History of Janakpurdham: A Study of Asceticism and the Hindu Polity*. Ph.D. thesis, The University of London, London 1978.

BURGHART 1978b = Burghart, Richard: 'Hierarchical Models of the Hindu Social System.' *Man (N.S.)* 13,4 (1978) 519–36.

BURGHART 1983 = Burghart, Richard: 'For a Sociology of Indias: An Intracultural Approach to the Study of "Hindu Society".' *Contributions to Indian Sociology (N.S.)* 17 (1983) 275–99.

BURGHART 1985 = Burghart, Richard: 'Introduction: Theoretical Approaches in the Anthropology of South Asia', in: BURGHART–CANTLIE (1985: 1–14).

BURGHART 1996 = Burghart, Richard: 'The Conditions of Listening: The Everyday Experience of Politics in Nepal.' C. J. Fuller, J. Spencer (eds.): *The Conditions of Listening. Essays on Religion, History and Politics in South Asia*. Oxford University Press, Delhi 1996: 300–318.

BURGHART–CANTLIE 1985 = Burghart, Richard; Cantlie, Audrey (eds.): *Indian Religion*. Curzon Press, London 1985.

CAILLAT 1984 = Caillat, Colette: 'Prohibited Speech and *Subhāsita* in the Theravāda Tradition.' *Indologica Taurinensia* 12 (1984) 61–73.

CAILLAT 1991 = Caillat, Colette: 'The Rules Concerning Speech (Bhāsā) in the Āyāranga- and Dasaveyāliya-Suttas', in: M. A. Dhaky, S. Jain (eds.): *Aspects of Jainology. Pt. Dalsukhbhai Malvania Felicitation Volume. Vol. 3*. P. V. Research Institute, Varanasi 1991: 1–15.

CARNAP 1931 = Carnap, Rudolph: 'Die Überwindung der Metaphysik durch die logische Analyse der Sprache.' *Erkenntnis* 2,4 (1931) 219–41.

CARRITHERS 1990 = Carrithers, Michael: 'Jainism and Buddhism as Enduring Historical Streams.' *Journal of the Anthropological Society of Oxford* 21,2 (1990) 141–63.

CARRITHERS 1991 = Carrithers, Michael: 'The Foundations of Community among Southern Digambar Jains: An Essay on Rhetoric and Experience.' CARRITHERS–HUMPHREY (1991: 261–86).

CARRITHERS 1992 = Carrithers, Michael: *Why Humans have Cultures: Explaining Anthropology and Social Diversity*. Oxford University Press, Oxford 1992.

CARRITHERS–HUMPHREY 1991 = Carrithers, Michael; Humphrey, Caroline (eds.): *The Assembly of Listeners: Jains in Society*. Cambridge University Press, Cambridge 1991.

CASSIRER 1923–1929 = Cassirer, Ernst: *Philosophie der symbolischen Formen*. I–III. Zweite Auflage. Wissenschaftliche Buchgesellschaft, Darmstadt 1994 [first edition: Darmstadt 1923–1929. English translation: *The Philosophy of Symbolic Forms*. I–III. Translated by Ralph Manheim. Yale University Press, New Haven 1953, 1955, 1957].

CHI 1974 = Chi, Richard S. Y.: 'Topics on Being and Logical Reasoning.' *Philosophy East and West* 24,3 (1974) 293–300.

CHOMSKY 1965 = Chomsky, Noam: *Aspects of the Theory of Syntax*. The M. I. T. Press, Cambridge (Massachusetts) 1965.

COLPE 1987 = Colpe, Carsten: 'Syncretism', in: Mircea Eliade (ed.): *The Encyclopaedia of Religion*, Vol. 14. Macmillan & Free Press, New York 1987: 218–27.

CORT 1989 = Cort, John E.: *Liberation and Wellbeing: A Study of the Mūrtipūjak Jains of North Gujarat*. Ph.D. dissertation, Harvard University, Harvard 1989.

CORT 1992 = Cort, John E.: 'Śvetāmbar Mūrtipūjak Jain Scripture in a Performative Context', in: J.R. Timm: *Texts in Contexts. Traditional Hermeneutics in South Asia*. State University of New York Press, New York 1992: 171–94.

CORT 1995 = Cort, John E.: '"Intellectual *Ahiṁsā*" Revisited: Jain Tolerance and Intolerance of Others.' *Philosophy East and West* 50,3 (2000) 324–47.

CORT 1995 = Cort, John E.: 'Genres of Jain History.' *Journal of Indian Philosophy* 23 (1995) 469–506.

CORT 2001 = Cort, John E.: 'The Intellectual Formation of a Jain Monk: A Śvetâmbara Monastic Curriculum.' *Journal of Indian Philosophy* 29 (2001) 327–49.

DAVIDSON 1984 = Davidson, Donald: 'Belief and the Basis of Meaning', in: D. Davidson: *Inquiries into Truth and Interpretation*. Clarendon Press, Oxford 1984: 141–154 [first published in: *Synthèse* 27 (1974) 309–23].

DAVIS 1998 = Davis, Wayne A.: *Implicature: Intention, Convention, and Principle in the Failure of Gricean Theory*. Cambridge University Press, Cambridge 1998.

DELEU 1970 = Deleu, Jozef: *Viyāhapannatti (Bhagavaī). The Fifth Anga of the Jaina Canon*. Introduction, Critical Analysis, Commentary & Indexes. Rijksuniversiteit de Gent, Brugge 1970.

DERRETT 1980 = Derrett, J. Duncan M.: 'Scrupulousness and a Hindu-Jain Contract.' *Journal of the Royal Asiatic Society of Great Britain and Ireland* (1980) 144–167.

DESHPANDE 1979 = Deshpande, Madhav M.: *Sociolinguistic Attitudes in India: An Historical Reconstruction*. With a Foreword by Murray B. Emmeneau. Karoma Publishers, Ann Arbor 1979.

DESHPANDE 1990 = Deshpande, Madhav M.: 'Changing Conceptions of the Veda: From Speech Acts to Magical Sounds.' *Adyar Library Bulletin* 54 (1990) 1–41.

DIXIT 1978 = Dixit, Krishna Kumar: *Jaina Ontology*. L. D. Institute of Indology, Ahmedabad 1978.

DÖBERT 1973 = Döbert, R.: *Systemtheorie und die Entwicklung religiöser Deutungssysteme*. Suhrkamp, Frankurt am Main 1973.

DONOVAN 1976 = Donovan, Peter: *Religious Language*. Sheldon Press, London 1976.

DRECHSEL 1994 = Drechsel, Paul: *Sozialstruktur und kommunikatives Handeln: Reflexionen über eine postmoderne Ethno-Soziologie*. Lit Verlag, Münster 1994.

DUMONT 1977 = Dumont, Louis: *Homo Aequalis*. Gallimard, Paris 1976 [English translation: *From Mandeville to Marx: The Genesis and Triumph of Economic Ideology*. Chicago University Press, Chicago 1977].

DUMONT 1980 = Dumont, Louis: *Homo Hierarchicus: The Caste System and its Implications*. Translated from the French by Mark Sainsbury, Louis Dumont and Basia Gulati. Complete Revised English Edition. University of Chicago Press, Chicago 1980 [first edition: *Homo hierarchicus: Le système des castes et ses implications*. Editions Gallimard, Paris 1966].

DUNDAS 1985 = Dundas, Paul: 'Food and Freedom: The Jaina Sectarian Debate on the Nature of the Kevalin.' *Religion* 15 (1985) 161–198.

DUNDAS 1996 = Dundas, Paul: 'Somnolent Sūtras: Scriptural Commentary in Śvetāmbara Jainism.' *Journal of Indian Philosophy* 24 (1996) 73–101.

DUNDAS 2007 = Dundas, Paul: 'The Non-Violence of Violence: Jain Perspectives on Warfare, Asceticism and Worship', in: J.R. Hinnells, R. King (eds.): *Religion and Violence in South Asia: Theory and Practice*. Routledge, London 2007: 41–61.

DURBIN 1970 = Durbin, M.: 'The Transformational Model of Linguistics and its Implications for an Ethnology of Religion: A Case Study of Jainism.' *American Anthropologist* 72 (1970) 334–42.

DVS = Ārya Sayyambhava: *Dasa-veyāliya-sutta* [*Daśa-vaikālika-sūtra*]. (1) Ernst Leumann (ed.), Walther Schubring (tr.): *The Dasaveyāliya Sutta*. Introduction and Notes, by Walther Schubring. The Managers of the Sheth Anandji Kalianji, Ahmedabad 1932. (2) Kustur Chand Lalwani (tr.): *Ārya Sayyambhava's Daśavaikālika Sūtra*. With Translation and Notes. Motilal Banarsidas, Delhi 1973. (3) Acārya Tulsī [Vācaka Pramukha], Muni Nathmal [Sampādaka aur Vivecaka] (eds.): *Dasaveāliyaṁ* (Mūlapāṭha, Saṁskṛt Chāyā, Hindī Anuvāda tathā ṭippaṇa). Jain Viśva Bhāratī, Lāḍnūṁ 1974 [first edition: 1964].

ELIAS 1983 = Elias, Norbert: *Die höfische Gesellschaft: Untersuchungen zur Soziologie des Königtums und der höfischen Aristokratie*. Suhrkamp, Frankfurt am Main 1983 [Submitted Habilitation 1933. First edition: Luchterhand, Darmstadt and Neuwied 1969. English translation: *The court society*. Translated by Edmund Jephcott. Blackwell, Oxford 1983].

FAUCONNIER 1981 = Fauconnier, Gilles: 'Social Ritual and Relative Truth in Natural Language', in: K. Knorr-Cetina, A.V. Cicourel (eds.): *Advances in Social Theory and Methodology*. Routledge & Kegan Paul, Boston 1981: 175–202.

FAURE 1991 = Faure, Bernard: *The Rhetoric of Immediacy: A Cultural Critique of Ch'an/Zen Buddhism*. Princeton University Press, Princeton 1991.

FAURE 1993 = Faure, Bernard: *Chan Insights and Oversights: An Epistemological Critique of the Chan Tradition*. Princeton University Press, Princeton 1993.

FERGUSON 1959 = Ferguson, Charles A.: 'Diglossia.' *Word* 15 (1959) 325–40 [reprinted: GIGLIOLI (1972: 232–51)].

FINDLEY 1989 = Findley, Ellison Banks: '*Māntra kaviśastā*: Speech as Performative in the Ṛgveda.' H.P. Alper (ed.): *Understanding Mantras*. State University of New York Press, Albany 1989: 15–48.

FISHMAN 1967 = Fishman, Joshua A.: 'Bilingualism with and without Diglossia; Diglossia with and without Bilingualism.' *Journal of Social Issues* 23,2 (1967) 29–38.

FISHMAN 2006 = Fishman, Joshua A.: 'A Decaloge of Theoretical Perspectives for a Sociology of Language and Religion', in: T. Omoniyi, J.A. Fishman (eds.): *Explorations in the Sociology of Language and Religion*. John Benjamins Publishing, Amsterdam 2006: 13–25.

FLÜGEL 1993 = Flügel, Peter: 'Worshipping the Ideal King: On the Social Implications of Medieval Jain Conversion Stories', Paper presented to the Jains in History and Culture Workshop, Amherst College, June 1993. Unpublished.

FLÜGEL 1994 = Flügel, Peter: *Askese und Devotion: Das Rituelle System der Terāpanth Śvetāmbara Jains*. Doctoral Dissertation, Johannes Gutenberg-Universität Mainz, Mainz 1994.

FLÜGEL 1995–1996 = Flügel, Peter: 'The Ritual Circle or the Terāpanth Śvetāmbar Jains.' *Bulletin D'Études Indiennes* 13 (1995–96) 117–76.

FLÜGEL 1997 = Flügel, Peter: 'Review: J. Laidlaw 1995: Riches and Renunciation.' *Journal of the Royal Anthropological Institute* 3,2 (1997) 401–2.

FLÜGEL 2000 = Flügel, Peter: 'Protestantische und Post-Protestantische Jaina Reformbewegungen: Zur Geschichte und Organisation der Sthānakavāsī I.' *Berliner Indologische Studien* 15–17 (2003) 149–240.

FLÜGEL 2005 = Flügel, Peter: 'The Invention of Jainism: A Short History of Jaina Studies.' *Journal of Jaina Studies* 11 (2005) 1–19 (Kyoto) [also: *International Journal of Jain Studies* 1 2005: www.soas.ac.uk/ijjs].

FLÜGEL 2006a = Flügel, Peter: 'Demographic Trends in Jaina Monasticism.' Peter Flügel (ed.): *Studies in Jaina History and Culture: Disputes and Dialogues*. Routledge, London 2006: 312–98.

FLÜGEL 2006b = Flügel, Peter: 'Jainism and Society [Review Article of J. E. Cort. 2002. Jains in the World. Religious Values and Ideology in India].' *Bulletin of the School of Oriental and African Studies* 69,1 (2006) 91–112.

FLÜGEL (forthcoming) = Flügel, Peter. 'The Power of Death: The Politics of Relic Worship Amongst the Jains', in: Peter Flügel; Gustaaf Houtman (eds.): *Asceticism and Power in South and Southeast Asia*. Routledge, London in press.

FOLKERT 1993 = Folkert, Kendall W.: *Scripture and Community: Collected Essays on the Jains*. Ed. J. E. Cort. Scholars Press, Atlanta 1993.

FOUCAULT 1981 = Foucault, Michel: *L'ordre du discours*. Gallimard, Paris 1971 [English translation: 'The Order of Discourse.' Translated by Ian McLeod. In: R. Young (ed.): *Untying the Text: A Poststructuralist Reader*. Routledge and Kegan Paul, London 1981: 48–78].

FRIED 1978 = Fried, C.: *Right and Wrong*. Cambridge (Massachusetts) 1978.

FUCHS 1989 = Fuchs, Peter: 'Die Weltflucht der Mönche: Anmerkungen zur Funktion des monastisch-asketischen Schweigens', in: P. Fuchs, N. Luhmann (eds.): *Reden und Schweigen*. Suhrkamp, Frankfurt am Main 1989: 21–45.

GADAMER 1993 = Gadamer, Hans-Georg: *Gesammelte Werke II*. J.C.B. Mohr (Paul Siebeck), Tübingen 1993.

GAEFFKE 1970 = Gaeffke, P.: 'On the Conception of the Dialogue in Hindi Narratives', *Wiener Zeitschrift für die Kunde Süd- und Ostasiens* 14 (1970) 33–38.

GANERI 1999 = Ganeri, Jonardon: *Semantic Powers: Meaning and the Means of Knowing in Classical Indian Philosophy*. Clarendon Press, Oxford 1999.

GANERI 2001 = Ganeri, Jonardon: *Philosophy in Classical India*. Routledge, London 2001.

GANERI 2002 = Ganeri, Jonardon: 'Jaina Logic and the Philosophical Basis of Pluralism.' *History and Philosophy of Logic* 23 (2002) 267–81.

GARFINKEL–SACKS 1970 = Garfinkel, Harold; Sacks, Harvey: 'On Formal Structures of Practical Actions', in: J.C. McKinney, E.A. Tiryakian (eds.): *Theoretical Sociology*. Appleton–Century–Crofts, New York 1970: 337–366.

GERT 1973 = Gert, Bernard: *The Moral Rules: A New Rational Foundation for Morality*. Harper & Row, New York 1973.

GHATAGE 1938 = Ghatage, A.M.: 'Parallel Passages in the Daśavaikālika and the Ācārāṅga.' *New Indian Antiquary* 1,2 (1938) 130–37.

GHATAGE 1996–2003 = Ghatage, A.M. (ed.): *A Comprehensive and Critical Dictionary of the Prakrit Languages with Special Reference to Jain Literature*. Vol. I–III.1–2. Bhandarkar Oriental Research Institute, Pune 1996–2003.

GIGLIOLI 1972 = Giglioli, P. P. (ed.): *Language and Social Context*. Penguin, Harmondsworth 1972.

GIRARD 1977 = Girard, R.: *La violence et le sacré*. Editions Bernard Grasset, Paris 1972 [English translation: *Violence and the Sacred*. Translated by P. Gregory. The Johns Hopkins University Press, Baltimore1977].

GLADIGOW 1997 = Gladigow, Burkhard: 'Erwerb religiöser Kompetenz. Kult und Öffentlichkeit in den klassischen Religionen', in: G. Binder, K. Ehrlich (eds.): *Religiöse Kommunikation—Formen und Praxis vor der Neuzeit: Stätten und Formen der Kommunikation im Altertum VI*. Wissenschaflicher Verlag Trier, Trier 1997: 103–118.

GLASENAPP 1915 = Glasenapp, Helmuth von: *Die Lehre vom Karma in der Philosophie der Jainas*. Otto Harrassowitz, Leipzig 1915 [English translation: *The Doctrine of Karman in Jain Philosophy*. Translated from the original German by B. Gifford and revised by the author. Ed. H. R. Kapadia. Bombay: Bai Vijibai Jivanlal Panalal Charity Fund, 1942].

GLUCKMAN 1955 = Gluckman, Max: *The Judicial Process among the Barotse of Northern Rhodesia*. University Press, Manchester1955.

GÖHLER 1995a = Göhler, Lars: *Wort und Text bei Kumārila Bhaṭṭa*. Peter Lang, Frankfurt am Main 1995.

GÖHLER 1995b = Göhler, Lars: 'Gab es im alten Indien eine Sprechakttheorie?' *Beiträge zur Geschichte der Sprachwissenschaft* 5 (1995) 65–89.

GOMBRICH 1971 = Gombrich, Richard: *Precept and Practice: Traditional Buddhism in the Rural Highlands of Ceylon*. Oxford University Press, Oxford 1971.

GOMBRICH 1988 = Gombrich, Richard: *Theravāda Buddhism: A Social History from Ancient Benares to Modern Colombo*. Routledge & Kegan Paul, London 1988.

GOMBRICH 1996 = Gombrich, Richard: *How Buddhism Began: The Conditional Genesis of the Early Teachings*. Athlone, London 1996.

GONDA 1959 = Gonda, Jan: 'Why are Ahiṁsā and Similar Concepts often Expressed in a Negative Form?' Jan Gonda: *Four Studies in the Language of the Veda*. Disputationes Theno-Trajectinaeis. Mouton, 'S-Gravenage 1959: 95–117.

GOONASEKERE 1986 = Goonasekere, Ratna Sunilsantha Abhayawardana: *Renunciation and Monasticism among the Jainas of India*. Ph.D. Dissertation. University of California, San Diego 1986.

GRANOFF 1992 = Granoff, Phyllis: 'The Violence of Non-Violence: A Study of Some Jain Responses to Non-Jain Religious Practices.' *The Journal of the International Association of Buddhist Studies* 15,1 (1992) 1–43.

GRANOFF 1993 = Granoff, Phyllis: 'Going by the Book: The Role of Written Texts in Medieval Jain Sectarian Conflicts.' *Jain Studies in Honour of Jozef Deleu*. In: SMET–WATANABE (1993: 315–38).

GRICE 1975 = Grice, H. Paul: 'Logic and Conversation.' P. Cohen, J. L. Morgan (eds.): *Syntax and Semantics*. Vol. 3. Academic Press, London 1975: 41–58.

GRICE 1978 = Grice, H. Paul: 'Further Notes on Logic and Conversation.' P. Cole (ed.): *Syntax and Semantics*. Vol. 9. Academic Press, New York 1978: 113–28.

GRIFFITHS 1981 = Griffiths, Paul: 'Concentration or Insight: The Problematic of Theravāda Buddhist Meditation-Theory.' *Journal of the American Academy of Religion* 49,4 (1981) 605–624.

GUMPERZ 1961 = Gumperz, John J.: 'Speech Variation and the Study of Indian Civilization.' *American Anthropologist* (*N.S.*) 63,5,1 (1961) 976–88.

GUMPERZ 1964 = Gumperz, John J.: 'Linguistic and Social Interaction in Two Communities.' *American Anthropologist* (*N.S.*) 66,6,2 (1964) 137–53.

GUMPERZ 1972 = Gumperz, John J.: 'The Speech Community.' D.L. Shils (ed.): *International Encyclopedia of the Social Sciences*. Macmillan, London 1968: 381–86 [reprinted: GIGLIOLI (1972: 219–31)].

GUMPERZ 1995 = Gumperz, John J.: *Discourse Strategies*. Cambridge University Press, Cambridge 1995 [first edition: Cambridge 1982].

GUMPERZ–HYMES 1986 = Gumperz, John J.; Hymes, Dell (Eds.): *Directions in Sociolinguistics: The Ethnography of Communication*. Holt, Rinehart, & Winston, New York1972: 35–71 [reprinted: Basil Blackwell, Oxford 1986].

GUNARATNE 1980 = Gunaratne, R. D.: 'Understanding Nāgārjuna's *catuṣkoṭi*.' *Philosophy East & West* 30,2 (1980) 211–239.

GUNARATNE 1986 = Gunaratne, R. D.: 'The Logical Form of *catuṣkoṭi*: A New Solution.' *Philosophy East & West* 36,3 (1986) 213–234.

GÜNTHER 1988 = Günther, Klaus: *Der Sinn für Angemessenheit: Anwendungsdiskurse in Recht und Moral*. Suhrkamp, Frankfurt am Main 1988.

HAACK 1974 = Haack, Susan: *Deviant Logic: Some Philosophical Ideas*. Cambridge University Press, Cambridge 1974.

HABERMAS 1975 = Habermas, Jürgen: *Zur Entwicklung der Interaktionskompetenz*. Gesellschaft zur Förderung der Wissenschaft, Frankfurt am Main 1975.

HABERMAS 1980–1981 = Habermas, Jürgen: *Theorie des kommunikativen Handelns*. 2 Bände. Suhrkamp, Frankfurt am Main 1980–1981 [English translation: HABERMAS (1984–1987)].

HABERMAS 1983 = Habermas, Jürgen: *Moralbewußtsein und kommunikatives Handeln*. Suhrkamp, Frankfurt am Main 1983 [English translation: HABERMAS (1990)].

HABERMAS 1984–1987 = Habermas, Jürgen: *The Theory of Communicative Action*. Vol. 1–2. Translated by Thomas McCarthy. Polity Press, Cambridge 1984–1987 [English translation of HABERMAS (1980–1981)].

HABERMAS 1984 = Habermas, Jürgen: *Vorstudien und Ergänzungen zur Theorie des kommunikativen Handelns*. Suhrkamp, Frankfurt am Main 1995 [first edition: 1984].

HABERMAS 1985 = Habermas, Jürgen: *Der philosophische Diskurs der Moderne*. Suhrkamp, Frankfurt am Main 1985.

HABERMAS 1986 = Habermas, Jürgen: 'Entgegnung.' A. Honneth, H. Joas (eds.): *Kommunikatives Handeln. Beiträge zu Jürgen Habermas' 'Theorie des kommunikativen Handelns*.' Suhrkamp, Frankfurt am Main 1986: 327–405.

HABERMAS 1988 = Habermas, Jürgen: *Nachmetaphysisches Denken*. Suhrkamp, Frankfurt am Main 1988.

HABERMAS 1990 = Habermas, Jürgen: *Moral Consciousness and Communicative Action*. Translated by Christian Lenhardt and Shierry Weber Nicholson. The M.I.T. Press, Cambridge (Massachusetts) 1990 [English translation of HABERMAS (1983)].

HABERMAS 1991 = Habermas, Jürgen: *Erläuterungen zur Diskursethik*. Suhrkamp, Frankfurt am Main 1991 [English translation: *Justification & Application: Remarks on Discourse Ethics*. Translated by Ciaran P. Cronin. The M.I.T. Press, Cambridge (Massachusetts) 1993].

HABERMAS 1993 = Habermas, Jürgen: 'Comments on John Searle: "Meaning, Communication, and Representation".' LEPORE–VAN GULICK (1993: 17–30).

HABERMAS 1996 = Habermas, Jürgen: 'On the Cognitive Content of Morality.' *Proceedings of the Aristotelian Society* 96,3 (1996) 335–358.

HABERMAS 1998 = Habermas, Jürgen: 'Reply to Symposium Participants, Benjamin N. Cardozo School of Law.' M. Rosenfeld, A. Arato (eds.): *Habermas on Law and Democracy: Critical Exchanges*. University of California Press, Berkeley 1998: 381–452.

HABERMAS 2004 = Habermas, Jürgen: *Wahrheit und Rechtfertigung: Philosophische Aufsätze. Erweiterte Ausgabe.* Suhrkamp, Frankfurt am Main 2004 [first edition: Frankfurt am Main 1999. English translation: *Truth and Justification.* Translation of the First Edition by Barbara Fultner. Polity Press, Cambridge 2003].

HABERMAS 2005 = Habermas, Jürgen: *Zwischen Naturalismus und Religion: Philosophische Aufsätze.* Suhrkamp, Frankfurt am Main 2005.

HACKER 1985 = Hacker, Paul: *Grundlagen Indischer Dichtung und Indischen Denkens.* Aus dem Nachlass herausgegeben von Klaus Rüping. Publications of the De Nobili Research Libarary 12. Sammlung de Nobili, Wien 1985.

HANDIQUI 1968 = Handiqui, Krishna Kanta: *Yaśastilaka and Indian Culture. Or Soma deva's Yaśastilaka and Aspects of Jainism and Indian Thought and Culture in the Tenth Century.* Jīvarāja Jaina Granthamālā No. 2, Jaina Saṁskṛti Saṁrakṣaka Saṅgha, Sholapur 1968 [first edition: 1949].

HARE 1972 = Hare, Richard Mervyn. 'Wrongness and Harm.' *Essays on Moral Concepts*, 92–109. Macmillan, London 1972.

HARE 1981 = Hare, Richard Mervyn: *Moral Thinking: Its Levels, Method, and Point.* Clarendon Press, Oxford 1981.

HARNAD 1999 = Harnad, Stevan: 'Re: Are Axioms Empirical?' 19 February (1999) 1 [http://www.ecs.soton.ac.uk/~harnad/Hypermail/Advanced.AI99/0009.html].

HAYNES 1991 = Haynes, Douglas E.: *Rhetoric and Ritual in Colonial India: The Shaping of a Public Culture in Surat City, 1852–1928.* University of California Press, Berkeley 1991.

HEGEL 1981 = Hegel, Georg Wilhelm Friedrich: *Phänomenologie des Geistes.* Suhrkamp, Frankfurt am Main 1981 [first edition: 1807].

HEIDEGGER 1927 = Heidegger, Martin: *Sein und Zeit.* Max Niemeyer Verlag, Tübingen 1927 [English translation: *Being and Time.* Translated by J. Macquarrie & E. Robinson: Harper, New York 1962].

HERTEL 1922 = Hertel, Johannes: *On the Literature of the Shvetambaras of Gujarat.* Sächsische Forschungsinstitute in Leipzig. Forschungsinstitut für Indogermanistik Indische Abteilung Nr. 1, Merkert & Petters, Leipzig 1922.

HICK 1969 = Hick, John: 'Religious Faith as Experiencing-As.' G.N.A. Vesey (ed.): *Talk of God.* Macmillan, London 1969.

HOERNLE 1989 = Hoernle, A. F. Rudolf. See UD.

HORN 1973 = Horn, Laurence R.: 'Greek Grice: A Brief Survey of Proto-Conversational Rules in the History of Logic.' *Chicago Linguistic Society* 9 (1973) 205–14.

HORN 1985 = Horn, Laurence R.: 'Metalinguistic Negation and Pragmatic Ambiguity.' *Language* 61,1 (1985) 121–74.

HORN 2001 = Horn, Laurence R.: *A Natural History of Negation*. CSLI Publications, Stanford: 2001 [first edition: Chicago University Press, Chicago 1989].

HORN–WARD 2004 = Horn, Laurence R.; Ward, Gregory L. (eds.). *The Handbook of Pragmatics*. Oxford: Blackwell, 2004.

HÖSLE 1997 = Hösle, Vittorio: *Die Krise der Gegenwart und die Verantwortung der Philosophie*. 3. Auflage. Beck, München 1997.

HOUTMAN 1999 = Houtman, Gustaaf: *Mental Culture in Burmese Crisis Politics: Aung San Suu Kyi and the National League for Democracy*. Institute for the Study of Languages and Cultures of Asia and Africa, Tokyo 1999.

HUMPHREY–LAIDLAW 1994 = Humphrey, Caroline; Laidlaw, James: *The Archetypal Actions of Ritual: A Theory of Ritual Illustrated by the Jain Rite of Worship*. Clarendon Press, Oxford 1994.

HYMES 1972a = Hymes, Dell: 'On Communicative Competence', in: J. Pride, J. Holmes (eds.): *Sociolinguistics*. Penguin, Harmondsworth 1972 [first edition: 1971].

HYMES 1972b = Hymes, Dell: 'Models of the Interaction of Language and Social Life', in: GUMPERZ–HYMES (1986: 35–71).

JACOBI 1884 = Jacobi, Hermann: *Jaina Sūtras I. Sacred Books of the East* Vol. 22 Oxford University Press, Oxford 1884.

JACOBI 1895 = Jacobi, Hermann: *Jaina Sūtras II. Sacred Books of the East* Vol. 45 Oxford University Press, Oxford 1895.

JACOBI 1903 = Jacobi, Hermann: 'Über den nominalen Stil des wissenschaftlichen Sanskrit.' *Indogermanische Forschung* 14 (1903) 236–251.

JAFFRELOT 1993 = Jaffrelot, Christophe: 'Hindu Nationalism: Strategic Syncretism in Ideology Building.' *Economic and Political Weekly* 20–27 March (1993) 517–24.

JAIN 1929 = Jain, Campat Rāy: *Faith, Knowledge and Conduct*. The Indian Press, Allahabad 1929.

JAIN 1981 = Jain, Jagdish Chandra: *Prakrit Narrative Literature: Origin and Growth*. Manohar, Delhi 1981.

JAINI 1974 = Jaini, Padmanabh S.: 'Jain Ṛṣabha as an Avatāra of Viṣṇu.' *Bulletin of the School of Oriental and African Studies* 40,2 (1974) 321–37.

JAINI 1979 = Jaini, Padmanabh S.: *The Jaina Path of Purification*. University of California Press, Berkeley 1979.

JAINI 1991 = Jaini, Padmanabh S.: 'Is there a Popular Jainism?' In: CARRITHERS–HUMPHREY (1991: 187–200).

JAMES 1982 = James, William: *The Varieties of Religious Experience*. Penguin, London 1982 [first edition: 1902].

JAYATILLEKE 1967 = Jayatilleke, K.N.: 'The Logic of Four Alternatives.' *Philosophy East & West* 17,1/4 (1967) 69–83.

JOHNSON 1995a = Johnson, William J.: *Harmless Souls: Karmic Bondage and Religious Change in Early Jainism with Special Reference to Umāsvāti and Kundakunda*. Motilal Banarsidas, Delhi 1995.

JOHNSON 1995b = Johnson, William J.: 'The Religious Function of Jaina Philosophy: *Anekāntavāda* Reconsidered.' *Religion* 25 (1995) 41–50.

JOHNSON 1999 = Johnson, William J.: 'Kundakunda: Two-Standpoints and the Socio-Religious Function of Anekāntavāda', in: N. K. Wagle, Olle Qvarnström (eds.): *Approaches to Jain Studies: Philosophy, Logic, Rituals and Symbols*. [Proceedings of the International Conference on Approaches to Jaina Studies: Philosophy, Logic, Rituals and Symbols, 31.03–2.04.1995 Toronto], University of Toronto: Center for South Asian Studies, Toronto 1999: 101–12.

JONES 1978 = Jones, Richard Hubert: 'The Nature and Function of Nāgārjuna's Arguments.' *Philosophy East and West* 28,4 (1978) 485–502.

KANNOOMAL 1917 = Kannoomal, Lala: *The Saptabhangi Naya or the Pluralist Aspects of the Jaina Dialectics*. Atmanand Jain Pustak Pracharak Mandal, Agra 1917.

KANT 1974 = Kant, Immanuel: *Kritik der reinen Vernunft*. Hrsg. Wilhelm Weischedel. Suhrkamp, Frankfurt am Main 1974 [first edition: 1787].

KANTOROWICZ 1957 = Kantorowicz, Ernst Hartwig: *The King's Two Bodies: A Study in Mediaeval Political Theology*. Princeton University Press, Princeton 1957.

KEENAN 1976 = Keenan, Ellnor Ochs: 'On the Universality of Conversational Implicatures.' *Language and Society* 5 (1976) 67–80.

KOKOSZYNSKA 1936 = Kokoszynska, M.: 'Über den absoluten Wahrheitsbegriff und einige andere semantische Begriffe.' *Erkenntnis* 6 (1936) 143–65.

KS = Bhadrabāhu: *Kappa-sutta* [*Kalpa-sūtra*]. Walther Schubring (tr.): *Das Kalpa-sūtra. Die alte Sammlung jinistischer Mönchsvorschriften*. Einleitung, Text, Analysen, übersetzung, Glossar. Indica 2. Hg. E. Leumann. Otto Harrassowitz, Leipzig 1905 [English Translation of the revised German translation: J.A.S. Burgess: 'The Kalpa-Sūtra. An Old Collection of Disciplinary Rules for Jaina monks.' *The Indian Antiquary* 39 (1910) 257–267].

LA BOÉTIE 1983 = La Boétie, Étienne de: *Discours de la Servitude volontaire*. Flammarion, Paris 1983.

LAIDLAW 1985 = Laidlaw, James: 'Profit, Salvation and Profitable Saints.' *Cambridge Anthropology* 9,3 (1985) 50–70.

LAIDLAW 1995 = Laidlaw, James: *Riches and Renunciation: Religion, Economy and Society among the Jains*. Clarendon, Oxford 1995.

LALWANI 1973 = Lalwani, Kustur Chand: *Ārya Sayyambhava's Daśavaikālika Sūtra*. Translation and Notes. Motilal Banarsidas, Delhi 1973.

LALWANI 1973–85 = Lalwani, Kustur Chand: *Sudharma Svāmī's Bhagavatī Sūtra*. Prakrit Text with English Translation of śatakas 1–11. Vol. 1–4. Jain Bhawan, Calcutta 1973–1985.

LAMOTTE 1992 = Lamotte, Étienne: 'The Assessment of Textual Interpretation in Buddhism', in: D.S. Lopez (ed.): *Buddhist Hermeneutics*. Studies in East Asian Buddhism 6. University of Hawaii Press, Honolulu 1992: 11–27 [first edition: 1949].

LEPORE–VAN GULICK 1993 = Lepore, E.; Van Gulick, R. (eds.): *John Searle and his Critics*. Blackwell, Oxford 1993 [first edition: Blackwell, Oxford 1991].

LEUMANN 1885 = Leumann, Ernst: 'Die alten Berichte von den Schismen der Jaina.' *Indische Studien* 17 (1885) 91–135.

LEVINSON 2000 = Levinson, Stephen C.: *Presumptive Meanings: The Theory of Generalized Conversational Implicature*. MIT Press, Cambridge (Mass.) 2000.

LÉVI-STRAUSS 1970 = Lévi-Strauss, Claude. *Mythologiques: le cru et le cuit*. Plon, Paris 1970 [first edition: 1964. English translation: *The Raw and the Cooked: Introduction to a Science of Mythology: I*. Translated by John and Doreen Weightman. Jonathan Cape, London 1970].

LINKENBACH 1986 = Linkenbach, Antje: *Opake Gestalten des Denkens: Jürgen Habermas und die Rationalität fremder Lebensformen*. Fink Verlag, München 1986.

LORENZEN 1995 = Lorenzen, David N.: 'Introduction.' David N. Lorenzen (ed.): *Bhakti Religion in North India: Community Identity and Political Action*. SUNY, Albany 1995.

LUHMANN 1988 = Luhmann, Niklas: *Macht*. 2. durchgesehene Auflage. Enke Verlag, Stuttgart 1988 [first edition: 1975. English translation: *Trust and Power: Two Works by Niklas Luhmann*. With an introduction by Gianfanco Poggi. Translated by Howard Davis, John Raffan & Kathryn Rooney. John Wiley,Chichester 1979].

LUHMANN 1982 = Luhmann, Niklas: *Funktion der Religion*. Suhrkamp, Frankfurt am Main 1982 [first edition: 1977].

LUHMANN 1990 = Luhmann, Niklas: *Die Wissenschaft der Gesellschaft*. Suhrkamp, Frankfurt am Main 1990.

LUHMANN 2002 = Luhmann, Niklas: *Das Recht der Gesellschaft*. Suhrkamp, Frankfurt am Main 2002.

MĀc = Vaṭṭakera: *Mūlâcāra*. See: OKUDA (1975).

MAHIAS 1985 = Mahias, Marie-Claude: *Délivrance et convivialité: Le système culinaire des Jaina*. Éditions de la Maison des Sciences de l'Homme, Paris 1985.

MALAMOUND 1982 = Malamoud, Charles: 'On the rhetorics and semantics of puruṣārtha.' *Contributions to Indian Sociology* (*N.S.*) 15 (1982) 33-54.

MĀLVAṆIYĀ 1968 = Mālvaṇiyā, Dalsukh D.: 'Introduction', in: Muni Puṇyavijaya, Pt. Dalsukh Mālvaṇiyā, Pt. Amritlāl Mohanlāl Bhojak (eds.): *Nandisuttaṁ and Aṇuyogaddārāiṁ*. Jaina-āgama-Series No. 1. Mahāvīra Jaina Vidyālaya, Bombay 1968: 1–127.

MĀLVAṆIYĀ 1971 = Mālvaṇiyā, Dalsukh. D.: 'Introduction', in: Muni Puṇyavijaya, Pt. Dalsukh Mālvaṇiyā, Pt. Amritlāl Mohanlāl Bhojak (ed.): *Paṇṇavaṇāsuttaṁ*. Jaina-āgama-Series No. 9, Part 2. Mahāvīra Jaina Vidyālaya, Bombay 1971: 201–487.

MĀLVAṆIYĀ 1996 = Mālvaṇiyā, Dalsukh. D.: 'The Jain Agamas.' Translated by Nagin Shah. Published on the 'Jain World' website (1996), http://sunsite.unc.edu/jainism/philosophy/smlbooks/agamdm.txt

MARRIOTT 1976 = Marriott, McKim: 'Hindu Transactions: Diversity without Dualism', in: B. Kapferer (ed.): *Transaction and Meaning. Directions in the Anthropology of Exchange and Symbolic Behaviour*. Institute of Human Issues, Philadelphia 1976: 109–42.

MATILAL 1981 = Matilal, Bimal Krishna: *The Central Philosophy of Jainism (Anekānta-Vāda)*. L.D. Institute of Indology, Ahmedabad 1981.

MATILAL 1999 = Matilal, Bimal Krishna: *The Character of Logic in India*. Eds. J. Ganeri & H. Tiwari. Oxford University Press, New Delhi 1999 [1st ed.: 1998].

MDhŚ = *Mānava-dharma-śāstra* [*Manu-smṛti*]. Wendy Doniger, Brian K. Smith (English tr.): as *The Laws of Manu*. Penguin, London 1991.

MEHTA 1991 = Mehta, Digish: *Shrimad Rajachandra: A Life*. Rajchandra Janma Shatabdi Mandal, Ahmedabad 1991.

MISRA 1972 = Misra, R.: 'The Jains in an Urban Setting.' *Bulletin of the Anthropological Survey of India* 21,1 (1972) 1–67.

MMK = Nāgārjuna: *Mūla-madhyamaka-kārikā*. Jay L. Garfield (tr.): *The Fundamental Wisdom of the Middle Way*. Translation and Commentary by J.L. Garfield, Oxford University Press, Oxford 1995.

MONE 1987 = Mone, Neelima N.: 'A Jaina View of the Kīcaka-Episode in the *Mahābhārata*.' *Oriental Conference* 32 (1987) 319–25.

MONIER-WILLIAMS 1986 = Monier-Williams, Monier: *Sanskrit-English Dictionary*. New Edition, Greatly Enlarged and Improved. Oxford University Press, Oxford 1899 [reprinted: Marwah Publications, New Delhi 1986].

MOSCOVICI 1985 = Moscovici, Serge: 'Social Influence and Conformity.' G. Lindzey, E. Aronson (eds.): *The Handbook of Social Psychology*. 3rd Edition, Vol. II. Random House, New York 1985: 347–412.

MURTI 1955 = Murti, Tirupattur Ramaseshayyar Venkatachala: *The Central Philosophy of Buddhism: A Study of the Mādhyamika System*. Allen and Unwin, London 1955.

NSā = Kundakunda: *Niyama-sāra*. Uggar Jain (ed., tr.): *Niyamasāra of Kundakunda*. Sacred Books of the Jainas Vol. 9, Jagmandarlal Jaini Memorial Series 5, The Central Jaina Publishing House, Lucknow 1931.

NYAYAVIJAYA 1998 = Nyayavijaya: *Jaina Philosophy and Religion*. Translated by Nagin J.Shah. Motilal Banarsidas, Delhi 1998 [Gujarātī Original: *Jaina Darśana*. Jainasahityamandira, Pune 1935].

OETKE 1991 = Oetke, Klaus: *Zur Methode der Analyse Philosophischer Sūtratexte: Die Pramāṇa Passagen der Nyāyasūtras*. Verlag für Orientalistische Fachpublikationen, Reinbeck 1991.

OETKE 1997 = Oetke, Klaus: 'Pragmatic Principles and Maxims of Interpretation.' *Studien zur Indologie und Iranistik* 21 (1997) 133–52.

OHIRA 1994 = Ohira, Suzuko: *A Study of the Bhagavatīsūtra. A Chronological Analysis*. Prakrit Text Society, Ahmedabad 1994.

OKUDA 1975 = Okuda, Kiyaoaki. *Eine Digambara-Dogmatik: Das fünfte Kapitel von Vaṭṭakeras Mūlācāra herausgegeben, übersetzt und kommentiert*. Franz Steiner Verlag, Wiesbaden 1975.

PAINE 1981 = Paine, Robert: 'Introduction', in: Robert Paine (ed.): *Politically Speaking: Cross-Cultural Studies of Rhetoric*. Institute for the Study of Human Issues, Philadelphia 1981: 1–6.

PANDHARIPANDE 2006 = Pandharipande, Rajeshwari V.: 'Ideology, Authority, and Language Choice: Language of Religion in South Asia', in: Tope Omoniyi, Joshua A. Fishman (eds.): *Explorations in the Sociology of Language and Religion*. John Benjamins Publishing, Amsterdam 2006: 141–64.

Paṇṇ = *Paṇṇavaṇā-sutta* [*Prajñāpanā-sūtra*]. Muni Puṇyavijaya, Pt. Dalsukh Mālvaṇiyā, Pt. Amritlāl Mohanlāl Bhojak. (eds.): *Paṇṇavaṇā (Prajñāpanā)*. Jaina-āgama-Series No. 9, Part 1–2. Mahāvīra Jaina Vidyālaya, Bombay 1969–1971. See also: PaṇṇṬ, PaṇṇV.

PaṇṇṬ = Malayagiri: *Prajñāpanā-ṭīkā*. (1) *Śrīmac-chyāmâcārya-dṛbdhaṁ śrīman-malayagiryâcārya-vihita-vivaraṇa-yutaṁ śrī-prajñāpanôpāṅgaṁ (Pūrvârddhaṁ)*. Agamôdāya-samiti, Mehasāna 1918, 1919 [printed: Nirṇaya-Sāgara Press, Bombay]. (2) Paṇḍit Bhagavānadāsa Harṣacandra [Anuvādaka ane Saṁśodhaka] (ed.): *Vācakavara-Bhagavad-ārya-śyāmâcārya-viracita. Mūla tathā śrīmad-āçārya-Malayagiri-viracita ṭīkānā Anuvāda-sahita*. Bhāg I–III. Jaina Sosāyaṭī, Amadāvāda (Ahmedabad) 1935.

PaṇṇV = Haribhadra-sūri: *Prajñāpanā-vyākhyā* (*Pūrvabhāgaḥ*). Ṛṣabha-deva-kesarī-malajī [Mudrayiśrī] (ed.): *Su-vahita-dhurandhara-sāhitya-saudhānanya-staṁbhôpama-śrī-Haribhadra-Sūri-sūtrita-pradeśa-vyākhyā-saṁkalitaṁ*. Phakīrcanda Maganalāla Badāmī, Jaina-vijayânanda Priṇṭiṅg Pres, Surat 1947.

PASU = Amṛtacandra-sūri: *Puruṣârtha-siddhy-upāya*. Ajit Prasada (ed., tr.): *Purushartha-Siddhyupaya (Jaina-pravachana-rahasya-kosha), with an Introduction, Translation and Original Commentaries in English*. J.L. Jaini Memorial Seiries VI, Abhinandan Prasada Jindal, The Central Publishing House, Ajitashram, Lucknow 1933.

PEUKERT 1984 = Peukert, Helmut: *Science, Action, and Fundamental Theology: Toward a Theology of Communicative Action*. Translated from the original German by James Bohman. MIT Press, Cambridge (Massachusetts) 1984 [first edition: *Wissenschaftstheorie – Handlungstheorie – fundamentale Theologie: Analysen zu Ansatz und Status theologischer Theoriebildung*. Patmos, Düsseldorf 1976].

PEUKERT 1992 = Peukert, Helmut: 'Fundamental Theology and Communicative Praxis as the Ethics of Universal Solidarity', in: REIMER (1992: 221–46).

PH = Aristotle: *Peri Hermeneias*. E.M. Edghill (tr.); *On Interpretation*. In: W.D. Ross (ed.): *The Works of Aristotle*, Volume 1: *Logic*. Clarendon Press, Oxford 1928 [http://classics.mit.edu/Aristotle/-interpretation.html].

PIAGET 1937 = Piaget, Jean: *La construction du rēel chez l'enfant*. Delachaux et Niestlé, Paris 1937.

PIATIGORSKY 1985 = Piatigorsky, Alexander: 'Some Phenomenological Observations on the Study of Indian Religion', in: BURGHART–CANTLIE (1985: 208–58).

POTTER 1970 = Potter, Karl: 'Realism, Speech-acts, and Truth-gaps in Indian and Western Philosophy.' *Journal of Indian Philosophy* 1,1 (1970) 13–21.

POTTER 1984 = Potter, Karl: 'A Speech-Act Model for Understandig Navya-Nyāya Epistemology', in: Bimal Krishna Matilal, Jaysankar Lal Shaw (eds.): *Analytical Philosophy in Comparative Perspective*. D. Reidel, Dordrecht 1984: 213–230.

PRATT 1986 = Pratt, Mary Louise. 'Ideology and Speech-Act Theory.' *Poetics Today* 7,1 (1986) 59–72.

PRETS 2004 = Prets, Ernst: 'Theories of Debate, Proof and Counter-Proof in the Early Indian Dialectical Tradition', in: Piotr Balcerowicz, Marek Mejor (eds.): *Essays in Indian Philosophy and Literature*. Motilal Banarsidas, Delhi 2004: 435–448.

PRIEST 2006 = Priest, Graham: *In Contradiction: A Study of the Transconsistent*. Second Edition. Oxford University Press, Oxford 2006 [first edition: Martinus Nijhoff, Leiden 1987].

PRIEST–ROUTLEY 1989 = Priest, Graham; Routley, Richard. 'First Historical Introduction: A Preliminary History of Paraconsistent and Dialethic Approaches.' G. Priest, R. Routley, J. Norman (eds.): *Paraconsistent Logic: Essays on the Inconsistent*. Philosophia Verlag, München 1989: 3–75.

PRINCE 1982 = Prince, Ellen F. 'Grice and Universality: A Reappraisal.' [ftp://babel.ling.upenn.edu/papers/faculty/ellen_prince/grice.ps].

PYE 1994 = Pye, Michael: 'Syncretism versus Synthesis.' *Method & Theory in the Study of Religion* 6–3 (1994) 217–29.

PYE 2003 = Pye, Michael: *Skilful Means: A Concept in Mahayana Buddhism*. Second Edition. Routledge, London 2003 [first edition: 1978].

RAJU 1954 = Raju, P. T.: 'The Principle of Four-Cornered Negation in Indian Philosophy.' *Review of Metaphysics* 7 (1954) 694–713.

RAMSEY 1967 = Ramsey, Ian Thomas: *Religious Language: An Empirical Placing of Theological Phrases*. SCM Press, London 1967 [first edition: 1957].

RATNACANDRA 1988 = Ratnacandra, Muni: *Sacitra Ardhamāgadhī Koṣa*. Bhāg 1–5. Motilal Banarsidas, Delhi 1988 [first edition: 1923].

REIMER 1992 = Reimer, A. James (ed.): *The Influence of the Frankfurt School on Contemporary Theology: Critical Theory and the Future of Religion*. Dubrovnik Papers in Honour of Rudolph J. Siebert. The Edwin Mellon Press, Lewiston 1992.

RENOU 1955 = Renou, Louis: 'Les pouvoirs de la parole dans le *Ṛg Veda*.' *Études Védiques et Panineennes* 1 (1955) 1–27.

ROBINSON 1957 = Robinson, Richard H.: 'Some Logical Aspects of Nāgārjuna's System.' *Philosophy East & West* 6,4 (1957) 291–308.

RUDOLPH–RUDOLPH 1984 = Rudolph, Susanne Hoeber; Rudolph, Lloyd I.: *Essays on Rajputana: Reflections on History, Culture and Administration*. Concept Publishing, New Delhi 1984.

RUSSELL 1905 = Russell, Bertrand: 'On Denoting.' *Mind* 14 (1905) 479–93.

RYAN 1998 = Ryan, James: 'Erotic Excess and Sexual Danger in the *Civakacintāmaṅi*.' J. E. Cort (ed.): *Open Boundaries: Jain Communities and Culture in Indian History*. State University of New York Press, Albany 1998: 67–84.

SAMARIAN 1969 = Samarian, William J.: 'Introduction', in: William J. Samarian (ed.): *Language in Religious Practice*. Newbury House Publiahers, Rowley 1969: 1–13.

SANGAVE 1980 = Sangave, Vilas A.: *Jaina Community*. 2nd Revised Edition. Popular Prakashan, Bombay 1980 [first edition: 1959].

SCHARF 1995 = Scharf, Peter M.: 'Early Indian Grammarians on a Speaker's Intention.' *Journal of the American Oriental Society* 115,1 (1995) 66–76.

SCHAYER 1933 = Schayer, Stanisław: 'Altindische Antizipationen der Aussagenlogik.' *Bulletin International de l'Academie Polonaise des Sciences et des Lettres, Classe de Philologie* (1933) 90–96 [English translation: by Joerg Tuske (tr.): 'Ancient Indian Anticipations of Propositional Logic.' Jonardon Ganeri (ed.): *Indian Logic: A Reader*. Curzon Press, London 2001: 96–101].

SCHMITHAUSEN 1981 = Schmithausen, Lambert: 'On some Aspects of Descriptions or Theories of Liberating Insight" and "Enlightenment" in Early Buddhism.' Klaus Bruhn, Albrecht Wezler (eds.): *Studien zum Jainismus und Buddhismus. Gedenkschrift für Ludwig Alsdorf*. Franz Steiner Verlag, Wiesbaden 1981.

SCHOPENHAUER 1977 = Schopenhauer, Arthur: *Parerga und Paralipomena II.1*. Diogenes Verlag, Zürich 1977 [first edition: 1850. English translation: *Parerga and Paralipomena*. Translated by E.F.J. Payne. Clarendon, Oxford 1974].

SCHROEDER 2000 = Schroeder, John: 'Nāgārjuna and the Doctrine of "Skillful Means".' *Philosophy East and West* 50,4 (2000) 559–583.

SCHUBRING 1932 = Schubring, Walther, see: DVS_1.

SCHUBRING 2000 = Schubring, Walther: *The Doctrine of the Jainas: Described after the Old Sources*. Translated from the Revised German Edition by Wolfgang Beurlen. With the Three Indices Enlarged and Added by Willem Bollée and Jayandra Soni. Motilal Banarsidas, Delhi 2000 [first German edition: 1935].

SEAL 1968 = Seal, Anil: *The Emergence of Indian Nationalism. Competition and Collaboration in the Later Nineteenth Century*. Cambridge University Press, Cambridge 1968.

SEARLE 1979 = Searle, John E.: *Expression and Meaning: Studies in the Theory of Speech Acts*. Cambridge University Press, Cambridge 1979.

SEARLE 1989 = Searle, John E.: *Intentionality: An Essay in the Philosophy of Mind*. Cambridge University Press, Cambridge 1989 [first edition: 1983].

SEARLE 1993 = Searle, John E.: 'Response: Meaning, Intentionality, and Speech Acts.' LEPORE–VAN GULICK (1993: 81–102).

SEYFORT RUEGG 1977 = Seyfort Ruegg, David: 'The Uses of the Four Positions of the *Catuṣkoṭi* and the Problem of the Description of Reality in Mahāyāna Buddhism.' *Journal of Indian Philosophy* 5 (1977) 1–71.

SEYFORT RUEGG 1985 = Seyfort Ruegg, David: 'Purport, Implicature and Presupposition: Sanskrit *Abhipraya* and Tibetan *Dgons Pa/Dgons Gzi* as Hermeneutical Concepts.' *Journal of Indian Philosophy* 13,4 (1985) 309–25.

SHAH 1966 = Shah, Nagin J.: 'Jainas on Testimony.' *Vishweshwarānand Indological Journal* 4,2 (1966) 209–27.

SHARF 1995 = Sharf, Robert H.: 'Buddhist Modernism and the Rhetoric of Meditative Experience.' *Numen* 42,3 (1995) 228–83.

SHARP 1960 = Sharp, Gene: *Gandhi Wields the Weapon of Moral Power: Three Case Histories*. Navajivan Publishing, Ahmedabad 1960.

SHARP 1973 = Sharp, Gene: *The Politics of Nonviolent Action*. 3 Vols, Porter Sargent, Boston 1973.

SINGER 1961 = Singer, Marcus George: *Generalization in Ethics: An Essay in the Logic of Ethics, with the Rudiments of a System of Moral Philosophy*. Alfred A. Knopf, New York 1961.

SMART 1964 = Smart, Ninian: *Doctrine and Argument in Indian Philosophy*. Allen and Unwin, London 1964.

SMART 1965 = Smart, Ninian: 'Interpretation and Mystical Experience.' *Religious Studies* 1 (1965) 75–87.

SMET–WATANABE 1993 = Smet, Rudy; Watanabe, Kenji (eds.): *Jain Studies in Honour of Jozef Deleu*. Hon-no-Tomosha, Tokyo 1993.

SN = *Sutta-nipāta*. Michael Viggo Fausböll (tr.): *The Sutta-Nipāta. A Collection of Discourses Being One of the Collection of the Canonical Books of the Buddhists*. Translated from the Pāli. The Sacred Books of the East X, Part II. The Clarendon Press, Oxford 1881.

SONTHEIMER 1991 = Sontheimer, Günther D. 'Hinduism: The Five Components and their Interaction.' G.D. Sontheimer, H. Kulke (eds.): *Hinduism Reconsidered*. New Manohar, Delhi 1991: 197–212 [first edition: 1989].

SPERBER & WILSON 1986 = Sperber, Dan; Wilson, Deidre: *Relevance: Communication and Cognition*. Basil Blackwell, Oxford 1986.

SSā = Kundakunda: *Samaya-sāra*. A. Chakravarti (ed., tr.): *Āchārya Kundakunda's Samayasāra, with English translation and commentary based upon Amṛtacandra's Ātmakhyāti*. Bharatiya Jnanpith, New Delhi, 1989.

STCHERBATSKY 1958 = Stcherbatsky, Fedor Ippolitovich: *Buddhist Logic*. 2 vols, Mouton, Gravenhage 1958 [first edition: *Bibliotheca Buddhica* 26, Издательство Академии Наук СССР, Ленинград / Leningrad I: 1930, II: 1932.]

STRAWSON 1950 = Strawson, Peter F.: 'On Referring.' *Mind* 59 (1950) 320–344.

STRECKER 1988 = Strecker, Ivo: *The Social Practice of Symbolization*. The Athlone Press, London 1988.

SUNAVALA 1922 = Sunavala, A.J.: *Vijaya Dharma Suri: His Life and Work*. Cambridge University Press, Cambridge 1922.

Sūy = *Sūya-gaḍaṁga* [*Sūtra-kṛtâṅga*]. English translation: JACOBI (1895: 235–435).

ŚrPr = Umāsvāti: *Śrāvaka-prajñapti*. Balacandra Sastri (ed.): *Haribhadra-sūri-viracita-vṛtti-samanvita; hindī anuvāda, prastāvanā, tathā anukramaṇikā-sahita sampādana-anuvāda*. Bhāratīya Jñānapīṭha, Nayi Dilli 1999.

STAAL 1962 = Staal, J. Frits: 'Negation and the Law of Contradiction in Indian Thought: A Study.' *Bulletin of the School of Oriental and African Studies* 25,1/3 (1962) 52–71.

TABER 1989 = Taber, John: 'Are Mantras Speech Acts? The Mīmāṁsā Point of View', in: Harvey P. Alper (ed.): *Understanding Mantras*. State University of New York Press, Albany 1989: 144–164.

TAMBIAH 1968 = Tambiah, Stanley J.: 'The Magical Power of Words.' *Man* (*N.S.*) 3 (1968) 175–208.

TAMBIAH 1977 = Tambiah, Stanley J.: *World Conqueror and World Renouncer: A Study of Buddhism and Polity in Thailand against a Historical Background*. Cambridge University Press, Cambridge 1977 [first edition: 1976].

TAMBIAH 1985 = Tambiah, Stanley J.: 'A Performative Approach to Ritual', in: Stanley J. Tambiah (ed.): *Culture, Thought and Social Action: An Anthropological Perspective*. Harvard University Press, Cambridge (Massachusetts) 1985 [first edition: 1979].

TANNEN 1984 = Tannen, Deborah: *Conversational Style: Analyzing Talk Among Friends*. Ablex Publications, Norwood (New Jersey) 1984.

TATIA 1951 = Tatia, Nathmal: *Studies in Jaina Philosophy*. Jain Cultural Research Society, Varanasi 1951.

TATIA–KUMAR 1981 = Tatia, Nathmal & Muni Mahendra Kumar: *Aspects of Jaina Monasticism*. Jain Vishva Bharati, Ladnun 1981.

Ṭhāṇ = *Ṭhāṇaṁga-sutta* [*Sthānâṅga-sūtra*]. (1) Acārya Tulsī [Vācaka Pramukha], Muni Nathmal [Sampādaka Vivecaka], Acārya Mahāprajña (eds.): *Thāṇaṁ (Mūl Pāṭh, Saṁskṛt Chāyā, Hindī Anuvāda tathā Ṭippaṇa)*. Jaina Viśva Bhāratī, Lāḍnūṁ 1976. (2) Muni Jambūvijaya [Sampādak] (ed.): *Sthānâṅga-sūtram. Navāṅgī-ṭīkā-kāra-śrī-Abhayadeva-sūri-viracita-vivaraṇa-sametaṁ*. Bhāg I–III. Jaina-āgama-Granthamālā 19 (1–3). Mahāvīra Jaina Vidyālaya, Muṁbaī 2002–2003. (3) Uttara Bhāratīya Pravartaka Amar Muni [Pradhāna Sampādaka], Śrīcand Surānā 'Saras' [Saha-Sampādaka] (eds.): *Sacitra Sthānâṅga Sūtra*. Bhāg I–II. Mūla Pāṭh-Hindī-Aṅgrezī Anuvāda, Vivecana evaṁ Raṅgīna Citroṁ Sahita. Padma Prakāśa, Dillī 2004.

TÖNNIES 1887 = Tönnies, Ferdinand. *Gemeinschaft und Gesellschaft: Abhandlung des Communismus und des Socialismus als empirischer Cultur-*

formen. Leipzig 1887 [English translation: *Community and Society*. Translated by Charles P. Loomis. The Michigan State University Press, East Lansing 1957].

TS = Umāsvāti / Umāsvāmin: *Tattvârtha-sūtra*. Nathmal Tatia (tr.): *That Which Is*. With the combined commentaries of Umāsvāti / Umāsvāmī, Pūjyapāda and Siddhasenagani. Harper Collins, New York 1994.

TULSĪ 1985 = Tulsī, Ācārya: *Illumination of Jaina Tenets* (*Jaina-Siddhānta-Dīpikā*). Translated by Satakari Mookerjee. Jain Vishva Bharati, Ladnun 1985 [first edition: 1945].

TURNER 1986 = Turner, Victor: *The Forest of Symbols*. Cornell University Press, Ithaca 1986 [first edition: 1967].

TYLER 1978 = Tyler, Stephen A.: *The Said and the Unsaid: Mind, Meaning, and Culture*. Academic Press, New York 1978.

UD = *Uvāsaga-dasāo* [*Upāsaka-daśāḥ* / *Upāsakâdhyayana-daśāḥ*]. A.F. Rudolf Hoernle (tr.): *The Uvāsaga-dasāo or the Religious Profession of the Uvāsaga Expounded in Ten Lectures Being the Seventh Anga of the Jains Translated from the Original Prakrit with Copies and Notes*. The Asiatic Society, Calcutta 1885–1890.

UPADHYAYA 1987 = Upadhyaya, Amrut M.: *The Kavyanusasana of Acharya Hemacandra: A Critical Study*. Ahmedabad 1987.

Uttar = *Uttarajjhayaṇa-sutta* [*Uttarâdhyayana-sūtra*]. (1) Upa-Pravartaka Amar Muni [Sampādaka], Śrīcand Surānā 'Saras' [Saha-Sampādaka] (eds.); Bṛj Mohan Jain [Aṅgrezī Anuvāda] (tr.): *Sacitra Uttarādhyayana Sūtra Mūla Pāṭha, Hindī-Aṅgrezī Anuvāda, Viśeṣa ṭippaṇa tathā Bhāvapūrṇa Citroṁ Sahit*. Ātmā Jñān Pīṭh, Mānasā Maṇḍī 1992. (2) English Translation: JACOBI (1895: 1–232).

VANDERVEKEN 1993 = Vanderveken, Daniel: 'Non-Literal Speech Acts and Conversational Maxims', in: LEPORE–VAN GULICK (1993: 371–84).

VELUTHAT 1978 = Veluthat, Kesavan: 'Royalty and Divinity: Legitimisation of Monarchical Power in South India.' *39th Session of the Indian History Congress, Hyderabad* (1978) 241–49.

VĀBh = Jinabhadra: *Viśeṣâvaśyaka-bhāṣā*. Dalasukha Malavaniya (ed.): *Śrī-jinabhadra-gaṇi-kṣamā-śramaṇa-viracitaṁ Viśeṣâvaśyaka-bhāṣyam. Svopajña-vṛtti-sahitam*. Lālabhai Dalapatabhai Bhāratīya Saṁskṛti Vidyāmandira, Amadavada 1966–1968.

Viy = *Viyāha-pannatti* [*Bhagavatī-sūtra*]. (1) DELEU (1970). (2) Kustur Chand Lalwani (tr.): *Sudharma Svāmī's Bhagavatī Sūtra*. Prakrit Text with English Translation of śatakas 1–11. Vol. 1–4. Jain Bhawan, Calcutta 1973–1985.

WAARDENBURG 1979 = Waardenburg, Jacques: 'The Language of Religion and the Study of Religions as Sign Systems', in: L. Honko (ed.): *Science of Religion: Studies in Methodology*. E.J. Brill, Leiden 1979: 441–457.

WAYMAN 1977 = Wayman, Alex: 'Who Understands the Four Alternatives of the Buddhist Texts.' *Philosophy East and West* 27,1 (1977) 3–21.

WEBER 1972 = Weber, Max: *Wirtschaft und Gesellschaft: Grundriß der verstehenden Soziologie*. 5. von Johannes Winckelmann revidierte Auflage. J.C.B. Mohr (Paul Siebeck), Tübingen 1972 [first edition: 1922. English translation: *Economy and Society: An Outline of Interpretive Sociology*. Edited by Guenther Roth and Claus Wittich. Translated by Ephraim Fischoff et al. Bedminster Press, New York 1968].

WEBER 1978 = Weber, Max: *Gesammelte Aufsätze zur Religionssoziologie II*. J.C.B. Mohr (Paul Siebeck), Tübingen 1978 [first edition: 1920].

WEBER 1988 = Weber, Max: *Gesammelte Aufsätze zur Wissenschaftslehre*. J.C.B. Mohr (Paul Siebeck), Tübingen 1988 [first edition: 1922].

WELLMER 1986 = Wellmer, Albrecht: *Ethik und Dialog: Elemente des moralischen Urteils bei Kant und in der Diskursethik*. Suhrkamp, Frankfurt am Main 1986.

WHEELOCK 1982 = Wheelock, Wade T.: 'The Problem with Ritual Language: From Information to Situation.' *Journal of the American Academy of Religion* 50,1 (1982) 49–71.

WILLIAMS 1983 = Williams, Robert: *Jaina Yoga*. Motilal Banarsidas, Delhi 1983 [first edition: 1963].

WINTERNITZ 1920 = Winternitz, Moritz: *Geschichte der Indischen Literatur. Zweiter Band. Die Buddhistische Literatur und die Heiligen Texte der Jainas*. C.F. Amelangs Verlag, Leipzig 1920.

WITTGENSTEIN 1953 = Wittgenstein, Ludwig: *Philosophische Untersuchungen—Philosophical Investigations*. Translated by G. E. M. Anscombe. Blackwell, Oxford 1953 [first edition: 1945].

YŚ = Hemacandra-sūri: *Yoga-śāstra*. Olle Qvarnström (tr.): *The Yoga-śāstra of Hemacandra. A Twelfth Century Handbook on Śvetāmbara Jainism*. Harvard Oriental Series Vol. 61, Cambridge (Massachusetts) 2002.

YT = Somadeva-sūri: *Yaśas-tilaka*. See HANDIQUI (1968).

God
Vis-à-Vis
Proof and Belief

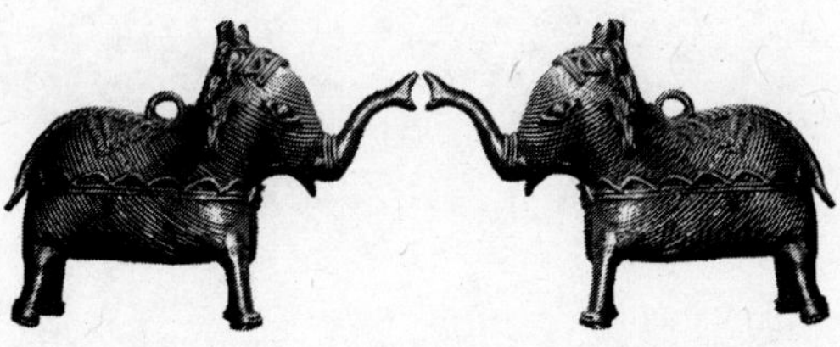

The Distinction *in intellectu / in re* in the Ontological Proof and in Bhartṛhari

FERNANDO TOLA and CARMEN DRAGONETTI

In our book *On the Myth of the Opposition between Indian Thought and Western Philosophy* (TOLA–DRAGONETTI (2004a)), reviewed by Ernst STEINKELLNER (2004), we have developed the four following theses and applied them to the *Veda*s, the *Veda*s, and the philosophical system of Sāṁkhya:

1. Up to the 16th century at least, in India on the one hand and in Greece and Europe on the other, there was frequent reflection on the same philosophical subjects ('thematic coincidences'), and it was carried out in the same way ('methodological coincidences').
   In support of this thesis we have quoted a number of Indian and Western texts containing parallel philosophical ideas.
2. In the history of Greek and European philosophies are found manifestations of irrationality, limitations in the exercise of the free use of reason and submission of philosophical thinking to interests or purposes alien to philosophy, in many forms and as numerous as they are in the history of Indian thought.
3. Philosophy did exist in India as in the West with the same expectations, with the same weaknesses.
4. The comparison between Indian and Western philosophical thought must limit itself to confront both as they manifested themselves before the end of the 17th century, or even in the centuries that followed, but in this last case only when and if they maintained certain forms of the philosophies previous to that date, prolonging them.
   From the 16th century onwards, a series of factors appeared in the West, such as the coming forth of modern science and the modern scientific mind, the discovery of the New World, the increase of European economic and military power, the weakening of ecclesiastical authority and the limitations it imposed on thinking, and the consciousness of the equality of individual rights and liberties. These factors gave a new course to universal history and led to modern

Logic and Belief in Indian Philosophy
Warsaw Indological Studies 3 (2010) 221–235.

culture. From the 17th century onwards, Western culture in all its expressions began to adopt a wholly novel form, which was different from all previously known forms, many times extraordinarily valuable. India was able to take part in this transformation in a profound way only since the middle of the 20th century due to historical circumstances.

In this article we deal with the so-called ontological proof of the existence of God in Western Philosophy (as proclaimed by Saint Anselm in 11th century) as well as with its refutation by three Western philosophers (Gaunilo, Saint Thomas Aquinas and Immanuel Kant) that were opposed to it, because that will give us the opportunity to indicate an interesting point of coincidence between the basis of the rejection of that proof and a principle of Indian thought expounded by Bhartṛhari, the great Indian philosopher of language. This point of coincidence is constituted by the distinction between *existence in re* (in reality) and *existence in intellectu* (in mind). We present a selection of texts that relate to the ontological proof and its refutation, and also to Bhartṛhari's principle in order to point out the similar function that the distinction *in intellectu / in re* has in both.

Moreover the ontological proof gives a good idea of the nature of what we call cultural dogmas in our book mentioned above. By 'cultural dogmas' we understand fundamental principles which, in general, are at the basis of any philosophical thinking in any culture as, for instance, (1) in the West: the existence of God, the immortality of the soul and a first cause, (2) in India: reincarnation and beginninglessness, and (3) in both cultures: the absolute value of the Scriptures, either the Bible or the *Veda*.

These cultural dogmas or basic principles in general are not founded in truly valid rational arguments as the example of the ontological proof clearly shows. This proof lies at the very foundation of all the other principal demonstrations of the existence of God in the West, which we consider the most important cultural dogma in the West.

The ontological proof obviously lacks any proving value or, at least, is of a very precarious and questionable value, and as such has been rejected by powerful minds, such as Saint Thomas or Kant. Nevertheless, the Western cultural dogma of God, based on arguments which in their turn are based on the ontological proof, was characterised, at least up to seventeenth century, by an unshakeable general adhesion in common belief and was the ultimate criterion for the acceptance of philosophical theories or ideas by thinkers who did not want to go beyond the limits of the orthodoxy. If we have to discard a rational basis for the cultural dogmas we must accept that, in a final analysis, their true foundation is faith. And although faith may be worthy of all respect and provide the support for human conduct and philosophical thought, it in no way belongs to the field of rational processes, which are claimed to be the core of philosophy.

We have purposely begun our study of the distinction *in intellectu* / *in re* in the systems of Bhartṛhari and of the Western thinkers with the latter ones, although such a procedure goes against chronology. We think that to show first the great and lasting interest in the West in the ontological proof that was once developed by Saint Anselm with the purpose to demonstrate the existence of God—despite its evident rational weakness lying in the fact that it overlooks the essential distinction between existence *in intellectu* and existence *in re*—and then to contrast it with the clear and direct way in which Bhartṛhari, five centuries earlier than Saint Anselm, refers to the distinction of the existence *in intellectu* / existence *in re* with full awareness of their essential opposition and presents that distinction as an obvious rational principle that cannot be left aside, allows us a better appreciation of the merit, importance and modernity of Bhartṛhari's thought in the history of philosophy.

Moreover the vitality the ontological proof enjoyed in the West, disregarding the fact that it is not logically possible to derive the existence in reality from the mere existence in mind—in order to maintain at any cost a cultural dogma or basic principle, God, to which philosophers were traditionally attached by faith—is another instance of our thesis (TOLA–DRAGONETTI (2004a)) that irrationality has been as strong in the West as it was in India, even within philosophy.

Thus the comparative study of Indian and Western philosophical ideas facilitates a better understanding and evaluation of intellectual products of both traditions. At the end of this article we shall briefly refer to some important consequences that the application of the Western ontological proof to some Indian beliefs has for both the proof itself and for Indian beliefs. It can serve as an example of the usefulness or even underlines the necessity of comparing Western and Indian philosophical thoughts, which helps eliminate the barrier that ethnocentric prejudices have built between them.

The Ontological Proof in the West

The ontological proof, also called 'proof of Saint Anselm' or 'Cartesian proof', has no parallel in Indian philosophy at all, which nevertheless did develop a number of proofs for the existence of the Īśvara (God). [1]

Saint Anselm's famous ontological proof of the existence of God amounts to affirming that God is a being that is more perfect than which nothing can be thought, i.e. he is by definition the most perfect being; to exist is more perfect that not to exist; to exist is a perfection; consequently, God cannot be only an idea; God must

[1] On the proofs of the existence of God in Nyāya and Vaiśeṣika philosophical systems of Indian philosophy, see C. BULCKE (1968: Chap VI).

really exist; God, if he can be thought, must possess the perfection of a real existence; otherwise another being as perfect as he is and, besides, really existing could be thought of; in that case God would not be a being which is more perfect than which nothing can be thought, which is contradictory to the initial assertion.

This proof had numerous defenders among outstanding philosophers who admitted it with some variants and for diverse reasons: Alexander of Hales (1185–1245), Bonaventura (1221–1274), William of de Auxerre (died 1231), Duns Scotus (1266–1308), Descartes (1596–1650), Leibniz (1646–1716), Malebranche (1638–1715) and Hegel (1770–1831). The proof had also many opponents, for instance Gaunilo (a monk in an abbey near Tours, died in 1083), Saint Thomas Aquinas (1225–1274), Gassendi (1592–1655), Locke (1632–1704), Hume (1711–1776), and Kant (1724–1804).

A. Sertillanges (1863–1948), one of the most active and influential modern neo-Thomist philosophers, points out that the evidence of God was approached by Saint Anselm 'more philosophically' but 'a little sophistically', due to the inclusion of existence in the notion of God itself (SERTILLANGES (1928: 55)).

The ontological proof was expounded by Saint Anselm (1035–1109) in Chapter II of *Proslogion*. In this exposition Saint Anselm makes use of the distinction of existence *in re* and existence *in intellectu*, without taking into account that it is not possible to derive the first from the second:

> 'And indeed we believe that You are something greater than which nothing can be thought. Or does such a nature not exist, because "the fool said in his heart: God does not exist" (*Psalm* 14.1; 53.1)? But certainly when the same fool hears what I say: "Something greater than which nothing can be thought", he understands what he hears; and what he understands exists *in* his *intellect*, even if he does not know that it exists. For one thing is that the object exists *in intellect*, and quite another is to know that the object exists [*in reality*]. When a painter for example thinks in advance what he is going to do, he certainly has *in* his *intellect* what he has not yet done, but he knows that [it] does not yet exist [*in reality*]. But once he has painted it, he has *in* his *intellect* what he has already done, and knows that it exists [*in reality*]. So even the fool is convinced that something greater than which nothing can be thought actually exists *in* his *intellect*, because he understands this when he hears [it], and whatever is understood exists *in* the *intellect*. And certainly that something greater than which nothing can be thought cannot exist only *in intellect*. For if it actually exists only *in intellect*, it can be thought that [it] exists also *in reality*—what would be greater than [that which exists only *in intellect*]. Consequently, if that greater than which nothing can be thought exists

> only *in intellect*, [then] that greater than which nothing can be thought is [at the same time] something greater than which something can be thought. But that is clearly impossible [since it is contradictory]. Therefore, there is no doubt that something greater than which nothing can be thought exists *in intellect as well as in reality*.'[2]

Refutation of the ontological proof: Gaunilo, Saint Thomas, Kant

Many important philosophers in the West have argued, as we have said, against Saint Anselm's proof. We shall briefly indicate the arguments developed by three of them, viz. the monk Gaunilo, Saint Thomas Aquinas and Immanuel Kant. All of them in their reasoning against the proof took recourse to the insurmountable distinction *in re* / *in intellectu*, which thus becomes the criterion of truth in this matter.

1. The monk Gaunilo, in his small treatise *Quid ad haec respondeat quidam pro insipiente*, begins his refutation with a synthesis of Saint Anselm's reasoning to demonstrating the existence of God as follows:

> 'Someone who either doubts or denies that there is any such nature greater than which nothing can be thought is told that it is proved that it exists, first because he himself, on denying or doubting about it (sc. that nature), has it already *in intellect*, since on hearing it spoken of he understands what is said; further, because what he understands must exist not only *in intellect*, but also *in reality*. And this is proved thus: since to exist [*in intellect* and] also *in reality* is greater than [to exist] only *in intellect*, and if that (sc. the mentioned nature) exists only *in*

[2] ANSELM (1986: 244–246): 'Et quidem credimus te esse aliquid quo nihil maius cogitari possit. An ergo non est aliqua talis natura, quia «dixit insipiens in corde suo: non est deus»? Sed certe ipse idem insipiens, cum audit hoc ipsum quod dico: 'aliquid quo maius nihil cogitari potest', intelligit quod audit; et quod intelligit *in intellectu* eius est, etiam si non intelligat illud esse. Aliud enim est rem esse *in intellectu*, aliud intelligere rem esse. Nam cum pictor praecogitat quae facturus est, habet quidem *in intellectu*, sed nondum intelligit esse quod nondum fecit. Cum vero iam pinxit, et habet in intellectu et intelligit esse quod iam fecit. Convincitur ergo etiam insipiens esse vel *in intellectu* aliquid quo nihil maius cogitari potest, quia hoc cum audit intelligit, et quidquid intelligitur *in intellectu* est. Et certe id quo maius cogitari nequit, non potest esse *in* solo *intellectu*. Si enim vel *in* solo *intellectu* est, potest cogitari esse et *in re*, quod maius est. Si ergo id quo maius cogitari non potest, est *in* solo *intellectu*: id ipsum quo maius cogitari non potest, est quo maius cogitari potest. Sed certe hoc esse non potest. Existit ergo procul dubio aliquid quo maius cogitari non valet, *et in intellectu et in re*.' In all the quotations of this article emphasis is ours.

> *intellect*, [then] greater than that will be whatever also would exist *in reality*. And thus the greater than anything else will be less than something else and will not be greater than everything else [as it has been claimed], which is of course a contradiction. And so what is greater than everything else, which has already been proved to exist *in intellect*, must exist not only *in intellect* but also *in reality*, since otherwise it could not be greater than everything else.'[3]

Gaunilo makes then the following remark, in which he succinctly expresses the central idea of his refutation:

> 'And, could I not also be said to have similarly *in* my *intellect* [ideas corresponding to] things that are false and not existing at all in themselves, since when someone speaks of them, I would understand whatever he could say?'[4]

The fact of a word being understood by somebody, which implies the existence in intellect (*in intellectu*) of an idea, does not guarantee the real (*in re*) existence of the thing designated by that word, i.e. *in intellect* can exist ideas that have false correlates or no correlates at all *in reality*, and that are nevertheless fully understood.

But the very nucleus of Gaunilo's refutation of Anselm's demonstration of the existence of God is found in sections 5 and 6 of his Treatise (GAUNILO (1986: 292–294). His reasoning is as follows:

> '... to that [argument] I reply: If it must be said that something exists *in intellect* that cannot be thought according to the truth (sc. true nature) of anything whatever, then I do not deny that this thing exists also *in* my [*intellect*]. But since from this [affirmation of the sole existence *in intellect*] it is not at all possible to infer the existence also *in reality*, [then] I do not concede at all to him (sc. the opponent) that this thing [that exists only *in intellect*] exists [also *in reality*] until [such a

[3] GAUNILO (1986: 288): 'Dubitanti utrum sit vel neganti quod sit aliqua talis natura, qua nihil maius cogitari possit, cum esse illam hinc dicitur primo probari, quod ipse negans vel ambigens de illa iam habeat eam *in intellectu*, cum audiens illam dici id quod dicitur intelligit; deinde quia quod intelligit, necesse est ut non *in* solo *intellectu* sed etiam *in re* sit, et hoc ita probatur quia maius est esse et *in re* quam *in* solo *intellectu*, et si illud *in* solo est *intelectu*, maius illo erit quidquid etiam *in re* fuerit, ac sic maius omnibus minus erit aliquo et non erit maius omnibus, quod utique repugnat; et ideo necesse est ut maius omnibus, quod esse iam probatum est *in intelectu*, non *in* solo *intellectu* sed et *in re* sit, quoniam aliter maius omnibus esse non poterit ...'

[4] GAUNILO (1986: 288): 'Nonne et quaecumque falsa ac nullo prorsus modo in seipsis existentia *in intellectu* habere similiter dici possem, cum ea dicente aliquo, quaecumque ille diceret, ego intelligerem?'

thing] is proved to me by an indubitable argument. For he who says: "That [greater than which nothing can be thought] exists [not only *in intellect* but also *in reality*] since otherwise that which is greater than everything else will not be greater than everything else"—he does not fully realise whom he is speaking with. For I do not say—even more, I even deny or doubt—that this [greater than everything else] is greater than any real thing, nor do I concede to it an existence [if it is possible to speak of "existence"] different from that [existence one has in mind] when the soul tries to imagine from a word that has been only heard a thing completely unknown to it. How, then, is it proved to me that this greater [than everything else] really exists simply because that is greater than everything else, when until this moment I am denying or doubting that this (sc. the fact of being greater that everything else) has been established, so that I do not [even] say that this greater than everything else exists *in* my *intellect* or *in* my *thought* at least in the way that many doubtful and uncertain things exist [*in* my *intellect*]? For it is necessary that first I become certain that greater [than everything] exists somewhere *in* true *reality*, and only then, due to the fact that it is greater than everything else, it will not be doubtful that it also exists in itself.'[5]

Next Gaunilo gives his well-known example of 'the Lost Island' in order to make clear his thought and to ridicule the position of a sustainer of such a proof:

'Some say that somewhere in the ocean exists an island, which, because of the difficulty or rather impossibility to find what does not exist, some call "[The] Lost [Island]". And they narrate that this island thrives much more than what it is said of the Blessed Islands with an inestimable abundance of riches and delights, and that, not having possessor or inhabitant, it is superior to all the other lands that human be-

[5] GAUNILO (1986: 5): '... ad hoc respondeo: Si esse dicendum est *in intellectu*, quod secundum veritatem cuiusquam rei nequit saltem cogitari: et hoc in meo sic esse non denego. Sed quia, per hoc, esse quoque *in re* non potest ullatenus obtinere: illud ei esse adhuc penitus non concedo, quousque mihi argumento probetur indubio. Quod qui esse dicit hoc, quod maius omnibus aliter non erit omnibus maius: non satis attendit cui loquatur. Ego enim nondum dico, immo etiam nego vel dubito ulla re vera esse maius illud, nec aliud ei esse concedo quam illud, si dicendum est 'esse', cum secundum vocem tantum auditam rem prorsus ignotam sibi conatur animus effingere. Quomodo igitur inde mihi probatur maius illud rei veritate subsistere, quia constet illud maius omnibus esse, cum id ego eo usque negem adhuc dubitemve constare, ut ne *in intellectu* quidem vel cogitatione mea eo saltem modo maius ipsum esse dicam, quo dubia etiam multa sunt et incerta? Prius enim certum mihi necesse est fiat re vera esse alicubi maius ipsum, et tum demum ex eo quod maius est omnibus, in seipso quoque subsistere non erit ambiguum.'

ings inhabit, because of the redundancy of all things worthy to be possessed. If somebody tells me that it is so, I will easily understand what he says—in this there is no difficulty. But if then, as it were a logical consequence, he would add and say: "You cannot any longer doubt that this island, more pre-eminent than all other lands, and which you do not doubt to exist *in* your *intellect*, truly exists somewhere *in reality*. And, since to exist not only *in intellect* but also *in reality* is more pre-eminent [than to exist only *in intellect*], therefore, this island must exist so (sc. also *in reality*), because if it did not exist [also *in reality*], any other land which exists also *in reality* would be more pre-eminent than it; and thus this same [island], which has been recognised by you to be the most pre-eminent, would not be the most pre-eminent." If—I say—by these [arguments] he would try to demonstrate to me that, in regard to this island, it is not possible to doubt anymore that it truly exists, either I would think he is joking or I do not know whom I ought to think more foolish, myself if I accept [his proof], or him, if he thinks that he has demonstrated with any certainty the existence of that island, without having instructed me before that the pre-eminence of that [island] exists *in* my *intellect* as a real and undoubtedly existing thing only, and not at all as something false and uncertain.'[6]

2. Saint Thomas Aquinas, the most prominent philosopher in the European Middle Ages, did not accept the ontological proof to establish the existence of God. As Battista MONDIN (1990: 161) of the Pontificia Università Urbaniana says,

---

[6] GAUNILO (1986: 6): 'Aiunt quidam alicubi oceani esse insulam, quam ex difficultate vel potius impossibilitate inveniendi quod non est, cognominant aliqui 'perditam', quamque fabulantur multo amplius quam de fortunatis insulis fertur, divitiarum deliciarumque omnium inaestimabili ubertate pollere, nulloque possessore aut habitatore universis aliis quas incolunt homines terris possidendorum redundantia usquequaque praestare. Hoc ita esse dicat mihi quispiam, et ego facile dictum in quo nihil est difficultatis intelligam. At si tunc velut consequenter adiungat ac dicat: non potes ultra dubitare insulam illam terris omnibus praestantiorem vere esse alicubi in re, quam et in intellectu tuo non ambigis esse; et quia praestantius est, non in intellectu solo sed etiam esse in re; ideo sic eam necesse est esse, quia nisi fuerit, quaecumque alia in re est terra, praestantior illa erit, ac sic ipsa iam a te praestantior intellecta praestantior non erit;—si inquam per haec ille mihi velit astruere de insula illa quod vere sit ambigendum ultra non esse: aut iocari illum credam, aut nescio quem stultiorem debeam reputare, utrum me si ei concedam, an illum si se putet aliqua certitudine insulae illius essentiam astruxisse, nisi prius ipsam praestantiam eius solummodo sicut rem vere atque indubie existentem nec ullatenus sicut falsum aut incertum aliquid in intellectu meo esse docuerit.'

'It is something universally admitted that Saint Thomas is resolutely against the ontological argument of the Anselmian type, argument that intends to prove the existence of God starting from the definition of His essence (*id cuius maius cogitari nequit*). According to Saint Thomas this way of proceeding is incorrect, because it is founded on the false assumption that human reason has a pure (and not simply nominal) concept of the divine essence even before it has known His existence.'

Saint Thomas, in his *Summa Theologiae* (*Prima Pars*, *Qu.* 2, A, I, *Resp. ad secundum*), expresses his view on the ontological argument and confines his criticism to two aspects of the argument, which he clearly marks as separate. Herwy RIKHOF (1990: 137), in 'A theological analysis of Aquinas' criticism', included in the already quoted work *L'argomento ontologico*, indicates which are these two aspects:

1. '... not everybody does understand that the word *God* means "that greater than which nothing can be thought"', and
2. 'The logical argument that from thinking something it does not follow its existence in reality, but only its existence in the mind.'

Saint Thomas contends thus:

'... it must be said that perhaps he who hears this word *God*, does not understand that it means :something greater than which nothing can be thought", since some have believed that God is a body. Even if it is conceded that anybody understands that what is meant by this word *God* is that what is said, i.e. that greater than which nothing can be thought, nevertheless from this fact does not follow that anybody thinks[7] that what is signified by the word exists—but only that it is not possible to argue that it exists, unless it is [previously] proved that something greater than which nothing can be thought exists, which is not accepted by those who affirm that God does not exist.'[8]

[7] Battista MONDIN (1990: 161) translates: *non segue ... la persuasione*: 'does not follow ... the conviction.'

[8] THOMAS AQUINAS (1988: 12): '... dicendum quod forte ille qui audit hoc nomen Deus, non intelligit significari aliquid quo maius cogitari non possit, cum quidam crediderint Deum esse corpus. Dato etiam quod quilibet intelligat hoc nomine Deus significari hoc quod dicitur, scilicet illud quo maius cogitari non potest; non tamen propter hoc sequitur quod intelligat id quod significatur per nomen, esse *in rerum natura*; sed *in apprehensione intellectus* tantum. Nec potest argui quod sit *in re*, nisi daretur quod sit *in re* aliquid quo maius cogitari non potest: quod non est datum a ponentibus Deum non esse.'

3. Immanuel Kant (1724–1804) all along his work was interested in the problem of the ontological proof of the existence of God, always adopting an attitude of rejection, characterised by—as in the case of Gaunilo and Saint Thomas—the contraposition of *existence in intellectu* and *existence in re*. Kant also makes manifest the absurd consequences that derive from the intent of passing without any other argument from the *existence in intellectu* to the *existence in re*.

We quote a selection of relevant passages of Kant, taken from his *Kritik der reinen Vernunft* and *Der einzig mögliche Beweisgrund zu einer Demonstration des Daseins Gottes*:

> [a] 'Notwithstanding this urgent necessity of reason of presupposing something (i.e. an Absolute Being, God) that could fully serve the understanding as a ground for the complete determination of its concepts [in order not to incur in a *regressus ad infinitum*], however reason notices *the idealistic* and *merely fictitious* [nature, i.e. existing only *in intellect*] of such a presupposition too easily to be persuaded by that alone to assume as *an actual being* [existing *in reality*] a *mere creation of its own thinking* [existing only *in intellect*]...'[9]
>
> [b] 'From what precedes it can easily be seen that the concept of an absolutely necessary being (sc. God) [that reason needs, looks for and constructs] is *a pure concept of reason*, i.e. *a mere idea* [existing *in intellect*], whose *objective reality* (sc. existence *in reality*) is not at all proved by the fact that reason needs it ...'[10]
>
> [c] 'Our *concept* of an object may thus contain whatever and however much it wants, nevertheless we must go out of it in order to provide it with *existence*.'[11]
>
> [d] 'Thus, all effort and labour given to this famous ontological (Cartesian) proof of the existence of a Supreme Being from *concepts* is lost, and a person could from *mere ideas* become richer in insight, not

[9] KANT (1998: 662)= A 583–584): 'Ungeachtet dieser dringenden Bedürfnis der Vernunft, etwas vorauszusetzen, was dem Verstande zu der durchgängigen Bestimmung seiner Begriffe vollständig zum Grunde liegen könne, so bemerkt sie doch das Idealische und bloss Gedichtete einer solchen Voraussetzung viel zu leicht, als dass sie dadurch allein überredet werden sollte, ein blosses Selbstgeschöpf ihres Denkes sofort für ein wirkliches Wesen anzunehmen...'

[10] KANT (1998: 668 = A 592): 'Mann siehet aus dem bisherigen leicht: dass der Begriff eines absolut notwendigen Wesens *ein reiner Vernunftbegriff*, d.i. *eine blosse Idee* sei, deren *objective Realität* dadurch, dass die Vernunft ihrer bedarf, noch lange nicht Bewiesen ist ...'

[11] KANT (1998: 675 = A 601): 'Unser *Begriff* von einem Gegestände mag also enthalten, was und wie viel er wolle, so müssen wir doch aus ihm heraugehen, um diesem die *Existenz* zu erteilen.'

much more than a merchant in money, if he, in order to improve his economic situation, would add a few zeros to his cash balance.'[12]

[e] 'However, we have a famous proof, which is based on that principle (sc. from the *concept* of something possible its *existence* is deduced), i.e. the so-called Cartesian [proof]. One conceives firstly the *concept* of a possible *thing* in which one imagines that all true perfection is reunited. Now one assumes that *existence* is also a perfection of things, so from the possibility of a most perfect being one deduces its *existence*. Equally from the *concept* of anything, which is also imagined as the most perfect of its kind—as for instance, only from the fact that a most perfect world is thought—one could deduce its *existence*.'[13]

The distinction *in intellectu* / *in re* in Bhartṛhari

As it is seen in the texts quoted in the previous sections, the central point of the problem of the ontological proof and its refutation lies in the admission of two types of existence, one *in intellectu* and the other *in re*, and in the impossibility to pass from the first to the second one without an adequate proof. The opposition of these two types of existence constitutes the ground for the construction of the ontological proof and its rejection.

It is interesting to remind what Bhartṛhari (6th century CE), says in relation to the same subject of the two levels of existence. For Bhartṛhari this distinction between both types of existence is an obvious fact, which constitues a fundamental principle of rational philosophical thinking outside any theological preoccupation.

According to Bhartṛhari's view expressed in his *Vākyapadīya* (*Sambandhasamuddeśa* 39–51), there are two types of existence (*sattā*), one is the 'principal' (*mukhya*), 'direct' (*saṁprati*) or 'external' (*bāhya*) existence, which corresponds

[12] KANT (1998: 676 = A 602): 'Es ist also an dem so berühmten ontologischen (cartesianischen) Beweise, vom Dasein eines höchten Wesens, aus *Begriffen*, alle Mühe und Arbeit verloren, und ein Mensch möchte wohl eben so wenig aus *blossen Ideen* an Einsichten reicher werden, als ein Kaufmann an Vermögen, wenn er um seinem Zustand zu verbessern, seinem Kassenbestande einige Nullen anhängen wollte.'

[13] KANT (1998: 730 = A 191–192): 'Indessen haben wir einen berühmten Beweis, der auf diesen Grund erbauet ist, nämlich den so gennanten Kartesianischen. Man erdenket sich zuvörderst einen *Begriff* von einem möglichen *Dinge*, in welchem man alle wahre Vollkommenheit sich vereinbart vorstellt. Nun nimmt man an, das *Dasein* sei auch eine Vollkommenheit der Dinge; also schliesst man aus der Möglichkeit eines vollkommensten Wesens auf seine *Existenz*. Eben so könnte man aus dem *Begriffe* einer jeden Sache, welche auch nur als die vollkommenste ihrer Art vorgestellt wird, z. E. daraus allein schon dass eine vollkommenste Welt zu gedenken ist, auf ihr *Dasein* schliessen.'

to the things of the external world, and the other is the 'secondary' or 'metaphorical' (*aupacāriki*, *upacāra*°) existence of all what is expressed by words. The commentator Helārāja *ad Sambandha-samuddeśa* 48.3.1 (VPP, p. 158.10), gives this second type of existence the epithet of *bauddha* ('mental'). Bhartṛhari's 'principal existence' is the 'existence *in re*' of Western philosophers, the 'metaphorical existence' is the 'existence *in intellectu*'.

In the following, we present the relevant verses of VP 3.3.39, 50d–51:

> 'When something is named, there is another existence, the metaphorical one, which is proper of things designated by words; it shows the form of all things in all situations.'[14]

Bhartṛhari (VP 3.3.49–51) refers to the metaphorical existence (*aupacārikī*), pointing out some of its characteristics in *kārikā*s 49 and 50. But the *kārikā*s 50d and 51 are those which directly concern the distinction between existence *in intellectu* and existence *in re*:

> 'Nothing expressed by a word can go beyond this metaphorical [or mental] existence. And in the *Bhāṣya* it has been taught that it is different from the principal existence.'[15]

The existence to which this stanza refers (*etaṁ sattām*) is, as we said, the *aupacārikī* or 'metaphorical' existence that Bhartṛhari characterises in *kārikā*s 49 and 50 and attributes several epithets to it. The notion or idea that a word expresses can never pretend to have an existence other than the metaphorical one, i.e. *in intellectu*; it is constrained to remain within the limits of mere 'metaphorical', 'secondary' or 'mental' existence, which by essence corresponds to it. Obviously, the 'principal' or 'external' *in re* existence can be attributed to the object, which is expressed by the notion or idea the word refers to, *if and only* if those who affirm that existence adduce solid arguments in support of it, as the commentator Helārāja expresses in his introductory remarks to *kārikā*s 40 and 41.

The existence of something (for instance: God) *in intellectu* does not by itself alone guarantee its existence *in re*. The existence of God or any other existence

[14] VP 3.3.39:

vyapadeśe padârthānām anyā sattâupacārikī /
sarvâvasthāsu sarveṣām ātma-rūpasya darśikā //

[15] VP 3.3.50d–51:

... aupacārikīm //50//
etāṁ sattāṁ padârtho hi na kaścid ativartate /
sā ca samprati-sattāyāḥ pṛthag bhāṣye nidarśitā //

supposed to be *in re* would have to be demonstrated by other means of proof, and not only by the fact that the corresponding notion or idea exists *in intellectu*.

Bhartṛhari in *kārikā* 51cd and Helārāja in the beginning of his commentary *ad locum* indicate that the foundation of the theory of the two types of existence is found in the *Mahā-bhāṣya* or 'Great Commentary', written by Patañjali around 150 BCE.

Let us add, as another, more ancient, antecedent in India of the distinction between the existence *in intellectu* and the existence *in re*, viz. a distinction that appears in the oldest Buddhist texts between an existence *dravyataḥ* ('as a real entity'), and an existence *prajñaptitaḥ* ('as [a mere] concept', i.e. 'without objective reality') that correspond to Bhartṛhari's principal, external, *in re* existence and the secondary, metaphorical, mental, *in intellectu* existence respectively.[16]

The ontological proof and its consequences for Indian theism

For Hindus, Śiva for some, Viṣṇu for others, is the Supreme Being, conceived by Indian philosophy and religion as the most pre-eminent and excellent God, endowed with all the possible perfections in their utmost degree, enhanced with the most excellent qualities, infinite, omnipotent, omniscient etc.[17]

Applying the reasoning of the ontological proof, utilised in the West for demonstrating the existence of God, to the Supreme Being as conceived in Indian philosophy—either under the name of Śiva or under the name of Viṣṇu—one could affirm that Śiva and/or Viṣṇu, conceived as Beings endowed with all the perfections, must possess, among these, also that of *real existence*. This conclusion cannot be but disturbing for any monotheist religion or culture, which pretends that its God not only *exists* but *is unique*.

Similarly, as in the case of the examples devised by Gaunilo ('the Lost Island') and by Kant ('a most perfect world'), the *real existence* of the magnificent worlds or paradises of Viṣṇu or Śiva conceived as the most excellent of their kind, ought to be admitted, if one accepts the ontological proof as a valid argument for establishing the existence of anything that is conceived as the most perfect or pre-eminent in its kind.

These consequences of the ontological proof, when applied to religious beliefs outside the limits of Christian world, should be taken into account together with the logical and epistemological reasons that are adduced when one examines the validity of that 'proof'.

---

[16] Cf. TOLA–DRAGONETTI (2004b: XXXII–XXXIV).

[17] See BULCKE (1968).

BIBLIOGRAPHY

ANSELM 1986 = Anselm: *Proslogion*. In: Michel Corbin, S.J. (ed.): *L'Oeuvre d'Anselme de Cantorbéry*. Tome Premier, Les Éditions du Cerf, Paris 1986: 209–287.

BULCKE 1968 = Bulcke, C., S.J.: *The Theism of Nyaya-Vaisesika. Its Origin and Early Development*. Motilal Banarsidass, Delhi 1968.

GAUNILO 1986 = Gaunilo: *Quid ad haec respondeat quidam pro insipiente*. In: ANSELM (1986: 288–297).

KANT 1996 = Kant, Immanuel: *Der einzige mögliche Beweisgrund zu einer Demonstration des Daseins Gottes*. In: Immanuel Kant: *Werkausgabe*, in 12 volumes, Suhrkamp Verlag, Frankfurt am Main, Vol. II: 1996.

KANT 1998 = Kant, Immanuel: *Kritik der reinen Vernunft*. Herausgegenen von Jens Timmermann, Felix Meiner Verlag, Hamburg 1998.

MBhā = Patañjali: *Vyākaraṇa-mahā-bhāṣya*. Kielhorn, Lorenz Franz (ed.): *The Vyākaraṇa-mahābhāṣya of Patañjali, third edition, revised and furnished with additional readings, references and select critical notes by K.V. Abhyankar*. 3 Vols, Bhandarkar Oriental Research Institute, Poona 1985.

MONDIN 1990 = Mondin, Battista: 'L'argomento <ontologico> nella metafisica dell'essere di San Tommaso d'Aquino', in: OLIVETTI (1990: 161–171).

OLIVETTI 1990 = Olivetti, M.M. (ed.): *L'argomento ontologico*. Cedam, Padova 1990.

RIKHOF 1990 = Rikhof, Herwy: 'Aquinas and the «ratio Anselmi»', in: OLIVETTI (1990: 137–159).

SCHARFE 1977 = Scharfe, Hartmut: *Grammatical literature*. In: Jan Gonda (general ed.): *A History of Indian Literature*. Vol. 5, fasc. 2, Otto Harrassowitz Verlag, Wiesbaden 1977.

SERTILLANGES 1928 = Sertillanges, Antoine, R.P.: *Les grandes thèses de la philosophie thomiste*, Bloud et Gay, Bibliothèque Catholique des Sciences Religieuses, France 1928.

STEINKELLNER 2004 = Steinkellner, Ernst: 'Anzeige' [of TOLA–DRAGONETTI (2004a)], *Wiener Zeitschrift für die Kunde Südasiens* 48 (2004) 224–225.

SUBRAMANIA IYER 1963 = Subramania Iyer, K.A.: *Vākyapadīya of Bhartṛhari with the Commentary of Helārāja, Kāṇḍa III, Part 1*. Deccan College Monograph Series 21, Deccan College, Poona 1963.

THOMAS AQUINAS 1988 = Sancti Thomae de Aquino: *Summa Theologiae*. Edizioni Paoline, Milano 1988.

TOLA–DRAGONETTI 2004a = Tola, Fernando; Dragonetti, Carmen: *On the Myth of the Opposition between Indian Thought and Western Philosophy*. Olms Verlag, Hildesheim 2004.

TOLA–DRAGONETTI 2004b = Tola, Fernando; Dragonetti, Carmen: *Being as Consciousness. The Yogācāra Philosophy of Buddhism*. Motilal Banarsidass, Delhi 2004.

VP = Bhartṛhari: *Vākyapadīya*. Wilhelm Rau (ed.): *Bhartṛharis Vākyapadīya: Die Mūlakārikās nach den Handschriften herausgegeben und mit einem Pāda-Index versehen.* Abhandlungen für die Kunde des Morgenlandes XLII, 4., Franz Steiner Verlag, Wiesbaden 1977.

VPP = Helārāja: *Vākyapadīya-prakāśa*. See: SUBRAMANIA IYER (1963).

Theism—The Culmination of Nyāya Logic

JOHN VATTANKY, S. J.

It is usually stated that the section on inference is the most important part of Nyāya works in general and of Navya-nyāya treatises in particular. What however is not so well known is that the inner dynamism of the logical topics finds its high point in what is usually called *Īśvara-vāda* or *Īśvarânumāna*. In the most fundamental work of Navya-nyāya, *Tattva-cintā-maṇi*, Gaṅgeśa begins his *Īśvara-vāda* with the following words: 'When inference is thus established, the existence of a supreme person who is the creator of the universe is thereby established.'[1] Here each word, even the smallest one has its own particular purpose. For instance the word, thus (*evam*) implies that according to Gaṅgeśa the connection between the treatise on inference in general and inference for the existence of God is more than casual. It is only on the basis of the nature of inference as examined and established in the earlier sections of *Tattva-cintā-maṇi* that it is possible to offer any proof for the existence of God. Therefore it implies also that the short phrase 'when inference is thus examined' (*evam anumāne nirūpite*) means that what follows is not lined up merely in chronological succession but also in logical consequence. The purpose of this essay is to examine and substantiate this claim, in other words to show that Nyāya logic culminates in a vigorous proposal and defence of theism.

Gaṅgeśa's *Īśvarânumāna* is the most sustained logical argumentation in the Nyāya tradition to uphold theism. It also is the final culmination of centuries of argumentations in the development of Nyāya thought in this regard. Therefore in order to appreciate fully the achievement of Gaṅgeśa and to grasp the full force of the Nyāya theistic arguments, it would be appropriate to examine a little the history of these ideas in the Nyāya tradition. Already in the *Nyāya-sūtra*s of Gautama we find three aphorisms (NS 4.1.19–21) which deal directly with God. These *sūtra*s are the following:

> '[19] God is the cause because we find fruitlessness in the actions of men. [20] It is not so because no fruit appears without the actions of

[1] TCM$_{I}$ 1,1–2: *evam anumāne nirūpite tasmj jaganirmātṛ-puruṣa-ghaureya-siddhiḥ*.

Logic and Belief in Indian Philosophy
Warsaw Indological Studies 3 (2010) 237–248.

> men. [21] This reasoning is not correct since they [the actions of men] are influenced by him (i.e. God).'[2]

I have given an elaborate commentary on these *sūtra*s in my work *Gaṅgeśa's Philosophy of God.*[3] It is not necessary to repeat all that I have developed in this commentary. Suffice to point out here that the early commentators like Vātsyāyana Pakṣilasvāmin and Uddyotakara consider these *sūtra*s as proposing the view that God is the cause of the world, and there is no rational justification to reject the opinion of these classical interpreters. It may be noted also that Uddyotakara not only comments on these three *sūtra*s but at the end of his commentary on the third of these theistic *sūtra*s adds a relatively long section on *Īśvara-prakriyā*. In concluding this part Uddyotakara gives an inference to establish the existence of God with *kāryatva* ('being-an-effect') as the reason. This has remained in its various formulations by different Nyāya authors the central argument for establishing the existence of God.

Vācaspati gives decisive logical interpretations to these *sūtra*s and rejects the arguments advanced by the Buddhists against the existence of God. I have also shown in my work that Vācaspati's contribution is seminal in the most important respect of showing the limitations and, ultimately, the untenability of the logical positions of the Buddhists, especially of Dharmakīrti. And Gaṅgeśa borrows freely from Vācaspati and, therefore, the conclusions drawn at the end of this essay after the discussions on Vācaspati are equally valid with regard to the contribution of Gaṅgeśa also.

Udayana also treats about the existence of God in his *Ātma-tattva-viveka*, *Nyāya-kusumâñjali* and *Kiraṇâvalī.* The *Nyāya-kusumâñjali* is entirely devoted to establishing the reality of God. It is probably the first authoritative, systematic and independent work as different from the *sūtra*s and their commentaries, to establish with rigorous arguments the main doctrines of the Nyāya system, especially the existence of God, as the culmination of this philosophical enterprise. In the fifth and final chapter of this work Udayana elaborates various proofs for the existence of God. Naturally the most significant proof is the inference with *kāryatva* ('being-an-effect') as the reason (*hetu*). Whatever may be the meagreness of Nyāya literature on the existence of God prior to Udayana, the situation is radically changed after his

---

[2] NS 4.1.19–21: [19] *īśvaraḥ kāraṇaṁ puruṣa-karmâphalya-darśanāt.* [20] *na, puruṣa-karmâbhāve phalâniṣpatteḥ.* [21] *tat-karitatvād ahetuḥ.*

[3] VATTANKY (1984: 4–11). As an introduction to the translation and interpretation of Gaṅgeśa's *Īśvara-vāda* I have also given an extended treatment on the contribution of various subsequent Naiyāyikas to the problem of God. The arguments of these Naiyāyikas were developed against the Buddhist philosophers who brought in a variety of objections against the existence of God; cf. VATTANKY (1984: 1–150). I have also treated the same subject matter in a different work, see VATTANKY (1993).

work *Nyāya-kusumâñjali*, for it is a voluminous and central work in the development of Nyāya system.[4]

Leaving less known Nyāya authors who have contributed to the doctrine of God like Śaśadhara and others I come to the great Gaṅgeśa in whose magisterial work *Tattva-cintā-maṇi* there is a very significant section, *Īśvarânumāna*, establishing the existence of God. Perhaps the towering personality of Udayana and his magnificent work, *Nyāya-kusumâñjali*, overshadowed the *Īśvarânumāna* of Gaṅgeśa and so earlier scholars like Jacobi argued that everything that could be said about God in the Nyāya tradition has already been stated by Udayana in his *Nyāya-kusumâñjali*; but in the light of the studies undertaken in recent times (VATTANKY (1984) and (1993)), it is no more possible to hold such an opinion. In fact a detailed and careful study of the text of Gaṅgeśa's *Īśvarânumāna* shows the considerable originality of the author not only in the organisation of the matter in the Nyāya tradition but also in the developments of the arguments especially in as far as their logical rigour is concerned. The whole work of Gaṅgeśa's *Īśvarânumāna* is a logical and epistemological defence of the basic Nyāya inference: 'The earth and so on have an agent, because they have the characteristic of being-an-effect'[5], the standard Nyāya inference to establish the existence of God. The defence of this inference is carried out by Gaṅgeśa with such philosophical depth and logical acumen that his *Īśvarânumāna* can easily be ranked as one of the finest philosophical text in any tradition, Indian or Western. But to appreciate the philosophical significance of this statement one should have carefully analysed each sentence and phrase and reflected over them for long. That is the only way to have even an inkling of the philosophical depth and logical acumen of Gaṅgeśa.

We can therefore conclude this section of the present essay pointing out that although the literature on God in the early Nyāya confines itself to the three theistic *sūtra*s and the commentaries on them, still the contributions of Uddyotakara and Vācaspati are so significant from the point of view of logic and epistemology that in no way can one assert that the idea of God plays only a minimal role in early Nyāya. With the advent of Udayana and Gaṅgeśa the whole philosophical scene changes and substantial independent works such as the *Nyāya-kusumâñjali* and *Īśvarânumāna* (*Tattva-cintā-maṇi*) establish God as the philosophical and logical culmination of the Nyāya system. In doing so these authors display philosophical and logical skills of the highest order and naturally they use precisely defined technical terms. Just to

[4] Interested readers may refer to the translations and interpretations of the *Ātma-tattva-viveka* and the *Nyāya-kusumâñjali* by the distinguished scholar, N.S. DRAVID (1995) and (1996).

[5] TCM_I 1.2–3: *kṣity-aṅkurâdikaṁ sakartṛkaṁ kāryatvāt*. For easy comprehension this inference is phrased in a way slightly different from the version found in TCM_I.

assert that these refinements are mere subtleties and to dismiss them as Nyāya paraphernalia would be just non-sense. It would be like the statements of Arthur Berriedale KEITH (1977: 35) who dismissed Navya-nyāya as a 'vast mass of perverted ingenuity'.

We now enter the basic argument itself of the Naiyāyikas to establish the existence of God. The most important proof for the existence of God in the Nyāya tradition is one which makes use of *kāryatva* ('being-an-effect') as the reason in the inference. Historically we find such a reason for the first time in the inference proposed by Uddyotakara (4th century CE). The whole proof runs as follows:

> 'Likewise one should bring "being-an-effect", as the reason, when grass etc. are the subject, since these are objects of sight and touch. Likewise, whenever a difference of opinion is given and "being-an-effect" is also seen, one should prove the existence of God with the same argument, with the same example of axe etc., after something has been taken as the subject.'[6]

The full form of the proof must have been something like this: the different things in nature like grass, earth, shoots etc., must have an agent just as things like a pot etc., have an agent, viz., potter. And the cause of the effect like grass, earth etc., is God. It may be noted here that while Uddyotakara explains in detail the other proofs which he brings forward for the existence of God, he does not go into the details of this proof. Hence it is reasonable to conclude that this proof may not be his original contribution but it may have been current at the time of Uddyotakara in the Nyāya school and he just mentioned it as if it were known to all.

But it is Vācaspatimiśra (10th century CE) who really defended this proof against the attack of Buddhist philosophers, especially Dharmakīrti, and drew its philosophical and logical implications. Vācaspati, Udayana (11th century CE) and Gaṅgeśa developed the philosophical and logical aspects of this proof. And it is to these dimensions of the proof for the existence of God that we shall turn our attention but such a discussion on the philosophical, especially the logical aspects of the question presupposes a fairly good acquaintance with the terms and techniques of Nyāya logic especially those concerning the validity of the reason. If a reason is false then the whole syllogism falls. That is why Nyāya theory of logic has elaborate, accurate and profound discussions on the nature and the kinds of fallacies. I shall not enter into any detailed discussion of this topic but mention only two of

[6] NBh 957.11–13: *evaṁ kāryatvāt tṛṇâdīni pakṣī-kṛtya darśana-sparśana-viṣayatvād iti vaktavyam. evaṁ yatra yatra vipratipattiḥ kāryatvaṁ ca tat tad anenâiva nyāyenânena dṛṣṭāntena vāsyâdinā pakṣayitvā sādhayitavyam.*

them which are essential to follow properly the discussions on the inference to establish the existence of God, viz. the unestablished invariable concomitance (*vyāpyatvâsiddhi*) and counter-thesis (*sat-pratipakṣa*).

The fallacy of unestablishedness of invariable concomitance occurs in such inferences as 'it has fire because it has blue smoke'; here blue smokeness is not the determinant of the state of being reason because of cumbersomeness. Hence there is the fault of unestablishedness of invariable concomitance. In other words, in the inference 'it has fire because it has blue smoke', the determinant of the state of being reason is blue smokeness. This is a cumbersome property and so this cannot be accepted as the real determinant of the state of being reason. The reason is that when there is a property which is less cumbersome, a cumbersome property cannot be accepted as the determinant of the state of being reason and here blue smokeness is cumbersome in comparison with mere smokeness which can really be accepted as the determinant of the state of being reason. Hence in the inference 'it has fire because it has blue smoke', there is the fault of unestablishedness of invariable concomitance (*vyāpyatvâsiddhi*).

The fallacy of counter-thesis is the subject which has that which is pervaded by the absence of *sādhya*. As for example, when one argues that 'the earth and so on have an agent because they are effects' (*kṣity-aṅkurâdikaṁ sakartṛkaṁ karyatvāt*) the opponent argues that 'the earth and so on have no agent because they are not produced by someone having a body' (*kṣity-aṅkurâdikaṁ na sakartṛkaṁ śarīrâjanyatvāt*) and so according to the opponent the reason 'being-an-effect' (*kāryatva*) suffers from the fallacy of counter-thesis. Here the fallacy of counter-thesis is that the earth and so on have the characteristic of not being produced by someone having a body and such a characteristic is pervaded, according to the opponent, by the absence of having an agent.

The Naiyāyikas defend their syllogism to establish the existence of God against all the possible attack of the opponents especially the Buddhists. But first of all let us recall the simpler form of the syllogism which the Naiyāyikas bring forward to establish the existence of God: 'the earth and so on have an agent because they are effects.' The Buddhists argued that there is no invariable concomitance of 'having an intelligent agent' with 'being an effect in general', but only with that class of things which although one has not seen being made by someone, but which when seen after having been made, one immediately knows that that thing has been made by someone. The heart of this Buddhist objection has already been explained by Dharmakīrti (PV 1.12–18) and Śāntarakṣita (TSa 12.61–65). In short, it means only that after having seen a jar being made by a potter, when we see a similar jar we can infer that this jar also has been made by a potter, although we have not actually seen this jar being made by a potter. But by the same sort of process we cannot conclude that the earth is produced by someone. And if one similarly infers the existence of an agent also for the earth, one could infer fire from any white substance as well, though one has never seen any instance of such a substance produced by fire.

Vācaspati's answer (NS 955.14–956.2; NVTṬ 4.1.21) to this objection has been seminal in the sense that later Naiyāyikas such as Udayana and Gaṅgeśa developed only the details of the answer, but the basic elements of the reply remained the same. Vācaspati asks the opponent: in order to have the invariable concomitance of having an intelligent agent, is it enough that the class of things should actually have an agent or should this agent be actually seen? If it is the first alternative, then the Naiyāyika has no objection: he holds that there is actually an intelligent agent for such things as the earth and so on. But if the Buddhist insists that this agent be visible, which is the second alternative, then the Buddhist is denying his own principle. In no instance at all of an effect would one have the knowledge of an intelligent agent if the agent is not actually seen. Therefore, when we see a palace which we did not actually see being built, we cannot conclude that this palace was also built by someone for the simple reason that we did not see someone building it, or to use the example which Vācaspati himself gives, because this cloth which one saw being produced by someone has a maker, one cannot conclude that the piece of cloth in the textile shop is also produced by somebody. This, obviously, the Buddhist also does not admit.

What follows (NS 955.18–21; NVTṬ 4.1.21) is an extremely vital but succinct series of objections on the part of the Buddhists and equally penetrating series of answers by the Naiyāyikas. In fact, all the basic questions about the inference to establish the existence of God are raised and answered here by Vācaspati. The Buddhist objects: that class of things which is established to have an intelligent agent will certainly imply that any member belonging to that class and not any other thing will have an intelligent agent. But to this Vācaspati answers that the class of things having a beginning, e.g. jars, have an intelligent agent; certainly trees and so on belong to the class of things having a beginning. Therefore, they also have an agent.

But of course, the Buddhist does not admit this answer (NS 955.21–23; NVTṬ 4.1.21): he insists that only such a class of things which have been actually perceived as having an agent does have an agent and not others. As for example, we know that individual things in the class of jar have an agent; from this, it does not follow that palaces have agents since they do not belong to the class of things which is perceived to have agents, since they do not belong to the class of jar. Therefore the Buddhist concludes, only such a class of things which is perceived to have an agent can enable us to infer that a member of that class has an intelligent agent, even though we do not actually perceive the agent. This is the final and definitive position of the Buddhist. It shows clearly the nature and limitation of his epistemology and logic. Whatever details and argumentations may have been developed by subsequent authors, in essence, this is the position of Dharmakīrti (PV 1.13, also commentary of Manorathanandin on this *kārikā*).

Now, Vācaspati definitely destroys this edifice of Buddhist arguments by a decisive blow of his logic (NS 955.23–24; NVTṬ 4.1.21); in fact, Vācaspati meets his adversary on his own and shows him that the class of things which are effects are perceived to have an intelligent agent. A palace is an effect and we know from perception that this palace has an agent; therefore, whenever we see a thing which has the characteristic of an effect, we can conclude that, that thing also has an intelligent agent since that thing also belongs to the class of things which are effects. Thus the earth and so on are also perceived by us as effects. Hence they also have an intelligent agent.

As to the Buddhist objection (NS 956.1–2; NVTṬ 4.1.21) that in that case an anthill should also be produced by a potter, the answer is that we cannot conclude that a potter is the maker of an anthill, since we do not see potters making anthills; but from the fact that the anthill is an effect, we can conclude that it is produced by intelligent agents which are not seen by us. As we have noted already, later Naiyāyikas, including even Udayana and Gaṅgeśa, have only developed the details of this answer.

Further, according to the opponents (TCM_I 58.19–71.3, see also VATTANKY (1984: 221–229, 361–383)), the reason of the establishing inference has the fault of having a counter-reason. The counter-inference itself is as follows: the world and so on are not produced by an agent since they are not something produced by someone having a body. The main objection against the reason of 'not being produced by body' is that in comparison with this reason, 'being not produced' is simpler and so it has the real invariable concomitance of not having an agent. Hence 'not being produced by body', does not have the invariable concomitance of 'having no agent'. The opponent tries to answer this objection trying to show that there is actually no useless qualification since the qualification here is helpful for producing the knowledge that the reason actually exists in the subject. Further, it is objected that only when the determinant of qualificandness is not the determinant of invariable concomitance, is the qualification such a determinant. In the case of instances such as 'not produced by body', 'blue-smoke' and so on, the qualificandness alone could be the determinant of the invariable concomitance in question. The opponent rejects this and says that even in the instances mentioned, there is invariable concomitance in the sense of 'having no deviation' or 'having no additional condition'.

All these objections of the opponent are rejected and it is established that such reasons as 'not being produced by body'; and 'blue-smoke' cannot be used as valid reasons, though they have the invariable concomitance of the respective *sādhya*s.

They cannot be used as valid reason because of the general principle that the determinant of invariable concomitance is itself the determinant of 'being reason'. Accordingly in reasons such as 'blue-smoke', the determinant of invariable concomitance is not 'being blue smoke', but simply 'smokeness' because of logical simplicity and so blue smoke cannot be used as a valid reason. Similarly, in the reason of 'produced by body' the determinant of the state of being reason is the 'state of being produced by body'. Therefore 'being produced by body' cannot be used as a valid reason.

From what we have been explaining it is easy to see that the intrinsic nature of the basic principles of Nyāya logic lead ineluctably to God as the culmination of philosophical and epistemological enterprise. What are the basic epistemological principles on which these subtle arguments are based? In Nyāya studies in general, and in Navya-nyāya studies in particular, it is very easy for one to miss the wood for the trees. There are so many different topics in Navya-nyāya that one can easily get lost in particulars, though of course a detailed and exact knowledge of the individual topics is a prerequisite for an appreciation of Navya-nyāya as a whole. What then is the basic concern of Navya-nyāya? Its overriding concern is in its sustained effort to study with unparalleled rigour and exactitude the nature, dimensions and conditions of human knowledge; and, as we know, the philosophical problem *par excellence* is the problem of knowledge. With rare insight Navya-nyāya examines the problems connected with human knowledge and sets forth in detail the exact conditions in which valid knowledge is possible. It should be borne in mind that in and through the analysis of human knowledge Navya-nyāya mediates also a self-understanding of human beings which deserves close examination and probably even unqualified appreciation. Thus its definition of *vyāpti*, invariable concomitance, is not a sterile definition of the concept but an exploration of a profound aspect of human knowledge itself and it may plausibly be argued that its true significance comes out in the *Īśvara-vāda*.

In order to make the problem still clearer let us pose the following question; we know that the logical proof for the existence of God is developed by Vācaspatimiśra, Udayana and Gaṅgeśa against the logical and philosophical arguments of their opponents, especially the Buddhists. What however is most intriguing is that none of these authors nor even later commentators on Gaṅgeśa's work like Jayadeva, Pragalbha or Rucidatta ask the question why is it that according to Nyāya logic it is possible to establish the existence of God? On the other hand neither Dharmakīrti nor any of his followers like Jñānaśrīmitra or Ratnakīrti raise the question why in the Buddhist logical system it is not possible to establish the existence of God? It is also to be noted that none of the modern scholars who studied these texts raise this question, much less answer it. The question has also escaped the attention of general philosophers who know broadly that the Buddhist tradition does not believe in God, whereas Nyāya is theistic, at least as far as the great works of Vācaspatimiśra, Udayana and Gaṅgeśa are concerned. But they never ask the question what is the reason for this difference?

An adequate answer for this question lies naturally in the concept of knowledge in the different systems and hence in the possibilities and limitations of their logic. Therefore it could be asserted without much hesitation that the Nyāya proof for the existence of God presupposes a theory of knowledge according to which it is possible to raise the question of God whereas the Buddhists of Dharmakīrti school propose a theory of knowledge according to which it is radically impossible not only to prove the existence of God but even to conceive an idea of him. Thus the Nyāya system has as horizon a theory of knowledge which renders possible the proofs for the existence of God. That is why it could be validly asserted that in the Nyāya theory of knowledge the Absolute becomes the horizon of all knowledge and therefore also of all human activities. This aspect of the Nyāya theory of knowledge in all its details is not developed explicitly in Nyāya treatises but implied in them. But of course it does not mean that such an interpretation is purely subjective. On the contrary an interpretation of this kind is based on the very foundation of the system itself.

In order to explain this it is necessary to refer to some of the very basic theories of Nyāya epistemology. Intimately connected with it is the fundamental Nyāya theory about what is usually known as invariable concomitance (*vyāpti*). In simple terms invariable concomitance is the invariable relationship of the reason with that which is to be established by the syllogism. Thus, when you establish fire by means of smoke, you presuppose an invariable relation of smoke with fire. But the concept is not as simple as that. In fact a large part of Nyāya discussions on the theory of knowledge and inference in general is all about this concept of invariable concomitance. Further this concept is of primary importance in all the major systems of classical Indian thought. In fact prolonged and persistent controversies ranged among the different schools on this point precisely because they sought to justify their different metaphysical positions on the basis of this aspect of the theory of knowledge. The controversy was acute between the Buddhists, especially of the Dharmakīrti school, and the Naiyāyikas. And the point of difference between these two schools is that in Nyāya it is possible from what we have known to assert also what we have not known, whereas the Buddhists tend to deny this. But this of course is an oversimplified statement.

In slightly more technical terms, the Buddhist position would be the following: we know a thing whose existence we have not directly perceived only if that thing belongs to the class of things which could be the object of direct experience. And the Naiyāyikas on the contrary hold that we can, on the basis of the experience of the class of things about which we have direct knowledge, assert the existence of a thing even if that thing does not strictly belong to the class of things that could be perceived. This in fact in simplified terms is the crux of the problem in the Buddhist and Nyāya theories of knowledge and of invariable concomitance. Consequently the arguments regarding the existence of God became the centre of heated controversies. Nyāya holds that it is possible for us to know the unknown from what we have known. It also means that this unknown need not necessarily belong to the class of things which are already known, but according to the Buddhist system as represented in the school of Dharmakīrti it is necessary that this unknown thing should belong to the class of things that are already known. Otherwise we cannot make any affirmation whatever about this unknown thing.

From what has been said it follows that the epistemological presupposition of Nyāya theory of inference involves by implication first of all the capacity of human intelligence to rise above what is of immediate experience. We could further draw the important conclusion that this Nyāya theory implies that human beings cannot think except in the context of an Absolute. No theory of knowledge is possible without implying at the same time the existence of an Absolute and the inherent capacity of human intellect somehow to grasp this Absolute. And such an explanation of the basis of Nyāya theory of knowledge particularly with reference to the concept of invariable concomitance is quite legitimate. An interpretation of this kind is based on sound philosophical and philological analysis of the texts concerned (VATTANKY (1984: 153 ff.)). This implies therefore that the Nyāya theory of knowledge can be explained and validated only against the background of the basic and inherent capacity of the human intellect to rise above the mere phenomena which are directly perceived by it.

This is also the basic reason why it is asserted that the God of the Naiyāyikas is a transcendent one. The dynamism of knowledge that is implicitly affirmed in the Nyāya theory of inference cannot simply stop at an anthropomorphic God who is immanent to the system itself.[7] If the God of the Naiyāyikas is just one of the categories admitted by the system then there would not be much point in elaborating the theory of inference which tries to establish objects beyond sense experience. In fact

[7] Of course this interpretation is not fully in line with the usual idea of God in the Nyāya-Vaiśeṣika system according to which, in the beginning of creation, God produces movement in the atoms according to the various *adṛṣṭa*s of souls. The *adṛṣṭa* itself is insentient and therefore God is needed to activate it. In such an interpretation of the Nyāya-Vaiśeṣika idea of God, he is not a transcendent reality but he is one of the categories within the system, but does not stand above it. My point here is that although this is the traditional interpretation of God in the Nyāya-Vaiśeṣika system, still the theory of knowledge in general and of inference in particular by its inherent dynamism demands the existence of a transcendent God.

as we have explained the dynamic nature of the Nyāya theory of knowledge and inference can be fully understood only in the context of the infinite capacity of the human intellect to reach out to the ultimate.

It is quite possible that some one may disagree with the above interpretation of the Nyāya theory of knowledge and inference on the one hand, and of the Buddhist theory of knowledge and inference on the other, and with the conclusions drawn from such interpretations. But then it is incumbent on the one who disagrees to propose another plausible answer to the question which was raised: why is it that according to the Nyāya logic it is possible to establish the existence of God? On the other hand why is it that in the Buddhist logical system of Dharmakīrti it is not possible to establish the existence of God? The classical authors and their commentators do not give any explicit answer to this question. We have to reflect long on their texts themselves and their implications. I have given one interpretation based on which a plausible answer to this question is given. It is for other scholars either to accept my answer or to challenge it with adequate reasons.

From these discussions, the conclusion seems to force itself upon us. In comparison with the literature on the other topics of the Nyāya system, works on *Īśvara-vāda* are significant. The three theistic *sūtra*s and the commentaries on them especially by Uddyotakara and Vācaspatimiśra, the *Nyāya-kusumâñjali* of Udayana and the *Īśvara-vāda* of Gaṅgeśa stand out as major contributions to philosophical and logical thought. Gaṅgeśa's *Īśvara-vāda* in particular is a work composed with considerable ingenuity, though dependent on Vācaspati for some of the basic arguments. It is as succinct as it is subtle, as we have seen in the discussion on the fallacy of counter-thesis with reference to the inference to establish the existence of God. But when we study in depth each section of the work analysing each sentence and each expression we can marvel at the subtlety and depth of the author. In a sense concealing his art, Gaṅgeśa deploys various important elements of Nyāya logic, such as the concept of invariable concomitance, the notion of fallacies etc. to substantiate his claims in the sphere of theism. And in doing so he is also communicating a profound understanding of human knowledge and of human being itself, firmly upholding that Theism is an integral element of genuine philosophical anthropology (VATTANKY (1984) and (1993)). Considered in this perspective, it can be asserted on sound principles of textual exegesis and philosophical hermeneutics that theism is the culmination of Nyāya logic.

BIBLIOGRAPHY

DRAVID 1995 = Dravid, N.S.: *Ātma-tattva-viveka by Udayanācārya. With translation, explanation etc.* Indian Institute of Advanced Study, Shimla 1995.

DRAVID 1996 = Dravid, N.S.: *Nyāya-kusumāñjali by Udayanācārya. With translation, explanation etc.* Indian Council of Philosophical Research, New Delhi 1996.

KEITH 1977 = Keith, Arthur Berriedale: *Indian Logic and Atomism.* Munshiram Manoharlal, New Delhi 1977.

NS = Akṣapāda Gautama: *Nyāya-sūtra.* Nyaya-Tarkatirtha, Taranatha [Chap. 1, Sec. 1]; Tarkatirtha, Amarendramohan [Chap. I-ii–V]; Tarkatirtha, Hemantakumar [Chap. IV–V] (eds.): *Nyāya-darśanam. With Vātsyāyana's Bhāṣya, Uddyotakara's Vārttika, Vācaspati Miśra's Tātparyaṭīkā and Viśvanātha's Vṛtti.* With an Introduction by Narendra Chandra Vedantatirtha. 2 Vols, Second edition, Munshiram Manoharlal Publishers, New Delhi 1985 [first edition: Calcutta Sanskrit Series 18, 29, Metropolitan Printing & Publishing House, Calcutta 1936, 1944].

NV = Uddyotakara: *Nyāya-vārttika.* See: NS.

NVTṬ = Vācaspatimiśra: *Nyāya-vārttika-tātparya-ṭīkā.* See: NBh.

PV = Dharmakīrti: *Pramāṇa-vārttika.* Swami Dwarikadas Shastri (ed.): *Pramāṇavārttika of Acharya Dharmakirtti with the Commentary 'Vṛtti' of Acharya Manorathanandin.* Bauddha Bharati Series, Varanasi 1968.

TCM = Gaṅgeśa: *Tattva-cintā-maṇi.* Pandit Kāmākhyanātha Tarkavāgīśa (ed.): *Tattva-cintā-maṇi of Gaṅgeśa, iśvarânumānam.* Vol. 2, Pt. 1: *Anumāna-khaṇḍà, with the commentary Āloka of Jayadevamiśra.* Chaukhamba Sanskrit Pratisthan, Delhi 1990 [first edition: Calcutta 1897].

TSa = Śāntarakṣita: *Tattva-saṁgraha.* Swami Dwarikadas Shastri (ed.): *Tattvasaṁgraha of Ācārya Shāntarakṣita with the Commentary 'Pañjikā' of Shri Kamalshīla.* 2 Vols, Bauddha Bharati Series 1, Bauddha Bharati, Varanasi 1981.

VATTANKY 1984 = Vattanky, J.: *Gaṅeśa's Philosophy of God.* The Adayar Library and Research Centre, Adayar, Madras 1984.

VATTANKY 1993 = Vattanky, John: *Development of Nyāya Theism.* Intercultural Publications, New Delhi 1993.

What Exists for the Vaiśeṣika?[*]

PIOTR BALCEROWICZ

1.1. Introduction: the knowability thesis *249*
1.2. Other examples of the knowability thesis *251*
2. The structure of Praśastapāda's argument *252*
2.1. Possible formulations and loss of ontology ... *252*
2.2. Possible readings of Praśastapāda's statement .*253*
2.3. Existentiality and existence *256*
2.4. How do existentiality and existence differ? ... *262*
2.5. Existentiality, existence and non-existence ... *266*
3.1. Do the properties overlap? *273*
3.2. Coextensiveness of meta-categories? *276*
3.3. The Nyāya-Vaiśeṣika knowability thesis and Fitch's Paradox of Knowability *281*
4.1. Knowability thesis and the 'knowability thesis package' *291*
4.2. Knowability thesis and god's existence *292*
4.3. Knowability thesis and god's omniscience ... *297*
4.4. Knowability thesis and supernatural perception *308*
4.4.1. Supernatural perception of the *yogins* *308*
4.4.2. Supernatural perception of the seers *314*
4.4.3. Supernatural perception and moral law *315*
4.4.4. Supernatural perception and the gradual development argument *318*
5. Conclusion *330*
5.1. God's incompatibility with the system of Nyāya-Vaiśeṣika *330*
5.2. The Vaiśeṣikas, the Pāśupatas and god *341*
5.3. Final word *348*

1.1. Introduction: the knowability thesis

In his *Padârtha-dharma-saṁgraha* (PBh), Praśastapāda ascribes three common properties to all ontological categories: existentiality[1] (*astitva*), nameability (*abhidheyatva*) and cognisability (*jñeyatva*). The well-known and often debated passage of PBh$_1$ 2.3, p. 16 = PBh$_2$ 11 reads:

T° *ṣaṇṇām api padârthānām astitvâbhidheyatva-jñeyatvāni*.

[*] I gratefully acknowledge the feedback I have received from Stephen Phillips on the notion of *astitva* and related issues and thank him for all his comments on the paper.

[1] To translate *astitva*, I deliberately choose 'existentiality', which might appear odd at first, in order not to project any ready-made ideas on the term, the semantics of which first requires proper analysis. Its meaning will become clear in the sequel, esp. p. 256 ff.

Logic and Belief in Indian Philosophy
Warsaw Indological Studies 3 (2010) 249–360.

> 'All the six ontological categories have [the following three properties in common]: existentiality, nameability and cognisability.'

This idea is sometimes simplified to the statement that 'whatever exists is nameable and knowable;'[2] however, such a rendering occurs not without a semantic loss of the original statement and prejudging the exact relation, such as co-extension or partial overlap, between the three properties, a relation that should first be studied more carefully. We can call it the Nyāya-Vaiśeṣika thesis of the knowability of everything, or the knowability thesis for short.

The present paper will take up the question again,[3] whether these three properties were thought to be coextensive or not, by supplying some additional material, and will demonstrate how far the issue is related to the idea of omniscience accepted by the Vaiśeṣika. I will also argue that the triad of existentiality (*astitva*), nameability (*abhidheyatva*) and cognisability (*jñeyatva*) entered the system of Vaiśeṣika in the late fifth century CE at the earliest in a package of four interrelated concepts that necessarily complement each other. The other three ingredients are: the belief in god's existence[4], belief in god's omniscience and belief in supernatural perception. What is important, the paper is an attempt to reconstruct early historical developments in the tradition of Nyāya-Vaiśeṣika and not to engage the subsequent development of these ideas. I deliberately avoid discussing such philosophers as Udayana or Gaṅgeśa or ideas (e.g. *upādhi*) that were later developed as, perhaps, a response to some problems also posed by issues discussed in the present paper in order to avoid a methodological error of projecting later ideas onto an early phase of the system.

[2] See Karl H. POTTER (1968: 275): 'to be is to be knowable and nameable', and POTTER (1995: 48): 'whatever is, is knowable and nameable'.

[3] The issue was dealt with already in such works, for example, as POTTER (1968), SHAW (1978), HALBFASS (1989), HALBFASS (1992: 158), POTTER (1995), PERRETT (1999).

[4] I consistently translate *īśvara* as 'god' for a few reasons. First, *īśvara* should be distinguished from *deva* ('divine being') in translation. Second, I consider it a better practice to translate Indian Sanskrit terms into English rather than leave them untranslated, because otherwise, in extreme cases, a translation would purely consist of Sanskrit terms embedded in English morphology and be a case of a 'Sanskritic new speech', and because even a rough English translation approximates the idea of how we understand a given Sanskrit term, albeit it does not always convey the meaning in a most adequate manner. Third, the Indian concept of *īśvara* does not really overlap with what is understood under 'God' in monotheistic traditions of Judaism, Christianity or Islam. Fourth, to an extent the meaning of *īśvara* partially relates to theistic concept of Western-Asian and European traditions, I consider the term 'god' (unlike Yahveh/Jehovah, Allah, Śiva etc.) a common noun (albeit with necessarily only one instantiation for the monotheists), not a proper name, and as such it should be consistently written lower case, despite the tradition.

1.2. Other examples of the knowability thesis

Praśastapāda was not unique in the tradition of Nyāya-Vaiśeṣika. At more or less the same time Uddyotakara alludes to these ideas in the *Nyāya-vārttika* with similar words,[5] taking the idea of the three properties as already well-known and necessitating no additional explanation.

Likewise Candramati (Maticandra?) refers to these ideas at the end of his *Daśa-padârtha-śāstra* (DPŚ)—now preserved only in Chinese translation,[6] that presents the Vaiśeṣika system partly independent of the *Vaiśeṣika-sūtra*s—which is cited here in two different English renderings:

> 'Which of these (five kinds of *abhāva*—P.B.) are objects of perception; which are not objects of it? All the five non-existences are not objects of perception. On the other hand, even those which exist without being supported by other things are altogether objects of inference. [Section 11.—*Conclusion*]
> Which of these ten categories are knowable; which are not knowable? All are knowable and also causes of their recognitions'[7];

> '[253] Among these five [kinds of absences], how many are the objects of direct cognition, and how many are not the objects of direct

[5] NV₁ 1.1.5, p. 56.21 = NV₂ 1.1.5, p. 50.17: *sattva-pra*[§]*meyatvâbhidheyatvâdy-anumānaṁ prāptam.*

[§] NV₂. The passage is quoted in HBṬĀ, p. 317.26.

Worth noting is that Uddyotakara uses the term *astitva* not in the Vaiśeṣika sense of 'existentiality', which is discussed in the present paper, as it stands in triad of *astitva–abhidheyatva–jñeyatva*, but in the sense of ontological existence, e.g. in such phrases and contexts as 'the existence of soul' (NV₁ 1.1.10, p. 66.17–18 = NV₂, p. 60.11–12: *icchâdīnāṁ pratisandhānam ātmâstitva-pratipādakam*; NV₁ 1.1.34, p. 119.8–9 = NV₂ 1.1.33, p. 109.21–22: *tad yathā ātmano 'stitva-nāstitva-vicāraṇāyām iti. ātmano 'stitva-nāstitva-saṁśayaḥ iti*, etc.) or 'the existence of god' (NV₁ 4.1.21, p. 461.4–7 = NV₂, p. 433.7 ff.: *īśvara eva nyāyam. tatra hi pramāṇāny avighātena pravartante iti. astitvâsiddhiḥ iti cet atha manyase siddhe īśvarasyâstitve kāraṇântara-nirākaraṇaṁ nimitta-kāraṇa-bhāvaś ca siddhyet*, etc.).

[6] After a first fragmentary attempt by Paramārtha, DPŚ was eventually fully translated into Chinese by Xuanzang (Hsuan-tsang, 600–664) under the title *Shengzong shijuyi lun* (a rendering of *Vaiśeṣika-nikāya-daśa-padārtha-śāstra*) in 648 (or between 646 and 648), after his return to China from Nālandā; see UI (1917: 1) and BAGCHI (1944: 151).

[7] Translated by UI (1917: 119). Cf. also a relevant note of UI (1917: 224): '"Knowable" represents *jñeyatva*, while *astitva* and *abhidheyatva* are included in "causes of their recognition".'

> cognition? [254] Any [kind of absence] is not the object of direct cognition. But all [kinds of absences], which exist without having any locus other [than their own], are the objects of inference. [255] Among these ten categories of entities, how many are cognizable and how many are non-cognizable? [256] All are cognizable and are the cause of expressions'[8] (emphasis—P.B.).

The idea is also expressly echoed in the *Praśastamati-ṭīkā* passages quoted in DNC (p. 517.5–7; see below, p. 274) by Mallavādin, albeit it does not seem to be known to the original author(s) of the *Vaiśeṣika-sūtra*.[9]

2. The structure of Praśastapāda's argument

Let us first take a closer look at the structure of Praśastapāda's statement.

2.1. Possible formulations and loss of ontology

As it is well-known, in the Vaiśeṣika ontology, the structure of the world is described as reducible to atomic facts, analysable as follows:

> A property (*dharma*, *q*) is related to its substratum (*dharmin*, *p*) with a particular relation (*sambandha*, *R*): *R* (*q*, *p*).

One of the relations possible in Vaiśeṣika, the relation of inherence (*samavāya*), acquired a predominant role and was classified as the sixth ontological category. Praśastapāda defined it as 'the relationship between the locus and the located property'[10]. Others defined it later as 'the qualifier-qualificand relationship' (*viśeṣaṇa-viśeṣya-bhāva*)[11].

---

[8] Translated and reconstructed into Sanskrit by MIYAMOTO (1996: 206), DPŚ$_2$ 253–256: [253] *etādṛśāṇāṁ pañcâbhāvānāṁ kati dṛṣṭa-viṣayāḥ katy adṛṣṭa-viṣayāḥ?* [254] *sarve 'dṛṣṭa-viṣayāḥ. kiṁ tu ananyâśritya vartamānāḥ sarve 'numāna-viṣayaḥ.* [255] *eteṣāṁ darśa-padârthānāṁ kati jñeyāḥ katy ajñeyāḥ?* [256] *sarva eva jñeyāḥ. te câivâbhidhāna-hetuḥ.* Cf. also MIYAMOTO (1996: 251): *praśastapāda-bhāṣya-dravya-granthe sādharmya-vaidharmya-nirūpaṇānām ṣaṇṇām api padârthānām astitvâbhidheya-jñeyatvāni.*

[9] Cf. n. 23.

[10] PBh$_1$ 12, p. 326.1 = PBh$_2$ 375: *adhikaraṇâdhikartavyayor eva bhāva[ḥ].*

[11] Uddyotakara, e.g. NV$_1$ 1.1.4, p. 32.16.

In the Vaiśeṣika-specific terminology, the Western-type predicate proposition of the form

> '*x* is *P*':
> *P* (*x*)

would thus correspond to:

> 'The property *P*-ness is related to its substratum *x* with the relation of inherence *I*':
> *I* (*P*-ness, *x*),

which can be simplified to:

> '*x* possesses the property *P*-ness.'[12]

This is why the idea expressed by Praśastapāda's statement: 'anything that possesses the property of existentiality, also possesses the property of nameability and cognisability', could be logically converted to a typical predicate statement: 'whatever is existent is also nameable and cognisable'.

That would not, however, happen without consequence. The transformation would, first, involve the obvious loss of the specific ontological relation between subject and predicate typified by the relation of inherence, and, second, would reduce the property-substratum relation of inherence to a predicate-subject relation. What remains intact is the logical relation between the subject and the predicates, or between the substratum and its properties. In the paper, I shall occasionally use the shorthand 'whatever is existent is also nameable and knowable', or similar expressions, for the complete proposition: 'among all the six categories anything that possesses the property of existentiality, also possesses the property of nameability and cognisability'.

2.2. Possible readings of Praśastapāda's statement

We notice that the three properties can, theoretically, be coextensive, partially overlap or be in the relation of inclusion. To save paper, I will not discuss all the theoretical possibilities, but only refer to those that are contextually most plausible.

Accordingly, Praśastapāda's complete statement: 'All the six ontological categories have [the following three properties, inherently related to them, in common]:

[12] For instances cf. PBh_1 2.3, p. 19 = PBh_2 15 (n. 26 below), and DNC, p. 517.5 f.: *yat punaḥ dravyâdīnāṁ svata evâbhidhāna-pratyaya-viṣayatvaṁ sattvāt sattâdivat* (see n. 30 below).

existentiality, nameability and cognisability', which assumes the reality of the relation of inherence, can be converted to one of the following predicate statements:

F1° 'Among the six ontological categories, whatever is existent, is also nameable which is in turn cognisable': *astitva* $\subseteq$ (*jñeyatva* $\subseteq$ *abhidheyatva*), or

F2° 'Among the six ontological categories, whatever is existent, is also cognisable which is in turn nameable': *astitva* $\subseteq$ (*abhidheyatva* $\subseteq$ *jñeyatva*), or

F3° 'Among the six ontological categories, whatever is nameable, is also existent which is in turn cognisable' *abhidheyatva* $\subseteq$ (*jñeyatva* $\subseteq$ *astitva*), or

F4° 'Among the six ontological categories, whatever is nameable, is also cognisable which is in turn existent' *abhidheyatva* $\subseteq$ (*astitva* $\subseteq$ *jñeyatva*), or

F5° 'Among the six ontological categories, whatever is cognisable, is also existent which is in turn nameable': *jñeyatva* $\subseteq$ (*astitva* $\subseteq$ *abhidheyatva*), or

F6° 'Among the six ontological categories, whatever is cognisable, is also nameable which is in turn existent': *jñeyatva* $\subseteq$ (*abhidheyatva* $\subseteq$ *astitva*).[13]

What needs to be clarified is also the exact relation between the sets of properties, i.e. the equation/inclusion sign $\subseteq$ should be diambiguated as either = or $\subset$, e.g.:

jñeyatva = *astitva* = *abhidheyatva*, or
astitva $\subset$ (*jñeyatva* $\subset$ *abhidheyatva*), or
jñeyatva $\subset$ *astitva* $\subset$ *abhidheyatva*, or
jñeyatva $\subset$ (*astitva* = *abhidheyatva*), etc.

The relation between nameability (*abhidheyatva*) and cognisability (*jñeyatva*) does not seem to pose much difficulty due to the e v e n t u a l l y[14] verbal character of cognition, accepted by the Nyāya-Vaiśeṣika, but also because the commentators take them both as coextensive: *jñeyatva* = *abhidheyatva*.

For instance at a much later period, in the *Kiraṇâvalī*, Udayana singles them out and treats in the same manner:

> '[Objection:] "But these two [categories of nameability and cognisability] exist even with respect to [the seventh ontological category of] absence". They do, indeed. However, what is intended to be expressed

[13] The possibilities of formal notation are larger depending on how we use the parentheses, e.g. F2* (*astitva* $\subseteq$ *jñeyatva*) $\subseteq$ *abhidheyatva*, F2* (*astitva* $\subseteq$ *abhidheyatva*) $\subseteq$ *jñeyatva*, etc. For our purposes the issue is of no practical importance.

[14] By 'eventually' I mean that, even in the case of the contents of the non-conceptual (indeterminate) perception (*nirvikalpaka-pratyakṣa*), one becomes aware of it only at a subsequent stage of conceptual (determinate) perception (*savikalpaka-pratyakṣa*), which in principle can be verbalised.

[here in the *Praśastapāda-bhāṣya*] is not the difference [between all the ontological categories] with respect to this [absence], but the similarity with respect to six ontological categories.'[15]

Similarly, in the *Nyāya-kandalī* (NKan), Śrīdharamiśra says that:

'Nameability is indeed the intrinsic nature of the real thing, i.e. it is nothing but the intrinsic nature of something that exists; and, in view of the difference of [the particular] condition [of the real thing], nameability is called cognisability.'[16]

What remains problematic is how the pair nameability–cognisability actually relates to existentiality, viz. whether it is the equation: *astitva* = (*jñeyatva* = *abhidheyatva*), or the inclusion of either of two kinds: nameability–cognisability is the proper subset of existentiality, viz. *astitva* ⊂ (*jñeyatva* = *abhidheyatva*), or the other way round, viz. (*jñeyatva* = *abhidheyatva*) ⊂ *astitva*.

Researchers interpreted Praśastapāda's thesis in diverse ways. Karl H. POTTER, for instance, took it for granted that all the three properties are coextensive:

'"To be is to be knowable and nameable". The Naiyāyika reads this as fully reversible: whatever exists (in the broadest sense) can be known and can be spoken of, named; furthermore, if something is known, or if it is named, then it exists. Likewise, if something is nameable, it is knowable, and vice-versa. The three abstract nouns in the Sanskrit motto apply to each and every thing in the universe' (1968: 275),

as well as

'whatever is, is knowable and nameable' (1995: 48).

Also Roy W. PERRETT (1999: 401) echoed the thought: 'Whatever exists is knowable and nameable'. The same interpretation was expressed several decades earlier by Gaṅgānātha JHĀ (1982: 37):

'Though "beingness" would seem to belong to Abhāva also, and as such the mention of "six" categories only would appear incorrect,—yet when we bear in mind the fact that our author has enumerated only six categories, the incongruity ceases; as to mention "six" categories, as having "beingness" is as much as to say that it belongs to *all things*.

[15] KA, p. 19.5–7: *nanv etad eva dvayam abhāve 'py astîti cet, astu, na hi tad-apekṣayā vaidharmyam idaṁ vivakṣitam, api tu ṣad-apekṣayā sādharmyam*.

[16] NKan$_1$, p. 16: *tac ca vastunaḥ svarūpam eva bhāva-svarūpam evâvasthā-bhedena* ***jñeyatvam*** *abhidheyatvaṁ côcyate*.

> And a n y t h i n g t h a t e x i s t s i s a l s o c a p a b l e o f b e i n g " p r e d i c a t e d " ' (emphaisis—P.B.).

And in the same spirit Jaysankar Lal SHAW (1978: 259–260) asserted that:

> 'To exist is to be knowable and nameable. It is claimed that if something has one of the three properties, it has the remaining two properties as well. ... Every object has the property of being communicable through language. ... This amounts to saying that an object can be an object of knowledge of cognition.'

However, Wilhelm HALBFASS (1992: 158) was far more cautious in his judgements:

> '"All six categories possess is-ness, nameability, and knowability" (*ṣāṇṇāṁ api padārthānāṁ astitvābhidheyatvajñeyatvāni*).[110] Praśastapāda's short statement is elusive; its simplicity is deceptive. It does not clarify the relationship between *astitva*, on the one hand, and predicability and knowability or objectifiability, on the other. The fact that he coordinates them as common attributes (*sādharmya*) of the six categories does not necessarily mean that he considers them to be coextensive.[111] The commentators usually include nonbeing (*abhāva*) under *abhidheyatva* and *jñeyatva*, but are reluctant to do so with regard to *astitva*; although we may know and speak of nonbeing, nothing knowable or speakable exists (or "is there") apart from the six positive categories.[112] [[110] PBh, p. 16.].'

I will return to this important question whether the three properties are coextensive or not in § 3 below (p. 273 ff.).

2.3. Existentiality and existence

Praśastapāda, Candramati and Uddyotakara are too laconic to judge the way they conceived of the relation of the three properties. Not only do they not define them, but also treat them as meta-categories[17] that underlie the system and its categories and are

[17] Cf. HALBFASS (1992: 1945): '*Astitva* is not part of the fundamental "nomenclature of the world.' It is not "listed" and "named" among the categories, but used to describe and analyze them. I is a second-order concept, an abstraction.' Indeed, the problem of the property of *astitva* to be considered a separate category is pointed out by Śāntarakṣita in TSaP 572:

> *saṁjñāpaka-pramāṇasya viṣaye tattvam iṣyate /*
> *ṣaṇṇām astitvam iti cet ṣaḍbhyo 'nyas te prasajyate //*

too well known to be defined or explained. They must have already become a 'common assumption' of the discourse at that time. All Praśastapāda says about them is, for instance, that they apply to all the six categories to which the universe is reducible, i.e. they apply to everything. Most importantly, *astitva* is clearly distinguished from the highest universal (*sāmānya*) of existence (*sattā*), which is possessed only by the first three categories of 'concrete things' (*artha*): substances (*dravya*), qualities (*guṇa*) and movements (*karman*). Existentiality (*astitva*) along with two other meta-categories, in their turn, are predicated of everything. Only 'concrete' things need 'existence' (*sattā*) for their existence, whereas the remaining three categories—i.e. universals (*sāmānya*), individuators (*viśeṣa*)[18] and inherence (*samavāya*)—do not and cannot; they do possess, however, existentiality (*astitva*).

Some clarification with respect to the actual relation between the concepts of *sattā* and *astitva* can be found in PBh. In the chapter on the relation of inherence, Praśastapāda explains that

> 'Just as the presence (sc. the universal existence, *sattā*) of substances, qualities and movements, which consists in [their] being existent,[19] has no additional association with the universal existence (sc. it needs no second-order universal of existence), similarly inherence, consisting in occurrence has no additional (*sc.* second order) occurrence; therefore [inherence] occurs in itself.'[20]

In other words, the highest universal of existence that characterises substances, qualities and movements, does not need any second-order universal of existence; it does need though the quality of 'being existent', or 'having the nature of something existent' (*sad-ātmaka*), i.e. existentiality (*astitva*).

Thus, the highest universal of existence (*sattā*) is inherently related—through the relation of *samavāya*—to only those entities and all those which can ostensively be referred to as denotata with specific terms denoting them. Accordingly, the extension, or application, of *sattā* is narrower than that of *astitva*.[21] This contention finds further

[18] An idea that only partially resembles Duns Scotus' notion of haecceity ('thisness'), the main difference being that for Duns Scotus it was the notion of a particular non-qualitative property or aspect of a thing responsible for its distinct individuality or essence, whereas for Vaiśeṣika it is a separate category.

[19] Cf. VS(C) 1.2.4 (*bhāvaḥ sāmānyam eva*) and VSV(C) ad loc.

[20] PBh_1 12, p. 328 = PBh_2 384: *yathā dravya-guṇa-karmaṇāṁ sad-ātmakasya bhāvasya nânyaḥ sattā-yogo 'sti, evam avibhāgino vṛtty-ātmakasya samavāyasya nânyā vṛttir asti tasmāt svâtma-vṛttiḥ.*

[21] This was eventually perceived as problematic by some. See for instance Bhaṭṭa Vādīndra who, in his *Vaiśeṣika-sūtra-vārttika* (VSV), equates *astitva* with *sattā* to avoid a range of

support in Praśastapāda's following statement which indirectly associates the property of being related to the universal existence (*sattā-sambandha*) with the property of being nameable according to a linguistic convention that governs the process of conventional naming of the first three categories (substances, qualities and movements):

> 'All three [categories, viz.] substance etc. (sc. qualities and movements), possess the relation with [the universal] existence, [possess] the status of [entities] that are endowed with intermediate universals, [possess] the status of [entities] that are nameable with [the help of] speech elements that [express their] denotata [in accordance] with the convention [that applies] to them[22].'[23]

We can see that for Praśastapāda there are two different strategies to denote entities, or—to put it differently—different categories are all amenable to being denoted in two different ways. All the six categories, which are also possessed of existentiality (*astitva*), are nameable (*abhidheya*), whereas the first three of them, which are pos-

difficulties, see ISAACSON (1995: 28–29): 'What Bhaṭṭa Vādīndra does here is attempt to solve an inherent difficulty in Vaiśeṣika ontology by equating what originally was a "second-order concept," which fell outside of the supposedly all-inclusive categories, with the highest universal. This attempt to make the description and classification of really existing things as complete as possible with a small set of first-order concepts and avoiding the use of concepts at a higher (meta-) level as far as possible, inevitably entails infinite regress, circularity or *ātmāśrayaḥ* at some key points; how persuasive Bhaṭṭa Vādīndra is in arguing that this does not invalidate his proposals I shall leave to philosophers to debate. No Indian thinker, as far as I know, has followed Bhaṭṭa Vādīndra in this.'

[22] This is in accordance with VS(C) 7.2.24: *sāmayikaḥ śabdād artha-pratyayaḥ*.—'The understanding of the meaning [takes place] by virtue of the speech element governed by a convention.'

A reference to such an understanding of the meaning of a word, which denotes concrete entities (substances and their qualities) as well as their movements, which expresses both the universal and the particular aspect—and only these first three categories possess universals (*sāmānya*) and individuators (*viśeṣa*), may earlier have been referred to by Bhartṛhari in VP 2.125, which is slightly cryptic:

> *niyatās tu prayogā ye niyataṁ yac ca sādhanam /*
> *teṣāṁ śabdâbhidheyatvam aparair anugamyate //*
>
> 'Others conclude that specific application [of words] (sc. universals) and means [to apply them] (sc. particulars) are what is expressed by the speech element.'

[23] PBh₁ 2.3, p. 17 = PBh₂ 14: *dravyâdīnāṁ trayāṇām api sattā-sambandhaḥ, sāmānya-viśeṣavattvaṁ, sva-samayârtha-śabdâbhidheyatvaṁ, dharmâdharma-kartṛtvaṁ ca*.

It is generally accepted by later Vaiśeṣika authors that the idea goes back to Praśastapāda, which further implies that the first to adopt the three properties (*astitva–abhidheyatva–jñeyatva*) common to all ontological categories was Praśastapāda, see VSU 8.2.3, p. 370.3–4: *tad uktaṁ praśastadevâcāryaiḥ "trayāṇām artha-śabdâbhidheyatvaṁ ca" iti*.—'It was stated by the esteemed preceptor Praśasta that the three [categories possess] the status of [entities] that are nameable with [the help of] speech elements that [express their] denotata.'

sessed of the highest universal of existence (*sattā*), are in addition nameable through speech elements that express their denotata following the convention that applies to these categories (*sva-samayârtha-śabdâbhidheya*). Such an interpretation is additionally strengthened by a mediaeval commentary called *Praśastapāda-bhāṣya-samālocana*:

> '[All first three categories, viz. substances, qualities and movements,] possess the relation with [the universal] existence, which (sc. the relation) consists in inherence. Intermediate universals are substantiality etc. (i.e. qualitativeness (*guṇatva*) and mobility (*karmatva*)). [These three categories also possess] the status of [entities] endowed with these [intermediate universals]. Only three [categories, viz.] substance etc., are named with the help of an independent (sc. not connected with a subordinate word) speech element that [expresses] its denotatum (object), not any other [category]. This precisely is the convention, [expressed] in the own literature of the Vaiśeṣikas, to facilitate practice, just as [the statement] of *The Instruction on Yoga* (YBh): "The triad of meditation, contemplation and concentration with respect to one [object constitute] restraint".'[24]

Thus, only the first three ontological categories can be related through inherence to existence, whereas such categories as intermediate universals (*dravyatva*, *guṇatva*, *karmatva*), individuators and inherence are excluded; they possess *astitva* ('existentiality') instead. Praśastapāda explicitly states that they are not nameable in the same way as the first three categories. In other words, universals etc. are not ostensively nameable, i.e. cannot be ostensively indicated with an accompanying verbal expression:

> '[The subsequent] three categories such as universals etc. (i.e. individuators and inherence) [possess] the status of [entities] that are existent in their own essence (sc. are self-existent), [possess] the status of [entities] that are characterised (or: recognised) by cognition[25], [possess] the status of [entities] that are not effects, [possess] the status of [entities] that are not causes, [possess] the status of [entities] that do not possess

[24] PBhS, p. 10.15–20 (ad PBh_2 14): *sattā-sambandhaḥ samavāya-lakṣaṇaḥ sāmānya-viśeṣā dravyatvâdayaḥ tadvattvaṁ nirupapadenârtha-śabdena dravyâdayas traya evâbhidhīyante nâpare. eṣa eva samayo vaiśeṣikāṇāṁ sva-śāstre vyavahāra-lāghavāya yathā "dhyāna-dhāraṇā-samādhi-trayam ekatra saṁyama"*[§] *iti yogânuśāsane.*

[a] YBh 3.4: *dhāraṇā-dhyāna-samādhi-trayam ekatra saṁyamaḥ.*

[25] As regards the ambiguity of the expression *buddhi-lakṣaṇa* ('those whose characteristic is cognition' or 'those who are recognised through cognition') cf. VyV, p. 40.21–22: *tathā buddhir lakṣaṇaṁ yeṣāṁ buddhyā lakṣyanta iti vā buddhi-lakṣaṇās teṣāṁ bhāvo buddhi-lakṣaṇatvam.*

> any intermediate universals (i.e. subtypes), [possess] the status of [entities] that are permanent and [possess] the status of [entities] that are not nameable with [the help of] speech elements that [express their] denotata.'[26]

Centuries later, Śaṅkaramiśra restates the idea slightly differently:

> '... even though [universals, individuators and inherence] are bereft of existence, [which is the highest universal], they are the contents of cognition that [they are] existent...'[27]

All that means is that all the six categories of the classical Vaiśeṣika can become the contents of both verbal expressions (*abhidhāna*) and cognitive acts (*pratyaya*), but only first three of them can be indicated directly (by pointing) as well as both named (with either general or non-abstract singular terms, or names) and veridically thought of as concrete objects, whose qualities or states are spatio-temporarily limited and which are potentially observable directly.

Worth noting is that the same idea is paraphrased (quoted?) and ascribed to Praśastamati by Mallavādin in DNC, where he introduces a longer quotation from the *Praśastamati-ṭīkā*:

> 'Further, one may object: "[All three categories, viz.] substance etc. (sc. qualities and movements), are the contents of verbal designation and cognition <as something existent>[28] only by their own force, because they are existent (or: because of their existentiality), just as the existence and other [universals are the contents of verbal designation and cognition because they are existent by their own force]. Just as there is verbal designation and cognition of the existence and other [universals] by their own force, not because of their union with [the universal] existence, similarly there is verbal designation and cognition also of [the three categories of] substance etc. (sc. qualities and movements) by their own force, not because they are endowed with [the universal] existence". That is not correct, because [substance, qualities and movements] do not share the na-

[26] PBh$_1$ 2.3, p. 19 = PBh$_2$ 15: *sāmānyâdīnāṁ trayāṇāṁ svâtma-sattvaṁ buddhi-lakṣaṇatvam akāryatvam akāraṇatvam asāmānya-viśeṣavattvaṁ nityatvam artha-śabdânabhidheyatvaṁ cêti.*

[27] PBhṬS, p. 177.3–7: *sāmānya-viśeṣa-samavāyānāṁ svâtma-sattvam. tac ca sattā-śūnyatve sati sat-pratyaya-viṣayatvam. buddhi-lakṣaṇatvaṁ cânuvr̥tta-buddhi-vyāvr̥tta-buddhi-hetu-buddhi-viṣayatvam eva lakṣaṇaṁ sāmānyâdīnāṁ trayāṇām ity uktam.*

[28] The edition reads: *dravyâdīnāṁ svata evâbhidhāna-pratyaya-viṣayatvaṁ*, but—in view of the recurring reading *sad-abhidhāna-pratyayau* in DNC, p. 517.6, p. 517.6–7 and p. 519.7—we should perhaps read *dravyâdīnāṁ svata eva sad-abhidhāna-pratyaya-viṣayatvaṁ*.

ture of it (i.e. of universal existence). Since substance etc. (sc. qualities and movements) do not have the nature of this [universal existence],[29] [their] verbal designation etc. (i.e. cognition) as something existent is based on [the universal] existence, like [the ideas] "the one with no stick" and "the one with a stick" are based on [the idea of] "a stick".'[30]

Thus, what renders the first three categories ostensibly expressible and cognisable as concrete denotata, i.e. as objects or phenomena that can be directly indicated, seems to be the universal existence that is related to them. The remaining three categories, including universals (the primary of them being existence (*sattā*)), can neither be expressed ostensibly (sc. pointed to) nor be directly cognised in the same manner, i.e. as potentially spatio-temporarily determinable objects that that are related to particular qualities, albeit they can be spoken and veridically thought of as general objects or ideas. Praśastamati rejects an unidentified opponent's opinion that the first three categories (substance, qualities and movements) would not need any additional factor or determinant to be expressed and cognised as existent entities, the way the remaining three categories can, on the grounds that the idea of existence as a universal is already entailed in any statement that addresses an object that exists or an object that does not exist. While Mallavādin subsequently rejects the idea, he nonetheless refers to Praśastamati's formulations:

'What has been said, viz. "Since they do not share the nature of it (i.e. of universal existence), verbal designation and cognition of substance etc. (sc. qualities and movements) as something existent is [possible]

---

[29] See remark [b] in n. 30. With the reading *asad-ātmatvāt*, as it is (wrongly) printed, we would have to read: 'Since substance etc. (sc. qualities and movements) do not have the nature of something existent [on its own]'.

In addition, the idea of *sad-ātmakatva*/ *sad-ātmatva* corresponds to *astitva* (see p. 257), and what is meant here is the idea that the three categories of substances etc. need the third category to be amenable to verbal expression etc.

[30] DNC, p. 517.5–518.1 (Vol. II): *yat punaḥ "dravyâdīnāṁ [dravya-guṇa-karmaṇāṁ[a]] svata evâbhidhāna-pratyaya-viṣayatvaṁ sattvāt sattâdivat. yathā sattâdeḥ sad-abhidhāna-pratyayau svata eva, na sattā-yogāt, evaṁ dravyâdīnām api sad-abhidhāna-pratyayau svata eva, na sattā-yogād" ity ukte ucyate—nâitad, atādātmyāt. dravyâdīnām asad-ātmatvāt[b] sattā-nimittaṁ sad-abhidhānâdi daṇḍa-nimittâdaṇḍa-daṇḍitvavad iti.*

[a] DNC, p. 517.3: *teṣāṁ trayaṇām*

[b] Read: *atad-ātmatvāt* in view of (1) the preceding *atādātmyāt*, (2) DNC, p. 519.7: *atad-ātmatvād dravyâdīnāṁ*... (see n. 31), and (3) DNCV, p. 519.26–27: ***atad-ātmatvād*** *ity-ādy asattâtmakatvād dravya-guṇa-karmaṇāṁ sad-abhidhāna-pratyayau sattā-yogāt.*

Cf. MŚVṬ, III, p. 29.5–8: *tad yadi daṇḍa-puruṣa-sambandho daṇḍi-śabdasyâbhidheyaḥ, tathā sati tan-niṣkarṣe daṇḍitvaṁ daṇḍitêti tva-talor anuśāsanam upapadyate. yathā go-śabdâbhidheyaṁ sāmānyaṁ gotvam iti tv apratyayena niṣkṛṣyate.*

> only because they are endowed with [the universal] existence, it is not possible by their own force", that too is not [correct].'[31]

We can further notice that members of the compound *sad-abhidhāna-pratyaya*—resolved as *sad-abhidhāna* ('verbal designation [of *x*] as existent') of Praśastamati and *sad-pratyaya* ('cognition [of *x*] as existent')—correspond to the triad *astitva–abhidheyatva–jñeyatva* of Praśastapāda.[32]

2.4. How do existentiality and existence differ?

The comparison of Praśastapāda's vocabulary (*astitva–abhidheyatva–jñeyatva*) and that of Uddyotakara (*sattva–abhidheyatva–prameyatva*, quoted in n. 5) reveals that the terms *astitva* and *sattva* can, at least on some occasions, be treated as interchangeable, depending on the choice of authors. The specific character of *astitva* ('existentiality') and the way it differs from *sattā* ('existence') will become clearer when we compare the usage of still another term, viz. *bhāva*, which may at first appear to cover some of the semantics of 'existence' and which occurs in selected passages of Praśastapāda's work and of the *Praśastamati-ṭīkā* as quoted by Mallavādin and Siṁha-sūri. The term *bhāva* occurs in at least the following meanings in both works:

---

[31] DNC, p. 519.7–520.1: *yad apy uktam "atad-ātmatvād dravyâdīnāṁ sad-abhidhāna-pratyayau sattā-yogāt, na svataḥ" tad api na.*

[32] In his criticism Mallavādin directly refers to Praśastamati's ideas. This also throws additional light on the relations between the three properties (existentiality, nameability and cognisability): DNC, p. 521.7–522.1: *yataś câivaṁ tasmāt sato bhāvaḥ sattêti vyutpattir dravyâdy-vyatirikta-sattârthâiva kartari ṣaṣṭhī-vṛtteḥ. yat tat sadbhir bhūyate ... sad ity-abhidhāna-pratyaya-kāraṇaṁ sarvatra.*—'Since it is so, [viz. the universal existence of substances etc. is there by its own force,] therefore the presence of that which is existent [is the universal] existence—such is the etymological formation the meaning of which is nothing but [the universal] existence as something different from substances etc., inasmuch as the genitive case is used [to indicate] the agent. ... That which obtains by virtue of existent [entities] (sc. the fact that existent entities occur as such) is the cause of verbal designation and cognition of the form: "[it] is existent" with respect to everything.' Cf. DNCV, p. 521.20–522.–11: ***yataś câivam*** *ity-ādi, yasmāt svata eva sattā dravyâdīnāṁ yuktā tasmāt sato bhāvaḥ sattêti yā śabda-vyutpattir bheda-ṣaṣṭhy-āpādanârthā sā dravyâdy-avyatirikta-sattârthâiva jñāyate satāṁ bhāvaḥ sattêti. kiṁ kāraṇam?* ***kartari ṣaṣṭhī-vṛtteḥ****. tad-vyākhyānam—****yat tat sadbhir*** *ity-ādi gatârthaṁ yāvat* ***sad ity-abhidhāna-pratyaya-kāraṇaṁ sarvatrêti****.* Comp. also DNCV, p. 535.23–24: *yat tat tena bhūyate sa sattā "bhū sattāyām"* [*PāDhā* 1] *iti pāṭhāt sāmānyam.*

(1) *bhāva* in the sense of 'presence', 'occurrence', where it is equivalent to *sadbhāva*, viz. '*x* is there', '*x* is present here';[33]
(2) *bhāva* in the sense of 'existence [of]', viz. 'there is', 'there exists';[34]
(3) *bhāva* in the copulative meaning of 'is', viz. '*x* is *P*'[35];[36]
(4) *bhāva* in the sense of *sattā-sāmānya*, viz. the highest universal.[37]

The last meaning is technical, and thus relevant to our discussion, whereas the first three express the ideas of 'being' (i.e. 'being there', 'being a *P*' etc.) in a rather lose sense, especially in ontological, existential or predicative senses respectively. Most importantly, *bhāva* in the fourth meaning is equated with the universal existence, which is in agreement with an earlier tradition of the *Vaiśeṣika-sūtra*[38], and it is nowhere associated with the idea of *astitva*, whereas the term *sattva* is. We see that, in other words, existentiality (*astitva*, *sattva*) corresponds neither to the highest universal (*sattā-sāmānya*) nor to existence (*bhāva*) in the ontological sense as 'presence', or 'being there' etc., nor to the copulative meaning of the verb 'to be' (√*as*, √*bhū*).

What is existentiality (*astitva*, *sattva*) then, and how does it differ in its meaning and application from the universal existence (*sattā*, *bhāva*)? It is, in my opinion, the

---

[33] PBh_1, p. 238 = PBh_2 270: *ubhayâsiddho 'nyatarâsiddhas tad-bhāvâsiddho 'numeyâsiddhaś cêti. ... tad-bhāvâsiddho yathā dhūma-**bhāvena**âgny-adhigatau kartavyāyām upanyasyamāno bāṣpo* [PBh_1: *vāṣpe*] *dhūma-bhāvenâsiddha iti*. Cf. VNṬ, p. 14: *vāsa-gṛhâdiṣu tarhi dahanâbhāve 'pi dhūma-**sadbhāvād** vyabhicāra iti cet.*

[34] PBh_1 10, p. 312 = PBh_2 364–365: *aparaṁ dravyatva-guṇatva-karmatvâdy anuvṛtti-vyāvṛtti-hetutvāt sāmānyaṁ viśeṣaś ca **bhavati**. ... prāṇy-aprāṇi-gatānām anuvṛtti-vyāvṛtti-hetutvāt sāmānya-viśeṣa-**bhāvaḥ** siddhaḥ*. See also DNC, p. 518.1–2: *katham idaṁ tādātmyam* (of *dravyâdi* and *sattā*)? *kiṁ sato **bhāvāt** uta sat-karatvāt?*

[35] In one of its two meanings, either = or ⊂, viz. ∈ ; cf. BOCHEŃSKI (1956: 357; § 40.16).

[36] PBh_1 9.5, p. 308.1 = PBh_2 356: *ākāśa-kāla-dig-ātmanāṁ saty api dravya-**bhāve** niṣkriyatvaṁ sāmānyâdivad amūrtatvāt.*

[37] PBh_1 8, p. 187.3–7 = PBh_2 171: *buddhi-sukha-duḥkhêcchā-dveṣa-prayatnānām dvayor ātma-manasoḥ saṁyogād upalabdhiḥ. **bhāva**-dravyatva-guṇatva-karmatvâdīnām upalabhyâdhāra-samavetānām āśraya-grāhakair indriyair grahaṇam ity etad asmad-ādīnāṁ pratyakṣam*. Comp. the paraphrase in $NKan_2$, p. 454.9: *sattā-dravyatvâdīnāṁ sāmānyānām āśrayo...* See also PBh_1 12, p. 326.12 ff. = PBh_2 376–377: *sa ca dravyâdibhyaḥ padârthântaraṁ, **bhāva**val lakṣaṇa-bhedāt. yathā **bhāvasya** dravyatvâdīnāṁ svâdhāreṣu ātmânurūpa-pratyaya-kartṛtvāt svâśrayâdibhyaḥ parasparataś cârthântara-**bhāvaḥ**, tathā samavāyasyâpi pañcasu padârtheṣv ihêti-pratyaya-darśanāt tebhyaḥ padârthântaratvam iti. na ca saṁyogavan nānātvaṁ, **bhāva**val liṅgâviśeṣād viśeṣa-liṅgâbhāvāc ca. tasmād **bhāva**vat sarvatrâikaḥ samavāya iti*. [here: *bhāva* = *sattā-sāmānya*. Comp. the paraphrase in in $NKan_1$, p. 236.21.

[38] VS(C) 1.2.4: *bhāvaḥ sāmānyam eva*. Cf. VSV(C) ad loc.: *bhāvaḥ sattā sāmānyam eva, triṣv api dravyâdiṣv anuvartamānatvāt na viśeṣaḥ*.

capability of any category of the Vaiśeṣika system to enter the ontological structure of the word and to relate to other categories, viz. it is that peculiar capacity that enables any category to be a part of the atomic facts (see § 2.1., p. 252) down to which the world structure is analysable. In other words, in terms of extension, the property of existentiality of entities that can be parts of atomic facts concerns primarily such entities that are subjects of existential statements '*x* exists'/ 'there is *x*', and as such the property seems to be characterised by existential entailment, controversial as it may seem (especially having taken into consideration Kant's argument). This aspect is highlighted centuries later by Śaṅkaramiśra, who avails himself of Navya-Nyāya terminology to make it unequivocally clear that *astitva* attaches to absolutely everything that is there, can be thought of and accordingly categorised:

> 'With respect to these [six categories] existentiality means precisely the fact [that all these categories] are referred to as "*x* exists". Further, this [property of existentiality] is indeed traditionally [considered] as something different, i.e. as [a property] common to absences. Accordingly, one should understand that everything, whether having the status of a property or a property-possessor, shares a common property of being universally present.'[39]

If my understanding of the above is correct, existentiality is, consequently, such a property that typifies a reification of the ontological commitment expressed in existential statements.

Precisely such reification is questioned by the Buddhist opponent Kamalaśīla, who—while referring to T° (PBh_1 2.3, p. 16 = PBh_2 11)—argues that to postulate such a property lacks any objective basis insofar as it never occurs separately from and as something separate from all the six categories; to say that '*x* possesses existentiality' and 'there is *x*' is one and the same thing and the difference is merely linguistic, but not ontological:

> 'In such [statements as] "the six ontological categories have existentiality" and "there is a group of six [categories]", even though there is no real difference [in what they express], the genitive form is used. For you do not admit existentiality as something over and above the six categories.'[40]

[39] PBhṬS, p. 175.4–7: *tatra câstitvam astîti-viṣayatvam eva tac câbhāva-sādhāraṇam anyad yathā-śrutam eva. evaṁ ca dharmatva-dharmitvâdikam api sarvaṁ kevalânvayi sādharmyam iha pratyetavyam.*

[40] TSaP 572, p. 192.9–10: *ṣaṇṇāṁ padârthānām astitvaṁ teṣāṁ ca ṣaṇṇāṁ varga ity-ādāv asaty api vāstave bhede ṣaṣṭhy-ādi bhavaty eva. nahi bhavadbhiḥ ṣaṭ-padârtha-vyatiriktam astitvâdîṣyate.*

The property of *astitva* singles entities as a part of the ontological framework, whereas the property of *sattā* ('existence') turns them into elements of our concrete experiences. The latter thus concerns merely entities that are potentially[41] amenable to ostension, i.e. they are capable of being demonstrated e.g. by pointing, and are relata, i.e. the loci of relations. At the same time, *sattā* points to the entities' capability of being subjects of predicative sentences of the type '*x* is P' as entities that are loci of relations and thus are predicated of as being endowed with properties, i.e. as related to other entities by a relation different than a relation of inherence (*samavāya*). Accordingly, we can predicate of qualities (*guṇa*) and movements (*karman*) of substances (*dravya*), and of other properties or relations (but not qualities) of qualities and movements, whereas we cannot predicate of any properties of the remaining three categories that do not possess *sattā*, but only possess *astitva*.

The relation between *astitva* and *sattā* is, therefore, additive in the sense that all the six categories possess the former, and some (i.e. the first three) are, in addition, endowed with the latter: *sattā* adds to *astitva* in some cases, but the converse of the relation does not hold. We could also use the term 'bare existence' for *astitva* in a very particular sense to imply that an entity is merely there at least as an object of thought in its bare form, divested of all its possible properties and relations; however it would not imply that the entity a c t u a l l y and o b j e c t i v e l y exists as an observable part of atomic facts, i.e. that it is endowed with various relations and properties. What is important, *astitva* i n n o w a y implies an object's existence in mind or an intentional content of a thought (*vide supra*, p. 269). Further, we could use the term 'actual existence' for *sattā* in the sense that an entity actually and objectively is a part of an atomic fact and, therefore, is possessed of particular properties and is related to other relata, i.e. that it is actually instantiatable. Since *sattā* only attaches to entities of which we can predicate properties and relations, we could also call it 'predicative existence'.

Interestingly, what we might thus provisionally call 'bare existence' will be described by subsequent authors exclusively and emphatically in positive terms, e.g. as '[the property of] being endowed with intrinsic nature' by Śrīdharamiśra (*sva-*

---

[41] In the Nyāya-Vaiśeṣika ontology, not all concrete entities are directly perceptible to an ordinary eye, e.g. atoms are not, being of infinitesimal size beyond ordinary perception. Similarly, qualities and movements of such entities are not directly perceptible to an ordinary eye, e.g. the vibrating movement of atoms (*spandana*) is not, unless—as the Naiyāyika-Vaiśeṣika believed—one is endowed with a kind of suprasensory perception (*yogi-pratyakṣa*) or the so-called seers' perception (*ārṣa-pratyakṣa*), known also as intuition (*pratibha* or *pratibhā*), see VS(C) 9.28 (see n. 162) and PBh_1 8.12, p. 258 = PBh_2 288 (see n. 161). However, all these objects are potentially amenable to ostention, provided one is endowed with a special kind of suprasensory perception, or adequate sensory apparatus to perceive them.

rūpavattva[42]), 'the ability to be cognised in a cognitive act primarily through affirmation' by Śaṅkaramiśra (*vidhi-mukha-pratyaya-vedyatva*)[43], 'the ability to become the datum for a cognitive act primarily as affirmation' by Udayana (*vidhi-mukha-pratyaya-viṣayatva*[44]) as well as 'the existence of the thing in its intrinsic nature' and 'the ability to become the datum for a cognition primarily as affirmation' by Jagadiśa Tarkālaṅkāra in his *Praśastapāda-bhāṣya-sūkti* (*svarūpa-sattva vidhi-mukha-pratīti-viṣayatva*[45]).

Thus, the usage of the term *astitva* as well as its subsequent paraphrases highlight the affirmative aspect of all the ontological categories and accentuate the opposition to the Buddhist *apoha* theory: all categories are amenable both to cognitive and verbal acts d i r e c t l y , as they are, not via the semantic exclusion (*apoha*).

2.5. Existentiality, existence and non-existence

If, as it seems, by ascribing a property of existence (*sattā*) to an entity that belongs to one of the first three categories, one is ontologically committed, how would it harmonise with the non-existence of such objects as a hare's horn (*śaśa-viṣāṇa*) or sky flower (*kha-puṣpa*) that we can think of and speak of?

To answer this, we should first see how the ascription of a property of existentiality (*astitva*) to such non-existent entities is compatible with its ontological commit-

---

[42] NKan$_1$ p. 16: ***astitvaṁ*** *svarūpavattvaṁ ṣaṇṇām api sādharmyaṁ yasya vastuno yat svarūpaṁ tad eva tasyâstitvam.* ***abhidhyeyatvam*** *apy abhidhāna-pratipādana-yogyatvaṁ, tac ca vastunaḥ svarūpam eva bhāva-svarūpam evâvasthā-bhedena* ***jñeyatvam*** *abhidheyatvaṁ côcyate.*

[43] PBhṬS, p. 174.14–175.3: *nirūpitā ṣaṭ-padārthī vairdhamyam* (recte: *vaidharmyam*) *api nirūpitam eva lakṣaṇa-prasaṅgena samprati sādharmyaṁ nirūpyate.* ***ṣaṇṇām astitvam abhidheyatvaṁ jñeyatvam****. tatrâstitvaṁ vidhi-mukha-pratyaya-vedyatvam. nanu abhāvo 'stîty abhāve 'py etat sādharmyaṁ gatam iti cet na nañ-uparāgena vidhitva-pratikṣepāt. tamo 'stîti pratītir astîti cet na nañ-arthântar-bhāveṇâiva tamaḥ-pada-pravṛtteḥ bhâbhāvo hi tama iti.* ***abhidheyatvam*** *abhidhāna-karma-bhāvatvaṁ sat-padâbhidheyatvaṁ vârthâbhidheyatvaṁ vā.* ***jñeyatvam*** *api sattā-prakāraka-jñāna-viṣayatvaṁ jñāna-viṣaya-bhāvatvaṁ vā.*

[44] KA, p.19.3–7: ***astitvam****—vidhi-mukha-pratyaya-viṣayatvam; pratiyogy-anapekṣa-nirūpaṇatvam iti-yāvat.* ***abhidheyatvam****—abhidhāna-yogyatā. śabdena saṅgati-lakṣaṇaḥ sambandhaḥ.* ***jñeyatvam****—jñāna-yogyatā, jñāpya-jñāpaka-lakṣaṇaḥ sambandhaḥ. nanv etad eva dvayam abhāve 'py astîti cet, astu, na hi tad-apekṣayā vaidharmyam idaṁ vivakṣitam, api tu ṣaḍ-apekṣayā sādharmyam.*

[45] PBhSū, p. 114: [*Sūkti*] ***astitvaṁ*** *svarūpa-sattvaṁ tac côbhayâvṛtti-dharmavattvam. abhāvasyâlakṣyatve tu tādṛśa-bhāvatvaṁ vācyam. evam agre 'pi.* ***astitvaṁ*** *vidhi-mukha-pratīti-viṣayatvam. tac ca—pratiyogy-anapekṣa-nirūpaṇa-viṣayatvam ity ācārya-vyākhyānantu cintyam. nirūpaṇaṁ hi tatra yadi sākṣāt-kāras tadâtīndriye dravyâdāv avyāptiḥ. yadi ca jñāna-mātraṁ tarhy abhāve 'ti vyāptiḥ, anapekṣânta-vaiyarthyaṁ ca syād iti.* ***abhidheyatvaṁ*** *pada-śakyatvam.* ***jñeyatvaṁ*** *jñāna-viṣayatam.*

ment within the Nyāya-Vaiśeṣika framework, insofar as it is the property of existentiality that carries the ontological commitment, whereas the property of existence (*sattā*), that applies to a narrower set of things, merely inherits it.

It seems that the latter three categories of universals (*sāmānya*), individuators (*viśeṣa*) and inherence (*samavāya*) do not pose any significant difficulty once their existence is accepted within the ontological framework of the Nyāya-Vaiśeṣika system. This is precisely what the list of the ontological categories (*padârtha*) is all about: it offers a catalogue of all that is there. Since the three categories, by definition, have no properties, they cannot function as subjects of predicative sentences that predicate a mismatched quality of, say, movement of them. Such sentences would suffer from defective construction of faulty ascription of a incompatible property. The problem, therefore, is with the first three categories that seem to allow for such entities as a hare's horn (*śaśa-viṣāṇa*), a sky flower (*kha-puṣpa*), a trembling of the hands etc. of the son of a barren woman[46], a colourless paint, or immovable wind. They 'allow' in the sense that it is only in the context of these first three categories that we can face the problem of a combination of incompatible or contradictory constituents into one contradictory, impossible or empirically unattested whole.

We should remember that, *generally* (there might be some exceptions though), the philosophers of the Nyāya-Vaiśeṣika do not distinguish between non-existent objects, such as 'Pegasus', a hare's horn (*khara-viṣāṇa*) or a crow's teeth (*kāka-danta*), that are generally not impossible but are merely not attested in experience, i.e. are empirically not instantiated, on the one hand, and, on the other, purely fictitious objects, such as 'the present king of the Republic of India' or 'a barren woman's son' (*vandhyā-suta*), that contain contradictory properties, which makes them logically impossible. All of these are subsumed in the Nyāya-Vaiśeṣika under the same category of absolute non-existence, or absence (*atyantâbhāva*, *sāmānyâbhāva*, see VS(C) 9.5). It seems that such a two-fold distinction is conceived of only by Candramati in his DPŚ 1.11, where he additionally speaks of relational non-existence, or absence (*saṁsargâbhāva*), i.e. the absence of (at least) two (or more) particular constituents that are not related in a particular place.[47]

So, the question arises whether, for the early Naiyāyika-Vaiśeṣika, the property of existentiality (*astitva*) can also be predicated of such fictitious, non-existent objects?

---

[46] The example is taken from NBhū, p. 109: **vandhyā-putrasya pāṇy-ādi-kampa-°*.

[47] DPŚ$_1$, p. 101: 'Natural non-existence is that whereby existence, substances, ad so on do not yet come either to conjoin with or entirely to abide in one another', DPŚ$_2$ 1.11 [81], p. 181: 'Relational absence: That in which the highest universal, substances and so on are neither connected with nor inherent in some place is called relational absence (*saṁsargābhāva iti yasmin sattā-dravyādīny ekaikapradeśe 'samyuktāny asamevatāni vā sa eva saṁsargābhāva ity ucyate*).'

Or, does it attach to existent objects only? If it does, what is the status of fictitious objects? Do they possess existentiality or not? If they do not, how is it possible to claim, as Praśastapāda does, that all the six ontological categories, including fictitious entities, have the property 'existentiality'? Further, how does existentiality relate to the fact that something exists or to the fact that something does not exist? Some light is on the problem is shed by the pre-Dharmakīrtian[48] Naiyāyika Aviddhakarṇa, whose view is referred in passing to by Śāntarakṣita (inexplicitly) and Kamalaśīla (explicitly) as follows:

> 'Aviddhakarṇa, however, formulated the following reasoning to prove the permanence (eternality) of atoms: indivisible atoms do not possess anything that can be accepted as [their] producer which is [at the same time] furnished with a property [that attaches] to something existent, because it is not a datum [that can be cognised] by cognitive criteria which demonstrate existence, like a hare's horn. [To explain word for word:] A property [that attaches] to something existent [means] a property of a thing in existence, [and this property is] existentiality; something that is furnished with this [property of existentiality] means something that is endowed with it; [the above statement] is the negation of such [a property that attaches to something existent]. [All this means] that there is no cause that produces atoms.'[49]

If we accept the veracity of Kamalaśīla's testimony—and Kamalaśīla generally proves quite reliable in this regard—that this is Aviddhakarṇa's view, and he was probably not unique, we can see the Nyāya-Vaiśeṣika considered existentiality to be a property of real or potentially existent entities (*sad-dharma*). Existentiality cannot therefore attach to such entities as a hare's horn (*śaśa-viṣāṇa*), a sky flower (*kha-puṣpa*) etc.[50]

That would be an indirect reply to a query whether it is at all conceivable that a fictitious compounded entity, e.g. a hare's horn, which does not possess the highest universal of existence (*sattā*), could be endowed with existentiality (*astitva*). Theoretically it could, the way universals, individuators and inherence do: they possess *astitva* but not *sattā*. Aviddhakarṇa seems to suggest that such a fictitious com-

[48] His proof of god ('from the unique structure', *saṁsthāna-viśeṣa, saṁniveśa-viśiṣṭa*), is referred to by Dharmakīrti in PV 1.12 ac (*Pramāṇa-siddhi*).

[49] TSaP 553, p. 187.3–7: *aviddhakarṇas tv aṇūnāṁ nityatva-prasādhanāya pramāṇam āha—paramâṇūnām utpādakâbhimataṁ sad-dharmôpagataṁ na bhavati, sattva-pratipādaka-pramāṇâviṣayatvāt khara-viṣāṇavad iti. sato vidyamānasya dharmaḥ sad-dharmo 'stitvaṁ tenôpagataṁ prāptam astîty arthaḥ. tasya pratiṣedho 'yam. aṇûtpādakaṁ kāraṇaṁ nâstîty arthaḥ.*

[50] It does, however, attach to their absences, see p. 278 ff.

pounded entity possesses neither. That conclusion is further strengthened by the series of paraphrases referred to above (p. 265), such as: '[the property of] being endowed with intrinsic nature', 'the ability to be cognised in a cognitive act primarily through affirmation', 'the ability to become the datum for a cognitive act primarily as affirmation', 'the existence of the thing in its intrinsic nature' or 'the ability to become the datum for a cognition primarily as affirmation'. Clearly, such descriptions would hardly apply to fictitious entities. Since such fictitious entities simply do not exist in any way, they can be possessed neither of existentiality nor of existence. Their 'existence' even as a content of thought or as an idea is merely an illusion which is a result of erroneous ascription of real properties to a real thing: a hare exists, a horn exists, a relation of a horn to a particular animal likewise exists; however such a property–substance–relation compound does not hold in the case of a hare.[51] That explains why *astitva* is not merely 'existence in mind' (*vide supra*, n. 265).

In addition, it is well-known that the Naiyāyika-Vaiśeṣika claimed that words do refer to existent things only, i.e. to things that possess existentiality (*astitva*). That is confirmed e.g. by Praśastapāda's statement that to say that 'a speech element does not denote an object' is a contradiction in terms[52]. That is perfectly in line with what Uddyotakara says elsewhere:

> 'For we do not find any single term which is non-denoting. Even if you considered that the term "soul" has the body etc. as its contents (referent), also in that case the inconsistency would not be eliminated. Why [not]? Because then what becomes the contents of the statement "there is no soul" is the following: "there is no body etc.". [If you say]: "What you imagine to be the soul does not exist", [we reply]: we do not imagine the soul, inasmuch as what the imagination [of a certain object *x*] is is a cognition of such [an object *x* which is formed] through wrong attribution of the properties of a certain [object onto another object] due to the [imagined] similarity of a certain [object *x*] which is not of that kind to [objects *y*] which are to be of such kind. However, we do not consider that the soul is of that kind. [If] you say: "[We consider the soul to be of such kind] as you imagine the soul", then you are confronted with the following query: In what way do we imagine the soul? [Do we imagine it] as something existent or as something non-existent? If [we imagine it] as something existent, then what is the affinity between something non-existent and some-

[51] See p. 271 ff., and nn. 57, 58.

[52] PBh_1 8.12, p. 234 = PBh_2 267: *na śabdo 'rtha-pratyāyaka iti sva-vacana-virodhī*. Praśastapāda mentions it in the context of logical fallacies (*ābhāsa*).

thing existent (sc. what is the shared property), on the basis of which the soul is the contents of the imagination? And [the existence of] the soul has already been accepted by anyone who advocates the affinity (sc. the shared property) of the soul and non-soul, because there is no affinity between something non-existent and something existent.
If [you] first imagine, in the soul, some personal identity the contents (sc. referent) of which is the body[53] and then [you] contradict it, [you do] not eliminate the inconsistency, because in such a way [you] accept the existence of the contents (referent) which is the personal identity as something different from the body etc. If you think that there can by no means exist an object for a single term, for instance the void, darkness etc., that is not [correct], because it [still] does not eliminate the inconsistency. The [denoted] object for the term "the void", to begin with, is the following: such a substance for which there exists no occupant, because it is [an empty space] fit for dogs (?)[54], is called "the void". Likewise, [the denoted object that corresponds] to the term "darkness" is the data such as substances, qualities and movements in the case of which the conditions [that make them amenable] to apprehension have not been reached[55]. Substances etc. (sc. qualities and movements) [found] in all such cases wherever there is absence of light are called "darkness". Someone (i.e. the Buddhist) who says that the term "darkness" is non-denoting contradicts his own doctrine because darkness consists in the four kinds of clinging [admitted in Buddhism]. Therefore there is no single term which is non-denoting.'[56]

---

[53] I.e. 'if you, although you deny the existence of soul, claim that, while using the word "soul", we in fact use the word as referring to a body…'

[54] The phrase *śvabhyo hitatvāt* is a bit unclear to me; it certainly relates to the etymology of both *śūnya* and *śvan*, traditionally derived from the verb √*śū* / √*śvi* ('to swell, to grow, to become inflated'). It definitely relates to the uselessness of things given dogs, an idea we find e.g. in MDhŚ 8.90:

> *janma-prabhṛti yat kiṁcit puṇyaṁ bhadra tvayā kṛtam /*
> *tat te sarvaṁ śuno gacched yadi brūyās tvam anyathā //*
>
> 'Whatever merit you have done since your birth, my dear, all that will go to the dogs, if you speak untruth.'

[55] Sc. 'invisible'; for the expression *(an)upalabdhi-lakṣaṇa-prāpta* see KELLNER (1999: 195-198) and BALCEROWICZ (2005).

[56] NV_1 3.1.1, p. 340.7–341.6 = NV_2 3.1.1, p. 320.16–321–9: *na hy ekaṁ padaṁ nirathakaṁ paśyāmaḥ. athâpi śarīrâdi-viṣayam ātma-śabdaṁ pratipadyethāḥ, evam apy anivṛtto vyāghātaḥ katham iti? na asty ātmêti vākyasya tadānīm ayam artho bhavati śarīrâdayo na santîti. atha yaṁ bhavanta ātmānaṁ kalpayanti sa nâstîti na vayam ātmānaṁ kalpayāmaḥ. kalpanā hi nāmâtathā-*

Clearly, such descriptions as 'a hare's horn' or 'a sky flower'—and, similarly, names (expressing complex ideas) such as 'Pegasus' or such compounded descriptions as 'the present King of the Republic of India'—do not denote any real entity taken as a whole, and are non-denoting expressions. On the other hand, these expressions do connote, inasmuch they represent particular cognitive states or intentional objects, albeit non-existent as a whole.[57] The solution of the problem how such non-denoting expressions are meaningful utterances lies in their composite nature.[58]

In a nutshell, a lucid explanation of the problem is given by Uddyotakara in his commentary on NS 3.1.1, where he defends the existence of soul:

> 'Even if the following [argument] is brought up: "[The concept «the soul»] is like [the concept] «the hare's horn», that too is an unproved example. Why? Because the statement "a hare's horn" has [a particular] relation as its contents (sc. refers to a particular relation). [Therefore] we negate the relation [of the horn to the hare, but] we do not negate the horn [as such]. [The opponent:] "Let the example be: «the re-

---

bhūtasya tathā-bhāvibhiḥ sāmānyāt tad-dharmâdhyāropeṇa[a] *tad-pratyayaḥ*[b]. *na câtmānam evaṁbhūtaṁ pratipadyāmahe. yaṁ bhavanta ātmānaṁ kalpayantîti bruvāṇo*[c] *bhavān praṣṭavyo jāyate, kathaṁ vayam ātmānaṁ kalpayāma iti. kiṁ sattvenâthâsattvena vā? yadi sattvena kim asataḥ satā sādharmyaṁ yena kalpanā-viṣaya ātmā*[d], *ātma-sāmānyaṁ cânātmano bruvatā ātmâbhyupagato bhavatîti. na hy asataḥ satā sāmānyam astîti.*

atha śarīrâdi-viṣayam ahaṁkāram ātmani kalpayitvā viparyeti[e] *evaṁ*[f] *śarīrâdi-vyatirikta-ahaṅkāra-viṣaya-sattva-abhyupagamād anivṛtto vyāghātaḥ. atha manyase eka-padasya nâvaśyam arthena bhavitavyam iti yathā śūnyaṁ tama iti*[g] *tan na, vyāghāta-anivṛtteḥ. śūnya-śabdasya tāvad ayam artho yasya rakṣitā dravyasya na vidyate tad dravyaṁ śvabhyo hitatvāc chūnyam ity ucyate. tamaḥ-śabdasyâpy anupalabdhi*[h]*-lakṣaṇa-prāptāni dravya-guṇa-karmāṇi viṣayaḥ. yatra yatrâsannidhis tejasaḥ tatra tatra dravyâdi tamaḥ-śabdenâbhdhīyate*[i]. *tamaḥ-śabdaś cânarthaka iti bruvāṇaḥ sva-siddhāntaṁ bādhate caturṇām upādāna*[j]*-rūpatvāt tamasa iti tasmān nânarthakam ekaṁ*[k] *padam iti.*

[a] NV_1: °*-dharmâropeṇa.* [b] NV_1: °*-pratyaya-viṣayatvam.* [c] NV_1: *bruvāṇo.* [d] NV_1: *ātmanā.* [e] NV_1: *viparyasyati.* [f] NV_2: *evaṁ ca.* [g] NV_2: *iti ca.* [h] NV_2: °*-śabdasyânupalabdhi-*°. [i] NV_1: °*-śabdenôcyate.* [j] NV_1: °*-upādeya.* [k] NV_1 omits *ekaṁ*.

Some portions of the section NV 3.1.1 have been translated by CHAKRAVARTI (1982: 230–231), albeit the references to the Buddhists are not.

[57] See e.g. SHAW (1974: 336).

[58] Much has been written on how such non-denoting expressions can be meaningful utterances, and how the analysis of such compounded expressions on the Nyāya-Vaiśeṣika account—to the excitement of a number of scholars—compares to various Western logicians, mostly Bertrand Russell; see e.g. MCDERMOTT (1970), MATILAL (1970), MATILAL (2005: 92 ff., Chapt. '4. Empty Subject Terms in Logic'), SHAW (1974), SHAW (1978), SHAW (1980), CHAKRAVARTI (1982), PERSZYK (1983), PERSZYK (1984), MATILAL (1985: 78–88), CHAKRABARTI (1985). Most of these authors focus, however, on later Nyāya tradition.

lation of the hare and the horn»". That too is not correct, because sometimes there can occur a relation of a hare and a horn, [e.g. we can tie a real horn to a real hare]. [The opponent:] "[But] that stands in contradiction with what people know. If you maintain that there is a horn on a hare, [you] contradict what people [know, i.e. you commit a formal fallacy called «a faulty example»]". We do not contradict, because the activity of people [occurs] by way of the denial of the cause-effect relation (sc. what the people are concerned with is the denial of the causal relation between the hare and the horn). People, to begin with, deny that the hare has a horn either as its effect or its cause. There is no cause-effect relation between a hare and a horn the way there is cause-effect relation between a cow and a horn. And, by [merely] denying a cause-effect relation [between the two, we do] not [assert] non-existence [of either of them], because it is not the case that if *x* is neither the effect nor the cause of *y*, *x* does not exist, like in the case of Devadatta's blanket (sc. we can deny that Devadatta has a blanket, but we do not have to assert the non-existence of the blanket as such or the non-existence of Devadatta as such, even though there is no causal relation or possessorship between the two). Further, if [you] say that a hare's horn does not exist, then you [have to] answer the query: is it a generic (absolute) denial or a specific (partial) denial? If it is a generic (absolute) denial, then it is a not correct, because it is not possible. [From the statement] "the hare does not have a horn" also follows that "the hare does not have any horns of a cow etc.", and that [thesis] is not possible [to assert], because it is not the case that the [horns of a cow] do not exist [or that one cannot tie a cow's horn onto a hare's head]. If it is a specific (partial) denial, then [we] deny a particular horn of a [particular] hare, [such a horn] of which the hare is not the effect and which is not the cause of the hare. What [we] deny is precisely such a cause-effect relation [between the hare and the horn]. On the other hand, a cause-effect relation that is found in other cases is denied here [in this particular hare-horn case]. Therefore, the example [of a hare's horn] is not applicable when you [want to] prove the absolute non-existence [of something]. By the same token the non-existence of a sky flower is understood to have been explained.'[59]

---

[59] NV_1 3.1.1, p. 343.3–20 = NV_2 3.1.1, p. 322.20–323.11: *yad apîdam ucyate śaśa-viṣāṇavad ity ayam apy asiddho dṛṣṭāntaḥ. katham iti śaśa-viṣāṇa-śabdasya sambandha-viṣayatvāt. sambandha-pratiṣedho na viṣāṇa-pratiṣedhaḥ. śaśa-viṣāṇa-sambandha udāharaṇaṁ bhaviṣyatîti so 'pi na yuktaḥ,*

Accordingly, the Naiyāyika-Vaiśeṣika do not assert the reality, in any sense, of such non-existent entities as a hare's horn (*śaśa-viṣāṇa*) or a sky flower (*kha-puṣpa*), which, it seems, can neither possess the property of existentiality (*astitva*) nor the property of existence (*sattā*). In the case of a non-existent object of this kind, all the three elements exist, viz. the hare, the horn and a causal relation. However, what is non-existent is a compound of all the three.[60]

For the above reason, such compounded fictitious entities cannot apparently possess the property of existentiality (*astitva*). Likewise, the expressions that seem to refer to them do not turn out to be non-denoting terms, possessing neither *astitva* nor *sattā*, but what they actually denote are existent components of such a compound, albeit causally or factually unrelated. It follows that the Naiyāyika-Vaiśeṣika neither postulate that such expressions may refer to fictitious, non-existent objects, the way MEINONG (1904), PARSONS (1980) or ZALTA (1983) and (1988) did, nor do they claim that these expressions are meaningful, albeit they cannot be assigned any truth-value, the way STRAWSON (1950) did.

What still remains unclear is the status of such fictitious entities and how they can be thought of if they are denied existentiality and, with this, a place within an ontological framework of entities that can be thought of.

3.1. Do the properties overlap?

After we (have gained an impression that we) have understood the meaning of the property of existentiality (*astitva*) and the way it differs from the highest universal of existence (*sattā*), we should return to the issue brought up in § 2.2, namely whether ex-

---

kadācid viṣāṇena śaśasya sambandhôpapatteḥ. loka-virodha iti cet. atha manyase yadi śaśe viṣāṇam asti nanu loko viruddhyata iti. na viruddhyate kārya-kāraṇa-bhāva-pratiṣedha-dvāreṇa laukika-pravṛtteḥ. lokas tāvat kāryaṁ kāraṇaṁ vā śaśasya viṣāṇaṁ nâstîty evaṁ pratiṣedhati. yaṭhā gor viṣāṇasya ca kārya-kāraṇa-bhāvaḥ, nâivaṁ[a] *śaśasya viṣāṇasya ca kārya-kāraṇa-bhāvaḥ. na ca kārya-kāraṇa-bhāva-pratiṣedhād asattvaṁ na hi yad yasya na kāryaṁ na kāraṇaṁ tan nâsti. yathā devadattasya paṭa*[b] *iti. idaṁ ca śaśa-viṣāṇaṁ nâstîti bruvāṇaḥ praṣṭavyaḥ kim ayaṁ sāmānya-pratiṣedho 'tha viśeṣa-pratiṣedha iti. yadi sāmānya-pratiṣedhaḥ tan nâ yuktam aśakyatvāt. śaśasya viṣāṇaṁ nâstîti gav-ādi-viṣāṇāny api śaśasya na santîti prāptam etac câśakyam. na hi tāni na santi. atha viśeṣa-pratiṣedhaḥ kiṁcid viṣāṇaṁ śaśasya pratiṣiddhyate yasya śaśo na kāryaṁ yac*[c] *ca śaśasya na kāraṇam iti. so 'yaṁ kārya-kāraṇa-sambandha eva pratiṣidhyate. kārya-kāraṇa-sambandhas tv anyatra*[d] *dṛṣṭa iha pratiṣidhyata iti nâtyantâsattva-pratipādane dṛṣṭānto bhavati. etena kha-puṣpâdy-asattvaṁ vyākhyātaṁ veditavyam.*

[a] NA_1: *na câivaṁ*. [b] NA_1: *ghaṭaḥ*. [c] NA_1: *tac*. [d] NA_1: °*-sambandhaś cânyatra*.

The passage has also been translated in CHAKRAVARTI (1982: 232–233).

[60] The issue whether fictitious, non-existent objects have *sattā* or *astitva* is different from the question whether the *absences* of such fictitious objects have either of them; see p. 278 ff.

istentiality, nameability and cognisability are coextensive properties or whether they partially overlap. A useful hint as regards the relationship between the three properties as they were understood in the sixth century can be found in the *Praśastamati-ṭīkā* passage, already quoted above (see p. 261 and n. 30) and reproduced in DNC, p. 517.5–7.

I leave aside the question whether the author of the *Praśastamati-ṭīkā* is the same person as the author of the *Praśastapāda-bhāṣya*, or whether 'Praśastamati' is just another name for Praśastapāda.[61] What is beyond doubt is, however, that both the

[61] A number of scholars opted for Praśastamati being different from Praśastapāda, e.g. B. BHATTACHARYYA (1926: lxv): "Śāntarakṣita[2] refers to the opinions held by another Naiyāyika scholar who is called Praśastamati. This author seems to be different from the Vaiśeṣika. Like his compeer Aviddhakarṇa we have no information about him, his doctrines, opinions and his time. All that we can hazard to say is that he flourished before Śāntarakṣita, and the latest date that can be assigned to him is *cir.* 700 A.D.' Also Surendranath DASGUPTA (1922–1955: I: 306, n. 1) assigns Praśastapāda to '5th or 6th century A.D.' and, following B. BHATTACHARYYA (1926), Praśastamati to 'A.D. 700' (1922–1955: II: 172), implying that these two were different authors. Some other scholars claim that Praśastamati and Praśastapāda are one and the same person, e.g. Anantalal THAKUR (1961: 14–16, esp. 14/15): 'This goes to prove that this Praśastamati is identical with Praśastapāda', George CHEMPARATHY (1970), Wilhelm HALBFASS (1989: 555), (1992: 170), and Johannes BRONKHORST (1996), (2000).

The question of the identity of Praśastamati and Praśastapāda does not seem conclusively settled to me, though, for various reasons. In the most comprehensive analysis of the question so far, CHEMPARATHY (1970: 249–251, §§ 9, 10) lists a number of quotations ascribed to Prāśastamat / Praśastamati in various sources, and tries to find either their direct source or equivalents in PBh. Of the largest portion of them (§ 9, § 10, (a)–(g)), he himself opines that 'It is to be observed that none of these fragments from the TSP [= TSaP] mentioned hitherto can be traced in PDS' (1970: 250). The remaining instances (§ 10, (h)–(i)), he cites, are indeed fragments found its TSaP 'slight modifications and the order of the sentences being changed', 'or leaving out of phrases or short sentences of the original' (1970: 250). CHEMPARATHY (1970: 251) arrives at his conclusion that 'Of the ten names under which we have classified these references and quations, all, except that of Prāśastamat, are clearly identical with Praśastapāda, either because they are associated with the *Padārthadharmasaṁgraha* as author or because the fragments handed down under these names have been traceable in the *Padārthadharmasaṁgraha*.' However, CHEMPARATHY's methodology follows the (logically faulty!) scheme:

P1 If passagges acribed to authors named 1. Praśasta, 2. Praśastācāra, 3. Praśastadeva, 4. Praśastadevācārya, 5. Praśastadevapāda, 6. Praśastakara, 7. Praśastakaradeva, 8. Praśastakāra, 9. Prāśastamat, 10. Praśastamati, are found in PBh, then all of these authors are identical with Praśastapāda.

P2 Indeed some passages are traceable to PBh.

C *Ergo*, all these authors are identical with Praśastapāda.

Indeed, most (if not all the authors 1–8) seem identical with Praśastapāda, a l s o because their quotations are traceable to PBh. However, it is not the case with Praśastamati. Close similarities of Praśastamati's fragments to passages of PBh may be simply due to the fact that both Praśastapāda and Praśastamati (if we suppose they are two distinct persons) were propounders of the same modified system of Vaiśeṣika and, naturally, expressed their ideas in similar words. That

texts belong to more or less the same period and to the same philosophical system. For practical reasons and out of cautiousness, I will treat Praśastamati, an important exponent of the Vaiśeṣika system, as different from Praśastapāda. My argument will, however, be equally valid in case Praśastapāda and Praśastamati are one and the same person.

Clearly, what Praśastamati (DNC, p. 517.5–7) calls 'being the scope for verbal designation' (*abhidhāna-viṣayatva*) and 'being the scope for cognition' (*pratyaya-viṣayatva*) corresponds to Praśastapāda's nameability (*abhidheyatva*) and cognisability (*jñeyatva*); similarly, Praśastamati's *sattva* is equivalent to Praśastapāda's *astitva*.[62]

The following passage contains a proof formula (*prayoga*) that shows exact logical relations between the terms:

> Thesis (*pratijñā*): 'Substance etc. (sc. qualities and movements) are the contents of verbal designation and cognition as something existent only by their own force' (*dravyâdīnāṁ svata evâbhidhāna-pratyaya-viṣayatvaṁ*).
> Logical reason (*hetu*): 'Because they are existent' (*sattvāt*).
> Example (*dṛṣṭānta*): 'Like existence and other universals' (*sattâdivat*).
> Invariable concomitance (*vyāpti*): 'Just as there is verbal designation and cognition of the universal existence and other universals by their own force, not because of their union with the universal existence, similarly there is verbal designation and cognition also of the three categories of substance etc. by their own force, not because they are endowed with the universal existence' (*yathā sattâdeḥ sad-abhidhāna-pratyayau svata eva, na sattā-yogāt, evaṁ dravyâdīnām api sad-abhidhāna-pratyayau svata eva, na sattā-yogāt*).[63]

---

should not surprise anybody who knows how much similar ideas are expressed in very similar terms by philosophers of the same school who are not so distant in time. And both Praśastapāda and Praśastamati lived sometime between 450-550 CE. A decisive proof of the identity of the two would be based on (1) an exact quote of Praśastamati that is traceable word for word in PBh, and supported by (2) a certain opinion propounded by Praśastapāda and Praśastamati, but rejected by other followers of the Vaiśeṣika system. On the other hand, a conclusive argument to prove that these two were different authors would be Praśastamati's opinion that stands in contradiction with views held by Praśastapāda and expressed in PBh. And there are still reasons (see n. 62) that make the identity of the authors improbable. I for myself consider it not unlikely that the two are one and the same person, however as far as I can see the reasons presented heretofore to assume such identity are insufficient.

[62] Also Uddyotakara has *sattva* instead of astitva, see n. 5. The difference of vocabulary might be one of such hints that point to different identity of Praśastamati and Praśastapāda.

[63] For the complete text see n. 39.

It does not bear on the cogency of my argument that the above proof is subsequently rejected by Praśastamati, because the reasons for the rejection are of different nature (i.e. faulty relation of the invariable concomitance (*vyāpti*)) and thus irrelevant to the ontological framework in which the argument is formulated; they concern neither the structure of the proof formula as such nor the relations between the members of the formula.

Both the properties of 'being the contents of verbal designation' (*abhidhāna-viṣayatva*) and 'being the contents of cognition' (*pratyaya-viṣayatva*), which correspond to nameability (*abhidheyatva*) and cognisability (*jñeyatva*) respectively, are the pervaders (*vyāpaka*) and stand in the same relation to existentiality (Praśastamati: *sattva* = Praśastapāda: *astitva*), which is thereby implied to be the pervaded property (*vyāpya*). In other words, the extension of *abhidheyatva* and *jñeyatva* is either identical with or larger than the extension of *astitva*. Accordingly, the passage clearly and logically eliminates other options listed in § 2.2 above and stipulates that it is existentiality that is the subset or proper subset of nameability–cognisability:

T1[0] *astitva* ⊆ (*jñeyatva* = *abhidheyatva*).

It is still left to be decided whether the set covered by existentiality (*astitva*) and the set covered by both nameability (*abhidheyatva*) and cognisability (*jñeyatva*) are coextensive or whether the former is a subset of the latter.

3.2. Coextensiveness of meta-categories?

Before I return to this problem, let us first examine the question whether for the Vaiśeṣika of the sixth century (Praśastamati, Praśastapāda, Candramati) there were indeed things which possessed nameability (*abhidheyatva*) and cognisability (*jñeyatva*), but would not possess existentiality (*astitva*). The problem boils down to the question which of the alternatives of the sentence 'whatever is existent is also nameable and knowable' holds true in the Vaiśeṣika system:

Q1 *astitva* ⊂ (*jñeyatva* = *abhidheyatva*),
'*x* is existent only if it is nameable and cognisable',

or

Q2 *astitva* = (*jñeyatva* = *abhidheyatva*),
'*x* is existent if and only if it is nameable and cognisable.'

Through conversion by contraposition, the two propositions yield the following statements, both equivalent to the assertion 'whatever is neither nameable nor knowable is non-existent':

Q1* (*ajñeyatva* = *anabhidheyatva*) ⊂ *anastitva*, or
'*x* is neither nameable nor cognisable only if it is non-existent',

or

Q2* (*ajñeyatva* = *anabhidheyatva*) = *anastitva*,
'*x* is neither nameable nor cognisable if and only if it is non-existent.'

The bold claim of the Vaiśeṣika that follows propositions Q1, Q2, Q1* and Q2* would seem to be not only that anything which can, potentially, enter the conceptual framework can at the same time be known and referred to in language,[64] but also—which is a much stronger claim—that anything which exists can at the same time be known and referred to in language.

The difference between the pairs Q1/Q1* and Q2/Q2* is that the former expresses the idea that the set of things that are nameable and cognisable is larger than the set of things that are existent, whereas the latter postulates that there are no existent things which are not amenable to cognition and not amenable to verbal designation: there is a concept and a name for everything, and there exists nothing for which there would be no name and which would remain beyond all cognition.

Most importantly, the latter claim of the pair Q2/Q2* is not ontological, but should be understood merely within the conceptual framework of Vaiśeṣika categories that help us to analyse the world.

The first implication of the pair Q1/Q1* would therefore be that some entities could both be named and cognised without being existent in the Vaiśeṣika framework of categories; in other words, something could have its verbal denotation and could function as an idea, but it would not be a category of the system. And we are not talking here merely of compounded entities that happen to be at the same time

[64] This claim would not only be uncontroversial, but to a certain degree even tautological, given the Indian context in which anything that is conceptualised can be referred to by speech. The context was greatly influenced by 'the grammarian paradigm' of Indian philosophy. In contradistinction to Western philosophy, which took recourse to mathematics in search of the paradigm of philosophising and science, Indians turned to grammar, and the grammatical way of thinking, linguistic structurising of the world etc., greatly influenced Indian philosophy, including logic. A good example of the grammarian paradigm in the realm of Indian logic is the development of the grammatical relations *anvaya* and *vyatireka* and their impact on Indian philosophy, cf. CARDONA (1967).

fictitious (see pp. 271–273) but of primary entities, e.g. individuals (*avāntara-viśeṣa*, intermediate particular), that are further unanalysable.

The consequence of such a claim would be disastrous for the system: the carefully designed fabric of a complete[65] set of categories and relations to optimally and economically describe the universe, viz. the primary design of the Vaiśeṣika to name all the irreducible categories, and only such categories that are absolutely necessary to accurately represent all the phenomena of the world by eliminating any other potential, redundant category that can be reduced to or which overlaps with another category, would be in ruin.

The second implication of the pair Q1/Q1* would be that things could have a name and a concept the mind corresponding to them without actually having any kind of existence in mind, which would be a contradiction.

For the above reasons I consider the interpretation Q1/Q1*—according to which, first, the set of existent entities is a subset of entities that can be named and cognised, and, secondly, a set of entities without a name and concept for them is smaller than the set of entities that do not exist (*ergo* there are 'non-existential' entities for which we have a name and concept)—as a genuine exegesis of the Nyāya-Vaiśeṣika system highly unlikely, and would rather advocate the interpretation Q2/Q2*, viz. to treat the three properties (or meta-categories) as coextensive: *astitva* = *abhidheyatva* = *jñeyatva*.

My conjecture that the meta-categories of existentiality, nameability and cognisability are coextensive seems to gain support in Candramati's statement of DPŚ$_2$ 254 (*vide surpa*, p. 251), which pertains to the extended system of ten ontological categories:

> 'Any [kind of absence] is not the object of direct cognition. But all [kinds of absences], which exist without having any locus other [than their own], are the objects of inference.'[66]

According to Candramati, even the fivefold category of absence (*abhāva*) should ultimately possess existentiality (*astitva*) in order to become nameable and cognisable. The two properties of nameability (*abhidheyatva*) and cognisability (*jñeyatva*) are implied in the passage by the fact that absences (*abhāva*) are not directly perceived, but are inferred, i.e. are expressible as a concept (i.e. are cognisable) endowed with verbal dimension (i.e. are expressible).

---

[65] Cf. NKan$_1$ (p. 230): *ṣaṭ-padârthebhyo nânyat prameyam asti.*—'There is no cognoscible thing other than the six ontological categories.'

[66] Translated and reconstructed by MIYAMOTO (1996: 206), *sarve 'dṛṣṭa-viṣayāḥ. kiṁ tu ananyâśritya vartamānāḥ sarve 'numāna-viṣayaḥ.*

This conclusion is corroborated also by Praśastamati's statement quoted in DNC (p. 517.5–518.1) by Mallavādin (see p. 30 above), who explains that that predicative existence (see p. 265) of entities, such as substances, qualities and movements, which are known to primarily possess existentiality (*astitva*) and to be elements of the ontological structure of the world, attaches to them only secondarily by virtue of their possessing the highest universal of existence (*sattā*), which renders them predicable:

> 'Since substance etc. (sc. qualities and movements) do not have the nature of this [universal existence], [their] verbal designation etc. (i.e. cognition) as something existent is based on [the universal] existence, like [the ideas:] "the one with no stick" and "the one with a stick" are based on [the idea of] "a stick".' (*dravyâdīnām atad-ātmatvāt sattā-nimittaṁ sad-abhidhānâdi daṇḍa-nimittâdaṇḍa-daṇḍitvavad iti*.)

The passage would, therefore, lead us to accept the following conclusion of co-extensiveness of all the three meta-categories:

T2° (*jñeyatva* = *abhidheyatva*) $\subseteq$ *astitva*.

In addition, the passage shows that it is the idea of universal existence (*sattā*) that introduces a relational character by virtue of which the first three categories become invested with predicative existence, i.e. they can be referred also in other sentences than existential ones. Just the way compounded, relational concepts, such as 'a person without a stick' (*adaṇḍa*) and 'a person with a stick' (*daṇḍin*),[67] involve a relation that links them to another entity, e.g. to a stick (*daṇḍa*), in the same manner substances, qualities and movements, which are possessed of existentiality (*astitva*), become predicable, i.e. 'acquire'[68] their nameability (*abhidheyatva*), when they are linked to universal existence (*sattā*).

Also Śaṅkaramiśra, who explicitly claims that existentiality attaches to absence (*abhāva*)[69] as well, lends some support to my interpretation. He relates the pair of nameability and cognisability to existentiality in a similar manner, taking the pair as logically subordinate to, i.e. subsets of, existentiality:

---

[67] Of course, such objects as 'a person' and 'a stick' (*daṇḍa*) exist independently of other entities and, as such, are not relational concepts, at least on this level of description.

[68] Clearly, this is purely conceptual and, generally speaking, atemporal, i.e. it is not the case that some entities first exist without their existence (*sattā*), and at a certain point of time they acquire it through some process that extends in time. On this problematic relation of entities with the universal existence (*sattā-sambandha*) in the context of the Vaiśeṣika theory of causality see: HALBFASS (1989).

[69] See n. 39.

> 'Nameability is the capacity to become an object of verbal designation, which is either the capacity to be named with a word that refers to something existent or the capacity to be named as a concrete thing. Also cognisability is the ability to be an object of cognition that reproduces [the object's] existence or the ability to become the contents of cognition.'[70]

In both cases, i.e. Praśastamati's and Śaṅkaramiśra's, the manner of exposition is very alike: for nameability (*abhidheyatva*) we have 'verbal designation etc. as something existent' (*sad-abhidhānâdi*) and 'the capacity to be named with a word that refers to something existent' (*sat-padâbhidheyatva*), respectively; and cognisability (*jñeyatva*) corresponds to '[cognition] as something existent' (*sad-jñāna*)[71] and 'the ability to be an object of cognition that reproduces [the object's] existence' (*sattā-prakāraka-jñāna-viṣayatva*), respectively.

We can easily see that one and the same author Praśastamati, on one occasion (see p. 39 and 274), expresses the ideas that entail thesis T1°:

T1° *astitva* $\subseteq$ (*jñeyatva* = *abhidheyatva*),

and, on another occasion (see pp. 30 and 279), he implies thesis T2°, which is supported also by Śaṅkaramiśra's reading:

T2° (*jñeyatva* = *abhidheyatva*) $\subseteq$ *astitva*.

The conjunction of T1° and T2° yields the only conclusion possible:

T3° *astitva* = *abhidheyatva* = *jñeyatva*.

The controversial character of the equation *astitva* = *abhidheyatva* = *jñeyatva*—which is a statement of the Nyāya-Vaiśeṣika thesis of the knowability of everything—could be considered to be delusive. First, the equation implies that any thought or idea can be formulated with words and that its elements are existent as entering into relations with other elements of the idea.

Interestingly, the equation *astitva* = *jñeyatva* corresponds to what is nowadays called 'knowability principle' PK, which claims that all truths are knowable:[72]

---

[70] PBhṬS, p. 175.1–3: ***abhidheyatvam*** *abhidhāna-karma-bhāvatvaṁ sat-padâbhidheyatvaṁ vârthâbhidheyatvaṁ vā.* ***jñeyatvam*** *api sattā-prakāraka-jñāna-viṣayatvaṁ jñāna-viṣaya-bhāvatvaṁ vā.*

[71] This is, of course, implied by the °*ādi* in *sad-abhidhānâdi*.

[72] Although it is the case that truths are not things, but to say 'all truths are knowable' is equivalent to the claim that we can know all of everything, which is the gist of the equation *astitva* = *jñeyatva*. If everything can be known, it means that it is possible to the contents of all true statements about everything and to know that they are true.

KP $\forall p\,(p \rightarrow \Diamond Kp)$,

where the symbol '◊' is the modal operator: 'it is possible that …'. The principle, frequently taken for granted also in Western science, states that for everything that exists it is possible that one can, in principle, know it. In other words, there are no logical limits to our cognition, except for factual limits: we just happen not to know some (perhaps: most?) truths, but there is intrinsically logically nothing that could prevent one from knowing these truths at some time.

Secondly, it is an obvious condition for meaningfulness of philosophical reflection: we can know and sensibly predicate of things that exist, and there is nothing in the world which could not, even potentially, become the contents of our judgements. It does not, however, have to imply that our knowledge has no limits in the sense that we will eventually know everything. Conversely, absolutely non-existent things cannot become the contents of our thoughts and utterances;[73] even dreams and illusions are made up of real things. That would be an unequivocal statement of realism of the Vaiśeṣika system.

The most troubling problem, however, is how to account for such an equation (*astitva* = *jñeyatva* = *abhidheyatva*), also within the conceptual framework of Nyāya-Vaiśeṣika, and whether there could be anyone who might practically attest that indeed all that exists can be known and expressed, or whether it is a matter of (rather optimistic) belief[74]. What the equation actually called for in Indian context presently discussed was a being who would epitomise all the cognitive faculties needed to validate the Nyāya-Vaiśeṣika claim.

3.3. The Nyāya-Vaiśeṣika knowability thesis and Fitch's Paradox of Knowability

This brings us to a strictly logical-epistemic problem which eventually, since the publication of a seminal and much debated paper by Frederic Brenton FITCH (1963)[75],

[73] When absolutely non-existent, fictitious things are claimed to become the contents of our cognition all that means is either that the contents are compounded wholes that consists of reals components related in a *fictitious* way or that names we use are empty terms the contents of which is analysable to a set of real elements.

[74] For one thing is to know that something is logically not impossible and another thing is to know that something is *actually* the case.

[75] FITCH's paper seemed to be neglected for some time and received wider recognition much later, after the Paradox of Knowability was revived in HART (1979: esp. 164–165, n. 3.). A handy account of the paradox is given by BROGAARD–SALERNO (2004).

came to be known as Fitch's Paradox of Knowability. In it, FITCH (1963: 139) formulates THEOREM 5, relevant for our discussion, which states that

> 'If there is some true proposition which nobody knows (or has known or will know) to be true, then there is a true proposition which nobody can know to be true.'

He bases his THEOREM 5, first, on an general notion of a truth class α of propositions for which every member of it is true, symbolically expressed as $(p)\ [(\alpha p) \rightarrow p]$ (where '$\rightarrow$' stands for strict implication), which later serves him as a model to substitute a range of operators that map what he calls value concepts ('striving for', 'doing', 'believing', 'knowing', 'desiring', 'ability to do', 'obligation to do', 'value for'). One of such operators, 'knowing', corresponds to what is now generally known as the epistemic operator K: 'somebody at some time knows that ...', or 'it is known by someone at some time that ... '. Thus, with the epistemic operator K instantiating α (other such instantiations are 'truth', 'causal necessity', 'logical necessity', 'doing', 'proving' etc.), one arrives at the assumption: $\forall p\ (\mathrm{K}p \rightarrow p)$ ('for all propositions p, if one knows that p, then it is the case that p'). Second, the theorem rests on his THEOREM 1:

> 'If α is a truth class which is closed with respect to conjunction elimination, then the proposition, $[p\ \&\ {\sim}\alpha p]$, which asserts that p is true but not a member of α (where p is any proposition), is itself necessarily not a member of α.'[76]

Again, using the epistemic operator K, one can reformulate the theorem to say if there is truth p which is unknown, $(p\ \&\ {\sim}\mathrm{K}p)$, then it is itself unknowable that it is an unknown truth.

The condition for both the theorems, and further proofs which FITCH lays down, is the idea of closure with respect to conjunction elimination: 'a class of propositions ... will be said to be closed *with respect to conjunction elimination* if (necessarily) whenever the conjunction of two propositions is in the class so are the two propositions themselves'[77], i.e. $(p)\ (q)\ [(\alpha(p\ \&\ q) \rightarrow (\alpha p)\ \&\ (\alpha q)]$. Again, what it means in our context of the epistemic operator K is that, for instance, if one knows both that Vincent d'Indy was French (p) and that Sigismondo d'India was Italian (q), then one also knows that Vincent d'Indy was French (p) *and* one knows that that Sigismondo d'India was Italian (q): $\mathrm{K}(p\ \&\ q) \rightarrow (\mathrm{K}p\ \&\ \mathrm{K}q)$.

[76] FITCH (1963: 138).

[77] FITCH (1963: 136).

Accordingly, what THEOREM 5 eventually states is that from the assertion that there are truths that merely happen to be unknown, $\exists p\ (p\ \&\ {\sim}\mathrm{K}p)$, it follows that ultimately there are necessarily unknowable truths, $\exists p\ (p\ \&\ {\sim}\Diamond\mathrm{K}p)$, which is a paradox. Further, the conclusion that there are truths that c a n n o t be known is in conflict with the knowability principle PK: $\forall p\ (p \rightarrow \Diamond\mathrm{K}p)$, according to which any truth can, in principle, be known.

As I have pointed out above (p. 281), the knowability principle corresponds to the (Praśastapāda and post-Praśastapāda) Nyāya-Vaiśeṣika equation: existentiality = nameability = cognisability. Consequently, FITCH's conclusions seem to threaten precisely this equation.

It was Nicholas RESCHER (1984: 150 ff.) who took up FITCH's conclusions and devised a proof[78] that has stimulated a prolonged debate, to the effect that there are logical limits for science and any cognitive enquiry, provokingly adding that 'perfected science is a mirage; completed knowledge a chimera'. And RESCHER's elaborated proof that not every truth can be known seems directly relevant to the (in)validity of the Nyāya-Vaiśeṣika equation, inasmuch as it seems to invalidate the latter. A rather similar line of reasoning based on FITCH's proof is applied by Roy W. PERRETT (1999) to the Nyāya-Vaiśeṣika equation.

Following RESCHER, let us consider four elementary theses of epistemic logic which all seem perfectly acceptable:

K1° 'Authentic knowledge is inherently veridical: $\mathrm{K}p \rightarrow p$.'
In other words, it is not possible to know anything that is false. K1° would also be a thesis accepted by the Naiyāyika-Vaiśeṣika realists who claimed that all that enters our minds and all we know is a result of something that is factual: if we know a proposition, then it is true.

K2° 'A conjunction can only be known if both its conjuncts are known: $\mathrm{K}(p\ \&\ q) \rightarrow (\mathrm{K}p\ \&\ \mathrm{K}q)$.'
If we know a conjunction of two propositions to be true, then we also know both the conjuncts. This corresponds to FITCH's (1963: 136) closure with respect to conjunction elimination (*vide supra*, p. 282).

[78] The proof is also reproduced and discussed for instance in SCHLESINGER (1986), which is later incorporated *in extenso* in SCHLESINGER (1988: 36 ff.), as well as in ZEMACH (1987), who attempts to demonstrate that RESCHER's, and thus also FITCH's, proof is valid only when taken in *de re* reading, not in *de dicto* (*vide supra*, p. 286 f.). A different approach, taking into account intuitionistic approach, to defend the Paradox of Knowability to the effect that not all truths can be known is found in FLORIO–MURZI (2008). See also Rafał PALCZEWSKI (2007: 460 ff.).

K3° 'Some truth is not known: $\exists p\ (p \ \&\ {\sim}\mathrm{K}p)$.'[79]
It is a premise of FITCH's THEOREM 5. Since there are a vast number of propositions which we do not know, it is a thesis that nobody would seriously question, lest we boldly declare we know everything. It is also Nyāya-Vaiśeṣika thesis that some truths are not known to humans. In fact, it is the condition for transmigration (*saṁsāra*) to persist that transmigrating beings do not know all the truth[80]. K3° follows from the fundamental tenet of both systems that the cognition of the true nature of all the categories, either epistemic, in case of Nyāya[81], or ontological, in case of Vaiśeṣika[82], leads to liberation. As long as

---

[79] As regards PERRETT's (1999: 405 ff.) analysis (*vide infra*, n. 84), in itself an inspiring and valuable endeavour, of the Nyāya-Vaiśeṣika equation and his attempt to demonstrate that 'the human knowability thesis is demonstrably false', he asks us to 'consider first the following pair of theses:

Human Knowability: All truths are knowable by humans.

Human Knownness: All truths are known by humans.

Indeed, as he rightly points out, 'Nyāya *affirms* human knowability and *denies* human knownness.' Further, he asks us to 'symbolize these two Nyāya theses thus:

T_1: $p \to \Diamond \mathrm{K}p$.

T_2: ${\sim}(p \to \mathrm{K}p)$.'

PERRETT's T_1 is, of course, an instantiation of our knowability principle PK: $\forall p\ (p \to \Diamond \mathrm{K}p)$, arrived at by universal instantiation.

We may have doubts whether PERRETT's T_2 is an accurate description of the Naiyāyika-Vaiśeṣika's denial of the *Human Knownness* thesis. What the *Human Knownness* thesis states actually is:

T_{HK}: $\forall p\ (p \to \mathrm{K}p)$.

Therefore, its denial by the Nyāya-Vaiśeṣika school should merely state:

D_{HK}: ${\sim}\forall p\ (p \to \mathrm{K}p)$,

which is equivalent to

$\exists p\ {\sim}(p \to \mathrm{K}p)$,

and to

$\exists p\ (p \ \&\ {\sim}\mathrm{K}p)$,

which is our K3°. From K3° one can easily obtain, by existential instantiation, PERRETT's T_2, which is a much stronger claim, however, not vice versa. I am not quite sure whether the application of the inference rule of existential elimination is at all legitimate here. On some problems concerning the existential instantiation in this proof—i.e. from $\exists p\ (p \ \&\ {\sim}\mathrm{K}p)$ deriving $(p \ \&\ {\sim}\mathrm{K}p)$ —see ZEMACH (1987: 529). Having this in view, one would have to redraft the whole argumement, albeit the flaw does not render PERRETT's demonstration pointless.

[80] *Vide infra*, p. 290.

[81] NS 1.1.1: *pramāṇa-prameya-saṁśaya-prayojana-dṛṣṭānta-siddhāntâvayava-tarka-nirṇaya-vāda-jalpa-vitaṇḍā-hetv-ābhāsa-cchala-jāti-nigraha-sthānānāṁ tattva-jñānān niḥśreyasâdhigamaḥ.*

[82] PBh_1 2.1, p. 6 = PBh_2 2, p. 1.6–7: *dravya-guṇa-karma-sāmānya-viśeṣa-samavāyānāṁ ṣaṇṇāṁ padârthānāṁ sādharmya-vaidharmya-tattva-jnānaṁ niḥśreyasa-hetuḥ.* See p. 295, n. 111.

we do not know the categories, which is tantamount to saying that there are some truths unknown to us, we transmigrate and endure existential pangs.

K4° 'All truths are knowable: $p \rightarrow \Diamond \mathrm{K}p$.'
This is precisely an instantiation of the knowability principle PK (pp. 281, 283), and is also admitted by Naiyāyika-Vaiśeṣika in the equation *astitva* = *jñeyatva*.

RESCHER's demonstration that the above four rules are inconsistent runs in nine steps as follows:

1.	$\mathrm{K}{\sim}\mathrm{K}p \rightarrow {\sim}\mathrm{K}p$	substitution in K1° [K*p*/*p*].
2.	${\sim}(\mathrm{K}{\sim}\mathrm{K}p \;\&\; \mathrm{K}p)$	from 1 by the definition of '→' $[(P \rightarrow Q) \equiv {\sim}(P \rightarrow {\sim}Q)]$.[83]
3.	$\mathrm{K}({\sim}\mathrm{K}p \;\&\; p) \rightarrow (\mathrm{K}{\sim}\mathrm{K}p \;\&\; \mathrm{K}p)$	substitution in K1° [K*p*/*q*].
4.	${\sim}\mathrm{K}({\sim}\mathrm{K}p \;\&\; p)$	from 2, 3 by *modus tollens*.
5.	$\Box{\sim}\mathrm{K}({\sim}\mathrm{K}p \;\&\; p)$	from 4 by the rule of necessitation RN (anything derivable from necessary truths is a necessary truth).
6.	${\sim}\Diamond\mathrm{K}({\sim}\mathrm{K}p \;\&\; p)$	from 5 by the equivalence: $\Box\phi \leftrightarrow {\sim}\Diamond{\sim}\phi$.
7.	${\sim}({\sim}\mathrm{K}p \;\&\; p)$	from 6, K4° by *modus tollens*.
8.	$\forall p\, {\sim}({\sim}\mathrm{K}p \;\&\; p)$	from 7 by generalisation.
9.	${\sim}\exists p\, ({\sim}\mathrm{K}p \;\&\; p)$	from 8.

Since step 9 contradicts K3°, therefore the set of theses K1°–K4° is incongruous, because they lead to a contradiction. Theses K1°–K3° appear to be legitimate, and therefore it is thesis K4° that should be rejected. 'We must concede that some truths are unknowable', concludes RESCHER (1984: 150).[84]

---

[83] Cf. an inspiring discussion in BENETT (2003: esp. 20 ff.).

[84] PERRETT's (1999: 405–407) demonstration applied to Nyāya-Vaiśeṣika is based on a rather similar, with some reservations (see n. 79) though, set of assumptions K1°–K4°, and he likewise dismisses thesis K4° (in his notation T_1), that corresponds to knowability principle PK.

His argument in full starts with the following theses and assumptions as follows (PERRETT (1999: 406)):

T_1:	$p \rightarrow \Diamond\mathrm{K}p$	Nyāya's *Human Knowability* thesis ('All truths are knowable by humans').
T_2:	${\sim}(p \rightarrow \mathrm{K}p)$	Nyāya's denial of *Human Knownness* thesis ('It is not the case that all truths are known by humans').
A_1:	$\mathrm{K}p \rightarrow p$	Assumption one ('what is known is true').
A_2:	$\mathrm{K}(p \;\&\; q) \rightarrow \mathrm{K}p \;\&\; \mathrm{K}q$	Assumption two ('knowledge distributes over conjunction').

Should we, therefore, completely dimiss the Nyāya-Vaiśeṣika equation: *astitva* = *jñeyatva* = *abhidheyatva* as illogical and invalid? There are two issues involved here. Firstly, it is whether FITCH's / RESCHER's argument indeed is correct or, granted that it is, under what conditions it is correct. Secondly, supposing that the logical structure of the Paradox of Knowability is in principle right, how far does it invalidate Nyāya-Vaiśeṣika claims?

There is here no room even for a brief discussion of (in)validity, lest for a mere review of numerous supporters and critics, of FITCH's/RESCHER's argument.[85] What is, however, vital to note is that Paradox of Knowability[86] does not merely boil down to SCHLESINGER's (1986: 26) observation that 'The final conclusion "(∃p) p&~PKp" states nothing more noteworthy than that there is some true proposition which at the present time is in principle unknowable'. It is not simply about some empirical observation that our knowledge, or science for that matter, faces some practical or technical limits at a given point of time, but it declares that it is *principally and logically impossible* to know some true proposition. This point seems to have been far too often misunderstood.

A possible way to defend against the paradox would be, for instance, the one taken by Eddy M. ZEMACH (1987) who proposes to distinguish two readings of the

---

Next, 'the *reductio* proof of the inconsistency of the premise set (T_1, T_2, A_1, A_2) goes through as follows:

(1)	$p \rightarrow \sim Kp$	From T_2
(2)	$\Diamond K(p \mathbin{\&} \sim Kp)$	From (1) & T_1
(3)	$\Diamond(Kp \mathbin{\&} K{\sim}Kp)$	From (2) & A_2
(4)	$\Diamond(Kp \mathbin{\&} \sim Kp)$	From (3) & A_1

Since (4) is a contradiction, we know that at least one of our original assumptions is false. ... Hence the conclusion to be drawn is that T_1 is false.'

Steps (1)–(4) in PERRETT's arguments are *identical* to MACKIE (1980: 90), reproduced in EDGINGTON (1985: 558), to an extent which does not seem coincidental. See also PALCZEWSKI (2007: 460), in which the premisses are extended.

[85] Just to mention a few critics, on different grounds: George N. SCHLESINGER (1988: 39 ff.), E.M. ZEMACH (1987), Michael DUMMETT (2007: 348–350), cf. for a brief review: BROGAARD–SALERNO (2004), and most recently Rafał PALCZEWSKI (2007), who makes use of additional operators and applies the idea of group knowledge and group knowability; this, althouth the author does not states it explicitly and may even not be aware of, presupposes Karl R. POPPER's (1970), (1972) notion of 'the third world', the world of the products of the human mind as a group knowledge.

[86] Which is basically an off-shot of Gödel's first incompleteness theorem, just as its opposite, verificationism (i.e. a view that all meaningful/true statements are verifiable) is related to what Gödel's first incompleteness theorem invalidates (i.e. a view that we can construct a consistent and complete theory).

epistemic operator K, *de dicto* and *de re*.[87] To illustrate the distinction, let us take one of the opacity verbs that cause some interpretation problem in the following sentence:

S1° Jago believes that someone is faithful.

This ambiguous sentence could be interpreted either (syntactically) *de dicto* ('of word'):

S2° Jago believes that there are faithful women. $B_{Jago}\ \exists x\ (Fx)$,

or (syntactically) *de re* ('of thing'):

S3° Jago believes of a particular woman that she is faithful. $\exists x\ (B_{Jago}\ Fx)$.

Now, let us suppose that Barbie once learnt Thales' theorem in a TV talk show, but has forgotten its contents the very next morning and all she knows now is that Thales' theorem is true. Is the statement asserting of Barbie that she knows Thales' theorem true or not? In other words, is $K_{Barbie}\, p$ (where p stands for 'Thales' theorem') true, and if it is, is it true unconditionally? If we read it *de re* ('Of a proposition called «Thales' theorem», Barbie knows that it is true') $K_{Barbie}\, p$ is true. However, if we read it *de dicto* ('Barbie knows that if A, B and C are points on a circle where the line AC is a diameter of the circle, then the angle ABC is a right angle'), $K_{Barbie}\, p$ turns out to be false. We can see that Kp may yield two different results when read it either *de re* or *de dicto*.

Let us now see whether the statement 'Barbie knows that she does not know Thales' theorem' is true or not? This is the case of the proposition K~Kp, which occurs in RESCHER's argument. Under what conditions is K~Kp true of Barbie and Thales' theorem? Indeed, we can justifiably claim that 'Barbie knows that she does not know Thales' theorem', but that can make sense only when read *de re*: 'Barbie knows that she does not know what «Thales' theorem» is all about'. It would not be very understandable when read *de dicto*: 'Barbie knows that she does not know that if A, B and C are points on a circle where the line AC is a diameter of the circle, then the angle ABC is a right angle'. This shows that K~Kp in RESCHER's argument may not be as unproblematic as it seems at first. Even taken intuitively, to claim that 'I know that I do not know that I am listening to music', in which p is 'I am listening to music', may seem puzzling. As ZEMACH (1987: 530) and EDGINGTON (1985: 560 ff.) point out, 'although "~Kp" may be read *de dicto*, if it is embedded in an-

[87] For the distinction see Willard Van Orman QUINE (1956), Alvin PLANTINGA (1969), that also contains some brief historical sketch of the distinction, Ernest SOSA (1970) and Roderick CHISHOLM (1976). Thomas MCKAY (2005) highlights some additional points by distinguishing three different conceptions of the *de re* / *de dicto* distinction: syntactically, semantically and metaphysically.

other *de dicto* epistemic operator relative to the same person, it must be read *de re*. "$K_S{\sim}K_J$p" (i.e., "Smith knows that Jones does not know that the car is stolen") is true iff Smith knows the contents of *p*, and that Jones does not know it. ... But for "$K_J{\sim}K_J p$" to be true, it is not required that Jones knows the content of *p* (that the car is stolen) and that he does not know it.'[88] Taking the *de re* / *de dicto* distinction into account, we will see that RESCHER's argument stalls at a certain point.[89]

The same strategy that distinguishes between *de re* and *de dicto* readings may cast doubt on assumption K2°: $K(p \,\&\, q) \rightarrow (Kp \,\&\, Kq)$, instead on K4°.[90] Suppose Barbie heard from a reliable source, say, her boyfriend Ken the arithmetician, that Gödel's theorems are true. Hence Barbie knows that both Gödel's incompleteness theorems are true[91]: $K_{\text{Barbie}}\,(p \,\&\, q)$. Does it follow from $K_{\text{Barbie}}\,(p \,\&\, q)$ that Barbie knows both that (*p*), i.e. that it is not possible to construct an effectively strong arithmetic theory which is both consistent and complete, because one can construct an arithmetical statement that is true, but not provable in the theory, and that (*q*), i.e. that the consistency of an arithmetic theory cannot be proved in the arithmetic itself, because the theory could contain a statement of its own consistency only if the theory were inconsistent? In other words, does it follow from $K_{\text{Barbie}}\,(p \,\&\, q)$ that $K_{\text{Barbie}}\,p \,\&\, K_{\text{Barbie}}\,q$? Suppose Barbie has, surprising as it may be, never heard anything more detailed about Kurt Gödel and has never studied arithmetic and logic. Read *de dicto*, the statement $K_{\text{Barbie}}\,(p \,\&\, q) \rightarrow (K_{\text{Barbie}}\,p \,\&\, K_{\text{Barbie}}\,q)$ is true, because Barbie does not have to know the contents of both *p* and *q* to have a justified true belief (thanks to Ken the arithmetician) that *p* and *q* are true. However, when read *de re*, the assumption $K_{\text{Barbie}}\,(p \,\&\, q) \rightarrow (K_{\text{Barbie}}\,p \,\&\, K_{\text{Barbie}}\,q)$ is plainly false, because Barbie neither knows what a theorem is nor what consistency and completeness of an arithmetic theory are, etc. She probably would not even be able to genuinely grasp the difference between Gödel's completeness theorem and his two incompleteness theorems at all.

Under the *de dicto* reading, assumption K2° would also bring us to an undesired conclusion that if we know something of *p* and if a piece of information *r* is logically entailed by *p* ($p \rightarrow r$) or is a part of *p* ($r \subset p$), we would automatically know *r*.

---

[88] In ZEMACH's convention, roman 'p' is a schematic letter substituting for propositions, whereas italicised *p* is taken as a name of a proposition, not a proposition itself; in my notation, it is *p* and '*p*' respectively.

[89] For details see ZEMACH (1987: 530–531).

[90] Cf. ZEMACH (1987: 531–532).

[91] That her knowledge is indeed a case of justified true belief can be seen on various counts, e.g. it fulfils Fred DRETSKE's (1971) conclusive reasons or the conditions of Robert NOZICK's (1981: 172–178) truth-tracking account (1. *p* is true; 2. S believes that *p*; 3. if *p* weren't true, S wouldn't believe that *p*; 4. if *p* were true, S would believe that *p*) etc.

Suppose Barbie knows that Thales' theorem is true, astonishing as it sounds, she even knows that if A, B and C are points on a circle where the line AC is a diameter of the circle, then the angle ABC is a right angle. However, does she also automatically know that the sum of the angles in a triangle is equal to two right angles (180°) and that the base angles of an isosceles triangle are equal, which is knowledge entailed by Thales' theorem? This does not automatically follow and she does not have to have such knowledge. Applied consistently on reading it *de dicto*, assumption K2° would lead us to an undesired consequence that one would know everything conceivable, whether already known to somebody at one point in history or so far never discovered by anybody, of *p*. That would approximate something like '*p*-bound omniscience'.[92]

Therefore it seems far from proven that one would have to, on purely logical grounds, e.g. by applying Fitch's Paradox of Knowability, reject Nyāya-Vaiśeṣika claim that all truths are, in principle, knowable and expressible.

Now, there is another problem, reflected in Roy W. PERRETT's (1999: 405 ff.) analysis of the Nyāya-Vaiśeṣika equation. He takes it for granted that what the equation refers to is what he calls 'Human Knowability' thesis, viz. that all truths are k n o w a b l e b y h u m a n s .

Throughout his paper Roy W. PERRETT, assumes that what the Nyāya-Vaiśeṣika equation, as an expression of the knowability of everything, comprises is not only god's but also human knowability: 'I suggest instead that this omission is because the scope of the knowability thesis is not supposed to be restricted just to knowability by God, but is supposed also to include knowability by humans' (1999: 402). Precisely such a postulate of unrestricted human knowability, viz. the knowability of everything p o t e n t i a l l y by every human being, can be problematic within the system of Nyāya-Vaiśeṣika. My point is that what the Nyāya-Vaiśeṣika knowability thesis actually expresses is knowability o n l y by god and, perhaps, by a select group of (super-)humans, in other words: the Nyāya-Vaiśeṣika knowability

---

[92] Cf. NOZICK's (1981: 204 ff., 227 ff.) discussion of non-closure and criticism of the subjunctive principle $K(p \rightarrow q)$ & $Kp \rightarrow Kq$ ('if S knows that *p* and he knows that *p* entails *q*, then he also knows that *q*') and his rejection of the claim that if a person S knows a conjunction, then he also knows the conjuncts, which is our K2°. PERRETT (1999: 407 ff.) considers an intutionist line of defence, following Timothy WILLIAMSON (1982), for the Nyāya-Vaiśeṣika thesis of the knowability of everything. This seems to be completely unecessary at least for the most of Nyāya-Vaiśeṣika till, perhaps, the 16th century and Raghunātha Śiromaṇi, for the system of Nyāya-Vaiśeṣika throughout its classical and mediaeval history admitted the elimination of double negation: $\sim\sim p = p$, viz. that that the negation of the negation of *p* is identical with *p*, the denial of which is both one of the fundaments of intuitionistic logic and necessary to evaluate and defend the Nyāya-Vaiśeṣika equation from the standpoint of intuitionistic logic.

thesis directly entails the acceptance of omniscience of god and, perhaps in addition, of certain humans, i.e. most spiritually advanced adepts of Nyāya-Vaiśeṣika or *yogin*s whose knowledge, for all practical reasons, equals omniscience (*vide infra*, §§ 4.3 and 4.4). Most importantly, Nyāya-Vaiśeṣika knowability thesis does not concern o r d i n a r y humans at all and, therefore, it loses some of its attractive flavour to a philosopher.

As I have already pointed out (p. 284), the theoretical edifices of both the systems rest on the assumption that their systems provide us with a scheme of all sufficient categories that comprehensively cover all that exists and with a method to cognise all of them.[93] The pragmatic and ethical relevance of such bold claims lay in the fact that the comprehensive scheme mapping all that exists onto a system of categories and relations was both a sufficient and necessary tool to bring transmigration to its end. As long as we do not achieve, apparently complete, knowledge of the categories and what they entail, we are going to endure hardships of *saṁsāra*. This is the salvific aspect of cognition within Nyāya-Vaiśeṣika.[94] Religious life in conformity with moral law (*dharma*) may secure mundane prosperity and better next birth (*abhyudaya*), but it is the cognition of the true nature of the categories that results in liberation.[95]

There is no doubt that, on logical analysis, the set of premisses K1°–K4° are inconsistent. Usually it is either premiss K2° (p. 288 f.) or the knowability principle K4° (p. 285), or the validity of K~K*p* (steps 1–3, p. 285 f., viz. the validity of the substitution of either '~K*p*'[96] or '*p* & ~K*p*'[97] for '*p*'), when read *de dicto*, that are

---

[93] A view expressed in the introductory *sūtra*s of Nyāya (n. 81) and Vaiśeṣika (n. 82).

[94] See NS 1.1.1: *pramāṇa-prameya-saṁśaya-prayojana-dṛṣṭânta-siddhântâvayava-tarka-nirṇaya-vāda-jalpa-vitaṇḍâhetv-ābhāsa-cchala-jāti-nigraha-sthānānāṁ tattva-jñānān niḥśreyasâdhigamaḥ*, and NBh 1.1.1: *ātmādeḥ khalu prameyasya tattva-jñānān niḥśreyasâdhigamaḥ*.—'The attainment of well-being is [possible] by means of the cognition of the true nature of [such categories as] cognitive criterion, the cognoscible …'

[95] Cf. VS(C) 1.1.2, see p. 292 f., n. 104. The tradition of Nyāya lays more stress on the cognition of one of the cognoscibles (*prameya*), i.e. the soul (*ātman*), see NS/NBh 4.2.1 ff. However, even that being the case, Vātsyāyana Pakṣilasvāmin's introduction to NS 4.2.1 reveals that it is not only the cognition of the soul and the imperfections responsible for erroneous attribution of the idea of self (*ahaṁkāra*, NS 4.2.1) that is important but also the cognition of other categories. Even the lengthy discussion on the whole and on the atoms which starts with NS 4.2.3 shows how important is the cognition of the environment in which the idea of the soul can be assessed. Further, Vātsyāyana Pakṣilasvāmin emphasises the role of cognition as the means to liberation: 'The cognition of the true nature of [the cognoscibles as the second category] is the means to achieve this [liberation]' (NBh 4.2.0, p. 259.1: *tasyâdhigamôpāyas tattva-jñānam*).

[96] Questioned in ZEMACH (1987: 530 ff.)

[97] Questioned in EDGINGTON (1985: 560 ff.).

blamed for the inconsistency. However, the validity of the thesis of the limits of human knownness— $\exists p\ (p\ \&\ {\sim}\mathrm{K}p)$, equivalent to $\exists p\ {\sim}(p \rightarrow \mathrm{K}p)$ —i.e. that there are some truths that happen not to be known, has never been questioned in the analyses of the Paradox of Knowability, also applied to the Nyāya-Vaiśeṣika equation.

Whether various strategies taken to defend against Fitch's Paradox of Knowability (see n. 85) prove indeed successful or not[98] is rather irrelevant to the Nyāya-Vaiśeṣika thesis of the knowability of everything, because—in view of omniscience asserted of god and of certain elevated individuals—the premiss rejected by Nyāya-Vaiśeṣika is K3°.[99] In other words, since Nyāya-Vaiśeṣika admit the existence of at least one being, i.e. god, that knows everything, it rejects the thesis that 'Some truth is not known'. The Nyāya-Vaiśeṣika system explicitly admits a thesis, contrary to K3°, that all truths can be, and actually a r e known: $\forall p\ (p \rightarrow \mathrm{K}p)$, which is equivalent to $\forall p\ {\sim}(p\ \&\ {\sim}\mathrm{K}p)$, or rather, more specifically, that there is someone α (god, a *yogin*) who knows all truths: $\exists\alpha\,\forall p\ (p \rightarrow \mathrm{K}_{\alpha}p)$, equivalent to $\exists\alpha\,\forall p\ {\sim}(p\ \&\ {\sim}\mathrm{K}_{\alpha}p)$. Therefore, for the proponents of the system, around and after the times of Praśastapāda at the latest, i.e. after the admittance of god into the system, the Paradox of Knowability simply, when based on premisses K1°, K2° and K4°, does not arise.[100]

Nevertheless, even seen on purely logical grounds, what the Nyāya-Vaiśeṣika equation requires is the elimination of assumption K3°, i.e. the acceptance of a being that is omniscient. We can easily see that Nyāya-Vaiśeṣika equation seemed controversial on various grounds, and that also includes modern interpretations of anti-realist claims. Indeed, the equation seems to be most defensible in the context of omniscience, and at first sight the equation of the knowability of everything smacks of omniscience (*vide supra*, p. 307).[101]

4.1. Knowability thesis and the 'knowability thesis package'

The idea of the three meta-categories, i.e. the properties *astitva–abhidheyatva–jñeyatva*, must have entered the system of Vaiśeṣika at a later date, most probably in

[98] There have been many attempts undertaken. See for instance a rejoinder to EDGINGTON's (1985) Timothy WILLIAMSON's (1987) arguments in favour of Paradox of Knowability.

[99] For a fruitful analysis of the idea of (un)knowability in the context of (god's) omniscience see Jonathan L. KVANVIG (1989: 488 ff.).

[100] Cf. Jonathan L. KVANVIG (1989) for the analysis of the untenability of the claim that unknowable truths may exist vis-à-vis the doctrine of omniscience, and Charles TALIAFERRO's (1993) rejoinder to KVANVIG.

[101] Logically, however, the statement '... can know everything' does not entail '... knows everything', whereas the latter does entail the former.

the fifth century, insofar as it is not present in the extant text of the *Vaiśeṣika-sūtra* itself. However, it must have become a part of the system of beliefs either slightly before or, which is much less likely, at the time of Praśastapāda, otherwise it would be hardly difficult to account for its relatively widespread presence in other works such as those of Praśastamati (granted that he is different from Praśastapāda), Candramati and Uddyotakara Bhāradvāja (550–610 CE) around the same time, i.e. in the first half of the sixth century, i.e. after Diṅnāga (480–540 CE) and before Mallavādin (c. 600 CE), or even earlier, i.e. in the second half of the fifth century, i.e. the time of Vātsyāyana Pakṣilasvāmin[102].

I shall now argue that the reasons that prompted Nyāya-Vaiśeṣika philosophers to adopt such a controversial claim were of different nature than philosophical analysis and purely rational concerns.

My thesis is that (1) the idea expressed in the equation *astitva* = *abhidheyatva* = *jñeyatva* was adopted by Vaiśeṣika thinkers simultaneously along with three other concepts at approximately the same period: (2) the idea of god's existence, (3) the idea of god's omniscience and (4) the idea of twofold supernatural perception (*ārṣa-pratyakṣa* and *yogi pratyakṣa*), which were absent in the original *Vaiśeṣika-sūtra*, as it existed prior to Praśastapāda[103]. Further, all these latter three ideas were indispensable to justify each other. To wit, it was a package of four tenets that entered Nyāya-Vaiśeṣika system in the late fifth century CE.

4.2. Knowability thesis and god's existence

Let me start with the idea of god, which was a foreign body to and incompatible with the system of early Nyāya-Vaiśeṣika. It hardly needs any additional prove now, since it is widely accepted, that the idea of god was absent in the original text of the *Vaiśeṣika-sūtra*. There are no references to that idea in VS, and the only passage of VS into which the existence of god is read into by later tradition is VS 1.1.3, which reads in a concrete context:

> '[2] That from which [results] the attainment of mundane prosperity and the highest good is moral law. Vedic tradition possesses cognitive validity, because of **its** statement.'[104]

[102] Cf. p. 298, n. 125.

[103] See WEZLER (1982), ISAACSON (1993) and HONDA (1988) and p. 308 ff.

[104] VS(C) 1.1.2–3: *yato 'bhyudaya-nihśreyasa-siddhiḥ sa dharmaḥ. tad-vacanād āmnāya-prāmāṇyam*. VS(C) 1.1.3 is explicitly quoted in PBh$_1$ 8.12.2.2, p. 213 = PBh$_2$ 257, see p. 297, n. 123.

The expression 'because of **its** statement' (***tad**-vacanāt*)—which was later interpreted as referring to god[105]—could be, in this particular context, interpreted either as:

(a) 'because [Vedic tradition] communicates moral law' (*tad* = *dharma*), or

(b) 'because [Vedic tradition] speaks of the attainment of mundane prosperity and the highest good' (*tad* = *abhyudaya-nihśreyasa-siddhiḥ*), or

(c) 'because [Vedic tradition] speaks of mundane prosperity and the highest good' (*tad* = *abhyudaya-nihśreyasa*).

All the interpretations could be linguistically plausible here. The idea connoted roughly by the interpretations (a), (b) or (c) is echoed by Candramati with the statement that 'the *Veda*s and sacred texts proscribe moral law and prohibit unrighteousness [respectively]' (**śruti-smṛti-vihita-pratiṣiddha-dharmâdharma*) in the passage of DPŚ:

> 'Of merit and demerit, the cause is the connection of mind with soul after [the production of] desire and aversion, assisted by both pure and impure intention on those means for performing merit and demerit which are ordered and prohibited by the *Veda*s and the authoritative sacred texts.'[106]

The anonymous author of the commentary *Vaiśeṣika-darśana-vyākhyā* clearly interprets the statement in the sense (c):

> 'Because of the statement, or the teaching about these two, viz. heaven and liberation, which produces knowledge, Vedic tradition, viz. the *Veda*s, sacred texts, historic stories etc., possess cognitive validity, viz. they are the causes of knowledge.'[107]

---

[105] Cf. e.g. Candrānanda and his VSV(C) 1.1.3: *tad iti hiraṇya-garbha-parāmarśo hiraṇyaṁ reto 'syêti kṛtvā bhagavān mahêśvara evôcyate.*—'The [pronoun] "that" invokes the idea of the golden egg (sc. Brahman). Having taken this to mean "that whose golden [egg] is progeny" it refers to the Supreme Lord.' See BRONKHORST (1996).

[106] DPŚ$_2$ 154 (reconstructed): *dharmâdharmayor icchā-dveṣa-purvakaḥ śruti-smṛti-vihita-pratiṣiddha-dharmâdharma-sādhana-śuddhâśuddhâbhisandy-ubhayâpekṣa ātma-manaḥ-saṁyogaḥ kāraṇam.* = DPŚ$_1$ 2.2.5.25, p. 110: 'Merit and demerit are preceded by desire and aversion, and have their causes in contact of self with mind, caused by hearing and reflecting on, or by disregarding the fact that merit and demerit (severally) bring about a pure or impure state in the future life.'

[107] VSV(D) 1.3, p. 2: *tayoḥ svargâpavargayor vacanāt pratipādanāt pramiti-jananād āmnāyasya śruti-smṛtîtihāsâdeḥ prāmāṇyaṁ pramiti-kāraṇatvam.*

However, against any philologically possible interpretation of the VS passage, Praśastapāda gives an entirely new sense to VS 1.1.3, by taking *tad-°* to mean 'god' (*īśvara-°*):

> 'Vedic tradition is based on the cognitive validity of the speaker' (*vaktṛ-prāmāṇyâpekṣaḥ*),[108]

in which 'the speaker' for Praśastapāda is the only ultimately reliable and indisputably trustworthy speaker, i.e. god.

With his novel interpretation, Praśastapāda overrides the original meaning of VS 1.1.3 at the very outset of his *Padârtha-dharma-saṁgraha*, by stating that

> 'This [cognition, operating by way of positive procedure and by way of negative procedure, of the true nature of the six ontological categories] is [attained] because of moral law revealed by god's injunction.'[109]

Interestingly, Praśastapāda's statement fulfils a double role.

First, it gives a new meaning to VS 1.1.3, as against the original purport of the *sūtra*. Most importantly for the present issue, in the context of moral law (*dharma*) related to Vedic tradition that is considered to be a valid and reliable source of knowledge, Praśastapāda takes Kaṇāda's phrase *tad-vacanāt* to eventually connote the meaning: *īśvara-codanâbhivyaktād dharmāt*. It becomes conspicuous when we compare the argumentative structure of relevant portions of VS(C) and PBh. We obtain the following either causal or explanatory dependence, which is very similar in both cases:

Kaṇāda, VS(C):[110]

dharma → *abhyudaya-nihśreyasa*

1. Moral law leads to prosperity and liberation.

tad-vacana → *āmnāya-prāmāṇya* → *dharma*

2a. The utterance of/by 'this' leads to cognitive validity of Vedic tradition.

2b. Vedic tradition leads to moral law.

---

[108] See PBh$_1$ 8.12.2.2, p. 213 = PBh$_2$ 257: *śruti-smṛti-lakṣaṇo 'py āmnāyo vaktṛ-prāmāṇyâpekṣaḥ* ***tad-vacanād āmnāya-prāmāṇyam****, liṅgāc cânityo, buddhi-pūrvā vākya-kṛtir vede buddhi-pūrvo dadātir ity uktatvāt*. For the translation of the whole passage see p. 297.

[109] PBh$_1$ 2.1, p. 7 = PBh$_2$ 2, p. 1.8: *tac cêśvara-codanâbhivyaktād dharmād eva*. [***tat*** = *ṣaṇṇāṁ padârthānāṁ sādharmya-vaidharmya-****tattva-jñānam***].

[110] VS(C) 1.1.2–3: *yato 'bhyudaya-nihśreyasa-siddhiḥ sa dharmaḥ. tad-vacanād āmnāya-prāmāṇyam*.

Praśastapāda, PBh:[111]

dharma → tattva-jñāna → nihśreyasa

1a. Moral law leads to the cognition of the true nature of the categories.

1b. The cognition of the true nature of the categories leads to liberation.

īśvara-codanâbhivyakti → dharma

2. The demonstration of the injunction by god leads to moral law.

In both cases it is ultimately *dharma* ('moral law') that leads, either in one or two steps, to liberation (or mundane prosperity) and in both cases *dharma* is communicated this way or another. Praśastapāda leaves no doubt that the source is the injunction revealed by god.

Second, Praśastapāda's above statement expresses, at the same time, a criticism directed against the Mīmāṁsaka and Jaimini's well-known claim that 'Moral law is something characterised by injunction'[112], viz. moral law is known directly from Vedic injunction without the mediation of anyone, including god. It cannot be a coincidence that Praśastapāda avails himself of a rather unusual term for the Vaiśeṣika, which is nowhere attested in VS and occurs only once in PBh. For Jaimini, the atheist, and for his tradition, people's adherence to *dharma* was due to a very special character of the language of Vedic revelation, which was characterised by injunction and therefore required no author or authority, being self-explanatory, or self-enforcing. That was the Mīmāṁsaka strategy to explain what provided the imperative character of Vedic statements that communicated *dharma* without taking recourse to god's authority and reliability. Praśastapāda the theist seems do deliberately refer to Jaimini's thesis, to modify it and augment it with the new element *īśvara-°*:

Jaimini:

**codanā-lakṣaṇo dharmaḥ*

Moral law is characterised by injunction, *ergo* n o t r e v e a l e d .

Praśastapāda:

**īśvara-codanâbhivyakto dharmaḥ*

Moral law is manifested through injunction r e v e a l e d b y g o d .

Praśastapāda, with his two-purpose comment, made therefore a statement: an unequivocal manifestation of his conviction as a theist.

---

[111] PBh_1 2.1, p. 6–7 = PBh_2 2, p. 1.6–8: *dravya-guṇa-karma-sāmānya-viśeṣa-samavāyānāṁ ṣaṇṇāṁ padârthānāṁ sādharmya-vaidharmya-tattva-jnānaṁ* [PBh_1, n. 5 = PBh_2, n. 2: °*-vaidharmyābhyāṁ tattva-*°] *niḥśreyasa-hetuḥ. tac cêśvara-codanâbhivyaktād dharmād eva.*

[112] MS 1.1.2: *codanā-lakṣaṇo 'rtho dharmaḥ.*

There is one more Kaṇāda's passage that was later interpreted in the theistic sense:

> '[1] The composition of sentences in the *Vedas* is preceded by conscious design. [2] And it does not [come] from our conscious designs. It is the inferential sign of a seer's [conscious design].'[113]

What Kaṇāda says is that behind the rational structure and meaningful contents of the *Vedas* stands a conscious design of a seer, who composed them. The phrasing and contents of Kaṇāda's words contains nothing that would allude to god as such. He merely says that it was a product of a consciousness higher than that of an ordinary being. The expression he uses is *na câsmad-buddhibhyaḥ* ('not ... from our conscious designs') bears a resemblance to Praśastapāda's wording *asmad-viśiṣṭānāṁ yogināṁ* (PBh 241, 370: '*yogins* ... who are superior to us', pp. 311, 312)[114]. It is hardly feasible that what he meant was god.[115]

However, Candrānanda, in his *Vṛtti*, offers a completely different exposition in the purely theistic spirit:

> 'For our [human] cognition is not of this kind [to know the *Vedas*], having as its scope [only] objects that are present, not concealed [from sight] and [directly] connected [to our sense organs][116]. Of such kind is only the cognition of god. For this reason god's cognition has as its scope extrasensory objects.'[117]

Also Bhaṭṭa Vādīndra (c. 1230–1250[118]), the author of *Vaiśeṣika-sūtra-vārttika* (*Tarka-sāgara*), gives a purely theistic exposition of the *sūtra*: '<And this> vener-

[113] VS(C) 6.1.1–2: *buddhi-pūrvā vākya-kṛtir vede. na câsmad-buddhibhyo liṅgam ṛṣeḥ.*

[114] Cf. Bhartṛhari's expression: *asmad-viśiṣṭānāṁ* (VP 3.1.46: 'those who are superior to us', p. 321).

[115] There existed an idea of *īśvara* being a kind of superman, a powerful superhuman being, 'a particular kind of soul, untainted by afflictions, *karman* and karmic fruition [caused by subliminal disposition' (YS 1.24: *kleśa-karma-vipākâśayair aparāmṛṣṭaḥ puruṣa-viśeṣa īśvarah.*) in the tradition of the *Pātañjala-yoga-śāstra* (ca 325 to 425 CE?, for the dating see MAAS (2006: xii–xix) and (2009: 383)). However, that idea is not what Kaṇāda or Praśastapāda refer to.

[116] This cognition is exactly the opposite of the *yogin*'s supernatural perception described, e.g., in VSV(C) 1.15, see n. 150.

[117] VSV(C) 6.1.2, p. 45.9–11: *na hi yādṛśam asmad-vijñānaṁ vartamānâvyavahita-sambaddhârtha-viṣayaṁ tādṛśam eva bhagavatọ vijñānam. ataḥ sambhavati bhagavato 'tīndriyârtha-viṣayaṁ vijñānam.*

[118] ISAACSON (1995: 4).

able seer is god'[119]. Clearly, such reinterpretations of Kaṇāda's intention presuppose Praśastapāda's theistic innovation in the system.

4.3. Knowability thesis and god's omniscience

Since, prior to Praśastapāda and his contemporaries, the Vaiśeṣika system as such knew no idea of god's existence[120], there could neither be any idea of god's omniscience known to the system before that time either. However, the idea of god's omniscience—as a corollary of the belief in god's existence—is present, which is my contention, as early as Praśastapāda's afore-mentioned statements that explicitly refer to god,[121] or even earlier, i.e. at the time of Vātsyāyana Pakṣilasvāmin (after c. 450).

There are at least two ideas that, when combined, lead us to the conclusion that Praśastapāda, while accepting the existence of god, also admitted of his omniscience.

First, it is his conviction that the composition of the *Veda*s, which reliably communicate all the knowledge and describe the whole world in its entirety, (a) entails the existence of their author and (b) presupposes prior knowledge of their contents in the author's consciousness:

> 'Vedic tradition, consisting in Vedic revelation (*śruti*) and authoritative testimony (*smṛti*), is based on the cognitive validity of the speaker: "Vedic tradition possesses cognitive validity, because of «its»[122] statement (here: because of god's statement)" [VS 1.1.3]. And [the word (*śabda*)] is [proved to be] impermanent on the basis of the inferential sign, because it has been said [in VS 6.1.1]: "The composition of sentences in the *Veda*s is preceded by conscious design", [and in VS(C) 6.1.1 = VS(Ś) 6.1.3]: "Benefaction is preceded by conscious design".'[123]

[119] VSV$_2$ *ad loc.*, p. 57: <*sa ca*> *bhagavān ṛṣir īśvaraḥ*. VSV$_1$ *ad loc.*, p. 298.11 = VSV(D), p. 58.11: <*veda-kartā*> *bhagavān ṛṣir īśvaraḥ*.

[120] I don't mean to say that theistic views were altogether unknown to Kaṇāda but that he did not subscribe to them.

[121] See PBh$_1$ 2.1, p. 7 = PBh$_2$ 2, p. 1.8 (*tac ceśvara-codanâbhivyaktād dharmād eva*) and PBh$_1$ 8.12, p. 213 = PBh$_2$ 257; see nn. 109 & 111, and n. 108 respectively.

[122] See § 4.2, p. 292 ff.

[123] PBh$_1$ 8.12.2.2, p. 213 = PBh$_2$ 257: *śruti-smṛti-lakṣaṇo 'py āmnāyo vaktṛ-prāmāṇyâpekṣaḥ* "*tad-vacanād āmnāya-prāmāṇyam*" (VS 1.1.3), *liṅgāc cânityo,* "*buddhi-pūrvā vākya-kṛtir vede*" (VS 6.1.1), "*buddhi-pūrvo dadātir*" (VS(C) 6.1.4 = VS(D) 6.1.4 = VS(Ś) 6.1.3) *ity uktatvāt*. Passage partially cited above on p. 294, n. 108.

Secondly, the admission of the idea of a complete knowledge of all the categories, which is indispensable to construct an exhaustive ontology attempted by the Vaiśeṣika, necessitates the acceptance of the idea of knowledge that embraces all the elements of the universe; and that is eventually tantamount to omniscience.

By the time of Praśastapāda the idea of omniscience as such, i.e. either human or divine, had already entered the body of beliefs professed by the representatives of Nyāya-Vaiśeṣika, and it is already present in the *Nyāya-bhāṣya*, just to quote two examples:

> 'Out of these [twelve cognoscible categories, the first one, viz.] the soul is the perceiver of everything, the experiencing subject of everything, the omniscient, the sensor of everything.'[124]

and

> '[It is known] through scriptural testimony [that] god is the perceiver, the knower, the omniscient. And who could possibly explain god, who is inexpressible [and] beyond the scope of perception, inference and scriptural testimony, by means of the soul's attributes, such as sentience etc.?!'[125]

These two instances demonstrate that the *Nyāya-bhāṣya* related the idea of omniscience to two categories of the soul (*ātman*). Firstly, it was a potential property of the soul as such, being its dormant innate aptitude that was correlated to its omnipresence and spatial infinity, features that, for Praśastapāda, the soul shared with three other substances.[126] Secondly, it was an actual property of god, a supreme kind of soul. This twofold division of the souls was later expressed in plain terms, e.g. by Udayana in his *Lakṣaṇâvalī*: 'Soul is twofold: god and non-god.'[127]

Even though Praśastapāda nowhere mentions god's omniscience directly, apparently taking it for granted and as something that necessitates no further proof, he does make use of the idea on a few occasions. The first is the description of the act of (re)construction of the world:

> 'Now the principle of the construction and dissolution of the four [atomic] material elements is described in the following. At the end of

[124] NBh 1.1.9: *tatrâtmā sarvasya draṣṭā sarvasya bhoktā sarva-jñaḥ sarvânubhāvī.*

[125] NBh 4.1.21, p. 228.13: *āgamāc ca draṣṭā boddhā sarva-jñātā īśvara iti. buddhy-ādibhiś câtma-liṅgair nirupākhyam īśvaraṁ pratyakṣânumānâgama-viṣayâtītaṁ kaḥ śakta upapādayitum.*

[126] PBh_1 3, p. 22 = PBh_2 19: *ākāśa-kāla-dig-ātmanāṁ sarva-gatatvaṁ, parama-mahattvaṁ, sarva-saṁyogi-samāna-deśatvaṁ ca.*

[127] LA 114 (p. 70): *sa dvividha īśânīśa-bhedāt.*

a hundred years [measured] by Brahma units, at the time of liberation of the current divine being Brahman—simultaneously with the wish of supreme god, the lord of the whole universe, to dissolve [the universe] in order to give rest during the [period of Brahma] night to all living creatures wearied by transmigration—the activity of invisible moral principles, which are present in all souls and which govern [the souls'] bodies, sense-organs and material elements, comes to halt. Then the suspension of the connection between these [atomic particles] occurs by means of the separations of the atomic particles which are the causes of bodies and sense-organs, [the separations being] accomplished through the actions that result from the connection of supreme god's wish, the souls and the atomic particles. Subsequently, the dissolution of these [atomic particles takes place] up to the indivisible atoms.'[128]

After the period of the world's dissolution comes to an end, god performs his role through a divine being Brahman and launches the world again to a new round of active manifest existence, having in the first step introduced motion into the universe anew and having brought the first two atoms together to form a particle[129]:

'And this [divine being] Brahman—being entrusted by supreme god [and] being endowed with cognition characterised by absolute excellence (sc. omniscience), and with passionlessness and divine might—gets to know the fruition of the deeds of living creatures (*sc.* souls), [first] begets [his] sons who are made of his mind and are lords of the creatures, [and then he creates] law-givers, divine beings, seers and classes of forefathers, the four social strata that sprung from [Prajāpati's] mouth, arms, thighs and feet, as well as other higher and lower [corporeal] living beings—so that the knowledge, experience and life span [of all these beings] correspond to their previous deeds. [In these acts of construction, divine Brahman] endows [all the created beings]

[128] PBh_1 5, p. 48.7 ff. = PBh_2 57: *ihêdānīṁ caturṇāṁ mahā-bhūtānāṁ sṛṣṭi-saṁhāra-vidhir ucyate. brāhmeṇa mānena varṣa-śatânte vartamānasya brahmaṇo 'pavarga-kāle saṁsāra-khinnānāṁ sarva-prāṇināṁ niśi viśrāmârthaṁ sakala-bhuvana-pater mahêśvarasya saṁjihīrṣā-samakālaṁ śarīrêndriya-mahā-bhūtôpanibandhakānāṁ sarvâtma-gatānāṁ adṛṣṭānāṁ vṛtti-nirodhe sati mahêśvarêcchâtmâṇu-saṁyoga-ja-karmabhyaḥ śarīrêndriya-kāraṇâṇu-vibhāgebhyas tat-saṁyoga-nivṛttau teṣām ā paramâṇv-anto vināśaḥ.*

[129] PBh_1 5, p. 48.19 ff. = PBh_2 58: *tataḥ punaḥ prāṇināṁ bhoga-bhūtaye mahêśvara-sisṛkṣânantaraṁ sarvâtma-gata-vṛtti-labdhâdṛṣṭâpekṣebhyas tat-saṁyogebhyaḥ pavana-paramâṇuṣu karmôtpattau teṣāṁ paraspara-saṁyogebhyo dvy-aṇukâdi-prakrameṇa mahān vāyuḥ samutpanno nabhasi dodhūyamānas tiṣṭhati.* etc.

with their [respective] moral duty, knowledge, passionlessness and divine might that conform to their potencies stored [as their *karman*].'[130]

Clearly, such an arduous task, as it probably would have to be, of putting the universe of all living beings together along with their respective *karmans*, to be accomplished by divine Brahman, would have to necessitate absolute and supreme knowledge (*atiśaya-jñāna*), which is consigned, or subcontracted, to Brahman by god (*mahêśvareṇa viniyuktaḥ*) as an act of divine outsourcing.

Another indirect reference to god's omniscience, or at least some kind of extraordinary cognition, is found in the section that describes how dimensions larger than atomic size as well as the idea of plurality in the world originate:

> 'Impermanent [dimensions] of all four kinds have their source in number, dimension and multitude. Out of these [dimensions, the idea of] the plural number arises thanks to god's mind with respect to atomic dyads, made of indivisible atoms; [the said plural number] produces [the qualities of] magnitude and length—simultaneously with the formation of colour and other [secondary qualities]—in [complex] substantial things, understood as atomic triads (i.e. particles composed of three pairs of atoms) and as other [larger macroscopic bodies], which are effects brought about by these [atomic dyads].'[131]

In other words, it is god's mind that stores the idea of two-atom particles as well as the notion of complex wholes based on the idea of plurality (plural number), inherent in the composition of atomic triads, that are composed of six atoms (i.e. three pairs). Praśastapāda wants us to believe that without that notion present in god's mind complex wholes could not emerge.

Three questions immediately arise here. First, what does the idea of plurality, or duality, have to do with atomic dyads (*dvy-aṇuka*)? Second, what does god have to do with it? And, third, what does it all have to do with god's omniscience?

To answer the first question, i.e. what relates the idea of plurality with two-atom particles, we have to take a closer look at the idea of the cognition of recurrent con-

[130] PBh_1 5, p. 49.11 ff. = PBh_2 59: *sa ca mahêśvareṇa viniyukto brahmâtiśaya-jñāna-vairāgyâiśvarya-sampannaḥ prāṇināṁ karma-vipākaṁ viditvā karmânurūpa-jñāna-bhogâyuṣaḥ sutān prajāpatīn mānasān manu-deva-ṛṣi-pitṛ-gaṇān mukha-bāhûru-pāda-taś caṭuro varṇān anyāni côccâvacāni bhūtāni ca sṛṣṭvā, āśayâṇurūpair dharma-jñāna-vairāgyâiśvaryaiḥ saṁyojayatîti.*

[131] PBh_1 8.7, p. 131 = PBh_2 155–156: *anityaṁ catur-vidham api saṁkhyā-parimāṇa-pracaya-yoni. tatrêśvara-buddhim apekṣyôtpannā paramâṇu-dvy-aṇukeṣu bahutva-saṁkhyā tair ārabdhe kārya-dravye try-aṇukâdi-lakṣaṇe rūpâdy-utpatti-samakālaṁ mahattvam dīrghatvaṁ ca karoti.*

tinuity (*apekṣā-buddhi*)[132], sometimes called enumerative knowledge, and the process through which our mind forms the notion of the number 'two' and larger numbers, as was understood by Praśastapāda, who surprisingly devoted a lot of space to the problem:

> '[130] The [number "two" and numbers larger than "two"] arise, as one should realise, from many [single instances] of oneness combined with the idea of a multiple object, and disappear with the disappearance of the cognition of recurrent continuity. [131] How [does it take place]? 'When it comes to a contact of the perceiver's eye with two individual substantial things, belonging either to the same class or to a different class (i.e. two homogeneous or heterogeneous things), there arises the cognition of generality of oneness which inheres in each [individual substantial thing] that is in contact with the [eye; and it has the form: "This is one. This is one"]; then from [three] acts of cognition: one of the generality of oneness and [two] of the relation [of the two single things] to this [oneness], there arises one single notion of two single-instantiated [things] with respect to a multiple object [made of these two individual substantial things]. Then, contingent on this [single notion of two single-instantiated things], the notion of duality emerges with respect to (sc. instantiated in the form of) these two onenesses, each of which having their respective substrata (i.e. the single-instantiated things). And, subsequently, with respect to this [singular notion of duality instantiated in the form of the two onenesses] there arises the cognition of generality of duality. As a consequence of this cognition of generality of duality the cognition of recurrent continuity (here: the cognition of duality dependent on two instantiations) gradually disappears and, from the acts of cognition: of the generality of duality, of the relation [of the two onenesses] to this [duality] and of [this singular] duality, there gradually arises one single notion of the quality of duality—[these two processes take place at] the same time. [132] Then, immediately on the disappearance of the cognition of recurrent continuity (here: the cognition of duality dependent on two instantiations), the quality of duality disappears. [Since] the cognition of the quality of duality is the cause of the disappearance of cognition of the generality of duality, there gradually arises—because of the quality of duality, its cognition and its relation—the notion of [two] individual substantial things of the form: "two individual substantial things";

[132] On *apekṣā-buddhi* see e.g. MIYAMOTO (1996: 78–84).

> [these processes take place at] the same time. [133] Immediately afterwards there arises the cognition of [two] individual substantial things of the form: "two individual substantial things", the duality disappears, the notion of the quality of duality gradually disappears; from the cognition of individual substantial thing subliminal impression gradually arises; [these processes take place at] the same time. [134] Immediately afterwards from the cognition of individual substantial thing the notion of the quality of duality disappears; also the notion of individual substantial thing [disappears] due to the subliminal impression. [135] In this way [we] have also described how [the notion of] the number "three" etc. originates. [Their] production proceeds from many [single instances] of oneness combined with the idea of a multiple object, and [their] disappearance follows the disappearance of the cognition of recurrent continuity.'[133]

This lengthy account on number two, and similar procedures, apply also to numbers larger than two, and shows that to conceive of a notion of number was maintained by Praśastapāda to be a highly complex process that involved a sequence of stages and a special cognitive ability called the cognition of recurrent continuity (*apekṣā-buddhi*). Equally easily can we see that Praśastapāda thought a clearly formed notion of the number 'two', or 'duality', and that of larger numbers as well, was indispensable for the existence of compounded entities, which by nature are aggregates consisting of numerous (at least two) parts, for instance for the existence of two-atom particles. In other words, the existence of a whole consisting of two ele-

---

[133] PBh_1 8.6, p. 111–112 = PBh_2 130–135: [130] *tasyāḥ* (= *sāṁkhyāyāḥ*) *khalv ekatvebhyo 'neka-viṣaya-buddhi-sahitebhyo niṣpattir apekṣā-buddhi-vināśād vināśa iti.* [131] *katham. yadā boddhuś cakṣuṣā samānâsamāna-jātīyayor dravyayoḥ sannikarṣe sati tat-saṁyukta-samaveta-samavetâikatva-sāmānya-jñānôtpattāv ekatva-sāmānya-tat-sambandha-jñānebhya eka-guṇayor aneka-viṣayiṇy ekā buddhir utpadyate tadā tām apekṣyâikatvābhyāṁ svâśrayayor dvitvam ārambhyate. tataḥ punas tasmin dvitva-sāmānya-jñānam utpadyate. tasmād dvitva-sāmānya-jñānād apekṣā-buddher vinaśyattā dvitva-sāmānya-tat-sambandha-taj-jñānebhyo dvitva-guṇa-buddher utpadyamānatêty ekaḥ kālaḥ.* [132] *tata idānīm apekṣā-buddhi-vināśād dvitva-guṇasya vinaśyattā dvitva-guṇa-jñānaṁ dvitva-sāmānya-jñānasya vināśa-kāraṇaṁ dvitva-guṇa-taj-jñāna-sambandhebhyo dve dravye iti dravya-buddher utpadyamānatêty ekaḥ kālaḥ.* [133] *tad-anantaraṁ dve dravye iti dravya-jñānasyôtpādo dvitvasya vināśo dvitva-guṇa-buddher vinaśyattā dravya-jñānāt saṁskārasyôtpadyamānatêty ekaḥ kālaḥ.* [134] *tad-anantaraṁ dravya-jñānād dvitva-guṇa-buddher vināśo dravya-buddher api saṁskārāt.* [135] *etena tritvâdy-utpattir api vyākhyātā. ekatvebhyo 'neka-viṣaya-buddhi-sahitebhyo niṣpattir apekṣā-buddhi-vināśāc ca vināśa iti.*

On the process of conceiving the idea of the number 'two', the way Praśastapāda understood it, see MIYAMOTO (1996: 59–77) and THAKUR (2003: 203–207): 'Duality (*dvitva*)'.

ments (e.g. a two-atom particle) entails prior existence of the notion of 'two' and a respective design based on this notion.

To understand why—and this is a reply to the second question: what is god's role in the process—we must recall that for Praśastapāda all movements and actions in the universe ultimately proceed from conscious entities, viz. the souls[134] of two kinds[135], because atoms, hence all other material entities composed of atoms alike, are not capable of autokinesis on their own. Further, movement and action is indispensable to produce a whole, therefore any compounded whole is thus a result of a series of events that eventually go back to the first mover, clearly an idea that was used to formulate one of a number of arguments for the existence of god, the argument from the first mover:

> 'Material substratum, atoms and *karman* operate, because—as they were put in motion earlier—they are superintended by a cause endowed with cognitive awareness (sc. god), insofar as they [themselves] are unconscious, like an axe etc., viz. just like an axe and other [tools] operate being superintended by a carpenter endowed with cognitive awareness, because they [themselves] are unconscious ...'[136]

Even to combine elements into a smallest possible whole, viz. an atomic dyad (*dvyaṇuka*), it takes a conscious being that would capacitate atoms to conjoin by applying his cognition of recurrent continuity (*apekṣā-buddhi*) to separate elements. We can

---

[134] Cf. e.g. PBh_1 6.4, p. 69.6 ff. = PBh_2 76: *tasya saukṣmyād apratyakṣatve sati* [PBh_1, n. 5: *'pi*] *karaṇaiḥ śabdâdy-upalabdhy-anumitaiḥ śrotrâdibhiḥ samadhigamaḥ kriyate. vāsyâdīnām* [PBh_1, n. 7: *vāsyâdīnām iva*] *karaṇānāṁ kartr̥-prayojyatva-darśanāc chabdâdiṣu prasiddhyā ca prasādhako 'numīyate.*—'Since due to its subtlety the [soul] is imperceptible, it is made known through sensory organs such as the organ of hearing whose [existence] is inferred through [the existence of sensory data] such as sound etc. Similarly, since instruments, such as axe etc., are empirically attested to [entail] that they are employed by an agent [with a purpose], and [sensory instruments] are well established to [be employed] with respect to sound and other [data, the soul] is inferred [to exist] as an executor [of all actions].'

[135] See p. 298, n. 127.

[136] NV_1 4.21, p. 461 11–13: *pradhāna-paramâṇu-karmāṇi prāk pravr̥tteḥ buddhimat-kāraṇâdhiṣṭhitāni pravartanta 'cetanatvād vāsy-ādivad iti yathā vāsy-ādi buddhimatā takṣṇā adhiṣṭhitam acetanatvāt pravartate* ... Cf. n. 229. The argument was frequently repeated by subsequent authors, e.g. by Udayana in NKA 5, p. 503.15: *paramâṇv-ādayo hi cetanā-yojitāḥ pravartante acetanatvād vāsy-ādivat.*—'Indivisible atoms etc. operate when propelled by consciousness, because they are unconscious, like an axe etc.' Jayanta-bhaṭṭa devotes a longer passage to the argument in NMa_1 I: 488–490. Cf. NS 1.1.11: *ceṣṭêndriyârthâśrayaḥ śarīram.*—'The body is a seat of action, sense organs and objects.'

speak here of something resembling Aristotelian final cause (*causa finalis*)[137], i.e. of a particular design god has while bringing about a combination of two atoms. Since in the (endlessly cyclical) beginning of the world after the period of its dissolution all other conscious beings are each time dormant, the only conscious agent is god who needs to have a well-formed notion of the number 'two' etc. in order to initiate the process of the composition of the universe, from finest particles to large macroscopic wholes.

The problem remains, which is our third question, what does god's omniscience have to do with all this? After a period of a complete dissolution of the world (*pralaya*), when all conscious beings are dormant and all matter has dissolved into separate, uncombined atoms in rest, god requires—in order to bring the world into existence back again—the ideas of the number 'two' etc. in order to initiate the union of two atoms and to induce the process of forming larger wholes. However, as Praśastapāda's account suggests, the notions of duality and plurality are as such an abstract synthesis derived from experience that requires elements somehow linked together with the help of the cognition of recurrent continuity (*apekṣā-buddhi*). To form a complex whole, necessarily based on notions of duality and plurality, requires a prior knowledge of such an idea of number larger than one. In the world emerging from the dissolution, in the first stage, there is nothing that could serve as a source for an experience that could subsequently trigger the conception of such numbers, because all objects are unitary and no objects are combined in pairs. Therefore, it has to be postulated that god must be possessed of such knowledge that is not derived from experience at all. His knowledge of this sort does not necessarily have to amount to omniscience, however, it certainly remains outside the scope of any experience or ordinary knowledge derived from experience.[138] No doubt it must be regarded as some kind of extraordinary knowledge: it is beyond the capability of any ordinary being to have knowledge which is not derived from experience of any form, including testimony communicated by another agent, which also entails some kind of experience. To put it plainly, the existence of wholes compounded of atoms rests on the notion of 'two' along with a respective design based on this notion; and that presupposes extra-empirical, perfect and, probably, omniscient mind of god, the (re)constructor, in which all such notions are stored.

---

[137] *Met* 983^{a}31-32: τετάρτην δὲ τὴν ἀντικειμένην αἰτίαν ταύτῃ, τὸ οὗ ἕνεκα καὶ τἀγαθὸν (τέλος γὰρ γενέσεως καὶ κινήσεως πάσης τοῦτ᾽ ἐστίν).—'The fourth [cause] is the opposite of the latter (i.e. of efficient cause), namely that for sake of which something happens (sc. purposefulness) and goodness, for it is the purpose of all that arises and moves.'

[138] An argument that god acquired such a knowledge empirically, i.e. before the dissolution, while the complex world was still there in developed form, and therefore, while the world is re-emerging after the dissolution, god's knowledge of duality and plurality would merely be a case of memory from previous, i.e. pre-dissolution experience, would lead to infinite regress.

Consequently, to postulate such a knowledge of simple numbers, as trivial as it may sound at first, in the context where the universe offers no observable data for one to empirically derive such a knowledge from it, is tantamount to asserting that god possesses at least some kind of supernatural cognition that transcends all a mundane soul could possibly know.

A very similar indication of the same kind of supreme knowledge, which exceeds everything known in the universe, is found in the following passage quoted in Abhayadeva-sūri's *Tattva-bodha-vidhāyinī* and ascribed to Praśastamati:

> 'Praśastamati, on the other hand, says: "In the beginning of (re)construction [of the world, verbal] usage of people is preceded by someone else's instruction, because later on [people's usage] awakened [after the dissolution of the world] is [properly] delimited with respect to their specific objects[139], just as verbal usage of children, who have not learnt verbal usage yet, [when properly] delimited with respect to their specific objects, is preceded by the instruction of [their] mothers and other [people].'

In his comment immediately following the passage, Abhayadeva-sūri explicates what is actually self-evident in the quote, that, first, that what Praśastamati has in mind as the primary source of verbal usage, when no knowledge yet exists, is god, and secondly, what lies at the core of god's capability of bestowing upon the humankind linguistic skills is his supreme cognition:

> '... It is proved that the one by whose instruction [verbal] usage [of people] is preceded in the beginning of [re]construction [of the world] is god; indeed, he is not deprived of excellence of cognition during the dissolution [of the world].'[140]

Further, Abhayadeva-sūri either recapitulates or quotes what Praśastamati apparently has to say on god's omniscience (*sarva-jñatva*), as being related to god's act

---

[139] I.e. people correctly use words and denote objects. The same expression occurs in PBh_1 8.12, p. 171= PBh_2 212: *buddhir upalabdhir jñānaṁ pratyaya iti paryāyāḥ. sā câneka-prakārârthânantyāt praty-artha-niyatatvāc ca.*—'Cognitive awareness [of an object], apprehension, cognition, comprehension—these are synonyms. This [cognitive awareness] has numerous varieties, because objects are infinite and it is delimited with respect to its specific objects.'

[140] TBV, p. 101.19–23: *praśastamatis tv āha: "sargâdau puruṣāṇāṁ vyavahāro 'nyôpadeśa-pūrvakaḥ, uttara-kālaṁ prabuddhānāṁ praty-artha-niyatatvād, aprasiddha-vāg-vyavahārāṇāṁ kumārāṇāṁ gav-ādiṣu praty-artha-niyato vāg-vyavahāro yathā mātrâdy-upadeśa-pūrvakaḥ" iti. prabuddhānāṁ praty artha-niyatatvād iti prabuddhānāṁ satāṁ praty arthaṁ niyatatvād ity arthaḥ. yad-upadeśa-pūrvakaś ca sa sargâdau vyavahāraḥ sa īśvaraḥ pralaya-kāle tu alupta-jñānâtiśaya iti siddham.*

of composition or construction (not an act of creation *ex nihilo*, of course!) of the world:

> '"Now, on the basis of this [argumentation] it must be taken as proven that god, consisting in multiple causes, is the cause of all the world. But how can it be proved that he is omniscient, so that he could become the object of devotion for all those [people] desirous of the highest good and mundane prosperity[141]? We say it is because it has been proved beyond doubt that [god] is the constructor of the world." And this is what Praśastamati and others said along these lines: "[{1. Thesis:} God is omniscient], {Logical reason:} because [he as] the agent has the knowledge of the product, of its material cause, of the tools (assisting causes) [to produce it], of the purpose [of the product] and of its recipient. {Invariable concomitance and example:} For in this world, whoever is the agent [producing] something, he has the knowledge of the material cause of the material cause etc. of that [thing]. For instance the potter, being the agent [producing] a pot [as the product] etc., has the knowledge of a clod of clay, which is the material cause [of the pot]; [he has the knowledge of] the potter's wheel, which are the tools [to produce the pot]; [he has the knowledge of] the fetching of water etc., which is the purpose [of the pot]; and [he has the knowledge of] the householder as the recipient. That is obvious. {Application:} Similarly, god is the agent [producing] all the world layers, he has the knowledge of their material causes, consisting in atoms etc.; [he has the knowledge of] the tools (immediate assisting causes) [to produce them], i.e. the moral law, space, time etc.; [he has the knowledge of] factual tools [to produce them], consisting in universals, individuators and inherence; [he has the knowledge of] the purpose, i.e. the benefit and [he has the knowledge of] people who are technically called recipients. {Conclusion:} Therefore it is proved that he is omniscient".'[142]

---

[141] Two goals mentioned in VS(C) 1.1.2 (*v* n. 104); *nota bene* the sequence of both the goals is interchanged.

[142] TBV, p. 101.27–35: *atha bhavatv asmād dhetu-kadambakâdîśvarasya sarva-jagad-dhetutva-siddhiḥ, sarva-jñatvaṁ tu kathaṁ tasya siddhaṁ yenâsau niḥśreyasâbhyudaya-kāmānāṁ bhakti-viṣayatāṁ yāyāt? jagat-kartṛtva-siddher evêti brūmaḥ. tathā câhuḥ praśastamati-prabhṛtayaḥ: "kartuḥ kāryôpādānôpakaraṇa-prayojana-saṁpradāna-parijñānāt. iha hi yo yasya kartā bhavati sa tasyôpādānâdīni jānīte, yathā kulālaḥ kuṇḍâdīnāṁ kartā, tad-upādānaṁ mṛt-piṇḍam, upakaraṇāni cakrâdīni, prayojanam udakâharaṇâdi, kuṭumbinaṁ ca saṁpradānaṁ jānīta*

What we find embedded in the passage as a quote is a full-fledged, five-membered proof formula of god's omniscience and its authorship is ascribed either to Praśastamati or to his immediate tradition. What is missing in the proof formula is an explicit formulation of the thesis; however, the context is so unequivocal that one can phrase it as follows beyond a shadow of doubt: **īśvarasya sarva-jñatvaṁ* ('god is omniscient').

Whether the Vaiśeṣika author of the above argument for god's omniscience was Praśastamati himself or his immediate disciples, or whether Praśastamati was Praśastapāda or not, the passage attests to the fact that around the time when Praśastamati and Praśastapāda flourished the idea of god's omniscience not only circulated but attempts were undertaken to prove it. The contention holds valid even when the above five-membered proof formula is not an original formulation but merely a paraphrase: it still attest to the fact that the Vaiśeṣikas attempted to prove their theistic stance. And that renders a strong support to my thesis that what Praśastapāda himself spoke of as supreme knowledge (*atiśaya-jñāna*, n. 130; or *jñānâtiśaya*, n. 140), which was beyond this world and did not undergo the process of dissolution when everything else was temporarily dissolved, was in fact omniscience.

To recup, we can see that although Praśastapāda did not make any consistent attempt, at least in his only extant work, to characterise the essence of god or to prove either his existence or his omniscience, he did, for all practical purposes, use the notion of god and god's omniscience as self-evident. These reservations will not hold if he indeed were the same person as Praśastamati, of course. For, as regards Praśastamati, granted he is different from Praśastapāda, we may not know whether at all or how he defined god's essence, but we do know that either he or someone of his direct disciples conceived of god as an omniscient being and, in addition, provided what he thought to be a valid proof formula for that. In any case, what is beyond doubt is that by the end of the fifth century a clear idea of god as an omniscient constructor of the world was a well-established doctrine of the Nyāya-Vaiśeṣika system.

Although they did not have all the theoretical apparatus of modern logic (*vide supra*, p. § 3.3), the intuition of the Naiyāyika-Vaiśeṣika seemed quite appropriate to relate the belief in omniscience to either god or to select humans of extraordinary qualities. It is therefore not at all surprising to find the knowability thesis enter their system. It would be too far-reaching to claim that the philosophers thought that the ability to know everything was really applicable to ordinary humans. It must

---

ity etat siddham. tathêśvaraḥ sakala-bhuvānāṁ kartā, sa tad-upādānāni paramâṇv-ādi-lakṣaṇāni, tad-upakaraṇāni dharma-dik-kālâdīni, vyavahārôpakaraṇāni sāmānya-viśeṣa-samavāya-lakṣaṇāni, prayojanam upabhogam, saṁpradāna-saṁjñakāṁś ca puruṣān jānīta iti. ata siddham asya sarvajñatvam iti.

have therefore been correlated with the idea of divine omniscience and yogic experience, which warranted their systems completeness and (seeming) consistency.

4.4. Knowability thesis and supernatural perception

The third and last idea that entered the body of tenets upheld by later Vaiśeṣika philosophers simultaneously with the equation 'existentiality = nameability = cognisability' (*astitva* = *abhidheyatva* = *jñeyatva*), and was complementary to it was the belief in supernatural perception. It eventually came to be believed to be of two kinds: the *yogin*'s perception (*yogi-pratyakṣa*) and the seer's perception (*ārṣa-pratyakṣa*).

4.4.1. Supernatural perception of the *yogin*s

We may safely assume that the admission of some sort of supernatural powers, including extrasensory perception, was quite a widespread popular 'folk-religious' belief at quite an early age also in India. However, it was not until the first half of the first millennium CE that the actual term for such a phenomenon, e.g. either *yogi-pratyakṣa* ('the *yogin*'s perception') or *ārṣa-pratyakṣa* ('the seer's perception'), was coined and found its way into philosophical treatises in general. Attempts to prove the existence of such a belief-based concept are generally even later.

Both the concept and the term are absent in earliest versions of the *Vaiśeṣika-sūtra*; their addition must have taken place later, about the turn of 4th/5th centuries at the earliest, and antedate Praśastapāda, as WEZLER (1982), HONDA (1988) and ISAACSON (1993) convincingly argued. The latter (ISAACSON (1993: 141-142)) also draws attention to the following passage of Vātsyāyana Pakṣilasvāmin's *Nyāya-bhāṣya*,[143] which directly mentions the idea and explicitly quotes VS(C) 9.13, apparently the earliest Vaiśeṣika reference to supernatural perception.[144]

---

[143] NBh 1.1.3 (p. 9.8–9): *pratyakṣaṁ yuñjānasya yoga-samādhijam "ātmany ātma-manasoḥ saṁyoga-viśeṣād ātmā pratyakṣaḥ" iti.*—'[Another proof of the existence of soul, beside verbal testimony of an authority or inference, is] perception of a [*yogin*] temporarily [engrossed] in meditation, which is born in the state of concentration in *yoga* [in accordance with] the following [*sūtra*]: "Due to particular connection of the self and the mind in the self [there arises] perception of the self".'

[144] Indeed, there is a reference to *samādhi* in NS 4.2.38: *samādhi-viśeṣâbhyāsāt.*—'[The cognition of the true nature of imperfections (see NS 4.2.1 and 1.1.18)] arises due to rehearsed exertion of a particular kind of concentration.' However, one should not take such a reference to

Accordingly, the section into which the discussion of supernatural perception is some time later inserted is VS(C) 9.13–17 and actually, in the version we have in front of us, deals with two kinds of it[145]:

> '[A: The state of a *yogin* temporarily engrossed in meditation (*yukta*, lit. "connected" or "disciplined, concentrated"[146]):]
> [13] Due to particular connection of the self and the mind in the self [there arises] perception of (through?) the self.[147]
> [14] [This perception] also [grasps] other substances, [*sc.* atoms[148] of five elements, time, space, mind].

meditative concentration (*samādhi*) as an indication that Akṣapāda Gautama accepted supernatural perception because there is no necessary link between the two. The explanation of Pakṣilasvāmin Vātsyāyana in NBh ad loc. is a clear indication that what *samādhi* meant was a process that has nothing to do with supernatural perception but was a process of withdrawal of the self's attention from the sense-data: 'This [concentration is a connection of the mind with the soul [only, the mind being] withdrawn (sc. disconnected) from sense-organs and held under control by a restraining effort, and [this connection] is characterised by a desire to understand the true nature [of the categories]' (*sa tu pratyāhṛtasyêndriyebhyo manaso vidhārakeṇa prayatnena dhāryamāṇasyâtmanā saṁyogas tattva-bubhutsā-viśiṣṭaḥ*).

[145] We should be aware, though, that this two-fold division—achieved through the later insertion of VS(C) 9.15—was most probably subsequently imposed on an earlier interpolation which did not know the two kinds of supernatural perception, and that happened under Praśastapāda's influence, see FADDEGON (1918: 293), HONDA (1988: 468–469) and ISAACSON (1993: 144–148), cf. WEZLER (1982: 667).

[146] It corresponds to *yuñjāna* ('connecting' or 'disciplining himself, concentrating') of NBh 1.1.3 (see n. 147).

[147] It is quoted in NBh 1.1.3 (p. 9.8–9) as a proof of the existence of the soul: *pratyakṣaṁ yuñjānasya yoga-samādhijam "ātmany ātma-manasoḥ saṁyoga-viśeṣād ātmā pratyakṣaḥ" iti.*—'[Another proof of the existence of soul, beside verbal testimony of an authority or inference, is] the perception of a [*yogin*] temporarily engrossed in meditation, which is born in the state of concentration in *yoga* [in accordance with] the following: "Due to particular connection of the self and the mind in the self [there arises] perception of the self".' VS(C) 9.13 is also quoted in RVār 5.2, p. 440.9 (as indicated by Muni Jambuvijaya in VS(C), n. 15, p. 234.26–27), and not in RVār 5.22, as ISAACSON (1993: 141) indicates.

Also Kauṇḍinya the Pāśupata accepts this kind of supernatural perception as different from ordinary, sensory variety, see PABh 1.1, p. 7.1–8: *tatra pratyakṣaṁ dvividham indriya-pratyakṣam ātma-pratyakṣaṁ ca. indriya-pratyakṣam indriyârthāḥ śabda-sparśa-rūpa-rasa-gandha-ghaṭâdyāḥ, vyākhyāna-tāpa-mūtra-purīṣa-māṁsa-lavaṇa-prāṇâyāmaiḥ siddham. ātma-pratyakṣaṁ tad-upahāra-kṛtsna-tapo-duḥkhântâdi-vacanāt siddham. yathā prasthena mito vrīhiḥ prasthaḥ. paramârthatas tv indriyârtha-sambandha-vyañjaka-sāmagryaṁ dharmâdharma-prakāśa-deśa-kāla-codanâdy-anugṛhītaṁ sat pramāṇam utpadyate. ātma-pratyakṣaṁ tu cittântaḥ-karaṇa-sambandha-sāmagryam.* See also PABh 3.19, p. 88.20–21: *kṛtsnasya tapaso lakṣaṇam ātma-pratyakṣaṁ veditavyam* (for the translation see n. 173).

[B: The state of a *yogin* no longer engrossed in meditation (*viyukta*, lit. "disconnected" or "undisciplined, no longer concentrated"):]
[15, interpolation:[149]] And [also] due to the contact of the self, sense-organ, mind and object [there arises supernatural perception].[150]
(ŚM: And [also] those whose internal organ (mind) is no [longer] concentrated, whose concentration has been interrupted, [acquire perception] of these [other substances].)
[16] And [there is also supernatural perception] of actions and qualities, since they inhere in [the other substances].
[17] And [also there is supernatural perception] of qualities of the self, since they inhere in the self.'[151]

However, as FADDEGON (1918: 293) suspected—on the basis of *tat-°* in *tat-samavāyāt* of VS(C) 9.16 = (VS(Ś) 9.14) referring naturally to VS(C) 9.14 = (VS(Ś) 9.12), not to the preceding *sūtra*—and as ISAACSON (1993: 144 ff., § 4) demonstrated, VS(C) 9.15 (= VS(Ś) 13) is still a later interpolation and its insertion introduced a two-fold division (known to Praśastapāda) of *yogi-pratyakṣa* into *yukta* and *viyukta*, apparently not known to the author of the earlier passage VS(C) 9.13–14

[148] Thus acc. to Candrānanda, VSV(C): ...*vyāpaka-dravyeṣv ātmanâsaṁyukteṣv apratiṣiddhâtma-saṁyogeṣu ca paramâṇv-ādiṣûbhābyāṁ saṁyukteṣu*...

[149] See ISAACSON (1993) and HONDA (1988).

[150] Cf. VSV(C) 1.15: *sūkṣma-vyavahita-viprakṛṣṭeṣv artheṣu teṣāṁ catuṣṭaya-sannikarṣād api pratyakṣaṁ jāyate. tathâsmad-ādi-pratyakṣeṣu.*—'For these [*yogins* no longer engrossed in meditation] there arises perception of objects which are subtle, concealed [from sight] and distant due to the contact of these four [viz. the self, sense-organ, mind and object][a]. And also of things perceptible to people like us.'

[a] On *catuṣṭaya* (as well as on *traya* and *dvaya*) see also DPŚ$_2$ 146 (p. 191–2): ... *yad jñānaṁ tasyâtmêndriya-mano-'rtha-catuṣṭaya-sannikarṣaḥ karaṇam*. Cf. also the sequence of connection in NBhū, p. 170 (apropos of NSā: *viprayuktâvasthāyāṁ catuṣṭaya-traya-dvaya-sannikarṣād grahaṇaṁ yathā-saṁbavena yojanīyam*): [*catuṣṭaya*:] *tatra rasana-cakṣus-tvācām ... ātmā manasā saṁyujyate, mana indriyeṇa, indriyam arthenêti.* [*traya*:] *śrotreṇârtha-grahaṇe trayāṇām ātma-manaḥ-śrotrāṇāṁ sannikarṣaḥ.* [*dvaya*:] *manasârtha-grahaṇe dvayor ātma-manaso sannikarṣa iti.*

[151] VS(C) 9.13–17 ≈ VS(Ś) 9.1.11–15 ≈ VS(D) 9.11–13:

	13:	*ātmany ātma-manasoḥ saṁyoga-viśeṣād ātma-pratyakṣam.*
[VS(D)	:	absent]
	14:	*tathā dravyântareṣu.*
[VS(Ś)	12:	*tathā dravyântareṣu pratyakṣam.*]
[VS(D)	:	absent]
	15:	*ātmêndriya-mano-'rtha-sannikarṣāc ca.* [= VS(D)]
[VS(Ś)	13:	*asamāhitântaḥ-karaṇā upasaṁhṛta-samādhayas teṣāṁ ca.*]
	16:	*tat-samavāyāt karma-guṇeṣu.* [= VS(D)]
	17:	*ātma-samavāyād ātma-guṇeṣu.* [= VS(D)]

and 16–17. Indeed, when we eliminate *sūtra* 15, we obtain a more consistent, uninterrupted reading, without the unnatural jump in the textual structure.

Praśastapāda's full-fledged description of both kinds of supernatural perception of a *yogin*, either directly engrossed in the practice of *yoga* (*yukta*) or not (*viyukta*), that influenced the later insertion of VS(C) 9.15 into the *Vaiśeṣika-sūtra* section on *yogi-pratyakṣa*, runs as follows:

> '[240] The grasping of the highest universal (i.e. *mahā-sāmānya*) and of [intermediate universals such as] substantiality, qualitativeness, and mobility etc., inherent in a perceptible substratum, through sense-organs which grasp [their] substratum is the [ordinary] perception of people like us. [241] However, in *yogin*s who are temporarily engrossed in meditation (*yukta*) [and] who are superior to us, through the mind influenced by moral excellence (*dharma*) produced by [the practice of] *yoga*, there arises an unerring perception of the intrinsic nature with respect to [such invisible substances as] their own self, the self of others, ether, space, time, air, atoms, mind as well as qualities, actions, universals, individuators which are inherent in these [substances]. [242] On the other hand, in [*yogin*s who are] no longer engrossed in meditation (*viyukta*) due to the contact of the four [viz. the self, sense-organ, mind and object and] thanks to the efficacy of the influence of moral law produced by [the practice of] *yoga*, there arises perception with respect to objects which are subtle, concealed (from sight) and distant[152].'[153]

Just as Praśastapāda's references to god implied the existence of an antecedent Vaiśeṣika tradition, albeit of quite a fresh date, in which that idea had already been established, also in the case of Praśastapāda's mature and particularised description of supernatural perception it seems that the idea of *yogi-pratyakṣa* had already been established in the system for quite some time and it was not Praśastapāda's own innovation.

---

[152] Cf. n. 150.

[153] PBh_1 8.12, p. 187 = PBh_2 240–242: [240] *bhāva-dravyatva-guṇatva-karmatvâdīnām upalabhyâdhāra-samavetānām āśraya-grāhakair indriyair grahaṇam ity etad asmad-ādīnāṁ pratyakṣam.* [241] *asmad-viśiṣṭānāṁ tu yogināṁ yuktānāṁ yoga-ja-dharmânugṛhītena manasā svâtmântarâkāśa-dik-kāla-paramâṇu-vāyu-manaḥsu tat-samaveta-guṇa-karma-sāmānya-viśeṣeṣu samavāye câvitathaṁ svarūpa-darśanam utpadyate.* [242] *viyuktānāṁ punaś catuṣṭaya-sannikarṣād yoga-ja-dharmânugraha-sāmarthyāt sūkṣma-vyavahita-viprakṛṣṭeṣu pratyakṣam utpadyate.*

What attests to a mature state of development of the idea of the *yogin*'s supernatural perception is not only the double division mentioned in the above section of PBh, but also the fact that Praśastapāda finds an additional role for *yogi-pratyakṣa* to play in the Vaiśeṣika ontology. For him it serves as an additional tool, or even a direct, perceptual proof of the existence of the individuators (*viśeṣa*), perhaps the most controversial and debatable ontological postulate of the school, and also of the atoms. This is how he attempts to prove the existence of the individuators by taking recourse to supernatural perception:

> '[370] Similarly to people like us who experience the differentiation in cognition occasioned by equal shapes, qualities, actions, parts or relations, with reference to cows, etc. [as different] from horses, etc.—[e.g. in the form] "[this] cow is white, of swift pace, with a fat neck hump, with a large bell"—in a similar manner *yogin*s, who are superior to us, [experience] the differentiation in cognition with reference to permanent [entities like] atoms as well as minds and souls of liberated people that [all] have identical shapes, qualities and actions. Since there is no other factor [that would make such a differentiation between seemingly identical things possible], the factors thanks to which [the *yogin*s are able to distinguish] each and every substratum [of qualities and actions in the form]: "this is different, that is different", and [thanks to which in those *yogin*s] a recognition arises: "this is that [atom]" with regard to an atom in distant place and time, are ultimate individuators.[154] [371] Suppose, on the other hand, without [postulating the existence of] ultimate individuators, that the *yogin*s possessed such a discrimination through cognition as well as recognition [of individual atoms, which they could acquire] through moral law (*dharma*) produced by [the practice of] *yoga*, what would happen then? It would not be possible [for them to distinguish between atoms etc.] in this

[154] Interestingly, while quoting the passage PBh_1 11, p. 321–322 = PBh_2 370 in his *Nyāya-viniścaya-vivaraṇa*, Vādirāja-sūri omits the above phrase *deśa-kāla-viprakarṣe ca paramâṇau sa evâyam iti pratyabhijñānaṁ ca bhavati*, see NViV 1.121, vol. 1, p. 452.1–3: *tato yad uktam* <> *yogināṁ nityeṣu tulyâkṛti-guṇa-kriyeṣu paramâṇuṣu muktâtma-manaḥsu cânya-nimittâsambhava ebhyo nimittebhyaḥ pratyādhāraṁ vilakṣaṇo 'yaṁ* <> *iti pratyaya-vyāvṛttiḥ* <> *te 'ntyā viśeṣāḥ*. (The dotted underline shows *varia lectio*, the square brackets <> indicate that some portions preserved in the edited text of PBh are missing in NViV).

That could either mean that Vādirāja-sūri omitted phrase *deśa-kāla-viprakarṣe*... deliberately, for it was not relevant to his critique of the *viśeṣa* category (although his way of quoting other work is generally quite faithful), or the phrase was not present in the manuscripts of PBh Vādirāja-sūri used, which might further imply that the phrase is a latter addition to PBh.

> way, [i.e. merely through such a supernatural perception]. Just like a cognition of white in something which is not white or a recognition of something completely invisible does not arise through moral law produced by [the practice of] *yoga*, and if it could [arise] it would be false, in the same manner the *yogin*s can possess neither discrimination through cognition nor a recognition through moral law born of [the practice of] *yoga* without [the existence of] ultimate individuators[155].[156]

The above account apparently refers primarily to *yogin*s who are temporarily engrossed in meditation (*yukta*, *yuñjāna*), because what is at stake is the *yogin*s' capability of perceiving atoms, viz. the competence Praśastapāda reserves for them[157]. Praśastapāda's strategy is to liken, by analogy[158] (*yathâsmad-ādīnāṁ ... tathâsmad-viśiṣṭānāṁ yogināṁ*), the operation and scope of supernatural perception, allegedly possessed by *yogin*s, to commonplace perception of ordinary humans. At the same time supernatural perception functions as a vital tool for 'the cognoscenti' to access the layers of reality which are beyond the scope or ordinary cognitive apparatus and which is at the same time the ontological fundament of Vaiśeṣika universe and metaphysics. We will subsequently see that it is not the sole role assigned to supernatural perception.

---

155 The idea of the individuators that make it possible for the *yogin*s to distinguish between various atoms is recapitulated in YBh 3.53 (p. 313.7).

156 PBh_1 11, p. 321–322 = PBh_2 370–371: [370] *yathâsmad-ādīnāṁ gav-ādiṣv aśvadibhyas tulyâkṛti-guṇa-kriyâvayava-saṁyoga-nimittā pratyaya-vyāvṛttir dṛṣṭā gauḥ śuklaḥ śīghra-gatiḥ pīna-kakudmān mahā-ghaṇṭa iti, tathâsmad-viśiṣṭānāṁ yogināṁ nityeṣu tulyâkṛti-guṇa-kriyeṣu paramâṇuṣu muktâtma-manaḥsu cânya-nimittâsambhavād yebhyo nimittebhyaḥ pratyādhāraṁ vilakṣaṇo 'yaṁ vilakṣaṇo 'yam iti pratyaya-vyāvṛttiḥ, deśa-kāla-viprakarṣe ca paramâṇau sa evâyam iti pratyabhijñānaṁ ca bhavati te 'ntyā viśeṣāḥ.* [371] *yadi punar antya-viśeṣam antareṇa yogināṁ yoga-jād dharmāt pratyaya-vyāvṛttiḥ pratyabhijñānaṁ ca syāt tataḥ kiṁ syāt? nâivaṁ bhavati. yathā na yoga-jād dharmād aśukle śukla-pratyayaḥ saṁjāyate atyantâdṛṣṭe ca pratyabhijñānam, yadi syān mithyā bhavet, tathêhâpy antya-viśeṣam antareṇa yogināṁ na yoga-jād dharmāt pratyaya-vyāvṛttiḥ pratyabhijñānaṁ vā bhavitum arhati.*

157 PBh_1 8.12, p. 187 = PBh_2 241, see above p. 311 and n. 153.

158 Analogy (*upamāna*) is a cognitively valid procedure also for the Vaiśeṣika, albeit it is not classified as a separate cognitive criterion (*pramāṇa*) but merely a subvariety of testimony of an authoritative person, see PBh_1, p. 220 = PBh_2 259: *āptenâprasiddhasya gavayasya gavā gavaya-pratipādanād upamānam āpta-vacanam eva.*—'Analogy based on explanation, by an authoritative person, [what the animal] gayal (Bos Gavaeus) [is like by comparing] the unknown gayal to [well known] cow is nothing but a testimony of an authoritative person.' It is considered different from inference, even such that is based on recognition of the whole from the perception of its parts, see VS(C) 2.1.8: *viṣāṇī kakudmān prānte vāladhiḥ sāsnāvān iti gotve dṛṣṭaṁ liṅgam.*—'The visible

4.4.2. Supernatural perception of the seers

Supernatural perception acquired through the practice of *yoga* is not the only kind of such an extrasensory faculty admitted by Praśastapāda. The other kind is *ārṣa-pratyakṣa*[159], or perception of the seers (*ṛṣi*) who are endowed with it 'genetically',[160] viz. they are apparently born with it by virtue of their past good deeds. However, not only seers have it, as Praśastapāda maintains:

> 'The seer's perception is described as such a cognition which makes things known as they are (*sc.* in correspondence to truth) and which arises, by virtue of the contact of the soul and the mind and due to special moral endowment (*dharma*), in the seers, who are revealers of the Vedic lore, as the insight into past, future and present, and into extrasensory things such as moral law etc., which are expounded in the scriptures and which are not expounded [at all]. This [supernatural perception] is possessed by divine beings and seers in an extensive form, [but] also sometimes by ordinary people, for instance when a girl says: "My heart tells [me] that tomorrow my brother will come".'[161]

The new element here is, first, purely extrasensory domain of this supernatural perception and, second, the inclusion of *dharma* in its domain; further it extends to things past and future, rendering predictions, fortune telling, authoritative religious accounts entrusted to scriptural word etc. possible. The seer's perception, which attracts much less attention in PBh, necessarily requires the contact of the self (*ātman*) and the mind (*manas*), and is considered a tool whereby one can directly, or 'perceptually', cognise moral law.

---

inferential sign [necessary for inference] with respect to "cow" [to be inferred] is that it has horns, it has a hump, it has bristled tail at its end, it has a dewlap.'

[159] The Vaiśeṣika distinguish it from *yogi-pratyakṣa*, even though the critics of the idea (the Mīmāṁsaka and the Cārvāka) take these two varieties, *yogi-pratyakṣa* and *ārṣa-pratyakṣa*, as one and the same phenomenon.

[160] The idea of 'genetically' induced supernatural perception is found also in Jainism, see e.g. TS 1.21–22: *dvividho 'vadhiḥ. bhava-pratyayo nāraka-devānām.*—'Clairvoyance is two-fold. [Clairvoyance] occasioned by birth is [possessed] by hell-beings and divine beings.'

[161] PBh_1, p. 258 = PBh_2 288: *āmnāya-vidhātṝṇām ṛṣīṇām atītânāgata-vartamāneṣv atīndriyeṣv artheṣu dharmâdiṣu granthôpanibaddheṣv anupanibaddheṣu câtma-manasoḥ saṁyogād dharma-viśeṣāc ca yat pratibhaṁ yathârtha-nivedanaṁ jñānam utpadyate tad ārṣam ity ācakṣate. tat tu prastāreṇa deva-ṛṣīṇāṁ, kadācid eva laukikānāṁ, yathā kanyakā bravīti śvo me bhrātâgantêti hṛdayaṁ me kathayatîti.*

The idea of the seer's perception (*ārṣa-pratyakṣa*), occasionally called intuition (*pratibha* or *pratibhā*), is mentioned as a special kind of supernatural perception also in *Vaiśeṣika-sūtra* in three recensions: 'The seer's [perception] and the perception of perfected beings [arises] from merits.'[162] This *sūtra* must be again a later interpolation, albeit we find it in all three recensions[163], because in all of them the *sūtra* is entirely mechanically appended at the very end of the respective chapters, without any direct connection to the preceding portion. The reason for such an insertion was most probably the need to accommodate the two-fold division of supernatural perception (*yogi-pratyakṣa* and *ārṣa-pratyakṣa*) found in the *Praśastapāda-bhāṣya*, but not in an earlier version of the *Vaiśeṣika-sūtra*, and to verbalise a reaction to the claims of the Mīmāṁsā school denying the existence of such a perception.

On the other hand, we have clear indications that even at the time of Praśastapāda the belief in supernatural perception did not belong to the Vaiśeṣika canon of convictions accepted universally by all proponents of the school. A section of *Daśapadârtha-śāstra* (DPŚ$_1$, p. 108–109 = DPŚ$_2$ 145–148) unmistakably shows that Candramati did not admit the existence of any supernatural perception, for he explicitly asserts that such categories as atoms, qualities of atoms etc., which are considered by Praśastapāda to be accessible to *yogi-pratyakṣa*, fall in the category of the imperceptibles. Likewise, in no way does he allude to the existence of or to the mere idea of liberation (*mokṣa*). Hakuju UI (1917: 11–12) rightly observes that

> 'The treatise has no mention of Īśvara, as in the case of *V.S.* (*Vaiśeṣika-sūtra*—P.B.); there is also no description of the way to emancipation (*mokṣa*); even if the second sort of merit (*dharma*, one of the twenty-four attributes) corresponds to it, it is only a definition of it. As a consequence, the author does not allude to *yoga*, *yogin*, or anything supernatural.'

4.4.3. Supernatural perception and moral law

Both accounts of supernatural perception, i.e. that of a *yogin* and that of a seer, associate it, either directly or indirectly, with moral law (*dharma*) and liberation (*mokṣa*). In the case of *ārṣa-pratyakṣa*, the link is immediate: those who are endowed with this kind of supernatural perception are capable of cognising *dharma* directly. In the

---

[162] VS(C) 9.28 = VS(Ś) 9.2.18 = VS(D) 9.22: *ārṣaṁ siddha-darśanaṁ ca dharmebhyaḥ*.

[163] Candrānanda in his exposition (VSV(C), p. 71) recapitulates PBh$_1$ 8.12, p. 258 = PBh$_2$ 288.

case of the *yogin*'s supernatural perception the link is a bit less obvious and not so explicit.

To understand it better, we should first see how Praśastapāda defines moral law (*dharma*):

> '[308] Moral law is a quality of the human being. It is the cause of pleasure, good and liberation for the agent;[164] it is extrasensory … [315] The practice of *yoga* is the moral law (i.e. obligation) [to be followed by] anyone who has [so far] been in any of the [first] three [life stages (*āśrama*)], who has acquired faith, after he has granted (sc. taken the single vow of) permanent amiability (lit. fearlessness) to all creatures [and] has laid down his [mundane] duties, who is not negligent as regards rules (*yama*) and restraints (*niyama*)[165] [and] becomes, due to constant rumination over the six ontological categories, a renouncer [in the last life stage of *saṁnyāsin*]. [316] Moral law arises through the contact of the soul and mind in dependence on these [above-mentioned] means and through purity of intention with no regard of any visible goal.'[166]

This succinct account first states that *dharma*, although a quality of the soul (*puruṣa-guṇa*), is not amenable to sense organs (*atīndirya*) and one therefore requires special faculty to cognise it directly or is forced to rely on another person's account who has seen it directly himself. Since *dharma* is the quality of the soul and under normal circumstances the soul, at least for the Naiyāyika-Vaiśeṣika, is incapable of self-cognition, or self-illuminating cognition (*sva-saṁvitti*, *sva-saṁvedana*), what is required for the perception of *dharma* is a direct contact of the soul and mind (*ātma-manasoḥ saṁyogād dharmôtpattiḥ*). Further, Praśastapāda declares that there exists the means to cognise the moral law, which is the practice of *yoga* (*yoga-prasādhana*), being at the same time the moral duty of a renouncer. Commenting on

[164] This is a reference to two-fold goal of moral law as expressed in VS(C) 1.1.2: *yato 'bhyudaya-nihśreyasa-siddhiḥ sa dharmaḥ.*—'That from which [results] the attainment of mundane prosperity and the highest good is moral law.'

[165] These are the well-know first two steps of the eight-fold path of *yoga*, see YS 2.29: *yama-niyamâsana-prāṇâyāma-pratyāhāra-dhāraṇā-dhyāna-samādhayo 'ṣṭāva aṅgāni.* It is certainly not a coincidence to find these two categories of the Yoga school in Praśastapāda's passage, which attests to the influence of *yoga* practice and belief on the latter.

[166] PBh_1, p. 272 = PBh_2 308, 315–316: [308] *dharmaḥ puruṣa-guṇaḥ. kartuḥ priya-hita-mokṣa-hetur atīndiryo* … [315] *trayāṇām anyatamasya śraddhāvataḥ sarva-bhūtebhyo nityam abhayaṁ dattvā saṁnyasya svāni karmāṇi yama-niyameṣv apramattasya ṣaṭ-padârtha-prasaṁkhyānād yoga-prasādhanaṁ pravrajitasyêti.* [316] *dr̥ṣṭaṁ prayojanam anuddiśyâitāni sādhanāni bhāva-prasādaṁ câpekṣyâtma-manasoḥ saṁyogād dharmôtpattir iti.*

the passage, Vyomaśiva makes the idea explicit by adding that the practise of *yoga* is the only means to achieve *dharma*.[167] The adept of *yoga* who is engaged in preliminary stages of the eight-fold path of *yoga* (*yama-niyameṣv apramattasya*) has one aim: liberation, which is achieved by virtue of knowing moral law (*kartuḥ* ... *mokṣa-hetuḥ*).

An additional support for the thesis that Praśastapāda did view the yogic path as a means to liberation is the expression 'permanent amiability', or 'constant fearlessness' (*nityam abhayaṁ*), which has its parallel in *Nyāya-bhāṣya* defining the state of liberation (*apavarga*):

> 'This is [the state of] amiability (lit. fearlessness), without decay, a state of immortality, the absolute, the attainment of tranquillity.'[168]

Moreover, the idea of 'granting permanent amiability to all living beings' (*sarva-bhūtebhyo nityam abhayaṁ dattvā*) is not an invention of proponents of the Nyāya-Vaiśeṣika systems but is an echo of an earlier expression, i.e. *sarva-bhūtâbhaya-pradāna*, well anchored in the tradition of the *Yoga-bhāṣya*:

> 'Being [continuously] roasted on dreadful coals of transmigration, I take the refuge in moral rules of *yoga* by granting amiability (lit. fearlessness) to all creatures.'[169]

Thus, the direct link between a *yogin*, who acquires supersensory faculties through the practice of *yoga*, and *yogi-pratyakṣa*, being precisely such a supersensory faculty, is therefore quite well established. Similarly well authenticated is the relation between the practice of *yoga*, understood as one's ultimate duty, and liberation (*mokṣa*). Thus, the explicit link between supernatural faculty and the perception of *dharma*, which was straightforwardly expressed in the case of the seer's perception (*ārṣa-pratyakṣa*), also holds in the case of the first kind of supernatural perception, that of a *yogin*. Consequently, such a supernatural perception of any form (either *yogi-*° or *ārṣa-pratyakṣa*) is ultimately related to the purpose of achieving the final goal, liberation.[170]

---

[167] VyV *ad loc.*, vol. II, p. 234.24: *yoga eva tasya dharma-sādhanam*.

[168] NBh 1.1.22, p. 22.3: *tad abhayam ajaram amṛtyu-padaṁ brahma kṣema-prāptir iti*.

[169] YBh 2.33, p. 217.10–11: *ghoreṣu saṁsārâṅgāreṣu pacyamānena mayā śaraṇam upāgataḥ sarva-bhūtâbhaya-pradānena yoga-dharmaḥ*.

[170] The salvific goal does not exhaust all possible motivations why *yoga* was practised: there are other traditions the adepts of which seek supernatural perception and other powers (*siddhi*, *ṛddhi*) for their own sake, not for the sake of liberation, but such a siddhi-tradition is not relevant to the present issue.

The direct link between *yogi-pratyakṣa* of the *yukta-yogins* and *dharma* is embedded in Praśastapāda's statement: "in *yogins* who are temporarily engrossed in meditation (*yukta*) [and] who are superior to us, through the mind influenced by moral excellence (*dharma*) produced by [the practice of] *yoga*"[171], which relates moral excellence to the practice of *yoga*, resulting in the superiority of *yogins* and in their inner excellence of supernatural perception that eventually grasps invisible substances such as their own selves, the selves of others, ether, space, time, air, atoms, mind as well as qualities, actions, universals, individuators which are inherent in these substances. A similar dependence between the acquisition of supernatural perception and moral law is expressed by Praśastapāda in another passage[172] which postulates that *yogins* can supernaturally perceive ultimate individuators inherent in atoms, accordingly discriminate between the atoms and recognise them after some time thanks to moral endowment (*dharma*) achieved thanks to their engagement with the practice of *yoga*.

The above passages dealing with supernatural perception as well as the recurrent expression *yoga-ja-dharma*[173] additionally demonstrate that the practice of *yoga* was conceived of as being instrumental in moral upliftment and inner (spiritual) progress.

4.4.4. Supernatural perception and the gradual development argument

I shall now attempt to demonstrate that the acceptance of supernatural perception eventually entails, in the tradition of Praśastapāda and/alias Praśastamati, the acceptance the idea of omniscience, or supreme knowledge (*atiśaya-jñāna, jñānâtiśaya*), to which the concept is indirectly and logically related. I would even venture to assert that it was a necessary corollary of the omniscience claim.

In his descriptions of *yogi-pratyakṣa*, Praśastapāda indirectly follows at least two lines of reasoning that may count as hidden arguments for omniscience, already referred to above:

---

[171] PBh_1 8.12, p. 187 = PBh_2 241, see above p. 311 and n. 153.

[172] PBh_1 11, p. 322 = PBh_2 371, see above p. 313, n. 156.

[173] Altogether five occurrences of *yoga-ja-dharma* in PBh_1 8.12, p. 187 = PBh_2 241–242 (n. 153) and PBh_1 11, p. 322 = PBh_2 371 (n. 156). A parallel is found in a commentary on the *Pāśupata-sūtra*, in which Kauṇḍinya explains that supernatural perception arises thanks to ascetic practices, see PABh 3.19, p. 88.20–21: *kṛtsnasya tapaso lakṣaṇam ātma-pratyakṣaṁ veditavyam.*— 'One should know the defining feature of all the austerities is [supernatural] perception of (through?) the self.'

A1° 'This [supernatural perception] is possessed by gods and seers in an extensive form, [but] also sometimes by ordinary people, for instance when a girl says: "my heart tells [me] that tomorrow my brother will come".'[174]

A2° 'Similarly to people like us who experience the differentiation in cognition occasioned by equal shapes, qualities, actions, parts or relations, with reference to cows, etc. [as different] from horses, etc.—[e.g. in the form] "[this] cow is white, of swift pace, with a fat neck hump, with a large bell"—in a similar manner *yogin*s, who are superior to us, [experience] the differentiation in cognition with reference to permanent [entities like] atoms and minds and souls of liberated people that have identical shapes, qualities and actions.'[175]

Both these descriptions rely on what I would call 'gradual development argument' for omniscience, well attested in Indian philosophical literature.

The underlying structure of such an argument could be phrased as follows:

T4° 'Supreme knowledge (omniscience) is possible, because we observe a gradual development of cognitive faculties',[176]

or, alternatively, more universally:

T5° 'An invisible perfect condition x (e.g. liberation, omniscience, extrasensory perception) is possible, because there is a gradation of the respective faculty".

A classical and lucid formulation of the argument can be found some time later in Jayanta-bhaṭṭa's *Nyāya-mañjarī*, who merely recapitulates an older version of it as follows:

> 'The proof [of supernatural perception] is the excellence (culmination) of perception. For it is as follows: a person like us whose sight relies [on light] notices a number of things placed in proximity. Cats[177], on the other hand, can recognise even [a thing] that has fallen into a place covered with a layer of mud in the thickest possible darkness. Fur-

[174] PBh$_1$, p. 258 = PBh$_2$ 288. *Vide supra*, p. 314, n. 161.

[175] PBh$_1$ 11, p. 321 = PBh$_2$ 370. *Vide supra*, p. 313, n. 156.

[176] Cf. BALCEROWICZ (2005: 180–181 and n. 133).

[177] The rare expression *undura-vairin* ('enemies of mice') is explained by Jayanta-bhaṭṭa himself later as *vṛṣa-daṁśa*, see NMa$_1$, Vol. 1, p. 269.6–10 = NMa$_2$, Vol. 1, p. 157.17: *sampāti-vṛṣa-daṁśa-dṛśoḥ*. The term *vṛṣa-daṁśa* ('having strong teeth'), i.e. 'the cat', is listed, e.g., in the *Amara-kośa* as one of the synonyms of 'the cat', see AmK 2.5.6ab, p. 242:

otur biḍālo mārjāro vṛṣa-daṁśaka ākhu-bhuk /

thermore, one learns from the *Rāmâyaṇa* epic that the king of vultures named Sampāti could even see Sītā (lit. the spouse of Daśaratha's son) in the distance of a hundred miles. This precisely is the excellence (culmination) of perception, just like the culmination of such qualities as white etc., which is based on gradation. Hence it is understood that there is the highest culmination without any higher culmination. And therefore those in whom there is the highest intensity of this [perception] are praised as *yogin*s. So the topmost culmination means that [*yogin*s'] perception has as its domain [things] that are subtle, concealed [from sight], distant, past, future etc.'[178]

At first glance, one might say that the above passage only deals with supernatural perception of *yogin*s (*yogi-pratyakṣa*), not with omniscience. Jayanta, however, dispels such doubts by himself making a direct link to omniscience, first by quoting Kumārila-bhaṭṭa's criticism of the idea, in which the term *sarva-jña* expressly occurs,[179] and subsequently by himself referring to the 'all-perceiving *yogin*s'.[180] Accordingly, what Jayanta-bhaṭṭa says is the following: some creatures can only see things in proximity when illuminated by light, some can also see objects in the dark, while others can perceive things in distance, and still others can grasps extremely remote objects, etc.; therefore there must be a limit to this gradual increase of perceptive powers which is their complete consummation in the form of omniscience.

The argument rests on an almost universally Indian fear of infinite regress (*anavasthā*), the literally meaning of which is 'lack of foundation', the designation itself quite suggestive of such a fear. Alternatively, what was generally considered a

---

[178] NMa$_1$, Vol. 1, p. 268.3–11 = NMa$_2$, Vol. 1, p. 157.1–7: *darśanâtiśaya eva pramāṇam. tathā hy asmad-ādir apekṣitâloko 'valokayati nikaṭa-sthitam artha-vṛndam, undura-vairiṇas tu sāndra-tama-tamaḥ-paṅka-paṭala-vilipta-deśa-patitam api saṁpaśyanti. sampāti-nāmā ca gṛdhra-rājo yojana-śata-vyavahitām api daśaratha-nandana-sundarīṁ dadarśêti rāmâyaṇe śrūyate, so 'yaṁ darśanâtiśayaḥ śuklâdi-guṇâtiśaya iva tāra-tamya-samanvita iti gamayati param api niratiśayam atiśayam. ataś ca yatrâsya paraḥ prakarṣas te yogino gīyante. darśanasya ca paro 'tiśayaḥ sūkṣma-vyavahita-viprakṛṣṭa-bhūta-bhaviṣyad-ādi-viṣayatvam.*

[179] MŚV 2.112 quoted in NMa$_1$, Vol. 1, p. 269.13–14 = NMa$_2$, Vol. 1, p. 158.1–2:

ekena tu pramāṇena sarva-jño yena kalpyate /
nūnaṁ sa cakṣuṣā sarvān rasâdīn pratipadyate iti //

[180] NMa$_1$, Vol. 1, p. 1.271.1–2 = NMa$_2$, Vol. 1, p. 158.11–12:

satyaṁ sāhasam etat te mama vā carma-cakṣuṣaḥ /
na tv eṣa durgamaḥ panthā yogināṁ sarva-darśinām //

'Surely it would be rash [to claim that] this moral law (*dharma*) [is visible] to physical eyes of you or me. But this is not an impossible path for all-perceiving *yogin*s.'

logical fallacy was occasionally[181] also called 'unreachable limit' (*alabdha-pariniṣṭha*). Any assumption that allows for such an infinite regress must *ex definitione* be wrong. Therefore, while admitting of any gradation of supernatural faculties, one has to admit an upper limit of the gradation, or apex, when the faculties reach their maximum.[182]

Such an argument is not completely new and we find it as early as in Bhartṛhari's *Vākyapadīya*:

> 'It is known that the cognition, encompassing all senses,[183] of those who are superior to us[184] with respect to [imperceptible universals stems] from repeated practise, just like [the knowledge] of specialists as regards certain [objects such as] gems, silver coins etc.[185,186]

The same idea of gradual progression, or growth, up to the climax, which underlies the above verse, is explicitly expressed by Bhartṛhari elsewhere:

> '[64/63] Whatever common quality *P* of an object (model, standard) *x* to which another object *y* is compared and of the object *y* that is compared to the object (model, standard) *x* is resorted to, some [other] property *R*, different from *P*, stands out that characterises the objects *x*, *y* etc. to which other objects are compared. [65/64] Whatever quality *P*, which is the cause of culmination (the highest degree) [in an object *x*], is specified as independent (topmost), the fact that this

[181] Cf. e.g. NAV 29.23, p. 457.4–5.

[182] Apparently one distinguished infinite regress as logical fallacy from actual infinity such as the infinity of the world, which is limitless or endless (*anādi*, *ananta*).

[183] The expression *sarvêndriyaṁ* implies extrasensory cognition which transcends all the conventional limitations of sensory organs that are perceptive only of their particular type of sensory data (*viṣaya*), cf. VP 1.155. In other words, the cognition is not sense-dependent and therefore grasps conventionally imperceptible objects.

[184] Cf. VS(C) 2.1.18 [p. 13]: *saṁjñā-karma tv asmad-viśiṣṭānāṁ liṅgam*, and PBh_1 8.12, p. 187 = PBh_2 241, see above p. 311 and n. 153.

[185] See VP 1.35:

pareṣām asamākhyeyam abhyāsād eva jāyate /
maṇi-rūpyâdi-vijñānaṁ tad-vidāṁ nânumānikam //

'The knowledge of specialists as regards certain gems, silver coins etc., which is not communicable to others, comes about only through repeated practise, it is not inferential.'

[186] VP 3.1.46:

jñānaṁ tv asmad-viśiṣṭānāṁ tāsu sarvêndriyaṁ viduḥ /
abhyāsān maṇi-rūpyâdi-viśeṣeṣv iva tad-vidām //

> [quality *P*] is of the highest degree can be known only through [still another] quality *R* that subsists in it.'[187]

Bhartṛhari's idea is that any comparison, which in itself entails gradation, of two items *x* and *y* rests on a property *P*, which we can call first-level property, shared by the two items, and the degree of the property *P* in both of the items *x* and *y* is assessed against still another property *R*, let us say a second-level property, being the criterion for the comparison. What may seem a little ambiguous in the above succinct verses is borne out in the commentary of Harivṛṣabha as follows:

> '[63] In the [verse], the following triad is laid down: (1) an object (model) *x* to which another object *y* is compared, (2) an object *y* that is compared to object *x* and (3) a common property of these two. That being the case, a common quality, which is ascertained in an object of comparison [expressed in the sentence:] "The *kṣatriya* studies recitation like a *brāhmaṇa*", is understood also with respect to the object (model) *x* to which the other object *y* is compared. However, when [in the comparison:] "The recitation study of the *kṣatriya* is similar to the recitation study of a *brāhmaṇa*", both the students are presented as the relata [of the relation] between an object (model) *x* to which another object *y* is compared and an object *y* that is compared to object *x*, then [first-level] properties such as competence etc. of two such recitation study practices, which are differentiated according to their respective substrata, [i.e. the *kṣatriya* and the *brāhmaṇa*], are ascertained as common properties [of these two substrata]. [That being the case], there are [additional second-level] properties such as absolute perfection etc. [that characterise the first-level properties such as] competence etc., which [in their turn] are relata [of the relation] of both the recitation study practices [accomplished by the *kṣatriya* and by the *brāhmaṇa*]. Hence, there is no limit to differentiation, [because also the second-level properties can be compared by taking recourse to a third-level property]. [64] As long as [anything] is presented [in the form] "this" [or] "that" as the main thing, it is the substance. However, the substance [as such] does not have any higher degree or lower degree. Therefore, an object, with respect to which one intends to express

[187] $VP_{1,2}$ 1.64–65 = VP_3 1.63–64:
sāmānyam āśritaṁ yad yad upamānôpameyayoḥ /
tasya tasyôpamāneṣu dharmo 'nyo vyatiricyate //
guṇaḥ prakarṣa-hetur yaḥ svātantryeṇôpadiśyate /
tasyâśritād guṇād eva prakṛṣṭatvaṁ pratīyate //

culmination (high degree), is graded by way of factors (sc. attributes) which subsist [in it], which are the causes of differentiation, which are dependent on it, which are associated with it, [and] which are instrumental in [manifesting] the culmination (high degree). ... As long as one expresses culmination (high degree) of something which subsists as the main thing of the expression "this" [or] "that", so long this [process of] expression [of the gradation] has no end, as having the undesired consequence that one can imagine [still] another factor (sc. attribute) [of higher grade].'[188]

The undesired consequence (*prasaṅga*), mentioned by Harivṛṣabha, indicates a conviction that a process of gradation must have an end: unlimited gradation is the undesired consequence (*prasaṅga*). What was in $VP_{1,2}$ 1.64–65 primarily a linguistic analysis of suffixes *taraP* and *tamaP* that express comparative and superlative degrees of adjectives or substantives was subsequently, in VP 3.1.46, projected onto metaphysics.

The logical structure of the argument of culmination ('gradual development argument'), based on a gradation of degree until it reaches a maximum point, has the following structure:

$$(\forall x\, \exists y\, (y \rightarrow x)) \rightarrow (\exists y\, \forall\, x\, (y \rightarrow x)),$$

If, for any thing x there exists some thing y which is higher in degree, then there exists some thing y which is highest in degree with respect to all things x.

The symbol $\rightarrow$ in the formula denotes any sort of antecedence (logical, causal, physical, spatial etc.).[189]

---

[188] VPV 1.63–64 ad VP 1.64/63–65/64: [63] *ihôpamānam upameyaṁ tayoś ca sādhāraṇo dharma iti tritayam etat siddham. tatra "brāhmaṇavad adhīte kṣatriyaḥ" ity upameye śrūyamāṇaṁ sāmānyam upamāne 'pi pratīyate. yadā tu brahmāṇâdhyayanena tulyaṁ kṣatriyâdhyayanam ity adhyetārau upamānôpameyayoḥ sambandhitvenôpādīyete, tadâdhyayanayor āśraya-viśeṣa-bhinnayoḥ sauṣṭhavâdayo dharmāḥ sādhāraṇatvena pratīyante. sauṣṭhavâdīnām apy adhyayana-sambandhināṁ pariniṣpatty-ādayo dharmā iti nâsti vyatirekasyâvacchedaḥ.* [64] *yāvad idaṁ tad iti prādhānyenôpādīyate tad dravyam. na ca drayasya prakarṣâpakarṣau sta ity aśritair bheda-hetubhiḥ para-tantraiḥ saṁsargibhir nimittaiḥ prakarṣe savyāpāraiḥ pracikīrṣito 'rthaḥ prakṛṣyate. ... yāvad idaṁ tad iti-vyapadeśasya prādhānyenâśritasya prakṛṣṭa-vyapadeśaḥ kriyate, tāvad vicchinno 'yaṁ nimittântara-parikalpanā-dharma-prasaṅga*[a] *iti.*

[a] Recte: *avicchinno* and °*-parikalpanā-prasaṅga*, cf. VPA ad loc., p. 113.28: *tāvad avicchinno 'yaṁ tatra tatra nimittântara-parikalpanā-dharma-prasaṅga*[*ḥ*].

[189] The structure of this proof resembles the proof of god's existence which we find in Thomas Aquinas' *Summa Theologiae* classified as 'the forth way', or the argument 'from the degrees of

A very similar structure relying on which Praśastapāda's acceptance of supernatural perception leads him to the acceptance of god's omniscience is found on a number of occasions in arguments for the existence or perfection of god, which attests to the fact that the logical argumentative structure was quite widespread in India. The first such type is the arguments which correspond to the cosmological argument: from the first cause (*kāraṇa*), known to Uddyotakara[190] and later to Jayanta[191], as well as from the first mover, likewise known both Uddyotakara[192] and to Jayanta[193].

Still before Uddyotakara, we come across an argument from perfection (**guṇa-viśiṣṭa-saṁpad*), which proves most relevant for our discussion. It is an Indian version of the well-known argument that there must be a real standard of perfection to make any hierarchy of beings possible. The argument underlies Vātsyāyana Pakṣilasvāmin's formulation of god's qualities:

> 'God is something more than soul, being distinguished by his special qualities. When one examines the notion of the soul, it is not possible to conceive of this [god] as anything else [other than as a kind of soul]. Since he is something distinguished by complete absence of evil,

perfection'. The logical flaw of this argument is structurally similar to two other arguments of god's existence ('from the movement' and 'from the efficient cause'), for the first time formulated by Aristotle at the beginning of his *Metaphysics*, at least in one respect. What the argument says is that we can order a set of, say, all possible white things in such a way that there will always be another thing greater in degree (whiter), until we reach the maximum white, or the most perfect white, or we reach the most perfect being in the hierarchy of all entities in the world which is god (which would be Thomas Aquinas's argument). Similarly, we can order all acts of perception so that it will culminate in the most perfect perception (*yogi-pratyakṣa* or *sarva-jñāna*), for which there will be other perfection that is better in degree. The grave logical flaw in the argument is that is not logically permissible to validly interchange the places of the quantifiers in a formula as follows: $\forall x\ \exists y\ (T(x, y)) \rightarrow (\exists x\ \forall y\ (T(x, y))$, whereas the following is a tautology: $\exists x\ \forall y\ (T(x, y)) \rightarrow \forall y\ \exists x\ (T(x, y))$. Besides, there is nothing logically binding that would force us to accept the termination of an infinite succession in a chain of events. In other words, one could admit a gradual quantitative growth of clearness of perception without any qualitative change.

[190] NV_1 4.1.21, p. 460.16 = NV_2, p. 433.1: *tad-kāritatvāt ... nimitta-kāraṇam īśvaraḥ.*

[191] NMa_1, Vol. 1, p. 492.2–3, com., Vol. 1, p. 502.10–13.

[192] NV_1 4.21, p. 461.10–14 = NV_2, p. 433.13–16: *pradhāna-paramâṇu-karmāṇi prāk pravr̥tteḥ buddhimat-kāraṇâdhiṣṭhitāni pravartante acetanatvād vāsy-ādivad iti. yathā vāsy-ādi buddhimatā takṣṇā adhiṣṭhitam acetanatvāt pravartate tathā pradhāna-paramâṇu-karmāṇy acetanāni pravartante tasmāt tāny api buddhimat-kāraṇâdhiṣṭhitāni iti.*

[193] NMa_1, Vol. 1, p. 488–490.

> wrong cognition and torpidity and by the perfection of righteousness, cognition and concentration, god is something more than soul.'[194]

The expression *dharma-jñāna-samādhi-saṁpad* ('the perfection of righteousness, cognition and concentration') is a clear verbalisation of the conviction, that god stands at the top of the hierarchy of entities with respect to all good qualities. Also humans, or other beings for that matter, are possessed of some degree of righteousness, cognition or concentration. However, what distinguishes god from all other individual souls is that he is the only such a substance in which all virtuous qualities find their perfect completion. He corresponds to what Thomas Aquinas would call *maxime ens*. Interestingly, Vātsyāyana applies the same argument by way of diminution of all negative qualities: it is god in whom all the negative qualities, present in all other individual souls in greater or lesser degree, find their complete annihilation.

This harmonises well with a similar reasoning found in Kauṇḍinya's *Pañcârtha-bhāṣya* (PABh, c. 500?) comment on the *Pāśupata-sūtra* thesis that 'there is god of all beings'[195]:

> 'In the [*sūtra*] god is [understood] as someone with respect to whom there is nothing supreme.'[196]

There is still another relevant argument for the existence of god, the structure of which is in fact a slight modification of the previous argument, embedded in the following rhetorical question posed by Vātsyāyana Pakṣilasvāmin:

> 'Who could possibly manage to prove, by way of attributes (inferential signs) of the soul such as cognition etc., that god is not recognisable [or] is beyond [all cognitive criteria]: perception, inference and scriptural testimony?'[197]

The obvious (albeit not really logically sound) reply to the quandary, which is supposed to rectify the doubt, would be the following argument: 'There is god, because he is inferred trough such perceptible attributes as cognition etc.' And this involves a gradation of (the intensity of) the attribute, i.e. of perception. Also such an argument would have to rely on the same idea of gradation: we prove the exis-

---

[194] NBh 4.1.21, p. 228.6–7: *guṇa-viśiṣṭam ātmântaram īśvaraḥ. tasya ātma kalpāt kalpântarânupapattiḥ. adharma-mithyā-jñāna-pramāda-hānyā dharma-jñāna-samādhi-saṁpadā ca viśiṣṭam ātmântaram īśvaraḥ.*

[195] PS 5.43, p. 145.1: *īśvaraḥ sarva-bhūtānām.*

[196] PABh 5.43, p. 145.2: *atra niratiśaya aiśvaryeṇa īśvaraḥ.*

[197] NBh 4.1.21, p. 228.14: *buddhyâdibhiś câtma-liṅgair nirupākhyam īśvaraṁ pratyakṣânumānâgama-viṣayâtītaṁ kaḥ śakta upapādayitum.*

tence of ordinary souls through the observation of their ordinary attributes, and we know of the existence of god, super-soul, through his extraordinary attributes.

The argumentative structure was well-known among the Jainas, even prior to Praśastapāda, a good example being Kundakunda's *Pavayaṇa-sāra* (ca 4th–5th centuries) and his 'proof' of liberation in which he applies the same gradual development argument, that rests on the idea of gradual purification, or natural development, till one reaches a perfectly pure condition, or perfection (*siddhatva*), tantamount to liberation, characterised by perfect omniscience (*kevala-jñāna*) and perfect 'omni-perception' (*kevala-darśana*):[198]

> '[45] Perfected souls (saints) [achieve their condition] as a result of merit (or: auspicious *karman*). Their activity is, however, a natural development, which is free from [inauspicious *karman* such as] confusion etc., and therefore it is known as "resulting from the destruction [of karman]" (*kṣāyika*)[199]. [46] If the soul itself could not become either good or bad by virtue of its own essential nature alone, there would be no mundane world (transmigration) for all the bodies endowed with a soul.'[200]

Also Samantabhadra (contemporary with Dharmakīrti) avails himself of the same argument in the *Āpta-mīmāṁsā*:

> '[4] A complete destruction of defects and karmic veils is possible, because a complete consummation [of the gradual purification process] is [possible], just like a [complete] annihilation of both external and internal blemishes in particular cases with the help of respective

[198] Kundakunda also makes use of what we could call a reverse gradual development argument in his *Samaya-sāra* 222–223, in which the development towards perfection of the soul is compared to a conch which is step by step turning into black until it becomes completely black and dirty.

[199] Cf. TS 10.1: *moha-kṣayāj jñāna-darśanâvaraṇântarāya-kṣayāc ca kevalam.*—'Absolute knowledge [arises] from the destruction of [the *karman* called] confusion and from the destruction of the *karmans* obstructing and veiling [innate] cognition and perception/conation.'

[200] PSā 1.45–46:

puṇṇa-phalā arahaṁtā tesiṁ kiriyā puṇo hi odaiyā /
mohâdīhiṁ virahiyā tamhā sā khāiga tti madā //
jadi so suho va asuho ṇa havadi ādā sayaṁ sahāveṇa /
saṁsāro vi ṇa vijjadi savvesiṁ jīva-kāyāṇaṁ //

Comp. also SSā 204.

> causes.[201] [5] Objects that are subtle, concealed [from sight] and distant remain [always] directly perceptible to someone, because they are inferable, just as fire etc. [is inferable from visible smoke]—such is a proof of the omniscient [Jina].'[202]

Similar arguments based on the idea of the gradation of attributes can be found also in Buddhist works, e.g. with Dharmakīrti:

> 'The *yogin*'s cognition is produced by the ultimate consummation (intensity) of contemplation of existing objects.'[203]

Dharmakīrti's description of supernatural perception achievable to an adept of *yoga* supplies a nucleus of a proof of *yogi-pratyakṣa* which in its crudest form would assume the formulation: 'Supernatural perception is possible, because it can be achieved by consummation (perfection) of practice (meditation).' In other words, uninterrupted spiritual practice and meditation have to necessarily lead to their culmination in the form of omniscience. Of course, such an argument in Buddhist (or Jaina) context did not lead one to accept the existence of a divine being endowed with perfect qualities but to accept the possibility of the existence a perfect cognition in a human form (that of Buddha, Bodhisattva or Tīrthaṁkara). Dharmakīrti's commentator, Dharmottara explains that 'contemplation (meditation) of an entity is the perpetual (lit. again and again) reflection on it'[204], and emphasises the gradual development that finally leads to supernatural perception, by emphatically dividing the process into three stages:[205] the consummation (intensity) of contemplation (*bhāvanā-prakarṣa*)[206], the apogee of the intensity (*prakarṣa-paryantâvasthā*)[207] and, ultimately, the *yogin*'s perception (*yogi-pratyakṣa*) as the final stage[208 209].

---

[201] For the analysis of the verse, being a formulation of a proof of liberation, and its soteriological implications see BALCEROWICZ (2005).

[202] ĀMī 4–5:

doṣâvaraṇayor hānir niḥśeṣâsty atiśāyanāt /
kvacid yathā sva-hetubhyo bahir antar mala-kṣayaḥ //
sūkṣmântarita-dūrârthāḥ pratyakṣāḥ kasyacid yathā /
anumeyatvato 'gny-ādir iti sarva-jña-saṁsthitiḥ //

[203] NB 1.11: *bhūtârtha-bhāvanā-prakarṣa-paryantajaṁ yogi-jñānaṁ cêti.*

[204] NBṬ 1.11, p. 67.5: *bhūtasya bhāvanā punaḥ punaś cetasi viniveśanam.*

[205] Cf. NAGASAKI (1988: 349–350).

[206] NBṬ 1.11 (p. 67.5–6): *bhāvanāyāḥ prakarṣo bhāvyamānârthâbhāsasya jñānasya sphuṭâbhatvârambhaḥ.*—'The consummation (intensity) of contemplation is the beginning of [the process in which] cognition [the contents of which is] the image of the object being contemplated represents [this object] in a clear way.'

[207] NBṬ 1.11 (p. 67.6–68.2): *prakarṣasya paryanto yadā sphuṭâbhatvam īṣad asaṁpūrṇaṁ bhavati. yāvad dhi sphuṭâbhatvam aparipūrṇaṁ tāvat tasya prakarṣa-gamanam. saṁpūrṇaṁ tu*

It is difficult at this stage to say when, where or with whom the gradual development argument originated. One of the earliest sources is certainly *Yoga-bhāṣya*:

> 'Further, his (god's) supremacy is without any equal excellence [that could compare with it]. To begin with, [his] excellence is not exceeded by any other excellence, [because] that very thing which would be excelling over [it] would necessarily be this very excellence [of god]. Therefore, where the excellence reaches its upper limit that is god. Moreover, there is no excellence that is equal to his. Why? [Because] when out of two [seemingly] equal things one thing is desired at the same time [and] and the thing is selected (lit. established) as follows: "This one must be new; that one must be old", then it is automatically follows that the other is inferior because it falls short of [satisfying] the desired expectation.[210] And it is not the case that for two [seemingly] equal things both are achieved as the desired object simultaneously, because of the contradiction in terms. Therefore the one whose supremacy is without any [seemingly equal excellences is god.'[211]

In view of the usage of the term *atiśaya* or *niratiśaya* in the *Praśastapāda-bhāṣya*, the *Pañcârtha-bhāṣya* and the *Yoga-bhāṣya*, it is quite possible that both the for-

---

yadā tadā nâsti prakarṣa-gatiḥ. tataḥ saṁpūrṇâvasthāyāḥ prāktany avasthā sphuṭâbhatva-prakarṣa-paryanta ucyate.—'The apogee of the intensity [in such a contemplation] is when the representation of [the object] in a clear way with ultimate intensity is almost complete. For as long as the representation of [the object] in a clear way is not absolutely complete, this is the progress of the consummation (intensity) of such a [contemplation]. But when [it is] complete, then there is no progress [any more]. Therefore, the state prior to the state of complete [representation] is called the apogee of the intensity of the representation of [the object] in a clear way.'

[208] NBṬ 1.11 (p. 68.2–3): *tasmāt paryantād yaj jātaṁ bhāvamānasyârthasya sannihitasyêva sphuṭatarâkāra-grāhi jñānaṁ yoginaḥ pratyakṣam.*—'Such a cognition which is produced by this apogee [of intensity and] which grasps more clear form of the object that is being contemplated as if it were immediately present [in front of the contemplator] is the *yogin*'s perception.'

[209] For further description of the three stages see NBṬ 1.11 (pp. 68.4–69.2). However, Vinītadeva in his *Ṭīkā* distinguishes four stages, see STCHERBATSKY (1930 II: 31, n. 2) and NAGASAKI (1988: 350–354).

[210] In my rendering and understanding of the passage I consciously go counter the interpretation of the *Vivaraṇa*.

[211] YBh 2.24, p. 56.2–57.4: *tac ca tasyâiśvaryaṁ sāmyâtiśaya-vinirmuktam. na tāvad aiśvaryântareṇa tad atiśayyate, yād evâtiśāyi syāt tad eva tat syāt. tasmād yatra kāṣṭhā-prāptir aiśvaryasya sa iśvara iti. na ca tat-samānam aiśvaryam asti. kasmat? dvayos tulyayor ekasmin yugapat kāmite 'rthe navam idam astu purāṇam idam astu ity ekasya siddhau itarasya prākāmya-vighātād ūnatvaṁ prasaktam. dvayoś ca tulyayor yugapat kāmitârtha-prāptir nâsti, arthasya viruddhatvāt. tasmād yasya sāmyâtiśayair vinirmuktam aiśvaryaṁ sa evêśvaram.*

mulations of the gradual development argument phrased by Kauṇḍinya and Praśastapāda go back to the *Yoga-bhāṣya* or to some common source from which the three traditions stem.

What is beyond doubt in all the passages of the number of authors quoted above is that we come across the very same structure of the argument that grades a particular attribute up to its ultimate perfection. The argument is well known also to the Mīmāṁsā school, which refers to it and criticises it.[212]

Consequently, in view of the logical structure of the argument, consistently applied in India to prove a 'perfect apex', it seems justified to hold that Praśastapāda, and/alias Praśastamati for that matter, saw supernatural perception as pointing to the existence of supreme knowledge, or omniscience. My contention gets additional strength in the fact that it was already Vātsyāyana Pakṣilasvāmin who spoke not only of god as such but also of his omniscience, the conviction unambiguously indicated in the statement that 'god is distinguished by the perfection of cognition (*jñāna-saṁpad*)'[213], thus paving the way for Praśastapāda and his tradition to admit of god also in the system of Vaiśeṣika.

I would further maintain that the acceptance of supernatural perception as such was not merely dictated, at least in part, by religious and extra-philosophical convictions of Praśastapāda and of the generation of Vaiśeṣika thinkers around his time,[214] but it was also an essential rational corollary of his belief in god's perfect powers, including his omniscience. In other words, to explain the process of how the idea of god entered the body of convictions of Nyāya-Vaiśeṣika, *yogi-pratyakṣa* was both a corollary of the belief in god's omniscience and a intermediary step in an argument for its existence. It was probably a conscious decision of the philosophers to avail themselves of an idea that was well-known to them from the tradition of Yoga.

---

[212] See e.g. Sucaritamiśra's MŚVṬ *ad* MŚV 4.27, p. 215.15 ff., Pārthasārathi Miśra in NRĀ *ad* MŚV 4.26, p. 102.15-16.

[213] See p. 324, n. 194.

[214] Perhaps the major philosophical function of supernatural perception was to prove the existence of atoms (an idea intimated in the interpolated VS(C) 9.14, see above p. 145, and expressly mentioned in PBh_1 8.12, p. 187 = PBh_2 241, see above p. 311 and n. 153) and individuators (mentioned in PBh_1 8.12, p. 187 = PBh_2 241, and PBh_1 11, p. 321–322 = PBh_2 370–371, see above 312 f.).

5. Conclusion

5.1. God's incompatibility with the system of Nyāya-Vaiśeṣika

Having analysed all the four components of the 'knowability thesis package', viz. (1) the equation *astitva = abhidheyatva = jñeyatva*, (2) the belief in god's existence, (3) the belief in god's omniscience and (4) the belief in supernatural perception, we see that all of them played an important role in justifying the three remaining ones, and it must have been a consistent step to accept them all.

The problematic and controversial equation (*vide supra*, p. 281 and § 3.3 ff.), a rational proof for which seemed entirely lacking, n e e d e d some additional strong support and eventually found it in the new dogmatics of the Vaiśeṣika school. It was god's unlimited cognition which came to be believed to account for the conviction that everything that exists is expressible and cognisable. In other words, god's omniscience was to guarantee that the Vaiśeṣika system was complete and logically consistent in the light of the knowability thesis: anything that is existent enters god's mind, and therefore can always be cognised at least by one person, i.e. god; likewise, it can also be expressed by him. It was god who indirectly provided people with the *Veda*s, that were supposed to contain the gist of all the knowledge about the world. Seen from this perspective, Praśastapāda's equation existentiality = nameability = cognisability' (*astitva = abhidheyatva = jñeyatva*) turns out to be much less controversial. We should remember that this explanation is only partial: it only explains how the Naiyāyikas and Vaiśeṣikas a s philosophers built the idea into their philosophical system. The other important part of the explanatory scheme is their extra-philosophical conviction, i.e. their religious belief which they entertained on account of reasons that were other than philosophical or rational (see below, p. 341 ff.).

The philosophical meaning of strictly religious believe in supernatural perception (§§ 4.4.1–2) lay in the demonstrative force and structure of the 'gradual development argument' (§ 4.4.4), and supernatural perception was merely an indispensable component of the premisses to proof that omniscience was at all possible.

In addition, the admittance of god into the ontology of Nyāya-Vaiśeṣika was no longer a philosophical stance, but a religious belief: all the universe, starting from the indivisible atoms as building blocks of the universe, along with the relations that bind atoms into atomic dyads and triad particles, up to all the ontological categories, is present in god's mind. It is god's mind that stores the design (*vide supra*, p. 297) which precedes the (re)construction of the universe after cyclical periods of dissolution. We know that god is omniscient, because we see the gradation of cognitive faculties in the world, and (faulty) logic, mostly based on the fear of *anavasthā* ('infinite regress'), tells us that the gradation must have its apex somewhere. And, indeed, it does find it in god's mind. Since god can know everything, as the Naiyāyikas and Vaiśeṣikas came to believe, the thesis that everything that exists can be also named and cognised is easily defensible.

The idea of god's existence and omniscience was indispensable in order to accept the equation: existentiality = nameability = cognisability, and *vice versa* the equation was an obvious consequence entailed by the idea of god's omniscience. Even though each of the four components was problematic in itself, they all when taken together, and thus rendering mutual support to each other, made Praśastapāda's decision to introduce all four a consistent move. At the same time the decision demonstrates how philosophical reason eventually capitulated before religious conviction.

What is important, there was nothing in the earlier, pre-Praśastapāda and pre-Vātsyāyana tradition of Nyāya-Vaiśeṣika that could foreshadow such a development and that would eventually prompt the philosophers to accept the contentious equation as a logical consequence of some ancient teachings. Neither was there anything in the system that would, on purely philosophical or logical grounds, impel the philosophers to accept the doctrine of god's existence and omniscience. What is even more significant, the acceptance of god went against 'the logic' of the Nyāya-Vaiśeṣika system, which was strictly realistic.

The theistic shift, correlated with the acceptance of the knowability thesis, eventually proved disastrous to the logical consistency of the Nyāya-Vaiśeṣika system of ethics. In the first place it was the objectivity and impersonality of the workings of *karman* that suffered most.

Prior to that, the workings of karmic retribution were essentially mechanistic, automatic and objective, i.e. not influenced by any extraneous controlling agent. Deeds of transmigrating beings, including humans, were directly translated into their fate in the form of the invisible moral principle (*adr̥ṣṭa*).[215] It was believed to comprise two aspects: a positive element, merit (*dharma*) and a negative element, demerit (*adharma*). These two were qualities of the soul (*ātman*) and inhered in it,[216] being connected via the relation called inherence (*samavāya*), the sixth category (*padârtha*) in the system. These joint properties of merit and demerit had both individual and cosmic dimension: they determined the fate of the soul they inhered in (e.g. the future birth and social status);[217] the fate after death, the movements of

[215] On *adr̥ṣṭa* see FADDEGON (1918: 341–354). On *adr̥ṣṭa* in early Vaiśeṣika see THAKUR (2003: 14–19), who takes *adr̥ṣṭa* in early Vaiśeṣika to mean merely 'unknown factor'.

[216] PBh_1 6, p. 70 = PBh_2 79: *tasya* [= *ātmanaḥ*] *guṇā buddhi-sukha-duḥkhêcchā-dveṣa-prayatna-dharmâdharma-saṁskāra-saṁkhyā-parimāṇa-pr̥thaktva-saṁyoga-vibhāgāḥ*.

[217] NV_1 1.1.1, p. 19.14.

the atomic mind, its egress from the dead body at the moment of death and its ingress into a new body at a new birth etc., digestion, development of the foetus etc.,[218] emotional states such as passion,[219] but also—as a cumulated, collective principle of all souls—they determined the course of world, including the movements of atoms, the attraction of iron particles by the magnet,[220] the circulation of liquids and juices in plants and trees,[221] the upward motion of the fire, the sideward motion of wind etc.,[222] untypical movements in the world, different from basic categories of movement enumerated in VS(C) 5.2.1,[223] all movements of water different than its falling down (e.g. rainfall) as a result of weight in the absence of contact, or support (mentioned in VS(C) 5.2.3), e.g. positive and negative results of rainfalls etc., or absence of rain,[224] and other phenomena of the physical world. The invisible moral principle was thus responsible for all phenomena that would not follow ordinary and known physical rules of the world. People could influence the workings of the invisible moral principle (*adṛṣṭa*) by various kinds of morally relevant behaviour, including rituals, religious activities etc.:

> 'Bath consecration (i.e. bathing in places of pilgrimage), fasting, celibacy, residing in the family of the preceptor, living in a forest [as a renouncer in the third stage of life (*āśrama*)], sacrifice, charity, purification by sprinkling[225], observances regarding cardinal points, constellations, sacrificial formulas and time contribute to the invisible moral principle'[226].

These two properties of all the souls, when combined, could directly affect the material world, without the agency of the souls themselves, because they were in contact with atoms; at the same time the invisible moral principle was believed to

---

[218] VS(C) 5.2.19: *apasarpaṇam upasarpaṇam aśita-pīta-saṁyogaḥ kāryântara-saṁyogāś cêty adṛṣṭa-kāritāni.*

[219] VS(C) 6.2.15.

[220] VS(C) 5.1.15: *maṇi-gamanaṁ sūcy-abhisarpaṇam ity adṛṣṭa-kāritāni.*

[221] VS(C) 5.2.8: *vṛkṣâbhisarpaṇam ity adṛṣṭa-kāritam.*

[222] VS(C) 5.2.14: *agner ūrdhva-jvalanaṁ vāyoś ca tiryak-pavanam aṇu-manasoś câdyaṁ karmêty adṛṣṭa-kāritāni.*

[223] VS(C) 5.2.2: *tad-viśeṣeṇâdṛṣṭa-kāritam.*

[224] VS(C) 5.2.4: *tad-viśeṣeṇâdṛṣṭa-kāritam.*

[225] Cf. MDhŚ 5.115c, 118a, 122a.

[226] VS(C) 6.2.2: *abhiṣecanôpavāsa-brahmacarya-guru-kula-vāsa-vāna-prasthya-yajña-dāna-prokṣaṇa-diṅ-nakṣatra-mantra-kāla-nigamāś*[a] *câdṛṣṭāya.*

[a] VSV(C) *ad loc.* consistently reads °*-niyama-*°: *diṅ-niyamâdayo 'nye viśeṣāḥ. diṅ-niyamaḥ ... nakṣatra-niyamaḥ ... mantra-niyamaḥ ... kāla-niyamaḥ.* Also VSV adopts the reading °- *niyamāś.*

inhere in the souls which were omnipresent, and therefore the results of past deeds stored as subliminal impressions (*saṁskāra*) could in theory be activated, it seems, basically anywhere.[227] The ambiguous term *saṁskāra* ('accumulation') pertained to both material/objective and mental/subjective plains: it comprised physical factors resulting from previous actions and triggering subsequent events, e.g. velocity (VS(C) 5.1.17) of an arrow put in motion, as well as subconscious determinants that were causes activating remembrance (VS(C) 9.22) or as causes, impeding cognitive faculties, of nescience (VS(C) 9.25) etc. Thus, the subliminal impressions mediated in causal relations.

Furthermore, in the causation theory of Nyāya-Vaiśeṣika, the cause—be it efficient cause (*nimitta-kāraṇa*) or the 'trigger' of a causal complex (*kāraṇa-sāmagrī*)—was thought to immediately precede the effect.[228] Also karmic retribution was explained as a part of such a rigid causal system, and a delay in either punitive or rewarding sanction, which one would expect to progress immediately after a respective demeritorious or meritorious deed, was mediated by subliminal impressions that temporarily stored the moral potential of the deed in order to activate it in an appropriate future moment. This mechanistic causal system of deeds committed in the past and future retribution for them required no additional agency. It functioned the way atoms could join or molecules could split without anybody's supervision, once a motion was there in the world. And it was there, because souls were believed to be such sources of motion.

The introduction of god brought confusion to the mechanistic principles of the system of karmic retribution and postulated an additional, supervising moral agent, next to moral agents proper, i.e. humans. God came to play a role of the Grand Moral Accountant, or the ultimate supervisor (*adhiṣṭhātṛ*) and supreme co-ordinator of how merit and demerit are distributed over to moral agents. The idea of supervision of moral law was immediately used by Uddyotakara to devise an argument from moral law to prove god's existence:

---

[227] PBh$_1$, p. 107, 266 = PBh$_2$ 127, 300: *ātmâṇu-saṁyogāt*; PBh$_1$ 5, p. 48.7 ff. = PBh$_2$ 57: *sarvâtma-gata-vṛtti-labdhâdṛṣṭâpekṣebhyas tat-saṁyogebhyaḥ pavana-paramâṇuṣu karmôtpattau*...

[228] Cf. POTTER (1995: 57): 'One, suggested perhaps by Uddyotakara, has it that the supreme cause is the most effective cause, the event which immediately precedes and brings about the production of the effect.' Early Vaiśeṣika sources do not provide too much information of how causality was conceived. The only passages of the *Vaiśeṣika-sūtra* on causality are the following ones: VS(C) 1.2.1–2: *kāraṇâbhāvāt kāryâbhāvaḥ. na tu kāryâbhāvāt kāraṇâbhāvaḥ.*—'From the absence of cause follows the absence of effect. However, it is not the case that from the absence of effect follows the absence of cause'; and VS(C) 4.1.3: *kāraṇa-bhāvād dhi kārya-bhāvaḥ.*—'[The effect of that which is eternal is an inferential sign for its existence,] because from the existence of cause follows the existence of effect.' On causality in Nyāya-Vaiśeṣika and the development of the idea see also Sadananda BHADURI (1975: 271–319) and MATILAL (1975).

> 'Merit and demerit, being superintended by a cause endowed with cognitive awareness, cause retribution of a human being, because they are ultimate causes (instruments), like an axe.'[229]

In other words, since differentiation into morally good and bad actions is, for whatever reasons, accepted as a matter of fact, and if the freedom of human conduct is to be constrained by some principles entailed by some established convention or moral law ('if not everything is permitted'), and if moral law is to be carried out m e a n i n g f u l l y , then a source of morality must exist (sc. 'god exists'). Uddyotakara's reasoning is a counterpart of Immanuel Kant's argument from morality. Absolute god's mind is, therefore, a warrant for moral order and truth in the world. Otherwise, and Uddyotakara would certainly subscribe to Fyodor Dostoevsky's paradox, 'if god does not exist, everything is permitted'.

However, there is nothing binding in Uddyotakara's (or Kant's) argument that would compel us to draw a conclusion that 'god exists' from premisses that there is the *summum bonum* and some rules of conduct, called moral order, exist in a society. Or, which is logically equivalent, from a statement that 'there is no god' it does not follow that moral law does not exist and human conduct is not liable to ethical judgement. From the same premiss, which so much troubled Dostoevsky and probably Uddyotakara, that 'god does not exist', we can draw a contrary conclusion, just as Jean-Paul Sartre did: 'we are alone, with no excuses'. If there is no god, we have to accept that there are no divine regulations which could coerce humans to act accordingly, and often uncritically (merely on the basis of divine authority), and no superhuman commandments which humans could adhere to mechanically and unreflectively in the hope of eternal bliss. 'Man is condemned to be free' and nobody can tell what is good and what is wrong, what alleviates the pain of nothingness and what can ease the fear of extinction. Man is condemned to be 'responsible for everything he does', to find his own way between good and wrong. And that means full responsibility for one's own deeds which no authority has jurisdiction to absolve one from.

Similarly, the earlier concept of karmic retribution implied full responsibility of human agents for their actions, albeit some clearly defined moral principles existed, determined by moral law (*dharma*). It was the individual, and nobody else, who was wholly accountable for all he had done. The consequences of his actions would inevitably return to him, and to nobody else, and in the degree proportional to the extent of good or wrong earlier committed by him. That was possible precisely be-

[229] NV_1 4.1.21, p. 463.13–14 = NV_2, p. 435.5–6: *dharmâdharmau buddhimat-kāraṇâdhiṣṭhitau puruṣasyôpabhogaṁ kurutaḥ karaṇatvād vāsy-ādivad iti*. Cf. n. 136 and VSV(C) 1.1.3: *īśvaraś ca sādhitas tanu-bhuvanâdīnāṁ kāryatayā ghaṭâdivad buddhimat-kartṛkatvânumānena*.

cause there was no extraneous agency which would remove the burden of responsibility from him or exculpate him, or suspend the workings of moral law by dint of grace, mercy or caprice.

Seen in this light, admission of god by the Naiyāyikas and Vaiśeṣikas involves a breach in the consistency of the moral law and undermines inevitability of karmic retribution. Uddyotakara's step brings the philosophers closer to strictly religious views and ethical reflection steers them towards devotion to god (*bhakti*), the highest superhuman instance on whose supervision of karmic retribution human fate partly relies. Clearly, such a theistic approach seriously undermined human ethical agency and moral responsibility, rendering the theory of karmic retribution ultimately ineffectual. Alternatively, assuming that the mechanism of karmic retribution retained its force, god's superintendence would become meaningless, because the only role to play for god would merely be that of an uninvolved and completely inactive observer, which would stand in contradiction with the initial premise of his supervision of the process of redistribution of merit and demerit to moral agents.

No wonder such an approach provoked criticism from various opponents who were keen to point out that god is n o t compatible with *karman*. A Buddhist thinker Vimalamitra (fist half of the sixth century?) observed in his *Abhidharmadīpa* that 'The cause of the world is these [human] deeds, not god etc.'[230]. Even earlier, Vasubandhu opined in the often-quoted verse in the same spirit:

> 'The diversity of the world comes from action (*karman*). This [action] consists in volitional consciousness and all that it brings about'[231].

The same criticism was expressed by the Jainas. Abhayadeva-sūri (TBV, p. 105) was not unique among them to point out that Uddyotakara's argument in support of god's supervision contradicts the original view found in the *Vaiśeṣika-sūtra* that

> 'The upward motion of the fire and the sideward motion of wind etc.,
> the first movement of the atom and of the mind—all this is caused by
> the invisible principle.'[232]

Among numerous arguments against the existence of god found in his *Mīmāṁsā-śloka-vārttika* (MŚV 5.16.42ab–117), Kumārila-bhaṭṭa directly refers to the problem faced by Uddyotakara and other theistic Naiyāyikas and Vaiśeṣikas and points out, in the latter part of the argument below (83cd), that the existence of god as a moral controller renders merit and demerit, to wit moral law, superfluous:

[230] APr [155], p. 118.13: *karmāṇi etāni lokasya kāraṇaṁ nêśvarâdayaḥ.*

[231] AK 4.1ab: *karma-jaṁ loka-vicitryam cetanā tat-kṛtaṁ ca tat.*

[232] VS(C) 5.2.14, see n. 222.

> 'There cannot be any impure (evil) creation [accomplished] by a pure (good) person (sc. god). And since merit and [demerit] were dependent on [god] himself, any distress resulting from them would be inconceivable. On the other hand, if the course [of the world] were determined by these [merit and demerit], then it would imply a different [agency than god's].'[233]

If the fate of humans, their rebirth, social status and happiness are determined by merit and demerit, that nullifies god, a thesis which is by transposition equivalent to saying that if god exists, he nullifies merit and demerit. Kumārila exposes the same paradox even more explicitly elsewhere:

> 'If you accept that it is god's will [to activate the accumulated *karman*s of living beings at the time of recreation of the world after its dissolution], then precisely this [will] is the [ultimate] cause of the world, [not the *karmans*]. However, if it is god's will that determines [the world], then to assume [any role for the accumulated] karman is pointless.'[234]

Therefore, if one is to take human responsibility and ethics seriously, one is compelled to reject the existence of god: the two notions are not compatible.[235]

That this critical judgement concerning the relation between the idea of karmic retribution and god's incompatibility with it was not restricted to philosophers is attested in a popular passage of the *Bhāgavata-purāṇa*:

> '[13] [Every] living being is born by the force of *karman*, and it is by the force of *karman* alone that he expires. Happiness, suffering, fear and tranquillity occur by the force of *karman* alone. [14] Even if there

---

[233] MŚV 5.16.82cd–83:

puruṣasya ca śuddhasya nâśuddhā vikṛtir bhavet //
svâdhīnatvāc ca dharmâdes tena kleśo na yujyate /
tad-vaśena pravṛttau vā vyatirekaḥ prasajyate //

[234] MŚV 5.16.72:

īśvarêcchā yadîṣyeta sâiva syāl loka-kāraṇam /
īśvarêcchā-vaśitve hi niṣphalā karma-kalpanā //

[235] The question how to exculpate god of all the evil in the world, he himself has created (or has been supervising) occurs as early as during the Kuṣāna reign and is found in the so-called Spitzer Manuscript, tentatively dated ca. 250 (FRANCO (2003: 21)). There (*folio* 284, *fragm.*: Sp. 19) we read: 'Living beings experience undesirable births. Did they offend God, so that he causes them to suffer?' (FRANCO (2003: 24)).

is some god who assumes the form of (sc. supervises) the results of the *karmans* of others, he himself engages as an agent, for he has no power over someone who is not an agent. [15] What is the use here of a controller of beings propelled by their own respective *karmans*, who is incapable of modifying what has been determined by people's own nature? [16] For the man, dependent on his own nature, follows his own nature. All this [universe], along with divine beings, demons and humans, is founded on [their] own nature. [17] Living being obtains and casts off bodies of low and high status by force of *karman*. It is nothing but *karman* that is [the living being's] enemy, friend, indifferent bystander, the teacher and god. [18] Therefore a person who is firmly settled in (sc. dependent on) his own nature and performs his own *karman* [alone] should worship *karman*. That alone by the force of which he is instantly propelled is his deity.'[236]

'Taking m o r a l rights seriously', to invoke Ronald Dworkin's famous work, was not the only concern. The first part of Kumārila's above argument (MŚV 5.16.82cd–83ab) highlights another important problem, that of theodicy[237]. At first sight, it would be the idea of karmic retribution, involving merit and demerit, which could help the Naiyāyika-Vaiśeṣika avoid the paradox of evil. Taking recourse to the idea of purpose (*prayojana*), one could argue that god—omnipotent, good and omniscient—merely creates initial environment into which all living beings are cast. It would precisely be the invisible moral principle (*adṛṣṭa*) of the individuals, or the law of karmic retribution, that exonerate god of all moral responsibility because, after the initial moment of recreation of the world, humans experience (*bhoga*) what

[236] BhāgP 10.24.13–18:
karmaṇā jāyate jantuḥ karmaṇâiva pralīyate /
sukhaṁ duḥkhaṁ bhayaṁ kṣemaṁ karmaṇâivâbhipadyate // 13 //
asti ced īśvaraḥ kaścit phala-rūpy anya-karmaṇām /
kartāraṁ bhajate so 'pi na hy akartuḥ prabhur hi saḥ // 14 //
kim indreṇêha bhūtānāṁ sva-sva-karmânuvartinām /
anīśenânyathā kartuṁ svabhāva-vihitaṁ nṛṇām // 15 //
svabhāva-tantro hi janaḥ svabhāvam anuvartate /
svabhāva-stham idaṁ sarvaṁ sadevâsura-mānuṣam // 16 //
dehān uccâvacāñ jantuḥ prāpyôtsṛjati karmaṇā /
śatrur mitram udāsīnaḥ karmâiva gurur īśvaraḥ // 17 //
tasmāt sampūjayet karma svabhāva-sthaḥ sva-karma-kṛt /
anjasā yena varteta tad evâsya hi daivatam // 18 //

[237] On theodicy, or the problem of evil in the world created by omnipotent and omniscient god see the excellent Chapter 9 'The Problem of Evil' in John L. MACKIE (1982), perhaps the best analysis so far of the problem.

they have sown, an argument used much later by Udayana (ĀTV, 410.2–411.5). The major flaw inherent in this argument, and present in the Nyāya-Vaiśeṣika system from the moment it admitted of god as the Grand Moral Accountant, who supervises merit and demerit, was the contradiction how to explain how morally good, omnipotent and omniscient god, who has a purpose and knows the consequences of his act of creation, creates or supervises a world in which also demerit, or evil, exists and, besides, its workings are beyond his control. This paradox was plainly and succinctly pointed out several decades before Kumārila by the anonymous author of the *Yukti-dīpikā*:

> 'Moreover, [the world could not be created by someone endowed with cognitive awareness], **because [the world] is full of utmost suffering**[238]. If ‹this› [world], being a special product, were preceded (sc. caused) by cognitive awareness, then the creator would not have any purpose in furnishing it with utmost suffering. And since the [creator is said to be] omnipotent, he would furnish it with utmost happiness. ... [If you argue that utmost suffering in the world] **is not the fault of god**, [but is there] **because it is occasioned by merit and demerit**, would the following be the opinion [of yours:] "Even though this [world as] a special product is preceded (sc. caused) by god, nevertheless living beings like us, who were brought into existence with utmost happiness at the moment of the initial creation, acquire (lit. come into contact with) lower, intermediate and higher [ranks] of life, caste, character etc. under the influence of merit and demerit. Therefore that is not the fault of god"? **Also this** [argument] **is not correct**. Why? **Because there is no logical reason to** [explain] **the origination of demerit** [in the world in this way]. If god had any authority over merit and demerit, he would create only merit, because [it alone] is the cause of happiness for living beings. [He would] not [create] demerit, because [demerit] has no purpose. Or [perhaps the following is your] opinion: "The origination of merit and demerit is natural, following their own causes, [independently of god]?" [Then you face] a contradiction with what you have said [earlier, namely,] that all manifest (sc. the world) is preceded by god's cognitive awareness (design). Therefore god cannot be the cause [of the world].'[239]

[238] The bolded text marks the *vārttika*s, following the convention of Albrecht Wezler amd Shujun Motegi, the editors of YDī.

[239] YDī 15d, p. 158.13–15, 19, 23–28: *kiṁ ca* **duḥkhôttaratvāt**. *buddhi-pūrvakaś ced ‹ayaṁ›*[a] *kārya-viśeṣaḥ syāt kartur duḥkhôttara-vidhāne prayojanaṁ nâsti, śaktimāṁś çâyam iti*

Another blow to an initial consistency of the karmic retribution dealt by the admission of god to the system was connected with the causal theory of Nyāya-Vaiśeṣika, according to which the effect immediately follows its ultimate cause (*vide supra*, p. 333). There opponents were likewise quick to utilise the incongruity. One of the classical formulations is again found in Kumārila's writings:

> 'Further, it is not consistent [to assume that] for [beings that] have accumulated *karman* there is a period of existence during which there is no [possibility to] experience the [accumulated *karman*], insofar as the results [of the accumulated *karman*] cannot be [temporarily] withheld by another *karman* on account of some other action [e.g. undertaken by god]. And a state in which all [actions exist] without [producing] a result is not possible. Moreover, such a want of fruition [of living beings' accumulated *karman*] cannot be a result of any *karman* at all. On the one hand, if all *karman* were destroyed [during the dissolution of the world], then no [future] creation [of the world] would be conceivable [because there would be no *karman* to determine the course of the new world]. On the other hand, [if the *karman* were not destroyed completely], what would be the causal factor during the time [of recreation of the world] to activate the [accumulated] *karman*s [of living beings, if all *karman*s were dormant]?'[240]

---

sukhôttaram eva vidadhyāt ... ***dharmâdharma-nimittatvād adoṣa iti cet***. *syān matam. yady apîśvara-pūrvako 'yaṁ kārya-viśeṣas tathâpy ādi-sarge sukhôttarāṇām ‹asmād-›*[a]*-utpannānāṁ prāṇināṁ dharmâdharma-parigrahād dhīna-madhyamôtkṛṣṭa-vayo-jāti-svabhāvâdi-yogo bhavati. tataś ca nâparādho 'yam īśvarasyêti.* ***etad apy ayuktam****. kasmāt.* ***adharmôtpatti-hetv-abhāvāt****. īśvaraś ced dharmâdharmayor utpattāv īṣṭe dharmam eva prāṇināṁ sukha-hetutvād utpādayet. nâdharmaṁ prayojanâbhāvāt. atha mataṁ svābhāvikī dharmâdharmayoḥ sva-kāraṇād utpattiḥ. yad uktaṁ sarvam īsvara-buddhi-pūrvakaṁ vyaktam iti [tu]*[c] *tasya vyāghātaḥ. tasmād īśvaro na kāraṇam.*

[a] 'All the Mss read *asya*' (note 2 in YDī, p. 158).

[b] 'All the Mss read *asmad-utpannānāṁ*' (note 3 in YDī, p. 158).

[c] According to the convention of Albrecht Wezler amd Shujun Motegi (YDī, p. XXX), the editors of YDī, the square brackets mark the text to be deleted.

[240] MŚV 5.16.69–71:

na ca karmavatāṁ yuktā sthitis tad-bhoga-varjitā /
karmântara-niruddhaṁ hi phalaṁ na syāt kriyântarāt //
sarveṣāṁ tu phalâpetaṁ na sthānam upapadyate /
na câpy anupabhogo 'sau kasyacit karmaṇaḥ phalam //
aśeṣa-karma-nāśe vā punaḥ sṛṣṭir na yujyate /
karmāṇāṁ vâpy abhivyaktau kiṁ nimittaṁ tadā bhavet //

The idea of karmic retribution demanded that there be no intermediate period when accrued *dharma* and *adharma* are suspended by anyone or anything. And that perfectly harmonised with causal contiguity adopted by the two systems. One might at first read Kumārila's argument as formulated against the idea of the cosmic dissolution (*pralaya*) . And so it was, in part. The context, however, shows that the reasoning was formulated in a line of arguments to disprove the existence of god. In addition, Kumārila's statement that 'the results [of the accumulated *karman*] cannot be [temporarily] withheld by another *karman* on account of some other action [e.g. taken by god]' (5.16.69cd) demonstrates that what is at stake is god's possible power to suspend the workings of *karman*: no one is omnipotent enough to bring the fruition of the accumulated *karman* to a halt, even for a short while. Any other solution yields inconsistency.

The above arguments formulated by the critics of Nyāya-Vaiśeṣika reveal the inherent contradictions involved by the admission of god into the ontology and ethics and indicate that god was indisputably a 'foreign body' in the system.

The critics of the system confirm that the reasons to accept the equation 'existentiality = nameability = cognisability', along with the existence of god the other two elements of the 'knowability thesis package', could not have been prompted by strictly rational enquiry of the philosophers but must have been motivated by their extra-philosophical and, in essence, non-philosophical religious beliefs. The introduction of the equation alone would have been unwarranted and difficult to defend had it not have come along with god, the guarantor of the completeness of doctrine and attestation to the validity of the equation.

In addition to the above survey of systemic difficulties the creation of god in the world of Nyāya-Vaiśeṣika engendered, a handy account of two more serious incompatibilities that the admission of god that the admission of god into the system involved is given by the author of the author of the *Yukti-dīpikā*:[241] god cannot be included in any of the six categories admitted by the Vaiśeṣika and Kaṇāda did not mention god as a separate category[242]; further, god's supervision of the final immobility of atoms during the dissolution of the world and their initial motion after the *pralaya* is problematic.

Why did then the Naiyāyikas and Vaiśeṣikas adopt the notion of god, if there was neither any rational need for him in the philosophical system (sc. nothing internal or logical necessitated such an improvement of the philosophical doctrine) nor any comfortable room for him in the universe of the categories (sc. such an idea stood in conflict with a range of doctrinal points)?

---

[241] Cf. CHEMPARATHY (1965: 130).

[242] YDī 15d, p. 160.3 ff.

5.2. The Vaiśeṣikas, the Pāśupatas and god

We know that it was probably around the fifth century when religious ideas of the Pāśupatas and other Śaiva movements started to penetrate into the doctrine of Nyāya and Vaiśeṣika.[243]

The influence was apparently mutual because we find a number of doctrinal or philosophical points among the tenets held by the Pāśupatas that are of strictly Nyāya-Vaiśeṣika origin, next to Sāṁkhya and Yoga influences.[244] A good example is the enumeration of four constituents of the process of cognition, viz. cognitive criterion (*pramāṇa*), the cogniser (*pramātṛ*), the cognoscible, or the object of valid cognition (*prameya*) and the resultant cognition (*pramiti*). These well-known four elements are found at the beginning of the *Nyāya-bhāṣya*.[245] Exactly the same quadruplet is also found in Kauṇḍinya's *Pañcârtha-bhāṣya*:

> 'Thus all three are the cognitive criteria (*pramāṇa*). ... The soul is the cogniser (*pramātṛ*). The five categories, viz. the effect, the cause etc. are the cognoscibles (*prameya*). The resultant cognition is knowledge (*pramiti*).'[246]

Another instance of such influence concerns the proofs of the existence of the soul. We know that it was already Akṣapāda Gautama who, in order to proof this claim, availed himself of the idea that no substance can exist without its properties, and *vice versa* no property is possible without its substratum, the substance. Thus, by observing mental phenomena, such as desire, aversion, effort, pleasure, pain,

---

[243] On the Pāśupatas (and also on the relation between the Pāśupatas and the Vaiśeṣikas) see HARA (1958), SCHULTZ (1958), INGALLS (1962), CHEMPARATHY (1965), HARA (2002), BISSCHOP (2005). There are, of course, numerous elements borrowed from *yoga* practise.

[244] Some of them are mentioned by THAKUR (1957: 16): Praśastapāda's 'classification of inference into Dṛṣṭa and Sāmanyato-dṛṣṭa bears striking resemblance with that in the Pañcārtha-bhāṣya of Kauṇḍinya on the Pāśupatasūtras. Kauṇḍinya's classification of perception into indriya-pratyakṣa and ātmapratyakṣa (P. 7) may equally be compared with the ordinary perception (asmadādīnāṁ pratyakṣam) and the perception of the Yogin (Yogipratyakṣa) of Praśasta°. The Pāśupatas according to Kauṇḍinya accept three means of knowledge, viz. perception, inference and authority and we find a similar classification in the Vyomavatī, though the Vaiśeṣikas generally accept the first two only' (*vide supra*, n. 147, p. 309). For another similarity between Vaiśeṣika and the Pāśupatas in the realm of the nature of supernatural perception, understood as resulting from ascetic practices see n. 173. See also HARA (1992).

[245] NBh 1.1.1: *tatra yasyêpsā-jihāsā-prayuktasya pravṛttiḥ sa pramātā, sa yenârthaṁ pramiṇoti tat pramāṇam, yo 'rthaḥ pramīyate tat prameyam, yad artha-vijñānaṁ sā pramitiḥ.*

[246] PABh 1.1, p. 7.19–22: *evam etāni trīṇi pramāṇāni. ... pramātā puruṣaḥ. prameyāḥ kārya-kāraṇâdayaḥ pañca padârthāḥ. pramitiḥ saṁvit.*

cognition, we conclude that they must have some substratum, which is the soul.[247] Akṣapāda described these mental phenomena as inferential signs on the basis of which one infers the existence of the soul.[248] The argument was also well known to Praśastapāda.[249] Precisely the same reasoning and the same mental phenomena, with slight modification (change in the sequence and 'consciousness' for 'cognition') is found in Kauṇḍinya's work:

> 'One accepts the soul's [existence] on the basis of such inferential signs as pleasure, pain, desire, aversion, effort, consciousness.'[250]

That in this case it was the influence of the Nyāya-Vaiśeṣika tradition on the Pāśupatas can be proved by the fact that the idea to which Akṣapāda refers to is also found in the *Caraka-saṁhitā,*[251] historically closely associated with the development of the system of Nyāya-Vaiśeṣika.

Moreover, it is also known that Indian philosophers were quite well aware of the links between the Pāśupatas and the Vaiśeṣikas and the fact that the latter had taken over the belief in god from the former. A clear evidence, and perhaps the earliest evidence, to corroborate this is offered by the author of the *Yukti-dīpikā* in the sixth century:

> 'The Pāśupatas and the Vaiśeṣikas hold that "God therefore exists";'[252]
> 'In such a way this [thesis] of the Vaiśeṣikas [that] "god exists" was taken over from the Pāśupatas;'[253]

[247] On the structure of the argument see CHAKRABARTI–CHAKRABARTI (1991).

[248] NS 1.1.10: *icchā-dveṣa-prayatna-sukha-duḥkha-jñānāny ātmano liṅgam.*

[249] See his enumeration of the qualities of the soul: PBh_1 6, p. 70 = PBh_2 79 (*vide supra*, n. 216).

[250] PABh 5.3, p. 112.1–2: *tasya sukha-duḥkhêcchā-dveṣa-prayatna-caitanyâdibhir liṅgair adhigamaḥ kriyata ity arthaḥ.*

[251] $CarS_2$ 8.43, p. 260A = $CarS_1$ 3.8.39: *atha pratyakṣaṁ—pratyakṣaṁ nāma tad yadâtmanā pañcēndriyaiś*[a] *ça svayam upalabhyate, tatrâtma-pratyakṣāḥ sukha-duḥkhêcchā-dveṣâdayaḥ, śabdâdayas tv indriya-pratyakṣāḥ.*

[a] $CarS_1$: *cêndriyaiś.*

[252] YDī 15d, p. 157.13: *asty evam īśvara iti pāśupata-vaiśeṣikāḥ.*

[253] YDī 15d, p. 160.29–30: *evaṁ kāṇādānām īśvaro 'stîti pāśupatôjñam etat.*

The editors of YDī, Albrecht Wezler and Shujun Motegi, conjecture that this passage may be a later interpolation by hand of a copyist. Even if it were the case, there are numerous similar passages in YDī itself that indicate the Pāśupatas' theistic influence on the Vaiśeṣikas and, besides, even if the passage does not originate from the sixth century, but a later addition, it still evidences that it was generally a known fact in India that the Vaiśeṣika adopted the idea of god under the influence of the Pāśupatas.

> 'Therefore, there is no [room for] god in the system of the author of the *Vaiśeṣika-sūtra*;'[254]

and

> 'Thus, this is the [logical] error committed by the Pāśupatas when it comes to the acceptance of god. And this also is the error committed by the Vaiśeṣikas.'[255]

Certain doctrinal elements of the Pāśupatas would make it extremely easy and self-evident to formulate some arguments for the existence of god, e.g. the cosmological argument (*vide supra*, p. 324). Among the five categories (*padârtha*) that the Pāśupatas distinguished, two of them have a direct bearing on the question of god and rational arguments to prove his existence. These are (1) the category of effect (*kārya*), understood as all the creation, that comprises consciousness, material entities and living beings, and (2) the category of cause (*kāraṇa*), i.e. god (*īśvara*, Śiva), who is the foundation (*pradhāna*) of the creation, from whom all creation takes its origin, 'who was in the beginning' (PABh 5.47, pp. 146–148). Kauṇḍinya the Pāśupata devotes considerable space to causal relations: those between the cause and the effect as well as those between god and his creation (PABh 2.1–27, pp. 55–77). Suppose one accepts a strict cause-effect relation between god and the world, the way the Pāśupatas did, and assumes that on the basis of (1) any relation between a and b (e.g. $a \rightarrow b$), and on the basis of (2) an act of perception of a, one can justifiably infer b, precisely the way the Vaiśeṣika would infer[256] an inferential sign-possessor (*liṅgin*) on the basis of the perceived inferential sign (*liṅga*). Consequently, to come up with an argument for the existence of god based on such an idea of causality is but a natural step.

Another easily discernible influence of the Pāśupatas, relevant for our discussion, is found in the idea of god's supervision and in Uddyotakara's moral argument for the existence of god (*vide supra*, p. 334, n. 229) as well as in Praśastapāda's statement that the divine being Brahman, under the supervision of god (*īśvara*), 'endows all the created beings with their respective moral duty, knowledge, passionlessness and divine might that conform to their potencies stored as their *karman*' (*vide supra*, p. 300, n. 130). Precisely such a belief is expressed in Kauṇḍinya's *Pañcârtha-bhāṣya*:

---

[254] YDī 15d, p. 160.15: *tasmāt sūtra-kāra-mate nâstîśvaraḥ.*

[255] YDī 15d, p. 160.2: *evaṁ tāvat pāśupatānām īśvara-parigrahe doṣaḥ. vaiśeṣikāṇāṁ câyaṁ doṣaḥ.*

[256] VS(C) 9.18: *asyêdaṁ kāryaṁ kāraṇaṁ sambandhi ekârtha-samavāyi virodhi cêti laiṅgikam.*

'What is called [god's] facility to recreate [the word] means the uniting of individual souls[257] with the constituents that bear the name of the effects and the instruments[258] and with the merit, knowledge, detachment, power, demerit, nescience, absence of detachment, absence of power etc. in agreement with combined net force of the positioning in life, body, sense organs, sensory data [which the soul deserves according to the accumulated *karman*] and according to dimension, division and individual character.'[259]

We see that god's authority is to supervise the process of distribution of merit and demerit as well as other positive and negative qualities related to *dharma* at the moment of the creation of the world after its dissolution. This power is called by Kauṇḍinya 'facility to recreate', or 'the production of modification'[260] (*vikaraṇatva*).

The author of the *Yukti-dīpikā* quotes, or at least paraphrases, two arguments for god's existence which were formulated by the Pāśupatas, and accepted by the Vaiśeṣikas:

'The Pāśupatas and the Vaiśeṣikas hold that "Thus god exists". Why? [They have two arguments.]
[First argument:] **Because a special product must be preceded** (sc. caused) **by a supreme cognitive awareness**.[261] In this world, a special product, such as a palace, a vehicle etc., is seen to be preceded (sc. caused) by a supreme cognitive awareness. And indeed this [world],

[257] See PABh 2.24, p. 74.2–3, 6–7: *atra kalā nāma kārya-karaṇâkhyāḥ kalāḥ. tatra kāryâkhyāḥ pṛthivy āpas tejo vāyur ākāśaḥ. ... tathā karaṇâkhyāḥ śrotraṁ tvak cakṣuḥ jihvā ghrāṇaṁ pādaḥ pāyuḥ upasthaḥ hastaḥ vāk manaḥ ahaṁ-kāro buddhir iti.*—'Here what are called "the constituents" are the constituents that bear the name of the effects and the instruments. Among these, [the constituents] having the name "effect" are [the elements:] earth, water, fire, air, ether. ... Next, what have the name of instruments are: ear, skin, eye, tongue, nose, foot, anus, sex organs, hand, mouth, mind, the centre of personal identity and consciousness.' Comp. also PABh 1.1, p. 5.5–6: *tatra pāśā nāma kārya-karaṇâkhyāḥ kalāḥ.*—'What are called here individual transmigrating souls are constituents that bear the name of effect and instrument.'

[258] The terms *kṣetra* and *kṣetra-jña* are clearly of the Sāṁkhya-Yoga origin, see YS 2.4, YBh 2.17 (p. 175.2), 3.49 (p. 306.1), BhG Chap. 13, MDhP 12.206.8. See also LARSON (1979: 131 f.).

[259] PABh 2.24, p. 74.9–11: *vikaraṇatvaṁ nāma sthāna-śarīrêndriya-viṣayâdi-saṁniveśena vistara-vibhāga-viśeṣataś ca kārya-karaṇâkhyābhiḥ kalābhir dharma-jñāna-vairāgyâiśvaryâdharmâjñānâvairāgyânaiśvaryâdibhiś ca kṣetra-jña-saṁyojanam.* Cf. CHEMPARATHY's (1965: 128) translation of the passage.

[260] CHEMPARATHY's (1965: 128).

[261] See n. 337.

being characterised by a complex structure made from the elements, sense organs, creatures etc., is a special product. Therefore, it must be preceded by a supreme cognitive awareness. That by which this [world] is preceded is god. Therefore, god exists.
What else?
[Second argument:] **Because the conjunction of a conscious [being] and an unconscious [thing] is brought about by a conscious [being].** In this world, the conjunction of a conscious [being] and an unconscious [thing] is seen to be brought about by a conscious [being], for instance [the conjunction] of ox and cart. And indeed this [world] is a conjunction of bodies and souls. Therefore, it must be brought about by a conscious [being]. That by which this [world] is brought about [as a conjunction] is god. Therefore, god exists as the cause.'[262]

The first of the arguments is a version of cosmological argument, i.e. the argument from the first cause (*kāraṇa*), which was known also to Uddyotakara (*vide supra*, p. 324). Interestingly, the structure of this argument is a combination of a typical cosmological argument and an argument from perfection (*vide supra*, p. 324), based on the idea of a hierarchy of qualities, such as cognitive qualities. The expression 'supreme cognitive awareness' (*atiśaya-buddhi*) comes very close to 'absolute and supreme knowledge' (*atiśaya-jñāna*) found in *Padârtha-dharma-saṁgraha* (*vide supra*, p. 300, n. 130), or to Praśastamati's expression 'excellence of cognition' (*jñānâtiśaya*), quoted in TBV by Abhayadeva-sūri (*vide supra*, p. 305, n. 140), or to the phrase 'the excellence of perception' (*darśanâtiśaya*, p. 320, n. 178), found later with Jayanta-bhaṭṭa.

It is very likely that precisely such an argument, probably its earlier formulation, was devised within the ranks of the Pāśupatas and later adopted by Uddyotakara and taken for granted by both Praśastamati and Praśastapāda, who not only adopted logical, argumentative structure but also verbal phrasing.

That Kauṇḍinya may indeed have known the argument, although he does not refer to it explicitly, is attested by a passage from his *Pañcârtha-bhāṣya*:

---

[262] YDī 15d, p. 157.13 ff.: *āha—asty evam īśvara iti pāśupata-vaiśeṣikāḥ. kasmāt.* ***kārya-viśeṣasyâtiśaya-buddhi-pūrvakatvāt****. iha kārya-viśeṣaḥ prāsāda-vimānâdir atiśaya-buddhi-pūrvako dṛṣṭaḥ. asti câyaṁ mahā-bhūtêndriya-bhavana-vinyāsâdi-lakṣaṇaḥ kārya-viśeṣaḥ. tasmād anenâpy atiśaya-buddhi-pūrvakeṇa bhavitavyam. yat-pūrvako 'yaṁ sa īsvaraḥ. tasmād astîśvara iti. kiṁ cânyat.* ***cetanâcetanayor abhisambandhasya cetana-kṛtatvāt****. iha cetanâcetanayor abhisambandhaś cetana-kṛto dṛṣṭas tad yathā go-śakaṭayoḥ. asti câyaṁ cenanâcetanayoḥ śarīra-śarīriṇor abhisambandhaḥ. tasmād anenâpi cetana-kṛtena bhavitavyam. yat-kṛto 'yaṁ sa īśvaraḥ. tasmād astîśaraḥ kāraṇam.*

> 'Inference, in its turn, is preceded (sc. caused) by perception, and its causal complex is made from consciousness, internal organ (mind) and [respective logical] relations; it is effected by the remembrance of [such factors as] merit, demerit, explanation, place, time, injunction etc.; [it concerns] origination, subsistence, disappearance, time etc. And by their means one infers of a cause that it is an agent that accomplishes the subsequent creation [of the world].'[263]

While describing the nature of inference, he refers to certain categories on the basis of which we can infer that there is a creator of the world. This would support the above evidence of the *Yukti-dīpikā* attesting to the doctrinal influence the Pāśupatas exercised on the system of Vaiśeṣika.

The second of the above arguments is not found in the early writings of Nyāya-Vaiśeṣika in precisely this form. However, its logical structure in the form the author of the *Yukti-dīpikā* relates it, makes a rather curious and cryptic impression: it states that if we have a material, unconscious thing and a conscious being that come into union, there must be another conscious being to put these two together. One thing is certain, namely that the argument relies on a conviction, widespread not only in India[264] but also in ancient Greece,[265] that any movement and activity has soul, or a conscious being, as it source. That is why, the Pāśupatas are said to maintain that there must be some conscious agent ('meta-soul') to bring these two elements (unconscious thing and conscious being) into union. However, if there is already a conscious being (soul) in conjunction with the unconscious thing, then the second conscious agent ('meta-soul'), as a source of action or movement that brings these two elements together, turns out to be redundant, insofar as the conscious being (soul) is already capable of coming into union with the material thing without any extraneous agent. Why should then the argument mention the second conscious agent ('meta-soul') at all? The argument, aiming at proving god's existence, would not make any sense because all one would require for a conjunction of, say, a man and a stick, would be the man alone who can take hold of the stick; similarly, oxen

---

[263] PABh 1.1, p. 7.8–11: *anumānam api pratyakṣa-pūrvakaṁ cittâtmântaḥ-karaṇa-sambandha-sāmagryaṁ ca dharmâdharma-prakāśa-deśa-kāla-codanâdi-smr̥ti-hetukam utpatty-anugraha-tiro-bhāva-kālâdi. taiś côttara-sr̥ṣṭi-kartr̥tvam anumīyate kāraṇasya.*

[264] See e.g. NV_1 4.21, p. 461.11–13 (*vide supra*, n. 136).

[265] See Plato's belief that planets must have a soul, or a conviction shared by the Ionians. According to what Aristotle relates, 'Also Thales, according to what is recorded about him, seems to have held that soul is a mover, since he said that the lodestone has a soul because it moves the iron.'—*De Anima*, 1.2; 405a19: ἔοιε δὲ καὶ Θαλῆς ἐξ ὧν ἀπομνημονεύουσι κινητικόν τι τὴν ψυχὴν ὑπολαβεῖν, εἴπερ τὴν λιθον ἔφη ψυχὴν ἔχειν, ὅτι τὸν σίδηρον κινεῖ.

can easily approach a cart on their own and push it (not draw it, though). In this way, one could easily dispense with any higher agent, and the argument would fail.

My hypothesis is, however, that what we really have here is a version of the argument from the first mover (*vide supra*, p. 303). It states that, indeed, any conjunction (which by definition requires movement), including that of an unconscious thing and a conscious being, is initiated by the conscious being; a series of such events of conjunctions brings us to an initial situation when the souls are, for whatever reason it might be (here it is the *pralaya*), inactive and cannot exercise their capacity to bring about any conjunction. Therefore, there must be a first mover that initiates first motion and capacitates the souls. Accordingly, the argument begins to make a perfect sense when interpreted in the context of the dissolution of the world, when souls' all capacities are dormant. Also the example of the ox and cart would make perfect sense under this view: it is not merely about a n y conjunction of the ox and cart, but the yoking of the ox, which requires some p r i o r d e s i g n of the agent that accomplishes it. Thus, god is the initial agent who brings movement into the world.

Again, also here we may speak of a direct exchange between the Naiyāyika-Vaiśeṣika and the Pāśupatas. What was already taken for granted by Praśastapāda as requiring no explicit proof finds its formulation in the two anonymous arguments cited by the author of the *Yukti-dīpikā*.

This brief review of mutual influences between the doctrine of the Pāśupatas and Nyāya-Vaiśeṣika shows that the admission of god, alongside the package of the corollaries, was no coincidence or inner development in the Nyāya-Vaiśeṣika schools but one of such influences from the theistic partner.

A good summary of the above discussion could be the opinion of George CHEMPARATHY (1965: 124–125):

> '... [H]e (i.e. the author of YDī—P.B.) then passes on to refute the Īśvara doctrine of the Vaiśeṣikas, where he shows that the author of the Vaiśeṣikasūtras did not accept the doctrine of Īśvara, but that it was introduced by the Pāśupatas into the system. ... Further it seems reasonable to conclude that these proofs, though they appear in formulations foreign to the Vaiśeṣika terminology, might have been accepted by the early Vaiśeṣikas as proofs for the existence of Īśvara, when as we learn from the Yuktidīpikā, the Īśvara doctrine was accepted into the system from the Pāśupatas...'

Perhaps, the attenuation of the rigidity, or mechanicity, of moral law was not felt as a genuine problem by the Naiyāyika-Vaiśeṣika because they had already adopted to the idea of the transfer of merit and demerit, which also seems to stand in opposition to rigour of karmic retribution. Obviously such a concept of the ceding, to or from others, of one's moral responsibilities and retributions for committed deeds was not in accord with the doctrine of *karman* conceived by the early Nyāya-Vaiśeṣika philosophers. It did harmonise, however, with the new idea that the accrued *karman* could be suspended. It seems also that such a belief in the transfer of merit and demerit paved the way to the latter idea.

It is especially the third chapter of the *Pāśupata-sūtra* which describes how a Pāśupata adept can absorb another person's merit and give away his own demerit and take hold of the merit of others by his provoking, obscene or otherwise unusual behaviour that arouses contempt (*avamāna*) for him in, say, bystanders.[266] Again, the idea was that one can manipulate one's own *karman* through various ascetic practices, and merit as well demerit may be, respectively, appropriated from and ceded to others, even without their knowledge or consent. Such unusual practices of the Pāśupatas might have made the philosophers of Nyāya-Vaiśeṣika receptive of the laxity of the system of karmic retribution, which had apparently been treated as rigid. They no longer saw it problematic that accumulated *karman* could be transferred by them or its operation simply withheld for some time, during the dissolution of the world, by god.

5.3. Final word

To conclude, the knowability thesis—i.e. the equation: 'existentiality = nameability = cognisability'—was adopted by the Vaiśeṣika at the time of, or slightly prior to Praśastapāda. Its necessary complements were the following three ideas: god's existence, god's omniscience and supernatural perception, and these two entered Vaiśeṣika around the same time, i.e. late fifth century, although the belief in god's existence became a tenet of the Nyāya dogmatics slightly earlier since it was known already to Vātsyāyana Pakṣilasvāmin.

It seems rather certain that the main reason for the Vaiśeṣika to adopt the knowability thesis were not philosophical concerns but their religious belief in god and the knowability thesis was principally an o f f s h o o t of their theistic belief, not a result of purely rational, philosophical enquiry. The theistic influence came from the side of the Pāśupatas: most probably some thinkers of Nyāya-Vaiśeṣika were primarily followers of the Pāśupata doctrine and took the existence of god as something obvious that needed no rational proof (probably being something 'perceived'

[266] See Daniel H.H. INGALLS (1962): 'The Pāśupata Sūtra lays stress on the transfer of sin and merit' (p. 293). INGALLS (1962: 285–291) provides a translation of the third chapter of PāśS.

or sensed through ascetic practices). Perhaps the influence was possible thanks to their family or regional background. A conceivable possibility is that, having been brought up, or having grown up, in a religious environment influenced by the worldview of the Pāśupatas they underwent some training in methodology and logic under the supervision of a Nyāya-Vaiśeṣika master and eventually joined the ranks of Nyāya-Vaiśeṣika philosophers. But this is just a hypothesis, albeit a very probable on in Indian social context, for which I have no irrefutable proof at present.

BIBLIOGRAPHY

AK = Vasubandhu: *Abhidharma-kośa*. (1) Swami Dwarikadas Shastri (ed.): *Abhidharmakośa and Bhāṣya of ācārya Vasubandhu with Sphuṭārthā Commentary of Ācārya Yaśomitra*. Bauddha Bharati Series 5, 6, 7, 9, Bauddha Bharati, Vārāṇasī 1987. [1. ed.: 1970: Part I (1 and 2 *Kośa-sthāna*); 1971: Part II (3 and 4 *Kośa-sthāna*); 1972: Part III (5 and 6 *Kośa-sthāna*); 1973: Part IV (7 and 8 *Kośa-sthāna*)]. (2) P. Pradhan (ed.): *Abhidharm-koshabhāṣya of Vasubandhu*. Tibetan Sanskrit Works Series 8, Bauddha Bharati, Patna 1967. [2nd revised edition: A. Haldar: Tibetan Sanskrit Works Series 8, Bauddha Bharati, Patna 1975].

ĀMī = Samantabhadra: *Āpta-mīmāṁsā*. (1) Pannālāl Jain (ed.): *Āpta-mīmāṁsā* of Samantabhadra Svāmi, with two commentaries: *Aṣṭa-śatī* of Bhaṭṭākalaṅka and *Devāgama-vṛtti* of Vasunandi. Sanātana Jaina Granthamālā 10(7), Kāśī (Benares) 1914.

AmK = Amarasiṁha: *Amara-kośa* (*Nāma-liṅgânuśāsana*). Pt. Haragovinda Śastrī (ed.): *Nāmaliṅgānuśāsana or Amarakośa of Amarasiṁha, with the Rāmāśramī (Vyakhyāsudhā) Commentary of Bhānuji Dīkṣita (Rāmāśrama)*. Chaukhamba Sanskrit Pratishtan, Varanasi 1970.

APr = Vimalamitra (?): *Abhidharma-(pra)dīpa*. Padmanabh S. Jaini (ed.): *Abhidharmadīpa With Vibhāshāprabhāvṛtti*. Critically Edited with Notes and Introduction. Kashi Prasad Jaysawal Research Institute, Patna 1959.

ĀTV = Udayana: *Ātma-tattva-viveka*. Pandit Dhundhirāja Śāstri (ed.): *Ātmatattvaviveka of Śrī Udayanāchārya with the (Nārāyaṇī) Commentary of Śrī Nārāyaṇāchārya Ātreya & the (Bauddhadhikāra) Dīdhiti Commentary of Śrī Raghunātha Śiromaṇi, with Bauddhādhikāra Vivṛti of Śrī Gadādhara Bhaṭṭāchārya*. Chowkhambā Sanskrit Series 84, Vārāṇasī 1940.

BAGCHI 1944 = Bagchi, Prabodh Chandra: *India and China. A Thousand Years of Sino-Indian Cultural Contact*. China Press, Calcutta 1944.

BALCEROWICZ 2001 = Balcerowicz, Piotr: *Jaina Epistemology in Historical and Comparative Perspective. Critical Edition and English Translation of Logical-Epistemological Treatises: Nyāyâvatāra, Nyāyâvatāra-vivṛti and Nyāyâvatāra-ṭippaṇa with Introduction and Notes*. 1–2 Vols., Alt- und Neu-Indische Studien 53, 1–2, Franz Steiner Verlag, Stuttgart 2001 [to be reprinted: 2008].

BALCEROWICZ 2005 = Balcerowicz, Piotr: 'Akalaṅka und die buddhistische Tradition: Von der Nichtwahrnehmung von Unsichtbarem (*adṛśyānupalabdhi*) zu Allwissenheit', *Wiener Zeitschrift für die Kunde Südasiens* 49 (2005) 151–226.

BENETT 2003 = Benett, Jonathan: *A Philosophical Guide to Conditionals*. Clarendon Press, Oxford 2003.

BHADURI 1975 = Bhaduri, Sadananda: *Studies in Nyāya-Vaiśeṣika metaphysics*. Bhandarkar Oriental Series 5, Bhandarkar Oriental Research Institute, Poona 1975.

BhG = *Bhagavad-gītā. The Bhagavadgītā with an Introductory Essay, Sanskrit text, English Translation and Notes* by S. Radhakrishnan, Bombay 1977.

BhāgP = *Bhāgavata-purāṇa. Śrīmad-bhāgavata-mahāpurāṇa*. 2 Vols., Gita Press, Gorakhpur (U.P.) 1951.

BHATTACHARYYA 1926 = Bhattacharyya, B.: 'Foreword' to TSa_1, p. i–cxvii.

BISSCHOP 2005 = Bisschop, Peter: 'Pañcārthabhāṣya on Pāśupatasūtra 1.37–39 Recovered from a Newly Identified Manuscript', *Journal of Indian Philosophy* 33 (2005) 529–551.

BOCHEŃSKI 1956 = Bocheński, I.M.: *Formale Logik*. Verlag Karl Alber, Freiburg–München 1956.

BROGAARD–SALERNO 2004 = Brogaard, Berit; Salerno, Joe: 'Fitch's Paradox of Knowability', in: Zalta, Edward N. (ed.): *Stanford Encyclopedia of Philosophy*. Center for the Study of Language and Information, Stanford University, Stanford (CA) 2004: http://plato.stanford.edu/entries/fitch-paradox

BRONKHORST 1996 = Bronkhorst, Johannes: 'God's Arrival in the Vaiśeṣika System', *Journal of Indian Philosophy* 24 (1996) 281–294.

BRONKHORST 2000 = Bronkhorst, Johannes: *Karma and Teleology. A problem and its solutions in Indian philosophy*. Studia Philologica Buddhica, Monograph Series XV, The International Institute for Buddhist Studies, Tokyo 2000.

CARDONA 1967 = Cardona, George: 'Anvaya and Vyatireka in Indian Grammar', Adyar Library Bulletin (Madras) 31–32 (1967–68) 313–352.

CarS = *Caraka-saṁhitā* [*vi* = *Vimāna-sthāna*]. (1) Vaidya Jādavaji Trikamji Āchārya (ed.): *The Charakasaṇhitā of Agniveśa. Revised by Charaka and Dṛidhabala. With the Āyurveda-Dīpikā Commentary of Chakrapāṇidatta*. 3rd ed., Nirṇaya Sagar Press (Nirṇaya-sāgara Pres), Bombay (Muṁbaī) 1941 [reprinted: Munshiram Manoharlal Publishers, New

Delhi 1981]. (2) Āyurvedâcārya Śrī Jayadeva Vidyālaṅkāra (ed., Hindi transl.): *Carakasaṁhitā. Maharṣiṇā Bhagavatâgniveśena praṇītā*. 2 Vols, Motīlāl Banārsīdās, Dilli 1974 [reprinted: 1994].

CHAKRABARTI 1985 = Chakrabarti, Arindam: 'Plato's Indian Barbers: Classical Indian Approaches to the Problem of Singular Existence Denials', in: Matilal, B.K.; Shaw, J.L. (eds.): *Analytical Philosophy In Comparative Perspective*. D. Reidel, Dordrecht 1985: 299–326.

CHAKRABARTI–CHAKRABARTI 1991 = Chakrabarti, Kisor Kumar; Chakrabarti, Chandana: 'Toward Dualism: The Nyāya-Vaiśeṣika Way', *Philosophy East and West* 41,4 (1991) 477–491 [The Sixth East-West Philosophers' Conference].

CHAKRAVARTI 1982 = Chakravarti, Arindam: 'The Nyāya proofs for the existence of the soul', *Journal of Indian Philosophy* 10 (1982) 211–238.

CHEMPARATHY 1965 = Chemparathy, George: 'The testimony of the Yuktidīpika considering the Īśvara Doctrine of the Pāśupatas and Vaiśeṣikas', *Wiener Zeitschrift für die Kunde Süd- und Ostasiens* 9 (1965) 119–146.

CHEMPARATHY 1970 = Chemparathy, George: 'Praśastapāda and his other names', *Indo-Iranian Journal* 12,4 (1970) 241–253.

CHISHOLM 1976 = Chisholm, Roderick: 'Knowledge and belief: "De dicto" and "de re"', *Philosophical Studies* 29 (1976) 1–20.

DASGUPTA 1922–1955 = Dasgupta, Surendranath: *A History of Indian Philosophy*. Vols. 1–5, Calcutta 1922–1955 [reprinted: Motilal Banarsidass, Delhi 1975].

De Anima = 'Αριστοτέλους: *Περὶ Ψυχῆς*. Ross, David (ed.): *Aristotle: De Anima*. Edited with Introduction and Commentary. Clarendon Press, Oxford 1961.

DhPr = Durvekamiśra: *Dharmottara-pradīpa*. Pt. Dalsukhbhai Malvania (ed.): *Paṇḍita Durveka Miśra*'s *Dharmottara-pradīpa* [*being a sub-commentary on Dharmottara's Nyāya-bindu-ṭīkā, a commentary on Dharmakīrti's Nyāya-bindu*]. Kashi Prasad Jayaswal Research Institute, Patna 1955 [reprinted: 1971].

DNC = Mallavādin Kṣamāśramaṇa: *Dvādaśâra-naya-cakra*. Muni Jambūvijayajī (ed.): *Dvādaśāraṁ Nayacakraṁ of Ācārya Śrī Mallavādī Kṣamāśramaṇa. With the commentary Nyāyāgamānusāriṇī of Ācārya Śrī Siṁhasūri Gaṇi Vādi Kṣamāśramaṇa*. Edited with critical notes by .... Pt. I (1–4 Aras), Śrī-Jaina-Ātmânaṁda-sabhā, Bhāvnagar 1966 [reprinted: Bhāvnagar 2000]; Pt. II (5–8 Aras): Bhāvnagar 1976; Pt. III (9–12 Aras): Bhāvnagar 1988.

DNCV = Siṁha-sūri: *Nyāyâgamânusāriṇī Dvādaśâra-naya-cakra-vṛtti*. See: DNC.

DPŚ = Candramati (Maticandra): *Daśa-padârtha-śāstra* / *Daśa-padârthī*. (1) UI (1917). (2) MIYAMOTO (1996).

DRETSKE 1971 = Dretske, Fred: 'Conclusive Reasons', *Australasian Journal of Philosophy* 49 (1971) 1–22.

DUMMETT 2007 = Dummett, Michael: 'Reply to Wolfgang Künne', in: Auxier, R. E.; Hahn, L.E. (eds.): *The Philosophy of Michael Dummett*. Open Court, Chicago 2007.

EDGINGTON 1985 = Edgington, Dorothy: 'The paradox of knowability', *Mind* 94 (1985) 557–568.

FADDEGON 1918 = Faddegon, B.: *The Vaiçeṣika-System, described with the help of the oldest texts*. Verhandelingen der Koninklijke Akademie van Wetenschappen te Amsterdam, Afdeeling Letterkunde, Nieuwe Reeks, Deel XVIII no. 2, Amsterdam 1918.

FITCH 1963 = Fitch, Frederic B.: 'A Logical Analysis of Some Value Concepts', *The Journal of Symbolic Logic* 28,2. (1963) 135–142.

FITCH 1963 = Fitch, Frederic Brenton: 'A Logical Analysis of Some Value Concepts', *The Journal of Symbolic Logic* 28,2. (1963) 135–142.

FLORIO–MURZI 2008 = Florio, Salvatore; Murzi, Julien: 'The Paradox of Idealization', paper presented to 11th Oxford Graduate Conference, Oxford, November 2007; version February 12, 2008; j.murzi.googlepages.com/PI_12-02-08.pdf

FRANCO 2003 = Franco, Eli: 'The Oldest Philosophical Manuscript in Sanskrit', in: Piotr Balcerowicz (ed.): *Proceedings of the International Seminar 'Argument and Reason in Indian Logic' 20–24 June, 2001 — Kazimierz Dolny, Poland. Journal of Indian Philosophy* 1–3 (2003): 21–31.

HALBFASS 1989 = Halbfass, Wilhelm: 'Observations on Sattāsambandha and the History of Vaiśeṣika Ontology', *Journal of the American Oriental Society* 109, 4 (1989) 553–557.

HALBFASS 1992 = Halbfass, Wilhelm: *On Being and What There Is. Classical Vaiśeṣika and the History of Indian Ontology*. State University of New York Press, Albany 1992.

HARA 1958 = Hara, Minoru: 'Nakulīśa-pāśupata-Darśanam', *Indo-Iranian Journal* 2,1 (1958) 8–32.

HARA 1992 = Hara, Minoru: 'Pāśupata Studies (1)', in: Teun Goudriaan (ed.): *Ritual and Speculation in Early Tantrism. Studies in Honour of André Padoux*. SUNY Series in Tantric Studies, State University of New York Press, Albany 1992: 210–226.

HARA 2002 = Hara, Minoru: *Pāśupata Studies*. Edited by Jun Takashima, Publications of the De Nobili Research Library 30, Sammlung de Nobili, Wien 2002.

HART 1979 = Hart, W. D.: 'The Epistemology of Abstract Objects', *Proceedings of the Aristotelian Society Supplementary Volume* 53 (1979) 153–165.

HBṬĀ = Durvekamiśra: *Hetu-bindu-ṭīkâloka*. Sukhlalji Sanghavi and Muni Shri Jinavijayaji (eds.): *Hetubinduṭīkā of Bhaṭṭa Arcaṭa with the Sub-Commentary entitled Āloka of Durveka Miśra*. Baroda Oriental Institute, Baroda 1949.

HONDA 1988 = Honda, Megumu: 'Vaishēshika Sūtora oboegaki II. [Notes on the Vaiśeṣikasūtra II]', *Indogaku Bukkyōgaku Kenkyū* (*Journal of Indian and Buddhist Studies*) 37,1 (1988) 472–467 [cited after ISAACSON (1993)].

INGALLS 1962 = Ingalls, Daniel H.H.: 'Cynics and Pāśupatas: The Seeking of Dishonor', *The Harvard Theological Review* 55,4 (1962) 281–298.

ISAACSON 1993 = Isaacson, Harunaga: 'Yogic perception (yogipratyakṣa) in early Vaieṣika', *Studien zur Indologie und Iranistik* 18 (1993) 139–160.

ISAACSON 1995 = Isaacson, Harunaga: *Materials for the study of the Vaiśeṣika system*. Proefschrift ter verkrijging van de graad van Doctor aan de Rijksuniversiteit te Leiden, 1995 [unpublished doctoral dissertation].

JHĀ 1982 = Jhā, Gaṅgānātha: *Padārthadharmasaṅgraha of Praśastapāda with Nyāyakandalī of Śrīdhara translated into English*. Reprinted. Chaukhambha Oriental Studies 4, Chaukhambha Orientalia, Varanasi-Delhi 1982 [first edition: 1903, 1915].

KA = Udayana: *Kiraṇâvalī*. Jitendra S. Jetly (ed.): *Praśastapādabhāṣyam With the Commentary Kiraṇāvalī of Udayanācārya*. Oriental Institute, Baroda 1971.

KELLNER 1999 = Kellner, Birgit: 'Levels of (im)perceptibility. Dharmottara on the *dṛśya* in *dṛśyānupalabdhi*', in: Shoryu Katsura (ed.): *Dharmakīrti's Thought and its Impact on Indian and Tibetan Philosophy. Proceedings of the Third International Dharmakīrti Conference, Hiroshima, November 4-6, 1997*. Beiträge zur Kultur- und Geistesgeschichte Asiens 32, Verlag der Österreichischen Akademie der Wissenschaften, Wien 1999: 193–208.

KVANVIG 1989 = Kvanvig, Jonathan L.: 'Unknowable Truths and the Doctrine of Omniscience', *Journal of the American Academy of Religion* 57,3 (1989) 485–507.

LA = Udayana: *Lakṣaṇâvalī*. See: TACHIKAWA 1981.

LARSON 1979 = Larson, Gerald J.: *Classical Sāṁkhya – An Interpretation of its History and Meaning*. Second revised edition, Ross-Erikson, Santa Barbara = Motilal Banarsidass, Delhi 1979.

MACKIE 1980 = Mackie, John Leslie: 'Truth and Knowability', *Analysis* 40,2 (1980) 90–92.

MACKIE 1982 = Mackie, John L.: *The Miracle of Theism: Arguments for and against the Existence of God*. Clarendon Press, Oxford 1982.

MAAS 2006 = Maas, Philipp André (ed.): *Sāmadhipāda. Das erste Kapitel des* Pātañjalayogaśāstra *zum ersten Mal kritisch ediert. / The First Chapter of the* Pātañjalayogaśāstra *for the first Time Critically Edited*. Studia Indologica Universitatis Halensis, Geisteskultur Indiens: Texte und Studien 9, Shaker Verlag, Aachen 2006.

MAAS 2009 = Maas, Philipp André: 'Valid Knowledge and Belief in Classical Sāṁkhya-Yoga', in: Piotr Balcerowicz (ed.): *Logic and Belief in Indian Philosophy*. Motilal Banarsidass, Delhi 2009.

MATILAL 1970 = Matilal, Bimal Krishna: 'Reference and Existence in Nyāya and Buddhist Logic', *Journal of Indian Philosophy* 1 (1970) 83–110.

MATILAL 1975 = Matilal, Bimal Krishna: 'Causality in the Nyāya-Vaiśeṣika School', *Philosophy East and West* 25,1 [*The Problems of Causation: East and West*] (1975) 41–48.

MATILAL 1985 = Matilal, Bimal Krishna: *Logic, Language and Reality: Indian Philosophy and Contemporary Issues*. Motilal Banarsidass, Delhi 1985.

MATILAL 2005 = Matilal, Bimal Krishna: *Epistemology, logic, and grammar in Indian philosophical analysis*. Ed. By. Jonardon Ganeri, Oxford University Press, New Delhi 2005 [first edition: Mouton, Paris 1971].

MCDERMOTT 1970 = McDermott, A. C. S.: 'Empty subject terms in late Buddhist logic', *Journal of Indian Philosophy* 1 (1970) 22–29.

MCKAY 2005 = McKay, Thomas: 'The De Re/De Dicto Distinction. Supplement to Propositional Attitude Reports', in: Zalta, Edward N. (ed.): *Stanford Encyclopedia of Philosophy*. Center for the Study of Language and Information, Stanford University, Stanford (CA) 2005: http://plato.stanford.edu/entries/prop-attitude-reports/dere.html

MDhP = *Mokṣa-dharma-parvan*. In: V.S. Sukthankar et al. (ed.): *The Mahābhārata for the first time critically edited*. Bhandarkar Oriental Research Institute, Poona 1971: 12.168–353.

MDhŚ = *Mānava-dharma-śāstra* [*Manu-smṛti*]. Olivelle, Patrick (tr., ed.); Olivelle, Suman (ed.): *Manu's Code of Law: A Critical Edition and Translation of the Mānava-Dharmaśāstra*. With the editorial assistance of Suman Olivelle. Oxford University Press, New York 2005.

MEINONG 1904 = Meinong, Alexius: 'Über Gegenstandstheorie', in: *Untersuchungen zur Gegenstandstheorie und Psychologie*. Barth, Leipzig 1904: 1–50 [English translation: 'The Theory of Objects', in: *Realism and the Background of Phenomenology*, ed. by R.M. Chisholm, Free Press, New York 1960: 76–117].

Met = 'Αριστοτέλους: *Τῶν Μετὰ τὰ Φύσικά*. Jaeger, Werner (ed.): *Aristotelis Metaphysica*. Oxford Classical Texts, Clarendon Press, Oxford 1957.

MIYAMOTO 1996 = Miyamoto, Keiichi: *The Metaphysics and Epistemology of the Early Vaiśeṣikas. With An Appendix: Daśapadārthī of Candramati (A Translation with a Reconstructed Sanskrit Text, Notes and a Critical Edition of the Chinese Version)*. Bhandarkar Oriental Series 28, Bhandarkar Oriental Research Institute, Poona 1996.

MS = Jaimini: *Mīmāṁsā-sūtras*. See: ŚBh.

MŚV = Kumārila Bhaṭṭa: *Mīmāṁsāślokavārttika*. Dvārikādāsa Śāstrin (ed.): *Ślokavārttika of Śrī Kumārila Bhaṭṭa with the Commentary Nyāyaratnâkara of Śrī Pārthasārathi Miśra*. Ratnabharati Series, Tārā Publications 3, Varanasi 1978.

MŚVṬ = Sucaritamiśra: *Mīmāṁsā-śloka-vārttika-ṭīkā* [*Kāśikā*]. Sāmbaśiva Śāstri; V.A. Rāmasvāmi Śāstri (eds.): *Ślokavārttikaṁ Sucaritamiśra-praṇītayā Kāśikākhyayāṭīkayā sametam*. 3 Vols., *Trivandrum Sanskrit Series* 23, 29 and 31, CBH Publications, Trivandrum 1926–1943.

NAGASAKI 1988 = Nagasaki, Hojun: *A Study of Jaina Epistemology*. [With appendixes: 1. 'Transcendent Perception in Jaina Logic with Special Reference to Buddhist Logic.' 2. 'Perception in Yogācāra-bhūmi.' 3. 'A Study of the Pramāṇa-mīmaṁsā: An Incomplete work on Jaina Logic']. Heirakuji–Shoten, Kyoto 1988.

NB = Dharmakīrti: *Nyāya-bindu*. See: DhPr.

NBh = Vātsyāyana Pakṣilasvāmin: *Nyāya-bhāṣya*. See: NS.

NBhū = Bhāsarvajña: *Nyāya-bhūṣaṇa*. Svāmī Yogīndrānanda (ed.): *Śrīmad-ācārya-Bhāsarvajña-praṇītasya Nyāya-sārasya svôpajñaṁ vyākhyānaṁ Nyāya-bhūṣaṇam*. *Ṣad-darśana-prakāśana-grantha-mālā* 1, Vārāṇasī 1968.

NKA = Udayana: *Nyāya-kusumâñjali*. Uttamur T. Viraraghavacharya (ed.) *Nyāya Kusumāñjali of Udayanācārya with the Kusumāñjalivistara*. Kendriya Sanskrit Vidyapeetha, Tirupati 1980.

NKan = Śrīdharamiśra: *Nyāya-kandalī*. (1) See: PBh_1. (2) Jitendra S. Jetly (ed.): *Nyāyakandalī, being a commentary on Praśastapādabhāṣya, with three subcommentaries*. Gaekwad's Oriental Series No. 174, Oriental Institute, Vadodara 1991.

NMa = Jayanta Bhaṭṭa: *Nyāya-mañjarī*. (1) K.S. Varadacharya (ed.): *Nyāya-mañjarī of Jayantabhaṭṭa with Ṭippaṇi-nyāya-saurabha by the editor*. Vol. 1 & 2, *Oriental Research Institute Series* 116, 139, University of Mysore, Mysore 1969, 1983. (2) Gaurinath Sastri (ed.): *Nyāyamañjarī of Jayanta Bhaṭṭa with the Commentary of Granthi-bhaṅga by Cakra-dhara*. Part 1–3, M. M. Śivakumāraśāstri-Granthamālā 5, Sampūrṇānand Saṁskṛta Viśvavidyālaya, Vārāṇasī 1982, 1983, 1984.

NOZICK 1981 = Nozick, Robert: *Philosophical Explanations*. Clarendon Press, Oxford 1981.

NRĀ = Pārthasārathi Miśra: *Nyāyaratnākara*. See: MŚV.

NṢ = Akṣapāda Gautama: *Nyāya-sūtra*. Anantalal Thakur (ed.): *Gautamīya-nyāyadarśana with Bhāṣya of Vātsyāyana*. Indian Council of Philosophical Research, New Delhi 1997.

NV = Uddyotakara: *Nyāya-*[*bhāṣya*]*-vārttika*. (1) Pt. Vindhyeśvarī Prasāda Dvivedin (ed.): *Nyāya-vārttika*. Kashi Sanskrit Series 33, Haridas Gupta, Benares 1916–18 [reprinted: Eastern Book Linkers, Delhi 1986]. (2) Anantalal Thakur (ed.): *Nyāyabhāṣyavārttika of Bhāradvāja Uddyotakara*. Indian Council of Philosophical Research, New Delhi 1997.

NViV = Vādirāja-sūri: *Nyāya-viniścaya-vivaraṇa*. (2) Mahendra Kumar Jain (ed.): *Nyāyaviniścaya-vivaraṇa of Śrī Vādirāja Sūri, the Sanskrit Commentary on Bhaṭṭa Akalaṅkadeva's Nyāyaviniścaya*. Vol. 1 & 2, Bhāratīya Jñānapīṭha Prakāśana, Vārāṇasī 1949, 1955. [2nd edition: Bhāratīya Jñānapīṭha Prakāśana, New Delhi 2000].

PABh = Kauṇḍinya: *Pañcârtha-bhāṣya*. See: PāśS.

PALCZEWSKI 2007 = Palczewski, Rafał: 'Distributed Knowability and Fitch's Paradox', *Studia Logica* 86 (2007) 455–478.

PARSONS 1980 = Parsons, T.: *Nonexistent Objects*. Yale University Press, New Haven 1980.

PāśS = *Pāśupata-sūtra*. Ananthakrishna Sastri (ed.): *Pasupata Sutras with Pancharathabhashya of Kaundinya*. Trivandrum Sanskrit Series 143, Oriental Manuscript Library of the University of Travancore, Trivandrum 1940.

PBh = Praśastapāda: *Praśastapāda-bhāṣya* (*Padârtha-dharma-saṁgraha*). (1) Vindhyeśvarī Prasāda Dvivedin (ed.): *The Praśastapāda Bhāṣya with Commentary Nyāyakandalī of Śrīdhara*. Vārāṇasī 1895 [2. Ed.: Sri Satguru Publications, Delhi 1984]. (2) Johannes Bronkhorst, Yves Ramseier (ed.): *Word index to the Praśastapādabhāṣya: a complete word index to the printed editions of the Praśastapādabhāṣya*. Motilal Banarsidass, Delhi 1994. (3) See: $NKan_2$.

PBhS = *Praśastapāda-bhāṣya-samālocana*. Vindhyeśvarī Prasāda Dvivedin (ed.): *Praśastapāda-bhāṣya-samālocanam Tarkâlaṅkāra-bhāṣya-parīkṣaṇaṁ ca*. Chowkhambā Sanskrit Series Nos. 231, 255, Benares 1917.

PBhSū = Jagadiśa Tarkālaṅkāra: *Praśastapāda-bhāṣya-sūkti*. Gopinath Kavirāj (ed.): *The Praśastapādabhāṣyam by Praśasta Devāchārya with Commentaries (up to Dravya): Sūkti – by Jagadiśa Tarkālaṅkāra, Setu – by Padmanābha Miśra and Vyomavatī by Vyomaśivāchārya (to the end)*. Chowkhambā Sanskrit Series Nos. 316, 342, 354, 374, 375, 384, 396, Benares 1930.

PBhṬS = Śaṅkaramiśra: *Praśastapāda-bhāṣya-ṭīkā-saṁgraha*. Vindhyeśvarī Prasāda Dvivedin (ed.): *Praśastapāda-bhāṣya-ṭīkā-saṁgrahaḥ, tatra kaṇāda-rahasyam, śrī-śaṅkaramiśra-viraçitam*. Chowkhambā Sanskrit Series Nos. 231, 255, Benares 1917.

PERRETT 1999 = Perrett, Roy W.: 'Is Whatever Exists Knowable and Nameable?', *Philosophy East and West* 49, 4 (1999) 401–414.

PERSZYK 1983 = Perszyk, Kenneth J.: '"Virtue is not blue": Navya-Nyāya and some Western views', *Journal of Indian Philosophy* 11 (1983) 325–338.

PERSZYK 1984 = Perszyk, Kenneth J.: 'The Nyāya and Russell on Empty Terms', *Philosophy East and West* 34,2 (1984) 131–146.

PLANTINGA 1969 = Plantinga, Alvin: 'De Re et De Dicto', *Noûs* 3,3 (1969) 235–258.

POPPER 1970 = Popper, Karl R.: 'Eine Objektive Theorie des historischen Verstehens', *Schweizer Monatshefte* 50,3 (1970) 207–215 [Reprinted in: *Auf der Such nach einer besseren Welt: Vortrage und Aufsätze aus dreissig Jahren*. Piper Verlag, München 1984].

POPPER 1972 = Popper, Karl R.: *Objective Knowledge: An Evolutionary Approach*. Oxford University Press, London–New York 1972.

POTTER 1968 = Potter, Karl H.: „Astitva Jñeyatva Abhidheyatva", in: *Festschrift für Erich Frauwallner*, *Wiener Zeitschrift für die Kunde Süd- und Ostasiens* 12–13 (1968) 275–280.

POTTER 1995 = Potter, Karl H.: *Encyclopedia of Indian Philosophies*. Vol. II: *Indian Metaphysics and Epistemology: The Tradition of Nyāya-Vaiśeṣika up to Gaṅgeśa*. Princeton University Press, Princeton–New Jersey 1977 [Indian edition: Motilal Banarsidass, Delhi 1977; reprinted: 1995].

PV = Dharmakīrti: *Pramāṇa-vārttika*. (1) Rāhula Sāṅkṛtyāyana (ed.): *Pramāṇavārttikam Ācārya-Manorathanandi-kṛtayā vṛttyā saṁvalitam* [*Dharmakīrti's Pramāṇavārttikam with a commentary by Manorathanandin*]. Parts I–II, Appendix to *Journal of the Bihar and Orissa Research Society* 24–26, Patna 1938–1940. (2) Ram Chandra Pandeya (ed.): *The Pramāṇa-vārttikam of Ācārya Dharmakīrti with Sub-commentaries: Svôpajña-vṛtti of the Author and Pramāṇa-vārttika-vṛtti of Manorathanandin*. Motilal Banarsidass, Delhi 1989.

QUINE 1956 = Quine, Willard Van Orman: 'Quantifiers and propositional attitudes', *The Journal of Philosophy* 53,5 (1956) 177–187.

RESCHER 1984 = Rescher, Nicholas: *The Limits of Science*. University of California Press, Berkeley (CA) 1984. [Revised edition: University of Pittsburgh Press, Pittsburgh (PA) 1999].

RVār = Akalaṅka: *Tattvârtha-vārttika* (*Rāja-vārttika*). Mahendra Kumar Jain (ed.): *Tattvārtha-vārttika* [*Rāja-vārttika*] *of Śrī Akalaṅkadeva*. Edited with Hindi Translation, Introduction, Appendices, Variant Readings, Comparative Notes etc. Parts I–II. First edition, Jñānapīṭha Mūrtidevī Jaina Grantha-mālā 10, 20 [Sanskrit Grantha], Bhāratīya Jñānapīṭha Prakāśana, Delhi 1953–1957. [2. ed.: Delhi 1982].

SCHLESINGER 1986 = Schlesinger, George N.: 'On the Limits of Science', *Analysis* 46,1 (1986) 24–26.

SCHLESINGER 1988 = Schlesinger, George N.: *New Perspectives on Old-time Religion*. Clarendon Press, Oxford 1988.

SCHULTZ 1958 = Schultz, Friederich August: *Die philosophisch-theologischen Lehren des Pāśupata-Systems nach dem Pañcārthabhāṣya und der Ratnaṭīkā*. Beiträge zur Sprach- und Kulturgeschichte des Orients, Heft 10, Walldorf-Hessen 1958.

SHAW 1974 = Shaw, Jaysankar Lal: 'Empty terms: the Nyāya and the Buddhists', *Journal of Indian Philosophy* 2 (1974) 332–343.

SHAW 1978 = Shaw, Jaysankar Lal: 'The Nyāya on existence, knowability and nameability', *Journal of Indian Philosophy* 5 (1978) 255–266.

SHAW 1980 = Shaw, Jaysankar Lal: 'The Nyāya on Cognition and Negation', *Journal of Indian Philosophy* 8 (1980) 279–302.

SOSA 1970 = Sosa, Ernest: 'Propositional attitudes de dicto and de re', *The Journal of Philosophy* [*Sixty-Seventh Annual Meeting of the American Philosophical Association Eastern Division*] 67,21 (1970) 883–896.

STCHERBATSKY 1930/1932 = Stcherbatsky, Theodor: *Buddhist Logic*, 2 vols, *Bibliotheca Buddhica* 26, Издательство Академии Наук СССР, Ленинград / Leningrad I: 1930, II: 1932.

STP = Siddhasena Divākara: *Saṁmati-tarka-prakaraṇa*. (1) Sukhlāl Saṅghavi; Becardās Dośi (ed.): *Saṁmatitarka-prakaraṇam by Siddhasena Divākara with Abhayadevasūri's Tattva-bodha-vidhāyinī. Gujarāt-purā-tattva-mandir-granthâvalī* 10, 16, 18, 19, 21, Gujarāt-purā-tattva-mandir, Amdāvād 1924–1931 [reprinted: 2 Vols., *Rinsen Buddhist Text Series* VI–1, 2; Kyoto 1984].

STRAWSON 1950 = Strawson, Peter Frederick: 'On Referring', *Mind* 59 (1950) 320–334.

ŚBh = Śabarasvāmin: *Mīmāṁsā-śābara-bhāṣya*. Yudhiṣṭhira Mīmāṁsaka (ed.): *Mīmāṁsā śābara bhāṣyam*. Vols. 1–6, Śrī Śāntisvarūp Kapūr, Rāmalāl Kapūr Trust Press, Bahālgaḍh Sonīpat—Haryāṇā I: 1987, II: 1990, III: 1980, IV: 1985, V: 1986, VI: 1990.

TACHIKAWA 1975 = Tachikawa, Musashi: *The Structure of the World in Udayana's Realism. A Study of Lakṣaṇāvalī and the Kiraṇāvalī*. D. Reidel Publishing Company, Dordrecht–Boston–London 1981.

TALIAFERRO 1993 = Taliaferro, Charles: 'Unknowable Truths and Omniscience: A Reply to Kvanvig', *Journal of the American Academy of Religion* 61,3 (1993) 553–566.

TBV = Abhayadeva-sūri: *Tattva-bodha-vidhāyinī*. See: STP.

THAKUR 1957 = Thakur, Anantalal: 'Introduction' to VS(D): 1–22.

THAKUR 1961 = Thakur, Anantalal: 'Introduction' to VS(C): 1–23.

THAKUR 2003 = Thakur, Anantalal: *Origin and Development of the Vaiśeṣika System*. In: D.P. Chattopadhyaya (general editor): *History of Science, Philosophy and Culture in Indian Civilization*. Vol. 2, Part 4. Centre for Studies in Civilizations, New Delhi 2003.

TS = Umāsvāmin: *Tattvârtha-sūtra*. M.K. Mody (ed.): *Tattvārthādhigama by Umāsvāti being in the Original Sanskrit with the Bhāṣya by the author himself.* Bibliotheca Indica 1044, 1079, 1118, Asiatic Society of Bengal, Calcutta 1903, 1904, 1905. [= Śvetāmbara Recension].

TSaP = Kamalaśīla: *Tattva-saṁgraha-pañjikā*. (1) Embar Krishnamacharya (ed.): *Tattvasaṁgraha of Śāntarakṣita with the commentary of Kamalaśīla*. 2 Vols., Gaekwad's Oriental Series 30–31, 1926 [reprinted: 1984, 1988]. (2) Dvarikadas Shastri (ed.): *Tattvasaṅgraha of Ācārya Shāntarakṣita with the Commentary 'Pañjikā' of Shri Kamalashīla*. 2 Vols. BBS 1, Vārāṇasī 1981–1982.

UI 1917 = Ui, Hakuju: *The Vaiśeṣika Philosophy according to the Daśapadārtha-śāstra: Chinese Text with Introduction, Translation, and Notes*. The Royal Asiatic Society, London 1917.

VNṬ = Śāntarakṣita: *Vāda-nyāya-ṭīkā*. Rāhula Sāṅkṛtyāyana (ed.): *Ācaryya-Dharmakīrtteḥ Vāda-nyāyaḥ ācāryya-Śāntarakṣita-praṇitayā Vipañcitârthâbhidhayā ṭīkayā saṁvalitaḥ*. Appendix to J.B.O.R.S., Vols. XXI & XXII, Patna 1935–36.

VP = Bhartṛhari: *Vākyapadīya*. (1) Wilhelm Rau: *Bhartṛharis Vākyapadīya. Die Mūlakārikās nach den Handschriften herausgegeben und mit einem Pāda-Index versehen*. Abhandlungen für die Kunde des Morgenlandes XLII, 4. Franz Steiner Verlag, Wiesbaden 1977. (2) Wilhelm Rau: *Bhartṛharis Vākyapadīya. Versuch einer vollständigen deutschen Übersetzung nach der kristischen Edition der Mūla-kārikās*. Hrsg. von Oskar von Hinüber. Akademie der Wissenschaften und der Literatur – Mainz, Franz Steiner Verlag, Stuttgart 2002. (3) Bhāgīratha Prasāda Tripāṭhī Vāgīśa Śāstrī (ed.): *Vākyapadīyam [Part I] (Brahmakāṇḍam) With the commentary Svopajñavṛtti by Harivriṣabha & Ambākartrī by Raghunātha Śarmā*. Sarasvatī-bhavana-granthamālā 91, Sampurnanand Sanskrit Vishvavidyalaya, Varanasi 1976. (4) Bhāgīratha Prasāda Tripāṭhī Vāgīśa Śāstrī (ed.): *Vākyapadīyam [Part II] (Vākyakāṇḍam) by Bhartṛhari, With the Commentary of Puṇyarāja & Ambākartrī by Raghunātha Śarmā*. Sarasvatībhavana-granthamālā 91, Sampurnanand Sanskrit Vishvavidyalaya, Varanasi 1980.

VPA = Raghunātha Śarman: [*Vākyapadīya-*]*Ambā-kartrī*. See VP_3.

VPV = Harivṛṣabha: *Vākyapadīya-vṛtti*. See VP_3.

VS(C) = Kaṇāda: *Vaiśeṣika-sūtra* [Candrānanda's recension]. Muni Jambuvijaya (ed.): *Vaiśeṣikasūtra of Kaṇāda with the Commentary of Candrānanda*. With the Introduction by Anantalal Thakur. Gaekwad's Oriental Series 136, Oriental Institute, Baroda 1961.

VS(D) = Kaṇāda: *Vaiśeṣika-sūtra*. Anantalal Thakur (ed.): *Kaṇāda-kṛtaṁ vaiśeṣika-darśanam avijñāta-kṛta-pracīna-vyākhyayā samalaṅkṛtam—Vaiśeṣikadarśana of Kaṇāda with an Anonymous Commentary*. Mithila Institute of Post-Graduate Studies and Research in Sanskrit Learning, Darbhanga 1957.

VS(Ś) = Kaṇāda: *Vaiśeṣika-sūtra* [Śaṅkaramiśra's recension]. (1) Jayanārāyaṇa Tarkapañcānana (ed.): *Vaiśeṣika-darśana of Kaṇāda with the Commentaries Vaiśeṣika-sūtrôpaskāra of Śaṅkara Miśra and Kaṇāda-sūtra-vivṛti of Jayanārāyaṇa Tarkapañcānana*. Bibliotheca Indica 34, Asiatic Society of Bengal, Calcutta 1861. (2) A.E. Gough (ed. tr.): *Vaiśeṣika-sūtras. Edited and Translated with Sections of Śaṁkara Miśra's Upaskāra and Jayanārayana Vivṛti Thereon*. E.J. Lazarus & Co., Vāraṇasī 1873.

VSU = Śaṅkaramiśra: *Vaiśeṣika-sūtrôpaskāra*. See VS(Ś)1.

VSV = Bhaṭṭa Vādīndra: *Vaiśeṣika-sūtra-vārttika* (*Tarka-sāgara*). (1) Anantalal Thakur (ed.): *Bhaṭṭa-vādīndra-racita-vaiśeṣika-vārtika-kṛṣṇa-bhūpala-racita-trisūtrī-prakāśâjñāta-kartṛka-vṛttibhir vilasitam maharṣi-kaṇāda-praṇītam vaiśeṣika-darśanaṁ*. Mithilā Institute Series, Darbhanga Press, Darbhaṅgā 1985. (2) Selected sections in: ISAACSON (1995).

VSV(C) = Candrānanda: *Vaiśeṣika-sūtra-vṛtti*. See: VS(C).

VSV(D) = [Anonymous:] *Vaiśeṣika-darśana-vyākhyā* (*Vaiśeṣika-sūtra-vyākhyā*?). See: VS(D).

VyV = Vyomaśiva: *Vyomavatī*. (1) Gopinath Kaviraj, Dhundhiraj Śāstrin (ed.): *Vyomavatī of Vyomaśiva*. Chowkhambā Sanskrit Series, Vārāṇasī 1930. (2) Gaurinath Sastri (ed.): *Vyomavatī of Vyomaśivācarya*. 2 Vols., M. M. Śivakumāraśāstri-Granthamālā 6, Sampūrṇānand Saṁskṛta Viśvavidyālaya, Vārāṇasī 1983–1984.

WEZLER 1982 = Wezler, Albrecht: 'Remarks on the definition of "yoga" in the Vaiśeṣikasūtra', in: L. A. Hercus et al. (eds.): *Indological and Buddhist Studies. Volume in Honour of Professor J.W. de Jong on His Sixtieth Birthday*. Australian National University, Faculty of Asian Studies, Canberra 1982: 643–686.

WILLIAMSON 1982 = Williamson, Timothy: 'Intuitionism Disproved?', *Analysis* 42 (1982) 203–207.

WILLIAMSON 1987 = Williamson, Timothy: 'On the paradox of knowability', *Mind* 96 (1987) 256–261.

YBh = [Vyāsa (ascribed):] *Yoga-bhāṣya*. Polakam Sri Rama Sastri and S.R. Krishnamurthi Sastri (eds.): *Pātāñjala-yogasūtra-bhāṣya Vivaraṇam of Śaṅkara-bhagavatpāda*. Government Oriental Manuscripts Library, Madras 1952.

YDī = *Yukti-dīpikā*. Wezler, Albrecht; Motegi, Shujun (eds.): *Yukti-dīpikā—The Most Significant Commentary on the Sāṁkhyakārikā*. Vol. 1, Alt- und Neu-Indische Studien 44, Franz Steiner Verlag, Stuttgart 1998.

YS = Patañjali: *Yoga-sūtra*. See: YBh.

ZALTA 1983 = Zalta, Edward E.: in Jaakko Hintikka (ed.): *Abstract Objects: an Introduction to Axiomatic Metaphysics*. Synthese Library 160, D. Reidel (Kluwer), Dordrecht 1983.

ZEMACH 1987 = Zemach, E.M.: 'Are There Logical Limits for Science?', *The British Journal for the Philosophy of Science* 38,4 (1987) 527–532.

Logic and Belief in Sāṁkhya and Yoga

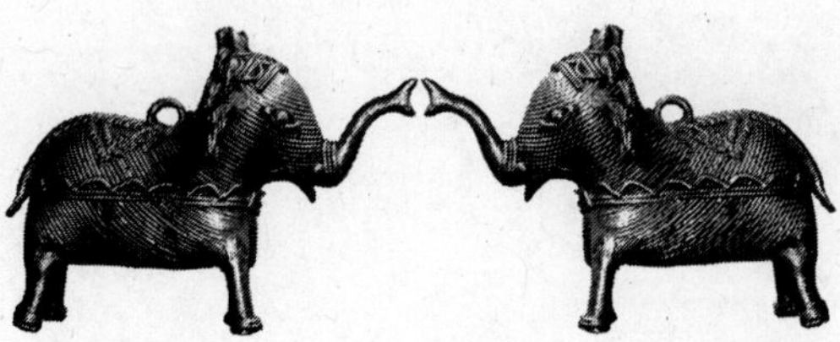

Early Concepts of Logic in Sāṁkhya

SHUJUN MOTEGI

vītâvīta-viṣāṇasya pakṣatā-vana-sevinaḥ /
pravādāḥ sāṁkhya-karinaḥ sallakī-ṣaṇḍa-bhaṅgurāḥ //
[YDī 1.3–4, 2.6–7][1]

Though its originality remains uncertain, the *Yukti-dīpikā* (YDī) starts with this verse which tells us that the Sāṁkhya argue with other schools by means of *vīta* and *avīta* (or *āvīta*) to defend the Sāṁkhya's standpoint and to win disputes. The concepts of *vīta* and *avīta*, therefore, seem to have played an important role in the history of the Sāṁkhya thought.

As these terms are not found in the *Sāṁkhya-kārikā* (SK), the compendium of the Sāṁkhya thought, and the oldest extant text of the school, some modern scholars have examined the concepts of *vīta* and *avīta* mainly in terms of their inclusion in the literature of other schools, especially in Buddhist literature. However, as YDī, a commentary on SK, refers to these terms rather frequently[2], I shall examine the treatment of the terms found in YDī, that is, their usage in an extant piece of Sāṁkhya literature.

1.1. In YDī, these terms are defined in the description of inference. The Sāṁkhya maintains, at least after SK, that there are three kinds of inference, namely *pūrvavat* (a priori), *śeṣavat* (a posteriori) and *sāmānyato-dṛṣṭa*. Among these three types, the existence of invisible beings is inferred by a method called *sāmānyato-dṛṣṭa anumāna* (inference based on the observation of similarity). This inference is, again,

[1] 'Accusations against the elephant of Sāṁkhya possessing the direct inference (*vīta*) and inference by elimination (*avīta*) as the tusks and rejoicing in the forest of subject (*pakṣatā*) are fragile like a group of *sallaki* trees' (translated by KUMAR–BHARGAVA (1990–1992: 1)).

[2] The author of YDī often refers to such old concepts as *ṣaṭ siddhi*, *karma-yoni*, old definitions of *anumāna*s, which are rarely referred to in other commentaries on SK. His wide knowledge of old theory is reflected in the frequent citation of the various theories of earlier teachers of the Sāṁkhya, by which some light may be shed on the days before SK.

Logic and Belief in Indian Philosophy
Warsaw Indological Studies 3 (2010) 363–382.

divided into two subcategories, due to differences in application. They are called *vīta* and *avīta*.[3] Their essential nature is described in the following verse:

> 'When a reason is used with its own specific sign in order to establish probandum, the reason is *vīta*. The other reason is used to establish probandum as the only remainder through exclusion of the other possible entities.'[4]

The author of YDī further explains both terms along with the meaning of the verse. On the term *vīta* his explanation is as follows:

> 'When a reason is used appropriately, with its own specific sign for the establishment of probandum, without reliance upon the standpoint of opponents, the reason is called *vīta*.'[5]

On the other hand, for the term *avīta*, the explanation is:

> 'On the contrary, by removing other possible entities, if it is proved that the probandum remains as the only possible entity, [the reason is] called *avīta*. For example, if the world does not originate from atoms, a cosmic person, a creator, conduct, destiny, time, nature, then it originates from the remainder: primordial matter.'[6]

Here, we see that both the terms of *vīta* and *avīta* are ways in which the inference based on general observation (*sāmānyato-dṛṣṭa*) is applied, and their difference is the manner in which the reason is treated. In the *vīta* inference, the proponent is supported by the nature of the reason. However, in the *avīta* inference, the validity of the reason is examined by means of entities which can substitute for the entity maintained by the proponent. It can be said that, while the *vīta* inference is positive in nature, the *avīta* inference is negative in nature. Judging from the general definition of the previously mentioned phrases, both methods of inference may be applied to any topic.

---

3 YDī 88.20–89.1: *tasmāt siddhaṁ sāmānyato-dṛṣṭād atīndriyāṇām arthānāṁ samadhigamaḥ. tasya prayoga-mātra-bhedād dvaividhyaṁ vīta avīta iti.*

4 YDī 89.2–3:

> *yadā hetuḥ sva-rūpeṇa sādhya-siddhau prayujyate /*
> *sa vīto 'rthântara-kṣepād itaraḥ pariśeṣataḥ //*

5 YDī 89.7–9: *tatra yadā hetuḥ para-pakṣam anapekṣya yathârthena svarūpeṇa sādhya-siddhāv apadiśyate tadā vītâkhyo bhavati.*

6 YDī 89.9–12: *yadā tu sva-sādhyād arthântara-bhūtānāṁ prasaṅgināṁ kṣepam apohaṁ kṛtvā pariśeṣataḥ sādhya-siddhāv apadeśyate tad-āvītâkhyo bhavati tad yathā na cet paramâṇu-puruṣêśvara-karma-daiva-kāla-svabhāva-yadṛcchābhyo jagad-utpattiḥ sambhavanti prariśeṣataḥ pradhānād iti tadā punar avītâkhyo bhavati.*

1.2. This general characteristic of the concepts of *vīta* makes it possible for it to be discussed in the context of the verbal explication (*vākya-bhāva*) of logic, or in syllogistic expressions. Though SK does not refer to any kind of syllogism, the *vīta* inference is connected with syllogistic formulas. In the Nyāya school of logic the syllogistic formula is said to consist of five parts.

The logical expression is said to consist of definite parts common to both sides, thus enabling the attainment of a conclusion acceptable to both sides.[7] The author of YDī provides us with two kinds of syllogistic expression. The first is utilised for obtaining the right knowledge, which is described as follows:

> 'The parts of explanation are desire for knowledge, doubt, purpose, attainment of possibility and negation of doubt.'[8]

The second is syllogistic parts to persuade others, which are common to the five parts of the Naiyāyika:

> 'The parts of persuading others are proposition, probans, example, application and conclusion.'[9]

As a result the *vīta* inference is said to have ten parts (YDī 97.5: *daśâvayavo vītaḥ*). In this context the concept *vīta* is partially connected with the five-part syllogism which is developed in Naiyāyikas. However, although each part of the syllogism is further explained or defined, an occurrence of the *vīta* inference expressed with the syllogism formula is not found. Although it is not expressed with the syllogism formula, the essential nature of the *vīta* is, together with *avīta*, in the persuasion of opponents.[10]

1.3. In contrast to *vīta*, the author of YDī does not refer to the syllogistic expression of the *avīta* inference.[11] But he provides us with the following example of the usage

---

[7] YDī 89.12–15: *tatra yadā vīto hetuḥ sva-buddhāv avahita-vijñāna-svarūpaṁ vijñānântaram ādadhānena vaktrā pratipādyâdau vākya-bhāvam upanīyate vākyam antareṇârthasya buddhy-antare saṁkrāmayitum aśakyatvāt, tad-āvayavi vākyaṁ parikalpyate.*

[8] YDī 89.16–17: *tasya punar avayavā jijñāsā-saṁśaya-prayojana-śakya-prāpti-saṁśaya-vyudāsa-lakṣaṇaś ca vyākhyâṅgam.*

[9] YDī 89.18: *pratijñā-hetu-dṛṣṭānta-upasaṁhāra-nigamanāni para-pratipādanâṅgam iti.*

[10] In the argument concerning the trustworthy words (*apta-vacana*) accepted by the Sāṁkhya as the valid means of cognition, an opponent exposed the contradiction within the Sāṁkhya thought. He knew the term *vītâvīta* and interpreted it as the reason to make something known to others verbally, see YDī 71.16–17: *vītâvītāv api hetū para-pratipādanârtham upadīyamānau śabda-vyāpāram apekṣete, tayor apy āpta-vacanatva-prasaṅgaḥ.*

[11] In the argument concerning example (*dṛṣṭānta*), the author of YDī mentions why examples in support of *avīta* are not mentioned, see YDī 90.23–91.2: *vyatirekas tv avītasya prasaṅgi-*

of the *avīta* inference, which is the only example of the *avīta* inference, that is, the only instance of its application seen in YDī.

In the explanation of *śeṣavat anumāna* (a posteriori inference), the author of YDī resorts to the *vītâvīta* inference. The opponent raises the objection that there can be supposed some reasons for the *nadī-pūra* other than the rainfall, for example, melted snow (*hima-vilayana*), the destruction of banks (*setu-bhaṅga*), the play of elephants (*gaja-krīḍa*) and so on. Hence, we cannot infer the rain fell upriver from the fact that the river water increased. The author of YDī here resorts to the *avīta* reason in order to make up for the insufficiency of a posteriori inference. Here we see a kind of definition and application of *avīta*. The role of *avīta* is to remove the other possible reasons in order to establish the validity of a conclusion. The author of YDī classifies the application of *avīta* into three aspects, namely from the viewpoint of place (*deśatas*), from the viewpoint of time (*kālatas*) and from the viewpoint of characteristics (*lakṣaṇatas*). By the removal of other possible reasons, the *śeṣavat anumāna* become valid.[12] The author of YDī uses *avīta* in inference in general to compensate for insufficiencies in the method of *vīta*, which are not connected with the inference designed to prove the existence of primordial matter.

1.4. Furthermore, in YDī, the term *vīta* appears in the argument to prove the existence of primordial matter (*prakṛti*).

The Sāṁkhya seem to make a great effort to prove the existence of primordial matter. The reason is that the concept of primordial matter is not derived from traditional philosophical thinking, being the basic concept on which the whole system of the Sāṁkhya school of thought is grounded. As the most characteristic theory of the school is based on this very concept, great efforts were made to prove its existence and to make its validity known to other schools of thought.

dharmântara-nivṛtti-rūpatvād antar-bhūta iti na tad-arthaṁ vaidharmya-dṛṣṭānta ucyate.—'A counter-example which excludes [the position of opponents] is not mentioned here because exclusion is included in the *avīta*, having a nature which denies possible characteristics of other entities.'

[12] YDī 84.19–85.3: *vītâvīta-sāmarthyāt. vītâvītābhyāṁ hetu-bhūtābhyām abhipretârtha-siddhir iti vakṣyāmaḥ. prasaṅgi-dharmântara-nivṛtti-mukhena câvīta-prayogaḥ. tatra yadā prasaṅgināṁ hima-vilayanâdīnāṁ deśa-kāla-liṅgaiḥ pratiṣedhaḥ kriyate tadā mukta-saṁśayaṁ pratipattir bhavati. deśatas tāvat tad yathā dakṣiṇā-pathe nâsti hima-vilayana-sambhavaḥ. kālato yathā prāvṛṭ-kāle. liṅgato 'pi yasmān mudga-gavedhuka-śyāmaka-kāṣṭha-tṛṇa-mūtra-śakṛt-prabhṛtīnām anupalambhas tathôṣma-kaluṣatvâdīnām upalabhāḥ. tasmāt pariśeṣato meghyā evâpa iti.*

In the argument of ten main topics (*cūlikârtha*)[13] in the sixty topics, the author of YDī refers to the term *vīta* as the means to prove the existence and uniqueness of primordial matter.

> 'Among them the existence and uniqueness of it is proved by five *vīta* reasons.'[14]

The author of YDī enumerates five kinds of *vīta*.[15] The five kinds of *vīta* are the five reasons which prove the existence of primordial matter. They are enumerated in SK 15:

> '[Primordial matter exists,] because (1) specific objects are finite, (2) they possess homogeneity, (3) they act according to their potency, (4) there is distinction between cause and effect, and (5) because of the merging of the world.'[16]

These five reasons in SK15 are named *vīta*. Here we see the concept that the term *vīta* denotes a group of five reasons for the proof of the existence of primordial matter.[17]

The term *avīta* appears in connection with the proof of the existence of primordial matter in its definition as seen above (p. 364). The same usage is again found in YDī as follows:

> 'This word (i.e. the term *prakṛti-kṛtaḥ* in SK 56) is used to end the argument. The existence of primordial matter is established by the *vīta-avīta* inference. It depends on the exclusion of atoms, and so on.'[18]

---

[13] The concept *cūlikârtha* is the ten topics of the sixty which constitute the *Ṣaṣṭi-tantra* of Vārṣagaṇya. Ten topics are found in YDī 2.12–13. These are: *pradhānâstitva, ekatva, arthavattva, anyatā, pārārthya, anaikya, viyoga, yoga*.

[14] YDī 6.14: *tatrâstitvam ekatvaṁ pañcabhir vītaiḥ siddham*.

[15] The five kinds of *vīta*s are seen again in YDī 154.11, which reads as follows:

evam etaiḥ pañcabhir vītair vyaktasya kāraṇam asty avyaktam iti siddham / (YDī 154.11–12)

[16] SK 15:

bhedānāṁ parimāṇāt samanavayāc chaktitas pravṛtteś ca /
kāraṇa-kārya-vibhāgād avibhāgād vaiśva-rūpasya //

[17] The same concept is seen in the argument raised by an opponent who doubts the validity of the reason. The opponent criticises the concept that the five reasons form a group called *vīta*, saying that each individual reason cannot be deemed valid if it is considered independently outside the group of five reasons. This opposition presupposes the concept that *vīta* is composed of five reasons, see YDī 92.26–27: *tatrâpi vītaḥ pañca-prabheda ity ataḥ samudāyān niṣkṛṣṭasyâikasya liṅgatvam aśakyaṁ vaktum iti.*—'If the *vīta* reason consists of five kinds, one reason extracted from the collection cannot be said to be an independent reason.'

[18] YDī 261.19–20: *anena vākya-parisamāpty-arthaṁ vītâvītābhyāṁ siddhaṁ pradhānâstitvam aṇv-ādi-pratiṣedhaṁ câpekṣate.*

The author of YDī (89.11–12) tries to show that the existence of primordial matter has been established by the *vīta* and *avīta* inference, in which the exclusion of other possible entities like atoms is also established. The *avīta* inference plays this part of exclusion in the whole inference.

1.5. In the previously cited phrase, we see the concept that both of *vīta* and *avīta* are applied together.[19] If *vīta* and *avīta* are used at the same time, it is said that *vīta* must be used first. The author of YDī (97.5–6, see n. 22) shows that this concept has been widespread.

This is easily understood, as the *vīta* inference has a positive probandum, without which nothing can be excluded.[20] The concept that both must be applied together implies that both are not independent methods of inference.

---

[19] The same concept that both of *vīta* and *avīta* must be used together is seen in the argument of SK 8ab which runs as follows:

> *saukṣmyāt tad-anupalabdhir nâbhāvat kāryatas tad-upalabdhiḥ* /
>
> 'The non-perception of primordial matter is due to its subtlety, not due to its non-existence. Because it is actually known through its effects.'

An opponent raises the objection that it is unnecessary to mention the term *nâbhāvāt*, because the Sāṁkhya's position is adequately expressed by the reason *saukṣmyāt*. The author of YDī responds to this objection by resorting to *vīta* and *avīta*. His point is that the reason *saukṣmyāt* is that of *vīta*. The reason *nâbhāvāt* is the application of *avīta*, because it denies other possible entity *abhāva*. If primordial matter is not perceived due to its non-existence then, as the remainder, it is not perceived due to its subtlety. First, the reason *vīta* is mentioned, followed by the reason *avīta* for the completeness of the reasoning process. Using this argument, the author of YDī justified SK 8, which enumerates two reasons for the one theme. The theme here is not about the existence of primordial matter.

The same concept is seen in YDī 244.4–5: *yadā vītâvītaiḥ pradhānam adhigamya tat-pūrvaktvaṁ ca mahad-ādīnāṁ vikārāṇām.*—'Understanding primordial material by the *vīta* and *avīta*, and understanding that the evolutes, *mahad* and so on, presuppose it, [a *yogin* is satisfied].'

We further find the same concept in the opinion raised by others (*tantrântarīya*), in YDī 107.2–3: *yat uktaṁ tantrântarīyaḥ "na pr̥thak-pratipatti-hetū vītâvītau" iti tad iṣṭam eva saṅgr̥hītaṁ bhavati.*

[20] The author of YDī (97.6 ff.) explains the reason why the *avīta* reason comes after *vīta* as follows: The characteristics of *avīta* support the probandum through exclusion. If a conclusion is drawn from the negation of opposites, there is nothing from which an exclusion can be made. If, as in the *avīta* inference, negation comes first, the following inference is possible: if [we know that] things (*vyakta*) did not originate from atoms etc., on the ground that the reason which supports the atoms etc., is negated, likewise [we know that] things did not appear from primordial matter because of the lack of a positive reason for its existence. It must, therefore, be established that things appears from primordial matter by the *vīta* reasons. Here again the function of *avīta* is to exclude other possible entities after the establishment of the existence of primordial matter.

1.6. Let us now summarise the previously cited occurrences of the terms *vīta* and *avīta* in YDī, according to their usages. The term *vīta* is generally used as (1) an inferential reason, connected with the syllogism of ten parts (§ 1.2), and as (2) connected with five reasons that prove the existence of primordial matter seen in SK 15 (§ 1.4). The term *avīta* is generally used as an inference to exclude other possible entities, but specifically to exclude other possible entities which could occupy the position of primordial matter. Both of them must be applied together, first *vīta*, then *avīta*, for the completeness of the inference. Keeping these different usages in mind, let us examine the usage of the terms in the literature older than YDī in order to clarify the concepts associated with them.

2.1. Prof. FRAUWALLNER (1958) made a great contribution to the inference theory of the early Sāṁkhya. In his paper, he analysed the argument of inference found in the *Pramāṇa-samuccaya* (PS), in its commentary by Jinendrabuddhi, in the *Dvādaśāra-naya-cakra* and its commentary, the *Nyāyâgamânusāriṇī* (NAA), by Siṁha-sūri, assuming that the inference theory referred to in these texts is that of the *Ṣaṣṭi-tantra* (ST) of Vārṣagaṇya and of two commentaries on ST. He finally presented a part of the text of ST which dealt with valid means of cognition, including inference. The presented text, which consists of Sanskrit and Tibetan, includes the following topics:

(1) The definition of inference (*anumāṇa*): *sambandhād ekasmāt śeṣa-siddhir anumānam*.

(2) Seven kinds of definite connections (*sambandha*) in the definition of inference: their designations and two examples for each kind.

(3) The definition and explanation of direct perception (*pratyakṣa*): *śrotrâdi-vṛttiḥ*.

(4) A short explanation of a trustworthy person (*āpta*).

(5) Two kinds of inference (*anumāna*): the analogical inference based on particularity (*viśeṣato-dṛṣṭa*) and the analogical inference based on similarity (*sāmānyato-dṛṣṭa*).

(6) Two kinds of analogical inference based on similarity (*sāmānyato-dṛṣṭa*): *pūrvavat* (a priori) and *śeṣavat* (a posteriori).

(7) Two kinds of application of *śeṣavat*: *vīta* and *avıta*.

(8) Parts of verbal expression, or the syllogism of *vīta*: *pratijñā*, *hetu*, *dṛṣṭānta*, *upasaṁhāra*, *nigamana*.

(9) Proof of the existence of primordial matter (*prakṛti*): An example of *vīta* and *āvīta*.

2.2. In the reconstructed text of ST (RST), *vīta* and *avīta* appear first as two ways of applying the *śeṣavad anumāna*. The relevant portion is as follows:

> 'Among them, the inference based on similarity is used as posteriori inference, the reason of posteriori inference is used for cognition of things beyond the range of sense organs. It is divided into two categories by difference in application, that is, *vīta* and *āvīta*. The *vīta* reason is established by the nature of probandum itself. When reason is used for the completion of probandum by its own nature, without depending on the opposite side, then it is called *vīta*. The establishment by *āvīta* is through the remainder. When this reason is used for the completion of probandum, being decided that, as it does not come into existence in any other way, but that it exists, the only reason possible becomes the remainder, and it is called *āvīta*.'[21]

Here, as seen in YDī, the *vīta* and *avīta* are two ways of applying inference, known as *śeṣavad anumāna*. However, their definitions are not described in connection with an attempt to prove the existence of primordial matter. As seen again in YDī, *vīta* is a reason based on the nature of probandum. Conversely, *avīta* is a kind of reason that excludes other possible entities as probandum. A kind of general expression of both concepts is continued in the next description of the five-part syllogism, which is regarded as the verbal statement of *vīta*. The relevant text of RST runs as follows:

> 'The verbal expression of *vīta* consists of five parts: proposition, reason, example, application and conclusion. Proposition is the assertion of probandum. Reason is the description of probans. Example is its presentation. Application is the union of probans and example. Con-

---

[21] RST, after FRAUWALLNER (1958: 44.3–4): *teṣāṁ yad etat sāmānyato-dṛṣṭam anumānaṁ śeṣavat, eṣa hetur atīndriyāṇāṁ bhāvānāṁ samadhigame, tasya prayogôpacāra-viśeṣād dvaividhyam, vīta āvīta iti. svarūpād vīta-siddhiḥ. yadā hetuḥ para-pakṣam avyapekṣya svenâiva rūpeṇa kārya-siddhāv apadiśyate, tadā vītâkhyo bhavati. pariśeṣād āvīta-siddhiḥ. yadā nêdam ato 'nyathā sambhavati, asti cêdam, tasmāt pariśeṣato hetur evâyam ity avadhārya kārya-siddhāv apadiśyate, tad-āvītâkhyo bhavati.*

The relevant texts of NAA 313.8–314.3, runs with slight differences: *teṣāṁ vītâvītānāṁ lakṣaṇaṁ tad yathā—prāg anumānaṁ saprabhedaṁ vyākhyāya teṣāṁ yad etat sāmānyato-dṛṣṭaṁ śeṣavad eṣa hetur atīndriyāṇāṁ bhāvānāṁ samadhigame, tasya prayogôpacāra-viśeṣād dvaividhyam. vīta iti sāmānyena, viśeṣeṇa tu svarūpād vīta-siddhiḥ, yadā hetuḥ para-pakṣam avyapekṣya svenâiva rūpeṇa kārya-siddhāv apadiśyate, tadā vītâkhyo bhavati. pariśeṣād āvīta-siddhiḥ, yadā nêdam ato 'nyathā sambhavaty asti cêdam, tasmāt pariśeṣato "hetur evâyam" ity avadhārya kārya-siddhāv apadiśyate, tad-āvītâkhyo bhavatîti prayoga-lakṣaṇam, sva-lakṣaṇaṁ tv asya para-pakṣa-pratiṣedhena sva-pakṣa-parigraha-kriyā āvīta iti.*

> clusion is the repetition of proposition. [Teachers] think that it is proper to use *vīta* first, and then *āvīta*.'[22]

From the previously quoted statement we know that the five-part syllogism is called *vīta* in RST. The five parts are *pratijñā* and so on, not including *jijñāsā* and so on as in YDī.

2.3. Following the previously mentioned general description of *vīta* and *avīta*, we can see their real usages in RST. Prof. FRAUWALLNER took the *vīta* inference out of a group of five to cite an example of its use, which is as follows:

> 'Primordial matter exists. Because one sees homogeneity in things. One sees the homogeneity of one sort in inner things consisting of effect and cause. <We will explain inner [things which] consists of effect and cause.> Inner things, which are essentially made of effect, are five in number. They are sound, touch, taste, form and smell. They are nothing but combination of three constituents, that is, pleasure, pain and bewilderment. Why? Because these five respectively make one effect. While sound, touch, taste, form and smell are in pleasure, they make, as effect, brightness, lightness, generation, affection, happiness and pleasure. [While these five are] in pain, the effect is dryness, separation (?, *apabheda*), excitement, regret and hate (?, *apadveṣa*). [While these five are] in bewilderment, the effect is covering, exhaustion, concealment, hate (?, *baibhatsya*, FRAUWALLNER: 'Abscheu'), misery and heaviness, and so on.'[23]

---

[22] RST, after FRAUWALLNER (1958: 44.10–14): *vītasya vākya-bhāvaḥ pañca-pradeśaḥ, pratijñā hetur dṛṣṭānta upasaṁhāro nigamanam iti. tatra sādhyâvadhāraṇaṁ pratijñā sādhana-samāsa-vacanaṁ hetuḥ, tan-nidarśanaṁ dṛṣṭāntaḥ, sādhya-dṛṣṭāntayor eka-kriyôpasaṁhāraḥ, pratijñâbhyāso nigamanam iti purastād vītasya prayogaṁ nyāyyaṁ manyante, paścād āvītasya*.

The relevant text of NAA, 314.4–6, runs again with slight differences: *vītasya [āvītasya] vā bhāvaḥ pañca-pradeśaḥ—pratijñā hetuḥ dṛṣṭānta upasaṁhāro nigamanam iti. tatra sādhyâvadhāraṇaṁ pratijñā sādhana-samāsa-vacanaṁ hetuḥ, tan-nidarśanaṁ dṛṣṭāntaḥ, sādhya-dṛṣṭāntayor eka-kriyôpasaṁhāraḥ, pratijñâbhyāso nigamanam iti* ***purastād vītasya prayogaṁ nyāyyaṁ manyante, paścād āvītasyêti***.

Here, regarding the order of application (bolded part), we notice almost identical phrase in YDī 97.5–6: *tasmāt sūktaṁ daśâvayavo vītaḥ. tasya purastāt prayogaṁ nyāyyam ācāryā manyante.*

[23] RST, after FRAUWALLNER (1958: 44.16–24): *asti pradhānam, bhedānām anvaya-darśanāt. ādhyātmikāṇāṁ bhedānāṁ kārya-karaṇâtmakānām eka-jāti-samanvayo dṛṣṭaḥ, <ādhyātmikānāṁ kāryâtmakānāṁ vakṣyāmaḥ>*[a] *ādhyātmikāḥ kāryâtmakā bhedāḥ śabda-sparśa-rasa-rūpa-gandhāḥ pañca trayāṇāṁ sukha-duḥkha-mohānāṁ sanniveśa-mātram. kasmāt? pañcānāṁ pañcānāṁ eka-kārya-bhāvāt, sukhānāṁ śabda-sparśa-rasa-rūpa-gandhānāṁ prasāda-lāghava-prasavâbhi-*

The reason *anvayāt* corresponds to *samanvayāt* in SK 15. In the *Nyāyâgamânusāriṇī*, on which Prof. FRAUWALLNER depends for reconstruction of ST, there is a somewhat lengthy description of *vīta* and *āvita*. After this inference, there follow four more *vīta* inferences in NAA, to which Prof. FRAUWALLNER refers by means of the sign '*usw.*'. The following reasons are the same as those in SK 15. The second reason is *parimāṇāt* (because of finiteness or limited measure).[24] Though the argument to support the first reason is similar to that found in YDī, the argument for the second reason is quite different, and will be briefly summarised in the following paragraph.

To show examples of things of finiteness (*parimāṇa*), the author divides finiteness into three categories: the finiteness of form (*rūpa-parimāṇa*), the finiteness of behaviour (*pravṛtti-parimāṇa*) and the finiteness of result (*phala-parimāṇa*). He further divides the finiteness of behaviour and finiteness of result into two categories. The finiteness of behaviour is divided into two categories according to two purposes, that is, obtaining welfare and avoiding misfortune. Or it is divided into four categories by the purposes of rightness (*dharma*) etc., that is, men who have purpose of satisfaction (*dhṛti*), good behaviour (*sad-ācāra*), love and pleasure (*kāma-sukha*) and cessation (*vinivṛtti*). Again it may be divided into five kinds, due to the nature of breath etc. The third finiteness, that is, the finiteness of result, is divided into two categories, visible and invisible (*dṛṣṭa* and *adṛṣṭa*). The finiteness of unseen result possesses two kinds of potency (*śakti*), that is, supreme power (? *prabhuśakti*) and omnipotent power (? *vibhuśakti*). In opposition to this, there are two kinds of impotency (*aśakti*). The beings with potency are god, *gandharva*, *yaksa*, *raksas*, *pitṛ* and *piśāca* (cf. SK 53). The beings with impotency are human beings, cows, deer, birds, serpents and plants. The nature of potency is the cause of body. (On the contrary the nature) of impotency is to be born by means of womb, egg, sprout and wettish heat (*saṁśoka*). The beings born by means of womb or egg, are generated by a mother and

---

ṣvaṅgôddharṣa-prītayaḥ kāryam, duḥkhānāṁ śoṣatâpabhedadôpaṣṭambhôdvegâpadveṣāḥ, mūḍhānāṁ varaṇa-sadanâpadhvaṁsana-baibhatsya-dainya-gauravāṇi etc.

[a] The relevant portion of NAA 314.7–8, runs as follows: *eka-jāti-samanvayo dṛṣṭa iti candana-śakalâdi-dṛṣṭāntaṁ vakṣyati*. In the original text of ST, an example of *candanaśakalâdivat* might have been present.

The relevant text of NAA, 314.4–6, runs again with slight differences: *vītasya* [*āvītasya*] *vā bhāvaḥ pañca-pradeśaḥ—pratijñā hetuḥ dṛṣṭānta upasaṁhāro nigamanam iti. tatra sādhyâvadhāraṇaṁ pratijñā sādhana-samāsa-vacanaṁ hetuḥ, tan-nidarśanaṁ dṛṣṭāntaḥ, sādhya-dṛṣṭāntayor eka-kriyôpasaṁhāraḥ, pratijñâbhyāso nigamanam iti* ***purastād vītasya prayogaṁ nyāyyaṁ manyante, paścād āvītasyêti.***

Here, regarding the order of application (bolded part), we notice almost identical phrase in YDī 97.5–6: *tasmāt sūktaṁ daśâvayavo vītaḥ. tasya purastāt prayogaṁ nyāyyam ācāryā manyante.*

[24] NAA 314.15: *itaś câsti pradhānaṁ bhedānāṁ parimāṇāt. ādhyātmikānāṁ kārya-kāraṇâtmakānāṁ parimāṇaṁ dṛṣṭam.*

father. They have six receptacle (? *ṣaṭ-kośikam*). By the earth are born plants (*udbhidja*). By the heat of earth and water are born worms. (Cf. *Manu-smṛti* 1.43) This is the finiteness of invisible result. The finiteness of visible result contains four kinds. They are *śakti*, *siddhi*, *tuṣṭi*, *indriya-vadha*. Additionally, *atuṣṭi* and *asiddhi* are enumerated, which correspond to fifty topics found in ST, being referred to as 'the creation of consciousness' (*pratyaya-sarga*) in SK 46–50. (NAA 314. 15–318.6).

The author seems to show that all the extant beings in the world have finiteness in themselves, by which even their ethical behaviour is limited. And, by this description of the many finite beings, he seems to indicate the existence of something beyond finite beings. This argument as a whole gives impression of being rather unrefined, or old fashioned at least.

In the same way, three more *vīta* inferences continue. The reasons are the same ones as those found in SK 15. However, the interpretation of each reason is rather unique and rather unsophisticated, as it does not appear in the commentaries of SK.[25] Observing the function of these inferences using rather simple examples, we

---

[25] The third reason is 'because of the cause-effect relationship' (*kārya-kāraṇa-bhāvāt*). An outline of the interpretation of this reason is as follows:

The constituents of *sattva*, *rajas* and *tamas*, existing in sound etc., help each other through illumination, stimulation and obstruction. The *sattva*, as the essence of sound etc., illuminates (*khyāpayati*) the activity of other two. In the same way, *rajas* stimulates the activity of other two, and *tamas* stops the activity of other two.

In this way, the author continues to enumerate other examples, in an effort to prove that all existing beings are in a relationship of mutual help (*upakārya-upakāraṇa*), which is the paraphrase of *kārya-kāraṇa*. With this notion of the mutual relationship among all existing beings, he perhaps tries to prove one existent being that makes this mutual relationship possible. He concludes this inference with the word that things are made by one creator (*eka-kartṛkā bhedāḥ*). (NAA 318.7–319.6).

The fourth reason is 'because potencies are nothing but the state of having potency' (*śaktimad-avasthā-mātratvāc chaktīnām*).

Potency, which can create its own effects, exists in three stages. Observing that a thing (*vyakta*) has beginning and end, one can infer that it possesses potency. This is because, if potency does not exist, it is impossible for a thing to have a beginning, like a sky-flower. The fact that a thing has a beginning means that it possesses potency. From the fact that the activity of the potency of a thing is seen, that potency, that is, primordial matter, exists. (NAA 319.7–11).

The fifth reason is 'because of attainment of dissolution of the multi-formed' (*vaiśva-rūpyasyâvibhāga prāpteḥ*). The explanation of this reason is as follows: Juice etc., which is changed form of water and earth, has manifold form, and is seen in plants. Then the changed form of plants is seen in animals. Then the changed form of animals is seen in plants. Then of plants in plants, of animals in animals. In this way, everything is seen in everything, because the barriers between the species are not fixed. However, as they are anchored by place, time, appearance and occasion, they do not take the same form at the same time. We think that the manifold form of juice is the one transformed from of water and earth. For other material elements, there are other transformation. In the same way, for other elements there are again other transformation. By ne-can safely infer that these must have been discussed in earlier literature of the Sāṁkhya school, for example, in ST.

With regards to syllogism, the first line of all the five inferences starts with a syllogistic expression, for example: *pradhānam asti bhedānām anvaya-darśanāt*. After this statement, we see long description of an example or interpretation of reason. Finally the last three inferences end with the expression: *tasmād asti pradhānam*. It is, therefore, difficult to postulate that these inferences are formed from the five-part syllogism scheme.

2.4. By such five *vīta* reasons as (1) *samanvaya*, (2) *pramāṇa*, (3) *upakāra*, (4) *śakti-pravṛtti*, (5) *vaiśvarūpya-gati*, the existence of primordial matter is established. Next, in order to strengthen the conclusion of the five *vīta* inferences, five *āvīta* inferences are mentioned. The essence of the concept of *āvīta* is said to be in denial of the concept propounded by an opponent, by which the standpoint of a proponent is established. The opponents are those who regard cosmic man, God and atoms as the cause of the world, and those whose mind are wicked, and Buddhist. Among these opponents, Buddhists are said to be criticised first.[26] These reasons are called *āvīta*. The first argument, which is clearly mentioned as *āvīta*, and is taken as an example of the *āvīta* inference by Prof. FRAUWALLNER (1958: 45), is as follows:

> 'If things are born from non-existence, as there is no cause (*yoni*), things come to be one and the same. As primordial matter does not exist, things of the world become equal without distinction. Why? Because we see that individual things presuppose the existence of equality. For example, such individual things as yoghurt, sour cream, curds, fresh butter, clarified butter, buttermilk, coagulated milk and inspissated milk presuppose milk. In non-existence, there exists no existential being (*bhāva*) which is presupposed to exist in any individual thing. Hence, things would come to be one and the same. But this is not the case. Therefore, a thing is not born from non-existence. The world does not originate from existence.[27] As a result, this individual

cessity, there is a state of non-separation, and it is in primordial matter that this non-separation occurs, because the one that has all the shape presupposes the state of non-separation. Therefore the primordial matter exists. (NAA 320.1–8).

[26] NAA 321.6–7: *tasyâsya pratipakṣāḥ sarvâikāntinaḥ puruṣêśvarâṇu-pravādāḥ vikāra-puruṣā vaināśikāś ca. teṣāṁ vaināśika-pratiṣedham agre vakṣyāmaḥ*. The similar opponents are enumerated in the beginning of YDī 2.2–3.

[27] This phrase is not understood. Prof. FRAUWALLNER (1958: 45.8) omits this sentence from his RST.

thing is born from nothing but primordial matter, which is the one remaining possibility. Therefore, primordial matter exists. This is the *āvīta* inference which corresponds to *vīta* reason of homogeneity (*anvaya*).'[28]

This *āvīta* inference first aims to deny the originality of things from non-existence. Second, it attempts to show the contradiction in the assumption of the non-existence of primordial matter. In order to highlight the contradiction they assume that primordial matter does not exist. Another characteristic is that it is connected with one of the *vīta* reasons. It can therefore be said that this *āvīta* inference attempts to show the existence of primordial matter from the reverse viewpoint of the *vīta* inference.

This *āvīta* inference does not deny or exclude the existence of any entities that might substitute for primordial matter, which are enumerated by name (such as God and so on), just before the real application of this *āvīta* inference. That is to say, this inference does not aim to exclude any other entities which might substitute for primordial matter. This is the case with a set of four *āvīta* inferences in NAA. All the four *āvīta* inferences deny that things could have originated from non-existence (*nêdaṁ vyaktam asata utpadyate*).[29]

---

[28] NAA 321.12–18: *kiṁ cânyat. yadi*[a] *vyaktasyâsata utpattir yony-abhāvād ekatva-prasaṅgaḥ, pradhānâbhāvāt sāmānya-mātram idaṁ vyaktaṁ niviśeṣam ity etat prasajyeta. kasmāt? sāmānya-pūrvakatvād viśeṣāṇām, sāmānya-pūrvakā hi loke viśeṣā dṛṣṭāḥ, tad yathā—kṣīra-pūrvakā dadhi-mastu-drapsa-nava-nīta-ghṛtâriṣṭa-kilāṭa-kūrcikâbhāvāḥ. na tv asati bhāvaḥ kaścid asti yat-pūrvakā vyakti-viśeṣāḥ syuḥ. tasmāt sāmānya-mātram idaṁ vyaktaṁ nirviśeṣam ity etat, na tv idaṁ tādṛk. tasmād nêdaṁ vyaktam asata utpadyate. na cêdaṁ sata utpadyate. pāriśeṣyāt pradhānād evêdaṁ vyaktam utpadyata*[b] *ity etad yuktam. tasmād asti pradhānam iti. eṣo 'nvaya-vītasyâvītaḥ.*

[a] Prof. FRAUWALLNER (1958: 45.1) starts RST with this term *yadi*. In NAA 321.10–12, before this inference, another inference is drawn which can be regarded as an *āvīta* inference, which runs as follows: *kiṁ cânyat, yadi vyaktasyâsata utpattir bhavaty arthârhtibhis tṛṇa-pāṁśu-vālukāḥ muktā-maṇi-rajata-suvarṇāni kriyeran, kasmāt? abhāva-kriyā guru-kāryā bhāva-kriyā laghvîti. na tv evaṁ kriyate, tasmād ayuktam ity ādi yāvad uktôttaratvād asamyag-vidhiḥ.*—'Moreover, if a thing is born from non-existence, pearls, diamonds, silver and gold are made from a grass, dust and sand by those who wish to make things. Why? Because the action of non-existent things makes a heavy matter with the help of light existent things (?). This actually does not happen. Therefore that is not right. As far as the answer is concerned, the standpoint is not right.'

Though it is not related to any *vīta* reason, from the nature of its meaning, it must be related to homogeneity (*anvaya*). This inference might be another example of the *āvīta* inference corresponding to one of the five *vīta* reasons, that it, homogeneity (*anvaya*). There is the possibility that more than five *āvīta* reasons are contrived before the number was fixed at five.

[b] Here Prof. FRAUWALLNER ends RST with the word *utpadyate*.

[29] The following *āvīta* inferences are summarised in the follows:

The reason called *yony-abhāvāt*, which is found in the previous *āvīta* inference, is again used for the next *āvīta* inference which corresponds to *vīta* reason called *parimāṇāt*. Finiteness is in-

Each argument has a somewhat regular expression at the end to show its relation to the *vīta* reasons, which are as follows:

NAA 323.2: *eṣo 'nvaya-vītasyâvītaḥ prasaṅgo vyākhyātaḥ.*
NAA 323.4: *tatra kārya-kāraṇa-vītasya āvītas tāvat.*
NAA 323.11: *kārya-kāraṇa-vītasya āvītaḥ.*
NAA 323.12: *iti śakti-vītasya āvītaḥ.*
NAA 323.17: *vaiśvarūpyâvibhāga-gati-vītasya āvīto draṣṭavya iti.*

In NAA, each *āvīta* inference is considered to correspond to the relevant *vīta* reason. The purpose of the *āvīta* inference is to support the relevant *vīta* reason by ob-

---

evitably connected with the creation of the world. If primordial matter does not exist, an individual thing will exist without finiteness. Why? Because things in the world are seen to be measured by the rod, measure, hand, fathom, string and one's height (*tulā-māna-hasta-vyāma-rajjv-ātmôpacayaiḥ*) (NAA 322.3). If primordial matter does not exist, anything known by measuring will not exist. Therefore things must have come into existence without being measured. This is not the case. Therefore, a thing does not originate from non-existence, and a thing does not originated from existence. It is born from primordial matter as the only remaining possible being. Therefore, primordial matter exists.

After this inference we encounter another *āvīta* inference connected with the first *vīta* reason called *anvaya* (NAA 322.6–323.2)

Subsequently, in connection with the *vīta* reason called *kārya-kāraṇa-bhāvāt*, the *āvīta* inference is mentioned. In the world, things are divided into two categories, cause and effect. If things are born from non-existence, they cannot be related to cause and effect, because they work neither simultaneously nor successively. In the world we see a thing is made, works and perishes. This is impossible without mutual dependence between cause and effect, like an axle and wheel. Therefore, it is impossible to postulate a relationship of cause and effect in things born from non-existence. But things in the world are related to cause and effect. Therefore, they are not born from non-existence. As a result, things are born from nothing but primordial matter, as the one remaining possibility. Therefore, primordial matter exists. This is the *āvīta* inference which corresponds with *vīta* reason called *kārya-kāraṇa* (NAA 323.4–11).

Next in connection with the *vīta* reason called *śakti*, the *āvīta* inference is made as follows. If a thing originates by chance without cause (*nirbījam akasmāt*), that is, from non-existence, it originates without any relationships to others. But, as a matter of fact, a thing originates when it is connected with others. Therefore, a thing does not originate from non-existence. This is the *āvīta* inference of the *vīta* reason called *śakti* (NAA 323.11–12)

As regards the last *āvīta* inference, it occupies the rest of the chapter, exploring the examination of result and its result (?) (*prasakta* and *anuprasakta*). These should be considered as the *āvīta* inference, which corresponds to the *vīta* reason called *vaiśvarūpyâvibhāva-gati* (NAA 323.12–14) Though the text is not so clear, the purpose of the rest of the chapter is to deny origination from absolute non-existence by showing that everything merges into everything else (*vikārasya vināśitvam*), but the primordial matter does not (*pradhānasya vināśitvam iti etad ayuktam*). The means for this proof seem to have been enumerated: recognition, the effect of an act, restriction of cause and result (?, *pratyabhijñānârtha-kriyā-hetu-kārya-niyamâdibhiś ca hetubhir*) (NAA 323.16).

serving the situation from the opposite standpoint, that is, by the assumption of the non-existence of primordial matter.[30]

3. Another commentary of SK, i.e. the *Sāṁkhya-tattva-kaumudī* (STK), explains the term *vīta* and *avīṭa* in relation to the classification of inference (*anumāna*). The author Vācaspatimiśra classifies inference into two categories, *vīta* and *avīta*, providing a definition for both: the function of *vīta* is affirmation, and that of *avīta* is negation. He then connects this classification with the three kinds of inference. While *vīta* consists of two kinds: *pūrvavat* and *sāmānyato-dṛṣṭa*, *avīta* is only *śeṣavat*.[31] In any case, when he refers to *vīta* and *avīta*, the interest of Vācaspatimiśra is in the well arranged classification of inference. His interest has nothing to do with the proof of primordial matter.

4. Concerning the relationship between the *vīta* inference and a syllogistic expression, an argument in YDī raises the question whether or not ST includes the five-part syllogism. At the beginning of YDī, the elements of *tantra* are discussed to prove that YDī is entitled to be called *tantra*. The author of YDī seems to believe that all ST, SK and YDī are authoritative treatise (*tantra*). They are entitled to be

---

[30] After the final *āvīta* inference we encounter a phrase that acts as a kind of summary of the *āvīta* inference, NAA 323.17–324.6: *evam eṣāṁ pradhānâstitvâikyâdi-sādhanârthaṁ vītānāṁ tat-sadbhāvasya anyathā vyaktâsambhavasya vā darśanena try-ātmaka-yoni-hetutvam avaśyam ity etad avadhāraṇârthānāṁ câvītānām atathârthatvam ukta-vidhinā pratipāditam.*—'In this way, while the *vīta* inference is used in order to prove the existence and uniqueness etc. of primordial matter, the *āvīta* inference is used to confirm that the cause is made of three constituents, that is, primordial matter. For this purpose, the *āvīta* inference will show that things never originate otherwise, and that things do not exist as they do, if the primordial matter does not exist.'

[31] STK on SK 5: *tatra prathamaṁ tāvad dvividham—vītam avītaṁ ca. anvaya-mukhena pravartamānaṁ vidhāyakaṁ vītam. vyatireka-mukhena pravartamānaṁ niṣedhakam avītam.* Vācaspatimiśra refers to the proofs of the non-difference of cause and effect in SK 9, calling them *avīta*. Here, all the proofs end in *nârthântaratvam* ('being not different from'). By means of this negative expression the proofs are regarded as *avīta*.

The view that *avīta* is the negation of an opponent is found in Uddyotakara and Dignāga, see:

> NV on NS 1.1.35, vol.1, p.211: *so 'yam avītaḥ para-pakṣa-pratiṣedhârtha eva bhavati. tāv etau vītâvita-hetū lakṣaṇābhyāṁ pṛthag-abhihitāv iti. tatra svarūpeṇârtha-paricchedakatvaṁ vīta-dharmaḥ, avītaḥ punaḥ para-pakṣa-pratiṣedhenâiva pravatata iti.*
>
> PS, Sde dge 56a1–2: *kun gyi rjes thog ma las bsal te ḥoṅs pa ḥgrub po shes pa la gshan gyi ḥdod pa so sor bkag nas raṅ gi phyogs yoṅs su gzuṅ baḥi bya ba ni bsal te ḥoṅs paḥo shes grag go / so sor ḥgegs paḥi thabs ni gñis te, dpe daṅ ḥgal ba daṅ khas blaṅs pa daṅ ḥgal ba shes so /*

called *tantra*, if they are possessed of necessary elements. The *tantra* is defined as follows:

> 'A philosophical work (*tantra*) is excellent if it contains: suitability of aphorisms, means of gaining knowledge and parts [of a logical syllogisms], no deficiencies [of principles], a description of doubt and decision, a brief statement and detailed explanation, the correct order [of the enumeration of principles] and appellations and [their] exposition.'[32]

The author of YDī explains all the terms in the above verse, and tries to prove the three texts are *tantra*. In the explanation of 'part' (*avayava*), the author of YDī 4.7 defines that the part consists of two kinds: *jijñāsâdayaḥ pratijñâdayaś ca*. An opponent raises a question: the parts must not be mentioned, because they are not taught in the treatise, that is, SK. The author of YDī tries to justify his mention of the parts, even if the term does not appear in SK. The third reason that the author of YDī uses in support of his justification is the fact that parts are taught in other authoritative texts (*tantrântarôkteḥ*). He explains this reason in the following way: teachers like Vindhyavāsin and so on taught the parts in their authoritative texts. These teachers are our criteria (*pramāṇa*). We can, therefore, said the author of YDī, mention the parts, even if they do not appear in SK. Here the author of YDī does not refer to ST to quote a description of the *avayava*, instead, he has recourse to other treatise written by Vindhyavāsin and so on to show that the Sāṁkhya had a tradition of logical expression. The author of YDī here does not refer to Vārṣagaṇya, even though he seems to have a good knowledge of him and his ST.[33] This fact suggests that ST itself did not refer to syllogism consisting of five or ten parts.

The second reason which may support this suggestion is the method of description of NAA, where a five-part syllogism is certainly included, but in a compact and well-ordered form. On the other hand, the real application of the *vīta* inference does not match the syllogistic expression. Taking long and undeveloped descriptions found throughout the whole section of the *vīta* inference, there seems to be a wide gulf between the description of the five-part syllogism and that of the five *vīta* inference. This contrasted description gives the impression that they were not written by the same person. This impression is strengthened by the fact that we encounter two different kinds of the *āvīta* inference in NAA. One postulates origination from non-existence and non-existence of primordial matter. The other is said to exclude pos-

---

[32] YDī 3.10–11:

sūtra-pramāṇâvayavôpapattir anyūnatā saṁśaya-nirṇayôktiḥ /
uddeśa-nirdeśam anukramaś ca saṁjñôpadeśāv iti tantra-sampat //

[33] Cf. Oberhammer (1961).

sible entities other than primordial matter, but without any real application. Thus it seems that the description found in NAA is not based on a single source, and that the portion of the syllogism and the real application of the *vīta* inference do not originate from the same source. It is therefore possible that this portion of the syllogism should be ascribed not to ST, but to Vindhyavāsin.[34] This again leads to a possibility that the syllogism is employed first in Sāṁkhya by Vindhyavāsin.[35]

5. As seen above, there are several different meanings or usages in the *vīta* and *avīta*. Here I would like to explain the different usages of the same expression in terms of a historical change. Based on a description of NAA and YDī, both of which contain real applications of the *vīta-avīta* inference, I shall conclude this paper with the following hypothesis.

The Sāṁkhya made a great effort to prove the existence of primordial matter, which is a unique concept of the school. They contrived various reasons in an effort to prove its existence. Finally, five reasons were contrived. They are considered to be a group sharing the same function, called *vīta*. To strengthen their position, the Sāṁkhya thinkers tried to highlight the contradiction in the assumption of non-existence of primordial matter. They tried to show that each *vīta* reason does not hold true if primordial matter does not exist. In accordance with the number of *vīta* reasons, this kind of inference is also five or more in number. As they are considered to

---

[34] Prof. FRAUWALLNER (1958: 34.3–5) (= *Kleine Schriften*: 254.3–5) takes a portion referred to by Jinendrabuddhi to be a part of the commentary on ST written by Vindhyavāsin.

[35] When we think of influence of Vindhyavāsin, we should perhaps be reminded of the fact that the concept of *viśeṣato-dṛṣṭa anumāna*, which Prof. FRAUWALLNER ascribes to ST, is referred to in the *Mīmāṁsā-śloka-vārttika* 5.4 (*Anumāna-pariccheda*) 143 and ascribed to Vindhyavāsin; see MŚV 5.4 (*Anumāna-pariccheda*) 142–143 (p. 86):

> *tad-deśâsthena tenâiva gatvā kālântare 'pi tam* /
> *yadâgnir budhyate tasya parva-bodhāt punaḥ punaḥ* // 142 //
> *sandihyamāna-sadbhāva-vastu-bodhāt pramāṇatā* /
> *viśeṣa-dṛṣṭam etac ca likhitaṁ vindhyavāsinā* // 143 //

Translation of the two verses by Ganganatha JHA (1900–1908: 202):

> 'On account of his former cognition (of the concomitance of "Fire" and "Smoke") such a person suspects the existence of "fire" whenever he sees any "smoke", and finds (on inspection) that in every case, (his suspicion is justified and) "fire" does exist.
> The frequent repetition (of such suspicion and its subsequent verification) gives rise to a definite general premise (that "the existence of smoke is always accompanied by the existence of fire"). It is the cognition of such particular relations that has been laid down by Vindhyavāsin.'

These verses, with slightly differences, are again cited in the TSa 1445–1446 (p. 422).

have the same function as the case of *vīta*, they are called *avīta* or *āvīta* as a group. By the application of both *vīta* and *avīta*, the existence of primordial matter was considered to have been completely proved. This is possibly the original concepts of *vīta* and *avīta*.

Being treated as a pair, a set of *vīta* and *āvīta* is considered to be the typical method of reasoning employed by the Sāṁkhya school. However, over time there occurred some changes in the meaning of both terms. An inference based on these five *vīta* reasons also called *vīta*. There is no substantial difference between the *vīta* reasons and the *vīta* inference. With this change, the *vīta* inference is criticised by opponents in relation to syllogistic expressions. But it is not certain that the Sāṁkhya had an interest in syllogism in earlier periods. Even if they had, it seems that the syllogism consisted at most of three parts, not of five parts as found in Vindhyavāsin. Regarding the concept of *avīta*, there occurred a change in its meaning, perhaps during the course of discussions with other schools. It came to mean the exclusion of other possible entities of other schools which might have the same function as primordial matter. As a result an original nature of *avīta* came to be emphasised, that is, *pariśeṣa*, which became a characteristic of the *avīta* inference. With this change *avīta* lost the relationship with five *vīta* reasons.

Both concepts finally came to be regarded as the two ways of reasoning that the Sāṁkhya generally used, distinct from the proof of the existence of primordial matter. At this stage, *vīta* is regarded as positive reasoning, and *avīta* is regarded as negative reasoning through exclusion.

The most important thing for the Sāṁkhya is to prove the existence of primordial matter. It is necessary for them to contrive methods of reason in order to attain this purpose. The concepts of *vīta* and *avīta* are a result of this effort. This is the only thing that concerned the Sāṁkhya, with some exceptions like Vindhyavāsin. As a whole they seemed little interested in the logic itself and they did not make further efforts to elaborate on the terms of inferential logic.

BIBLIOGRAPHY

FRANCO 1999 = Franco, Eli: 'Avīta and āvīta', *Asiatische Studien / Études Asiatiques* 53,3 (1999) 563–577.

FRAUWALLNER 1958 = Frauwallner, Erich: 'Die Erkenntnislehre des klassischen Sāṁkhya-Systems', *Wiener Zeitschrift für die Kunde Süd- und Ost-Asiens* 2 (1958) 84–139 [= *Kleine Schriften*, Herausgegeben von Gerhard Oberhammer und Ernst Steinkellner, Glasenapp-Stiftung 22, Franz Steiner Verlag, Wiesbaden 1982: 223–278].

HADANO 1944 = Hadano, Hakuyu: 'Suron gakuha no ronri setsu, vīta avīta ni tsuite (on vīta and avīta, logical theory of the Sāṁkhya)', *Bunka* 11/3 (1944) 177–219, 11/4 (1944) 306–36 (= Hakuyu Hadano: *Collective Works of Tibetan and Indian Studies*. Vol. 4, Hozokan, Kyoto 1988: 34–90).

JACOBI 1927 = Jacobi, Hermann: 'Vīta und Avīta', in: Julius von Negelein (ed.): *Aus Indiens Kultur. Festgabe Richard von Garbe, dem Forscher und Lehrer zu seinem 70. Geburtstag.*Palm & Enke, Erlangen 1927: 19–133 [= *Kleine Schriften*. Herausgegeben von Bernhard Kölver, 2 Vols, Glasenapp-Stiftung 22, Franz Steiner Verlag, Wiesbaden 1970: 613–621].

JHA 1900–1908 = Jha, Ganganatha (tr.): *Çlokavārtika, translated from the original Sanskrit with extracts from the commentaries 'Kasika' of Sucarita Misra and 'Nyāyaratnākara' of Partha Sarthi Misra*. Sri Harib Das Oriental Series No.8, Calcutta 1900–1908 [reprinted: Sri Satguru Publications, Delhi 1983].

JHA 1965 = Jha, Ganganatha (tr.): *The Tattvakaumudī, Vācaspati Miśra's Commentary on the Sāṁkhya-Kārikā*. Poona Oriental Series 10, Poona 1965.

KUMAR–BHARGAVA 1990–1992 = Kumar, Shiv; Bhargava, D.N. (ed., tr.): *Yuktidīpikā*. Eastern Book Linkers, Delhi, I: 1990, II: 1992.

MŚV = Kumārila Bhaṭṭa: *Mīmāṁsā-śloka-vārttika*. V.A. Ramaswami Sastri (ed.): *The Mīmāṁsāślokavārttika of Kumārilabhaṭṭa with the commentary Kāśikā of Sucaritamiśra*. Part III. Trivandrum Sanskrit Series 150, Trivandrum 1943.

NAA = Siṁha-sūri: *Nyāyâgamânusāriṇī*. Muni Jambūvijayajī (ed.): *Dvādaśāraṁ Nayacakraṁ of Ācārya Śrī Mallavādī Kṣamāśramaṇa. With the commentary Nyāyāgamānusāriṇī of Ācārya Śrī Siṁhasūri Gaṇi Vādi Kṣamāśramaṇa*. Edited with critical notes. Pt. I (1–4 Aras), Śrī Ātmānand Jain Granthamālā Serial 92, Śrī-Jaina-Ātmānaṁda-sabhā, Bhāvnagar 1966.

NV = Uddyotakara: *Nyāya-vārttika*. Nyaya-Tarkatirtha, Taranatha [Chap. 1, Sec. 1]; Tarkatirtha, Amarendramohan [Chap. I-ii–V]; Tarkatirtha, Hemantakumar [Chap. IV–V] (eds.): *Nyāya-darśanam. With Vātsyāyana's Bhāṣya, Uddyotakara's Vārttika, Vācaspati Miśra's Tātparyaṭīkā and Viśvanātha's Vṛtti*. With an Introduction by Narendra Chandra Vedantatirtha. 2 Vols, Rinsen Sanskrit Text Series I-1, Kyoto, 1982 [first edition: Calcutta Sanskrit Series 18, 29, Metropolitan Printing & Publishing House, Calcutta 1936, 1944].

OBERHAMMER 1961 = Oberhammer, Gerhard: 'On the Śāstra Quotations of the Yuktidīpikā', *The Adyar Library Bulletin* 25/1–4 (1961) 131–172.

PS = Dignāga: *Pramāṇa-samuccaya*. J. Takasaki; Z. Yamaguchi; Y. Ejima (eds.): *sDe dge Tibetan Tripiṭaka bsTan ḥgyur—preserved at the Faculty of Letters, University of Tokyo*. Tshad Ma (Ce). Tokyo 1981–1984.

RST	= Vārṣagaṇya: *Ṣaṣṭi-tantra*—Reconstructed text, after FRAUWALLNER (1958).
ST	= Vārṣagaṇya: *Ṣaṣṭi-tantra*.
STK	= Vācaspatimiśra: *Sāṁkhya-tattva-kaumudī*. See: JHA (1965).
TSa	= Śāntarakṣita: *Tattva-saṁgraha*. Embar Krishnamacharya (ed.): *Tattvasaṅgraha of Śāntarakṣita With the Commentary of Kamalaśīla*. 2 Vols, Oriental Institute, Baroda 1984.
YDī	= *Yukti-dīpikā*. Albrecht Wezler; Shujun Motegi (ed.): *Yukti-dīpikā—The Most Significant Commentary on the Sāṁkhyakārikā*. Vol. 1, Alt- und Neu-Indische Studien, Franz Steiner Verlag, Stuttgart 1998.

Valid Knowledge and Belief in Classical Sāṁkhya-Yoga*

PHILIPP A. MAAS

This paper is composed of three parts, starting with a brief description of the textual basis of Sāṁkhya-Yoga. The second part is concerned with the concept of three kinds of valid knowledge; it discusses the relationship between the definitions of valid knowledge in the *pramāṇa*-section of the *Pātañjala-yoga-śāstra* (PYŚ) 1.7 and notions of valid knowledge apparent in various other passages of the text. This relation is shown to be a complicated one., since the views on valid knowledge applied in the body of the text more than once differ considerably from those which one would expect against the backdrop of the *pramāṇa* section. This result leads to the conclusion that the theories of valid knowledge as expounded in the *pramāṇa* section are probably innovations to the classical Sāṁkhya-Yoga. The third and final part of this paper deals with the role of the *pramāṇa*-section in the PYŚ. I argue that this passage does not, in the first place, aim at a philosophical clarification. Patañjali upholds his special *pramāṇa*-theories in order to create acceptance for—or belief in—the soteriological efficiency of Sāṁkhya-Yoga.

As is well known, very few primary texts of classical Sāṁkhya-Yoga have survived. Almost all we have is the *Yoga-sūtra* of Patañjali together with its oldest commentary, the so-called *Yoga-bhāṣya*. According to manuscript colophons and secondary evidence, both texts taken collectively bear the common title *Pātañjala-yoga-śāstra*. In the introduction to my critical edition of its first chapter, I have argued—in accordance with BRONKHORST (1985: 191–203), but for different reasons—that probably one single author named Patañjali collected the *sūtra*s from different sources and furnished them with explanations which in later times came to be known as the *Yoga-bhāṣya*. The date of the work is still uncertain, but a time span reaching from 325 to 425 CE seems to be most likely.[1]

* Many thanks to Susanne Kamüller for having a close look at my English.

[1] MAAS (2006: xii–xix).

Logic and Belief in Indian Philosophy
Warsaw Indological Studies 3 (2010) 383–392.

For an appropriate understanding of difficult passages of the PYŚ—the number of which could be reduced by critically editing the first chapter, but which are still by no means rare—we can draw upon three sub-commentaries of different value. The most important, i.e. the one being the most faithful to classical Sāṁkhya-Yoga thought, is without doubt the *Pātañjala-yoga-śāstra-vivaraṇa* (YVi). The question of whether or not it is to be attributed to the famous Advaita-Vedāntin Śaṅkara is still open,[2] and I cannot enter into this discussion here. For my present purpose it may be sufficient to recall that the YVi's basic text, i.e. the version of PYŚ commented upon by the author of YVi, definitely goes back to quite an early stage of the transmission. The YVi's basic text not infrequently transmits correct readings which are lost in all manuscripts of the PYŚ available to me.[3] As the YVi does not cite any source younger than Kumārila,[4] accumulative evidence hints to a proximity of the YVi to its basic text not only with regard to its content, but also with regard to its time of composition. An exact dating is difficult to establish, but I can see no reason why the YVi should not go back to the late 7th or early 8th century CE. This, of course, does not mean that we may follow blindly Śaṅkara's interpretations, for the considerable gap of time between the composition of the PYŚ and its oldest surviving commentary will surely have had an impact on the development of philosophical ideas.

Due to limitations of space and time, this paper is mainly based upon Śaṅkara's interpretations, but Vācaspatimiśra's *Tattva-vaiśāradī* (TVś) has been consulted throughout. I did not, however, use the explanations provided by the *Yoga-vārttika* of Vijñānabhikṣu, which, in any case, is not a work of classical Sāṁkhya-Yoga.

PYŚ 1.7, the *pramāṇa*-section, contains a series of definitions of three kinds of valid knowledge. It starts with perception (*pratyakṣa*):

> 'Perception as valid knowledge is a mental process (*vṛtti*) which—because the *citta* is coloured (or: affected) by an outer entity by means of the sense-capacities as channels—has this [entity] as its object (*tad-viṣayā*). [Its] main task is to determine particularities of a sense object which consists of generic properties as well as of individual properties. The result is a uniform (*aviśiṣṭa*) awareness of the mental process (*citta-vṛtti*) belonging to the self. I shall explain later [how] the self experiences its mental organ (*buddhi*).'[5]

---

[2] Cf. HALBFASS (1991: 223 f.).

[3] Cf. MAAS (2006: lxix).

[4] HALBFASS (1983: 120).

[5] PYŚ 1.7.2 f.: *indriya-praṇāḍikayā cittasya bāhya-vastûparāgāt tad-viṣayā sāmānya-viśeṣâtmano 'rthasya viśeṣâvadhāraṇa-pradhānā vṛttiḥ pratyakṣaṁ pramāṇam. phalam aviśiṣṭaḥ pauruṣeyaś citta-vṛtti-bodhaḥ. "pratisaṁvedī buddheḥ puruṣaḥ", ity upariṣṭād darśayiṣyāmaḥ.*

This definition states that an entity of the outer world (*bahya-vastu*) creates a content of consciousness. The *citta* is related to the outside world by means of the well-known set of sense capacities, i.e. hearing, feeling, smelling, tasting and seeing. These sense capacities provide the *citta* with a representation of the outer entity, the sense object (*artha*).

Patañjali is not very specific as to the kind of involvement of the self. He merely hints at it by using the *vṛddhi*-derivative *pauruṣeya* 'belonging to the self' and postpones a more thorough explanation to a later portion of the PYŚ. The passage referred to, i.e. PYŚ 2.20, is not concerned with perception as valid knowledge, but with the generation of mental events in general.[6]

the author of YVi, provides illustrations. The perception of a blue colour includes the perception of two kinds of properties: the individual property (*viśeṣa*) of being blue, and the generic property (*sāmānya*) of being a colour. Although both kinds of properties are subject to perception, the perception of the generic property, viz. 'colourness' is subordinate to the perception of the individual property, viz. blueness.[7]

The determination of generic properties in direct perception therefore accounts for the recognition of class membership and for the application of a linguistic term to the perceived entity. The determination of *viśeṣa*, on the other hand, provides information on an entity as being individual. Śaṅkara's example clearly shows that *sāmānya* and *viśeṣa* are relative notions, and not—like in Praśastapāda's Vaiśeṣika—'real factor[s] in the real world'[8], which, of course, would have no place in Sāṁkhya-Yoga metaphysics.[9] On the whole, the information provided by the PYŚ is too scarce to allow a more thorough examination of these concepts, and, moreover, their discussion is beyond the scope of this paper.

Having in view the metaphysical and soteriological dimension of Sāṁkhya-Yoga, the absence of any discernible reference to specifically yogic perceptions within the definition of perception is surprising.

The author of YVi allows an opponent to formulate objections against the exclusion of yogic perception and introspection from the definition of perception:

> '[Objection:] The vision (*darśana*) of *yogin*s, which is generated in meditative concentration being free from conceptual thinking (*vikalpa*),

[6] YS 2.20, p. 87.6 f., defines the role of the self in cognition: *draṣṭā dṛśi-mātraḥ śuddho 'pi pratyayânupaśyaḥ*.

[7] YVi 177.2–4: *na sāmānyaṁ nâvadhāryate, guṇa-bhūtaṁ tu gṛhyata eva. yathā nīlaṁ rūpam iti nīlâvadhāraṇa-prādhānye saty api rūpam eva nīlam iti guṇa-bhūtam avadhārayati …*

[8] Halbfass (1992: 117).

[9] Cf. YVi 177.9–11: *sarvam eva hi vastu vastv-antarâpekṣayā sāmānyaṁ viśeṣaś ca.*

> because it does not conform to this definition, as well as the knowledge of joy, passion etc., which does not require the sense capacities as channels etc., should either be acknowledged as different means of knowledge, or [the definition of *pratyakṣa*] should have stated that they too are means of knowledge.
> [Answer:] [This is] not [true], because [this objection has already been] ruled out by [the definition itself, which states that perception] is dependent on the self's cognition. It is well known (*hi*), that perception is not a mental process without cognition. [The mental process] having cognition obtains its [status of] being perception only because of the appearance of [pure] consciousness (i.e. the self). ... The use of [the expression] "the sense capacities as channels" is only [meant to be] a clarifying explanation (*anuvāda*) for the coming into being of ordinary perception, because otherwise the knowledge possessed by *yogin*s and by the supreme lord, which is independent from sense capacities, would not be perceptions. But simultaneous grasping of fine, remote, and other [objects that are imperceptible to ordinary perception] exists by means of the mind-*sattva* which has everything as its object and refers to everything, when it is not restricted by taints, [*karman*, its fruition] and [latent deposits].'[10]

These objections deal with two kinds of mental events which allegedly are not included in the definition of *pratyakṣa*, as both are independent from sense capacities. The first one is specifically yogic perceptions, the second kind is introspections. If one would deny both kinds of mental events to be valid knowledge at all, the consequences would be severe. The refutation of yogic perceptions would render Sāṁkhya-Yoga meaningless.[11] Moreover, the rejection of introspection as valid knowledge would be tantamount to the rejection of the foundations of everyday life.

Although the YVi's dismissal of these objections all in all is not convincing, it seems—at least in part—to be in line with classical Sāṁkhya-Yoga. We can leave its relegation of the definition's opening section to the status of a mere explanation (*anuvāda*) out of consideration. It is not convincing, simply because it is very un-

[10] YVi 178.7–179.1: *nanu ca, yogināṁ nirvikalpa-samādhi-jaṁ darśanam, tasyânevaṁ-lakṣaṇatvāt, tathā sukha-rāgâdi-vijñānasya cânindriya-praṇāḍikā-pūrvatvāt, pramāṇântaratvam abhyupetavyam, pratyakṣatvaṁ vā vaktavyam, ucyate—na, pramāṇasya puruṣa-pratyayâpekṣatvena parihṛtatvāt. na hy apratyayā vṛttiḥ pratyakṣam, caitanyôdaya-hetor eva sapratyayāyāḥ pratyakṣatvam. ... indriya-praṇāḍikâgrahaṇaṁ laukika-pratyakṣôdbhāvanânuvāda eva; anyathā hîndriya-nirapekṣasya yogîśvarayor jñānasyâpratyakṣatā syāt. asti hi kleśâdi-pratibandhâbhāve sarvârthena citta-sattvena sarva-viṣayeṇa yugapat-sūkṣma-vyavahitâdi-grahaṇam.*

[11] Cf. below, p. 391.

likely that the author of the PYŚ would have expressed himself so misleadingly. If his intention had been to solely provide a definition of worldly perception, which excludes yogic and other forms, he would have had to particularly mention a distinction.

The second argument, on the other hand, deserves more attention. The acceptance of all kinds of mental events providing consciousness of individual properties as valid knowledge is in line with the final part of the definition, which refers to the discussion of the relationship of *puruṣa* and *citta* in PYŚ 2.20 and similar passages. As stated above, the passage is not primarily concerned with the perception of entities in the outside world. On the whole, the involvement of sense capacities and the distinction between external and internal entities is not even mentioned.

The final argument, which seems to aim at the unity of the PYŚ, is obviously circular. It proves the agreement of the definition with other parts of the PYŚ only under the condition that this agreement is already taken for granted. There are, indeed, a number of passages which evidently accept yogic states of consciousness as *pratyakṣa*. For example, with regard to 'the attainment without conceptual thinking' (*nirvikalpa-samāpatti*) we read: 'This is the highest perception' (PYŚ 1.42.9: *tat paraṁ pratyakṣam*). According to the perspective of the author of YVi on the PYŚ as a unified whole, this and similar passages prove the inclusion of yogic perception into the above definition. From a more critical point of view, of course, we cannot but notice that the endeavours of the commentator to establish harmony is ultimately futile. The definition of perception seems to be alien at least to the more *yoga*-specific parts of Sāṁkhya-Yoga epistemology.

In turning to inference (*anumāna*), we do not need to concern ourselves with the details of its definition, which according to TfphSI (Vol. 1: 47, col. 2, s.v. *anumāna*) point to a 'peculiar development of the teaching of *anumāna*' in the history of Indian philosophy. For the present purpose it is sufficient to notice a parallel to the definition of direct perception. PYŚ 1.7,7 runs: '... inference is a mental process which mainly determines universals ...' (... *sāmānyâvadhāraṇa-pradhānā vṛttir anumānam* ...). In spite of the obvious fact that °*-pradhāna* at the end of the compound, here as well as in the definition of *pratyakṣa*, means 'being chiefly concerned with', the commentator as well as later passages in the PYŚ support a different interpretation. They regard inference as being restricted exclusively to the determination of generic properties, leaving no room at all for the capacity to determine individual properties. The following two passages sufficiently illustrate this point. PYŚ 1.25.6 f. reads: 'Inference exhausts itself by only drawing together generic properties. It is not able to determine individual properties' (*sāmānya-mātrôpasaṁhāre kṛtôpakṣayam anumānaṁ na viśeṣa-pratipattau samartham*). A similar statement is met with in PYŚ 1.49.4: *tathânumānaṁ sāmānya-viṣayam eva.*

The author of the *pramāṇā*-passage—although we do not know any details—must have held a different position. If in his opinion *anumāna* had no capacity at all to determine individual properties, he would not, again, have expressed himself so misleadingly.

Similar to the treatment of direct perception, the commentaries, also with regard to verbal testimony or authoritative teaching (*āgama*), give interpretations which go far beyond the wording of the definition, but which are in harmony with later passages of the PYŚ. The definition of *āgama* runs:

> 'A trustworthy person (*āpta*), communicates an object, which he himself has perceived (literally: seen) [or] inferred, in order to transfer his own awareness to another person by means of a verbal expression (*śabda*). The mental process of the listener, which because of [the] words [uttered] refers to this object, is verbal testimony (or: authoritative tradition). Verbal testimony (or: authoritative tradition) is unreliable, if [it is given by] a speaker whose objects of speech are unbelievable, [and/or who] has not perceived or inferred the objects of his speech [himself]; but if he is an original speaker who [himself] has seen or inferred the object, there is no unreliability.'[12]

This passage quite clearly refers to the transmission of information from one human being to another. The inclusion of verbal testimony into the set of means of knowledge must presumably be seen against the backdrop of verbal communication of *yoga* teachers to their pupils. The instructions, advice and descriptions of mental contents to be encountered in meditation would have been taken as supplementary and subsidiary valid knowledge. The interpretations provided by Śaṅkara and Vācaspati are much more comprehensive. Both take *āgama* not as 'valid verbal testimony' but as 'authoritative tradition'. Therefore they interpret the word *mūla-vaktṛ* ('original speaker') as designating the supreme lord, Īśvara.[13] The interpretation of *āgama* as 'authoritative tradition' seems to be an attempt to bring the definition into harmony with the bulk of the PYŚ, as it is exactly this meaning of *āgama*—and its synonym *śruta*—which is used throughout the PYŚ. Moreover, even the interpretation of *mūla-vaktṛ* to mean 'Īśvara' is not as far fetched as it might seem on first sight. In PYŚ 1.25 we find a citation from the Sāṁkhya teacher Pañcaśikha,[14] which desig-

[12] PYŚ 1.7,9–12: *āptena dṛṣṭo 'numito 'rthaḥ paratra sva-bodha-saṁkrāntaye śabdenôpadiśyate. śabdāt tad-artha-viṣayā vṛttiḥ śrotur āgamaḥ. yasyâśraddheyârtho vaktā na dṛṣṭânumitârthaḥ, sa āgamo viplavate. mūla-vaktari tu dṛṣṭânumitârthe nirviplavaḥ syāt.*

[13] Cf. TVś ad PYŚ 1.7 (= YS, p. 12.20 f.): *mūla-vaktā tatrêśvaro dṛṣṭânumitârtha ity arthaḥ*, and YVi 195.9: *mūla-vaktari tv ādi-vaktarîśvare.*

[14] According to TVś ad PYŚ 1.25 (= YS, p. 31.16).

nates Īśvara is as the 'first knower' who, as the founder of the Sāṁkhya lineage of teachers and pupils, expounds the teaching of Sāṁkhya-Yoga to Āsuri.

> 'The first knower, having taken possession[15] of a mental capacity of magical transformation (*nirmāṇa-citta*)[16], out of compassion, [being] the venerable, most excellent seer [Kapila], taught [the teaching of Sāṁkhya-Yoga] to Āsuri, who was desirous to know.'[17]

Although the interpretation of *mūla-vaktṛ* as Īśvara is in line with the thought of Sāṁkhya-Yoga, it clearly goes beyond the wording of the *pramāṇa*-passage. Moreover, it even seems to contradict this passage, which states that 'the original speaker has perceived [and/or] inferred himself'. It is hard to imagine how and why the Īśvara, being capable of a direct perception of everything by means of his perfect (*utkṛṣṭa*) *citta*, should acquire knowledge by means of inference. Therefore, the definition cannot have been composed with the conveyance of knowledge from the Īśvara to a human being in mind. It refers exclusively to interpersonal communication. If this is true, we are obliged to diagnose a tension between the definition of *āgama* and the concept of authoritative teaching as it is accepted in different passages of the PYŚ.

Within the first chapter of the PYŚ we find, moreover, two statements dealing with the aptitude of authoritative tradition to determine truth which clearly contradict each other. PYŚ 1.25 denies the capacity of inference to provide knowledge of individual properties and ascribes this capacity to authoritative tradition:

> '... Inference is not able to [provide] knowledge of particularities, therefore knowledge of particularities—as for example [the Īśvara's] omniscience—have to be gained from authoritative tradition.'[18]

In PYŚ 1.49, on the other hand, the capacity of *āgama* to provide knowledge of particularities is boldly denied.

> 'Authoritative tradition ... has generic properties as its objects, since authoritative tradition cannot convey a an individual property.'[19]

---

[15] For the meaning of *adhiṣṭhāya* cf. BHSD: 12, col. 2, s.v. *adhitiṣṭhati*.

[16] Cf. BHSD: 302, col. 1, s.v. *nirmāṇa*.

[17] PYŚ 1.25.9–11: *ādi-vidvān nirmāṇa-cittam adhiṣṭhāya kāruṇyād bhagavān parama ṛṣir āsuraye jijñāsamānāya provāca.*

[18] PYŚ 25.6 f.: ... *anumānaṁ na viśeṣa-pratipattau samartham iti tasya sarva-jñatvâdi-viśeṣa-pratipattir āgamataḥ paryeṣyā.*

[19] PYŚ 49.2 f.: ... *āgama-jñānam ... sāmānya-viṣayam. na hy āgamena śakyo viśeṣo 'bhidhātum.*

These statements could only be reconciled if they would either deal with two different kinds of authoritative tradition or with different kinds of individual properties, but I have not been able to find a hint to such a distinction.

These observations show that the *pramāṇa*-section does not form a unified whole with the remaining part of PYŚ. We find unexplained and inexplicable extensions and limitations of their definitions. With regard to *āgama* we do not only have to ascertain an extension of the definition of verbal testimony to authoritative tradition. We even meet with contradicting statements regarding its aptitude to provide valid knowledge.

If one was asked to account for these findings, historical explanations and the compilatory nature of the text would, of course, be the first things to come to one's mind. The final part of this paper elaborates this explanation.

The PYŚ was compiled at a time when the teaching of the *pramāṇa*s had become a fixed part of philosophical treatises. The importance of *pramāṇa*-theories for the various systems of philosophical thought cannot even be touched upon here. We may just briefly recall that it is not a mere coincidence that '*pramāṇa*' is the first word in Gautama Akṣapāda's *Nyāya-sūtra*, which is supposedly older than the PYŚ.[20]

Although theories of valid knowledge in pre-classical Yoga may not have played a very prominent part, Patañjali includes a *pramāṇa*-theory into his *Yoga-śāstra*. His motives presumably were not exclusively of a philosophical, but also of a strategic nature. He did not only aim at the clarification of the concept of valid knowledge, but was probably at least as much concerned about the acceptance of the soteriological potential of Sāṁkhya-Yoga. Therefore Patañjali not only places the *pramāṇa*-theory at the beginning of his work, but also puts perception at the head of the *pramāṇa*s.[21]

On the other hand, Patañjali in his own terms has good reasons for deviating from the outline of direct perception in the bulk of the text. The definition of *yoga* in YS 1.2 calls for the 'shut down of all kinds of mental processes' (*citta-vṛtti-nirodha*), which, of course, includes the shut down of valid knowledge.

With the exception of the *pramāṇa*-section, Patañjali is conspicuously silent about the concepts of inference and verbal testimony. He almost exclusively refers to them when stressing their dependence upon—and inferiority to—perception.[22] But the concept of perception in the *pramāṇa*-section is not identical with the concept of perception in the rest of the text. While the former is concerned with a theory of ordinary knowledge dealing with outside objects which cause the content of con-

[20] NS 1.1.1, p. 28.2.

[21] In contrast to the PYŚ's emphasis on perception, the older *Ṣaṣṭi-tantra* holds inference to be the most important means of knowledge. Cf. TfphSI, Vol. 3: 69, col. 1, s.v. *pramāṇa*, which cites FRAUWALLNER's (1958: 265) reconstruction of the *Ṣaṣṭi-tantra*.

[22] Cf. PYŚ 1.42.9: *ta[t pratyakṣaṁ ś]rutânumānayor bījam. tataḥ śrutânumāne prabhavataḥ.*

sciousness, the latter deals with supernatural knowledge and cognitions in meditation. The acceptance of these cognitions as valid knowledge is of fundamental importance for Sāṁkhya-Yoga. If 'knowledge of the difference' (*viveka-khyāti*) between the self (*puruṣa*) and matter (*prakṛti*) was denied the status of valid knowledge, Sāṁkhya-Yoga would loose its soteriological potential. Therefore, one aim of the theory of valid knowledge apparently is to foster the belief into the teachings of authoritative tradition; a belief that leads to the support of followers as well as to acceptance with practitioners. With an initial belief once secured, the teachings of tradition and advice of the teacher lead the practitioner to *yoga*-specific cognitions in meditation. These cognitions, if seen as valid knowledge, cause a deepening of the belief in tradition.[23] From this perspective, valid knowledge and belief in classical Sāṁkhya-Yoga both embrace the cause of spiritual progress.

BIBLIOGRAPHY

BHSD = Edgerton, Franklin: *Buddhist Hybrid Sanskrit Grammar and Dictionary*. Volume II: Dictionary. William Dwight Whitney Linguistic Series, Yale University Press, New Haven 1953.

BRONKHORST 1985 = Bronkhorst, Johannes: 'Patañjali and the Yoga Sūtras', *Studien zur Indologie und Iranistik* 10 (1985) 191–212.

FRAUWALLNER 1958 = Frauwallner, Erich: *Kleine Schriften*, Hrsg. von Gerhard Oberhammer und Ernst Steinkellner, Glasenapp-Stiftung 22, Franz Steiner Verlag, Wiesbaden 1982.

[23] For the interdependence of specifically yogic preceptions and spiritual progress see PYŚ 35,6–10: *yady api śāstrânumānâcāryôpadeśair avagatam artha-tattvaṁ tathā-bhūtam eva bhavati, teṣāṁ yathā-bhūtârtha-pratipādana-sāmarthyāt, tathâpi yāvad eka-deśo 'pi kaścit sva-karaṇa-saṁvedyo na bhavati, tāvat sarvaṁ parokṣam iva, āpavargāt sūkṣmeṣv artheṣu na dṛḍhāṁ buddhim utpādayati. tasmāc chāstrânumānâcāryôpadeśôpodbalanârtham avaśyaṁ kaścid viśeṣaḥ pratyakṣī-kartavyaḥ. tatra tad-upadiṣṭârthâika-deśa-pratyakṣatve sati, sarvaṁ sūkṣma-viṣayam apy âpavargāc chraddhīyate.*—'Even if [a *yogin*] understands by means of authoritative tradition, inference, and the instruction of the teacher, that an object in reality is of such qualities as these [means of knowledge] are able to provide knowledge of the object as it really is, everything seems [still] to be beyond the range of cognition and does not bring forth a firm understanding of subtle objects up to liberation, as long as [the *yogin*] is not able to perceive [at least] in part (*eka-deśa*) something with his own sense capacities. Therefore, in order to strengthen authoritative tradition, inference, and the instruction of the teacher, something particular has to be brought to perception. If one of these (*tatra*) [objects], which has been taught by [authoritative tradition, inference, and the instruction of the teacher], becomes direct perceptible [at least] in part, [the *yogin*] beliefs the whole [teaching of Sāṁkhya-Yoga] even with reference to subtle objects, up to liberation.'

HALBFASS 1983 = Halbfass, Wilhelm: *Studies in Kumārila and Śaṅkara*. Studien zur Indologie und Iranistik, Monographie 9, Inge Wezler Verlag, Reinbek 1983.

HALBFASS 1991 = Halbfass, Wilhelm: *Tradition and Reflection. Explorations in Indian Thought*. State University of New York Press, Albany (New York) 1991.

HALBFASS 1992 = Halbfass, Wilhelm: *On Being and What There Is. Classical Vaiśeṣika and the History of Indian Ontology*. State University of New York Press, Albany (New York) 1992.

MAAS 2006 = Maas, Philipp André (ed.): *Sāmadhipāda. Das erste Kapitel des* Pātañjalayogaśāstra *zum ersten Mal kritisch ediert. / The First Chapter of the* Pātañjalayogaśāstra *for the first Time Critically Edited.* Studia Indologica Universitatis Halensis, Geisteskultur Indiens: Texte und Studien 9, Shaker Verlag, Aachen 2006.

NS = Akṣapāda Gautama: *Nyāya-sūtra*. Nyaya-Tarkatirtha, Taranatha [Chap. 1, Sec. 1]; Tarkatirtha, Amarendramohan [Chap. I-ii–V]; Tarkatirtha, Hemantakumar [Chap. IV–V] (eds.): *Nyāya-darśanam. With Vātsyāyana's Bhāṣya, Uddyotakara's Vārttika, Vācaspati Miśra's Tātparyaṭīkā and Viśvanātha's Vṛtti*. With an Introduction by Narendra Chandra Vedantatirtha. 2 Vols, Second edition, Munshiram Manoharlal Publishers, New Delhi 2003 [first edition: Calcutta Sanskrit Series 18, 29, Metropolitan Printing & Publishing House, Calcutta 1936, 1944].

PYŚ = Patañjali: *Pātañjala-yoga-śāstra* (*Yoga-sūtra* and *Yoga-bhāṣya*). For the first chapter (*Samādhi-pāda*), see: MAAS (2006). For the remaining chapters see: YS.

TfphSI = Oberhammer, Gerhard; Prets, Ernst; Prandstetter, Joachim (eds.): *Terminologie der frühen philosophischen Scholastik in Indien. Ein Begriffswörterbuch zur altindischen Dialektik, Erkenntnislehre und Methodologie.* 3 Vols, ÖAW, philosophisch-historische Klasse, Denkschriften, 223, 248 und 343; Beiträge zur Kultur- und Geistesgeschichte Asiens 9, 17 und 49, Verlag der Österreichischen Akademie der Wissenschaften, Wien 1991 (Vol. 1: *A–I.*), 1996 (Vol. 2: *U–Pū*), 2006 (Vol. 3: *Pra–H*).

TVś = Vācapatimiśra: *Tattva-vaiśaradī*. See YS.

YS = Patañjali: *Pātañjala-yoga-sūtra. Pātañjalayogasūtrāṇi. Vācaspatimiśra-viracita-ṭīkā-sameta-Śrī-Vyāsa-bhāṣya-sametāni. Āśramasya paṇḍitaiḥ saṁśodhitam*... 4. edition, Ānanda Āśrama Sanskrit Series 47, Puṇyapattana (= Pune) 1978 [first edition: 1904]. Cf. PYŚ.

YVi = Śaṅkara (?): *Pātañjala-yoga-śāstra-vivaraṇa*. Kengo Harimoto (ed.): *A Critical Edition of the Pātañjala-yoga-śāstra-vivaraṇa. First Part.* Samādhipāda *with an Introduction.* A Dissertation in Asian and Middle Eastern Studies. University of Pennsylvania, Philadelphia 1999 (unpublished).

Language, Grammar and Belief

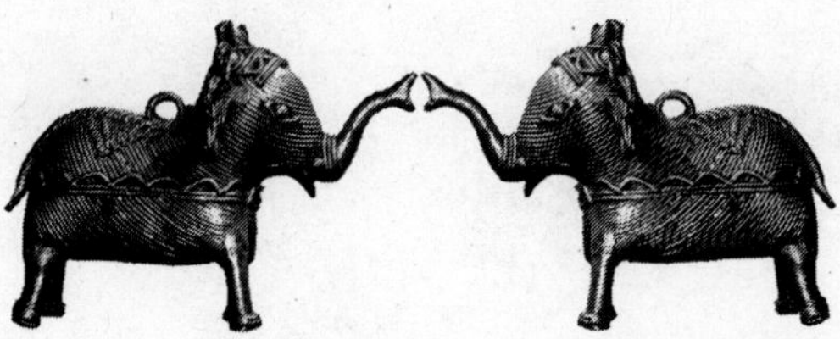

Grammarians' Leaving Logic at the Door*

ASHOK AKLUJKAR

— 1 —

1.1. It would not be illogical to think of the Bhartṛhari-authored passage, *Trikāṇḍī* (later commonly but inexactly referred to as *Vākyapadīya*) 1.30–42, that I am about to discuss, as a piece written, with unbelievable foresight, to serve as the basis for a discussion focusing on logic and belief. The confrontation between willingness to be satisfied with received wisdom, knowledge or information and the insistence on asking for proof, reasoning or critical inquiry that is recurrently witnessed in life has found an explicit and extended expression in this passage. Further, parts of it, particularly verses 34 and 42, namely,

> *yatnenânumito 'py arthaḥ kuśalair anumātṛbhiḥ /*
> *abhiyuktatarair anyair anyathâivôpapādyate //*

and

> *hasta-sparśād ivândhena viṣame pathi dhāvatā /*
> *anumāna-pradhānena vinipāto na durlabhaḥ //*
> (translated under (d) and (f) in the appendix below, p. 405 ff.)

belong to the body of verses that later Indian philosophers quote again and again when they respond to questions such as: What are the relative strengths of the com-

---

* My thanks to George and Jody Cardona for their observations on the first version.

In the following, I will use 'logic' in its loose, colloquial sense, not as a technical term standing for a specific branch or mode of philosophising. Reflecting the reality of my sources and of the ordinary English usage, I will let 'logic' stand for any activity of the human mind in which inferring, deducing, guessing, speculating, theorising, reasoning, arguing etc. of any kind is involved for what we sometimes express with 'thinking rationally, reasoning, non-faithbased argument.' Moving from a piece of knowledge (whatever is believed to be true at a given time) to another piece of knowledge on the assumption that the two pieces are related to each other through a çause-and-effect relationship would suffice for me as a definition of 'logic' in the present context.

Logic and Belief in Indian Philosophy
Warsaw Indological Studies 3 (2010) 395–414.

monly accepted *pramāṇas*? Is a *pratyakṣa*, thought to generate a piece of knowledge directly or to provide empirical confirmation, always more reliable than an *anumāna*, which brings knowledge of the world to us in a roundabout way? Do the *pramāṇas* always operate in dependence on each other, or, to ask the same question differently, should we think of the *pramāṇas* as capable of being related to validity in isolation from each other (see AKLUJKAR (1988))?

1.2. In TK 1.30–42, Bhartṛhari's argument consists of the following six steps (see the correspondingly marked points in the appendix (p. 405 ff.) toward the end for supporting textual evidence):

(a1) For matters or objects falling beyond perception and inference one needs *āgama* 'received knowledge'.

(a2) An *āgama* in this context starts with persons having extraordinary cognitive capabilities or experiences.[1]

(a3) If one wishes to explain logically why these persons had the capabilities or experiences they are said to have had, one must assume that there was something different from the ordinary in their backgrounds—i.e. one must admit that the roots of the extraordinary capabilities or experiences must be non-ordinary.

(a4) This non-ordinary cannot be something utterly undefined or unprecedented, for, then, in putting it forward, one will not really be giving the expected precise cause-and-effect statement; one will, in effect, be saying that anything can result from anything whatsoever. This means that, in a proper explanation, the background in the form of the extraordinary roots or causes must be in accordance with some *āgama*, prescribing a method for certain cognitive cultivation.

(b) So far in human history, reasoning has failed to impede what people do in the case of religio-spiritual merit, the other world etc. Empirical evidence would not support any assertion of overpowering or displacing role to rationality or logic.

(c) Inference is a shaky business. Predictions fail to come true as the situational elements change.

(d) If one logician establishes a thesis carefully through inference, another logician accounts for it in a very different way. There is no uniqueness about the manner of logical establishment (and therefore there is no constancy of philosophical presuppositions or implications).

(e) Jewellers, musicians etc., through practice, come to possess cognitive abilities, the nature of which they cannot explain to others, no matter how hard

[1] Note the expressions *ṛṣi, śiṣṭa, āvir-bhūta-prakāśa* and *anupapluta-cetas* occurring in the passages cited in the Appendix.

they think about the situation. The abilities make their cognition content, which has a directness or vividness, indistinguishable from the content of perceptions. Further, the directness or vividness is such that neither they nor those who believe in their abilities would allow inference to override what they say.

(f) Life being what the points made in (a)–(e) indicate it to be, relatively little business of the world is run or can be run by relying solely on one's inferential ability.

1.3. As in the case of many prophetic, programmatic or repeatedly useful passages, TK 1.30–42 analysed above has a rather specific and relatively narrow context, namely to argue that the Vaiyākaraṇas or grammarians should not be faulted for teaching what expressions one should use, by resting their preference on the *Veda* and the *smṛti*s receiving corroboration in the conduct of the spiritual elite.

Beginning with Kātyāyana (not later than the third century BCE), the second authoritative figure in the Pāṇinian grammatical tradition, we have evidence to the effect that the Pāṇinīyas connected grammatical usage (*sādhu-śabda*s) with religio-spiritual merit (*dharma*). They considered alternative modes of this connection—whether knowing such *śabda*s was sufficient or one must also employ them—and concluded that employment backed by knowledge of the rules of grammar (*śāstra-pūrvaka prayoga*) was required.

The question of whether merit was acquired or simply revealed also engaged their minds. To judge by what Bhartṛhari tells us, they voted in favour of the latter alternative.

The accessed merit could lead to worldly elevation (*abhyudaya*) or serve to cleanse the mind as a preliminary to *brahma-prāpti* or *mokṣa* 'spirit liberation, liberation of the worldly self or personality'.[2]

— 2 —

2.1. The Pāṇinian statement, given above in a summary form, is a mission statement. Like the university administrators of our time, almost every Indian system of knowledge issued a mission statement, initially as a list of *prayojana*s and later as a part of what came to be known as *anubandha-catuṣṭaya*. However, the Pāṇinīyas, in making a case for the branch of knowledge they were pursuing, appear to have gone

[2] I have dealt with the issues of understanding the grammarians' concepts of *dharma*, *abhivyakti* ('revelation, manifestation'), *abhyudaya* and *brahma-prapti*/*mokṣa* in AKLUJKAR (2004). References to earlier discussions of the issues can be found in the same article.

too far to most modern minds. To connect grammar with worldly elevation seems reasonable enough. Those who speak or write a grammatical form of a language—those who place themselves close to the standard, respectable dialect—do seem to have access to better economic opportunities in most settled or organised societies. But in claiming as much as 'our branch of study can enlighten you about brahman', implying 'we can land you on brahman', the grammarians appear to have overstated their usefulness. Many witnesses to their claim begin to view them as slavishly imitating systems like the Vedānta or as incapable of shaking off a traditionally received assertion—as sacrificing reasonableness on the altar of belief. Even a grammarian like Bhaṭṭoji-dīkṣita feels compelled to offer the clarification that Bhartṛhari's elucidation of Brahman is incidental and resembles the gifting of the wish-fulfilling jewel (*Cintā-maṇi*) to a cowrie-seeking reader (cf. ŚK, p. 12).

2.2. However, Bhartṛhari, as the grammarian-philosopher giving us the earliest available and sufficiently detailed statement on the issue, seems to be aware of the possible negative reaction or criticism. In fact, he knew of thinkers who differed radically from him. In the *Vṛtti* on TK 1.182, he refers to anitya-vādins who were quite satisfied in reading a social etiquette, a convention, in the '*sādhu* : *asādhu*' distinction. They did not see any reason for saddling the grammatical or *sādhu* expressions with the additional responsibility of leading to *dharma*. For these thinkers, our approbation of some speech forms and our denigration of some other speech forms were not different from the expectations made of wrestlers etc., namely that the wrestlers should behave only in a certain way when training or competing, should not hold the opponent with this or that part of his body and observe an honour code. All language was natural and, therefore, not blameworthy in itself. It was a human act that some realisations of language were given a position of honour and some not.[3]

2.3. Bhartṛhari did not have to pulverise this view with blows of counter-arguments. There was no great or absolute loss even if it was followed by the society. It contained an easily verifiable reality.[4] While thus choosing not to lose his credibility by going for a knockout punch, however, he had to be mindful of the need for cohesion and comprehensiveness in his own philosophy. He knew that, as other considera-

[3] TKV 1.182: *anitya-vādinas tu ye sādhūnāṁ dharma-hetutvaṁ na pratipadyante, mallạ-samayādi-sadṛśīṁ [ca sādhv-a]sādhu-vyavasthāṁ manyante, te prākṛtaṁ sarvaṁ [/ prakṛtyâivam …] sādhūnāṁ śabdānāṁ samūhạm ācakṣate. vikāras tu paścād vyavasthāpito yaḥ saṁbhinna-buddhibhiḥ puruṣaiḥ svara-saṁskārādibhir ni[rṇī]yata iti.*

[4] The structural similarity between depending on a *śiṣṭa* for *sādhu* determination and on an Oxford professor for the determination of acceptable English usage is pointed out in AKLUJKAR (2004: § 6.1). The subsequent sections of the same article may be helpful in understanding the differences.

tions led him to posit the language-principle as Brahman and the *Veda* as the first accessible manifestation or image (*anukāra*) of that Brahman, his philosophy would be better off by locating all languages in the stream that started with the language of the *Veda* (what we call Vedic Sanskrit or Sanskrit). Thinking in terms of mutually exclusive languages or language families, each having a different point of origin, was going to be inimical to theoretical economy—causing *gaurava* and losing *lāghava*. Besides, since independent arguments could establish that language can have no beginning in philosophy or logical theory (as distinct from any biological or evolutionary beginning it might have had) and that, for this reason, each system had to depend on *āgama* (that there could be no system that did not invoke anything outside of itself), there was a considerable theoretical advantage in accepting the *Veda* as the most fundamental *āgama* from which all *āgama*s, including those of the Buddhists, Jains etc., sprang.[5] For this configuration of theses in his thinking, as well as because, he lived in an ethos in which any act involving restraint or self-discipline could be viewed as a Yoga that purified one's personality and made one more eligible for attainment of Brahman (AKLUJKAR (2004: § 6.6)), Bhartṛhari's preferred view had to be that grammatical expressions had *dharma*-potential.

2.4. Bhartṛhari was aware even of the more general and basic problem we would now articulate with such words or phrases as 'textual authority versus empiricism' or 'need for empirical verification in scientific determination'. He knew that there would be opposition to claims such as 'grammatical words have a merit-generating nature' (with or without the qualification that the user of such words must know grammar) if the claimant had no reasoning to back up the claim. A discussion of how a particular property of something is known had taken place before his time. This discussion covered (even or especially) the issue of knowledge of a property (or outcome) thought to be nonmundane or otherworldly (*adṛṣṭa*). On such a background, he would not have been able to proceed by assuming a gullible or unquestioning reader even if he so wished. In fact, as I show in a forthcoming article on the concept of *Veda* revelation, Bhartṛhari preserves for us some precious early evi-

[5] This reconstruction of Bhartṛhari's reasoning—of how Bhartṛhari could have thought—is mine. It would be too much to expect that he would give us an explicit statement on our question—a historical possibility that was unlikely to occur to him, given the different concerns of his works. However, only the configuration is mine and it falls within the bounds of charitable or creative reading that we owe to any ancient thinker. For every component of the configuration there is explicit support in Bhartṛhari's words. For the language-principle and the *Veda*, see AKLUJKAR (forthcoming): 'Veda revelation according to Bhartṛ-hari'; for one language stream, see AKLUJKAR (2003: § 5), (2004: § 6.1); for beginningless language, see AKLUJKAR (1970: § 4.19, § 5.26); for Bhartṛhari's acceptance of *Veda* as the basis of even the unorthodox philosophies; see AKLUJKAR (1991: § 2.1).

dence of engagement with the issue of need for empirical support. This evidence is precious because it establishes that not only the issue was felt and tackled but also that a refined philosophical theory developed in early India to get over the problem of circularity to which any effort to handle the issue led.[6] The crucial expression in the evidence is *sākṣat-kṛta-dharman* taken over from Yāska's *Nirukta* in TKV 1.5 and the most revealing reason statement of it is *tatra kecid ācāryā manyante ... parāṇudyate* found in TKV 1.172 (SUBRAMANIA IYER (1966: 224–225)). I have translated the passage in AKLUJKAR (2004: § 2.4) and, in the fifth section of the forthcoming article to which I just referred, I have explained how the notion of *sākṣāt-kṛta-dharman ṛṣis* is, philosophically, a recognition of the need to have empirical evidence of properties attributed to things, as well as an attempt to get over the problem created by the impossibility of getting such evidence in a conception-free or language-free world.

— 3 —

3.1. We have now seen how something appearing in a narrow specific concern can have its antecedents or roots in the whole complex of an author's philosophy. Accurate translations would further enlighten us that, unlike Hajime NAKAMURA (1960), we should not view Bhartṛhari as unqualifiedly holding *āgama* or testimony to be weightier than *pratyakṣa* and *anumāna* (cf. AKLUJKAR (1970)) or read him as a narrowly Brahmanical philosopher reacting to the logic-loving Buddhists mainly on the strength of his faith in the Brahmanical way of life. In fact, Bhartṛhari is a proponent of the view that there is a constant interplay between *pratyakṣa*, *anumāna* and *āgama*. His model is not one in which valid cognition has three independent routes leading to it, but one in which three routes conjointly take us to validity.[7] A

[6] This theory serves also to explain how the *mantra* phenomenon is to be logically understood and how the *ṛṣi* institution has an epistemological justification in addition to any sociological or socio-political justification it may have.

[7] Following Mokṣākaragupta, one could also speak of two routes, *pratyakṣa* and *śābda/āgama*. Although Bhartṛhari frequently speaks in terms of *pratyakṣa*, *anumāna* and *śabda/āgama* and thus gives us justification to speak of three routes as acceptable to him, we could view that talk of his as a concession to philosophers of other persuasions made in order to make the dialogue possible. As *pratyakṣa* and *anumāna* are infused with *śabda* according to Bhartṛhari, attributing to him the view that ultimately *śabda* alone is the *pramāṇa* at our disposal would also be justified. Those who state that the grammarians accept only *pratibhā* as the *pramāṇa* essentially give expression to the same view.

comparison with Nyāya as presented in the *Tarka-saṁgraha*, for example, may serve to clarify the difference:[8]

Nyāya division:	Validity comes from a valid *pratyakṣa*, a valid *anumāna*, a valid *upamāna* or a valid *śabda* (= the same as Bhartṛhari's *āgama* to a significant extent) as the case may be.
	Invalidity is that which has a form different from any of these—*saṁśaya* ('doubt'), *viparyaya* ('perception not matching its claimed object') and *tarka* ('asserting the broader from the narrower')—or which results from a means recognised by some as capable of leading to knowledge (*pramā*) but not given such recognition in Nyāya (that is, everything other than a valid *pratyakṣa*, *anumāna*, *upamāna* and *śabda*).
Bhartṛhari's division:	Validity rests on *pratyakṣa* etc., contributing collectively, but it may appear to have a single source such as *pratyakṣa*, if that source is dominant in a given instance.
	Invalidity has the form of a *pratyakṣa* etc., depending on the circumstances, but our determination of validity comes from what we learn collectively from all means of knowing.

3.2. Bhartṛhari's validity, naturally, has a dynamic nature. It goes on changing its constituent elements, very much like the conceptual scheme described by the American philosopher Willard van Orman Quine. As in Quine's conceptual scheme, it has some central, normally unchangeable elements (e.g. expectation of cause-and-effect relationships and I-awareness) and some not so central or permanent elements (AKLUJKAR (1988: §§ 2.6–9)). Accordingly, the tussle between logic and belief or between the means of knowing that are generally more amenable to objectivity and the means that are more prone to losing objectivity has less intensity in Bhartṛhari's thinking than in the thinking of some other philosophers.

3.3. Consonant with the preceding is also the fact that, in the relevant contexts, Bhartṛhari speaks more of *āgama* than of *śabda* and that his *āgama* concept has at least three layers or strata. As established in my 1970 Ph.D. dissertation and as summarised in my (1971) critique of NAKAMURA's (1960) presentation, the most general meaning of *āgama* in the TK is 'inherited lore', 'conceptual inheritance',

---

[8] I have not yet studied how older Nyāya and other systems of Indian philosophy viewed, in comparative and collective terms, the relationship of *pramāṇa*s to what a person comes to accept as valid.

'knowledge that one inherits because of birth in a particular biological species or linguistic community', 'lore of the forefathers'. Next, in those contexts in which awareness and preservation of knowledge is assumed, come the meanings: 'tradition', 'traditionally inherited body of knowledge', 'traditional instruction of conduct', 'sources of testimony', 'authoritative literature', 'imbibed or internalized results of the activity of systematization', 'body of knowledge and views preserved by the adherents of a system' and 'a single view or piece of knowledge preserved in a system'. Most particularly, in sufficiently specific contexts, *āgama* denotes the *śruti* and *smr̥ti*. Given this, it follows that, according to Bhartr̥hari, we should not flatter ourselves and think that inheriting belief is something under our control. We are probably better than other animate forms, but they and we are not essentially different. Only the spaces or positions we occupy on the spectrum of animate entities are different.[9]

3.4. The kind of thinking delineated above allows Bhartr̥hari to connect *āgama* and, through it, belief with induction, which connecting, in turn, serves to reduce the gap between the rational and the non-rational (or emotive) parts of our personalities. Induction, in the sense of 'outcome or content of the act or process of induction' (e.g. the concept/universal *gotva* or applicability of the same word *go* to all cows), is essentially indistinguishable from belief. Its genesis is inexplicable in the usual logical ways. The genesis is close to a burst of inspiration and to happenstance. There is no certainty that it will take place after a certain number of steps or recurrences or that we will be able to feel the gradual progression toward an epistemological destiny. Its validity or usefulness is established after the process has taken place. Like belief, we have to take it as a given and then examine, *if the question occurs to us,* if it fits what we expect in the case of a valid piece of knowledge. In the form, especially of universals (or words used for sets of things), we receive instances of induction much in the same manner as beliefs. Language consists of (a) signifiers which extend beyond the individual objects that gave rise to them and (b) signata which sacrifice a part or range of their individualities in finding themselves expressed. Together the signifiers and signata, as it were, add another plane of being (*upacāra-sattā*) that we must hold on to, even if our logical analysis tells us that this additional plane does not exist in the same way as the plane of physical objects and events—that it is a belief infiltrating the very means of our thinking and communication, a situation immune to logical dislodging, an entity which falls short of being a belief only because most of us are not aware of it most of the time.

[9] In this respect, Bhartr̥hari is closer to the general Indian view of man as it is stated in HALBFASS (1991, particularly page 268).

3.5. It would not take much time to realise that the features of induction specified above are largely present also in the phenomenon of intuition and the intuited content. Why a woman staying in her husband's or in-laws' house suddenly gets the 'feeling' that tomorrow her brother will come (to take her to her parents' house to enjoy some festivities and to get relief from her responsibilities in the husband's or in-laws' house) is inexplicable exclusively in terms of inference,[10] whether inference is understood in a well-defined technical sense (*anumāna*, *anumiti*) or loosely as a process of guessing (akin to *ūha*, *tarka*, *saṁbhava*, *arthâpatti* etc.). What happens is more like what the English-speaking world articulates through such words as 'gut-feeling' or 'vibes/vibrations'. There is no awareness of process or moving from thought T_1 to thought T_2. At the most something can be said to take place subconsciously. Also, the occurrence of the thought is frequently sudden, and the thought is not uncommonly borne out by the brother's actual arrival.

3.6. It is thus not surprising that Bhartṛhari's notion of *pratibhā* combines in itself the elements of what we call induction, intuition and linguistic content (sentence meaning and word meaning) and, in the last, bestows prominence on *kriyā* 'action (inclusive of state, primarily as language conveys it and only secondarily as it actually takes place on the physical plane)'. Literally meaning 'what appears on the other side (in front, opposite of the mind's eye)', *prati* √*bhā* has in it a suggestion of involuntariness, of initiative resting with the content or object rather than with the observing subject, of intuition/induction and inspiration, of arising from something within the subject but not being fully explicable in terms of that something, of being (at least partly) a mysterious phenomenon, of being primarily inherited (without losing the amenability for cultivation), and of leading to a 'know-how' with regard to realisation of the content, goal or object that presents itself.

3.7. It is also not surprising, on the background delineated so far, that the distance between hermeneutics or language-based logic applied to a text (found primarily in Mīmāṁsā or Pūrva-mīmāṁsā) and inference on the factual or physical plane (found primarily in Nyāya-Vaiśeṣika) is ultimately eliminated in Bhartṛhari.[11] Another way

[10] The example (*śvo me bhrātâgantā*) given here comes from a traditional Indian social set-up in which women went to live with the families of in-laws after marriage and social customs were developed to enable them to return to the houses of their mothers at least in the first few years of marriage. A culturally Western and modern example can be found in the following 'Quotation of the Day', in the New York Times issue of 11 July 2007. The quotation is attributed to Scott Podsednik, an outfielder for the White Sox baseball team, who was talking about the magic of a perfect bat: 'You can't describe if it's a feel. When you pick it up and take a couple of swings with it, you just know.'

[11] TK 1.153: *śabdānām eva sā śaktis tarko yaḥ puruṣâśrayaḥ.*

of stating this would be that Bhartṛhari would distinguish between analytic and synthetic truths only provisionally and only at the lower levels of his philosophising or only while conducting a dialogue with other philosophical schools.

— 4 —

4.1. To return to the passage with which I began in § 1.1–2, the following should be noted: It is with logic or disciplined reasoning that Bhartṛhari argues for the limitations of that reasoning, just as one argues for the definition of *pramāṇa* or for a particular number of *pramāṇa*s by using the *pramāṇa*s themselves. There is a variety of philosophers in India, as well as elsewhere, which considers this circularity to be the longest nail that can be driven into the heart of philosophy, understood as thinking ambitious enough to aim at certainty about the world.[12] However, Bhartṛhari should be thought of as a thinker holding the view that not all circularity or mutual dependence is a fault in reasoning. His statements asserting that we do not come to this world with a clean slate[13] or that all philosophers must, at some point, accept a certain given nature of a thing or a postulate[14] make sense only on the assumption that, in his view, the mutual dependence that every philosopher has to face at some juncture in his/her attempt to provide a structure to 'understand' the world is not to be taken as proof of the attempt's failure—as sufficient basis to claim that the attempt should not be made in the first place and that a laissez-faire state should be allowed to prevail in philosophy. Even to make this final claim, logic is used, which presupposes a decision regarding what is logical or what can be a *pramāṇa*. Thus, circularity is not avoided even in advocating abandonment of the endeavour of philosophers. If such is the case, why should the philosophers not be permitted to live with circularity at the deepest or highest level? To say this is just another way of admitting that no system of philosophy is complete in itself; it must accept something for which it has not made a case on its own criteria—which, in other words, is accepted as a belief would be.

---

[12] The variety I have in mind consists of philosophers who maintain scepticism or agnosticism at a very fundamental level of epistemology, not directing it to particular entities or issues.

[13] TK 1.129–130 and the *Vṛtti* thereto: *yāṁ* [= *iti-kartavyatāṁ*] *pūrvâhita-saṁskāro bālo 'pi pratipadyate … samāviṣṭa-vācāṁ ca sva-jātiṣu bālānam api … ādyaḥ karaṇa-vinyāsaḥ … na vinā śabda-bhāvanām. anādiś câiṣā śabda-bhāvanā …*

[14] Cf. TKV 1.30: *sarve 'pi hi vādino dūram api gatvā sva-bhāvaṁ na vyativartante*—'Every philosopher ultimately comes to a stage at which he/she has no alternative but to say that "such is the nature of things".'

4.2. True, a part of Bhartṛhari's argumentation pointing out the limitations of logic is based on his observation of the world (cf. § 1.2b, p. 396, and the corresponding TK and TKV passages in the appendix below) and would not be exactly philosophical (and hence proved or respectable enough) in the view of some. Viewed, however, in the light of his (a) emphasis on the importance of context and (b) other philosophical views, his argumentation can and should be deemed as making a good case for not thinking of logic and belief as a 'twain' that shall never meet but as a twain or twins joined at birth and having no alternative to joint survival. When Bhartṛhari advises us not to take logic too far—to leave logic at the door as one would leave one's footwear while entering an Indian or Japanese household or temple, he is in fact establishing that, in some contexts, we logically have no choice but to take the recommended position and that we need to be sensitive to context, in a linguistic sense as well as in the sense of the whole that a theory forms. This stance or awareness of his may even be the very basis of his perspectivism and linguistic approach to philosophical issues.

APPENDIX[15]

Text of TK 1.30–42 summarised in § 1.2.

(a1) TK 1.30ab:

na cāgamād ṛte dharmas tarkeṇa vyavatiṣṭhate /

'What is good (and what is bad) cannot be settled through reasoning divorced from inherited knowledge.'

[15] Fairly literal and largely reliable translations of the Sanskrit passages I cite below are available in BIARDEAU (1964) and SUBRAMANIA IYER (1965). For this reason, as well as because not all the details in the passages are directly relevant to the main points of the paper, I will not translate each passage. For some passages, I will provide a summarising comment and only cite the part providing examples. Even where I translate, I will aim at making the point clear and not losing the emphasis of the original—not at sticking to the order or each individual word of the original.

The readings adopted, including indications of text definitely or possibly lost provided in bracket or rectangular parentheses, come from my TK critical edition in the making. The variants listed are sometimes reflected in the translation, and sometimes not. They do not make any difference to the theses of the article.

TKV 1.30: ... *sarve 'pi hi vādino dūram api gatvā sva-bhāvaṁ na vyativartante. adṛṣṭârthānāṁ ca karmaṇāṁ phala-niyame sva-bhāva-saṁvid āgama-pratibaddhā. ko hy anavasthita-sādharmya-vaidharmyeṣu nityam alabdha-niścayeṣu puruṣa-tarkeṣu viśvāsaḥ.*—'... For all discussants (of a particular philosophical or theoretical topic) cannot ultimately escape (the prospect of having to appeal to) own natures (of things). In delimiting the actions intended for non-mundane outcomes to certain outcomes, one must come to know the natures (of the actions). This knowing is tied to (or rests on) inherited knowledge. How can one put one's confidence (in this area or context) in the inferences of humans—inferences in which the similarities and dissimilarities (that are appealed to) are open to questioning (and therefore) bereft of certainty!'

(a3) TKV 1.30: ... *tarkâtītaḥ ... kaścid anuttaraḥ puruṣa-dharmaḥ*...—'... some extraordinary human quality, impervious to (common) ways of making sense ...'

(a4) TK 1.30cd:

> *ṛṣīṇām api yaj jñānaṁ tad apy āgama-pūvakam //*
>
> 'Even in the case of seers, knowledge is preceded by inherited knowledge (that is, by traditionally handed-down guidance as to how one should cultivate oneself in order to transcend the ordinary limitations of senses).'

TKV 1.30: ... *yeṣv api tarkâtītaḥ pṛthag-vidyā-caraṇa-parigraheṣu kaścid anuttaraḥ puruṣa-dharmaḥ śrūyate, teṣv api* [*tat-*]*tad-artha-jñānam ārṣam ṛṣīṇām āgamikenâiva dharmeṇa saṁskṛtâtmanām āvir-bhavatīty ākhyāyate. svābhāvike hi tasmin, prayatnaḥ phalād vyatiricyeta, sva-bhāvataś ca pratyavāyo 'pi tathā-bhūtaḥ prasajyeta.*—'Even in those mutually differing schools[16] in which we hear the talk of some extraordinary human quality, impervious to (common) ways of making sense, the seers' knowledge of this or that thing, to the extent it is born of a mystical or transforming experience,[17] is said to occur when the seers' personalities are modified by a quality found (i.e. recommended for cultivation) in the *āgama*. If such knowledge were to be something

[16] The meaning of the expression *vidyâcaraṇa-parigraha* is not clear as commentator Vṛṣabha's offering of two possible meanings (*caryā ācāraḥ siddhānto vā*) of *caraṇa* indicates. In fact, one cannot even be certain about reading *caraṇa;* the expression would make a contextually plausible sense even if *ācaraṇa* is read in it. Further, the nature of the compound *vidyâcaraṇa* is uncertain. Should we take it as a *dvandva* or as a genitive *tat-puruṣa*?

[17] Following Vṛṣabha, one could accommodate *ārṣam* and *ṛṣīṇām* in the somewhat convoluted manner indicated by my translation (the intention could have been to convey 'not everything a seer knows, only what he/she is said to have acquired in a moment or experience of enlightenment'). A stylistically comparable construction is found in *prākṛtam aprākṛta-gamyam* of TKV 1.32. However, one should not rule out the possibility that a redundant *ārṣam* could have entered the manuscripts under the influence of *ṛṣīṇām* or TK 1.38.

natural—something not requiring cultivation, the effort will exceed (i.e. divorce itself from) the outcome, and even an impediment may come about as an unwelcome outcome from (that) nature (or by the very nature of things).'

(b) TK 1.31:

> *dharmasya câvyavacchinnāḥ panthāno ye vyavasthitāḥ /*
> *na tāṁl loka-prasiddhatvāt kaścit tarkeṇa bādhate //*
>
> 'And, no one invalidates (i.e. can prove to be wrong or unneeded), through reasoning, the uninterrupted pathways of what is good that have come to be established, as they are well-known in the world.'

TKV 1.31: *bahu-vikalpeṣv api śiṣṭānāṁ caraṇeṣu santi sādhāraṇāḥ prasiddhāḥ puruṣa-hita-pratipatti-mārgāḥ, yeṣv anyathā pravṛttir loka-virasā. na ca te tarkeṇa kadācid api vyudasta-pūrvāḥ. kāmam āgamôddeśa-niśrayaṇenâiva* [/°*śrayeṇâiva*] *kecid vininditam api loka-samācāra-viruddham ācaraṇaṁ pratipadyante.*—'Although the schools of the learned spiritual elite contain many options, there indeed are certain shared and well-known ways of attaining the good of humans, in the case of which proceeding in any other way turns off people. Reasoning (i.e. mere reasoning) has never been able to uproot them. This is so, even though there are some (persons) who take to behaviour going against what people consider to be proper by resorting to a part of that very inherited knowledge (i.e. by selectively appealing to or quoting out of context parts of the time-honoured written or oral texts and thus temporarily bringing the *āgama* into disrepute).'[18]

(c) TK 1.32:

> *avasthā-deśa-kālānāṁ bhedād bhinnāsu śaktiṣu /*
> *bhāvānām anumānena prasiddhir atidurlabhā //*
>
> 'It is very difficult (i.e. well-nigh impossible) to establish through inference that things have such and such nature when what they can do differs with a change in phase, place or time.'

The following three paragraphs illustrate how, with a change in phase, place or time, the properties things exhibit change, making one wonder if there indeed is anything that one can take as the constant part or true nature of things:

TKV 1.32: *ihâvyabhicaritâbhimata-sāhacaryasya* [→ °*ritatvâbhi*°] *dṛṣṭasya sambandhinas tat-sadṛśasya vā darśanād adṛṣṭe sambandhini yaj jñānam utpadyate, tenâpratyakṣasyârthasya prasiddhir duravasānā.*

---

[18] The reference is to situations that are frequently summed up with an expression like 'Devil quoting the Bible' in English and kindred languages.

tathā hi. avasthāntareṣu viniścita-bala-sattvâdīnāṁ punar avasthāntareṣu puruṣa-gamyeṣv apuruṣa-gamyeṣu vā dṛśyante sva-bhāvā vyabhicāriṇaḥ. bāhyānām api bījâuṣadhi-prabhṛtīnām avasthā-bhedād upalabhyate śakti-vyabhicāraḥ.
tathā deśa-bhedād api. atiśīto haimavatīnām apāṁ sparśaḥ. sa tu balāhakâgni-kuṇḍâdiṣu tad-rūpāṇām evâtyuṣṇa upalabhyate. tatra rūpa-sāmānyād apahṛta-buddhiḥ parokṣa-viśeṣo durjñānaṁ bhedam arvāg-darśano darśana-mātreṇâgamyam āgamenâiva pratipadyate.
kāla-bhedād api. grīṣma-hemantâdiṣu kūpa-jalâdīnām atyanta-bhinnāḥ sparśādayo gṛhyante. tatra sūkṣmam avasthāna-viśeṣaṁ prākṛtam [?] *aprākṛta-gamyam āgama-cakṣur* [/*āgamika-cakṣur*] *antareṇâpratyakṣam anumāna-mātreṇâniścitaṁ* [/°*treṇa niścitya*] *kaḥ sādhayitum asaṁmūḍhaḥ prayatate* [→ *prayateta*].

These three paragraphs are followed by:

TK 1.33:

> *nirjñāta-śakter dravyasya tāṁ tām artha-kriyāṁ prati /*
> *viśiṣṭa-dravya-sambandhe sā śaktiḥ pratibadhyate //*
>
> 'Even if we come to know for sure that substance S_1 performs action A_1 revealing of its existence, we find that S_1's capability to perform A_1 is blocked if it comes into contact with certain other substances (and we are thus prevented from making an absolute or universalistic statement about its nature).'

The following provides illustrations in support of the preceding statement:

TKV 1.33: *agny-ādīnāṁ kāṣṭhâdi-vikārôtpādane dṛṣṭa-sāmarthyānām abhra-paṭalâdiṣu dravyeṣu tathā-bhūtaṁ* [/°*thā-vidhaṁ*] *sāmarthyaṁ pratibadhyate.*[19] *tathā mantrâuṣadhi-rasâdibhir yogyeṣv api dravyeṣu dāhâdikaṁ pratibadhyate. tatrâikasmin viṣaye dṛṣṭa-sāmarthyānāṁ punar viṣayântareṣu dravyāṇāṁ dur-avasānāḥ śaktayaḥ.*

(d) TK 1.34:

> *yatnenânumito 'py arthaḥ kuśalair anumātṛbhiḥ /*
> *abhiyuktatarair anyair anyathâivôpapādyate //*
>
> 'If a proficient inferer exerts to infer x, there comes along an even more proficient knowledge-master who accounts for that very x in an altogether different way.'

TKV 1.34 reproduced below shows how reasoning is used to settle a philosophical issue in different ways—how one side picks holes in an argument that seems valid

[19] Compare the use of asbestos as a fire resistant in modern times.

to the other. The issue mentioned as an example has a long history in philosophy: Should we think of substance as distinct from qualities? Is there an essence which is over and above the associated qualities and which, therefore, should be acknowledged in a separate philosophical category called 'substance'? However, while the issue taken up for illustration is clear and while it is natural that the debate about it should result in a discussion about associated linguistic usage, the precise nature of the arguments on the two (or more?) sides is not always clear, partly due to reading problems and partly due to the loss of literature presupposed by Bhartṛhari. UNEBE (2006) is helpful in understanding a part historically.

TKV 1.34: ... *anyad dravyaṁ guṇebhyo, vyapadeśāt* [→ °*bhyo 'py apa*°?]. [...?] *tad yathā. sati viśeṣaṇa-viśeṣya-bhede rājñā rāṣṭraṁ viśeṣyate, na parivrājakena. viśeṣyate* [*ca*] *candanena gandhaḥ, na rūpâdibhiḥ. tasmād, anyad dravyaṁ guṇebhya ity anumānena dravye vyavasthāpite, nâyam apadeśo yukta ity āhuḥ.* [...?] *viśiṣṭâviśiṣṭâbhidheya-nibandhanatvāt. katham candana-śabdena hi viśiṣṭa-rūpâdi-vacanena viśeṣaṇam arthavad gandhâdīnām. rūpâdi-mātra-vacanatvāt tu rūpâdīnāṁ, tāvato 'rthasya nirjñātatvād anarthakaṁ viśeṣaṇam. tathā hi. kasyâyaṁ puruṣa iti praśne, viśeṣântarâvacchedârthaṁ rājña iti vyapadiśyate, na tu nirjñātatvāt puruṣasyêti.*

apara āhuḥ. pada-samūhâika-deśa-bhāve 'pi padam ṛcā vyapadiśyate, na padena ṛk.

apara āha. ekatvâbhyupagamenâiva candanena vyapadeśo gandhâdīnām, rūpâdibhir avyapadeśa [...] *iti viruddhatvād asiddham* [→ *asiddhi-dvayam*?] *etat. śruti-viśeṣa-saṁnidhānâsaṁnidhāna-kṛtas tu pūrva-pakṣôpanyāsaḥ.*

tasmād dṛṣṭād adṛṣṭam anugamyata ity avirodhāt siddham etat.

tathā pākâdy-anumānârthāni kriyā-viśeṣeṣu pratiniyatāny aṅgāni vipralambhârthāny [→ °*mbhârtham*] *api kaiścit kathaṁcid upādīyante.*

(e) TK 1.35:

> *pareṣām asamākhyeyam abhyāsād eva jāyate /*
> *maṇi-rūpy-ādi-vijñānaṁ* [/°*diṣu jñā*°] *tad-vidāṁ nânumānikam //*
>
> 'Those who know jewels, precious metals etc. perceive those objects in their distinctiveness (i.e. with their individual good features and bad features) only through constant practice. (If others ask them, 'How did you figure out the merits or blemishes of this diamond, and so on?') they cannot give expression to their (experience or process of) knowing. (This sort of knowing) is not an outcome of inference (it is like perception in its directness, but it is not ordinary perception either, as it perceives what most others cannot).'

TKV 1.35, while restating the point clarified in the preceding translation, adds the example of persons who have musical ears. Such persons perceive subtle differences of notes that even the persons who dedicate their lives to mastering other branches of learning cannot perceive, no matter how attentive they are, until they have sufficient practice.

TKV 1.35: *na hi rūpa-tarkâdayaḥ sūkṣmān aprasiddha-saṁvijñāna-padān kārṣâpaṇâdīnāṁ kalpayitvâpi samadhigama-hetūn parebhya ākhyātuṁ śaknuvanti. ṣaḍja-ṛṣabha-gāndhāra-dhaivatâdi-bhedaṁ vā pratyakṣa-pramāṇa-viṣayam apy abhyāsam antareṇâbhiyuktāḥ praṇidhānavanto 'pi na pratipadyante.*

TK 1.36:

> *pratyakṣam anumānaṁ ca vyatikramya vyavasthitāḥ /*
> *pitṛ-rakṣaḥ-piśācānāṁ* [/*rakṣaḥ-pitṛ-pi°*] *karmajā eva siddhayaḥ* //[20]

TKV 1.36: *svapne hi* [/*°pne 'pi*] *badhirâdīnāṁ śabdâdi-pratipādanam, ghana-saṁniviṣṭâvayavānāṁ ca kuḍy-ādīnām avayava-vibhāgam antareṇântar-veśmâdiṣu sūkṣmāṇām arthānāṁ darśanaṁ yat sarva-pravâdeṣu siddham* [→ *°vāda-prasi°?*], *tatra kathaṁ-bhūtāni sādhanānîty adṛsta-śaktim acintyāṁ hitvā nânyāni sādhanāny ākhyātuṁ śakyante* //

The following two verses and the *Vṛtti* thereto touch upon manners of knowing that cannot be subsumed under ordinary perception or inference and yet have the immediacy and power to convince that perception or direct personal experience has in all epistemologies. The first mentions determination of material cause-and-effect relationships even when neither the 'effect-is-inherent-in-the-cause' view nor the 'effect-is-something-newly-produced' view are free from logical difficulties. The second points out the postulation by philosophers or theoreticians of entities (such as mind or an inner controlling subject, atoms, Brahman, phases of action outcomes or consequences, subtle transmigratory bodies etc.) that ordinary persons cannot see or infer. In short, if one were to summarise the content of the two verses in modern terminology, they refer to genesis of philosophical or theoretical insights—moments in which something probably based on sustained and concentrated thought but

[20] The *siddhis* TK 1.36 speaks of belong to 'persons' different from ordinary human beings and are a matter of belief, at least for many modern human beings. It may, therefore be argued that the verse should be grouped with the next two. But if justice is to be done to the emphasis in *karmajā eva,* it should form a group with TK 1.35. If we agree to do so then we should understand that the author's intention was not to argue for the existence of ghosts etc. or the capabilities attributed to them (which he may accept elsewhere) but to state that the capabilities attributed to ghosts etc. make sense only as entities born of something analogous to *abhyāsa*—as arising out of actions they performed, the inclinations they cultivated, as humans.

lacking a definite or demonstrable causal connection to it flashes forth and is found to have considerable explanatory value.

TK 1.37:

> *āvir-bhūta-prakāśānām anupapluta-cetasām /*
> *atītânāgata-jñānaṁ pratyakṣān na viśiṣyate //*

TKV 1.37: [...] *tatrôtpatti-pakṣe tāvat katham apadam avastu nirātmakam adṛṣṭâpratiniyata-kāraṇa-śakti-parigraham adhigantuṁ śakyate. pakṣântare* [/°*re 'pi*] *ca viśiṣṭa-vyakti-rūpa-tiro-bhāvād vyavahāraṁ prati tad avijñeyaṁ vastu nirupākhyair eva tulyam. atha ca tapasā nirdagdha-doṣā nirāvaraṇa-khyātayaḥ śiṣṭāḥ pratibimba-kalpena pratyakṣam iva svāsu khyātiṣu saṁkrāntâkāra-parigraham avyabhicaritaṁ sarvaṁ paśyanti.*

TK 1.38:

> *atīndriyān asaṁvedyān paśyanty ārṣeṇa cakṣuṣā /*
> *ye bhāvān vacanaṁ teṣāṁ nânumānena bādhyate //*

TKV 1.38: *antaryāmiṇam, aṇu-grāmam, abhijāti-nimitta-nibandhanam, anabhivyaktaṁ śabda-brahma, śakty-adhiṣṭhānaṁ* [→ ?] *devatāḥ, karmaṇām anubandha-pariṇāma-śakti-vaikalyāni, sūkṣmam ātivâhikaṁ śarīraṁ, pṛthag anyāṁś ca tīrtha-pravādeṣu prasiddhān arthān, rūpâdivad indriyair agrāhyān, sukhādivac ca pratyātmam asaṁvedyān, ye śiṣṭā vyāvahārikād anyenâiva cakṣuṣā mukta-saṁśayam upalabhante, teṣām anumāna-viṣayatâtītaṁ vacanaṁ vyabhicāribhir anumānair apākartum aśakyam. jāty-andhâdīnāṁ hi "rūpâdi-grahaṇam evam utpadyata" iti* [*yā*]*sā*[*v a*]*vasthā nâivānubhūta-pūrvā kadācit, tasyāṁ katham anumānaṁ pravarteta.*

The persons who have faith in the insights or statements of persons with extraordinary capabilities, that is, of persons spoken of in the preceding two verses, are not swayed by rationalistic criticisms. For them, what the *śiṣṭa*s say is as unquestionably valid as something they themselves witnessed:

TK 1.39:

> *yo yasya svam iva jñānaṁ darśanaṁ nâbhiśaṅkate /*
> *sthitaṁ pratyakṣa-pakṣe taṁ katham anyo nivartayet //*

TKV 1.39: *santi prati-caraṇaṁ prati-puruṣaṁ câptāḥ, yeṣāṁ vacanam avicāritaṁ svam iva darśanam atyantam anabhiśaṅkanīyaṁ, yeṣāṁ câdṛṣṭam api śilā-plāvanâdi pratyayena śakyaṁ śrad-dhātum. tathā hi. karmaṇām iha kṛtānām, ūrdhvaṁ dehād, iṣṭâniṣṭa-phala-prāptir āpta-vacana-parigraheṇâiva loke prasiddhā, vinâpi śāstrôpadeśena, prāyeṇa manuṣyair anugamyate.* [...]

> *"idaṁ puṇyam idaṁ pāpam ity etasmin pada-dvaye /*
> *ācaṇḍālaṁ* [/*ācāṇḍā°*] *manuṣyāṇām alpaṁ śāstra-prayojanam //*"[21]

[...?] *tasmāt pratyakṣam ārṣaṁ ca jñānaṁ, saty api virodhe, bādhakam anumānasya.*

The same observation applies to *āgama*, or received traditional wisdom. It is as ingrained in the being of most persons as their very sentience or life force. Accepted by the spiritual learned, it not given up by the majority simply because philosophers or intellectuals disagree among themselves. In fact, those who do not give it up, usually escape social censure:

TK 1.41:

> *caitanyam iva yaś câyam avicchedena vartate /*
> *āgamas tam upāsīno hetu-vādair na bādhyate //*

TKV 1.41: *yathā hy aham asmîty evam-ādi-pratyayânugataṁ sahajam anādī yac caitanyaṁ tan nâsmi, na mamêty-evam āptôpadeśe saty api, loke rūḍhatvān muktâtmanām api vyavahāraṁ prati na vyavacchidyate* [→ *vicchi°*], *tathâivâyaṁ śruti-smṛti-lakṣaṇaḥ sarvaiḥ śiṣṭaiḥ parigṛhīta āgamaḥ kāryâkārya-bhakṣyâbhakṣya-gamyâgamyâdiṣu* [/*bhakṣyâ°*] *yo bhinnānām api pravādināṁ prāyeṇânātilaṅghanīyaḥ. tam itthaṁ-bhūtam anādim upasevitaṁ vṛddhaiḥ samyag upāsīno na tārkika-pravādaiḥ kaiścin* [→ *kaścin*] *nyāyyād apanīyate vartmanaḥ. tatrasthaś cânindyo loke bhavati.*

(f) TK 1.42:

> *hasta-sparśād ivândhena viṣame pathi dhāvatā /*
> *anumāna-pradhānena vinipāto na durlabhaḥ //*
>
> 'It is not difficult to find that a person who puts store by guessing and deducing falls like a blind person running on an uneven path merely on the basis of what the touch of his hand revealed earlier.'

TKV 1.42 restates the preceding more precisely:

yasya hi sthālī-pāka-pulāka-nyāyenâika-deśaṁ [/*°lī-pu°*] *dṛṣṭvā śiṣṭe 'rthe pratipattiḥ, so 'ndha iva, viṣame giri-mārge, cakṣuṣmantaṁ nêtāram antareṇa, tvarayā* [→ *tarasā*] *paripatan kaṁcid eva mārgâika-deśaṁ hasta-sparśenâvagamya samatikrāntas tat-pratyayād aparam api tathâiva pratipadyamāno, yathā vināśaṁ labhate, tadvad āgama-cakṣuṣā vinā tarkânupātī, kevalenânumānena kvacid āhita-pratyayo dṛṣṭâdṛṣṭa-phaleṣu karmasv āgamam utkramya pravartamāno niyataṁ mahatā pratyavāyena saṁyujyate.*

---

[21] The preceding verse is found in the TK *kārikā* manuscripts and hence has been included and numbered as *kārikā* 40 in Rau's edition. In my judgement, it was originally a quotation in the *Vṛtti* of verse 39.

BIBLIOGRAPHY

AKLUJKAR 1970 = Aklujkar, Ashok: *The Philosophy of Bhartṛ-hari's Trikāṇḍī*. Ph.D. dissertation. Harvard University, Cambridge (Massachusetts) 1970 (unpublished).

AKLUJKAR 1971 = Aklujkar, Ashok: 'Nakamura on Bhartṛ-hari', *Indo-Iranian Journal* 13 (1971) 161–75.

AKLUJKAR 1988 = Aklujkar, Ashok: 'Prāmāṇya in the philosophy of the Grammarians', in: Avanindra Kumar et al. (eds.): *Studies in Indology: Professor Rasik Vihari Joshi Felicitation Volume*. Shree Publishing House, New Delhi 1988: 15–28.

AKLUJKAR 1991 = Aklujkar, Ashok: 'Bhartṛ-hari's concept of the Veda', in: Johannes Bronkhorst (ed.): *Panels of the VIIth World Sanskrit Conference*. Volume IV–V, E.J. Brill, Leiden 1991: 1–18.

AKLUJKAR 2003 = Aklujkar, Ashok: 'A different sociolinguistics for Brahmins, Buddhists and Jains', in: Bhudev Sharma (ed.): *Contemporary Views on Indian Civilization*. World Association for Vedic Studies, India and USA 2003: 54–69.

AKLUJKAR 2004 = Aklujkar, Ashok: 'Can the grammarians' dharma be a dharma for all?' *Journal of Indian Philosophy* 32 (2004) 687–732.

AKLUJKAR (forthcoming) = Aklujkar, Ashok: 'Veda revelation according to Bhartṛ-hari', to be published in: Mithilesh Chaturvedi, Kanshiram (eds.): *Proceedings of the International Seminar on Language, Meaning and Reality in Bhartrihari*. Motilal Banarsidass Publishers, New Delhi.

BIARDEAU 1964 = Biardeau, Madeleine (ed., tr.): *Vākyapadīya Brahmakāṇḍa avec la Vṛtti de Harivṛṣabha*. Publications de l'Institut de Civilisation Indienne. Série in-8°, Fascicule 24, Éditions E. de Boccard, Paris 1964.

HALBFASS 1991 = Halbfass, Wilhelm: *Tradition and Reflection: Explorations in Indian Thought*. State University of New York Press, Albany (New York) 1991.

NAKAMURA 1960 = Nakamura, Hajime: 'Bhartṛ-hari the scholar', *Indo-Iranian Journal* 4 (1960) 282–305.

RAU 1977 = Rau, Wilhelm (ed.): *Bhartṛharis Vākyapadīya: Die Mūlakārikās nach den Handschriften herausgegeben und mit einem Pāda-Index versehen*. Abhandlungen für die Kunde des Morgenlandes XLII, 4., Franz Steiner Verlag, Wiesbaden 1977.

ŚK = Bhaṭṭoji-dīkṣita: *Śabda-kaustubha*. Edited and revised by Rama Krishna Shastri, alias Tatya Shastri Patwardhana. Chowkhamba Sanskrit Series, Chowkhamba Sanskrit Book-depot, Benares 1898.

SUBRAMANIA IYER 1965 = Subramania Iyer, K.A. (tr.): *The Vākyapadīya of Bhartṛhari with the Vṛtti. Chapter I*. Deccan College Building Centenary and Silver Jubilee Series. No. 26, Deccan College, Poona 1965.

SUBRAMANIA IYER 1966 = Subramania Iyer, K.A. (ed.): *Vākyapadīya of Bhartṛhari with the Vṛtti, and the Paddhati of Vṛṣabhadeva*. Deccan College Monograph Series No. 32, Deccan College Postgraduate and Research Institute, Poona 1966.

TK = Bhartṛhari: *Trikāṇḍī kārikā*s, also known as *Vākyapadīya*. See: SUBRAMANIA IYER (1966) and RAU (1977).

TKV = Bhartṛhari: *Trikāṇḍī-vṛtti*, traditionally taken to be an integral part of TK. See: SUBRAMANIA IYER (1966) and footnote 13 above.

UNEBE 2006 = Unebe, Toshiya: 'Inference based on vyapadeśa: Bhartṛ-hari's remark and related discussions in Nyāya and Buddhist treatises', in: Ujjwala Jha, Toshihiro Wada, Nirmala Kulkarni and Arun Ranjan Mishra (eds.): *Nyaya-Vasiṣṭha: Felicitation Volume of Prof. V.N. Jha*. Sanskrit Pustak Bhandar, Kolkata 2006: 478–495.

Bhartṛhari on Unnameable Things*

HIDEYO OGAWA

0. In his *Mahā-bhāṣya* Patañjali declares that for grammarians what words express is their authority[1]. Later Pāṇinīyas from Bhartṛhari onwards illustrate this principle by stating that grammarians are not concerned with things as they are (*vastv-artha*) but as they are spoken of (*śabdârtha*). It is interesting that they recognise that there are things which are unnameable, beyond verbalisation. In his *Vṛtti* on the *Vākya-padīya* Bhartṛhari calls them *asaṁvijñāna-pada*s—'those which have not words to convey themselves'. In this paper I shall show how Bhartṛhari accounts for the existence of a thing defined as *asaṁvijñāna-pada* and what philosophical significance he attaches to the issue of whether a certain thing has a word defined as *saṁvijñāna-pada*.

1. To begin with, let us consider how the term *saṁvijñāna-pada* is to be interpreted. HOUBEN (1995: 340, n. 564), who translates this term as 'specific designation', gives the following explanation:

> '*saṁvijñānapada*, literally "word of thorough understanding". The translation "specific designation" was suggested to me by Professor Aklujkar. The word is also used in the Vṛtti on 1.94 (Biardeau: "mot qui donne une connaissance complète"; Iyer: "special name") in the context of the stages of a continuous process, of which some have a *saṁvijñāna-pada*, and others don't.'

Bhartṛhari and his commentators do not give an etymological explanation of this term. But Vṛṣabha's comments on VP 1.94 furnish useful hints.

In his *Vṛtti* on VP 1.94 Bhartṛhari, who mentions the transformation of milk into clarified butter and its specific stages (*avasthā-viśeṣa*), describes specific stages

* I gratefully acknowledge helpful discussions with Professor Brendan S. Gillon and my student Jaehyung Yi on several points in the paper.

[1] MBhā 1.11.1–2; 1.366.12–13: *śabda-pramāṇakā vayam. yac chabda āha tad asmākaṁ pramāṇam.*

Logic and Belief in Indian Philosophy
Warsaw Indological Studies 3 (2010) 415–430.

such as curds as *saṁvijñāna-pada-nibandhana*, i.e. 'those which depend on *saṁvijñāna-pada*', and transformation stages within them as *asaṁvijñāna-pada*, i.e. 'those for which there are no *saṁvijñāna-pada*s'.[2] According to Vṛṣabha, specific stages such as curds have words (*pada*) like *maṇḍaka*, while the specific stages within them have no words to signify them (*vācaka*).[3] Thus, it becomes clear that the term *saṁvijñāna-pada* means: (as a *karma-dhāraya* compound) 'a word which consists in being that from which a certain thing is understood', that is, a word to convey something.

It may be worth pointing out, in passing, that, to my knowledge, the term *saṁvijñāna-pada* and its derivatives are not so commonly used by Indian theorists. I could only find the use of the negative compound *asaṁvijñāna-pada* in the *Bhāvanā-viveka* of Maṇḍanamiśra.[4] This might suggest that Bhartṛhari's use of the term in question manifests the characteristics of his own philosophy of language.

2. Bhartṛhari does not use the term *saṁvijñāna-pada* in the *kārikā* text but in the *Vṛtti*. Moreover, in the *Vṛtti* he uses it only in two contexts: (1) in connection with the determination of the distinction among things (*bheda*, *viśeṣa*) and (2) in connection with the denotation of something essentially dependent (*paratantra*) as something independent (*svatantra*).[5]

---

[2] VPV 1.94: *yathā kṣīram utpatti-pakṣe 'bhivyakti-pakṣe vā sarpir-ādi-vikāra-prayuktaṁ niyata-krama-rūpair maṇḍakâdibhir avasthā-viśeṣair viśiṣṭa-saṁvijñāna-pada-nibandhanair asaṁvijñāna-padaiś ca yujyamānaṁ ...*

[3] PDh ad VPV 1.94: *saṁvijñāna-pada-nibandhanaiḥ iti. etāny eva maṇḍakâdīni teṣām avasthā-viśeṣāṇāṁ padāni. eteṣām eva ca ye 'ntar-āla-vibhāgāḥ sūkṣmā avasthā-viśeṣāḥ, na teṣāṁ vācako 'stîty asaṁvijñāna-padāḥ.*

[4] BhViṬ 45.7–46.2: *yukta evôttare sāmānya-nirdeśaḥ; anyathā praśna-gataṁ tad-apekṣaṇīyaṁ syāt, viśeṣatas tu bhāvanāyā asaṁvijñāna-pada-bhedatvāt parôpadhāna-vyajyamāna-sphuṭa-viśeṣāyāḥ.*

[5] It is interesting that Maṇḍanamiśra describes *bhāvanā*, or the act of bringing about as having the property of being *asaṁvijñāna-pada-bheda*. This description gives the idea that *bhāvanā* has no word to convey its own distinction, which closely reflects the idea Bhartṛhari advances in the former context.

For the sake of reference, here I mention the interpretations of the word *asaṁvijñāna-pada-bheda* given by Umbeka and Nārāyaṇa:

BhViṬ 46.14–16: *bhāvanāyās tu pacaty-ādi-pade viśeṣeṇa sāmānya-nirdeśa eva kartavyaḥ, na hi tatra bhāvanā-viśeṣa-pratipādakaḥ kaścic chabdo 'sti.*

BhViṬ 88.8–11: *samyak viśeṣâkāreṇa jñāyate 'rtho yena padena tat saṁvijñāna-padam, tasya bhedo viśeṣaḥ saṁvijñāna-pada-bhedaḥ, na sa vidyate yasyā bhāvanāyās sêyam asaṁvijñāna-pada-bhedā, tad-bhāvo 'saṁvijñāna-pada-bhedatvam. na kaścid api śabdo bhāvanā-viśeṣeṇa gṛhīta-sambandho 'stîty arthaḥ.*

3. Let us first consider the former context (§ 2.1).

3.1. In his *Vṛtti* on VP 1.35 Bhartṛhari says the following:

> (a) Connoisseurs of things such as coins can determine for some reasons that the things examined by them are a *kārṣâpaṇa* and the like in weight. But, even conceiving of the reasons, they cannot communicate those reasons to others.[6]
> (b) For, the reasons are subtle (*sūkṣma*) and hence imperceptible, so that they have no well-established words to convey them.[7]
> (c) Without repeated practice, even experts, extremely attentive, do not understand the distinction (*bheda*) among musical notes such as *ṣaḍja*, *ṛṣabha*, *gāndhāra*, *dhaivata*, even if such distinction comes within the range of perception.[8]

The musical notes mentioned in (c) and the distinction among them will also be characterised as 'those which have no fixed and well-established words to convey them' (VPV 1.123: *anavasthitâprasiddha-saṁvijñāna-pada*).

The points made in (b) is this: the reasons connoisseurs of coins find for determining the weight of the coins (*samadhigama-hetu*) are, as Vṛṣabha explains, imperceptible (*apratyakṣa*), non-inferable (*anānumānika*) and incommunicable (*anāgamika*; in Bhartṛhari's words, *asamākhyeya*).[9]

According to Umbeka, when *bhāvanā* is spoken of as *asaṁvijñāna-pada-bhedā*, it is implied that there is no word to convey a specific *bhāvanā* (*bhāvanā-viśeṣa-pratipādaka*). According to Nārāyaṇa, the term *saṁvijñāna-pada-bheda* means 'a specific word to properly convey its meaning in a specific form', so that, when *bhāvanā* is spoken of as *asaṁvijñāna-pada-bhedā*, it is implied that *bhāvanā* has no specific word by which it is conveyed in a specific form, namely that there is no word which has signification relation with a specific *bhāvanā*.

[6] VPV 1.35: *na hi rūpa-tarkâdayaḥ sūkṣmān aprasiddha-saṁvijñāna-padān kārṣâpaṇâdīnāṁ kalpayitvâpi samadhigama-hetūn parebhya ākhyātuṁ śaknuvanti.*

[7] See n. 6 above.

[8] VPV 1.35: *ṣaḍja-ṛṣabha-gāndhāra-dhaivatâdi-bhedaṁ vā pratyakṣa-pramāṇa-viṣayam apy abhyāsam antareṇâbhiyuktāḥ praṇidhānavanto 'pi na pratipadyante.*

[9] VP 1.35:

pareṣām asamākhyeyam abhyāsād eva jāyate /
maṇi-rūpyâdi-vijñānaṁ tad-vidāṁ nânumānikam //

PDh ad VPV 1.35: *sūkṣmān iti viśeṣaṇaṁ, samadhigama-hetūnām, duravadhānatvād* [read: *duravadhāraṇatvād*] *apratyakṣatvam. ata evânumānâbhāvaḥ. aprasiddha iti. prasiddhaṁ saṁvijñāna-padaṁ nâsti teṣāṁ samadhigama-hetūnām ity ākhyānasyâśakyatayânāgamikatvaṁ samam.*

The point made in (c) is that the distinction among musical notes, which is imperceptible since it exists in a subtle form, comes to be perceived and determined through repeated practice.

It is important to note here the following two points. First, even if a thing has no corresponding word to convey it (*asaṁvijñāna-pada*), nonetheless the things exists, that is, it comes within the range of perception. Repeated practice, therefore, can make it possible to perceive and determine the thing. Secondly, it is simply because such a thing has no well-established word to convey it that it cannot be communicated to others.

However, a question arises: How does a subtle thing come to be perceived and determined through repeated practice? In order to answer this question, we have to consider what Bhartr̥hari states in VP 1.123 and the *Vr̥tti* thereupon.

3.2. VP 1.123 is very important in this regards, for Bhartr̥hari declares there that the denotative power of the word (*śabda-mātrā*, *śabda-śakti*) is the cause for understanding the distinction among things:

> 'The distinction among things such as *ṣaḍja* is determined when conveyed through words; therefore, all kinds of entities depend upon the powers of words (*śabda-mātrā*).'[10]

Bhartr̥hari elaborates the point here as follows:

> (a) Indeed, any entity depends on a word to convey it, so that it enters into discourse when determined through recollection-determination, muttering-determination and form-determination.[11]
>
> (b) But, the distinction among the musical notes, *ṣaḍja*, *r̥ṣabha*, *gāndhāra*, *dhaivata*, *niṣāda*, *pañcama*, and *madhyama*, which have no fixed and well-established words to convey them, is not determined without understanding the words on which the determination of the distinction depends.[12]

---

[10] VP 1.123:

ṣaḍjâdi-bhedaḥ śabdena vyākhyāto rūpyate yataḥ /
tasmād artha-vidhāḥ sarvāḥ śabda-mātrāsu niśritāḥ //

RAU (1977: 48) reads *pāda* a as *śabdâdibhedaḥ śabdena*. I follow IYER's (1966: 182) reading. The term *śabda-mātrā* is glossed by Vr̥ṣabha by the term *śabda-śakti*.

[11] VPV 1.123: *saṁvijñāna-pada-nibandhano hi sarvo 'rthaḥ smr̥ti-nirūpaṇayâbhijalpa-nirūpaṇayâkāra-nirūpaṇayā ca nirūpyamāṇo vyavahāram avatarati.*

[12] VPV 1.123: *ṣaḍja-r̥ṣabha-gāndhāra-dhaivata-niṣāda-pañcama-madhyamānāṁ cânavasthitâprasiddha-saṁvijñāna-padānāṁ viśeṣo 'vadhāraṇa-nibandhana-pada-pratyayam antareṇa nâvadhāryate.*

(c) For, cowherds, shepherds, and others also, who have invented (*prakalpya*) the words which serve as the cause for the determination of distinction, undertake to make a discourse with reference to the distinction among cows and others.[13]
(d) Therefore, a distinct entity, when imposed on words,[14] is manifested, picked out, and received by the cognition which is united with the denotative power of the word, which is impregnated with the word, and which is identical with the word (*śabdâtmikā*).[15]
(e) Words whose meanings are incommunicable are called 'incommunicable'; terms such as *ṣaḍja* are among such words; they are defined as 'general term'. On the other hand, words whose meanings are communicable are called 'communicable'; terms such as 'cow' are among such words; they are defined as 'specific term'.[16]

There are several points to note. Let us first note (b) and (c). There exists the distinction among musical notes and musicians can grasp the distinction. Similarly, there exists the distinction among cows and cowherds can grasp the distinction. It is highly important to note the point that since a word is the basis for the determination of the distinction among things, it is not until the word is understood that the distinction is determined. This clearly implies that the determination of the distinction among things, as Vṛṣabha says, presupposes the application of specific words to them.[17] To explain. When a certain musical note is known as 'This is *ṣaḍja*' or 'This is named *ṣaḍja*' and another as 'This is *ṛṣabha*' or 'This is named *ṛṣabha*', the distinction between these two musical notes is determined. Similarly, when, by inventing the names A and B, a certain cow is named A and known as 'This is A' and

[13] VPV 1.123: *gopālâvipālâdayo 'pi hi nibandhana-padāni prakalpya gavādiṣu viśeṣa-viṣayaṁ vyavahāram ārabhante.*

[14] According to Vṛṣabha, this amounts to saying that a specific word appears as if engraved on a specific meaning. PDh ad VPV 1.123: *tasminn arthe sa śabda utkīrṇa ivêti.*

[15] VPV 1.123: *tasmāt samākhyeyeṣv asamākhyeyeṣu ca sāmānya-viśeṣa-śabdeṣv adhyārūḍho bhedavān arthaḥ śabda-śakti-saṁsṛṣṭayā śabdânuviddhayā śabdâtmikayā buddhyā prakāśyata, upagṛhyate, svīkriyate.*

[16] See n. 15 and PDh ad VPV 1.123: *samākhyeyeṣu iti. samākhyeyārthaḥ gavâdi-piṇḍeṣu ye śabdāḥ pratyasyante te samākhyeyā ity uktam. asamākhyeyârthatvād asamākhyeyāḥ ṣaḍjâdayaḥ. samākhyeyā iti śakyârthe kṛtyaḥ, samākhyātuṁ śakyā iti. gavâdīnām arthānāṁ sphuṭataraṁ paricchedyatayā śakyatvam. ṣaḍjâdīnāṁ tu durākhyānā arthā iti. sāmānya-viśeṣa-śabdeṣu iti. sāmānya-viśeṣa-śabdāḥ* [read: *sāmānya-śabdāḥ*] *ṣaḍjâdayaḥ. viśeṣa-śabdāḥ sanniveśitā ye gopālakaiḥ piṇḍeṣu.*

[17] PDh ad VPV 1.123: *viśeṣâvadhāraṇāya śabda-viśeṣa-niveśam āśrayante.*

another cow is named B and known as 'This is B', the distinction between these two cows is determined.

Let us next note (a) and (d). Bhartṛhari has stated that any entity depends on a word to convey it. Words such as *ṛṣabha* are the words to convey specific musical notes and names such as A are also the words to convey specific cows. As shown above, an entity (*artha*) is known as a specific one (*bhedavān arthaḥ*) when, depending on a word to convey it (word *x*), it is known as 'This is *x*' or 'This is named *x*'. This is precisely what is meant by statement (d). What is more, according to Bhartṛhari, the cognition 'This is *x*' is the cognition (1) in which the entity referred to by 'this' is identified with the word *x*,[18] (2) which is united with the denotative power of *x*, (3) which is impregnated with *x*, and (4) which is identical with *x*. It is to be noted in passing that, according to Vṛṣabha, *smṛti-nirūpaṇā* is the recollection of the cognition 'This is *x*', or the determination of the cognition; *abhijalpa-nirūpaṇā* is the awareness of the word *x* and its meaning as identical with each other, or the determination of the word; *ākāra-nirūpaṇā* is the determination of the *x*'s meaning as *sādhana* (*kāraka*) or as *sādhya* (*kriyā*, act) to have a sentence meaning, or the determination of the meaning.[19]

Let us finally note (e). Bhartṛhari characterises words such as *ṣaḍja* and words such as *go* are respectively as *asamākhyeya* 'incommunicable' and as *samākhyeya* 'communicable', according to whether they are fixed and well-established words. In addition, he describes the former type of word as *sāmānya-śabda* 'general term' and the latter type of word as *viśeṣa-śabda* 'specific term'. The underlying idea is this. When the word *ṣaḍja* is uttered by a speaker, the hearer to whom this word is unfamiliar can only understand that something is meant by the speaker but cannot specify what it is. On the other hand, when the word *go* is uttered, the hearer to whom this word is familiar can understand that an entity as excluded from non-cows is meant by the speaker.[20]

---

[18] The identity between a word and its meaning is established when they are imposed on each other. See (d) and n. 14.

[19] PDh ad VPV 1.123: *tat tu tathā paricchidyôttaraṁ śabdânuviddhayā buddhyā smaryate idam evaṁ ca iti smṛti-rūpeṇa. śabdârthayor abheda-darśanam abhijalpa-nirūpaṇā. idam asyāḥ sādhanam, iyam eṣāṁ sādhyā ity ākāra-nirūpaṇā. ... athavā smṛti-nirūpaṇayā iti jñānasya nirūpaṇam āha. abhijalpa-nirūpaṇayā iti śabdasya. ākāra-nirūpaṇayā ity arthasyâha.*

[20] It is to be noted that the word called *viśeṣa-śabda* denotes an entity excluded from others (*vyāvṛttârthâbhidhāyin*), referring to the exclusion (*vyāvṛtti*), see VP 3.5.4cd:

> *viśeṣa-śabdair ucyante vyāvṛttârthâbhidhāyibhiḥ* /

Cf. VPP 3.5.4: *ekâika-vyāvṛtti-niṣṭhā hi bahavaḥ śabdā vastuni pravartante. tathā ca te tatra viśeṣa-śabdā ity ucyante...*

Such is an outline of what Bhartṛhari states in his *Vṛtti* on VP 1.1.23. All of this amounts to saying that, as said above, one cannot cognise distinct things without resorting to the words which are capable of conveying them. The question has arisen how a subtle thing comes to be perceived and determined through repeated practice. Now the answer to this question is: By means of coming to be cognised as 'This is *x*' by the cognition which is impregnated with the word *x* capable of conveying the thing referred to by 'this'.

3.3. As shown, in Bhartṛhari's view, verbalisation is an essential factor of cognition. We have to note, however, that he has said that the musical note *ṣaḍja*, even if it comes within the range of perception, cannot be determined without being cognised as 'This is *ṣaḍja*'. The next question to consider is how verbalisation is associated with cognising existent things. To this question, the *Vṛtti* on VP 1.131 will give an answer:

(a) Things are to be known by a person according to the person's *śabda-bhāvanā*, or the residual traces of linguistic ability, which consist in being such in which things to be verbalised are merged.[21]
(b) Even if a non-conceptual cognition (*avikalpakaṁ jñānam*) arises of such things, no effect is brought about by it.[22]
(c) For instance, when one walks quickly and touches things such as grass and pebbles, a cognition arises.
(d) But even if such a cognition arises, the state of the cognition is a specific one.
(e) For, in this state of cognition which contains an about-to-sprout seed of the residual traces of linguistic ability (*abhimukhī-bhūta-śabda-bhāvanā-bījā*), when denotative powers of words manifest themselves, the cognition gets impregnated with words (*śabdânuviddha*) and follows the denotative powers of the words to determine its object (*śabda-śakty-anupātin*).
(f) The entity itself (*vastv-ātman*) which is the object of such a cognition is said to be cognised (*jñāyata ity abhidhīyate*) when it is obtained through its cognitive image (*ākriyamāṇa*)[23] and picked out by that cognition.

---

[21] VPV 1.131: *yathâsya saṁhṛta-rūpā śabda-bhāvanā tathā jñeyeṣv artheṣûtpannenâpy avikalpakena jñānena kāryaṁ na kriyate.*

[22] For (b)–(h), see note 25 below.

[23] PDh ad VPV 1.131: *ākriyamāṇaḥ iti. viśiṣṭenâkāreṇa śabdânuviddhena spaṣṭena labhyamānaḥ.* When an entity is definitely cognised by the cognition impregnated with a word to which a specific image of the entity appears, it is spoken of as *ākriyamāṇa* 'being obtained through its cognitive image'.

(g) Under this condition, the entity is understood by the cognition (*jñānânugata*) and appears clearly in it (*vyakta-rūpa-pratyavabhāsa*).
(h) Words that pick out meanings (*arthôpagrāhin*)[24] are of two types: 'communicable' words such as *go* and 'incommunicable' words such as *ṣaḍja*.[25] The denotative power of words is fixed for each of their meanings.[26]

Statement (a) is made under Bhartṛhari's well-known thesis that verbalisability is immanent in our cognitive faculty.[27] A part of (e), (f), and (g) say the same thing as (d) in the previous section. What is stated in (h) overlaps with what is stated in (e) in the previous section. We have to note here (b)–(e). What Bhartṛhari argue there is this.

When one walks quickly and touches grass, a cognition, i.e. a tactile sensation, arises of it. This cognition is a non-conceptual cognition. Even if the grass is cognised, practically nothing is cognised. For, in that state of cognition, the function of the seed of the residual traces of linguistic ability has not been activated. The grass is said to be cognised when it is cognised by the cognition which is impregnated with the word for it. It is not until the function of the seed is activated that the denotative power of the word manifests itself.[28]

It is important to note two points. One is that an entity is said to be cognised when it is cognised through a cognition which is impregnated with the word for it; if it is not cognised through such a cognition, practically nothing is cognised. The other is

---

[24] That is, words which convey meanings, see PDh ad VPV 1.131: *arthôpagrāhiṇām iti. artha-pratipādakānām.*

[25] PDh ad VPV 1.131: *ākhyeya-rūpāṇām iti. ākhyātuṁ śakyate rūpaṁ yeṣāṁ gavâdi-śabdavat. anākhyeya-rūpāṇām iti. ṣaḍjâdivat. yato na teṣām arthaḥ paryāyântareṇâkhyātuṁ śakyate.*

[26] VPV 1.131: *tad yathā. tvaritaṁ gacchatas tṛṇa-loṣṭâdi-saṁsparśāt saty api jñāne kācid eva sā jñānâvasthā yasyām abhimukhī-bhūta-śabda-bhāvanā-bījāyām āvir-bhūtāsv arthôpagrāhiṇām ākhyeya-rūpāṇām anākhyeya-rūpāṇāṁ ca śabdānāṁ praty-artha-niyatāsu śaktiṣu śabdânuviddhena śabda-śakty-anupātinā jñānenâkriyamāṇa upagṛhyamāṇo vastv-ātmā jñānânugato vyakta-rūpa-pratyavabhāso jñāyata ity abhidhīyate.*

[27] VPV 1.130: *anādiś câiṣā śabda-bhāvanā prati-puruṣam avasthita-jñāna-bīja-parigrahā. na hy etasyāḥ kathañcit pauruṣeyatvaṁ sambhavati.* According to Bhartṛhari, the residual traces of linguistic ability contain the seed of cognition, which is established in each human being; and, such residual traces of linguistic ability are beginningless, for they can never be artificial.

[28] Saying that a word has the power to convey its meaning amounts to saying that the word is capable of determining an entity. Note Vṛṣabha's following comments in PDh ad VPV 1.131: (1) *śabdasya śaktir artha-pratipādanam, tad-upadarśane 'rtha-rūpa-pratipatteḥ, gaur ayam aśvo 'yam iti*; (2) *pratiniyatârtha-paricchedôpayoginyo hi tāḥ. artha-nirūpaṇa-yogata* [read: *artha-nirūpaṇa-yogyatā*] *śabdasya śaktir ity uktā. tasyāṁ hi prabuddhāyāṁ taj-jñānaṁ tayârthaṁ nirūpayati.*

that there is a case in which the seed of the residual traces of linguistic ability does not come up.

The first point will remind us of what Bhartṛhari says in his *Vṛtti* on VP 1.129:

> 'Even if it exists as a thing to be cognised, an entity is as good as non-existent as long as it is not picked out by a verbal expression.'[29]

According to Bhartṛhari, even an existent thing is regarded as non-existent, for what is said to exist is just what enters into discourse (*vyavahārâṅga*). As shown, what enters into discourse is only an entity which is cognised by a cognition impregnated with the word for it.

The second point is explained by Bhartṛhari in his *Vṛtti* on VP 1.132 as follows:

> (a) Speech-element (*vāg-rūpa-mātrā*) inheres in all cognitions, just as the essential property of being an illuminator inheres in fire and that of being consciousness in the mind (*antar-yāmin*). The subtle penetration of speech (*vāg-rūpa*) recurs even in the state which lacks ostensible mental activity.[30]
>
> (b) The illumination (*prakāśa*) which first comes into relation with external objects makes the bare essence of an entity shine forth, since the causes for the use of the word cannot be apprehended because of the function, which cannot be designated as this or that, of the seed of the residual traces of linguistic ability (*śabda-bhāvanā-bīja*).[31]

According to Vṛṣabha, it is said that the function of the seed of the residual traces of linguistic ability cannot be designated as this or that as long as this function is not activated.[32] In the light of Bhartṛhari's denotation theory, the cause for applying a word to an entity must be the delimiting factor (*upādhi*) of the entity.[33] Conse-

[29] VPV 1.129: *sad api vāg-vyavahāreṇânupagṛhītam artha-rūpam asatā tulyam.*

[30] VPV 1.132: *yathā prakāśakatvam agneḥ sva-rūpaṁ caitanyaṁ vântar-yāmiṇas tathā jñānam api sarvaṁ vāg-rūpa-mātrânugatam. yâpy asañcetitâvasthā tasyām api sūkṣmo vāg-rūpânugamo 'bhyāvartate.*

[31] VPV 1.132: *yo 'pi prathamôpanipātī bāhyeṣv artheṣu prakāśaḥ sa nimittānām aparigraheṇa vastu-svarūpa-mātram idaṁ tad ity avyapadeśyayā vṛttyā pratyavabhāsayati.*

[32] PDh ad VP 1.132: *vyapadeśyayā iti. śabda-bhāvanā vidyamānâpi sā kāryâbhāvān na tatra vṛttiṁ labheta.* Bhartṛhari says that when an entity is cognised by the cognition which is impregnated with a word, it appears clearly in that cognition (*vyakta-rūpa-pratyavabhāsa*); see (g). Vṛṣabha remarks that in this situation the entity is what can be designated as this or that. PDh ad VP 1.131: *vyakta-rūpa iti. vyakta-rūpaḥ pratyavabhāso 'smin. idaṁ tad iti vyapadeśa-rūpatvāt.*

[33] VP 3.5.2abc: *dravyasyâvyapadeśasya ya upādīyate guṇaḥ. bhedako vyapadeśāya...* According to Vṛṣabha, what Bhartṛhari means by the term *nimitta* ('cause') here is a qualifier (*viśeṣaṇa*) connected with an entity; see PDh ad VPV 1.132: *teṣāṁ vastu-sambandhināṁ gotvâdīnāṁ*

quently, when such a cause is not apprehended, it is natural that the entity is beyond verbalisation. In this situation, it has to be said that such a cognition manifests the entity as a bare entity, in an unqualified form,[34] and hence that it is not distinctly perceived.

All these things make it clear that in Bhartṛhari's view what is beyond verbalisation, namely what is beyond conceptualisation, is beyond the reach of ordinary cognitive states and thoughts, practically a non-existent thing. This is the underlying view on which Bhartṛhari argues that the musical note *ṣaḍja*, even if it comes within the range of perception, cannot be determined without being cognised as 'This is *ṣaḍja*'.

3.4. In view of what has been said, let us then consider another case in which it is argued that the determination of the distinction among things depends upon the word. The instance is an expression of excellence (*prakṛṣṭa-vyapadeśa*), such as *śuklataraṁ rūpam asya*—'The colour of this is whiter'.

3.4.1. Let us first of all keep in mind a basic framework for the expression of excellence. Bhartṛhari says:

> 'A quality is the cause to convey excellence [in respect of a substance (*dravya*)]. If the quality is presented as an independent thing (i.e. as a substance), the excellence in respect of it is understood only on the basis of its quality which resides in it.'[35]

The point here is this. In order to convey excellence in respect of a substance, one has to resort to a quality which resides in the substance. The quality is susceptible to substantialisation. When one wishes to convey excellence in respect of a quality, which one has substantialised, one has to resort to the quality which resides in the substantialised quality.

Now Bhartṛhari says the following in regard to the utterance *śuklataraṁ rūpam asya*:

---

viśeṣāṇām. In Bhartṛhari's denotation theory, the terms *guṇa*, *viśeṣaṇa*, and *upādhi* are synonymous with one another.

[34] PDh ad VPV 1.132: *tato viśeṣaṇa-rahitam eva vastu pratyāyati*.

[35] VP1.65:

guṇaḥ prakarṣa-hetur yaḥ svātantryeṇopadiśyate /
tasyâśritād guṇād eva prakṛṣṭatvaṁ pratīyate //

(a) In the utterance in question there does not occur any word to convey the distinction among white colours (*saṁvijñāna-padântarâbhāva*) other than the word *śukla*.[36]

(b) Therefore, what are understood to be the causes of the expression of excellence (*prakṛṣṭa-vyapadeśa-hetu*) are the differentiators (*viśeṣa*) characterised as follows:[37]

(c) They are other than what is denoted by an affix which signifies the cause for the occurrence of the word (*bhāva-pratyaya*).

(d) They are understood from the word *śukla* which denotes a white colour in general (*tulya-śruty-upagṛhīta*).

(e) They reside in the colour white which is spoken of as a substance, just as the colour white resides in a substance such as a cloth (*śaukalyavad eva rūpâśritāḥ*).

(f) Insofar as the expression of excellence is made in respect of a quality which resides in a substance and which can be referred to by 'this' or 'that' and hence can be denoted as something principal, there is no end to the resulting of the abstraction of a property, which takes place when another cause for the expression of excellence is assumed.[38]

Let us first note (c). Concerning the question of what the cause for excellence in the utterance *śuklataraṁ rūpam asya* is, Bhartṛhari, first of all, points out that the generic property whiteness (*śaukalya*, *śvaitya*), which is denoted by the affix *śyaÑ*, cannot serve as the cause for excellence in being white because the generic property 'whiteness' resides in all white colours and cannot serve to distinguish among white colours. Then he submits the alternative solution presented here.[39]

It is important to note (a). Bhartṛhari states that, in the given utterance, there is no word to convey the distinction among white colours. His idea here is this. One can have different shades of white. If one wishes to specify the colour white more pre-

---

[36] VPV 1.65: *saṁvijñāna-padântarâbhāvād vā bhāva-pratyayair anirdeśyās tulya-śruty-upagṛhītāḥ śauklyavad eva rūpâśritā viśeṣāḥ prakṛṣṭa-vyapadeśa-hetavo vijñāyante.*

Suppose that there are white and non-white substances. The quality white serves to differentiate the white substance from the non-white one. In this respect the item *śukla* which conveys the distinction among colours is considered to be a *saṁvijñāna-pada* with respect to that distinction.

[37] For (b)–(e), see note 36.

[38] VPV 1.65: *yāvac cêdaṁ tad iti vyapadeśyasya prādhānyenâśritasya prakṛṣṭa-vyapadeśaḥ kriyate tāvad avicchinno 'yaṁ nimittântara-parikalpanā-dharma-prasaṅga iti.*

[39] VPV 1.65: *śuklataraṁ rūpam asyêtra* [read: *asyêty atra*] *tu rūpasya dravyatvenôpādāne kriyamāṇe rūpâśrita-nimittāt prakṛṣṭa-vyapadeśaḥ prakalpate. na ca guṇa-sāmānyaṁ śveta-samavāyi śvaitryam ekatvād bheda-hetuḥ sambhavatîti saṁsargi-dharmântarâśrayo 'vântarasyâikasyâpi bhedaḥ parikalpyate.*

cisely, one can use a modifier, such as 'bright'. One can seek differentiating properties such as *bhāsvaratva* or brightness to have this kind of utterance. In the utterance in question, obviously, a term such as *bhāsvara*, which denotes the property brightness, is not used. The term *bhāsvara* is properly described as *saṁvijñāna-pada* with respect to brightness, since it signifies 'brightness'.[40] It goes without saying that this property is considered to reside in the white colour functioning as a substance (e).

As (d) states, the meaning 'brightness' in question lies within the domain of the word *śukla*. This is because this word denotes different white colours with different shades. It can denote a bright white colour.

Let us note (f). Bhartṛhari maintains that a quality is the cause for denoting excellence in respect of a substance; when excellence in respect of the quality is to be denoted, the quality of that quality is sought. Even if, theoretically, there would be no end to this process of abstracting some quality or other, it is natural that when one has no knowledge of the word to convey the differentiating property, one cannot have any further utterance. It is significant that in the given context Bhartṛhari considers the word *bhāsvara* as *saṁvijñāna-pada*. For, this shows that he holds that one who uses the utterance in question must have obtained the knowledge of the word which serves as the cause for determining the distinction among white colours in respect of brightness and must have determined the distinction. We have to recall that Bhartṛhari regards *saṁvijñāna-pada* as *avadhāraṇa-nibandhana-pada*.[41] Therefore, if, with a certain word, one can determine the distinction among bright white colours, one can have the utterance *rūpam asya bhāsvarataram*—'This is of a brighter white.' But this implies that if one cannot determine the distinction in question due to the lack of the knowledge of *saṁvijñāna-pada* for it, one cannot have such an utterance.[42]

4. Let us turn now to the context in which Bhartṛhari uses the term *saṁvijñāna-pada* to deal with the denotation of something essentially dependent as something independent (§ 2. (2)). The context is the one in which he discusses the unsignifiability of the relation (*sambandha*). What I mean by 'the unsignifiability of the relation' is what Bhartṛhari asserts in VP 3.3.3–4.

> '[3] When the utterance "This is the signifier of that" or "That is the significand of this" is used, the relation between word and meaning is

[40] PDh ad VPV 1.65: *na hi teṣāṁ kiṁcit saṁvijñāna-padaṁ bhāsvarâdi-śabdavad ihâsti.*

[41] See § 3.2.

[42] Helārāja explains as follows in VPP 3.5.3: *tatrâpi dharmântarasya prādhānye tad-aparâśrita-dharma-nimitta eva prakarṣa iti yāvat sambhavati śabda-vyāpāras tāvad aparyavasānam eva dharmāṇām iti ... yadā tu śabda-vyāpārôparamas tadā dharmântara-paryeṣaṇā paryavasyati.*

understood from the genitive ending. On the basis of this [relation] the identity (*tattva*) of word and meaning is also expressed. [4] There is no word to denote a relation in terms of its own property. Because it is absolutely dependent, its form cannot be referred to by its own word.'[43]

There are two points to note here. First, a relation (*yoga*, *sambandha*) between word and its meaning enters into our consciousness through the use of genitive endings. Secondly, there is no nominal term which signifies a relation qua relation: a relation is absolutely dependent (*atyanta-paratantratva*); its characteristic form is not referred to by any particular nominal term.

Now, on this assumption, Bhartṛhari describes a relation using the term *saṁvijñāna-pada* in his *Vṛtti* on VP 2.439:[44]

(a) In the utterance 'There is a contact of two fingers' (*aṅgulyoḥ saṁyogaḥ*), the contact (*saṁyoga*), even if it is a relation, is denoted as something independent (*svatantra*) by a *saṁvijñāna-pada* such as *saṁyoga* ('contact').
(b) The contact is understood here as what has the property of being a relatum (*sambandhin*), just like the servant in the utterance 'the king's servant' (*rājñaḥ puruṣaḥ*), even if it is a relation.
(c) In the utterance 'There is inherence between the contact and its holder' (*saṁyoga-saṁyoginoḥ samavāyaḥ*), on the other hand, the relation with the contact, understood to be a relatum, becomes the cause for the occurrence of the genitive ending.

The point made in (a) is that with reference to the relation contact (*saṁyoga*), the term *saṁyoga*, a nominal term, is a *saṁvijñāna-pada*. Besides, the point made in (b) is that the term *saṁyoga* denotes this relation as being independent (*svatantra*) and hence as being a relatum with respect to its property (*sambandhin*), but not in its own property.

---

[43] VP 3.3.3–4:

... vācya iti ṣaṣṭhyā pratīyate /
yogaḥ śabdârthayos tattvam apy ato vyapadiśyate //
nâbhidhānaṁ sva-dharmeṇa sambandhasyâsti vācakam /
atyanta-paratantratvād rūpaṁ nâsyâpadiśyate //

[44] VPV 2.439: *aṅgulyoḥ saṁyoga iti sambandho 'pi saṁyoga[ḥ] saṁvijñāna-padena svatantro 'bhidhīyamānaḥ puruṣâdivat sambandhidharmâbhidhīyate / sambandhi-sambandhas tu ṣaṣṭhyā nimittatvāya kalpate /* My special thanks are due to Professor Ashok Aklujkar for permission to use his unpublished edition of the *Vṛtti* to read this passage. See Ogawa (forthcoming).

What all this implies is the following: contact qua relation cannot be denoted by the term *saṁyoga* and, with reference to contact qua relation, this term is not a *saṁvijñāna-pada*. These points are stressed by Helārāja in his *Prakāśa* on VP 3.3.4.[45] According to him, when, extracting a relation from its relatum, one speaks of the relation using the term *sambandha*, one cannot refer directly to the relation qua relation with that term, since in this case one can only speak of the relation in question as something dependent (*sva-pradhāna*). Helārāja clearly states that a relation qua relation is *asaṁvijñāna-pada*, or what has no word by which it can be conveyed; and that it is to be understood from the effect of the occurrence of the genitive ending (*kāryâika-gamya*). It is to be noted that when Helārāja says that a relation qua relation is *asaṁvijñāna-pada*, he implies that it has no term which, entering into its own essence, conveys it (*tat-svarūpa-niveśi-saṁvijñāna-pada*).[46]

As shown above, one cannot have a discourse on a relation without resorting to a *saṁvijñāna-pada*, such as '*sambandha*'. But 'relation' has no *saṁvijñāna-pada* of its own by which one could capture its essence. 'Relation' as a substantialised entity has its *saṁvijñāna-pada*, while 'relation' per se has no corresponding *saṁvijñāna-pada*. That is characteristic of what is in essence of a dependent nature, such as relation.[47] And that is why in (c) Bhartṛhari has to say *ṣaṣṭhyā pratīyate*, namely that the relation is understood from the use of the genitive ending. The point is that there does exist a relation and it is determined as a distinct entity, but it has to be indicated with the genitive ending.

5. A close look at what is called *asaṁvijñāna-pada* has revealed the following points: First, a thing characterised as *asaṁvijñāna-pada* exists in an indistinct way. Secondly, the word called *saṁvijñāna-pada* denotes a distinct entity; but, in some cases, not in its own form.

---

[45] VPP 3.3.4: *tato niṣkṛṣya sambandha-śabdena sva-pradhānaḥ sambandhi-rūpatayâbhidhīyamāno na sākṣāt spraṣṭuṁ śakyata ity asaṁvijñāna-padaḥ kāryâika-gamyaḥ.*

[46] Regarding the term *samavāya* ('inherence'), the following idea is expressed by Helārāja in VPP 3.3.19: *nitya-paratantra-rūpaś câsau samavāya-śabdād api nâvadhāryate prayoktṛ-pratipattṛbhyām iti na tat-svarūpa-niveśi-saṁvijñāna-padaṁ kiṁcanâsti ity avācya eva bhāvato 'yam. sambandhi-rūpatayā tu svatantraḥ samavāyaḥ śabdād avagamyate.*

[47] According to Bhartṛhari, the nominal terms *diś* ('direction'), *sādhana* ('accomplisher'), *kriyā* ('action') and *kāla* ('time') signify their meanings as substances, so that they do not refer to the essence of being a power (*śakti*) the direction and others have; see VP 3.6.1:

dik sādhanaṁ kriyā kāla iti vastv-abhidhāyinaḥ /
śakti-rūpe padârthānām atyantam anavasthitāḥ /

In Bhartṛhari's view, power consists in being what renders service (*upakārin*) and hence in being something dependent. See OGAWA (forthcoming).

As shown above, the word called *saṁvijñāna-pada* is the word called *avadhāraṇa-nibandhana-pada* which, denoting a distinct entity differentiated from others, serves to determine the distinction among things. This clearly shows that Bhartṛhari argues that the world we experience is segmented into distinct things by virtue of our language. The word characterised as *saṁvijñāna-pada* is involved in such segmentation, and what is signified by such a word is precisely what enters into discourse. This means that we have to depend on *saṁvijñāna-pada* for a thing so that we may speak of the thing. To speak of a relation, for example, we have to use the nominal term *sambandha* which is a *saṁvijñāna-pada* with respect to a relation as a substantialised entity. It is noteworthy that verbalisation presupposes substantialisation in Bhartṛhari's denotation theory. But we also have to note that how it is spoke of is different from how it is. The most important point to keep in mind with respect to Bhartṛhari's philosophy of language is that only the world as we speak of it is existent, namely that an entity is said to be existent only when it becomes a meaning of a word.

BIBLIOGRAPHY

BhVi = Maṇḍanamiśra: *Bhāvanā-viveka*. (1) Ganganatha Jha (ed.): *The Bhāvanā Viveka of Mandana Misra with the Commentary of Bhatta Umbeka*. 2 parts. Princess of Wales Saraswati Bhavana Texts 6, Government Press, Allahabad 1922–23. (2) V.A. Ramaswami Sastri, K.A. Sivaramakrishna Sastri (eds.): *Bhavanaviveka with Viṣamagranthibhedika*. Annamalai University Sanskrit Series 16, Annamalai University, Annamalainagar 1952.

BhViV = Nārāyaṇa: *Bhāvanā-viveka-viṣama-granthi-bhedika*. See: $BhVi_2$.

BhViṬ = Umbeka Bhaṭṭa: *Bhāvanā-viveka-ṭīkā*. See: $BhVi_1$.

HOUBEN 1995 = Houben, Jan E.M.: *The Saṁbandha-samuddeśa (Chapter on Relation) and Bhartṛhari's Philosophy of Language: A Study of Bhartṛhari Saṁbandha-samuddeśa in the context of the Vākyapadīya with a translation of Helārāja's commentary Prakīrṇaprakāśa*. Gonda Indological Studies, Vol. II, Egbert Forstein, Groningen 1995.

MBhā = Patañjali: *Vyākaraṇa-mahā-bhāṣya*. Kielhorn, Lorenz Franz (ed.): *The Vyākaraṇa-mahābhāṣya of Patañjali, third edition, revised and furnished with additional readings, references and select critical notes by K.V. Abhyankar*. 3 Vols, Bhandarkar Oriental Research Institute, Poona I: 1962, II: 1965, III: 1972.

OGAWA (forthcoming) = Ogawa, Hideyo: 'On Bhartṛhari's notion of "power" (*śakti*).'

PDh = Vṛṣabhadeva: *Pad-dhati*. See: SUBRAMANIA IYER (1966).

RAU 1977 = Rau, Wilhelm (ed.): *Bhartṛharis Vākyapadīya: Die Mūlakārikās nach den Handschriften herausgegeben und mit einem Pāda-Index versehen*. Abhandlungen für die Kunde des Morgenlandes XLII, 4., Franz Steiner Verlag, Wiesbaden 1977.

RAU 2002 = Rau, Wilhelm (ed.): *Bhartṛharis Vākyapadīya: Versuch einer vollständigen deutschen Übersetzung nach der kritischen Edition der Mūla-Kārikās*. Herausgegeben von Oskar von Hinüber. Akademie der Wissenschaften und der Literatur, Abhandlung der Geistes- und Sozialwissenschaftlichen Klasse, Einzelveröffentlichung Nr. 8. Akademie der Wissenschaften und der Literatur, Mainz, Franz Steiner Verlag, Stuttgart 2002.

SUBRAMANIA IYER 1963 = Subramania Iyer, K.A.: *Vākyapadīya of Bhartṛhari with the Commentary of Helārāja, Kāṇḍa III, Part 1*. Deccan College Monograph Series 21, Deccan College, Poona 1963.

SUBRAMANIA IYER 1965 = Subramania Iyer, K.A.: *The Vākyapadīya of Bhartṛhari with the Vṛtti: Chapter I, English Translation*. Deccan College Building Centenary and Silver Jubilee Series 26, Deccan College, Poona 1965.

SUBRAMANIA IYER 1966 = Subramania Iyer, K.A.: *Vākyapadīya of Bhartṛhari with the Commentaries Vṛtti and Paddhati of Vṛṣabhadeva*. Deccan College Monograph Series 32, Deccan College, Poona 1966.

SUBRAMANIA IYER 1971 = Subramania Iyer, K.A.: *The Vākyapadīya of Bhartṛhari, chapter III, part 1; English translation*. Deccan College Building Centenary and Silver Jubilee Series 71, Deccan College, Poona 1971.

SUBRAMANIA IYER 1977 = Subramania Iyer, K.A.: *The Vākyapadīya of Bhartṛhari, Kāṇḍa II: English Translation with Exegetical Notes*. Motilal Banarsidass, Delhi 1977.

SUBRAMANIA IYER 1983 = Subramania Iyer, K.A.: *The Vākyapadīya of Bhartṛhari (An Ancient Treatise on the Philosophy of Sanskrit Grammar), Containing the Ṭīkā of Puṇyarāja and the Ancient Vṛtti, Kāṇḍa II, with a Foreword by Ashok Aklujkar*. Motilal Banarsidass, Delhi 1983.

VP = Bhartṛhari: *Vākyapadīya*. See: (1) Rau; (2) SUBRAMANIA IYER (1963), (1965), (1966), (1971), (1977), (1983). [The numbering of the *kārikā*s follows RAU (1977).]

VPP = Helārāja: *Vākyapadīya-prakāśa*. See: SUBRAMANIA IYER (1966).

VPV = Bhartṛhari: *Vākyapadīya-vṛtti*. See SUBRAMANIA IYER (1966), (1983).

Logic and Belief in Interpretation and Translation

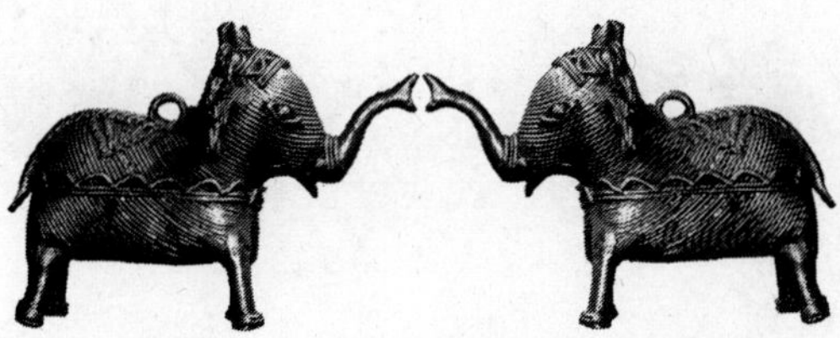

Major Points of Vācaspati's Disagreement with Maṇḍana*

DIWAKAR ACHARYA

The first two works of Vacaspatimiśra I, the *Nyāya-kaṇikā* and *Tattva-samīkṣā*[1], are commentaries on Maṇḍanamiśra's works. This indicates that Vācaspati initially studied Mīmāṁsā, focusing especially on Maṇḍana. His study of Maṇḍana's Mīmāṁsā works made him gradually develop his interest further in the latter's Vedānta work, the *Brahma-siddhi* (BSi), before he found his way to Nyāya. As a result, Vācaspati's tenets are influenced by Maṇḍana's thought, particularly insofar as they reflect Mīmāṁsā and Vedānta[2]. The *Bhāmatī*, which establishes a distinct school of interpretation of the *Brahma-sūtra-śāṅkara-bhāṣya* (BSŚBh), is mainly based on the foundation of the *Brahma-siddhi* and Vācaspatimiśra's commentary thereon, the *Tattva-samīkṣā* (TSam). It is not unknown to the scholars of Indian philosophy that most of distinctive features of the *Bhāmatī*-school have their roots in Maṇḍana's views as set forth in the *Brahma-siddhi*. In the *Bhāmatī*, Vācaspatimiśra resorts to the *Brahma-siddhi* whenever he faces unclear points in the *Śāṅkara-bhāṣya*, and so invariably explains the text convincingly. Therefore, Vācaspatimiśra is blamed by some traditional authors for following Maṇḍanamiśra blindly.

My impression, however, is that this is not always true, at least in the final stage of his writing career. It is true that Vācaspatimiśra appears to have been heavily

* I would like to express my gratitude to Prof. Ashok Aklujkar (University of British Columbia), Prof. Harunaga Isaacson and Prof. Emeritus Albrecht Wezler (Universität Hamburg) for their critical comments on an earlier draft of this paper. I am grateful to Prof. Akihiko Akamatsu (Kyoto University) for his offer to present this issue in the VAADA lecture series of the 21st century COE Program at Kyoto University in October 2005. I am also grateful to Mr. Philip Pierce (Nepal Research Centre) for going over my English.

[1] On chronological order of Vācaspati's works, see ACHARYA (2006: xxxi–xxxiii).

[2] Following the line of Maṇḍanamiśra and further developing it, Vācaspatimiśra brings together the Mīmāṁsā and Nyāya theories of error as two dimensions of a combined theory of error in Vedānta, which, if observed from two different angles, is equally acceptable to all these three schools (see ACHARYA (2006: lxvii-lxviii)). I intend to compare concerned passages at some other occasion in near future.

Logic and Belief in Indian Philosophy
Warsaw Indological Studies 3 (2010) 433–445.

influenced by Maṇḍanamiśra's ideas but, at the same time, we find him reconsidering the latter's positions and refining them in the *Bhāmatī*. There it appears that he developed further arguments or even new ideas from simple points made by Maṇḍana and blended them with the ideas of Śaṅkara. Not only that, Vācaspatimiśra in the *Bhāmatī* seems to differ from Maṇḍanamiśra on a number of crucial points. I shall reflect upon them here briefly.

1. Levels of Brahman Realisation

Firstly, Vācaspati does not agree with Maṇḍana on the levels of realisation of Brahman. At the beginning of the *Niyoga-kāṇḍa*, Maṇḍana mentions three possible levels of Brahman realisation: verbal knowledge, meditative knowledge and the final intuitive knowledge. In the *Tattva-samīkṣā*, Vācaspati briefly comments on the passage, saying nothing specific from his side, but in the *Bhāmatī* he delimits the third as the profound meditation (*nididhyāsana*) in the form of continuity of the mind (*citta-santati-maya*) and identifies the intuitive knowledge as a fourth form at the top, and proceeds to justify its necessity. This fourth level of realisation is an original idea on the part of Vācaspati; however, his speculation is grounded in Maṇḍana's discourse. Let us compare the following passages from the *Brahma-siddhi* and *Bhāmatī*:

> 'There are three [levels of] realisation with regard to Brahman. The first comes from verbal knowledge (lit. word). Another is the realisation variously known as meditation, contemplation and cultivation, which is a continuation of the first realisation from the verbal knowledge, and the other takes the form of intuitive perception, when the state of completion occurs and all mental fabrications have ceased.'[3]

> 'There are four [levels of] realisation with regard to Brahman. The first is reached by merely studying sentences from the Upaniṣads; this is known as the "act of hearing". The second is reached by studying of the same Upaniṣadic sentences but at the same time reflecting on them; this is known as the "act of reflection". The third is the profound

[3] BSi 1.74: *tisraś ca pratipattayo brahmaṇi. prathamā tāvac chabdāt, anyā śabdāt pratipadya tat-santānavatī dhyāna-bhāvanôpāsanâdi-śabda-vācyā, anyā tato labdha-niṣpattir vigalita-nikhila-vikalpā sākṣāt-karaṇa-rūpā*, see ACHARYA (2006: 156).

Vācaspatimiśra's commentary on this passage runs as follows (ACHARYA (2006: 156–157)): "*ātmā jñātavyaḥ*" *iti hi kila brahmaṇi pra*[*ti*](*pattir vidhīyate, ti*)*sraś ca tāḥ sambhavantîty āha—tisraś cêti. anyā tataḥ santānavatyāḥ pratīter ādara-nairantarya-dīrgha-kālâsevana-labdha-paripākāyā* (*labdha-niṣpattir viga*)*lita-nikhila-vikalpā, viśeṣaṇa-viśeṣya-bhāva-nirbhāso 'vacchinna-viṣaya-pratyayo vikalpaḥ, tad-rahitêty arthaḥ.*

meditation in the form of a continuation of the mind, and the fourth is the state of the intuitive perception in the form of a particular mode of the mind. Absolute unity is an inherent property of this fourth state.'[4]

In the above passage from the *Bhāmatī*, Vācaspati clearly states that verbal knowledge continues up to the second level, and on the third level merely continuity of thought prevails, while on the fourth level intuitive realisation occurs from a particular operation of mind.[5]

Thus, according to him, a particular operation of the mind following upon impressions of 'hearing' (*śravaṇa*), 'reflection' or 'spiritual cultivation' (*manana*) and 'meditation' (*nididhyāsana*) causes the final and direct realisation of Brahman. For the followers of the *Vivaraṇa*-school of Śaṅkara Vedānta, the latter is caused by the hearing of the Upaniṣadic sentences being perfected by spiritual cultivation and meditation. This is one of the major points of difference between the two schools of interpretation among the followers of Śaṅkara Vedānta.

This question is of great importance because it involves another controversial point of debate concerning the capacity of the Upaniṣadic sentences. In Vācaspati's scheme, spiritual cultivation is fundamental and necessary; the Upaniṣadic sentences can produce only indirect knowledge of Brahman, and without spiritual cultivation direct realisation of Brahman is not possible. This is not acceptable to the followers of the *Vivaraṇa*-school, since it limits the capacity of the Upaniṣadic sentences.

In Maṇḍana's three-level scheme, the third level is already the final stage of intuitive perception and is said to be a culmination of the second level and free of all fabrications and diversities.[6] This level is already the level of final culmination, and there is no scope for the fourth in this scheme.

In the *Brahma-sūtra-śāṅkara-bhāṣya* there is not the slightest allusion to a fourth level or a passage that would admit such a stage. In the *Pañca-pādikā* (PP) and *Vivaraṇa*, there is no mention of the fourth level either. Therefore, we must say that

---

[4] *Bhāmatī* ad BSŚBh 3.4.26: *catasraḥ pratipattayo brahmaṇi. prathamā tāvad upaniṣad-vākya-śravaṇa-mātrād bhavati yāṁ kila ācakṣate śravaṇam iti. dvitīyā mīmāṁsā-sahitā tasmād eva upaniṣad-vākyād yām ācakṣate mananam iti. tṛtīyā citta-santati-mayī, yām ācakṣate nididhyāsanam iti. caturthī sākṣāt-kāravatī vṛtti-rūpā, nântaryaṁ hi tasyāḥ kaivalyam iti.*

[5] This operation of the mind in later Vedānta texts is identified as being in a pure and undifferentiated state.

[6] It is not clear from Maṇḍana's passage, however, whether or not the verbal knowledge which is continued in the second level continues till the third, where it is culminated. This can be interpreted either way: Ānandapūrṇa in BhŚu thinks that this final culmination takes place by means of hearing (*śravaṇa-dvārā*); and if he is right, Prakāśātman is closer to Mandana. In any case, Maṇḍana's stance is less disputable than that of Vācaspati's.

this is an original idea on the part of Vācaspati which is not in agreement with Maṇḍana's thought.

2. Liberation in life

Once Brahman is realised, what happens to the realised person? Does his body immediately collapse, that is, does he die, due to the total annihilation of ignorance (*avidyā*) and *karman* brought about by the realisation of Brahman? If not, how does his body remain functional after such an annihilation?

Maṇḍana says that it all depends either upon leftover traces of the cause of the body (*avidyā*), which was once in operation (*labdha-vṛtti*), or upon the residual effect of this cause, or upon both of them.[7] The bodies of those who have no such traces may immediately collapse, but those who have such traces may persevere in a bodily state for some time, this state being termed 'liberation in life' (*jīvan-mukti*). Maṇḍana holds a person in this state to be a man of stable insight (*sthita-prajña*) and explains that he might not be a *siddha*, one who has already attained the goal, but still a *sādhaka*, one who has reached a highly advanced stage in spiritual cultivation and is waiting for the final realisation. He writes:

> 'We say, first of all, the man of stable insight is not a *siddha* (i.e. one who has accomplished the goal), for whom *avidyā* has entirely disappeared, but a *sādhaka* (i.e. one who is still progressing towards the goal) who has reached a particular state, and we do not say that the body is dropped immediately after the realisation of Brahman. He awaits the extinction of the *karman* whose effects are still in motion. Here the one enjoys immediate liberation, whereas the other suffers some delay.'[8]

On this point, Vācaspati does not follow Maṇḍana, and indeed even refutes him, following Śaṅkara. According to Śaṅkara, a question like whether a realised person dies or continues to live is not a matter of debate, for the realisation of Brahman brings about annihilation of only that portion of *karman* which has not fructified and begun to produce results (*anārabdha*) but not of that which has begun to produce results (*prārabdha*). Śaṅkara writes:

---

[7] Maṇḍanamiśra's preference seems to be for the second alternative (see below, p. 437). As commentators think, inasmuch as differences in the mind produce impressions and the body continues to exist.

[8] BSi_1 130–131: *ucyate—sthita-prajñas tāvan na vigalita-nikhilâvidyaḥ siddhaḥ, kiṁ tu sādhaka evâvasthā-viśeṣaṁ prāptaḥ syāt. na ca brūmaḥ—brahma-vedanânantara eva deha-viyogaḥ. ārabdha-kārya-karma-kṣayaṁ bhogena pratīkṣata iti tatra kasya cit tat-kālo 'pavargaḥ, kasya cit kiyāṁś cit kṣepaḥ.*

'Moreover, one should not debate in this point whether a realised person bears his body for some time or not. How could the realisation of Brahman, a conception of one's mind, negate endurance of a body affected by some other [conception]? This point is explained in both the *śrutis* and *smṛtis* by describing the characteristics of a man of stable insight. Therefore, it can be concluded that on the strength of realisation there is extinction only of those vices and virtues the effects of which are not yet in motion.'[9]

As already stated, Vācaspatimiśra in the *Bhāmatī* not only accepts the position of Śaṅkara on this issue but also refutes Maṇḍanamiśra's position by stating that a *sthita-prajña* or *jīvan-mukta* cannot be a *sādhaka* awaiting the final realisation but must be a *siddha*, and that there is no higher state than this to be accomplished. Here is Vācaspatimiśra's commentary on the above excerpt from the *Brahma-sūtra-śāṅkara-bhāṣya*:

'On the *mūla* expression **one should not debate...**: the man of stable insight is not one who is still progressing towards the goal (*sādhaka*), for there is not any more primal conception that could be based on the supremacy of even further meditation. Rather, the man of stable insight is without a superior and is one who has already accomplished the goal (*siddha*).'[10]

It should also be noted that Maṇḍanamiśra does not think that the realised person has to consume the *prārabdha-karman* by experiencing its results; he seems to say that what remains even in the state of *jīvan-mukti* is merely an impression of *prārabdha-karman* but not the residue itself. Thus he mentions the contrary position and refutes it:

[9] BSŚBh 4.1.15: *api ca naîvâtra vivaditavyam—brahma-vidā kaṁ cit kālaṁ śarīraṁ dhriyate na vā dhriyata iti. kathaṁ hy ekasya sva-hṛdaya-pratyayaṁ brahma-vedanaṁ deha-dhāraṇaṁ câpareṇa pratikṣeptuṁ śakyeta? śruti-smṛtiṣu ca sthita-prajña-lakṣaṇa-nirdeśenâitad eva nirucyate. tasmād anārabdha-kāryayor eva sukṛta-duṣkṛtayor vidyā-sāmarthyāt kṣaya iti nirṇayaḥ.*

[10] *Bhāmatī* ad BSŚBh 4.1.15: ***api ca naîvâtra vivaditavyam*** *iti. sthita-prajñaś ca na sādhakaḥ; tasyôttarôttara-dhyānôtkarṣeṇa pūrva-pratyayânavasthitatvāt. niratiśayas tu sthita-prajñaḥ. sa ca siddha eva.*

Interestingly enough, Amalānanda in commenting upon this passage expressly states that Vācaspati has here refuted Maṇḍana, see KT on *Bhāmatī* ad BSŚBh 4.1.15: *bhāṣye sthita-prajña-lakṣaṇa-nirdeśo jīvan-mukti-sādhaka uktaḥ. tatra sthita-prajñaḥ sādhako na sākṣāt-kāravān iti maṇḍana-miśrair uktaṁ dūṣaṇam uddharati—****sthita-prajñaś*** *cêti.*—'In the *Bhāṣya*, a mention of the characteristics of the man of stable insight [found in the Upaniṣadic and *smṛti* texts] is said to be the proof of "liberation in life". In this context, Vācaspati takes out the fault Maṇḍana [pointed out] that the man of stable insight is one who is still progressing (*sādhaka*) but not one who has obtained the intuitive perception, and writes "**The man of stable insight**...".'

> 'Some people, however, think that cessation of the *karman* set for fruition is not possible, just as in the case of an arrow impetuous [in its course] or a wheel [in motion], and that for this reason it is necessary to wait for the cessation of such *karman*. That is not true. An arrow can certainly be stopped by setting a wall or the like in its way, and can also be destroyed by cutting it off [in flight] or by other means. In our case, too, there are pacifying rituals which are capable of destroying *karman* bound for consumption, as indicated in a dream or the like. Therefore, it is sure that the endurance of the body is due to impressions (*saṁskāra*).'[11]

However, both Śaṅkara and Vācaspati are opposed to this view and regard what is destroyed after realisation as only the *karman* which is not yet bound to have repercussions but not the *karman* which is set for fruition.[12] Thus Vācaspati not only differs from Maṇḍana on this issue but even accepts a position refuted by him.

3. The Relationship between *karman* and Realisation

Another controversial view of Maṇḍanamiśra that Vācaspati discards in the *Bhāmatī* concerns the relationship between *karman* and realisation. According to Maṇḍana, *karman* has a vital role to play even in the process of realisation of Brahman, the former being closely associated with the latter. Maṇḍana presents seven possible theories on this issue and affirms two of them. For him, either *karman* by virtue of its bi-functional nature is conducive to the realisation of *ātman* alongside the production of its direct result; or else it exists for the purification of the individual and perfects him so as to prepare him for Brahman realisation. Maṇḍana presents these two views as follows:

> 'Others, however, say that all types of *karman* are finally governed by the realisation of *ātman* due to the property of separateness-with-conjunction, for it is stated in the *śruti* that "they desire to know by performing sacrifice" and "by whatever means he makes sacrifice, his mind becomes pure after the concluding *darvī-homa*". Some others describe the relationship between *karman* and the governing authority of Brahman realisation with the words that "by means of sacrifices and

---

[11] BSi$_1$ 132–133: *ye tu manyante—pravṛtta-bhogānāṁ karmaṇāṁ pravṛtta-vegasyêṣor iva cakrasyeva vā na śakyaḥ pratibandhaḥ, ato bhogena kṣaya-pratīkṣêti. tad asat. śakyo hīṣuḥ pratibandhuṁ kuḍyâdibhiḥ, nāśayituṁ ca cchedâdibhiḥ. svapnâdi-sūcitôpasthita-vipāka-varttamāna-deha-bhogya-karma-kṣayârthāni ca śāntikāni karmāṇi. tasmāt saṁskārād eva sthitiḥ.*

[12] See ACHARYA (2006: cxxi).

great sacrifices this body is made ready for [realisation]" and "to whom the forty rites of purification and the eight virtues [apply]".'[13]

Later, after presenting all possible views, he returns to these two views and affirms them in the following way:

> 'It is logical that that *karman* which is not dependent on some other action is subordinate to realisation according to the property of separation-with-conjunction, even as the *śruti* states that "those who contemplate Brahman desire to know it by means of sacrifice". It is called subordinate, inasmuch as it is instrumental in attaining [realisation] but does not contribute to producing it the way *prayāja* and the like do, for realisation has no other effect to be produced. Alternatively, the other position of purification is acceptable because of the testimony of the *smṛti* and also because of the fact that realisation comes only to a purified person. Thus it is said: "and since it is prescribed, the *karman* of a particular *āśrama*, too, [is helpful in realisation]".'[14]

Thus Maṇḍana not only claims usefulness of *karman* in the course of realising Brahman but also says that the accumulation of *karman* accelerates the process of realisation and so should be continued until the final intuitive stage of realisation (*sākṣāt-kāra*)[15].

Vācaspati criticises this view of Maṇḍana and accepts that of Śaṅkara, who believes that *karman* and Brahman realisation are quite opposed to each other and a reconciliation of the two is impossible. Though Vācaspati accepts that *karman* purifies and qualifies a person for the realisation of *ātman*, he says it is effective as long as a desire for such knowledge (*vividiṣā*) is not produced. He writes:

> 'For [fear of] entering into a cumbersome assumption, it is not logical to agree upon the position which postulates that the obligatory duties have a direct relation to realisation via separation-with-conjunction,

[13] BSi_1 27 = BSi_2 21–22: *anye tu saṁyoga-pṛthaktvena sarva-karmaṇām evâtma-jñānâdhikārânupraveśam āhuḥ "vividiṣanti yajñena" iti śruteḥ, "yena kenacana yajetâpi darvi-homenânupahata-manā eva bhavati" iti ca. anye tu puruṣa-saṁskāratayâtma-jñānâdhikāra-saṁsparśaṁ karmaṇāṁ varṇayanti—"mahā-yajñaiś ca yajñaiś ca brāhmīyaṁ kriyate tanuḥ", "yasyâte catvāriṁśat-saṁskārā aṣṭāv ātma-guṇāḥ" iti ca.*

[14] BSi_1 36: *idaṁ tu yuktam—kāryântara-nirākāṅkṣāṇām api karmaṇāṁ saṁyoga-pṛthaktvāt "tam etaṁ vedânuvacanena brāhmaṇā vividiṣanti yajñena" iti vidyâṅga-bhāvaḥ. so 'py upapatty-arthatayā, na prayājâdivat kāryôpayogena, vidyāyāḥ kāryântarā-bhāvāt. saṁkāra-pakṣo vā, smṛteḥ; saṁskṛtasya hi vidyôtpatteḥ. tad uktam—"vihitatvāc câśrama-karmâpi" iti.*

[15] See the passage quoted below, p. 441.

whereas these duties can be related easily with realisation [in another way], inasmuch as they purify a person by regularly disposing accumulated vice. Thus virtues are in fact acquired from the performance of the obligatory duties, whence vice goes away. Vice alone pollutes one's mind by casting an antithetic view of eternity, purity and pleasure on this mortal, impure and sorrowful world. So when vice is removed and the doors of perception and reasoning are opened, one understands by perception and reasoning the nature of this world beyond doubt as mortal, impure and sorrowful. Then a disliking for this world known as displeasure is developed, and then rises a desire to abandon it. Then one searches for the means to do so, and in this search, hearing that the knowledge of the self is the means being searched for, one desires to know the self. Thereafter, one comes to know it by following the due course, beginning with "hearing". Because of all this, it is logical to agree that the purification of the mind by *karman* is indirectly contributive to the process of realising the truth.'[16]

In brief, then, according to Śankara and Vācaspati, once the desire for knowledge is produced and one is minded to listen to the Upaniṣads, *karman* has no further role to play and must be dropped entirely.[17]

---

[16] *Bhāmatī* ad BSŚBh 1.1.1: *kḷptenâiva ca nityānāṁ karmaṇāṁ nityêhitenôpātta-durita-nibarhaṇena puruṣa-saṁskāreṇa jñānôtpattāv aṅga-bhāvôpapattau na saṁyoga-pṛthaktvena sākṣād aṅga-bhāvo yuktaḥ, kalpanā-gauravâpatteḥ. tathā hi nitya-karmânuṣṭhānād dharmôtpādaḥ, tato pāpmā nivartate, sa hy anityâśuci-duḥkha-rūpe saṁsāre nitya-śuci-sukha-khyāti-lakṣaṇena viparyāsena citta-sattvaṁ malīnayati. ataḥ pāpani-vṛttau pratyakṣôpapatti-dvārâpāvaraṇe sati pratyakṣôpapattibhyāṁ saṁsārasyânityâśuci-duḥkha-rūpatām apratyūham avabuddhyate, tato 'syāsminn anabhirati-saṁjñaṁ vairāgyam upajāyate, tatas taj-jihāsôpāvartate, tato hānôpāyaṁ paryeṣate, paryeṣamāṇaś câtma-tattva-jñānam asyôpāya ity upaśrutya tat jijñāsate, tataḥ śravaṇâdikrameṇa taj jānātîty ārād upakārakatvaṁ tattva-jñānôtpādaṁ prati citta-sattva-śuddhyā karmaṇāṁ yuktam.*

[17] In commenting on Śaṅkara's interpretation of the Upaniṣadic sentence *kurvann evêha karmāṇi*... ('one should aspire to live a full life by performing *karman*'), Vācaspatimiśra follows Śaṅkara in admitting the point that a realised person can continue accumulating *karman* but states that even so he is not afflicted by it. However, his inclination is to take the above statement as a recommendation to an unrealised person, and so for him it is a secondary solution, *Bhāmatī* ad BSŚBh 3.4.13–14: "*kurvann evêha karmāṇi jijīviṣed*" *ity-evam-ādiṣu niyama-śravaṇeṣu na viduṣa iti viśeṣo 'sti, aviśeṣeṇa niyama-vidhānāt.* "*kurvann evêha karmāṇi*" *ity-atrâparo viśeṣa ākhyāyate. yady apy atra prakaraṇa-sāmarthyād vidvān eva kurvann iti sambandhyeta, tathâpi vidyā-stutaye karmânuṣṭhānam etad draṣṭravyam.* "*na karma lipyate nare*" *iti hi vakṣyati. etad uktaṁ bhavati—yāvaj-jīvaṁ karma kurvaty api viduṣi puruṣe na karma lepāya bhavati vidyā-sāmarthyād iti tad evaṁ vidyā stūyate.*—'In the case of the statement of rules like "One should aspire to live in this world by performing *karman*", there underlies the special point that such a

Contrary to this, Maṇḍana thinks that the process of Brahman realisation is accelerated if it is accompanied by *karman*, even though plodding on towards realisation without accumulating *karman* is also possible. In support of his view, he quotes *Brahma-sūtra* 3.4.26 (*sarvâpekṣā ca yajñâdi-śruter aśvavat*) and elaborates the idea that, even as it is possible to reach a destination without a horse, although one is desirable for reaching there quickly or for the sake of convenience, in the same way *karman* is desirable in the process of Brahman realisation for the same reason. He writes:

> 'In the case of ascetics living in chastity, the rise of pure knowledge could be expected even without [the performance of] those duties; still, there is difference in terms of time. Thanks to these particular means, pure knowledge is revealed quickly, [much] more quickly, while in the absence of these means it is revealed slowly, [much] more slowly. It is said: "the requirement of all types of *karman* is admitted, for the *śruti* teaches sacrifice and so on [as a means of attaining Brahman], but [these duties are] like a horse". This is the meaning of this *sūtra*: the performance of duties is required for realisation, which is to be attained through repeated practice, as the *śruti* teaches through sacrifice and charity, just as a horse is required in order to reach a village swiftly and conveniently, even though it is possible to reach there without a horse.'[18]

Śaṅkara's interpretation of the same *sūtra* is quite different, and seemingly a bit distorted. He says that as a horse is employed to draw a chariot but not to plough fields, so too *karman* is required in order to produce a desire for knowledge (*vividiṣā*), not to accomplish the final goal of Brahman realisation (*brahma-jñāna*):

prescription is not for a realised person. For this statement is made without any specification, [so that a clarification is needed]. However, in the case of this particular statement, "One should aspire…", it is further necessary to make another point, that though depending on the context a realised person may be an agent who accumulates *karman*, the accumulation of *karman* should be viewed as something for the sake of praising the realisation of [Brahman]. Later it is said that "*karman* does not defile a [realised] person". This amounts to saying the following: even though a realised person accumulates *karman* for his whole life, his *karman* will not cause any defilement in him, given his realisation, and thus [Brahman] realisation is praised.'

[18] BSi$_1$ 36–37: *ūrdhva-retasāṁ câśramiṇāṁ vinâpi tair viśuddha-vidyodaya iṣyate. kiṁ tu kāla-kṛto viśeṣaḥ. sādhana-viśeṣād dhi sā kṣipraṁ kṣiprataraṁ ca vyajyate, tad-abhāve cireṇa ciratareṇa ca. tad uktam—sarvâpekṣā ca yajñâdi-śruter aśvavat. eṣo 'rthaḥ—"yajñena dānena" iti śravaṇāt karmāṇy apekṣante vidyāyām abhyāsa-labhyāyām api, yathântareṇâśvaṁ grāma-prāptau siddhyantyāṁ śaighryâyākleśāya vāśvo 'pekṣyate.*

> 'The right knowledge, once attained, requires nothing towards accomplishing the goal, but it requires means towards its [own] rise. How so? Because the *śruti* teaches sacrifice and so on as the means thereto. ... Given their connection with the desire to know [the self], they are regarded as the means whereby [the right knowledge] arises. The expression "like a horse" in the *sūtra* points at ability. Even as a horse, because of its ability, is employed to pull a chariot but not to plough, similarly the ritual duties of [the earlier] *āśrama*s are not required by the right knowledge towards accomplishing the goal, but only towards its [own] rise.'[19]

Maṇḍana strongly criticises this position. He postulates that *karman* and Brahman realisation are hardly opposed to each other, and repeatedly states that the former is conducive not only to a desire for knowledge (*vividiṣā*) but also to the final intuitive realisation of Brahman.[20]

For his part, Vācaspati rejects any positive relation between the two:

> 'In this way, for a person who has not performed *karman* in this life but whose mind has been purified by his actions in the previous life and an aversion to this world has arisen in him through an apprehension of its worthlessness, there is no use performing *karman*, that is fit and favourable for the rise of aversion. For its purpose has already been served by his having performed *karman* in his previous life.'[21]

Thus neither of the two views concerning the relation between *karman* and realisation affirmed by Maṇḍanamiśra is acceptable to Vācaspatimiśra in this matter.

4. The Significance of Renunciation (*saṁnyāsa*)

The above view of Maṇḍanamiśra regarding the relationship between *karman* and Brahman realisation has a direct impact on the question of the significance of

[19] BSŚBh 3.4.26: *utpannā hi vidyā phala-siddhiṁ prati na kiṁ cid apekṣate, utpattiṁ prati tv apekṣate. kutaḥ? yajñâdi-śruteḥ. ... vividiṣā-saṁyogāc câiṣām utpatti-sādhana-bhāvo 'vasīyate. ... aśvavad iti yogyatā-nidarśanam. yathā ca yogyatā-vaśenâśvo na lāṅgalâkarṣaṇe yujyate, ratha-caryāyāṁ tu yujyate. evam āśrama-karmāṇi vidyayā phala-siddhau nâpekṣyante, utpattau câpekṣyanta iti.*

[20] See BSi_1 32–36.

[21] *Bhāmatī* ad BSŚBh 1.1.1: *evaṁ cânanuṣṭhita-karmâpi prāg-bhavīya-karma-vaśād yo viśuddha-sattvaḥ saṁsārâsāratā-darśanena niṣpanna-vairāgyaḥ, kṛtaṁ tasya karmânuṣṭhānena vairāgyôt-pādôpayoginā, prāg-bhavīya-karmânuṣṭhānād eva tat-siddheḥ.*

saṁnyāsa. Since *karman* is conducive to the final realisation and is effective till the end of one's life, *saṁnyāsa* should not really be necessary. A householder who continues with the performance of *karman*, specifically the obligatory duties (*nitya-karman*), should reach the goal rather earlier than an ascetic who renounces everything. Indeed, according to Maṇḍana, a householder gallops towards the goal while an ascetic is still plodding on.[22] This idea would in no way have been acceptable to Śaṅkara and his followers, who champion *saṁnyāsa* with almost propagandist fervour.

According to Śaṅkara, *saṁnyāsa* is a necessary condition for Brahman realisation. For him, abiding in Brahman (*brahma-saṁsthatā*), in complete surrender to Brahman, is possible only for a renunciant, not for others in any of the other three stages of life. These have to perform their specific duties; if they stop performing the recommended duties, they will be committing sin. A renunciant, however, is different; he does not acquire sin by not performing *karman*, inasmuch as he has renounced all *karman*.[23]

Śaṅkara states that renunciation is part and parcel of the maturity leading to Brahman realisation and is recommended for a qualified person. One is called upon to renounce all *karman* after listening to the Upaniṣads:

> 'As renunciation is part of the maturity leading to Brahman realisation, it is not for people other than allotted ones. And the *śruti* teaches this: "Now a mendicant with his head shaved, pale-dressed, without possessions, clean, free from malice and living on alms is [ready] for Brahmanhood".'[24]

Here too, Vācaspati follows Śaṅkara, not Maṇḍanamiśra, as his commentary on the above *Brahma-sūtra-śāṅkara-bhāṣya* passage makes clear:

> 'This is what is taught: Brahman[hood] is renunciation characterised by the abandonment of all types of longing through devotion to Brahman. Therefore, such a special [way of life] characterised by renunciation and abiding in Brahman is only for the mendicant, not for people in the

[22] See ACHARYA (2006: cxv).

[23] BSŚBh 3.4.20: *atrôcyate—brahma-saṁstha iti hi brahmaṇi parisamāptir ananya-vyāpāratā-rūpaṁ tan-niṣṭhatvam abhidhīyate. tac ca trayāṇām āśramāṇāṁ na sambhavati, svâśrama-vihita-karmânanuṣṭhāne pratyavāya-śravaṇāt. parivrājakasya tu sarva-karma-saṁnyāsat pratyavāyo na sambhavaty ananuṣṭhāna-nimittaḥ. śama-damâdis tu tadīyo dharmo brahma-saṁsthatāyā upodbalako na virodhī. brahma-niṣṭhatvam eva hi tasya śama-damâdy-upabṛṁhitaṁ svâśrama-vihitaṁ karma.*

[24] BSŚBh 3.4.20: *brahma-jñāna-paripākâṅgatvāc ca pārivrājyasya nânadhikṛta-viṣayatvam. tac ca darśayati—"atha parivrāḍ vivarṇa-vāsā muṇḍo 'parigrahaḥ śucir adrohī bhaikṣāṇo brahma-bhūyāya bhavati" iti.*

other stages of life. Intuitive perception, the maturity of Brahman realisation arising from verbal knowledge, is the only means of emancipation. Renunciation is prescribed as part of this maturity, and is not for people to whom it has not been allotted.'[25]

According to Vācaspati, one should renounce as soon as desires have fallen away;[26] and thus he appears to assume that *saṁnyāsa* is a prerequisite for Brahman realisation.

Vācaspati generally takes the liberty to introduce new ideas and add extra remarks. Thus, though he appears to follow Śaṅkara in the last three instances above, it is important to note that he does so while refuting or discarding Maṇḍana's views. As to the first instance, it is a revised presentation of an idea found in the *Brahmasiddhi*; still, it is perfect and effective in its own way, and even leads to new avenues of philosophic pursuit.

BIBLIOGRAPHY

ACHARYA 2006 = Acharya, Diwakar: *Vācaspatimiśra's Tattvasamīkṣā: The Earliest Commentary on Maṇḍanamiśra's Brahmasiddhi*. Nepal Research Centre Publications 25, Franz Steiner Verlag, Stuttgart 2006.

Bhāmatī = Vācaspatimiśra I: *Bhāmatī*. See: BSŚBh.

BhŚu = Ānandapūrṇa: *Bhāva-śuddhi*. N.S. Anantakrishna Sastri (ed.): *Two Commentaries on Brahmasiddhi: Bhāvaśuddhi of Ānandapūrṇa Muni and Abhiprāyaprakāśikā of Citsukha Muni*. Madras Government Oriental Series 161, Government Oriental Manuscript Library, Madras 1963.

BSŚBh = Śaṅkara: *Brahma-sūtra-śāṅkara-bhāṣya*. Anantakṛṣṇa Śāstrī (ed.): *The Brahmasūtra Śānkara Bhāṣya, with the Commentaries Bhāmatī, Kalpataru and Parimala*. Second edition by Bhārgav Śāstrī, Nirṇāya Sāgara Press, Bombay 1938.

[25] *Bhāmatī* ad BSŚBh 3.4.20: *etad uktaṁ bhavati—brahma-paratayā sarvêṣaṇā-parityāga-lakṣaṇo nyāso brahmêti. tathā cêdṛśaṁ nyāsa-lakṣaṇaṁ brahma-saṁsthatva-lakṣaṇaṁ bhikṣor evâsādhāraṇaṁ nêtareṣām āśramiṇām. brahma-jñānasya śabda-janitasya yaḥ paripākaḥ sākṣāt-kāro 'pavarga-sādhanaṁ tad-aṅgatayā pārivrājyaṁ vihitam, na tv anadhikṛtaṁ pratīty arthaḥ.*

[26] *Bhāmatī* ad BSŚBh 1.1.1: "*yadi vetarathā brahmacaryād eva pravrajed gṛhād vā vanād vā*" *ity etāvatā hi vairāgyam upalakṣayati. ata eva* "*yadahar eva virajet tadahar eva pravrajed*" *iti śrutiḥ.*

BSi	= Maṇḍanamiśra: *Brahma-siddhi.* (1) S. Kuppuswami Sastri (ed.): *Brahmasiddhi of Maṇḍana Miśra with Śaṅkhapāṇi's Commentary (vyākhyā).* Madras Government Oriental Series No. 4. Government Press, Madras 1937. [Photographic reprint" Sri Satguru, Delhi 1984]. (2) See: ACHARYA (2006).
KT	= Amalānanda: *Kalpa-taru.* See: BSŚBh.
NK	= Vācaspatimiśra: *Nyāya-kaṇikā.* See VV.
PP	= Padmapāda: *Pañca-pādikā.* S. Śrīrāma Śāstrī, S. R. Krishnamurthi Śāstrī (eds.): *Pañcapādikā of Padmapāda with Prabodha-pariśodhinī of Atmasvarūpa and Tātparyārthadyotinī of Vijñānātman and Pañcapādikāvivaraṇa of Prakāśātman with Tātparyadīpikā of Citsukha and Bhāvaprakāśikā of Nṛsiṁhāśrama.* Madras Government Oriental Series. Madras Government Oriental Manuscripts Library, Madras 1958.
TSam	= Vācaspatimiśra I: *Tattva-samīkṣā.* See: ACHARYA (2006).
VV	= Maṇḍanamiśra: *Vidhi-viveka.* Mahaprabhu Lal Gosvami (ed.): *The Vidhi-viveka of Maṇḍanamiśra with the Commentary Nyāya-kaṇikā of Vācaspatimiśra.* Tara Publications, Varanasi 1978.

From the *Tattva-cintā-maṇi* by Gaṅgeśa
The *Kevala-vyatireki-prakaraṇam*

NEGATIVE-ONLY INFERENCE

Annotated Translation and Commentary

STEPHEN H. PHILLIPS

Introduction

Much of the outstanding work in epistemology and logic of the Navya-nyāya school remains inaccessible except to traditional scholars in India. N.S. Ramanuja Tatacharya, a traditional scholar of great accomplishment, read with me this section of the masterwork of Gaṅgeśa (c. 1300) in February of 2000. This translation and commentary have benefited much from his guidance and an occasional correction of the text. Unlike with some of our previous work, however, we are not this time co-authors and mistakes of interpretation belong only to me. Before attempting to translate the section, which concerns a thorny area of logic, I did much work in Western sources (including a graduate course in philosophical logic) and my reading and comments are informed, hopefully, as much by contemporary understandings as by Gaṅgeśa's Nyāya inheritance. Gaṅgeśa is a first-rate philosopher and tools of contemporary logic help enormously in tracing his thought.

The text is taken from the Tirupati Vidyapeetha edition of the inference chapter of the *Tattva-cintā-maṇi*, part one (TCM_T).[1] In the present edition, compounds are indicated by hyphens and *sandhi* is broken but letters dropped or changed are not restored. A circumflex indicates a vowel *sandhi* at the word junction of a compound, overriding the usual hyphen. Beyond indicating *sandhi* breaks, no effort has been made to improve the representation of *sandhi*. The Tirupati edition is here practically mirrored and violations of *sandhi* are left as they appear. Some punctua-

---

[1] RAMANUJA TATACHARYA (1982: 441–487). The edition includes the *Prakāśa* commentary by Rucidatta Miśra and a subcommentary by Dharmarājādhvarin, both of which have proved helpful.

Logic and Belief in Indian Philosophy
Warsaw Indological Studies 3 (2010) 447–517.

tion has been simplified and there are no paragraph indentations or designations other than the big breaks for translation and comment. In this way my transliterated text is an edition distinct from the Tirupati edition, representing how I read Gaṅgeśa. All non-punctuation emendations are indicated in notes. References (e.g. TCM_T 442) are to pages of the editions.

For the convenience of Sanskritists who possess only the older Calcutta Asiatic Society edition (1991 reprint), page references to it too are given (TCM_C).[2] No attempt has been made to edit the text critically or systematically to compare the two published editions. But in a few places I have followed a clearly preferable phrase of the Calcutta edition, marking the emendation in a note. The commentary, moreover, by Mathurānātha, published there, sometimes proved helpful.

Let us review a minimal set of logical terms, ones that are standard across Nyāya and most of the other classical schools:

pakṣa	(*a*)	the inferential subject, e.g. 'the mountain' in the stock example;
sadhana	(H)	the prover (*hetu* is a synonym), e.g. 'smokiness';
sādhya	(S)	the probandum, the property to be proved, e.g. 'fieriness';
vyāpti	$(x)(Hx \rightarrow Sx)$	the inference-grounding pervasion, e.g. 'Wherever smoke, there fire'.

Inductive support is presumed, a basis for the proper formation of the inference-informing *saṁskāra* or 'mental disposition', which is called the 'example'.

dṛṣṭānta	a pervasion-supportive example, a locus known to exhibit both the prover and the probandum, e.g. 'a kitchen hearth'; and with respect to the negative method, e.g. 'a lake', known as a locus of both the absence of the probandum and absence of the prover.

A stock five-step proof formula runs as follows:

1. [The 'proposition' to be proved:] That mountain is fiery.
2. [The 'reason':] That mountain is smoky.
3. [The 'example' generating the general rule:] Like a kitchen hearth. [Or, in the case of the negative method:] Unlike a lake.

[2] TARKAVAGISH (1991: 582–625).

4. [The 'application':] And this is likewise.
5. [The 'conclusion':] Therefore, that mountain is fiery.

The five steps are to be construed as a single statement governed by grammatical and semantic rules, a formal presentation of an 'inference for others' (*parârthânumāna*).

'Inference for oneself' (*svârthânumāna*) may be represented:

$$(K)(^{Sp}Ha) \rightarrow (K)Sa$$

If a person comes to know that H-as-qualified-by-being-pervaded-by-S (*sādhya-vyāpaka-pakṣa-dharmatā-viśiṣṭa-hetu*) qualifies *a*, then that person comes to know that S*a*.

In wide overview, negative-only inference was highly controversial among the classical schools.[3] Two co-extensional terms (e.g. 'being earthen' and 'having smell') present an epistemological puzzle when the one is used to pick out the inferential subject (*pakṣa*) and the other the prover (*hetu*): inference as a knowledge source normally requires a positive inductive basis from which extrapolation proceeds to inference-warranting knowledge of pervasion. An objector will say as much in the very first passage of our text (see below, p. 452). And since the inferential subject cannot be used itself as such support—otherwise, inference would be pointless—a putative prover's extensional equivalence to the subject would mean that there could be no positive support, no correlations of a positive variety of the S and the H. Correlations of absences, the objector will suggest (in line with many of like philosophical prejudice), are problematic.

Clearly, the form seems invalid without restriction, since it would prove too much: given merely that '*a* is H', with no known H outside the *pakṣa* (*a*), it would appear from the correlation of ~S and ~H, then, that we could prove of *a* any S known not to reside outside the *pakṣa*. For example, 'Martian-made' (S) could be proved of every cow (*a*) by the prover cowhood (H). Everywhere we find something that is not a cow, there we find something that is not Martian-made, e.g. a rock. Thus, since every cow has cowhood, it is Martian-made. (See below p. 501, TCM_T 500, for a similar point concerning the name 'Ḍittha'.) It is true that Gaṅgeśa would rule this inference out as having an 'unfamiliar' probandum (*aprasiddha*). And other Nyāya logicians would reject it as falling to the counter-inference, *sat-pratipakṣa*, 'Every cow is non-Martian-made, *since* it is a cow, unlike a rock.' Nev-

[3] Excellent discussion of Dharmakīrti, the great Buddhist logician (c. 650), who dismisses the form, and Uddyotakara and company, who defend it, is: MATILAL (1998: 108–26). Another excellent introduction concentrating on Pracīna ('Old') Nyāya is: CHAKRABARTI (1999: 79–91).

ertheless, if the form is to have validity *prima facie*—an epistemological interpretation consonant with Gaṅgeśa's overall view[4]—it appears we'll have to be especially good at countering in this way pseudo-inferences. Better would appear to be the way of the Buddhists to reject the form entirely.

Furthermore, negative correlations would not seem strictly relevant, as is brought out by the 'ravens paradox' well-known to students of inductive logic.[5] An evidence basis supporting the generalisation, 'All ravens are black', benefits from the sight of an additional black raven. But to flip the pages of a book, noting that one after another is neither a raven nor black, seems irrelevant. In Nyāya terms, a pervasion of being-black (H) by being-a-raven (S) would seem to require positive evidence. Negative correlations, being practically everywhere, shouldn't count. Of course, Gaṅgeśa would view the pervasion of being-a-raven by being-black as known by both the positive and negative methods. The problem is nevertheless plain.

On the other hand, if the absence of the probandum (~S) is grasped as having the same or an inclusive extension with the absence of the prover (~H), the presence of the prover (H), which is an absence of the absence of itself (~~H), proves the absence of the absence of the probandum (~~S), which is the probandum itself (S). This seems to be how Gaṅgeśa understands the logic of the 'negative-only' inference, (*kevala-*)*vyatirekin*. He will point to the logical rule of transposition as underpinning his position on the negative-only (below, TCM_T 442). A pervasion expressed negatively is equivalent to one expressed positively.

Furthermore, all things H being things S may be evident only from the ramification that everything that is not an S is not an H. Positive correlations may be hidden. A double absence is equivalent to a positive presence, that is, with respect to two 'mutual absences' or 'distinctnesses' (*a*'s distinctness from being-distinct-from-*a* is equivalent to *a*'s identity), as opposed to 'relational absences'. All these points surface in the section.

Finally concerning the content of the knowledge generated. In consideration of the knowledge that would be the result of negative-only inferences, the deepest worry concerns definitions of fundamental categories. The fundamental truths of things (*tattva*), which are captured by philosophical definitions, seem accessible only through knowledge of fundamental distinctions. For example, a standard inference to self (*ātman*) as a fundamental category of substance is negative-only:

a (*pakṣa*)	=	every-living-body
S (*sādhya*)	=	has-a-self
H (*sādhana*)	=	has-breath

[4] Phillips–Ramanuja Tatacharya (2004: 7–12 and 20).

[5] Cf. Hempel (1965: 12–25).

Thus, 'Every living body has a self, *since* every living body has breath, unlike a pot (a pot being qualified by both absence-of-self and absence-of-breath).' The inferential subject includes all living bodies and so there is no *sapakṣa*, no examples of the probandum known outside the set of things that are living bodies. Thus, the inference has to be *kevala-vyatirekin*, based solely on correlations of absences, 'unlike a pot', a pot having neither breath nor a self.

This inference, analysis of which is probably the most interesting portion of the section (beginning below, TCM_T 488), was in part presented by me at the International Seminar, 'Logic and Belief in Indian Philosophy', May 2006, organised by the Institute of Oriental Studies, Warsaw University. I wish to thank all the participants for helpful feedback and in particular the conference organisers, Piotr Balcerowicz, Marek Mejor and Monika Nowakowska.

* * *

kevala-vyatireky-anumāna
atha kevala-vyatireki-prakaraṇam

Now examination of the exclusively negative inference.

Text (TCM_T 441 and TCM_C 582) and Translation

> *kevala-vyatirekī tv asat sapakṣaḥ. yatra vyatireka-sahacāreṇa vyāpti-grahaḥ. nanu vyatirekī na anumānam, vyāpti-pakṣa-dharmatā-jñānasya tad-dhetutvāt. atra vyatireka-sahacārāt tatra vyāptir anvayasya pakṣa-dharmatā*[6].

Gaṅgeśa: [Of the three types of inference, (a) that having a prover whose pervasion by the probandum is known by both positive and negative correlations, (b) that where the prover's being pervaded is known only by positive correlations and (c) that where the pervasion is known only by negative correlations, this last], the prover's being known as pervaded [by the probandum] only through negative correlations works without a *sapakṣa* [known instances of the probandum property other than the inferential subject]. The pervasion is grasped by the method of negative correlation [where the probandum S is not, there the prover H is not, too].

[6] Deleting the *na* in line with the correct reading of TCM_C.

Objection: The 'exclusively negative' pattern [as you have it] is not inference, (i.e. the 'prover' whose relation to a probandum is grasped in such a manner of negative correlation is not a *pramāṇa*). For, inferential awareness is caused by cognition (*parāmarśa*) of a prover's being a property of an inferential subject as qualified by an awareness of pervasion [by a probandum]. Here [in your pseudo-inferential pattern] where the correlation is with an absence [absence of the prover], the pervasion is also so (i.e. a correlation with an absence). But the inferential subject's exhibiting a [genuine] prover is an exhibiting [not of absence but] of a positive presence.

Comments

Gaṅgeśa's division of inferences into three types—according to the inference-warranting pervasion being known (a) by both positive and negative correlations, (b) only by positive correlations and (c) only by negative correlations—is not found in the *Nyāya-sūtra* (NS, c. 150) or Vātsyāyana's commentary, the NBh (c. 400). Uddyotakara (c. 600) introduces it in his 'elaboration' (*vārttika*) of Vātsyāyana's *bhāṣya*. However, near the end of Vātsyāyana's comments on the so-called inference *sūtra* (NS 1.1.5), there occurs the 'negative-only' inference—to the existence of self, *ātman*—that will become the centre of discussion in the second half of our text (TCM_T 488 ff.). There Vātsyāyana also disparages any final or natural system of inference types. Nevertheless, in Uddyotakara's subcommentary, Gaṅgeśa's issues are raised in connection with the *sāmānyato-dṛṣṭa* type of inference mentioned in NS 1.1.5 and illustrated by Vātsyāyana's proof of a self, including the objection here.[7]

This objection, which is not definitively answered until several other arguments are out on the table, targets the negative form of the inference rule, absences of the probandum correlating with absences of the prover. A good inference not only requires knowledge of pervasion (*vyāpti*) along with knowledge of the prover as qualifying the inferential subject (*pakṣa-dharmatā*). A good inference also requires, the objector alleges, a match between, so to say, the quality of the variables in the general and singular requirements (where H, there S; *a* is H). Such a singular qualifying (H*a*) is always positive, the objector claims, and thus could not match the negative variable (~H) of the 'negative-only'. Furthermore, the conclusion is positive (S*a*).

Text (TCM_T 441 and TCM_C 585) and Translation

> *na ca vyāpta-pakṣa-dharmatvaṁ sādhyâbhāva-vyāpakâbhāva-pratiyogi-sattvam ubhayam apy anumiti-prayojakam iti vācyam. ananugamāt. na*

[7] NYAYA-TARKATIRTHA–TARKATIRTHA–TARKATIRTHA (1985: 156–57).

> *ca anyataratvaṁ tathā, eka-pramāṇa-pariśeṣâpatteḥ. na ca tṛṇâraṇi-maṇi-nyāyena anumiti-viśeṣe tad-kāraṇatvam iti vācyam. vyatireki-sādhye 'numititvâsiddheḥ, ubhaya-siddha-kḷpta-tat-kāraṇasya abhāvāt. na ca sādhyâbhāva-vyāpakâbhāva-pratiyogitvam eva anumiti-prayojakam iti vācyam. gauravāt. kevalânvayiny abhāvāc ca.*

Objection 2 (to the original objector 1): Both the two initiate the process resulting in inferential awareness, both, that is, the prover's being a property of the inferential subject that is pervaded (by the probandum) and the prover's being the counter-correlate (or absentee) of the absence that pervades the probandum's absence.

Answer (by objector 1): That should not be said. For in that case inference would not be uniform (i.e. would divide into two distinct *pramāṇa*). And being-the-one-or-the-other [as you describe the dual or alternative types of prover] is not the uniformity required, since if it were only one type of *pramāṇa* would remain.

Objector 2: [But the sort of uniformity required is not what you presume.] By the maxim of '[Fire can be produced] from straw, tinder sticks, or a jewel', we should think of the causes of an inferential awareness as varying with the instance.

Objector 1: That also should not be said. It is not accepted [by us] that any inferential awareness is the result of such a prover establishing its probandum negatively, since there is no agreement between our two sides that there is such a negative cause of inference beyond the factors that we both do accept and work with [namely, the prover's qualifying the inferential subject and its being pervaded by the probandum].

Objector 2: [Then] 'the prover's being the counter-correlate [or absentee] of the absence that pervades the probandum's absence [indirectly]' alone initiates the process resulting in inferential awareness (i.e. the alternative characterisation is not necessary).

Objector 1: You can't say that. For, it is a cumbersome conception [in its trying to turn a relation between positive presences into a relation between absences] and it leaves out inferences based exclusively on positive correlations [such as, 'This is nameable, *since* it is knowable'].

Comments

Inference is a process with more unity than the proposal by Objector 2 would entail. By the quirky logic of alternation we could reduce all *pramāṇa* to one. Given that we are concerned with pertinent factors in the generation of veridical awareness, if a veridical inferential awareness is said to result from inference specified as such-and-such *or* whatever (generator of veridical awareness), then perception, analogy and testimony will all be the same as inference.

The cumbersomeness of the final proposal is shown simply by its being a few words that are used in the standard expression, '[cognition of] the prover on the inferential subject etc.', *vyāpti-pakṣa-dharmatā*, compared to the long expression, '[cognition of] the prover's being the counter-correlate of the absence that pervades the probandum's absence'. But the latter expression is of course awkward as well, with its mention of the word 'absence' (*abhāva*) twice.

A second fault of the proposal is that some of its terms would fail to refer when the type of inference is plugged in that is 'based exclusively on positive correlations', *kevalânvayin*. This is the fault that eliminates, Gaṅgeśa has shown in the first section of his *anumāna* chapter, several well-known contenders for a definition of pervasion itself, *vyāpti*.

Text (TCM_T 442 and TCM_C 588) and Translation

> *atha sādhyâbhāva-vyāpakâbhāva-pratiyogitvena sādhya-vyāpyatvam anumīyate. evaṁ vyatireka-vyāptyânvaya-vyāptim anumāya yatra anumitiḥ sa eva vyatirekī ity ucyata iti. tan na. anvaya-vyāpter gamakatve vyatireka-vyāpty-upanyāsasya arthântaratâpatteḥ. anvaya-vyāpty-anukūlatayā ca tad-upanyāse 'nvaya-vyāptim anupanyasya tad-upanyāsasya aprāpta-kālatvād iti.*

Objection (by Objector 2): By means of a prover that is the counter-correlate of an absence that pervades an absence of the probandum ($\sim S \rightarrow \sim H$), it is inferred that it is pervaded by the probandum ($H \rightarrow S$). In this way, having inferred by means of a pervasion between absences (*vyatireka-vyāpti*) that there is a pervasion between presences, one goes on to arrive at the [standard] inferential awareness [of the inferential subject as possessing the probandum]—where this occurs there alone is there a case of '[exclusively] negative inference' (not where there is no prior step involving the relation of absences, though all inferences involve a relation of presences).

Answer (by Objector 1): That's wrong. For, this faces the objection that the mention of the negative pervasion becomes pointless (a kind of 'switching meaning', *arthântara*) since a positive pervasion is what makes an inference.

Furthermore, if the mention of the negative pervasion is because it conforms to the positive pervasion, then one not mentioning the positive pervasion commits the 'mistimed' fallacy in mentioning the negative pervasion.

Comments

Objector 2 now points out that the 'negative-only' inference (*vyatirekin*) is really two inferences: it is concluded, first, from the relation between the absences that the probandum pervades the prover (which qualifies the inferential subject); from this it is concluded, second, that the inferential subject possesses the probandum. In response, Gaṅgeśa's original objector claims that this view has two faults against it, both of which amount to equivocation. Only the positive form is meant.

Text (TCM_T 442 and TCM_C 591) and Translation

> *ucyate. nirupādhi-vyatireka-sahacāreṇa anvaya-vyāptir eva gṛhyate pratiyogy-anuyogi-bhāvasya niyāmakatvāt anvaya-vyatireka-vat.*

Gaṅgeśa: We answer. By means of the method of negative correlation (no S and no H) insofar as there is no inferential undercutting condition, a pervasion between positives [H and S] is grasped. For, there is an invariable rule regulating the relation between the two terms, as in the case of an inference based on both positive and negative correlations.

Comments

Let us put in mind again, here at the beginning of a *siddhānta* statement, the standard inference to self (*ātman*). As mentioned, this comes to be centre stage only much later, after a long discussion of an inference to earth as a fundamental substance. But we can appreciate Gaṅgeśa's present points in its terms.

a	(*pakṣa*)	every-living-body
S	(*sādhya*)	has-a-self
H	(*sādhana*)	has-breath
b	(*dṛṣṭānta*)	a pot (~S*b* and ~H*b*)

Thus,

> Every living body has a self (S*a*), *since* a living body has breath (H*a*), unlike a pot ((x)(~Sx → ~Hx)).

Gaṅgeśa endorses a version of the law of contraposition (or transposition):

$$(x)(\sim Sx \rightarrow \sim Hx) \equiv (x)(Hx \rightarrow Sx)$$

Therefore, S*a*, since H*a* and (x)(Hx → Sx).

The inferential subject includes all living bodies, and so there is no *sapakṣa*, no examples of the probandum known outside the set of things that are living bodies. It is based solely on negative correlations, 'unlike a pot', a pot having neither breath nor a self. Of course, it is also true that a pot is not clever. Does this mean that every living body is? To repeat some of our opening remarks, the inference form seems by itself too powerful, generating false inferential awarenesses.

Thus one is tempted to interpret the qualification included here, 'so long as there is no inferential undercutting condition' (*nirupādhi*), as terrifically significant, in restricting appropriately (it might be hoped) the negative-only method. An *upādhi* is an 'inferential undercutter' because it entails a counter-example, to wit, that there is something or other that is both an H and a ~S.

An *upādhi* is (according to a standard definition which although refined by Gaṅgeśa suits our purposes here) a property U such that

(1) U pervades the probandum S (*sādhya*, i.e. anything that is an S is a U, *sādhya-vyāpaka*): 'Everything clever is human', and

(2) U does not pervade the prover H (*sādhana* or *hetu*, i.e. there is something that is an H but not a U, *sādhanâvyāpaka*): 'e.g. my cat'.

(1) $(x)\,(Sx \rightarrow Ux)$

(2) $(\exists x)\,(Hx \cdot {\sim}Ux)$

It follows then that

(3) $(\exists x)\,(Hx \cdot {\sim}Sx)$.

(There is something that exhibits the prover without exhibiting the probandum: 'e.g. my cat'.)

Thus, there is 'deviation' and no relation of pervasion:

(4) ${\sim}(x)\,(Hx \rightarrow Sx)$

Thus in the present passage, Gaṅgeśa would seem to state a relevance condition, a requirement that we consider the possibility of a counter-example in extrapolating from correlations of absences in particular, that we be duly diligent in checking for an undercutter—the ramifications of something's being an S—to make sure that any such thing would also pervade the H, the prover. If we would prove that 'every living body is clever' from the prover, 'having-breath', the undercutter (*upādhi*), 'being-human', would show the error of our ways. Being-human pervades cleverness, but some things that have breath are not clever.

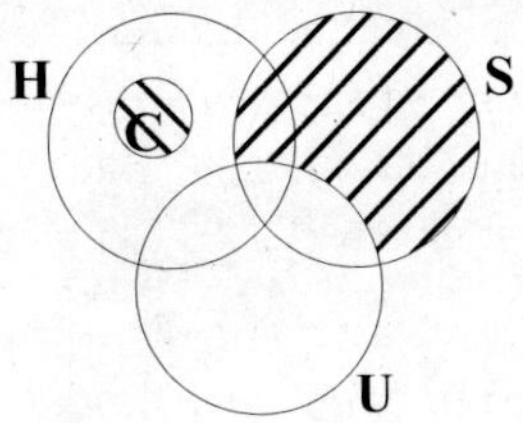

H = having breath
S = being clever
U = being human
C = my cat

(1) (x) (Sx → Ux)
Everything clever is human

(2) (∃x) (Hx · ~Ux)
e.g. my cat, which has breath but is not human

However, undercutting is not Gaṅgeśa's focus in this section, which is, rather, the epistemic requirement that the probandum property be understood or 'familiar' (*prasiddha*) in some way. There may seem, then, to be an interpretative issue in the question of how much work is supposed to be done by the *nirupādhi* requirement over and above the requirement of familiarity, but my view is that it does none in particular. One may ask whether Gaṅgeśa needs the *nirupādhi* requirement given his restrictions on term introduction that he will emphasise until the very end. Note that this is the only place where he mentions *upādhi*s in the entire section. How diligently would we have to search to make sure that an inference is *upādhi*-frei?

The *upādhi* makes a distinction, showing that while there may be some Hs that are Ss not all of them are. Unfortunately, there is no prophylactic to protect us from actual *upādhi*-infection of what we quite rightly take to be good inferences. But though imitated by cognitive patterns that turn out to be wrong, some negative-only inferences remain *bona fide*. Indeed, we have every right to assert the conclusion of such an inference so long as we are unaware of *upādhi*s. In other words, I take sensitivity to *upādhi*s to be a general epistemic requirement. I may well infer the cleverness of living beings from their having-breath—until you remind me that non-human animals have breath but are not commonly clever. To think of living beings as clever may be absent-minded but nevertheless not simply wrong. Inference is prolific and looking for *upādhi*s is a general epistemic duty that is more or less pressing depending on circumstances.[8]

Note finally that the special domains of philosophy, the general topics of metaphysics and epistemology, all involve controversy and thus call for argument and due consideration of opposing views. Thus the epistemological requirements are much higher than those of everyday life, *laukika* knowledge being automatically acquired without special preparations. With philosophy, in contrast, we bring to the table mastery of fallacies and other common flaws of reasoning and would have the

[8] This epistemological incorporation is argued in PHILLIPS–RAMANUJA TATACHARYA (2002). Helping us to appreciate the epistemic nature of *upādhi* consideration by way of arguing that the concluding of S*a* is monotonic is: SIDERITS (2004: 302–21). An excellent paper showing that the issue of the nature of the logic (as opposed to the epistemology) is not clear-cut, however, is: OETKE (2004: 23–38).

responsibility to prove, for instance, that an alleged undercutter (*upādhi*) is only pseudo (*ābhāsa*). This is the reason that we study, Gaṅgeśa says, *upādhy-ābhāsa* and *hetv-ābhāsa*, in advance of philosophical engagement *(kathā)*.[9]

Text (TCM_T 447 and TCM_C 592) and Translation

> *nanv*[10] *evaṁ vyāpti-graha eva pr̥thivī itara-bhinnā iti bhāsitaṁ niyata-sāmānâdhikaraṇya-rūpatvāt vyāpter iti cet, satyam. gandha-vattvâvacchedena itara-bhedasya sādhyatvāt. ata eva ācāryaḥ pakṣatâvacchedake na hetutvam anumene. pr̥thivītvam itara-bheda-vyāpyam iti pratītāv api sarvā pr̥thivī itara-bhinnā iti pr̥thivī-viśeṣyaka-buddher vyatireki-sādhyatvāc ca.*

Objection: Only if the pervasion has already been grasped will there appear to cognition [the conclusion of your standard 'negative-only inference', namely] that earth is distinct from the other things (i.e. the other substances, water and the rest, along with things belonging to non-substance categories, according to Nyāya-Vaiśeṣika ontology and so you would commit the fallacy of trying to prove what is already established, *siddha-sādhana*). For, a pervasion takes the form of a rule-bound presence [of the prover and probandum] in the same loci.

Gaṅgeśa: That's true [to an extent, but there is no fallacy of *siddha-sādhana* for two reasons]. (1) The probandum is 'distinctness from the other things' as specified by the having of smell. This is why our teacher [Udayana] has not accepted inferences whose provers are the specifiers of the subjecthood. And (2) although a person already has the notion that being-earth (earthhood, the universal resting in all earthen things) is pervaded by distinctness-from-the-other-things, [to make the inference is nevertheless useful in that] the cognition that *everything* earthen is distinct from the other things [in our ontology], which is a cognition that has as its qualificandum [not earthhood or earth in general but] earth [in particular], is proved [only] by a inference based on negative correlations.

---

[9] RAMANUJA TATACHARYA (1999: 1). This is not a new position. Vātsyāyana, in explaining why the word *saṁśaya* ('doubt') appears in *Nyāya-sūtra* 1.1.1, reminds us that it is neither certainty nor ignorance but rather doubt that provokes the employment of *nyāya* ('philosophical method'). This latter, *nyāya*, amounts to inferential demonstration of a thesis and refutation of a counter-thesis: *pakṣa-pratipakṣau nyāya-pravr̥tti*; *arthâvadhāraṇaṁ nirṇayas tattva-jñānam iti*. In the translation by JHA (1984: 44): '..."considering of the two sides" constitutes the process of reasoning [*nyāya*]; and "ascertainment of the reality of things", which is "Demonstrated Truth" [*nirṇaya*, a word that also appears in *Nyāya-sūtra* 1.1.1]; forms the knowledge of the real nature of things.'

[10] Reading *nanv* instead of *na ca*, with TCM_C.

Comments

The fault of *siddha-sādhana* hovers above all the discussion of the inference based on negative correlations, the *vyatirekin*. If the inferential subject is known as qualified by the probandum, there would be no point in inferring that proposition from a sign, a prover property. One would not take the trouble for oneself. But if the predicate to be proved, i.e. the probandum property, is not familiar, then there can be no inferring that the subject has the property. Proper 'consideration', *parāmarśa*, requires that the probandum be available.

Here is the first mention of the inference about earth as category:

S	(*sādhya*)	has-distinctness-as-a-substance
H	(*sādhana*)	has-smell
a	(*pakṣa*)	earth

Thus,

Earth is a distinct substance, *since* it has smell, unlike water.

If the specifier of the inferential subject—the property or concept through which the inferential subject is nailed down, in Sanskrit, the *pakṣatâvacchedaka*—is the same as the prover property, then the fault of *siddha-sādhana* would occur, according to Udayana as reported by Gaṅgeśa here. Inference would be pointless, as with 'Earth is distinct etc., *since* it has *earthhood*.' But if the 'specifier of subjecthood' is distinct from the prover—as it is with earth's being distinct etc. where the prover is *having-smell*—then this fault is not committed and the inference proceeds 'based on negative correlations'. Similarly for the inference, 'Things having smell are distinct from the things that are substances other than earth along with everything in the non-substance categories, *since* they have earthhood.'

Gaṅgeśa implicitly disagrees with Udayana, however, in pointing out the difference between a predicate being known in general and being known, so to say, distributively. Thus, the inference, 'Earth is distinct from the other things [etc.], *since* it has earthhood', is not, according to Gaṅgeśa, a faulty inference, although it commits the *siddha-sādhana* fallacy in the view of his 'teacher'.

Text (TCM_T 448 and TCM_C 593) and Translation

yad vā vyatireka-vyāpter eva anvayena gamya-gamaka-bhāvaḥ. sādhyâbhāva-vyāpaka-sādhanâbhāvâbhāvena sādhanena pakṣe sādhyâbhāvâbhāvasya sādhyasya sādhanāt. vyāpakâbhāvena vyāpyâbhāvâvaśyam-bhāvāt.

(**Gaṅgeśa** continues:) Alternatively, a pervasion between absences is itself inferential by reason of a pervasion between presences. For, an absence (A) of a prover that is the pervader of an absence of a probandum, well, by its absence (i.e. by A's absence, e.g. the absence of the absence of smoke), which absence is the prover, there is proved the probandum (fire) as an absence of an absence of itself. By reason of an absence which is a pervader, there has to be an absence of that which it pervades.

Comments

For example, as fieriness pervades smokiness ('wherever smoke, there fire'), so an absence of smokiness pervades an absence of fieriness ('wherever no fire, there no smoke'). Here the logic of the absences is that of double negation, which holds of absences of the 'mutual' (*anyonya*) variety, not necessarily of relational absences.

Problems about absences occupied a large place in the earlier section on the nature of inference grounding pervasion (*vyāpti*) and further discussion follows a bit below (p. 461). Note that mutual absences and the other types—absolute absence, prior absence and posterior absence, which are called 'relational absences' (*saṁsargâbhāva*)—are differentiated according to knowability conditions by later Navya-Naiyāyika philosophers, for example, by Viśvanātha in his *Muktâvalī*. The mainstream position is that with the relational absences the perceptibility of the countercorrelate is a causal factor. The perceptibility of the substratum is a cause, a necessary condition, only with mutual absences. Gaṅgeśa will endorse the point about mutual absence a bit below.

Text (TCM_T 453 and TCM_C 594) and Translation

atha evaṁ sânumitiḥ kḷpta-tad-dhetu-liṅga-parāmarśâbhāvāt, anyathânanugama iti cen, na. anumiti-mātre vyāpti-jñānasya prayojakatvāt. na ca evam atiprasaṅgaḥ, anumiti-sāmānya-sāmagryāṁ satyām apy anumiti-viśeṣa-sāmagrī-virahād[11] *anumiti-anutpatteḥ, viśeṣa-sāmagrī-sāpekṣāyā eva sāmānya-sāmagryā janakatvāt. anvayi-vyatireki-viśeṣa-dvaya-sāmagrī ca na asty eva.*

Objection: If your view were correct, the 'negative-only' inference would not result in inferential awareness, since there would be no correct appreciation of the inferential mark (i.e. no 'correct reflection', *parāmarśa*) which as an established

[11] Adding *viśeṣa-sāmagrī-°*, with TCM_C.

explanatory category [in the form of a positive prover or mark, not as an absence] is a cause of any inferential awareness. Or, if there were that result, then there would be no unitary conception of 'inferential awareness'.

Gaṅgeśa: Wrong. With respect to inferential awareness in general, [simply] awareness of a pervasion is the instigator. And this view does not have too wide an application. For, although all the general factors necessary for an inferential awareness to arise are in place, there would be no inferential awareness if the collection of particular causal factors is missing anything. General factors (e.g. time, space, God, *karman*) are causal only as members of a collection of causal factors including some that are unique. And there simply is no collection of causal factors that includes the particular factors necessary for both the 'positive-only' and 'negative-only' inferences.

Comments

To produce a pot, time, space and a few other, quite universal conditions stand as necessary factors. If they did not hold, the pot would not be produced. But they are not causal factors independently of other factors that are not so general but particular to the production of the pot, to wit, the potter, the clay and so forth.

Similarly, cognition of an inferential subject as possessing a prover that one is also aware of as pervaded by a probandum *produces* an inferential awareness—so long as one is speaking in general terms. More specifically, the awareness of a pervasion takes one of three specific forms, 'positive-only', 'negative-only', and 'based on both positive and negative correlations'. And no inferential awareness would be produced if there were not one of these three types of particular awareness of pervasion.

Gaṅgeśa's last statement is not be taken as denying that there can be awareness of a pervasion based on both positive and negative correlations, but as denying that the conditions sparking the positive-only variety of inference are anything but mutually exclusive of those that spark the negative-only variety.

Text (TCM_T 455 and TCM_C 596) and Translation

> *nanu pr̥thivī itarebhyo bhidyate pr̥thivītvād iti vyatirekiṇi sādhyâsiddham, tathā ca na vyatireki-nirūpaṇaṁ na vā pakṣatvaṁ na vā liṅga-janya-sādhya-viśiṣṭa-taj-jñānaṁ teṣāṁ sādhya-jñāna-janyatvāt. atha sādhyaṁ prasiddhaṁ tadā yatra prasiddhaṁ tatra hetor avagame 'nvayitvam anavagame asādhāraṇyam.*

Pūrva-pakṣin (objecting to Gaṅgeśa's position): The probandum in the 'negative-only' inference (*vyatirekin*), 'Earth is distinct from the other things [accepted in the ontology], *since* it has earthhood', is not known [outside the inferential context]. And so (1) it cannot be determined [to belong to the inferential subject] by a negative inference. Nor (2) would there be a proper inferential subject (*pakṣatva*, which requires doubt whether the probandum is its qualifier, whereas here that is already known). Nor (3) would there be generated by means of the prover a cognition of the inferential subject as qualified by the probandum. For, these three are generated by (i.e. require) cognition of the probandum [prior to and outside the inferential context].

Alternatively, let us say the probandum is so known. This being the case, we would have a positive inference [based on positive correlations] if the prover is known to occur there where the probandum is known to occur. If the prover is not known to occur there, we would have the 'no similar instance' fallacy (i.e. 'no prover in the *sapakṣa*', *asādhāranya*).

Comments

The *Pūrva-pakṣin* adversary challenges the form's validity by claiming that its advocate faces a trilemma, three bad options, three apparently exhaustive alternatives, none of which appears unobjectionable. (1) If there are other known instances of the probandum, the inference would be (a) based on positive correlations (and not be 'negative-only'), (b) fallacious if a counter-example were known, or (c) fallacious as based on knowledge of the *sapakṣa* without an example of the prover (*asādhāraṇya*). This fallacy (the 'not common to the *sapakṣa*') is committed when there is no known example of the prover in the *sapakṣa*, i.e. the set of things where the probandum is known to occur. Given a *sapakṣa*, we expect to find at least a single instance of positive correlation. 'Sound is eternal, since it has soundhood' commits the fallacy since the prover, soundhood, is not found in the *sapakṣa*, ether, atoms and other things known to be eternal. (2) If there are no known instances of the probandum at all, the probandum term cannot be available for inference, period. One cannot make an inference where one does not understand the terms it trades on. (3) If the probandum is known to occur on the subject or *pakṣa* itself, there would be no point to the inference (*siddha-sādhana*).

Concerning good inferences that seem to be 'negative-only', the best option, the *Pūrva-pakṣin* insinuates, is (1a): these genuine inferences that seem to be based only on negative correlations are really informed by positive knowledge. There is no 'negative-only' type of inference.

To avoid the unwanted options, Gaṅgeśa will concentrate on (2), the familiarity requirement. He accepts (3) and appears to accept (1) as well. He will concede with respect to (1) that in some cases a negative-only inference need not have been *only* negative, there being available positive correlations that were, for some reason or other, not relied on, while the negative inference remains correct. In other circumstances, one might have made an inference based on both types of evidence. Nevertheless, it is Gaṅgeśa's qualifying of (2)—the requirement that the probandum be exampled—that is his core response.

To consider the earth inference with respect to the trilemma: (1) there is no example of *is-distinct-from-the-other-things* outside of earth, the inferential subject and so the inference is 'negative only'. (2) This probandum *is* known prior to the inference *in particular*—for instance, a pot, something earthen, is so known—and so the term is available. (3) The probandum is not known *in general* to apply to all earth prior to the negative-only inference and so the *siddha-sādhana* fallacy is not committed. The inference makes something new known through a generalisation that proceeds on the basis of negative evidence ('This pond is both not-distinct-etc. and not smelly').

Gaṅgeśa holds, as we shall see, that prior to inference the probandum ('Earth is distinct from the other things') is known only distributively, only with respect to particular instances. Post inference, it is known also in general; that is to say, one knows that *everything* earthen is distinct from the other substances and non-substance entities. Perception introduces the term. By negative-only inference, we can learn about very general truths and the deep categorial joints of the universe.

Text (TCM_T 455 and TCM_C 597) and Translation

> *kiṁ ca itara-bhedo na sva-rūpam adhikaraṇa-pratiyoginoḥ pṛthivī-jalâdyor anumānāt prāg eva siddheḥ. na api vaidharmyaṁ jalâdi-niṣṭâtyantâ bhāva-pratiyogimattvam, tad dhi pṛthivītvâdikaṁ tac ca siddham eva. na ca jalâdi-niṣṭhâtyantâbhāva-pratiyogitvena pṛthivîtvam na siddham iti vācyam. jalâdau pṛthivītvâtyantâbhāva-graha-daśāyāṁ pṛthivîtve 'pi tat-pratiyogitva-grahāt.*

(The ***Pūrva-pakṣin*** continues:) Furthermore, the probandum 'distinct from the other things' [which is a kind of absence, a mutual absence or distinctness], is not by its very nature [as some hold] the locus—earth—or [as others say] the loci where it is absent—water and the rest. For, in that case it would be known even before any inference [and inference would be pointless].

Nor is it 'difference of property' *(vaidharmya)* understood as the having of a property that is absolutely absent in water and so on, (i.e. exhibiting the counter-correlate of an absolute absence that rests in water and so on, as, say, earthhood is the counter-correlate of the absolute absence of earthhood that rests in water and so on). For, in that case the things that have earthhood and so on and this (i.e. difference of property) would be indeed known [and again there would be no prompting of inference].

Objection: Earthhood, [although known with respect to earthen things,] is not known *as* the counter-correlate of an absolute absence resting in water and so on, [and so there is a point to the inference that would establish that it is distinct from the other things, with 'other' being understood as 'difference in property'].

Pūrva-pakṣin: That move should not be tried. For [earthhood would be known in that way, in that with the inference, 'Earth is distinct from the other things, *since* it has earthhood', there would be required—by the lights of those who advocate the 'negative-only' as a type of inference—cognition of the places where both the distinctness and earthhood do not occur, in water and so on, namely], concerning water and so on, at the time any absolute absence of earthhood were grasped (an absence that would be grasped as in water and so on which have no earthhood), earthhood would also be grasped as being the counter-correlate of the absence.

Comments

The commentators (Rucidatta, TCM_T 456 in particular) along with my teacher N.S. Ramanuja Tatacharya are responsible for restoring the elided ideas. The point is that one has to be familiar with the predicate, being-earth.

We may add that being-odorous *(gandhavattva)* is commonly identified within Nyāya-Vaiśeṣika as a distinctive property of earth, in that all earthen things have odour but nothing else does. Thus having-earthhood can be established for anything that smells, by inference of the usual sort, based on both positive and negative correlations. Of course, that does not mean that the negative-only is useless, as will be further explained.

Text (TCM_T 456 and TCM_C 598) and Translation

> *anyonyâbhāvas tu bhedo yady api sādhyaṁ sambhavati vaidharma-jñāna-sādhyatvād anyonyâbhāva-grahasya, tathā api jalâdi-pratiyogikânyonyâbhāvasya aprasiddhiḥ. na ca jalâdi-pratyekânyo-nyâbhāvaḥ sādhyaḥ, asādhāraṇya-prasaṅgāt.*

(The ***Pūrva-pakṣin*** continues:) But even if the distinctness understood as 'mutual distinctness' (or, 'mutual absence', *anyonyâbhāva*) is the probandum of the inference ['is *distinct* from the others'], inasmuch as a mutual absence is grasped as the probandum in the [required] cognition of a difference of property [such that the probandum would be known in general as such an absence], still [it would not be known in particular, i.e.] the mutual absence whose counter-correlate is water and so on would be unknown [and so for this reason inference could not proceed].

And it is not the case that the probandum is the mutual absence of each of the set of water and so on. For, if so, the unfortunate consequence would be that we would have a case of the fallacy of 'no similar instance', [since there would be a *sapakṣa*].

Comments

Why would the probandum be unknown? The knowledge is not precluded by the inferential context, since such an absence exists only in earth which is the inferential subject (though this seems a problem as well). Rather, the difficulty is that the probandum is so all-inclusive, 'distinctness from all those other things'. Thus the objector to the *Pūrva-pakṣin* tries to understand the probandum distributively. But in that case the inference would not be 'negative-only' in that there would be a *sapakṣa*: to wit, all the instances of the 'being-other' except the one in focus, e.g. the fiery element and the rest, given that water is mentioned in the statement of the probandum.

Text (TCM_T 456 and TCM_C 599) and Translation

atha pṛthivī tejo-bhinnā na vā iti saṁśayena tejo-bhinnatve 'vagame pṛthivī tejo-bhinnā satī jalâdi-dvā-daśa-bhinnā na vā iti saṁśaye tejo-bhinnatve sati jalâdi-dvā-daśa-bhinnatvaṁ prasiddhaṁ tad eva sādhyaṁ, eka-viśeṣaṇa-viśiṣṭe viśeṣaṇântara-buddher eva viśiṣṭya-jñānatvāt, evaṁ ca saṁśaya-prasiddhaṁ sādhyam ādāya vyatirekâdi-nirūpaṇam. yad vā pṛthivī jalâdi-bhinnā na vā iti pratyekaṁ trayo-daśa-saṁśaya-viṣayāṇāṁ trayo-daśânyonyâbhāvānāṁ samudāyaḥ pṛthivyām avagato vyatirekâdi-nirūpakaḥ. na ca evaṁ pṛthivyām eva sādhya-prasiddher vyatireki-vaiyarthyam, sādhya-niścayârthaṁ vyatireki-pravṛtteḥ. na ca asādhāraṇyam, samuditânyonyâbhāvānāṁ sādhyatve sapakṣâbhāvād iti cen. na.

Objection: By means of a *question* [or doubt whose object or content is the probandum as known well enough to be proved to belong to the *pakṣa* by means of inference, e.g.], 'Is earth distinct from the fiery or not?', a distinctness from the fiery is understood; [and then] in [other] questions, 'Given that earth is distinct from the fiery, is it distinct or not from water and the rest, the twelve other things (i.e. the other substances and things belonging to non-substance categories)?' a distinctness from the twelve other things is known well [enough for inference to proceed (*prasiddha*)]. That alone (i.e. the collective object of the questioning) is the probandum [in the inference at issue]. For, a cognition of a qualified entity as [again] qualified (e.g. 'The staff-bearing person', where a qualificandum qualified by personhood is also qualified by staff-bearingness) is generated just from a cognition of another qualifier with respect to something qualified by a single qualifier. And in this way, taking the probandum to be that which is well-known from the questioning, one proceeds with negative-only correlation and the rest of the inference.

Alternatively, 'Is earth distinct from water or not' and a series of like questions each contribute to a collection of thirteen mutual absences that are the objects of thirteen questions. The collection is understood just with respect to earth and determines the negative-only correlation and the rest of the inference.

And it is not the case that the probandum being known in this way just with respect to earth makes the negative-only inference pointless. For, one proceeds with it in order to be certain about the probandum [as belonging to the subject, whereas prior to the inference the probandum was known only through being the object of a doubt or question].

Nor [on this analysis] would the inference commit the 'no similar instance' fallacy, since there would be no *sapakṣa* (i.e. no places where the probandum is known definitely to occur) given that the collected mutual absences stand as its probandum.

Pūrva-pakṣin: Wrong.

Comments

The non-substance categories are six in number: quality, motion, universal, ultimate individuator, inherence and absence. There are eight substances in addition to earth (nine in all): water, the fiery element, air, ether, time, space, *manas* and self. Not counting the fiery element since it is mentioned in the *sādhya* statement, thirteen instead of twelve should be said. N.S. Ramanuja Tatacharya suggested to me that the category absence is not counted because it is already included in the mention of distinctness, which is a kind of absence, a mutual absence.

The 'no similar instance' fallacy requires that (1) there be a *sapakṣa* as well as (2) the prover be unknown as occurring anywhere there, that is, that there be no things known to be both S and H outside the inferential context while there are things known to be S. No negative-only inference could commit this fallacy since the *sapakṣa* is empty. So again the more serious problem would seem to be how the probandum can be available, given that the inferential context requires that it not be known to occur on the *pakṣa*.

Text (TCM_T 459 and TCM_C 601) and Translation

> *sādhya-niścaye hi sādhya-vyatireka-niścayo bhavaty eva sādhya-sandehe tad-vyatireka-saṁśayasya vajra-lepāt, tathā ca saṁśaya-rūpā*

sādhya-siddhir iti śiṣya-bandhanam, etena pṛthivī jalâdibhyo bhinnā iti vipratipatti-rūpa-vādi-vākyād ākāṅkṣâdimato 'pūrvârtha-pratipādakāt sādhya-prasiddhir iti parāstam. vākyād eva pṛthivyāṁ sādhya-siddher vyatireki-vaiyārthāt. na ca tad-buddhau vādi-vākya-janyatvena aprāmāṇya-saṁśayāt niścaye 'pi saṁśaya iti tan-niścayârthaṁ vyatireki iti vācyam. tarhi saṁśaya-prasiddhaṁ sādhyam, tasya ca na vyatireka-niścayakatvam uktatvāt, svârthânumāne tad-abhāvāc ca.

Pūrva-pakṣin: [You are wrong.] For if the probandum is known with certainty [in correlations elsewhere], there will indeed be certainty about its absence [in negative correlations]. If the probandum is cognised with doubt [as in your questions], then it is cemented in diamond that there will be doubt about its absence [in negative correlations, whereas inference requires that a pervasion be cognised with certainty]. And, therefore, the 'proving' of the probandum in the form of something dubious, well, it's to torture and imprison students.

Objection: The probandum is ['introduced' (*prasiddhi*) or] made well-known from the statement of a debater taking the form of a [doubt-provoking] counter-contention meeting the conditions of syntactic expectancy etc., which would make understood something not previously understood, [e.g.] 'Earth is distinct from water and the rest.'

Pūrva-pakṣin: By the reasoning just given, this is rejected, too. For, the establishment of the probandum as in earth just from a statement would make the negative-only inference pointless.

Objection: Given that the idea of that is generated from the debater's statement, because of a [contrary] doubt about its non-veridicality [given a context of debate], there would be doubt even with respect to something [initially] certain. Thus, the negative-only inference would proceed for the purpose of [maintaining] its certainty.

Pūrva-pakṣin: That also should not be said. For in that case the probandum would be introduced (*prasiddhi*) by the doubt and [so] it could not be made certain by a negative-only inference, as has been stated already. And with respect to inference for oneself, such would not occur.

Comments

Doubt or questioning is no way to introduce a probandum such that it could be proved by a negative-only inference. For, inference requires certainty concerning all of its terms and relations.

kevala-vyatireki-siddhântaḥ

The right view of the exclusively negative inference.

Text (TCM_T 463 and TCM_C 604) and Translation

> *ucyate. ghaṭādāv eva itara-sakala-bhedasya pratyakṣataḥ prasiddhiḥ ghaṭo na jalâdir iti pratīteḥ.*

Gaṅgeśa: We answer. An entire distinctness from the other things is made well-known (i.e. introduced and made known sufficiently well for inference to proceed) by perception with respect to just a pot and the like, that is to say, from such a [perceptual] cognition as, 'The pot is not water and the rest' [the probandum is 'well-known'].

Comments

Gaṅgeśa's position is that prior to inference the probandum mentioned in the inference being discussed ('Earth is distinct from the other things') is known only distributively, only with respect to particular instances. Posterior to inference, it is known also in general, that is to say, one knows that *everything* earthen is distinct from the other substances and non-substance entities. Perception introduces the term. As explained, by negative-only inference we can learn about very general truths and the deep categorial joints of the universe.

Towards the end of the section, Gaṅgeśa reminds us of the negative-only inference that figured crucially in the section of the previous chapter on knowing veridicality (*jñapti*). Let us rehearse that discussion with an eye to this one. The inference explained how one could know for the very first time that a cognition with such-and-such objecthood (e.g. 'That line in the distance is a river') is veridical.[12] The success of drinking from the stream as guided by the sighting is the prover in the negative-only inference (wherever I have had non-veridical cognition, there no such success as this drinking water from the stream at first only distantly perceived). The prover correlates negatively with non-veridicality (every cognition known to be non-veridical is also known not to have sparked such success). Although the veridicality of the first-time cognition has no *sapakṣa*—there has been no cognition with such objecthood before, the objecthood of which it is meaningful to talk of veridicality—the successful subject infers, thirst quenched, 'That cognition is (was) a veridical river-water cognition, *since* it produced successful effort [what is not so, is not so, for example, a non-veridical cognition of water].'

[12] PHILLIPS–RAMANUJA TATACHARYA (2004: 102–19).

Perhaps the most interesting point about this in the current context is that there the probandum—veridicality—is understood as known in general prior to the inference and not known in particular. This is just the opposite of the order of knowing here where earth is the inferential subject. The veridicality of the type of cognition that has not been had before (*anabhyāsa-daśāyām*) has no *sapakṣa*. This is because veridicality is not a true universal, but a makeshift to serve our purposes.[13] The veridicality known prior to inference (the probandum as *prasiddha* ('well-known') in the technical sense that permits inference) is said to be what non-veridical cognitions, which are revealed as non-veridical through frustration of effort, are opposed to, namely, the common way they all fall short. But let us not be distracted by the ontological wriggling; my point is that the reasoning proceeds from the general to the particular.

Here the order of knowing begins with the particular and moves to the universal. Earth in general is known to be distinct from the other things in the ontology. Gaṅgeśa takes the negative-only inference to be of an interestingly ontological variety, the sort of inference whose conclusion reveals a very general fact, here, that earth is a distinct type of substance, different not only from all the things that are not substances (colours etc.) but also from all other types of substance. Earthhood is a true universal (*jāti*) and this seems to be the way we learn that fact.

Furthermore, there seems a certain plausibility to the argument voiced in the current passage. Perception does seem to tell us that the pot is not water or any of the other non-earthen types of thing. But perception does not tell us that everything earthen is distinct from the other fundamental types. We have to be prompted to the appropriate reflection (*parāmarśa*) and infer this. We have to wonder whether earth in general is distinct in this way and we infer that it is by a method of negative correlation.

Gaṅgeśa should not be misunderstood as saying that we actually know about everything we encounter perceptually whether it is distinct or not from non-earthen things. Being-earthen or not is not something that he thinks can invariably be read off of perceptual experience. But presumably we do have a wide enough negative sample of things not-S (the *vipakṣa*, places where the probandum is known not to be) and things not-H (here, absence of the specific quality, 'having-smell', or, in an alternative inference, absence of the universal, 'earthenhood') to cognise a pervasion. We reflect on numerous individuals where we know the probandum is not and we find that none of them has smell (or is earthen). And so we arrive at the veridical cognition of everything earthen—or earth in general—as distinct from the other things.

---

[13] PHILLIPS–RAMANUJA TATACHARYA (2004: 210–16).

Text (TCM_T 463 and TCM_C 604) and Translation

> *nanv ayam anyonyâbhāvo na pratyakṣaḥ atīndriya-pratiyogikâbhāvatvāt paramâṇu-saṁsargâbhāva-vat yogyânupalabdher abhāva-grāhakatvāt nayanônmīlanânantaraṁ stambhaḥ piśāco na bhavati iti pratīter bādhaka-balena vāyur vāti iti-vat liṅga-grahôpakṣīṇatvāt cet. na. yo hy anupalambho 'dhikaraṇe pratiyogi-sattva-virodhī*[14] *so 'bhāvaṁ grāhayati na tu yogyânupalabdhi-mātram, anyathā vāyau rūpâbhāva-pratīti-vat jala-paramâṇau pṛthivītvâbhāva-graha-prasaṅgāt. adhikaraṇe pratiyogi-sattvaṁ ca tarkitaṁ yadi hi stambhaḥ piśācaḥ syāt stambha-vad upalabhyeta na piśācânupalambhaḥ syāt.*

Objection: This 'mutual absence' (mutual distinctness) is not perceptual. For [in the midst of the list of things that are other than earth] things that are beyond the reach of the senses would be the counter-correlate to that absence (that mutual absence mentioned in the probandum expression). Like the absence of contact with an ultimate atom [of earth in a mass of water, an absence that clearly is not perceptual], the condition of 'non-perception of something perceptible' governs the grasping of the absence (i.e. if the counter-correlate is not perceptible, its absence is not perceptible).

[This view about the perceptibility of absences is correct despite certain evidence:] immediately after opening one's eyes, one has the cognition, 'The stump is not a demon' [where it seems that the absence of the demon is perceptual even though the demon is not]. This evidence is countered by the force of a defeater [and the cognition is inferential in fact]. As with 'The wind is blowing', the senses exhaust themselves in the grasping of the inferential mark (the touch of the air, not the air itself, which is imperceptible and similarly in cases of being-other-than-earth).

Gaṅgeśa: No. For, [the rule is] that a non-perception [of *x*] that is *opposed* to [a perception of] the entity [*x*], the counter-correlate, at a particular spot [as, for instance, a non-perception of a pot is blocked by the perception of a pot at a particular spot] makes the absence grasped, not simply the non-perception of something capable of being perceived. Otherwise, there would be the unfortunate consequence that, like a cognition of the absence of colour in air, there would be a [perceptual] grasping of the absence of earthhood in ultimate atoms of water. Furthermore, the [possible] existence [and perception] of the counter-correlate in the locus is arrived at through counterfactual reasoning (*tarka*): 'If the stump were a demon, then like the stump it would be perceived. It is not the case that the demon would not be perceived' [for instance].

[14] Here I follow the suggestion of N.S. Ramanuja Tatacharya to emend to *pratiyogi-sattva-virodhī* from *pratiyogimattva-virodhī*. Both editions have the latter.

Comments

Presumably, no demon has previously been seen. But one sees immediately the distinctness (the mutual absence) that rests in the stump. (One sees the stump as in this way distinct.) Gaṅgeśa's objector views this as an illusion, asserting that the phenomenological evidence is overridden by the principle that the only absences that are perceptible are those whose absentees are perceptible (thus an absence of a horn on a rabbit is perceptible, but not an absence of a rabbit's horn wherever). Gaṅgeśa contends that there is an additional requirement concerning the *locus* of the absence. This principle asserts that an absence is perceptible or not according to whether or not the presence of the absentee at the particular spot would normally force its perception and thus block perception of its absence. This is shown by a little reflection on cases where the substrata are imperceptible, as revealed by 'counterfactual reasoning' (*tarka*).

For example, colour is perceptible. So its absence should be perceptible, according to the principle that an absence is perceptible if its counter-correlate is perceptible. But we do not perceive an absence of red in watery atoms. Since the substratum is imperceptible, there is no opposition between the non-perception of colour there and the perception. It's not true that given the right circumstances including its actual presence we would perceive it (in fact watery atoms do house an absence of red). So this new principle explains why the absence of colour in atoms is not perceptually grasped: the locus is imperceptible.

The new principle—the perceptibility of the absence's locus—handles the stump-demon case, as shown by *tarka*. Reflecting, 'If that were a demon instead of a stump, the demon would be perceived', we see that the absence in this case is perceptible since the demon in the counterfactual worlds would also be perceived. This accords both with the appearance and how people speak, 'That's not a demon!' for instance.

If air were coloured, the colour would be perceived. Therefore, according to Gaṅgeśa, its absence is directly grasped. But the more common opinion among his philosophic contemporaries—both within Nyāya and outside—was that air is imperceptible and known by inference from its touch (the touch alone being perceived and not also its locus or substratum). So, by the light of this new principle, an absence of air would be imperceptible.[15]

In the current context, the thrust of the objector's position is to challenge the introduction of a probandum in a negative-only inference. Gaṅgeśa is trying to escape from the impossible options laid out by the *Pūrva-pakṣin* by having the probandum

---

[15] PHILLIPS–RAMANUJA TATACHARYA (2004: 491 ff.).

perceptually introduced but not in such a way as to make inference pointless (and committing the error of *siddha-sādhana*, 'trying to prove what is already granted'). So, how can the probandum be perceptually introduced—and indeed introduced only, it seems (though this may be where the trick lies), in cases included within the *pakṣa*, the inferential subject, which are illicit as bracketed in the inferential context—in such a manner that the question is not begged? Finally, it bears repeating, if one manages to introduce a probandum properly referring to places where it occurs *outside* the inferential context, then any inference, it would seem, would be positive in character and not 'only-negative'.

Text (TCM_T 464 and TCM_C 609) and Translation

> *na ca pṛthivī jalād bhidyate jalâvṛttir dharmavattvāt tejo-vat evam anyebhyo 'pi bheda-siddhau dvā-daśa-bhinnā iti viśeṣaṇaṁ dattvā samavāya-bheda-sādhanād anvayina eva pṛthivyāṁ trayo-daśa-bheda-siddhir iti kiṁ vyatirekiṇā iti vācyam. jalâdi-bhinnā satī samavāya-bhinnā iti buddhāv api trayo-daśa-bhinnā iti buddher vyatireki-sādhyatvāt.*

Objection: The inference, 'Earth is distinct from water, *since* it has a property that does not occur in water, like *tejas*, the fiery element', is the way that its distinctness is established with respect to the others [on the list, *tejas*, ether etc.], too: 'distinct from twelve [in the series, water, *tejas*, air, ether and so on through the first four non-substance categories]' is then a qualifier kept in mind as one establishes inferentially earth's distinctness from inherence [the thirteenth member of the set of 'the other things']. Thus by an inference based on positive correlations distinctness from the thirteen [other types of thing] is proved. How, then, is there any use for the 'negative-only?'

Gaṅgeśa: This too should not be said. For, even though the cognition that earth is distinct from inherence given its being distinct from water and so on [could be established by positive correlations], the cognition that it is distinct from the thirteen is established veridically by a negative-only inference.

Comments

We can prove that earth is distinct from water straightforwardly by positive and negative correlations making the pervasion known: 'Whatever is distinct from earth does not have smell, like fire and unlike sandalwood.' So we can prove serially that earth is distinct from each substance (and everything composed of those substances) and from the things in the non-substance-categories, too, without resorting to a negative-only inference. But, Gaṅgeśa contends, what about the final inference, where the probandum is not some one or another non-earthen thing but rather everything non-earthen, all entities other than those that are earthen? In that case, the probandum would not be known outside the inferential subject and so the only cases to be considered would be places where the probandum is not. And in none of those places do we find the prover. Thus we conclude—on the basis of a *vyatirekin* inference—that earth is distinct from the other things, where we understand 'the other things' to be everything mentionable other than earth.

Other fundamental categories could be revealed in similar fashion, as we shall see, in the second half of the section, in particular concerning the self (*ātman*), which is another fundamental category.

Text (TCM_T 465 and TCM_C 612) and Translation

> *na ca ghaṭasya api pakṣatvād aṁśataḥ siddha-sādhanam, sarvā pṛthivī itara-bhinnā ity uddeśya-pratīter abhāvāt. pakṣatâvacchedaka-nānātve hi tat, ata eva anitye vāṅ-manasī*[16] *ity atra anityā vāg iti buddheḥ uddeśyāyāḥ siddhatvād aṁśataḥ siddha-sādhanam, anyathā anumāna-mātrôcchedāt pakṣasya siddhasya sādhyatvāt.*

(**Gaṅgeśa** continues:) And it is not the case that the pot [pointed to show that the predicate 'is distinct from the others' is known well enough to be available as probandum in the negative-only inference] belongs to the inferential subject, such that, bit by bit, there would be the error of trying to prove what is already known. There is no such idea in what we want to prove, namely, '*All* earth is distinct from the other things.'

For [there occur cases of bit by bit trying to prove what is already known but] they are cases where the [final] inferential subject is specified by variety (i.e. where it is conceived distributively, in contrast to universally, as our subject is specified by the universal, being-earth). Just for this reason, the inference, 'Non-eternal are speech and mind [*since* they are products]' is an example of this kind of 'proving what is already known': bit by bit the designated cognition [of the *pakṣa*] is known [prior to the inference, e.g.] 'Speech [is non-eternal]' (i.e. is known to be non-eternal prior to the inference). If this were not how the inferential error should be understood, then the whole system of inference would break down, since an inferential subject [so understood] may well be previously known as the probandum [with respect to some one or more of its 'parts'].

[16] Again I follow the suggestion of N.S. Ramanuja Tatacharya, changing *manase* to *manasī*.

Comments

The probandum is introduced by such perceptions as 'This pot, which is earthen, *is distinct from water and so on*.' But apart from the *vyatirekin* inference, the probandum is not known to be true of everything earthen. Therefore, this is not a case of 'trying to prove what is already known.'

The specifiers of the inferential subject in a case where it is 'various' (*nānā*) will be multiple, more than one in number. For example, in the inference about speech and mind as non-eternal, speechhood and mindhood (*manastva*) are the specifiers (*avacchekas*) of being-the-inferential-subject (*pakṣatā*). In Gaṅgeśa's negative-only inference, in contrast, the specifier of the *pakṣatā* is singular: earthhood. Thus, such a speech-mind inference could commit the error of 'bit-by-bit trying to establish what is already known', but not Gaṅgeśa's in that the inferential subject is understood as non-composite.

Text (TCM_T 470 and TCM_C 614) and Translation

> *na ca ghaṭaḥ kathaṁ pakṣaḥ sādhya-niścayena saṁśaya-siṣādhayiṣayoḥ abhāvād iti vācyam. sarvā pṛthivī itara-bhinnā na vā iti saṁśayasya tat-prakāraka-siṣādhayiṣāyāś ca sāmānyato ghaṭa-viṣayatvāt ghaṭatvena viśeṣa-darśanaṁ siddhir vā, atas tena rūpeṇa saṁśaya-siṣādhayiṣe na sthaḥ, pṛthivītvena tu bhavata eva dhūmavān vahnimān iti dhūmavattvena vahni-niścaye 'pi parvate vahni-saṁśaya-vat.*

Objection: How is it that the pot [which is something earthen] can be [part of] the inferential subject, since as known with certainty to possess the probandum there is no doubt about its possessing it nor a desire to infer that it possesses it?

Gaṅgeśa: That, too, should not be asked. The question, 'Is all earth distinct from the other things or not?' and a desire to infer whose predication content is the pot as object as a generality [not as a particular, i.e. as something earthen, not as a pot]. As a pot, it is either perceived as a particular or it is established as that [but as a pot is not the way it is included in the *pakṣa* of the current inference nor is it the way it is the object of the desire to infer]. Thus, not in that way (i.e. taking it as a pot) do the question and/or the desire to infer occur but as earth as their object alone do they occur. This is similar to the case of 'That having smoke is that having fire' where [*in general*, prior to the inference that would prove that yonder mountain has fire], it is known with certainty that there is fire on whatever has smoke but there is doubt [prior to the inference] whether there is fire on the particular mountain.

Comments

The objector claims that the conditions for being a proper *pakṣa* are not met by Gaṅgeśa's example of a negative-only inference since a pot, for example, which is supposed to be included in the *pakṣa* (it is something earthen), is not something about which there would be either a question or a desire to infer of the appropriate sort. Gaṅgeśa responds by making clear that in the case of any known pervasion by things S of things H anything known as H would be in general known as S in advance of the inference that would infer of some particular thing, e.g. a mountain, that it is S because it is H. The doubt that prompts the inference is about a particular as S, not about the relation between things S and H in general. Thus, the mountain of the stock example is a proper *pakṣa*, as is, too, the *pakṣa* of Gaṅgeśa's negative-only inference.

Text (TCM_T 474 and TCM_C 615) and Translation

> *yad vā sarvatvena rūpeṇa na pakṣatā sarvatra avipratipatteḥ. ghaṭâdy-eka-deśe itara-bhedasya pratyakṣa-siddhatvāt. tathā ca eka-deśe vipratipattau sāmānye pṛthivītvena yāvad eva vipratipatti-viṣayas tāvatām eva pakṣatā viśeṣyânanugamāt.*

(**Gaṅgeśa** continues:) Alternatively, [in this case] being-the-inferential-subject is not specified by 'all' or 'everything' [but rather by 'being-earth'] in that everything is not the object of the doubt [that prompts the inference]. For, the several parts [of the inferential subject], the pot and the rest, are established by perception as 'being distinct from the other things' [prior to the final inference and so there would be no doubt about it being true of them].

And so if the doubt were about one or another part [of that which is the inferential subject] and the inference proceeded to prove distinctness from the other things *in general*, the fault of 'switching meaning' (*arthântara*) would be committed. However, my inference [is free from that fault in that] just in that the object of the inference-prompting doubt [which becomes the inferential subject] is understood in general as being-earth. If one takes those parts of it to be [the object of the doubt and] the inferential subject, one would indeed fail to think uniformly of the qualificandum (and thus to make the *arthântara* error).

Comments

Under whatever concept or 'predicate' (*prakāra*) a doubt is borne concerning something, that something becomes an inferential subject (*pakṣa*) under that *prakāra*—it is this rule that Gaṅgeśa invokes to make his point. If there were a doubt: 'Is everything distinct from the other things', then there would be an inferential subject determined by a notion of everything. However, the inference at issue has its *pakṣa* specified by earthhood.

If we change what we are referring to in a proof, our inferences are *eo ipso* vitiated, as in the Aristotelian fallacy of equivocation or 'four terms'. Vātsyāyana, however, explains *arthântara* as a kind of irrelevance, the additional meaning being beside the point.

Text (TCM_T 474 and TCM_C 616) and Translation

> *tarhi pṛthivī itara-bhinnā pṛthivītvāt ghaṭa-vad ity anvayinā eva itara-bhedasya siddhatvāt kiṁ vyatirekiṇā, ghaṭa-sādhāraṇa-pakṣatve 'py abhedânumāna-vat pakṣasya api dṛṣṭântatva-virodhāt pakṣânyatvaṁ hi tatra atantram. kiṁ tu sādhyavattayā niścitatvaṁ prayojakam. na ca pṛthivītvâgrahe pūrvaṁ gṛhītaṁ yatra sādhyaṁ paścāt smaryate tatra hetu-sādhya-sāmānâdhikaraṇyâgrahād vyatireky-avatāra iti vācyam. hetor eva pakṣatâvacchedakatvena ghaṭe pṛthivītva-graha-daśāyām itara-bheda-sāmānâdhikaraṇya-grahâvaśyam-bhāvād iti cet. satyam. anvayi-tulyatayā vyatirekiṇo 'pi sāmārthyāt. anvayâpratisandhāna-daśāyāṁ vyatireky-upanyāsasya aparyanuyojyatvāt. tad uktam, "āstāṁ tāvad ayaṁ suhṛd-upadeśaḥ, kevala-vyatireki lakṣaṇaṁ tāvan nirvyūḍham".*

Objection 1: In that case, the inference, 'Earth is distinct from the other things, *since* it has earthhood, like a pot, proceeds based simply on positive examples [such as the pot that you have excluded from the *pakṣa*], in proving the distinctness from the others. So what's the point of your negative-only inference?

Even if the pot [cited as an example] is [in a sense] common to the *pakṣa*, like a 'non-distinctness' inference [such as, 'This is the pot that I experienced yesterday, *since* it has the shape and so on of the pot that I experienced yesterday', where the supporting example can be nothing other than the pot itself], there is no contradiction in the inferential subject itself being offered as a supporting example. For, the principle [governing the citing of an example] does not apply there. Rather, the criterion is that the example helps make the having of the probandum certain.

Objection 2 (against Objector 1): At first, when the probandum is grasped [in a pot and so on which are known by perception to be 'distinct from the others'], earthhood is not grasped [since the pot and so on are grasped through their pothood, for example, not as examples of earth]. In cases where the probandum has been grasped later, it is remembered as being there. But there is no grasping of [pervasion defined as] the prover's having the same loci as the probandum [in that the examples not being grasped as earthen are not grasped as exhibiting the prover, earthhood]. From this, there is room for the entry of the negative-only inference.

Answer (by Objector 1): That should not be alleged. For, it is just the prover that specifies how the inferential subject is understood in the case of the pot: at the time that it is understood as being-earth [in the context of the inference under discussion] necessarily is there grasped [a pervasion in] the prover's having the same loci as [the probandum] distinctness-from-the-other-things. [Therefore, positive correlations can be had and the inference need not be 'only negative'.]

Gaṅgeśa (responding to Objector 1): What you say is true [to an extent]. For the capability of the negative-only is, though negative, the equivalent of positive inference. On an occasion when positive correlations are not brought to mind, that negative correlations are mentioned is not to be worried about. So it has been said [by Vācaspatimiśra]: '"Away with it" (i.e. with the negative-only, given an accomplished positive inference)—such is the teaching of a friend. [But without a positive inference] an inference whose nature is negative-only is itself indeed an accomplished method.'

Comments

The objector complains that Gaṅgeśa can't have it both ways. He can't exclude such earthen things as a pot from the inferential subject and then pretend that he has an inference based on negative correlations alone. For, the pot is an example of *sapakṣa*, a place known to exhibit the probandum, and the method of positive correlation checks such places for the presence of the prover. One might also check the *vipakṣa*, places known to be bereft of the probandum, to make sure that the prover is not there. But relying on both positive and negative correlations is not to make an inference that is 'negative-*only*', as Gaṅgeśa seems to pretend.

The objector then weakens his case with a comparison to 'non-distinctness' inferences, opening the possibility that something can be both an inferential subject and a supporting example in the same inference. But the inference on the table is different. Here the example is *sapakṣa*. It helps 'make the probandum certain'. Note that the standard convention is to cite an instance of *sapakṣa* where the prover is also known to occur. A negative example is an instance of *vipakṣa* (where the probandum is known definitely not to occur) where the prover, too, is known to be absent. According to the paradigm, then, an example has to be something outside the *pakṣa* (the inferential subject). But some good inferences break the rule, for example, so-called 'non-distinctness' inferences, an example of which is given in parentheses here.

Gaṅgeśa admits that his example could be reconstructed such that the same inferential awareness would be produced by a positive inference, with positive examples, in the fashion of Objector 1, whose point about the example in a 'non-distinctness' inference Gaṅgeśa does not contend. His current point seems to be, then, that negative-only inference may be used if we like or if we do not see positive correlation. But it need not be defended as indispensable.

Text (TCM_T 475 and TCM_C 618) and Translation

> *athavā jalâdīnāṁ trayo-daśânyonyâbhāvāḥ trayo-daśasu prasiddhāḥ pṛthivyāṁ sādhyante. ata eva ākāśe vyatirekiṇā jalâdi-milita-pratiyogikânyonyâbhāvâpratītāv api trayo-daśânyonyâbhāvāḥ sādhyā iti na anvayitvâsādhāraṇye.*

(**Gaṅgeśa** continues:) Alternatively, thirteen mutual absences of water and the rest (or thirteen 'mutual distinctnesses', *anyonyâbhāva*), which are well-known in thirteen types of entity (each one of a total of fourteen types of entity would appear to be mutually distinct from the others), are established in earth (i.e. earth is proved mutually distinct from the thirteen other types of entity). Just for this reason, in ether [which has no parts] thirteen mutual absences are established by a negative-only inference, although there is no notion of a mutual absence whose counter-correlate is the collection of water and the rest [prior to the inference]. Therefore, [the inference] is not [based] on positive correlations and there is no [fallacy of] 'no similar instance'.

Comments

To this point Gaṅgeśa has claimed his sample negative-only inference meets the requirement of having a probandum that has been properly introduced (*prasiddha*, 'well-known') by being known in a part (*eka-deśa*, 'one spot') of the inferential subject, for example, a pot which as something earthen is included in the inferential subject earth in general but not as a pot. This analysis, we have seen, has resulted in an admission that the inferential awareness ('Earth is distinct from the other things') that is the result could be generated by a positive inference just as well (or better, it would seem) as by the method at issue. So the objector's complaint about usefulness stings a bit still. So now Gaṅgeśa tries a different tact, switching our focus from earth to ether and other potential inferential subjects for which 'being distinct from the others' is surely known. These entities, or categories (*padârtha*, 'types of thing to which words refer'), have no parts or instances. Ether is non-atomic, unlike earth, water and air. Similarly, a self is a partless unit as are other fundamental entities such as inherence.

In the case of ether, which is the inferential subject in the current passage ('Ether is distinct from the other things, *since* it is the substratum of sound'), each of thirteen mutual absences are known prior to the inference. But unlike the case of the earthen pot where the probandum, a summational mutual absence ('being distinct from the other things'), is introduced through the pot, which is an earthen thing, here with ether the probandum is not well-known, since ether has no parts. How, then, is the probandum available? Gaṅgeśa does not answer here and the question drives much of the subsequent discussion.

Let us take stock. Putting aside the availability issue, we see that with a previously unknown probandum, there cannot be inference based on positive correlations (as Gaṅgeśa will point out at the end). Nor can there be the 'no common instance' fallacy, which requires that there be a *sapakṣa*. The defence so far of the usefulness of negative-only inference has been pretty minimal. In other words, Gaṅgeśa is now occupied with knowledge that has no source other than inference of the negative-only variety. In some cases, it *is* indispensable.

Finally, it seems pretty plausible in itself that the mind make a leap to a new term in the conclusion or result of a negative inferential process, at least as Gaṅgeśa has us picture it in his example. All that is unknown prior to the inference is the combined absence, the mutual distinctness that is a composite of other mutual distinctnesses already known. The leap is from the particular not so much to the general but to the collection, the very general collection of all things other than earth.

Text (TCM_T 477 and TCM_C 619) and Translation

> *yad vā jalaṁ tejaḥ-prabhr̥ti-dvā-daśa-bhinna-pratiyogikânyonyâbhāva-vat dravyatvāt tejo-vat ity anumānāt trayo-daśa-bhinnasya sāmānyataḥ siddhau pr̥thivyāṁ trayo-daśa-bhinnatvaṁ sādhyam. na ca anvayitvam asādhāraṇyaṁ vā, pakṣād anyatra sādhyâprasiddhiḥ. vastu-gatyā pr̥thivyām eva sādhya-siddheḥ kiṁ vyatirekiṇā iti cet, na. pr̥thivī trayo-daśa-bhinnā iti vyatirekiṇaṁ vinā apratīteḥ.*

(**Gaṅgeśa** continues:) Alternatively, one could say that the inference, 'Water possesses the mutual distinctness whose counter-correlate is [itself not only distinct from water but also] distinct from the twelve sorts of entities beginning [on the standard list] with *tejas* (the fiery element), *since* it is a substance, like *tejas*', establishes its probandum in general as belonging to something distinct from the thirteen (i.e. the twelve distinct from water's distinctness from X plus water's distinctness from X). This being-distinct-from-the-thirteen is the probandum with respect to earth [as inferential subject].

And here there is neither an inference based on positive correlations nor the fallacy of 'no similar instance', because the probandum is unknown outside the inferential subject (i.e. there is no *sapakṣa*).

But in reality the answer to the 'It's *already established* for earth' challenge to the usefulness of negative-only inference is to say: no, without the negative-only inference there would be no knowledge, 'Earth is distinct from the thirteen.'

Comments

Once we have X, we have also the absence of X available to be inferred. All inference extends the scope, so to say, of a probandum. So it is no objection that the absential term gets new meaning through the negative-only inference.

Text (TCM_T 478 and TCM_C 619) and Translation

> *nanv evaṁ pṛthivī jalâdi-trayo-daśa-bhinna-pratiyogikânyonyâbhāvavatī dravyatvād iti pṛthivī-bhinna-tad-bhinnâdi-siddhiḥ syād iti cet, na. aprayojakatvāt. prakṛte ca anubhūyamāna-jalâdi-vaidharmyasya pṛthivītva-śabdâśrayatvâder atiriktaṁ vinā anupapatteḥ.*

Objection: In this way, 'Earth possesses the mutual distinctness whose countercorrelate is [itself not only distinct from earth but also] distinct from the *thirteen* sorts of entities beginning [on the standard list] with water, *since* it is a substance' is an inference that would prove not only something to be distinct from earth but also as distinct from that and on on [*ad infinitum*].

Gaṅgeśa: Wrong. For that inference [unlike mine] would be unmotivated [by favourable counterfactual reasoning (*tarka*)]. And in the case of my inference, such entities as earth in general or the substratum of sound [ether], which are experienced as having different properties from water and so on, would not be known without something in addition [to the experience, to wit, my negative-only inference].

Comments

The favourable counterfactual reasoning is that if there were not something distinct from, say, water, then things that have properties that water does not have would not be experienced. And of course we do experience earth and the rest.

Text (TCM_T 479 and TCM_C 620) and Translation

nanv itara-bhedo yady anyonyâbhāvas tadâbhāvād[17] *na sidhyet. abhāvasya abhāvântarâbhāvāt. yadi ca tena samaṁ sva-rūpa-bheda eva sādhyaḥ, tadânanugamād anumānâpravṛttiḥ. bhāvo 'bhāvo*[18] *na bhavati ity abādhita-pratīti-balād abhāvasya api anyonyâbhāvo 'sti iti kecit. tan na. apasiddhântāt. anatiprasaktâdhikaraṇa-sva-rūpa-mātreṇa eva abhāva-pratīty-upapattau ca adhikâbhāve mānâbhāvāc ca iti cet, na. itara-bhāvânyonyâbhāvasya sādhyatvāt. na ca evam abhāvād aviveka-tādavasthyam. tena samaṁ sva-rūpa-bhedasya anvayinā vyatirekiṇā vā sādhyatvāt.*

Objection: If 'distinctness from the others' [as employed in your inference] were [as you say] a mutual absence, then distinctness from [the seventh category on the traditional list of things] absence would not be proved [by it]. For there is no other type of absence that would be an 'absence of absence'. [Rather, that is a presence, but your inference requires an absence of absence to make sense of earth's distinctness from absence as a category.]

And if along with that [distinctness that is the probandum in your inference] there is the distinctness that is something's 'very nature' (*sva-rūpa*, i.e. absence reduced to the substratum), then, because there would not be the uniformity necessary, inference could not proceed.

Answer (by a Naiyāyika faction): A presence is not an absence (i.e. absence is a separate category)—a thesis that holds by force of being undefeated. So absence [as a fundamental category], too, is a mutual absence.

Gaṅgeśa: So say some. But they're wrong. For, the position is inconsistent with our overall view.

Objection: The notion of absence is explained just by the 'very nature' of the locus or substratum, which is a view that faces no [such] untoward consequence. Furthermore, there is no argument that there is any other type of absence.

Gaṅgeśa: No. For, the probandum [with the current inference], the *being* other [which is a presence], is proved [by a separate inference] to be mutually distinct [from absence].

And it is not the case that in this way earth's being the way it is would be indistinguishable from absence. [My sample inference does not purport to prove earth's dis-

[17] Emending to *abhāvād* (i.e. *tadâbhāvād*) from *bhāvād* (i.e. *tadā bhāvād*).

[18] Deleting *vā*.

tinctness from absence.] Equally for absence, earth's distinctness is by its very nature to be proved by either a positive or a negative inference.

Comments

If earth were not different from absence, then its very nature would be an absence. But this is ridiculous. On the other hand, it seems that we have to have a new type of absence.

Text (TCM_T 482 and TCM_C 621) and Translation

> *anye tu pṛthivītva-bhinna-dharmâtyantâbhāva eva sādhyaḥ jalâdi-pratiyogikās tāvanto 'tyantâbhāvā vā tat-tad-asādhāraṇa-tat-tad-dharmâtyantâbhāva-yogo vā. ete ca abhāvā jalatvaṁ na ghaṭâdau ghaṭâdi jalatvâtyantâbhāva-vad iti pratyakṣâdeḥ kvacit tat-tad-vaidharmyād eva prasiddhā iti na aprasiddhiḥ. tāvatām abhāvānāṁ vaiśiṣṭyaṁ na prasiddham iti cet, kim etāvatā. na hi tāvad-vaiśiṣṭyam atra sādhyate. kiṁ tu jalatvâdināṁ yāvanto 'bhāvā iha sādhyās te ca tatra tatra prasiddhā eva. tāvad-vaiśiṣṭya-dhīs tu phalam. anyathā siddha-sādhanāt. nimilitānām api sādhyatve na aprasiddhiḥ. kiñcid eka-dharmâvacchedako hi balâdi-van melakârthaḥ, sa ca na asiddhiḥ. na ca hetor asādhāraṇyam. tāvad abhāva-yogī hy atra sapakṣo bhavati, na tu tad-eka-deśa-katipayâbhāvavān. sādhyatāyās tāvaty aparyāpteḥ.*

(**Gaṅgeśa** continues:) But others hold the following.

Naiyāyika faction: What's to be proved [by the sample inference is not a *mutual absence* from earth, it] is simply an *absolute absence* of a property distinct from earthhood [*in* earth]. Or [to frame the inference more specifically], what's to be proved is [in earth] the absolute absences whose counter-correlates are waterhood and company. Or, it is the relation [in earth] to absolute absences of this and that 'specific property', i.e. a property not the same as just this or that property [of earth].

And these absences are well-known such that there is no issue concerning introduction (*prasiddhi*). 'Waterhood does not exist in a pot and so on' [and] 'A having of an absolute absence of [e.g.] waterhood in a pot and so on' are produced by perception and the rest, (i.e. by inference and testimony). Thus, with respect to some things these absences are well-known just from this or that difference of property.

Objection: The relationality of those absences [to earth] is not well-known.

Naiyāyika faction: What would be the use of that being known [prior to the inference]? For, it is not the case that such relationality is to be proved here first. Rather, such absences as of waterhood and so on are to be proved and then these absences being here and there well-known indeed inform such a cognition of relationality [that takes them all, so to say, in summation], which is the [final] fruit [of the inference as a knowledge source]. Otherwise, there would be the fault of 'trying to prove what is already established'.

Even though [in the final inference] the probandum consists of them taken together, there is no issue of introduction (*prasiddhi*). For, there is specification by some single property or other for the purpose of a combining, like power [in combining men into an army] and the like. And this is not unfamiliar. Nor is there the 'no similar instance' fallacy of the prover. For, here the *sapakṣa* (places where the probandum is known definitely to occur) is: being-related-to-such-a-[collective]-absence, not possessing-the-absence-of-a-*few*-properties-in-some-one-or-another-part, [the former not occurring other than in the inferential subject, whereas the latter is well-known to occur in various things made of the element earth]. No formulation of the probandum would be sufficient [for what we want to prove] that was in such a way limited (i.e. limited in the manner of the second formulation in its mention of a 'few').

Comments

'Earth has an absolute absence of a property distinct from earthhood, *since* it has earthhood' is how the sample inference would be reconstructed by the Naiyāyika faction in the first formulation. The second formulation of the probandum, which is in terms of the absences' counter-correlates, waterhood and company, suggests the solution to the problem of the availability of the probandum. And the third switches from the universals proper to the elements to 'specific properties' such as viscosity (*sneha*) for water. These properties, which are themselves not universals (*jāti*) but tropes (*guṇa*) in Nyāya-Vaiśeṣika ontology, are, like universals, exhibited by the one type of thing and nothing else, as being-smelly by all things earthen and nothing else. A further, more minor change in the third formulation is the mention of the qualificative relation, the being-qualified by such absences to the probandum: 'Earth is qualified by the absolute absence of this and that specific property etc.'.

As before, the probandum is known prior to the inference in a portion of the inferential subject, for example, a pot.

The solution to the availability problem is, then, like counting, which, according to Nyāya, can create a new property in the things counted (*apekṣā-buddhi*, which is a kind of mental perception, not an inference, brought about by the *manas*, the internal organ). Putting all the absences together would be an act of the *manas* making the collectivity known prior to the inference that would establish it as qualifying earth. It is the collective absence, as opposed to an absence of a few properties, that makes the probandum provable only by a negative-only inference.

Text (TCM_T 485 and TCM_C 623) and Translation

yad vā jalatvâtyantâbhāvas tejastvâtyantâbhāvâdhikaraṇa-vr̥ttiḥ atyantâbhāvatvāt ghaṭatvâtyantâbhāva-vat. evam atyantâbhāvântara-sāmānâdhikaraṇyam api tatra sādhyam iti kva aprasiddhiḥ. kiṁ ca itare tāvat prasiddhā eva. te ca bheda-pratiyogino meyatvāt iti itara-bhedo 'pi sugraha eva.

(The **Naiyāyika faction** continues:) Alternatively, in the manner of the following inference it is shown that the probandum becomes for other absolute absences, [e.g. of airhood,] the having of the same substratum: 'An absolute absence of waterhood rests in the substratum of the absolute absence of *tejas*-hood [or, being-the-fiery-element], *since* it is an absolute absence, like the absolute absence of pothood [in e.g. a cloth].' So where is the not being familiar?

Furthermore, 'the others' are, in the first place, familiar indeed. And they are the counter-correlates of the distinctness, [that is, earth's from the other things], *since* they are knowable. So 'distinctness from the others', too, is easy to grasp, quite easy.

Comments

Bit by bit the probandum is aggregated, in each case being 'familiar' (*prasiddha*, 'well-known') in a particular instance.

Text (TCM_T 486 and TCM_C 624) and Translation

nanu pr̥thivī na itara-bhedavatī gurutvâdibhyo jala-vad iti pratirodha iti cet, na. itara-bheda-niṣedho hi itarâbhedaḥ na tu tejaḥ-prabhr̥ty-abhedo jala iti dr̥ṣṭāntasya sādhya-vaikalyāt. catur-daśâbhedānāṁ ca ekatra virodhena asambhavāt. catur-daśa-bhedānāṁ ca ekatra vr̥ttau na virodhaḥ.

Objection: [Your inference is defeated because it faces a counter-inference (*sat-pratipakṣa*):] 'Earth is *not* distinct from the others, *since* it is heavy and the like, like water' contradicts your inference [and is equally well-supported].

Naiyāyika faction: No. For, a denial of distinctness from the others amounts to [an assertion of] non-distinctness with the others, but not to non-distinctness [in some respect] with members of the list beginning with the fiery element. So the example given, 'water', commits the fault called 'probandum infirmity', (i.e. an instance of the probandum's absence since water though possessing some properties in common with other types of thing is clearly not non-distinct with the others as a group). And there is no possibility of fourteen *non*-distinctnesses at a single spot because they would be mutually opposed, whereas fourteen *distinctnesses* occurring at a single spot would not be mutually opposed.

Comments

The fault of the example required in a presentation of an inference for others called 'infirmity of the probandum' (*sādhya-vaikalya*) applies to an example that does not exhibit the probandum: 'There is smoke on yonder mountain, *since* there is fire, like a lake.' Water does not exhibit the probandum, 'non-distinctness from the others'.

Furthermore, a thing has a single identity. It is non-distinct only with itself. There is only the single entity. But a single thing, a pot, for instance, is distinct from many other things, such that the idea that there be fourteen distinctnesses resting in it is quite plausible. 'Fourteen', of course, is the number in the text because it is the number of earth's distinctnesses from the other fundamental types of thing, substances and non-substances (counted by fundamental category of non-substances and fundamental sub-category of substance0, all the things that are not earth.

Text (TCM_T 487 and TCM_C 625) and Translation

> *yat tu sādhya-prasiddhau pṛthivī itara-bhinnā tat-sādhyâdhikaraṇa-tad-anadhikaraṇa-pṛthivy-anyataratvāt*[19] *tad-adhikaraṇavat pṛthivyāṁ tat-sādhyam anvayina eva 'setsyati iti. tan na. anyataratvasya aliṅgatvād ity uktatvāt. liṅgatve vā jalâdāv api tat-siddhi-prasaṅgāt. evaṁ tarhi pṛthivī jalaṁ pṛthivītvāt yan na jalaṁ tan na pṛthivī yathā teja iti sat-pratipakṣo 'stv iti cet, na. ajalasya ghaṭâdeḥ pratyakṣata eva pṛthivītva-niścaye vyatireka-vyabhicārād asya nyūnatvāt. tad-anavadhāraṇe tu sat-pratipakṣatvam iṣṭam eva.*

Objection: Given that the probandum is introduced as you have explained (i.e. bit by bit), the inference, 'Earth is distinct from the others, *since* earth is either (a) the probandum's substratum (i.e. earthen things such as a pot where distinct-from-the-others has been already determined to occur) or (b) the substratum of its absence (i.e. where it has not been determined to occur), like the probandum's substratum', that probandum will be proved just by a positive inference. [So your example of a negative-only inference disintegrates.]

Gaṅgeśa: That's wrong. It has already been explained that being-one-or-the-other [of a property and its absence] cannot be a true inferential mark. Or if it can be, then

[19] N.S. Ramanuja Tatacharya suggests the addition, *tad-anadhikaraṇa-°*, although both editions leave the string out.

the predicament is that being-distinct-from-non-earthen-things could be established for water and so on, too.

Objection: Let there be in this way, then, the counter-inference [showing your inference to be fallacious], 'Earth is water, since it has earthhood—what is not water, that is not earth—like *tejas*, the fiery element.'

Gaṅgeśa: No. It is just by perception that a pot and the like, which are not water, are known to be earthen [to possess earthhood]. This being so, your so-called counter-inference falls to the fallacy of deviation in negative correlations, [that is to say, there is a counter-example, a place that exhibits the prover but not the probandum]. It [also] commits the debate error known as 'leaving something out' (*nyūna*, failing to mention or formulate correctly one or another of the five steps required in a proper 'inference for others', *parârthânumāna*). But if such is not determined [by perception], then your [crazy] counter-inference would be welcome indeed!

Comments

Here we move from the availability problem back to the usefulness of the negative form of inference. Granting that the probandum is available for inference in the way that has been sketched, we see that the inference proceeds by generalising over cases where it is known to occur. Thus, the inference looks pretty normal, that is to say, based on positive correlations as well as negative ones.

But the attempt to formulate a positive inference involves a trick prover, '*since* it is *one or the other of*...', which invokes the logic of alternation in a way that could prove anything if such a prover were legitimate. However, something being's either F or not-F cannot be used as a significant prover, Gaṅgeśa points out.

What counts as a genuine inference is in part determined by what we know is true. If an apparent inference form could be used to prove something false, then it is in reality non-genuine. 'This four-headed creature is from Mars, since it has four heads—what is not from Mars, that does not have four heads—like a pot.' Of course, the counter-inference proposed by the objector is defective in its example, i.e. in the third of the five specified steps, which is supposed to show the pervasion between the prover and probandum but does not. But Gaṅgeśa's final counterfactual reasoning shows just what we would have to swallow were a pot's being earthen, for instance, not known perceptually.

We turn now to a negative-only inference with a rather momentous conclusion, to judge by the classical controversy, a proof of self, *ātman*, an enduring substratum of psychological properties. That there is such a thing is hotly disputed by Buddhists and Cārvāka materialists and is a primary issue for all the schools.

Text (TCM_T 488 and TCM_C 626) and Translation

nanu jīvac-charīraṁ sātmakaṁ prāṇâdimattvāt icchâdi-kāryavattvād vā iti vyatirekiṇi sādhyâprasiddhau kathaṁ vyatirekâdi-nirūpaṇam. nairātmyaṁ ca na ghaṭasya pratyakṣa-vedyam, tasya tatra asāmarthyāt. na anumāna-gamyam, nairātmyâpratītāv anvayino 'bhāvāt. sātmakatva-pratītiṁ vinā vyatirekiṇo ' nupapatteḥ.

Objection (by a new *Pūrva-pakṣin*): Consider another so-called negative-only inference: 'A living body has a self, *since* it has breath and the like, or *since* it has as effects [inhering in itself] desire and the like.' Given that the probandum is not known, how can there be such an inference as that which you understand to be 'negative-only?' (i.e. How is it that having-a-self is something known and thus available for inference?)

And not-having-a-self is not to be known perceptually for [e.g.] a pot, because perception is not capable there of making that known. Nor is it arrived at through inference [because the required pervasion cannot be established]. Given that there is no cognition of not-having-a-self, there can be no positive correlations; without cognition of having-a-self, negative correlations are impossible.

Comments

Like his Nyāya predecessors, Gaṅgeśa views a self as knowable both by perception and by inference. But for present purposes, we must bracket the perceptual position in order to explore the method of negative-only inference.

As mentioned at the beginning, this stretch of text seems practically a subcommentary on the *Bhāṣya* of Vātsyāyana (c. 400) on *Nyāya-sūtra* (NS) 1.1.5, where he proves the existence of the self as the locus of psychological properties by way of an inference type called *sāmānyato-dṛṣṭa*. He says: 'The self is known inferentially by means of [the marks of] desire and the like. Desire and the like are qualities and qualities have as their foundations substances. That which is the foundation of desires and the like is the self.'[20] Note that the NS has a long stretch of *sūtra*s at the beginning of chapter three on the self, its character and how it is known (NS 3.1.1–25).

Despite the elucidations of the subcommentaries (and of Udayana's independent treatise on the self[21]), one might wonder how precisely to reconstruct Vātsyāyana's

---

[20] NYAYA-TARKATIRTHA–TARKATIRTHA–TARKATIRTHA (1985: 156–57): *icchâdibhir ātmā, guṇāḥ, guṇāś ca dravya-saṁsthānāḥ, tad yad eṣāṁ sthānaṁ sa ātmā.*

[21] The richness within the commentarial tradition notwithstanding, it is Udayana's *Ātma-tattva-viveka* ('Discrimination of Truth (from Falsehood) concerning the Self'), with its mind-boggling array of arguments, that is the outstanding Nyāya treatise on the self and self-knowledge. Never-

reasoning. For instance, if an inference is proffered, what is the *pakṣa*? More than one argument, moreover, seems to be implicit. A primary issue for Gaṅgeśa is the nature of our knowledge of the inferential subject prior to the inferential process or act. In the current passage, the *pakṣa* is the collection of living bodies (*śarīra*—a word used primarily for the human body but which here includes animals and presumably plants, which have their own type of *prāṇa* or breath).

Now although liberated selves are not embodied, clearly a dead body does not exhibit the prover here, breath, as also do not all other non-living things. Then presupposing that having-a-self is not revealed to the senses (otherwise inference would not be required), how could the absence of having-a-self, to wit, not-having-a-self, be known? Is it known perceptually? No. We do not directly observe that a pot, for instance, has no self. Nor is the probandum known by inference. If not-having-a-self is not made available by perception, it could not be grasped by an inference based on positive correlations, since perceptual evidence would be required. And with 'not-having-a-self' as probandum, the *vipakṣa* would be things that 'have a self'. Of course, that predicate is unavailable.

Text (TCM_T 488 and TCM_C 626) and Translation

> *atha icchā samavāyi-kāraṇa-janyā kāryatvāt. tac ca samavāyi-kāraṇaṁ pṛthivy-ādy-aṣṭa-dravya-bhinnaṁ pṛthivy-āditve bādhaka-sattvād iti pṛthivy-ādi-bhinnâtma-siddhau tadvattvaṁ jīvac-charīre sādhyata iti cet, yadi sātmakatvaṁ ātma-saṁyogavattvam, tadā ghaṭâdau tad asti iti tato hetu-vyāvṛttāv asādhāraṇyam. jñāna-samānâdhikaraṇa-jñāna-kāraṇī-bhūta-saṁyogâśraya-kāryatvaṁ sātmakatvaṁ, śarīrâtma-saṁyogasya jñāna-kāraṇatvāt, ātma-manasos tathātve 'py akāryatvād iti cet, na. śarīrād anyatra asiddheḥ. tatra prasiddhau siddha-sādhanam.*

Objection (to the *Pūrva-pakṣin*, by a Naiyāyika defender of the separate utility of *kevala-vyatirekin* inference): [First there is established an inherent cause of psychological qualities:] Desire has origins in an inherent cause, *since* it is an effect [like a pot]. And [then it is established that] the inherent cause is distinct from the eight substances [on the traditional list] beginning with earth, because there are de-

theless, Gaṅgeśa most directly follows Vātsyāyana and the NS commentaries, not his 'teacher's' *Ātma-tattva-viveka*. The latter is, by the way, a long work. The edition DVIVEDIN–DRAVIḌA (1986), with a commentary by Saṅkara Miśra that takes up about half, runs almost a thousand pages. And despite his focus, it is safe to assume that overall Gaṅgeśa takes a position that is pretty much the same as Udayana's. (The *Ātma-tattva-viveka* is organised around refutation of rival views, and wanders to inferences to God and to the authority of scripture, departing dramatically from the order of the NS discussion.)

featers that rule out earth and the rest. Given that self has been established as distinct from earth and the rest, the having of that [a self] is proved [by negative correlations] for a living body.

Pūrva-pakṣin: If 'having a self' amounts to 'being conjoined with a self', then that occurs in the case of a pot and so on (too, since, according to Nyāya, a self is ubiquitous in size, i.e. all-pervasive, such that everything would be in a sense 'conjoined' with it). Therefore, the prover being excluded (from the *sapakṣa*), the fallacy of 'no common instance' is committed.

Objection: [The probandum predicate] 'having a self' amounts to something's (i.e. a living body's) 'being an effect and a substratum that supports the conjunction (i.e. body-self conjunction or connection) that is a cause of cognition and that has the same substratum [namely, a self] as cognition.' For, body-self conjunction is a cause of cognition. Although self-*manas* conjunction is such a cause, too, *manas* ('mind' or the 'internal organ') is not an effect [and so the predicate does not overapply to *manas*].

Pūrva-pakṣin: Wrong. For it is unknown elsewhere than with respect to the body (i.e. the *pakṣa*). [And] if it is known there, then [you've got a case of] 'trying to prove what is already known'.

Comments

Following Vātsyāyana under *Nyāya-sūtra* 1.1.5 (the so-called inference *sūtra*), Gaṅgeśa puts forth a two-step argument. First, desires are proved to have a locus, a substance in which to inhere, like all qualities. In step two, self is proved to be that locus, a distinct substance, different from earth, water, *tejas* and so on down the traditional list, by eliminative argument. Note that all that we know about the self hereby is that it is the locus of certain properties, on analogy to the way, say, the lotus is a locus of blue.

The defeaters for the proposition that desire and the like belong to earth or the rest consists of counterfactual reasoning such as the following. If desire were a property of earth (or water and so on down the list), then like the colour that exists in earthen things, it too would be perceived. Surveying pots and so on, we find that nothing material has desire, cognition etc., outside of living bodies, bodies conjoined, on the Nyāya theory, with selves.

Next, instead of advancing inquiry about the main concern of how the probandum is available, the new *Pūrva-pakṣin* tries to exploit bits of incoherence within the overall Nyāya picture of mind-body relation. By a separate eliminative argument concerning substances and size, a self is proved to be ubiquitous: all substances are supposed to be of ubiquitous, intermediate, or atomic size (with examples in ether, a pot and an earthen atom, respectively). Thus, the *Pūrva-pakṣin* points out, a pot is conjoined with a self as ubiquitous on the Nyāya view, and so such a non-living thing too would be qualified by the probandum. But the prover, having-breath, does not qualify a pot. So there is no evidence for the required pervasion and the 'no common instance' fallacy is committed. There should be evidence, but there isn't any.

Two conjunctions, or connections, are viewed in Nyāya as necessary for cognitive occurrences: body-self conjunction and *manas*-self conjunction. The *manas*, or 'internal organ', is of course itself a controversial posit—both within Nyāya, we should note, as well as outside. (There is a section on *manas* in Gaṅgeśa's perception chapter.[22]) By separate arguments, *manas* (along with the self) is properly excluded as qualified by the property, having-a-self, by its 'being an effect' (neither self nor *manas* is an effect). So Gaṅgeśa qualifies the probandum term of his inference, specifying that conjunction of self and body is an *avacchedaka* or condition for the self's being the locus of desires, cognitions and so on, as effects.

Thus the objection is met (our having been reminded of the many problems attaching to the conception of *manas* notwithstanding). Unfortunately, there remains the main problem, the *Pūrva-pakṣin* points out: where have we encountered this now, on the objector's analysis, highly complex property, having-a-self? The probandum cannot be both unknown and available for inference, nor both known and needing to be proved.

Text (TCM$_T$ 490 and TCM$_C$ 627) and Translation

> *icchāyā asamavāyi-kāraṇa-saṁyogâvacchedakatvasya abhāvo ghaṭâdau dṛṣṭaḥ, tad-vyatirekaḥ śarīre sādhyata iti cet, na. icchāyā asamavāyi-kāraṇa-saṁyogâvacchedakatvasya śarīra eva prasiddheḥ siddha-sādhanam. anyathā asiddhi-vyatirekâdy-anirūpaṇāt. aprasiddha-sādhya-saṁsargam iva sādhyam aprasiddaṁ sādhayati vyatirekī iti cet, na. vyatirekâdy-anirūpaṇād asādhāraṇa-dharmeṇa apratīta-padârthânumāne ghaṭatvâdinā api svêcchā-kalpita-ḍitthâdy-anumāna-prasaṅga iti.*

Objection: In a pot and so forth there is experienced no specifier of the emergent cause, which is conjunction [of self and body], with respect to desire [as effect, i.e. it is only living bodies that have desires, not things like pots]. Its absence (i.e. the absence of the absence) is [thereby] proved with respect to the living body. (That is to say, the property, living-body-as-specifying-the-conjunction-etc., which is what having-a-self amounts to, is proved to belong to a living body.)

---

[22] PHILLIPS–RAMANUJA TATACHARYA (2004: 537–74).

Pūrva-pakṣin: No. [Your absence's counter-correlate, namely] the specifier of the emergent cause, which is conjunction [of self and body], with respect to desire, is well-known just with the living body and so this is a case of 'trying to prove what is already known'. Otherwise, the problem is that its not being present could not be determined by a negative method or the like (i.e. by another method of knowledge: it would be unavailable to all knowledge-generative processes).

Objection: The way that the probandum that the negative inference proves is unknown is like the relation to the probandum that is unknown [with respect to the *pakṣa*, prior to inference].

Pūrva-pakṣin: No. For, it could not be determined by a negative method or the like (as has been said).

If inference could prove an uncognised something by way of the thing's uncommon property, [as 'having-breath' is a property possessed only by living bodies], then a pot too could be inferred to have, by its [uncommon property] pothood or the like, such arbitrarily imagined properties as 'Ḍittha' (a name normally used only for persons)—this is the difficulty.

Comments

The suggestion is that, since no difficulty attaches the probandum's being unknown with respect to the *pakṣa* prior to inference, the unknownness or unfamiliarity of the probandum is nothing to be concerned with. No matter what the method of correlation establishing *vyāpti*, the probandum is unknown as qualifying the *pakṣa* prior to inference, and so with negative-only inference we have a similar unknownness in the case of the probandum itself prior to inference.

'This distinctive-in-this-way creature is from Mars, *since* it is distinctive-in-this-way.' Imagining invariable concomitance between (a) whatever marks something as of a certain type of thing and (b) any far-flung predicate we like, we can prove the far-flung predicate to occur in that sort of thing. Thus, 'Pots have ghosts, *since* they have pothood', and 'Earthen things are from Mars, *since* they have smell.' Such 'negative-only' inference would be way too powerful an engine. The problem is supposed to be solved by limitations on probandum availability. The suggestion in the objection would undermine the solution and we could prove way too much, says the *Pūrva-pakṣin* in response.

Text (TCM_T 490 and TCM_C 629) and Translation

> *ucyate. icchā-samavāyi-kāraṇa-siddhāv icchātvaṁ saṁyogâsamavāyi-kāraṇaka-vṛtti, nityêndriya-grāhya-viśeṣa-guṇa-vṛtti-guṇatva-sākṣād-vyāpya-jātitvāt śabdatva-vat. sa ca asamavāyi-kāraṇaṁ saṁyogaḥ*

kiñcid-avacchinnaḥ saṁyogatvāt ātma-saṁyoga-mātrasya icchā-janakatve atiprasaṅgād iti icchâsamavāyi-kāraṇa-saṁyogâvaccheda-katvaṁ[23] *sātmakatvaṁ śarīre sādhyate.*

Gaṅgeśa: We answer. Given that desire has been proved to have an inherent cause [by the inference previously stated, 'Desire has origins in an inherent cause, *since* it is an effect', we formulate a second inference], being-a-desire occurs in that [namely, desire] which has as emergent cause a conjunction, *since* being-a-desire is a universal directly pervaded by, [i.e. whose instances are all instances of the wider universal of,] being-a-quality-occurring-in-specific-qualities-grasped-by-an-eternal-organ (i.e. *manas* or the organ of hearing), like being-a-sound (i.e. soundhood, the universal of sound). And this emergent cause, which is a conjunction, is specified by something, since it is a conjunction. (That 'something', of course, is the living body.) If merely conjunction with a self were the origins of desire [without requiring something else, something delimiting it], then ramifications would overextend. Therefore, having-a-self, which is the specifier of the conjunction that gives rise to desire, is proved with respect to the living body. (That is, every living body is 'enselved', *sātmaka*.)

Comments

Conjunction is a two-term relation. It does not occur on its own but simultaneously in two loci. The point here, however, is that as a property of each of its terms it is not a locus-pervading property, like, say, cowhood, which pervades every part of the cow. Thus it has to be specified or delimited in order to make inference predicating it possible. That is, since a conjunction between, for instance, a monkey and a tree occurs in the tree's branches but not at its roots, the tree both has and does not have monkey-conjunction. That a single thing is qualified by both a property and its absence presents an obvious problem for logic, to be resolved by specification of precisely where in the tree the property occurs. Similarly, the conjunction necessary for desire makes us ask, 'Where, precisely, does it occur?' The answer is not everywhere in the self but only where there is conjunction with the living body. A self, we must keep in mind, is ubiquitous in size and so a 'conjunction' (of sorts) of self with a pot does occur. But a pot does not have desire. Desire occurs only in a self as connected to a living body. Indeed, desire is itself a non-locus-pervading property—given that the self is ubiquitous. So, the specifier—or delimiter (*avacchedaka*)—of the conjunction that makes desire possible is the living body.

[23] Adding *atiprasaṅgād iti icchā-samavāyi-kāraṇa-saṁyogâvacchedakatvaṁ*, with TCM_C.

The conjunction is proved by Gaṅgeśa at the beginning of the passage by some complicated reasoning centring on second-order properties, or symmetries, within the system of Nyāya-Vaiśeṣika categories, specifically, a desire's being an effect like a colour. Thus desire and the like not only demand posit of an inherent cause whereof they would be 'specific properties' (exhibited only by that type of thing), but also posit of a conjunction as their 'emergent cause', as conjunctions among threads are emergent causes of the colour of a piece of cloth. More on this after the next passage.

Gaṅgeśa apparently shares the view of his Nyāya predecessors that between incarnations a self does not have desire, cognition and other psychological properties had by living persons. Although it is disputable whether he sees a self as in every way unconscious between birth and death, clearly without a body a self has no cognition (*jñāna*). At several places it is evident that this is Vātsyāyana's position.[24] 'Awareness' (*anubhava*, which is the experiential subset of 'cognition', *jñāna*, which divides into awareness and memory) is dependent on embodiment. Though normally reborn after death, a self has no cognition etc., between incarnations, that is, not until it is reconjoined with a body—this is the mainstream position.

Uddyotakara is, notably, one who occasionally suggests otherwise. Vātsyāyana's 'elucidator' seems to see detached cognition of self as possible without embodiment.[25] Furthermore, God is thought of as having cognition without having a body.[26]

Theology aside, the thesis that the body is required for cognition and other psychological properties feeds Gaṅgeśa's analysis of 'having-a-self'. Thus the conclusion of his negative-only inference to self as locus of desire and the like is restricted to self as conjoined with a living body.

Like the current argument, which we see draws deep on Nyāya psychology, next we have a formally constructed negative-only inference couched in what are really technical terms that also have everyday meanings.

Text (TCM_T 493 and TCM_C 629) and Translation

> *yad vā, ātmani icchâdhāratā mahat-saṁyogâavacchedyā janya-vibhu-viśeṣa-guṇâdhāratātvāt vāyv-ādi-saṁyogâvacchedya-śabdâdhāratva-*

[24] For example, NBh 1.1.2, 1.1.22 and 4.2.38: see NYAYA-TARKATIRTHA–TARKATIRTHA–TARKATIRTHA (1985: 76.227 ff. and 1090–91).

[25] Otherwise, we would not have the authoritative teaching, which of course we do have, of the 'living liberated', see NV 1.1.2 in NYAYA-TARKATIRTHA–TARKATIRTHA–TARKATIRTHA (1985: 67–8).

[26] There are, on the other hand, contrary positions on this; see, e.g. Udayana's *Ātma-tattva-viveka* in DVIVEDIN–DRAVIḌA (1986: 808–09).

vad iti sāmānyataḥ siddham icchâdhāratā-ghaṭakêcchâsamavāyi-kāraṇa-dravya-saṁyogavattvaṁ sātmakatvam. ata eva jñāna-samānâdhikaraṇa-jñāna-kāraṇī-bhūta-saṁyogâśraya-kāryatvaṁ vā sātmakatvam. sva-śarīre prāṇâdimattvasya icchâdimattvasya ca ceṣṭâvayavôpacayâdi-vyāpyatva-grahāt. ghaṭâdau ceṣṭâdi-viraheṇa prāṇâdimattvêcchâdimattva-virahânumānam, icchâdi-virahāt icchâdi-prayojakêcchâdy-ādhāratā-ghaṭakêcchâdy-asamavāyi-kāraṇa-saṁyoga-virahânumānaṁ kāryâbhāvavati kāraṇâbhāva-niyamāt.

(**Gaṅgeśa** continues:) Alternatively, 'The abstract property of a desire's locus being a self [is only half right, i.e. it] requires specification by a conjunction with something of intermediate size [neither ubiquitous like a self nor atomic like an earthen atom, i.e. a living body], *since* it is an abstract property of the 'specific qualities' (i.e. desire, cognition, pleasure, pain and so on) that are both generated and belong to something ubiquitous [namely, a self], like the abstract property of sound's locus [ether, which, like a self, is ubiquitous] requiring specification by the likes of a conjunction with air or something of the sort [having intermediate size].' This inference proves *in general* that 'having-a-self' amounts to the 'having of a conjunction with another substance, this conjunction being an emergent cause of desire that specifies its locus.'

Just for this reason, an alternative analysis of 'having-a-self' [is all right for such a proof in general]: 'having-a-self' is [as I have said above] something's (i.e. a living body's) 'being an effect and a substratum that supports the conjunction (i.e. body-self conjunction) that is a cause of cognition and that has the same substratum [namely, a self,] as cognition.'

A pervasion is grasped between (a) having-breath and so on in the case of a person's own body [and others] along with having-desire and so on and (b) voluntary bodily movement along with becoming fat or thin on the part of various [bodily] parts (i.e. one's waist and so on). From this grasping, an inference proceeds [targeting a *vipakṣa* (places where the probandum is known definitely to be absent), namely] with respect to a pot and the like, which do not have voluntary movement and so on, establishing the absence there of both having-breath and having-desire-and-the-like. From the absence of desire etc., an inference proceeds to establish [in that same *vipakṣa*, viz., a pot and the like,] the absence of the conjunction that is the emergent cause of desire and the like, a conjunction that specifies their locus and counts among their causes. For, [with emergent causality] the rule is that without showing the effect no such cause is to be supposed.

Comments

An 'emergent cause', *asamavāyi-kāraṇa*, is a causal condition only with respect to certain effects; e.g. the colour of a piece of cloth has an emergent cause in the colour of the threads. Considering the cloth as effect, the conjunction of the threads is an emergent cause.[27] Similarly here with a desire, there is an emergent cause in the connection between a self and a living body.

Text (TCM_T 494 and TCM_C 631) and Translation

> *na ca sātmakatvaṁ śarīra-vṛtti śarīra-vṛttitve*[28] *bādhakâbhāvāt śarīratva-vad iti anvayinā eva sādhya-siddheḥ kiṁ vyatirekiṇā iti vācyam. śarīraṁ sātmakam iti śarīra-viśeṣyaka-buddher vyatirekiṇaṁ vinā anupapatteḥ. upāyântarasya upāyântarâdūṣakatvāc ca.*

Objection: The inference, 'Having-a-self has its occurrence in the body, *since* with respect to its occurring there that there is no defeater [or counter-consideration], like being-a-body', establishes the probandum simply by positive correlations. Hence, what's the use of your negative-only inference?

Gaṅgeśa: And that should not be asked. For, 'A [living] body has a self'—a cognition whose qualificandum is the body—would not be possible without the negative method. Furthermore, one means [of knowledge] does not vitiate another.

Comments

In the objector's inference, having-a-self is the inferential subject, whereas in Gaṅgeśa's it is the living body. Gaṅgeśa apparently accepts the objector's inference and accepts that it is based on positive correlations. But one valid means of knowing does not cancel out another, he says. What's the loss in accepting both as reliable sources? 'Those delighting in reasoning' (e.g. TCM_C 977, *tarka-rasika*) sometimes prove things even though they are already known by perception. And if one takes the living body as inferential subject, one has no *sapakṣa* for one's inference (no instance of 'having-a-self' outside the set of living bodies) and thus no possibility to prove that 'A living body has a self' except by a negative-only inference.

---

[27] See PHILLIPS–RAMANUJA TATACHARYA (2004: 540 ff.) for further explanation of emergent causality, as well as the causality section in the introduction (23–25).

[28] Emending *śarīre* to *śarīra-vṛttitve*.

Text (TCM_T 494 and TCM_C 632) and Translation

yad vā ceṣṭā saṁyogâsamavāyi-kāraṇikā saṁskārâjanya-kriyātvād iti ceṣṭāyā asamavāyi-kāraṇa-saṁyoga-siddhau prayatnavad ātma-saṁyoga eva paryavasyati prayatnânvaya-vyatirekânuvidhāyitvāt. evaṁ ca ceṣṭāyāḥ asamavāyi-kāraṇa-saṁyogâśrayatve sati śarīratvaṁ sātmakatvaṁ jīvac-charīre sādhyam, ceṣṭāvattvād iti hetuḥ. ceṣṭā-virahaś ca ghaṭâdau pratyakṣa-siddhiḥ. ceṣṭā-virahāt tad-asamavāyi-kāraṇa-saṁyoga-virahe 'pi sugrahaḥ.

(**Gaṅgeśa** continues:) Alternatively, voluntary bodily movement has an emergent cause in a conjunction [of something with the body], *since* it is action not generated by a disposition. Given that this conjunction is established—the conjunction, that is, that is an emergent cause of voluntary bodily movement—it is concluded that it is a conjunction [of the body] with a self, i.e. something capable of effort, by positive and negative correlations with effort.

And in this way, given that there is a [dual] substratum of the conjunction that is an emergent cause of voluntary bodily movement [which amounts to a general understanding of 'having a self'], that to be a [living] body is to be 'enselved' (*sātmaka*) is to be proved (i.e. it is the probandum in an inference) targeting living bodies, and it is proved, *since* a living body exhibits voluntary bodily movement—the prover.

Moreover, absence of voluntary bodily movement is known in a pot and the like by perception. From this absence of voluntary bodily movement, it is easy to grasp that there is also an absence of the conjunction [we have been talking about] that is an emergent cause of it. [Thus, we prove that living bodies are enselved by a negative-only inference.]

Comments

Here 'disposition' (*saṁskāra*) includes the impetus of a moving object and the like.

A standard example of action born of a conjunction is striking a tree branch with a stick such that a piece of fruit falls. The conjunction of stick with branch is an emergent cause of the falling of the fruit. This example contrasts with disposition-impelled action that does not require conjunction or disjunction.

The main idea behind the argument is that action that is not *saṁskāra*-impelled, not something dropping because of weight or inherently active such as wind or air (according to the traditional physics), is generated by conjunction or disjunction, which are themselves qualities with substrata, two substrata, to be precise. One substratum of the conjunction that is an emergent cause of voluntary bodily movement is the body; the other has to be capable of initiating effort and action, to wit, a self 'capable of effort'.

Text (TCM_T 495 and TCM_C 633) and Translation

> *yad vā jīvac-charīraṁ tad-avayavo vā ātma-bhinnatve saty ātma-viśeṣa-guṇa-kāraṇa-bhogânadhikaraṇâvṛtti-saṁyogavat prāṇânyatve sati jñāna-kāraṇī-bhūta-prāṇa-saṁyogavattvāt yan na evaṁ tan na evaṁ yathā ghaṭaḥ. ātma-prāṇa-saṁyogaḥ prāṇa-manas-saṁyogo vā śarīra-prāṇa-saṁyogena eva anyathā-siddhaṁ na kāraṇam. bhogâdhāratvaṁ bhoga-samavāyi-kāraṇâtirikta-vṛtti sakala-bhogâdhikaraṇa-vṛttitvāt prameyatvâdi-vad iti tārkikī rītiḥ.*

(**Gaṅgeśa** continues:) Alternatively, the living body or one of its parts exhibits a conjunction that is a cause of the 'specific qualities' (i.e. desire, cognition, pleasure and so on) of a self, given that the living body and its parts are distinct from selves. They exhibit a conjunction, [furthermore,] that does not occur in what is not the substratum of pleasure, *since* the living body or the part exhibits a conjunction with breath that is a cause of cognition, given that it is other than breath. What is not so, is not so, like a pot.

The conjunction between self and breath and the conjunction between breath and *manas* (the 'internal organ') are not such causes in that they are rendered irrelevant (*anyathā-siddha*) just by [the emergent cause we have targeted as the prover, namely] conjunction between body and breath.

To be a pleasure's substratum is to be something over and above [the other term of self-body conjunction] an inherent cause of a pleasure, *since* it is to be a substratum of every pleasure [but not the only one], like such pervasive properties as being-knowable—to use the logical style [of those who like formally formulated inferences].

Comments

This new inference contains an expression that qualifies the probandum, 'given that a living body and its parts are distinct from selves', which is required because otherwise a self would be proved to 'have a self', too, since both self and body exhibit the conjunction—i.e. the connection between these two—that is a cause of desire and the like. A second qualifier, 'a conjunction, [furthermore,] that does not occur in what is not a substratum of pleasure', eliminates *manas* as a candidate for being 'enselved', since the internal organ is not a locus of pleasure, although its connection with a self is a causal factor in the appearance of psychological qualities. Thus, of the two emergent causes, body-self conjunction and *manas*-self conjunction, only the former is key to the inference (and indeed to the meaning of 'being enselved').

The qualification to the prover, 'given…', is added because the second term of the conjunction of body and breath is of course breath. The inference proceeds based on negative correlations only: 'What is not so, is not so, like a pot.' The example, which is negative, exhibits both the absence of the probandum, in effect, 'not having a self', and the absence of the prover, 'not having breath'.

In the second paragraph, Gaṅgeśa addresses the worry that there might be deviation in the case of breath inasmuch as the first two conjunctions with breath mentioned would also be emergent causes of psychological qualities. However, they are not to be regarded as such, because they are 'rendered irrelevant' by the connection between breath and the body. In brief, without the body-breath connection that marks a living body, there would not be the connections with the other two substances.

According to both Mathurānātha and Rucidatta, the final paragraph concerns the question of how the probandum is known. The living body is known to be both a locus of psychological qualities and something distinct from the other term of the required 'mind-body' connection. Psychological qualities occur in a self only as conjoined with a body, and in a body only through causal processes involving *manas* and self. A body as so known allows us to avoid the dilemma of (a) an unavailable probandum or (b) an unnecessary inference. We know what a substratum of a pleasure is in knowing the living body as such a substratum and we know it as something over and above a second inherent cause. We know that it is not the only causal factor. But prior to the inference we do not know the self as either such a substratum or as something over and above the body. Unfortunately, just how we know the body is not the only causal factor is not explained here. The inference is framed formally, presupposing knowledge of the entire Nyāya-Vaiśeṣika system.

Text (TCM_T 499 and TCM_C 633) and Translation

> *atha icchā aṣṭa-dravyâtirikta-dravyâśritā aṣṭa-dravyânāśritatve sati guṇatvāt yan na evaṁ tan na evaṁ yathā anāśritam aṣṭa-dravyâśritaṁ vā kathaṁ vyatirekī. aṣṭa-dravyâtirikta-dravyasya tad-vṛttitvasya ca apratīter vyatirekâdy-anirūpaṇāt. syād etat. icchāyāḥ dravyâśritatve 'numite pṛthivyâdau bādhânavatāra-daśāyāṁ vipratipatti-vākyād āśritatvâdi-sādhāraṇa-dharma-darśanād vā tad-dravyam aṣṭa-dravyâtiriktaṁ na vā iti sandehena aṣṭa-dravyâtirikta-dravyôpasthitiḥ.*

(New) ***Pūrva-pakṣin***: [Reconsider your inference:] 'Desire rests in a substance over and above the eight substances [mentioned on the traditional list, earth and the rest], *since*, given that it does not rest in any of the eight, it is a quality [and all qualities rest in, or qualify, substances]; what is not so, is not so, like something that does not reside anywhere [for example, ether, which does not have a substratum] or like something that resides in one or another of the eight substances [for example, a smell].'

How is it that this is [a *bona fide* inference, as you say] a negative-only inference? A substance that is over and above the eight substances [mentioned on the traditional list] is unknown, as is something that would occur in something like that [as opposed to one of the eight or a combination of them], unless they are determined by your negative inference or the like [which is precisely what is in question].

A **Naiyāyika faction**: That may be. [What you say is right in part.] Desire may have been inferred to reside in a substance [on the grounds that it is a quality], but until the realisation of the patent falsehood of its resting in earth or the rest [of the eight], a question is provoked by a statement of a debater or questioner or by an experience of a common property such as of [qualities all] resting in something or other: 'Such a substance, is it over and above the eight or is it not?' The question (or 'doubt', *saṁdeha*) puts the probandum into awareness [that is to say, makes it available for inference, the probandum, to wit], a substratum that is over and above the eight substances.

Comments

The probandum 'rests in a substance over and above the eight substances (mentioned on the traditional list, earth and the rest)' is asserted of desire. Desire may well be known, but it is not to be assumed that self as a ninth substance is known. The inference is one of a set that target psychological qualities and infer a self as their bearer. Thus selves are not to be assumed in the context and the inference has to be 'negative-only'. A smell, for example, does *not* rest in a substance over and above the eight, since smells rest in things earthen. It is not an example of the probandum nor of the prover as precisely specified, 'given that it does not rest in any of the eight.'

The Naiyāyika faction argues that the ways that a probandum can be introduced and made available for inference are not as narrow as some apparently think. Under certain conditions, a debater's statement or a mere question can make a term known well enough to be used in inference. And there are several alternative formulations of doubts or questions—or more precisely an ordered series of questions—that make the probandum in the negative-only inference about the self 'well-known' (*prasiddha*).

Text (TCM_T 499 and TCM_C 634) and Translation

> *yad vā icchā aṣṭa-dravyâtiriktâśritā na vā iti saṁśayāt icchāyāḥ aṣṭa-dravyâtiriktâśrayôpasthitau paścād icchâśrayo 'ṣṭa-dravyâtirikta-dravyaṁ na vā iti saṁśayād aṣṭa-dravyâtirikta-dravyôpasthitiḥ. atha*

> *vā dravyâśritā icchā aṣṭa-dravyâtirikta-dravya-vṛttir na vā pūrva-vat saṁśayāt aṣṭa-dravyâtirikta-dravya-vṛttitvaṁ prasiddham icchāyāḥ sādhyate. saṁśaya-prasiddham api sādhyaṁ vyatirekâdi-nirūpakam, sādhya-jñāna-mātrasya kāraṇatvāt. na ca evaṁ saṁśayād eva pakṣe sādhya-siddher vyatireki-vaiyarthyam. niścayârthaṁ tat-pravṛtter.*

(The **Naiyāyika faction** continues:) Alternatively, from the question [or doubt]: 'Does desire reside in *something* over and above the eight or not?' [the fact] that desire rests in such a substance over and above the eight is set in awareness. Later [having concluded that it does], one questions, 'Is the substratum of desire a *substance* over and above the eight or not?' Thereby, that there is substance over and above the eight gets set in awareness.

Alternatively, 'Does desire, which resides in a substance, reside in a substance that is over and above the eight or not?' is a question, as explained above, that makes an occurrence in a substance over and above the eight known [well enough for inference (*prasiddha*)]—a probandum that is [then] proved of desire. Although the probandum is introduced (*prasiddha*) by a question, it is determined to hold [for the inferential subject] by a process involving its absence and so on, since simply cognition of the probandum [not veridical awareness of it] is the relevant causal factor [for inference].

And it is not the case that just from the doubt there would be, on this view, knowledge of the probandum as qualifying the inferential subject such that negative-only [or any] inference would be pointless. For, the inference is carried out to gain certainty.

Comments

Understanding a debater's statement, asking a question, or entertaining a doubt do not require previous knowledge of the precise terms employed. Furthermore, prior cognition—understanding of an opponent's statement etc.—of a probandum term, not knowledge, is required. Gaṅgeśa does not appear himself to accept this position.

Text (TCM_T 499 and TCM_C 635) and Translation

> *mā evam. saṁśayena sādhya-prasiddhāv api tad-vyatireka-niścayâsambhavāt sādhya-vyatireka-tad-vyāpti-niścayasya sādhya-niścaya-sādhyatvāt sādhya-sandehe tad-vyatirekâdi-saṁśayâvaśyambhāvāt.*

[New] ***Pūrva-pakṣin***: Don't think like that. For, were a probandum indeed 'well-known' by means of a doubt [or a question], there would be no possibility of the certainty about its absence. For, certainty about the absence of the probandum along with certainty about its pervasion [by the absence of the prover] is [or becomes] the certainty about the probandum [qualifying the inferential subject that is the result of inference]. If doubt about the probandum is what we have, necessarily will there be doubt about the absence of the probandum et cetera (i.e. doubt about the pervasion, doubt that blocks inference).

Comments

Gaṅgeśa or any advocate of negative-only inference would concede that the absence of the probandum has to be known with certainty to occur in at least one instance of correlation with the absence of the prover and normally with many. And if there is doubt about the pervasion from any (reasonable) quarter, then inference does not proceed. If all we know about some probandum term is that it dubiously applies to the subject, then we do not know enough about it to infer anything. And the very nature of the proposed negative-only method requires that it not be known to hold of anything; otherwise, inference could proceed based on positive correlations. Again, the old bind.

Text (TCM_T 500 and TCM_C 635) and Translation

> *kiṁ ca saṁśayôpasthita-sādhyasya vyatireki-nirūpaṇaṁ na yogyânupalambhāt, sādhya-niścayaṁ vinā yogyânupalambhâsambhavāt. na api vyāpakâbhāvāt, sādhya-niścayaṁ vinā tad-vyāpakatva-niścayâbhāvāt. na ca yadi icchā aṣṭa-dravyâtirikta-dravyâśritā na syād aṣṭânāśritā satī dravyâśritā na syāt rūpa-vad iti sādhya-viparyaya-koṭau pratikūla-tarka-saha-kṛtaḥ sādhya-saṁśaya eva niścaya-kāryaṁ karoti. ata eva etādṛśa-saṁśayôpasthita-kalpita-ḍitthâdi-sādhanam apy apāstam. tad-viparyaye pratikūla-tarkâbhāvād iti vācyam. sādhya-niścayaṁ vinā sādhya-vyatireka-niścaya-tan-mūla-tarkânavatārāt. anyathā aṣṭa-dravyâtirikta-dravya-vṛttitva-nirūpaṇe tarkôdayas tarkôdaye ca tat-saha-kṛta-sādhya-saṁśayasya sādhya-vyatireka-niścāyakatvam iti.*

(The new ***Pūrva-pakṣin*** continues:) Furthermore, determination by a negative inference of a probandum [to qualify an inferential subject, i.e. a probandum] set in awareness through a doubt [or question] cannot derive from the probandum's not being experienced while being capable of being perceived. For, without certainty about the probandum, there could be no 'non-perception of something as capable of being perceived' (i.e. where that 'something' would be the probandum).

Nor could it derive from an absence of something that pervades it [from your negative prover, that is], because without certainty about the probandum there would be no certainty about its having something as its pervader.

Objection: 'If desire did not reside in a substance that is over and above the eight substances, then, not residing in any of the eight, it would not reside in a substance, like colour'—this is unfavourable counterfactual reasoning on the assumption of the probandum's opposite. So it is the doubt about the probandum accompanied by such reasoning that renders the effect of certainty.

Just for this reason, an earlier objection is also thrown out, the objection, namely, that such arbitrarily imagined properties as 'Ḍittha' (a name normally used for persons) could also be established [for a pot, say] through the probandum being set in awareness by a doubt [or question]. For, there would be no such unfavourable counterfactual reasoning on the assumption of the probandum's opposite.

New ***Pūrva-pakṣin***: That should not be said. For, without certainty about the probandum, there could be no entry either for certainty about the absence of the probandum [as would be required by your negative-only inference] or for counterfactual reasoning which is based in that [certainty, too]. Otherwise, [there would be the fault of 'mutual dependence' (*anyonyâśraya*):] given knowledge that there is an occurrence in a substance over and above the eight substances, counterfactual reasoning would be employed, on the one hand, and, on the other, given the use of the counterfactual reasoning, the absence of this probandum would be made certain by a doubt about it 'accompanied' by such counterfactual reasoning!

Comments

A pot whose absence is known by perception to occur on the floor ('The pot is not on the floor') has been encountered previously or at least learned about through a trustworthy statement. The pot's being capable of being perceived is a requirement for its absence to be known perceptually, but so too must it as absentee be previously known. Otherwise, the memory of it could not inform the sort of perception that some call 'non-perception of something capable of being perceived'. Simply put, nothing not known perceptually could be known to be 'capable of being perceived'.

Counterfactual reasoning can distinguish proper and improper conclusions drawn using a term introduced solely through a doubt or a question—says the objector to the new *Pūrva-pakṣin*—and thus eliminate fallacious inferences. It is not true that if the pot were not named 'Ḍittha' any untoward consequence would ensue.

The rebuttal by the new *Pūrva-pakṣin* of the view that questioning and so forth can make a probandum available for inference leaves us with the unresolved bind of how the probandum of a negative inference would be known well enough for the inference to proceed, given that it is not known outside the inferential subject and that the inference would not prove something that is already known.

Text (TCM_T 501 and TCM_C 636) and Translation

ucyate. icchâśraya-dravya-siddhau pṛthivy-ādāv icchâdhāratâbhāve tad-dravyaṁ pṛthiyâdy-aṣṭa-dravya-bhinnam aṣṭa-dravyâvṛtti-dharmavattvāt pṛthiyâditve bādhaka-sattvād vā ity aṣṭa-dravyâtirikta-dravya-siddhau icchāyām aṣṭa-dravyâtirikta-dravyavattvam aṣṭa-dravyâtirikta-dravya-vṛttitvaṁ vā sādhyate. sādhya-prasiddhir dravyatve. icchā-viśeṣyakâṣṭa-dravyâtirikta-dravya-vṛttitva-pratīter vyatireki-sādhyatvāt.

Gaṅgeśa: We answer. With it established that desire resides in a substance, that substance—in the absence of a locus for it in earth and the rest [of the eight]—is *distinct* from the eight substances [on the list] beginning with earth, *since* it possesses a property that does not occur in the eight or *since* there are counter-considerations ('defeaters') that rule out earth and the rest [of the eight]—thus is there established a substance over and above the eight. Given that establishment, there is proved—with respect to desire [as inferential subject]—a having of (i.e. a resting in) a substance that is over and above the eight, or, an occurring in a substance that is over and above the eight. Either probandum [such a having or such an occurring] is 'well-known' (*prasiddha*) in the case of substancehood (the universal of substances). The cognition of an occurrence in a substance that is over and above the eight substances has as its qualificandum desire. That is proved true by an inference based on negative correlations.

Comments

Gaṅgeśa here appears to defend—and to emend slightly as well as to unpack with a stepwise analysis of how the probandum is introduced—the negative-only inference stated by the new *Pūrva-pakṣin* at the beginning of this stretch of text: 'Desire rests in a substance over and above the eight substances (mentioned on the traditional list, earth and the rest), *since*, given that it does not rest in any of the eight, it is a quality (and all qualities rest in, or qualify, substances); what is not so, is not so, like something that does not reside anywhere (for example, ether, which does not have a substratum) or like something that resides in one or another of the eight substances (for example, a smell).'

First an inference establishes that desire resides in a substance, e.g. 'Desire and the like rest in a substance, *since* they are qualities, like colour.' Next it is proved that that substance is not earth or another on the list of eight (earth, water, *tejas*, air, ether, time, space and *manas*) since various counter-considerations rule each of them out (e.g. 'If earth possessed desire as a property, then it would be experienced there, like colour'). Finally, it is concluded that desire (and the like) rest in a ninth substance. The extrapolation is from things that do not reside in a ninth substance, all of which are not qualities or are items that rest in one or more of the eight substances or their combinations, universals of substances, for example. Everything we encounter outside the inferential subject, which consists of all psychological qualities, is not something that rests in a ninth substance. For, everything is either something that does not, by nature, rest in a substance (e.g. ether, an earthen atom), or does rest in one or more of the eight (e.g. the universal of substances).

Since the second inference establishes that there is a substance over and above the eight, we also know that as a substance it is a locus of substancehood, the common character running through earth and the rest. Thus, there is an example of the second-order property (which will presently serve as probandum) 'occurring in a substance that is over and above the eight.' It qualifies substancehood, since substancehood 'occurs in a substance etc.' as was just proved.

The reason I add a parenthetical 'and the rest' to the first inference is that if desire alone is the inferential subject, it does not seem as though we could prove this of it by an inference based only on negative correlations as Gaṅgeśa asserts. Rather obviously there would be a *sapakṣa*, places other than the inferential subject where the probandum is known to occur, namely, pleasure, pain, cognition and other psychological qualities. This objection is addressed next, though instead of pain or the like an abstract property is used as an example of *sapakṣa*.

Text (TCM_T 502 and TCM_C 637) and Translation

> *tathā api icchā aṣṭa-dravyâtirikta-dravyâśritā aṣṭa-dravyânāśritatve sati dravyâśritatvāt aṣṭa-dravyâtirikta-dravyatva-vad iti sādhya-prasiddhyā eva dṛṣṭānta-prasiddher anvayī hetuḥ syād iti cet, na. anvaya-vyāpty-apratisandhāne vyatireka-vyāpti-pratisandhāna-daśāyāṁ vyatireki-sambhavāt.*

Objection: So, too, then, would the prover be positive, [i.e. based on positive as well as negative correlations], inasmuch as the probandum would be indeed 'well-known' through knowledge of an example: 'Desire resides in a substance that is over and above the eight substances, *since*, given that it does not reside in any of the eight, it rests in a substance, *like* the property, being-a-substance-over-and-above-the-eight.'

Gaṅgeśa: Wrong. [Even if the inference could be based on positive correlations as well as negative ones] insofar as one has not seen the pervasion as based on positive correlations, there is the possibility that one make a negative inference on an occasion where one sees a pervasion among absences.

Comments

Gaṅgeśa is talking about *svârthânumāna* ('inference for oneself'). A cogent 'inference for others' (*parârthânumāna*) would group desire with all psychological properties, with the inferential subject as 'desire and the rest', as explained just above.

Text (TCM_T 503 and TCM_C 637) and Translation

> *na ca dravyatvâdeḥ sapakṣāt vyāvṛttāv asādhāraṇyam. tad dhi sādhya-tad-abhāvôbhaya-sādhakatvena sat-pratipakṣôtthāpakatayā doṣâvaham. prakṛte ca na hetoḥ sādhyâbhāva-sādhakam, vipakṣe bādhakâbhāvāt sādhya-sādhakatve tat-sattvāc ca. ata eva yāvad ekatra anukūla-tarko na avatarati tāvad eva daśā-viśeṣe 'sādhāraṇyaṁ doṣa ity uktaṁ suvarṇa-taijasatva-sādhaka-vyatirekiṇi śabdo 'nityaḥ śabdatvāt ity-ādāv api tathā.*

(**Gaṅgeśa** continues:) And it is not the case that since there is a *sapakṣa* (places where the probandum is known to occur), for example, substancehood and the like [which, like desire, would rest in a substance over and above the eight], the fallacy 'no similar instance' would be committed [by our negative inference] in the exclusion of the prover there. For, the criterion of that fallacy is that an inference at fault would establish both the probandum and its absence in the manner of the working of the fallacy of 'counter-inference'. And in the current case, the prover does not establish the absence of the probandum [but rather its presence, in desire, by an inference where only negative correlations are found], since there is no counter-consideration (i.e. counterfactual reasoning) placing it in the *vipakṣa* (loci known to be lacking the probandum), whereas there is a counter-consideration (i.e. favourable counterfactual reasoning) for its establishment [by being pervaded by] the probandum.

Just for this reason is it said that 'no similar instance' is the fallacy that occurs insofar as no favourable counterfactual reasoning presents itself with respect to the one side [favouring it over the other, given no *sapakṣa* (counterfactual reasoning could suggest that the prover is either present or absent in the *vipakṣa*, but without it there is the fallacy)]—just as such is 'no similar instance' a fault (an epistemic defect pertinent to inference, *doṣa*) sometimes [only]. The inference that would prove by negative correlations that gold is made out of the fiery element succumbs to this fault, as does 'Sound is non-eternal, *since* it has soundhood [the universal of sound]', and the like.

Comments

The difference between 'no similar instance' and 'counter-inference' as fallacies is that in the first case there is a single prover whereas in the second there are two. The problem with both is nevertheless the same in that with equal force both a probandum and its opposite would be proved.

The 'no similar instance' fallacy occurs when there is a *sapakṣa* and we are unable to find an instance of the prover there. It is classified as a 'person-relative' fallacy, one that is 'non-eternal' or 'non-constant' (*anitya-doṣa*), in contrast with a fallacy such as 'deviation' (the prover's being known to occur where the probandum does not). Depending on whether there is in a given epistemic context reasonable doubt (including whether or not there are pertinent counterfactual considerations that favour a proposition or its opposite), lack of a *sapakṣa* may be a reason why this fallacy occurs or a mark of a cogent negative-only inference.

For example, 'Sound is non-eternal, *since* it has soundhood', is a pseudo-inference whose prover has as much force for the eternality of sounds as it does for their non-eternality as asserted. There is no supporting co-locatedness of non-eternality and soundhood since there is no locus of soundhood anywhere outside of the inferential subject, which is to be construed as all sounds. The wider context of doubt required to motivate inference means that we are supposing that the non-eternality is in question. But favourable or unfavourable *tarka* could change the epistemic default.

The translation of the second paragraph's final sentence follows Mathurānātha. Another possible rendering of the 'whereas' clause at the very end: 'whereas [to consider the counter-inference] there would be a counter-consideration (i.e. unfavourable counterfactual reasoning) to its establishing [by being pervaded by] the [counter]probandum.' The upshot would remain the same.

Text (TCM$_T$ 503 and TCM$_C$ 638) and Translation

> *atha aṣṭa-dravya-bādhânantaram icchâdau guṇatvād eva aṣṭa-dravyâtirikta-dravya-vṛttitvaṁ sidhyati pakṣa-dharmatā-balāt. prasiddha-viśeṣa-bādhe sāmānya-jñānasya tad-itara-viśeṣa-viṣayatva-niyamāt. ata eva asarva-viṣayânitya-jñāna-bādhânantaraṁ kṣityâdau kāryatvena jñāna-janyatvaṁ siddhyat nitya-sarva-viṣayatvaṁ jñānasya ādāya eva sidhyati iti cet, na. bādhânantaram aṣṭa-dravyâtirikta-dravya-viṣayā apy anumitir dravyâśritatva-prakārikā syāt. anumiter vyāpakatâvacchedaka-mātra-prakārakatva-niyamāt. na tv aṣṭa-dravyâtirikta-dravya-vṛttitva-prakārikā, tasya pūrvam apratītatvena prakāratvâsambhavād iti tat-prakārikânumitir vyatirekiṇā eva. anādy-ananta-dvy-aṇukâdi-yāvat-pakṣīkaraṇe 'nādy-*

ananta-tāvad-upādāna-gocarâparokṣa-jñānatvam eva nitya-sarva-viṣayakatvam, etad-anya-nitya-sarva-viṣayatvaṁ vyatirekiṇa eva sidhyati. pakṣa-dharmatā-balena api vyāpakatâvacchedaka-prakāreṇa sādhya-siddhir bhavati na tu sādhya-gata-viśeṣa-prakārikā, atiprasaṅgāt.

Objection: Right after realising that counter-considerations rule out the eight substances, one proves that desire and the like occur in a substance that is over and above the eight, just by their being qualities—by force of the inferential subject possessing the prover property. For, well-known particulars being eliminated [such as a pot as an earthen thing and so on], the cognition of the generality (namely, that there is some sort of substance over and above the eight, its precise nature not being known) has by rule as its object only that the particular (i.e. the self) is distinct from those others [that have been ruled out].

Just for this reason, [in the case of the inference to God] right after realising that counter-considerations rule out cognition that has as its object less than everything—non-eternal cognition, namely—proving that this world and the like as effects are generated by cognition proves it *understanding* the [generating] cognition to be precisely a cognition that is eternal and whose object is everything. (Thus there is no need for a negative-only inference in that the first inference that you sketch out, the inference to the probandum in general, is embedded, so to say, with the desired conclusion.)

Gaṅgeśa: Incorrect. Right after realising the ruling out, one would make an inference that—albeit its object would be a substance over and above the eight—would have as its predication content [or probandum] residence in a substance [and nothing else]. For, the rule with veridical inferential awareness is that its predication content is restricted to that which specifies the pervading [of the prover by the probandum, as fieriness specifies the pervading of smoke by fire, not, e.g. fire's being-a-substance]. It is not an inferential awareness whose predication content is the occurrence [of particular properties] in the substance that is over and above the eight, since, as not having been previously cognised, that cannot serve as predication content (i.e. as a probandum). Thus the inferential awareness that has that as its predication content comes about by means of a negative-only inference alone.

[To consider the inference to God:] Insofar as the beginningless and endless series of things right up from the dyads [though not ether, for example, or the ultimate atoms, which are eternal and uncreated] are taken as the inferential subject, what is proved [on the basis of these things being effects] is only [God's] immediate cognition as restricted to the substrata of the beginningless and endless list of things. Beyond this, cognition that is [truly] eternal and having [truly] everything as its object is proved by [another inference, namely] a negative-only inference alone. Though [of course] it is by force of the inferential subject possessing the prover property, the probandum is proved through the predication content that specifies the pervading [of the prover by the probandum]. What is proved (i.e. the inferential awareness brought about) does not have as its predication content particularities included in the probandum, because that would have consequences that are too wide.

Comments

Perception—or more precisely, non-perception—is one of the defeaters that rule out earth and so on as candidates for the locus of desire and similar properties. In a pot, for example, which is an earthen thing, no desire is evident.

Agency requires cognition, desire to do and action, in that order. Everything produced, from dyads (ultimate atoms are not produced) to planets and stars, implies agency. From all those things that are produced by the limited cognition and desire of the likes of women and men we know, it follows that things that are produced but do not fall within the limitedly-created set (such as dyads and planets) are produced by God whose cognition is not limited, at least not in the ways with which we are familiar. The inference is negative-only because the inferential subject is taken to be everything produced but not by the likes of humans. There is no *sapakṣa* but no matter. The *vipakṣa*, which consists of all those things brought about by limited humans etc., do not exhibit the property-to-be-proved, 'brought about by one whose cognition is unlimited.'

The inference does not have implications that are too wide, since God's cognition is to be supposed unlimited only in the sense that is required for the production of things not produced by humans etc. We have little idea about what this involves. Similarly, a locus of fire as known by inference from smoke seen is not known in its utter particularity but rather only in general, as an instance of fieriness.

Text (TCM_T 503 and TCM_C 639) and Translation

> *nanv aṣṭa-dravyânāśritā icchā dravyâśritā iti yadi sādhyate tadā-aṣṭa-dravyâtirikta-dravyâśritatvam antareṇa pratijñârtha eva na upapadyate. satyam. evam apy aṣṭa-dravyânāśritā icchāyāṁ dravyâśritatvaṁ sidhyatu, tasya aṣṭa-dravyâtirekyaṁ kutaḥ sidhyet.*

Objection: If desire, which does not reside in the eight substances, is proved to reside in a substance ('*since* it is a quality'), then, without its residing in a substance over and above the eight, there would be no meaning to the proposition to be proved.

Gaṅgeśa: That's true. So, too, let it be proved that residing-in-a-substance applies to desire, which does not reside in any of the eight substances. Why should that substance's being over and above the eight [need to] be proved [too]?

Comments

Gaṅgeśa apparently sees the two expressions as extensionally equivalent and practically as intensionally equivalent, too, varying only in which part of the two assertions is in the foreground, so to say, and which immediately behind.

Text (TCM_T 504 and TCM_C 640) and Translation

> *atha sāmānyâvyabhicāram ādāya mānântarôpanītaṁ tat-tad-anyatvam upajīvya aṣṭa-dravyânya-dravya-vṛttitā eva icchâdeḥ paricchidyate. jñānântarôpasthāpita-viśeṣaṇa-viśiṣṭa-jñānasya surabhi candanam ity-ādau darśanād iti cet, na. mānântarān niyamena anupasthiteḥ. ye ca icchâśraye pṛthivy-ādi-bhinnatvaṁ na jānanti icchāyāś ca pṛthivy-ādy-anāśritaṁ na jānanti teṣām apy anumānād ity apy āhuḥ.*

Objection: [With regard to the inference, 'Desire, which does not reside in the eight substances, resides in a substance, *since* it is a quality, like colour',] we take [let us grant] the prover not to deviate from the probandum considered *in general*. [How then do we get the particular content that you say is provided by a separate negative-only inference?] That non-deviating prover is informed by other means of knowledge that reflect the substance's being other than this or that. This (such a 'laden' prover) makes it known that desire and the like occur in a substance other than the eight. For, we do find such experiences as 'Fragrant is the sandalwood' [where the information carried by the visual organ gets fused with, or informed by, a memory of sandalwood's fragrance, such that there is a perception of smell without the operation of the olfactory organ], which is a cognition of an entity as qualified by a qualifier set in awareness by another cognition (i.e. by the cognition that formed the memory-impression of the fragrance which has been revived).

Gaṅgeśa: No. For, it does not become set in awareness from another source by rule.

And so too they (i.e. our teachers) say: for those who do not know desire as residing in something distinct from earth and the rest (e.g. Cārvākas who say the self is the living body or Buddhists who deny a self altogether or a student who is confused by the rival teachings) and who do not know that desire does not reside in earth and the rest, for them the inference generates the knowledge.

Comments

The objector is opposed to the utility of negative-only inference and the two-step proof that Gaṅgeśa has laid out. We could look at it instead as a variety of 'impregnated' perception. In rejecting the proposal, Gaṅgeśa invokes what he sees as the default, namely, that this kind of knowledge is generated by inference, not perception. Such 'impregnated' perception is itself controversial, especially in a debate about the self, and we had better make all of our sources clear, we might read between the lines.

At the very end of the section, Gaṅgeśa differentiates his position from the one voiced here, which is that of his teachers, especially Udayana, who do of course try to prove the existence of the self against opposition. The disagreement provides drama for the section's close.

Text (TCM_T 505 and TCM_C 641) and Translation

> *atha vyatirekī na anumānam, sarvatra prameyatvâdinā sat-pratipakṣa-grastatvād iti cet, na. vipakṣa-bādhakena vyatirekiṇo balavattvāt.*

Objection: The negative-only is not a valid form of inference, since in every case it is eaten up by the 'counter-inference' fallacy by means of [a 'counter-prover', e.g.] knowability and the like.

Gaṅgeśa: Wrong. For, the negative-only has force [and would have greater cogency than such a counter-inference] because of considerations excluding the prover from the *vipakṣa* (places where the probandum is known definitely not to occur).

Comments

For example, the inference to the self would face a counter-inference that ran as follows: 'Desire does not reside in a substance over and above the eight, *since* it is knowable, like a colour.'

Gaṅgeśa implies that when a negative-only inference is cogent, exclusion of a counter-prover from the *vipakṣa* would not face cogent counter-considerations (*tarka*).

Text (TCM_T 505 and TCM_C 641) and Translation

> *anye tu vyatirekiṇy abhāva eva sādhyaḥ, sa ca aprasiddha eva sidhyati. yasya abhāvasya vyāpako hetv-abhāvo gṛhītaḥ tasya abhāvaḥ pakṣe vyāpakâbhāvâbhāva-rūpeṇa hetunā sidhyati. vyāpakâbhāvavattayā jñāte vyāpyâbhāva-jñānâvaśyam-bhāvāt. tathā hi pṛthivī itarebhyo bhidyate pṛthivītvād ity atra itarasya jalâder vyāpakaḥ pṛthivītvâbhāvo*

gṛhīta iti pṛthivītvâbhāvâbhāva-rūpeṇa pṛthivītvena pṛthivyām itarânyonyâbhāvo 'prasiddha eva sidhyati, pratiyogi-jñānasya vṛttitvāt, pratyakṣeṇa bhūtale ghaṭâbhāva-vat.

(**Gaṅgeśa** continues:) But others hold the following.

Naiyāyika faction: In the case of a negative-only inference, the probandum is nothing but an absence and this, which is indeed not known [prior to the inference], is what is proved [on the following principle]. An absence of a prover (~H) is grasped as pervading the absence of just that *x* (~S) whose absence is proved to qualify the inferential subject by that prover (H), which [as itself qualifying the inferential subject] is an absence (~~H) of the pervading absence (~H) (i.e. H ≡ ~~H)—if something is cognised as having an absence of a pervader (e.g. an absence of a pervading absence), necessarily is it cognised as lacking the pervaded [too].

For example, there are 'Earth is distinct from the other things [on the traditional list], *since* it has earthhood' and other such inferences. Here an absence of earthhood (~H) is grasped as pervading the absence of the others (~S) beginning with water [and so on down the list]. By that earthhood (H), which is an absence (~~H) of the absence of earthhood (H ≡ ~~H), a *mutual* absence of the others is proved to qualify [the inferential subject, namely] earth. That is to say, a mutual absence ('mutual distinctness', here, a mutual absence from the others beginning with water) that is itself unknown (i.e. prior to the inference) is proved. This is like an absence of a pot on the floor known by perception because a cognition of the absentee (the pot) has previously occurred [forming a memory-impression that in turn supplies the absentee in the absential perception].

Comments

This principle about the pervasion of absences explains why even though a probandum has not been known before, so long as its absentee, or counter-positive, *pratiyogin*, has been known before, it can be proved by a negative-only inference. This means the probandum would have to be an absence. And presumably insofar as ~H's pervading ~S is grasped, S's pervading H would be grasped.

Do not be mislead by the example of the absential perception involving an absolute absence, not a mutual absence. ('The pot is not on the floor' would express a locative or 'absolute' absence, whereas 'The pot is not the floor' would express a 'mutual' absence.) The point is that the cognition of the absentee would be a causal factor responsible, along with other factors, for generating the absential cognition.

Text (TCM_T 507 and TCM_C 642) and Translation

evam anyatra apy avyāpya-vṛttîcchāyāḥ sāśrayatve[29] *siddhe svâśraye yo 'tyantâbhāvas tad-avacchedakaṁ ghaṭâdi sarvam, tad-avacchedena icchânupalambhāt. tathā ca icchâtyantâbhāvâśrayatâvacchedakatva-rūpasya nairātmyasya ghaṭâdau prāṇâdimattvâbhāvo vyāpako gṛhīta iti jīvac-charīre prāṇâdimattvena icchâtyantâbhāvâśrayatvâvaccheda-katvasya abhāvaḥ sātmkatvaṁ sādhyate. evaṁ prāmāṇya-sādhaka-vyatirekiṇy api vyadhikaraṇa-prakārâvacchinnatvasya vyāpakaḥ samartha-pravṛtti-janakatvâbhāvo apramāyāṁ gṛhīto 'to vivādâsitânubhave samartha-pravṛtti-janakatvena vyadhikaraṇa-prakārâvacchinnasya abhāvaḥ siddhyati vyadhikaraṇa-prakārânavacchinnatvam*[30] *eva pramātvam.*

(The **Naiyāyika faction** continues:) Elsewhere, too, it is this way. Given the proof that desire has a substratum (i.e. that it is located in a substance, '*since* it is a quality')—desire, that is, that as a property does not pervade its locus (a self being omnipresent, a desire occurs in a self only as delimited by the living body)—the absolute absence [of desire] has as its specifier a pot and so on, everything namely [except the living body which specifies instead desire's occurrence in a self]. For, there is no experience of desire by means of specification by any of those things (a pot and so on). But the living body is not like that. For, there is experience of desire by means of that specification of its locus (i.e. a delimitation of a self's being a locus by the specifier, being-a-living-body).

And so, not-being-a-self (or 'not-enselved' (*nairātmya*) contrasting with 'enselved' (*sātmya*)), which is to be (~S) a specifier of the locus of an absolute absence of desire, is grasped as absent in things where having-breath and the like are absent (~H), namely, in a pot and the like. That is to say, it is grasped as having that absence as its pervader (~S → ~H: the absence of the prover is grasped as pervading the absence of the probandum). Therefore, with respect to the living body [as inferential subject], an *absence* of [what we just said, i.e. *not* being] a specifier of the substratum of an absolute absence of desire (~~S)—which is what it is to be 'enselved' (or, having-a-self, *sātmya* or *sātmakatva*)—is proved by [the negative-only prover] having-breath or the like.

In this way, there is also the negative-only inference that establishes veridicality [to wit, the veridicality of a cognition arising in unfamiliar circumstances]. [~H, an

[29] Emending *svâśrayatve* to *sāśrayatve*.

[30] Reading *vyadhikaraṇa-prakārânavacchinnatvam* instead of *vyadhikaraṇa-prakārâvacchinnatvam*, with TCM_C.

absence of H, i.e.] an absence of a generating of successful effort, which is an absence that pervades [~S, non-veridicality, i.e.] that which is specified by predication content whose locus or substratum is not the thing cognised—such an absence having been grasped in the case of a non-veridical cognition—there is, then, proved with respect to an awareness whose veridicality has been drawn into question [which is the inferential subject] an absence of the cognition's being specified by predication content whose locus is not the thing cognised, by [the prover in the form of an absence of an absence of itself, ~~H, to wit] being a generator of successful effort. [And so it is an *absence* that is proved. This is the same as veridicality, the positive property, in that] veridicality is just an awareness' not being specified by predication content that belongs to a different locus than the thing cognised (~~S).

Comments

The inference is: 'This cognition is veridical, *since* it is a generator of successful effort; what is not so, is not so (~S → ~H), like a non-veridical cognition [of silver, say, as mother-of-pearl].'[31]

Text (TCM_T 514 and TCM_C 643) and Translation

> *nanu sādhyâprasiddhau katham sādhya-viśiṣṭa-jñānam, viśeṣaṇa-jñāna-janyatvād viśiṣṭa-jñānasya iti cet, na. pakṣe sādhyânumiti-sāmagrī-sattvāt pakṣa-viśeṣaṇakaḥ sādhya-viśeṣyaka eva pratyayo jāyate, bhū-tale ghaṭo nâsti ity abhāva-viśeṣyaka-pratyaya-vat.*

Objection: Given that the probandum is not known, [that is, prior to the inference, as you apparently hold], how can a cognition of an entity as qualified by the probandum come to be, since [there is the rule that] a cognition of an entity as qualified is generated [in part] by a [prior] cognition of the qualifier.

Gaṅgeśa: No. Because of the collection of causal conditions coming together that are sufficient to produce a [veridical] inferential awareness with respect to the inferential subject, a cognition arises that has the [eventual] inferential subject as the qualifier (i.e. predication content) and the [eventual] probandum just as its qualificandum, [there being no rule that a cognition of an entity as qualified is generated even in part by a prior cognition of the qualificandum]. This is like the [absential] cognition, 'On the floor the pot is not', which has the absence as the qualificandum.

[31] See PHILLIPS–RAMANUJA TATACHARYA (2004: 99–105), where the inference is first put forth in Gaṅgeśa's book, in the section on 'knowing veridicality' (*jñapti-vāda*). It figures crucially in Gaṅgeśa's account of knowledge and is discussed there at length.

Comments

For example, 'Fire is on the mountain' is a cognition with the probandum fire as qualificandum and 'on the mountain' as qualifier. Similarly, since a given absence of a pot on the floor would not have been experienced before, properly speaking an absential cognition has, first of all, the absence itself as qualificandum and 'on the floor' as qualifier. The qualifier-qualificandum relation can be converted by inference.[32]

Thus does Gaṅgeśa appear to hold that with the negative-only inference about earth being other than those other things (on the traditional list) the probandum is first cognised as the qualificandum of an awareness and 'from earth' or 'in earth' as first the qualifier. 'Difference from those other things is in earth' converts to 'Earth is different from those other things.'

Text (TCM_T 515 and TCM_C 643) and Translation

> *tathā api sādhyâbhāva-vyāpakâbhāvâbhāva-rūpa-hetumattayā pakṣa-jñānaṁ vyatirekiṇi gamakatâupāyikam. na ca sādhya-prasiddhaṁ vinā etādṛśa-pratisandhānaṁ sambhavati. na ca vastu-gatyā yaḥ sādhyâbhāvaḥ tad-vyāpakâbhāva-pratiyogimattayā jñānaṁ mṛgyata iti vācyam. vyatireky-ābhāsânupapatter iti cet, na. yo 'bhāvo yasya bhāvasya vyāpakatvena gṛhītaḥ tad-abhāvâbhāvena tasya vyāpyasya abhāvaḥ pakṣe sādhyata ity anugatânatiprasaktasya gamakatâupāyikatvāt. ayaṁ ca vyatireki-prakāraḥ svârtha eva. paraṁ prati sādhyâprasiddhyā pratijñâdy-asambhavād iti sarvaṁ samañjasam.*

Objection (by Objector 1): So, too, in the case of the negative-only inference there has to be [as you have urged, 'consideration' or 'correct reflection' (*parāmarśa*) which is] cognition of the inferential subject as possessing the prover in the form of an absence of the pervading absence (~~H along with the rule ~S → ~H), the absence that pervades the absence of the probandum: such is the method of inference. [So you must still tell us how the probandum is available to such *parāmarśa*, as you say.] And it is false that somehow without knowledge of the probandum [prior to the inference], such correct reflection or putting it all together is possible.

Objection (by Objector 2 against Objector 1): [But] in reality, the cognition [we have been talking about] is not only looked for but found: a having of the counter-correlate (or absentee, i.e. the prover) to an absence (i.e. ~H) that pervades (~S) that

---

[32] The analogy to absential cognition is discussed in the perception chapter, PHILLIPS–RAMANUJA TATACHARYA (2004: 113).

which will be [with every negative-only inference] an *absence* of the probandum [as we have explained].

Objector 1 (responding to Objector 2): That should not be said. For, it would not be possible in that case that an inference look like a negative-only inference but be an error. [And so the problem of the unknown probandum has not been solved.]

Gaṅgeśa: No. That absence (~H) grasped as pervasive of its presences (i.e. as uniform throughout a set, as earthhood is absent in water in so on) is such that by its absence (~~H) the absence (~~S) of that which it (~H) pervades (~S → ~H) is proved (by *modus tollens*) for the inferential subject. For, [in this way] the negative inference as uniform (all such inferences that are correct take this form) and as free of untoward consequences is a method of inference.

And this way [of correct reflection in a negative inference making a probandum well-known for the first-time] works only in 'inference for oneself'. For, in inference presented for another, since the probandum would not be known, presenting the 'proposition to be proved' [as the first member of a formal five-membered demonstration] would not be possible.

Comments

The outstanding problem is to account for the cognition of pervasion without which no veridical inferential awareness could occur. Objector 2 used the expression, 'an absence of the probandum', in explaining how there is a cognition of pervasion in the case of a negative inference. Gaṅgeśa's formulation, in contrast, does not mention the probandum and would thereby avoid the problem of an unavailable term. The probandum is a generalisation made in the very process of making the inference. For example, prior to inference, the probandum, 'distinct from the others', is not known in its full generality, but its counter-correlate—the distinctness is an absence—namely, the others (water and so on) are known prior to the inference. Indeed, they form the stock of negative examples that the proof draws upon. In other words, water and so on are not specified through the property having-an-absence-of-the-*probandum* but rather as presences specified by waterhood and so on. The negative inference requires a correct consideration that generalises for the first time, i.e. introduces, a new property made apparent by the prover, both of which are absences.

What a concession to the Buddhists to admit that in 'inference for others' the negative-only fails because the probandum is not understood! It's a concession because this is the nature of several key 'religious' inferences, concerning a self and God. In other words, by pointing out that his discussion has been restricted to 'inference for oneself' (*svârthânumāna*) Gaṅgeśa signals a sense of need for some kind of perceptual knowledge of self in the way that a pot known as earthen is crucial to the inference that renders definitional knowledge of earth. Otherwise, we might as well call the ninth substance proved as the locus of psychological properties something else, not 'self' (*ātman*).

Gaṅgeśa does not say this explicitly, but he uses the *svârtha/parârtha* distinction to differentiate his position from that of his teachers, especially Udayana, who do of course try to prove the existence of the self against opposition. Indeed, Udayana takes as his principal interlocutor the Buddhist stream-theorist who denies Nyāya's whole approach to ontology as a matter of properties, some of which are short-lived and property-bearers enduring through some types of change. For the Buddhist opponent, 'self' is a 'convenient fiction', bundling momentary *dharma* or properties that have no property-bearers but are causally ordered in sequences. Gaṅgeśa holds that the inferences we have been discussing are *bona fide* only as 'inference for oneself' (*svârthânumāna*) not 'inference for others' (*parârthânumāna*) and thus would have no force against the Buddhist for whom the probandum would make no sense. This is a sharp departure from tradition. The engine of the negative-only inference seems quite severely restricted by Gaṅgeśa if it is to be applied only to noncontroversial predicates.

BIBLIOGRAPHY

CHAKRABARTI 1999 = Chakrabarti, Kisor Kumar: *Classical Indian Philosophy of Mind.* State University of New York Press, Albany 1999.

DVIVEDIN–DRAVIḌA 1986 = Dvivedin, Vindhyeśvarī Prasāda; Draviḍa, Lakṣmaṇa Sastri (eds.): *Ātmatattvaviveka of Udayanācarya with the commentaries of Śaṅkara Miśra, Bhagiratha Thakkura and Raghunatha Tarkikaśiromaṇi.* Bibliotheca Indica 170, Asiatic Society, Calcutta 1986 [first edition: 1907–1939].

HEMPEL 1965 = Hempel, Carl: *Aspects of Scientific Explanation.* Macmillan, New York 1965.

JHA 1984 = Jha, Ganganatha (tr.): *The Nyāya-sūtras of Gautama: With the Bhāṣya of Vātsyāyana and the Vārtika of Uddyotakara.* Vol. 1. Motilal Banarsidass, Delhi 1984.

MATILAL 1998 = Matilal, Bimal Krishna: 'Dharmakīrti and the Problem of Induction in India', in: Jonardon Ganeri (ed.): *The Character of Logic in India.* State University of New York Press, Albany 1998: 108–26.

NBh = Vātsyāyana Pakṣilasvāmin: *Nyāya-bhāṣya.* See: NYAYATARKATIRTHA–TARKATIRTHA–TARKATIRTHA (1985).

NS = Akṣapāda Gautama: *Nyāya-sūtra*. See: NYAYA-TARKATIRTHA–TARKATIRTHA–TARKATIRTHA (1985).

NV = Uddyotakara: *Nyāya-vārttika*. See: NYAYA-TARKATIRTHA–TARKATIRTHA–TARKATIRTHA (1985).

NYAYA-TARKATIRTHA–TARKATIRTHA–TARKATIRTHA 1985 = Nyaya-Tarkatirtha, Taranatha [Chap. 1, Sec. 1]; Tarkatirtha, Amarendramohan [Chap. I-ii–V]; Tarkatirtha, Hemantakumar [Chap. IV–V] (eds.): *Nyāya-darśanam. With Vātsyāyana's Bhāṣya, Uddyotakara's Vārttika, Vācaspati Miśra's Tātparyaṭīkā and Viśvanātha's Vṛtti*. With an Introduction by Narendra Chandra Vedantatirtha. 2 Vols, Munshiram Manoharlal, New Delhi 1985 [first edition: Calcutta Sanskrit Series 18, 29, Metropolitan Printing & Publishing House, Calcutta 1936, 1944].

OETKE 2004 = Oetke, Claus: 'In which sense are Indian theories of inference non-monotonic?', *Horin* 11 (2004) 23–38.

PHILLIPS–RAMANUJA TATACHARYA 2002 = Phillips, Stephen H.; Ramanuja Tatacharya, N.S.: *Gaṅgeśa on the Upādhi, the 'Inferential Undercutting Condition': Introduction, Translation, and Explanation*. Indian Council of Philosophical Research, New Delhi 2002.

PHILLIPS–RAMANUJA TATACHARYA 2004 = Phillips, Stephen H.; Ramanuja Tatacharya, N.S.: *Epistemology of Perception: The Perception Chapter of Gaṅgeśa's Tattva-cintā-maṇi, Transliterated Text, Translation, and Philosophical Commentary*. American Institute of Buddhist Studies, New York 2004.

RAMANUJA TATACHARYA 1982 = Ramanuja Tatacharya, N.S.: *Tattva-cintā-maṇi of Gaṅgeśa*. Vol. 2: *Anumāna-khaṇḍa*, Part One. Kendriya Sanskrit Vidyapeetha Series 33, Tirupati 1982.

RAMANUJA TATACHARYA 1999 = Ramanuja Tatacharya, N.S.: *Tattva-cintā-maṇi of Gaṅgeśa*. Vol. 2, *Anumāna-khaṇḍa*, Part Two. Kendriya Sanskrit Vidyapeetha, Tirupati 1999.

SIDERITS 2003 = Siderits, Mark: 'Deductive, Inductive, Both or Neither?', *Journal of Indian Philosophy* 31 (2003) 302–21.

TARKAVAGISH 1991 = Tarkavagish, Kamakhyanath: *Tattva-cintā-maṇi of Gaṅgeśa*, vol. 2, pt. 1, anumāna-khaṇḍa, with the commentary of Mathurānātha. Asiatic Society, Calcutta (reprint) 1991, 582–625.

TCM_C = Gaṅgeśa: *Tattva-cintā-maṇi*. See: TARKAVAGISH (1991).

TCM_T = Gaṅgeśa: *Tattva-cintā-maṇi*. See: RAMANUJA TATACHARYA (1982).

Logic,
Reality and Belief
in
Buddhist Tradition

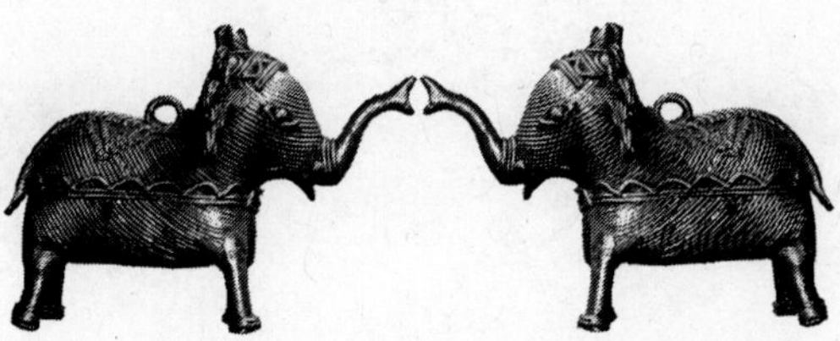

A Hot Dispute About Lukewarm Air
Dignāga on *Āpta-vāda*[1]

HORST LASIC

Buddhism has often been associated with a strong leaning towards rationality, as well as a high esteem for and strong belief in the words of the Buddha. These two features might be regarded as indicating incompatible attitudes, and therefore one may feel the need for justification.

Within the Buddhist *pramāṇa* tradition, the relation between empirically gained knowledge and knowledge based on the words of the Buddha is a recurrent theme. The passage constantly referred to in this connection is Dharmakīrti's *Pramāṇa-vārttika-sva-vṛtti* 108 ff., where the statements of a trustworthy person (*āpta-vāda*) are given the status of a source of correct knowledge. An interesting point is that the statements of a trustworthy person have been classified as inference, although the status of inference has been accepted only because there is no other way to enable Buddhist practice.

The discussion in the PVSV takes a line of verse from Dignāga's *Pramāṇa-samuccaya* as its starting point:

PS 2.5ab: *āpta-vādâvisaṁvāda-sāmānyād anumānatvam* /

There are several variants of this line. The one presented here is attested in Jinendrabuddhi's *Pramāṇa-samuccaya-ṭīkā*.

Modern scholars have interpreted this line of verse in various ways. I refer here in particular to Richard Hayes, Tom Tillemans, Hideomi Yaita, Vittorio van Bijlert and John Dunne. These scholars agree that the main proposition is that something is (or, respectively: is to be subsumed under; is to be regarded as; is classified as; is a sort of) *anumāna*. The question of what the word *anumāna* means in this passage is closely related to the question of what is intended to be identified as being a sort of *anumāna* here. At this point the different contexts in which this line of verse occurs have to be taken into account. HAYES (1980: 252), (1987: 238), TILLEMANS (1986: 32), (1990: 20 and 24) and VAN BIJLERT (1989: 122), who treat this passage in its

---

[1] I would like to express my thanks to Cynthia Peck-Kubaczek, who kindly improved my English.

Logic and Belief in Indian Philosophy
Warsaw Indological Studies 3 (2010) 521–537.

own right as part of Dignāga's work, hold that it is *āpta-vāda* which is said to be *anumāna*.

In PVSV this line of verse occurs twice. First, in PVSV 108.1–2, it is cited by an opponent in order to point out a contradiction in Dignāga's as well as in Dharmakīrti's statements:[2]

> *yat tarhîdam* ***āpta-vādâvisaṁvāda-sāmānyād anumānatêty*** *āgamasyânumānatvam uktam, tat katham.*

The line has its second entry as part of verse PV 1.216:

> ***āpta-vādâvisaṁvāda-sāmānyād anumānatā /***
> *buddher agatyâbhihitā parokṣe 'py asya gocare //*

In the first passage, the opponent's rendering of that part of the verse line he considers important to his argument, namely *āgamasyânumānatvam*, seems to say that in PS 2.5ab, it is *āgama* that is identified as *anumāna*. If it is admissible to equate *āgama* with *āpta-vāda*, this understanding fits well with the above-mentioned interpretation. The second passage however takes 'cognition' (*buddhi*) to be that which is *anumāna*.

Concerning this question, namely, what precisely does *anumāna* mean here, Professor YAITA (1987: 4) cautions in his article 'Dharmakīrti on the Authority of Buddhist Scriptures (*āgama*)', that

> 'in this context we have to be careful with the word *anumāna*. "*Anumāna*" in PS 2.5ab and PV 1.216b etc. seem to mean an inferential cognition as a result, so to speak, *anumānaphala*. On the other hand, "*anumāna*" in sentences as "*āgamasya anumānatvam*" (108.1–2 etc.) seems to mean an inferential source, like *liṅga*.'

In a footnote he then points to the fact that Jinendrabuddhi explains *anumāna* in the sense of *liṅga*. To be sure, Jinendrabuddhi's explanation[3] refers to the '*anumānatvam*' of PS 2.5b, or to be more precise, to its restatement in PSV, and not to the opponent's rendering in PVSV 108.1–2. In the same footnote, Professor YAITA says that

> 'H. Kitagawa (op. cit., p. 92) following J[inendrabuddhi], properly translates the word "anumānatā" in PS 2.5b into "its being the producer [of the inferential cognition]".'

---

[2] For the context, see the synopsis in YAITA (1987: 2–3).

[3] PSṬ 64a5.

Combining all this information, I understand that according to Professor Yaita, *anumāna* means 'inferential source' in PS 2.5ab, but that—in an attempt, as I see it, to harmonise this passage with PV 1.216—he opts to understand it in the sense of an inferential cognition when the same line of verse is cited by the opponent in PVSV 108.1. Concerning its paraphrase by the opponent, however, YAITA keeps, so to speak, to the original meaning.

Facing the same problem, Prof. John DUNNE (2004) seems cautiously indecisive in his translation of the verse line. On p. 239, introducing his readers to Dharmakīrti's treatment of scriptural inference, he translates PS 2.5ab as it occurs in PVSV 108.1 in the following way:

> 'Since the statements of a credible person are generally trustworthy, a cognition arising from them is an instrumental inference.'

In a footnote thereon, he explains his motivation for adding the phrase 'a cognition arising from them' with a reference to PV 1.216, which shows, so he says, that 'Dharmakīrti clearly understand(s) this statement in that fashion.' In the appendix of the same book (2004: 361), however, DUNNE restrains from harmonising this passage with verse 216 and translates,

> 'The testimony of a credible person is the source for an inference because it is generally trustworthy.'

In his translation of Śākyabuddhi's commentary, he renders this sentence in the same manner. His rendering of *luṅ*[4] / *āgama,* which corresponds to *āgama* of PVSV 108.2, with '[knowledge derived from] scripture', however, again takes account of Dharmakīrti's understanding as expressed in PV 1.216.

The interpretations of *āpta-vādâvisaṁvāda-sāmānyāt* diverge even more than those related to the expression *anumānatvam* / °*tā*. Of greatest interest are the interpretations of *sāmānyāt*. With the exception of Prof. HAYES (1980: 252), (1987: 238) and VAN BIJLERT (1989: 122), both of whom render the ablative with 'insofar / in so far',[5] modern scholars interpret it as expressing cause or reason, rendering it by 'since', 'as' and 'because'. We will later encounter still another possibility for interpreting this ablative.

A major interpretative difference concerns the expression *sāmānya*. One interpretation, offered by HAYES, TILLEMANS (1986) and VAN BIJLERT, understands *āpta-*

[4] PVṬ Je 242b4.

[5] For a criticism of this translation and especially of HAYES' portrayal of Dignāga as a sceptic, with which it is connected, see TILLEMANS (1990: 18–22).

vāda to have something in common with inference or to be similar[6] to it, the common character or, respectively, the *tertium comparationis* being *avisaṁvāda*. Later, TILLEMANS (1990) modified his translation, rendering it more ambiguous. This new translation also allows it to be understood in line with Jinendrabuddhi's commentary.[7] According to this understanding, the similarity is not between *āpta-vāda* and common *anumāna*, but between different *āpta-vāda*s. As for Dignāga's intended meaning, however, TILLEMANS sticks to his interpretation of 1986.[8]

YAITA (1987: 6, 8), (2005: 443, 447) and DUNNE (2004: 239, 361, 363), on the other hand, translate '*sāmānya*' with 'generally'. DUNNE (2004) refers to this interpretation twice, once in his description of Dharmakīrti's treatment of scriptural inference (p. 239) in connection with the PVSV 108.1 quotation. His reason for preferring this interpretation over the 'interpretation of *sāmānya* as "the same as" or "similar to"' is that this reading renders 'the comments by Jinendrabuddhi, Karṇakagomin and Śākyabuddhi more intelligible.'[9] In his translation in the Appendix, DUNNE (2004: 363–4, n. 10) returns anew to the question of how to understand *sāmānya*, here in connection with PV 1.216. He rejects a possible understanding of *sāmānya* in the sense of 'sameness', which would imply 'that the trustworthiness (*avisaṁvāda*) of a credible person's statements about observable objects is *the same* as the trustworthiness of those statements with regard to unobservable objects', with the argument that only two verses later Dharmakīrti would then contradict himself. He informs us, however, that the rejected reading 'appears to be the interpretation taken by Śākyabuddhi.' Discussing his preferred understanding of *sāmānya* in the sense of 'generally', DUNNE explains that on this interpretation, Dharmakīrti's 'argument is that, since the statements of a particular author have been observed to be trustworthy in terms of observable objects, this general trustworthiness may be extended to unobservable objects.' As the obvious problem with this second interpretation, he points out 'that it uses a type of reasoning that Dharmakīrti explicitly rejects, namely, *śeṣavad* evidence.' 'However', he continues, 'since Dharmakīrti is not concerned with rendering scriptural inferences fully instrumental, this tentative reasoning may be adequate for his purposes.' Indeed, when Dharmakīrti criticises the Mīmāṁsaka's proof of validity of the *Veda* on account of being a *śeṣavad*-

[6] To support the interpretation of *sāmānya* as 'similarity', TILLEMANS refers to *mtshungs pa'i phyir* (*tulyatvāt*) in PSV as Dignāga's paraphrase of *sāmānya*.

[7] TILLEMANS (1986: 32): 'Because authoritative speech (*āpta-vāda*) is similar [to an inference] in being infallible …', and TILLEMANS (1990: 20): 'Because authoritative words are similar in not belying …'

[8] TILLEMANS (1990: 22): '[Authoritative statements] are similar to normal inference because they too are non-belying with regard to the real particular.'

[9] DUNNE (2004: 239, n. 25).

anumāna, he is confronted with the accusation that he uses the same kind of reasoning in his own treatment of *āgama*. Dharmakīrti seems to accept this claim, and in accordance with PV 1.216 to 217 and his commentary thereon he points out that his approach is nevertheless the best option.[10]

From DUNNE's remarks we learn that Śākyabuddhi provides two different explanations of *āpta-vādâvisaṁvāda-sāmānyāt*: one that is rendered 'more intelligible', as DUNNE says, when *sāmānya* is understood as 'generally', and one that evidently relies on an interpretation that implies *sāmānya* being understood in the sense of 'sameness'.

According to Śākyabuddhi's first explanation, the relation expressed in *āpta-vādâvisaṁvāda-sāmānyāt* implies that whatever is an *āpta-vāda* is trustworthy.[11] According to the second explanation, the relation is such that as an *āpta-vāda* has trustworthiness with regard to empirically verifiable things, it also, in the same way, has trustworthiness with regard to empirically non-verifiable things.[12] The ideas expressed in these two explanations do not explicitly contradict one another, but they are certainly different. Śākyabuddhi's second explanation is in the context of PV 1.216, and as we would expect, it is influenced by Dharmakīrti's treatment. The first explanation, however, is in the context of PVSV 108.1–2. Here Dignāga's line of verse stands in its own right and is explicitly marked as a quotation. Would it be absurd to suspect that here, in the context of the opponent's reproach, Śākyabuddhi has deliberately chosen to explain this line of verse differently in order not to anticipate Dharmakīrti's interpretation? And could it be conceivable that this non-Dharmakīrtian interpretation is not just something invented by the commentator for dramaturgical purposes, but that it renders a pre-Dharmakīrtian understanding?

I would like to refer here to yet another reading of PS 2.5ab, which displays an understanding similar to Śākyabuddhi's first explanation regarding the relation of *āpta-vāda* and *avisaṁvāda*. In the MŚV *śabda-pariccheda*, Kumārila makes use of the expression *āpta-vādâvisaṁvāda-sāmānyāt*. In Sucaritamiśra's commentary, ŚVṬ 111.20–23, we read:

> *ayam arthaḥ—yathā dhūmâdiṣu bheda-hānena sāmānya-dharmayor vyāptir avadhāryate, evaṁ śābde 'py āpta-vādâvisaṁvāda-sāmānayor*

[10] PVSV 173.16–174.2.

[11] PVṬ Je 242b3: *gang dang gang nyes pa zad pa'i tshig de dang de ni mi slu ba yin te*; cf. PVSVṬ 390.16: *yo ya āpta-vādaḥ so 'visaṁvādī*.

[12] PVṬ Je 245a7: *ci ltar mngon sum dang rjes su dpag pas mi slu ba'i don* yongs su gcod par nus pa la nyes pa zad pa'i tshig mi slu ba de ltar shin tu lkog tu gyur pa yang yin te* (* read *don* instead of *mi slu ba'i don*); cf. PVSVṬ 393.25–26: *yathā śākya-paricchede 'rtha āpta-vādasyâvisaṁvādas tathâtyanta-parokṣe 'pi*.

vyāptir avagatā. (āpta-vādâvisaṁvādêti?). evaṁ ca viditvā vede 'pîśvarâpta-vādatvād avisaṁvādo 'numīyate, ato 'numānam evêdam.

'The meaning [of this argument] is as follows: Just as one, leaving aside the differences, ascertains the pervasion of two universal properties in the case of smoke and so on, in the same way the pervasion of the two universals of "a credible person's statement" and of "trustworthiness" is cognised. Knowing it thus, one infers trustworthiness also in the case of the *Veda* on account of its being a statement of the credible *Īśvara*. Therefore it is precisely *anumāna*.'

Sucaritamiśra continues[13] by emphasising that a statement is not an instrument of knowledge as long as its trustworthiness has not been inferred, and then gives a grammatical explanation of '*āpta-vādâvisaṁvāda-sāmānyāt*'. Of particular interest is his understanding of the ablative. He says that the word *sāmānya* has to be construed twice: once with *āpta-vāda,* once with *avisaṁvāda* (*sāmānya-śabdaḥ pratyekam abhisambadhyate*). The ablative case is explained in such a way that *āpta-vādâvisaṁvāda-sāmānya* is to be understood as the object of a verb in its gerund-form, the gerund-form being elided (*lyab-lope pañcamī*). He then restates PS 2.5ab: 'Even if one cannot recognise a connection between particular instances of statements by credible persons and particular instances of trustworthiness, one can nevertheless call [a credible person's statement] an *anumāna*, after one has cognised the universal [of each] of those two, since pervasion is possible between two universals.'

These various readings of PS 2.5ab display a variety of ideas associated with this line of verse and thereby may suggest possibilities for our own understanding of it. It is noteworthy, however, that none of the Sanskrit authors gives the slightest hint that *āpta-vāda* is to be classified as *anumāna* on account of trustworthiness being a common character of both, or on account of their similarity in being trustworthy.

In the following, I will attempt to clarify the structural position of PS 2.5ab in Dignāga's text and will reflect on how this might influence our understanding of this line of verse.

There will probably not be much disagreement that the understanding of the *Pramāṇa-samuccaya* poses some extraordinary difficulties. A large disadvantage is that we do not have access to the Sanskrit original. Another cause for our difficulties

[13] ŚVṬ 111.24–112.10: *yāvat tv avisaṁvādo nânumīyate tāvad artha-gocaraṁ jñānam utpannam apy aniścāyakatvād apramāṇam eva. sāmānya-śabdaḥ pratyekam abhisambadhyate. lyab-lope pañcamī. tad ayam anvayo bhavati—yady apy āpta-vādâvisaṁvāda-viśeṣāṇāṁ bhedān na sambandho 'vagantuṁ śakyate, tathâpi tayoḥ sāmānya<ṁ> pratītyânumānatā śakyate vaktum, sāmānyayor vyāpti-sambhavād iti.*

is that there is evidently no reliable commentarial tradition. Generally speaking, many of the śāstric texts can only be interpreted and evaluated with the help of the commentarial literature, which, if carefully used, often provides information about the background of an argument, thereby helping us to better understand the problems addressed in the text. The closer the commentator is to the author, both in terms of time and of personal acquaintance, the better it is for our purposes. And, of course, the commentator should not be endowed with too much innovative energy.

The only available commentary on the *Pramāṇa-samuccaya*, i.e. Jinendrabuddhi's *Ṭīkā*—long known only in its Tibetan translation—has fortunately finally surfaced in the Sanskrit original.[14] However, it was composed considerably later than Dignāga's lifetime. As is clear on almost every page of the *Ṭīkā*, Jinendrabuddhi's understanding of the *Pramāṇa-samuccaya* has been influenced by concepts developed or adopted by the highly creative philosopher Dharmakīrti and by his commentators. Therefore, I would not place too much weight in Jinendrabuddhi's interpretation of Dignāga, at least with regard to those teachings of Dignāga that Dharmakīrti has dealt with.

Nevertheless, the value of Jinendrabuddhi's commentary must not be underestimated. When dealing with opponents' views, Jinendrabuddhi evidently had access to and at times quotes verbatim some of the very texts referred to by Dignāga. To a certain extent, this fact compensates for our otherwise meagre knowledge of Dignāga's philosophical environment. And, of course, Jinendrabuddhi's commentary provides us with words and phrases of the *Pramāṇa-samuccaya*, which together with the hitherto known fragments permit us to gain a much clearer picture of what the original Sanskrit text looked like.

Aside from the lack of a complete text in the original language and the missing background information, both made up for only partially by Jinendrabuddhi's commentary, there might still be another point that makes an understanding of the *Pramāṇa-samuccaya* difficult. I hesitate, but nevertheless suggest that perhaps the work was not well composed. One explanation for the text of the *Pramāṇa-samuccaya* seeming sometimes less clear and less coherent than one would hope for might be based on the fact that Dignāga produced his *samuccaya* by recycling some of his earlier works. And my impression is that he often did not bother to reformulate passages in order to embed them smoothly into the new context, but rather favoured the method of copy-and-paste.

As far as the section under consideration is concerned, the work that has been recycled might well be the *Vāyu-prakaraṇa*. Śākyabuddhi, Karṇakagomin, Vibhūticandra and Jinendrabuddhi mention the title *Vāyu-prakaraṇa* in connection with

[14] Chapter 1 has already been published, see STEINKELLNER–KRASSER–LASIC (2005). The remaining five chapters are under preparation.

passages and ideas found in the said section. To my knowledge, modern scholars consider it simply to be the title of the section of the *Pramāṇa-samuccaya* we are dealing with. Tibetan sources, however, speak of the *Vāyu-prakaraṇa* as an independent work of Dignāga's.[15] These Tibetan sources also suggest that the *Vāyu-prakaraṇa* consisted of verses with commentary. This information fits well into the picture. In the section of the *Pramāṇa-samuccaya* in question, there are at least two passages that are possibly identifiable as parts of verses; however they do not belong to the verses of the *Pramāṇa-samuccaya*.

This said we may turn to the analysis. The discussion starts[16] with a criticism of Dignāga's opinion that each and every inference has a universal (*sāmānya*) for its object. One can, so the argument runs, indeed observe inferences that have non-universals for their object. To exemplify this, the inference of air (*vāyu*) from temperature (*sparśa*) is cited, an inference that is used in the *Vaiśeṣika-sūtra*s. Dignāga does not say exactly what distinguishes the inference of air from the inferences of fire etc., making the object of the first an *asāmānya* and the objects of the others *sāmānya*. Nevertheless, one difference that comes to my mind is that, at least according to the Vaiśeṣika's opinion, air is not perceptible. Therefore, if one were to infer air, this would be the first time one cognises air. Since in this case one would not be able to relate the object of this cognition to something one has previously perceived (**pūrva-dṛṣṭânusandhāna*), it may not be classified as a *sāmānya*. At least PS 2.2ab and the *Vṛtti* thereon seem to point in this direction.[17]

Thanks to Jinendrabuddhi's *Ṭīkā* we know that Dignāga, when discussing *Vaiśeṣika* tenets, often makes use of direct and indirect commentaries on the *Vaiśeṣika-sūtra*s and even includes verbatim passages from these texts. It is also clear that at least one of these commentaries is somehow genetically related to Candrānanda's *Vṛtti*. It is plausible that Candrānanda knew this *Vaiśeṣika-sūtra* commentary either directly or via intermediate works, or that his *Vṛtti* and the commentary used by Dignāga had a common source, again either direct or indirect.

Although there is no hint that Dignāga is quoting verbatim from one of these commentaries in the present discussion, I think it is methodologically justifiable to

[15] In his commentary on Sa skya paṇḍita's *Tshad ma rigs pa'i gter*, Go rams pa (b. 1429, d. 1489) mentions the *Vāyu-prakāraṇa* together with its *Vṛtti* among a list of the works by Dignāga that had been translated into Tibetan (RTZM 3a2–3). He mentions the title for the second time in a list of the works that Sa kya paṇḍita had learned from Śākyaśrībhadra (RTZM 5b2).

[16] PSV 450.9.

[17] In PS(V) 2.2ab, Dignāga argues that 'touch' (*sparśa*), otherwise a particular and a typical object of perception, is a *sāmānya* when inferred, on account of its being associated with a previously perceived 'touch'. Cf. also PSṬ 58a1–2: *tat-prathamataḥ sparśa-viśeṣeṇa grahaṇād ity asāmānya-viṣayam anumānam*.

use the passage of the commentary that we can access via Jinendrabuddhi to get an idea of that understanding of the *Vaiśeṣika-sūtra*s Dignāga refers to, taking recourse in Candrānanda's *Vṛtti* if required. In the following, I will try to lay out the structure and the content of the *vāyu*-discussion as I understand it, as based on these materials.

To recapitulate, an opponent holds the opinion that an inference can also have a non-universal as its object, as seen in the inference of air from temperature—more precisely, the inference of the existence of air from a specific temperature,[18] namely one that is neither hot nor cold.

Dignāga's first response[19] is that the opponent has misunderstood the object of the cited inference. It does not refer to air, but rather what it indicates is that temperature, being a quality, is supported by something. Since 'being supported' (*āśritatva*) is a general property, there is no chance of the object being a non-universal. As an alternative, Dignāga proposes that this inference indicates that temperature is supported by a substance. Since the state of being supported by a substance is also a general property, there is again no chance for this inference to have a non-universal as its object. This second reply gives the opponent an opportunity to begin a new line of argumentation.[20] Starting from the understanding that temperature must be supported by a substance, and moreover, that according to *Vaiśeṣika* ontology there are only nine substances, it would be possible to infer air by eliminating (*pariśeṣa*) the other eight substances as possible substrata of the temperature in question.

Dignāga replies[21] that the procedure of elimination is generally not applicable in such cases. If we suppose that air is known to exist and that one can successfully eliminate the other substances as substrata of the specific temperature in question, it would be possible to establish air as its substratum. However, it is exactly the existence of air that one is attempting to prove by this inference. Therefore the necessary conditions for this procedure have not been fulfilled.

On top of this, Dignāga shows that it would not even be possible to exclude the eight other substances as substrata of the temperature in question. These eight substances fall in two groups: perceptible substances[22] and imperceptible substances.[23] As far as the first group is concerned, the opponent supposedly uses mere non-per-

---

18 According to the commentary quoted in PSṬ 57b6, this temperature is particular insofar as it is *śītôṣṇatva-viśeṣa-rahita*; according to Karṇakagomin (PVSVṬ 66.23) it is *apākajânuṣṇāśīta*, cf. PBh 8.8–9.

19 PSV 450.17–451.5.

20 PSV 451.5–9.

21 PSV 451.9–452.6.

22 Namely *pṛthivī, āp, tejas*.

23 Apart from *vāyu*, these are *ākāṣa, kāla, diś, ātman* and *manas*.

ception to establish the absence of the temperature in question in them, a procedure that is not acceptable to Dignāga. Nor does he accept the opponent's manner of excluding the imperceptible substances as possible substrata.

The opponent's argument may somehow be outlined as follows: Only substances that are corporeal (*mūrtiman*) can offer physical resistance (*abhighāta*) and can therefore serve as substrata of temperature.[24] Other than air, of the group of imperceptible substances only the internal organ (*manas*) fulfils this requirement. Since the qualities of the internal organ must all be inferred, that is, since they are not perceptible,[25] temperature, being perceptible, cannot be a quality of the internal organ and therefore, one can exclude it as a possible candidate. Dignāga counters that temperature, in general, is observed in perceptible substances. Merely because one cannot decide which of those substances the temperature in question belongs to, it is not possible to eliminate them as its possible substrata. Therefore one cannot infer the existence of air by means of elimination. Lacking any other means, the opponent must rely on *āgama*.[26] Having first inferred a substance in general, he establishes the existence of air by eliminating the other substances. This last process is possible, since the authorities correctly gave names to things (*āpta-sañjñā-prāmāṇyāt*), and therefore there are exactly nine substances and air is one of them.

If we now look at the *Vaiśeṣika-sūtra*s, we discover a skeleton form of this discussion:

> VS 2.1.9 (*vāyoḥ sparśaś ca*) says that temperature is an indicator of air. The commentary explains the *ca* as implying that temperature is only one of several indicators.[27]
>
> VS 2.1.10 (*na ca dṛṣṭānāṁ sparśa ity adṛṣṭa-liṅgo vāyuḥ*) states that the temperature in question does not belong to the other perceptible substances. Therefore, air has as its indicator a temperature which is not observed in the perceptible substances.[28] The commentary explains

---

[24] Cf. VSV 13.17: *vibhūnāṁ sparśavattve bhāvānāṁ pratighāta(ḥ)*, and NKan 129.2–5: *nâpy amūrtteṣv ākāśa-kāla-dig-ātmasu varttate, sparśasya mūrttâvyabhicārôpalambhāt. manasāñ ca sparśavattve paramâṇūnām iva teṣāṁ sajātīya-dravyârambhakatvaṁ syāt, na câivam, tasmāt teṣām api na bhavati, ato yatrâyam āśritaḥ sa vāyur iti pariśeṣaḥ.*

[25] See VS 2.1.25: *paratra samavāyāt pratyakṣatvāc ca nâtma-guṇo na mano-guṇaḥ.*

[26] PSV 452.6–14.

[27] The other indicators are *śabda, dhṛti* and *kampa*, see PSṬ 57b6–7 and PBh 9.1.

[28] The commentary (PSṬ 58b1) explains: *na câyaṁ dṛṣṭānāṁ kṣity-ādīnām. ca-śabdān na câdṛṣṭānām ākāśâdīnām. ato dṛṣṭâdṛṣṭeṣv adṛṣṭatvāt sparśa-viśeṣo 'dṛṣṭaḥ. so 'sya liṅgam ity adṛṣṭa-liṅgo vāyuḥ*. The understanding of the compound *adṛṣṭa-liṅgaḥ*, that is indicated, here may be rendered in a more conventional form as *dṛṣṭeṣv [adṛṣṭeṣu ca] dravyeṣv adṛṣṭaḥ sparśo liṅgaṁ yasya sa tathôktaḥ* ('that which has for its mark a temperature that has not been perceived in per-

the *ca* as indicating that the temperature in question also does not belong to the imperceptible substances.[29]

VS 2.1.16 (*sāmānyato dṛṣṭāc câviśeṣaḥ*) and 2.1.17 (*tasmād āgamikam*) object that since temperature, in general, is seen in various substances, a specific temperature cannot be an indicator of air. Therefore, so says the opponent, air is known by tradition, by 'mere telling' as paraphrased by Candrānanda.

To this point it is clear that Dignāga has based his discussion very closely on a discussion from the Vaiśeṣika tradition. Dignāga's ostensible reason for presenting this discussion, the alleged inference of a non-*sāmānya*, however, is not addressed in VS. Whether the Vaiśeṣika commentary used by Dignāga referred to this problem is unclear. When Jinendrabuddhi presents the assumption that this is an inference of a non-*sāmānya*, one cannot decide, based on formal reasons, whether he is stating an opinion actually expressed in the commentary or whether he is just showing a possible consequence—as expressed by Dignāga—of what the commentary says. Since I see no hints elsewhere that this topic was treated in the Vaiśeṣika tradition, I prefer the second possibility.[30]

Next,[31] the opponent tries to save his argument that the cognition of air is an inference by saying that there is no difference between inference and verbal testimony (*āgama*). Dignāga responds by arguing that there is a difference between inference and *śābda*. Jinendrabuddhi, of course, emphasises that this is not Dignāga's real opinion. This discussion, which is quite long, ends with the statement that inference and *śābda* are said to be different from each other merely because of a tiny difference.

At this point, the reader of the *Pramāṇa-samuccaya* might ask: What should this mean? Is the difference so small that verbal testimony might be treated as inference? Then the Vaiśeṣika would have made his point and would be ready to fight another round. Or is the difference small, but nonetheless decisive? Then the alleged infer-

ceptible [nor in imperceptible] substances'). This solution seems to me more convincing than WEZLER's (1983: 53) proposal, *adṛṣṭe* or *adṛṣṭasya liṅgaṁ yasya saḥ*, which to his mind is 'the only one that really makes sense in the narrower and wider context.'

[29] Interestingly, Kanakavarman's translation renders this *sūtra* as if it explicitly were to say that the temperature in question does not belong to the imperceptible substances either (PSV 451.8–10: *ji skad du mthong ba rnams la reg bya yod pa ma yin la / ma mthong ba rnams la yang ma yin no zhes bya ba la sogs pa lta bu yin no*).

[30] In fact, it is extremely implausible that the question whether the inference of air has a non-*sāmānya* for its object could have been discussed prior to Dignāga. But theoretically, of course, the Vaiśeṣika commentary may have referred to this topic. In that case its author must have been a contemporary of Dignāga and must have already been acquainted with some of his teachings.

[31] PSV 452.15–454.5/8.

ence of air would not be an inference and should therefore not be cited as an example of an inference with a non-*sāmānya* for its object, and Dignāga's position that each and every inference has a *sāmānya* for its object would not be endangered, at least not by the quoted example. Of course, this position would contradict PS 5.1, in which Dignāga says that *śābda* is not a different instrument of knowledge than *anumāna*.

In the first case, this means that if verbal testimony were to be accepted as inference,[32] we would expect Dignāga to show in the remaining discussion why verbal testimony, as a sort of inference, also can only have a *sāmānya* for its object. One way to do so would be to reject that statements which assert the existence of air and so on are in fact verbal testimonies.

Professor TILLEMANS' (1990: 22) interpretation of the next paragraph[33] of Dignāga's discussion might be understood as hinting in this direction. I will try to summarise his explanation: 'The general underlying principle in Dignāga' is, according to TILLEMANS, 'that the object of inference is not a real particular, or *svalakṣaṇa*, but that, nonetheless, via these mentally created objects we do gain knowledge about *svalakṣaṇa*.' Dignāga distinguishes 'two types of inference', one having an empirical object, the other a non-empirical. 'In the latter case we only have a concept (*rnam par rtog pa* = *vikalpa*) and do not cognize the *svalakṣaṇa* object.' Against the reproach 'that in that case authoritative statements about imperceptible objects would just express the conceptually invented object and not the real particular at all', Dignāga would reply 'that authoritative statements about heaven and the like do not express *just* the conceptually invented object: they are similar to normal inference because they too are non-belying with regard to the real particular. For, although the heavens and so forth are beyond our sense range, authoritative people have directly seen them and hence were able to apply the words "heaven", etc.' Explaining the final part of the discussion TILLEMANS states: 'Dignāga then says, "This position refutes inferences with regard to natures such as *pradhāna* and so forth." In other words, the word "*pradhāna*" has never been applied by an authoritative person to a real particular. His conclusion from all this is to restate his general view, now safe from attack: "therefore, the object of inference is not a *svalakṣaṇa*".'

In addition to many other interesting points in this explanation, we learn that Dignāga denies the status of an inference to statements that have been made by credible persons, as held by other schools, simply by saying that these allegedly credible persons have never directly seen what they are talking about. The primordial nature, so TILLEMANS tells us, 'is an example of something which does not exist, and where the scriptures describing it are bogus.'

---

[32] This position seems more likely and so I will treat only this option.

[33] PSV 454.5/8–455.7.

Admittedly it might be possible that this conforms to Dignāga's private opinion. However, could he really have bluntly said that only those statements that refer to things he himself believes to exist are trustworthy? And how could this contribute to the question of whether there are inferences that have a *sva-lakṣaṇa* for their object or not? Besides, at this point of the discussion Dignāga does not yet speak of the primordial nature. He is still talking about the inference of air. Only at the end of the discussion does he add that one should refute inferences with regard to the primordial nature and other *sva-bhāva*s in the same manner as he has refuted the inference of air.[34] I doubt whether Dignāga would have impressed his contemporary Vaiśeṣika opponents just by saying: 'Your Great Lord has not seen a thing he could justifiably call air.'

I also hesitate to believe that Dignāga aims here at openly discrediting the scriptures adhered to by his opponents. This is because of the fact that the passage Professor TILLEMANS understands as an argument against them—namely that an acceptable verbal testimony must refer to something the speaker has perceived—is actually a *Vaiśeṣika-sūtra*, namely

VS 2.1.19: *pratyakṣa-pūrvakatvāt sañjñā-karmaṇaḥ*.

Let us look at the context: With VS 2.1.18 (*sañjñā-karma tv asmad-viśiṣṭānāṁ liṅgam*), the proponent of the Vaiśeṣika opinion counters the reproach expressed in VS 2.1.17. According to Candrānanda, VS 2.1.18 states that the assignment of names by those who are distinct from ourselves—this meaning the Great Lord (*mahêśvara*)—is a reason for knowing that there are exactly nine substances, and consequently, that the temperature in question definitely belongs to the air. VS 2.1.19, still according to Candrānanda's explanation, answers the question of how the Lord is known: He must exist, because the assignment of names is preceded by perception.

Of course, we do not know how far Candrānanda's interpretation of these two *sūtra*s agrees with the interpretation of the commentary used by Dignāga, but I think there is no risk in saying that in his opinion, too, the one who assigned the name '*vāyu*' to the air had really had a perception of it. Dignāga would not gain much in a discussion by just denying this.

What I would like to emphasise here is that Dignāga's discussion at this point still seems to follow the one he met in the Vaiśeṣika literature of his time, possibly enriching it with related ideas from the same tradition.

[34] PSV 455.4–6/5.

This presumption may be supported by another source. If we look at a passage from the *Yukti-dīpikā* that refers to PS 2.5ab,[35] the explanation given there seems to associate PS 2.5ab with the Vaiśeṣikas rather than with the Buddhists, who would not state that the *mahêśvara* and the *ṛṣi*s are trustworthy. As the *Yukti-dīpikā* suggests, the question answered by PS 2.5ab is how verbal testimony that refers to things imperceptible by common people can be related to a *sāmānya* and, therefore, be classified as *anumāna*. The answer is that a credible person's statement is an inference since it can be thought of as having a universal for its object. This is because it has the universal feature of trustworthiness (*avisaṁvāda-sāmānya*).

The argument's representation in the *Yukti-dīpikā* may be oversimplified so that it can be easily refuted. And sure enough, the argument is rejected by pointing to the fact that the universal is shared by the *pramāṇa*, but not by the *prameya*.[36] Nonetheless, the *Yukti-dīpikā*'s discussion might well hint to a certain view that existed at the time. Relying on the presented material and its interpretation that I have used so far, I am tempted to identify this view with Dignāga's reading of the Vaiśeṣikas' advocacy of verbal testimony as a kind of inference, a reading that includes their discussion on *vāyu* and expands upon it with arguments prompted by his own contributions in the field of *pramāṇa*. At a certain point, the hypothetical proponent of the Vaiśeṣika tenet would have to admit that even if the *śābda* type of inference of air were acceptable (which of course is not the case), its object could not be an *asāmānya*.[37] And this is, I would like to suggest, the main conclusion of Dignāga's discussion. To prove that scriptures referring to air as a substance or claiming the existence of a primordial nature and so on are bogus, other arguments would be needed, arguments that would most likely question their qualification for *āpta-vāda*. In this discussion, however, Dignāga seems not to have been concerned with the question of which criteria a statement has to fulfil to be acceptable as an *āpta-vāda*. The question was going to receive more attention from Dharmakīrti and from the tradition that followed him.

---

[35] YDī 100.21–101.3: *ucyate—svargâdīnāṁ tarhi katham anumānatvam iti. āha—āpta-vādâvisaṁvāda-sāmānyāt. yathā hairaṇyaka-prabhṛtīnām āptānāṁ vākyam avyabhicāry evam, īśvara-maha-rṣayo 'pi câptāḥ. tasmād eṣām api vākyam avyabhicārîti śakyam atrâpi sāmānya-viṣayatvaṁ kalpayitum. evam anumānam evâgama iti.*

[36] YDī 103.15–104.4.

[37] The statement that a credible person has perceived air, for instance, before having given a name to it could somehow be used to show that a word like 'air' or 'heaven' refers to a *sāmānya*, even if the listener has never cognised such a thing before and is therefore not able to connect the present mental image in a generalising way to a previously perceived *sva-lakṣaṇa*.

BIBLIOGRAPHY

D = Takasaki, Jikido; Yamaguchi, Zuiho; Hakamaya, Noriaki (eds.): *sDe dge Tibetan Tripiṭaka, Bstan 'gyur—preserved at the Faculty of Letters, University of Tokyo*. Sekai Seiten Kankō Kyōkai, Tokyo 1977–1981.

DUNNE 2004 = Dunne, John D.: *Foundations of Dharmakīrti's Philosophy*. Wisdom Publications, Boston 2004.

HAYES 1980 = Hayes, Richard P.: 'Diṅnāga's Views on Reasoning (*svārthānumāna*)', *Journal of Indian Philosophy* 8 (1980) 219–277.

HAYES 1987 = Hayes, Richard P.: *Dignaga on the Interpretation of Signs*. Kluwer Academic Publishers, Dordrecht–Boston–London 1987.

MŚV = Kumārila Bhaṭṭa: *Mīmāṁsā-śloka-vārttika*. V.A. Ramaswami Sastri (ed.): *The Mīmāṁsāślokavārttika of Kumārilabhaṭṭa with the commentary Kāśikā of Sucaritamiśra*. Part III. Trivandrum Sanskrit Series 150, Trivandrum 1943.

NKan = Śrīdhara: *Nyāya-kandalī*. J.S. Jetly, Vasant G. Parikh (eds.): *Nyāyakandalī. Being a Commentary on Praśastapādabhāṣya, with three sub-commentaries*. Oriental Institute, Baroda 1991.

PBh = Praśastapāda: *Praśastapāda-bhāṣya* (*Padârtha-dharma-saṁgraha*). Johannes Bronkhorst, Yves Ramseier (eds.): *Word Index to the Praśastapādabhāṣya: A complete word index to the printed editions of the Praśastapādabhāṣya*. Motilal Banarsidass, Delhi 1994.

PSṬ = Jinendrabuddhi: *Pramāṇa-samuccaya-ṭīkā* [photocopies of a palmleave manuscript]. See: Anne Macdonald's Manuscript Description in Ernst Steinkellner, Helmut Krasser, Horst Lasic (eds): *Jinendrabuddhi's Viśālāmalavatī Pramāṇasamuccayaṭīkā. Chapter 1, Part II: Diplomatic Edition. With a Description by Anne MacDonald*. China Tibetology Publishing House and Austrian Academy of Sciences Press, Beijing–Vienna 2005.

PS = Dignāga: *Pramāṇa-samuccaya*. See: PSV.

PSV = Dignāga: *Pramāṇa-samuccaya-vṛtti*. See: Hidenori Kitagawa: *Indo koten rongigaku no kenkyū—Jinna no taikei*. Appendix B: Tibetan Texts of the *Pramāṇasamuccaya*. Suzuki Gakujutsu Zeidan, Tōkyō 1965.

PV 1 = Dharmakīrti: *Pramāṇa-vārttika* (chapter 1). Raniero Gnoli (ed.): *The Pramāṇavārttikam of Dharmakīrti. The First Chapter with the Autocommentary. Text and Critical Notes*. Istituto Italiano per il Medio ed Estremo Oriente, Rome 1960.

PVSV = Dharmakīrti: *Pramāṇa-vārttika-svôpajña-vṛtti*. See: PV 1.

PVSVṬ = Karṇakagomin: *Pramāṇa-vārttika-svavṛtti-ṭīkā*. Rāhula Saṅkṛtyāyana (ed.): *Ācārya-Dharmakīrteḥ Pramāṇa-vārttikaṁ* (*svârthânumānaparicchedaḥ*) *svôpajña-vṛttyā, Karṇakagomi-viracitayā taṭ-ṭīkayā ca sahitam*. Kitāb Mahal, Ilāhābād (Allahabad) 1943.

PVṬ = Śākyabuddhi: *Pramāṇa-vārttika-ṭīkā*. D 4220 Je 1b1–Ñe 282a7

RTZM = Kun mkhyen Go rams pa bSod nams seng ge: *tshad ma'i dka' ba'i gnas rnam par bshad pa sde bdun gyi dgongs pa rab tu gsal ba'i nyi ma, rigs pa'i gter gyi gzugs la lta ba'i me long yang dag rigs pa'i gzhan phan 'byung ba'i rnga sgra*. In: *The Collected works of Kun-mkhyen Go-rams-pa Bsod-nams-seng-ge. Sa-skya-pa* (*Sect*). *Vol. 3*. Sakya College, Dehra-Dun 1979.

STEINKELLNER–KRASSER–LASIC 2005 = Steinkellner, Ernst; Krasser, Helmut; Lasic, Horst (eds): *Jinendrabuddhi's Viśālāmalavatī Pramāṇasamuccayaṭīkā. Chapter 1, Part II: Critical Edition*. China Tibetology Publishing House and Austrian Academy of Sciences Press, Beijing–Vienna 2005.

ŚVṬ = Sucaritamiśra: *Śloka-vārttika-ṭīkā*. See: MŚV.

TILLEMANS 1986 = Tillemans, Tom J.F.: 'Dharmakīrti, Āryadeva and Dharmapāla on Scriptual Authority', *Tetsugaku* 38 (1986) 31–47.

TILLEMANS 1990 = *Tillemans, Tom J.F.: Materials for the Study of Āryadeva, Dharmapāla and Candrakīrti. The Catuḥśataka of Āryadeva, Chapters XII and XIII, with the Commentaries of Dharmapāla and Candrakīrti: Introduction, Translation, Sanskrit, Tibetan and Chinese Texts, Notes. Vol. 1*. Arbeitskreis für Tibetische und Buddhistische Studien Wien, Wien 1990.

TILLEMANS 1993 = Tillemans, Tom J.F.: *Person of Authority. The* sTson pa tshad ma'i skyes bur sgrub pa'i gtam *of A lag sha Ngag dbang bstan dar. A Tibetan Work on the Central Religious Questions in Buddhist Epistemology*. Franz Steiner Verlag, Stuttgart 1993.

VAN BIJLERT 1989 = van Bijlert, Vittorio A.: *Epistemology and Spritual Authority. The Developement of Epistemology and Logic in the Old Nyāya and the Buddhist School of Epistemology with an Annotated Translation of Dharmakīrti's Pramāṇavārttika II (Pramāṇasiddhi) vv. 1–7*. Arbeitskreis für Tibetische und Buddhistische Studien Wien, Wien 1989.

VS = Honda, Megumu: 'A Reading in the Vaiśeṣika Sūtra.' *Dōhō Daigaku Kiyō* 4 (1990) 1–94.

VSV = Candrānanda: *Vaiśeṣika-sūtra-vṛtti*. Muni Śrī Jambuvijayaji (ed.): *Vaiśeṣikasūtra of Kaṇāda with the Commentary of Candrānanda*. Gaekwad's Oriental Series 136, Oriental Institute, Baroda 1961.

WEZLER 1983 = Wezler, Albrecht: 'A note on concept *adṛṣṭa* as used in the *Vaiśeṣikasūtra*', in: B. Datta (ed.): *Aruṇa-Bhāratī. Professor A.N. Jaini Felicitation Volume* (*Essays in contemporary indological research*). Baroda 1983.

YAITA 1987 = Yaita, Hideomi: 'Dharmakīrti on the Authority of Buddhist Scriptures (*āgama*). An Annotated Translation of the Pramāṇavārtika-svavṛttiḥ ad v. 213–217.' *Kyōto Bukkyō* 58 (1987) 1–17.

YAITA 2005 = Yaita, Hideomi: *Three Sanskrit Texts from the Buddhist Pramāṇa-Tradition—The Hetu-vidyā Section in the Yogācārabhūmi, the Dharmottaraṭippanaka, and the Tarkarahasya.* Naritasan Shinshoji, Narita 2005.

YDī = Albrecht Wezler, Shụjun Motegi (eds.): *Yuktidīpikā. The Most Significant Commentary on the Sāṁkhyakārikā.* Vol. I. Franz Steiner Verlag, Stuttgart 1998.

On (Non-semantically) Remembering Conventions: Dharmakīrti and Dharmottara on *Saṁketa-kāla*[*]

DAN ARNOLD

> '... a theory of meaning for a particular language should be conceived by a philosopher as describing the practice of linguistic interchange by speakers of the language without taking it as already understood what it is to have a language at all: that is what, by imagining such a theory, we are trying to make explicit.'
>
> Michael DUMMETT (2004: 31)

1. Introduction

In the subtitle of a recent article, Mark SIDERITS (2001) asked: 'Is the Eightfold Path a Program?' What SIDERITS thus wants to know is whether persons, on the Buddhist analysis thereof, can be understood as analogous to computers. More precisely, Siderits wonders whether Indian Buddhist philosophy might finally be reconcilable with the sort of physicalism currently exemplified by the contemporary research programs of 'cognitive science'. This is a large and flourishing field of inquiry comprising various approaches, and Siderits does not specify any particular instance of it; he simply wonders whether or not the strong dualist tendencies of Indian Buddhist philosophy are really integral to the Buddhist project—or whether, instead, the basic Buddhist commitment to selflessness might be compatible with *physicalism*, of which cognitive science is widely thought to advance a uniquely cogent version. Siderits argues that the basic Buddhist project is, in fact, thus compatible.

[*] I would like to thank Charles Goodman and Mark Siderits for their helpful comments on an earlier version of this paper. In addition, I would like to thank the participants in the International Seminar on Logic and Belief in Indian Philosophy (Poland, May 2006) for their comments on a different but related paper—and, especially, Piotr Balcerowicz for providing the opportunity for my presentation of that work. For a full development of the related paper, see ARNOLD (2006).

The constitutively Buddhist concern to advance a basically causal-reductionist account of the person surely makes it natural to ask whether Buddhist thought might be compatible with contemporary cognitive science. But despite this, it seems to me that SIDERITS is wrong to argue that the characteristically Buddhist form of dualism is not really integral to the Buddhist project. It seems, in particular, that the role and significance of rebirth in the Buddhist project commit Buddhists to refuting physicalism.[1] Paul GRIFFITHS (1986: 112) is right, I think, to stress 'just how radical a dualism' was advanced particularly by the Abhidharma and Yogācāra trajectories of Buddhist thought. 'Physicalism', GRIFFITHS argues, 'in any form (identity theory, epiphenomenalism and so forth) is not an option' for this tradition of Buddhist thought.

But that is not the point I want to defend here. What I want to suggest here is, I hope, finally a more interesting point: that while Indian Buddhist thought is not (contra SIDERITS) reconcilable with physicalism, central strands of Buddhist philosophy nevertheless turn out to be vulnerable to precisely the same kinds of critiques that can be brought to bear against physicalism. Attention to this can help us appreciate the extent to which the category of *intentionality* is problematic for Buddhist philosophers.[2] Chief among the questions faced by contemporary philosophers of mind is whether it is possible to give an exhaustively *causal* account of *intentionally* describable states or events.[3] It is, then, to the extent that theirs is an exhaustively causal account that many Buddhists share what is arguably the most im-

[1] A well-known elaboration of such an argument (developed precisely in the context of arguing for rebirth) comes in the *Pramāṇa-siddhi* chapter of Dharmakīrti's *Pramāṇa-vārttika*; for useful analyses of that argument, see FRANCO (1997: 95–132), HAYES (1993), and TABER (2003).

[2] It should be said at the outset that in using variations on the word 'intentionality' here, I have in mind a usage (common among Anglo-American philosophers) according to which intentionality is a constitutively semantic phenomenon. This usage follows Wilfrid Sellars in taking it that mental events should be understood on the model of a thought's *meaning* something. In other words, the kind of *aboutness* that is typically taken to define 'intentionality' is here taken to be inextricably related to the sense in which linguistic items are *about* what they mean. SELLARS's 'Empiricism and the Philosophy of Mind' can, in this regard, be read as chiefly meant to advance the conclusion that 'the categories of intentionality are, at bottom, semantic categories pertaining to overt verbal performances' (1963: 180). Cf., as well, CHISHOLM–SELLARS (1957); and SEARLE (1982: 260), who similarly urges that '[i]ntentional states represent objects and states of affairs in exactly the same sense that speech acts represent objects and states of affairs.' SEARLE (1982: 260) emphasises, however, that 'Language is derived from Intentionality, and not conversely. The direction of pedagogy is to explain Intentionality in terms of language. The direction of analysis is to explain language in terms of Intentionality.'

[3] Proponents of such causal accounts are often characterised as undertaking a project in 'naturalising' mental content, and the question is whether such a project can succeed; for a cogent argument to the effect that such a project cannot, in principle, succeed, see BAKER (1987).

portant presupposition of contemporary cognitive science—and that Buddhists are, like cognitive scientists, therefore at pains to account particularly for the 'intentional' phenomena that are propositional attitudes.

I want to suggest some ways in which this point plays out particularly in the trajectory of thought stemming from Dignāga and Dharmakīrti. In hopes of being brief, I would here like simply to suggest two issues—central to that philosophical trajectory—that are usefully characterised vis-à-vis the category of intentionality, and in ways that show this Buddhist program to be vulnerable to critiques that have identified intentional phenomena as what are most intractable for contemporary physicalists.

First, I want to suggest that the doctrine of *apoha* can be understood not only in terms of familiar debates regarding the status of universals, but more generally as an attempt at a *non-intentional, non-semantic*—a purely *formal* or *syntactic*—account of mental content.[4] Here, however, I want to approach this point indirectly. In particular, I want to suggest what I mean simply by considering an interesting problem case that is briefly addressed by Dharmakīrti's commentator Dharmottara: that of the *perceptual* experience of any (necessarily unique) *utterance* of a word. Consideration of an utterance under this description—that is (as Dharmottara says), as a perceptible *śabda-sva-lakṣaṇa*—then raises the question of how we get from this perceptual experience of a *noise*, to the discursive awareness of a *sentence*. The question then becomes: can the transition from one level of description to the other *itself* be described in non-intentional terms?

The problem that Dharmottara thus addresses represents a special case of what is a more general problem for Buddhist philosophers of this trajectory of thought: that of how to go from (causally describable) sense perceptions to (semantically evaluable) propositional awareness.[5] I will suggest that in this form, we can appreciate this case as a point of access to what the contemporary cognitive scientist Jerry FODOR identifies as the 'disjunction problem'—and despite Dharmottara's relatively brief treat-

---

[4] In my use of the terms 'semantic' and 'syntactic', I particularly have in mind the usage exemplified by Jerry FODOR. In his early formulations of a computational theory of mind, FODOR proposes the computer model as most basically meant to advance our understanding of how a process can be (like the workings of a computer) exhaustively describable in physical (causal, 'formal') terms, and yet yield semantically 'meaningful' outputs: 'Computers are a solution to the problem of mediating between the causal properties of symbols and their semantic properties' (1985: 94). And '[w]hat makes syntactic operations a species of formal operations is that being syntactic is a way of *not* being semantic. Formal operations are the ones that are specified without reference to such semantic properties of representations as, for example, truth, reference, and meaning ... formal operations apply in terms of the, as it were, shapes of the objects in their domains' (1982: 279).

[5] For a development of this point with reference to Dharmottara's revisions of Dharmakīrti's epistemology, see ARNOLD (2005) 42–48. Something precisely like the problem characterised there is usefully stated in BRANDOM (1997: 126–28).

ment of the problem, I will suggest, as well, that this way of framing the issue can help us to appreciate what is, in point of fact, a very significant problem for Buddhist Apoha-vādins. This can be appreciated by briefly considering the extent to which a line of argument associated with the Mīmāṁsakas (but one not ordinarily brought to bear on discussions of *apoha*) turns out to have some purchase here.

Second, I want to suggest that another doctrine important to these thinkers—that of *sva-saṁvitti*, reflexive cognition or 'apperception'—is important to understanding why these Buddhists may not, in principle, be able to address the issues raised by consideration of the first point. It is, I suggest, the characteristically Buddhist emphasis on *sva-saṁvitti* that makes this trajectory of Buddhist thought an instance of what Vincent DESCOMBES (2001) characterises as *cognitivism*—that is, of those philosophies of mind that take the locus of the 'mental' to be exhaustively internal to the subject, in the way, for example, that Jerry FODOR (1982) does in commending 'methodological solipsism' as a necessary 'research strategy in cognitive psychology'. It is, according to a line of argument that I will sketch sympathetically, chiefly the 'cognitivism' or 'methodological solipsism' of contemporary projects in physicalism that makes it finally impossible for physicalists to account for the semantic content of intentional states—and I will suggest that arguments to this effect may have considerable purchase, as well, with regard to Dignāga and Dharmakīrti's *sva-saṁvitti*.

Before turning to these Buddhist thinkers, then, let us consider briefly what motivates and characterises at least some of the influential examples of cognitive-scientific physicalism, and some of the lines of critique that have been developed against them.

2. The Problem of Semantics in Cognitive-scientific Physicalism

Cognitive science is heralded by its proponents as a revolutionary breakthrough, capable of solving the historically intractable 'mind-body' problem. It is particularly the characteristically cognitive-scientific appeal to the analogy of computers—to the idea, as proponents of this project often say, that thought is *computational*—that promises this.

The basic problem is familiar: human bodies are manifestly material objects, and so subject to whatever laws of physics we take to govern the behaviours of other such objects. But despite the possibility of seemingly exhaustive descriptions of bodily actions in physical terms, we *experience* at least a great many such actions as governed by our *intentional states*—by our beliefs, reasons, fears, intentions, and so forth. The question arises: How can we understand the content of such mental events to be causally efficacious with respect to the physically described actions of our bodies, so that intentional states (like *having a belief*) can be thought to play some explanatory role in our behaviour?

The 'cognitive-scientific' approach to this problem involves an appeal to the model of computers to argue that *thought is computational*. There are reasons to think this characterisation can achieve what had eluded all previous versions of physicalism: namely, an intelligible characterisation of intentional states at the same time in *syntactic* and *semantic* terms. To accomplish this would be to answer the question, put by Vincent DESCOMBES (2001: viii–ix): 'How can a mechanical sequence of mental states also be a chain of reasoning?'

Consider, in this regard, the operation of a simple calculator. The calculator's execution of an algorithm can be described entirely in causal terms: the completion of each instruction causes the machine to pass into a consequent electrical state, with the series determined entirely by the algorithm. What is remarkable is that the end result of this physically describable process—in the form of a numeric display on a screen—is at the same time also a meaningful *sign*. With the example of a calculator, then, we seem to find an instance of a 'sign' that can also be completely described as the effect of certain causal transactions. So what is really advanced by the computer analogy is a way to imagine describing a semantically meaningful occurrence (like *having an idea*) as simply the effect of a series of causally efficacious, physical events.

This basic picture is expressed by Jerry FODOR's (1982: 279) representative claim that 'computational processes are both *symbolic* and *formal*. They are symbolic because they are defined over representations, and they are formal because they apply to representations, in virtue of (roughly) the syntax of the representations.' For FODOR, then, cognitive science is defined by its attempt to elaborate this idea that states of mind simultaneously have semantically meaningful *content*, and yet are *formal* in the sense that 'they apply to representations by virtue of their non-semantic (e.g. syntactic, computational, functional, physical) properties.'

But it is, on this view, finally only under a causal-syntactic description that mental representations can really be thought to play any explanatory role. This is because FODOR thinks that a properly 'scientific' psychology can involve reference only to causally efficacious particulars with specifiable identity criteria—in this case, individual tokens of what FODOR figuratively calls a 'language of thought': representations or neurologically 'inscribed' correlates to the propositions that we experience as 'contentful'.[6] And it is only to these that we can refer if we are to explain

[6] Chief among the upshots of this is that this 'language of thought' would consist *only* in unique particulars; this is the point of GARFIELD's (1988: 51) characterisation of FODOR as treating not *propositional* attitudes (which is Russell's term for referring, basically, to intentional states), but *sentential* attitudes; that is, on FODOR's account, the propositional attitudes, 'like overt utterances, are biologically instantiated relations *of individuals* to concrete inscriptions of sentence

how intentional attitudes relate to our physically described actions; for a rigorously causal account requires reference only to processes that are (like the neuro-electrical and -muscular transactions that figure in the description of bodily actions) internal to the body.

Thus, the passages here quoted from FODOR all come from his influential article 'Methodological Solipsism Considered as a Research Strategy in Cognitive Psychology' (1982). FODOR (1982: 283) argues that the cognitive-scientific hypothesis is 'tantamount to a sort of methodological solipsism. If mental processes are formal, they have access only to the formal properties of such representations of the environment as the senses provide. Hence, they have no access to the *semantic* properties of such representations, including the property of being true, of having referents, or, indeed, the property of being representations *of the environment*.'

It is chiefly this commitment that is attacked by critics who argue that intentional phenomena cannot finally be explained in entirely non-semantic terms. Lynne Rudder BAKER (1987: 27), for example, has argued that 'description of states in terms of content at all is incompatible with the presupposition that nothing exists other than the subject.' There are several lines of argument behind this point, many of them finally supporting a basically Wittgensteinian point against the coherence of a 'private language'—though it is something like Hilary Putnam's 'semantic externalism' (advanced with reference to numerous thought experiments that basically resemble Putnam's 'Twin Earth' case) that BAKER explicitly invokes. BAKER's (1987: 41) argument, then, is one to the effect that, among other things, '[t]he identity of ... beliefs depends in part upon the language-using community of the believer; so even considered apart from semantic properties of truth and reference, such beliefs are not wholly "in the head." Therefore, if behavior is to be explained only by what is in the head, it is not to be explained by belief.'

The physicalist's case only becomes more problematic if we then factor in the additional 'semantic properties of truth and reference'—as we must if his own analysis is to be taken as possibly true.[7] The argument here is that intentional descriptions

tokens' (my emphasis). The 'objects' of intentional states, then, are on this account nothing like, say, Fregean 'thoughts' or Husserlian '*noemata*' (which are both fundamentally *abstract* ideas, akin to 'propositions'); rather, the objects of intentional states are invariably *particular*. Dharmakīrti, as we will see, is after the same thing, and emphasises, in his account of the cognitive 'representations' (*pratibhāsa*) that are produced by perception, that they, like their putatively object referents, are *sva-lakṣaṇa*s. More on this in due course.

[7] The argument that the intentionality of mental content thus necessarily involves the idea of *reference* is one that is made by SELLARS in the section of his 'Empiricism and the Philosophy of Mind' devoted to considering 'The logic of "looks".' Against characteristically representationalist attempts to show that knowledge is built on the foundations of what incorrigibly *seems* to a subject to be the case, SELLARS (1963: 142) argues that '*being red* is logically prior, is a logically simpler

are presupposed *even by those accounts that aim to explain away intentionality*. Thus, it is not a trivial point to ask what analysis we are to give, on the cognitivist's own account, of the phenomenon of giving reasons in support of a belief. Suppose, for example, that we want to give reasons to justify the belief that *beliefs are reducible to brain states*. If the claim itself is true, what difference can it be thought to make to adduce reasons for it? What could it mean, in other words, for someone to *understand the meaning* of a cognitive scientist's argument, given that intentional states like 'understanding' are said by this program to consist in the kinds of physical events that, *ex hypothesi*, do not *mean* anything at all? To press this question is basically to make a transcendental argument—one to the effect that intentional descriptions are necessarily presupposed even by the very arguments that claim to explain them away.[8]

While it may yet be—as SIDERITS (2001: 307) says—that contemporary cognitive-scientific iterations of physicalism are 'more difficult to resist' than earlier versions, these lines of critique make clear, at least, the kinds of problems that it is in principle difficult for physicalist accounts of mental content to accommodate. Thus, intentionally described situations—like *being persuaded by an argument* or *believing in physicalism*—may be intractable even for those physicalists who have suggestively exploited computer analogies. Physicalists can here be said to face a dilemma: it is arguably the case that the semantic content of mental events (the description of what it is that intentional states are *about*) necessarily involves factors external to the subject, such as truth conditions and the norms of a linguistic community; but to the extent that FODOR rightly takes a purely formal (causal, syntactic, computational) description of mental tokens to compel 'methodological solipsism', such physicalists cannot consider all of the factors that thus constitute mental content as being *about* what it's about. The failure thus to vindicate intentionally described mental content cannot, however, coherently be taken to show that such semantic content is superfluous; for the very attempt to *argue* this necessarily turns out to presuppose intentional descriptions. And if that is right, then it is not intentional descriptions that are dispensable; rather, it is putatively exhaustive causal explanations thereof that we can coherently do without.

---

notion, than *looking red*'—given which, 'it just won't do to say that *x is red* is analysable in terms of *x looks red to y*.' FODOR (1982: 279) can be understood to refuse just this notion with his contention that what is required is an account of the mental that involves only terms 'that are specified without reference to such semantic properties of representations as, for example, truth, reference, and meaning.'

[8] This is the basic argument in Part II of BAKER (1987); see also GARFIELD (1988), whose sixth chapter comprises a similar approach.

3. Buddhist Epistemology and the Disjunction Problem

Let us now consider whether these lines of arguments against the program of cognitive-scientific physicalism have any purchase against the Buddhist tradition of thought stemming from Dignāga and Dharmakīrti—and thus, whether this Buddhist program might, despite its clear rejection of physicalism, share something of the deep structure of physicalist arguments. Let me begin by briefly characterising the epistemological and ontological commitments that create the conceptual problems to be addressed by the Buddhist doctrine of *apoha*—which, I have said, I propose we understand not simply as an account of the referents of words, but more generally as a non-intentional, non-semantic account of mental content.

As is well known to students of Indian philosophy, Dignāga and Dharmakīrti admit only two reliable epistemic warrants, i.e. two *pramāṇa*s: perception and inference.[9] These have as their respective objects the only two kinds of things that are held by these Buddhists to exist: 'unique particulars' (*sva-lakṣaṇa*s) and 'abstractions' (*sāmānya-lakṣaṇa*s). Only the former, though, are to be admitted into a final ontology—in characteristically Buddhist terms, only these are 'ultimately existent' (*paramârtha-sat*), whereas abstractions are merely 'conventionally existent' (*saṁvṛti-sat*). And what qualifies unique particulars as thus 'real', on Dharmakīrti's view, is that they alone possess causal efficacy.[10]

To the ontological claim that only causally efficacious particulars are 'real', there is the epistemological corollary that only cognitions that bear on (that are *caused by*) such particulars are finally warranted. More precisely, only cognitions that are themselves the *effects* of causally efficacious particulars[11] can be said to be (in Dharmakīrti's term) 'inerrant' (*abhrānta*). This is the point advanced by the claim——made alike by Dignāga and Dharmakīrti—that perception is constitutively 'free

[9] For a fuller development of my understanding of the epistemology of Dignāga and Dharmakīrti (and of its problems), see ARNOLD (2005: Part I).

[10] So, for example, PV_I 3.3, p. 112:

> *artha-kriyā-samarthaṁ yat tad atra paramârtha-sat /*
> *anyat saṁvṛti-sat proktaṁ te sva-sāmānya-lakṣaṇe //*

[11] See, for example, PV_I 3.224ab, p 186:

> *hetu-bhāvād ṛtte nânyā grāhyatā nāma kācana /*
>
> 'Other than being a *cause*, there is nothing at all that can be called being *apprehendable*.'

As we will see, it is finally only subjectively occurrent cognitions that are the relevant 'effects' thus produced—a point of great significance for understanding Dharmakīrti's project.

of conceptual elaboration' (*kalpanâpoḍha*). The 'conceptual elaboration' that perceptual cognitions thus lack consists, we might say, in *propositional attitudes*—in 'association with name and genus and so forth' (as Dignāga defined it), or (with Dharmakīrti) in thought whose phenomenological content is suitable for association with such linguistic items.[12]

Dignāga and Dharmakīrti thus maintain that discursive thought constitutively involves reference to things that are *not actually present*. A genuine 'perception' of, say, a book will consist only in a sensory impingement caused by some particular object, yielding a cognition whose appearance is itself *caused* by the object. But if one then entertains the propositional belief that 'this is a book', one's thought now includes reference to something not actually present—for example, the generic image of a book, knowledge of the conventions for the use of the word 'book', and so forth. What distinguishes perceptual encounters as uniquely warranted, then, is that only these cognitions are *causally constrained by actually present objects*. Inferential cognitions are not so constrained, and therefore 'add' something to the uninterpreted data of perception. This amounts to a radical critique of naive realism; for insofar as perceptual cognitions are really thus constrained only by fleeting sense data, it turns out that whenever we think we experience a more or less enduring token *of some type*, we are deeply mistaken about what is really present.[13]

I do not think it too much of a stretch to understand this program as roughly analogous to cognitive science at least in the minimal sense that we have here a systematic *redescription* of our common-sense intuitions about our epistemic situation. Thus, while we typically experience ourselves as confronted with a world of intentionally described objects—which is to say, a world of things *under familiar descriptions*—the claim here being made is that objects *as thus described* do not really exist; rather, we are only really warranted in believing there to be uniquely particular and fleeting sensations, such as will, by definition, not admit of any predication.[14]

Moreover, this Buddhist approach thus admits of comparison with cognitive-scientific physicalism insofar as the privileged level of description involves only *causal* transactions; just as on FODOR's account it is finally only under a formal or

[12] So, for example, NB 1.5, p. 47: *abhilāpa-saṁsarga-yogya-pratibhāsā pratītiḥ kalpanā*.——'Conception is a thought whose phenomenological content is suitable for association with discourse.'

[13] Here, it is helpful to recall the basically Buddhist point that is ultimately advanced by this epistemology: all that is finally warranted by the kind of cognition that is uniquely in contact with really existent phenomena is the conclusion that *there are sensations*—which does not also warrant the inferential belief that these must be the states of a 'self.'

[14] This is what Dignāga meant in saying of *sva-lakṣaṇa*s only that they are 'inexpressible' (*avyapadeśya*); see HATTORI (1968: 24, and p. 81, n. 1.19).

'syntactic' description that mental representations can be thought to have any explanatory role, so, too, it is affirmed by Dharmakīrti that only the world of causally efficacious sensibilia consists in 'ultimately existent' (*paramârtha-sat*) things. And the problem for Dharmakīrti, just as for FODOR, is whether and how the non-privileged level of description—the level consisting in those 'conventionally' described things (*saṁvṛti-sat*) that involve the kinds of 'abstractions' (*sāmānya-lakṣaṇa*s) that alone are *semantically* evaluable—can be brought into contact with this.

But here is the problem: if perceptual cognition is defined by its independence from conceptual thought, and if the latter is held to be the point of ingress for cognitive error, then how could one ever be certain *that* the (propositional) judgement that follows a perception is in fact properly related to the perception in question? More precisely, if perception's privileged status is a function of its having been caused by its object, and if discursive cognitions are defined by their adding something, then how can one ever be sure that what one is thinking *about*, when entertaining some proposition, is in any sense the same thing that was *perceived*? How can perceptual data—which is exhaustively explicable in non-intentional (causal, formal, or syntactic) terms—be made available as the content of thought? In the terms suggested by FODOR, then, we have here a process that meets the *formality* condition, but it is not clear how it can also meet the *content* condition.

One way to address this problem is to redescribe thought and its contents in the same kind of non-intentional (causal, formal, or syntactic) terms here used to explain perception. And this is, I suggest, precisely the kind of answer that is elaborated by Dignāga and Dharmakīrti and their followers in the form of the doctrine of *apoha*. While space will not permit me here to give a full account of this as an attempt at an entirely non-intentional re-description of intentional phenomena,[15] I want to suggest an oblique but revealing angle of approach to the issue. If the doctrine of *apoha* is to succeed at what I thus take to be its aims, it must provide an account that explains the conceptual construction of (semantic) mental content without any reference to semantic descriptions (since these are what this account proposes to explain)—it must, instead, finally make reference only to *subjectively appearing particulars*[16] in explaining how it is that the abstractions or universals that are the objects of thought are constructed.

One problem for such an account is that it turns out to be very difficult at once to provide a non-semantic description of the comprehension of a linguistic utterance, *and* to distinguish that from a perception. We can see this if we consider that any

[15] See ARNOLD (2006) for a fuller development of many of the relevant points.

[16] The significance of its finally being *subjectively appearing* particulars that are in play here will be considered in due course.

particular utterance of a word or sentence is—considered as a unique, perceptible acoustic event—in a sense precisely the kind of thing of which we can (these Buddhists have urged) have a wholly non-conceptual *perception*. Given, then, that the utterance of a sentence can be appropriately described as a perceptible acoustic event that, as such, is no different from the sound of, say, thunder, the task is to explain how in one such case (but not the other) the sound also *means* something——which involves the further question of how (or whether) the transition from one level of description to the other can *itself* be described in non-intentional terms. That is, the case of a speaker's uttering a sentence presents us with an event that is describable in two very different kinds of terms: what is 'conventionally' (*saṁvṛtitas*) taken as the expression of a meaningful proposition is, 'ultimately' (*paramârthatas*), nothing but the causation of particular noises that in turn have among their effects the production of certain cognitions. But insofar as it is only terms from the latter level of description that have a place in the final ontology (which is just what it means to characterise them as *paramârtha-sat*), the *relation between* these two descriptions must itself be explicable in terms that are *paramârtha-sat*—which is just to say that the process of understanding *sāmānya-lakṣaṇa*s must, as Apoha-vādins want to argue, finally be explicable with reference only to *sva-lakṣaṇa*s.

The problem I thus pose is closely related to what Jerry FODOR (1990: 89) has identified as the 'disjunction problem', which arises from the fact that 'it's just not true that Normally [sic] caused intentional states ipso facto mean whatever causes them.' That this is a problem is clear from attempts to give thoroughly causal accounts even of perception; when, for example, one has a visual perception of a tree, all manner of brain events are surely among the *causes* of the resultant cognition——but these are not among the things that we say are thus *seen*. A tenable causal theory of perception requires, then, that there be some principled way to explain which of the relevant causes of any perception is at the same time *what is perceived*.

If (as I think is the case) it turns out to be a not entirely straightforward matter to provide such an account, the problem is even more difficult in the case of the specifically semantic version of the disjunction problem: 'What the disjunction problem is really about deep down is the difference between *meaning* and *information* ... Information is tied to aetiology in a way that meaning isn't ... By contrast, *the meaning of a symbol is one of the things that all of its tokens have in common, however they may happen to be caused. All* 'cow' tokens mean *cow*; if they didn't, they wouldn't be 'cow' tokens' (FODOR (1990: 90); emphasis original). In this way, FODOR distinguishes between, as it were, artefacts that are efficiently precipitated by their causes ('information'), and those that somehow manage to 'refer' to something other (or something *more*) than the particulars that cause them; the latter he calls conveyors of 'meaning', and he characterises the relatively unconstrained nature of these in terms of the 'robustness' of signifying tokens.

The problem that FODOR thus identifies is the same as the problem of how innumerable uniquely particular acoustic events—such as those that occur when countless speakers of English make the sound conventionally represented by the letters *c-o-w*—can commonly be taken as utterances *of the same word.* Insofar as the uniqueness (the contingency, temporality) of any such event can (as with anything capable of being represented in space and time) be understood to consist in its being causally describable, the problem is invariably that of how to relate the causal level of description to the intentionally describable abstraction.[17]

Something like the same question is anticipated by Dharmakīrti's commentator Dharmottara in his commentary to verse 5 of the first chapter of Dharmakīrti's *Nyāya-bindu.* It is in this verse that Dharmakīrti stipulates that the 'conceptual thought' (*kalpanā*) of which perception is constitutively devoid consists in 'a thought whose phenomenological content is suitable for association with discourse.'[18] This definition significantly revises Dignāga's earlier characterisation of conceptual thought as simply 'association with name and genus and so forth', making it possible to infer conceptual thought even in pre- or non-linguistic creatures—even, that is, in the absence of any *actual* use of language.

But it raises various questions to argue, in this way, that constitutively discursive thought can be inferred even in the absence of any overt use of discourse. Dharmottara elaborates on the situation:

---

[17] The problem here characterised is one of the most prominently recurrent issues addressed in HUSSERL's *Logical Investigations.* 'What in general', HUSSERL (1970: 567 [Investigation V, §13]) asks, 'is the surplus element distinguishing the understanding of a symbolically functioning expression from the uncomprehended verbal sound?' And his answer is: '…we do not, *qua* expressing it, live in the acts constituting the expression as a physical object—we are not interested in this object—but we live in the acts which give it sense: we are exclusively *turned* to the object that appears in such acts, we *aim* at it, we *mean* it in the special, *pregnant* sense' (1970: 584 [Investigation V, §19]). Again, 'The ideality of the relationship between expression and meaning is at once plain in regard to both its sides, inasmuch as, when we ask for the meaning of an expression, e.g. "quadratic remainder", we are naturally not referring to the sound-pattern uttered here and now, the vanishing noise that can never recur identically: we mean the expression *in specie.* "Quadratic remainder" is the same expression by whomsoever uttered. The same holds of talk about the expression's meaning, which naturally does not refer to some meaning-conferring experience.' (1970: 284 [Investigation I, §11]). HUSSERL's point here (which is an expression of his ongoing critique of psychologism in logic) could, I think, serve just as well as a critique of Dharmakīrti's account of meaning, according to which utterances *are*, in the final analysis, to be understood as referring to 'some meaning-conferring experience'; more on this shortly.

[18] See n. L.

> 'There are some thoughts whose phenomenological appearance (*ābhāsa*) is [actually] associated with discourse, such as the conception of a jar on the part of someone by whom the [relevant linguistic] convention has been learned—[such a thought is one] whose phenomenological content [specifically] involves the word "jar". But some [thoughts] have phenomenological content that is [simply] *suitable* for association with discourse, even though [they are in fact] un-associated with discourse—like the conception of a child by whom the [relevant linguistic conception] has not been learned.'[19]

While this passage raises various questions, I am most interested in Dharmottara's references to those who have learned the conventional usage of a word whose utterance is being heard (those who are, as Dharmottara says, *vyutpanna-saṁketa*), and those who have not. Dharmottara recurs to this idea when he gets around to considering the following objection:

> 'An auditory cognition [that is, a *sensory perception* of the auditory sort] apprehends a unique particular which is a sound. And since some audible particulars are *referents* and some are *signifiers*,[20] [it therefore follows that cognition of an audible particular] would be one whose phenomenological content is suitable for association with discourse—and thus, it would be *conceptual*.'[21]

The objection, then, is that insofar as it is a unique, perceptible acoustic event, any particular utterance of a word would seem to count as a *sva-lakṣaṇa*—that is, as the kind of unique particular that can be the object of a constitutively non-conceptual perception; and yet, insofar as the thing that is thus uttered is a *word*, it seems that we must allow that we here have a cognition that, though describable as a perception, is *conceptual*.[22] In order to avoid this unwanted consequence, Dharmottara must find

[19] NBṬ, p. 48: *tatra kācit pratītir abhilāpa-saṁsṛṣṭâbhāsā bhavati, yathā vyutpanna-saṁketasya ghaṭârtha-kalpanā ghaṭa-śabda-saṁsṛṣṭârthâvabhāsā bhavati. kācit tv abhilāpenâsaṁsṛṣṭâpy abhilāpa-saṁsarga-yogyâbhāsā bhavati, yathā bālakasyâvyutpanna-saṁketasya kalpanā.*

[20] I find Dharmottara's use of the pair *vācya* and *vācaka* a bit counterintuitive here, since, in fact, *both* of these would seem to denote abstractions (precisely parallel to Saussure's 'signified' and 'signifier', respectively). But it seems clear that what is wanted here is a dichotomy one of whose terms is a *particular*; hence, I render *vācya* here as 'referent', rather than as 'signified'.

[21] NBṬ, p. 52: *śrotra-jñānaṁ tarhi śabda-sva-lakṣaṇa-grāhi; śabda-sva-lakṣaṇaṁ ca kiñcid vācyaṁ kiñcid vācakam ity abhilāpa-saṁsarga-yogya-pratibhāsaṁ syāt; tathā ca savikalapakaṁ syāt.*

[22] Dharmottara's commentator Durvekamiśra introduces this whole discussion by noting the following assertion 'by previous commentators' (*pūrva-vyākhyātṛbhiḥ*; I do not know whom he is quoting), which makes explicit the contradiction that Dharmottara is trying to avoid: DhPr, p. 52: *iha pūrva-vyākhyātṛbhiḥ "asāmarthya-vaiyarthābhyāṁ sva-lakṣaṇasya saṁketayitum aśakyatvād*

some way to keep these two descriptions of the same event distinct from one another (so that the true 'perception' of the utterance can, as Dharmakīrti's definition of perception requires, still count as non-conceptual); but he must do so in a way that allows us to understand how we can, as users of language, effortlessly go from the perceptual to the semantic (i.e. the *conceptual*) description.[23] This is, then, another case of the same problem that recurrently bedevils the philosophical program of Dignāga and Dharmakīrti: how to bring these two sharply distinct levels of description together.

4. Recollection of Conventions as Culminating in *Sva-saṁvitti*

In response to the foregoing problem, Dharmottara elaborates the following account:

> 'This is not a problem. Even if a unique particular can be a referent or a signifier, the unique particular can be apprehended as referent or signifier [only insofar as it is] being apprehended as having been experienced at the time [when one learned the relevant linguistic] convention. And a thing's being an object of experience does not now exist as occurring at the time [when one learned the relevant linguistic] convention. And just as the perception that existed at the time [one learned the relevant linguistic] convention has now ceased, in the same way a thing's also being an object of that [experience] does not now exist. Thus, a [purely perceptual] auditory cognition, not registering the fact of having been previously seen, does not [itself] apprehend a signifier-signified relation.'[24]

avācya-vācakatvam; avācyâvācaka-sva-lakṣaṇa-grāhitvāc cêndriya-jñānam avikalpakam iti" vyākhyātam.—'Since, as lacking both [intrinsic] significance and *in*-significance, it cannot be involved in a linguistic convention (*saṁketayati*), a unique particular is not a signifier or a signified; and a sensory cognition, because of [its] being the apprehender of a unique particular that is neither signifier nor signified, is non-conceptual.'

[23] Dharmottara's task here would be further complicated by consideration of the phenomenology of such a situation; for in fact, we do not experience ourselves as *moving* from one level of description to the other, but simply as *understanding the sentence*. Cf. HUSSERL (1970: I: 282–84, §10)—a discussion that DUMMETT (2004: 11) summarises as attending to the fact that 'we hear or read the words *as* saying whatever it is that they say; only by a heroic effort can we hear them as mere sounds or see them as mere shapes.'

[24] NBṬ, pp. 52–53: *nâiṣa doṣaḥ; saty api sva-lakṣaṇasya vācya-vācaka-bhāve, saṁketa-kāla-dṛṣṭatvena gṛhyamāṇaṁ sva-lakṣaṇaṁ vācyaṁ vācakaṁ ca gṛhītaṁ syāt. na ca saṁketa-kāla-bhāvi darśana-viṣayatvaṁ vastunaḥ sampraty asti; yathā hi saṁketa-kāla-bhāvi-darśanam adya niruddham, tadvat tadviṣayatvam apy arthasyâdya nâsti. tataḥ pūrva-kāla-dṛṣṭatvam apaśyac chrotra-jñānaṁ na vācya-vācaka-bhāvi-grāhi.*

Let us first develop the idea that what Dharmottara is here addressing is something like FODOR's 'disjunction problem'—and in so doing, gain a more complete picture of the account that Dharmottara's references to *saṁketa-kāla* here presuppose. Recall that the disjunction in question is between what FODOR referred to as 'information' and 'meaning'. 'Information', on FODOR's usage, is carried by the kinds of events that are only 'about' what *causes* them; and his account is one according to which all instances of *meaning* must in the final analysis be explicable with reference to some particular occasion on which the use of a signifying convention was in some sense *caused* by an interaction with some ostensible particular. *Meaning*, then, is for FODOR explicable in terms of *information*—in terms of particular cognitions that are 'about' their causes.[25] And FODOR needs thus to bring the processes of signification to rest in some causally describable transaction with unique particulars since his account of semantics, like that of Dignāga and Dharmakīrti, just is an account of how it is that semantically meaningful states are constructed out of the causally efficacious particulars that alone are really existent.[26]

Now, what thus causes foundational utterances on Dharmakīrti's view is ultimately that kind of *sva-lakṣaṇa* (if it makes sense to talk of *kinds* of *sva-lakṣaṇa*s!) that is some particular, subjectively occurrent 'intention' (*abhiprāya* or *vivakṣā*). Here it is important, then, to attend briefly to Dharmakīrti's elaboration of another view commonly held by Buddhist philosophers in this trajectory of thought: specifically, the claim that cognitions engendered by testimony (*śābda-jñāna*) are not themselves *pramāṇa*s just insofar as such cognitions are reducible to some other *pramāṇa*—namely, inference. On Dharmakīrti's account, the inference involved here is specifically one to the fact *that* the speaker has some 'intention' (*abhiprāya*). As Dharmakīrti says at PV 1.213,

> 'Since words have no inherent connection with things, there is no proof of objects based on them; for they [merely] express a speaker's intention.'[27]

---

[25] See ARNOLD (2006) for a fuller elaboration of FODOR's arguments here.

[26] It should be said, in this regard, that FODOR claims to be a realist about propositional attitudes, which suggests that he might not endorse this characterisation of his project; but I am persuaded by such critiques as that of BAKER (1987) that, notwithstanding FODOR's avowed realism, his reductionist position reduces, in the end, to an *eliminativist* one, insofar as the only real explanatory work is done at the 'syntactic' level of description. To that extent, the semantic level of description basically becomes epiphenomenal, which makes it hard to retain the claim that one is a 'realist' about things at this level.

[27] PV_2, p. 107:

nāntarīyakatâbhāvāc chabdānāṁ vastubhiḥ saha /
nârtha-siddhis tatas te hi vaktr-abhiprāya-sūcakāḥ //

Note, however, that Dharmakīrti thus credits only the inference to the fact *that* a speaker has some intention, but cannot get at *what* that intention is; for the 'intentions' Dharmakīrti thus imagines must be understood not as anything like 'propositions' (not, that is, as concerning objective states of affairs), but only as *subjectively occurrent representations*. This is the salient point of Dharmakīrti's saying (as he does at PV 2.2) that 'language is a reliable warrant[28] [only] in regard to *that object which appears in thought, which is the speaker's object of engagement*; it is not grounded in the reality of the object [itself].'[29] And again, in the autocommentary on PV 1.227, Dharmakīrti explains:

> 'An utterance is impelled by an intention regarding a particular point; for one who knows that this [utterance thus] comes from that [intention,] *the point expressed* [*by the utterance*] *is the phenomenal appearance which is its proper cause*. Hence, there is a cause-effect relation between [an intention] *whose form is mental*, and its expression in speech.'[30]

The inference to a speaker's intention, then, is an inference based on a *kārya-hetu* (that is, an inference from an effect to its cause).[31] And the cause in question is a subjectively occurrent representation (*ābhāsa*) appearing to the speaker. For Dharmakīrti, to say that such a representation is thus the *cause* of the utterance is in effect to say that the 'intention' in question must be a unique particular, since only *sva-lakṣaṇa*s, on his view, are causally efficacious.[32] Indeed, Dharmakīrti has it that the 'intention' in question—a mental representation that is itself causally produced by what it is 'about'—is, like any such representation, itself a *sva-lakṣaṇa*.[33]

But *that* means that this 'intention' must in some sense be *perceptible*, since *sva-lakṣaṇa*s are the objects only of perception—although as a subjectively occurrent representation, it would of course be 'perceptible' only to the subject to whom it was appearing. This is not, however, a problem for Dharmakīrti, and the attractive-

---

[28] More literally, 'language has reliability' (*śabdasya prāmāṇyaṁ*).

[29] PV_1 1.4:

> *vaktṛ-vyāpāra-viṣayo yo 'rtho buddhau prakāśate /*
> *prāmāṇyaṁ tatra śabdasya nârtha-tattva-nibandhanam //*

[30] PV_2, p. 113–114: *artha-viśeṣa-samīhā-preritā vāg ata idam iti viduṣaḥ sva-nidānâbhāsinam arthaṁ sūcayatîti buddhi-rūpa-vāg-vijñaptyor janya-janaka-bhāvaḥ sambandhaḥ*. Cf. DUNNE (2004: 146).

[31] As Kamalaśīla says in expressing this point, 'the intention is understood from the utterance because of [the utterance's] being the effect of that [intention], but not as being [directly] expressible' (TSaP, p. 376: *sā ca vivakṣā tat-kāryatvād vacanāt pratīyate, na tu vācyatayā.*).

[32] Cf. n. J.

[33] On this point, DUNNE (2004: 116) says, 'Since each image is an effect, it as much a particular' as the *sva-lakṣaṇa*s which they represent; cf. DUNNE (2004: 121).

ness of this picture becomes clear when we then factor in one of the other central commitments of Dharmakīrti and his philosophical fellow-travellers: the commitment to the view that *sva-saṁvedana* or *sva-saṁvitti* (reflexive cognition or 'apperception') is not only to be reckoned as a type of immediate, preconceptual awareness—which is to say, as a kind of *pratyakṣa*—but in the final analysis, as the *only* such cognition.[34] That is, the only truly non-conceptual, non-discursive cognition——the only kind whose status as 'inerrant' (*abhrānta*) is such as to make it *indubitable*—is the awareness we have of the contents of our own mental events. This, then, is the account that is in play when Tom TILLEMANS (2000: 163), explicating PV 4.109, thus summarises what he calls Dharmakīrti's 'fundamental position' with regard to the role of a speaker's intentions: 'words are used according to the speaker's wishes and designate anything whatsoever which he might intend. The speaker is thus an authority as to what he is referring to in that he can ascertain his own intention by means of a valid cognition (*pramāṇa*), viz., reflexive awareness (*sva-saṁvedana*).'

Now, however, we are in a position to see all the more clearly how problematic is this account of inferences to a speaker's intention; for precisely insofar as our inference is thus to a particular, subjectively occurrent representation, there remains the question of how the speaker's 'intention' itself relates to what that intention is *about*. That is, if the only inference involved here is one to the bare fact of 'some speaker's having an intention', we are no closer to understanding *what* that intention is.[35] Indeed, the account we have just surveyed would seem to undermine whatever claim Dharmakīrti has on giving an account of the *reference* of words; for insofar as the 'reference' thus becomes a subjectively occurrent representation, what we are 'explaining' seems no longer to be the constitutively intersubjective phenomenon of language, but rather, something eminently subjective and psychological.[36] Against such a view, understanding what a speaker's intention is *about* arguably requires reference to a universal such as a *proposition*—something with Husserlian 'ideality',[37] or what the grammarian Bhartṛhari called *upacāra-sattā* ('figurative reality').[38] Whatever it is we can thus be thought to require, the salient point is that it must, if it is to explain how it is that thoughts and utterances can be about objective states of affairs, be something other than the efficient causes of any particular mental event.[39]

[34] Dignāga first made this point in elaborating on *Pramāṇa-samuccaya* 1.8; see ARNOLD (2005: 34–36).

[35] For a highly illuminating development of this and related points, see NANCE (2004: 42–67).

[36] DUNNE (2004: 139 ff.) has made a similar point.

[37] See n. Q, above.

[38] Cf. HOUBEN (1995: 257–262).

[39] In fact, Dharmottara is arguably striving for precisely such an account of intentionality when he revises Dharmakīrti's account of perception. Thus, in commenting on the first chapter of the *Nyāya-*

Here, then, we can begin to see how the specifically semantic kind of 'aboutness' exemplified by linguistic items can be considered inextricably related to the 'intentionality' of mental events;[40] for giving any account that takes *thoughts or sentences* to be *about* anything at all arguably requires reference to precisely the kinds of abstractions that pointedly do not figure in Dharmakīrti's account of speakers' intentions—requires reference, that is, to (what FODOR's methodological solipsism is precisely meant to exclude) the '*semantic* properties of such representations, including the property of being true, of having referents, or, indeed, the property of being representations *of the environment*' (FODOR (1982: 283)). This nicely discloses, I think, the main reason why Dharmakīrti's epistemology can move so easily between realist[41] and idealist commitments; for on one reading of the Dharmakīrtian account of *sva-saṁvitti*, the whole point just is to bracket from consideration the question of whether our mental events have the property of 'being representations *of the environment*.'[42]

5. Mīmāṁsakas on the Impossibility of a Non-intentional Account of Linguistic Conventions

To the extent that is right, the *sva-saṁvitti* of Dignāga and Dharmakīrti can be understood to play a role precisely analogous to the 'methodological solipsism' that underlies FODOR's project—given which, we can say that the Buddhist commitment to *sva-saṁvitti* figures prominently in the difficulty of their giving a semantic account of mental content; for the view that all of our higher-order awareness has its foundations in indubitably occurrent, uniquely particular episodes of reflexive cognition[43] just is the view that an account of the mental cannot finally make reference to the semantic properties of mental representations.

---

bindu, Dharmottara is concerned to reverse Dharmakīrti's exhaustively causal account of perception, with an eye towards allowing that perception must, after all, yield something like propositional content; cf. ARNOLD (2005: 42–48). But of course, Dharmottara (as a commentator who claims exegetical adequacy to the texts of Dharmakīrti) tries to do so while yet maintaining that perception is *kalpanâpoḍha*.

[40] Cf. n. B.

[41] Here, I mean 'realist' in the ordinary sense that pertains to a world of external objects.

[42] Thus, these ideas put Dharmakīrti in a good position to take the further, idealist step of arguing that *there is no* 'environment' thus to be 'represented'; but insofar as this 'bracketing' does not by itself commit Dharmakīrti to taking that step, he also remains in a good position to argue (as he usually does) as a 'Sautrāntika'.

[43] Which is just the view SELLARS (1963) attacks when he considers 'the logic of "looks"'; cf. n. G.

Now, I have been trying to argue that these considerations (to recur, finally, to our passages from Dharmottara) represent the kind of thing that is presupposed by talk of *saṁketa-kāla*. Recall, then, that what makes a cognition 'conceptual', for Dharmakīrti and his ilk, is its not being causally constrained by an actually present object—by its involving, that is, reference to (or *recollection of*) something that is not presently there. When we hear (i.e. *perceive*) someone speaking, all that is presently occurring is the causally or 'syntactically' describable utterance of noises. The relevant non-present thing that is then recalled is the 'linguistic convention' (*saṁketa*) that governs the use of the word. Thus, on this way of describing the 'computation' (as it were) of a linguistic expression, the initial perception of the acoustic event that is someone's utterance can be described as the effect of a causally efficacious, unique particular (namely, the sound emitted by the speaker). The sound's being taken as *meaningful* (i.e. as '*vācaka*') is then attributed to a stimulated *recollection* of an arbitrary convention—and if we are to avoid question-begging, the initial devising or acquisition[44] of the relevant convention, as well as the recollection thereof, must itself be causally describable.

But can this picture work? What I want to suggest is that at least this part of the Buddhist proposal cannot, in the end, coherently be given a non-semantic, non-intentional description; for the picture that Dharmottara has sketched here presupposes precisely the intentional level of description that it is meant to explain. To see this, the question to ask is: how are we to explain—in non-semantic, non-intentional terms—the linkage between the sound that is immediately perceived, and the 'convention' (*saṁketa*) one is thereby prompted to recall? More compellingly, how are we to describe *the making of this convention itself* in non-intentional terms?

It is here that it becomes relevant to consider a Mīmāṁsaka argument that has not, so far as I am aware, been much considered with regard to the doctrine of *apoha*. Here, I have in mind not the characteristically Mīmāṁsaka arguments that were developed specifically against *apoha*, but rather, one of the arguments deployed to support the quintessentially Mīmāṁsaka claim that—as affirmed at *Mīmāṁsā-sūtra* 1.5—'the relation between a word and its referent is primordial' (MS, p. 28: *autpattikas tu śabdasyârthena sambandhaḥ...*). Among the arguments marshalled in support of this claim is the following, which Śabara—in his lengthy commentary on *Mīmāṁsā-sūtra* 1.5—quotes from the earlier commentary of the unnamed Vṛtti-kāra ('author of the *Vṛtti*'):

---

[44] Note that the expression *saṁketa-kāla* is ambiguous in this regard; it could mean 'the time of [*the devising of*] the convention'—a translation that is recommended by the understanding of *saṁketa* as 'agreement' (for we can then simply translate 'at the time of the agreement [i.e. between the creators of the convention]')—or 'the time of [*the learning of*] the convention.' For further reflections on this ambiguity, see ARNOLD (2006).

> 'There is no period whatsoever without a relation [between words and their referents, no period] in which not a single word was related to any referent. How so? Because the very act of making a relation does not [otherwise] stand to reason. Some language must be used by the one who is creating the relation; who created [the relations constitutive] of that [language] by which he would [thus] do so? If [that was done] by someone else, then who created [linguistic relations] for him, and who, [in turn,] for him? There is no end [to the series]. Therefore, someone who is [ostensibly] creating [any linguistic] relation must presuppose some words whose relations are unmade, established according to the usage of elders.'[45]

The Vṛtti-kāra's argument is straightforward but compelling: the fundamental connection (*sambandha*) of language with non-linguistic fact cannot coherently be imagined without presupposing precisely the intentional, semantic level of description that is supposed to be *explained* by positing the creation of precisely such a connection. This is, the Vṛtti-kāra argues, because we can only imagine an act of meaning-assignment—an act such as that consisting in the utterance 'this [accompanied by an act of ostension] is to be called a *cow*'—as *itself* a linguistic act. Hence, the very act of creating such a 'relation' does not stand to reason unless we presuppose that both the agent and the audience of this act already have (what we are here trying to understand) the idea of *meaning* something—already find intelligible, that is, the very idea that the utterance that accompanies some act of ostension ('this is called a cow') *means* what is ostended.

This argument brings to mind one made by WITTGENSTEIN, who nicely gets at what all is involved in knowing a language by criticising Augustine's account of language-acquisition by children. Thus, against the view that children require only to learn the names of things by attending to the 'bodily movements' of adults—'as it were the natural language of all peoples'[46]—WITTGENSTEIN says:

> 'Augustine describes the learning of human language as if the child came into a strange country and did not understand the language of the

---

[45] ŚBh 1.5, p. 68: *na hi sambandha-vyatiriktaḥ kaścit-kālo 'sti, yasmin na kaścid api śabdaḥ kenacid arthena saṁbaddha āsīt. katham? sambandha-kriyâiva hi nôpapadyate. avaśyam anena sambandhaṁ kurvatā kenacic chabdena kartavyaḥ. yena kriyeta, tasya kena kṛtaḥ? athânyena kenacit kṛtaḥ, tasya kenêti, tasya kenêti, nâivâvatiṣṭhate. tasmād avaśyam anena sambandhaṁ kurvatā akṛta-sambandhāḥ kecana śabdā vṛddha-vyavahāra-siddhā abhyupagantavyāḥ*. This line of argument is further elaborated by Kumārila in the *Saṁbandhâkṣepa-parihāra* chapter of the *Śloka-vārttika*; see ARNOLD (2006).

[46] Augustine, *Confessions*, 1.8; quoted at WITTGENSTEIN (1958: § 1).

> country; that is, as if it already had a language, only not this one. Or again: as if the child could already think, only not yet speak. And "think" would here mean something like "talk to itself."'[47]

Similarly, the Mīmāṁsakas have argued that to presuppose the intelligibility of a proposed convention's *meaning* what is ostended is to presuppose that the audience for this act of creation 'already had a language, only not this one.' The challenge to the would-be nominalist here is a significant one: What must be imagined is how anybody could *explain* to someone—how they could, that is, *tell* them—what it means to *mean* something. This must be imagined, moreover, without presupposing that the parties to this eminently intentional act can already 'think', where that means (with Wittgenstein) something like *talk to themselves*.

6. Conclusion

It is this basically Wittgensteinian point that Vincent DESCOMBES (2001) develops in his critique of 'cognitivism';[48] for ultimately the problem with all instances of cognitivism—with all philosophical programs, that is, that take the locus of the 'mental' as entirely internal to the subject—is that the *normative, rule-governed, semantic* character of thought requires reference to a constitutively *social* dimension. This fact, DESCOMBES (2001: 58–59) suggests, applies to the explanation and understanding of all constitutively social practices and institutions:

---

[47] WITTGENSTEIN (1958: § 32). Interestingly, Jerry FODOR (1975: 63–64) quotes this passage from WITTGENSTEIN at the conclusion to an argument almost precisely like that of the Vṛtti-kāra: 'Learning a language (including, of course, a first language) involves learning what the predicates of the language mean. Learning what the predicates of a language mean involves learning a determination of the extension of these predicates. Learning a determination of the extension of the predicates involves learning that they fall under certain rules (i.e. truth rules). But one cannot learn that *P* falls under *R* unless one has a language in which *P* and *R* can be represented. So one cannot learn a language unless one has a language. In particular, one cannot learn a first language unless one already has a system capable of representing the predicates in that language *and their extensions*. And, on pain of circularity, that system cannot be the language that is being learned. Bur first languages *are* learned. Hence, at least some cognitive operations are carried out in languages other than natural languages.' FODOR thus agrees with the Mīmāṁsakas that trying to imagine a first creation (or acquisition) of linguistic conventions seems to confront us with an infinite regress; it's just that FODOR, thinking the regress intolerable, takes the argument as a *reductio*, and argues that it is therefore necessary to posit what he figuratively calls a 'language of thought.' For a much lengthier development of the role of that argument in FODOR's project, and of the Mīmāṁsaka argument briefly sketched here, see ARNOLD (2006).

[48] Of which FODOR's 'methodological solipsism' is a paradigm case—as would be Dharmakīrti's *sva-saṁvitti*, to the extent that (as I have suggested) this plays a role comparable to that of FODOR's guiding principle.

> '... there can be no formal rules where there are no preexisting practices and customs... What we require, then, is an explanation that provides the institution's intellectual principle, but without seeking it in an individual consciousness...'

But insofar as they take causally describable instances of *sva-saṁvitti* to be foundational—to be, as Dharmakīrti argues, all that is finally expressed by (because they are the *causes of*) any linguistic utterance—Buddhist philosophers in the tradition of Dharmakīrti are unable to look to anything *other* than the mental representations occurring within an individual consciousness.

To be sure, there are characteristically Buddhist commitments that are well served by this account. Chief among these, of course, is (what all Buddhist philosophy is finally concerned to elaborate) the cardinal Buddhist doctrine of selflessness; Dharmakīrti's account of a speaker's 'intention' is, then, one among the many arguments meant to block any inference from the experience of sensations to the conclusion that these must be the properties or states of an enduring subject (a 'self'). Dignāga and Dharmakīrti can be understood to have recognised that even to allow that thoughts or utterances could be *about* something other than their proximate causes—that they could be about such enduring realities as 'objective states of affairs'—is already to clear the way for the view that our experiences could be related to something (a *self*) other than their manifestly episodic causes. Accordingly, these thinkers developed a radically thoroughgoing sort of empiricism, which is concomitant with a broadly nominalist account (such as they elaborated with the doctrine of *apoha*) in which the only existents to be admitted into a final ontology are causally efficacious particulars. The refusal that thoughts or utterances are really *about* anything so abstract as 'objective states of affairs' thus serves the goal of taking the only properly indubitable belief to be that *there are sensations*.

But the price to be paid for this is that the locus of *truth* becomes just subjectively appearing representations; and this is precisely the view that Husserl, in his ongoing struggle against psychologism, criticised by saying that an expression's *meaning* 'naturally does not refer to some meaning-conferring experience.' For these Buddhists, in contrast, utterances *are* finally to be understood as referring simply to some 'meaning-conferring experience'—specifically, to the reflexive cognitions (*sva-saṁvitti*) of some particular speaker. Husserl's argument against such a route, however, is compelling, and has ultimately to do with the very idea of *truth*; for it is only by taking expressions (and thoughts) to be, in general, *about* something other than their proximate causes that it is possible to make sense of the fact that (as Husserl says) '[q]uadratic remainder' is the same expression by whomsoever uttered'—which is a condition of the possibility of our holding (what must be held by anyone who would make use of the idea of *truth*) that '[t]he state of affairs is what it is whether we assert that it obtains or not.'[49]

The difficulties with holding a contrary view are clear in the Buddhist account that can be elaborated as relevant to understanding Dharmottara's brief references to the recollection, by someone who perceives a speaker uttering sounds, of '*saṁketa-kāla*'—of the 'time of [one's learning] a convention'. As we saw, Dharmottara needs to give such an account if he is to allow that we can appropriately describe the hearing of a *śabda-sva-lakṣaṇa* (an audible particular) as the non-conceptual *perception* of a unique acoustic event, while yet explaining how an event so described can also be understood in terms of the auditor's *understanding what the speaker means*. On the view Dharmottara sketches, such an occasion is indeed describable as a true perception, and the semantic level of description is brought in only by the recollection that is stimulated thereby—the recollection, that is, of some bygone '*saṁketa-kāla*'.

But in order for such an account to succeed—in order, that is, for it to *explain* the emergence of a semantic level of description without at any point *presupposing* one—it must be possible to imagine both this recollection itself, and the '*saṁketa-kāla*' so recalled, in constitutively non-semantic terms. And I have suggested that a characteristically Mīmāṁsaka argument for the eternality of linguistic relations can be understood as cogently calling into question precisely this possibility. Thus, Mīmāṁsakas have argued, at least since the time of the Vṛtti-kāra, that we can only imagine an act of meaning-assignment as *itself* a linguistic act. I have suggested that among the things the Mīmāṁsakas can be said thus to have recognised is (with Vincent Descombes) that we require 'an explanation that provides the institution's intellectual principle, but without seeking it in an individual consciousness.' And among the things that make it impossible for Buddhists like Dharmakīrti to look anywhere other than to an individual consciousness is their deployment of the idea of *sva-saṁvitti*—which, we saw, lies at the root of characteristically Buddhist claims that we are entitled to infer from anyone's utterance of words only that some subjectively occurrent representation (some object, Dharmakīrti says, that 'appears in thought', *buddhau prakāśate*)[50] has caused the noise we perceive.

It is, among other things, to the extent that these Buddhists in this way uphold something like FODOR's 'methodological solipsism' that this Buddhist program is vulnerable particularly to those critiques of physicalism that argue for 'semantic externalism'—that argue, in other words, that an intentional level of description cannot be reduced to an efficient-causal level of description just insofar as the for-

[49] Cf. n. Q.

[50] Cf. n. CC.

mer involves reference to something constitutively *social*. And the more compelling argument is then one to the effect that these Buddhist philosophers cannot forego such reference without also compromising their belief that their own account is intelligibly proposed as *true*.

Whether or not, then, arguments such as those developed by Lynne Baker and Vincent Descombes are finally convincing in showing the program of cognitive-scientific physicalism to be problematic, I hope to have suggested at least that they apply as well to the thought of Dignāga and Dharmakīrti and Dharmottara as they do to the accounts of mental content developed under the contemporary program of cognitive science. I have not, then, here tried to argue that physicalism is false (though I find the arguments sympathetically developed here to be cogent); only that many of the important critiques that have been brought to bear upon physicalism can also be brought to bear against certain Buddhist arguments—and this despite the fact that these Buddhists are emphatically not physicalists.

BIBLIOGRAPHY

ARNOLD 2005 = Arnold, Dan: *Buddhists, Brahmins, and Belief: Epistemology in South Asian Philosophy of Religion*. Columbia University Press, New York 2005.

ARNOLD 2006 = Arnold, Dan: 'On Semantics and *Saṁketa*: Thoughts on a Neglected Problem with Buddhist *Apoha* Doctrine', *Journal of Indian Philosophy* 34 (2006) 415–478.

BAKER 1987 = Baker, Lynne Rudder: *Saving Belief: A Critique of Physicalism*. Princeton University Press, Princeton 1987.

BRANDOM 1997 = Brandom, Robert: 'Study Guide [to Wilfrid Sellars's *Empiricism and the Philosophy of Mind*]', in: Wilfrid Sellars: *Empiricism and the Philosophy of Mind: With an Introduction by Richard Rorty and a Study Guide by Robert Brandom*. Harvard University Press, Cambridge 1997: 119–181.

CHISHOLM–SELLARS 1957 = Chisholm, Roderick M.; Sellars, Wilfrid: 'Intentionality and the Mental: Chisholm-Sellars Correspondence on Intentionality', in: H. Feigl, M. Scriven, and G. Maxwell (eds.): *Minnesota Studies in the Philosophy of Science*. Vol. 2, University of Minnesota Press, Minneapolis 1957: 521–539.

DESCOMBES 2001 = Descombes, Vincent: *The Mind's Provisions: A Critique of Cognitivism*. Translated by Stephen Adam Schwartz, Princeton University Press, Princeton 2001.

DhPr = Durvekamiśra: *Dharmottara-pradīpa*. Paṇḍita Dalsukhbhai Malvania (ed.): *Paṇḍita Durveka Miśra*'s *Dharmottara-pradīpa* [*being a subcommentary on Dharmottara's Nyāya-bindu-ṭīkā, a commentary on Dharmakīrti's Nyāya-bindu*]. Second edition, Tibetan Sanskrit Works Series 11, Kashiprasad Jayaswal Research Institute, Patna 1971 [first edition: Patna 1955].

DUMMETT 2004 = Dummett, Michael: *Truth and the Past*. Columbia University Press, New York 2004.

DUNNE 2004 = Dunne, John D.: *Foundations of Dharmakīrti's Philosophy*. Wisdom Publications, Boston 2004.

FODOR 1975 = Fodor, Jerry: *The Language of Thought*. Harvard University Press, Cambridge 1975.

FODOR 1982 = Fodor, Jerry: 'Methodological Solipsism Considered as a Research Strategy in Cognitive Psychology', in: Hubert L. Dreyfus (ed.): *Husserl, Intentionality, and Cognitive Science*. MIT Press, Cambridge 1982: 277–303.

FODOR 1985 = Fodor, Jerry: 'Fodor's Guide to Mental Representation: The Intelligent Auntie's Vade-Mecum', *Mind* (New Series) 94 /373 (1985) 76–100.

FODOR 1990 = Fodor, Jerry: *A Theory of Content and Other Essays*. MIT Press, Cambridge 1990.

FRANCO 1997 = Franco, Eli: *Dharmakīrti on Compassion and Rebirth*. Wiener Studien zur Tibetologie und Buddhismuskunde, Heft 38. Arbeitskreis für Tibetische und Buddhistische Studien Universität Wien, Wien 1997.

GARFIELD 1988 = Garfield, Jay. *Belief in Psychology: A Study in the Ontology of Mind*. MIT, Cambridge 1988.

GRIFFITHS 1986 = Griffiths, Paul: *On Being Mindless: Buddhist Meditation and the Mind-Body Problem*. Open Court, LaSalle (IL) 1986.

HATTORI 1968 = Hattori Masaaki: *Dignāga, On Perception, being the Pratyakṣa-pariccheda of Dignāga's Pramāṇa-samuccaya from the Sanskrit fragments and the Tibetan versions*. Harvard University Press, Cambridge 1968.

HAYES 1993 = Hayes, Richard: 'Dharmakīrti on Rebirth', in: Egaku Mayeda (ed.): *Studies in Original Buddhism and Mahāyāna Buddhism*, Vol. 1, Nagata Bunshodo, Kyoto 1993: 111–129.

HOUBEN 1995 = Houben, Jan E.M.: *The Saṁbandha-samuddeśa (Chapter on Relation) and Bhartṛhari's Philosophy of Language: A Study of Bhartṛhari Saṁbandha-samuddeśa in the context of the Vākya-padīya with a translation of Helārāja's commentary Prakīrṇa-prakāśa*. Gonda Indological Studies, Vol. 2, Egbert Forsten, Groningen 1995.

HUSSERL 1970 = Husserl, Edmund: *Logical Investigations*. Translated by J.N. Findlay, 2 Vols, Humanity Books, Amherst (NY) 1970 [translated from editions of 1900, 1913].

MS = Jaimini: *Mīmāṁsā-sūtra*. K.V. Abhyankar (ed.): *Mīmāṁsā-darśanam, Vol. I: Śrīmajjaiminipraṇīte Mīmāṁsādarśane Prathamādhyāyasya Tarkapādanāma Prathamapāda.* (*Jaimini's sūtras with Śābarabhāṣyam, commentary Prabhā by Śrī Vaidya-nāthaśāstri*). Ānandāśrama Sanskrit Series 97, Trivandrum 1976 [first edition: 1929–1934].

NANCE 2004 = Nance, Richard F.: *Models of Teaching and the Teaching of Models: Contextualizing Indian Buddhist Commentary*. Ph.D. dissertation, University of Chicago, Chicago 2004.

NB = Dharmakīrti: *Nyāya-bindu*. See: DhPr.

NBṬ = Dharmottara: *Nyāya-bindu-ṭīkā*. See: DhPr.

PV = Dharmakīrti: *Pramāṇa-vārttika*. (1) Rāhula Sāṅkṛtyāyana (ed.): 'Dharmakīrti's *Pramāṇavārttika* with a Commentary by Manorathanandin', *Journal of the Bihar and Orissa Research Society* 24 /3–26 /3, Patna 1938–40. (2) Raniero Gnoli (ed.): *The Pramāṇavārttikam of Dharmakīrti: The First Chapter with the Autocommentary: Text and Critical Notes*. Serie Orientale Roma XXIII, Istituto Italiano per il Medio ed Estremo Oriente, Rome 1960.

SEARLE 1982 = Searle, John: 'What Is an Intentional State?', in: Hubert L. Dreyfus (ed.): *Husserl, Intentionality, and Cognitive Science*. MIT Press, Cambridge 1982: 259–276.

SELLARS 1963 = Sellars, Wilfrid: *Science, Perception and Reality*. Ridgeview, Atascadero (CA) 1963.

SIDERITS 2001 = Siderits, Mark: 'Buddhism and Techno-Physicalism: Is the Eightfold Path a Program?', *Philosophy East & West* 51 /3 (2001) 307–314.

ŚBh Śabara-svāmin: *Mīmāṁsā-śābara-bhāṣya*. See: MS.

TABER 2003 = Taber, John: 'Dharmakīrti against Physicalism', *Journal of Indian Philosophy* 31 (2003) 479–502.

TILLEMANS 2000 = Tillemans, Tom J.F. *Dharmakīrti's Pramāṇavārttika: An Annotated Translation of the Fourth Chapter (parārthānumāna), volume 1 (k.1–148)*. Philosophisch-Historische Klasse Sitzungsberichte, 675. Band, Verlag der Österreichischen Akademie der Wissenschaften, Wien 2000.

TSaP = Kamalaśīla: *Tattva-saṁgraha-pañjikā*. Swami Dwarikadas Shastri (ed.): *Tattvasaṅgraha of Ācārya Shāntarakṣita with the Commentary 'Pañjikā' of Shri Kamalashīla*. 2 Vols, Bauddha Bharati, Varanasi 1997. [first edition: 1981–1982].

WITTGENSTEIN 1958 = Wittgenstein, Ludwig: *Philosophical Investigations*. Translated by G.E. M. Anscombe. Macmillan, New York 1958.

Studies in Dharmakīrti's Religious Philosophy: 4. The *Cintā-mayī Prajñā*[*]

VINCENT ELTSCHINGER

1. From *cintā-mayī prajñā* to *hetu-vidyā*

— 1.1 —

In the sixth chapter of his AK(Bh), Vasubandhu presents us with the following statement about the sequence of the three traditional *prajñā*s ('insights', 'wisdoms', 'discernments'):

> 'Whoever desires to see the Truths should first of all keep the Precepts. Then he reads the teaching upon which his Seeing of the Truths depends, or he hears their meaning. Having heard, he correctly reflects. Having reflected, he gives himself up to the cultivation of meditation. With the wisdom arisen from the teaching (*śruta-mayī*) for its support, there arises the wisdom arisen from reflection (*cintā-mayī*); with this for its support, there arises the wisdom arisen from meditation (*bhāvanā-mayī*).'[1]

After criticising a Vaibhāṣika conception of the *prajñā*s,[2] Vasubandhu gives his own explanation:

---

[*] I wish to express my most sincere gratitude to Helmut Krasser, Cristina Pecchia and Ernst Steinkellner, who looked at this paper and made useful comments on it, as well as to Cynthia Peck-Kubacek, who kindly corrected my English.

[1] AKBh 334.16–19 on AK 6.5ab: *satyāni h[i] draṣṭu-kāma ādita eva śīlaṁ pālayati. tataḥ satya-darśanasyânulomaṁ śrutam udgṛhṇāty arthaṁ vā śṛṇoti. śrutvā cintayaty aviparītaṁ cintayitvā bhāvanāyāṁ prayujyate. samādhau tasya śruta-mayīṁ prajñāṁ niśritya cintā-mayī jāyate. cintā-mayīṁ niśritya bhāvanā-mayī jāyate.* English translation of POUSSIN (1980: VI,142–143) in PRUDEN (1991: III,911–912). On the three *prajñā*s, see LAMOTTE (1976: 48) and SCHERRER-SCHAUB (1981: 195–197).

[2] AKBh 334.22–24 on AK 6.5cd: *nāmâlambanā kila śruta-mayī prajñā. nāmârthâlambanā cintā-mayī. kadācid vyañjanenârtham ākarṣati kadācid arthena vyañjanam. arthâlambanâiva*

Logic and Belief in Indian Philosophy
Warsaw Indological Studies 3 (2010) 565–603.

'[T]he wisdom arisen from the teaching is a certitude which arises from a means of correct knowledge termed "the word of a qualified person"; the wisdom arisen from reflection is a certitude born of rational examination; and the wisdom arisen from meditation is a certitude arisen from absorption.'[3]

According to Saṅghabhadra, Vasubandhu's criticism falls in line with the so-called Sūtra-master, i.e. it matches the Sautrāntika doctrine.[4] Although KRITZER (2005: 346–347) states that he is not aware of any parallel passages in the BoBh, I think there is enough evidence to hold Vasubandhu's interpretation of the *cintā-mayī prajñā* as grounded in Yogācāra literature. First and foremost, the expression *yukti-nidhyāna* ('rational examination') itself occurs in an interesting MSABh account of the three aforementioned wisdoms.[5] Second, most[6] Yogācāra sources interpret *cintā-mayī prajñā*, or simply *cint(an)ā*, in terms of reasoning. The ŚrBh distinguishes between two forms of reflection (*cintanā*). Whereas the first has an enumerative aspect (*gaṇanâkārā*), the second is accounted as having an evaluative aspect (*tulanâkārā*), and is further described as an 'examination of qualities and defects through reasoning' (*yuktya guṇa-doṣôpaparīkṣaṇâkārā*).[7] The same holds true of the BoBh's depiction of a Bodhisattva's correct reflection (*samyak-cintanā*):

'Engaged in reflection, the Bodhisattva analyses and penetrates [the *dharma*s as he has heard them before] by means of reasoning.'[8]

And a few lines later:

---

bhāvanā-mayī. sā hi vyañjana-nirapekṣā 'rthe pravartate.—'According to the Vaibhāṣikas, wisdom arisen from the teaching has the name for its object; wisdom arisen from reflection has the name and the thing for its object: in fact, sometimes it grasps the thing by means of the name, and sometimes it grasps the name by means of the thing. Wisdom arisen from meditation has the thing for its object; it goes to the things as an abstraction made from its name.' English translation of POUSSIN (1980: VI,143) in PRUDEN (1991: III,912).

[3] AKBh 335.4–6 on AK 6.5cd: *āpta-vacana-prāmāṇya-jāta-niścayaḥ śruta-mayī. yukti-nidhyāna-jaś cintā-mayī. samādhi-jo bhāvanā-mayîti.* English translation of POUSSIN (1980: VI,143–144) in PRUDEN (1991: III,912–913).

[4] Following POUSSIN (1980: VI,143, n. 4) and KRITZER (2005: 346).

[5] See MSABh 82.1–4 on MSA 12.14–15. MSAVBh D *Mi* 240a7–b3 does not provide any explanation of *yukti-nidhyānāt.*

[6] SNS 8.24 (105.7–31) being a notable exception.

[7] See ŚrBh 117*.15 = 140.12–14 (ŚrBh$_T$ D57a5–6 = Q67b3–4); °*ôpaparīkṣaṇâ*° according to ŚrBh$_T$ (*ñe bar brtag pa*) and ŚrBh 121*.2 = 143.19–20.

[8] BoBh$_D$ 76.11–12 = BoBh$_W$ 108.8–9 (BoBh$_T$ D58b4 = Q68a7–8, BoBhVy D128b7 = Q157a7–8, BoBhVṛ D175b7 = Q222b1): *bodhisattvaś cintā-prayukto yuktyā vicārayaty anupraviśati.*

'As he discerns, penetrates and analyses something through reasoning, [the Bodhisattva] does not rely on anyone else with regard to the *dharmas* he examines by means of reasoning.'[9]

Later Yogācāra sources such as the ASBh[10] present us with equivalent interpretations of *cintā-mayī prajñā* /*cint(an)ā*.

— 1.2 —

Yogācāra texts provide us with a fourfold analysis of the reasoning (*yukti*) which bridges the gap between the servile learning of texts (*śruta-mayī prajñā*) and the sustained meditation on their rationally worked out contents (*bhāvanā*-[*mayī prajñā*]):

'How is one to reflect on the teaching of the *skandhas* by means of the reflection consisting (°*âkāra*) of an examination through reasoning? One is to examine [it] by means of four [types of] reasoning.—Which four?—By means of *apekṣā-yukti*, *kārya-karaṇa-yukti*, *upapatti-sādhana-yukti*, and *dharmatā-yukti*.'[11]

Three of these four *yuktis* share common features, namely the *apekṣā-yukti*, the *kārya-karaṇa-yukti*, and the *dharmatā-yukti*. In contrast to the *upapatti-sādhana-yukti*, all of them have the character of an investigation into causal processes, which they intend to reflect upon on a logical level.[12] Let me first summarise the ŚrBh's

---

[9] BoBh$_D$ 76.18–19 = BoBh$_W$ 108.18–20 (BoBh$_T$ D58b7 = Q68b3, BoBhVy D129a5 = Q157b7, BoBhVṛ D176a3 = Q221b6): *yuktyā punaḥ kiṁcit pravicinvan praviśayan vicārayan na para-pratyayo bhavati teṣu yukti-parīkṣiteṣu dharmeṣu*. BoBhVṛ D176a3 = Q221b6 explains BoBh$_T$ D58b7 = Q68b3 (*gźan gyi driṅ mi 'jog pa = na para-pratyayaḥ*) as: *gźan la mi ltos pa źes bya ba'i don to* //, to be compared with POUSSIN (1980: IX,246, n. 2).

[10] See ASBh 150.10–12.

[11] ŚrBh 118*,10–13 = 141.7–10 (ŚrBh$_T$ D57b2–3 = Q68a1–2): *kathaṁ yukty-upaparīkṣâkārayā cintayā skandha-deśanāṁ cintayati. catasṛbhir yuktibhir upaparīkṣate. katamābhiś catasṛbhiḥ. yad utâpekṣā-yuktyā kārya-karaṇa**-*yuktyôpapatti-sādhana-yuktyā dharmatā-yuktyā*.

* As SAKUMA (1990: II,8, n. 36) has rightly pointed out, one must read °-*karaṇa*-° instead of °-*kāraṇa*-°.

On the four *yuktis*, see respectively TfphSI (1991: 74b–76a), (1996: 77a–78b), (1996: 40b–42b), (1996: 124a–125b), and (2006: 93a–96b); see also MSABh 58.5–12 on MSA 19.43–46. On *yukti* in general, see SCHERRER-SCHAUB (1981), SAKUMA (1990: II,99–102, nn. 596–605), YOSHIMIZU (1996: 114–119, n. 85), DELEANU (2006: II,494–495, n. 74).

[12] Buddhist theoreticians have tried to supply these expressions with an ontological foundation: a given event *x* is the reason (*yukti*), device (*yoga*) or means (*upāya*) for a given event *y* to occur (ŚrBh 119*,2–3 = 141.17–142.2 [ŚrBh$_T$ D57b5–6 = Q67b6–7], ŚrBh 119*,11–12 = 142.9–11

account of these three *yukti*s. (1) In order to be produced (*utpatti*), a given *skandha* depends (*apekṣā*) on particular causes (*hetu*) and conditions (*pratyaya*); coining the verbal designation '*skandha*' (*skandha-prajñapti*) depends on various linguistic factors such as names (*nāma-kāya*), phrases (*pada-kāya*) and syllables (*vyañjana-kāya*). The *apekṣā-yukti* investigates both of these dependences.[13] (2) Arisen (*utpanna*) from the aforementioned causes and conditions, our *skandha* is bound (*viniyoga*) by them to produce such and such an effect of its own (*tasmiṁs tasmin sva-kārya-karaṇe*). The *kārya-karaṇa-yukti* investigates this generation of effects.[14] (3) That the said *skandha* is so and so (*tathā-bhūta*), say, impermanent (*anitya*), is due to its nature (*prakṛti*), to its own being (*svabhāva*), and to its fundamental nature (*dharmatā*). The *dharmatā-yukti* investigates this fundamental nature.[15]

Although the ŚrBh took the *skandha-deśanā* as its main example, i.e. a core Buddhist doctrine, it also brought some more 'profane' or ordinary examples into discussion. Sthiramati presents us with a more sharply delineated account of the *yukti*s in that he distinguishes between an 'ordinary' and, say, a 'religious' way of accounting for them.[16] On an ordinary level, the *apekṣā-yukti* is concerned with the fact

[ŚrBh$_T$ D58a1 = Q68a2–3], ŚrBh 120*,9–10 = 143.11–14 [ŚrBh$_T$ D58a6–7 = Q69a2–3]). From an ontological point of view, then, these terms must be construed as *karma-dhāraya* compounds: the reason consisting in a [given event *x*'s] dependence [on the previous event *y*] (*apekṣā-yukti*), the reason consisting in [the fact that *x*] brings about an effect [*z*] (*kārya-karaṇa-yukti*), and the reason consisting in [the fact that it is due to their] fundamental nature [that events are what they are] (*dharmatā-yukti*). Since, as (psycho)logical events (*causae cognoscendi*), our *yukti*s question these ontological reasons or causes (*causae fiendi*), let me render them as follows: reasoning about dependence (*apekṣā-yukti*), reasoning about the production of an effect (*kārya-karaṇa-yukti*), and reasoning about the fundamental nature [of events/things] (*dharmatā-yukti*).

[13] See ŚrBh 118*,15–119*,4 = 141.11–142.2 (ŚrBh$_T$ D57b3–6 = Q67b2–7); see also SNS 10.7 (155.17–19), with *rjes su tha sñad gdags pa* instead of *prajñapti*.

[14] See ŚrBh 119*,6–12 = 142.3–11 (ŚrBh$_T$ D57b6–58a1 = Q67b7–68a3); see also SNS 10.7 (155.20–22).

[15] See ŚrBh 120*,3–13 = 143.4–16 (ŚrBh$_T$ D58a4–b1 = Q68b6–69a4), and WAYMAN (1961: 79–80); see also SNS 10.7 (158.28–30), with an interesting explanation of *dharmatā-yukti* through the famous formula: *utpādād vā tathāgatānām anutpādād vā dharmāṇāṁ sthitaye dharmatā-dhātu-sthititā*.

[16] Respectively MSAVBh D *Tsi* 202a5 (*'jig rten gyi tshul gyis*) and 202b2 (*chos kyi don daṅ sbyar ba*) on MSA 19.44cd. The scope of these three *yukti*s covers such transempirical (but by no means less 'natural') states of affairs as the structure and sequence of the Buddhist path to salvation. In his rather lengthy commentary on MSA 19.43–46, Sthiramati exemplifies it as follows: In the *adhimukti-caryā-bhūmi*, a Śrāvaka, a Pratyeka-buddha or a Bodhisattva thoroughly concentrates (*yoniśo manas-kāraḥ*) on the *dharma*s' being impermanent, unsatisfactory, empty and unsubstantial. Depending on that *yoniśo manas-kāraḥ*, for the Śrāvaka or Pratyeka-buddha who has entered the stream (*srota-āpanna*), the right view (*samyag-dṛṣṭi*) that perceives *pudgala-nairātmya* will arise at the time of the path of vision (*darśana-mārga*); depending on that same

that 'a visual cognition (*cakṣur-vijñāna*) arises in dependence on an eye (*cakṣus*) and a visible [object] (*rūpa*), and [that] a sprout (*aṅkura*) arises in dependence on a seed (*bīja*).'[17] As for the *kārya-karaṇa-yukti*, it investigates the fact that 'entities bring about their own effects (*sva-kārya*) after they have arisen in dependence on causes and conditions.'[18] Finally, the *dharmatā-yukti* devotes itself to the fact that 'in the world (*loka*), fire is hot (*uṣṇa*) by its own nature and water is liquid (*drava*) by its own nature.'[19]

Whereas the three *yukti*s discussed above are of an investigating character, the *upapatti-sādhana-yukti* has a mere probative or argumentative character, and aims at rationally establishing the essentials of Buddhist doctrine. The ŚrBh defines it as follows:

> 'By means of the three *pramāṇa*s, viz. scriptures of a trustworthy [person], direct perception and inference, [a monk and /or a Bodhisattva] examines [the fact] that the *skandha*s are impermanent, [and /or] that they are produced in dependence [on causes and conditions], unsatisfactory, empty and unsubstantial. By means of those three *pramāṇa*s, which are subordinate to [particular] arguments (*upapatti*) [and] convince wise [people], one carries out probative determinations, viz. of the *skandha*s' being impermanent, or produced in dependence [on

yoniśo manas-kāraḥ, the supramundane (right) view (*lokôttarā* [*samyag-*]*dṛṣṭiḥ*) that realises both *pudgala-* and *dharma-nairātmya* will arise for a Bodhisattva at the time of *darśana-mārga*, in the first stage (*bhūmi*). In that case, the *apekṣā-yukti* examines this sequence by focusing upon the *dṛṣṭi*s' dependence on *yoniśo manas-kāraḥ* (see MSAVBh D *Tsi* 202b2–5 on MSA 19.47a; MSAVBh D *Tsi* 205a6–8 on MSABh 168.7–8). As for the *kārya-karaṇa-yukti*, it will examine the *dṛṣṭi*s' being endowed with a fruit/effect (*phalânvita*), viz. the liberation (*vimokṣa*/ *vimukti*) = *nirvāṇa* that is brought about by the *samyag-dṛṣṭi* born in the path of vision (see MSAVBh D *Tsi* 202b5–6 on MSA 19.47b). Finally, the *dharmatā-yukti* will investigate the very naturality of the fact that, once the *samyag-dṛṣṭi* has arisen, one will reach those (presently) inconceivable (*acintya*) states of affairs that consist e.g. in the true reality (*dharmd-dhātu*) and the *nirvikalpaka-jñāna* or non-conceptual insight (see MSAVBh D *Tsi* 203a3–5 on MSA 19.45c_2d_1; MSAVBh D *Tsi* 205a8–b3 on MSABh 168.10).

[17] MSAVBh D *Tsi* 202a5 on MSA 19.44cd: *mig daṅ gzugs la ltos nas mig gi rnam par śes pa skye ba daṅ / sa bon la ltos nas myu gu skye ba* [*ni ltos pa'i rigs pa źes bya'o*] // .

[18] MSAVBh D *Tsi* 202a5–6 on MSA 19.44cd: *de ltar dṅos po rnams rgyu daṅ rkyen la ltos nas skyes pa'i 'og tu raṅ gi las byed pa* [*ni bya ba byed pa'i rigs pa źes bya ste*] / .

[19] MSAVBh D *Tsi* 202b1–2 on MSA 19.44cd: *'jig rten na me raṅ bźin gyis tsha ba daṅ / chu raṅ bźin gyis gśer ba* [*ni chos ñid kyi rigs pa źes bya'o*] // . ŚrBh 120*,4–5 = 143.4–7 ($ŚrBh_T$ D58a4–5 = Q68b6–7, WAYMAN (1961: 79)) contains numerous examples of the like.

causes and conditions], or unsatisfactory, or empty, or unsubstantial. This is termed a reasoning that proves by means of arguments[20].'[21]

Or, as the MSABh has it,[22] 'the *upapatti-sādhana-yukti* is an examination [that one carries out] by means of *pramāṇa*s such as direct perception.'

— 1.3 —

According to Sthiramati, *upapatti-sādhana-yukti* is not only an (*upa*)*parīkṣā*, but also a kind of knowledge that ascertains (*dbab* = *nirṇaya*?) and causes one to attain (*yoṅs su sgrub pa* = *samprāpaṇa*?) the objects it deals with,[23] the latter property being reminiscent of Pakṣilasvāmin's conception of a *pramāṇa*.[24] Sthiramati's account presents us with other interesting features. First, *upapatti-sādhana-yukti* is concerned with two kinds of objects only, namely *pratyakṣa* and *parokṣa*; accordingly, this *yukti* makes use of only two *pramāṇa*s, viz. *pratyakṣa* and *anumāna*, thus leaving no room for the third *pramāṇa* Buddhists traditionally agreed upon, viz. *āptâgama*.[25] Second, and more importantly, the vocabularies of *pramāṇa*s and *yukti*s tend to intermingle, as is testified to by such 'hybrid' expressions as

[20] On the different translations of *upapatti-sādhana-yukti*, see STEINKELLNER (1988: II 18, n. 43). STEINKELLNER translates: 'Argumentationsweise (*yukti*), die im Nachweis (*sādhana*) durch Argumente (*upapatti*) besteht.'

[21] ŚrBh 119*,14–120*,1 = 142.12–143.3 (ŚrBh$_T$ D58a1–4 = Q68b3–6): *upapatti-sādhana-yuktiḥ katamā. anityāḥ skandhā iti pratītya-samutpannā duḥkhāḥ śūnyā anātmāna iti tribhiḥ pramāṇair upaparīkṣate yad utâptâgamena pratyakṣeṇânumānena ca. ebhis tribhiḥ pramāṇair upapatti-yuktaiḥ satāṁ hṛdaya-grāhakair vyavasthāpanā sādhanā kriyate yad uta skandhânityatāyā vā pratītya-samutpannatāyā vā duḥkhatāyā vā śūnyatāyā vā 'nātmatāyā vā. iyam ucyata upapatti-sādhana-yuktiḥ.*

[22] MSABh 168.9–10 on MSA 19.43–46: *upapatti-sādhana-yuktiḥ pratyakṣâdibhiḥ pramāṇaiḥ parīkṣā*. See also SNS 10.7 (155.23–25): *so so'i śes pa daṅ / bśad pa daṅ / smras pa'i don sgrub pa daṅ legs par khoṅ du chud par bya ba'i rgyu gaṅ dag yin pa daṅ / rkyen gaṅ dag yin pa de ni 'thad pas sgrub pa'i rigs pa yin no //*, and SNS 10.7 (157.30–32): *de ltar 'thad pa'i sgrub pa'i rigs pa de ni mṅon sum gyi tshad ma daṅ / rjes su dpag pa'i tshad ma daṅ / yid ches pa'i luṅ gi tshad mas mtshan ñid lṅa po dag gis yoṅs su dag pa yin no //* . On the SNS's understanding of *upapatti-sādhana-yukti*, see STEINKELLNER (1988: II,14–19).

[23] See MSAVBh D *Tsi* 202a7 on MSA 19.44cd, MSAVBh D *Tsi* 202b7 on MSA 19.47c$_1$. *dbab pa* = *nirṇaya* (but also *āveśa*) in TSD$_{LCh}$ 1701b *s.v.* and TSD$_{LCh\text{-}s}$ 1313a *s.v.*; *yoṅs su 'grub par bya ba* = *samprāpaṇa* in TSD$_{LCh}$ 2174a *s.v.* On *samprāpaṇa*, see BHSD 579a *s.v.*

[24] See NBh 1.6–11.

[25] See MSAVBh D *Tsi* 202a7, MSAVBh D *Tsi* 202b6–7.

pratyakṣânumāna-yukti, *pratyakṣa-yukti* and *upapatti-sādhana-pramāṇa*,[26] which are used side by side with *pratyakṣânumāna-pramāṇa*, *pratyakṣa-pramāṇa* and *upapatti-sādhana-yukti*.[27] Third, none of the examples Sthiramati adduces is concerned with the Buddhist path to salvation (this being in turn explicable by Sthiramati's ruling out of supersensuous objects): perception of a pot (*ghaṭa*) in a given place (*pradeśa*),[28] direct perceptual experience of pain (*duḥkha*) such as being bound (*bandhana*) or beaten (*tāḍana*) for having committed an evil act like murder (*prāṇâtipātâdi-duṣkarman*) in a previous life;[29] inference of fire from smoke,[30] the visual faculty /organ (*cakṣur-indriya*) from the arising of a visual cognition (*cakṣur-vijñānôtpatti*),[31] or impermanence (*anityatā*) from the property of being brought about by causes and conditions (*hetu-pratyaya-kṛtakatā*).[32] The lexical confusion that prevails in Sthiramati's account of the *upapatti-sādhana-yukti* mirrors the fact that the latter's properties and range have been transferred from the *definiens* (the *pramāṇas*) to the *definiendum* (the *upapatti-sādhana-yukti*).

— 1.4 —

More interesting is the fact that Sthiramati's interpretation of *upapatti-sādhana-yukti* is indeed very close to his own understanding of *hetu-vidyā* ('logic', lit. 'science of reasons'), one of the five traditional 'sciences' or 'branches of knowledge' (*vidyā-sthāna*).[33] Like the *upapatti-sādhana-yukti*, the *hetu-vidyā* is mainly

---

[26] See MSAVBh D *Tsi* 202a6–7 (*mṅon sum daṅ rjes su dpag pa'i rigs pa*), MSAVBh D *Tsi* 202a7 (*mṅon sum gyi rigs pa*), MSAVBh D *Tsi* 202b7 (*'thad pa sgrub pa'i tshad ma*).

[27] See MSAVBh D *Tsi* 202b6 (*mṅon sum daṅ rjes su dpag pa'i tshad ma*), MSAVBh D *Tsi* 202b1 (*mṅon sum gyi tshad ma*), MSAVBh D *Tsi* 202a6 (*'thad pa sgrub pa'i rigs pa*).

[28] See MSAVBh D *Tsi* 202a7–b1.

[29] See MSAVBh D *Tsi* 202b7–203a1.

[30] See MSAVBh D *Tsi* 202b1.

[31] See MSAVBh D *Tsi* 203a1–2.

[32] See MSAVBh D *Tsi* 203a2.

[33] The five branches of knowledge constituting a Bodhisattva's *śāstra-jñatā* (MSA 18.26a) are *adhyātma-vidyā* ('soteriology', 'scriptural science'), *hetu-vidyā* ('logic', 'epistemology', lit. 'science of reasons'), *śabda-vidyā* ('grammar', 'linguistics'), *cikitsā-vidyā* ('medicine') and *śilpa-karma-sthāna-vidyā* ('science of fine arts and crafts', see GRIFFITHS (1990: 99)). For a useful overview, see SEYFORT RUEGG (1995: 101 ff.), and also GRIFFITHS (1990: 99–101). Note also that Sthiramati's commentary on MSA(Bh) provides valuable pieces of information in the three following passages: MSAVBh D *Tsi* 91b5–93b6 (on MSA 18.25–26 and MSABh 136.21 ff.), MSAVBh D *Mi* 202b3–203b6 (on MSA 11.60 and MSABh 70.14–18), MSAVBh D *Tsi* 201b6–206b1 (on MSA 19.43–46 and MSABh 167.28–168.16). *Adhyātma-vidyā* consists in the mastery over the Tathāgata's twelvefold word, and leads to the knowledge of the noble path (*ārya-mārga*)

concerned with investigation *and* demonstration by means of (mostly two) *pramāṇa*s, as is testified to by the following definition:

> 'We term "*hetu-vidyā*" as being the mastery (*mkhas pa* = *kauśal*[*y*]*a*?) over the treatises (*gźuṅ* = *grantha*?) [bearing] upon [such] reasoning (*tarka*) [that are] supported by the *pramāṇa*s direct perception and inference.'[34]

There is at least one passage in the MSAVBh that testifies to the fact that in Sthiramati's opinion *yukti*s and *hetu-vidyā* somehow correspond or even coincide:

> 'In that [case], we [shall] term "*adhyātma-vidyā*" the Mahāyāna itself. Having included the *hetu-vidyā*, the *śabda-vidyā*, the *cikitsā-vidyā* and the *śilpa-karma-sthāna-vidyā* in the *Mahāyāna-sūtra*s, the Blessed One taught [them] to the Bodhisattvas. For instance, in *Sūtra*s like the *Laṅkâvatāra* and the *Saṁdhi-nirmocana*, he taught the *pramāṇa*s direct perception and inference, which form/constitute (*lta bu* = *bhūta*?) the *hetu-vidyā*. In the *Saṁdhi-nirmocana-sūtra*, he said: "*Yukti* should be known as fourfold, that is, *apekṣā-yukti*, *kārya-karaṇa-yukti*, *upapatti-sādhana-yukti*, and *dharmatā-yukti*".'[35]

as well as of the true reality (*tattvârtha*), which in turn bring about the destruction of passions (*kleśa*). *Śabda-vidyā* consists in the mastery of grammar (*byā ka ra ṇa*, MSAVBh D *Tsi* 92a4); skilfulness in Sanskrit (*saṁ skri ta'i skad*, MSAVBh D *Mi* 203a7–b2; see BoBh$_D$ 74.13 = BoBh$_W$ 105.17: *saṁskr̥ta-lapita*-°) allows a Bodhisattva not to resort to *apabhraṁśa* (*tshig zur chags pa*) when teaching. As for *cikitsā-vidyā* and *śilpa-karma-sthāna-vidyā*, they consist in conversancy with such treatises as the *Caraka*-[*saṁhitā*] (*ca ra ka la sogs pa sman dpyad kyi gtsug lag*, MSAVBh D *Tsi* 92a4–5; see also Sthiramati's statement to the effect that medicine was taught by the Tathāgata in the *Suvarṇa-prabhās*[*ôttam*]*a-sūtra*, MSAVBh D *Tsi* 203b7) and the *Bhārata-śāstra* (*bha ra ta'i gtsug lag*, MSAVBh D *Tsi* 92a5).

[34] MSAVBh D *Mi* 205b6 on MSA 11.60: *mṅon sum daṅ rjes su dpag pa tshad mas ni zin pa'i tar ka'i gźuṅ la mkhas pa ni rgyu rig pa źes bya'o //*. See also MSAVBh D *Tsi* 92a4 on MSA 18.26bd: *tar ka'i phyogs la mkhas pa ni gtan tshigs śes pa źes bya'o //*. 'We term "*hetu-vidyā*" the mastery over the field (*phyogs*) of reasoning.'

[35] MSAVBh D *Tsi* 203b3–6 on MSABh 168.2: *de la theg pa chen po ñid ni naṅ rig pa źes bya'o // rgyu rig pa daṅ / sgra rig pa daṅ / gso ba rig pa daṅ / bzo'i las kyi gnas rig pa dag kyaṅ chen po'i mdo sder bsdus nas / bcom ldan 'das kyis byaṅ chub sems dpa' rnams la bśad de / dper na rgyu rig pa lta bu yaṅ mṅon sum daṅ / rjes su dpag pa'i tshad ma* Laṅ ka ra gśegs pa *daṅ* dGoṅs pa ṅes par 'grel ba *la sogs pa mdo sde'i naṅ nas bśad de /* dGoṅs pa ṅes par 'grel ba'i mdo *las / rig pa ni rnam pa bźir śes par bya ste / ltos pa'i rigs pa daṅ / bya ba byed pa'i rigs pa daṅ / 'thad pa sgrub pa'i rigs pa daṅ / chos ñid kyi rigs pa'o źes bya ba la sogs pa gsuṅs pa'o //*. The passage quoted is SNS 10.7 (155.14–16).

In the BoBh as well as in the MSA(Bh),[36] a Bodhisattva cannot reach omniscience unless he gives himself up to the five *vidyā-sthānas*. Studied separately, however, each *vidyā-sthāna* has a purpose of its own. So whereas *cikitsā-vidyā* and *śilpa-karma-sthāna-vidyā* aim at benefiting (*anugrahaṇa*) others, *hetu-vidyā* and *śabda-vidyā* mainly aim at defeating (*nigraha*) others, i.e. non-Buddhist heretics (*tīrthika, tīrthya*). Let us consider first Sthiramati's (rather simple) commentary on MSA 11.60:

> 'The Bodhisattva devotes himself to *hetu-vidyā* and *śabda-vidyā*.—Why [so]?—He devotes himself [to these two sciences] in order to defeat the heretics who boast of knowing (*śes par rlom pa*) the *hetu-vidyā-śāstra* and *śabda-vidyā-śāstra*.'[37]

In another passage, Sthiramati makes a somewhat more explicit statement about the identity of the heretics and the polemic aim of *hetu-vidyā*:

> 'By means of the [*hetu-vidyā*, the Bodhisattva] recognises that the heretics make errors that infringe the *pramāṇa*s [when they] invoke the *pramāṇa*s direct perception and inference as [well-]established reasons to [prove] such [doctrines] as *ātman* or permanence (*rtag par yod pa*) [; he identifies these errors] and, defeating, by means of *pramāṇa*s like direct perception and inference, opponents (*para-vādin*) such as the heretics who discard the *Buddha-dharma*, he refutes the heretics' substantialist treatises.'[38]

From the time of the BoBh on, however, the purpose of *hetu-vidyā* had by no means been restricted to merely defeating non-Buddhist challengers. As the following passage testifies, it was correlatively connected with missionary aims:

---

[36] See BoBh$_D$ 74.19–21 = BoBh$_W$ 105.25–106.2 (BoBh$_T$ D57a7–b1 = Q67a1–2). On the MSA(Bh)'s doctrine of omniscience in relation to the *vidyā-sthāna*s, see GRIFFITHS (1990: 99–101); see also KRASSER (2005: 135–137).

[37] MSAVBh D *Mi* 203a3 on MSA 11.60: *rgyu rig pa daṅ / sgra rig pa la byaṅ chub sems dpa' brtson par byed do // ci'i phyir že na / mu stegs rgyu rig pa'i gtsug lag śes par rlom pa daṅ / sgra rig pa'i gtsug lag śes par rlom pa de dag tshar gcad par bya ba'i phyir brtson par byed do //* See also MSAVBh D *Mi* 203a6–7 on MSABh 70.16–17.

[38] MSAVBh D *Tsi* 92b2–3 on MSABh 136.23–24: *des ni mu stegs pa la sogs pa bdag daṅ rtag par yod pa la sogs par grub pa'i gtan tshigs su mṅon sum daṅ / rjes su dpag pa'i tshad ma dag smra ba la / tshad mar mi ruṅ ba'i ñes pa yod par rtog pa daṅ / mu stegs la sogs pa'i phas kyi rgol ba rnams saṅs rgyas kyi chos la sun 'byin pa dag mṅon sum daṅ rjes su dpag pa la sogs pa'i tshad mas tshar gcod ciṅ mu stegs pa'i bdag tu smra ba'i gžuṅ sun 'byin par byed de /.*

> '[The Bodhisattva gives himself up to *hetu-vidyā*] in order that those who have no faith [develop] faith in the [Buddhist] Teaching, and that those who [already] have faith strengthen [it].'[39]

According to Sāgaramegha's commentary, *hetu-vidyā* helps those who have already developed faith in Buddhism (whom he also terms *źugs pa rnams*) to strengthen (**sthāpana*?) their own Buddhist position (*sva-pakṣa*).[40] In his MSAVBh, Sthiramati borrows from the BoBh with only one slight change:

> '[The Bodhisattva] gives himself up [to *hetu-vidyā*] in order that those who have no faith develop faith in the [Buddhist] Teaching, and that those who have [already] developed faith [in it] intensify [their] faith.'[41]

So according to Sthiramati, the *yukti/hetu-vidyā* enterprise was expected to shape arguments in order (1) to found and support key Buddhist doctrines, (2) to defeat the non-Buddhist intellectuals' hostility towards Buddhism; (3) to convert them to the Buddhist *sad-dharma* or *śāsana*, (4) to strengthen the coreligionists' adherence to Buddhism.

— 1.5 —

Sthiramati's text testifies to the circumstance that, by the middle of the sixth century, two structures that had long been kept separate and were meant to meet very different theoretical and religious needs had merged with one another. On the one hand, the *yukti*s which the *cintā-mayī prajñā* mainly consisted of had been shaped as a hermeneutic tool aiming at demonstrating and investigating key Buddhist doctrines by means of reasoning. However, their purpose was strictly 'internal', and met the need of subjecting scriptural contents to critical analysis before these were passed on to cultivation/meditation.[42] On the other hand, *hetu-vidyā* as an episte-

[39] BoBh$_D$ 74.11–13 = BoBh$_W$ 105.13–16 (BoBh$_T$ D57a3–4 = Q66b3–5): *hetu-vidyāṁ bodhisattvaḥ paryeṣate ... aprasannānām asmiṁś chāsane prasādāya prasannānāṁ ca bhūyo-bhāvāya.* See also MVy 255.5–6: 5. *anabhiprasannānām abhiprasādāya.* 6. *abhiprasannānāṁ bhūyo-bhāvāya.*

[40] See BoBhVy D126a2–3 = Q153b5–6.

[41] MSAVBh D *Mi* 203a7 on MSABh 70.16–17: *bstan pa 'di la ma dad pa rnams dad pa bskyed pa daṅ / dad pa bskyed pa rnams dad pa'i phyir źiṅ 'phel bar bya ba'i phyir brtson par byed do //* . It is not easy to determine whether the second *dad pa bskyed pa* represents something like **utpanna-prasāda* (as a *bahu-vrīhi* compound), or if it just reflects the Tibetan translators' understanding of *prasanna*. At any rate, Sthiramati's Sanskrit is likely to have read **prasāda-bhūyo-bhāvāya*.

[42] It is no wonder that of the many objects the *upapatti-sādhana-yukti* is reputed to deal with, impermanence (*anityatā*) is quoted by far the most often (see ŚrBh 119*,14 = 142.12–13 and 119*,18 = 143.1 [ŚrBh$_T$ D58a1–2 and 3 = Q68a3 and 5]; SNS 10.7 [156.6]; MSAVBh D *Tsi*

mological and methodological device had long been connected with the primarily 'external' ambition to defend the Buddhist Dharma,[43] and to defeat (*nigraha*) and convert non-Buddhist opponents by means of *pramāṇa*-related reasoning (*tarka*). In the sixth century, theoretical as well as religious needs changed[44] to such an extent that what had long been kept separate, because of reflecting different concerns, was brought to coincide or coalesce. Dogmatics and dialectics, both of which had been using *pramāṇas*, came to merge and develop into a new apologetic and 'heresiological' enterprise. The gradual involvement of Buddhist dogmatics into the *hetu-vidyā* was made possible by Dignāga's achievements in the field of logic and by his re-shapement of the traditional *hetu-vidyā* into a powerful epistemological enterprise. Dignāga's strong defence of Buddhist epistemological doctrine in the *Pramāṇa-samuccaya* both served as an example and paved the way for his successors' endeavours in order to include key Buddhist doctrines like momentariness or Buddhology in the jurisdiction of *hetu-vidyā*. Buddhist *hetu-vidyā* specialists were now also in charge of the former concern and scope of *cint(an)ā*, in its *upapatti-sādhana-yukti* form especially, which they developed into a large-scale intellectual project committed to protection from outside hostility as well as the redefinition of Buddhist identity. Dharmakīrti stands out as the most prominent representative of this restructured Buddhist intellectual activity. But true to the traditional delineation between *hetu-vidyā* and *adhyātma-vidyā*, Buddhist epistemologists denied any soteriological relevance to epistemology as such, which, they contend, has no other *raison d'être* than to discard the heretics' misguiding epistemological doctrines. We can easily understand why this task was deemed an important one: if the soteriologically valued *cint(an)ā* exhausts itself in rational enquiry by means of *pramāṇas*, wrong epistemological doctrines can only be detrimental to the Buddhist path. Epistemology has no soteriological relevance whatsoever, but makes the intellectual turning-point between *śruta-mayī prajñā* and *bhāvanāmayī prajñā* possible.

203a2 on MSA 19.47c_1); next in importance come those properties Buddhist intellectuals regarded as closely connected with impermanence, namely, unsatisfactoriness (*duḥkhatā*), selflessness (*anātmatā*), dependent origination (< *pratītya-samutpannatā*), emptiness (*śūnyatā*) and momentariness (*kṣaṇikatva*) (see ŚrBh 119*,14–15 = 142.13–14 and 119*,18–120*,1 = 143.1–2 [ŚrBh$_T$ D58a2 and 3 = Q68a3 and 5]; SNS 10.7 [156.6–8]); mention can further be made of such *apratyakṣa* topics as the existence of the other world (*para loka-sattā*), or the non-destruction of good and evil actions (*śubhâśubha-karmâvipraṇāśa*) (see SNS 10.7 [156.10–12] and [156.16]; see also STEINKELLNER (1988: II,14–19)).

[43] See MSA 18.25–26 and MSABh 137.3 (*sad-dharma-*[*dh*]*āraṇāya*), where a Bodhisattva's *śāstra-jñatā*, i.e. his conversancy with different sciences /scientific treatises, aims at preserving (*dhāraṇa*) the Buddhist *sad-dharma*. Sthiramati's commentary is located at MSAVBh D *Tsi* 93b5–6.

[44] See ELTSCHINGER (2007: 25–64).

2. The Buddhist Epistemologists' account of *cintā-mayī prajñā*

— 2.1 —

Dharmakīrti concludes the first chapter of his PVin with the following remark:

> 'And it is this nature of the conventional means of valid cognition that has been explained. [Not only with regard to the ultimate means of valid cognition, but] also with regard to this [conventional cognition], others who are confused lead the world astray. Those, however, who cultivate the very wisdom born of reflection realise the ultimate *pramāṇa*, which is devoid of error, immaculate [and] without return.'[45]

In this passage, conventional means of valid cognition (*sāṁvyavahārika-pramāṇa*, i.e. ordinary perception and inference) and ultimate means of valid cognition (*pāramārthika-pramāṇa*) are contrasted sharply. It is also suggested that Dharmakīrti only elaborates on epistemology because dull-witted opponents develop and propagate misconceptions regarding conventional *pramāṇa*s. Since conventional *pramāṇa*s are instrumental in the path to liberation insofar as the whole process of *cintā-mayī prajñā* resorts to them, Dharmakīrti considers it his duty to refute these misconceptions so that people are not laid astray. In other words, epistemology or *hetu-vidyā* as a theoretical concern has no direct bearing on the path to salvation, but misconceived *pramāṇa*s ensure one's failure to achieve liberation, and hence epistemology is a necessary science.

A symmetrical contrast may be observed in the following statement by Kamalaśīla:

> 'Because he is endowed with such a perfection of qualities, the Blessed One causes the world to obtain elevation and *summum bonum*, and hence is the Teacher. ... Now it is by teaching dependent origination that the Blessed One causes [people] to attain such [human goals] as elevation. Indeed, [both elevation and *summum bonum* originate] from the correct teaching of dependent origination. [First,] firm conviction (*sampratyaya*) concerning the correct relation between action and result etc., which is the cause of good destinies, arises from the determination of its meaning; and [second,] the [proper] understanding

---

[45] PVin 1.44.1–4: *sāṁvyavahārikasya câitat pramāṇasya rūpam uktam, atrâpi pare mūḍhā visaṁvādayanti lokam iti. cintā-mayīm eva tu prajñām anuśīlayanto vibhrama-viveka-nirmalam anapāyi pāramārthika-pramāṇam abhimukhī-kurvanti*. Translation in KRASSER (2005: 143). On this passage and Dharmottara's important comments on it, see KRASSER (2005: 142–144), and ELTSCHINGER (2005b: 154–162).

> of *pudgala-* and *dharma-nairātmya*, which is the cause of *summum bonum*, arises through the sequence of hearing, reflection and cultivation, for once it has arisen, ignorance, which is the cause of *saṁsāra*, ceases, and once it has ceased, all the obstacles [consisting] of passions and [the obstacles that are screens] to the knowable, which are rooted in this [ignorance], cease. One will therefore attain liberation due to the cessation of all obstacles. ... But opponents hold this dependent origination to be an unsuitable cause (?*viṣama-hetu*, Tib. *mi mthun pa'i rgyu*) and to bear upon (°*-adhikaraṇa*, Tib. *brten pa*) entities that are contradicted by *pramāṇa*s. Therefore, both in order to show, by refuting them, that [dependent origination] has been correctly explained by the Blessed One, and in order to hint at the identity of the topics that must be dealt with by the whole treatise that is to be composed, [Śāntarakṣita] enumerates the many attributes of dependent origination as it was explained [by the Blessed One].'[46]

The epistemological endeavour here serves both a polemical and apologetic purpose in refuting challengers to Buddhist soteriology and reaffirming the pristine truth of Buddhism. But for meeting (mainly outward) objections, Śāntarakṣita could have spared himself the trouble of composing a treatise as impressive as the TSa. Learning, reflecting and meditating upon dependent origination in order to realise the two types of unsubstantiality is indeed enough (if I may say so) to ensure liberation.

First, both Dharmakīrti and Kamalaśīla hold theoretical epistemology (i.e. the composition of treatises such as the PVin or TSa) to meet polemical needs, in the case of Dharmakīrti, those pertaining to misconceptions with regard to conventional *pramāṇa*s and, in the case of Kamalaśīla, objections raised against *pratītya-samutpāda*. Dharmakīrti and Kamalaśīla agree in denying that epistemology itself has any soteriological value whatsoever provided one is not under the sway of mis-

[46] TSaP$_{K}$ 10.12–23 = TSaP$_{Sh}$ 13.1–12 (TSaP$_{T}$ D *Ze* 141a4–b3 = P *'e* 170a4–b5): [*t*]*athâbhūta-guṇa-sampad-yogād abhyu*[*]*daya-niḥśreyasa-prāpaṇato jagataḥ śāstā bhavati bhagavān ... pratītya-samutpāda-deśanayā câbhyudayâdi-samprāpako bhagavān. tathā hy aviparīta-pratītya-samutpāda-deśanātas*[**] *tad-arthâvadhāraṇāt sugati-hetur aviparīta-karma-phala-sambandhâdi-sampratyayôpajāyate. pudgala-dharma-nairātmyâvabodhaś ca niḥśreyasa-hetuḥ śruta-cintā-bhāvanā-krameṇôtpadyate. tad-utpattau hy avidyā saṁsāra-hetur nivartate. tan-nivṛttau ca tan-mūlaṁ sakalaṁ kleśa-jñeyâvaraṇaṁ nivartata iti sakalâvaraṇa-vigamād apavarga-samprāptir bhavati ... sa câyaṁ pratītya-samutpādaḥ parair viṣama-hetuḥ pramāṇa-vyāhata-padārthâdhi-karaṇaś cêṣyate. atas tan-nirāsena yathā-vad eva bhagavatā ukta iti darśanârthaṁ vakṣyamāṇa-sakala-śāstra-pratipādyârtha-tattvôpakṣepârthaṁ ca bahūnāṁ yathôkta-pratītya-samutpāda-viśeṣaṇānām upādānam...*

[*] TSaP$_{K}$, TSaP$_{T}$: °*yogād abhyu*°, TSaP$_{Sh}$: °*yogâdy-abhyu*°. [**] TSaP$_{Sh}$, TSaP$_{T}$: °*deśanā*°, TSaP$_{K}$ om. °*deśanā*°.

conceptions. Second, both of them consider the traditional sequence of *prajñā*s as a self-sufficient means of securing enlightenment.

Let us now have a closer look at the various dimensions of *cintā-mayī prajñā* in the Buddhist epistemological tradition. Five topics are worth considering in this respect: the *cintā-mayī prajñā* as a definitional prerequisite for the cognition of *yogin*s (§ 2.2), the removal of nescience as the aim of a *yogin*'s endeavour (§ 2.3), the initial philosophical reflections of the Buddha-to-be (§ 2.4), the appraisal of scriptural authority (§ 2.5) and the issue of practical rationality (§ 2.6).

— 2.2 —

As is well known, a given cognition must meet two conditions in order to be termed a '(direct) perception' (*pratyakṣa*) and thus a means of valid cognition: first, it must be free of any intellectual/linguistic content whatsoever (*kalpanâpoḍha*); second, it must be non-erroneous (*abhrānta*).[47] This holds true of the so-called 'perception of mystics' (*yogi-pratyakṣa*).[48] According to ordinary understanding (*loka, loka-prasiddhi*), a *yogin* is one who devotes himself to psychic concentration (*samādhi*) or mental one-pointedness (*cittâikāgratā*);[49] according to (Buddhist) treatises (*śāstra, śāstra-sthiti*), a *yogin* is one who is endowed with tranquillity (*śamatha*, i.e. *samādhi*) and discernment (*vipaśyanā*, i.e. *prajñā*), the latter being also described as the 'discrimination' of the (true) reality (**tattva-pravicaya*?).[50] Since mystics' cognition has a nearly endless mental cultivation (*bhāvanā*) for its cause (°-*maya*),[51] it is non-conceptual (*vidhūta-kalpanā-jāla, akalpa, avikalpaka*) and

---

[47] See PVin 1, p. 7.2, NB 1.5.

[48] See PV 3.281–286, PVin 1, p. 27.7sq, NB 1.11. On the cognition of mystics (*yogi-pratyakṣa*), see ELTSCHINGER (forthcoming 2).

[49] According to PVinṬ D117b2 /Q135b1 (*'jig rten na ni mñam par gźag pa la rnal 'byor ba yin*), NBṬ$_{Ś}$ 12.8–9 = NBṬ$_{M}$ 70.2 (*yogaḥ samādhiḥ. sa yasyâsti sa yogī*) and DhPr 70.19–20 thereon (*yogi-śabdasya vyutpattim āha—yoga iti. samādhiś cittâikāgratā. iha dharmottareṇa loka-prasiddhir āśritā*).

[50] According to PVinṬ D117b2–3 = Q135b1–2 (*bstan bcos las ni tiṅ ṅe 'dzin daṅ śes rab kyi bdag ñid źi gnas daṅ lhag mthoṅ la yin te / rnal 'byor ba de dag la yod pa de dag ni rnal 'byor bas te / rtag tu mñam par gźag pa daṅ / de kho na rnam par 'byed pa la* [D: P *las*] *brtson pa'o //*) and DhPr 70.20–22 (*viniścaya-ṭīkāyāṁ tu śāstra-sthitis tenâvirodhaḥ. yad vā samādhi-grahaṇa-syôpalakṣanatvāt prajñā ca viveka-karaṇa-śaktir draṣṭavyā. s*[*ā*?] *yasyâsti sa nitya-samāhito viveka-karaṇa-tatparaś ca yogī*).

[51] Commented upon as °-*hetu-niṣpattika* (PVA 326.23–24), °-*hetuka* (PVV 203.1–2), °*rdzogs pa las skyes pa* (PVP D210b4 /Q246b7–8). For a grammatical explanation of °-*maya*, see AKBh 335.6 (*hetau mayaṭ-vidhānāt*) and POUSSIN (1980: VI,144, based on AKVy 525.8–16).

therefore presents a vivid or distinct image of its object.[52] The first necessary condition is thus met. But contrary to other types of meditative experiences (*aśubhā, pṛthivī-kṛtsnâyatana* etc.) or to dream-images, which present a vivid picture of an *unreal* (*abhūta*) object, the mystics' cognition Dharmakīrti describes is reliable/non-belying (*saṁvādin, avisaṁvādin*),[53] i.e. bears upon a real (*bhūta*) object.[54]

Cintā-mayī prajñā is the factor Dharmakīrti holds to be responsible for a cognition's meeting the second defining condition and thus being a *pramāṇa*. In PVin 1, p. 27.9–11, Dharmakīrti presents us with the following sequence of cultivation (*bhāvanā-krama*[55]):

> 'The *yogin*s cultivate objects after they have [first] grasped [them] through a cognition born of listening [to treatises that are favourable to cultivation], and [then] ascertained [them] through a [cognition] born of reflecting [upon them] by means of reasoning (*yukti*) [, i.e. by means of *pramāṇa*s; of these *yogin*s,] the [cognition] which, at the completion of this [cultivation], appears as vividly as in cases such as fear [or sorrow, and hence is] non-conceptual [but also] has a true object [because it bears upon an object that has been formerly ascertained by *pramāṇa*s], this is also the *pramāṇa* [that consists in direct] perception.'[56]

Here, *yukti-cintā-maya* ('born from reflection by means of[57] reasoning') already points to Dharmakīrti's indebtedness to the Yogācāra/Sautrāntika interpretation of *cintā-mayī prajñā /cint(an)ā*. Dharmottara's explanations, which clearly borrow from the AKBh, confirm this impression: whereas *śruta-maya* is commented upon as 'having for its cause the hearing of treatises that are suitable for /conducive to mental cultivation',[58] *yukti-cintā-maya* is explained as 'reflection (*cintā*), i.e. exami-

[52] See PV 3.281 (*spaṣṭam evâvabhāsate*), PVin 1.28 (*spaṣṭaṁ bhāsate*), PVin 1, p. 27.10 (*spaṣṭâvabhāsin*).

[53] See PV 3.286, PVin 1.28.

[54] *Bhūta* in PV 3.285 = PVin 1.31; *bhūtârtha* in NB 1.11.

[55] *Bhāvanā-krama* in PVinṬ D117b1–2 and 3 = Q135b1 and 3, DhPr 68.5.

[56] PVin 1, p. 27.7–8: *yogināṁ api śruta-mayena jñānenârthān gṛhītvā yukti-cintā-mayena vyavasthāpya bhāvayatāṁ tan-niṣpattau yat spaṣṭâvabhāsi bhayādāv iva tad avikalpakam avitatha-viṣayaṁ pramāṇaṁ pratyakṣam.*

[57] Contrary to PVin 1_V, p. 72.30–31 (*rigs pa sems pa*), PVinṬ$_{Jñ}$ D195a5 = Q238a1 and PVinṬ's *pratīka* (D117b4 = Q135b4) read: *rigs pas sems / bsams pa.*

[58] According to PVinṬ D117b3–4 /Q135b3–4: *thos pa las byuṅ bas bsgoms pa daṅ rjes su mthun pa'i bstan bcos mñan pa'i rgyu can gyis bzuṅ ba'i ṅes pa'i don*… Cf. AKBh 334.16–17 (*satya-darśanasyânulomaṁ śrutam udgṛhṇāti*). Dharmakīrti's *gṛhītvā* is also reminiscent of Vasubandhu's formulation.

nation (*nidhyāna*) by means of reasoning (*yukti*), i.e. by means of *pramāṇas*.'[59] According to Dharmakīrti, the objects of the *yogin*'s perception are *bhūta* or *bhūtârtha*, 'real', which Dharmottara comments upon as 'grasped by means of a *pramāṇa*.'[60] Similarly, the reason why this perception is reliable/ non-belying is, according to Jñānaśrībhadra, that 'it cognises an object that has been [previously] determined ([*b*]*źag*) by means of reasoning.'[61] It is thus clear that the reliability of the *yogin*'s perception rests on the fact that its objects have been submitted to a rational analysis carried out by means of *pramāṇas*. As an example of such objects, Dharmakīrti refers his reader back twice to (the vision of) the Noble Truths (*ārya-satya*) as he has ascertained (*nirṇīta, gtan la pheb pa*) them in his PV.[62] Dharmottara adduces the same example,[63] whereas all of Dharmakīrti's commentators interpret the latter's use of *prāk* ('previously') as a reference to the *satya-vicāra*-section of PV 2.[64] Other examples are Prajñākaragupta's *para-loka* and Devendrabuddhi's impermanence (*anityâdi*).[65]

---

[59] According to PVinṬ D117b4 = Q135b4: *rigs pas te tshad mas sems śiṅ ṅes par rtog pa ni rigs pa sems pa'o //* . Cf. AKBh 335.5 (*yukti-nidhyāna-jaś ca cintā-mayī*), n. 4 above. On the equivalence *ṅes par rtog pa* = *nidhyāna*, see HIRAKAWA (1973: 209) *s.v. nidhyāna*. AKVy 525.9 glosses *nidhyāna* with *nitīraṇa*, which also can be found as *ṅes par rtog pa* in Tibetan translations (see TSD_{LCh} *s.v. ṅes par rtog pa*).

[60] According to $NBṬ_Ś$ 11.18 = $NBṬ_M$ 67.3: *bhūtaḥ sad-bhūto 'rthaḥ. pramāṇena dṛṣṭaś ca sad-bhūtaḥ*.

[61] According to $PVinṬ_{Jñ}$ D195a5–6 /Q231b1: *rigs pas* [*b*]*źag pa'i don rtogs pa'i phyir bslu ba med pa…*

[62] PVin 1, p. 27.11–12: *ārya-satya-darśanavad yathā nirṇītam asmābhiḥ pramāṇa-vārttike*; PV 3.286b_2: *prāṅ-nirṇīta-vastuvat*.

[63] See $NBṬ_Ś$ 11.18 = $NBṬ_M$ 67.4 (*yathā catvāry ārya-satyāni*) and DhPr 70.15–16 thereon; PVinṬ D118a4–6 = Q136a5–8.

[64] See PVP D210b4 = Q246b7 and D211b5 = Q248a5; PVA 327.32–33; PVV 204.12. In addition, mention should be made of the fact that all commentators interpret PV 3.281a (*prāg uktaṁ yogināṁ jñānam*) as: '[As to] the cognition of *yogins*, [it has already been] presented above [as bearing upon the four Noble Truths]' (PVP D210b4 = Q246b7: *'phags pa'i bden pa bźi'i yul can du bśad pa*; PVA 326.23: *catur-ārya-satya-viṣayam ... uktam*; PVV 203.1: *satya-viṣayam uktam*).

[65] See PVA 327.32–33; PVP D211b2 = Q247b8–248a1. In his first BhK, Kamalaśīla also addresses the issue of the *cintā-mayī prajñā*. By means of the *cintā-mayī prajñā*, a *yogin* is supposedly able to penetrate (*nirvedhayati*) the explicit as well as intentional meanings (*nīta-neyârtha*), and to ascertain (*niś√ci*) the real object (or: meaning) in order to dispel any possible doubts (*vicikitsā*) before proceeding to mental cultivation (see BhK 1 p. 508/198.11–16). Kamalaśīla says (BhK 1 p. 508–509/ 198.21–199.2): *cintā-mayyā prajñayā yukty-āgamābhyāṁ pratyavekṣya bhūtam eva vastu-rūpaṁ bhāvanīyam. vastūnāṁ svarūpaṁ ca paramârthato 'nutpāda evâgamato yuktitaś ca niścitam.*—'The real nature of entities alone should be cultivated [by the *yogin*], after he has pondered [on it] by means of the *cintā-mayī prajñā*, i.e. through reasoning and scriptures. Now through reasoning and scriptures, the proper nature of entities has been ascertained (*niścita*) as consisting ultimately of mere non-origination.' A few pages later, Kamalaśīla concludes, BhK 1, p. 514/204.11–13: *tad evaṁ*

In order to grasp at the metaphysical as well as soteriological relevance of a *yogin*'s making use of *pramāṇa*s at the *cintā-mayī prajñā*-level, some explanations may not be out of place.

— 2.3 —

According to Dharmakīrti and Vasubandhu,[66] *avidyā* ('nescience', 'ignorance') is neither something other than *vidyā* ('knowledge'), nor is it the mere absence of *vidyā*.[67] *Avidyā* can therefore only be some kind of 'anti-*vidyā*', i.e. a cognition that counteracts or opposes (*pratipakṣa*, *vipakṣa*) *vidyā*.[68] Moreover, *avidyā* must be 'cognitional' since it is a mental factor (*caitta*-[*dharma*]).[69] Dharmakīrti sums up this rather technical discussion in the following way:

> 'Since [ignorance] is the opposite of *vidyā* [and] is a perception (*upalabdhi*) because it is a mental factor, ignorance consists in erroneous perception (*mithyôpalabdhi*).'[70]

Here (1) *vidyā* is defined as the perception (*darśana*) or grasping (*grahaṇa*) of a real object (*bhūtârtha*);[71] we may then expect *avidyā* to grasp an unreal object

---

cintā-mayyā prajñayā niścitya bhūtam arthaṁ tasya pratyakṣī-karaṇāya bhāvanā-mayīṁ prajñām utpādayet.—'Therefore [the *yogin*], having ascertained (*niścitya*), in the [above-mentioned] way (*evam*), the real object by means of the *cintā-mayī prajñā*, should generate the *bhāvanā-mayī prajñā* in order to realise [this object] directly.' Keywords are here the gerund and past passive participle of *niś√ci*, 'to ascertain', a term we have already met in Durvekamiśra's interpretation of *pramāṇena dṛṣṭam* as *pramāṇena niścitam*. According to Kamalaśīla, the function of *cintā-mayī prajñā* is to ascertain a real object (and meaning), the real or true nature ([*sva*]*rūpa*) of entities (*vastu*).

[66] See AKBh 140.26–141.5, POUSSIN (1980: III,88–89), translated in PRUDEN (1991: II,419–420).

[67] If *avidyā* were something other than *vidyā*, then it would ensue that *rūpa* ('corporeity') would also be *avidyā*; since *nirvāṇa* puts an end to, or coincides with the elimination of (defiled) ignorance, mere *asamprakhyāna* ('lack of clarity') cannot define *avidyā*, because it may still characterise an Arhat. See PVP D91a7–b1 = Q105b3–5, PVA 145.16–21, PVV 85.5–7.

[68] See PVP D91b1–2 = Q105b5–6.

[69] Abhidharma defines mental factors as associated (*samprayukta*) with *citta* ('mind'), i.e. sharing the latter's support (*āśraya*), object (*ālambana*), aspect (*ākāra*), time (*kāla*) and (number of) *dravya*s. Since *asamprakhyāna* is mere absence (*abhāva*), it can have no support, object, aspect etc., and therefore can be neither a mental factor nor a cognition. See AK 2.34b_2d and AKBh, p. 62.5–10, POUSSIN (1980: II,177–178) translated in PRUDEN (1991: 205–206), PVP D91b7–92a2 = Q106a5–7, PVA 146.3–4, PVV 85.8–10.

[70] PV 2.213ac: *vidyāyāḥ pratipakṣatvāc caittatvenôpalabdhitaḥ / mithyôpalabdhir ajñānam.*

[71] PVP D91a7 = Q105b3: *yaṅ dag pa'i don mthoṅ ba ni rig pa yin la /* ; PVṬ *Je* D113b7 = Q134b2 = ṔVSVṬ 209.20–21: *bhūtârtha-grahaṇaṁ vidyā /* .

(*abhūtârtha*) or, as Devendrabuddhi has it, to 'grasp aspects that are contrary (*viparīta*) to the aspects grasped by *vidyā*.'[72] (2) Unlike Vasubandhu, Dharmakīrti defines *avidyā* as the false view of Self (*sat-kāya-darśana*, *ātma-dṛṣṭi*) or the belief in/adherence to a Self (*ātma-graha*, °-*abhiniveśa*).[73] Erroneous perception/ignorance then turns out to consist in the superimposition of ego-related aspects on a reality that is devoid of them. As Manorathanandin puts it, '*avidyā* is opposite to *vidyā*, the perception of unsubstantiality (*nairātmya-darśana*).' To sum up: whereas *vidyā* grasps the *bhūtârtha*, i.e. real aspects like impermanence, unsubstantiality etc., *avidyā* as erroneous perception grasps superimposed aspects like Self (*ātman*).

Vidyā is nothing but the 'normal' or 'natural' operation of the mind. In this respect, the mind naturally has *tattva-darśana* ('perception of the [true] reality') or *vipaśyanā* ('discernment') as its own nature. This is the way Dharmakīrti interprets the canonical *topos* of the mind's natural luminosity (*prakṛtyā prabhāsvaram*) in PV 2.208ab.[74] However, it is the very nature of human beings' saṁsāric existence to be under the sway of *avidyā*, i.e. to superimpose erroneous aspects on the unsubstantial, unsatisfactory and impermanent reality. In other words, the erroneous cognition that defines *avidyā* represents a distortion of the mind's 'natural' operation or *vipaśyanā*-nature. But there is a way out, as Dharmakīrti himself puts it:

> 'Owing to another cause[, i.e. to a cause of error], the [mind] moves away from this [own nature, and with regard to its object engages in the superimposition of unreal aspects such as permanence; but as] unsettled [in this distortion] as the cognition of a serpent [instead of a rope, the mind stands] in need of a condition in order to get rid [of such deviations].'[75]

The condition the mind depends upon in order to rid itself of that distortion consists in the *pramāṇa*s, as is made clear by Devendrabuddhi.[76] Commenting on PV 2.209, the same author holds direct perception and inference to be causes that annul

---

[72] According to PVP D91b1–2 = Q105b5–6: *de ltar na rnam pa gaṅ rig pas gzuṅ ba de las phyin ci log pa'i rnam pa 'dzin pa can ni ma rig pa źes bya bar 'gyur ro //* . Note also PVP D91b5–6 = Q106a2–3: *rigs pas gzuṅ bar bya ba rnams las phyin ci log tu rtogs pa'i ṅo bo ñid ni ma rig pa'o //* .

[73] Among numerous other passages, see PVSV 111.11–112.5 and PV 2.212d.

[74] See ELTSCHINGER (2005b: 180, 184–197 and n. 133) for *vipaśyanā* as the nature of the mind.

[75] PV 2.207a_2d:

... asyās tan nimittântarataḥ skhalat /
vyāvṛttau pratyayâpekṣam adṛḍhaṁ sarpa-buddhivat //

On this stanza, see also ELTSCHINGER (2005b: 187–190).

[76] PVP D89a3 = Q102b6: *'khrul pa gnod pa can gyi tshad ma la ltos pa daṅ bcas pa yin no //* .

(*bādhaka-nimitta*) the mind's distortion.[77] But whereas Devendrabuddhi remains silent about the way *pramāṇa*s may neutralise or oppose error, Śākyabuddhi provides us with an interesting explanation:

> 'For example, at the time of the elimination [of error], one perceives another phase (*kṣaṇa*) that is entirely dissimilar (*ativilakṣaṇa*?) to the preceding one; therefore, by means of the [kind of] perception (*pratyakṣa*) called "non-perception" (*anupalabdhi*), one establishes (*vyavasthāp-*?) the impermanence (*anityatā*) of the cause, and on account of this, unsubstantiality (*nairātmya*). Then, once the sequence of cultivation has taken place, perception turns out to be the annulling cause (*bādhaka-nimitta*) which consists of (°-*lakṣaṇa*) the perception of unsubstantiality (*nairātmya-darśana*). And when one successively undertakes such [stages] as reflection (*cintā*) and cultivation (*bhāvanā*) after having determined unsubstantiality on the [logical] ground (*liṅga*) of being a product (*kṛtakatva*), then inference (*anumāna*) also turns out to be an annulling cause.'[78]

As this passage makes clear, *pramāṇa*s are asked to establish or ascertain the real aspects that will help cognitions oppose erroneous superimpositions and will thus gradually correct the mind's distortion.

The cognitions that take these aspects for their objects are regularly described as 'agreeing with/corroborated by (a) means of valid cognition' (*pramāṇa-saṁvādin*). According to Devendrabuddhi and Śākyabuddhi, a cognition (first and foremost *nairātmya-darśana*) that bears upon such aspects as impermanence or unsubstantiality is termed *pramāṇa-saṁvādin* (but also 'correct' [*aviparīta*], 'true' [*satya*]), and as such may successfully oppose and finally overcome the *ātmâtmīya-dṛṣṭi*. Conversely, an erroneous cognition that functions (*pravṛtta*) on the basis of superimpositions (or bears upon superimposed aspects such as the Self) is described as 'disagreeing with /non-corroborated by (a) means of valid cognition' (*pramāṇâsaṁvādin*), and is nothing but a condition that is entirely adventitious (*āgantuka-pratyaya*) to the

---

[77] PVP D89b5–6 = Q103b4: *mṅon sum daṅ rjes su dpag pa'i rkyen ji lta ba bźin du gnod pa can gyi rgyu mtshan khas blaṅs pa'i phyir ro //* .

[78] PVṬ *Ñe* D134a6–b1 = Q165b4–5: *rgyun rnam par 'chad pa'i dus na / sṅa ma las śin tu mtshan ñid mi 'dra ba'i skad cig ma gźan mṅon sum du byed pa'i phyir / mi dmigs pa źes bya ba'i mṅon sum gyis rgyu mi rtag pa ñid daṅ / de'i stobs kyis bdag med pa ñid rnam par 'jog par byed do // de nas bsgom pa'i rim pa yin pa de'i tshe mṅon sum ni bdag med pa ñid mthoṅ ba'i mtshan ñid can gyi gnod pa can rgyu mtshan ñid yin no // gaṅ gi tshe byas pa ñid la sogs pa'i rtags kyis bdag med pa rnam par* [*b*]*źag nas / bsam pa daṅ bsgom pa la sogs pa rim bźin rtsom pa de'i tshe / rjes su dpag pa yaṅ rgyu mtshan ñid yin no //* .

mind.[79] As for Dharmottara, he holds the objects of the *yogin*'s perception to have been 'purified' ([*pari*]*śuddha*) by, i.e. to be correct in virtue of (a) *pramāṇa*(s). According to him, the *yogin*s' perception[80] 'is non-belying because it grasps an object that has been purified (*śuddha*) by the *pramāṇa*s', or because[81] 'it bears upon something that has been 'purified' (*pariśuddha*) by the *pramāṇa*s.' To put it in other words, it is the very function of *yukti-cintā-mayī prajñā* to provide the *yogin*'s cultivation with *pramāṇa-(pari)śuddhârtha*, to make it **pramāṇa-pariśuddha-vastu-viṣayā*.[82]

[79] According to PVP D58b3 = Q66b7–8 (*bdag med pa mthoṅ ba ni bdag daṅ bdag gir lta ba'i gñen po daṅ / phyin ci ma log pa daṅ tshad ma'i grogs can yin no //*), PVP D58b4–5 = Q67a1–2 (*bdag med pa mthoṅ ba ni bdag daṅ bdag gir lta ba 'joms par byed pa yin no // gaṅ gi phyir bden pa daṅ tshad ma'i grogs can ñid yin pa…*), PVP D90a4 /Q104a4 (*mi rtag pa la sogs pa'i rnam pa'i yul can ñid yin pa'i phyir ro // des ni tshad ma'i grogs can ñid yin par bśad do //*), PVṬ *Ñe* D133a5 /Q164a4–5 (*rgyu mtshan 'ga 'źig las bdag la sogs par sgro btags pas 'jug pa'i 'khrul pa'i śes pa ni glo bur gyi rkyen yin te / de ni tshad ma'i grogs ma yin pa ñid kyi phyir ro //*), PVP D89a7 /Q103a3–4 ([concerning *dri ma*] *sgro btags pa'i rnam pa'i sgo nas dṅos po med pa'i stobs kyis źugs pa'i phyir daṅ tshad ma'i grogs med pa ñid kyi phyir ro //*). See also PVV 86.24.

[80] $NBṬ_Ś$ 12.8 = $NBṬ_M$ 70.1: *pramāṇa-śuddhârtha-grahitvāc ca saṁvādakam*. Note also Durvekamiśra's explanation (DhPr 67.15–16): *pramāṇâdhigato 'rthaḥ pramāṇa-śuddha ity ucyate*.

[81] According to PVinṬ D117b1 = Q135a8: *tshad mas yoṅs su dag pa'i dṅos po'i yul can yin pa'i phyir ma 'khrul pa yin pas…* Note also PVinṬ D123a1–2 = Q142a2–3: *tshad mas yoṅs su dag pa'i don can ñid kyis kyaṅ mi slu ba ñid yin te /* . For a similar use of *pariśuddha*, see the passage of the SNS quoted in n. 22 above, and compare PVSV 109.3–4.

[82] The following two stanzas also make the sequence between *cintā* and *bhāvanā* quite clear, PV 2.252–253:

> *saṁskāra-duḥkhatāṁ matvā kathitā duḥkha-bhāvanā /*
> *sā ca naḥ pratyayôtpattiḥ sā nairātmya-dṛg-āśrayaḥ //*
> *muktis tu śūnyatā-dṛṣṭes tad-arthāḥ śeṣa-bhāvanāḥ /*
> *anityāt prāha tenâiva duḥkhaṁ duḥkhān nirātmatām //*
>
> 'The meditation on [such an aspect as] suffering has been stated thinking [not of suffering qua suffering, but] of [that] suffering [that is] essential to conditioned factors as such (*saṁskāra-duḥkhatā*), and this [very suffering] is for us [Buddhists] the arising through conditions, this [being in turn] the basis of the [right] view of unsubstantiality. [As for] the liberation [from the bondage in *saṁsāra*, it] is due to the [right] view of emptiness, [all] the remaining meditations aiming at this [view of emptiness]; this is the reason why [the Blessed One] taught suffering out of impermanence [and] selflessness out of suffering.'

That *sā nairātmya-dṛg-āśrayaḥ* pertains to *yukti* is made clear by Devendrabuddhi's commentary on this *pāda* (PVP D108b4–5 = Q126a1–3): *bdag med lta rten yin / bdag med pa ñid mthoṅ ba skye ba'i thabs yin te / skad cig mar zad pa can gyi dṅos po mi rtag pa rigs pas ṅes par byas pas mi rtag pa gaṅ yin pa de ni rgyu'i gźan dbaṅ skad cig ma re rer 'jig pa can byed pa med par 'jug par 'gyur ro // de bas na 'di ni bdag gam bdag gi ma yin no źes bsgoms pa na / gaṅ zag stoṅ pa ñid du rtogs pa 'gyur ro //* —'[Suffering which is essential to conditioned factors as such] is the basis of the right view of unsubstantiality, viz., is the means (*upāya*) for the rise of the perception

Though unable to uproot ignorance by themselves, *pramāṇa*s do more than just pave the way toward the Path to liberation. In being responsible for the arising of right views that (still on a theoretical level) counteract the most visible and gross manifestations of *avidyā*, they form the turning point that makes the Path toward salvation *possible*. This is I think exactly what Śākyabuddhi and Karṇakagomin intend to say when they state that[83] 'the *pramāṇa*s, which grasp real aspects such as impermanence, induce (*āvahanti*) the counteracting path (*pratipakṣa-mārga*)' a *yogin* will have to go through in order to reach liberation, i.e. to have his mind freed from the adventitious defilements that hinder its 'natural' operation.

— 2.4 —

Dharmakīrti's PV 2 presents us with a sketchy account of the main stages in the Bodhisattva's long career, from the prerequisite of compassion (*jagad-dhitâiṣitva*, PV 2.34–131ab) to the various intellectual and meditative achievements that constitute the religious Path (*śāstṛtva*, PV 2.131c–138), and from the Enlightenment (*sugatatva*, PV 2.139–144) to the (new) Buddha's teaching of the four Noble Truths (*tāyitva*, PV 2.145–279).[84] This chapter often provides an opportunity to fixate rather abstruse epistemological topics onto the general map of Dharmakīrti's Buddhism. In other words, PV 2 provides us with narrative equivalents of theoretical elaborations. The sequence between *cintā-mayī* and *bhāvanā-mayī prajñā* is no exception. Its 'biographical' account occurs in PV 2.131cd–136, where Dharmakīrti recounts the Bodhisattva's reflections and subsequent transition to cultivation:

> '[Wishing to calm other people's suffering,] the compassionate [Bodhisattva] engages in [the cultivation of] means to [calm suffering] in order to eradicate [his own] suffering: for whom the goal (*upeya*) and [its] cause remain imperceptible (*parokṣa*), it is indeed a difficult task to [correctly] teach [others about them]. Reflecting on [the means and the goal] through reasoning (*yukti*) and the Scriptures (*āgama*), [the compassionate Bodhisattva] inquires into the cause of the suffer-

of unsubstantiality. The ascertainment, by means of reasoning (*yukti*), that momentary entities are impermanent, [makes it clear that] what[ever] is impermanent exists as dependent on causes (*hetu-paratantra*), momentarily perishing ([*kṣaṇa-*]*kṣaṇa-kṣayin*) and bereft of an agent (*akartṛ*?). Therefore, the understanding of *pudgala-nairātmya* occurs when one has cultivated [the view] that the [impermanent] is neither I nor mine.'

[83] PVṬ *Je* D252a1–2 = Q299a8–b1 = PVSVṬ 401.12–13: *pramāṇāny anityâdi-bhūtâkāra-grāhīṇi pratipakṣa-mārgam āvahanti*.

[84] On this sequence of properties, see FRANCO (1997: 15–43), and ELTSCHINGER (forthcoming 1).

ing [that is to be eradicated] and, through the particularities of suffering itself, [he also inquires] into the impermanent nature etc., of the [cause in question]. Since in this way [he who wishes to eradicate suffering] sees that there is no end to the effect as long as the cause remains, he inquires into the antidote of the cause [of suffering] in order to eliminate it. [As for the *dharma* forming] the antidote to that [cause, it] is also ascertained by the [Bodhisattva's] knowledge of the nature of the cause [itself]. [That] cause [is] attachment to dispositions, [an attachment which] is due to the belief in Self and "one's own"; [as for] the antidote to that [cause, it is] the perception of unsubstantiality, [which is] incompatible with it. All the [respective] virtues and shortcomings of the [means and its antidote] become [very] clear to [the altruistic Bodhisattva] who practices the means [that he has ascertained, i.e. the perception of unsubstantiality] constantly, without interruption and for a [very] long time.'[85]

This passage presents us with no less than Dharmakīrti's account of the future Buddha's initial philosophical reflections, i.e. with an exemplary or paradigmatic case of *cintā-mayī prajñā*. Dharmakīrti's (and his commentators') terminology is typical for *cintā*: first, the Bodhisattva analyses (< *vimṛśan*, PV 2.132c) through *yukti* and *āgama*,[86] which we can safely interpret as the characteristic attitude gov-

[85] PV 2.131cd–136:

dayāvān duḥkha-hānârtham upāyeṣv abhiyujyate //
parokṣôpeya-tad-dhetos tad-ākhyānaṁ hi duṣkaram /
yukty-āgamābhyāṁ vimṛśan duḥkha-hetuḥ parīkṣate //
tasyânityâdi-rūpaṁ ca duḥkhasyâiva viśeṣaṇaiḥ /
yatas tathā sthite hetau nivṛttir neti paśyati //
phalasya hetor hānârthaṁ tad-vipakṣaḥ parīkṣate /
sādhyate tad-vipakṣo 'pi heto rūpâvabodhataḥ //
ātmâtmīya-graha-kṛtaḥ snehaḥ saṁskāra-gocaraḥ /
hetur virodhi nairātmya-darśanaṁ tasya bādhakam //
bahuśo bahudhôpāyaṁ kālena bahunāsya ca /
gacchanty abhyasyatas tatra guṇa-doṣāḥ prakāśatām //

On that passage, see in general ELTSCHINGER (2005a: 397–408).

[86] In his review of VETTER (1984) = (1990^2), FRANCO (1989: 86) has made a strong case of the former's 'belittling of the Buddha': VETTER's interpretation 'would leave no room for the Buddha to innovate anything, not even to improve a previously existing way to liberation' (1989: 85). According to FRANCO (1989: 88), Dharmakīrti's allusion to *āgama* in PV 2.132cd should be understood as referring to 'the time when the Buddha was not yet a Buddha, i.e. when he was still a Bodhisattva.' Moreover, it should be read against the background of the Buddhist 'traditional solution' (1989: 89) to the 'problem of the originality of the Buddha' (1989: 89), namely 'that there were many Buddhas, and they all have exactly the same teaching, but each of them discovers the way by himself' (1989: 90). In ELTSCHINGER (2005a: 399–400, n. 22), I partly interpreted

erning *cintā* in the light of the passages from Kamalaśīla's BhK quoted above; whereas Śākyabuddhi interprets *āgama* as actually consisting of a critical examination of the means taught in the scriptures (*des bstan pa = luṅ gis bstan pa*),[87] he explains *yukti* as being inference (*anumāna*) as well as the analysis (*vicāra*) one carries out by means of inference;[88] second, *yukty-āgamābhyāṁ vimarśaḥ* serves the end of a double examination (*parīkṣā*, PV 2.132d, 134b); third, both *parīkṣā*s function by way of proof/establishment (< *sādhyate*, PV 2.134a), which Manorathanandin as well as the Tibetan translators of PV understand as ascertainment (< *niścīyate*; *ṅes 'gyur*).[89] Now let us have a closer look at the structure and sequence of the double examination carried out by the Bodhisattva. First he inquires into the cause of suffering (*duḥkha-hetu*) as well as into the nature (*rūpa*) of this cause. By analysing causation (*hetu-mātra*), he makes certain that suffering cannot be without cause, and that it will be possible to put an end to it if its cause is not eternal;[90] as suffering itself is occasional (*kādācitka*), its cause must be occasional too, and hence impermanent and destructible (< *nivartana-yogyatā*).[91] Second, he inquires into the antidote (*vipakṣa*) to the cause of suffering, i.e. into the *dharma* which proves to be contradictory to that cause, for he knows that the resultant suffering (*phala*) will last as long as its cause; the cultivation (*abhyāsa*) or practice (*anuṣṭhāna*) of this oppo-

PV 2.132cd along the line suggested by FRANCO. I would now suggest an altogether different interpretation of PV 2.132cd, one that reads with a decidedly Mahāyānist perspective. Although virtually infinite in number in all places and times, Buddhas are extremely rare in one and the same world-system. At the beginning of their careers, they all learn Buddhist teachings under the kind guidance of such *kalyāṇa-mitra*s as fellow but more advanced Bodhisattvas or even Buddhas, and then proceed to reflect on these teachings in a rational and independent way. It is my contention that Dharmakīrti alludes here only to the *cintā-mayī* level: *yukty-āgamābhyām* does not refer in reversed order to *śruta-mayī* and *cintā-mayī*, but to the latter *only*, in much the same way as Buddhist, Yogācāra or Mādhyamika literature examines various topics *yukty-āgamābhyām*, i.e. first by demonstrating and then by quoting authoritative Buddhist scriptures. That *cintā-mayī prajñā* also consists of reasoning *yukty-āgamābhyām* is made clear by the passage of BhK 1 (see n. 65 above) quoted above, but also by some suggestive remarks by Kajiyama (see SCHERRER-SCHAUB (1981: 196–197)). If Dharmakīrti's half-verse is to be read against a Mahāyānist background, as I would suggest, the question of a Buddha's originality is no longer a problem: first, because all Buddhas have become Buddhas by first hearing *Buddhist* scriptures; second, because Buddhas are so rare that their uniform teaching is nevertheless always new to their audience, thus meeting the criterion of *ajñātârtha-prakāśatva*.

[87] See PVṬ *Ñe* D117a3–4 = Q143a4–7, and ELTSCHINGER (2005a: 398–400).

[88] PVṬ *Ñe* D117a2 = Q143a3–4: *rigs pa ni rjes su dpag pa yin la des rnam par dpyad pa ni rigs pa yin te* / .

[89] PVV 57.19.

[90] See PVP D55a4–5 = Q62b6–8.

[91] See PVP D55b1–2 = Q63a3–5 and PVV 57.8–10.

site *dharma* will destroy the cause of suffering.[92] Just as the Bodhisattva inferred the properties of the cause from the properties of its effect, he now identifies the antidote as that which presents an aspect (*ākāra*) of the object (*ālambana*) which is contrary to the aspect of the cause.[93] The cause of suffering can be identified as an attachment (*sneha*) (1) that bears upon (*gocara, viṣaya* = *ālambana*) the dispositions (*saṁskāra*), and (2) that itself arises from the belief in the Self and 'one's own', i.e. has *ātman* and *ātmīya* for its aspects. In other words, the ultimate cause of suffering is nothing other than *avidyā* = *sat-kāya-dṛṣṭi*, which in its turn gives rise to *tṛṣṇā*. The opposing or counteracting *dharma* can but consist in the perception of unsubstantiality (*nairātmya-darśana*).

This narrative account of *cintā-mayī prajñā* yields the same results as the materials we have been dealing with earlier. By means of reasoning (*yukti, vimarśa, parīkṣā, anumāna, vicāra, niścaya, sādhana*), the Bodhisattva first ascertains the cause of the suffering that must be eliminated, i.e. *sat-kāya-dṛṣṭi* or the superimposition of such erroneous aspects as *ātmâtmīya* on *saṁskāra*s, which are devoid of them.[94] Second, he determines *nairātmya-darśana* to be the antidote, i.e. the opposing or counteracting factor that is to be cultivated. Our investigation into Dharmakīrti's conception of *yogi-pratyakṣa* also showed that the four Noble Truths represent the most typical object of the *yogin*s' perception or mental cultivation. Now it is easy to show that the passage considered above describes the Bodhisattva's rational ascertainment of the Noble Truths. PV 2.131cd–132ab present us with a Mahāyānist account of the Bodhisattva's being struck by his own as well as the other living beings' suffering (*duḥkha-satya*). This of course needs not be further investigated since *duḥkha* is but an empirical fact. PV 2.132c–133ab and 135ac$_1$ account for the Bodhisattva's inquiry into the origin of suffering (*samudaya-satya*), whereas PV 2.134bd and 135c$_2$d describe his determination of the path leading to the destruction of suffering (*mārga-satya*). As to the destruction of suffering (*nirodha-satya*) itself, it cannot be made the object of an analysis, but merely be hinted at, which we can observe in PV 2.133cd–134a, with its characteristic allusion to *nivṛtti*.

— 2.5 —

Having thoroughly cultivated the means of salvation (*upāya*) he ascertained by way of reasoning, the Bodhisattva has rid himself of passions together with their traces (*vāsanā*) and has become a fully enlightened Buddha (or Sugata). He is now

[92] See PVP D56a2 = Q63b6 ≈ PVV 57.15–16 and PVP D56a4 = Q63b8–64a1.

[93] See PVP D56a5–6 = Q64a2–3, PVV 57.19–20 and 58.5–6.

[94] PVP D56b1 = Q64a5–6: *sdug bsṅal du gyur pa'i 'dus byas bdag daṅ bdag gi daṅ bral ba la /* .

endowed with the perfection of teaching (*śāstṛtva-sampad*) or miracle of instruction[95] (*anuśāsanī-prātihārya*) that enables him to teach what he had reflected upon myriads of rebirths earlier, i.e. the Path or the four Noble Truths:

> '[The Blessed Buddha's] protecting [of living beings consists in his] teaching [them] the Path he himself experienced [in order to rid himself of suffering]; he does not speak untruth for this would be useless, [both] because he is compassionate and because [it is but] for the others' sake [that] he has yoked himself to [that] whole [religious] enterprise; therefore, [the Blessed Buddha] is a *pramāṇa* [with regard to the means of salvation for those who seek salvation]. Or [his] protecting [them and hence being a *pramāṇa* consists in his] revealing the four Truths.'[96]

The next 133 stanzas of PV 2 present us with Dharmakīrti's own account of the four *ārya-satya*s.[97]

But to expound on his ideas pertaining to the Truths is by no means the only purpose Dharmakīrti assigns to PV 2.145–279.[98] As he himself suggests in PVSV 109.15–16, the inferential analysis to be carried out in PV 2 illustrates the way a *pravṛtti-kāma-puruṣa* ('a person who wishes to act /engage [religiously]') should proceed in order to make sure that the scriptures on which he intends to base his religious endeavour are trustworthy. To be more precise, PV 2.145–279 exemplifies how one is to ascertain the reliability of a given scripture (here the Buddhist *āgama*s) on empirical matters in order to transfer the said reliability to completely imperceptible objects.[99] Dharmakīrti first shapes the general contour of this legitimisation strategy:

---

[95] See PVP D61a2–3 = Q69b5–6 and PVV-Vibh 61, n. 3.

[96] PV 2.145–146ab:

tāyaḥ sva-dṛṣṭa-mārgôktir vaiphalyād vakti nânṛtam /
dayālutvāt parârthaṁ ca sarvârambhâbhiyogataḥ //
tataḥ pramāṇaṁ tāyo vā catuḥ-satya-prakāśanam /

The explanation is based on PVP D61a1–62b3 = Q69b4–71b2.

[97] *Duḥkha-satya* in PV 2.146c–178; *samudaya-satya* in PV 2.179–189; *nirodha-satya* in PV 2.190–204; *mārga-satya* in PV 2.205–279. See VETTER (1990: 53–168).

[98] On the location of the *tāyitva*/*satya-vicāra* section in the framework of Dharmakīrti's proof of the Buddha's *pramāṇa-bhūtatva*, see FRANCO (1997: 15–43).

[99] The strategy adopted here by Dharmakīrti is indeed an alternative to the one he develops in PVSV 108.16–109.11 (in PVSV 108.24–25, Dharmakīrti also resorts to the four Noble Truths in order to exemplify an 'objectively' inferable state of affairs). As I have argued elsewhere (see ELTSCHINGER (2007: 112–114)), the first model is heresiological, whereas the second is of a more apologetic character. For a short overview of the two strategies and their Tibetan developments, see TILLEMANS (1993: 9–17).

> 'Or, the principal point [viz. the four Noble Truths] is reliable, for the nature of what is to be rejected and what is to be realised as well as the means is established[, i.e. ascertained by means of a *pramāṇa*]. Therefore [the understanding arising from the Buddha's words can properly] be an inference in the case of other things [too, i.e. completely imperceptible objects].'[100]

Dharmakīrti next comments on his own stanza in the following way:

> 'Reliability consists in the correctness[, when analysed by means of inference,] of that which the [alleged authority] has taught, i.e. what is to be rejected and what is to be realised as well as their [respective] means. As an example, [we may adduce the reliability] of the four Noble Truths [when analysed] by the method (*nīti*) we shall present [in the second chapter].'[101]

In the passage of PVin 1 quoted above,[102] the four *ārya-satya*s as they have been dealt with in PV 2 also exemplify the kind of objects a *yogin* meditates on after having ascertained them by means of *yukti-cintā-mayī prajñā*. The consequence is easily drawn: the critique of authority that Dharmakīrti elaborates on in the PVSV clearly falls within the realm of *yukti-cintā-mayī prajñā*. This is not surprising in the least if we remember that to assess the reliability of scriptures on the empirical level was the defining feature of *cintanā* in the ŚrBh and especially in the BoBh: there, the Bodhisattva was advised to reflect upon (< *cintayitu-kāma*), evaluate (< *tulayitu-kāma*) and examine (< *upaparīkṣitu-kāma*) the *dharma*s as he had learnt them from the Buddhist *dvā-daśâṅga-pravacana*; to set inconceivable subjects (*acintya-sthāna*) aside from the very beginning;[103] to be intent on meaning alone; and to discriminate correctly between *kālâpadeśa* and *mahâpadeśa*.[104]

---

[100] PV 1.217:

heyôpādeya-tattvasya sopāyasya prasiddhitaḥ /
pradhānârthâvisaṁvādād anumānaṁ paratra vā //

Translation in TILLEMANS (1993: 15), slightly modified (i.a. on account of PVSVṬ 394.28: *pramāṇena prasiddhito niścayataḥ*).

[101] PVSV 109.15–16: *heyôpādeya-tad-upāyānāṁ tad-upadiṣṭānām avaiparītyam avisaṁvādaḥ. yathā catūrṇām ārya-satyānāṁ vakṣyamāṇa-nītyā*. Note PVSVṬ 395.15–16: *vakṣyamāṇayā nītyā vicāreṇa*.

[102] See § 2.2 above.

[103] The oldest Yogācāra layers warn the Bodhisattva from tackling the so-called inconceivable subjects (*acintya-sthāna*), which contradict the scope and operation of *cint(an)ā* by remaining

unfathomable (note the interesting [and quite rare] definition of *acintya* in Asvabhāva's MSaṅU D277a4–5 = Q335a7–b1 on MSaṅ 10.3.5: *bsam gyis mi khyab pa'i mtshan ñid ni de bźin ñid rnam par dag pa de so so raṅ gis rig par bya ba źes bya ba la sogs pa la / bsam pa źes bya ba ni rigs pa ṅes par sems pa las byuṅ ba'i śes pa ste / rtog ger gtogs* [P: D *rtogs*] *pa dper śes par bya ste / de'i spyod yul ma yin pas rtog ge'i sa la yaṅ dag par 'das pa'i phyir bsam gyis mi khyab pa ñid do //*; see LAMOTTE's (1973: II,274) translation of the Chinese equivalent of MSaṅU; for an analysis of '*acintya*', see also BoBhVṛ D175b4–6 = Q221a5–8). Let us consider first the following statement from $BoBh_D$ 76.8–10/$BoBh_W$ 108.3–7 ($BoBh_T$ D58b2–3/Q68a5–7, BoBhVy D128b3–7/Q157a2–b1, BoBhVṛ D175b4–7/ Q221a5–b1): *iha bodhisattva ekākī raho-gato yathā-śrutān dharmāṁś cintayitu-kāmas tulayitu-kāma upaparīkṣitu-kāma ādita evâcintyāni sthānāni vivarjayitvā dharmāṁś cintayitum ārabhate /* —'Wishing to reflect upon, evaluate and examine the *dharmas* as [he has] heard [them before], the lonesome and secluded Bodhisattva sets about reflecting on *dharmas* by setting aside the inconceivable subjects right from the outset.'

In its definition of *cintanā*, the ŚrBh is a little more explicit regarding these *acintyāni sthānāni*: ŚrBh 117*,8–12 /140.6–11 ($ŚrBh_T$ D57a3–5/ Q67a8–b3): *ekatyas tān eva yathā-śrutān dharmān ekākī raho-gataḥ ṣaḍ acintyāni sthānāni tad yathā ātma-cintāṁ sattva-cintāṁ loka-cintāṁ sattvānāṁ karma-vipāka-cintāṁ dhyāyināṁ dhyāyi-viṣayaṁ buddhānāṁ buddha-viṣayaṁ varjayitvā sva-lakṣaṇataḥ sāmānya-lakṣaṇataś ca cintayati /* —'Setting aside the six inconceivable subjects, viz. reflection on a self, reflection on a living being, reflection on a person (*loka*), reflection on the maturation of living beings' *karman*, reflection on the meditative range of those who meditate, and reflection on the Buddha-range of the Buddhas, a lonesome and secluded one reflects on the *dharmas* as [he has] heard [them before] from [the point of view of] their individual and general characteristics.'

As hinted at by Sāgaramegha (BoBhVy D128b5/Q157a5–6), these six *acintya-sthānāni* have their *locus classicus* in the *Śruta-mayī-bhūmi* of the VinSg. First, the VinSg (D190a6–b1/Q197b2–4) makes a sharp distinction between, on the one hand, *ātma-cintā*, *sattva-cintā* and *loka-cintā*, which all resort to the false view of Self (*sat-kāya-dṛṣṭi*, VinSg D190b5–6/ Q197b8), and *sattvānāṁ karma-vipāka-cintā*, *dhyāyināṁ dhyāyi-viṣayaḥ* and *buddhānāṁ buddha-viṣayaḥ*, which are all, of course, devoid of *sat-kāya-dṛṣṭi*. Next, the VinSg (D191a1–2/Q198a4–5) gives a threefold content to the *dhyāyināṁ dhyāyi-viṣayaḥ*, and a fivefold one to the *buddhānāṁ buddha-viṣayaḥ*: whereas the meditative range of those who meditate consists of *tathatā-mātrârtha* (*de bźin ñid zad pa'i don*), *vaśitā* (*?dbaṅ* [*b*]*sgyur ba*) and *anāsrava-dhātu* (*zag pa zad pa'i dbyiṅs*), the Buddha-range of Buddhas consists of these three plus two others, viz. *anāvaraṇa* (*sgrib pa med pa*) and *sattvârtha-kriyâkāra* (*?sems can gyi don bya ba mdzas pa*).) Why should a Bodhisattva who is giving himself up to reflection set these subjects aside? Because, as the BoBh has it, 'a Bodhisattva who sets the inconceivable aside will not lapse into confusion and mental perplexity.' ($BoBh_D$ 76.15–16/ $BoBh_W$ 108.13–14 ($BoBh_T$ D58b5–6/ Q68b1, BoBhVy D129a3–4/ Q157b4–5, BoBhVṛ D176a2 / Q221b3–4): *acintyaṁ varjayan bodhisattvaḥ sammohaṁ citta-vikṣepaṁ nâdhigacchati*). Put in other words: 'And when [merely] trusting something, he does not reject those profound *dharmas* that his intelligence does not fathom, [but simply says] so: "These *dharmas* are [within] the range of the Tathāgatas, [but] not [within] the range of our [ordinary] intelligence"; [in so doing,] he keeps himself uninjured and unimpaired, [and remains] beyond reproach.' ($BoBh_D$ 76.19–22/$BoBh_W$ 108.19–23 ($BoBh_T$ D58b7–59a1/Q68b3–4, BoBhVy D129b5–6/Q157b7–158a1, BoBhVṛ D176a3–4/ Q221b6–7): *kiṁcit punar adhimucyamāno yeṣv asya dharmeṣu*

— 2.6 —

We have seen how the Epistemologists' critique of authority as well as their account of the Bodhisattva's first philosophical steps relate to the issue of *cintā-mayī prajñā*. Now it should be noted that both themes are closely connected with the representation of the 'rational person' (*prekṣāvat-puruṣa*), a key normative figure in the Buddhist Epistemologists' anthropology.[105] Suffice it to say here that as a property of goal-oriented actions, practical rationality (*prekṣāvattva*) consists in one's using the best possible means for the achievement of his aims (*prayojana*). And since practical aims of the religious type (e.g. *sugati, nirvāṇa, bodhi*) are the highest goals one can strive for, it is but natural that practical rationality should first and foremost characterise the so-called *pravṛtti-kāma-puruṣa*, he who is most in need both of trustworthy scriptures and sound soteriological strategies.

---

gambhīreṣu buddhir nâvagāhate tathāgata-gocarā ete dharmā nâsmad-buddhi-gocarā ity evam apratikṣipaṁs tān dharmān ātmānam akṣataṁ cânupahataṁ ca pariharaty anavadyam).

[104] At the stage of the *cintā-mayī prajñā*, the Bodhisattva continues to concentrate on the meaning (*artha-pratisaraṇa*) of what he has already heard, i.e. the twelvefold teaching of the Tathāgata, and not on the letter (*vyañjana-pratisaraṇa*) alone (see ŚrBh 113*,4–117*,6 = 135.6–140-5 [ŚrBh$_T$ D55b3–57a3 = Q65b5–67a8], and LAMOTTE (1976: 159–161)); moreover, he proves able to discriminate between the so-called black teachings (*kālâpadeśa*), i.e. non-authoritative teachings, and great teachings (*mahâpadeśa*), i.e. authenticated Buddhist scriptures (see BoBh$_D$ 76.13–14 = BoBh$_W$ 108.9–11 [BoBh$_T$ D58b4–5 = Q68a8]; note BoBhVy D129a1–2 /Q157b1–2: *nag po bstan pa ni mdo sde la mi 'jug 'dul ba la mi snaṅ / chos ñid daṅ 'gal bar gnas pa'o // de las bzlog pa dkar po'i phyogs ni chen po bstan pa'o //* ; BoBhVṛ D175b7–176a1 = Q221b2–3: *nag po bstan pa daṅ chen po bstan pa rnams kyaṅ yaṅ dag pa ji lta ba bźin du rab tu śes so źes bya ba ni / gaṅ mdo sde la 'jug ciṅ 'dul ba la snaṅ la / chos ñid daṅ mi 'gal ba de ni chen po bstan pa yin la / de las bzlog pa ni nag po bstan pa'o //* ; on *kālâpadeśa* and *mahâpadeśa*, see LA VALLÉE POUSSIN (1938: 158–160) [who did not know of Sāgaramegha's and Guṇaprabha's explanations]). As the BoBh puts it, 'being concentrated on the meaning and not on the letter, the Bodhisattva will penetrate all the Blessed Buddhas' intentional sayings, [so that] in no [possible] way can anybody cause the Bodhisattva, who masters the black and the great teachings, to turn away and shrink from the [true] reality (*tattvârtha*).' (BoBh$_D$ 76.22–24 = BoBh$_W$ 108.23–109.2 [BoBh$_T$ D59a1–2 = Q68b4–6, BoBhVṛ D176a5 = Q221b8–222a1]: *arthaṁ pratisaran bodhisattvo na vyañjanaṁ buddhānāṁ bhagavatāṁ sarva-sandhāya-vacanāny anupraviśati. kālâpadeśa-mahâpadeśa-kuśalo bodhisattvas tattvârthān na vicalayituṁ na vikampayituṁ kenacit kathaṁcic chakyate*). That our text resorts to the traditional doctrines of the *apadeśa*s and *pratisaraṇa*s gives evidence to the fact that the exegetical function of *cint(an)ā* is not limited to the assessment of a text's proper meaning, but also covers critique of scriptural authenticity and authority (see LAMOTTE (1947: 218–222) and (1949); DAVIDSON (1990); POUSSIN (1980: IX,246–248)).

[105] See MCCLINTOCK (2002: 38–42) and ELTSCHINGER (2007b).

The connection between *prekṣāvat-puruṣa* and the critique of authority can already be found in Dharmakīrti's writings, most conspicuously in the following summary of his own position with regard to the authority of scriptures:

> 'Every [person] who wishes to act [religiously] as a rational agent and not by [mere blind] devotion examines [whether a given treatise] is an [authoritative] scripture or not[, thinking in the following way]: "May I be successful [in my endeavour], if I act after having learnt from [this authoritative scripture] what I ought to practice[, i.e. realise[106]]." This [person indeed] acts with regard to [objects of] another [type, i.e. imperceptible objects] on the ground of [a scripture's] reliability on [perceptually and inferentially] ascertainable[107] [objects], because ordinary practical activity usually [proceeds] that way.[108] But if one were to act by [first] inquiring into the [alleged trustworthy] person [himself], there would be no action at all, because such[109] [a person] is impossible to recognise, but not because [we would] not accept [that such a person exists], for such [persons assuredly] speak the truth.'[110]

However, the most striking expression of practical rationality is no doubt found in the entire career of the Bodhisattva itself. Driven by compassion, the Bodhisattva ultimately aims at alleviating other people's suffering; but in order to do so, he will have to teach them the goal (*upeya*) and its means (*upāya*); now since he will not be able to teach correctly unless he has experienced *upāya* and *upeya* himself, he sets about reflecting and meditating upon them in order to realise (*sākṣāt√kṛ*) them and hence remove his own suffering. To the best of my knowledge, we owe the first explicit mention of the *prekṣāvat-(puruṣa)* in this context to Devendrabuddhi:

> 'To set about [practising] the means of removing his own suffering is [for the Bodhisattva] the only [method] suited to [strive for] the well-being of others. Thus, by putting [its] means (*upāyârtha*), i.e. its cause into practice, those who must be [religiously] trained (*v[a]ineya*) will reach the goal (*tad-upeyârtha*). [But] for whom the goal and its cause

[106] According to PVSVṬ 396.19: *anuṣṭheyaṁ sākṣāt-kartavyam artham.*

[107] According to PVSVṬ 396.20: *śakyaṁ darśanaṁ niścayaḥ.*

[108] PVSVṬ 396.23: *evam ity eka-deśâvisaṁvāda-darśanenânyatra pravartanam.*

[109] PVSVṬ 396.26: *tasya puṁsas tathā-bhūtasya yathârtha-darśanâdi-guṇa-yuktasya.*

[110] PVSV 110.3–8: *sarva eva āgamam anāgamaṁ vā pravṛtti-kāmo 'nveṣate prekṣā-pūrva-kārī na vyasanena. api nāmânuṣṭheyam ato jñātvā pravṛtto 'rthavān syām iti. sa śakya-darśanâvisaṁvāda-pratyayenânyatrâpi pravartate. evaṁ-prāyatvāl loka-vyavahārasya. puruṣa-parīkṣayā tu pravṛttāv apravṛttir eva. tasya tathā-bhūtasya jñātum aśakyatvān nâniṣṭeḥ. tādṛśām avitathâbhidhānāt.*

> remain imperceptible, it is [indeed] a difficult task to teach them, i.e. to correctly explain the goal and its cause to the living beings who ought to be instructed, because one who is ignorant of the way [to go] is not qualified to show the correct way [to others]. [Hence] one who wishes to teach living beings that very [goal] and its cause as they really are[, if he is] rational, first realises [them himself].'[111]

The full-fledged version of this doctrinal complex can be found in Kamalaśīla, who harmonises broader Mahāyānist concerns (here drawn mainly from the BoBh) and epistemological issues, thus often bringing Dharmakīrti's doctrinal background to light. In his commentary on TSa no. 3337(/8), Kamalaśīla argues strongly in favour of the purposefulness (*arthitva*) and hence rationality of *bhāvanā*. But, contrary to Devendrabuddhi, he does not restrict practical rationality to the commitment to Mahāyāna, but takes into consideration the (admittedly lower) motives (*nimitta*) that drive Śrāvakas and Pratyeka-buddhas in the direction of *nirvāṇa*:

> 'And neither could [our opponent] say the following: "A [mental] cultivation that would result in a perceptual knowledge of the type [you assert] is not possible for anyone." [Our opponent would not be able to say this,] for he would [then] have to state the reason for [such] an impossibility. ... Here, since the practice of a rational [person always] implies purposefulness, the reason for not engaging in [mental] cultivation could be that [the mental cultivation of unsubstantiality] is not at all useful to anyone. ... First, among the [various reasons supposed to justify the fact that a rational person does not engage in mental cultivation], purposelessness is not established. Indeed, fear of *saṁsāra* is the reason why those who are limited to the Awakening of the Hearers or [Buddhas-for-themselves] cultivate unsubstantiality: [their] thoughts being tormented by the suffering of birth etc., [and their] mind being terrified by *saṁsāra*, they seek to calm it for themselves. But since [a person] to whom the goal and its cause [remain] imperceptible cannot

[111] PVP D54b5–7 = Q62a4–8, rather freely in order to avoid the commentarial style: *ñid ñid kyi sdug bsṅal rab tu źi ba'i thabs rtsom pa gaṅ yin pa 'di ñid gźan gyi don daṅ rjes su mthun pa yin no // de lta yin na thabs kyi don gaṅ yin pa de'i rgyu gaṅ yin pa nan tan du byas pa las de'i thabs las byuṅ ba'i don de gdul bya de dag gis 'thob par 'gyur ro // ... thabs byuṅ de rgyu lkog gyur can*[*] *no // sems can bstan par bya ba la de 'chad pa ste / thabs las byuṅ ba daṅ de'i rgyu phyin ci ma log par bstan par mdzad pa dka' ba yin te / lam mi śes pas phyin ci ma log pa'i lam ston pa'i skabs med pa'i phyir*[**] */ re źig rtogs pa daṅ ldan pa ñid sems can rnams la de ñid daṅ de'i rgyu ji ltar gnas pa bźin du 'chad par bźed pas mṅon sum du mdzad pa yin no //* .

[*] PV_T 2.132a. [**] PVV-Vibh 57, n. 2: *na hy amārga-jño 'viparīta-mārgôpadeśe 'dhikriyate.*

> teach them [to others properly], the reason why the [Bodhisattvas] proceed with the cultivation is compassion: having by nature, due to a specific *gotra*, the good of others as their sole delectation, they consider [this] world afflicted by the three sufferings of being conditioned etc.; suffering from its painfulness because they rely upon commiseration, they reject [all] self-interest; and considering all the [beings] who are caught in transmigration as themselves, they make the vow to come to their rescue.'[112]

— 2.7 —

On the level of the Epistemologists' religious anthropology, the wisdom born of (rational) reflection mirrors the concerns of a human 'type' who ideally has two properties: first, his desire to commit himself to and engage in a religious path, second, his practical rationality. Although the Bodhisattva, driven by compassion and acting for the sake of living beings, typically incarnates this ideal (Devendrabuddhi), other religious types such as Śrāvakas or Pratyeka-buddhas-to-be, albeit on an inferior level, are not denied those properties (Kamalaśīla). Desire to engage as well as practical rationality command one to critically assess the truth of scriptures on the empirical level in order to maximise the probability of their trustworthiness in transempirical matters too. The four Noble Truths which form the core or principal point of the Buddhist teachings, stand critical analysis by means of valid cognition and especially by inference: 'instrumental in [such] human goals [as *nirvāṇa*]', these Noble Truths can then be declared 'worthy of exertion[, i.e. of repeated practice/cultivation].'[113]

The Bodhisattva's philosophical reflections at the eve of his long career form a second complex closely connected with *cintā-mayī prajñā*. In a philosophical narra-

---

[112] $TSaP_K$ 871.12–15 and 872.1–7 = $TSaP_{Sh}$ 1054.19–22 and 1055.14–20 ($TSaP_T$ D *'e* 296a6–7 and 296b6–297a2 = P *Ye* 361b1–2 and 362a3–7): *na câpy evaṁ śakyaṁ vaktum—sâiva tādṛśī bhāvanā na kasyacit sambhavati, yā tathā-bhūta-pratyakṣa-jñāna-phalā bhaved iti, yato 'sambhave kāraṇaṁ vacanīyam. tathā hi bhāvanāyām aprayoge sarveṣām evânarthitvaṁ ... kāraṇaṁ bhavet, prekṣāvataḥ pravṛtter arthitayā vyāptatvāt. ... tatra na tāvad anarthitvaṁ siddham. tathā hi ye tāvaj jātyâdi-duḥkhôtpīḍita-mānasāḥ saṁsārād uttrasta-manasaṣ tad-upaśamam ātmanaḥ prārthayante, teṣāṁ śrāvakâdi-bodhaniyatānāṁ saṁsārād bhayam eva nairātmya-bhāvanā-nimittam. ye tu gotra-viśeṣāt prakṛtyâiva para-hita-karaṇâikâbhirāmāḥ saṁskārâdi-duḥkhatā tritaya-paripīḍitaṁ jagad avekṣya, kṛpā-paratantratayā tad-duḥkha-duḥkhinaḥ svâtmani vyapekṣām apāsya, sakalān eva saṁsāriṇa ātmatvenâbhyupagatās tat-paritrāṇāya praṇidadhate, teṣāṁ karuṇâiva bhāvanā-pravṛtti-nimittam, parokṣôpeya-tad-dhetos tad-ākhyānasya duṣkaratvāt.*

[113] According to PVSV 109.17 (*puruṣârthôpayogino 'bhiyogârhasyâvisaṁvāditvāt*) and Karṇakagomin's comment thereon (PVSVṬ 395.17–18: *puruṣârthôpayoginaḥ. puruṣârtho nirvāṇaṁ tatrôpayogaḥ kāraṇatvaṁ sa yasyâsti tathā. ata evâbhiyogârhasyâbhyāsârhasya…*).

tive, Dharmakīrti relates how the compassionate Buddha-to-be rationally ascertains both the cause of suffering and the antidote to that cause, viz. the false view of Self and the perception(/realisation) of unsubstantiality respectively. But in so doing, the Bodhisattva rationally determines the four Noble Truths and hence the path of unsubstantiality that, once duly cultivated, will lead him to Buddhahood. Both doctrinal structures lay strong emphasis on inferential analysis and ascertainment, the first one in the perspective of a critical appraisal of the already existent Truths, the second as the very means of their determination. In both cases, these Truths or unsubstantiality alone are made the object(s) of repeated practice, mental cultivation and exertion, i.e. of the counteracting path that leads ultimately to the definitive suppression of (passions together with their) traces.

On a more theoretical level, these objects perfectly match the ones Dharmakīrti himself as well as his commentators associate repeatedly with the so-called perception of *yogin*s. That the cognition of (Buddhist) mystics can be termed a perception and hence a valid cognition is not due only to the *bhāvanā*'s securing a vivid image, but also to the fact that its objects have been subjected to rational investigation (*parīkṣā*, *vicāra* etc.) and ascertainment (*niścaya, nirṇaya, vyavasthapana*, *nidhyāna* etc.) at the *yukti-cintā-mayī*-level. As the commentators have it, the truth or non-belying character of the *yogin*s' cognition consists in its being *pramāṇa-saṁvādin* (Devendrabuddhi, Śākyabuddhi, Manorathanandin) or bearing upon *pramāṇa-(pari) śuddhârtha*s (Dharmottara). In the stage of rational reflection, *pramāṇa*s (i.e. inference) ascertain or determine the real aspects (impermanence, unsatisfactoriness, unsubstantiality, selflessness) of entities and hence provide the reflecting *yogin*'s cognition with aspects and objects that contradict, oppose or counteract the superimpositions (Self, 'one's own', permanent etc.) ignorance as a generalised erroneous perception is responsible for. What the *yogin* does here is tantamount to the Bodhisattva's rational identification of unsubstantiality as the antidote to *sat-kāya-dṛṣṭi*. And what the *yogin* is intent upon is nothing other than a counteracting path that will enable him to remove the adventitious filth of passions and hence establish 'his' mind in its originally radiant and flawless condition.

3. Concluding remarks

Vasubandhu's Sautrāntika definition of *cintā-mayī prajñā* as *yukti-nidhyāna-jo niścayaḥ* testifies to his indebtedness to the Yogācāra tradition (ŚrBh, BoBh, MSA[Bh] etc.), which understands *cint(an)ā* as a rational appraisal-cum-examination (*tulanā*, *upaparīkṣā*, *vicāra* etc.) of scripture-based contents. Of the four *yukti*s resorted to by this tradition, the *upapatti-sādhana-yukti* is the only one endowed with a probative/demonstrative function: as a *vyavasthāpanā sādhanā* (ŚrBh), this *yukti* serves the function of establishing key Buddhist doctrinal contents (*anityatā, śūnyatā, kṣaṇikatva, duḥkhatā, pratītya-samutpannatā, para-loka, anātmatā* etc.) by means of *pramāṇa*s (*pratyakṣa, anumāna, āptâgama*). In sharp contrast to the exegetical as well as soteriological purpose of *cint(an)ā*, *hetu-vidyā* possesses a strong polemical/ dialectical character, aiming as it does at defeating (*nigraha*) non-Buddhist opponents with the help of *pramāṇa*s; *hetu-vidyā* is also traditionally assigned the apologetic and missionary function of defending (*dhāraṇa*) the *Sad-dharma* against outward hostility, converting non-Buddhists and strengthening the coreligionists' faith (**prasāda-sthāpana*). Although *cint(an)ā* and *hetu-vidyā* both give strong emphasis to *pramāṇa*s, they seem to have developed independently. This is in turn explainable in terms of their meeting religious needs that must have been felt quite distinct. Sthiramati's remarks may well testify to the fact that by the middle of the sixth century, the two structures and concerns started merging with one another, for the most part, I would suggest, not because of a growing awareness of their common resort to *pramāṇa*s, but rather, with the collapse of the Gupta empire, because social, economical and political factors made it necessary. Epistemological debate and the religious quest for exegetical and doctrinal certainty could no longer be kept separated as the communities faced an easily documentable hostility and concomitant lack of political and economical security.[114] This time coincides with the foundation of such centralised institutions as Valabhī and Nālandā, which probably mirrors on the institutional level what (the Valabhī-based) Sthiramati testifies to on the doctrinal level.

Dharmakīrti and his successors' ideas are in close consonance with older accounts of *cint(an)ā* and especially *upapatti-sādhana-yukti*, to which they assign the same function (cf. *vyavasthāpya* in PVin) and the same contents (the real aspects of entities, but also *para-loka* etc.). This consonance is best seen in two parallel but rhetorically distinct doctrinal complexes in Dharmakīrti, viz. the theoretical/ epistemological depiction of *yogi-pratyakṣa*, and the narrative account of the future Buddha's first philosophical reflections. Moreover, the works of Dharmakīrti as well as those of Śāntarakṣita or Kamalaśīla are remarkable representatives of the overlap between *para-nigraha*, *sad-dharma-dhāraṇa* and **prasāda-sthāpana* on the one hand, and *cint*(*an*)*ā*-like establishment of key Buddhist doctrinal contents on the other. Maybe some tentative explanations are necessary here. On the normative level of individual religious practice, no authority may substitute for a Bodhisattva's and /or *bhikṣu*(*ṇī*)'s beginning to reflect on scriptural contents (cf. BoBh: *na para-pratyayo bhavati teṣu yukti-parīkṣiteṣu dharmeṣu*) by means of reasoning. On a first institutional level, *hetu-vidyā*-specialists probably did not encroach upon the jurisdiction of the various competing dogmatists or *adhyātma-vidyā*-specialists. On a

[114] See ELTSCHINGER (2007: 25–64).

second institutional level, however, *hetu-vidyā*-specialists now seem to be concerned with dialectics and epistemology as well as with apologetics and doctrinal elaboration; by creating some kind of 'interface' between outward pressure and competing doctrinal interests within, they attempted to shape and propagate the non-ritual part of a renewed Buddhist identity. Note should be made, however, that authors like Dharmakīrti and Kamalaśīla maintained the traditional clear-cut distinction between the polemical precincts of *hetu-vidyā*, to which they denied any soteriological value whatsoever, and the salvational aims of *cint(an)ā*. One is of course free to consider whether these authors' playing down of epistemology (!) bears sincere testimony to their beliefs or was rather a concession imposed on them by the dominating institutional concerns.

BIBLIOGRAPHY

AK = Vasubandhu: *Abhidharma-kośa*. Prahlad Pradhan (ed.): *Abhidharma-kośabhāṣyam of Vasubandhu*. Tibetan Sanskrit Works Series 8, K.P. Jayaswal Research Institute, Patna 1975.

AKBh = Vasubandhu: *Abhidharma-kośa-bhāṣya*. See: AK.

AKVy = Yaśomitra: *Abhidharma-kośa-vyākhyā*. Unrai Wogihara (ed.): *Sphuṭārthā Abhidharmakośavyākhyā, the Work of Yaśomitra*. The Publishing Association of Abhidharmakośavyākhyā, Sankibo Buddhist Book Store, Tokyo 1989 [first edition: 1936].

ASBh = *Abhidharma-samuccaya-bhāṣya*. Nathmal Tatia (ed.): *Abhidharma-samuccayabhāṣyam*. Tibetan Sanskrit Works Series 17, K.P. Jayaswal Research Institute, Patna 1976.

BhK 1 = Kamalaśīla: First *Bhāvanā-krama*. Giuseppe Tucci (ed.): *Minor Buddhist Texts*. Motilal Banarsidass, Delhi 1986: 497/187–539/229.

BHSD = Edgerton, Franklin: *Buddhist Hybrid Sanskrit Grammar and Dictionary*. Volume II: *Dictionary*. Motilal Banarsidass, Delhi 1970 [first edition: Yale University Press, New Haven 1953].

$BoBh_D$ = *Bodhisattva-bhūmi*. Nalinaksha Dutt (ed.): *Bodhisattvabhūmiḥ* [*Being the XVth Section of Asaṅgapāda's Yogācārabhūmiḥ*]. Tibetan Sanskrit Works Series 7, K.P. Jayaswal Research Institute, Patna 1978.

$BoBh_T$ = D no 4037, *Wi* 1b1–213a7 = P no 5538, *Źi* 1b1–247a8.

BoBhVṛ = Guṇaprabha: *Bodhisattva-bhūmi-vṛtti*. D no 4044, *'i* 141a1–182a2 = P no 5545, *Yi* 176a3–229a6.

BoBhVy = Sāgaramegha: *Bodhisattva-bhūmi-vyākhyā*. D no 4043, *Yi* 1b1–338a7 = P no 5548, *Ri* 1b1–425a6.

$BoBh_W$ = *Bodhisattva-bhūmi*. Unrai Wogihara (ed.): *Bodhisattvabhūmi. A Statement of Whole Course of the Bodhisattva (Being Fifteenth Section of Yogācārabhūmi)*. Sankibo Buddhist Book Store, Tokyo 1971.

D = Takasaki, Jikido; Yamaguchi, Zuiho; Hakamaya, Noriaki (eds.): *sDe dge Tibetan Tripiṭaka bsTan 'gyur preserved at the Faculty of Letters, University of Tokyo*. Sekai seiten kankō kyōkai, Tokyo 1977–1981.

DAVIDSON 1990 = Davidson, Ronald M.: 'An Introduction to the Standards of Scriptural Authenticity in Indian Buddhism', in: Robert E. Buswell (ed.): *Chinese Buddhist Apocrypha*. University of Hawaii Press, Honolulu 1990: 291–325.

DELEANU 2006 = Deleanu, Florin: *The Chapter on the Mundane Path (Laukikamārga) in the Śrāvakabhūmi. A Trilingual Edition (Sanskrit, Tibetan, Chinese), Annotated Translation, and Introductory Study*. 2 vols, Studia Philologica Buddhica, Monograph Series 20b, The International Institute for Buddhist Studies, Tokyo 2006.

DhPr = Durvekamiśra: *Dharmottara-pradīpa*. See NBṬ$_M$.

ELTSCHINGER 2005a = Eltschinger, Vincent: 'Études sur la philosophie religieuse de Dharmakīrti: 1. Le Bouddha comme Śāstṛ et comme Sugata', *Études Asiatiques /Asiatische Studien* 59–2 (2005) 395–442.

ELTSCHINGER 2005b = Eltschinger, Vincent: 'Études sur la philosophie religieuse de Dharmakīrti: 2. L'*āśrayaparivṛtti*.' *Journal Asiatique* 293–1 (2005) 151–211.

ELTSCHINGER 2007a = Eltschinger, Vincent: *Penser l'autorité des Écritures. La polémique de Dharmakīrti contre la notion brahmanique orthodoxe d'un Veda sans auteur. Autour de PV 1.213–268 et Svavṛtti*. Verlag der Österreichischen Akademie der Wissenschaften, Vienna 2007.

ELTSCHINGER 2007b = Eltschinger, Vincent: 'On 7th and 8th century Buddhist accounts of human action, practical rationality and soteriology', in: Birgit Kellner; Helmut Krasser; Horst Lasic; Michael Torsten Much; Helmut Tauscher (eds.): *Pramāṇakīrtiḥ, Papers dedicated to Ernst Steinkellner on the occasion of his 70th birthday*. Wiener Studien zur Tibetologie und Buddhismuskunde 70–1, Arbeitskreis für tibetische und buddhistische Studien Universität Wien, Wien 2007: 135–162.

ELTSCHINGER (forthcoming 1) = Eltschinger, Vincent: 'Studies in Dharmakīrti's Religious Philosophy: 3. Compassion and its Place in PV II', to be published in the *Proceedings of the Fourth Dharmakīrti Conference (Vienna, August 2006)*, edited by Birgit Kellner, Helmut Krasser, Horst Lasic, Eli Franco.

ELTSCHINGER (forthcoming 2) = Eltschinger, Vincent: 'Studies in Dharmakīrti's Religious Philosophy: 5. On the Career and Cognition of Yogins.' To be published in the *Proceedings of the Symposium on Yogic Perception, Meditation and Altered States of Consciousness (Vienna, June 2006)*, edited by Eli Franco and Dagmar Eigner.

FRANCO 1989 = Franco, Eli: 'Was the Buddha a Buddha?', *Journal of Indian Philosophy* 17 (1989) 81–99.

FRANCO 1997 = Franco, Eli: *Dharmakīrti on Compassion and Rebirth*. Wiener Studien zur Tibetologie und Buddhismuskunde 38, Arbeitskreis für tibetische und buddhistische Studien Universität Wien, Wien 1997.

GRIFFITHS 1990 = Griffiths, Paul J.: 'Omniscience in the Mahāyāṇasūtrālaṅkāra and its Commentaries', *Indo-Iranian Journal* 33 (1990) 85–120.

HIRAKAWA 1973 = Hirakawa, Akira; *et al.*: *Index to the Abhidharmakośabhāṣya (P. Pradhan Edition)*. Part One: Sanskrit-Tibetan-Chinese. Daizo Shuppan Kabushikikaisha, Tokyo 1973.

KRASSER 2005 = Krasser, Helmut: 'Are Buddhist Pramāṇavādins non-Buddhistic? Dignāga and Dharmakīrti on the impact of logic and epistemology on emancipation', *Horin* 11 (2005) 129–146.

KRITZER 2005 = Kritzer, Robert: *Vasubandhu and the Yogācārabhūmi. Yogācāra Elements in the Abhidharmakośabhāṣya*. Studia Philologica Buddhica, Monograph Series 18, The International Institute for Buddhist Studies, Tokyo 2005.

LAMOTTE 1935 = Lamotte, Étienne: *Saṁdhinirmocana Sūtra, l'explication des mystères*. Université de Louvain, Bureaux du Recueil, Louvain–Paris 1935.

LAMOTTE 1947 = Lamotte, Étienne: 'La critique d'authenticité dans le bouddhisme', in: *India Antiqua. A Volume of Oriental Studies Presented by His Friends and Pupils to Jean Philippe Vogel on the Occasion of the Fiftieth Anniversary of His Doctorate by Kern Institute-Leyden*, Kern Institute, E.J. Brill, Leyden 1947: 213–222.

LAMOTTE 1949 = Lamotte, Étienne: 'La critique d'interprétation dans le bouddhisme', *Annuaire de l'Institut de Philologie et d'Histoire Orientales et Slaves (Université Libre de Bruxelles)* 9 (1949) 341–361 [*Mélanges Henri Grégoire*].

LAMOTTE 1973 = Lamotte, Étienne: *La Somme du Grand Véhicule d'Asaṅga (Mahāyānasaṅgraha)*. 2 Vols, Publications de l'IOL 8, Université de Louvain, Institut Orientaliste, Louvain-la-Neuve 1973.

LAMOTTE 1976 = Lamotte, Étienne: *Histoire du bouddhisme indien. Des origines à l'ère Śaka*. Publications de l'IOL 14, Institut Orientaliste, Université de Louvain, Louvain-la-Neuve 1976.

MCCLINTOCK 2002 = McClintock, Sara: *Omniscience and the Rhetoric of Reason in the Tattvasaṁgraha and the Tattvasaṁgrahapañjikā*. Ph.D. Thesis. Harvard University, Cambridge (Massachusetts) 2002 (unpublished).

MSA(Bh) = Asaṅga: *Mahāyāna-sūtrâlaṅkāra*. Sylvain Lévi (ed.): *Asaṅga. Mahāyāna-Sūtrālaṅkāra, Exposé de la doctrine du Grand Véhicule selon le système Yogācāra*. Tome 1: texte. Librairie Honoré Champion, Paris 1907.

MSaṅ = *Mahāyāna-saṁgraha*. See: LAMOTTE (1973: I).

MSaṅU = Asvabhāva: *Mahāyāna-saṅgrahôpanibandhana*. D no 4051, *Ri* 190b1–296a7 = P no 5552, *Li* 232b5–356b7. [For French translations of the quoted passages, see LAMOTTE (1973: II)].

MSAVBh = Sthiramati: *Mahāyāna-sūtrâlaṅkāra-vṛtti-bhāṣya*. D no 4034, *Mi* 1b1–*Tsi* 266a7.

MVy = *Mahā-vyutpatti*. I.P. Minaev (ed.): *Mahāvyutpatti*. Bibliotheca Indo-Buddhica Series 98, Sri Satguru Publications, Delhi 1992 [first edition: St. Petersburg 1911].

NB = Dharmakīrti: *Nyāya-bindu*. See: NB.

NBh = Vātsyāyana Pakṣilasvāmin: *Nyāya-bhāṣya*. Anantalal Thakur (ed.): *Gautamīyanyāyadarśana with Bhāṣya of Vātsyāyana*. Nyāyacaturgranthikā 1, Indian Council of Philosophical Research, New Delhi 1997.

NBṬ$_{M}$ = Dharmottara: *Nyāya-bindu-ṭīkā*. Paṇḍita Dalsukhbhai Malvania (ed.): *Paṇḍita Durveka Miśra's Dharmottarapradīpa (Being a subcommentary on Dharmottara's Nyāyabinduṭīkā, a commentary on Dharmakīrti's Nyāyabindu)*. Tibetan Sanskrit Works Series 2, K.P. Jayaswal Research Institute, Patna 1971.

NBṬ$_{\check{S}}$ = Dharmottara: *Nyāya-bindu-ṭīkā*. Th. I. Ščerbatskoj (ed.): *Nyāyabindu. Buddijskij učebnik logiki—sočinenie Dharmakirti i tolkovanie na nego Nyāyabinduṭīkā—sočinenie Darmottary*. Bibliotheca Buddhica 7, Biblio Verlag, Osnabrück 1970 [first edition: Petrograd 1918].

POUSSIN 1938 = Poussin, Louis de La Vallée: 'Buddhica', *Harvard Journal of Asiatic Studies* 3–2 (1938) 137–160.

POUSSIN 1980 = Poussin, Louis de La Vallée: *L'Abhidharmakośa de Vasubandhu*. 6 Vols, Mélanges Chinois et Bouddhiques 16, Institut Belge des Hautes Études Chinoises, Bruxelles 1980.

PRUDEN 1991 = Pruden, Leo M. (tr.): *Abhidharmakośabhāṣyam by Louis de La Vallée Poussin*. English Translation by Leo M. Pruden. 4 Vols, Asian Humanities Press, Berkeley 1991.

PV 1–4 = Dharmakīrti: *Pramāṇa-vārttika* (chapters 1–4). Yūsho Miyasaka (ed.): 'Pramāṇavārttika-kārikā (Sanskrit and Tibetan)', *Acta Indologica* 2 (1971–1972) 1–206. [For PV 1–4 see also: PVV; for PV 2–3, see also: PVA; for PV 1, see also: PVSV; for PV 2.131cd–285, see also: VETTER (1990). My numeration of the verses in PV 2 follows that of VETTER].

PVA = Prajñākaragupta: *Pramāṇa-vārttikâlaṅkāra*. Rāhula Sāṅkṛtyāyana (ed.): *Pramāṇavārttikabhāṣyam or Vārtikālaṅkāraḥ of Prajñākaragupta (Being a Commentary on Dharmakīrti's Pramāṇavārtikam)*. K.P. Jayaswal Research Institute, Patna 1953.

PVin 1 = Dharmakīrti: *Pramāṇa-viniścaya* (chapter 1: *pratyakṣa*). Ernst Steinkellner (ed.): *Dharmakīrti's Pramāṇaviniścaya. Chapters 1 and 2*. Sanskrit Texts from the Tibetan Autonomous Region 2, China Tibetology Publishing House / Austrian Academy of Sciences Press, Beijing / Vienna 2007.

PVin 1$_{V}$ = Tilmann Vetter: *Dharmakīrti's Pramāṇaviniścayaḥ. 1. Kapitel: Pratyakṣam*. Hermann Böhlaus Nachf., Kommissionsverlag der Österreichischen Akademie der Wissenschaften, Wien 1966.

PVinṬ = Dharmottara: *Pramāṇa-viniścaya-ṭīkā*. D no 4229, *Dze* 1b1–*Tshe* 178a3 = P no 5727, *Dze* 1b1–*We* 209b8.

PVinṬ$_{J\tilde{n}}$ = Jñānaśrībhadra: *Pramāṇa-viniścaya-ṭīkā*. D no 4228, *Tshe* 178b4–295a7 = P no 5728, *We* 209b8–355a6.

PVP = Devendrabuddhi: *Pramāṇa-vārttika-pañjikā*. D no 4217, *Che* 1–326b4 = P no 5717, *Che* 1–390a8.

PVSV = Dharmakīrti: *Pramāṇa-vārttika-svavṛtti*. Raniero Gnoli (ed.): *The Pramāṇavārttikam of Dharmakīrti. The First Chapter with the Auto-Commentary*. Serie Orientale Roma 23, Istituto Italiano per il Medio ed Estremo Oriente, Roma 1960.

PVSVṬ = Karṇakagomin: *Pramāṇa-vārttika-svavṛtti-ṭīkā*. Rāhula Sāṅkṛtyāyana (ed.): *Karṇakagomin's Commentary on the Pramāṇavārttikavṛtti of Dharmakīrti*. Rinsen Books Co., Kyoto 1982 [first edition: Kitāb Mahal, Ilāhābād (Allahabad) 1943].

PVṬ = Śākyabuddhi: *Pramāṇa-vārttika-ṭīkā*. D no 4220, *Je* 1b1–*Ñe* 282a7 = P no 5718, *Je* 1b1–*Ñe* 348a8.

PVV = Manorathanandin: *Pramāṇa-vārttika-vṛtti*. Rāhula Sāṅkṛtyāyana (ed.): *Pramāṇavārttikam Ācārya-Manorathanandi-kṛtayā vṛttyā saṁvalitam* [*Dharmakīrti's Pramāṇavārttikam with a commentary by Manorathanandin*]. Parts I–II, Appendix to *Journal of the Bihar and Orissa Research Society* 24–26, Patna 1938–1940.

PVV-Vibh = Vibhūticandra's notes to PVV. See: PVV.

Q = Suzuki, Daisetz T. (ed.): *The Tibetan Tripitaka, Peking Edition, Kept in the Library of the Otani University, Kyoto*. Tibetan Tripitaka Research Institute, Tokyo–Kyoto 1957.

Sakuma 1990 = Sakuma, Hidenori S.: *Die Āśrayaparivṛtti-Theorie in der Yogācārabhūmiḥ*. 2 Vols, Alt- und Neu-Indische Studien 40, Franz Steiner Verlag, Stuttgart 1990.

Scherrer-Schaub 1981 = Scherrer-Schaub, Cristina: 'Le terme *yukti*: première étude', *Études Asiatiques/Asiatische Studien* 25,2 (1981) 185–199 [*Hommage Régamey*].

Seyfort Ruegg 1995 = Seyfort Ruegg, David: *Ordre spirituel et ordre temporel dans la pensée bouddhique de l'Inde et du Tibet*. Publications de l'Institut de Civilisation Indienne, Série in–8°, Fascicule 64, Collège de France, Paris 1995.

SNS = *Saṁdhi-nirmocana-sūtra*. See: Lamotte (1935).

ŚrBh = *Śrāvaka-bhūmi*. (1) Śrāvakabhūmi Study Group (ed.): *Śrāvakabhūmi. Revised Sanskrit Text and Japanese Translation. The First Chapter*. The Insitute for Comprehensive Studies of Buddhism (Taishō University), Taishō University Sōgō Bukkyō Kenkyūjo Series 4, Sankibo Press, Tokyo 1988. (2) Karunesh Shukla (ed.): *Śrāvakabhūmi of Ācārya Asaṅga*. Tibetan Sanskrit Works Series 14, K.P. Jayaswal Research Institute, Patna 1973.

ŚrBh$_{T}$ = D no 4036, *Dzi* 1b1–195a7 = P no 5537, *Wi* 1b1–236a8.

Steinkellner 1988 = Steinkellner, Ernst: *Nachweis der Wiedergeburt. Prajñāsenas 'Jig rten pha rol sgrub pa*. 2 Vols, Beiträge zur Kultur- und Geistesgeschichte Asiens 1, Verlag der Österreichischen Akademie der Wissenschaften, Wien 1988.

T = Tibetan translation (in case of an extant Sanskrit text only).

TfphSI = Oberhammer, Gerhard; Prets, Ernst; Prandstetter, Joachim (eds.): *Terminologie der frühen philosophischen Scholastik in Indien. Ein Begriffswörterbuch zur altindischen Dialektik, Erkenntnislehre und Methodologie.* 3 Vols, ÖAW, philosophisch-historische Klasse, Denkschriften, 223, 248 und 343; Beiträge zur Kultur- und Geistesgeschichte Asiens 9, 17 und 49, Verlag der Österreichischen Akademie der Wissenschaften, Wien 1991 (Vol. 1: *A–I.*), 1996 (Vol. 2: *U–Pū*), 2006 (Vol. 3: *Pra–H*).

TILLEMANṢ 1993 = Tillemans, Tom: *Persons* of *Authority. The* sTon pa tshad ma'i skyes bur sgrub pa'i gtam of A lag sha Ngag dbang bstan dar, *A Tibetan Work on the Central Religious Questions in Buddhist Epistemology.* Tibetan and Indo-Tibetan Studies 5, Franz Steiner Verlag, Stuttgart 1993.

TSa = Śāntarakṣita: *Tattva-saṁgraha.* See: TSaP.

$TSaP_K$ = Kamalaśīla: *Tattva-saṁgraha-pañjikā.* Embar Krishnamacharya (ed.): *Tattvasaṅgraha of Śāntarakṣita With the Commentary of Kamalaśīla.* 2 Vols, Oriental Institute, Baroda 1984.

$TSaP_{Sh}$ = Kamalaśīla: *Tattva-saṁgraha-pañjikā.* Swami Dwarikadas Shastri (ed.): *Tattvasaṅgraha of Ācārya Shāntarakṣita with the Commentary 'Pañjikā' of Shri Kamalshīla.* 2 Vols, Bauddha Bharati Series 1, Bauddha Bharati, Varanasi 1981.

$TSaP_T$ = D no 4267, *Ze* 133b1–*'e* 331a7 = P no 5765, *'e* 159b2–*Ye* 405a7.

TSD_{LCh} = Chandra, Lokesh: *Tibetan-Sanskrit Dictionary.* Compact Edition, Rinsen Book Co., Kyoto 1990 [first edition: International Academy of Indian Culture, Delhi 1959].

$TSD_{LCh\text{-}s}$ = Chandra, Lokesh: *Tibetan-Sanskrit Dictionary, Supplementary Volumes.* International Academy of Indian Culture, Aditya Prakashan, Delhi 1992–1994.

VETTER 1990 = Vetter, Tilmann: *Der Buddha und seine Lehre in Dharmakīrtis Pramāṇavārttika. Der Abschnitt über den Buddha und die vier edlen Wahrheiten im Pramāṇasiddhi-Kapitel.* Wiener Studien zur Tibetologie und Buddhismuskunde 12, Arbeitskreis für tibetische und buddhistische Studien Universität Wien, Wien 1990 [first edition: 1984].

VinSg = *Viniścaya-saṅgrahaṇī* of the *Yogâcāra-bhūmi.* D no 4038, *Źi* 1b1–*Zi* 127a4 = P no 5539, *Zi* 1b1–*'i* 142b8.

WAYMAN 1961 = Wayman, Alex: *Analysis of the Śrāvakabhūmi Manuscript.* University of California Press, Berkeley–Los Angeles 1961.

YOSHIMIZU 1996 = Yoshimizu, Chizuko: *Die Erkenntnislehre des Prāsaṅgika-Madhyamaka nach dem Tshig gsal stoṅ thun gyi tshad ma'i rnam bśad des 'Jam dbyaṅs bźad pa'i rdo rje.* Wiener Studien zur Tibetologie und Buddhismuskunde 37, Arbeitskreis für tibetische und buddhistische Studien Universität Wien, Wien 1996.

The ‘Principle of True Nature’ (*dharmatā-yukti*) as a Justification for Positive Descriptions of Reality in Mahāyāna Buddhism[1]

KLAUS-DIETER MATHES

When looking for a suitable topic for my contribution to the seminar on logic and belief in Indian philosophy, I quickly settled on the *Tattva-daśaka* of Maitrīpa (ca. 1007–ca. 1085)[2], in which reality is not only ascertained to be neither existent nor non-existent, on the basis of common Madhyamaka logic, but also equated with luminosity as directly experienced in the *samādhi* of realising reality as it is (*yathā-bhūta-samādhi*). Ultimately, there is of course only one reality for Maitrīpa, but descriptions of it differ depending on one's approach: while reality escapes any category (ontological or otherwise) in analysis, it can be described in a more positive way on the basis of direct experience.[3] Madhyamaka analysis can and should be questioned on logical grounds, but the positive descriptions of reality as luminosity and the like must be first believed in, and can be verified by becoming a successful *yogin* or Buddha oneself.[4]

---

[1] Improvements to my English by Philip H. Pierce (Nepal Research Centre, Kathmandu) are gratefully acknowledged.

[2] TATZ (1994: 65).

[3] See MATHES (2006: 210–220).

[4] This is clear, for example, from the *Anūnatvâpūrṇatva-nirdeśa* (as quoted in the *Ratna-gotra-vibhāga-vyākhyā* on stanza 1.1), RGVV, p. 2.8–11: *tathāgata-viṣayo hi śāriputra ayam arthas tathāgata-gocaraḥ*[.] *sarva-śrāvaka-pratyeka-buddhair api tāvac chāriputra ayam artho na śakyaḥ samyak sva-prajñayā* [*jñātuṁ vā*][a] *draṣṭuṁ vā pratyavekṣituṁ vā*[b] *prāg eva bāla-pṛthag-janair anyatra tathāgata-śraddhā-gamanataḥ. śraddhā-gamanīyo hi śāriputra paramârthaḥ. paramârtha iti śāri*[*putra*] *sattva-dhātor etad adhivacanam.*—‘ Śāriputra, this [ultimate] meaning is the [cognitive] object of the Tathāgata; it comes under the range of the Tathāgata['s awareness]. Śāriputra, it cannot, to start with, be known, seen or examined correctly even by Śrāvakas or Pratyeka-buddhas on the basis of their own insight, much less by fools and ordinary people, unless they (i.e. Śrāvakas, Pratyeka-buddhas, fools and ordinary persons) realise it by faith in the Tathāgata. Śāriputra, that which must be realised by faith is the ultimate. Śāriputra, “ultimate” is an expression for the [Buddha]-element in sentient beings.’ [[a] Not readable in B (2a2) (several *akṣara*s are broken

Logic and Belief in Indian Philosophy
Warsaw Indological Studies 3 (2010) 605–616.

To grasp reality correctly is thus not only a philosophical discipline, but also a crucial soteriological pursuit. The long history of Mahāyāna Buddhism in India has witnessed a host of different views on what reality precisely is. For the Mādhyamikas it is the emptiness of all phenomena, while for the Yogācāras it is the mind empty of duality (to give only the generally accepted descriptions for the two main traditions in Mahāyāna). Whatever tenet was maintained, it is safe to say that nobody ever considered reality to be self-evident to ordinary sentient beings.

Thus reality must be either determined logically (usually to be something which is 'free from mental fabrications' (*niṣprapañca*)) or experienced directly in advanced *yoga* practices that mainly rely on non-conceptual types of insight. The latter approach enables, besides the definiens *niṣprapañca* or emptiness, such positive descriptions of reality as found in the *sūtra*s of and commentaries on the third *dharma-cakra* (i.e. the Yogācāra works, the *Ratna-gotra-vibhāga* and so forth). The division of the Buddhist doctrine into three sets or 'wheels' (*cakra*) of teachings was provided its chief doctrinal support in the *Saṁdhi-nirmocana-sūtra*, and became necessary in order to accommodate the philosophical tenets of the Mahāyāna schools within mainstream Buddhism. The Yogācāras in particular felt compelled to resolve the tensions they observed between the Abhidharma ontology of momentary 'factors of existence' (*dharma*s) and the Prajñāpāramitā's emptiness of all *dharma*s (these two forming the first two *dharma-cakra*s) by restricting emptiness to what has been wrongly projected onto the *dharma*s. A similar approach can be found among the proponents of a Buddha-nature (*tathāgata-garbha*) in all sentient beings.[5]

The reaction to such interpretative strategies was mainly twofold. While some Mādhyamikas, such as Candrakīrti (seventh century CE), refuted the Yogācāra and Tathāgata-garbha doctrines and dismissed their hermeneutics (which concluded that the third *dharma-cakra* has definitive meaning), Kamalaśīla (ca. 700–750)[6] tried to show that the last two *dharma-cakra*s do not contradict each other. Within such latter traditions, the differences between the second and third *dharma-cakra* were explained by distinguishing an analytical from a direct approach to one and the same reality.[7]

Positive descriptions of reality must at first simply be believed in, but the believer eventually acquires the means of verifying them as he progresses along the path. In other words, one has to trust a *yogin* that reality has the nature of luminosity, in the

away); A is not available. The gap is filled in according to the Tibetan. See also TAKASAKI (1966: 143). [b] B (2a2) reads *mvā*; A is not available. DE JONG (1979: 567) suggests reading *vā* without a following *daṇḍa*.]

[5] For a detailed explanation of the three *dharma-cakra*s see MATHES (1996: 155–163).

[6] NAKAMURA (1987: 281).

[7] Such a strategy can be discerned, for example, in 'Gos Lo tsā ba gZhon nu dpal's commentary on the *Ratna-gotra-vibhāga-vyākhyā*. See MATHES (2008: 375–377).

same way as one trusts a scientist that gamma rays reveal their nature of being both a wave and matter when hitting gold atoms in the Compton Experiment; with a laboratory of one's own one can then verify this. It is such a trust or belief in the true nature of the factors of existence (*dharmatā*) or reality that led to the coining of the 'principle of true nature' (*dharmatā-yukti*).

Dharmatā-yukti is the last in a group of four *yukti*s, which are as follows: (a) the principle of dependence (*apekṣā-yukti*), (b) the principle of cause and effect (*kārya-kāraṇa-yukti*), (c) the principle of proving on the basis of feasibility (*upapatti-sādhana-yukti*), and (d) the principle of true nature (*dharmatā-yukti*).[8] In the *Mahāyāna-sūtrâlaṁkāra*, stanza 19.45, the four *yukti*s respectively correlate to (a) correct mental engagement, (b) the right view accompanied by [its] fruit, (c) analysis based on valid cognition, and (d) the inconceivable.[9] In his *bhāṣya* on MSA 19.45 Vasubandhu comments:

> 'A proper presentation of principle [explains its] fourfold [nature]: The principle of dependence, the principle of cause and effect, the principle of proving on the basis of feasibility, and the principle of true nature… The principle of dependence is correct mental engagement on the three *yāna*s. Since the correct, supramundane view arises in virtue of that, that is, from that precondition, the principle of cause and effect is the right view accompanied by [its] fruit. The principle of proving on the basis of feasibility is an investigation on the basis of direct and the other types of valid cognition. The principle of true nature is an inconceivable subject. For the true nature is established and not something to be worried about—[worries] such as "From which correct mental engagement does the right view arise?" or "Is the abandonment of defilements because of that the fruit?"'[10]

While the first three principles are more or less based on logical analysis, *dharmatā-yukti* is considered to be a principle in the sense that reality is of a given nature

[8] See MSABh, p. 168.5–12.

[9] MSA 19.45, p. 167.24–25:

yoniśaś ca manas-kāraḥ samyag-dṛṣṭiḥ phalânvitā /
pramāṇair vicayo 'cintyaṁ jñeyaṁ yukti-catuṣṭayaṁ //

[10] MSABh, p. 168.5–12: *yukti-prajñapti-vyavasthānaṁ catur-vidhaṁ. apekṣā yuktiḥ. kārya-kāraṇa-yuktiḥ. upapatti-sādhana-yuktiḥ. dharmatā-yuktiś ca. ... tatrâpekṣā-yuktis triṣv api yāneṣu yoniśo-manas-kāraḥ. tam apekṣya tena pratyayena lokôttarāyāḥ samyag-dṛṣṭer utpādāt. kārya-kāraṇa-yuktiḥ samyag-dṛṣṭiḥ saphalā. upapatti-sādhana-yuktiḥ. pratyakṣâdibhiḥ pramāṇaiḥ parīkṣā. dharmatā-yuktir acintyaṁ sthānaṁ. siddhā hi dharmatā na punaś cintyā. kasmād*[a] *yoniśo-manas-kārāt samyag-dṛṣṭir bhavati. tato vā kleśa-prahāṇaṁ phalam ity evam-ādi.*

[a] According to Lévi's emendation, see BHATTACHARYA (2001: 14).

which can be as inconceivable as the fact that the building blocks of the universe do not only behave like billiard balls but also like waves, something which is difficult to grasp on purely logical grounds, but must be accepted as a result of experiments.

In the presentation of the four *yukti*s in the *Saṁdhi-nirmocana-sūtra*, *dharmatā-yukti* is taken in the following way:

> 'Whether Tathāgatas appear [in this world] or not, because the factors of existence (*dharma*s) must abide [in their true nature (*dharmatā*)] this very abiding in the sphere of *dharmatā* (i.e. the *dharma-dhātu*) is the principle of true nature (*dharmatā-yukti*).'[11]

In his *Ṭīkā* on the *Saṁdhi-nirmocana-sūtra* (Peking Tanjur No. 5517), Yüan-ts'ê (613–696)[12] explains that *dharmatā-yukti* implies the fact that things have a certain nature throughout beginningless time, just as fire burns, water moistens and wind moves.[13]

In the *Tathāgata-garbha-sūtra* we find a passage similar to the *dharmatā-yukti* passage in the *Saṁdhi-nirmocana-sūtra*. The true nature is here taken as the Buddha-nature in all sentient beings:

> 'Son of a noble family, the true nature (*dharmatā*) of the factors of existence is this: whether Tathāgatas appear [in this world] or not, these sentient beings always possess the Buddha-nature.'[14]

Asaṅga[15] comments:

> 'This true nature is here principle, argument and method: by virtue of which (i.e. true nature) this (i.e. contents of perception) is this way (i.e. an accurate realisation of mind), and not otherwise. Everywhere it is precisely the true nature which is what is relied upon,[16] the principle underlying an "accurate realisation" [and] a "correct knowledge" of

---

[11] SNS, p. 158.29–31: *de la de bzhin gshegs pa rnams byung yang rung / ma byung yang rung ste / chos gnas par bya ba'i phyir chos nyid dbyings gnas pa nyid gang yin pa de ni chos nyid kyi rigs pa yin no /* .

[12] A disciple of Hsüan-tsang, see STEINKELLNER (1989: 233).

[13] POWERS (1994: 369).

[14] As quoted in RGVV, p. 73.11–12: *eṣā kula-putra dharmāṇāṁ dharmatā. utpādād vā tathāgatānām anutpādād vā sadâivête sattvās tathāgata-garbhā iti.*

[15] For the sake of convenience, I simply follow the Tibetan tradition here in ascribing the *Ratna-gotra-vibhāga-vyākhyā* to Asaṅga.

[16] DRSM *rten*, D *rtogs*, NP *rtog*. Given Skt. *pratisaraṇa*, the reading must be *rton* [*pa*], which is, moreover, the *lectio difficilior*.

> mind. The true nature is inconceivable and unthinkable; it must rather be simply believed in.'[17]

To sum up, the true nature is taken as either luminosity (Yogācāra) or the Buddha-nature (*Tathāgata-garbha-sūtra* and *Ratna-gotra-vibhāga*). In justification of this it is claimed that reality is simply of such a nature. This must be believed in, and can be verified when one eventually becomes a Buddha.

In his commentary on the above-quoted passage from the *Ratna-gotra-vibhāga*, 'Gos Lo tsā ba gZhon nu dpal (1392–1481) makes it clear that the possibility to see the similarity between the mind of sentient beings and the *dharma-kāya* of the Buddhas (i.e. the Buddha-nature of all sentient beings) is established by *dharmatā-yukti* and not by a direct cognition obtained on the basis of familiarity with the content of inferences:

> 'Well then, one may ask, whether such a seeing is one that has become a direct [cognition] by virtue of first realising [what the Buddha-nature is] through an inferential valid cognition based on the principle of proving on the basis of feasibility (*upapatti-sādhana-yukti*), and [then] becoming continuously used to it (i.e. to the content of the inferential cognition); or whether it is a seeing that [occurs] without any special reason, [that is,] adventitiously? It is neither a seeing based on [the principle of] proving on the basis of feasibility nor a seeing without reason. It is a seeing based on the principle of true nature (*dharmatā-yukti*).'[18]

In other words, reality cannot be ascertained as luminosity or the Buddha-nature on logical grounds, for the simple reason that such a nature remains inconceivable even for somebody who relies on inferential valid cognitions. This leaves us with

---

[17] RGVV, p. 73.12–16: *yâiva câsau dharmatā sâivātra yuktir yoga upāyaḥ*[a]. *yayâivam*[b] *evâitat*[c] *syāt. anyathā nâivâitat*[c] *syād iti. sarvatra dharmatâiva pratisa(text:śa)raṇam. dharmatâiva yuktiś citta-nidhyāpanāya citta-saṁjñâpanāya. sā na cintayitavyā na vikalpayitavyā*[. *a*][d]*dhimoktavyêti*. [[a] Johnston inserts after *upāyaḥ*, against B (38a3), *paryāyaḥ* (A is not available), but neither the Tibetan nor the Chinese has an equivalent for *paryāyaḥ*. See TAKASAKI (1966: 295, n. 8).[b] According to DE JONG (1979: 575). [c] According to B (38a3); Johnston reads in both cases *eva tat*. [d] TAKASAKI (1966: 296, n. 14) inserts *kevalaṁ tv*, but the unemended phrase (that is, without TAKASAKI'S insertion, but an additional *daṇḍa*) is also found in ŚrBh, p. 377.6.]

[18] DRSM, p. 431.13–6: *'o na de ltar mthong ba de dang por 'thad pas sgrub pa'i rigs pa la brten nas rjes su dpag pa'i tshad mas rtogs te de'i rgyun goms par byas pa las mngon sum du gyur pa zhig gam / rgyu mtshan chen med par glo bur du mthong ba zhig yin zhe na / 'thad pas sgrub pa la brten nas mthong ba yang ma yin / rgyu mtshan med par mthong ba yang ma yin te / chos nyid kyi rigs pa la brten nas mthong ba yin no /* .

the path of the *yogin*, which starts with direct valid cognitions right from the beginning (as described in Sahajavajra's commentary on TD 7cd).[19]

One might object that working with direct cognitions right from the beginning does not reveal the luminous nature of reality either, for everybody has direct cognitions—for example, in the first moment of perceiving visual forms—without experiencing their luminous nature. A similar objection is raised in Śāntarakṣita's *Madhyamakâlaṁkāra*, stanzas 73:

> 'Now, since the nature of it (i.e. a vase etc.) is directly manifest
> By virtue of its having been realised,
> Why is it that unwise persons
> Do not similarly realise the nature (*dngos po*)[20] of entities?'[21]

The point here is that a direct cognition is non-conceptual and thus free from reifications and denials. Ordinary people should thus realise the object of a direct perception exactly as it is (in the context of the *Madhyamakâlaṁkāra*, as being empty of its own-being, which is emptiness that corresponds to luminosity in the *Tattvadaśaka*). Śāntarakṣita refutes this objection in stanza MA 74:

> '[In fact] they do not. Having a burdensome [mind]-stream without beginning,
> They are overpowered by [their habit of] of imagining entities as real;
> Therefore no living beings
> Directly realise it (i.e. the nature of entities).'[22]

In other words, even though direct perceptions enable the seeing of objects as they are, these sense data are immediately processed under the distorting influence of mental imprints. In his commentary on these two stanzas (MA 73–74) gZhon nu dpal explains:

> 'Moreover, [ordinary direct perception] is not very amazing. Even though the shapes of a vase, an ox and so forth, which are devoid [of any universal properties] of oxness and so forth, are clearly seen, those who have a

[19] See MATHES (2006: 219–220).

[20] Mi pham explains in his *dBu ma rgyan rtsa 'grel*, 383: *dngos rnams kyi dngos po* as: *dngos po rnams kyi dngos po'am ngo bo yin lugs*.

[21] MA, p. 244.10–13: *'o na de ni rtogs gyur pas // de yi rang bzhin mngon sum phyir // mi mkhas rnams kyang dngos rnams kyi // dngos po 'di 'dra cis mi rtogs /* .

ICHIGŌ (1985: 244) introduces this and the following two stanzas (MA 73–75) in the following way: 'By whom and how is the absence of intrinsic nature in all *dharma*s understood?' MA 73–74 are given the subtitle: 'Emptiness (*śūnyatā*) and unwise people'.

[22] MA, p. 246.9–12: *ma yin thog med rgyud lci bar // dngos por sgro btags dbang byas pas // de phyir srog chags thams cad kyis // mngon sum rtogs par mi 'gyur ro /* .

mistaken understanding, [viewing as they do things] according to the traditions of Kapila, Kaṇāda and the like, do not perceive [them] in this way (i.e. as being empty of universal properties). Thus all sentient beings possess a knowledge of [direct] appearances [even] on the basis of not having ascertained natural emptiness. Nevertheless, owing to the confusion which has arisen throughout beginningless time, ascertainment is lacking. It is like the Sāṁkhyas and others, who possess a knowledge [of things] which clearly appear to be devoid of real universal properties, and still a [corresponding] ascertainment does not arise [in them].'[23]

In the epistemological tradition of Dignāga and Dharmakīrti, reality consists of specifically characterised phenomena or particulars (*sva-lakṣaṇa*s), which are the object of direct valid cognition, but usually unreal universals are projected onto these particulars and this leads to a distorted knowledge of reality. This is most clear from *Pramāṇa-vārttika-kārikā* 1.68–70:[24]

'The other form is concealed
By [thought's] own form—[imputed] by the intellect,
Which, [while] basing itself on different entities,
Reflects a single object.

Through [such] a concealing [thought]
The concealed manifold objects appear—even though discrete in themselves—
As if they were not different entities,
In some form [suggestive of a universal property].[25]

Under the constraint of [such] thinking on the part of it (i.e. the intellect),
[This] universal is [then] declared to be [something] existent.
It does not exist in any ultimate sense,
As imagined by that [intellect].'[26]

---

[23] DRSM, p. 57.8–13: *gzhan yang 'di ni ngo mtshar mi che ste / 'di ltar bum pa dang ba lang nyid la sogs pas dben pa'i ba lang la sogs pa'i dbyibs gsal bar mthong yang / ser skya dang / gzegs ma spyod pa la sogs pa'i lugs kyis blo gros phyin ci log tu gyur pa dag de ltar rtogs par mi byed do // zhes sems can thams cad la rang bzhin stong pa nyid ma nges pa las snang ba'i she's pa ni yod la / de yod kyang thog ma med pa nas byung ba'i 'khrul pas nges su mi lter ba ni grangs can la sogs pa la spyi dngos po bas dben pa'i gsal bar snang ba'i shes pa yod kyang nges pa mi skye ba bzhin no /* .

[24] The numbering follows STEINKELLNER (1977).

[25] Even though concrete entities (i.e. particulars) are completely different from each other, certain entities can cause a perception whose image is the same. Such an image is usually mistaken for the concrete entity itself (see FRAUWALLNER (1932: 264–5) for a discussion of these stanzas).

gZhon nu dpal's commentary on these three stanzas is as follows:

> 'To a conceptual knowledge governed by direct cognition that takes in different entities, such as sandalwood and *nyagrodha* [trees], there appears the form of a single universal called "tree", into which all distinctive features of a tree are gathered. When it appears, one thinks that that form is external, and clings to the existence of a single object universal. Even though such objects do not relate to a single universal, the latter's non-existence becomes obscured by the thought's own form, and the [concrete] entities that are trees are looked upon as something not different from the single entity of the universal "tree". Since a great number of sentient beings possess such thoughts, the existence of universals is proclaimed in accordance with the ideas of the many. The intellect which harbours the form of a universal "tree" thus corresponds to the apparent [truth], concealing as it does the ultimate. Such a universal [form] of trees is a mere convention, but apart from that it does not exist in any ultimate sense. To sum up, it may be said that the universal [called] "tree" is imputed to the set of trees taken as the basis of imputation.'[27]

In other words, the initial non-conceptual moments in the process of ordinary perception cannot lead to a soteriologically relevant realisation of reality as long as one's mind is engaged in the usual process of false imagining. It goes without saying that in the eyes of the Mādhyamikas it is not only the adherence to a notion of

---

[26] PV 1.68–70 (ed. GNOLI (1960: 38.11–6)):

para-rūpaṁ sva-rūpeṇa yayā saṁvriyate dhiyā /
ekârtha-pratibhāsinyā bhāvān āśritya bhedinaḥ //
tayā saṁvṛta-nānârthāḥ[a] *saṁvṛtyā bhedinaḥ svayam /*
abhedina ivâbhānti bhāvā rūpeṇa kenacit //
tasyā abhiprāya-vaśāt sāmānyaṁ sat prakīrtitam /
tad asat paramârthena yathā saṁkalpitaṁ tayā //

[[a] Manorathanandin reads °-*nānātvāḥ*, which is supported by the Tibetan *tha dad pa nyid* (see the PV edition of Miyasaka (1972: 124–5)). My translation is based on Gnoli's edition.]

[27] DRSM, p. 57.20–26: *tsan dan dang nya gro dha sogs dngos po tha dad pa mthong ba'i mngon sum gyis drangs pa'i rtog pa'i shes pa la shing gi khyad par de dag gang du 'du ba'i shing zhes pa'i spyi gcig gi rnam pa shar zhing / de shar na rnam pa de phyi rol yin snyam nas don gyi spyi gcig pa zhig yod par 'dzin to / de 'dra ba'i don la spyi gcig pa med kyang med pa de rtog pa rang gi rnam pas bsgribs nas shing gi dngos po rnams shing gi spyi'i dngos po gcig tu tha mi dad par mthong la / rtog pa de 'dra ba sems can shin tu mang ba la yod pas mang po'i bsam pa dang mthun par spyi yod pa skad du bsgrags so // de bas na shing spyi'i rnam pa can gyi blo ni kun rdzob ste dam pa'i don la sgrib byed yin pa'i phyir ro // de lta bu'i shing gi spyi de ni tha snyad tsam las dam pa'i don du med de / don bsdu na shing gi tshogs pa gdags gzhir byas nas shing gi spyi 'dogs so zhes bya ba yin no / .*

really existing universals which distorts one's perception of reality, but also the adherence to particulars, for both particulars and universals lack an own-being. gZhon nu dpal makes the following claim:

> 'Likewise, all imputations that a nature of entities exists are made on the basis of different parts. All perceptions of permanence, such as the thought that "The man of last year is this one [here]", are merely imputations relating to different earlier and later parts. Therefore, [whereas] Dharmakīrti [applies this critique] only to how universals are [wrongly] imputed to be real, it is applied in the Madhyamaka treatises to assertions concerning particulars as well, and [then] it is determined that all entities are without their own-being.'[28]

Coming back to our principle of true nature: it has been shown why an ordinary conceptual mind does not experience reality as luminosity or the Buddha-nature (as taught in the teachings of the third *dharma-cakra*). Luminosity cannot be inferred by an inferential valid cognition, nor can it be ascertained on the basis of the first moments of a direct valid cognition. In this context it is of interest, how the Third Karmapa Rang byung rdo rje (1284–1339) defends his definition of apparent truth as being mere appearances in the *Zab mo nang don gyi rang 'grel*. Rang byung rdo rje claims that even though the duality of a perceived object and a perceiving subject does not exist, something appears which is not deceptive. In response to the objection that these mere appearances would then be the ultimate truth, he clarifies his understanding of the ultimate truth:

> 'These [mere appearances] are presented as the expressible ultimate (*paryāya-paramârtha*), whereas the ultimate truth [here] is that which is related to the principle of the true nature (*dharmatā-yukti*), [namely] the natural emptiness previously mentioned while presenting the eighteen great [types of] emptiness.'[29]

---

[28] DRSM, p. 58.23–26: *zhes gsungs pa ltar dngos po'i ngo bo yod snyam du btags pa thams cad cha tha dad pa la btags shing / na ning gi mi de 'di'o snyam pa la sogs pa'i rtag par 'dzin pa thams cad ni snga phyi'i cha tha dad pa la btags pa kho na yin pas chos kyi grags pas spyi dngos po bar btags pa'i tshul de kho na dbu ma'i bstan bcos rnams su rang gi mtshan nyid du 'dod pa rnams la yang sbyar nas dngos po thams cad rang bzhin med par gtan la phab bo / .*

[29] Rang byung rdo rje: *Zab mo nang don gyi rang 'grel*: 63a5–6: *'di yang rnam grangs kyi don dam par bzhag pa yod mod kyi / chos nyid kyi rigs pa'i rjes su 'brel pa dag ni stong pa nyid chen po bco brgyad kyi rnam par bshad pa'i rang bzhin stong pa nyid sngar smos pa de nyid don dam pa'i bden pa yin no / .*

In other words, the principle of true nature does not refer here to a correct perception of phenomenal reality (which yields apparent truth), but to the fact that the ultimate is of a given nature. Although its emptiness can be inferred on logical grounds, other aspects of it, such as luminosity, can only be verified after abandoning all wrong projections onto reality and the underlying process of false imagining. This is described in the *Nirvikalpa-praveśa-dhāraṇī*, for example, and referred to by Maitrīpa and Sahajavajra in the context of directly realising the luminous nature of reality.[30]

Conclusion

The positive descriptions of the ultimate in the third *dharma-cakra* are mainly justified on the basis of the principle of true nature. This principle is not taken to stand in contradiction to the analytic approach of the second *dharma-cakra*, the latter being viewed indeed as a possible preparation for overcoming false imagining, which is a necessary condition for experiencing reality as it is. Since reality is thus beyond the reach of an ordinary intellect, one has to believe that it is of a certain nature, and that one will eventually experience it this way.

BIBLIOGRAPHY

BHATTACHARYA 2001 = Bhattacharya, Kamaleshwar: 'For a New Edition of the *Mahāyānasūtrālaṁkāra*', *Journal of the Nepal Research Centre* 12 (2001) 5–16.

DE JONG 1979 = de Jong, Jan W.: 'Review of Takasaki 1966', in: Schopen, Gregory (ed.): *Buddhist Studies by J. W. de Jong*. Asian Humanities Press, Berkeley 1979: 563–82.

DRSM = 'Gos Lo tsā ba gZhon nu dpal: *Theg pa chen po rgyud bla ma'i bstan bcos kyi 'grel bshad de kho na nyid rab tu gsal ba'i me long*. Klaus-Dieter Mathes (ed.): *'Gos Lo-Tsā-ba Gzon-Nu-Dpal Gyis Mdzad Pai Theg Pa Chen Po Rgyud Bla Mai Bstan Bcos Kyi grel Bshad De Kho Na nid Rab Ru Gsal Ba'i Me Long Zhes Bya Ba Bzhugs So: 'Gos Lo-Tsā-Ba Gzhon-nu-dpal's Commentary on Ratnagotravibhaga-vyakhya* (*Theg Pa Chen Po Rgyud Bla Ma'i Bstan Bcos Kyi grel Bshad De Kho Na Nyid Rab Ru Gsal Ba'i Me Long*). Nepal Research Centre Publications 24, Franz Steiner Verlag, Stuttgart 2003.

FRAUWALLNER 1932 = Frauwallner, Erich: 'Beiträge zur Apohalehre', *Wiener Zeitschrift für die Kunde des Morgenlandes* 39 (1932) 247–85.

[30] See MATHES (2005: 23–27).

ICHIGŌ 1985 = Ichigō, Masamichi. See: MA.

MA = Śantarakṣita: *Madhyamakâlaṁkāra*. Masamaichi Ichigō (ed.): *Madhyamakālaṁkāra of Śantarakṣita with his own commentary or Vṛtti and with the subcommentary or Pañjikā of Kamalaśīla*. Kyoto Sangyo University, Kyoto 1985.

MATHES 1996 = Mathes, Klaus-Dieter: *Unterscheidung der Gegebenheiten von ihrem wahren Wesen* (*Dharmadharmatāvibhāga*). Indica et Tibetica 26, Indica et Tibetica Verlag, Swisttal–Odendorf 1996.

MATHES 2005 = Mathes, Klaus-Dieter: 'Gos Lo tsā ba gZhon nu dpal's Commentary on the *Dharmatā* Chapter of the *Dharmadharmatāvibhāga-kārikā*s', *Studies in Indian Philosophy and Buddhism, University of Tokyo* 12 (2005) 3–39.

MATHES 2006 = Mathes, Klaus-Dieter: 'Blending the Sūtras with the Tantras: The Influence of Maitrīpa and his Circle on the Formation of *Sūtra Mahāmudrā* in the Kagyu Schools', in: Ronald M. Davidson, Christian K. Wedemeyer (ed.): *Tibetan Buddhist Literature and Praxis: Studies in its Formative Period 900–1400*. [Proceedings of the Tenth Seminar of the IATS, Oxford 2003]. Brill's Tibetan Studies Library 10 /4, E.J. Brill, Leiden 2006: 201–227.

MATHES 2008 = Mathes, Klaus-Dieter: *A Direct Path to the Buddha Within: Gö Lotsawa's Mahamudra Interpretation of the Ratnagotravibhaga*. Studies in Indian and Tibetan Buddhism. Wisdom Publications, Boston 2008.

Mi pham = 'Ju Mi pham rgya mtsho: *dBu ma rgyan rtsa 'grel*. Si khron mi rigs dpe skrun khang, Chengdu 1992.

MSA = Asaṅga: *Mahāyāna-sūtrâlaṁkāra*. Sylvain Lévi (ed.): *Mahāyāna-Sūtrālaṁkāra. Exposé de la Doctrine du Grand Véhicule*. Vol. 1, Bibliothèque de l'École des Hautes Études. Sciences historiques et philologiques 159, Librairie Honoré Champion, Paris 1907.

MSABh = Vasubandhu: *Mahāyāna-sūtrâlaṁkāra-bhāṣya*. See MSA.

NAKAMURA 1987 = Nakamura, Hajime: *Indian Buddhism: A Survey with Bibliographical Notes*. Buddhist Tradition Series 1, Motilal Banarsidass, Delhi 1987 [first edition: 1980].

POWERS 1994 = Powers, John: *Wisdom of the Buddha: The Saṁdhinirmocanasūtra*. Translated by John Powers. Tibetan Translation Series 16, Dharma Publishing, Berkeley 1994.

PV = Dharmakīrti: *Pramāṇa-vārttika*. (1) Yūsho Miyasaka (ed.): 'Pramāṇavārttika-kārikā (Sanskrit and Tibetan)', *Acta Indologica* 2 (1971–1972) 1–206. (2) Raniero Gnoli (ed.): *The Pramāṇavārttikam of Dharmakīrti: The First Chapter with the Autocommentary: Text and Critical Notes*. Serie Orientale Roma XXIII, Istituto Italiano per il Medio ed Estremo Oriente, Rome 1960.

Rang byung rdo rje = [The Third Karmapa] Rang byung rdo rje (karma pa gsum pa): *Rang 'grel: Zab mo nang gi don gsal bar byed pa'i 'grel pa bzhugs so* (block print). No place, no date. [The work was composed at the O rgyan kyi mkhan po padma 'byung gnas kyi sgrub gnas in 1325 (fol. 92b6)].

RGV = *Ratna-gotra-vibhāga* [*Mahāyānôttara-tantra-śāstra*]. Edward H. Johnston (ed.): *The Ratnagotravibhāga Mahāyānottaratantra-śāstra*. Bihar Research Society, Patna 1950. [Includes the *Ratna-gotra-vibhāga-vyākhyā*].

RGVV = *Ratna-gotra-vibhāga-vyākhyā*. (1) See: RGV. [The manuscripts A and B on which Johnston's edition is based are described in RGV: vi–vii. (2) Frank Bandurski, Bikkhu Pāsādika, Michael Schmidt, Bangwei Wang: *Untersuchungen zur buddhistischen Literatur. Sanskrit-Wörterbuch der buddhistischen Texte aus den Turfan-Funden*, Beiheft 5, Vandenhoeck & Ruprecht in Göttingen, Göttingen 1994: 12–13.

SNS = *Saṁdhi-nirmocana-sūtra* [Tibetan translation from the Kanjur]. Étienne Lamotte (ed.): *Saṁdhinirmocana Sūtra, l'explication des mystères*. Université de Louvain, Bureaux du Recueil, Louvain–Paris 1935.

STEINKELLNER 1977 = Steinkellner, Ernst: *Verse-Index of Dharmakīrti's Works* (*Tibetan Version*). Wiener Studien zur Tibetologie und Buddhismuskunde 1, Arbeitskreis für tibetische und buddhistische Studien, Vienna 1977.

STEINKELLNER 1989 = Steinkellner, Ernst: 'Who is Byaṅ chub rdzu 'phrul? Tibetan and non-Tibetan Commentaries on the *Saṁdhi-nirmocana-sūtra*—A Survey of the Literature.' *Berliner Indologische Studien* 4 /5 (1989) 229–251.

ŚrBh = Asaṅga: *Śrāvaka-bhūmi*. Karunesh Shukla (ed.): *Śrāvakabhūmi of Ācārya Asaṅga*. Tibetan Sanskrit Works Series 14, K.P. Jayaswal Research Institute, Patna 1973.

TAKASAKI 1966 = Takasaki, Jikido: *A Study on the Ratna-gotra-vibhāga (Uttara-tantra) Being a Treatise on the Tathāgatagarbha Theory of Mahā-yāna Buddhism*. Rome Oriental Series 33, Istituto Italiano per il Medio ed Estremo Oriente, Rome 1966.

TATZ 1994 = Tatz, Mark: 'Philosophic Systems according to Advayavajra and Vajrapāṇi.' *The Journal of Buddhist and Tibetan Studies* 1 (1994) 65–120.

TD = Maitrīpa: *Tattva-daśaka*. (1) In: Haraprasad Shaṣtri (ed.): *Advaya-vajrasaṁgraha*. Gaekwad's Oriental Series 40, Oriental Institute, Baroda 1927: 59. (2) The 'Studying Group of Sacred Tantric Texts' / Mikkyō-seiten kenkyūkai (ed.): 'The Results of a Joint Study on the Buddhist Tantric Texts: Advayavajrasaṁgraha—New Critical Edition with Japanese Translation', *Annual of the Institute for Comprehensive Studies of Buddhism Taisho University* 13 (March 1991) (92)–(94) [= 245–243]. (3) See also: The Nepal-German Manuscript Preservation Project (NGMPP) reel no. B 22/ 24.

Tsong kha pa on the Three Times: New Light on the Buddhist Theory of Time*

HIROSHI NEMOTO

1. Introduction

— 1.1 —

For Buddhist philosophers, time is not a substance existing apart from entities such as colour/form, sound and so on. In the *Abhidharma-kośa* time, not being enumerated in the list of seventy-five factors (*dharma*), is considered to be a nominal designation of conditioned phenomena (*saṁskāra*).[1] In the *Abhidharma-samuccaya* it is included in the list of non-associated compositional factors (*viprayukta-saṁskāra*) and is not posited as a substantial entity but rather as a nominal designation of a causal stream (*hetu-phala-prabandha-pravṛtti*).[2] Not surprisingly, Mādhyamikas deny that time is intrinsically existent, as is shown by such texts as the *Mūla-madhyamaka-kārikā* (Chapter 19) and *Catuḥ-śataka* (Chapter 11).

While denying the substantiality or intrinsic nature of time, however, Buddhist philosophers admit time divisions: the future, present and past, in terms of conventional experience. For otherwise one could not account for the recollection of past events, for the law of *karman* and transmigration, for the fact that previous karmic actions are responsible for our present experiences and so on. In fact, we can find

* I wish to express my sincere gratitude to Prof. Tom Tillemans for his helpful remarks regarding an earlier version of this paper.

1 AKBh 212.13–14 (cf. POUSSIN (1937: 135)): *kālo nāma ka eṣa dharmaḥ. saṁskāra-paridīpanâdhivacanam etat.*—'What is this *dharma* called "time"? It is a nominal designation indicating *saṁskāras*.'). AKBh 180.23: *kalpaṁ kiṁ-svabhāvaḥ. pañca-skandha-svabhāvaḥ.*—'What is the essence of *kalpa*? [It has] the essence of being five aggregates.'

2 AS_1 19.8–9: *kālaḥ katamaḥ. hetu-phala-prabandha-pravṛttau kāla iti prajñaptiḥ.*—'What is time? It is a designation indicating the continuous succession of causes and effects.'

Logic and Belief in Indian Philosophy
Warsaw Indological Studies 3 (2010) 617–625.

the definitions of the three times given in Buddhist texts such as the *Madhyānta-vibhāga*, *Abhidharma-samuccaya* and *Catuḥ-śataka-ṭīkā*.[3]

Turning to Tibetan Buddhism, we notice that Tsong kha pa blo bzang grags pa (1357–1419), who flourished in Medieval Tibet and founded the dGe lugs pa sect, develops the Buddhist theory of time in an original way. He is unique, we have to say, in that he thinks that Prāsaṅgika-Mādhyamikas assert that all the three times (*dus gsum ga*) are effective things (*dngos po*), that is, future, present and past things are equally capable of producing their effects. While it may be a challenging task to discuss whether and how Prāsaṅgikas actually express such an idea, this paper focuses upon Tsong kha pa's own view of time which he presents in his *rTsa she Tik chen* (Chapter 19), as well as in the *mNgon sum le'u'i Tikka*, a memorandum of his lecture on the *Pramāṇa-vārttika* 3, compiled by his prominent student mKhas grub rje dge legs dpal bzang po (1385–1438). His unique interpretation of the idea of time, we may say, has had a great influence on later dGe lugs pa scholars to this day.[4]

Tsong kha pa seems to have formed his own view of time by considering how the views of time accepted by the Sautrāntika, Yogācāra and Mādhyamika schools differed from that of the Vaibhāṣika school. Thus the purpose of this paper is first to consider his exposition of the Vaibhāṣika's view on time and then to examine his understanding of the view of time accepted by the other three schools.

2. Tsong kha pa on the Vaibhāṣika's view of time

— 2.1 —

As is generally known, Vaibhāṣikas, alias Sarvāsti-vādins, advocate the doctrine that factors exist as real entities (*dravya*) in the three time periods of future, present and past. Sautrāntikas, on the other hand, argue that there is no future nor past and that factors exist only in the present. Such a divergence of opinion had already been known in Tibet before the arrival of Tsong kha pa. mChims 'jam pa'i dbyangs (13c.) says the following:

> 'Therefore, it is also stated by Ācārya Pūrṇavardhana as follows: "Those who admit the existence of [an entity in each of] the three times are Sarvāsti-vādins; those who admit the existence of present

[3] See MAVBh 47.8–11 (ad MAV 3.20cd), AS_1 22.25–23.5 (=AS_2 21.8–22), CṢṬ 171b6–7. Cf. *rTsa she Tik chen*, 197a3 ff.

[4] For example, *Sras bsdus grwa*, an elementary textbook used at Drepung Gomang Monastery (*'bras spungs sgo mang grwa tshang*), devotes to the topic 'Three Times' (*dus gsum*) one chapter, in which Tsong kha pa's view is propounded.

> things as well as that of past things which have not brought about effects are Vibhajya-vādins; and those who admit that [only] present things exist are Sautrāntikas".'[5]

mChims 'jam pa'i dbyangs already knew in this way that there is a divergence of opinion about the existence of a thing in the three time periods. According to him, in the Sarvāsti-vādins' view future, present and past things are equally existent; in the Vibhajya-vādins' view past things which have not yet brought about effects and present things are existent; in the Sautrāntikas' view only present things are existent. It is natural to assume that Tsong kha pa must have been aware of such a difference of opinion among Buddhist schools concerning the existence of the three times.

— 2.2 —

Tsong kha pa summarises the Vaibhāṣika's theory of time as follows:

> 'Vaibhāṣikas establish each [entity], e.g. a sprout, [as existent] in all of the three temporal periods. By doing so, they [intend to] say that a sprout exists even when the sprout has not yet come about and even when the sprout has passed away. They say the same thing about other entities also.'[6]

Tsong kha pa points out here that, in the Vaibhāṣika system, every entity is regarded as existing in each of the three temporal periods. This means that a single sprout, for example, continues to exist and remains constant throughout the three temporal periods. In Vaibhāṣikas' view, consequently, a single sprout can be established not only as a present sprout but also as a future sprout and a past sprout. Of course, this does not mean that a single entity can at the same time be a future thing, a present thing, as well as a past thing; for Vaibhāṣikas do accept time divisions. On the question of how the three times are distinguished from one another, there are four different views among Vaibhāṣikas: According to Dharmatrāta the three times are

---

[5] *mDzod 'grel mngon rgyan*, 513.19–22 (cf. AKLA Chu. 112b4–5): *de'i phyir slob dpon gang spel gyis kyang / dus gsum ga yod par smra ba dang / da ltar ba dang 'das pa 'bras bu ma bskyed pa yod par smra ba dang / da ltar byung ba yod par smra ba rnams ni go rim bzhin du thams cad yod par smra ba dang / rnam par phye ste smra ba dang / mdo sde pa yin no zhes bshad do //*

[6] *rTsa she Tik chen*, 198a3–4 (cf. SAMTEN—GARFIELD (2006: 400)): *bye brag tu smra ba rnams myu gu la sogs pa re re la dus gsum gsum du 'jog pas myu gu ma 'ongs pa dang 'das pa'i dus su yang myu gur yod par 'dod de dngos po gzhan la yang de ltar 'dod do //*

Comp. the parallel passages in *mNgon sum le'u'i Tikka*, 24b2 and *sTong thun chen mo*, 180a3–4; cf. CABEZÓN (1992: 307).

distinguished in terms of a change in nature (*bhāvânyathika*); according to Ghoṣaka, in terms of a change in characteristic (*lakṣaṇânyathika*); according to Vasumitra, in terms of a change in state (*avasthânyathika*); and according to Buddhadeva, through their mutual difference in state of affairs (*anyathânyathika*).[7] According to Tsong kha pa, however, all Vaibhāṣikas should accept that an entity exists even when it has not yet come about and even when it has passed away. This is precisely what the three times theory advocated by Vaibhāṣikas claims.

3. Tsong kha pa on the Sautrāntika, Yogācāra and Mādhyamika's view of time

— 3.1 —

Tsong kha pa, basing himself on such Indian Buddhist treatises as the *Madhyânta-vibhāga*, *Abhidharma-samuccaya* and *Catuḥ-śataka-ṭīkā,* attempts to grasp the point made by Sautrāntikas, Yogācāras and Mādhyamikas (including both Svātantrikas and Prāsaṅgikas), saying:

> 'Such being the case, the ceased sprout is the past sprout; the non-arisen sprout is the future sprout; the sprout which has arisen but which has not yet ceased is the present sprout. Therefore, with reference to three times, one has to take into consideration the following respective times of an entity like a sprout: the time of having ceased, that of having not yet arisen and that of having arisen but not yet ceased.'[8]

What Tsong kha pa means to say is as follows. First, when a sprout has ceased, it no longer exists; instead, there exists a ceased sprout (*myu gu zhig pa*). We should notice that the ceased sprout is not the sprout itself which has ceased (*zhig pa'i myu gu*). The sprout which has ceased is what existed before and what is hence not currently existent. The ceased sprout, on the other hand, refers to the state of the sprout's having ceased, which is considered to be existent. It is such a state of the sprout that is said to be 'a past sprout' (*myu gu 'das pa*). Secondly, when a sprout

[7] See *rTsa she Tik chen*, 198a4–b8 (cf. SAMTEN—GARFIELD (2006: 400–401); AKBh 296.9–297.3 ad AK V 26ab) and *sTong thun chen mo*, 180a4–b3; cf. CABEZÓN (1992: 307–308).

[8] *rTsa she Tik chen*, 197b6–198a1 (cf. SAMTEN—GARFIELD (2006: 400)): *de ltar na myu gu zhig pa ni myu gu 'das pa'i dus dang myu gu ma skyes pa ni myu gu ma 'ongs pa'i dus dang myu gu grub nas ma zhig pa ni myu gu da ltar ba'i dus yin pas / dus gsum char yang myu gu la sogs pa'i dngos po de'i zhig pa dang ma skyes pa dang skyes nas ma zhig pa'i dus gang yin pa de la rtsi ba yin gyi /...* Comp. the parallel passages in *mNgon sum le'u'i Tikka*, 25b6–26a1 and *sTong thun chen mo*, 183a5–b1; cf. CABEZÓN (1992: 311).

has not yet arisen, it does not exist; instead there exists a non-arisen sprout (*myu gu ma skyes pa*). Here again, we should notice that the non-arisen sprout is not the sprout itself which has not yet arisen (*ma skyes pa'i myu gu*). The sprout which has not yet arisen is what will exist later and hence is not currently existent. The non-arisen sprout, on the other hand, is the sprout's state of having not arisen, which is considered to be existent. And such a state of the sprout is said to be 'a future sprout' (*myu gu ma 'ongs pa*). Thirdly, when a sprout has come into existence but has not yet ceased, the sprout itself is spoken of as 'a present sprout' (*myu gu da ltar ba*). In this case, there is no need to posit any factor other than the currently existent sprout as a present sprout.[9]

This is how Tsong kha pa explains the view of time held by the Sautrāntika, Yogācāra and Mādhyamika schools. The points he wishes to emphasise are (1) that in the three schools' view a sprout is regarded as existent only when it is in the present state; (2) and that in their view a future sprout is not the sprout which will come about, nor is a past sprout the sprout which existed before. Of these two points, the first point is in stark contrast to the Vaibhāṣika school's view that a single sprout continues to exist and remains constant throughout the three temporal periods.

—3.2 —

Of the second point, Tsong kha pa goes on to say:

> 'That which does not exist at the present moment when a speaker is in the process of using temporal language can nonetheless be said to be present (*lit.* 'is not said to be non-present'), because the [moment at which the speaker is making a statement] is the present [only] in relation to the speaker.'[10]

---

[9] The same idea is expressed by dKon mchog 'jigs med dbang po (1728–1791) who defines the three times as follows: 'The past is defined as the factor of another thing's having ceased in its second moment after its own time [i.e. the moment at which it is existent]. The future is defined as the factor of another thing's having not yet arisen due to the incompletion of conditions within the context of a certain place and time even though causes producing it exist. The present is defined as that which has arisen but has not yet ceased.' (*Grub mtha' rin phreng*, 144.6–10: *dngos po gzhan zhig rang grub dus kyi skad cig gnyis par zhig pa'i cha de 'das pa'i mtshan nyid / dngos po gzhan zhig skye ba'i rgyu yod kyang rkyen ma tshang ba'i dbang gis yul dus 'ga' zhig tu ma skyes pa'i cha de ma 'ongs pa'i mtshan nyid / skyes la ma 'gag pa da ltar ba'i mtshan nyid /*).

[10] *rTsa she Tik chen*, 198a1–2 (cf. SAMTEN—GARFIELD (2006: 400)): *dus kyi tha snyad byed pa pos brjod bzhin pa'i da ltar ba'i dus su med pa la da ltar ba ma yin par smra ba ma yin te de ni brjod pa po de la ltos pa'i da ltar ba yin pa'i phyir ro //* Comp. the parallel passage in *mNgon sum le'u'i Tikka*, 26a1–2 and *sTong thun chen mo*, 183b1–b2; cf. CABEZÓN (1992: 311).

This statement requires clarification. According to Tsong kha pa, the word 'present' has two different senses. First, the word is used in the sense of the moment at which a person makes a statement about a certain entity. For example, when a sprout has not yet arisen, one may say: 'A sprout does not exist in the present.' We may say that this is just the way we use the word 'present' from a commonsensical point of view.[11] Tsong kha pa, however, rejects such a way of using the word. He, instead, defines the present as the state of having arisen but not yet ceased, which is not distinct from the thing in that state. In his view, consequently, even the object which will arise tomorrow is regarded as present, for the object satisfies the condition of being present in the sense that it will be in the state of having arisen tomorrow. For example, when one speaks of the sprout which will be in the state of having arisen tomorrow, one may say: 'It is a present sprout', instead of saying: 'It is a future sprout.' What is, then, a future sprout? As we have seen, the future is defined as a thing's state of having not arisen. Therefore, such a state of the sprout of tomorrow, today, yesterday, and so on, is spoken of as a future sprout. In the same manner, the object which existed yesterday is regarded as present. For example, when one speaks of the sprout which was in the state of having arisen yesterday, one may say: 'It is a present sprout', instead of saying: 'It is a past sprout.' What is, then, a past sprout? The past, under Tsong kha pa's definition, is a thing's state of having ceased. Therefore, such a state of the sprout of yesterday, today, tomorrow, and so on, is spoken of as a past sprout.

Tsong kha pa thus rejects the view that the present time is established in terms of a speaker's perspective. From his standpoint, both the sprout of yesterday and that of tomorrow are ever present and never become past or future. We can recognise from these things that he takes the fact of the sprout being present as an unchanging truth.[12]

---

[11] We may recall that Bertrand RUSSELL (1940: Chap. VII) considers the words 'past', 'present' and 'future' to be 'egocentric particulars', the denotation of which is relative to the speaker.

[12] Interestingly enough, gSer mdog paṇ chen Shākya mchog ldan (1428–1507), who argues against Tsong kha pa, seems to hold the view that the three times are established in terms of a speaker's perspective. He defines the three times as follows: 'The present is defined as that which has arisen but which has not elapsed at the present moment. This is illustrated by the harvest of this year. The past is defined as that which, in general, has arisen and then has gone away at the present moment. This is illustrated by the harvest of last year. The future is defined as that which, in general, has not yet arisen even though causes producing it exist. This is illustrated by the harvest of next year.' (*dBu ma rnam nges*, Ba. 13b5–6: *da ltar gyi dus su skyes zhing thal ma zin pa de / da ltar ba'i mtshan nyid / mtshan gzhi ni da lo'i lo thog lta bu'o // spyir skye myong zhing da ltar gyi dus las gzhan du song ba de / 'das pa'i mtshan nyid / mtshan gzhi ni / na ning gi lo thog lta bu'o // spyir 'byung ba'i rgyu yod cing ma byung ba de / ma 'ongs pa'i mtshan nyid / mtshan gzhi ni / sang phod kyi lo thog lta bu'o //*).

— 3.3 —

Let me stress again that, as Tsong kha pa understands it, in the view of the three schools in question the sprout which will exist is not a future sprout; and the sprout which existed before is not a past sprout. Tsong kha pa distinguishes the sprout of tomorrow from a future sprout and the sprout of yesterday from a past sprout. In his view, the sprout of tomorrow, called 'that which will come about' (*'ong rgyu*), is considered to be the sprout's present state which has not yet come about; and the sprout of yesterday, called 'that which would cease' (*zhig rgyu*), is considered to be the sprout's present state which once existed. Let us consider the following remarks:

> 'On account of this, we speak of the past king Mahā-saṁmata as a present person (*lit.* a present entity). This means that the king Mahā-saṁmata is a present person at his own time. And further, what will occur tomorrow is [said to be] a present entity since what will occur tomorrow is a present entity at its own time.'[13]

This might be explained as follows. A thing's own time (*rang dus*) is the moment at which the thing is existent, before which it has not arisen and after which it will cease. That something is a present entity at its own time means that it exists at such a moment. Consequently, when one uses the expression 'the sprout of tomorrow', if one intends to imply that the sprout will exist tomorrow, one may speak of it as a present entity in the sense that the sprout is tomorrow's 'present' sprout; and similarly, when one uses the expression 'the sprout of yesterday', if one intends to imply that the sprout existed yesterday, one may speak of it as a present entity in the sense that the sprout is yesterday's 'present' sprout. What all this shows is that the sprout which exists at any particular moment should always be described as present irrespective of when the statement concerning the sprout is made.

In everyday linguistic usage also, we can describe the sprout of yesterday as the present by using a past tense, as we say: 'The sprout was present'; and similarly, we can describe the sprout of tomorrow as the present by using a future tense, as we say: 'The sprout *will be* present.' But we should notice that Tsong kha pa, while analysing the expression of time, does not introduce the notion of verb tense at all. The fact of the sprout being present, as we have seen, is considered to be an unchanging truth. Accordingly, unlike in the case of ordinary language, the sprout is

[13] *mNgon sum le'u'i Tikka*, 26a2–4: *rgyu mtshan 'di nyid kyis na 'das pa'i rgyal po mang pos bkur ba da ltar ba'i dngos po yin par smras pa ni rgyal po mang pos bkur ba'i rang dus na da ltar ba'i dngos po yin pa'i don dang / sang nyin dngos po da ltar ba yin pa'ang sang nyin rang dus na dngos po da ltar ba yin pa'i don yin no //*

always described as present by using an atemporal verb 'is' (*yin*), as it is said: 'The sprout is present' (*myu gu da ltar ba yin*). Mutatis mutandis for the future and past. The non-arisen sprout and the ceased sprout are always described as future and past, respectively, by using the atemporal verb, as it is said: 'The non-arisen sprout is future' (*myu gu ma skyes pa ma 'ongs pa yin*), and 'The ceased sprout is past' (*myu gu zhig pa 'das pa yin*). We may say that Tsong kha pa is thus trying to formulate all statements concerning the three times in an atemporal fashion.

4. Concluding Remarks

As shown above, Tsong kha pa, while explaining the view of time shared by the Sautrāntika, Yogācāra and Mādhyamika schools, makes a unique interpretation of the idea of the three times. According to him, the future is not that which will come about, but a thing's state of having not arisen; the past is not that which existed before, but its state of having ceased; and the present is the thing which is in the state of having arisen at the moment at which it exists. Consequently, from his viewpoint, the words 'future', 'present', and 'past' are used to refer to such objects without depending on the context in which their utterance is made. It is interesting that, identifying the three states of an entity with the three times, he ends up with the existence of the three times. This is along the line where he holds that Prāsaṅgika-Mādhyamikas claim that the three times are effective things.

BIBLIOGRAPHY

AK = Vasubandhu: *Abhidharma-kośa*. See: AKBh.

AKBh = Vasubandhu: *Abhidharma-kośa*. Prahlad Pradhan (ed.): *Abhidharma-kośabhāṣyam of Vasubandhu*. Tibetan Sanskrit Works Series 8, K.P. Jayaswal Research Institute, Patna 1975.

AKLA = Pūrṇavardhana. *Abhidharma-kośa-ṭīkā-lakṣaṇânusāriṇī*. Tibetan sDe dge ed. Tohoku No. 4093.

AS = Asaṅga: *Abhidharma-samuccaya*. (1) V.V. Gokhale (ed.): *Fragments from the Abhidharmasamuccaya of Asaṅga*. Journal of the Royal Asiatic Society, Bombay Research, New Series 23, Bombay 1947. (2) P. Pradhan (ed.): *Abhidharma Samuccaya of Asanga*. Visva Bharati Studies 12, Santiniketan 1950.

dBu ma rnam nges = gSer mdog paṇ chen Shākya mchog ldan: *dBu ma rnam par nges pa'i chos kyi bang mdzod lung dang rigs pa'i rgya mtsho*. Collected Writings of gSer-mdog Paṇ-chen Sākya-mchog-ldan, Vol.14–15. Reprinted by Nagwang Topgyal, Delhi 1988.

CABEZÓN 1992 = Cabezón, José Ignacio: *A Dose of Emptiness, An Annotated Translation of the sTong thun chen mo of mKhas grub dGe legs dpal bzang*. State University of New York Press, Albany 1992.

CSṬ = Candrakīrti: *Catuḥ-śataka-ṭīkā*. Tibetan sDe dge ed. Tohoku No. 3865.

mDzod 'grel mngon rgyan = mChims 'jam pa'i dbyangs: *Chos mngon pa mdzod kyi tshig le'ur byas pa'i 'grel pa mngon pa'i rgyan*. Library of Gaden Shartse Monastic College, Mundgod 1992.

Grub mtha' rin phreng = dKon mchog 'jigs med dbang po: *Grub mtha'i rnam par gzhag pa rin po che'i phreng ba*. Drepung Gomang Library, 2005.

MAVBh = Vasubandhu: *Madhyānta-vibhāga-bhāṣya*. Gadjin Nagao (ed.): *Madhyānta-vibhāga-bhāṣya, A Buddhist Philosophical Treatise Edited for the First Time From a Sanskrit Manuscript*. Suzuki Research Foundation. Tokyo 1964.

mNgon sum le'u'i Tikka = Tsong kha pa blo bzang grags pa / mKhas grub rje dge legs dpal bzang po: *mNgon sum le'u'i Tikka*. Tohoku No. 5410. Zhol ed. Ma.

RUSSELL 1940 = Russell, Bertrand: *An Inquiry into Meaning and Truth: The William James lectures for 1940 delivered at Harvard University*. George Allen and Unwin Ltd., London 1940.

SAMTEN—GARFIELD 2006 = rJe Tsong Khapa. Translated by Geshe Ngawang Samten and Jay L. Garfield. *Ocean of Reasoning, A Great Commentary on Nāgārjuna's Mūlamadhyamakakārikā*. Oxford University Press. 2006.

sTong thun chen mo = mKhas grub rje dge legs dpal bzang po: *Zab mo stong pa nyid kyi de kho na nyid rab tu gsal ba'i bstan bcos skal bzang mig 'byed*. Tohoku No. 5459. Zhol ed. Ka.

POUSSIN 1937 = Poussin, L.D.L. Vallée: 'Note sur le moment (*kṣaṇa*) des Vaibhāṣikas et des Sautrāntikas', in *Mélanges Chinois et Buddhistiques*, Vol. 5: 134–158.

rTsa she Tik chen = Tsong kha pa blo bzang grags pa: *dBu ma rtsa ba'i tshig le'ur byas pa shes rab ces bya ba'i rnam bshad rigs pa'i rgya mtsho*. Tohoku No. 5401. Zhol ed. Ba.

The *Bodhi-caryâvatāra* and Its Monastic Aspects: On the Problem of Representation*

KAORU ONISHI

1. Introduction

— 1.1 —

Śāntideva, the author of the *Bodhi-caryâvatāra* (henceforth abbreviated BCA), is considered to have been active sometime between the mid-seventh century and the mid-eighth century.[1] If we are to believe the legendary accounts, he composed the BCA as a monk-scholar at the monastic university (*mahā-vihāra*) in Nālandā.[2] At the time of Śāntideva, Nālandā was one of the main *mahā-vihāra*s that came to be the centres of Buddhist monastic life in India. Nālandā was so prosperous and prestigious that many monks from various regions of India, Tibet, and China wanted to come and study there.[3] According to Xuanzang, who studied in Nālandā for six years (630–635 CE),[4] there were several thousand monks at the 'Nālandā

* I would like to thank Professor Robert Sharf (The University of California, Berkeley), Professor Donald Lopez and Professor Luis Gómez (both, The University of Michigan) for their helpful comments and suggestions on earlier versions of this paper, although of course I am solely responsible for any surviving errors.

1 According to BHATTACHARYA (1926: XXIII), the *terminus a quo* is suggested from the fact that Yijing, who left India in 695 CE, does not mention Śāntideva in his 'Record' (*Nanhai jigui naifazhuan*); the *terminus ad quem* is drawn from the fact that Śāntarakṣita, who visited Tibet in 743 CE, quotes two stanzas from the BCA (1.10 and 7.28) in his *Tattva-siddhi*. See PEZZALI (1968: 38; DE JONG (1975: 163, 179–80); SEYFORT RUEGG (1981: 82). Also see BENDALL (1992: III–VI), who, earlier than Bhattacharya, suggests that the *terminus a quo* is the middle of the seventh century and the *terminus ad quem* is 800 CE, depending mostly on the accounts of Tāranātha. Cf. SCHIEFNER (1869: 161–164).

2 OBERMILLER (1932: 162–63). Also see CHIMPA–CHATTOPADHYAYA (1970: 217), and SCHIEFNER (1869: 162–166).

3 DUTT (1962: 331–32).

4 LI (1959: 105, 120).

Logic and Belief in Indian Philosophy
Warsaw Indological Studies 3 (2010) 627–654.

saṅghârāma'.[5] Yijing, having stayed there for ten years (675–685 CE), also reports that there were more than three thousand monks and that there were eight halls and three hundred apartments in the monastery, for it was difficult for them all to assemble in one place.[6] We can imagine a highly organised and institutionalised community from these accounts.

The Buddhist monastic community[7] had, from early on, been regulated by the monastic codes: *vinaya*. It was the *vinaya* that prescribed the rules of discipline as well as rituals and behaviours of monks. The *vinaya* remained valid for the monastic communities regardless of whether they belong to 'Hīnayāna' or 'Mahāyāna'.[8] Śāntideva, who is believed to have been a 'Mahāyāna monk', was very well aware of the *vinaya* regulations and seems to have respected them, which we know from his direct mention of *Prātimokṣa* rules in the BCA.[9] And it is most probably in this local, cultural, and historical context that the BCA was produced by Śāntideva.

— 1.2 —

The BCA[10] has been very popular in Western Buddhist scholarship. This is probably one of the texts most often rendered into Western languages throughout the his-

[5] BEAL (1884: 170).

[6] TAKAKUSU (1966: 154).

[7] The word that refers to a Buddhist community in the broadest sense is *saṅgha*, which includes fully ordained monks and nuns (*bhikṣu*/*bhikṣuṇī*), male and female novices (*śrāmaṇera*/*śrāmaṇerī*), and laymen and laywomen (*upāsaka*/*upāsikā*). *Saṅgha* as a whole, which can be translated as 'Buddhist community', therefore, does not mean monastic community; however, the monks, nuns and novices constitute the community that is distinctive from lay people in terms of their social status. This community, which can be called '*saṅgha*' in the narrow sense of the word, can be conceived of as monastic; they left home and became wanderer (*parivrājaka*) or live in temporary retreats (*āvāsa*), or, later, they lived in monasteries (*vihāra*) or cave dwellings (*guhā*). See COLLCUTT (1987: 41–44) and GÓMEZ (1987: 57–60).

[8] We do not know whether a monk could be called definitively Hīnayāna or Mahāyāna. Even if it was possible to somehow distinguish them, we do not know exactly how or to what extent this distinction was made.

[9] ISHIDA (1993) details the correspondence between the stanzas and the *Prātimokṣa* rules. Together with other evidence, he suggests a hypothesis that the revision from Dunhuang version to the canonical version is a part of monachising process of the text.

[10] The first Sanskrit edition of the text was published in 1889 by MINAYEFF, based on three manuscripts, two now in London and another in his possession. This edition was reproduced by H. P. Shastri in 1894 but it is said to be full of mistakes (KANAKURA (1958: 244)). Based on two more manuscripts, now in Paris (Bibliothèque Nationale, Devanāgarī 78 and Burnouf 98), la Vallée POUSSIN edited the text, along with Prajñākaramati's *Pañjikā*, from 1901 to 1914, which I

tory of Buddhist Studies.[11] The introductions to these translations, and other numerous remarks on the BCA, show that this work has been read in various manners: it was once called a 'book of religious ardour (*enthusiasm*) and propaganda' (la Vallée POUSSIN (1892)); KERN (1989: 11) defined it as a 'poem breathing a truly pious spirit.' In their subtitles to their translations, BARNETT (1959) and SCHMIDT (1923) characterised it as a 'manual of Mahāyāna Buddhism' and a 'Buddhist didactic poem (*Lehrgedicht*) of the seventh century', respectively. MURTI (1980: 101) said that the BCA and the *Śikṣā-samuccaya* are 'our chief sources for the Mādhyamika path of spiritual realisation'; SEYFORT RUEGG (1981: 82–83) claimed that it presented 'the mystical aspects of Madhyamaka thought', but should be read as 'a philosophical treatise' rather than a 'religious and devotional poem'.

What is striking, however, is that most of these translators, as well as other scholars, have ignored its monastic aspects, which are especially evident in chapters five and six. It is only recently that its monastic character has been explicitly recognised and acknowledged. GÓMEZ (1995: 183) emphasised its monastic elements, such as ritual, demeanour, and monastic rules, by attributing importance to 'precepts'[12]. Further, in the 'General Introduction' to a recent English translation (CROSBY–SKILTON (1995)), WILLIAMS (1995: xi) imagines, based on the BCA, Śāntideva's everyday life in a monastery, which serves as an indication of its monastic provenance. The translators are also well aware of the monastic context of the BCA.[13] Despite this,

believe remains the best edition so far. V.S. Shastri (=Vidhushekhara BHATTACHARYA) also published an edition, together with the Tibetan translation, in 1960, probably based on the abovementioned H.P. Shastri's edition and perhaps revised depending on la Vallée Poussin's edition. Also in 1960, VAIDYA published another edition based on a manuscript in Nepalese script (all stanzas in ten chapters and *Pañjikā* on the first nine chapters) and another in Maithilī script (VAIDYA used this for the stanzas and *Pañjikā* of the ninth chapter); cf. KANAKURA (1958: 243–245); VAIDYA (1960: VII–VIII); PEZZALI (1968: 47–56); WALLACE (1997: 145–151).

[11] There have been two translations in French (from Sanskrit), two in German (from Sanskrit), eight in English (from either Sanskrit or Tibetan or both), one in Italian (partial), one in Spanish, one in Estonian. The BCA has been rendered into non-Western languages as well: two in Japanese (one from Sanskrit, one from Tibetan); one in each of four modern Indian languages—Hindi, Gujarati, Marathi, and Bengali; one in Mongol and Oirat (Kalmuk). Cf. VAIDYA (1960: x); PEZZALI (1968: 63–5); BATCHELOR (1994: 58); WALLACE (1997: 145–151).

[12] It is noteworthy that he presents selected passages from the BCA under the title of 'Mahāyāna Liturgy'. Here, he also mentions the problem of circulation or usage of texts, which has rarely been asked, noting that the BCA was very popular 'at least in monastic circles, during the later Mahāyāna period in India' (1995: 184).

[13] The translators repeatedly mention the importance of its monastic context. For example, CROSBY–SKILTON (1996: xxviii) say: 'Particularly pertinent to Śāntideva's work was the development of the monastic university at Nālandā, where it is said that he lived as a monk during the period at which he composed the *Bodhicaryāvatāra*.' Also see pp. xxvii, xxix, and xxxv.

perhaps because this translation is published as one of 'World Classics', the translators still try to present the BCA as a book not only for monks but also for lay people.[14]

In this paper, I consider how and why the BCA's monastic aspects had been largely neglected until recently and why its monastic characteristics tend to be underrepresented still today. In other words, I address the problem of cultural representation, which has been recently raised in Buddhist Studies—e.g. in ALMOND (1988), TUCK (1990), SCHOPEN (1991), LOPEZ (1996)—reflecting the recent development of other fields, notably history and literary studies. Although there have been numerous translations of the BCA, there is no critical research on the interpretations of the BCA as cultural representation. This essay would be the first contribution that links the BCA to a broader discussion about the question of the production of knowledge in Buddhist Studies.

— 1.3 —

Before starting to discuss how the BCA has been represented and why its monastic aspects have been ignored, however, I should make it clear what I mean by 'monastic'. The word 'monastic', when referring to people, generally means people living in a religious community who lead disciplined lives. Monasticism can be defined by its unique combination of social status, specific discipline, ritual and behaviour. The monastic leaves his lay household and dwells in a 'new' sacred home. His special status and self-identification are usually presented by his clothing, daily schedule, diet, all of which are distinctive from those of ordinary lay people. The monastic observes specific discipline, or monastic codes, in order to attain his religious goals. The monastic discipline also serves as the monastic identification by prescribing certain rituals and normative behaviours.[15] Bearing in mind this general

---

[14] In their comment on the monastic rules in the fifth chapter, CROSBY–SKILTON (1996: 33) note: 'Yet although Śāntideva uses the terms of the monastic discipline, he is not merely quoting rules which must be obeyed mechanically. By emphasising that this code of discipline is a means of developing mindfulness, in a sense he is bringing these rules to life, both for the monks, for whom they may have become banal from familiarity, and *for the layman who has no obligation to observe them.* ... and in this way implies the primacy of practice and attainment over and above mere clerical hierarchy and formalism' [my emphasis]. The prototype of this kind of view can be found in la Vallée Poussin's introduction to his translation of chapter five; see la Vallée POUSSIN (1896: 308). WILLIAMS (1995: xxvi), too, says: 'Though it was composed in India over a thousand years ago by a Buddhist monk for himself and a few like-minded friends, even allowing for the verses concerned with a Buddhist monastic environment, *the Bodhicaryāvatāra nevertheless presents us with a series of brilliant meditations directly relevant to our own present lives*' [my emphasis].

[15] Cf. WECKMAN (1987: 35–41).

usage of the word 'monastic', I will here use the word 'monastic aspects' to refer to these elements that are found in a text written by a monk, not by a lay person, composed for monks, not for lay people, and produced in a monastic community rather than in a lay community. In other words, monastic aspects are the features of a text as a product of monastic life. And, although the BCA is precisely this kind of work with many of these 'monastic' elements, it is these aspects that have received little attention in the study of, and in the production of knowledge about, the BCA.

2. Representations of the Text

The BCA has been represented in various manners but it would be useful, just for our discussion's sake, to classify these portrayals into four models according to their presupposed orientations: (1) a doctrinal history model, (2) a spirituality model, (3) a philosophy model and (4) a way of life model. I should note, however, that these models have been historically influenced by, and ideologically connected with, each other. I will discuss the representatives of these models basically in chronological order, but we should keep in mind that most 'portraits' of the BCA represented by a translator have elements of two or more models.

2.0. Four Models

— 2.1 —

The first model sees the BCA from the perspective of the history of doctrines as an exemplar of thought as opposed to religious practice. La Vallée POUSSIN's (1892) introduction to his first translation of the BCA (only chapters I–IV, and X) is an example of this strain; since his arguments presented there have influenced many other introductions, I will examine his introduction in greater detail.

La Vallée Poussin's introduction consists of three parts: (1) general Introduction; (2) Śāntideva and the composition of the BCA according to Tāranātha's history; and (3) Religious doctrine of the BCA. In the first part, he says that 'from the point of view of ideas and religious impression the BCA is similar to *Bhagavad-gītā* as a religious and philosophical song', and states that 'several chapters are devoted to metaphysical discussions of the school.'[16] After having explained the meaning of its title, he defines the BCA as a 'book of religious ardour (*enthusiasm*) and propa-

[16] POUSSIN (1892: 68–69). It is not very clear what he means by 'the school', but it probably means 'Mahāyāna Buddhism' because he does not mention Mādhyamika before this sentence but says that the BCA is the most interesting and suggestive 'parmi les textes Bouddhiques du Nord' (68).

ganda', for, according to him, 'all the flames of pious thought are expressed in it nobly and sincerely.' La Vallée POUSSIN (1892: 69) further maintains:

> 'We know the name of its author and the time of its composition, therefore, it is possible to construct the history of religion in India through the study of the dated document and through the history of the sects.'

Here we can see his excitement about a document of which he thought he could know the date somewhat precisely; at the same time, however, we must note that he is particularly interested in placing the BCA in 'the history of sects' (*l'histoire des sectes*), showing his personal inclination to the analysis of the different sects.[17] But it is not of course just a matter of personal preference. La Vallée Poussin's assumption that we can reconstruct the history of religion in India by tracing the history of sects is of great significance in thinking about the representation of the BCA in the West. This presupposition most probably comes from the nineteenth-century Zeitgeist: historicism, which is concerned primarily, if not solely, with the reconstruction of historical, objective, and therefore universal 'facts'. This historicist orientation led to the idea that the analysis of the doctrines of different sects can constitute the major part of the study of religion. We should not overlook that it is this idea, represented by la Vallée Poussin, that has played a key role in creating the privileged status of the ninth chapter in the research history of the BCA. After all, la Vallée POUSSIN (1898) published the Sanskrit edition of chapter nine of the BCA, with the corresponding section of the *Pañjikā*, before he published the complete edition of all nine chapters of the *Pañjikā*.

In the second part, la Vallée Poussin tries to place Śāntideva in the lineage of scholars at Nālandā by utilising secondary sources—mostly Chinese texts.[18] But he does not even mention Nālandā's local situation as a monastic university, despite the fact that we can see it, albeit indirectly, in Tāranātha's accounts la Vallée POUSSIN (1892: 72–5) introduces in the following part. This omission of the local context shows that he is only interested in 'universal' thoughts that are supposedly constructed from a philological reading of written texts. La Vallée Poussin only summarises the 'legend' told by Tāranātha and does not reflect upon the implication the legend carries. In other words, he deals with the legend only as a quasi-historical account, which he uses as external evidence to support his 'reconstructed' ideas, and does not fully consider the meaning of the legend in Indo-Tibetan tradition itself. Many other trans-

[17] DE JONG (1987: 45) says: 'He preferred to analyse the views of the different schools. No scholar has contributed more to our knowledge of Buddhist Abhidharma than La Vallée Poussin.'

[18] La Vallée POUSSIN (1892: 70) acknowledges three books as his sources: (1) *Bouddhisme* by Ryōon Fujishima, (2) *Buddhisme II* by H. Kern (Jacobi's translation), and (3) Minayeff's article (?): 'La doctrine du salut dans le Bouddhisme postérieur' (source unidentified).

lators follow la Vallée Poussin and, in almost the same manner, give a summary of the Tibetan historian's account in their introductions (e.g. Finot, Schmidt).

In the third part, la Vallée Poussin first declares that the BCA 'expounds the doctrine of Salvation' and is 'not a philosophical treatise but a vivid and sincere exhortation.' What is surprising is that, for him, 'philosophical treatise' means 'certain Buddhist works, the *Dhamma-pada* for example and the works of Southern (Buddhism) in general.' La Vallée POUSSIN (1892: 75) then goes on to the comparison of them with the BCA and claims:

> 'These Pāli treatises are completely unaware of the confidence of the faithful in its master, love and faith. In a word, it is Bhakti that characterises the Northern Buddhism and the Hindu religions (*les religions hindoues*).'

The subtext here is of course the dichotomy between Hīnayāna and Mahāyāna Buddhisms. It is originally an emic categorisation with highly polemical intentions, but, in the West, it was generalised to become a framework for conceiving Buddhism as an object of study. In this framework, Hīnayāna and Mahāyāna came to be considered sharply distinctive from each other with little overlaps, which we know is no longer true. This is obviously a result of too much emphasis on the doctrinal history in which the contention between the two is most evident.[19] Thus, while 'Pāli Buddhism' is restricted by 'philosophical' doctrines, la Vallée POUSSIN (1892: 77) maintains, we find in the BCA a 'living and warm religion.' And he concludes his discussion by noting as follows:

> 'Now we know that the doctrine of salvation, *which is the core (le tout) of Buddhism*, appears to us very differently in the books of Pali and in the books of Northern Buddhism. ... Buddhism sometimes assumes the character of philosophy and morality without God. This is the doctrine of

[19] In his article, 'Mahāyāna', la Vallée POUSSIN (1908–1926: 330–31) begins his 'Definition and Description' by noting that '[i]n order to define Mahāyāna, we must first notice certain characteristics of the Hīnayāna.' He then lists five points that he thinks define Hīnayāna: (1) the doctrine of salvation, which he calls a 'perfectly coherent mysticism' with 'philosophical' and 'ethical' dogmas; (2) the method of salvation, which, he notes, cannot be practised 'except by a person who observes ... 'morality' and, what is very important, 'a person who practises continence ... as a Buddhist monk'; (3) the view on Buddha, who is 'very different from other saints'; (4) the place of 'devotion (*bhakti*)' in the cult of the Buddha, which is 'useful and recommended ..., as penance (*tapas*) is, but is not essential'; (5) teachings on 'how to be re-born in heaven, in the world of *Brahmā*.' In contrast with these characteristics of Hīnayāna, la Vallée Poussin argues that Mahāyāna consists of three elements: (1) the practice of the virtues (*pāramitā*s) of a *bodhisattva* or future Buddha; (2) the wisdom or knowledge of vacuity; (3) devotion.

> Southern Buddhism, which became popular in the West (*en occident*). It sometimes assumes the character of ardent religion (*religion enthousiaśte*). This is Northern Buddhism with countless deities, tutelary Buddhas, and benevolent Bodhisattvas.' (1892: 82) [My emphasis].

Nevertheless, as the title of the third part, 'religious doctrine', shows, most of his argument there consists of 'doctrinal' and 'soteriological' issues such as views on Buddha and *nirvāṇa* and the philosophies of Yogācāra and Mādhyamika found mostly in the ninth chapter. On account of these almost exclusively doctrinal discussions, it should be noted, la Vallée Poussin came to the above conclusion. Even though he says that the BCA is not a 'philosophical treatise', he still perceives it only from the perspective of Buddhist doctrines, excluding the elements of religious practice that would have indicated the monastic context of the BCA. He published a complete translation of the BCA in 1906 and 1907 but again never explicitly mentioned its monastic aspects in his introduction.

La Vallée Poussin, however, was by no means indifferent to, nor of course ignorant of, Buddhist monastic rules. On the contrary, he was well aware of the fact that Śāntideva refers to the *Prātimokṣa* rules in the BCA, which we know from the footnotes in his translation (1906–1907) and his introduction to the translation of chapter five (1896) that was published between the two above-mentioned translations.[20] la Vallée POUSSIN (1896: 308) notes:

> '*Bodhicaryāvatāra* is a sort of *Vinaya* or *Dharmaśāstra* for the use of Buddhists: we read in the fifth chapter the series of precepts of a practical nature, (on the manner of eating, of sitting, of gesturing) (91, 92, 94, 95), general advice on purity, the rule which orders that one avoid what is disapproved of in society (93). The ascetic must have a smiling face, he must speak gently and clearly; he looks at creatures in the face, his step is silent, he encourages good people.—All these practices are dominated by a constant concern about "the purification of thought (*pensée*)": ... To realise this essential "*vrata*" (see 16, 18) one must read the books of *Dharma* (98).'[21]

But, at the same time, la Vallée POUSSIN (1896: 308) maintains that:

---

[20] It is not all clear to me why he published this chapter separately.

[21] He has a footnote to this passage: 'We must not forget that the practice is an inferior means of salvation: if intelligence is not illuminated by the supreme truth, nothing serves for taking vow of Bodhi and for observing the rules of conduct (rien ne sert de former vœu de Bodhi et d'observer les régles de vie) ...'

'Śāntideva does not address the *Bhikṣus*, members of a religious order with regular *Prātimokṣas*, but the lay Bodhisattvas, the faithful of a broader Church (see śl.93).'

The verse in question (5.93) does not talk about rules to address 'the lay Bodhisattvas' but about monastic codes laid down for ascetic monks, however.[22] As la Vallée Poussin himself explains, the second half of the verse is simply 'the rule which orders that one avoid what is disapproved of in society.' And the context of the verse makes it clear that 'one' here means an 'ascetic' (*yati*).[23] Still, as is evident in his discussions on 'religious doctrines of Bodhicaryāvatāra', la Vallée Poussin assumes that Mahāyāna is entirely different from Hīnayāna. And this assumption comes from his conception that 'the core of Buddhism' is 'the doctrine of salvation'. It thus seems that his limited interests in the doctrinal history prevented him from recognising the fact that these verses in chapter five are the rules for ascetic monks. He must have thought that he should present the BCA as an exclusively Mahāyāna text that is distinctive from Hīnayāna texts.[24]

— 2.2 —

The second model emphasises the 'spirituality' of the Bodhisattva practice. The examples are Louis FINOT's (1920) introduction and Auguste BARTH's (1893) remark that compares the BCA to the *Imitation of Christ* by Thomas à Kempis. FINOT

[22] BCA 5.93 reads:

nâikânya-striyā kuryād yānaṁ śyanam āsanaṁ /
lokâprasādakaṁ sarvaṁ dṛṣṭvā pṛṣṭvā ca varjayet //

'One should neither walk nor lay down nor sit down with any one women. By knowing and asking all the things that are considered disturbing by common people, one should avoid them.'

I have not identified the rule in *Prātimokṣa* corresponding to 93cd, but ISHIDA (1993: 8–9) points out that we can find the elements in 93ab in more than one *Prātimokṣa*s. Cf. la Vallée POUSSIN (1901–1914: 149). Also see CROSBY–SKILTON (1995: 163, a note to 5.93b).

[23] We find explicit references to *yati* twice (5.21 and 5.73). If you look at only the verse 5.93, it is not entirely impossible to take it as an exhortation to 'ascetise' lay people. But chapter five as a whole makes this interpretation very unlikely. Cf. ROBINSON (1965–66).

[24] In the introduction to his edition of the ninth chapter of the BCA and *Ādikarma-pradīpa*, la Vallée POUSSIN (1898: 1–161) opposes the views of the so-called Pāli school, represented by Oldenberg and Rhys Davids, that only the Pāli canon can be the source for the 'historical' study of Buddhism. He maintains that 'Pāli Buddhism' is a narrow doctrinal system and Mahāyāna Buddhism, which the BCA represents as a new text of the time, can provide much richer religious ideas. Cf. its review by Paul CARUS (1899).

(1920: 9) gives a literal translation of the title: 'Introduction to the Practice leading to Bodhi', and explains that 'the practice (*caryā*, the "course", or "career", in the etymological sense) is the set of spiritual exercises which lead the future Buddha toward his goal.' It seems that he uses the word 'spiritual exercises', which is of course a Catholic term,[25] to emphasise two elements of Buddhist practice that he thinks share their value with Christianity: piety and charity.[26] Interpreting the key words such as 'Buddha', Finot maintains that Śāntideva belongs to the 'Mahāyānist church', in which, according to him, 'the travellers' are led to the ideal state of 'Buddha, Saviour of the world' through the practice of charity. Although he does not attempt to detail the doctrinal history, he takes for granted the dichotomy between Hīnayāna and Mahāyāna. He certainly gives the impression that only Mahāyāna Buddhism can be 'spiritual'. FINOT 1920: (13–14) states:

> 'Although hagiography tells us very little about this person (*personnage*), his work is more instructive: it reveals an original and engaging physiognomy, where the characteristics of the Mahāyānist spirit dominate: piety and charity.'

In order to support this point, FINOT (1920: 14) quotes the following remark by Auguste BARTH (1893: 259–260):

> 'It is a very beautiful work, ... a kind of Buddhist equivalent to the *Imitation of Christ*, with which it shares its *humble renunciation and passionate charity*. An aspect in the Indian Buddhism of the seventh century, about which we had not known, is revealed to us: *the true spirit of the apostolic mission had not been extinguished* and, among its ranks, *it included not only bonze* (*il ne comptait pas que des bonzes*).' [My emphasis]

The BCA's similarity to *The Imitation of Christ* is one of the recurring themes in its representation, especially in the early stage of Western studies on the BCA (from 1890's to 1920's).[27]

---

[25] For Ignatius Loyola's well-known work, which has the very term, 'Spiritual Exercises', as its title, see, for example, an English translation by Anthony MOTTOLA (1989). Thomas à Kempis also wrote a book titled 'Spiritual Exercises'; see SHERLEY-PRICE (1952: 22).

[26] FINOT (1920: 19–20) is aware of Poussin's doctrinal inclination and seems to have tried to contrast his translation against it by emphasising spiritual aspects and the poetical beauty of the BCA. On its poetical beauty, also see WINTERNITZ (1987: 308, 313).

[27] On BARTH's remark, also see FOUCHER (1908: 241–42) and WINTERNITZ (1987: 313). MURTI (1980: 101) also regards the BCA in a similar way: 'A very high order of spiritual serenity and detachment pervades his works. One is invariably reminded of the *Imitation of Christ* in reading the *Bodhicaryāvatāra*, which is the stronger in appeal, as it is born of deep philosophical insight.

The Imitation of Christ (*Imitatio Christi*) is a fifteenth-century work that is usually, at least since the nineteenth century, included in the genre of 'devotional' literature (CREASY (1989: xiii)), or what is now called books of 'spirituality'. It has been traditionally attributed to Thomas à Kempis (c. 1379–1471), an Augustinian monk of Mount St. Agnes monastery (near Zwolle, Holland) that was associated with a religious movement called *Devotio Moderna*. The movement led to the formation of the Brethren of the Common Life, a group that stressed 'simplicity, humility and great faith', 'an intimate relationship with God', and 'personal piety grounded in devotion to Jesus and to prayer and meditation' (CREASY (1989: xliv)). As a monk of such a community, Thomas spent 72 years in the monastery in his 92 year-long life; he wrote as Novice Master his collection of sermons to the novices and other didactic works, one of which is the *Imitation*. It is therefore a well-known fact that this text was composed in a monastic context (SHERLEY-PRICE (1958: 11)): a monk composed it for novices in a monastic community. We should also note that it is primarily an ascetic work because, as a work of *Devotio Moderna* movement, its main themes are *contemptus mundi* and self-denial. Given that the *Imitation* thus has monastic and ascetic aspects, it seems curious that scholars who noticed its similarity to the BCA did not acknowledge the monastic and ascetic aspects of the BCA. In other words, why, despite *The Imitation*'s monastic provenance, was the BCA's monastic context ignored? Why did they think that the BCA and the *Imitation* had in common only such elements as 'piety and charity' or 'humble renunciation and passionate charity'?

We can probably find a clue to these questions if we consider how the *Imitation* has been recommended to and read by lay people in Christian countries. It is perhaps the case that lay readers have been attracted not so much by its monastic and ascetic roots and ideals as by its devotional and 'spiritual' aspects, that is, by those aspects of its message that can be taken out of their monastic contexts to become 'internalised', 'individualised' and 'universalised' private ideals. It also appears that the translators of the *Imitation* have tried to present it as a book from which not only monks but also laymen can learn something about their spiritual life.[28] It thus seems highly probable that in the time of secularisation, especially from the Victorian era onward, both groups of lay intellectuals, those who read the medieval Christian text from modern lay perspectives and those who introduced the Buddhist text from the 'Orient' to the West, have interpreted their texts on a similar set of presuppositions, seeing them as documents of private piety, or 'spirituality'. Such presuppositions reflect major changes that came with modernity but culminated in the late nine-

Devotion (*bhakti*) to the Buddhas and Bodhisattvas, and confession of one's transgressions (*pāpadeśanā*) before them are enjoined as part of spiritual purification. This is by no means an innovation; Nāgārjuna's *Catuḥstava* is in the same strain.'

[28] See in particular CREASY's (1989) introduction to his translation.

teenth century, and led to the secularising of religion in general and the laicising of monastic works in particular.[29]

The last sentence of BARTH's comment as well furnishes a clue to these questions. The word 'bonze' in particular seems to be suggestive in this context because this word had been used, since the late eighteenth century, in the 'rhetoric of indolent and decadent Chinese monasticism.'[30] As Almond explains, the nineteenth-century views on *contemporary* Buddhist monasticism were primarily negative ones. He suggests that severe criticism against Buddhist monasticism was motivated by 'an anti-Catholic bias in Victorian society' in general and 'Victorian gospel of work' in particular. Thus, Buddhist monasticism of the time came to be seen as 'pre-eminently selfish and anti-social.' Its similarity to the practice of Catholicism, says Almond, also played an important role in forming the negative evaluations of Buddhist monasticism.

In considering the origin of the spirituality model in the BCA's representation, it is even more significant that not only Protestant Victorians but also Catholic missionaries from earlier periods criticised Buddhist monasticism, particularly that of Chinese Buddhism, which came to produce the dominant 'image of a decadent Mahāyāna monasticism' (ALMOND (1988: 121)) in the Victorian era. This image therefore is not just a product of Protestant bias against other religions but a typical manifestation of Orientalism, which postulates the absolute difference between the West and the Orient, claiming the ultimate supremacy of the West over the Other. ALMOND (1988: 140) suggests that this 'fundamental mode of organising the East' provided Europeans with a 'conceptual filter through which acceptable aspects of Buddhism could be endorsed, unacceptable ones rejected.' It is of course difficult, from BARTH's brief remark quoted above, to determine whether or not he actually had this filter, or how strongly he held it even if he did. In other words, we cannot tell, depending only on the remark, whether or not he acknowledged the BCA's similarity to the *Imitation* in order to give his endorsement to the 'spirituality' of the BCA in the Orientalist discourse.

The context in which he made this remark, however, makes it clear that Barth was working within a massive textualisation of 'religions of India'. He commented on the BCA as one of the numerous Indian texts that were newly edited and translated in the West. In fact, his article entirely consists of the enumeration of such texts and his brief comments on them. And this article as a whole, we should note, is called

[29] For a useful account of 'laicisation', 'monachisation', 'secularisation', and 'asceticisation', see ROBINSON (1965–66).

[30] ALMOND (1988: 120). There have been much criticism of Almond's book and I agree that it poses certain problems we should be careful of. See, in particular, Charles HALLISEY's (1995: 31–32) critique on 'latent Orientalism'. Even so, I believe, Almond accounts on the nineteenth-century construction of Buddhism give much useful information for my present discussion.

'Bulletin des religions de l'inde'. This kind of textualisation of the Other, which has as its basis what SAID calls 'textual attitude', is one of the main features of Orientalism.[31] Seen from this perspective, it is perhaps not farfetched to interpret Barth's words as a part of Orientalist discourse. 'True spirit of the apostolic mission had not been extinguished'; in other words, it had survived in this eighth-century Indian *text*, which only we, Westerners, can read and understand to reconstruct the ideal of Mahāyāna Buddhism. It is we in the West, he would maintain, that speak for the true form of Mahāyāna that has been long lost, not they, the contemporary 'corrupt' Buddhists in the Orient.

On the surface level, the spirituality model can be seen as a reaction to the Victorian denigration of Mahāyāna monasticism. But on the deeper level, we should note, this type of admiration of the BCA is still in the same framework of Orientalist discourse. They share with the Victorians the Orientalist and textualist assumption that that true Buddhism can be found only in the text, not in the actual practices of 'fallen' Buddhists in Asia. Despite the fact that FINOT (1913), before his translation of the BCA, edited the *Prātimokṣa* of the Sarvāsti-vādins, which explains his often accurate understanding of stanzas referring to these rules in chapter five of the BCA, he never mentioned the monastic context of the BCA.[32] He dismissed it deliberately and emphasised its spirituality expressed in the text, since the image of Buddhist monasticism was too negative to be acknowledged as an aspect of a text that was supposed to represent 'true' Mahāyāna Buddhism. What we should remember here is that this negative image had largely been formed on account of the actual practice in contemporary Asian countries.

— 2.3 —

In the third place, partly as a reaction against the spirituality model and partly as a continuation of the doctrinal history model, the BCA is often seen as primarily, if not exclusively, a philosophical treatise. This tendency has been demonstrated by many Japanese scholars as well,[33] but the best examples are still Western. Consider, for instance, the following statement of D. SEYFORT RUEGG (1981: 83):

---

[31] On the textualisation of Buddhism, see ALMOND (1988: 3). On 'textual attitude', see SAID (1979: 92–95). Cf. HALLISEY (1995: 37 and n. 37).

[32] He does not mention the existence of these stanzas in his introduction and never gives reference to the rules in his translation of these stanzas.

[33] To discuss how Japanese scholars have seen the BCA is beyond the scope of this paper, but I should note here that most research in Japan have dealt only with chapter nine.

Privileging philosophical aspects of Buddhist texts as the object of study appears to have a lot to do with Japanese scholars' fear of being called 'sectarian'. By avoiding being explicitly

'Because it is concerned also with the religious side of Madhyamaka thought the *Bodhicaryāvatāra* has sometimes been described as a primarily religious and devotional poem rather than a philosophical treatise. Such a description however curiously neglects the ninth chapter—the longest in the whole work—dealing with the *prajñāpāramitā*, which clearly places the treatise in the main stream of Madhyamaka thought; and if due consideration is given to this chapter it becomes abundantly clear that the work is hardly more religious in any sense exclusive of philosophy than certain earlier works of the school attributed to Nāgārjuna, e.g. the *Ratnāvalī*, as well as important portions of Āryadeva's, Bhāvaviveka's and Candrakīrti's treatises.'

Notice first that he considers the BCA only in the context of Madhyamaka philosophical treatises. Chapter nine is the most important of all the chapters, he appears to think, just because it 'places the treatise in the main stream of Madhyamaka thought.'[34] Notice also his presupposition that 'philosophy' is different from the 'religious' side of thought; he even considers the 'religious' side as a side of 'Madhyamaka thought', not as an aspect of Buddhism as religion. In other words, he

'sectarian', they try not to 'taint' their supposedly scientific objectivity with their faith or religious commitment. Since the creation of 'Buddhist Studies' in the Meiji period, Japanese scholars, most of whom are Buddhist priests, have struggled to establish the discipline as a scientific field of study worthy of pursuing even in an increasingly modernised and secularised society. For instance, in the introduction to Nanjō Bunyū's autobiography, Hajime SAKURABE (1979: 327–8), a contemporary scholar of Abhidharma (now retired from Otani University), argues that 'modern Buddhist Studies' differ from sectarian studies in three aspects: (1) sources and materials, (2) method and (3) purpose or goal of study:

> 'They are different in terms of sources in that, while previous studies deal with Chinese and Japanese materials ..., modern Buddhist Studies, in addition to them, use Sanskrit and Pāli materials ... They are different in terms of method in that, while previous studies placed their main emphasis on the exposition of sectarian doctrines ..., modern Buddhist Studies, by introducing Western academic method, explore new research fields such as historical, philological, and doctrinal studies, *with liberal and critical attitude that is free from sectarian restrictions*. They are different in terms of purpose in that, if one can, or should, distinguish academic study of Buddhism which stems from *universal desire for knowledge* from following Buddhist path guided by *one's inner religious desire*, modern Buddhist Studies definitely fall into the first category.' [My translation and my emphasis].

[34] He assumes that the longer a chapter is the more important it is, but there is no ground for that assumption. Moreover, as for the number and length of *kārikā* themselves, chapter nine (168 *ślokas*) is merely the second longest after the eighth one (with 180 *ślokas* and 6 *triṣṭubhs*). Apparently SEYFORT RUEGG is wrong because it is Prajñākarmati's commentary that dedicates more space to the ninth chapter than to any other.

seems to be forgetting that Buddhist philosophy is a part of the religion and Buddhism is more than just a thought.

For SEYFORT RUEGG (1981: 82), Śāntideva is simply a 'great representative of the (Prāsaṅgika?) Madhyamaka school.' It is in a manner of speaking only natural, however, that he takes this point of view because his book is, after all, about the *Literature of the Madhyamaka Philosophy in India* published in a series called *A History of Indian Literature*. But the real problem is that, as LOPEZ (1995a: v) pointed out, this kind of book, or series, which focuses almost exclusively on philosophy or 'the religious expressions of elite groups', have until recently dominated Indology in general and Buddhist Studies in particular. Seyfort Ruegg claims that, 'if due consideration is given to this chapter', it becomes evident that the BCA is as philosophical as other earlier works of Madhyamaka school. But the question I am asking here is how, by what standard, one decides what is 'due' in the study of Buddhism. Who decides what is 'due' is also a critical question, of course, which appears to elude Seyfort Ruegg's 'philosophical' mind.

There seem to be a number of factors that have brought the special emphasis on philosophy into Buddhist Studies. One element among others would be the rationalism of the Enlightenment of the eighteenth century, which made Buddhism an object of 'reasoned analysis and study' and ultimately aimed at 'rational construction of Buddhism' (BATCHELOR (1994: 231, 246)). Romanticism of the nineteenth century appears to be another reason; as TUCK (1990: 10) suggests, Europeans have enthusiastically studied Buddhism to find 'answers to Western philosophical problems.' But the nature of modern scholarly tasks can be counted among the most important reasons for the privileged status of philosophy. Scholars in Buddhist Studies, and perhaps scholars in humanities in general as well, who undertake intellectual tasks as their profession, tend to pay more attention to intellectual activities, or 'high tradition', of Buddhists, thus granting a privileged status to 'philosophy', a culmination of intellectual practice. But they all too easily forget the fact that philosophy is for most Buddhists only a part of their religious life; the majority of people in Buddhist traditions, both the monastic and the lay who do not produce philosophical texts, are more concerned with 'mundane' things such as merit, right behaviour, rituals, and ceremonies in a community.[35]

What should be noted here, however, is that, among traditional Buddhists themselves, philosophy and 'philosophers' often claim authority over a whole religious tradition, trying to create the identity, consistency, and integrity of the tradition. This

[35] These aspects of Buddhism are clearly demonstrated in LOPEZ (1995a). SCHOPEN (1997) has also shown that monks and nuns in India were as well concerned with these 'mundane' matters as lay people.

point about the place of philosophy in Buddhist traditions is supported by the fact that the emphasis on philosophical aspects can also be found in Indian scholarship. As is well-known, Prajñākaramati (late tenth century to early eleventh century) comments more on the ninth chapter than on any other. Furthermore, the fact that there is a commentary on only chapter nine (P No. 5278) suggests that this chapter assumed a special meaning among Indian scholars already around the eleventh century.[36] This does not mean that the BCA as a whole was thought of as a philosophical work,[37] but it does mean that what might be called 'philosophical bias', which must have been pervasive in Indian Buddhist scholars' circles, began to be applied to the BCA rather soon after its production by Śāntideva. And it is this attitude that has been inherited in modern Buddhist Studies in the West.[38] As SEYFORT RUEGG's confusion about the length of the chapters (eight and nine) of the BCA implies,[39] he looks at the text only through the eyes of Prajñākaramati, who most certainly represents the 'religious expressions of elite groups' and, therefore, cannot be counted as one of the majority in Buddhist traditions at large.

It is thus not surprising at all that Western scholars who have been interested only in philosophy or in the thought of individual authors as the representatives of philosophical schools, have not taken into account the BCA's monastic aspects in their representation of the text. The purpose of studying a text, those scholars would maintain, is to reconstruct its author's thinking process as meticulously as possible in the historical development of 'Buddhist thought.' Their assumption is that philosophy is a purely intellectual entity that can be treated separately from other sides of religion. Monastic elements, such as the liturgical structure and allusions to the

[36] The Tibetan *Tri-piṭaka* also lists a commentary only on the ninth and tenth chapters (P No. 5279) as an independent work. But this commentary is actually an extract of the two chapters from another commentary on all chapters (P No. 5274). This confusion may suggest that chapter nine, together with chapter ten, in this case, had been circulated independently probably as a text for philosophical debates; cf. EJIMA (1966).

[37] On the contrary, clear evidence shows that the BCA had been used as liturgical manual as well as pedagogical device in Indo-Tibetan tradition. For its liturgical structure, see GÓMEZ (1995). As to a pedagogical usage of the text, see EIMER (1981), which contains the list of stanzas in a summary called *Piṇḍârtha*. The *Piṇḍârtha* is an abridgement of the text, but the inclusion of the first stanzas of some chapters gives an impression that these stanzas were chosen somewhat mechanically just to draw an outline of the BCA. Nevertheless, its selection of verses clearly shows that this work was meant to be a kind of introductory guide for novices.

[38] Considering the nature of any scholarly tasks and the place of philosophy in both Western and traditional Buddhist scholarships, it should be clear why the philosophical bias remains strong even today. For example, SEYFORT RUEGG (1995: 145), again, recently confirmed his conviction that 'philosophical thinking constitutes a major component in Buddhism.'

[39] See n. 34.

states of mind of monks in a community found in the BCA, is irrelevant to this reconstruction of the author's philosophy. For, an author's philosophy consists of his 'private' thoughts and, therefore, can be placed in the historical, and 'universal', development of philosophy. Accordingly, scholars who privilege philosophy tend to ignore social and cultural conditions in local and traditional communities, in which various thoughts were produced, accepted (or rejected), and transmitted over time.

— 2.4 —

At the almost exactly opposite pole of the philosophy model and, therefore, at least on one level, on somewhat closer side of the spirituality model, we find the fourth approach to the BCA: the 'way of life' model.[40] It is represented by modern Western scholars who sympathise with certain aspects of Tibetan Buddhism as their 'spiritual' ideal. It also serves as a model when the BCA is presented to Western audience by modern Tibetan scholars who appeal to Westerners to make them supporters of their endangered culture and religion in the current historical situation since 1959.[41] In this model the BCA is portrayed as a book that tells the way of life to modern everyday man in the West. Asking why the BCA has been popular in the Western intellectual world, BATCHELOR (1994: 58) maintains:

> 'What is it about A Guide to the Bodhisattva's Way of Life that makes it so appealing even today? ... It is the compelling *humanism* of the text, the author's intensely *personal tone*, that speaks across time and culture to the concerns and aspirations of our age.' [My emphasis]

In the chapter of his book that contains this passage, Batchelor describes the historical and cultural context in which the BCA was produced. He is probably right when he assumes that Śāntideva 'lived at a time of internal political conflict and disarray in the Indian subcontinent', noting that the time of the production of the

[40] Tenzin GYATSO (1994: 1), the Fourteenth Dalai Lama, notes: 'Shāntideva composed this text in the form of an inner dialogue. He turned his own weapons upon himself, doing battle with his negative emotions. Therefore, when we teach or listen to this text, it is important that we do so in order to progress spirituality, rather than making it simply a subject of academic study.' He seems to warn Western scholars and practitioners to avoid both the doctrinal history and philosophy models.

[41] For a brief account of Tibet's cultural and political relation to the West and China in the twentieth century, see SNELLGROVE–RICHARDSON (1995: Chap. 9, esp. 233–36, 242–45, 264–67; 268–71 ['Epilogue'] and 272–83 ['Aftermath']). As for Tibetans' as well as Westerners' struggle to keep Tibetan culture in exile and in the West after 1959, see in particular (1995: 274–77). For an account that places this cultural endeavour in the broader context of Orientalism, see LOPEZ (1995c: 251–52, 263–68).

BCA was 'renowned for its advances in scholarship and philosophical analysis' in 'vast monastic universities' that had replaced the 'freely wandering *bhikshus*' and it was therefore 'the time when Buddhism became top-heavy with institutions' (1984: 55). What makes me wonder, however, is his logic and rhetoric when BATCHELOR (1984: 57), interpreting the meaning of Śāntideva's legendary life in Tibetan historiographies, states:

> 'Whatever the historical legitimacy of these accounts, they confirm the underlying principles of Shantideva's legend. The example of Shantideva stands as a model Buddhist life of his times. He is a true individual, one who follows his own insights and intuition ..., first by rejecting the expectations of the world and then those of the monastic establishment. His life is a critique of the institutionalization of the Buddhist order, which he purifies, as it were, through his poem, by forcefully restating the principles of the Bodhisattva's Way of Life.'

It is now clear that he emphasises the 'institutionalization' of Buddhist orders in his description of the historical context of the BCA because he wants to claim that Śāntideva is, curiously enough, not only an exception but also a critic of that movement. BATCHELOR (1984: 57) goes on to say:

> '... the institutions were beyond salvation. The authentic Buddhist life was to be found outside the monastic walls, in a return to the world, to a practice based on a personal insight and expressed through protean forms of life, some of which might outwardly appear shocking.'

Here we see Batchelor's rather obvious agenda: he tries to create the autonomy of the individual author free of the institution of a monastic community, thus, in effect, explicitly laicising the BCA to include the Western lay people, the target audience of his book, into the BCA's audience as well. We, modern everyday people in the West, can learn the way of life from the BCA, he seems to say, because it is only based on Śāntideva's 'personal insight' and 'intuition'. However, it should be noted, Batchelor laicises the BCA by interpreting Śāntideva's legend in the historiographies in a Tibetan tradition, not by presenting an analysis of the discourse found in the BCA.

In societies with pre-modern culture, legends about authors are created and confirmed through the interpretation of texts attributed to them. An author's legend generally shows how his works have been interpreted in a given tradition during a certain period in history. But Batchelor here ignores that these interpretations often reflect not so much what is actually said in texts as Zeitgeist of later period in which they are interpreted. In Śāntideva's case, you could surely find some elements in his legend that could be interpreted as the 'critique of the institutionalization', reflecting the growth of Tantrism in the late stage of Buddhism in India. But we cannot find in the BCA's text itself any evidence indicating that Śāntideva actually criticised the so-called institutionalisation of Buddhist order. In other words, Batchelor deals with the legend in the same way as other scholars in that they all use it as external evidence to support their own readings of the BCA and their 'reconstructed' ideas about Buddhism. He does so only in a very different direction.

But why does he have to laicise the BCA to appeal to Western audience today? It is perhaps helpful to quote from SNELLGROVE–RICHARDSON (1995: 276) to answer the question from a broader perspective:

> '... the United States has now become the most sought after haven for Tibetan lamas intent on establishing a following amongst westerners. Following in the wake of Indian yoga schools and the very successful Zen Buddhist movement, they have learned rapidly how to best adapt their teachings to an American audience.'

Their observation that Tibetan Buddhists came to the West after 'Indian *yoga* schools' and 'Zen Buddhist movement' is important. This perspective would allow us to see the fact that Tibetan Buddhism in the West is another instance of the transmutation of a religion that tends to happen when it moves from one cultural realm to another, both geographically and historically (e.g. from pre-modern to modern). In other words, it would allow us to place the laicising process of Tibetan Buddhism in the historical context of the modern Western world.

The historically contingent combination of current political and cultural situation of Tibetan Buddhism and a modern Western myth about religion has undoubtedly played a major role in creating this laicising process. In the modern West, notably in the United States, people deeply and firmly believe that religion is, and should be, simply a matter of individual choice based on private experience and individual conscience.[42] Their antipathy toward overtly institutionalised religions is common and pervasive. Those who present a text to Westerners, especially to an 'American audience', necessarily try to underrepresent the monastic aspects of their religion in general and of their religious texts in particular. Acknowledging the BCA's monastic character, let alone emphasising it, is the last thing they would do if they want the BCA to be accepted by such an audience.

In considering more specifically how Tibetan scholars 'adapted' their teachings, it is suggestive that Batchelor chooses 'compelling humanism' and 'intensely personal tone' as the factors that have supposedly made the BCA 'appealing even today' in

---

[42] For the individualism in the United States based on the concept of Civil Religion, see BELLAH–TIPTON (1985: 220–27, 232–35, 243–46).

the West. These two factors represent the universalisation and internalisation of religion—the two sides of the coin—which are usually employed to construct an individual Self that is free from local communities, traditional discourse, and historicity, both sociologically and psychologically.[43] Indeed we find 'the author's intensely personal tone' in the BCA—many verses are presented in the first person voice. But it is questionable if we can call it 'compelling humanism' that 'speaks across time and culture'[44] that can be juxtaposed against institutionalised religions. Writing a text in a 'personal' tone at a monastic university in medieval India is most likely very different from doing so in a modern Western society in the twenty-first century. If we want to understand something the author wrote in his 'personal tone', we first have to ask what it meant to present a text in a 'personal' tone, or more generally, what it was to be 'personal' at a monastic university in the eighth-century India,[45] rather than universalising it as 'humanism'. The reality of the monastic community must have conditioned writing and being 'personal' in its own historicity. In other words, instead of trying to retrieve our modern values and ideals from the text, we should raise the various questions about the cultural representations of the Self to re think our modern presuppositions and values.

I am not saying that we, lay people in contemporary secular industrial society, can learn nothing 'spiritual' from the BCA. What I am saying is that we do not have to ignore nor dismiss its monastic aspects to maintain that we can learn something spiritual, 'the way of life'. Emphasising only the way of life, while ignoring these monastic elements, would be a gross distortion of the text, which is produced by not

---

[43] Two following remarks offer good examples of the universalisation and individualisation of religion. First, Tulku Pema WANGYAL (1994: vii), while referring to the Dalai Lama, says: 'For him, Buddhism is not a dogma or religion but *a way of life*, a source of happiness, *inner* peace, and *wisdom*. It awakens in us kindness and love, teaching us to protect every living thing on this earth. This is why he emphasises *universal* responsibility, the awareness that each one of us, as a member of *the human family*, can be a worker for peace and a protector of the environment' [my emphasis]. Second, Jonathan LANDAW (1989: xi) notes: 'In presenting his commentary Geshe Kelsang continually reminded his audience that despite the antiquity of the root text and the rigorously logical language in which certain of its sections (notably the ninth chapter) are couched, everything contained within Shantideva's work is meant to be taken as *personal advice* by the modern day practitioner interested in travelling the path leading to full spiritual awakening' [my emphasis].

[44] The word and the concept 'humanism' is only an 'invention' of nineteenth-century scholarship on the history of Renaissance, although Batchelor here seems to use the word in an extended meaning closer to 'humanitarianism' (also the nineteenth-century origin), which is more 'altruistic' in orientation; see NAUERT (1995: 8).

[45] GÓMEZ (1994) has raised this sort of question and discussed it from the perspective of autobiography. I believe that further exploration of this line is necessary and would be fruitful in the future study of the BCA.

taking critical steps in the representation of other cultures. 'The way of life' presented in the BCA is embedded in the monastic life in medieval India in its cultural and historical context.

I should also note here that my intention in this discussion is not to undermine the entire value of the effort of Tibetan people, including scholars, to desperately preserve their jeopardised religion and culture. It is easy to criticise the obvious connection between the political situation of Tibet and their apologetic production of knowledge under this circumstance. But the question about the role of scholars in this kind of condition remains to be answered. My point here is at least to suggest another, less obvious, but perhaps equally grave danger: namely, that modern Tibetan scholars, either consciously or unconsciously, adjust their own culture to the value of the modern West. Tibetans hope that politically strong power of the West would help them to restore the nation of Tibetan Buddhism. But the culture of the restored nation would inevitably be coloured by the ideology of the West.

3. Provisional Conclusion: Summary and Implications

The purpose of this paper has been to discuss how and why the monastic aspects of the BCA have largely been neglected, in the hope that this examination gives us ideas about what kinds of questions we could and should ask in the study of the BCA. Now, as a provisional conclusion, I summarise the discussion and consider some of its implications to link them to the question of the production of knowledge in Buddhist Studies.

In the first model, although la Vallée Poussin was very aware of the reference to monastic codes found in the BCA, he did not see its significance in presenting the text as a whole. He is concerned only with 'universal' thought and shows little interest in the local context for the production of meanings.[46] Seen in the broader intellectual context in the West, which I discussed in the second and third models, we can also see the doctrinal history model as another example of Orientalist textualisation. The process of this textualisation was intertwined with a traditional Buddhist discourse: the dichotomy between Hīnayāna and Mahāyāna. For him, the BCA must be a book of the doctrine of salvation representing Mahāyāna Buddhism. For, he thought, it offered richer and broader religious doctrines than the narrow philosophical system of Hīnayāna Buddhism. What has been overlooked, as the result of this doctrine-oriented textualisation, is the continuity between 'Mahāyāna' and 'Hīnayāna'. As the BCA clearly demonstrates, this continuity manifests par-

[46] Cf. HALLISEY (1995: 49–53).

ticularly in the lives of monks in monastic communities situated in the local, institutional, and cultural contexts.

Finot ignored the BCA's monastic aspects and emphasised the spirituality of Bodhisattva practice because he represented it as a text that speaks for Mahāyāna Buddhism. What makes his and Barth's representation problematic is that they did not find 'true' Mahāyāna Buddhism in religious practice found in contemporary Asia. From the nineteenth century on, Westerners had been constructing 'Buddhism' based on the philological elaboration, with Orientalist discourse working under this 'scientific' enterprise. Although Finot was critical of the philological and doctrinal orientation in its extreme, he was still working in the Orientalist discourse. He might have sincerely admired the spirituality of Bodhisattva practice expressed in the BCA. But he had to choose only that side of the text as the 'true' Mahāyāna Buddhism and suppress the monastic aspects also found in the text. For, thanks to the Orientalist and textualist construction of 'Buddhism' in the West, the actual practice found in monastic communities in the 'Orient' assumed too negative an image to be represented as 'true' Buddhism to a Western audience.

The third model offers yet another example of this textualisation of Buddhism, privileging philosophy as a purely intellectual entity that can be separated from other aspects of religion. Accordingly, chapter nine, which surely deals with philosophical issues, came to be considered the most significant of all. Several scholars have attempted to study some particular points in the BCA, rather than simply translating the entire text. But most of them have investigated, with few exceptions, only the ninth chapter from the perspective of the history of Buddhist philosophy, often with the help of philologically meticulous reading of commentaries. This kind of research has been legitimised by the dominant discourse of modern Buddhist scholarship. As long as one studies a philosophical text in a 'scientific' way, following the principles of philology, his research is valid and useful. It is therefore only natural that monastic aspects of the BCA have been ignored in this model. Scholars representing this model are only interested in the history of Buddhist philosophy that is reconstructed by philology-oriented 'scientific' method. They assume that philosophy is not a product of communal activities of monks but a product of individual authors' 'private' thinking process. It is entirely legitimate to investigate it without taking account of the local circumstances of the production of knowledge. Thus, monastic aspects that would help us to shed a light on the different sides of philosophical issues do not fall into the scope of their research.

The origin of the fourth model is found in a more general intellectual realm in the West. 'The way of life', is not a matter of a small number of scholars interested in Buddhism. To single out the way of life first and foremost results from Batchelor's historically contingent agenda that he has to effectively appeal to Western audience in general and American public in particular. His need to make the BCA more attractive for Western audience comes from the current political and cultural situation of Tibetan Buddhism since 1959. But the way he does so reflects more about modern Western values and ideals than about those of Tibetan Buddhism.

Batchelor not only neglects the BCA's monastic aspects but also explicitly laicises the BCA by creating an individual and autonomous author. His rhetoric of individualisation is evidently brought by the BCA's encounter with modern Western myth that religion is a matter of private experience and individual conscience. As a result, Tibetan Buddhism, represented by the BCA, has been transformed into an internalised and universalised religion free of local communities, traditional discourse, and its own historicity. When we conceive a religion as such, we necessarily make very little room for an institutional side of a traditional religion to be acknowledged in the representation of a text.

This universalisation and internalisation of religion raises the question of modernity in cultural representation. As the problem of the representation of the Self indicates, this question of modernity is most evident in the way of life model (§ 2.4.). But all other models are also the products of modernity, which in general underplays communal activities of believers (e.g. cosmology, ritual and ceremonies) in their local and institutional milieu, in favour of individual, rational, and therefore universal elements of religion.[47] Both the doctrinal history and philosophy models are the epitome of the rationalisation of religion. The spirituality and way of life models exemplify the internalisation and universalisation. In short, Orientalism, which has certainly played a significant role in shaping these models, is only one of the variations of the discourse of modernity.

This essay is meant to be a point of departure for more critical discussions on the research history of the BCA. As such, it only reconfirms a now well-known fact that Buddhist Studies has been dominated by Orientalist and modernist discourse. But one contribution of this paper on the problem of the production of knowledge would be to offer a specific example of a situation in which not only the selection of texts[48] but also the selection of aspects of a single text to be represented has been deeply affected in various ways by these modern, often ideological, presuppositions in the West. The BCA has been chosen as a text worthy of study in the West. Even so, it should be clear from what I have been discussing in this paper, only a part of the text has been represented and properly understood due to the assumptions of Western scholarship that have been ingrained in modernity.

[47] Cf. HALLISEY (1995: 49).

[48] Cf. LOPEZ (1995b: 7).

BIBLIOGRAPHY

ALMOND 1988 = Almond, Philip: *The British Discovery of Buddhism*. Cambridge University Press, Cambridge 1988.

BARNETT 1959 = Barnett, Lionel David: *The Path of Light: Rendered from the Bodhi-charyāvatāra of Shānti-Deva: A Manual of Mahāyāna Buddhism*. Grove Press Inc., New York 1959 [first edition: John Murray, London 1909].

BARTH 1893 = Barth, Auguste: 'Bulletin des religions de l'Inde', *Revue de l'histoire des religions* 28 (1893) 241–282.

BATCHELOR 1994 = Batchelor, Stephen: *The Awakening of the West*. Parallax Press, Berkeley 1994.

BCA = Śāntideva: *Bodhi-caryâvatāra*. See: POUSSIN (1901–1914).

BEAL 1884 = Beal, Samuel: *Si-yu-ki, Buddhist Records of the Western World*. 2 Vols, London 1884.

BELLAH–TIPTON 1985 = Bellah, Robert N.; Madsen, Richard; Sullivan, William M.; Swidler, Ann; Tipton, Steven M.: *Habits of the Heart: Individualism and Commitment in American Life*. University of California Press, Berkeley, Los Angeles, and London 1985.

BENDALL 1992 = Bendall, Cecill: 'Introduction' to: *Śikshāsamuccaya: A Compendium of Buddhistic Teaching, compiled by Śāntideva, chiefly from earlier Mahāyāna sūtras*. Bibliotheca Buddhica I, Motilal Banarsidass, Delhi 1992: I–XXX [first edition: John Murray, London 1897–1902].

BHATTACHARYA 1926 = Bhattacharya, B.: 'Preface' to: Embar Krishnamacharya (ed.): *Tattvasaṅgraha of Śāntarakṣita with the commentary of Kamalaśīla*. 2 Vols, Gaekwad Oriental Series 30, Baroda 1926.

BHATTACHARYA 1960 = Bhattacharya, Vidhushekhara (ed.): *Bodhicaryāvatāra of Śāntideva*. Bibliotheca Indica 280, The Asiatic Society, Calcutta 1960.

CARUS 1899 = Carus, Paul: 'Review of: "Louis de La Vallée Poussin: *Bouddhisme: Études et Matériaux I*"', *Monist* 9 (1899) 157–8 [The Open Court Publication Company, Chicago].

CHIMPA–CHATTOPADHYAYA 1970 = Chimpa, Lama; Chattopadhyaya, Alaka (tr.); Chattopadhyaya, Debi (ed.): *Tāranātha's History of Buddhism in India*. Motilal Banarsidass, Delhi 1970.

COLLCUTT 1987 = Collcutt, Martin: 'Monasticism: Buddhist Monasticism', in: Mircea Eliade (ed.): *The Encyclopedia of Religion*. Vol. 10, Macmillan, New York 1987.

CREASY 1989 = Creasy, William C.: 'Introduction' to: Thomas à Kempis: *The Imitation of Christ*. Translated by William C. Creasy. Ave Maria Press, New York 1989: xiii–xlix.

CROSBY–SKILTON 1996 = Crosby, Kate; Skilton, Andrew (tr.): *Śāntideva. The Bodhicaryāvatāra*. The World's Classics. Oxford University Press, Oxford–New York 1996.

DE JONG 1975 = de Jong, Jan W.: 'La légende de Śāntideva', *Indo-Iranian Journal* 16.3 (1975) 161–182.

DE JONG 1987 = de Jong, Jan W.: *A Brief History of Buddhist Studies in Europe and America*. Sri Satguru Publications, Delhi 1987.

DUTT 1962 = Dutt, Sukumar: *Buddhist Monks and Monasteries of India*. George Allen and Unwin, London 1962.

EIMER 1981 = Eimer, H.: 'Suvarṇadvīpa's Commentaries on the Bodhicaryāvatāra', in: Klaus Bruhn, Albrecht Wezler (ed.): *Studien zum Jainismus und Buddhismus: Gedenkschrift fur Ludwig Alsdorf*. Alt- und Neu-Indische Studien 23. F. Steiner, Wiesbaden 1981: 73–78.

EJIMA 1966 = Ejima, Yasunori: 'Nyūbodaigyōron no chūshakubunken ni tsuite', *Indogaku Bukkyōgaku Kenkyū* 14.2 (1966) 644–648.

FINOT 1913 = Finot, Louis: 'Le Prātimokṣasūtra des Sarvāstivādins, Texte Sanskrit par M. Louis Finot avec la version chinoies de Kumārajīva traduite en Français par Édouard Huber', *Journal Asiatique* XI série, tome II (novembre-décember 1913) 465–557.

FINOT 1920 = Finot, Louis: *La Marche à la Lumière: Bodhicaryāvatāra*. Les classiques de l'Orient vol. 2. Editions Bossard, Paris 1920.

FOUCHER 1908 = Foucher, A.: Review of: 'Louis de la Vallée Poussin: *Bodhicaryāvatāra, Introduction à la pratique des futurs Bouddhas*', *Revue de l'histoire des religions* 57 (1908) 241–42.

GÓMEZ 1987 = Gómez, Luis O.: 'Buddhism in India', in: Joseph M. Kitagawa, Mark D. Cummings (ed.): *Buddhism and Asian History*. Religion, History, and Culture: Readings from The Encyclopedia of Religion. Macmillan Publishing Company, New York 1987: 51–104.

GÓMEZ 1994 = Gómez, Luis O.: 'Presentations of Self: Personal Dimensions of Ritualized Speech', in: Phyllis Granoff, Koichi Shinohara (ed.): *Other Selves: Autobiography and Biography in Cross-Cultural Perspective*. Mosaic Press, Oakville–Buffalo 1994: 114–131.

GÓMEZ 1995 = Gómez, Luis O.: 'A Mahāyāna Liturgy', in: Donald S. Lopez, Jr. (ed.): *Buddhism in Practice*. Princeton University Press, Princeton, New Jersey 1995: 183–196.

GYATSO 1989 = Gyatso, Geshe Kelsang: *Meaningful to Behold: A Commentary to Shantideva's Guide to the Bodhisattva's Way of Life*. Tharpa Publications, London 1989.

GYATSO 1994 = Gyatso, Tenzin: *A Flash of Lightening in the Dark of Night: A Guide to the Bodhisattva's Way of Life*. Transated by The Padmakara Translation Group. Shambhala, Boston–London 1994.

HALLISEY 1995 = Hallisey, Charles: 'Roads Taken and Not Taken in the Study of Theravāda Buddhism', in: LOPEZ (1995b: 31–61).

ISHIDA 1988 = Ishida, Chikō: 'Some new remarks on the *Bodhicaryāvatāra* chapter V', *Indogaku Bukkyōgaku Kenkyū* 37.1 (1988) 479–476.

ISHIDA 1993 = Ishida, Chikō: '*Bodhicaryāvatāra* ni okeru haradaimokusha to zangehō—kaihen to kaiyaku no shōseki', *Bukkyō Shigaku Kenkyū* 36.2 (1993) 1–27.

KANAKURA 1958 = Kanakura, Enshō: *Satori e no michi*. Heirakuji-shoten, Kyoto 1958.

KERN 1989 = Kern, H.: *Manual of Indian Buddhism*. Motilal Banarsidass, Delhi 1989. [first edition: Strassburg 1898].

LANDAW 1989 Landaw, Jonathan: 'Preface to the First Edition' of Geshe Kelsang GYATSO (1989: xi–xv).

LI 1959 = Li, Yung-hsi (tr.): *The Life of Hsuan-Tsang: The Tripiṭaka-Master of the Great Tzu En Monastery, Compiled by Monk Hui-li*. The Chinese Buddhist Association, Peking 1959.

LOPEZ 1995a = Lopez, Donald S., Jr., ed.: *Buddhism in Practice*. Princeton Readings in Religions. Princeton University Press, Princeton, New Jersey 1995.

LOPEZ 1995b = Lopez, Donald S., Jr. (ed.): *Curators of the Buddha: The Study of Buddhism under Colonialism*. University of Chicago Press, Chicago and London 1995.

LOPEZ 1995c = Lopez, Donald S., Jr.: 'Foreigner at the Lama's Feet', in: LOPEZ (1995b: 251–295).

MINAYEFF 1889 = Minayeff. Ivan Pavlovitch (ed.): 'Bodhicaryāvatāra', *Zapiski* 4 (1889) 155–225.

MOTTOLA 1989 = Mottola, Anthony (tr.): *The Spiritual Exercises of St. Ingatius*. Image Books Doubleday, New York 1989 [first edition: Doubleday, New York 1964].

MURTI 1980 = Murti. T.R.V.: *The Central Philosophy of Buddhism: A Study of Mādhyamika System*. Unwin Paperbacks, London, Boston, and Sydney 1980 [first edition: Gerge Allen and Unwin, London 1955].

NAUERT 1995 = Nauert, Charles G., Jr.: *Humanism and the Culture of Renaissance Europe*. Cambridge University Press, Cambridge 1995.

OBERMILLER 1932 = Obermiller, E. (tr.): *History of Buddhism (Chos-ḥbyung) by Buston. II. Part—The History of Buddhism in India and Tibet*. Otto Harrassowitz, Heidelberg 1932.

P = Pekin Edition of the Tibetan *Tripiṭaka*.

PEZZALI 1968 = Pezzali, Amalia: *Śāntideva, mystique bouddhiste des 7e et 8e siècles*. Vallecchi Editore, Firenze 1968.

POUSSIN 1892 = Poussin, Louis de La Vallée: 'Bodhicaryāvatāra: Introduction à la Pratique de la Sainteté Bouddhique (Bodhi) par Śāntideva: Chapitres I, II, III, IV et X. Texte et Traduction' *Muséon* tome XI–N.I (1892). [French translation of chapters I, II, III, IV, and X].

POUSSIN 1896 = Poussin, Louis de La Vallée: 'Bodhisattvacaryāvatāra: Exposition de la pratique des Bodhisattvas.' *Muséon* tome XV–N.III (1896). [French translation of chapter V].

POUSSIN 1898 = Poussin, Louis de La Vallée: *Bouddhisme: Études et Matériaux I*. Bruxelles and London: Academie de Belgique and Luzac. [Sanskrit edition of chapter IX of the BCA and *Ādi-karma-pradīpa* with Introduction].

POUSSIN 1901–1914 = Poussin, Louis de La Vallée: (ed.): *Bodhicaryāvatārapañjikā, Commentary to the Bodhicaryāvatāra of Śāntideva*. Bibliotheca Indica no. 150. The Asiatic Society, Calcutta 1901–1914. [Sanskrit edition of chapters I–IX].

POUSSIN 1906–1907 = Poussin, Louis de La Vallée: 'Introduction à la Pratique des Futurs Bouddhas (Bodhicaryāvatāra) par Śāntideva', *Revue d'histoire et de littérature religieuses* tome XI (1906) 430–458 [chapters I–III], et tome XII (1907) 59–117 [chapters IV–VI], 389–463 [chapters VII–IX].

POUSSIN 1908–1926 = Poussin, Louis de La Vallée: 'Mahāyāna', in: James Hastings (ed.): *The Encyclopaedia of Religion and Ethics*. Vol. 8, Charles Scribner's Sons, New York 1908–1926.

ROBINSON 1965–66 = Robinson, Richard H.: 'The Ethics of the Householder Bodhisattva.' *Bhāratī* 9.2 (1965–66) 25–56.

SAID 1979 = Said, Edward W.: *Orientalism*. Vintage Books, New York 1979 [first edition: Routledge & Kegan Paul, London 1978].

SAKURABE 1979 = Sakurabe, Hajime: 'Introduction' to: Nanjō Bunyū: *Kaikyūroku*. Heibonsha, Tokyo 1979: 325–337.

SCHIEFNER 1869 = Schiefner, Anton (tr.): *Tāranātha's Geschichte des Buddhismus in Indien*. Academy of Sciences of St. Petersburg, St. Petersburg 1869.

SCHMIDT 1923 = Schmidt, Richard (tr.): *Der Eintritt in den Wandel in Erlechtung (Bodhicaryāvatāra). Von Śāntideva. Ein buddhistisches Lehrgedicht des VII. Jahrhunderts n. Chr. Aus dem Sanskrit übersetzt*. Dokumente der Religion vol. 5. Ferdinand Schöning, Paderborn 1923.

SCHOPEN 1991 = Schopen, Gregory: 'Archaeology and Protestant Presuppositions in the Study of Indian Buddhism', *History of Religions* 31.1 (1991) 1–23.

SCHOPEN 1997 = Schopen, Gregory: *Bones, Stones, and Buddhist Monks: Collected Papers on the Archaeology, Epigraphy, and Texts of Monastic Buddhism in India*. University of Hawai'i Press, Honolulu 1997.

SEYFORT RUEGG 1981 = Seyfort Ruegg, David: *The Literature of the Madhyamaka School of Philosophy in India*. A History of Indian Literature vol. VII, fasc. 1. Otto Harrassowitz, Wiesbaden 1981.

SEYFORT RUEGG 1995 = Seyfort Ruegg, David: 'Some Reflections on the Place of Philosophy in the Study of Buddhism', *Journal of International Association of Buddhist Studies* 18.2 (1995) 145–181.

SHERLEY-PRICE 1952 = Sherley-Price, Leo: 'Introduction' to: Thomas à Kempis: *The Imitation of Christ*. Transated by Leo Sherley-Price. Penguin Books, London 1952: 11–25.

SNELLGROVE–RICHARDSON 1995 = Snellgrove, David; Richardson, Hugh: *A Cultural History of Tibet.* Aftermath, Shambhala, Boston–London 1995 [first edition: George Wedenfeld and Nicolson, London 1968].

TAKAKUSU 1966 = Takakusu, Junjirō (tr.): *A Record of the Buddhist Religion as Practiced in India and the Malay Archipelago (A.D. 671–695) by I-Tsing.* Munshiram Manoharlal, Delhi 1966 [first edition: Clarendon Press, London 1896].

TUCK 1990 = Tuck, Andrew P.: *Comparative Philosophy and the Philosophy of Scholarship: On the Western Interpretation of Nāgārjuna.* Oxford University Press, New York and Oxford 1990.

VAIDYA 1960 = Vaidya, P.L. (ed.): 'Introduction' to: *Bodhicaryāvatāra of Śānti-deva with the Commentary Pañjikā of Prajñākaramati.* Buddhist Sanskrit Texts 12. The Mithila Institute, Darbhanga 1960: vii–xii.

WALLACE 1997 = Wallace, Vesna A.; Wallace, B. Alan (tr.): *A Guide to the Bodhisattva Way of Life (Bodhicaryāvatāra) by Śāntideva.* Snow Lion Publications, Ithaca–New York 1997.

WANGYAL 1994 = Wangyal, Tulku Pema: 'Foreword' to: GYATSO (1994: vii–viii).

WECKMAN 1987 = Weckman, George: 'Monasticism: An Overview', in: Mircea Eliade (ed.): *The Encyclopedia of Religion.* Vol. 10, Macmillan, New York 1987.

WILLIAMS 1995 = Williams, Paul: 'General Introduction' to: CROSBY–SKILTON (1995: vii–xxvi).

WINTERNITZ 1987 = Winternitz, M.: *History of Indian Literature. vol. II, part I. Buddhist Literature.* Translated and Revised by Bhaskara Jha. Bharatiya Vidya Prakashan, Delhi and Varansi 1987.

Belief, Hope and Gambling

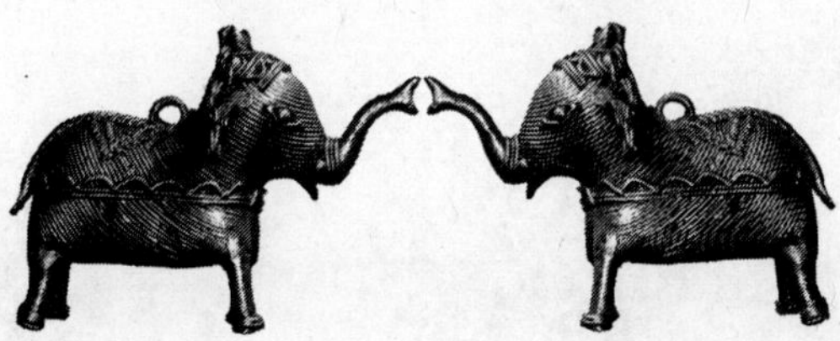

Sociological and Juridical Aspects of Dice-Play in Ancient India

IRMA PIOVANO

Society in ancient India was organised according to an ideal division of the individual's existence into four stages or subsequent phases (*āśrama-dharma*, i.e. *dharma* applied to the way of living): the stage devoted to study, characterised by the initiation ceremony (*upanayana*), known as *brahma-carya*; the stage devoted to practical life when the individual establishes a career for himself and forms a family (*gṛha-stha*); the stage characterised by retirement from active life and withdrawal to the forest (*vānaprastha*); the final stage when the individual devotes himself entirely to an ascetic life (*saṁnyāsa*). This structure highlights the all-pervading nature of the religious element and the constant aspiration to escape the cycle of rebirth (*saṁsāra*). At the age of seven or eight, children of the higher castes began the long stage devoted to study and lived with a teacher (*guru*) who was deeply knowledgeable of the Vedic texts—the inescapable foundation of all knowledge—consequently little time was left for playing. Indeed, classic literature contains but little reference to children's games and toys[1]. One of the children's most common and most cherished toys was a cart made either of metal—sometimes precious—or terracotta, and in fact 'The terracotta cart' was the title of a famous play which dates back to the fourth century CE and is attributed to Śūdraka. This play offers an insight into the social life in an Indian town at a time, when dice players contributed towards enlivening the realistic portrayal.[2]

Outdoor and indoor pastimes and games were numerous, the most popular being archery, playing ball, horse and chariot racing and several others.[3]

Bearing witness to often neglected playful spirit of the Indian people are the numerous festivals which offered an occasion to dice-playing. The latter was very popular

[1] ALTEKAR (1951: 273–275).

[2] See BOTTO (1969: 228–29); BASAK (1929: 299–325). It must be noted that OLEKSIW (1980–81: 415–435) expresses his regret about the fact that the part devoted to dicing in MṛK, while certainly remarkable, was not paid adequate attention by LÜDERS (1907), presenting an analysis and classification of the various types of dice-play.

[3] See RAY (1939: 240–26); BIARDEAU (1981: 875–881); GOKHALE (1959).

Logic and Belief in Indian Philosophy
Warsaw Indological Studies 3 (2010) 657–674.

and was practised both as a ritual, in order to interpret the will of the gods, and even more so as a gambling activity. According to anthropologists, the latter is the category to which it belongs, because it offers the opportunity to place bets and it generates in the player a deep sense of excitement which prompts him to increase his wagers.

Dicing has recently become an object of many studies, offering an analysis of its ritualistic and philosophical-religious aspects, as well as its technical components, the way in which the game is played and the various types of dice used. A vast diachronic analysis of the primary and secondary sources in Sanskrit literature that contain references to dice-play is to be found in the volume by C. PANDURANGA BHATTA (1985). Such analysis, however, is not within the scope of this article, which intends to examine a few sociological and juridical aspects of dice-play, as can be inferred from ancient Indian literature, particularly juridical-political writings.

Vedic texts contain many references to dice-play, that appears to have been popular among all the social classes. The famous 'Lament of the dicer' contained in the *Ṛg-veda*[4] not only bears witness to the popularity of the game in the Āryan society, but it reflects emblematically the influence dice-play exercised on social life, especially in terms of its negative consequences such as the loss of one's wealth—often also of one's wife—and the resultant social decline of the dice player: 'Now my mother-in-law hates me, my wife turns me out. The dicer is like a beggar for whom nobody feels any sympathy, claiming that «I cannot find any usefulness in a player, like an old horse put up for sale»'. And again 'The winning die yearned for his possessions and now others embrace his spouse. His father, his mother, and his brothers say of him, «We do not know him: take him away in chains!»'.

In some hymns the anguish emerges in all its dramatic clarity, the desire to escape the addiction to the game, that assumes almost 'erotic' contours: dice 'by their appeal on the player seem to be smeared with honey.'[5] The attraction of dicing is impellent: 'If I resolve not to play anymore with these dice and step aside when my friends go to play dice, none the less, those brown nuts[6], thrown on the table, call out for me, then I go to meet them, as a woman in love.'[7] As narrated in the *Mṛccha-kaṭika*, the same powerful pull of the dice makes the losing player Saṁvāhaka come out of the temple, where he was hiding, the same temple where the game supervisor and another player, who had been chasing him, had stopped to play, probably counting on his very weakness to flush him out. It is this weakness

[4] RV 10.34.3–4; see SANI (2000: 203).

[5] RV 10.34.7; see SANI (2000: 203). SANI (1989–1990: 239–260).

[6] The 'brown nuts' refer to the fruit of the *vibhīdaka* tree (*Terminalia bellerica*) that were used as dice and this term will also come to indicate the type of game played in the Vedic age.

[7] RV 10.34.5; see SANI (2000: 203) and BASHAM (1969: 207).

that makes him exclaim, 'The tinkling of the dice inflames the heart of a penniless person just like the beat of drums fills the heart of a king who has lost his kingdom!'[8]

The torment is such that the player abandons himself to exhort others to avoid this addiction: 'Do not play dice: plough your field, enjoy what you have and regard it as enough.'[9]

The player was not immune to hopes of increasing his wealth, the desire to tempt, to dominate fate, the attraction to risk, a sort of exaltation that took hold of the gamblers then as it does today and that transforms the game into a sort of total addiction and enslavement.

Prayers and rituals to bring luck to the game can be found in the *Atharva-veda.* In particular, hymn AV 4.38, contains a prayer to Apsaras, the deity who brings luck to gambling. It describes dancing with the dice and invoking the deity's propitious intervention to make the opponent lose: 'The winning Apsaras who arrives unexpectedly, who plays deftly, who wins at the gambling table, this Apsaras I hereby invoke', while in hymn AV 7.52, the invocation is addressed to Agni, the Maruts, Indra and lastly, directly to the dice urging them to concede a game as 'fruitful as a milk cow.'[10]

The way the winning player casts the dice is likened to the action of the god Varuṇa who sets down his laws: 'King Varuṇa can probe into what is between sky and earth and what is beyond. He also counts the battings of men's eyes: he does this in the same way as the player [does] with the dice.'[11] Centuries later, in the *Bhagavad-gītā*—where dice-playing is listed among human passions—the god Kṛṣṇa, addressing Arjuna and listing his prerogatives, declares himself to be the personification of dicing: 'I am the dicing of the deceivers, of the glorious I am the glory, I am the victory and the firm purpose, I am the courage of the braves.'[12]

The fact that the Vedic gods were even likened to the throwing of the dice and therefore were able to award or take away wealth, depending on whether the game was won or lost, was a belief that was based on social foundations. References to the distribution of wealth—a distribution that took place in the assembly hall (*sabhā, samiti*)—can be found in several passages of the *Ṛg-veda*, among which is the following, addressed to Agni: 'O Lord, for an equal fruition you have bestowed your wealth dividing it in parts in the assembly.'[13] Once determined that the function of the *sabhā* or *samiti*—two synonymous terms that indicate the assembly (the

[8] MṛK 2.5.

[9] RV 10.34.13; see SANI (2000: 204).

[10] For both extracts see ORLANDI–SANI (1992: 548–549).

[11] AV 4.16.5 (The literal translation of this extract is provided by Prof. Saverio Sani).

[12] BhG 10.36.

[13] RV 2.1.4; see OLDENBERG (1964: 186).

terms also refer to the assembly hall) of the clan or military chiefs in the *Ṛg-veda*—was to distribute wealth through a draw by casting the dice, N.N. BHATTACHARYA (1974: 297) wonders if dice-play, representing one of the most important characteristics of the coronation ceremonies known as *rāja-sūya* and *agny-ādheya*, is perhaps reminiscent of the drawing of the riches in pre-Vedic times, that is, the illusory representation of an ancient custom of equal distribution. The dice game played symbolically by the sovereign in the course of the *rāja-sūya*, is described as follows in the *Śatapatha-brāhmaṇa*: 'He then throws the five dice in his hand, reciting «You are the dominant one: may these five regions of yours prosper! Since there are indeed five regions, he thus determines their prosperity'[14] (the dice used in the ceremony of the *rāja-sūya* were made of gold and in numbers of over a hundred or over a thousand).

Moving away from the principle that every ritual is the symbolic representation of ancient social realities, N.N. BHATTACHARYA (1974) maintains that the dice game, mimed by the sovereign, contributes towards understanding the long phase of change from a tribe-based society to a society organised in classes and to the stabilisation of the figure of the elected sovereign—and therefore not yet hereditary—among the clan or military chiefs who had distinguished themselves particularly in the wars of conquest. The action of the sovereign symbolised therefore the application of an ancient norm of social justice of which the sovereign represented the highest ideal. He thus provided evidence of the adherence to ancient tribal customs linked to the collective ownership of wealth and the principle that required one not to keep it personally as this was contrary to the *ṛta* (justice)[15]. Drawing by casting dice was in fact the best method to distribute wealth because, without knowing the cost of the products amassed as collective wealth, it was impossible to determine its exact value. Dice play—the original tribal nature of which is demonstrated—takes, in this context, on significance that is deeply different from the one it will acquire later on, that is to say a high-betting game of chance.

The dice most commonly referred to in the texts are *kṛta*, *tretā*, *dvāpara* and *kali*, with decreasing values of four to one. The same terminology is used in the Hindu mythology to define the four times (*yuga*) or eras of the existence of the world.

The most feared dice is the one worth one point, known as *kali*, indicated in the *Atharva-veda*[16] as 'the lord of the dice', and later on in the *Śatapatha-brāhmaṇa*[17] referred to as 'the die dominating on the other (dice)', the die that sanctions the loss.

---

[14] ŚaT 5.4.4. See RAYCHAUDURY (1953: 165 f.).

[15] WINTERNITZ (1981–85, I: 154) regards it as the order of the universe, MACDONELL (1972: 75) as the physical and moral order, KEITH (1989: 248) as the cosmic, RADHAKRISHNAN (1996, I: 78–79) as, literally, the 'course of events', i.e. a law in general and the immanence of justice, the order of the world.

[16] AV 7.114.1; see ORLANDI–SANI (1992: 551).

[17] ŚaT 5.4, AŚ.4.6.

The game was played in rather a complex manner and several dice were used; one verse refers to no less than 150! This number probably refers to the most ancient period when *vibhīdaka* nuts were used.

Dice-play is absolutely forbidden to students (*brahma-carin*) and to the youth who have completed their student stage (*snātaka*)[18]. This concern to protect youth from the vice of gambling is clearly expressed in a few passages of the *Gṛhya-sūtra*s and the *Śrauta-sūtra*s (auxiliary and doctrinal handbooks pertaining to different Vedic schools of thought, containing norms and provisions of various nature) in which there are indications for the construction of buildings which state that assembly or meeting halls must be oriented southwards. Other authors believe instead that such an attitude leads the youth to indulge in gambling and, among them, Āśvalāyana in particular maintains that the people who frequent such halls will turn into gamblers, troublemakers and will have a short life.[19] Kātyāyana, for his part, suggests that the building where a gambling hall is located must have a special entrance in the shape of an arc (*dvārâvasthita-toraṇa*) so as to be recognisable by decent people, thus implying a negative judgement.[20] Instead an assembly hall is considered favourable and, more to the point, free from gambling when it is built on land[21] where the waters flow easily in all directions. According to Apastamba[22], it is up to the sovereign to see to the construction of an assembly hall where a gambling table (*adhidevana*) is to be positioned and dice in even numbers are made available to the devoted and trusted subjects so as to allow them to gamble. The assembly hall described in the *Mahā-bhārata*[23] is monumental and lavishly decorated with precious metals and stones, but this was the assembly hall of the palace of the sovereign. Also in the *Hari-vaṁśa* the hall where the dice game between Rukmin and Bālarāma takes place is adorned with golden columns and embellished with flowers and fountains from which sprinkle sandal-scented water[24], but in general the references contained in theatre works, in prose and also in the *Artha-śāstra* by Kauṭilya, refer to public and private gambling houses of a popular nature that existed in the larger towns[25].

The popularity enjoyed by dice-play in different historical times is witnessed by archaeological excavations that have brought to light several dice, some of which

[18] See GDhS 2.17,VSm 71.45 and MDhŚ 4.74.

[19] See PANDURANGA BHATTA (1985: 107).

[20] KMS 785.

[21] APTE (1954: 139).

[22] ĀDhS 2.10.25.12–13, no.11.

[23] MBh, *Sabhā-parvan* 56.18. See MANI (1984).

[24] See PANDURANGA BHATTA (1985: 108).

[25] AŚ 3.20; DKC, *dvitīyôcchvāsa*, pp. 76–77 (tr.: pp. 53–54).

with six faces, as well as gambling tables. In Mohenjo-daro dice were found that date back to the Civilisation of the Valley of the Indus (fig. 1)[26]. In Taxila instead were found dice dating back to the Greek and Schythian-Parthian period; in Kumrahar archaeological finds confirm the existence of dice-play, while in the famous Buddhist site of Andhra Pradesh, Nāgārjunakoṇḍa, several ivory dice were found with engraved pips, similar to those of the Vedic period[27]. Yet another testimony is represented by a bas-relief of Bharhut *stūpa* (2nd–1st century BCE) depicting two people engaging in a game that is presumably dice-play (fig. 2)[28].

According to the law texts (*dharma-śāstra*), the two authors Gautama and Baudhāyana strongly disapprove of dicing and gambling. Indeed, Gautama[29] regards the dice player as belonging to that group of people who must be avoided during the performance of the rites to honour ancestors (*śrāddha*); Manu goes as far as to forbid the company of players during such ceremonies and extends the same injunction also towards the managers of gambling houses,[30] while Baudhāyana[31] confines himself to judging gambling as a cause of impurity.

Manu[32] cites dice-play as the eighteenth and last category that can lead to a law suit. He considers dice-play as the act of earning money from the use of inanimate objects and wagers (*samāhvaya*) in the same way as if they were animated beings used for the same purpose[33].

Manu, whose vision of society is governed by balance and strict moral principles, is rather harsh in his appraisal of gambling and wagering. According to this author these are practices—or rather vices—that lead to the destruction of kingdoms and their sovereigns; they are blatant thefts and the sovereign should spare no efforts to suppress both and condemn to corporal punishment not only those who engage in gambling and wagering, but also those who make them possible. Since players are regarded as thieves, they should be banned from the town in order to prevent them from corrupting honest subjects. However the punishment to be inflicted, envisaged also for those who gamble in private, is left to the discretion of the sovereign and may simply consist of a fine.[34]

---

[26] See CITÉS (1988: 171).

[27] See KRISHNA MURTHY (1982: 69–70) and KRISHNA MURTHY (1961: 1–4).

[28] See COOMARASWAMI (1956: 93–94).

[29] GDhS 15.18.

[30] MDhŚ 3.151 and 159.

[31] BDhS 14.2.1.2–16.

[32] MDhŚ 8.7.

[33] MDhŚ 9.223.

[34] MDhŚ 9.221–228.

As if to justify his completely hostile position towards gambling, Manu recalls that in earlier times (*kalpa*) dice-play was the cause of great enmities and therefore the wise man would be well advised to refrain from it even if practised only for the purpose of entertainment[35]. These statements clearly refer, according to Georg BÜHLER (1984: lxxx), to two episodes contained in the *Mahā-bhārata*, and specifically to the one regarding the loss of King Nala's kingdom at dicing, and the tragic dice game between Yudhiṣṭhira and Śakuni, representing respectively the two warrior groups of the Pāṇḍava and the Kaurava. But if the loss of the kingdom caused by Nala's gambling led to the touching tale of the love and fidelity of his spouse Damayantī, Yudhiṣṭhira's fateful dice game triggered the bloody war among the cousins. From a juridical point of view, Yudhiṣṭhira's obstinacy in continuing his dice-playing which led to the loss of his kingdom, his brothers, himself and his spouse Draupadī, contains an important juridical issue to which M.A. MEHENDALE (1986: 179–194) devotes a vast and detailed analysis. The question is posed by Draupadī when, humiliated and at that point regarded as a slave by the winning cousins, addressing the two groups of contenders in the assembly hall where she has been led, leaves all those present speechless. The anguished question asked by Draupadī is: Was she lost at gambling by Yudhiṣṭhira before or after he wagered and lost himself? From this answer depends nothing less than her honour or her future as a slave. And the answer will be given by Arjuna, who affirms that Yudhiṣṭhira, having lost himself first at gambling, is no longer in a position to lose his spouse and thus Draupadī preserves her honour.

According to P.V. KANE (1930–62, III: 542), the intentions of the author of the *Mahā-bhārata* were to emphasise a condemnation of gambling regarded as a deplorable practice and so detrimental and degrading as to lead even the best and the greatest to lose all sense of duty, morals and even the ties of love and family life.

Both Nārada[36] and Bṛhaspati[37] declare that, in the same way as the worst criminals and even murderers, dice players cannot be called to testify, and the possessions, that is to say the winnings, obtained through gambling represent possessions of the lowest type[38].

The definition of dice players as blatant cheats put forth by Manu[39] is shared by Nārada, who puts them on the same level as alcoholics and those belonging to the lowest strata of society according to their work activity, and, in particular, those who use crooked dice are considered manifest thieves[40].

---

[35] MDhŚ 9.227.

[36] NāSm 12.1.159 and 14.178.

[37] BṛSm 7.30.

[38] BṛSm 1.47.

[39] MDhŚ 9.258.

[40] NāSm, Appendix 1.2, 12.45 and 22.3,9.

In his very strict view, Manu considers any art form and also gambling among the ten vices that derive from a love for entertainment that a sovereign should avoid[41].

Several contradictions appear evident in the *Manu-smṛti* due to the fact that the text dates back to a time characterised by the reaffirmation of the ideals of purity, which were set in the Vedic time and which represent the foundations of the theory of the *varṇa* and of the corresponding social hierarchy[42], a hierarchy which under the influence of the theories made popular by Buddhism, were rejected earlier on.

The theory of equality among the castes and the importance attached to work and to frugality preached by Buddhism had indeed determined the development of activities pertaining to industry and commerce, with a consequent affirmation of a prosperous social class which, concerned with the preservation of integrity and wealth, had promoted conservative values and punitive norms towards gambling. The latter was regarded as dangerous for society and one of the six ways in which to squander one's wealth. The *Dīgha-nikāya*, the Buddhist canonical text, maintains that there are six negative consequences of gambling: the winner is hated, the loser is saddened by the money lost, there is an evident loss of wealth, the player is not admitted to testify in a court of law, he is despised by his friends and is not taken in consideration by the parents of girls at a marriageable age because a scoundrel addicted to gambling is unfit to have a wife[43].

Consequently, if society in Buddhist times condemned gambling by virtue of the conservative values mentioned above, so did the society that developed in Manu's time a few centuries later, in the name of a return to the fundamental values of the Vedic world.

Nevertheless the commentators Mitramiśra and Nīlakaṇṭha, respectively the authors of the *Viramitrôdaya* and the *Vyavahāra-māyuka*, assert that the prohibition of gambling on the part of Manu extends only to cases in which crooked dice are used or the authorisation of the sovereign has not been obtained. Clearly the commentators tend to stress that no particular differences exist among the texts of the *smṛti*, precisely because these are texts belonging to a consolidated tradition and therefore are regarded as sacred[44].

On the other hand, the statement by Nārada is decidedly supportive in that it considers gambling as a form of entertainment that is completely legal as long as it is carried out in public gambling houses and is organised and managed by an official whose authority must be recognised by the players and to whom they must spontaneously pay a set sum amounting to 10% of the winnings. If gambling takes places

[41] MDhŚ 7.47.

[42] MDhŚ 12.95–96. See INDRA DEVA (1986: 115–119).

[43] See INDRA DEVA (1986: 46–47).

[44] See PANDURANGA BHATTA (1985: 126).

without the authorisation of the sovereign, the player has no right to receive his winnings and must instead pay a fine[45].

Already in the *Yajur-veda* a passing reference is made to a supervisor (*akṣa-vāpa*) who oversaw the gambling on behalf on his sovereign: a figure that will be found, centuries later, recognised and affirmed in the *Artha-śāstra* and the law texts. Thus a professional figure is consolidated, that of the *sabhika*, indicated clearly by Yājñavalkya[46] as the official in charge of overseeing games with specific duties and who, in the *Mitâkṣarā*[47], is identified with the manager and owner of the gambling house. The *sabhika* is assisted by an employee (*sabhā-pati*) whose task consists in making available to the players all that is necessary for the game, a task from which he earns his living. In this text there is a curious definition of the players who, while having lost everything and therefore are unable to continue gambling, are nevertheless incapable of leaving the gambling hall and remain watching the others play, as motionless as pillars (*sabhā-stāṇū*)[48].

According to Yājñavalkya the *sabhika* has the right to receive 10% of the wagers of the losers, and also 5% of the winnings if the bet was increased—fraudulently—by 100 times. He must pay the sovereign a set percentage and, after collecting what is owed by the defeated player, sees to the winner's payment. According to this author, in order to expose thieves, it is useful that the gambling houses be supervised by an appointed supervisor whose job it is to gather information on thieves also to visit gambling houses regularly. If the *sabhika* fails to make the losing player pay what he owes and if the game was played publicly in the presence of himself and other players, the sovereign may require the *sabhika* himself to pay off the sum owed by the loser, as well as what is owed to the state in taxes.[49]

The *sabhika* is also charged with collecting pledges, seeing to it that various articles are sold inside the gambling house, and he himself is subject to fines if he fails to prohibit cheating due to dexterity of hands during the game.[50]

If the losing player does not have the money to pay off his debt to the winner, Kātyāyana maintains that the *sabhika* must take it upon himself to pay the sum, granting the loser a 45-day respite, but he must demand to be paid back immediately when the possibility exists that he could lose the money. In a subsequent passage he

---

[45] NāSm 17.2.5.7.

[46] YDhŚ 2.202–203.

[47] PANDURANGA BHATTA (1985: 111) and BANERJI (1997: 361).

[48] MACDONELL (1912: 426): *sabhā-sthānu* is instead the game supervisor, called 'the pillar of the assembly' for his constant presence in the room. See also BHATTACHARYA (1974: 304–305).

[49] YDhŚ 2.202–206.

[50] AŚ 3.20.10–12.

is however more drastic and states that the wagers must be paid off immediately in the gambling house and that the *sabhika*, being the one who established the exact procedure to be followed for the game, is the person who has to compel the loser to pay, even by resorting to force[51]. The *Mṛccha-kaṭika* contains an emblematic scene when Saṁvāhaka, unable to settle his gambling debt amounting to 10 gold coins, runs away and is chased by the supervisor Māthura and another player. Saṁvāhaka complains and asks for a reduction of his debt, Māthura declares that he is under arrest in the name of the Association of Dicers and invites him to sell his own parents or himself. A third person intervenes to defend Saṁvāhaka and the quarrel degenerates into a fight with insults and blows[52].

In this text too the figure of the *sabhika* appears again as particularly significant[53]. Furthermore the game supervisor Māthura seems to have used a book where he recorded the winnings and the losses and the names of the players who had yet to settle their debts before being allowed to visit other gambling houses[54]. The *sabhika*, who was familiar with the habits of many of the subjects, could also become a precious informant for the sovereign[55].

The players who were unable to settle gambling debts were allowed to leave the house after submitting adequate guarantees. Gambling debts however were not transferable and therefore could not fall on heirs[56].

The powerful role of the *sabhika* in the society of the time is attested by the fact that he could also inflict punishments and for this reason, not infrequently, many a defaulting player ran away at the mere sight of him[57]. The *Kathā-sarit-sāgara* narrates of a *sabhika* so enraged that, after beating up with a stick a player who had not paid off his debt, he got other players to throw him into a well and personally committed himself to settling the debt to the winner[58].

Kauṭilya, who has a supervisor appointed even for the courtesans, has not appointed one for gambling (*dyūtâdhyakṣa*). He deems it necessary however to appoint a director whose responsibility it is to make available a clean dice, cup and the dice against a payment of 5% of the winnings, a percentage to which has to be added the rent for the cups, the dice, a supplement for water, the use of the premises

[51] KMS 783–792 (*dyūta-samāhvaya*).

[52] MṛK 2, p. 84–85.

[53] See BANERJEE (1994: 116).

[54] MṛK 2.2, p. 84–85.

[55] See PANDURANGA BHATTA (1985:.112).

[56] MDhŚ 8.159, BṛSm 11.51.

[57] MṛK 2.2, p. 84–85.

[58] KSS 92.19–22.

and the permit to play. The description of the fines is detailed and meticulous: 20 *paṇa* to replace the cup or the dice, while the fine for fraudulent gambling is as high as the lowest one implemented for an act of violence; confiscation of winnings and, in case of cheating, a fine for theft. In general terms, Kauṭilya, while regarding the players as cheats, seems to be more concerned about the economic aspects—that is, the increase in the state revenue—than about the moral issues related to the game[59].

The chance to make easy gains from gambling determined the adoption of fraudulent practices such as dice manipulation and many other expedients, not the least of which the possibility to swallow the unfavourable die. Cheating at dice play was a rather common practice, so much so that the terms *kitava* and *dhuta* that originally indicated dicers finally came to mean cheat and scoundrel respectively.[60]

In order to prevent frauds, it was decided that dice play should take place in especially selected sites, approved by the state. If however the game took place in secret locations and without authorisation, the players and the game supervisor could not collect their due and were also punished[61]. For cheats particularly harsh punishments were adopted, such as exile[62], those who used crooked dice could have their hands cut off and those who adopted other fraudulent practices to win risked losing their index finger and thumb[63]. And then there were also interesting punishments, intended to expose dishonest players to public contempt, like branding their foreheads with the shape of dog's pawn and sending them into exile[64] or the less ignominious one of wearing a dice collar around the neck[65]. Those who appeared reluctant to settle what they owed risked being beaten mercilessly by the managers of gambling houses and forced to 'sell' their parents or be tortured or hung upside down by their feet for one full day or be dragged on their backs on an uneven road[66].

The case list is vast and very detailed and suggests that players resorted to very sophisticated stratagems and shrewd ruses in order to win. This case history however also bears witness to the moral decay in which the dicers eventually fell, inveterate gamblers who regularly visited gambling houses where chaos and racket reigned undisturbed and talk was vulgar and indecent[67].

---

[59] AŚ 3.20.7–10.

[60] See PANDURANGA BHATTA (1985: 115).

[61] YDhŚ 2.204, NāSm 16.7.

[62] YDhŚ 2.205, BṛSm 28.8.

[63] VSm 5.135.

[64] YDhŚ 2.205.

[65] NāSm 16.6.

[66] See C. PANDURANGA BHATTA (1985: 115–116).

[67] DKC, *dvitīyôcchvāsa*, pp. 76–77 (tr.: pp. 53–54).

To resolve the disputes that arose among the players both Nārada and Yājñavalkya believe other players who would act as judges and witnesses, as the case required, should be called in[68]. The players were to be appointed by the sovereign. Bṛhaspati maintains very fairly that a judging panel made up of the *sabhika* and three players could also act as witnesses to settle a dispute related to the game and if the players were manifestly hostile to the disputants, it was up to the king to settle the issue. The losing players, if not aware of the rules of the game, had to be released, just like the players who were indeed familiar with the rules, but were defeated through cheating or using crooked dice. And if a player lost all his belongings in gambling, he was not required to relinquish them all[69]. As regards disputes between two players, based on the widespread belief that both are dishonest and therefore there is no distinction between winner and loser, Kauṭilya maintains that, if the contenders have gambled without authorisation, both must be punished, while if the winner of the game is nominated by the court, no fines are inflicted. Kauṭilya believes that the habit of accepting that, if the player who won the game by cheating also wins the dispute and therefore his fine is small, while the loser of the game and of the dispute is given a higher fine, only encourages more fraudulent behaviour at gambling[70].

The juridical writings of the different authors of the *smṛti* appear to contain a number of incongruities, justified by the fact that this type of norms was of a customary nature and was for a long time rooted in definitions that were totally informal and often contradictory; only later were they elaborated and systematised over the course of the centuries.

The variations and the contradictions in form and substance are nevertheless evidence of an effort to adjust to the historical context and of a constant commitment towards adapting the rules to a truth that proved very ephemeral in itself, before attaining the definition and the actual implementation of laws that adhered more closely to reality. The dissimilarities contained in the writings themselves speak eloquently of the commitment on the part of the legislator towards his quest for absolutes that, by their formulation, represent the cornerstones and the main lines of civil law[71].

These derogations originate from an analysis of the human behaviour, that is often animated by deep passions and ardent attraction of the imponderable. The gambler sets off for his own destruction, leaving it to the dice to decide about his future.

---

[68] NāSm 17.4; YDhŚ 2.205. This is an exception to the general rule that forbids players to testify in a court of law and be part of a jury.

[69] BṛSm 26.7–8.

[70] AŚ 3.20.3–7.

[71] See PIOVANO (1999: 158).

The examination of the gambler's behaviour reveals not only the purpose of improving his habits and restraining his wild passions but also an unusual aptitude to deep psychological investigation.

The dice game becomes the symbol of a fortuitousness that affects both the cosmic and the human world; both *ṛta* and *dharma*, albeit regulated by rigid laws and by a supratemporal and changeless order, can be impaired by events escaping the rule, or rather escaping human rationality.

Recourse to an irresponsible act and thus to irrationality consequently implies an unforeseen and deadly event but, as ancient Indian texts state, this is the fate of our age. These considerations lead legislators to recognise the difficulty, almost impossibility, of complying with all the norms of *dharma* and to accept, around the eleventh century, the theory of 'the actions forbidden in the Kali Age' (*kali-varjya*).

ILLUSTRATIONS

Fig.1

Cubic dice found during archaeological excavations in Mohenjo-daro. The position of the spots on the six faces follows the arithmetic progression and varies from one item to the next. The dice on the left is made of white limestone and on opposing faces presents the following pairs: one-three, two-five, four-(nought); the middle one is made of terracotta and has the following pairs: one-two, three-four, five-six; the one on the right is one of the finest and has the following pairs: one-two, three-five, four-six.

Source: CITÉS (1988: 171).

Fig. 2

Dice players depicted on the relief of the trabeation in the Bharhut *stūpa*.
Source: A.K. COOMARASWAMI (1956: 93–94, pl. XLVIII, fig 223).

Fig. 3

Pacīsī players depicted in the Zanana (Janana) Mahal of the Udaipur Royal Palace (by courtesy of Prof. Rosa Maria Cimino).

BIBLIOGRAPHY

ĀDhS = *Āpastamba-śrauta-sūtra*. See: BÜHLER (1986).

ALTEKAR 1951 = Altekar, A.S.: *Education in Ancient India*. Nand Kishore Brothers, Banaras 1951.

APTE 1954 = Apte, V.M.: *Social and Religious Life in the Grihya Sūtras* (*with brief surveys of social and religious conditions in pre-Grihya-sūtra Vedic literature and in early Avestan literature*). Popular book depot, Bombay 1954 [first edition: Ahmedabad 1939].

AŚ = Kauṭilya: *Artha-śāstra*. R.P. Kangle: *The Kauṭilīya Arthaśāstra*. Part II: *An English Translation with Critical and Explanatory Notes*. Motilal Banarsidass, Delhi 1986 [first edition: University of Bombay, Bombay 1963].

AV = *Atharva-veda*. K.L. Joshi (ed.): *Atharva-veda-saṁhitā*, Sanskrit text, English transl., notes and index of verses according to the translation of W.D. Whitney and Bhāṣya of Sāyaṇācarya (including 20th *kāṇḍa*) / edited and revised by ... Parimal Publications, Delhi 2000.

BANERJEE 1994 = Banerjee, B.: *King Śūdraka and his drama*. Orientalia, Collana di Studi Orientali del Cesmeo (directed by I. Piovano) 5, Torino 1994.

BANERJI 1997 = Banerji, S.Ch.: *Society in Ancient India*. D.K. Printworld, New Delhi 1997 [first edition: 1993].

BASAK 1929 = Basak, R.: 'Indian society as pictured in *Mṛcchakatika*', *Indian Historical Quarterly* 1 (1929) 299–325.

BASHAM 1969 = Basham, A.L.: *The wonder that was India: a survey of the history and culture of the Indian sub-continent before the coming of the Muslim*. 3rd edition, London 1969.

BDhS = *Baudhāyana-dharma-sūtra*. (1) *Baudhāyana-dharma-sūtra govinda-svāmi-praṇīta-vivaraṇa-sameta-saṭippaṇa – hindī-vyākhyôpetam*. Caukhambā Saṁskṛta Sīrīj Āphīsa, Vārāṇaṣī 1934. (2) Georg Bühler (tr.): *The Sacred Laws of the Āryas*, Part II: *Vāsistha and Baudhāyana*. Sacred Books of the East vol. 14, Motilal Banarsidass, Delhi 1984 [first edition: Delhi 1882].

BHATTACHARYA 1974 = Bhattacharya, N.N.: 'The King and the Dice, A Study in the Ritual of *Rājasūya*', *Journal of the Oriental Institute* Baroda 23/4 (1974) 288–307.

BhG = *Bhagavad-gītā*. (1) Swami Swarupananda (ed., tr.): *Śrīmad-Bhagavad-Gītā*, with text, word-for-word translation, English rendering comments and index. Advaita Ashrama, Calcutta 1956. (2) Raniero Gnoli (tr.): *Il canto del Beato*. Classici delle Religioni Orientali, directed by Oscar Botto, UTET, Torino 1976.

BIARDEAU 1981 = Biardeau, M.: 'The Ball-Game: Myth and Rite', *Ludwik Sternbach Felicitation Volume* (Akhila Bharatiya Sanskrit Parishad, Lucknow 1981) 875–881.

BṛSm = *Bṛhaspati-smṛti.* (1) K.V. Rangaswami Aiyangar: *Bṛhaspati-smṛti.* Gaekwad Oriental Series 85, Baroda 1941. (2) Tr.: JOLLY (1965).

BOTTO 1969 = Botto, O.: Letterature Antiche dell'India', *Storia delle Letterature d'Oriente* (Diretta da Oscar Botto) vol. III, Milano 1969: 1–350.

BÜHLER 1984 = Bühler, Georg (tr.): *The Laws of Manu.* Sacred Books of the East vol. XXV, Motilal Banarsidass, Delhi 1984 [first edition: 1886].

BÜHLER 1986 = Bühler, Georg (tr.): *The Sacred Laws of the Āryas.* Part I: *Āpastamba and Gautama.* Sacred Books of the East vol. II, Motilal Banarsidass, Delhi 1986 [first edition: 1879–1882].

CITÉS 1988 = *Les Cités Oubliées de l'Indus—Archéologie du Pakistan.* Association Française d'action artistique, Paris 1988.

COOMARASWAMI 1956 = Coomaraswami, A.K.: *La sculpture de Bharhut.* Annales du Musée Guimet, Bibliothèque d'Art (N.S.) 6, Paris 1956.

DKC = Daṇḍin: *Daśa-kumāra-carita.* R.M. Kale (ed., tr.): *The Daś-kumāra-carita of Daṇḍin. With commentary.* Edited with critical and explanatory notes and an introduction. Motilal Banarsidass, Delhi 1979 [first edition: 1917].

DUTT 1978 = Dutt, M.N. (ed., tr.): *The Dharma Shastra—Hindu Religious Codes,* Reprinted Edition, Vol. I, Cosmo publ., Delhi 1978.

GDhS = *Gautama-dharma-sūtra.* See: BÜHLER (1986).

GOKHALE 1959 = Gokhale, B.G.: *Ancient India—History and Culture.* 4th edition, Asia Publishing House, New York 1959 [first edition: 1952].

HUIZINGA 2002 = Huizinga, J.: *Homo Ludens, A Study of the Play Element in Culture.* Routledge & Kegan Paul, London 1939 [Italian edition: *Homo Ludens.* With introduction by U. Eco, Piccola Biblioteca Einaudi, Torino 2002].

INDRA DEVA 1986 = Indra Deva, Shrirama M.A.: *Traditional Values and Institutions in Indian Society.* Ram Nagar, New Delhi 1986.

JOLLY 1965 = Jolly, Julius (tr.): *The Minor Law Books.* Part I: *Nārada and Bṛhaspati.* Sacred Books of the East vol. XXXIII, Motilal Banarsidass, Delhi 1965 [first edition: 1889].

KANE 1930–62 = Kane, Pandurang Vaman: *History of Dharma-śāstra.* 5 Vols, Bhandarkar Oriental Research Institute, Pune 1930–62.

KEITH 1989 = Keith, A.B.: *The religion and philosophy of the Veda and Upaniṣad.* Motilal Banarsidass, Delhi 1989 [first edition: Harvard Oriental Series, Cambridge (Massachusetts) 1925].

KMS 1986 = Kātyāyana: *Kātyāyana-mata-saṁgraha.* N.Ch. Bandyopadhyaya (ed.): *Kātyāyana-mata-saṅgraha or A Collection of the Legal Fragments of Kātyāyana.* Sri Satguru Publications, Delhi 1986 [first edition: Calcutta 1927].

KOSAMBI 1965 = Kosambi, D.D.: *The Culture and Civilization of Ancient India in Historical Outline.* Routledge and Kegan Paul, London 1965.

KRISHNA MURTHY 1961 = Krishna Murthy, K.: 'Dice Play and its Archaeological corroboration at Nāgārjunakoṇḍa – Andhra Pradesh', *The Orissan Historical Research Journal* 10/1–2 (1961) 1–4.

KRISHNA MURTHY 1982 = Krishna Murthy K., *Social and Cultural Life in Ancient India*. Sundeep Prekashan, Delhi 1982.

KSS = Somadeva: *Kathā-sarit-sāgara*. (1) Hermann Brockhaus (ed.): *Kathā Sarit Sāgara: die Märchensammlung des Somadeva*. Sanskrit und deutsch, hrsg. von. F.A. Brockhaus, Leipzig 1839–66. (2) F. Baldissera, V. Mazzarino, M.P. Vivanti (tr.): *Somadeva, L'Oceano dei fiumi dei racconti*. 2 vols, Einaudi, Torino 1993.

LÜDERS 1907 = Lüders, Heinrich: *Das Würfelspiel in alten Indien*. Weidmannsche Buchhandlung, Berlin 1907.

MACDONELL 1912 = MacDonell, A.A.—Keith, A.B.: *Vedic index of names and subjects*. Rist. anast. 2 Vols, Motilal Banarsidass, Delhi 1982 [first edition: London 1912].

MACDONELL 1972 = Macdonell, A.A.: *History of Sanskrit Literature*. 3rd edition, Munshiram Manoharlal, New Delhi 1972 [first edition: 1958].

MANI 1984 = Vettam Mani: *Purāṇic Encyclopaedia*. Motilal Banarsidass, Delhi 1984 [first edition: 1975].

MBh = *Mahā-bhārata*. Ramchandrashastri Kinjawadekar (ed.): *The Mahābhāratam with the Bharata Bhawadeepa Commentary of Nilkantha*. 6 Vols, second edition, Munshiram Manoharlal Publishers, New Delhi 1979 [first edition: Chitrashala Press, Poona 1929–1933].

MDhŚ = *Mānava-dharma-śāstra* [*Manu-smṛti*]. (1) J. Jolly (ed.): *Mânava Dharma-sâstra. The code of Manu. Original Sanskrit Text Critically Edited According to the Standard Sanskrit Commentaries, with Critical Notes*. Trübner & Co., Ludgate Hill 1887. (2) Tr.: BÜHLER (1984).

MEHENDALE 1986 = Mehendale, M.A.: 'Draupadī's Question', *Journal of the Oriental Institute*, Baroda 35/3–4 (1986) 179–194.

MITRA 1965 = Mitra, V.: *India of Dharma-sūtras*. Arya Book Depot, New Delhi 1965.

MṛK = *Mṛccha-kaṭika*. M.R. Kale (ed., tr.): *Mṛcchakaṭika*. Revised edition, Motilal Banarsidass, Delhi 1972.

NāSm = *Nārada-smṛti*. (1) Richard W. Lariviere (ed., tr.): *The Nāradasmṛti. Critical Edition and Translation*. Motilal Banarsidass, Delhi 2003 [first edition: Part I & II, University of Pennsylvania, Philadelphia 1989]. (2) Tr.: JOLLY (1965).

OLDENBERG 1964 = Oldenberg, Hermann (tr.): *Vedic Hymns*. Sacred Books of the East vols XXXII, XLVI, Motilal Banarsidass, Delhi 1964 [first edition: 1891, 1897].

OLEKSIW 1980–81 = Oleksiw, S.: 'Dicing in the *Mṛcchakaṭika*', *The Adyar Library Bulletin* 44–45 [*Dr. Kunjunni Raja Felicitation Volume,* Madras] (1980–81) 415–435.

ORLANDI–SANI 1992 = Orlandi, Chatia; Sani, Saverio: *Atharva-veda: inni magici*. UTET, Classici delle Religioni Orientali (directed by Oscar Botto), Torino 1992.

PANDURANGA BHATTA 1985 = Panduranga Bhatta, C.: *The Dice Play in Sanskrit Literature*. Amar Prakashan, Delhi 1985.

PATKAR 1963 = Patkar, M.M.: 'The role of gambling in ancient Indian society and some Sanskrit words pertaining to the game', *Vishveshvaranand Indological Journal* 1/1 (1963) 141–153.

PIOVANO 1999 = Piovano, Irma: 'Il diritto di proprietà della donna secondo l'antico diritto indiano', in: *Atti del Convegno Internazionale 'La donna e i diritti umani—Aspetti religiosi e giuridici' (Agrigento, 26–28 November 1998),* Accademia di Studi Mediterranei 'Lorenzo Gioeni', Agrigento 1999: 149–162.

PURI 1968 = Puri, B.N.: *India in the time of Patañjali*. Bharatiya Vidya Bhavan, Bombay 1968.

RADHAKRISHNAN 1996 = Radhakrishnan, S.: *Indian Philosophy*. Oxford University Press, Delhi 1996.

RAY 1939 = Ray, T.N.: 'The Indoor and Outdoor Games in Ancient India', *Proceedings of the Indian History Congress*. Third Session, Calcutta 1939" 240–261.

RAYCHAUDURY 1953 = Raychaudury, H.C.: *Political History of Ancient India*. University of Calcutta, Calcutta 1953.

RV = F.M. Müller (ed.): *Rig-Veda-Saṁhitā. The Sacred Hymns of the Brāhmans together with the Commentary of Sāyaṇācārya*. 4 Vols, Krishnadas Academy, Varanasi 1983 [first edition: 1890, 1892]. (2) See: OLDENBERG (1964).

SANI 1989–1990 = Sani, S.: 'Madhuga ou la violence de la douceur', *Bulletin d'Etudes Indiennes* VII-VIII (1989–1990) 239–260.

SANI 2000 = Saverio Sani: *Ṛg-veda, Le strofe della sapienza*. Marsilio, Venezia 2000.

SHARMA 1977 = Sharma, R.N.: *Culture and civilization as revealed in the Śrauta-sūtras*. Nag publishers, Delhi 1977.

ŚaT = *Śatapatha-brāhmaṇa*. Julius Eggeling (tr.): *Śatapatha-Brāhmaṇa according to the text of the Mādhyandina school*. 5 parts, Sacred Books of the East, Vols XII, XXVI, XLI, XLIII, XLIV, Motilal Banarsidass, Delhi 1963 [first edition: 1882–1900].

VSm = *Viṣṇu-smṛti*. Julius Jolly (tr.): *The Institutes of Vishnu*. Sacred Books of the East vol. VII, Motilal Banarsidass, Delhi 1965 [first edition: 1880].

WINTERNITZ 1981–85 = Winternitz M.: *A History of Indian Literature*. Delhi 1981–85.

YDhŚ = *Yājñavalkya-dharma-śāstra*. (1) Ganapati Śastri (ed.): *The Yājñavalkya-smṛti, with the commentary Bālakrīda of Viśvarūpāchārya*. 2nd edition. Munshiram Manoharlal, Delhi 1982 [first edition: 1922–24]. (2) Tr.: DUTT (1978).

GENERAL INDEX

A

a posteriori inference, 363; 366; 369
ābhāsa, 72; 77; 269; 284; 327; 458; 551; 554
abhāva, 58; 251; 255; 256; 278; 279; 368; 375; 454; 470; 481; 482; 510; 512; 513; 514; 581. *See also* absence
abhaya, 149; 316; 317
Abhayadeva-sūri, 305; 335; 345
Abhayatilaka, 35
Abhidharma, 540; 581; 587; 606; 632; 640
Abhidharma-dīpa, 335
Abhidharma-kośa, 617
Abhidharma-kośa-bhāṣya, 37
Abhidharma-samuccaya, 617; 618; 620
abhidheyatva (nameability), 249; 250; 251; 254; 255; 256; 258; 262; 275; 276; 278; 279; 280; 281; 286; 291; 292; 308; 330
Abhinavagupta, 74
abhiprāya, 133; 553; 612
abhrānta, 75; 546; 555; 578
abhyudaya, 290; 293; 294; 397
abiding in Brahman (*brahma-saṁsthatā*), 443
absence, 26; 45; 67; 74; 76; 77; 143; 147; 148; 152; 189; 241; 251; 254; 255; 264; 267; 270; 278; 279; 324; 332; 333; 344; 385; 441; 448; 449; 450; 451; 452; 453; 454; 455; 456; 460; 461; 463; 464; 465; 466; 467; 469; 470; 471; 478; 479; 480; 481; 482; 483; 484; 485; 488; 490; 491; 492; 494; 496; 498; 500; 501; 502; 503; 504; 505; 511; 512; 513; 514; 515; 530; 550; 581; 610
absolute non-existence (*atyantâbhāva*, *sāmānyâbhāva*), 267; 272; 376
actual existence, 265
adharma, 77; 325; 331; 340
adhiṣṭhātṛ, 333
adhyāsa, 82
adhyātma-vidyā, 571; 572; 575; 597
adhyavasāya, 48
adṛṣṭa, 77; 252; 299; 331; 332; 337; 372; 399; 409; 410; 530
Advaita Vedānta, 35; 36; 37; 38
āgama, 7; 80; 130; 131; 132; 133; 153; 298; 325; 388; 389; 390; 396; 399; 400; 401; 402; 406; 407; 408; 412; 522; 523; 525; 530; 531; 534; 570; 580; 585; 586; 589; 593; 597
Aggañña-sutta, 27
ahiṁsā, 129; 131; 140; 141; 143; 144; 146; 148; 149; 151; 153; 154; 162; 181; 182; 194
air, 179; 311; 318; 344; 466; 470; 471; 472; 478; 494; 496; 503; 528; 529; 530; 531; 532; 533; 534
aiśvarya (supremacy), 328
ajñāna, 79; 344; 581
ākāṅkṣā, 65; 439; 467
akhyāti, 81
Akṣapāda Gautama, 341
akṣa-vāpa, 665
alaukika-pratyakṣa, 76
Amalānanda, 437
Amitagati, 29
Amṛtacandra, 147; 180; 185
anadhyavasāya, 48
anāgamika, 417. *See also asamākhyeya*
analogical inference based on particularity (*viśeṣato-dṛṣṭa*), 369; 379
analogical inference based on similarity (*sāmānyato-dṛṣṭa*), 369; 370

analogy (*upamāna*), 132; 159; 161; 313; 454; 489
anātman, 38; 271; 570; 575; 597
anekânta-vāda, 91; 97; 134; 165; 168; 186
anirvacanīya-khyāti, 81
Anitya-vādin, 398
Annambhaṭṭa, 78
Anselm, 222; 223; 224; 225; 226; 229
antaḥ-karaṇa, 73; 74; 79; 80
antaḥ-karaṇa-vṛtti, 73; 74
anti-realist claims, 291
anubandha-catuṣṭaya, 397
anubhava, 49; 76; 493
anumāna, 52; 66; 67; 70; 76; 132; 251; 346; 363; 366; 369; 370; 377; 379; 387; 388; 389; 395; 396; 400; 401; 403; 408; 410; 411; 412; 451; 454; 473; 487; 490; 510; 521; 522; 523; 524; 525; 526; 528; 532; 534; 570; 583; 587; 588; 590; 597
anumātṛ, 395; 408
anupalabdhi, 271; 368; 583
anuvāda, 386
anvaya, 277; 372; 374; 375; 376; 377; 454; 455; 504
apavarga, 76; 77; 317; 577
apekṣā-buddhi, 301; 302; 303; 304; 483
apekṣā-yukti (principle of dependence, reasoning from dependence), 567
apekṣā-yukti (principle of dependence, reasoning from dependence), 567; 568; 569; 572; 607
apoha, 266; 364; 541; 542; 546; 548; 549; 557; 560
Apoha-vādin, 542; 549
apperception, 186; 542; 555
apprehension, 57; 78; 133; 229; 270; 305; 442
apramāṇa, 139; 163; 526
āpta, 130; 131; 193; 313; 365; 369; 388; 411; 521; 522; 523; 524; 525; 526; 530; 534; 566
Āpta-mīmāṁsā, 326
āpta-vāda, 521; 522; 524; 525; 526; 534
argument from perfection, 324; 345
argument from the first mover. *See* first mover
Arhat, 581
Aristotle, 169; 171; 172; 324; 346
arithmetic progression, 669
Arjuna, 659; 663
ārṣa-pratyakṣa (seer's perception), 76; 265; 292; 308; 314; 315; 317
artha-kriyā, 75; 376; 408; 546; 591
artha-kriyā-kāritva, 75; 675
artha-kriyā-samartha, 546
arthāpatti, 403
Artha-śāstra, 661; 665
arthâvadhāraṇa, 50; 458
ārya-satya, 580; 589; 590
asamākhyeya (incommunicable), 321; 409; 417; 419; 420
asaṁvijñāna-pada. *See saṁvijñāna-pada*
asat-khyāti, 81
asat-khyāti-vāda, 81
assembly hall, 659; 660; 661; 663
astitva (existentiality, existence), 38; 249; 250; 251; 254; 255; 256; 257; 258; 259; 261; 262; 263; 265; 266; 267; 268; 269; 273; 275; 276; 278; 279; 280; 285; 286; 291; 292; 308; 330
Āsuri, 389
āśrama-dharma, 657
Atharva-veda, 659; 660
atheism, 36; 295
atiprasaṅga, 460; 491; 492; 507
atiśaya (excellence), 328
atiśaya-jñāna, 25; 26; 300; 305; 307; 318; 345
ātma-khyāti, 81
ātma-khyāti-vāda, 81
ātman, 30; 38; 50; 72; 73; 74; 76; 232; 251; 257; 260; 261; 262; 263; 270; 271; 293; 298; 299; 308; 309; 310; 312; 313; 314; 316; 318; 325; 331; 333; 341; 342; 371; 372; 377; 384; 406; 412; 421; 438; 439; 440; 450; 452; 455; 473; 486; 493; 516; 529; 530; 570; 571; 573; 582; 588; 591; 595
ātmâśraya (circularity), 258
Ātma-tattva-viveka, 238; 239; 338; 487; 493
atom, 26; 137; 268; 298; 299; 300; 303; 304; 306; 309; 311; 312; 313; 315; 318; 319; 330; 332; 333; 335; 340; 364; 367; 368; 374; 410; 462; 470; 471; 478; 489; 494; 504; 507; 508; 607

atomic dyad (*dvy-aṇuka*), 299; 300; 302; 303; 330; 507
atomic fact, 252; 264; 265
atomic size, 300; 489
atomic subject-predicate proposition, 49
atomic triad, 300; 330
atyantâbhāva, 267; 484
audible particular (*śabda-sva-lakṣaṇa*), 551; 561
Augustine, 558
Austin, John Langshaw, 93; 105; 106; 146; 170; 184
authoritative teaching (*āgama*), 388; 389; 493; 592
autokinesis, 303
avāntara-viśeṣa (intermediate particular), 278
āvaśyaka (obligatory rites), 98; 192
Aviddhakarṇa, 268; 273; 274
avidyā, 48; 436; 577; 581; 582; 585; 588
avīta anumāna, 363; 364; 365; 366; 367; 368; 369; 370; 371; 377; 379; 380
āvīta anumāna, 363; 369; 370; 371; 374; 375; 376; 378
avyapadeśya, 72; 423; 547
ayathârtha, 49; 58; 59; 76

B

bādhaka-nimitta, 583
bādhita, 65; 481
Baker, Lynne Rudder, 540; 544; 545; 553; 562
bare existence, 265
barren woman's son, 267
Barth, Auguste, 635; 636; 638; 639; 648
Batchelor, Stephen, 629; 641; 643; 644; 645; 646; 648; 649
Baudhāyana, 662
being. *See sat*
being-an-effect (*kāryatva*), 238; 239; 240; 241
beingness. *See* existentiality (*astitva*)
belief, 23; 27; 34; 35; 45; 46; 47; 48; 49; 50; 51; 52; 53; 54; 55; 56; 57; 58; 60; 61; 62; 63; 64; 66; 67; 68; 70; 77; 85; 87; 96; 100; 132; 142; 177; 222; 223; 233; 250; 281; 288; 292; 297; 298; 307; 308; 315; 329; 330; 340; 342; 343; 348; 383; 391; 398; 401; 402; 404; 521; 542; 543; 544; 545; 547; 560; 562; 582; 586; 588; 598; 605; 607; 659; 668
belief-acquisition, 49; 51; 52; 55; 56; 59; 61; 63; 69
Bhāgavata-purāṇa, 336
bhakti, 128; 306; 335; 633; 637
Bhāmatī, 433; 434; 435; 437; 438; 440; 442; 444
Bhāmatī-school, 433
Bhāratavarṣa, 32
Bharhut *stūpa*, 662; 670
Bhartṛhari, 222; 223; 231; 233; 258; 296; 321; 322; 395; 396; 397; 398; 399; 400; 401; 402; 403; 405; 409; 415; 416; 417; 418; 420; 421; 422; 423; 424; 425; 426; 427; 428; 429; 555
Bhāsarvajña, 36
bhāṣā-samiti, 144
Bhaṭṭa Vādīndra, 257; 258; 296
Bhaṭṭoji-dīkṣita, 398
bhāvanā-mayī prajñā, 565; 566; 581; 585
bhikṣu, bhikṣuṇī, 119; 597; 628; 635
bhūtākāra, 585
bhūtārtha, 391; 579; 580; 581; 582
bi-functional nature of *karman*, 438
Bṛhaspati, 663; 668
Bodhicaryāvatāra, 629; 630; 634; 635; 636; 640
Bodhisattva, 327; 566; 567; 568; 569; 571; 572; 573; 574; 575; 585; 586; 587; 588; 590; 591; 592; 593; 595; 596; 597; 633; 634; 635; 637; 643; 644; 648
body-self conjunction, 345; 489; 490; 494; 497
brahma-carya, 657
brahma-jñāna, 441; 443; 444
brahman, 38; 73; 78; 79; 299; 300; 343; 398; 399; 410; 434; 435; 436; 437; 438; 439; 441; 442; 443; 444
Brahman realisation (*brahma jñāna*), 434; 438; 441; 443; 444
Brāhmaṇa, 23; 24; 25; 27; 28; 29; 30; 35; 36; 96; 97; 98; 131; 132; 140; 151; 179; 180; 185; 322; 323; 439
Brahmanhood, 443
brahma-prāpti, 397

brahma-saṁsthatā (abiding in Brahman), 443
Brahma-siddhi, 433; 434; 444
Brahma-sūtra, 433; 435; 437; 441; 443
Brahma-sūtra-śāṅkara-bhāṣya, 433; 435; 437; 443
Brahmā, 26; 27; 28; 299; 327; 343; 633
Buddha, 20; 27; 149; 173; 521; 573; 578; 585; 586; 588; 589; 590; 594; 596; 597; 605; 606; 608; 609; 634; 636
Buddha's *pramāṇa-bhūtatva*, 589
Buddhadeva, 620
Buddha-dharma, 573
Buddha-nature (*tathâgata-garbha*), 606; 608; 609; 613
buddhi, 48; 49; 50; 76; 259; 260; 263; 294; 296; 297; 301; 302; 303; 304; 331; 338; 345; 384; 408; 483; 522; 554; 592
Buddhism, 35; 37; 38; 81; 85; 96; 97; 120; 133; 149; 150; 156; 270; 521; 574; 577; 585; 606; 618; 633; 635; 636; 638; 639; 640; 641; 642; 643; 644; 645; 646; 647; 648; 664
Buddhist Dharma, 575
Buddhist *pramāṇa* tradition, 521
Buddhist Studies, 629; 630; 640; 641; 642; 647; 649

C

Candrakīrti, 606; 640
Candramati, 251; 256; 267; 276; 278; 292; 293; 315
Candrānanda, 293; 296; 310; 315; 528; 529; 531; 533
Caraka-saṁhitā, 342
Carnap, Rudolph, 104
Cārvāka, 314; 486; 509
cat, 58; 319
categorical imperative, 151; 152
category, 48; 49; 50; 59; 71; 72; 77; 78; 91; 104; 108; 113; 115; 119; 132; 138; 144; 145; 146; 155; 157; 159; 161; 162; 163; 165; 167; 170; 172; 173; 174; 178; 246; 249; 250; 251; 252; 253; 254; 255; 256; 257; 258; 259; 260; 261; 264; 265; 266; 267; 268; 275; 276; 277; 278; 279; 284; 290; 294; 295; 298; 312; 315; 316; 330; 331; 332; 340; 341; 343; 346; 364; 370; 372; 376; 377; 409; 450; 458; 459; 461; 465; 466; 468; 472; 473; 478; 481; 485; 493; 540; 541; 605; 640; 658; 662
Catuḥ-śataka, 617; 618; 620
Catuḥ-śataka-ṭīkā, 618; 620
catuṣ-koṭi, 156; 157; 168; 176
causa finalis, 304
causal complex, 346
causal efficacy (*artha-kriyā-kāritva*), 75; 546
causal stream (*hetu-phala-prabandha-pravṛtti*), 617
causality, 38; 136; 272; 279; 282; 294; 323; 333; 339; 340; 343; 346; 411; 460; 461; 494; 495; 497; 498; 500; 511; 513; 540; 541; 542; 544; 545; 546; 547; 548; 549; 550; 553; 554; 556; 557; 560; 561; 567
causation theory, 333
cause, 73; 77; 141; 161; 162; 222; 237; 238; 240; 252; 262; 268; 272; 287; 293; 301; 303; 304; 306; 316; 321; 324; 333; 334; 335; 336; 338; 339; 341; 343; 345; 346; 367; 371; 372; 373; 374; 376; 377; 390; 395; 396; 401; 410; 419; 423; 424; 425; 426; 436; 441; 460; 461; 488; 489; 490; 491; 492; 493; 494; 495; 496; 497; 498; 523; 526; 546; 554; 576; 577; 578; 579; 582; 583; 585; 587; 593; 594; 596; 607; 662; 663
cause of karmic bondage, 161
cause of liberation, 77
cause of *saṁsāra*, 577
cause of suffering, 77; 587; 588; 596
cause of the world, 238; 335; 336; 374
cause-effect relation, 272; 343; 367; 373; 376; 377; 554; 607
chala, 77; 166; 284; 290
Chomsky, Noam, 89; 121
cintā, 132; 565; 566; 567; 574; 576; 577; 578; 579; 580; 581; 583; 584; 585; 586; 587; 588; 590; 591; 592; 595; 596
Cintā-maṇi, 398
cintā-mayī prajñā, 565; 566; 567; 576; 578; 579; 580; 581; 584; 585; 586; 587; 588; 590; 592; 595; 596
cintanā, 566; 590; 591
circularity, 57; 72; 75; 258; 400; 404; 559

citta, 384; 385; 386; 387; 389; 390; 434; 435; 440; 581; 591; 609
citta-vṛtti, 384; 390
citta-vṛtti-nirodha, 390
civil law, 668
Civilisation of the Indus Valley, 662
clarifying explanation (*anuvāda*), 386
closure with respect to conjunction elimination, 282; 283
codanā, 294; 295; 297; 309; 346
co-extension, 250; 449
coextensiveness, 250; 253; 254; 255; 256; 274; 276; 278; 279; 280
cognisability (*jñeyatva*), 249; 250; 254; 255; 262; 274; 275; 276; 278; 279; 280; 283; 331
cogniser (*pramātṛ*), 341
cognition of recurrent continuity (*apekṣā-buddhi*), 301; 302; 303; 304
cognitive criterion (*pramāṇa*), 268; 313; 325; 341
cognitive science, 539; 540; 541; 542; 543; 547; 562
comparison (*upamāna*), 68; 76; 161
complete, 404
complex whole, 300; 304
Compton Experiment, 607
computational, 541; 542; 543; 545
concentration, 259; 308; 309; 310; 325; 385; 578
concept of belief, 46; 48
conceptual content, 46
conceptual scheme, 401
conceptual thought, 550
conceptualisation, 75; 134; 185; 424
conclusion (*nigamana*), 82; 306; 365; 368; 370; 371; 449; 452; 457; 458; 469; 479; 486; 559
conflict, 27; 29; 31; 32; 89; 93; 104; 107; 112; 113; 114; 115; 116; 121; 122; 136; 151; 194; 283; 340; 643
conflict resolution, 89; 93; 107; 114; 116; 668
Confucius, 20
conjunct, 283; 289
conjunction, 280; 282; 283; 285; 289; 345; 346; 347; 438; 439; 489; 490; 492; 493; 494; 495; 496; 497; 498
consciousness of a means of knowing (*pramāṇa-caitanya*), 73
consciousness of an object (*viṣaya-caitanya*), 73; 74
consciousness of the knower (*pramātṛ-caitanya*), 73; 74
consciousness-centric error theory (*ātma-khyāti-vāda*), 81
contemplation, 259; 327; 328; 434
conventional time (*samaya*), 165
conveyor of a verbal message, 60
cosmological argument, 324; 343; 345
counterfactual reasoning (*tarka*), 49; 470; 471; 480; 486; 489; 502; 505; 506
counter-thesis, 50
counter-thesis (*sat-pratipakṣa*), 50; 247; 458
cūlikârtha, 367
cultural dogmas, 222
cultural representation, 630; 646; 649

D

d'India, Sigismondo, 282
d'Indy, Vincent, 282
Daśa-padârtha-śāstra, 251; 315
Daśaratha, 320
de dicto belief, 60; 283; 287; 288; 289; 290
de re belief, 59; 283; 287; 288
demerit, 77; 293; 331; 333; 334; 335; 336; 337; 338; 344; 346; 347; 348
Descombes, Vincent, 542; 543; 559; 561; 562
designation, 161; 260; 261; 262; 275; 276; 277; 279; 280; 320; 369; 415; 448; 568; 617
desire for knowledge, 365; 440; 441; 442; 640
destruction of banks (*setu-bhaṅga*), 366
determinate perception (*savikalpaka-pratyakṣa*), 76; 254
Devendrabuddhi, 580; 582; 583; 584; 593; 594; 595; 596
dharma, 26; 38; 77; 252; 268; 269; 290; 292; 293; 294; 295; 300; 307; 311; 312; 314; 315; 316; 317; 318; 320; 323; 325; 331; 334; 340; 344; 372; 377; 397; 398; 399; 406; 425; 426; 498; 516; 569; 574;

575; 577; 581; 586; 587; 588; 597; 606; 607; 608; 617; 634; 657; 669
dharma-cakra, 606; 613; 614
dharma-dhātu, 569; 608
dharma-kāya, 609
Dharmakīrti, 63; 65; 66; 67; 69; 75; 238; 240; 241; 243; 244; 245; 246; 247; 268; 326; 327; 449; 521; 522; 523; 524; 525; 527; 534; 540; 541; 542; 544; 546; 547; 548; 550; 552; 553; 554; 555; 556; 557; 559; 560; 561; 562; 575; 576; 577; 579; 580; 581; 582; 585; 586; 588; 589; 590; 593; 594; 596; 597; 598; 611; 613
dharma-nairātmya, 569; 577
Dharma-parīkṣā, 29
Dharmarāja Adhvarīndra, 73; 74; 75; 79; 80
dharma-śāstra, 662
dharmatā, 449; 451; 452; 454; 507; 567; 568; 569; 572; 607; 608; 609; 613
dharmatā-yukti, 567; 568; 569; 572; 607; 608; 609; 613
Dharmatrāta, 619
Dharmottara, 35; 327; 541; 550; 551; 552; 553; 555; 556; 557; 561; 562; 576; 579; 580; 584; 596
Dhūrtâkhyāna, 28
dialetheia, 167
dialethic approach, 167
dice, 657; 658; 659; 660; 661; 662; 663; 664; 666; 667; 668; 669; 670
Digambara, 96; 99; 100; 130; 132; 144; 149; 173; 177; 180
Dīgha-nikāya, 27; 664
Diṅnāga, 292; 377; 521; 522; 523; 524; 525; 526; 527; 528; 529; 530; 531; 532; 533; 534; 541; 542; 546; 547; 548; 550; 552; 553; 555; 556; 562; 575; 611
direct valid cognition, 610; 611; 613
disjunction, 159; 496; 541; 546; 549; 553
disjunction problem, 541; 549; 553
dissolution of the world (*pralaya*), 298; 299; 304; 305; 307; 330; 336; 339; 340; 344; 347; 348
distinction *in intellectu* / *in re*, 222; 223; 224; 225; 226; 227; 230; 231; 232; 233
dKon mchog 'jigs med dbang po, 621
dṛṣṭānta, 50; 141; 186; 240; 272; 275; 284; 290; 365; 366; 369; 371; 372; 448; 455; 476; 484; 504
Dostoevsky, Fyodor, 334
double meaning (*śleṣa*), 99
doubt, 48; 49; 51; 52; 65; 144; 158; 166; 170; 173; 179; 181; 225; 227; 228; 325; 365; 378; 458; 462; 465; 466; 467; 474; 475; 476; 500; 501; 502; 506; 593. *See also saṁśaya*
Draupadī, 663
dravya, 159; 160; 233; 252; 253; 257; 258; 259; 260; 261; 262; 263; 265; 266; 267; 271; 284; 295; 300; 302; 310; 311; 323; 408; 423; 424; 425; 487; 488; 494; 500; 501; 503; 506; 509; 530; 581; 618
dravyatva, 259; 263; 311; 425; 504
duḥkha, 48; 50; 76; 77; 263; 309; 331; 337; 338; 342; 571; 587; 588; 597
dualism, 134; 138; 539; 540
duality, 124, 300; 301; 302; 304; 606; 613
Dummett, Michael, 286; 539; 552
Dunne, John, 521; 523; 524; 525; 554; 555
Duns Scotus, 224; 257
Durkheim, Émile, 109; 112; 115; 125; 126
Durvekamiśra, 35; 551; 581; 584
Dvādaśâra-naya-cakra, 369
dveṣa, 48; 50; 77; 162; 263; 293; 331; 342; 371; 372
dvy-aṇuka. *See* atomic dyad

E

earth, 23; 26; 31; 32; 33; 239; 240; 241; 242; 243; 344; 373; 455; 458; 459; 461; 463; 464; 465; 466; 467; 468; 469; 470; 472; 473; 474; 475; 476; 477; 478; 479; 480; 482; 483; 484; 485; 486; 488; 489; 498; 499; 503; 504; 509; 511; 514; 516; 544; 646; 659
effect, 26; 87; 93; 101; 104; 105; 106; 107; 108; 109; 111; 113; 124; 142; 148; 162; 170; 174; 190; 191; 238; 239; 240; 241; 242; 243; 259; 272; 300; 333; 339; 341; 343; 344; 367; 368; 371; 373; 376; 377; 395; 396; 397; 401; 410; 421; 428; 436; 437; 439; 487; 488; 489; 490; 492; 493; 494; 495; 498; 502; 507; 540; 542; 543;

544; 545; 546; 549; 554; 557; 568; 569; 572; 586; 588; 607; 617; 618; 619
efficient cause, 304; 324; 555
emancipation. *See also* liberation
emancipation (*mokṣa*), 315; 444
emergent cause, 491; 492; 493; 494; 495; 496; 497; 498
empirical, 47; 52; 55; 67; 86; 92; 94; 96; 97; 104; 105; 107; 109; 111; 113; 114; 118; 119; 120; 121; 127; 132; 133; 134; 140; 145; 160; 172; 178; 190; 286; 304; 396; 399; 400; 532; 588; 589; 590; 595
empiricism, 540; 544; 560
emptiness (*śūnyatā*), 575; 584; 606; 610; 611; 613; 614
epiphenomenalism, 540; 553
epistemic logic, 283
epistemic operator K, 282; 287; 288
epistemology, 45; 51; 54; 55; 56; 67; 68; 70; 71; 74; 75; 78; 80; 90; 97; 134; 136; 233; 239; 242; 244; 245; 246; 387; 400; 402; 404; 410; 447; 449; 450; 457; 541; 546; 556; 571; 574; 575; 576; 577; 578; 585; 592; 594; 595; 597; 598; 611
equivocation, 169; 455; 476
error, 45; 49; 65; 69; 81; 343; 433; 456; 472; 473; 474; 475; 486; 515; 548; 573; 576; 582; 583; 627
error theory (*akhyāti*), 81
essentialism, 86; 87; 89; 118; 190; 194
ether, 311; 318; 344; 462; 466; 472; 478; 479; 480; 489; 494; 499; 503; 504; 507
ethicisation, 110
ethics, 86; 90; 94; 99; 102; 104; 107; 110; 120; 121; 125; 129; 130; 136; 139; 140; 142; 146; 148; 152; 153; 158; 162; 163; 165; 171; 177; 178; 181; 182; 193; 194; 290; 331; 334; 335; 336; 340; 373; 633
evil, 324; 336; 337; 338; 571; 575
evil, problem of, 336; 337; 338
example (*dṛṣṭānta*), 58; 64; 81; 240; 271; 272; 275; 306; 347; 365, 366; 369; 370; 372; 375; 403; 448; 456; 462; 463; 475; 476; 477; 483; 484; 485; 486; 496; 498; 499; 503; 504; 532; 619; 622
excellence (*atiśaya*), 328
existence *in intellectu*, 222; 223; 224; 230; 232; 233. *See also* existence in mind
existence in mind, 223; 229; 265; 269; 278. *See also* existence *in intellectu*
existence *in re*, 222; 223; 224; 230; 232; 233. *See also* existence in reality
existence in reality, 223; 229; 230. *See also* existence *in re*
existent (*sat*), 75; 81; 253; 254; 257; 259; 260; 261; 262; 266; 268; 269; 271; 273; 275; 276; 277; 278; 279; 280; 330; 373; 421; 423; 429; 547; 553; 596; 605; 611; 617; 619; 620; 621; 623
existentiality (*astitva*), 249; 250; 253; 254; 255; 256; 257; 258; 260; 262; 263; 264; 266; 267; 268; 269; 273; 276; 278; 279; 283; 308; 330; 331; 340; 348
extraordinary cognitive capabilities, powers, experiences, 300; 304; 307; 326; 396; 406; 411
extraordinary perception (*alaukika-pratyakṣa*), 76
extrasensory objects, 296; 314; 316
extrasensory perception, 308
extrinsic validity of proof (*parataḥ-prāmāṇya*), 72; 76

F

factual limits to cognition, 281
fallacy, 65; 66; 163; 165; 170; 240; 241; 247; 269; 272; 321; 454; 457; 458; 459; 462; 463; 465; 466; 476; 478; 479; 480; 483; 486; 489; 490; 502; 505; 506; 510
falsity, falsehood, 168; 170; 171; 179; 487; 499
fictitious entity, 268; 269; 273
final cause (*causa finalis*), 304
Finot, Louis, 633; 635; 636; 639; 648
fire, 26; 49; 58; 64; 65; 82; 241; 242; 245; 327; 332; 335; 344; 379; 408; 423; 453; 460; 472; 474; 485; 507; 508; 514; 528; 569; 571; 608
first cause, 222; 324; 345
first mover, 303; 324; 347
Fitch, Frederic Brenton, 281; 282; 283; 284; 286; 289; 291
Fitch's Paradox of Knowability. *See* Paradox of Knowability

fixed means of knowing (*pramāṇa-vyavasthā*), 81
Fodor, Jerry, 541; 542; 543; 544; 545; 548; 549; 550; 553; 556; 559; 561
Frege, Gottlob, 544
functionalism, 95; 125; 190
future, 106; 166; 171; 293; 331; 586; 597; 617; 620; 622; 624; 636; 646

G

gaja-krīḍa, 366
gambling, 658; 659; 661; 662; 663; 664; 665; 666; 667; 668
Gaunilo, 222; 224; 225; 226; 227; 228; 230; 233
gaurava, 372; 399; 440; 453
Gautama, 662
Gautama Akṣapāda, 36; 237; 341; 342; 390
Ghoṣaka, 620
Go rams pa, 528
god, 340
God of the Naiyāyikas, transcendent, 246
God, aphorisms (*sūtra*s) on, 239
God, as the logical culmination of the Nyāya system, 239
God, gods, 21; 23; 26; 28; 30; 33; 36; 60; 79; 98; 160; 167; 179; 222; 223; 224; 225; 226; 229; 230; 232; 233; 237; 238; 239; 240; 241; 242; 244; 245; 246; 247; 268; 289; 290; 291; 292; 293; 294; 295; 296; 297; 298; 299; 300; 303; 304; 305; 306; 307; 311; 314; 319; 324; 325; 328; 329; 330; 331; 333; 334; 335; 336; 337; 338; 339; 340; 342; 343; 344; 345; 347; 348; 372; 374; 375; 461; 488; 493; 507; 508; 515; 633; 658; 659
God, proof / argument against the existence of. *See* proof against the existence of God
God, proof / argument for the existence of. *See* proof for the existence of God
god's existence, 222; 223; 225; 226; 228; 229; 230; 232; 233; 237; 238; 239; 240; 241; 242; 244; 245; 246; 247; 250; 251; 292; 297; 303; 323; 324; 325; 326; 330; 331; 333; 335; 336; 340; 343; 344; 346; 348
Gödel, Kurt, 286; 288
Gödel's theorems, 286; 288
golden egg (*hiraṇya-garbha*), 293
'Gos Lo tsā ba gZhon nu dpal, 606; 609; 610; 612; 613
gradual development argument, 318; 319; 323; 326; 327; 330
gradual progression, 321; 402
grammarian paradigm, 277
grammarians, 36; 397; 398; 400; 415; 555
Gramsci, Antonio, 91
Grice, Herbert Paul, 90; 94; 104; 105; 107; 108; 111; 113; 114; 116; 117; 118; 124; 129; 144; 145; 146; 149; 151; 153; 154; 155; 170; 178; 179; 180; 181; 182; 190
Gricean maxims, 115; 116; 129; 144; 145; 146; 149; 170; 180; 181; 182
Griffiths, Paul, 91; 540; 571; 573
guṇa, 48; 99; 100; 160; 257; 261; 263; 265; 271; 284; 295; 302; 310; 311; 312; 313; 316; 320; 322; 324; 325; 331; 385; 423; 424; 425; 439; 483; 487; 492; 497; 498; 506; 530; 566; 577; 586; 593
guṇatva, 259; 263; 311; 491
gupti, 144; 154; 156; 158

H

Habermas, Jürgen, 86; 87; 88; 89; 90; 91; 92; 93; 94; 96; 102; 103; 104; 105; 106; 107; 108; 109; 110; 111; 112; 113; 115; 117; 118; 121; 123; 124; 126; 127; 129; 130; 133; 136; 142; 143; 144; 145; 146; 148; 151; 152; 153; 158; 166; 175; 178; 180; 182; 184; 185; 190; 193
haecceity, 257
happenstance, 402
happiness, 46; 80; 336; 338; 371; 646
Haribhadra, 29; 35; 37; 156; 160; 162; 173
Hariṣeṇa, 29
Harivṛṣabha, 322; 323
Hayes, Richard, 521; 523; 540
Hegel, Georg Wilhelm Friedrich, 91; 127; 152; 224
Helārāja, 232; 233; 426; 428
hermeneutics, 29; 90; 123; 124; 132; 134; 140; 150; 159; 165; 190; 247; 403; 606

hetu (logical reason, probans, prover, cause), 71; 238; 252; 260; 275; 285; 295; 317; 364; 365; 366; 369; 370; 371; 372; 376; 412; 417; 425; 448; 449; 456; 476; 488; 496; 504; 546; 554; 568; 571; 572; 573; 574; 575; 576; 577; 578; 585; 586; 587; 597; 617
hetu-phala-prabandha-pravṛtti, 617
hetu-vidyā, 571; 572; 573; 574; 575; 576; 597
hetv-ābhāsa, 77; 284; 458
hima-vilayana, 366
Hīnayāna, 628; 633; 635; 636; 647
Hinduism, 85; 95; 96; 97; 100; 101; 104; 134; 194
hiṁsā, 141; 151; 181; 192; 194
hiraṇya-garbha, 293
Hsuan-tsang. *See* Xuanzang
human knowability, 284; 285; 289
human knownness, 284; 285; 291
humanitarianism, 646
Husserl, Edmund, 89; 131; 544; 550; 552; 555; 560
hypothetical judgement, 49

I

I-awareness, 401
icchā, 48; 50; 170; 251; 293; 342; 487; 488; 490; 491; 492; 493; 498; 499; 501; 503; 504; 506; 508; 509; 512
idealism, 125; 148; 230; 556
identity (*tādātmya*), 78
identity (*tattva*), 427
illocutionary, 106; 107; 109; 115; 124; 154; 166; 171; 174; 178; 184
Imitatio Christi, 637
Imitation of Christ (*Imitatio Christi*), 635; 636; 637
implication, 46; 47; 78; 94; 99; 101; 102; 106; 111; 114; 117; 123; 124; 125; 126; 127; 129; 133; 135; 140; 141; 145; 146; 152; 156; 178; 179; 180; 185; 188; 191; 192; 194; 240; 277; 278; 282; 396; 508; 647
implicit knowledge, 46
inclusion, 49; 72; 96; 129; 224; 253; 254; 255; 314; 363; 387; 388; 642
incommunicable, 146; 192; 417; 419; 420; 422. *See also* unnameable, nameability, *abhidheyatva*
incompleteness, 108; 182; 286; 288. *See also*: complete
incompleteness of any system' view / theorem, 404
incompleteness theorem, 286; 288
indescribable theory of error (*anirvacanīya-khyāti-vāda*), 81
indeterminate perception (*nirvikalpaka-pratyakṣa*), 72; 75; 76; 78
Indian logic, 7; 45; 47; 51; 52; 53; 66; 67; 68; 69; 70
Indian tradition, 47; 51; 70; 119
individuator (*viśeṣa*), 257; 258; 259; 260; 267; 268; 306; 311; 312; 313; 318; 329; 466
induction, 402; 403
inductive logic, 448; 449; 450
Indus Valley Civilisation. *See* Civilisation of the Indus Valley
inference, 28; 48; 52; 53; 55; 62; 63; 64; 65; 66; 67; 68; 69; 70; 71; 76; 81; 108; 132; 187; 237; 238; 239; 240; 241; 242; 243; 245; 246; 247; 251; 252; 278; 284; 298; 308; 309; 313; 325; 341; 346; 363; 364; 365; 366; 367; 368; 369; 370; 371; 372; 373; 374; 375; 376; 377; 378; 379; 387; 389; 390; 391; 396; 397; 403; 406; 407; 409; 410; 447; 448; 449; 450; 451; 452; 453; 454; 455; 456; 457; 458; 459; 460; 461; 462; 463; 464; 465; 466; 467; 468; 469; 471; 472; 473; 474; 475; 476; 477; 479; 480; 481; 482; 483; 484; 485; 486; 488; 489; 490; 491; 492; 493; 494; 495; 496; 497; 498; 499; 500; 501; 502; 503; 504; 505; 507; 509; 510; 511; 512; 513; 514; 515; 516; 521; 523; 524; 528; 529; 531; 532; 534; 546; 553; 555; 560; 569; 571; 572; 576; 582; 583; 587; 590; 595; 596; 609
inference by elimination (*avīta*), 363
inferential cognition, 76; 522; 523; 547; 609
inferential reasoning, 54; 66
inferential sign (*liṅga*), 296; 297; 314; 325; 333; 342; 343
inferential valid cognition, 609; 613

information, 63; 90; 91; 108; 113; 114; 118; 140; 154; 174; 177; 182; 187; 288; 388; 395; 509; 527; 549; 553; 571; 638; 665
inherence (*samavāya*), 252; 253; 257; 259; 260; 265; 267; 268; 306; 331; 427; 428; 466; 472; 478
inherent cause, 488; 492; 493; 497; 498
initiation, 657
injunction, 80; 106; 141; 157; 170; 662
injunction (*codanā*), 30; 294; 295; 346
innate belief, 59
intention, 66; 69; 90; 102; 105; 106; 108; 112; 115; 116; 117; 132; 133; 134; 140; 142; 146; 150; 158; 162; 170; 174; 177; 178; 182; 185; 186; 188; 189; 293; 297; 316; 387; 406; 410; 542; 553; 554; 555; 556; 560; 633; 663
intentional content, 265
intentional description, 544; 545; 557
intentional state, 178; 542; 543; 544; 545; 549
intentionality, 88; 89; 131; 150; 540; 541; 544; 545; 555; 556
interaction, 86; 88; 89; 90; 93; 100; 101; 103; 105; 106; 107; 115; 116; 118; 119; 120; 121; 122; 124; 149; 152; 153; 191; 194; 553
interactional competence, 86; 90; 93; 103; 112; 121; 122; 123; 154
intermediate particular (*avāntara-viśeṣa*), 278
introspection, 385; 386
intuitionistic logic, 283; 289
invalidity, 175; 401
invariable concomitance (*vyāpti*), 241; 242; 243; 244; 245; 246; 247; 275; 276; 306; 491
invisible moral principle. *See adṛṣṭa*
Ionians, 346
irrationality, 7; 114; 221; 223; 669
īśvara, 79; 223; 237; 238; 244; 247; 251; 294; 295; 297; 298; 305; 306; 315; 324; 325; 334; 336; 337; 338; 342; 343; 345; 347; 386; 388; 389; 526; 534
Īśvarânumāna, 237; 239
Īśvara-prakriyā, 238
īśvara-sākṣin, 79
Īśvara-vāda, 237; 238; 244; 247

J

jahad-ajahad-lakṣaṇa ('quasi-inclusive implication'), 78
Jaimini, 295
Jaina, 28; 29; 35; 37; 38; 91; 97; 98; 100; 131; 156; 157; 168; 189; 190; 193; 326; 327; 335
Jainism, 37; 38; 85; 93; 95; 96; 97; 98; 99; 101; 102; 104; 113; 119; 121; 130; 131; 134; 141; 144; 154; 156; 173; 179; 181; 182; 191; 192; 194; 314
jalpa, 290
Jambūdvīpa, 32
Jayanta-bhaṭṭa, 81; 303; 319; 320; 324; 345
jijñāsā, 64; 65; 365; 371; 378
Jina, 86; 91; 98; 100; 132; 158; 191; 327
Jinabhadra, 173
Jinasena, 99
Jinendrabuddhi, 369; 379; 521; 522; 524; 527; 528; 529; 531
jīva, 31; 79; 138; 146; 160; 163; 164; 191; 194; 326; 440
jīvan-mukti, 30; 436; 437
jīva-sākṣin, 79; 80
jñāna, 26; 36; 48; 49; 58; 72; 73; 74; 76; 77; 78; 79; 80; 131; 132; 133; 156; 192; 266; 280; 284; 294; 295; 300; 302; 305; 307; 310; 314; 318; 321; 324; 325; 326; 327; 328; 329; 341; 342; 344; 345; 386; 389; 406; 407; 409; 410; 411; 420; 421; 422; 423; 439; 440; 441; 443; 444; 451; 458; 460; 461; 464; 465; 488; 493; 497; 500; 509; 511; 513; 514; 526; 551; 552; 553; 569; 579; 580; 581; 595
jñāna-gata-pratyakṣatva (perceptuality of knowledge), 73; 74
Jñānaśrīmitra, 244
jñeyatva (cognisability), 249; 250; 251; 254; 255; 256; 258; 262; 276; 278; 279; 280; 281; 285; 286; 291; 292; 308; 330
judgement, 48; 49; 69; 109; 121; 123; 126; 140; 179; 181; 183; 185; 256; 281; 334; 336; 412; 548; 661
Jupiter, 31; 32

K

kalpa, 147; 617; 663
kalpanā, 75; 270; 323; 336; 425; 440; 547; 550; 551; 556; 578
kalpanâpoḍha, 75; 547; 556; 578
Kamalaśīla, 264; 268; 554; 576; 577; 580; 587; 594; 595; 597; 598; 606
Kanakavarman, 531
Kant, Immanuel, 104; 109; 125; 130; 145; 146; 151; 222; 224; 225; 230; 231; 233; 334
Kapila, 389; 611
karman, 99; 137; 138; 141; 162; 184; 257; 261; 265; 300; 303; 326; 331; 335; 336; 339; 340; 343; 348; 386; 436; 437; 438; 439; 440; 441; 442; 443; 461; 571; 591; 617
karman and realisation, 438; 442
karman, bi-functional nature of, 438
karmatva, 259; 263; 311
karmic retribution, 331; 333; 334; 335; 336; 337; 339; 340; 348
Karṇakagomin, 524; 527; 529; 585; 595
kārya-hetu, 66; 554
kārya-kāraṇa-yukti / *kārya-karaṇa-yukti*, 607
kāryatva (being an effect), 238; 239; 240; 241; 260; 488; 493; 494; 506; 554
Kathā-sarit-sāgara, 666
Kātyāyana, 397; 661; 665
Kauṇḍinya, 309; 318; 325; 341; 342; 343; 344; 345
Kauṭilya, 661; 666; 667; 668
kevala-darśana, 326
kevala-jñāna (omniscience), 132; 133; 172; 326
kevalin, 132; 173
khyāti-vāda, 81
Kiraṇâvalī, 28; 238; 254
Kṛṣṇa, 659
knowability of everything thesis. *See* thesis of knowability of everything
knowability principle PK, 280; 283; 284; 285; 290
knowability thesis, 250; 251; 281; 284; 285; 289; 290; 291; 292; 297; 308; 330; 331; 340; 348
knower (*pramātṛ*), 71; 73; 74; 130; 131; 298; 389
knowledge, 22; 25; 26; 33; 35; 37; 45; 46; 47; 48; 51; 52; 53; 54; 55; 56; 57; 59; 60; 61; 62; 63; 64; 66; 67; 68; 69; 70; 72; 73; 74; 76; 78; 82; 89; 93; 103; 104; 110; 114; 118; 121; 122; 123; 124; 126; 130; 131; 132; 133; 135; 136; 146; 147; 156; 158; 162; 181; 185; 189; 190; 191; 192; 193; 242; 243; 244; 245; 246; 247; 256; 281; 283; 285; 286; 288; 289; 290; 293; 294; 297; 298; 299; 301; 304; 305; 306; 307; 318; 319; 321; 326; 329; 330; 341; 343; 345; 348; 363; 365; 378; 383; 384; 385; 386; 387; 388; 389; 390; 391; 395; 396; 397; 399; 401; 402; 405; 406; 407; 408; 415; 426; 434; 435; 439; 440; 441; 442; 444; 449; 450; 452; 457; 458; 462; 465; 479; 480; 483; 487; 488; 491; 495; 500; 502; 504; 509; 510; 513; 514; 515; 521; 523; 526; 527; 532; 544; 547; 566; 570; 571; 581; 586; 593; 594; 608; 611; 612; 630; 631; 632; 633; 640; 647; 648; 649; 657
knowledge about beliefs, 54; 55
knowledge of the difference (*viveka-khyāti*), 391
knowledge, concept of, 245
knowledge-acquisition, 51; 52; 54; 55; 56; 59; 60; 63; 64; 69
knows *p*, 46; 66
knows that *p*, 46; 282; 289
kriyā, 75; 99; 313; 339; 370; 375; 376; 403; 408; 409; 420; 428; 496; 546; 591
kṣaṇika, 75; 575; 597
kṣatriya, 25; 28; 161; 322; 323
Kumārila, 340
Kumrahar, 662
Kundakunda, 134; 146; 326

L

lāghava, 259; 372; 399
Lakṣaṇâvalī, 298
Lament of the dicer, 658
language of thought, 543; 559
language-acquisition, 558
laukika-pratyakṣa (ordinary perception), 76
legitimation, 88; 109; 126; 129; 150; 152

Ṛg-veda, 23; 658; 659; 660
liberation (*apavarga*, *mokṣa*), 35; 36; 74; 76; 77; 80; 142; 149; 152; 284; 290; 293; 294; 295; 299; 315; 316; 317; 319; 326; 327; 391; 397; 436; 437; 569; 576; 577; 584; 585
liberation in life (*jīvan-mukti*), 436; 437
limiting adjunct (*upādhi*), 73; 79
limits of human knowledge, 244; 291; 321
limits to cognition, factual, 281
limits to cognition, logical, 281; 283
linguistic convention, 115; 132; 138; 146; 159; 258; 559
linguistic convention (*saṁketa*), 557
liṅgin, 343
logic, 20; 45; 46; 47; 51; 52; 67; 68; 69; 70; 90; 91; 93; 109; 113; 129; 135; 145; 156; 167; 168; 171; 176; 237; 239; 240; 243; 244; 245; 247; 283; 288; 289; 307; 330; 365; 380; 395; 396; 400; 401; 403; 404; 405; 447; 450; 451; 453; 457; 460, 486; 492; 544; 550; 556; 575; 644
logical limits to cognition, 281
logical theory, 399
Lost Island, 227; 233
luminosity, 582; 605; 606; 609; 610; 613; 614

M

Madhyamaka, 38; 156; 605; 613; 617; 629; 640; 641
Madhyamakâlaṁkāra, 610
Mādhyamika, 133; 168; 587; 606; 612; 617; 618; 620; 621; 624; 629; 631; 634
Madhyânta-vibhāga, 618; 620
Mahā-bhārata, 24; 30; 661; 663
mahā-sāmānya, 311
mahā-vihāra, 627
Mahāvīra, 86; 131; 132; 139; 149; 169; 174
Mahāyāna, 37; 572; 594; 606; 607; 628; 629; 631; 633; 635; 636; 638; 639; 647; 648
Mahāyāna-sūtrâlaṁkāra, 607
mahêśvara, 25; 293; 299; 300; 533; 534
Maitrīpa, 605; 614
Mallavādin, 35; 252; 260; 261; 262; 279; 292
manas-self conjunction, 490; 497; 498
Maṇḍanamiśra, 416; 433; 434; 436; 437; 438; 442; 443
Manu, 26; 30; 31
Manu-smṛti, 25; 373; 664
many-valued logic, 90; 168; 176
Mars, 31; 32; 486; 491
material cause, 306
materialist, 486
mathematics, 91; 277
Maticandra. *See* Candramati
maxime ens, 325
mChims 'jam pa'i dbyangs, 618; 619
meaning, 22; 37; 50; 51; 59; 78; 79; 89; 92; 95; 105; 108; 114; 116; 117; 118; 119; 120; 124; 125; 126; 127; 131; 132; 133; 135; 137; 138; 142; 145; 159; 161; 163; 164; 167; 174; 175; 176; 177; 182; 184; 185; 188; 190; 191; 192; 258; 262; 263; 273; 294; 320; 330; 364; 375; 380; 388; 401; 403; 417; 419; 420; 422; 426; 427; 429; 441; 476; 480; 497; 508; 523; 524; 526; 533; 539; 540; 541; 545; 549; 550; 553; 558; 559; 560; 561; 565; 576; 580; 581; 590; 592; 605; 606; 631; 632; 642; 644; 646
meaning-nominalism, 108
means of knowledge (*pramāṇa*), 51; 53; 55; 57; 59; 61; 62; 66; 67; 68; 70; 132; 341; 386; 388; 390; 391; 509
meditation, 26; 91; 98; 131; 133; 134; 259; 308; 309; 310; 311; 313; 318; 327; 388; 391; 434; 435; 437; 565; 566; 567; 574; 584; 630; 637
melted snow (*hima-vilayana*), 366
mental content, 388; 540; 541; 544; 545; 546; 548; 556; 562
mental disposition (*saṁskāra*), 448
mental fabrication, 434; 606
mental fabrications, free from, 606
mental mode (*antaḥ-karaṇa-vṛtti*), 73; 74
mental organ (*buddhi*), 384
mental process (*citta-vṛtti*), 62; 86; 384; 386; 387; 388; 390; 544
merit, 335
meta-categories of Vaiśeṣika, 256; 257; 276; 278; 279; 291
metaphorical existence (*aupacārikī*), 232

metaphysics, 55; 74; 75; 78; 80; 191; 313; 323; 324; 385; 457
methodological coincidences, 221
methodological solipsism, 542; 544; 545; 556; 559
Mīmāṁsaka, 29; 30; 36; 295; 314; 524; 542; 557; 559; 561
Mīmāṁsā, 29; 30; 35; 36; 93; 315; 329; 335; 379; 403; 433; 435; 557
mind, 26; 38; 65; 68; 73; 74; 76; 77; 79; 80; 127; 132; 133; 142; 144; 156; 158; 161; 177; 183; 187; 221; 222; 223; 227; 229; 265; 269; 278; 286; 293; 299; 300; 301; 304; 305; 308; 309; 310; 311; 312; 314; 316; 318; 319; 330; 332; 334; 335; 344; 346; 374; 386; 389; 395; 397; 403; 410; 423; 434; 435; 437; 438; 440; 442; 473; 474; 477; 479; 489; 498; 540; 541; 542; 543; 544; 581; 582; 583; 584; 585; 594; 596; 606; 608; 609; 610; 612; 613; 641; 643
miṇd reading, 132; 133; 187
Mitâkṣarā, 665
Mitramiśra, 664
mKhas grub rje dge legs dpal bzang po, 618
Mṛccha-kaṭika, 658; 666
mobility (*karmatva*), 259; 311
modal operạtor, 281
modalisation, 185
modernity, 223; 637; 649
modus tollens, 285; 515
Mohenjo-daro, 662; 669
mokṣa, 86; 100; 315; 316; 317; 397; 568
Mokṣākaragupta, 400
momentary (*kṣaṇika*), 75; 516; 585; 606
monastic aspects, 629; 630; 631; 634; 642; 645; 646; 647; 648; 649
monastic university (*mahā-vihāra*), 627; 629; 632; 646
Mondin, Battista, 228; 229
monotheism, 233
moral endowment (*dharma*), 314; 318
moral law (*dharma*), 290; 292; 293; 294; 295; 306; 311; 312; 314; 315; 316; 317; 318; 320; 333; 334; 335; 347
moral responsibility, 110; 116; 334; 335; 336; 337; 398; 646
morality, 93; 129; 130; 151; 152; 153; 154; 177; 193; 334; 633
morality without God, 334; 335; 336; 633
Muktâvalī, 460
Mūla-madhyamaka-kārikā, 156; 617
mūla-vaktṛ (original speaker), 388; 389
mundane prosperity. *See* wealth, prosperity
musical notes, 417; 418; 419; 420; 421; 424. *See also ṣaḍja*

N

nairātmya, 487; 512; 568; 569; 577; 582; 583; 584; 585; 586; 588; 595
nairātmya-darśana, 582; 583; 586; 588
naive realism, 547
Naiyāyika, 35; 71; 72; 76; 77; 81; 238; 240; 241; 242; 243; 245; 246; 255; 265; 268; 269; 273; 274; 283; 284; 285; 307; 316; 335; 337; 347; 365; 460; 481; 482; 483; 484; 488; 499; 500; 511; 512
Nālandā, 251; 597; 627; 629; 632
nameability (*abhidheyatva*), 249; 250; 253; 254; 255; 256; 262; 274; 275; 276; 278; 279; 280; 283; 308; 330; 331; 340; 348
Nārada, 663; 664; 668
Navya-Naiyāyika, 35; 460
Navya-nyāya, 36; 76; 90; 120; 237; 240; 244; 264; 447
naya, 130; 133; 135; 139; 140; 159; 161; 165; 176; 369
Neo-Hinduism, 95
Neo-Kantian, 96; 125
nescience, 333; 344; 578; 581. *See also avidyā, ajñāna*
niḥśreyasa, 77; 284; 285; 295; 306; 577
nidhyāna, 566; 580; 596
nigamana (conclusion), 82; 365; 369; 371
nigraha-sthāna (points of defeat), 77; 284
Nīlakaṇṭha, 30; 31; 664
nirṇaya (ascertainment), 48; 50; 284; 378; 437; 458; 570; 596
nirvikalpaka-pratyakṣa, 72; 75; 76; 78; 79; 254
Nirvikalpa-praveśa-dhāraṇī, 614
niṣprapañca, 606
niścaya, 130; 134; 467; 500; 501; 566; 588; 590; 593; 596

Niśītha-sūtra, 29
nitīraṇa, 580
niyama, 50; 316; 332; 440
noble truths (*ārya-satya*), 580; 585; 588; 589; 590; 595; 596
noemata, 130; 544
noesis, 130
non-dualism, 30
non-existent error theory (*asat-khyāti-vāda*), 81
non-factive, 46; 49; 51; 58
non-perception, 368; 470; 471; 501; 502; 508; 530; 583
non-self (*anātman*, *ajīva*), 38; 77; 191
non-sensuous perception (*atīndriya*), 76
non-soul, 90; 270
non-violence (*ahiṁsā*), 90; 113; 131; 134; 141; 145; 146; 147; 148; 150; 176; 177; 178; 179; 183; 185; 193
Nozick, Robert, 288; 289
number two, 302. *See* duality
Nyāya, 281; 330; 340; 401
Nyāya epistemology, 245
Nyāya-bhāṣya, 49; 50; 51; 57; 59; 64; 65; 67; 298; 308; 317; 341
Nyāya-bindu, 550; 556
Nyāya-bindu-ṭīkā, 35
Nyāyāgamânusāriṇī, 369; 372
Nyāya-kandalī, 28; 255
Nyāya-kaṇikā, 433
Nyāya-kusumâñjali, 238; 239; 247
Nyāyâlaṁkāra, 35
Nyāya-mañjarī, 319
Nyāya-praveśa, 35
Nyāya-sūtra, 49; 166; 237; 390; 452; 458; 487; 489
Nyāya-vārttika, 37; 251

O

obligatory duties (*nitya-karman*), 439; 440; 443
obligatory rites (*āvaśyaka*), 98; 192
omnipotent, 233; 337; 338; 340; 372
omniscience (*sarva-jñatva*, *kevala-jñāna*), 132; 133; 136; 139; 250; 289; 290; 291; 292; 297; 298; 299; 300; 304; 305; 307; 308; 318; 319; 320; 324; 326; 327; 329; 330; 331; 348; 389; 573
omniscient (*sarva-jña*, *kevalin*), 131; 132; 136; 173; 191; 193; 233; 291; 298; 304; 305; 306; 307; 320; 327; 330; 337; 338; 389
ontological commitment, 82; 129; 264; 266; 267; 546
ontological proof, 222; 223; 224; 228; 230; 231; 233
ontological proof, refutation, 225
ordinary perception (*laukika-pratyakṣa*), 76; 265; 341; 386; 409; 410; 576; 612
Orientalism, 638; 639; 643; 649
Orientalist discourse, 638; 639; 647; 648; 649
original speaker (*mūla-vaktṛ*), 388; 389
ostension, 257; 259; 265; 558
overlap, 111; 154; 161; 174; 182; 187; 250; 253; 273; 274; 278; 422; 597; 633

P

padârtha, 264; 267; 316; 331; 343; 478
Padârtha-dharma-saṁgraha, 25; 26; 28; 249; 274; 294; 345
pakṣa, 50; 71; 160; 240; 363; 364; 370; 374; 377; 416; 439; 448; 449; 450; 451; 452; 454; 455; 458; 459; 462; 465; 466; 472; 473; 474; 475; 476; 477; 488; 489; 491; 506; 513; 514; 574; 581; 585; 586
Pāṇini, 397
Pāṇinian, 397
Pāṇinīya, 397; 415
Pañca-pādikā, 435
Pañcârtha-bhāṣya, 325; 328; 341; 343; 345
Pañcaśikha, 388
Paradox of Knowability, 281; 282; 283; 286; 289; 291
para-loka, 575; 580; 597
paramāṇu, 25; 268; 273; 299; 300; 303; 307; 310; 311; 312; 313; 324; 333; 364; 470; 530
paramârtha, 38; 251; 309; 546; 548; 549; 580; 605; 612; 613
paramârtha-sat, 546; 548; 549
pāramārthika, 130; 133; 149; 576

parataḥ-prāmāṇya (extrinsic validity of proof), 72; 76
partial overlap, 250; 253; 274
paryāya-paramârtha, 613
past, 19; 27; 85; 166; 179; 333; 620; 623; 624
Pāśupata, 26; 36; 309; 341; 342; 343; 344; 345; 346; 347; 348
Pāśupata-sūtra, 318; 325; 328; 341; 348
Pātañjala-yoga-śāstra, 383; 384
Pātañjala-yoga-śāstra-vivaraṇa, 384
Patañjali, 146; 233; 383; 385; 390; 415
Pavayaṇa-sāra, 326
penance, 154; 633
perception, 48; 50; 53; 55; 62; 64; 65; 67; 68; 70; 72; 73; 74; 75; 76; 78; 79; 80; 81; 132; 137; 192; 243; 250; 251; 254; 265; 292; 296; 298; 308; 309; 310; 311; 312; 313; 314; 315; 316; 317; 318; 319; 320; 324; 325; 326; 327; 328; 329; 330; 341; 343; 345; 346; 348; 369; 384; 385; 386; 387; 388; 389; 390; 391; 396; 397; 401; 409; 410; 417; 418; 421; 424; 434; 435; 437; 440; 444; 454; 463; 468; 469; 470; 471; 474; 475; 476; 482; 483; 486; 487; 488; 490; 495; 496; 502; 508; 509; 510; 511; 514; 528; 530; 533; 541; 544; 546; 547; 548; 549; 550; 551; 552; 554; 555; 556; 557; 561; 569; 570; 571; 572; 573; 576; 578; 579; 580; 581; 582; 583; 584; 586; 588; 596; 608; 610; 611; 613; 614
perception of *yogins* (*yogi-pratyakṣa*), 320; 385; 578; 580; 596
perceptual awareness, 80
perceptual awareness generated through verbal testimony (*śābda-janya-pratyakṣa*), 80
perceptual data, 62; 63; 548
perceptuality of knowledge (*jñāna-gata-pratyakṣatva*), 73; 74
perceptuality of object (*viṣaya-gata-pratyakṣatva*), 73; 74
perfect perception (*yogi-pratyakṣa*, *sarva-jñāna*), 324
perfected beings / souls, 315; 326; 435
perlocutionary, 87; 105; 106; 108; 111; 149; 162; 174; 190; 191
perlocutions, 93; 105
phenomenological theory, phenomenology, 87; 150; 471; 547; 550; 551; 552
physicalism, 539; 540; 541; 542; 543; 544; 545; 546; 547; 561; 562
Piṇḍârtha, 642
Plato, 346
plural number, 300. *See also* plurality
plurality, 69; 300; 304
points of defeat (*nigraha-sthāna*), 77
pole star, 31
Popper, Karl Raimund, 108; 133; 286
Popper's three world theory, 108; 286
Poussin, Louis de La Vallée, 565; 566; 567; 578; 581; 592; 617; 628; 629; 630; 631; 632; 633; 634; 635; 636; 647
practical rationality (*prekṣāvattva*), 578; 592; 593; 594; 595
pradhāna, 303; 324; 343; 364; 367; 368; 371; 372; 374; 375; 376; 377; 384; 387; 428; 532; 590
pragmatics, 92; 96; 102; 105; 107; 108; 109; 130; 132; 139; 140; 148; 178; 193
prajñā, 565; 566; 567; 574; 575; 576; 578; 579; 580; 581; 584; 585; 586; 587; 588; 590; 592; 595; 596
Prajñākaragupta, 580
Prajñākaramati, 628; 642
Prajñāpāramitā, 606
prajñā-pāramitā, 640
prajñapti, 174; 233; 568; 607; 617
prakṛti (primordial matter), 366; 367; 369; 391; 398; 568; 595
pralaya, 304; 305; 340; 347. *See also* dissolution of the world
pramāṇa, 7; 45; 46; 48; 51; 52; 53; 55; 56; 57; 59; 60; 61; 62; 63; 64; 66; 67; 68; 69; 70; 71; 72; 73; 76; 77; 78; 81; 82; 131; 132; 139; 163; 176; 251; 256; 268; 273; 284; 290; 309; 313; 320; 341; 374; 378; 379; 383; 384; 386; 389; 390; 396; 400; 401; 404; 410; 415; 417; 452; 453; 521; 534; 546; 553; 555; 569; 570; 571; 572; 573; 575; 576; 577; 579; 580; 581; 582; 583; 584; 585; 589; 590; 596; 597; 607
pramāṇa-(pari)śuddha, 584
pramāṇâbhāsa (pseudo-*pramāṇa*), 72
pramāṇa-caitanya, 73

pramāṇa-samplava, 81
Pramāṇa-samuccaya, 369; 521; 526; 527; 528; 531; 555; 575
Pramāṇa-samuccaya-ṭīkā, 521
pramāṇa-saṁvādin, 583; 596
Pramāṇa-siddhi, 268; 540
Pramāṇa-vārttika, 540; 611; 618
Pramāṇa-vārttika-sva-vṛtti, 521
pramāṇa-vyavasthā, 81
prāmāṇya, 72; 76; 292; 293; 294; 297; 467; 512; 554; 566
pramātṛ, 71; 73; 74; 341
pramātṛ-caitanya, 73; 74
prameya, 49; 71; 76; 77; 78; 82; 262; 275; 278; 284; 290; 341; 497; 510; 534
prameyatva, 262; 275; 497; 510
pramiti (resultant cognition, valid cognition), 64; 71; 293; 341
prāṇa, 309; 316; 488; 497
prāṇin, 25; 263; 299; 300; 338
prasaṅga, 28; 266, 323; 364; 365; 366; 375; 376; 425; 460; 464; 470; 485; 490; 492; 507
Prāsaṅgika, 618; 620; 624; 641
Praśastamati, 260; 261; 262; 274; 275; 276; 279; 280; 292; 305; 306; 307; 318; 329; 345
Praśastamati-ṭīkā, 252; 260; 262; 274
Prāśastamat, 274
Praśastapāda, 25; 26; 27; 29; 36; 37; 249; 251; 252; 253; 255; 256; 257; 258; 259; 262; 268; 269; 274; 275; 283; 291; 292; 294; 295; 296; 297; 298; 300; 302; 303; 304; 307; 308; 310; 311; 312; 313; 314; 315; 316; 317; 318; 324; 326; 329; 330; 331; 341; 342; 343; 345; 347; 348; 385
Praśastapāda-bhāṣya, 25; 48; 67; 252; 255; 274; 315
Praśastapāda-bhāṣya-samālocana, 259
Praśastapāda-bhāṣya-sūkti, 266
pratibhā, 265; 315; 400; 403
pratijñā (proposition, thesis), 82; 275; 365; 369; 371; 372; 378; 508; 514
Prātimokṣa, 628; 634; 635; 639
prātipadika, 79
pratyakṣa. *See also*: *yogi-pratyakṣa*; supernatural perception; sensory perception; perfect perception perception of *yogins*
pratyakṣa (perception), 50; 64; 72; 73; 74; 75; 76; 78; 79; 80; 81; 132; 254; 263; 265; 292; 298; 303; 308; 309; 310; 311; 312; 314; 315; 317; 318; 320; 324; 325; 327; 328; 329; 341; 342; 346; 369; 384; 386; 387; 390; 391; 396; 400; 401; 407; 408; 410; 411; 412; 417; 440; 468; 470; 475; 482; 485; 487; 496; 511; 530; 533; 555; 570; 571; 575; 578; 579; 580; 583; 588; 595; 597; 607
pratyaya, 48; 253; 258; 260; 261; 262; 263; 266; 270; 275; 276; 305; 312; 313; 314; 373; 385; 386; 418; 425; 434; 437; 513; 567; 568; 571; 576; 582; 583; 584; 593; 607
Pratyeka-buddha, 568; 594; 595; 605
pravṛtti-kāma-puruṣa, 589; 592
prayatna, 48; 50; 263; 331; 342; 406; 496
prayojana, 284; 290; 306; 316; 337; 338; 365; 397; 412; 592
predicative existence, 265; 279
prekṣāvat-puruṣa, 592; 593; 595
present, 133; 166; 267; 286; 618; 620; 621; 622; 623; 624
present king of France, 267; 271
primary entities, 278
primordial matter (*prakṛti*), 364; 366; 367; 368; 369; 370; 371; 373; 374; 375; 376; 377; 378; 379; 380
principal existence, 232
principle of cause and effect (*kārya-kāraṇa-yukti*), 607
principle of dependence (*apekṣā-yukti*), 607
principle of proving on the basis of feasibility (*upapatti-sādhana-yukti*), 607; 609
principle of true nature (*dharmatā-yukti*), 607; 608; 609; 613; 614
proof against the existence of God, 238; 335; 336; 340
proof for the existence of God, 222; 223; 225; 226; 228; 229; 230; 232; 233; 237; 238; 239; 240; 241; 242; 244; 245; 246; 247; 292; 297; 303; 325; 326; 335; 343; 348
proposition, atomic subject-predicate, 49

propositional attitude, 59; 541; 543; 547; 553
Proslogion, 224
pseudo-*pramāṇa* (*pramāṇâbhāsa*), 72
pseudo-reason (*hetv-ābhāsa*), 77
psychologism, 550; 560
pudgala-nairātmya, 568; 585
Purāṇa, 25; 31; 32; 33; 336
pure categories of understanding, 145
Pūrṇavardhana, 618
Puruṣa-sūkta, 23; 24; 25
Pūrva-mīmāṁsā, 403
pūrvavat anumāna, 363; 369; 377
Putnam, Hilary, 544

Q

qualificand (*viśeṣya*), 78; 243; 252; 458; 466; 475; 495; 503; 513; 514
qualifier (*viśeṣaṇa*), 78; 252; 423; 462; 466; 472; 497; 509; 513; 514
qualitativeness (*guṇatva*), 259; 311
quibble (*chala*), 77
Quine, Willard van Orman, 287; 401

R

rājanya, 23; 24
Rāmāyaṇa, 23; 24; 30; 320
Rang byung rdo rje, the Third Karmapa, 613
rational examination, 7; 566
rational examination (*yukti-nidhyāna*), 566
rationality, 55; 61; 97; 105; 114; 190; 192; 396; 521; 578; 592; 593; 594; 595; 669
Ratna-gotra-vibhāga, 605; 606; 608; 609
Ratnakīrti, 244
realism, 95; 162; 180; 281; 547; 553; 556
reasoning from dependence (*apekṣā-yukti*), 568; 569; 607
rebirth, 35; 76; 77; 336; 540; 589; 657
recollection, 418; 420; 557; 561; 617
reflection (*cintanā*), 566; 567; 576; 583
reflexive cognition (*sva-saṁvitti*), 542; 555; 556; 560
relational absence (*saṁsargâbhāva*), 267; 450; 460
relational non-existence (*saṁsargâbhāva*), 267
religious discourse, 87; 94; 101; 110; 119; 125; 132; 180; 192
remembrance (*smṛti*), 49; 69; 70; 333; 346
renunciation, 98; 104; 150; 151; 152; 153; 170; 442; 443; 636; 637
representation, 19; 85; 108; 142; 156; 158; 160; 179; 328; 385; 541; 543; 544; 545; 548; 554; 555; 556; 560; 561; 592; 630; 632; 636; 638; 642; 646; 647; 648; 649; 660
Rescher, Nicholas, 283; 285; 286; 287; 288
resolution of conflicts. *See* conflict resolution
restraint, 115; 120; 131; 140; 153; 154; 181; 183; 188; 259; 316; 399
resultant cognition (*pramiti*), 341; 549
Rikhof, Herwy, 229
ṛta (justice), 660; 669
Russell, Bertrand, 172; 176; 271; 543; 622

S

Sa skya paṇḍita, 528
sabhā, samiti, 659; 665
sabhika, 665; 666; 668
sacred violence, 150
sad-abhidhāna, 260; 261; 262; 275
sādhu, 123; 397; 398
ṣaḍja, 410; 417; 418; 419; 420; 421; 422; 424
sad-pratyaya, 262
Sahajavajra, 610; 614
Said, Edward W., 639
saint, 191; 222; 223; 224; 225; 228; 229; 230; 326; 633
sākṣāt-kṛta-dharman, 400
salvific violence, 149; 150
samādhi, 259; 308; 309; 325; 386; 566; 578; 605
samākhyeya (communicable), 419; 420. *See also asamākhyeya*
Samantabhadra, 326
sāmānya, 81; 257; 258; 259; 260; 261; 262; 263; 267; 271; 272; 285; 295; 302; 307; 311; 322; 323; 364; 370; 375; 384; 385; 387; 389; 416; 419; 420; 425; 460; 474;

479; 493; 523; 524; 525; 526; 528; 531; 532; 534; 546; 548; 549; 591; 612
sāmānyâbhāva, 267
sāmānya-lakṣaṇa, 81; 546; 548; 549; 591
sāmānyato-dṛṣṭa, 363; 364; 369; 370; 377; 452; 487
samavāya (inherence), 252; 257; 259; 260; 263; 265; 267; 284; 295; 307; 310; 311; 331; 343; 425; 427; 428; 472; 492; 530
Samaya-sāra, 134; 146; 180
sāmayika, 258
sambandha, 78; 252; 258; 259; 261; 266; 272; 279; 302; 309; 323; 343; 345; 346; 369; 416; 423; 426; 427; 428; 429; 440; 526; 554; 557; 558; 577
samiti. *See sabhā, samiti*
Sampāti, 320
saṁbhava, 67; 160; 162; 366; 403
Saṁdhi-nirmocana-sūtra, 572; 606; 608
saṁketa, 551; 552; 557
saṁketa-kāla, 552; 553; 557; 561
Sāṁkhya, 35; 36; 221; 363; 365; 366; 368; 369; 374; 378; 379; 380; 383; 384; 385; 386; 387; 388; 389; 390; 391; 611
Sāṁkhya-kārikā, 363; 365; 367; 368; 369; 372; 373; 377; 378
Sāṁkhya-tattva-kaumudī, 377
saṁnyāsa, 442; 443; 444; 657
saṁnyāsin, 316
saṁpratipatti, 51
saṁsāra, 284; 290; 299; 440; 577; 584; 594; 657
saṁsargâbhāva, 267; 460; 470
saṁskāra (impression, accumulation, disposition), 98; 302; 333; 438; 439; 448; 496; 584; 586; 588; 617
saṁśaya (doubt), 48; 49; 170; 173; 174; 251; 284; 365; 366; 378; 401; 411; 458; 465; 466; 474; 499; 501
saṁvijñāna-pada, 410; 415; 416; 417; 418; 425; 426; 427; 428; 429
saṁvṛti-sat, 546; 548
saṅgha, 88; 96; 110; 188; 628
Saṅghabhadra, 566
saṅghārāma, 628
sapta-bhaṅgī, 139; 168; 176; 178
Saptarṣi stars, 31
Sartre, Jean-Paul, 334
sarva-jñāna (omniscience), 298; 324
sarva-jñātṛ (omniscient), 298
Sarvāsti-vādin, 618; 619; 639
Ṣaṣṭi-tantra, 367; 369; 390
sat (being), 75; 191; 260; 263; 266; 280; 309; 546; 548; 549
sat-padābhidheyatva, 266; 280
sat-pratipakṣa, 65; 66; 241; 449; 484; 485; 510
sattā-sāmānya, 263
sattā-sambandha, 258; 259; 279
Saturn, 31; 32
Sautrāntika, 37; 556; 566; 579; 596; 618; 619; 620; 621; 624
savikalpaka-pratyakṣa, 254
scriptural testimony, 298; 325. *See also āgama*
Searle, John Rogers, 89; 93; 105; 106; 107; 108; 111; 112; 113; 115; 124; 146; 175; 178; 190; 540
seer's perception (*ārṣa-pratyakṣa*), 76; 265; 296; 308; 314; 315; 317; 406
selflessness, 539; 560; 575; 584; 596
Sellars, Wilfrid, 540; 544; 556
semantic externalism, 544; 561
semantic loss, 250; 253
semantics, 90; 96; 99; 102; 108; 114; 133; 134; 135; 139; 161; 178; 185; 262; 553
sense capacities, 385; 386; 387; 391
sense object (*artha*), 384; 385
sensory perception, 551
Sertillanges, Antoine, 224
setu-bhaṅga, 366
Seyfort Ruegg, David, 133; 146; 149; 150; 156; 186; 571; 627; 629; 639; 640; 641; 642
Shengzong shijuyi lun, 251
siddhi, 71; 72; 82; 237; 241; 292; 293; 294; 306; 316; 363; 366; 369; 370; 373; 409; 410; 442; 472; 474; 480; 485; 496; 507; 553
Siderits, Mark, 457; 539; 540; 545
signifier–signified relationship (*vācya-vācaka-bhāva*), 79
Siṁha-sūri, 262; 369
Sītā, 320
skandha, 567; 568; 569; 570; 617

smṛti, 49; 82; 132; 293; 294; 297; 346; 397; 402; 412; 418; 420; 437; 439; 664; 668
solipsism, 542; 544; 545; 556; 559; 561
soul, 50; 90; 91; 133; 134; 137; 138; 142; 147; 149; 165; 188; 222; 227; 246; 251; 269; 270; 271; 293; 298; 299; 303; 305; 308; 309; 312; 314; 316; 319; 324; 325; 326; 331; 332; 333; 341; 342; 344; 345; 346; 347
space, 73; 137; 270; 306; 309; 311; 318; 323; 461; 466; 503; 550
speech act, 92; 93; 104; 105; 106; 107; 111; 112; 113; 117; 123; 124; 142; 144; 145; 158; 162; 163; 170; 172; 174; 180; 182; 186; 194; 540
sphoṭa, 79
spiritual cultivation (*manana*), 435; 436
standpoint (*naya*), 132; 133; 135; 159; 168; 178
status-mobility, 98
stem (*prātipadika*), 79
sthita-prajña, 436; 437
strict implication, 282
sublation, 81
subliminal impression (*saṁskāra*), 302; 333
substantiality, 259; 311; 577; 582; 583; 584; 585; 586; 588; 594; 596; 617
Sucaritamiśra, 329; 525; 526
successful practice, 55
suffering, 76; 77; 80; 191; 336; 338; 584; 585; 586; 587; 588; 589; 593; 594; 595; 596
sukha, 48; 50; 263; 331; 337; 338; 342; 372; 386; 440
sūkṣma, 310; 311; 320; 327; 386; 391; 408; 411; 416; 417; 423
summum bonum, 334; 576; 577
superimposition (*adhyāsa*), 82; 582; 583; 588; 596
supernatural perception, 250; 265; 292; 296; 308; 309; 310; 311; 312; 313; 314; 315; 316; 317; 318; 319; 320; 321; 324; 327; 329; 330; 341; 348
supervision of moral law, 123; 303; 333; 334; 335; 336; 337; 338; 340; 343; 344
suprasensory perception (*yogi-pratyakṣa*), 265
supremacy (*aiśvarya*), 328
supreme knowledge (*atiśaya-jñāna*), 300; 305; 307; 318; 319; 329; 345
supreme lord (*īśvara*), 293; 386; 388
svabhāva-hetu, 66
sva-lakṣaṇa, 75; 81; 370; 532; 533; 534; 541; 544; 546; 547; 549; 551; 552; 553; 554; 561; 591; 611
sva-saṁvedana, 316; 555
sva-saṁvitti, 316; 542; 555; 556; 559; 560; 561
Svātantrika, 620
syād-vāda, 97; 134; 140; 156; 162; 165; 168; 186
syllogism, 240; 241; 245; 365; 369; 370; 371; 374; 377; 378; 380
syntactic, 181; 287; 467; 541; 543; 545; 548; 553; 557
syntactic expectancy, 467
synthetic truths, 404
system of beliefs, 292

Ś

Śabara, 29; 30; 557
śabda, 53; 60; 76; 79; 81; 124; 131; 133; 261; 262; 270; 271; 272; 297; 309; 365; 372; 388; 397; 398; 400; 401; 403; 404; 410; 411; 415; 418; 419; 420; 421; 422; 423; 426; 434; 444; 492; 505; 525; 526; 530; 541; 551; 554; 557; 558; 561; 571; 572; 573; 578
śabda-brahman, 79
śābda-janya-pratyakṣa, 80
Śabda-kaustubha, 398
śabda-sva-lakṣaṇa, 541; 561
śabda-vidyā, 571; 572; 573
Śaiva, 36; 37; 99; 100; 341
Śakuni, 663
Śākyabuddhi, 523; 524; 525; 527; 583; 585; 587; 596
Śākyaśrībhadra, 528
Śāntarakṣita, 241; 256; 268; 274; 577; 597; 610; 627
Śāntideva, 627; 628; 629; 630; 631; 632; 634; 635; 636; 641; 642; 643; 644
Śaṅkaramiśra, 260; 264; 266; 279; 280
Śaṅkarasvāmin, 35
Śāriputra, 605

śeṣavat anumāna, 363; 366; 369; 370; 377
śiṣṭa, 396; 398; 407; 411; 412
Śiva, 31; 36; 100; 233; 343
Śiva-purāṇa, 31
śrāddha, 662
śrāvaka, 86; 98; 128; 188; 568; 594; 595; 605
Śrāvaka-prajñapti, 184
śruta, 131; 132; 388; 565; 566; 567; 575; 577; 579; 587; 591
śruta-kevalin, 132
śruta-mayī prajñā, 565; 566; 567; 575; 587; 591
śruti, 80; 293; 294; 297; 402; 409; 412; 437; 438; 439; 441; 442; 443; 444
śūdra, 23; 24; 25; 28
Śūdraka, 657
śūnyatā, 81; 570; 575; 584; 597; 610
śūnyatā (voidness, emptiness), 81; 570; 575; 584; 597; 610
Śvetāmbara, 93; 129; 155; 160; 161; 173; 177; 178

T

tādātmya, 78; 263
tamaP suffix, 323
Tanjur, 608
tapas, 98; 188; 309; 318; 411; 633
taraP suffix, 323
tarka, 37; 49; 59; 284; 401; 403; 470; 471; 480; 495; 501; 506; 510; 572; 575
Tarka-sāgara, 296. *See Vaiśeṣika-sūtra-vārttika*
Tarka-saṁgraha, 49; 57; 58; 59; 60; 65; 401
tat tvam asi, 78; 79; 81
tathāgata, 571; 591; 592; 605; 606; 608
tathāgata-garbha, 606; 608
Tathāgata-garbha-sūtra, 608; 609
Tattva-daśaka, 605; 610
Tattva-samīkṣā, 433; 434
Tattva-vaiśāradī, 384
Taxila (Takṣaśila), 662
ten main topics (*cūlikârtha*), 367
Terāpanth, 102
Thales, 287; 289; 346
Thales' theorem, 287; 289
the present, 179; 534; 622
theism, 233; 237; 238; 239; 245; 247; 295; 296; 297; 307; 331; 335; 342; 347; 348
theistic shift, 331
thematic coincidences, 221
theodicy, 337
theorem, 61; 282; 283; 284; 286; 287; 288; 289
theory of error, 81; 433
Theravāda, 96; 97
thesis of knowability of everything, 250; 280; 289; 291
Thomas Aquinas, 222; 224; 225; 228; 229; 323; 324; 325
Thomas à Kempis, 635; 636; 637
three-atom particle. *See* atomic triad
Tillemans, Tom, 521; 523; 524; 532; 533; 555; 589; 590
time, 73; 76; 78; 131; 164; 165; 166; 167; 169; 176; 178; 179; 279; 286; 306; 309; 311; 312; 318; 339; 346; 364; 366; 373; 407; 441; 461; 466; 468; 503; 557; 561; 568; 581; 608; 611; 617; 618; 619; 620; 621; 622; 623; 624; 635
time, theory of, 169; 617; 618; 619
Tīrthaṅkara, 131; 191; 327
transcendental argument, 545
transcendental perception (*yogi-pratyakṣa*), 76
transfer of merit, 347; 348
transmigration, 180; 284; 290; 299; 317; 326; 595; 617. *See also saṁsāra*
Trikāṇḍī, 395; 396; 397; 398; 401; 403; 404; 405; 406; 407; 408; 409; 410; 411; 412
Trikāṇḍī-vṛtti, 398; 400; 404; 405; 406; 407; 408; 409; 410; 411; 412
trustworthiness, 60; 524; 525; 526; 534; 595
trustworthy person (*āpta*), 64; 82; 369; 388; 521
truth, 20; 22; 37; 38; 45; 47; 56; 57; 60; 62; 66; 67; 68; 70; 76; 82; 88; 93; 104; 107; 108; 131; 132; 133; 139; 141; 142; 144; 145; 146; 154; 155; 156; 157; 158; 159; 160; 161; 162; 163; 166; 167; 168; 169; 170; 171; 172; 175; 176; 177; 178; 179; 180; 181; 182; 183; 185; 187; 191; 192;

225; 226; 282; 283; 284; 285; 288; 314; 334; 389; 404; 440; 458; 487; 541; 544; 545; 559; 560; 561; 577; 593; 595; 596; 612; 613; 614; 622; 623; 634; 668
truth class, 282
truth conditions, 545
truth, unknowable. *See* unknowable truths
truth, unknown. *See* unknown truths
truth-value, 76; 140; 170; 273
try-aṇuka. *See* atomic triad
Tshad ma rigs pa'i gter, 528
Tsong kha pa blo bzang grags pa, 618; 619; 620; 621; 622; 623; 624
Twin Earth, 544

U

Udayana, 238; 239; 240; 242; 243; 244; 245; 247; 254; 266; 298; 303; 338; 458; 459; 487; 488; 493; 510; 516
Uddyotakara, 36; 37; 65; 238; 239; 240; 247; 251; 252; 256; 262; 269; 271; 275; 292; 324; 333; 334; 335; 343; 345; 377; 449; 452; 493
ūha, 403
undercutter (*upādhi*), 456; 458
undesired consequence (*prasaṅga*), 289; 323. *See also prasaṅga*
unestablished invariable concomitance (*vyāpyatvâsiddhi*), 241
unique singular (*sva-lakṣaṇa*), 75; 81
universal, 167; 175; 176; 257; 258; 259; 260; 261; 262; 263; 267; 268; 273; 275; 279; 284; 306; 311; 318; 321; 387; 402; 458; 466; 469; 473; 483; 492; 503; 504; 505; 526; 528; 529; 534; 541; 548; 555; 610; 611; 612; 613; 632
unknowable truths, 283; 291
unknown truths, 282
unnameable, 415. *See also* incommunicable; nameability; *abhidheyatva*
unsubstantiality (*nairātmya*), 577; 582; 583; 584; 585; 586; 588; 594; 596
upacāra, 232; 370; 402; 555
upacāra-sattā, 402; 555
upādhi (limiting adjunct, undercutter), 73; 79; 423; 424; 455; 456; 457; 458
upalabdhi, 48; 49; 50; 263; 270; 305; 581
upamāna, 76; 313; 401
upanayana, 657
Upaniṣad, 38; 78; 434; 435; 437; 440; 443
Upaniṣadic sentences, 434; 435
upapatti-sādhana-yukti, 567; 569; 570; 571; 572; 574; 575; 596; 597; 607; 609
upāsaka, *upāsikā*, 128; 188; 628
upasaṁhāra, 365; 369; 371; 372; 387

V

vācaka, 79; 416; 427; 551; 552; 557
Vācaspatimiśra, 35; 240; 244; 245; 247; 377; 384; 433; 434; 437; 440; 442; 477
vācya, 79; 80; 266; 427; 428; 452; 467; 472; 474; 476; 501; 514; 551; 552; 554
vācya-vācaka-bhāva (signifier–signified relationship), 79; 551; 552
Vādi Vāgīśvara, 37
Vaibhāṣika, 565; 566; 618; 619; 621
Vaiśeṣika, 25; 26; 28; 35; 36; 37; 48; 49; 50; 138; 223; 246; 250; 251; 252; 253; 254; 257; 258; 259; 260; 265; 267; 268; 269; 271; 273; 274; 275; 276; 277; 278; 279; 280; 281; 283; 284; 285; 286; 289; 290; 291; 292; 295; 297; 298; 307; 308; 311; 312; 313; 314; 315; 316; 317; 329; 330; 331; 333; 335; 337; 338; 339; 340; 341; 342; 343; 344; 346; 347; 348; 385; 403; 458; 464; 483; 493; 498; 528; 531; 533; 534
Vaiśeṣika-sūtra, 251; 252; 257; 263; 292; 296; 308; 311; 315; 333; 335; 343; 347; 528; 529; 530; 533
Vaiśeṣika-sūtra-vārttika (*Tarka-sāgara*), 257; 296
vaiśya, 23; 24; 97
Vaiyākaraṇa (grammarian), 397
vākya-bhāva, 365; 371
Vākyapadīya, 231; 321; 395; 415
Valabhī, 597
valid cognition (*pramiti*, *pramāṇa*), 71; 131; 341; 400; 555; 576; 578; 583; 595; 596; 607; 609; 611; 613
validity, 66; 72; 76; 93; 104; 105; 106; 107; 108; 109; 111; 112; 113; 117; 118; 121; 123; 124; 125; 126; 129; 132; 133; 142;

145; 146; 148; 152; 153; 157; 158; 175; 178; 182; 190; 192; 193; 233; 240; 283; 286; 290; 292; 293; 294; 297; 340; 364; 366; 367; 396; 400; 401; 402; 450; 462; 524
validity claims, 104; 105; 106; 107; 108; 109; 111; 112; 113; 118; 121; 123; 124; 125; 126; 129; 142; 145; 146; 148; 153; 178; 182; 190; 193
Vālmīki, 23
vānaprastha, 657
vandhyā-suta, 267
varṇa, 23; 24; 25; 26; 27; 160; 664
Vārṣagaṇya, 367; 369; 378
Vāseṭṭha, 27
Vasubandhu, 37; 335; 565; 566; 579; 581; 582; 596; 607
Vasumitra, 620
Vātsyāyana Pakṣilasvāmin, 71; 238; 292; 297; 308; 324; 325; 329; 331; 348; 452; 458; 476; 487; 488; 489; 493; 570
Vāyu-prakaraṇa, 527; 528
Veda, 29; 30; 31; 35; 54; 77; 98; 221; 222; 293; 296; 297; 330; 397; 399; 524; 526
Vedānta, 35; 36; 37; 38; 77; 398; 433; 435
Vedānta-paribhāṣā, 79
Venus, 31; 32
verbal communication, 53; 54; 60; 61; 64; 65; 67; 68; 69; 70; 388
verbal expression, 259; 260; 261; 369; 370; 388; 423
verbal testimony (*śabda*, *āgama*), 76; 80; 81; 132; 308; 309; 388; 390; 531; 532; 533; 534
verification, 87; 379; 399
vicāra, 251; 566; 567; 580; 587; 588; 589; 596
vidyā, 48; 406; 437; 439; 440; 441; 442; 565; 571; 572; 573; 574; 575; 576; 577; 581; 597; 598
Vijñānabhikṣu, 384
vikaraṇatva, 344
Vimalamitra, 335
Vindhyavāsin, 378; 379; 380
Vinītadeva, 328
violence, 94; 99; 103; 104; 111; 129; 141; 148; 149; 150; 155; 162; 183; 184; 185; 194; 667
violence (*hiṁsā*), 141; 142; 145; 148; 150; 151; 165; 192
vipakṣa, 469; 477; 488; 494; 505; 508; 510; 581; 586; 587
viparyaya, 49; 401; 501
viprakṛṣṭa, 310; 311; 320
viprayukta-saṁskāra, 617
Viramitrôdaya, 664
viṣaya-caitanya, 73; 74
viṣaya-gata-pratyakṣatva (perceptuality of object), 73; 74
Viṣṇu, 233
viśeṣa, 257; 258; 260; 263; 267; 268; 272; 278; 284; 295; 307; 312; 323; 338; 345; 379; 385; 387; 389; 391; 409; 415; 416; 417; 419; 420; 425; 440; 441; 460; 474; 492; 493; 497; 506; 529; 554
viśeṣaṇa (qualifier), 79; 252; 409; 417; 423; 424; 434; 465; 472; 509; 513; 586
viśeṣato-dṛṣṭa, 369; 379
viśeṣya (qualificand), 252; 409; 434; 458; 495; 503; 513
Viśvanātha, 76; 460
vīta anumāna, 363; 364; 365; 366; 367; 368; 369; 370; 371; 372; 373; 374; 375; 376; 377; 378; 379; 380
vitaṇḍā, 290
vītāvīta anumāna, 363; 365; 366; 367; 368
vivakṣā, 159; 553; 554
Vivaraṇa-school (Śaṅkara Vedānta), 435
viveka-khyāti, 391
vividiṣā, 439; 441; 442
viyukta, 310; 311
Vṛtti-kāra, 557; 558; 559; 561
voidness (*śūnyatā*), 81
vyāpyatvâsiddhi, 241
vyatireka, 277; 323; 336; 365; 377; 451; 454; 455; 459; 466; 485; 490; 500; 501; 504
vyavahāra, 130; 133; 134; 138; 146; 159; 160; 163; 169; 172; 188; 259; 305; 307; 411; 412; 418; 419; 423; 558; 593
Vyavahāra-māyuka, 664
vyavahita, 296; 310; 311; 320; 386
vyavasthāpanā, 570; 596
Vyomaśiva, 317
vyutpanna-saṁketa, 551

W

water, 74; 306; 332; 344; 366; 373; 458; 459; 463; 464; 465; 466; 467; 468; 469; 470; 472; 474; 478; 479; 480; 483; 484; 485; 486; 489; 503; 511; 515; 569; 661; 666
wealth, distribution of, 659
wealth, prosperity, 290; 292; 293; 294; 295; 306; 316; 658; 659; 660; 664
well-being (*niḥśreyasa*), 77; 101; 593
Western tradition, 47; 61
witness in God (*īśvara-sākṣin*), 79
witness in self (*jīva-sākṣin*), 79
Wittgenstein, Ludwig, 89; 176; 558; 559
world, most perfect, 231; 233

X

Xuanzang (Hsuan-tsang), 251; 627

Y

Yaita, Hideomi, 521; 522; 523; 524
Yājñavalkya, 665; 668
Yajur-veda, 665
yama, 316; 317
yathā-bhūta-samādhi, 605
yathârtha, 49; 58; 76; 314; 593
Yijing, 628
yoga, 158; 159; 161; 308; 309; 311; 312; 313; 314; 315; 316; 317; 318; 327; 367; 387; 388; 390; 391; 427; 567; 578; 606; 609; 645
Yoga-bhāṣya, 259; 317; 328; 329; 383
Yogācāra, 37; 540; 566; 567; 579; 587; 590; 596; 606; 609; 618; 620; 621; 624; 634
Yogâcāra-bhūmi, 37
yoga-ja-dharma, 311; 318
Yoga-sūtra, 383
Yoga-vārttika, 384
yogin, 291; 296; 308; 309; 310; 311; 312; 313; 315; 316; 317; 318; 319; 320; 327; 328; 341; 368; 385; 386; 387; 391; 578; 579; 580; 581; 584; 585; 588; 590; 596; 606; 610
yogin's perception (*yogi-pratyakṣa*), 308; 313; 315; 317; 327; 328; 386; 580; 584; 588
yogi-pratyakṣa (*yogin*'s perception), 76; 265; 292; 308; 310; 311; 312; 314; 315; 317; 318; 320; 324; 327; 329; 341; 578; 588; 597
Yüan-ts'ê, 608
Yudhiṣṭhira, 663
yuga, 660
yukta, 272; 309; 310; 311; 313; 318; 409; 416; 440. *See also yuñjāna*
yukti, 566; 567; 568; 569; 570; 571; 572; 574; 575; 579; 580; 584; 585; 586; 587; 588; 590; 596; 597; 607; 608; 609
Yukti-dīpikā, 338; 339; 340; 342; 343; 344; 345; 346; 347; 363; 364; 365; 366; 367; 368; 369; 370; 371; 372; 374; 377; 378; 379; 534
yukti-nidhyāna (rational examination), 566; 580; 596
yuñjāna, 308; 309; 313. *See also yukta*

Z

Zemach, E.M., 283; 284; 286; 287; 288; 290